# PRENTICE HALL
# LITERATURE

## BRONZE

Annotated Teacher's Edition
Teaching Portfolio
Novel Study Guides

## SILVER

Annotated Teacher's Edition
Teaching Portfolio
Novel Study Guides

## GOLD

Annotated Teacher's Edition
Teaching Portfolio
Novel Study Guides

## PLATINUM

Annotated Teacher's Edition
Teaching Portfolio
Novel Study Guides

## THE AMERICAN EXPERIENCE

Annotated Teacher's Edition
Teaching Portfolio
Novel Study Guides

## THE ENGLISH TRADITION

Annotated Teacher's Edition
Teaching Portfolio
Novel Study Guides

# PRENTICE HALL
# LITERATURE
## PLATINUM

PRENTICE HALL, Englewood Cliffs, New Jersey 07632

ISBN 0-13-698580-7

10 9 8 7 6 5 4 3 2

Art credits begin on page 1062.

COVER AND TITLE PAGE: **INDIAN IN CANOE**, 1922, Frank Schoonover, Private Collection

PRENTICE HALL
A Division of Simon & Schuster
Englewood Cliffs, New Jersey 07632

# ACKNOWLEDGMENTS

Grateful acknowledgment is made to the following for permission to reprint copyrighted material:

**Margaret Walker Alexander**
Lines from "I Want to Write" by Margaret Walker, originally published in *Crisis* magazine (NAACP), May 1934. Reprinted in *October Journey*, 1973, by Margaret Walker (Broadside Press). Reprinted here by permission of Margaret Walker Alexander.

**Samuel Allen**
"To Satch" by Samuel Allen, reprinted by permission of the author.

**American Council for Nationalities Service**
"Chee's Daughter" by Juanita Platero and Siyowin Miller. Originally published in *Common Ground*, 1948.

**American-Scandinavian Foundation**
"The Brothers" by Björnstjerne Björnson from *Norway's Best Stories* edited by Hanna Astrup Larsen. Copyright 1927 by the American-Scandinavian Foundation, published by W. W. Norton & Co. Reprinted courtesy of the American-Scandinavian Foundation.

**Arte Público Press**
Lines from "Napa, California" from *Women Are Not Roses* by Ana Castillo, 1987 (Second Edition), Arte Público Press, University of Houston. Reprinted by permission.

**Asian American Studies Center**
"Abalone, Abalone, Abalone" from *The Chauvinist and Other Stories* by Toshio Mori. Copyright © 1979 by The Regents of the University of California.

**Elizabeth Barnett, Literary Executor of the Estate of Norma Millay Ellis**
"Ebb" by Edna St. Vincent Millay. From *Collected Poems*, Harper & Row. Copyright © 1921, 1948 by Edna St. Vincent Millay. "I Shall Go Back Again to the Bleak Shore" and excerpt from "Counting-Out Rhyme" by Edna St. Vincent Millay. Copyright © 1923, 1928, 1951, 1955 by Edna St. Vincent Millay and Norma Millay Ellis. Reprinted by permission.

**Bilingual Press/Editorial Bilingüe**
Three lines from "Allí por la calle San Luís" by Carmen Tafolla from *Five Poets of Aztlán*, edited by Santiago Daydí-Tolson, © 1985 by Bilingual Press/Editorial Bilingüe. Reprinted by permission.

**Brandt & Brandt Literary Agents, Inc.**
"By the Waters of Babylon" from *The Selected Works of Stephen Vincent Benét*, Holt, Rinehart & Winston, Inc. Copyright 1937 by Stephen Vincent Benét; copyright renewed © 1964 by Thomas C. Benét, Stephanie B. Mahin, and Rachel Benét Lewis. "Shaving" by Leslie Norris. Copyright © 1977 by Leslie Norris. Reprinted by permission of Brandt & Brandt Literary Agents, Inc.

**Gwendolyn Brooks**
"Maud Martha Spares the Mouse" and "The Sonnet-Ballad" from *The World of Gwendolyn Brooks* by Gwendolyn Brooks, published by Harper & Row. Copyright © 1971 Gwendolyn Brooks, the David Company.

**The Christian Science Publishing Society**
Excerpt from "Unfolding Bud" by Naoshi Koriyama from *The Christian Science Monitor*, July 13, 1957. Copyright © 1957 by The Christian Science Publishing Society. Reprinted by permission from *The Christian Science Monitor*. All rights reserved.

(continued on page 1059)

# CONTENTS

## SHORT STORIES

READING ACTIVELY  2

MODEL

**Guy de Maupassant** . . . . . . . .    The Piece of String . . . . . . . . . . . . .3

Plot    **Jack Finney** . . . . . . . . . . . . . .    Contents of the Dead Man's Pocket . .15

**W. W. Jacobs** . . . . . . . . . . . .    The Monkey's Paw . . . . . . . . . . . . .29

**Carl Stephenson** . . . . . . . . . .    Leiningen Versus the Ants . . . . . . . .41

**O. Henry** . . . . . . . . . . . . . . . .    Hearts and Hands . . . . . . . . . . . . . .59

Characterization    **William Melvin Kelley** . . . . . .    A Visit to Grandmother . . . . . . . . . .65

**Juanita Platero and**

   **Siyowin Miller** . . . . . . . . . .    Chee's Daughter . . . . . . . . . . . . . . .73

**Kay Boyle** . . . . . . . . . . . . . . . .    The Soldier Ran Away . . . . . . . . . .85

**Mark Twain** . . . . . . . . . . . . . .    Luck . . . . . . . . . . . . . . . . . . . . . . . .99

Point of View    **Heinrich Böll** . . . . . . . . . . . . .    The Laugher . . . . . . . . . . . . . . . . .107

**Leslie Norris** . . . . . . . . . . . . .    Shaving . . . . . . . . . . . . . . . . . . . .111

**Gwendolyn Brooks** . . . . . . . .    Maud Martha Spares the Mouse . .119

**Virginia Woolf** . . . . . . . . . . . .    The Widow and the Parrot . . . . . . .123

Setting    **Ray Bradbury** . . . . . . . . . . . . .    There Will Come Soft Rains . . . . . .133

**Josephina Niggli** . . . . . . . . . .    The Street of the Cañon . . . . . . . . .139

**Stephen Vincent Benét** . . . . .    By the Waters of Babylon . . . . . . . .147

**Doris Lessing** . . . . . . . . . . . .    Through the Tunnel . . . . . . . . . . . .159

Symbol    **Toshio Mori** . . . . . . . . . . . . . .    Abalone, Abalone, Abalone . . . . . .169

**Edgar Allan Poe** . . . . . . . . . .    The Masque of the Red Death . . . .173

**Anne Tyler** . . . . . . . . . . . . . . .    With All Flags Flying . . . . . . . . . . .181

Tone and Irony    **Edward D. Hoch** . . . . . . . . . . .    The Last Unicorns . . . . . . . . . . . . .191

**Saki (H. H. Munro)** . . . . . . . . .    The Open Window . . . . . . . . . . . .195

**Isaac Asimov** . . . . . . . . . . . . .    The Machine That Won the War . .201

**Björnstjerne Björnson** . . . . . .    The Brothers . . . . . . . . . . . . . . . . .209

Theme    **Katherine Mansfield** . . . . . . . .    The Apple Tree . . . . . . . . . . . . . . .217

**Mark Helprin** . . . . . . . . . . . . .    White Gardens . . . . . . . . . . . . . . .223

**Sarah Orne Jewett** . . . . . . . .  The Hiltons' Holiday . . . . . . . . . . .227
**Frank R. Stockton** . . . . . . . . .  Old Pipes and the Dryad . . . . . . .241

PUTTING IT TOGETHER   254

*MODEL*
**Willa Cather** . . . . . . . . . . . . .  The Sentimentality of
                                                    William Tavener . . . . . . . . . . . . .255

FOCUS ON READING: Understanding Relationships   262
YOU THE WRITER   264
YOU THE CRITIC   265

# DRAMA

READING ACTIVELY   268

**Arnold Perl (based on
   Tevya stories of Sholom
   Aleichem)** . . . . . . . . . . . . . .  Tevya and the First Daughter . . . . .271
**Howard Koch** . . . . . . . . . . . . .  Invasion from Mars . . . . . . . . . . . .289
**Reginald Rose** . . . . . . . . . . . .  Twelve Angry Men  . . . . . . . . . . . .311

THE SHAKESPEAREAN THEATER   342
**William Shakespeare** . . . . . . .  The Tragedy of Julius Caesar  . . . .345

FOCUS ON READING: Mapping   434
YOU THE WRITER   436
YOU THE CRITIC   437

# NONFICTION

READING ACTIVELY   440

*MODEL*
**James Thurber** . . . . . . . . . . . .  The Dog That Bit People . . . . . . .441

**Biographies
and Personal
Accounts**

**Van Wyck Brooks** . . . . . . . . . .  Emily Dickinson . . . . . . . . . . . . . . .451
**Langston Hughes** . . . . . . . . . .  Marian Anderson: Famous
                                                    Concert Singer . . . . . . . . . . . . . .463
**Dylan Thomas** . . . . . . . . . . . .  A Child's Christmas in Wales . . . . .469
**Truman Capote** . . . . . . . . . . .  A Christmas Memory . . . . . . . . . . .479

| | | |
|---|---|---|
| **Types of Essays** | Harry Crews . . . . . . . . . . . . . . . | The Hawk Is Flying . . . . . . . . . . . 493 |
| | N. Scott Momaday . . . . . . . . | *from* The Way to Rainy Mountain . 501 |
| | Annie Dillard . . . . . . . . . . . . . | Flood . . . . . . . . . . . . . . . . . . . 509 |
| | Evan S. Connell . . . . . . . . . . | *from* The White Lantern . . . . . . . . 517 |
| | Lorraine Hansberry . . . . . . . . | On Summer . . . . . . . . . . . . . . . . 529 |
| | E. B. White . . . . . . . . . . . . . | *from* Some Remarks on Humor . . . 535 |
| | Calvin Trillin . . . . . . . . . . . . | Rural Literalism . . . . . . . . . . . . . 539 |
| **Essays in the Arts and Sciences** | Lewis Thomas . . . . . . . . . . . . | Notes on Punctuation (Language Arts) . . . . . . . . . . . . . . . . . . . . . 545 |
| | Theodore H. White . . . . . . . . | The American Idea (History) . . . . . . 549 |
| | Aaron Copland . . . . . . . . . . . | The Creative Process in Music (Music) . . . . . . . . . . . . . . . . . . . 553 |
| | Ann Beattie . . . . . . . . . . . . . | Alex Katz's *The Table* (Art) . . . . . . . 561 |
| | Rachel Carson . . . . . . . . . . . . | The Marginal World (Science) . . . . 565 |

PUTTING IT TOGETHER   572

*MODEL*

| | | |
|---|---|---|
| Thomas Boswell . . . . . . . . . . | Glove's Labor Lost . . . . . . . . . . . 573 |

FOCUS ON READING: Reading Charts and Tables   578
YOU THE WRITER   580
YOU THE CRITIC   581

## POETRY

READING ACTIVELY   584

*MODEL*

| | | |
|---|---|---|
| May Swenson . . . . . . . . . . . . | The Centaur . . . . . . . . . . . . . . . . . 585 |
| **Narrative Poetry** | John Keats . . . . . . . . . . . . . . . | La Belle Dame sans Merci . . . . . . . 591 |
| | Robert Frost . . . . . . . . . . . . . | Two Tramps in Mud Time . . . . . . . 595 |
| | Henry Wadsworth Longfellow . | The Wreck of the Hesperus . . . . . 601 |
| **Dramatic Poetry** | Rudyard Kipling . . . . . . . . . . . | Danny Deever . . . . . . . . . . . . . . 607 |
| | W. H. Auden . . . . . . . . . . . . . | O What Is That Sound . . . . . . . . . 611 |
| | Edgar Allan Poe . . . . . . . . . . . | Eldorado . . . . . . . . . . . . . . . . . . 615 |
| **The Speaker and Tone** | Gwendolyn Brooks . . . . . . . . | The Sonnet-Ballad . . . . . . . . . . . . 620 |
| | Dorothy Parker . . . . . . . . . . . | One Perfect Rose . . . . . . . . . . . . 622 |
| | Samuel Allen (Paul Vesey) . . | To Satch . . . . . . . . . . . . . . . . . 623 |

| Lyric Poetry | Conrad Aiken | Music I Heard | 629 |
| | Naomi Shihab Nye | Making a Fist | 630 |
| | Amy Lowell | Generations | 632 |
| | James Wright | A Blessing | 636 |
| | Octavio Paz (translated by Muriel Rukeyser) | The Street | 638 |
| | Mary Oliver | A Letter from Home | 639 |

| Figurative Language | Lucille Clifton | Miss Rosie | 644 |
| | Elizabeth Coatsworth | July Storm | 645 |
| | Eve Merriam | Metaphor | 646 |
| | Philip Booth | First Lesson | 647 |
| | Amy Lowell | Night Clouds | 650 |
| | Marianne Moore | A Jelly-Fish | 651 |
| | Marcie Hans | Fueled | 652 |
| | Emily Dickinson | The Wind—tapped like a tired Man | 654 |

| Imagery | Theodore Roethke | Big Wind | 658 |
| | A. R. Ammons | Loss | 659 |
| | John Ciardi | One Morning | 660 |
| | Jean Toomer | Reapers | 664 |
| | Elizabeth Bishop | The Fish | 665 |
| | Robert Francis | Pitcher | 668 |
| | John Masefield | Cargoes | 669 |

| Musical Devices | Robert Burns | My Heart's in the Highlands | 674 |
| | Alfred, Lord Tennyson | The Splendor Falls | 676 |
| | Christopher Morley | Nursery Rhymes for the Tender-Hearted | 678 |
| | Carl Sandburg | Jazz Fantasia | 680 |
| | John McCrae | In Flanders Fields | 682 |

| Forms | William Shakespeare | Shall I Compare Thee to a Summer's Day? | 686 |
| | Elinor Wylie | Puritan Sonnet | 688 |
| | Hyakuchi, Chiyojo, Bashō, and Issa | Four Haiku | 691 |
| | John Updike | Letter Slot | 696 |
| | Lawrence Ferlinghetti | Constantly Risking Absurdity | 697 |

| Themes | Frank Horne | To James | 702 |
| | Karl Shapiro | Auto Wreck | 704 |
| | Thomas Hardy | The Oxen | 706 |
| | Edna St. Vincent Millay | Ebb | 707 |

PUTTING IT TOGETHER  708

*MODEL*

**John Updike** . . . . . . . . . . . . . Ex-Basketball Player . . . . . . . . . . . 709

**FOCUS ON READING: Making Inferences  712**
**YOU THE WRITER  714**
**YOU THE CRITIC  715**

## THE LEGEND OF KING ARTHUR

**READING ACTIVELY  718**

**T. H. White** . . . . . . . . . . . . . . Arthur Becomes King of Britain . . . 721
**Thomas Malory** . . . . . . . . . . . The Marriage of King Arthur . . . . . . 733
**Thomas Malory** . . . . . . . . . . . The Adventures of Sir Launcelot . . 737
**Alfred, Lord Tennyson** . . . . . . Morte d'Arthur . . . . . . . . . . . . . . . 749
**Geoffrey Hill** . . . . . . . . . . . . Merlin . . . . . . . . . . . . . . . . . . . . . 764
**Edwin Muir** . . . . . . . . . . . . . Merlin . . . . . . . . . . . . . . . . . . . . . 766

**FOCUS ON READING: Reading Maps  768**
**YOU THE WRITER  770**
**YOU THE CRITIC  771**

## THE NOVEL

**READING ACTIVELY  774**

**John Steinbeck** . . . . . . . . . . . The Pearl . . . . . . . . . . . . . . . . . . . 779
**John Knowles** . . . . . . . . . . . . A Separate Peace . . . . . . . . . . . . . 831

**FOCUS ON READING: Making Generalizations  938**
**YOU THE WRITER  940**
**YOU THE CRITIC  941**


**HANDBOOK OF WRITING ABOUT LITERATURE  942**
**HANDBOOK OF LITERARY TERMS AND TECHNIQUES  1002**
**HANDBOOK OF CRITICAL THINKING AND READING TERMS  1024**

**GLOSSARY  1034**
**INDEX OF FINE ART  1044**
**INDEX OF SKILLS  1046**
**INDEX OF TITLES BY THEMES  1052**
**INDEX OF AUTHORS AND TITLES  1056**

**ACKNOWLEDGMENTS (continued)  1059**

**GIRLS ON THE JETTY**
*Edvard Munch*
Three Lions

# SHORT STORIES

Originally *fiction* meant anything made up, created, or shaped. Today we have refined the definition to mean a prose story based on the imagination of the author. While many writers of fiction may imitate the forms of nonfiction or may use true or historically accurate details in their stories, they write not to recreate reality but to entertain and perhaps to say something significant about human existence.

One of the most popular forms of fiction, the short story was first defined by Edgar Allan Poe. He was sure that "worldly interests" prevented most readers from concentrating on reading, so he felt that a short, concentrated tale that could be read in a single sitting and that created a single, powerful impression was the best type of fiction. Today, innumerable writers have followed Poe's recommendations, creating stories on a vast array of subjects. For instance, this unit presents short stories ranging from a tale of three wishes to a story of an empty house after a nuclear war.

As opposed to other types of fiction, short stories are characterized by a limited number of characters, restricted settings, and a narrow range of action, but short stories share common elements with other forms. Seven of those elements are examined in this unit—plot, characterization, point of view, setting, symbols, tone and irony, and theme. *Plot* refers to the series of events that make up the story. *Characterization* is the creation of reasonable facsimiles of human beings with all their warts and smiles. *Point of view* is the perspective of the story, the voice or speaker who is doing the narrating. *Setting* refers to the natural or artificial environment in which the story takes place, while a *symbol* is a thing that may be understood to mean something beyond itself. Every short story has a tone or attitude that the writer conveys toward the story itself and toward you, the reader. A special element sometimes used in creating tone is *irony,* in which writers use language or situations that are the opposite of what is expected to create impact. Finally, *theme* is what the short story reveals about life, the central idea presented throughout the work.

These, then, are the major tools short story writers have at their disposal. Understanding the elements of the story will help you discover the author's intentions and what is being said about life and the human experience. However, while you the reader might be studying one of the elements, it is important to realize that a short story is unified, that all elements happen at once in the tale. As you read, look for the whole as well as the parts.

# The Short Story

"Fiction is like a spider web," wrote Virginia Woolf, "attached ever so slightly perhaps, but still attached to life at all four corners." In other words, fiction has a certain verisimilitude, or resemblance to life. This means that when you read a short story, you can bring your own life experiences to it and become actively involved with it.

The following strategies will help you become an active reader. Remember that the more you put into a short story, the more you are likely to get out of it.

**Question**    Formulate questions as you read. Put yourself in the story and ask questions about what is happening. Try to determine what the characters are like and why they act as they do. Question the effect that setting has on the characters and the plot. Read between the lines and try to figure out the tone, or attitude, of the writer.

**Predict**    Make predictions as you read based on what you know about life. Use your knowledge of how a story works to guess at the way events will turn out. Take risks with your predictions. Although your predictions should be reasonable, they need not always turn out to be accurate.

**Clarify**    Monitor your reading. Take time to answer your questions and to check your predictions. When something in the story isn't clear to you, stop and try to clarify the confusion, even if this means rereading earlier parts of the story. Remember, though, that you will not always be able to clarify, because literature, like life, does not always have cut-and-dried answers.

**Summarize**    At appropriate points in the story, stop to review what has happened so far. Identify what seems to be important and try to determine how that piece of information works with everything else in terms of how the story is developing.

**Pull It Together**    Find the central idea of the story. The success of a short story depends on its effect on the reader. What did the story say to you? How did you react to it?

On the following pages is a model with comments in the margin showing how an active reader might read a short story.

# The Piece of String

### Guy de Maupassant

**Questions:** Why is this story called "A Piece of String"? Why would a piece of string be important?

Along all the roads around Goderville the peasants and their wives were coming toward the burgh[1] because it was market day. The men were proceeding with slow steps, the whole body bent forward at each movement of their long twisted legs; deformed by their hard work, by the weight on the plow which, at the same time, raised the left shoulder and swerved the figure, by the reaping of the wheat which made the knees spread to make a firm "purchase," by all the slow and painful labors of the country. Their blouses, blue, "stiff-starched," shining as if varnished, ornamented with a little design in white at the neck and wrists, puffed about their bony bodies, seemed like balloons ready to carry them off. From each of them a head, two arms and two feet protruded.

**Question:** Will this story be about one of the peasants?

**Clarification:** *Purchase* here means a hold on the ground to keep from slipping.

Some led a cow or a calf by a cord, and their wives, walking behind the animal, whipped its haunches with a leafy branch to hasten its progress. They carried large baskets on their arms from which, in some cases, chickens and, in others, ducks thrust out their heads. And they walked with a quicker, livelier step than their husbands. Their spare straight figures were wrapped in a scanty little shawl pinned over their flat bosoms, and their heads were enveloped in a white cloth glued to the hair and surmounted by a cap.

Then a wagon passed at the jerky trot of a nag, shaking strangely, two men seated side by side and a woman in the bottom of the vehicle, the latter holding onto the sides to lessen the hard jolts.

In the public square of Goderville there was a crowd, a throng of human beings and animals mixed together. The horns of the cattle, the tall hats, with long nap, of the rich peasant and the headgear of the peasant women rose above the surface of the assembly. And the clamorous, shrill,

---

**1. burgh** (berg) *n.*: Small town.

**THE MARKETPLACE IN FRONT OF THE TOWN HALL AT PONTOISE, 1876**
*Ludovic Piette*
Musées de Pontoise

screaming voices made a continuous and savage din which sometimes was dominated by the robust lungs of some countryman's laugh or the long lowing of a cow tied to the wall of a house.

All that smacked of the stable, the dairy and the dirt heap, hay and sweat, giving forth that unpleasant odor, human and animal, peculiar to the people of the field.

**Clarification:** It seems the story will be about Maître Hauchecome. And here is the piece of string mentioned in the title.

Maître[2] Hauchecome of Breaute had just arrived at Goderville, and he was directing his steps toward the public square when he perceived upon the ground a little piece of string. Maître Hauchecome, economical like a true Norman, thought that everything useful ought to be picked up, and he bent painfully, for he suffered from rheumatism. He took the bit of thin cord from the ground and began to roll it carefully when he noticed Maître Malandain, the harness maker, on the

---

**2. Maître** (me′ trə): Mister, a term of address.

threshold of his door, looking at him. They had heretofore had business together on the subject of a halter, and they were on bad terms, both being good haters. Maître Hauchecome was seized with a sort of shame to be seen thus by his enemy, picking a bit of string out of the dirt. He concealed his "find" quickly under his blouse, then in his trousers' pocket; then he pretended to be still looking on the ground for something which he did not find, and he went toward the market, his head forward, bent double by his pains.

He was soon lost in the noisy and slowly moving crowd which was busy with interminable[3] bargainings. The peasants milled, went and came, perplexed, always in fear of being cheated, not daring to decide, watching the vendor's eye, ever trying to find the trick in the man and the flaw in the beast.

The women, having placed their great baskets at their feet, had taken out the poultry which lay upon the ground, tied together by the feet, with terrified eyes and scarlet crests.

They heard offers, stated their prices with a dry air and impassive face, or perhaps, suddenly deciding on some proposed reduction, shouted to the customer who was slowly going away: "All right, Maître Authirne, I'll give it to you for that."

Then little by little the square was deserted, and the Angelus[4] ringing at noon, those who had stayed too long scattered to their shops.

At Jourdain's the great room was full of people eating, as the big court was full of vehicles of all kinds, carts, gigs, wagons, dumpcarts, yellow with dirt, mended and patched, raising their shafts to the sky like two arms or perhaps with their shafts in the ground and their backs in the air.

Just opposite the diners seated at the table the immense fireplace, filled with bright flames, cast a lively heat on the backs of the row on the right. Three spits were turning on which were chickens, pigeons and legs of mutton, and an appetizing odor of roast beef and gravy dripping over the nicely browned skin rose from the hearth, increased the jovialness and made everybody's mouth water.

**Prediction:** This action of hiding the string will cause some trouble later on.

**Prediction:** Here are people who do not trust one another. Suspicion and lack of trust will play a major role in this story.

---

**3. interminable** (in tur' mi nə b'l) *adj.*: Endless.
**4. Angelus** (an' jə ləs) *n.*: Bell rung to announce the time for a prayer said at morning, noon, and evening.

All the aristocracy of the plow ate there at Maître Jourdain's, tavern keeper and horse dealer, a rascal who had money.

The dishes were passed and emptied, as were the jugs of yellow cider. Everyone told his affairs, his purchases and sales. They discussed the crops. The weather was favorable for the green things but not for the wheat.

**Question:** What does this drumbeat mean?

Suddenly the drum beat in the court before the house. Everybody rose, except a few indifferent persons, and ran to the door or to the windows, their mouths still full and napkins in their hands.

After the public crier had ceased his drumbeating he called out in a jerky voice, speaking his phrases irregularly:

**Clarification:** The drumbeat announces the presence of the public crier. He tells the people of the lost pocketbook and the reward.

"It is hereby made known to the inhabitants of Goderville, and in general to all persons present at the market, that there was lost this morning on the road to Benzeville, between nine and ten o'clock, a black leather pocketbook containing five hundred francs[5] and some business papers. The finder is requested to return same with all haste to the mayor's office or to Maître Fortune Houlbreque of Manneville; there will be twenty francs reward."

Then the man went away. The heavy roll of the drum and the crier's voice were again heard at a distance.

Then they began to talk of this event, discussing the chances that Maître Houlbreque had of finding or not finding his pocketbook.

And the meal concluded. They were finishing their coffee when a chief of the gendarmes[6] appeared upon the threshold.

He inquired:

"Is Maître Hauchecome of Breaute here?"

Maître Hauchecome, seated at the other end of the table, replied:

"Here I am."

And the officer resumed:

**Prediction:** Here comes the trouble predicted earlier. Now Maître Hauchecome will be accused of finding the pocketbook.

"Maître Hauchecome, will you have the goodness to accompany me to the mayor's office? The mayor would like to talk to you."

The peasant, surprised and disturbed, swallowed at a draft his glass, rose and, even more bent than in the morning,

---

**5. francs** (franks) *n.*: Unit of money in France.
**6. gendarmes** (zhän' därmz) *n.*: French police.

for the first steps after each rest were specially difficult, set out, repeating: "Here I am, here I am."

The mayor was awaiting him, seated on an armchair. He was the notary of the vicinity, a stout, serious man with pompous phrases.

"Maître Hauchecome," said he, "you were seen this morning to pick up, on the road to Benzeville, the pocketbook lost by Maître Houlbreque of Manneville."

The countryman, astounded, looked at the mayor, already terrified by this suspicion resting on him without his knowing why.

"Me? Me? Me pick up the pocketbook?"

"Yes, you yourself."

"Word of honor, I never heard of it."

"But you were seen."

"I was seen, me? Who says he saw me?"

"Monsieur Malandain, the harness maker."

The old man remembered, understood and flushed with anger.

"Ah, he saw me, the clodhopper, he saw me pick up this string here, M'sieu[7] the Mayor." And rummaging in his pocket, he drew out the little piece of string.

But the mayor, incredulous, shook his head.

"You will not make me believe, Maître Hauchecome, that Monsieur Malandain, who is a man worthy of credence,[8] mistook this cord for a pocketbook."

The peasant, furious, lifted his hand, spat at one side to attest his honor, repeating:

"It is nevertheless the truth of the good God, the sacred truth, M'sieu the Mayor. I repeat it on my soul and my salvation."

The mayor resumed:

"After picking up the object you stood like a stilt, looking a long while in the mud to see if any piece of money had fallen out."

The good old man choked with indignation and fear.

"How anyone can tell—how anyone can tell—such lies to take away an honest man's reputation! How can anyone—"

**Summary:** Maître Hauchecome picks up a piece of string. When he sees his enemy Maître Malandain notice his action, he feels embarrassed and tries to cover up what he was doing. Later, after a pocketbook has been lost on the same road, Maître Malandain accuses Maître Hauchecome of having found the pocketbook and hiding it.

---

**7. M'sieu** (mə syʉr'): Monsieur, a French title used like Mister or Sir.
**8. credence** (krēd' ns) *n.*: Belief.

There was no use in his protesting; nobody believed him. He was confronted with Monsieur Malandain, who repeated and maintained his affirmation. They abused each other for an hour. At his own request Maître Hauchecome was searched; nothing was found on him.

Prediction: Maître Hauchecome will try to prove his innocence.

Finally the mayor, very much perplexed, discharged him with the warning that he would consult the public prosecutor and ask for further orders.

The news had spread. As he left the mayor's office the old man was surrounded and questioned with a serious or bantering curiosity in which there was no indignation. He began to tell the story of the string. No one believed him. They laughed at him.

He went along, stopping his friends, beginning endlessly his statement and his protestations, showing his pockets turned inside out to prove that he had nothing.

They said:

"Old rascal, get out!"

Clarification: Maître Hauchecome does try to clear his name, but no one believes him.

And he grew angry, becoming exasperated, hot and distressed at not being believed, not knowing what to do and always repeating himself.

Night came. He must depart. He started on his way with three neighbors to whom he pointed out the place where he had picked up the bit of string, and all along the road he spoke of his adventure.

In the evening he took a turn in the village of Breaute in order to tell it to everybody. He only met with incredulity.

It made him ill at night.

The next day about one o'clock in the afternoon Marius Paumelle, a hired man in the employ of Maître Breton, husbandman[9] at Ymanville, returned the pocketbook and its contents to Maître Houlbreque of Manneville.

Prediction: Now his name will be cleared.

This man claimed to have found the object in the road, but not knowing how to read, he had carried it to the house and given it to his employer.

The news spread through the neighborhood. Maître Hauchecome was informed of it. He immediately went the circuit and began to recount his story completed by the happy climax. He was in triumph.

---

**9. husbandman** (huz′ bənd mən) *n*.: Farmer.

**ROAD TO SIN LE NOBLE**
*Jean Baptiste Corot*
Three Lions

"What grieved me so much was not the thing itself as the lying. There is nothing so shameful as to be placed under a cloud on account of a lie."

He talked of his adventure all day long; he told it on the highway to people who were passing by, in the shop to people who were there and to persons coming out of church the following Sunday. He stopped strangers to tell them about it. He was calm now, and yet something disturbed him without his knowing exactly what it was. People had the air of joking while they listened. They did not seem convinced. He seemed to feel that remarks were being made behind his back.

**Question:** Is Maître Hauchecome imagining things or *are* people talking behind his back?

On Tuesday of the next week he went to the market at Goderville, urged solely by the necessity he felt of discussing the case.

Malandain, standing at his door, began to laugh on seeing him pass. Why?

He approached a farmer from Crequetot who did not let him finish and, giving him a thump in the stomach, said to his face;

"You big rascal."

Then he turned his back on him.

Maître Hauchecome was confused; why was he called a big rascal?

When he was seated at the table in Jourdain's tavern he commenced to explain "the affair."

A horse dealer from Monvilliers called to him:

"Come, come, old sharper, that's an old trick; I know all about your piece of string!"

Hauchecome stammered:

"But since the pocketbook was found."

But the other man replied:

"Shut up, papa, there is one that finds and there is one that reports. At any rate you are mixed with it."

**Clarification:** His name is not cleared. No one believes his story. People think he had a confederate return the pocketbook.

The peasant stood choking. He understood. They accused him of having had the pocketbook returned by a confederate, by an accomplice.

He tried to protest. All the table began to laugh.

He could not finish his dinner and went away in the midst of jeers.

He went home ashamed and indignant, choking with anger and confusion, the more dejected that he was capable, with his Norman cunning, of doing what they had accused him of and even boasting of it as of a good turn. His innocence to him, in a confused way, was impossible to prove, as his sharpness was known. And he was stricken to the heart by the injustice of the suspicion.

Then he began to recount the adventures again, prolonging his history every day, adding each time new reasons, more energetic protestations, more solemn oaths which he imagined and prepared in his hours of solitude, his whole mind given up to the story of the string. He was believed so much the less as his defense was more complicated and his arguing more subtle.[10]

"Those are lying excuses," they said behind his back.

He felt it, consumed his heart over it and wore himself out with useless efforts. He wasted away before their very eyes.

The wags now made him tell about the string to amuse them, as they make a soldier who has been on a campaign tell about his battles. His mind, touched to the depth, began to weaken.

Toward the end of December he took to his bed.

He died in the first days of January, and in the delirium[11] of his death struggles he kept claiming his innocence, reiterating:

"A piece of string, a piece of string—look—here it is, M'sieu the Mayor."

**Pulling It Together:** A man falsely accused becomes sick at heart when unable to clear his name and dies protesting his innocence.

---

**10. subtle** (sut′ ′l) *adj.*: Showing fine distinctions in meaning.
**11. delirium** (di lir′ ē əm) *n.*: State of extreme mental confusion.

**Guy de Maupassant** (1850-1893) was born in Normandy, a region along the English Channel in northwestern France. Gustave Flaubert, the famous French novelist, was de Maupassant's godfather. From Flaubert, de Maupassant learned much about writing. De Maupassant became one of the world's best short story writers. Writing in a simple, realistic style, de Maupassant often displayed a pessimistic view of life. In only ten years, he wrote over 300 stories, 6 novels, and 200 essays and articles.

## THINKING ABOUT THE SELECTION
### Recalling

1. Why does Maître Hauchecome pick up the string? Why does he disguise his action?
2. Explain why Maître Hauchecome is accused of finding the wallet.
3. Explain why Maître Hauchecome's name is not cleared, even after the wallet is returned.

### Interpreting

4. Describe Maître Hauchecome and Maître Malandain's relationship. How does this relationship help bring about Maître Hauchecome's problem?
5. Describe the characteristics of the people of Goderville. How do the characteristics bring about Maître Hauchecome's problem?
6. Describe Maître Hauchecome's chief characteristics. In what way do his characteristics prevent people from believing his story?

### Applying

7. Maître Hauchecome is upset because his reputation has been destroyed. Discuss why people put such value in their reputations.

## ANALYZING LITERATURE
### Understanding Paradox

A **paradox** is a statement that appears to be contradictory but in fact reveals an unexpected truth. For example, when George Bernard Shaw wrote that "youth is wasted on the young," he was presenting a paradox. The wisdom of age does help you appreciate the advantages of youth. By presenting what sounds impossible but is true, writers show the complexity of life.

First explain how the passage below presents a paradox. Then explain how it reveals a truth about life.

He went home ashamed and indignant, choking with anger and confusion, the more dejected that he was capable, with his Norman cunning, of doing what they had accused him of and even boasting of it as a good turn. His innocence to him, in a confused way, was impossible to prove, as his sharpness was known.

## CRITICAL THINKING AND READING
### Understanding Stereotypes

A **stereotype** is a generalization about a whole group of people that does not allow for individual differences. When Maupassant writes, "Maitre Hauchecome, economical like a true Norman, thought that everything useful ought to be picked up. . . . ," he is repeating a stereotype about the natives of Normandy, France.
1. Find one other stereotype about Normans that Maupassant includes in this story.
2. Explain why stereotypes in real life can be dangerous.

## UNDERSTANDING LANGUAGE
### Using Word Roots

The word *reputation* is based on the Latin word *putare,* meaning "to think." Your reputation consists of what others *think* about you. The word root *put* from *putare* gives us many other English words. Explain how each word below relates to the idea of thinking.
1. repute 2. reputed 3. dispute 4. putative

## THINKING AND WRITING
### Writing an Account

Imagine that you are a police inspector assigned to the case of the missing wallet. First list everything you know about the case based on the eye witness account of Maître Malandain and the testimony of Maître Hauchecome. Then write a report of the case relating the details and drawing your own conclusion based on these details. When you revise make sure you have recounted only the details you would have in your possession and that the conclusion you have drawn from these details is logical.

# Plot

**REGATTAS AT ARGENTEUIL, 1875**
*Claude Monet*
*Paris, Louvre/Giraudon/Art Resource*

## Contents of the Dead Man's Pocket

**Jack Finney** (1911–    ) was born in Milwaukee, Wisconsin. Finney has worked in advertising and in journalism in addition to writing fiction. In 1956 one of Finney's science-fiction stories was made into the movie *The Invasion of the Body Snatchers.* In most of his work, Finney creates suspense and makes his readers experience terror through his portrayal of the everyday world. This is the method he uses in "Contents of the Dead Man's Pocket."

**Plot**

The **plot** of a story is a series of related events moving from a problem to a solution. A plot often begins with **exposition,** which presents the characters and the situation, including the **conflict.** The conflict, the source of tension in a story, is the struggle between opposing forces. Tension builds to a **climax,** or turning point of this conflict. Following the climax, the **resolution** shows how the problems are worked out. The plot may also have **complications,** events that stand in the way of resolving the conflict. In "Contents of the Dead Man's Pocket," Tom faces a series of complications as he tries to complete one simple but dangerous task.

**Look For**

Ambition is usually considered a positive quality, but in this short story, Tom's ambition leads him into a terrifying situation. As you read the story, feel the many moments of tension. Try to decide at which moment the story reaches its climax.

**Writing**

In this story Tom becomes very frightened. Freewrite about how fear can affect a person physically and emotionally.

**Vocabulary**

Knowing the following words will help you as you read "Contents of the Dead Man's Pocket."

**convoluted** (kän və lo͞ot′ id) *adj.:* Intricate; twisted (p. 17)

**grimace** (gri mās′) *n.:* A twisted facial expression (p. 20)

**deftness** (deft′ nis) *adj.:* Skillfulness (p. 20)

**imperceptibly** (im pər sep′ tə blē) *adv.:* In such a slight way as to be almost unnoticeable (p. 21)

**reveling** (rev′ 'l iŋ) *v.:* Taking great pleasure in (p. 23)

**interminable** (in tur′ mi nə b'l) *adj.:* Seemingly endless (p. 24)

# Contents of the
# Dead Man's Pocket

## Jack Finney

At the little living-room desk Tom Benecke rolled two sheets of flimsy[1] and a heavier top sheet, carbon paper sandwiched between them, into his portable. *Interoffice Memo,* the top sheet was headed, and he typed tomorrow's date just below this; then he glanced at a creased yellow sheet, covered with his own handwriting, beside the typewriter. "Hot in here," he muttered to himself. Then, from the short hallway at his back, he heard the muffled clang of wire coat hangers in the bedroom closet, and at this reminder of what his wife was doing he thought: Hot, no—guilty conscience.

He got up, shoving his hands into the back pockets of his gray wash slacks, stepped to the living-room window beside the desk and stood breathing on the glass, watching the expanding circlet of mist, staring down through the autumn night at Lexington Avenue,[2] eleven stories below. He was a tall, lean, dark-haired young man in a pullover sweater, who looked as though he had played not football, probably, but basketball in college. Now he placed the heels of his hands against the top edge of the lower window frame and shoved upward. But as usual the window didn't budge, and he had to lower his hands and then shoot them hard upward to jolt the window open a few inches. He dusted his hands, muttering.

But still he didn't begin his work. He crossed the room to the hallway entrance and, leaning against the doorjamb, hands shoved into his back pockets again, he

---

**1. flimsy** (flim′ zē) *n.*: Thin typing paper for making carbon copies.
**2. Lexington Avenue:** A major avenue on New York City's East Side.

called, "Clare?" When his wife answered, he said, "Sure you don't mind going alone?"

"No." Her voice was muffled, and he knew her head and shoulders were in the bedroom closet. Then the tap of her high heels sounded on the wood floor and she appeared at the end of the little hallway, wearing a slip, both hands raised to one ear, clipping on an earring. She smiled at him—a slender, very pretty girl with light brown, almost blonde, hair—her prettiness emphasized by the pleasant nature that showed in her face. "It's just that I hate you to miss this movie; you wanted to see it too."

"Yeah, I know." He ran his fingers through his hair. "Got to get this done though."

She nodded, accepting this. Then, glancing at the desk across the living room, she said, "You work too much, though, Tom —and too hard."

He smiled. "You won't mind though, will you, when the money comes rolling in and I'm known as the Boy Wizard of Wholesale Groceries?"

"I guess not." She smiled and turned back toward the bedroom.

Tom sat at his desk again; then a few moments later Clare appeared, dressed and ready to leave. "Just after seven," she said. "I can make the beginning of the first feature."

He walked to the front-door closet to help her on with her coat. He kissed her then and, for an instant, holding her close, smelling the perfume she had used, he was tempted to go with her; it was not actually true that he had to work tonight, though he very much wanted to. This was his own project, unannounced as yet in his office, and it could be postponed. But then they won't see it till Monday, he thought once again, and if I give it to the boss tomorrow he

might read it over the weekend . . . "Have a good time," he said aloud. He opened the door for her, feeling the air from the building hallway, smelling faintly of floor wax, stream gently past his face.

He watched her walk down the hall, flicked a hand in response as she waved, and then he started to close the door, but it resisted for a moment. As the door opening narrowed, the current of warm air from the hallway, channeled through this smaller opening now, suddenly rushed past him with accelerated force. Behind him he heard the slap of the window curtains against the wall and the sound of paper fluttering from his desk, and he had to push to close the door.

Turning, he saw a sheet of white paper drifting to the floor in a series of arcs, and another sheet, yellow, moving toward the window, caught in the dying current flowing through the narrow opening. As he watched, the paper struck the bottom edge of the window and hung there for an instant, plastered against the glass and wood. Then as the moving air stilled completely the curtains swinging back from the wall to hang free again, he saw the yellow sheet drop to the window ledge and slide over out of sight.

He ran across the room, grasped the bottom edge of the window and tugged, staring through the glass. He saw the yellow sheet, dimly now in the darkness outside, lying on the ornamental ledge a yard below the window. Even as he watched, it was moving, scraping slowly along the ledge, pushed by the breeze that pressed steadily against the building wall. He heaved on the window with all his strength and it shot open with a bang, the window weight rattling in the casing. But the paper was past his reach and, leaning out into the night, he watched it scud steadily along the ledge to the south, half plastered against the building wall. Above the muffled sound of the street traffic far below, he could hear the dry scrape of its movement, like a leaf on the pavement.

The living room of the next apartment to the south projected a yard or more farther out toward the street than this one; because of this the Beneckes paid seven and a half dollars less rent than their neighbors. And now the yellow sheet, sliding along the stone ledge, nearly invisible in the night, was stopped by the projecting blank wall of the next apartment. It lay motionless, then, in the corner formed by the two walls—a good five yards away, pressed firmly against the ornate corner ornament of the ledge, by the breeze that moved past Tom Benecke's face.

He knelt at the window and stared at the yellow paper for a full minute or more, waiting for it to move, to slide off the ledge and fall, hoping he could follow its course to the street, and then hurry down in the elevator and retrieve it. But it didn't move, and then he saw that the paper was caught firmly between a projection of the convoluted corner ornament and the ledge. He thought about the poker from the fireplace, then the broom, then the mop—discarding each thought as it occurred to him. There was nothing in the apartment long enough to reach that paper.

It was hard for him to understand that he actually had to abandon it—it was ridiculous—and he began to curse. Of all the papers on his desk, why did it have to be this one in particular! On four long Saturday afternoons he had stood in supermarkets counting the people who passed certain displays, and the results were scribbled on that yellow sheet. From stacks of trade publications, gone over page by page in snatched half hours at work and during evenings at home, he had copied facts, quotations, and figures onto that sheet. And he had carried it with him to the Public Library on Fifth Avenue, where he'd spent a dozen lunch hours and early evenings adding more. All were needed to support and lend authority to his idea for a new grocery-store display method; without them his idea was a mere opinion. And there they all lay, in his own improvised shorthand—countless hours of work—out there on the ledge.

For many seconds he believed he was going to abandon the yellow sheet, that there was nothing else to do. The work could be duplicated. But it would take two months, and the time to present this idea was *now*, for use in the spring displays. He struck his fist on the window ledge. Then he shrugged. Even though his plan were adopted, he told himself, it wouldn't bring him a raise in pay—not immediately, anyway, or as a direct result. It won't bring me a promotion either, he argued—not of itself.

But just the same, and he couldn't escape the thought, this and other independent projects, some already done and others planned for the future, would gradually mark him out from the score of other young men in his company. They were the way to change from a name on the payroll to a name in the minds of the company officials. They were the beginning of the long, long climb to where he was determined to be, at the very top. And he knew he was going out there in the darkness, after the yellow sheet fifteen feet beyond his reach.

By a kind of instinct, he instantly began making his intention acceptable to himself by laughing at it. The mental picture of himself sidling along the ledge outside was absurd—it was actually comical—and he smiled. He imagined himself describing it; it would make a good story at the office and, it occurred to him, would add a special interest and importance to his memorandum, which would do it no harm at all.

To simply go out and get his paper was an easy task—he could be back here with it in less than two minutes—and he knew he wasn't deceiving himself. The ledge, he saw, measuring it with his eye, was about as wide as the length of his shoe, and perfectly flat. And every fifth row of brick in the face of the building, he remembered—leaning out, he verified this—was indented half an inch, enough for the tips of his fingers, enough to maintain balance easily. It occurred to him that if this ledge and wall were only a yard aboveground—as he knelt at the window staring out, this thought was the final confirmation of his intention—he could move along the ledge indefinitely.

On a sudden impulse, he got to his feet, walked to the front closet and took out an old tweed jacket; it would be cold outside. He put it on and buttoned it as he crossed the room rapidly toward the open window. In the back of his mind he knew he'd better hurry and get this over with before he thought too much, and at the window he didn't allow himself to hesitate.

He swung a leg over the sill, then felt for and found the ledge a yard below the window with his foot. Gripping the bottom of the window frame very tightly and carefully, he slowly ducked his head under it, feeling on his face the sudden change from the warm air of the room to the chill outside. With infinite care he brought out his other leg, his mind concentrating on what he was doing. Then he slowly stood erect. Most of the putty, dried out and brittle, had dropped off the bottom edging of the window frame, he found, and the flat wooden edging provided a good gripping surface, a half inch or more deep, for the tips of his fingers.

Now, balanced easily and firmly, he stood on the ledge outside in the slight, chill breeze, eleven stories above the street, staring into his own lighted apartment, odd and different-seeming now.

First his right hand, then his left, he carefully shifted his fingertip grip from the puttyless window edging to an indented row of bricks directly to his right. It was hard to take the first shuffling sideways step then —to make himself move—and the fear stirred in his stomach, but he did it, again by not allowing himself time to think. And now—with his chest, stomach, and the left side of his face pressed against the rough cold brick—his lighted apartment was suddenly gone, and it was much darker out here than he had thought.

Without pause he continued—right foot, left foot, right foot, left—his shoe soles shuffling and scraping along the rough stone, never lifting from it, fingers sliding along the exposed edging of brick. He moved on the balls of his feet, heels lifted slightly; the ledge was not quite as wide as he'd expected. But leaning slightly inward toward the face of the building and pressed against it, he could feel his balance firm and secure, and moving along the ledge was quite as easy as he had thought it would be. He could hear the buttons of his jacket scraping steadily along the rough bricks and feel them catch momentarily, tugging a little, at each mortared crack. He simply did not permit himself to look down, though the compulsion to do so never left him; nor did he allow himself actually to think. Mechanically—right foot, left foot, over and again—he shuffled along crabwise, watching the projecting wall ahead loom steadily closer . . .

Then he reached it, and, at the corner —he'd decided how he was going to pick up the paper—he lifted his right foot and placed it carefully on the ledge that ran along the projecting wall at a right angle to the ledge on which his other foot rested. And now, facing the building, he stood in the corner formed by the two walls, one foot on the ledging of each, a hand on the shoulder-high indentation of each wall. His forehead was pressed directly into the corner against the cold bricks, and now he carefully lowered first one hand, then the other, perhaps a foot farther down, to the next indentation in the rows of bricks.

Very slowly, sliding his forehead down the trough of the brick corner and bending his knees, he lowered his body toward the paper lying between his outstretched feet. Again he lowered his fingerholds another

foot and bent his knees still more, thigh muscles taut, his forehead sliding and bumping down the brick V. Half squatting now, he dropped his left hand to the next indentation and then slowly reached with his right hand toward the paper between his feet.

He couldn't quite touch it, and his knees now were pressed against the wall; he could bend them no farther. But by ducking his head another inch lower, the top of his head now pressed against the bricks, he lowered his right shoulder and his fingers had the paper by a corner, pulling it loose. At the same instant he saw, between his legs and

far below, Lexington Avenue stretched out for miles ahead.

He saw, in that instant, the Loew's theater sign, blocks ahead past Fiftieth Street: the miles of traffic signals, all green now; the lights of cars and street lamps; countless neon signs; and the moving black dots of people. And a violent instantaneous explosion of absolute terror roared through him. For a motionless instant he saw himself externally—bent practically double, balanced on this narrow ledge, nearly half his body projecting out above the street far below—and he began to tremble violently, panic flaring through his mind and muscles, and he felt the blood rush from the surface of his skin.

In the fractional moment before horror paralyzed him, as he stared between his legs at that terrible length of street far beneath him, a fragment of his mind raised his body in a spasmodic jerk to an upright position again, but so violently that his head scraped hard against the wall, bouncing off it, and his body swayed outward to the knife edge of balance, and he very nearly plunged backward and fell. Then he was leaning far into the corner again, squeezing and pushing into it, not only his face but his chest and stomach, his back arching; and his fingertips clung with all the pressure of his pulling arms to the shoulder-high half-inch indentation in the bricks.

He was more than trembling now; his whole body was racked with a violent shuddering beyond control, his eyes squeezed so tightly shut it was painful, though he was past awareness of that. His teeth were exposed in a frozen grimace, the strength draining like water from his knees and calves. It was extremely likely, he knew, that he would faint, to slump down along the wall, his face scraping, and then drop backward, a limp weight, out into nothing. And to save his life he concentrated on holding onto consciousness, drawing deliberate deep breaths of cold air into his lungs, fighting to keep his senses aware.

Then he knew that he would not faint, but he could neither stop shaking nor open his eyes. He stood where he was, breathing deeply, trying to hold back the terror of the glimpse he had had of what lay below him; and he knew he had made a mistake in not making himself stare down at the street, getting used to it and accepting it, when he had first stepped out onto the ledge.

It was impossible to walk back. He simply could not do it. He couldn't bring himself to make the slightest movement. The strength was gone from his legs; his shivering hands—numb, cold and desperately rigid—had lost all deftness; his easy ability to move and balance was gone. Within a step or two, if he tried to move, he knew that he would stumble clumsily and fall.

Seconds passed, with the chill faint wind pressing the side of his face, and he could hear the toned-down volume of the street traffic far beneath him. Again and again it slowed and then stopped, almost to silence; then presently, even this high, he would hear the click of the traffic signals and the subdued roar of the cars starting up again. During a lull in the street sounds, he called out. Then he was shouting *"Help!"* so loudly it rasped his throat. But he felt the steady pressure of the wind, moving between his face and the blank wall, snatch up his cries as he uttered them, and he knew they must sound directionless and distant. And he remembered how habitually, here in New York, he himself heard and ignored shouts in the night. If anyone heard him, there was no sign of it, and presently Tom Benecke knew he had to try moving; there was nothing else he could do.

Eyes squeezed shut, he watched scenes in his mind like scraps of motion-picture film—he could not stop them. He saw himself stumbling suddenly sideways as he crept along the ledge and saw his upper body arc outward, arms flailing. He saw a dangling shoestring caught between the ledge and the sole of his other shoe, saw a foot start to move, to be stopped with a jerk, and felt his balance leaving him. He saw himself falling with a terrible speed as his body revolved in the air, knees clutched tight to his chest, eyes squeezed shut, moaning softly.

Out of utter necessity, knowing that any of these thoughts might be reality in the very next seconds, he was slowly able to shut his mind against every thought but what he now began to do. With fear-soaked slowness, he slid his left foot an inch or two toward his own impossibly distant window. Then he slid the fingers of his shivering left hand a corresponding distance. For a moment he could not bring himself to lift his right foot from one ledge to the other; then he did it, and became aware of the harsh exhalation of air from his throat and realized that he was panting. As his right hand, then, began to slide along the brick edging, he was astonished to feel the yellow paper pressed to the bricks underneath his stiff fingers, and he uttered a terrible, abrupt bark that might have been a laugh or a moan. He opened his mouth and took the paper in his teeth, pulling it out from under his fingers.

By a kind of trick—by concentrating his entire mind on first his left foot, then his left hand, then the other foot, then the other hand—he was able to move, almost imperceptibly, trembling steadily, very nearly without thought. But he could feel the terrible strength of the pent-up horror on just the other side of the flimsy barrier he had erected in his mind; and he knew that if it broke through he would lose this thin artificial control of his body.

During one slow step he tried keeping his eyes closed; it made him feel safer, shutting him off a little from the fearful reality of where he was. Then a sudden rush of giddiness swept over him and he had to open his eyes wide, staring sideways at the cold rough brick and angled lines of mortar, his cheek tight against the building. He kept his eyes open then, knowing that if he once let them flick outward, to stare for an instant at the lighted windows across the street, he would be past help.

He didn't know how many dozens of tiny sidling steps he had taken, his chest, belly, and face pressed to the wall; but he knew the slender hold he was keeping on his mind and body was going to break. He had a sudden mental picture of his apartment on just the other side of this wall—warm, cheerful, incredibly spacious. And he saw himself striding through it, lying down on the floor on his back, arms spread wide, reveling in its unbelievable security. The impossible remoteness of this utter safety, the contrast between it and where he now stood, was more than he could bear. And the barrier broke then, and the fear of the awful height he stood on coursed through his nerves and muscles.

A fraction of his mind knew he was going to fall, and he began taking rapid blind steps with no feeling of what he was doing, sidling with a clumsy desperate swiftness, fingers scrabbling along the brick, almost hopelessly resigned to the sudden backward pull and swift motion outward and down. Then his moving left hand slid onto not brick but sheer emptiness, an impossible gap in the face of the wall, and he stumbled.

His right foot smashed into his left anklebone; he staggered sideways, began falling, and the claw of his hand cracked against glass and wood, slid down it, and his fingertips were pressed hard on the puttyless edging of his window. His right hand smacked gropingly beside it as he fell to his knees; and, under the full weight and direct downward pull of his sagging body, the open window dropped shudderingly in its frame till it closed and his wrists struck the sill and were jarred off.

For a single moment he knelt, knee bones against stone on the very edge of the ledge, body swaying and touching nowhere else, fighting for balance. Then he lost it, his shoulders plunging backward, and he flung his arms forward, his hands smashing against the window casing on either side; and—his body moving backward—his fingers clutched the narrow wood stripping of the upper pane.

For an instant he hung suspended between balance and falling, his fingertips pressed onto the quarter-inch wood strips. Then, with utmost delicacy, with a focused concentration of all his senses, he increased even further the strain on his fingertips hooked to these slim edgings of wood. Elbows slowly bending, he began to draw the full weight of his upper body forward, knowing that the instant his fingers slipped off these quarter-inch strips he'd plunge backward and be falling. Elbows imperceptibly bending, body shaking with the strain, the sweat starting from his forehead in great sudden drops, he pulled, his entire being and thought concentrated in his fingertips. Then suddenly, the strain slackened and ended, his chest touching the window sill, and he was kneeling on the ledge, his forehead pressed to the glass of the closed window.

Dropping his palms to the sill, he stared into his living room—at the red-brown davenport across the room, and a magazine he had left there; at the pictures on the walls and the gray rug; the entrance to the hallway; and at his papers, typewriter and desk, not two feet from his nose. All was as he had left it—this was past all belief—only a few minutes before.

His head moved, and in faint reflection from the glass before him he saw the yellow paper clenched in his front teeth. Lifting a hand from the sill he took it from his mouth; the moistened corner parted from the paper, and he spat it out.

For a moment, in the light from the living room, he stared wonderingly at the yellow sheet in his hand and then crushed it into the side pocket of his jacket.

He couldn't open the window. It had been pulled not completely closed, but its lower edge was below the level of the outside sill; there was no room to get his fingers underneath it. Between the upper sash and the lower was a gap not wide enough —reaching up, he tried—to get his fingers into; he couldn't push it open. The upper window panel, he knew from long experience, was impossible to move, frozen tight with dried paint.

Very carefully observing his balance, the fingertips of his left hand again hooked to the narrow stripping of the window casing, he drew back his right hand, palm facing the glass, and then struck the glass with the heel of his hand.

His arm rebounded from the pane, his body tottering, and he knew he didn't dare strike a harder blow.

But in the security and relief of his new position, he simply smiled; with only a sheet of glass between him and the room just before him, it was not possible that there wasn't a way past it. Eyes narrowing, he thought for a few moments about what to do. Then his eyes widened, for nothing occurred to him. But still he felt calm: the trembling, he realized, had stopped. At the back of his mind there still lay the thought that once he was again in his home, he could give release to his feelings. He actually *would* lie on the

floor, rolling, clenching tufts of the rug in his hands. He would literally run across the room, free to move as he liked, jumping on the floor, testing and reveling in its absolute security, letting the relief flood through him, draining the fear from his mind and body. His yearning for this was astonishingly intense, and somehow he understood that he had better keep this feeling at bay.

He took a half dollar from his pocket and struck it against the pane, but without any hope that the glass would break and with very little disappointment when it did not. After a few moments of thought he drew his leg up onto the ledge and picked loose the knot of his shoelace. He slipped off the shoe and, holding it across the instep, drew back his arm as far as he dared and struck the leather heel against the glass. The pane rattled, but he knew he'd been a long way from breaking it. His foot was cold and he slipped the shoe back on. He shouted again, experimentally, and then once more, but there was no answer.

The realization suddenly struck him that he might have to wait here till Clare came home, and for a moment the thought was funny. He could see Clare opening the front door, withdrawing her key from the lock, closing the door behind her, and then glancing up to see him crouched on the other side of the window. He could see her rush across the room, face astounded and frightened, and hear himself shouting instructions: "Never mind how I got here! Just open the wind—" She couldn't open it, he remembered, she'd never been able to; she'd always had to call him. She'd have to get the building superintendent or a neighbor, and he pictured himself smiling and answering their questions as he climbed in. "I just wanted to get a breath of fresh air, so—"

He couldn't possibly wait here till Clare came home. It was the second feature she'd wanted to see, and she'd left in time to see the first. She'd be another three hours or—He glanced at his watch; Clare had been gone eight minutes. It wasn't possible, but only eight minutes ago he had kissed his wife goodbye. She wasn't even at the theater yet!

It would be four hours before she could possibly be home, and he tried to picture himself kneeling out here, fingertips hooked to these narrow strippings, while first one movie, preceded by a slow listing of credits, began, developed, reached its climax and then finally ended. There'd be a newsreel next, maybe, and then an animated cartoon, and then interminable scenes from coming pictures. And then, once more, the beginning of a full-length picture—while all the time he hung out here in the night.

He might possibly get to his feet, but he was afraid to try. Already his legs were cramped, his thigh muscles tired; his knees hurt, his feet felt numb and his hands were stiff. He couldn't possibly stay out here for four hours, or anywhere near it. Long before that his legs and arms would give out; he would be forced to try changing his position often—stiffly, clumsily, his coordination and strength gone—and he would fall. Quite realistically, he knew that he would fall; no one could stay out here on this ledge for four hours.

A dozen windows in the apartment building across the street were lighted. Looking over his shoulder, he could see the top of a man's head behind the newspaper

he was reading; in another window he saw the blue-gray flicker of a television screen. No more than twenty-odd yards from his back were scores of people, and if just one of them would walk idly to his window and glance out. . . . For some moments he stared over his shoulder at the lighted rectangles, waiting. But no one appeared. The man reading his paper turned a page and then continued his reading. A figure passed another of the windows and was immediately gone.

In the inside pocket of his jacket he found a little sheaf of papers, and he pulled one out and looked at it in the light from the living room. It was an old letter, an advertisement of some sort; his name and address, in purple ink, were on a label pasted to the envelope. Gripping one end of the envelope in his teeth, he twisted it into a tight curl. From his shirt pocket he brought out a book of matches. He didn't dare let go the casing with both hands, but, with the twist of paper in his teeth, he opened the matchbook with his free hand; then he bent one of the matches in two without tearing it from the folder, its red-tipped end now touching the striking surface. With his thumb, he rubbed the red tip across the striking area.

He did it again, then again, and still again, pressing harder each time, and the match suddenly flared, burning his thumb. But he kept it alight, cupping the matchbook in his hand and shielding it with his body. He held the flame to the paper in his mouth till it caught. Then he snuffed out the match flame with his thumb and forefinger, careless of the burn, and replaced the book in his pocket. Taking the paper twist in his hand, he held it flame down, watching the flame crawl up the paper, till it flared bright. Then he held it behind him over the street, moving it from side to side, watching it over his shoulder, the flame flickering and guttering in the wind.

There were three letters in his pocket and he lighted each of them, holding each till the flame touched his hand and then dropping it to the street below. At one point, watching over his shoulder while the last of the letters burned, he saw the man across the street put down his paper and stand —even seeming, to Tom, to glance toward his window. But when he moved, it was only to walk across the room and disappear from sight.

There were a dozen coins in Tom Benecke's pocket and he dropped them, three or four at a time. But if they struck anyone, or if anyone noticed their falling, no one connected them with their source, and no one glanced upward.

His arms had begun to tremble from the steady strain of clinging to this narrow perch, and he did not know what to do now and was terribly frightened. Clinging to the window stripping with one hand, he again searched his pockets. But now—he had left his wallet on his dresser when he'd changed clothes—there was nothing left but the yellow sheet. It occurred to him irrelevantly that his death on the sidewalk below would be an eternal mystery; the window closed —why, how, and from where could he have fallen? No one would be able to identify his body for a time, either—the thought was somehow unbearable and increased his fear. All they'd find in his pockets would be the yellow sheet. *Contents of the dead man's pockets,* he thought, *one sheet of paper bearing penciled notations—incomprehensible.*

He understood fully that he might actually be going to die; his arms, maintaining his balance on the ledge, were trembling steadily now. And it occurred to him then with all the force of a revelation that, if he fell, all he was ever going to have out of life he would then, abruptly, have had. Nothing, then, could ever be changed; and nothing more—no least experience or pleasure —could ever be added to his life. He wished, then, that he had not allowed his wife to go off by herself tonight—and on similar nights. He thought of all the evenings he had spent away from her, working; and he regretted them. He thought wonderingly of his fierce ambition and of the direction his life had taken; he thought of the hours he'd spent by himself, filling the yellow sheet that had brought him out here. *Contents of the dead man's pockets,* he thought with sudden fierce anger, *a wasted life.*

He was simply not going to cling here till he slipped and fell; he told himself that now. There was one last thing he could try; he had been aware of it for some moments, refusing to think about it, but now he faced it. Kneeling here on the ledge, the fingertips of one hand pressed to the narrow strip of wood, he could, he knew, draw his other hand back a yard perhaps, fist clenched tight, doing it very slowly till he sensed the outer limit of balance, then, as hard as he was able from the distance, he could drive his fist forward against the glass. If it broke, his fist smashing through, he was safe; he might cut himself badly, and probably would, but with his arm inside the room, he would be secure. But if the glass did not break, the rebound, flinging his arm back, would topple him off the ledge. He was certain of that.

He tested his plan. The fingers of his left hand clawlike on the little stripping, he drew back his other fist until his body began teetering backward. But he had no leverage now—he could feel that there would be no force to his swing—and he moved his fist slowly forward till he rocked forward on his knees again and could sense that his swing would carry its greatest force. Glancing down, however, measuring the distance from his fist to the glass, he saw that it was less than two feet.

It occurred to him that he could raise his arm over his head, to bring it down against the glass. But, experimenting in slow motion, he knew it would be an awkward blow without the force of a driving punch, and not nearly enough to break the glass.

Facing the window, he had to drive a blow from the shoulder, he knew now, at a distance of less than two feet; and he did not know whether it would break through the heavy glass. It might; he could picture it happening, he could feel it in the nerves of his arm. And it might not; he could feel that too—feel his fist striking this glass and being instantaneously flung back by the unbreaking pane, feel the fingers of his other hand breaking loose, nails scraping along the casing as he fell.

He waited, arm drawn back, fist balled, but in no hurry to strike; this pause, he knew, might be an extension of his life. And to live even a few seconds longer, he felt, even out here on this ledge in the night, was infinitely better than to die a moment earlier than he had to. His arm grew tired, and he brought it down and rested it.

Then he knew that it was time to make the attempt. He could not kneel here hesitating indefinitely till he lost all courage to act, waiting till he slipped off the ledge. Again he drew back his arm, knowing this time that he would not bring it down till he struck. His elbow protruding over Lexington Avenue far below, the fingers of his other hand pressed down bloodlessly tight against the narrow stripping, he waited, feeling the sick tenseness and terrible excitement building. It grew and swelled toward the moment of action, his nerves tautening. He thought of Clare—just a wordless, yearning thought—and then drew his arm back just a bit more, fist so tight his fingers pained him, and knowing he was going to do it. Then with full power, with every last scrap of strength he could bring to bear, he shot his arm forward toward the glass, and he said, *"Clare!"*

He heard the sound, felt the blow, felt himself falling forward, and his hand closed on the living-room curtains, the shards and fragments of glass showering onto the floor. And then, kneeling there on the ledge, an arm thrust into the room up to the shoulder, he began picking away the protruding slivers and great wedges of glass from the window frame, tossing them in onto the rug. And, as he grasped the edges of the empty window frame and climbed into his home, he was grinning in triumph.

He did not lie down on the floor or run through the apartment, as he had promised himself; even in the first few moments it seemed to him natural and normal that he should be where he was. He simply turned to his desk, pulled the crumpled yellow sheet from his pocket and laid it down where it had been, smoothing it out; then he absently laid a pencil across it to weight it down. He shook his head wonderingly, and turned to walk toward the closet.

There he got out his topcoat and hat and, without waiting to put them on, opened the front door and stepped out, to go find his wife. He turned to pull the door closed and the warm air from the hall rushed through the narrow opening again. As he saw the yellow paper, the pencil flying, scooped off the desk and, unimpeded by the glassless window, sail out into the night and out of his life, Tom Benecke burst into laughter and then closed the door behind him.

## THINKING ABOUT THE SELECTION

### Recalling

1. Why does Tom go out on the ledge?
2. How is Tom's journey back different from the one to the corner of the ledge?
3. Describe the progression of Tom's thoughts as he attempts to return to his apartment.
4. How does Tom succeed in getting back into his apartment?

### Interpreting

5. Explain what the paper that flew out the window represents to Tom.
6. Explain how Tom's thoughts and feelings affect his physical ability to return to his apartment and therefore increase the tension.
7. Contrast Tom's attitude at the beginning of the story with his attitude at the end.
8. At the end of this story, why does Tom laugh?
9. Why is this story called "Contents of the Dead Man's Pocket"?

### Applying

10. Tom's perilous position causes him to examine his life. Do you think people can ever truly change after examining their lives? Explain your answer.

## ANALYZING LITERATURE

### Understanding Plot

The **plot** of a story is a series of events related to the solution of a problem or conflict. The plot includes **exposition,** which introduces the situation; **conflict,** or the struggle between opposing forces; a **climax,** or turning point; and the **resolution,** or outcome. It may also include complications that delay the resolution of the conflict. Without complications, "Contents of the Dead Man's Pocket" would progress like this: Tom edged his way along the ledge, picked up the paper, and returned home safely.

Study the plot diagram below.

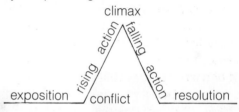

1. Describe the major conflict in the story.
2. What complicates the opening situation?
3. What is the moment of climax in the story?
4. Why does the story continue after Tom gets safely back into the apartment?

## UNDERSTANDING LANGUAGE

### Reading a Dictionary Entry

You can learn much more than just the meaning and spelling of a word from a dictionary. You can also find out how to pronounce a word, where the word comes from, and what part of speech it is.

Use your dictionary to answer the following questions.

1. Is the *ough* in *trough* usually pronounced like the *ough* in *rough, through,* or *cough*?
2. Which syllable in *spasmodic* is accented?
3. From what language does *absolute* come?

## THINKING AND WRITING

### Writing About Plot

A local book club is holding a contest to pick the best short story of the year. Write a statement to the nominating committee telling why you think "Contents of the Dead Man's Pocket" should (or should not) be a candidate for the award. Include an analysis of the plot, telling why it is special and why you were impressed (or not impressed) by it. When you revise your statement, make it as forceful and convincing as possible.

# GUIDE FOR READING

## The Monkey's Paw

**W. W. Jacobs** (1863–1943) was born in London, England, and lived as a child in a house on a Thames River dock. There, he had a chance to hear strange tales of foreign lands told by the passing seafarers. As an adult, Jacobs made use of this experience by writing strange tales of his own. Many of his stories artfully combine everyday life with elements of the supernatural. "The Monkey's Paw" is one such tale. First published in 1902, it was made into a successful play a year later.

### Suspense and Foreshadowing

**Suspense** is the quality of the story that keeps you reading to find out what will happen. Authors often use foreshadowing to help build suspense. **Foreshadowing** refers to the use of hints about what is going to happen. In "The Monkey's Paw," the hints are clear enough to let you know something frightening is in store but ambiguous enough to keep you guessing.

### Look For

As you read "The Monkey's Paw," look for hints that enable you to predict what will happen in the story.

### Writing

"The Monkey's Paw" is about having wishes granted. Some people say the worst thing that can happen to you is to have your wishes come true. Do you agree? Freewrite about how having a wish granted can be good or bad.

### Vocabulary

Knowing the following words will help you as you read "The Monkey's Paw."

**doughty** (dout′ ē) *adj.*: Brave; valiant (p. 30)

**talisman** (tal′ is mən) *n.*: Anything believed to have magical power (p. 32)

**antimacassar** (an′ ti mə kas′ ər) *n.*: A small cover on the arms or back of a chair or sofa to prevent soiling (p. 32)

**credulity** (krə dooʹ lə tē) *n.*: A tendency to believe too readily (p. 32)

**prosaic** (prō zā′ ik) *adj.*: Commonplace; ordinary (p. 33)

**avaricious** (av′ə rish′ əs) *adj.*: Greedy for riches (p. 33)

**bibulous** (bib′ yoo ləs) *adj.*: Given to drinking alcoholic beverages (p. 33)

**fusillade** (fyoo sə lād′) *n.*: Something that is like the rapid firing of many firearms (p. 38)

# The Monkey's Paw

## W. W. Jacobs

### I

Without, the night was cold and wet, but in the small parlor of Laburnam Villa the blinds were drawn and the fire burned brightly. Father and son were at chess, the former, who possessed ideas about the game involving radical changes, putting his king into such sharp and unnecessary perils that it even provoked comment from the white-haired old lady knitting placidly by the fire.

"Hark at the wind," said Mr. White, who, having seen a fatal mistake after it was too late, was amiably desirous of preventing his son from seeing it.

"I'm listening," said the latter, grimly surveying the board as he stretched out his hand. "Check."[1]

"I should hardly think that he'd come tonight," said his father, with his hand poised over the board.

"Mate,"[2] replied the son.

"That's the worst of living so far out," bawled Mr. White, with sudden and un-looked-for violence; "of all the beastly, slushy, out-of-the-way places to live in, this is the worst. Pathway's a bog, and the road's a torrent. I don't know what people are thinking about. I suppose because only two houses on the road are let, they think it doesn't matter."

"Never mind, dear," said his wife, soothingly; "perhaps you'll win the next one."

Mr. White looked up sharply, just in time to intercept a knowing glance between mother and son. The words died away on his lips, and he hid a guilty grin in his thin gray beard.

"There he is," said Herbert White, as the gate banged to loudly and heavy footsteps came toward the door.

The old man rose with hospitable haste, and opening the door, was heard condoling with the new arrival. The new arrival also condoled with himself, so that Mrs. White said, "Tut, tut!" and coughed gently as her husband entered the room, followed by a tall, burly man, beady of eye and rubicund of visage.[3]

"Sergeant Major Morris," he said, introducing him.

The sergeant major shook hands, and taking the proffered seat by the fire, watched contentedly while his host got out tumblers and stood a small copper kettle on the fire.

At the third glass his eyes got brighter, and he began to talk, the little family circle regarding with eager interest this visitor from distant parts, as he squared his broad shoulders in the chair and spoke of wild

---

**1. check** (c⁀hek) *n.*: A move in chess that threatens to capture the king.
**2. mate** (māt) *n.*: Checkmate, a chess move in which the king is captured and the game is over.

**3. rubicund** (roo′ bək ənd) **of visage** (viz′ ij): Having a red complexion.

scenes and doughty deeds; of wars and plagues and strange peoples.

"Twenty-one years of it," said Mr. White, nodding at his wife and son. "When he went away he was a slip of a youth in the warehouse. Now look at him."

"He don't look to have taken much harm," said Mrs. White, politely.

"I'd like to go to India myself," said the old man, "just to look round a bit, you know."

"Better where you are," said the sergeant major, shaking his head. He put down the empty glass, and sighing softly, shook it again.

"I should like to see those old temples and fakirs and jugglers," said the old man. "What was that you started telling me the other day about a monkey's paw or something, Morris?"

"Nothing," said the soldier, hastily. "Leastways nothing worth hearing."

"Monkey's paw?" said Mrs. White, curiously.

"Well, it's just a bit of what you might call magic, perhaps," said the sergeant major, offhandedly.

His three listeners leaned forward eagerly. The visitor absent-mindedly put his empty glass to his lips and then set it down again. His host filled it for him.

"To look at," said the sergeant major, fumbling in his pocket, "it's just an ordinary little paw, dried to a mummy."

He took something out of his pocket and proffered it. Mrs. White drew back with a grimace, but her son, taking it, examined it curiously.

"And what is there special about it?" inquired Mr. White as he took it from his son, and having examined it, placed it upon the table.

"It had a spell put on it by an old fakir," said the sergeant major, "a very holy man.

He wanted to show that fate ruled people's lives, and that those who interfered with it did so to their sorrow. He put a spell on it so that three separate men could each have three wishes from it."

His manner was so impressive that his hearers were conscious that their light laughter jarred somewhat.

"Well, why don't you have three, sir?" said Herbert White, cleverly.

The soldier regarded him in the way that middle age is wont to regard presumptuous youth. "I have," he said, quietly, and his blotchy face whitened.

"And did you really have the three wishes granted?" asked Mrs. White.

"I did," said the sergeant major, and his glass tapped against his strong teeth.

"And has anybody else wished?" persisted the old lady.

"The first man had his three wishes, yes," was the reply; "I don't know what the first two were, but the third was for death. That's how I got the paw."

His tones were so grave that a hush fell upon the group.

"If you've had your three wishes, it's no good to you now, then, Morris," said the old man at last. "What do you keep it for?"

The soldier shook his head. "Fancy, I suppose," he said, slowly. "I did have some idea of selling it, but I don't think I will. It has caused enough mischief already. Besides, people won't buy. They think it's a fairy tale; some of them, and those who do think anything of it want to try it first and pay me afterward."

"If you could have another three wishes," said the old man, eyeing him keenly, "would you have them?"

"I don't know," said the other. "I don't know."

He took the paw, and dangling it between his forefinger and thumb, suddenly

threw it upon the fire. White, with a slight cry, stooped down and snatched it off.

"Better let it burn," said the soldier, solemnly.

"If you don't want it, Morris," said the other, "give it to me."

"I won't," said his friend doggedly. "I threw it on the fire. If you keep it, don't blame me for what happens. Pitch it on the fire again, like a sensible man."

The other shook his head and examined

his new possession closely. "How do you do it?" he inquired.

"Hold it up in your right hand and wish aloud," said the sergeant major, "but I warn you of the consequences."

"Sounds like the *Arabian Nights*,"[4] said Mrs. White, as she rose and began to set the supper. "Don't you think you might wish for four pairs of hands for me?"

Her husband drew the talisman from pocket, and then all three burst into laughter as the sergeant major, with a look of alarm on his face, caught him by the arm. "If you must wish," he said, gruffly, "wish for something sensible."

Mr. White dropped it back in his pocket, and placing chairs, motioned his friend to the table. In the business of supper the talisman was partly forgotten, and afterward the three sat listening in an enthralled fashion to a second installment of the soldier's adventures in India.

"If the tale about the monkey's paw is not more truthful than those he has been telling us," said Herbert, as the door closed behind their guest, just in time for him to catch the last train, "we shan't make much out of it."

"Did you give him anything for it, Father?" inquired Mrs. White, regarding her husband closely.

"A trifle," said he, coloring slightly. "He didn't want it, but I made him take it. And he pressed me again to throw it away."

"Likely," said Herbert, with pretended horror. "Why, we're going to be rich, and famous and happy. Wish to be an emperor, Father, to begin with; then you can't be bossed around."

He darted round the table, pursued by the maligned Mrs. White armed with an antimacassar.

Mr. White took the paw from his pocket and eyed it dubiously. "I don't know what to wish for, and that's a fact," he said, slowly. "It seems to me I've got all I want."

"If you only cleared the house, you'd be quite happy, wouldn't you?" said Herbert, with his hand on his shoulder. "Well, wish for two hundred pounds,[5] then; that'll just do it."

His father, smiling shamefacedly at his own credulity, held up the talisman, as his son, with a solemn face somewhat marred by a wink at his mother, sat down at the piano and struck a few impressive chords.

"I wish for two hundred pounds," said the old man distinctly.

A fine crash from the piano greeted the words, interrupted by a shuddering cry from the old man. His wife and son ran toward him.

"It moved," he cried, with a glance of disgust at the object as it lay on the floor. "As I wished it twisted in my hand like a snake."

"Well, I don't see the money," said his son as he picked it up and placed it on the table, "and I bet I never shall."

"It must have been your fancy, Father," said his wife, regarding him anxiously.

He shook his head. "Never mind, though; there's no harm done, but it gave me a shock all the same."

They sat down by the fire again while the two men finished their pipes. Outside, the wind was higher than ever, and the old man started nervously at the sound of a door banging upstairs. A silence unusual and

---

**4. Arabian Nights:** A story collection from the ancient Near East.

**5. pounds** *n.*: English money.

depressing settled upon all three, which lasted until the old couple rose to retire for the night.

"I expect you'll find the cash tied up in a big bag in the middle of your bed," said Herbert, as he bade them good night, "and something horrible squatting up on top of the wardrobe watching you as you pocket your ill-gotten gains."

Herbert sat alone in the darkness, gazing at the dying fire, and seeing faces in it. The last face was so horrible and so simian[6] that he gazed at it in amazement. It got so vivid that, with a little uneasy laugh, he felt on the table for a glass containing a little water to throw over it. His hand grasped the monkey's paw, and with a little shiver he wiped his hand on his coat and went up to bed.

## II

In the brightness of the wintry sun next morning as it streamed over the breakfast table Herbert laughed at his fears. There was an air of prosaic wholesomeness about the room which it had lacked on the previous night, and the dirty, shriveled little paw was pitched on the sideboard with a carelessness which betokened no great belief in its virtues.

"I suppose all old soldiers are the same," said Mrs. White. "The idea of our listening to such nonsense! How could wishes be granted in these days? And if they could, how could two hundred pounds hurt you, Father?"

"Might drop on his head from the sky," said the frivolous Herbert.

---

6. **simian** (sim′ ē ən) *adj.*: Monkeylike.

"Morris said the things happened so naturally," said his father, "that you might if you so wished attribute it to coincidence."

"Well, don't break into the money before I come back," said Herbert, as he rose from the table. "I'm afraid it'll turn you into a mean, avaricious man, and we shall have to disown you."

His mother laughed, and following him to the door, watched him down the road, and, returning to the breakfast table, was very happy at the expense of her husband's credulity. All of which did not prevent her from scurrying to the door at the postman's knock, nor prevent her from referring somewhat shortly to retired sergeant majors of bibulous habits when she found that the post brought a tailor's bill.

"Herbert will have some more of his funny remarks, I expect, when he comes home," she said, as they sat at dinner.

"I dare say," said Mr. White, "but for all that, the thing moved in my hand; that I'll swear to."

"You thought it did," said the old lady soothingly.

"I say it did," replied the other. "There was no thought about it; I had just—What's the matter?"

His wife made no reply. She was watching the mysterious movements of a man outside, who, peering in an undecided fashion at the house, appeared to be trying to make up his mind to enter. In mental connection with the two hundred pounds, she noticed that the stranger was well dressed, and wore a silk hat of glossy newness. Three times he paused at the gate, and then walked on again. The fourth time he stood with his hand upon it, and then with sudden resolution flung it open and walked up the path. Mrs. White at the same moment placed her hands behind her, and hurriedly unfastening the strings of her apron, put that useful article of apparel beneath the cushion of her chair.

She brought the stranger, who seemed ill at ease, into the room. He gazed at her furtively, and listened in a preoccupied fashion as the old lady apologized for the appearance of the room, and her husband's coat, a garment which he usually reserved for the garden. She then waited patiently for him to broach his business, but he was at first strangely silent.

"I—was asked to call," he said at last, and stooped and picked a piece of cotton from his trousers. "I come from 'Maw and Meggins.'"

The old lady started. "Is anything the matter?" she asked, breathlessly. "Has anything happened to Herbert? What is it? What is it?"

Her husband interposed. "There, there, mother," he said, hastily. "Sit down, and don't jump to conclusions. You've not brought bad news, I'm sure, sir," and he eyed the other wistfully.

"I'm sorry—" began the visitor.

"Is he hurt?" demanded the mother, wildly.

The visitor bowed in assent. "Badly hurt," he said quietly, "but he is not in any pain."

"Oh, thank God!" said the old woman, clasping her hands. "Thank God for that! Thank—"

She broke off suddenly as the sinister meaning of the assurance dawned upon her and she saw the awful confirmation of her fears in the other's averted face. She caught her breath, and turning to her husband, laid her trembling old hand upon his. There was a long silence.

"He was caught in the machinery," said the visitor at length, in a low voice.

"Caught in the machinery," repeated Mr. White, in a dazed fashion, "yes."

He sat staring blankly out at the window, and taking his wife's hand between his own, pressed it as he had been wont to do in their old courting days nearly forty years before.

"He was the only one left to us," he said,

turning gently to the visitor. "It is hard."

The other coughed, and, rising, walked slowly to the window. "The firm wished me to convey their sincere sympathy with you in your great loss," he said, without looking round. "I beg that you will understand I am only their servant and merely obeying orders."

There was no reply; the old woman's face was white, her eyes staring, and her breath inaudible; on the husband's face was a look such as his friend the sergeant might have carried into his first action.

"I was to say that Maw and Meggins disclaim all responsibility," continued the other. "They admit no liability at all, but in consideration of your son's services they wish to present you with a certain sum as compensation."

Mr. White dropped his wife's hand, and rising to his feet, gazed with a look of horror at his visitor. His dry lips shaped the words, "How much?"

"Two hundred pounds," was the answer.

Unconscious of his wife's shriek, the old man smiled faintly, put out his hands like a sightless man, and dropped, a senseless heap, to the floor.

### III

In the huge new cemetery, some two miles distant, the old people buried their dead, and came back to a house steeped in shadow and silence. It was all over so quickly that at first they could hardly realize it, and remained in a state of expectation as though of something else to happen —something else which was to lighten this load, too heavy for old hearts to bear.

But the days passed, and expectation gave place to resignation—the hopeless resignation of the old, sometimes miscalled apathy. Sometimes they hardly exchanged a word, for now they had nothing to talk about, and their days were long to weariness.

It was about a week after that the old man, waking suddenly in the night, stretched out his hand and found himself alone. The room was in darkness, and the sound of subdued weeping came from the window. He raised himself in bed and listened.

"Come back," he said, tenderly. "You will be cold."

"It is colder for my son," said the old woman, and wept afresh.

The sound of her sobs died away on his ears. The bed was warm, and his eyes heavy with sleep. He dozed fitfully, and then slept until a sudden wild cry from his wife awoke him with a start.

*The paw!* she cried wildly. "The monkey's paw!"

He started up in alarm. "Where? Where is it? What's the matter?"

She came stumbling across the room toward him. "I want it," she said quietly. "You've not destroyed it?"

"It's in the parlor, on the bracket," he replied, marveling. "Why?"

She cried and laughed together, and bending over, kissed his cheek.

"I only just thought of it," she said hysterically. "Why didn't I think of it before? Why didn't *you* think of it?"

"Think of what?" he questioned.

"The other two wishes," she replied rapidly. "We've only had one."

"Was not that enough?" he demanded, fiercely.

"No," she cried triumphantly; "we'll have one more. Go down and get it quickly, and wish our boy alive again."

The man sat up in bed and flung the bedclothes from his quaking limbs. "You are mad!" he cried, aghast.

"Get it," she panted; "get it quickly, and wish—Oh, my boy, my boy!"

Her husband struck a match and lit the candle. "Get back to bed," he said unsteadily. "You don't know what you are saying."

"We had the first wish granted," said the old woman feverishly; "why not the second?"

"A coincidence," stammered the old man.

"Go and get it and wish," cried his wife, quivering with excitement.

The old man turned and regarded her, and his voice shook. "He has been dead ten days, and besides he—I would not tell you else, but—I could only recognize him by his clothing. If he was too terrible for you to see then, how now?"

"Bring him back," cried the old woman, and dragged him toward the door. "Do you think I fear the child I have nursed?"

He went down in the darkness, and felt his way to the parlor, and then to the mantelpiece. The talisman was in its place, and a horrible fear that the unspoken wish might bring his mutilated son before him ere he could escape from the room seized upon him, and he caught his breath as he found that he had lost the direction of the door. His brow cold with sweat, he felt his way round the table, and groped along the wall until he found himself in the small passage with the unwholesome thing in his hand.

Even his wife's face seemed changed as he entered the room. It was white and expectant, and to his fears seemed to have an unnatural look upon it. He was afraid of her.

*"Wish!"* she cried, in a strong voice.

"It is foolish and wicked," he faltered.

*"Wish!"* repeated his wife.

He raised his hand. "I wish my son alive again."

The talisman fell to the floor, and he regarded it fearfully. Then he sank trem-

bling into a chair as the old woman, with burning eyes, walked to the window and raised the blind.

He sat until he was chilled with the cold, glancing occasionally at the figure of the old woman peering through the window. The candle-end, which had burned below the rim of the china candlestick, was throwing pulsating shadows on the ceiling and walls, until, with a flicker larger than the rest, it expired. The old man, with an unspeakable sense of relief at the failure of the talisman, crept back to his bed, and a minute or two afterward the old woman came silently and apathetically beside him.

Neither spoke, but lay silently listening to the ticking of the clock. A stair creaked, and a squeaky mouse scurried noisily through the wall. The darkness was oppressive, and after lying for some time screwing up his courage, he took the box of matches, and striking one, went downstairs for a candle.

At the foot of the stairs the match went out, and he paused to strike another; and at the same moment a knock, so quiet and stealthy as to be scarcely audible, sounded on the front door.

The matches fell from his hand and spilled in the passage. He stood motionless, his breath suspended until the knock was repeated. Then he turned and fled swiftly back to his room, and closed the door behind him. A third knock sounded through the house.

"*What's that?*" cried the old woman, starting up.

"A rat," said the old man in shaking tones—"a rat. It passed me on the stairs."

His wife sat up in bed listening. A loud knock resounded through the house.

"It's Herbert!" she screamed. "It's Herbert!"

She ran to the door, but her husband was before her, and catching her by the arm, held her tightly.

"What are you going to do?" he whispered hoarsely.

"It's my boy; it's Herbert!" she cried, struggling mechanically. "I forgot it was two miles away. What are you holding me for? Let go. I must open the door."

"Don't let it in," cried the old man, trembling.

"You're afraid of your own son," she cried, struggling. "Let me go. I'm coming, Herbert; I'm coming."

There was another knock, and another. The old woman with a sudden wrench broke free and ran from the room. Her husband followed to the landing, and called after her appealingly as she hurried downstairs. He heard the chain rattle back and the bottom bolt drawn slowly and stiffly from the socket. Then the old woman's voice, strained and panting.

"The bolt," she cried, loudly. "Come down. I can't reach it."

But her husband was on his hands and knees groping wildly on the floor in search of the paw. If he could only find it before the thing outside got in. A perfect fusillade of knocks reverberated through the house, and he heard the scraping of a chair as his wife put it down in the passage against the door. He heard the creaking of the bolt as it came slowly back, and at the same moment he found the monkey's paw, and frantically breathed his third and last wish.

The knocking ceased suddenly, although the echoes of it were still in the house. He heard the chair drawn back and the door opened. A cold wind rushed up the staircase, and a long loud wail of disappointment and misery from his wife gave him courage to run down to her side, and then to the gate beyond. The street lamp flickering opposite shone on a quiet and deserted road.

## THINKING ABOUT THE SELECTION
### Recalling

1. According to the sergeant major, what power does the monkey's paw have?
2. In what way is Mr. White's first wish fulfilled?
3. What evidence from the story indicates that his other two wishes were fulfilled?

### Interpreting

4. How does the opening setting of the cold, wet night and the warm, cozy fire set the mood?
5. The sergeant major states that the wishes were granted so naturally that they seemed like coincidence. Explain the events of the story as coincidence.
6. Explain whether you think the events of the story prove the fakir's point that "fate ruled people's lives and those who interfered with it did so to their sorrow."

### Applying

7. Suppose someone gave you a talisman that would grant three wishes. After reading this story, what would you do?

## ANALYZING LITERATURE
### Understanding Suspense

**Suspense** is the quality of a story that keeps you reading to find out what will happen. In "The Monkey's Paw," the suspense arouses a feeling of dread as you wonder what terrible results Mr. White's wishes will have. Jacobs uses foreshadowing to build suspense.

Decide if each of these quotations from "The Monkey's Paw" is an example of foreshadowing. If so, explain how it helps build suspense.
1. "'If you keep it, don't blame me for what happens.'" (page 31)
2. "'Come back. . . . You will be cold.'" (page 36)
3. "'If he was too terrible for you to see then, how now?'" (page 36)

## CRITICAL THINKING AND READING
### Predicting Outcomes

As you read, you make predictions, or intelligent guesses, about what will happen next. At what point in the story did you first predict the following events, and what was the basis for your prediction?
1. Herbert is killed in an accident.
2. Mrs. White asks her husband to wish her son alive again.

## UNDERSTANDING LANGUAGE
### Choosing Meaning from Context

A word may have several meanings. The **context,** words and phrases around a word, can help you decide which meaning the author intended. Give the one meaning that best fits the context for the following italicized words.
1. ". . . putting his king into such *sharp* and unnecessary perils . . ." (page 29)
2. ". . . the old man . . . dropped, a *senseless* heap, to the floor." (page 35)
3. "The old woman with a sudden *wrench* broke free and ran from the room." (page 38)

## THINKING AND WRITING
### Writing About Mood

Suppose that you were asked to make suggestions for a television show based on "The Monkey's Paw." Write a memo to the director suggesting ways to create the proper mood. Suggest a location, the actors appropriate for each part, and music that will help create the mood. Give reasons for your choices. Revise to be sure your ideas are clear.

# GUIDE FOR READING

## Leiningen Versus the Ants

**Carl Stephenson** (1893–    ) was born in Germany and has lived there all his life. "Leiningen Versus the Ants" was first published in 1938, and it has been widely read ever since, appearing in numerous collections of short stories. According to Stephenson's literary agent, "Leiningen Versus the Ants" may be the only story that Stephenson will allow to be published during his lifetime.

### Internal and External Conflict

A short story generally contains a **conflict,** which is a struggle between opposing forces. A conflict can be internal or external. An **internal conflict** takes place within a character, as he or she struggles with two opposing thoughts, feelings, beliefs, or needs. An **external conflict** is one that occurs between two or more characters or between a character and a natural force.

### Look For

When man-eating ants threaten to take over his plantation, an official tells Leiningen, "They're not creatures you can fight—they're an elemental—an 'act of God!'" As you read, look for the ways in which Leiningen does fight the ants. Will he win?

### Writing

Imagine you have just learned that your community is in the path of man-eating ants. What would you do? Freewrite about steps you and your neighbors could take.

### Vocabulary

Knowing the following words will help you as you read "Leiningen Versus the Ants."

**saurians** (sôr´ ē əns) *n.*: Lizardlike animals (p. 41)

**pampas** (pam´ pəz) *n.*: Treeless plains in South America (p. 43)

**peons** (pē´ änz) *n.*: Laborers in Spanish America (p. 43)

**flout** (flout) *v.*: Show contempt for (p. 44)

**weir** (wir) *n.*: A low dam (p. 45)

**provender** (präv´ ən dər) *n.*: Food (p. 49)

**alluvium** (ə $\overline{oo}$´ vē əm) *n.*: Material such as sand or gravel deposited by moving water (p. 56)

**fomentations** (fō´ mən tā´ shəns) *n.*: Applications of warm, moist substances in the treatment of an injury (p. 56)

# Leiningen Versus the Ants

## Carl Stephenson

"Unless they alter their course, and there's no reason why they should, they'll reach your plantation in two days at the latest."

Leiningen sucked placidly at a cigar about the size of a corn cob and for a few seconds gazed without answering at the agitated District Commissioner. Then he took the cigar from his lips and leaned slightly forward. With his bristling gray hair, bulky nose, and lucid eyes, he had the look of an aging and shabby eagle.

"Decent of you," he murmured, "paddling all this way just to give me the tip. But you're pulling my leg, of course, when you say I must do a bunk. Why, even a herd of saurians couldn't drive me from this plantation of mine."

The Brazilian official threw up lean and lanky arms and clawed the air with wildly distended fingers. "Leiningen!" he shouted, "you're insane! They're not creatures you can fight—they're an elemental—an 'act of God!' Ten miles long, two miles wide—ants,

nothing but ants! And every single one of them a fiend from hell; before you can spit three times they'll eat a full-grown buffalo to the bones. I tell you if you don't clear out at once there'll be nothing left of you but a skeleton picked as clean as your own plantation."

Leiningen grinned. "Act of God, my eye! Anyway, I'm not going to run for it just because an elemental's on the way. And don't think I'm the kind of fathead who tries to fend off lightning with his fists, either. I use my intelligence, old man. With me, the brain isn't a second blind gut;[1] I know what it's there for. When I began this model farm and plantation three years ago, I took into account all that could conceivably happen to it. And now I'm ready for anything and everything—including your ants."

The Brazilian rose heavily to his feet. "I've done my best," he gasped. "Your obstinacy endangers not only yourself, but the lives of your four hundred workers. You don't know these ants!"

Leiningen accompanied him down to the river, where the government launch was moored. The vessel cast off. As it moved downstream, the exclamation mark neared the rail and began waving arms frantically. Long after the launch had disappeared round the bend, Leiningen thought he could still hear that dimming, imploring voice. "You don't know them, I tell you! *You don't know them!*"

But the reported enemy was by no means unfamiliar to the planter. Before he started work on his settlement, he had lived long enough in the country to see for himself the fearful devastations sometimes wrought by these ravenous insects in their campaigns for food. But since then he had planned measures of defense accordingly, and these, he was convinced, were in every way adequate to withstand the approaching peril.

Moreover, during his three years as planter, Leiningen had met and defeated drought, flood, plague, and all other "acts of God" which had come against him—unlike his fellow settlers in the district, who had made little or no resistance. This unbroken success he attributed solely to the observance of his lifelong motto: *The human brain needs only to become fully aware of its powers to conquer even the elements.* Dullards reeled senselessly and aimlessly into the abyss; cranks, however brilliant, lost their heads when circumstances suddenly altered or accelerated and ran into stone walls; sluggards drifted with the current until they were caught in whirlpools and dragged under. But such disasters, Leiningen contended, merely strengthened his argument that intelligence, directed aright, invariably makes man the master of his fate.

Yes, Leiningen had always known how to grapple with life. Even here, in this Brazilian wilderness, his brain had triumphed over every difficulty and danger it had so far encountered. First he had vanquished primal forces by cunning and organization, then he had enlisted the resources of modern science to increase miraculously the yield of his plantation. And now he was sure he would prove more than a match for the "irresistible" ants.

That same evening, however, Leiningen assembled his workers. He had no intention of waiting till the news reached their ears from other sources. Most of them had been born in the district; the cry, "The ants are coming!" was to them an imperative signal for instant, panic-stricken flight, a spring for life itself. But so great was the Indians' trust in Leiningen, in Leiningen's word, and in Leiningen's wisdom, that they received his curt tidings, and his orders for the imminent struggle, with the calmness with which they were given. They waited, unafraid, alert, as if for the beginning of a new game or hunt which he had just described to them. The ants were indeed mighty, but not so mighty as the boss. Let them come!

They came at noon the second day. Their approach was announced by the wild unrest of the horses, scarcely controllable now ei-

---

**1. blind gut:** Reference to the appendix, which may have no function.

ther in stall or under rider, scenting from afar a vapor instinct with horror.

It was announced by a stampede of animals, timid and savage, hurtling past each other; jaguars and pumas flashing by nimble stags of the pampas; bulky tapirs, no longer hunters, themselves hunted, outpacing fleet kinkajous; maddened herds of cattle, heads lowered, nostrils snorting, rushing through tribes of loping monkeys, chattering in a dementia[2] of terror; then followed the creeping and springing denizens of bush and steppe, big and little rodents, snakes, and lizards.

Pell-mell the rabble swarmed down the hill to the plantation, scattered right and left before the barrier of the water-filled ditch, then sped onwards to the river, where, again hindered, they fled along its banks out of sight.

This water-filled ditch was one of the defense measures which Leiningen had long since prepared against the advent of the ants. It encompassed three sides of the plantation like a huge horseshoe. Twelve feet across, but not very deep, when dry it could hardly be described as an obstacle to either man or beast. But the ends of the "horseshoe" ran into the river which formed the northern boundary, and fourth side, of the plantation. And at the end nearer the house and outbuildings in the middle of the plantation, Leiningen had constructed a dam by means of which water from the river could be diverted into the ditch.

So now, by opening the dam, he was able to fling an imposing girdle of water, a huge quadrilateral with the river as its base, completely around the plantation, like the moat encircling a medieval city. Unless the ants were clever enough to build rafts, they had no hope of reaching the plantation, Leiningen concluded.

The twelve-foot water ditch seemed to afford in itself all the security needed. But while awaiting the arrival of the ants, Leiningen made a further improvement. The western section of the ditch ran along the edge of a tamarind wood,[3] and the branches of some great trees reached over the water. Leiningen now had them lopped so that ants could not descend from them within the "moat."

The women and children, then the herds of cattle, were escorted by peons on rafts over the river, to remain on the other side in absolute safety until the plunderers had departed. Leiningen gave this instruction, not because he believed the noncombatants were in any danger, but in order to avoid hampering the efficiency of the defenders.

Finally, he made a careful inspection of the "inner moat"—a smaller ditch lined with concrete, which extended around the hill on which stood the ranch house, barns, stables, and other buildings. Into this concrete ditch emptied the inflow pipes from three great petrol[4] tanks. If by some miracle the ants managed to cross the water and reach the plantation, this "rampart of petrol" would be an absolutely impassable protection for the besieged and their dwellings and stock. Such, at least, was Leiningen's opinion.

He stationed his men at irregular distances along the water ditch, the first line of defense. Then he lay down in his hammock and puffed drowsily away at his pipe until a peon came with the report that the ants had been observed far away in the south.

Leiningen mounted his horse, which at the feel of its master seemed to forget its uneasiness, and rode leisurely in the direc-

---

**2. dementia** (di men' shə) *n*.: Insanity or madness.

**3. tamarind** (tam' ə rind) **wood:** A grove of leafy trees found in the tropics.
**4. petrol** (pet' rəl) *adj*.: Gasoline.

tion of the threatening offensive. The southern stretch of ditch—the upper side of the quadrilateral—was nearly three miles long; from its center one could survey the entire countryside. This was destined to be the scene of the outbreak of war between Leiningen's brain and twenty square miles of life-destroying ants.

It was a sight one could never forget. Over the range of hills, as far as eye could see, crept a darkening hem, ever longer and broader, until the shadow spread across the slope from east to west, then downward, downward, uncannily swift, and all the green herbage of that wide vista was being mown as by a giant sickle, leaving only the vast moving shadow, extending, deepening, and moving rapidly nearer.

When Leiningen's men, behind their barrier of water, perceived the approach of the long-expected foe, they gave vent to their suspense in screams and imprecations. But as the distance began to lessen between the "sons of hell" and the water ditch, they relapsed into silence. Before the advance of

that awe-inspiring throng, their belief in the powers of the boss began to steadily dwindle.

Even Leiningen himself, who had ridden up just in time to restore their loss of heart by a display of unshakable calm, even he could not free himself from a qualm of malaise. Yonder were thousands of millions of voracious jaws bearing down upon him and only a suddenly insignificant, narrow ditch lay between him and his men and being gnawed to the bones "before you can spit three times."

Hadn't his brain for once taken on more than it could manage? If the blighters decided to rush the ditch, fill it to the brim with their corpses, there'd still be more than enough to destroy every trace of that cranium of his. The planter's chin jutted; they hadn't got him yet, and he'd see to it they never would. While he could think at all, he'd flout both death and the devil.

The hostile army was approaching in perfect formation; no human battalions, however well drilled, could ever hope to rival the precision of that advance. Along a front that moved forward as uniformly as a straight line, the ants drew nearer and nearer to the water ditch. Then, when they learned through their scouts the nature of the obstacle, the two outlying wings of the army detached themselves from the main body and marched down the western and eastern sides of the ditch.

This surrounding maneuver took rather more than an hour to accomplish; no doubt the ants expected that at some point they would find a crossing.

During this outflanking movement by the wings, the army on the center and southern front remained still. The besieged were therefore able to contemplate at their leisure the thumb-long, reddish-black, long-legged insects; some of the Indians believed they could see, too, intent on them, the brilliant, cold eyes, and the razor-edged mandibles,[5] of this host of infinity.

It is not easy for the average person to imagine that an animal, not to mention an insect, can *think*. But now both the brain of Leiningen and the brains of the Indians began to stir with the unpleasant foreboding that inside every single one of that deluge of insects dwelled a thought. And that thought was: Ditch or no ditch, we'll get to your flesh!

Not until four o'clock did the wings reach the "horseshoe" ends of the ditch, only to find these ran into the great river. Through some kind of secret telegraphy, the report must then have flashed very swiftly indeed along the entire enemy line. And Leiningen, riding—no longer casually —along his side of the ditch, noticed by energetic and widespread movements of troops that for some unknown reason the news of the check had its greatest effect on the southern front, where the main army was massed. Perhaps the failure to find a way over the ditch was persuading the ants to withdraw from the plantation in search of spoils more easily attainable.

An immense flood of ants, about a hundred yards in width, was pouring in a glimmering black cataract down the far slope of the ditch. Many thousands were already drowning in the sluggish creeping flow, but they were followed by troop after troop, who clambered over their sinking comrades, and then themselves served as dying bridges to the reserves hurrying on in their rear.

Shoals of ants were being carried away by the current into the middle of the ditch, where gradually they broke asunder and then, exhausted by their struggles, vanished below the surface. Nevertheless, the wavering, floundering hundred-yard front was remorselessly if slowly advancing toward the besieged on the other bank. Leiningen had been wrong when he supposed the enemy would first have to fill the ditch with their bodies before they could cross; instead, they merely needed to act as steppingstones, as they swam and sank, to the hordes ever pressing onwards from behind.

Near Leiningen a few mounted herdsmen awaited his orders. He sent one to the weir—the river must be dammed more strongly to increase the speed and power of the water coursing through the ditch.

A second peon was dispatched to the outhouses to bring spades and petrol sprinklers. A third rode away to summon to the zone of the offensive all the men, except the observation posts, on the nearby sections of the ditch, which were not yet actively threatened.

The ants were getting across far more quickly than Leiningen would have deemed possible. Impelled by the mighty cascade

---

**5. mandibles** (man′ də b′lz) *n.*: Biting jaws.

behind them, they struggled nearer and nearer to the inner bank. The momentum of the attack was so great that neither the tardy flow of the stream nor its downward pull could exert its proper force; and into the gap left by every submerging insect, hastened forward a dozen more.

When reinforcements reached Leiningen, the invaders were halfway over. The planter had to admit to himself that it was only by a stroke of luck for him that the ants were attempting the crossing on a relatively short front: had they assaulted simultaneously along the entire length of the ditch, the outlook for the defenders would have been black indeed.

Even as it was, it could hardly be described as rosy, though the planter seemed quite unaware that death in a gruesome form was drawing closer and closer. As the war between his brain and the "act of God" reached its climax, the very shadow of annihilation began to pale to Leiningen, who now felt like a champion in a new Olympic game, a gigantic and thrilling contest, from which he was determined to emerge victor. Such, indeed, was his aura of confidence that the Indians forgot their fear of the peril only a yard or two away; under the planter's supervision, they began fervidly digging up to the edge of the bank and throwing clods of earth and spadefuls of sand into the midst of the hostile fleet.

The petrol sprinklers, hitherto used to destroy pests and blights on the plantation, were also brought into action. Streams of evil-reeking oil now soared and fell over an enemy already in disorder through the bombàrdment of earth and sand.

The ants responded to these vigorous and successful measures of defense by further developments of their offensive. Entire

clumps of huddling insects began to roll down the opposite bank into the water. At the same time, Leiningen noticed that the ants were now attacking along an ever-widening front. As the numbers both of his men and his petrol sprinklers were severely limited, this rapid extension of the line of battle was becoming an overwhelming danger.

➤ To add to his difficulties, the very clods of earth they flung into that black floating carpet often whirled fragments toward the defenders' side, and here and there dark ribbons were already mounting the inner bank. True, wherever a man saw these they could still be driven back into the water by spadefuls of earth or jets of petrol. But the file of defenders was too sparse and scattered to hold off at all points these landing parties, and though the peons toiled like mad men, their plight became momently more perilous.

One man struck with his spade at an enemy clump, did not draw it back quickly enough from the water; in a trice the wooden haft swarmed with upward scurrying insects. With a curse, he dropped the spade into the ditch; too late, they were already on his body. They lost no time; wherever they encountered bare flesh they bit deeply; a few, bigger than the rest, carried in their hindquarters a sting which injected a burning and paralyzing venom. Screaming, frantic with pain, the peon danced and twirled like a dervish.[6]

Realizing that another such casualty, yes, perhaps this alone, might plunge his men into confusion and destroy their morale, Leiningen roared in a bellow louder than the yells of the victim: "Into the petrol, idiot! Douse your paws in the petrol!" The dervish ceased his pirouette as if transfixed, then tore off his shirt and plunged his arm and the ants hanging to it up to the shoulder in one of the large open tins of petrol. But even then the fierce mandibles did not slacken; another peon had to help him squash and detach each separate insect.

Distracted by the episode, some defenders had turned away from the ditch. And now cries of fury, a thudding of spades, and a wild trampling to and fro, showed that the ants had made full use of the interval, though luckily only a few had managed to get across. The men set to work again desperately with the barrage of earth and sand. Meanwhile an old Indian, who acted as medicine man to the plantation workers, gave the bitten peon a drink he had prepared some hours before, which, he claimed, possessed the virtue of dissolving and weakening ants' venom.

Leiningen surveyed his position. A dispassionate observer would have estimated the odds against him at a thousand to one. But then such an onlooker would have reckoned only by what he saw—the advance of myriad battalions of ants against the futile efforts of a few defenders—and not by the unseen activity that can go on in a man's brain.

For Leiningen had not erred when he decided he would fight elemental with elemental. The water in the ditch was beginning to rise; the stronger damming of the river was making itself apparent.

Visibly the swiftness and power of the masses of water increased, swirling into quicker and quicker movement its living black surface, dispersing its pattern, carrying away more and more of it on the hastening current.

Victory had been snatched from the very jaws of defeat. With a hysterical shout of joy, the peons feverishly intensified their bombardment of earth clods and sand.

---

**dervish** (dər' vish) n.: One who performs a ritual Moslem whirling dance.

And now the wide cataract down the opposite bank was thinning and ceasing, as if the ants were becoming aware that they could not attain their aim. They were scurrying back up the slope to safety.

All the troops so far hurled into the ditch had been sacrificed in vain. Drowned and floundering insects eddied in thousands along the flow, while Indians running on the bank destroyed every swimmer that reached the side.

Not until the ditch curved toward the east did the scattered ranks assemble again in a coherent mass. And now, exhausted and half-numbed, they were in no condition to ascend the bank. Fusillades of clods drove them round the bend toward the mouth of the ditch and then into the river, wherein they vanished without leaving a trace.

The news ran swiftly along the entire chain of outposts, and soon a long scattered line of laughing men could be seen hastening along the ditch toward the scene of victory.

For once they seemed to have lost all their native reserve, for it was in wild abandon now they celebrated the triumph—as if there were no longer thousands of millions of merciless, cold and hungry eyes watching them from the opposite bank, watching and waiting.

The sun sank behind the rim of the tamarind wood and twilight deepened into night. It was not only hoped but expected that the ants would remain quiet until dawn. But to defeat any forlorn attempt at a crossing, the flow of water through the ditch was powerfully increased by opening the dam still further.

In spite of this impregnable barrier, Leiningen was not yet altogether convinced that the ants would not venture another surprise attack. He ordered his men to camp along the bank overnight. He also detailed parties of them to patrol the ditch in two of his motor cars and ceaselessly to illuminate the surface of the water with headlights and electric torches.

After having taken all the precautions he deemed necessary, the farmer ate his supper with considerable appetite and went to bed. His slumbers were in no wise disturbed by the memory of the waiting, live, twenty square miles.

Dawn found a thoroughly refreshed and active Leiningen riding along the edge of the ditch. The planter saw before him a motionless and unaltered throng of besiegers. He studied the wide belt of water between them and the plantation, and for a moment almost regretted that the fight had ended so soon and so simply. In the comforting, matter-of-fact light of morning, it seemed to him now that the ants hadn't the ghost of a chance to cross the ditch. Even if they plunged headlong into it on all three fronts at once, the force of the now powerful current would inevitably sweep them away. He had got quite a thrill out of the fight—a pity it was already over.

He rode along the eastern and southern sections of the ditch and found everything in order. He reached the western section, opposite the tamarind wood, and here, contrary to the other battle fronts, he found the enemy very busy indeed. The trunks and branches of the trees and the creepers of the lianas,[7] on the far bank of the ditch, fairly swarmed with industrious insects. But instead of eating the leaves there and then, they were merely gnawing through the stalks, so that a thick green shower fell steadily to the ground.

---

**7. lianas** (lē a′ nəz) *n.*: Climbing vines found in the tropics.

No doubt they were victualing columns sent out to obtain provender for the rest of the army. The discovery did not surprise Leiningen. He did not need to be told that ants are intelligent, that certain species even use others as milch cows, watchdogs, and slaves. He was well aware of their power of adaptation, their sense of discipline, their marvelous talent for organization.

His belief that a foray to supply the army was in progress was strengthened when he saw the leaves that fell to the ground being dragged to the troops waiting outside the wood. Then all at once he realized the aim that rain of green was intended to serve.

Each single leaf, pulled or pushed by dozens of toiling insects, was borne straight to the edge of the ditch. Even as Macbeth watched the approach of Birnam Wood in the hands of his enemies,[8] Leiningen saw the tamarind wood move nearer and nearer in the mandibles of the ants. Unlike the fey Scot, however, he did not lose his nerve; no witches had prophesied his doom,[9] and if they had he would have slept just as soundly. All the same, he was forced to admit to himself that the situation was now far more ominous than that of the day before.

He had thought it impossible for the ants to build rafts for themselves—well, here they were, coming in thousands, more than enough to bridge the ditch. Leaves after leaves rustled down the slope to the water, where the current drew them away from the bank and carried them into midstream. And every single leaf carried several ants. This time the farmer did not trust to the alacrity of his messengers. He galloped away, leaning from his saddle and yelling orders as he rushed past outpost after outpost: "Bring petrol pumps to the southwest front! Issue spades to every man along the line facing the wood!" And arrived at the eastern and southern sections, he dispatched every man except the observation posts to the menaced west.

Then, as he rode past the stretch where the ants had failed to cross the day before, he witnessed a brief but impressive scene. Down the slope of the distant hill there came toward him a singular being, writhing rather than running, an animallike blackened statue with a shapeless head and four quivering feet that knuckled under almost ceaselessly. When the creature reached the far bank of the ditch and collapsed opposite Leiningen, he recognized it as a pampas stag, covered over and over with ants.

It had strayed near the zone of the army. As usual, they had attacked its eyes first. Blinded, it had reeled in the madness of hideous torment straight into the ranks of its persecutors, and now the beast swayed to and fro in its death agony.

With a shot from his rifle Leiningen put it out of its misery. Then he pulled out his watch. He hadn't a second to lose, but for life itself he could not have denied his curiosity the satisfaction of knowing how long the ants would take—for personal reasons, so to speak. After six minutes the white polished bones alone remained. That's how he himself would look before you can —Leiningen spat once, and put spurs to his horse.

The sporting zest with which the excitement of the novel contest had inspired him the day before had now vanished; in its place was a cold and violent purpose. He would send these vermin back to the hell where they belonged, somehow, anyhow. Yes, but how was indeed the question; as

---

**8. Macbeth . . . enemies:** In William Shakespeare's play *Macbeth*, soldiers carried boughs from Birnam Wood to hide behind as they attacked a castle.
**9. fey** (fā) **Scot . . . doom:** "Fey Scot" refers to Macbeth, whose death was foretold by three witches.

things stood at present it looked as if the devils would raze him and his men from the earth instead. He had underestimated the might of the enemy; he really would have to bestir himself if he hoped to outwit them.

The biggest danger now, he decided, was the point where the western section of the ditch curved southward. And arrived there, he found his worst expectations justified. The very power of the current had huddled the leaves and their crews of ants so close together at the bend that the bridge was almost ready.

True, streams of petrol and clumps of earth still prevented a landing. But the number of floating leaves was increasing ever more swiftly. It could not be long now before a stretch of water a mile in length was decked by a green pontoon over which the ants could rush in millions.

Leiningen galloped to the weir. The damming of the river was controlled by a wheel on its bank. The planter ordered the man at the wheel first to lower the water in the ditch almost to vanishing point, next to wait a moment, then suddenly to let the river in again. This maneuver of lowering and raising the surface, of decreasing then increasing the flow of water through the ditch, was to be repeated over and over again until further notice.

This tactic was at first successful. The water in the ditch sank, and with it the film of leaves. The green fleet nearly reached the bed and the troops on the far bank swarmed down the slope to it. Then a violent flow of water at the original depth raced through the ditch, overwhelming leaves and ants, and sweeping them along.

This intermittent rapid flushing prevented just in time the almost completed fording of the ditch. But it also flung here and there squads of the enemy vanguard simultaneously up the inner bank. These seemed to know their duty only too well, and lost no time accomplishing it. The air rang with the curses of bitten Indians. They had removed their shirts and pants to detect the quicker the upward-hastening insects; when they saw one, they crushed it; and fortunately the onslaught as yet was only by skirmishers.

Again and again, the water sank and rose, carrying leaves and drowned ants away with it. It lowered once more nearly to its bed; but this time the exhausted defenders waited in vain for the flush of destruction. Leiningen sensed disaster; something must have gone wrong with the machinery of the dam. Then a sweating peon tore up to him:

"They're over!"

While the besieged were concentrating upon the defense of the stretch opposite the wood, the seemingly unaffected line beyond the wood had become the theater of decisive action. Here the defenders' front was sparse and scattered; everyone who could be spared had hurried away to the south.

Just as the man at the weir had lowered the water almost to the bed of the ditch, the ants on a wide front began another attempt at a direct crossing like that of the preceding day. Into the emptied bed poured an irresistible throng. Rushing across the ditch, they attained the inner bank before the Indians fully grasped the situation. Their frantic screams dumbfounded the man at the weir. Before he could direct the river anew into the safeguarding bed he saw himself surrounded by raging ants. He ran like the others, ran for his life.

When Leiningen heard this, he knew the plantation was doomed. He wasted no time bemoaning the inevitable. For as long as there was the slightest chance of success, he had stood his ground; and now any further resistance was both useless and dangerous. He fired three revolver shots into the air—the prearranged signal for his men to retreat instantly within the "inner moat." Then he rode toward the ranch house.

This was two miles from the point of invasion. There was therefore time enough to prepare the second line of defense against the advent of the ants. Of the three great petrol cisterns near the house, one had already been half emptied by the constant withdrawals needed for the pumps during the fight at the water ditch. The remaining petrol in it was now drawn off through underground pipes into the concrete trench which encircled the ranch house and its outbuildings.

And there, drifting in twos and threes, Leiningen's men reached him. Most of them were obviously trying to preserve an air of calm and indifference, belied, however, by their restless glances and knitted brows. One could see their belief in a favorable outcome of the struggle was already considerably shaken.

The planter called his peons around him.

"Well, lads," he began, "we've lost the first round. But we'll smash the beggars yet, don't you worry. Anyone who thinks otherwise can draw his pay here and now and push off. There are rafts enough and to spare on the river and plenty of time still to reach 'em."

Not a man stirred.

Leiningen acknowledged his silent vote of confidence with a laugh that was half a grunt. "That's the stuff, lads. Too bad if you'd missed the rest of the show, eh? Well, the fun won't start till morning. Once these blighters turn tail, there'll be plenty of work for everyone and higher wages all round. And now run along and get something to eat; you've earned it all right."

In the excitement of the fight the greater part of the day had passed without the men once pausing to snatch a bite. Now that the ants were for the time being out of sight, and the "wall of petrol" gave a stronger feeling of security, hungry stomachs began to assert their claims.

The bridges over the concrete ditch were removed. Here and there solitary ants had reached the ditch; they gazed at the petrol meditatively, then scurried back again. Apparently they had little interest at the moment for what lay beyond the evil-reeking barrier, the abundant spoils of the plantation were the main attraction. Soon the trees, shrubs and beds for miles around were hulled with ants zealously gobbling the yield of long weary months of strenuous toil.

As twilight began to fall, a cordon of ants marched around the petrol trench, but as yet made no move toward its brink. Leiningen posted sentries with headlights and electric torches, then withdrew to his office, and began to reckon up his losses. He estimated these as large, but, in comparison with his bank balance, by no means unbearable. He worked out in some detail a scheme of intensive cultivation which would enable him, before very long, to more than compensate himself for the damage now being wrought to his crops. It was with a contented mind that he finally betook himself to bed where he slept deeply until dawn, undisturbed by any thought that next day little more might be left of him than a glistening skeleton.

He rose with the sun and went out on the flat roof of his house. And a scene like one from Dante[10] lay around him; for miles in every direction there was nothing but a black, glittering multitude, a multitude of

---

**10. Dante** (dan' tā): Italian poet (1265–1321) who wrote *The Divine Comedy*, describing the horrors of hell.

rested, sated, but nonetheless voracious ants; yes, look as far as one might, one could see nothing but that rustling black throng, except in the north, where the great river drew a boundary they could not hope to pass. But even the high stone breakwater, along the bank of the river, which Leiningen had built as a defense against inundations, was, like the paths, the shorn trees and shrubs, the ground itself, black with ants.

So their greed was not glutted in razing that vast plantation? Not by a long chalk; they were all the more eager now on a rich and certain booty—four hundred men, numerous horses, and bursting granaries.

At first it seemed that the petrol trench would serve its purpose. The besiegers sensed the peril of swimming it, and made no move to plunge blindly over its brink. Instead they devised a better maneuver; they began to collect shreds of bark, twigs and dried leaves and dropped these into the petrol. Everything green, which could have been similarly used, had long since been eaten. After a time, though, a long procession could be seen bringing from the west the tamarind leaves used as rafts the day before.

Since the petrol, unlike the water in the outer ditch, was perfectly still, the refuse stayed where it was thrown. It was several hours before the ants succeeded in covering an appreciable part of the surface. At length, however, they were ready to proceed to a direct attack.

Their storm troops swarmed down the concrete side, scrambled over the supporting surface of twigs and leaves, and impelled these over the few remaining streaks of open petrol until they reached the other side. Then they began to climb up this to make straight for the helpless garrison.

During the entire offensive, the planter sat peacefully, watching them with interest, but not stirring a muscle. Moreover, he had ordered his men not to disturb in any way whatever the advancing horde. So they squatted listlessly along the bank of the ditch and waited for a sign from the boss.

The petrol was now covered with ants. A few had climbed the inner concrete wall and were scurrying toward the defenders.

"Everyone back from the ditch!" roared Leiningen. The men rushed away, without the slightest idea of his plan. He stooped forward and cautiously dropped into the ditch a stone which split the floating carpet and its living freight, to reveal a gleaming patch of petrol. A match spurted, sank down to the oily surface—Leiningen sprang back; in a flash a towering rampart of fire encompassed the garrison.

This spectacular and instant repulse threw the Indians into ecstasy. They applauded, yelled and stamped. Had it not been for the awe in which they held their boss, they would infallibly have carried him shoulder high.

It was some time before the petrol burned down to the bed of the ditch, and the wall of smoke and flame began to lower. The ants had retreated in a wide circle from the devastation, and innumerable charred fragments along the outer bank showed that the flames had spread from the holocaust in the ditch well into the ranks beyond, where they had wrought havoc far and wide.

Yet the perseverance of the ants was by no means broken; indeed, each setback seemed only to whet it. The concrete cooled, the flicker of the dying flames wavered and vanished, petrol from the second tank poured into the trench—and the ants marched forward anew to the attack.

The foregoing scene repeated itself in every detail, except that on this occasion less time was needed to bridge the ditch, for the petrol was now already filmed by a layer of ash. Once again they withdrew; once again petrol flowed into the ditch. Would the

creatures never learn that their self-sacrifice was utterly senseless? It really was senseless, wasn't it? Yes, of course it was senseless—provided the defenders had an *unlimited* supply of petrol.

When Leiningen reached this stage of reasoning, he felt for the first time since the arrival of the ants that his confidence was deserting him. His skin began to creep; he loosened his collar. Once the devils were over the trench there wasn't a chance for him and his men. What a prospect, to be eaten alive like that!

For the third time the flames immolated the attacking troops, and burned down to extinction. Yet the ants were coming on again as if nothing had happened. And meanwhile Leiningen had made a discovery that chilled him to the bone—petrol was no longer flowing into the ditch. Something must be blocking the outflow pipe of the third and last cistern—a snake or a dead rat? Whatever it was, the ants could be held off no longer, unless petrol could by some method be led from the cistern into the ditch.

Then Leiningen remembered that in an outhouse nearby were two old disused fire engines. The peons dragged them out of the shed, connected their pumps to the cistern, uncoiled and laid the hose. They were just in time to aim a stream of petrol at a column of ants that had already crossed and drive them back down the incline into the ditch. Once more an oily girdle surrounded the garrison, once more it was possible to hold the position—for the moment.

It was obvious, however, that this last resource meant only the postponement of defeat and death. A few of the peons fell on their knees and began to pray; others, shrieking insanely, fired their revolvers at the black, advancing masses, as if they felt their despair was pitiful enough to sway fate itself to mercy.

At length, two of the men's nerves broke: Leiningen saw a naked Indian leap over the north side of the petrol trench, quickly followed by a second. They sprinted with incredible speed toward the river. But their fleetness did not save them; long before they could attain the rafts, the enemy covered their bodies from head to foot.

In the agony of their torment, both sprang blindly into the wide river, where enemies no less sinister awaited them. Wild screams of mortal anguish informed the breathless onlookers that crocodiles and sword-toothed piranhas were no less ravenous than ants, and even nimbler in reaching their prey.

In spite of this bloody warning, more and more men showed they were making up their minds to run the blockade. Anything, even a fight midstream against alligators, seemed better than powerlessly waiting for death to come and slowly consume their living bodies.

Leiningen flogged his brain till it reeled.

Was there nothing on earth could sweep this devils' spawn back into the hell from which it came?

Then out of the inferno of his bewilderment rose a terrifying inspiration. Yes, one hope remained, and one alone. It might be possible to dam the great river completely, so that its waters would fill not only the water ditch but overflow into the entire gigantic "saucer" of land in which lay the plantation.

The far bank of the river was too high for the waters to escape that way. The stone breakwater ran between the river and the plantation; its only gaps occurred where the "horseshoe" ends of the water ditch passed into the river. So its waters would not only be forced to inundate into the plantation, they would also be held there by the breakwater until they rose to its own high level. In half an hour, perhaps even earlier, the plantation and its hostile army of occupation would be flooded.

The ranch house and outbuildings stood upon rising ground. Their foundations were higher than the breakwater, so the flood would not reach them. And any remaining ants trying to ascend the slope could be repulsed by petrol.

It was possible—yes, if one could only get to the dam! A distance of nearly two miles lay between the ranch house and the weir—two miles of ants. Those two peons had managed only a fifth of that distance at the cost of their lives. Was there an Indian daring enough after that to run the gauntlet five times as far? Hardly likely; and if there were, his prospect of getting back was almost nil.

No, there was only one thing for it, he'd have to make the attempt himself; he might just as well be running as sitting still, anyway, when the ants finally got him. Besides, there *was* a bit of a chance. Perhaps the ants weren't so almighty, after all; perhaps he had allowed the mass suggestion of that evil black throng to hypnotize him, just as a snake fascinates and overpowers.

The ants were building their bridges. Leiningen got up on a chair. "Hey, lads, listen to me!" he cried. Slowly and listlessly, from all sides of the trench, the men began to shuffle toward him, the apathy of death already stamped on their faces.

"Listen, lads!" he shouted. "You're frightened of those beggars, but I'm proud of you. There's still a chance to save our lives —by flooding the plantation from the river. Now one of you might manage to get as far as the weir—but he'd never come back. Well, I'm not going to let you try it; if I did, I'd be worse than one of those ants. No, I called the tune, and now I'm going to pay the piper.

"The moment I'm over the ditch, set fire to the petrol. That'll allow time for the flood to do the trick. Then all you have to do is to wait here all snug and quiet till I'm back. Yes, I'm coming back, trust me"—he grinned—"when I've finished my slimming cure."

He pulled on high leather boots, drew heavy gauntlets over his hands, and stuffed the spaces between breeches and boots, gauntlets and arms, shirt and neck, with rags soaked in petrol. With close-fitting mosquito goggles he shielded his eyes, knowing too well the ants' dodge of first robbing their victim of sight. Finally, he plugged his nostrils and ears with cotton-wool, and let the peons drench his clothes with petrol.

He was about to set off when the old Indian medicine man came up to him; he had a wondrous salve, he said, prepared from a species of chafer[11] whose odor was intolerable to ants. Yes, this odor protected

---

**11. chafer** (chāf′ ər) *n.*: Insects that feed on plants.

these chafers from the attacks of even the most murderous ants. The Indian smeared the boss's boots, his gauntlets, and his face over and over with the extract.

Leiningen then remembered the paralyzing effect of ants' venom, and the Indian gave him a gourd full of the medicine he had administered to the bitten peon at the water ditch. The planter drank it down without noticing its bitter taste; his mind was already at the weir.

He started off toward the northwest corner of the trench. With a bound he was over—and among the ants.

The beleaguered garrison had no opportunity to watch Leiningen's race against death. The ants were climbing the inner bank again—the lurid ring of petrol blazed aloft. For the fourth time that day the reflection from the fire shone on the sweating faces of the imprisoned men, and on the reddish-black cuirasses[12] of their oppressors. The red and blue, dark-edged flames leaped vividly now, celebrating what? The funeral pyre of the four hundred, or of the hosts of destruction?

Leiningen ran. He ran in long, equal strides, with only one thought, one sensation, in his being—he *must* get through. He dodged all trees and shrubs; except for the split seconds his soles touched the ground, the ants should have no opportunity to alight on him. That they would get to him soon, despite the salve on his boots, the petrol on his clothes, he realized only too well, but he knew even more surely that he must, and that he would, get to the weir.

Apparently the salve was some use after all; not until he had reached halfway did he feel ants under his clothes, and a few on his face. Mechanically, in his stride, he struck at them, scarcely conscious of their bites. He saw he was drawing appreciably nearer the weir—the distance grew less and less—sank to five hundred—three—two—hundred yards.

Then he was at the weir and gripping the ant-hulled wheel. Hardly had he seized it when a horde of infuriated ants flowed over his hands, arms, and shoulders. He started the wheel—before it turned once on its axis the swarm covered his face. Leiningen strained like a madman, his lips pressed tight; if he opened them to draw breath . . .

He turned and turned; slowly the dam lowered until it reached the bed of the river. Already the water was overflowing the ditch. Another minute, and the river was pouring through the nearby gap in the breakwater. The flooding of the plantation had begun.

Leiningen let go the wheel. Now, for the first time, he realized he was coated from head to foot with a layer of ants. In spite of the petrol, his clothes were full of them, several had got to his body or were clinging to his face. Now that he had completed his task, he felt the smart raging over his flesh from the bites of sawing and piercing insects.

Frantic with pain, he almost plunged into the river. To be ripped and slashed to shreds by piranhas? Already he was running the return journey, knocking ants from his gloves and jacket, brushing them from his bloodied face, squashing them to death under his clothes.

One of the creatures bit him just below the rim of his goggles; he managed to tear it away, but the agony of the bite and its etching acid drilled into the eye nerves; he saw now through circles of fire into a milky mist, then he ran for a time almost blinded, knowing that if he once tripped and fell. . . . The old Indian's brew didn't seem much good; it weakened the poison a bit, but didn't get rid of it. His heart pounded as if it

---

**12. cuirasses** (kwi ras′ əz) *n.*: Body armor; here, the ants' outer bodies.

would burst; blood roared in his ears; a giant's fist battered his lungs.

Then he could see again, but the burning girdle of petrol appeared infinitely far away; he could not last half that distance. Swift-changing pictures flashed through his head, episodes in his life, while in another part of his brain a cool and impartial onlooker informed this ant-blurred, gasping, exhausted bundle named Leiningen that such a rushing panorama of scenes from one's past is seen only in the moment before death.

A stone in the path . . . too weak to avoid it . . . the planter stumbled and collapsed. He tried to rise . . . he must be pinned under a rock . . . it was impossible . . . the slightest movement was impossible. . . .

Then all at once he saw, starkly clear and huge, and, right before his eyes, furred with ants, towering and swaying in its death agony, the pampas stag. In six minutes —gnawed to the bones. He *couldn't* die like that! And something outside him seemed to drag him to his feet. He tottered. He began to stagger forward again.

Through the blazing ring hurtled an apparition which, as soon as it reached the ground on the inner side, fell full length and did not move. Leiningen, at the moment he made that leap through the flames, lost consciousness for the first time in his life. As he lay there, with glazing eyes and lacerated face, he appeared a man returned from the grave. The peons rushed to him, stripped off his clothes, tore away the ants from a body that seemed almost one open wound; in some places the bones were showing. They carried him into the ranch house.

As the curtain of flames lowered, one could see in place of the illimitable host of ants an extensive vista of water. The thwarted river had swept over the plantation, carrying with it the entire army. The water had collected and mounted in the great "saucer," while the ants had in vain attempted to reach the hill on which stood the ranch house. The girdle of flames held them back.

And so, imprisoned between water and fire, they had been delivered into the annihilation that was their god. And near the farther mouth of the water ditch, where the stone mole had its second gap, the ocean swept the lost battalions into the river, to vanish forever.

The ring of fire dwindled as the water mounted to the petrol trench and quenched the dimming flames. The inundation rose higher and higher: because its outflow was impeded by the timber and underbrush it had carried along with it, its surface required some time to reach the top of the high stone breakwater and discharge over it the rest of the shattered army.

It swelled over ant-stippled shrubs and bushes, until it washed against the foot of the knoll whereon the besieged had taken refuge. For a while an alluvium of ants tried again and again to attain the dry land, only to be repulsed by streams of petrol back into the merciless flood.

Leiningen lay on his bed, his body swathed from head to foot in bandages. With fomentations and salves, they had managed to stop the bleeding, and had dressed his many wounds. Now they thronged around him, one question in every face. Would he recover? "He won't die," said the old man who had bandaged him, "if he doesn't want to."

The planter opened his eyes. "Everything in order?" he asked.

"They're gone," said his nurse. He held out to his master a gourd full of a powerful sleeping-draft. Leiningen gulped it down.

"I told you I'd come back," he murmured, "even if I am a bit streamlined."

## THINKING ABOUT THE SELECTION

### Recalling

1. What threat do the ants pose to Leiningen?
2. At what point in the story does it first seem that Leiningen has snatched victory "from the very jaws of defeat"? Explain how the ants snatch back victory.
3. How does Leiningen finally defeat the ants?

### Interpreting

4. Why do you think Leiningen was so determined to stay and fight the ants?
5. What qualities do you think make Leiningen well equipped to fight the ants? What qualities might make him dangerous to others?
6. What behavior of the ants makes them appear to be intelligent beings?
7. Early in the story, Leiningen's motto is stated: *The human brain needs only to become fully aware of its powers to conquer even the elements.* Explain how the events of the story either support or invalidate his motto.

### Applying

8. By staying to fight the ants, Leiningen risked other's lives as well as his own. Do you think he was justified? Why or why not?

## ANALYZING LITERATURE

### Examining Conflicts

An **internal conflict** is a struggle that takes place within a character who battles himself or herself over differing ideas and feelings. The peons have internal conflicts between their fear of the ants and their belief in Leiningen. An **external conflict** occurs between two or more characters or between a character and natural forces.

1. Give an example of an internal conflict that pits intellect against instinct.
2. Give an example of an external conflict that pits intellect against instinct.

## CRITICAL THINKING AND READING

### Recognizing Causes and Effects

Situations have both causes and effects. The **causes** are the reasons why something happens. The **effects** are the results or outcomes of the situation.

1. Describe each of Leiningen's lines of defense against the ants.
2. Explain the effect of each line of defense.

## UNDERSTANDING LANGUAGE

### Using Context Clues

You can use **context clues,** the words and phrases around a new word, to figure out its meaning. The words *floods* and *pouring* and the phrase *down the far slope* are clues that the meaning of the word *cataract* is *waterfall* in the sentence: "An immense flood of ants . . . was pouring in a glimmering black cataract down the far slope of the ditch."

Use context clues to figure out the meaning of each italicized word.

1. ". . . in a trice, the wooden *haft* swarmed with upward scurrying insects." (page 47)
2. ". . . a stretch of water a mile in length was decked by a green *pontoon* over which the ants could rush in millions." (page 50)

## THINKING AND WRITING

### Writing About Conflict

Imagine that you are a reporter covering Leiningen's war against the ants. To write your final, summary story, decide what the conflict was really about and why it was important. Also list some high points of the fighting. Write a story that helps your readers understand what went on. When you revise your story, be sure that it answers the questions: Who? What? Where? When? and How?

## Hearts and Hands

**O. Henry** (1862–1910) is the pen name of William Sydney Porter, who was born in Greensboro, North Carolina. O. Henry moved to Texas in 1886, where he held a number of jobs. While working as a bank teller, he was charged with embezzling funds. He fled to Honduras but eventually returned to face the charges and was sentenced to a three-year prison term. While in prison, O. Henry took up writing short stories. Perhaps his own journey to prison served as inspiration for "Hearts and Hands."

### The Surprise Ending

Sometimes you can predict the ending of a story while you are reading it. At other times you cannot tell for certain how the story will be resolved, but the ending seems in all ways the logical outcome of the events. Some stories, however, have **surprise endings—** unexpected twists at the end that you did not expect. Such endings startle you when you get to them. Authors build up to surprise endings by misleading you, as O. Henry does in "Hearts and Hands." No matter how surprising such an ending is, however, it must be believable. Therefore the author plants clues throughout that foreshadow the surprise.

### Look For

As you read "Hearts and Hands," pay attention to details. Try to figure out which ones point to the real ending and which ones are there to mislead you.

### Writing

Think of a friend whom you have not seen for a long time. If you were to run into this friend unexpectedly, what might your friend want to know about you? List information about yourself that you would want to tell your friend.

### Vocabulary

Knowing the following words will help you as you read "Hearts and Hands."

**influx** (in′ fluks′) *n*.: A coming in (p. 59)
**forestalled** (fôr stôld′) *v*.: Prevented by having done something ahead of time (p. 60)
**counterfeiting** (koun′ tər fit′ iŋ) *v*.: Making imitation money to pass off as real money (p. 60)
**sidled** (sī′ d'ld) *v*.: Moved sideways (p. 61)

# Hearts and Hands

## O. Henry

THE "LIGHTNING EXPRESS" TRAINS: "LEAVING THE JUNCTION"
*F. F. Palmer, Del/ lithograph by Currier & Ives, 1863*
The Harry T. Peters Collection, Museum of the City of New York

At Denver there was an influx of passengers into the coaches on the eastbound B. & M. express. In one coach there sat a very pretty young woman dressed in elegant taste and surrounded by all the luxurious comforts of an experienced traveler. Among the newcomers were two young men, one of handsome presence with a bold, frank countenance and manner; the other a ruffled, glum-faced person, heavily built and roughly dressed. The two were handcuffed together.

As they passed down the aisle of the coach the only vacant seat offered was a reversed one facing the attractive young woman. Here the linked couple seated themselves. The young woman's glance fell upon them with a distant, swift disinterest; then with a lovely smile brightening her countenance and a tender pink tingeing her rounded cheeks, she held out a little gray-gloved hand. When she spoke her voice, full, sweet, and deliberate, proclaimed that its owner was accustomed to speak and be heard.

"Well, Mr. Easton, if you *will* make me speak first, I suppose I must. Don't you ever recognize old friends when you meet them in the West?"

The younger man roused himself sharply at the sound of her voice, seemed to struggle with a slight embarrassment which he threw off instantly, and then clasped her fingers with his left hand.

"It's Miss Fairchild," he said, with a smile. "I'll ask you to excuse the other hand; it's otherwise engaged just at present."

He slightly raised his right hand, bound at the wrist by the shining "bracelet" to the left one of his companion. The glad look in the girl's eyes slowly changed to a bewildered horror. The glow faded from her cheeks. Her lips parted in a vague, relaxing distress. Easton, with a little laugh, as if amused, was about to speak again when the other forestalled him. The glum-faced man had been watching the girl's countenance with veiled glances from his keen, shrewd eyes.

"You'll excuse me for speaking, miss, but I see you're acquainted with the marshal here. If you'll ask him to speak a word for me when we get to the pen he'll do it, and it'll make things easier for me there. He's taking me to Leavenworth prison. It's seven years for counterfeiting."

"Oh!" said the girl, with a deep breath and returning color. "So that is what you are doing out here? A marshal!"

"My dear Miss Fairchild," said Easton, calmly, "I had to do something. Money has a way of taking wings unto itself, and you know it takes money to keep step with our crowd in Washington. I saw this opening in the West, and—well, a marshalship isn't quite as high a position as that of ambassador, but—"

"The ambassador," said the girl, warmly, "doesn't call any more. He needn't ever have done so. You ought to know that. And so now you are one of these dashing Western heroes, and you ride and shoot and go into all kinds of dangers. That's different from the Washington life. You have been missed from the old crowd."

The girl's eyes, fascinated, went back, widening a little, to rest upon the glittering handcuffs.

"Don't you worry about them, miss," said the other man. "All marshals handcuff themselves to their prisoners to keep them from getting away. Mr. Easton knows his business."

"Will we see you again soon in Washington?" asked the girl.

"Not soon, I think," said Easton. "My butterfly days are over, I fear."

"I love the West," said the girl irrelevantly. Her eyes were shining softly. She looked away out the car window. She began to speak truly and simply, without the gloss of style and manner: "Mamma and I spent the summer in Denver. She went home a week ago because father was slightly ill. I could live and be happy in the West. I think the air here agrees with me. Money isn't everything. But people always misunderstand things and remain stupid—"

"Say, Mr. Marshal," growled the glum-faced man. "This isn't quite fair. Haven't had a smoke all day. Haven't you talked long enough? Take me in the smoker now, won't you? I'm half dead for a pipe."

The bound travelers rose to their feet, Easton with the same slow smile on his face.

"I can't deny a petition for tobacco," he said lightly. "It's the one friend of the unfortunate. Goodbye, Miss Fairchild. Duty calls, you know." He held out his hand for a farewell.

"It's too bad you are not going East," she said, reclothing herself with manner and style. "But you must go on to Leavenworth, I suppose?"

"Yes," said Easton, "I must go on to Leavenworth."

The two men sidled down the aisle into the smoker.

The two passengers in a seat nearby had heard most of the conversation. Said one of them: "That marshal's a good sort of chap. Some of these Western fellows are all right."

"Pretty young to hold an office like that, isn't he?" asked the other.

"Young!" exclaimed the first speaker, "why— Oh! didn't you catch on? Say—did you ever know an officer to handcuff a prisoner to his *right* hand?"

---

## THINKING ABOUT THE SELECTION
### Recalling

1. Who are the three people talking together on the train?
2. How do Miss Fairchild and Mr. Easton know each other?
3. In what way does the marshal deceive Miss Fairchild?

### Interpreting

4. For what reasons do you think the marshal deceives Miss Fairchild?
5. Why is it significant that the prisoner's crime is counterfeiting?
6. Why do the two passengers who overhear the conversation have such different ideas about what is taking place?
7. Think of the title of this story. Explain what role hearts play in it. Explain what role hands play in it.

### Applying

8. Clarence Day has written "A moderate addiction to money may not be hurtful; but when taken in excess, it is nearly always bad for the health." Explain how this story proves the truth of this statement.

## ANALYZING LITERATURE
### Appreciating a Surprise Ending

A **surprise ending** is an unexpected twist at the end of a story. O. Henry is known for his surprise endings, and many readers try to outsmart him by looking for his clues to the real ending. In "Hearts and Hands," the fact that Mr. Easton has the handcuff on his right hand is one such clue.

1. What ending are you led to expect as you are reading the story?
2. At what point in the story did you realize that Mr. Easton was not the marshal?
3. Point out at least three clues in Mr. Easton's words and behavior that foreshadow the real ending.

## CRITICAL THINKING AND READING
### Making Inferences from Evidence

An **inference** is a conclusion based on given facts and past experience. Since authors tend to leave much unsaid, you often need to make inferences when you read. When you infer, you use the evidence the author provides.

What is the most likely inference you would draw from the evidence in each of the following scenes from the story? Does the inference turn out to be correct?

1. The description of the two men handcuffed together as they enter the car. (page 59)
2. The conversation between Mr. Easton and Miss Fairchild in which he explains how he became a marshal, saying it is not as high a position as ambassador, and she responds to his statement. (page 60)

## SPEAKING AND LISTENING
### Performing in a Reader's Theater

In a **Reader's Theater,** you act out stories without scenery or costumes, using only your voice, face, and gestures. You might, however, use a few simple props. For "Hearts and Hands," you might use a pair of toy handcuffs, or you might just act *as though* you had handcuffs on.

With two classmates, prepare a Reader's Theater presentation of "Hearts and Hands." Present it to your classmates.

## THINKING AND WRITING
### Writing a Surprise Ending

Write a letter to a friend or relative you have not seen in some time. You may want to use the list of information you wrote on page 58. Describe a situation with an unexpected outcome, creating a surprise ending for your letter. When you finish, revise to include details that will cause your reader to expect a different ending. Also include clues that make the real ending believable. Proofread your letter and share it with your classmates.

# Characterization

**EVENING, MONHEGAN ISLAND**
*Samuel Reindorf*

# GUIDE TO READING

## A Visit to Grandmother

**William Melvin Kelley** (1937–     ) was born in New York City. He was educated at Harvard University and has taught at several colleges. Kelley's stories focus on the problems of individuals, some of them black. Kelley has said, "I am not a sociologist or a politician or a spokesman. Such people try to give answers. A writer, I think, should ask questions." In "A Visit to Grandmother," Kelley shows members of a black family seeking answers to their own questions.

### Direct and Indirect Characterization

Characterization is the way a writer brings a character to life. Sometimes a writer uses **direct characterization**—directly telling you about the character's personality. More frequently a writer uses **indirect characterization,** revealing personality through a physical description of the character; through the character's thoughts, words, and actions; and through other characters' comments. Kelley uses indirect characterization in "A Visit to Grandmother," for example, when the grandmother tells a story that reveals a great deal about herself and one of her children.

### Look For

Seeing our parents with grandparents sometimes helps us understand parents better. As you read this story, look for what Chig learns about his father as they visit grandmother.

### Writing

"A Visit to Grandmother" concerns a reunion of some family members who have not seen one another in a long time. Imagine that you are part of a large family with many brothers and sisters. Think about how the size of your family makes it special. Freewrite about the advantages and disadvantages of being a child in a large family.

### Vocabulary

Knowing the following words will help you as you read "A Visit to Grandmother."

**indulgence** (in dul' jəns) *n.:* Leniency; forgiveness (p. 66)
**grimacing** (grim' əs iŋ) *v.:* Making a twisted or distorted facial expression (p. 66)
**lacquered** (lak' ərd) *adj.:* Coated with a varnish made from shellac or resin (p. 70)

# A Visit to Grandmother
### William Melvin Kelley

Chig knew something was wrong the instant his father kissed her. He had always known his father to be the warmest of men, a man so kind that when people ventured timidly into his office, it took only a few words from him to make them relax, and even laugh. Doctor Charles Dunford cared about people.

But when he had bent to kiss the old lady's black face, something new and almost ugly had come into his eyes: fear, uncertainty, sadness, and perhaps even hatred.

Ten days before in New York, Chig's father had decided suddenly he wanted to go to Nashville to attend his college class reunion, twenty years out. Both Chig's brother and sister, Peter and Connie, were packing for camp and besides were too young for such an affair. But Chig was seventeen, had nothing to do that summer, and his father asked if he would like to go along. His father had given him additional reasons: "All my running buddies got their diplomas and were snapped up by them crafty young gals, and had kids within a year—now all those kids, some of them gals, are your age."

The reunion had lasted a week. As they packed for home, his father, in a far too offhand way, had suggested they visit Chig's grandmother. "We this close. We might as well drop in on her and my brothers."

So, instead of going north, they had gone farther south, had just entered her house.

And Chig had a suspicion now that the reunion had been only an excuse to drive south, that his father had been heading to this house all the time.

His father had never talked much about his family, with the exception of his brother, GL, who seemed part con man, part

practical joker and part Don Juan;[1] he had spoken of GL with the kind of indulgence he would have shown a cute, but ill-behaved and potentially dangerous, five-year-old.

Chig's father had left home when he was fifteen. When asked why, he would answer: "I wanted to go to school. They didn't have a Negro high school at home, so I went up to Knoxville and lived with a cousin and went to school."

They had been met at the door by Aunt Rose, GL's wife, and ushered into the living room. The old lady had looked up from her seat by the window. Aunt Rose stood between the visitors.

The old lady eyed his father. "Rose, who that? Rose?" She squinted. She looked like a doll, made of black straw, the wrinkles in her face running in one direction like the head of a broom. Her hair was white and coarse and grew out straight from her head. Her eyes were brown—the whites, too, seemed light brown—and were hidden behind thick glasses, which remained somehow on a tiny nose. "That Hiram?" That was another of his father's brothers. "No, it ain't Hiram; too big for Hiram." She turned then to Chig. "Now that man, he look like Eleanor, Charles's wife, but Charles wouldn't never send my grandson to see me. I never even hear from Charles." She stopped again.

"It Charles, Mama. That who it is." Aunt Rose, between them, led them closer. "It Charles come all the way from New York to see you, and brung little Charles with him."

The old lady stared up at them. "Charles? Rose, that really Charles?" She turned away, and reached for a handkerchief in the pocket of her clean, ironed,

flowered housecoat, and wiped her eyes. "God have mercy. Charles." She spread her arms up to him, and he bent down and kissed her cheek. That was when Chig saw his face, grimacing. She hugged him; Chig watched the muscles in her arms as they tightened around his father's neck. She half rose out of her chair. "How are you, son?"

Chig could not hear his father's answer.

She let him go, and fell back into her chair, grabbing the arms. Her hands were as dark as the wood, and seemed to become part of it. "Now, who that standing there? Who that man?"

"That's one of your grandsons, Mama." His father's voice cracked. "Charles Dunford, junior. You saw him once, when he was a baby, in Chicago. He's grown now."

"I can see that, boy!" She looked at Chig squarely. "Come here, son, and kiss me once." He did. "What they call you? Charles too?"

"No, ma'am, they call me Chig."

She smiled. She had all her teeth, but they were too perfect to be her own. "That's good. Can't have two boys answering to Charles in the same house. Won't nobody at all come. So you that little boy. You don't remember me, do you. I used to take you to church in Chicago, and you'd get up and hop in time to the music. You studying to be a preacher?"

"No, ma'am. I don't think so. I might be a lawyer."

"You'll be an honest one, won't you?"

"I'll try."

"Trying ain't enough! You be honest, you hear? Promise me. You be honest like your daddy."

"All right. I promise."

"Good. Rose, where's GL at? Where's that thief? He gone again?"

"I don't know, Mama." Aunt Rose looked embarrassed. "He say he was going by the store. He'll be back."

---

**1. Don Juan** (dän' wän'): An idle, immoral nobleman who enjoyed a great appeal for women.

"Well, then where's Hiram? You call up those boys, and get them over here—now! You got enough to eat? Let me go see." She started to get up. Chig reached out his hand. She shook him off. "What they tell you about me, Chig? They tell you I'm all laid up? Don't believe it. They don't know nothing about old ladies. When I want help, I'll let you know. Only time I'll need help getting anywheres is when I dies and they lift me into the ground."

She was standing now, her back and shoulders straight. She came only to Chig's chest. She squinted up at him. "You eat much? Your daddy ate like two men."

"Yes, ma'am."

"That's good. That means you ain't nervous. Your mama, she ain't nervous. I remember that. In Chicago, she'd sit down by a window all afternoon and never say nothing, just knit." She smiled. "Let me see what we got to eat."

"I'll do that, Mama." Aunt Rose spoke softly. "You haven't seen Charles in a long time. You sit and talk."

The old lady squinted at her. "You can do the cooking if you promise it ain't because you think I can't."

Aunt Rose chuckled. "I know you can do it, Mama."

"All right. I'll just sit and talk a spell." She sat again and arranged her skirt around her short legs.

Chig did most of the talking, told all about himself before she asked. His father spoke only when he was spoken to, and then, only one word at a time, as if by coming back home, he had become a small boy again, sitting in the parlor while his mother spoke with her guests.

When Uncle Hiram and Mae, his wife, came they sat down to eat. Chig did not have to ask about Uncle GL's absence; Aunt Rose volunteered an explanation: "Can't never tell where the man is at. One Thursday morning he left here and next thing we knew, he was calling from Chicago, saying he went up to see Joe Louis[2] fight. He'll be here though; he ain't as young and footloose as he used to be." Chig's father had mentioned driving down that GL was about five years older than he was, nearly fifty.

Uncle Hiram was somewhat smaller than Chig's father; his short-cropped kinky hair was half gray, half black. One spot, just off his forehead, was totally white. Later, Chig found out it had been that way since he was twenty. Mae (Chig could not bring himself to call her Aunt) was a good deal younger than Hiram, pretty enough so that Chig would have looked at her twice on the street. She was a honey-colored woman, with long eyelashes. She was wearing a white sheath.

At dinner, Chig and his father sat on one side, opposite Uncle Hiram and Mae; his grandmother and Aunt Rose sat at the ends. The food was good; there was a lot and Chig ate a lot. All through the meal, they talked about the family as it had been thirty years before, and particularly about the young GL. Mae and Chig asked questions; the old lady answered; Aunt Rose directed the discussion, steering the old lady onto the best stories; Chig's father laughed from time to time; Uncle Hiram ate.

"Why don't you tell them about the horse, Mama?" Aunt Rose, over Chig's weak protest, was spooning mashed potatoes onto his plate. "There now, Chig."

"I'm trying to think." The old lady was holding her fork halfway to her mouth, looking at them over her glasses. "Oh, you talking about that crazy horse GL brung home that time."

---

2. **Joe Louis:** U.S. boxer (1914–1981), and the world heavyweight champion from 1937 to 1949.

"That's right, Mama." Aunt Rose nodded and slid another slice of white meat on Chig's plate.

Mae started to giggle. "Oh, I've heard this. This is funny, Chig."

The old lady put down her fork and began: Well, GL went out of the house one day with an old, no-good chair I wanted him to take over to the church for a bazaar, and he met up with this man who'd just brung in some horses from out West. Now, I reckon you can expect one swindler to be in every town, but you don't rightly think there'll be two, and God forbid they should ever meet —but they did, GL and his chair, this man and his horses. Well, I wished I'd-a been there; there must-a been some mighty high-powered talking going on. That man with his horses, he told GL them horses was half-Arab, half-Indian, and GL told that man the chair was an antique he'd stole from some rich white folks. So they swapped. Well, I was a-looking out the window and seen GL dragging this animal to the house. It looked pretty gentle and its eyes was most closed and its feet was shuffling.

"GL, where'd you get that thing?" I says.

"I swapped him for that old chair, Mama," he says. "And made myself a bargain. This is even better than Papa's horse."

Well, I'm a-looking at this horse and noticing how he be looking more and more wide awake every minute, sort of warming up like a teakettle until, I swears to you, that horse is blowing steam out its nose.

"Come on, Mama," GL says, "come on and I'll take you for a ride." Now George, my husband, God rest his tired soul, he'd brung home this white folks' buggy which had a busted wheel and fixed it and was to take it back that day and GL says: "Come on, Mama, we'll use this fine buggy and take us a ride."

"GL," I says, "no, we ain't. Them white folks'll burn us alive if we use their buggy. You just take that horse right on back." You see, I was sure that boy'd come by that animal ungainly.

"Mama, I can't take him back," GL says.

"Why not?" I says.

"Because I don't rightly know where that man is at," GL says.

"Oh," I says. "Well, then I reckon we stuck with it." And I turned around to go back into the house because it was getting late, near dinner time, and I was cooking for ten.

"Mama," GL says to my back. "Mama, ain't you coming for a ride with me?"

"Go on, boy. You ain't getting me inside kicking range of that animal." I was eying that beast and it was boiling hotter all the time. I reckon maybe that man had drugged it. "That horse is wild, GL," I says.

"No, he ain't. He ain't. That man say he is buggy and saddle broke and as sweet as the inside of a apple."

My oldest girl, Essie, had-a come out on the porch and she says: "Go on, Mama. I'll cook. You ain't been out the house in weeks."

"Sure, come on, Mama," GL says. "There ain't nothing to be fidgety about. This horse is gentle as a rose petal." And just then that animal snorts so hard it sets up a little dust storm around its feet.

"Yes, Mama," Essie says, "you can see he gentle." Well, I looked at Essie and then at that horse because I didn't think we could be looking at the same animal. I should-a figured how Essie's eyes ain't never been so good.

"Come on, Mama," GL says.

"All right," I says. So I stood on the porch and watched GL hitching that horse up to the white folks' buggy. For a while there, the animal was pretty quiet, pawing a little, but not much. And I was feeling a little better about riding with GL behind that crazy-looking horse. I could see how GL was happy I was going with him. He was scurrying around that animal buckling buckles and strapping straps, all the time smiling, and that made me feel good.

Then he was finished, and I must say, that horse looked mighty fine hitched to that buggy and I knew anybody what climbed up there would look pretty good too. GL came around and stood at the bottom of the steps, and took off his hat and bowed and said: "Madam," and reached out his hand to me and I was feeling real elegant like a fine lady. He helped me up to the seat and then got up beside me and we moved out down our alley. And I remember how black folks come out on their porches and shook their heads, saying: "Lord now, will you look at Eva Dunford, the fine lady! Don't she look good sitting up there!" And I pretended not to hear and sat up straight and proud.

We rode on through the center of town, up Market Street, and all the way out where Hiram is living now, which in them days was all woods, there not being even a farm in sight and that's when that horse must-a first realized he weren't at all broke or tame or maybe thought he was back out West again, and started to gallop.

"GL," I says, "now you ain't joking with your mama, is you? Because if you is, I'll strap you purple if I live through this."

Well, GL was pulling on the reins with all his meager strength, and yelling, "Whoa, you. Say now, whoa!" He turned to me just long enough to say, "I ain't fooling with you, Mama. Honest!"

I reckon that animal weren't too satisfied with the road, because it made a sharp right turn just then, down into a gulley and struck out across a hilly meadow. "Mama," GL yells. "Mama, do something!"

I didn't know what to do, but I figured I had to do something so I stood up, hopped down onto the horse's back and pulled it to a stop. Don't ask me how I did that; I reckon it was that I was a mother and my baby asked me to do something, is all.

"Well, we walked that animal all the way home; sometimes I had to club it over the nose with my fist to make it come, but we made it, GL and me. You remember how tired we was, Charles?"

"I wasn't here at the time." Chig turned to his father and found his face completely blank, without even a trace of a smile or a laugh.

"Well, of course you was, son. That happened in . . . in . . . it was a hot summer that year and—"

"I left here in June of that year. You wrote me about it."

The old lady stared past Chig at him. They all turned to him; Uncle Hiram looked up from his plate.

"Then you don't remember how we all laughed?"

"No, I don't, Mama. And I probably wouldn't have laughed. I don't think it was funny." They were staring into each other's eyes.

"Why not, Charles?"

"Because in the first place, the horse was gained by fraud. And in the second place, both of you might have been seriously injured or even killed." He broke off their stare and spoke to himself more than to any of them: "And if I'd done it, you would've beaten me good for it."

"Pardon?" The old lady had not heard him; only Chig had heard.

Chig's father sat up straight as if preparing to debate. "I said that if I had done it, if I had done just exactly what GL did, you would have beaten me good for it, Mama." He was looking at her again.

"Why you say that, son?" She was leaning toward him.

"Don't you know? Tell the truth. It can't hurt me now." His voice cracked, but only once. "If GL and I did something wrong, you'd beat me first and then be too tired to beat him. At dinner, he'd always get seconds and I wouldn't. You'd do things with him, like ride in that buggy, but if I wanted you to do something with me, you were always too busy." He paused and considered whether to say what he finally did say: "I cried when I left here. Nobody loved me, Mama. I cried all the way up to Knoxville. That was the last time I ever cried in my life."

"Oh, Charles." She started to get up, to come around the table to him.

He stopped her. "It's too late."

"But you don't understand."

"What don't I understand? I understood then; I understand now."

Tears now traveled down the lines in her face, but when she spoke, her voice was clear. "I thought you knew. I had ten children. I had to give all of them what they needed most." She nodded. "I paid more mind to GL. I had to. GL could-a ended up swinging if I hadn't. But you was smarter. You was more growed up than GL when you was five and he was ten, and I tried to show you that by letting you do what you wanted to do."

"That's not true, Mama. You know it. GL was light-skinned and had good hair and looked almost white and you loved him for that."

"Charles, no. No, son. I didn't love any one of you more than any other."

"That can't be true." His father was standing now, his fists clenched tight. "Admit it, Mama . . . please!" Chig looked at him, shocked; the man was actually crying.

"It may not-a been right what I done, but I ain't no liar." Chig knew she did not really understand what had happened, what he wanted of her. "I'm not lying to you, Charles."

Chig's father had gone pale. He spoke very softly. "You're about thirty years too late, Mama." He bolted from the table. Silverware and dishes rang and jumped. Chig heard him hurrying up to their room.

They sat in silence for awhile and then heard a key in the front door. A man with a new, lacquered straw hat came in. He was wearing brown and white two-tone shoes with very pointed toes and a white summer suit. "Say now! Man! I heard my brother was in town. Where he at? Where that rascal?"

He stood in the doorway, smiling broadly, an engaging, open, friendly smile, the innocent smile of a five-year-old.

## THINKING ABOUT THE SELECTION

### Recalling

1. What is the reason Chig's father, Charles, gives for visiting Chig's grandmother?
2. What reasons does Charles give for leaving home when he was fifteen?
3. What is Charles's reaction to the story that Mama tells about the horse?
4. How does Mama explain the difference in the way she treated her children?

### Interpreting

5. Why is there "fear, uncertainty, sadness, and perhaps even hatred" in Charles's eyes when he kisses his mother?
6. Describe Charles's attitude toward GL.
7. Why is GL the center of attention?
8. Why do you think Charles has not visited his mother before? What draws him back now?
9. What do you think Charles's relationship with his mother will be like in the future?

### Applying

10. What are some possible effects of not clearing up misunderstandings?

## ANALYZING LITERATURE

### Understanding Characterization

With **direct characterization,** the author tells you directly what a character is like. With **indirect characterization,** the author allows you to discover what a character is like through the dialogue and action of the character or through other characters' comments. In "A Visit to Grandmother," Kelley uses indirect characterization to present GL. Even though GL doesn't appear until the end of the story, you know a great deal about him from what other characters say.

1. List three things you learn about GL indirectly.
2. Explain how the author reveals each of the details you listed.

## CRITICAL THINKING AND READING

### Making Inferences About Characters

When authors reveal characters indirectly, you make **inferences,** or reasonable conclusions based on evidence, to know what the characters are like. For example, when Aunt Rose offers to cook dinner, you might infer that she is a considerate person.

What inferences about the characters can you make from the following statements?

1. Mama: "Only time I'll need help getting anywheres is when I dies and they lift me into the ground."
2. Charles: ". . . spoke only when he was spoken to . . . as if by coming back home, he had become a small boy again . . ."

## UNDERSTANDING LANGUAGE

### Appreciating Dialect

**Dialect** refers to the speech patterns of people in a particular group or region. Dialects may include pronunciation, grammar, or vocabulary that differs from standard English. The family in "A Visit to Grandmother" speaks in a dialect.

Explain whether or not you think this story would have been as effective if the dialogue had been written in standard English.

## THINKING AND WRITING

### Writing a Character Sketch

Think of somebody you know who is an unusually interesting or memorable character. Write an article for a magazine in which you show the special qualities of the person. Include examples of things the person has done and said to illustrate your statements about what he or she is like. Try to get across the sense that the person is truly special. Revise your article, making sure your points are clear.

## Chee's Daughter

**Juanita Platero** and **Siyowin Miller** met in 1929, when Platero was living on a Navaho reservation in New Mexico and Miller was living in California. The two women collaborated on the novel *The Winds Erase Your Footprints,* which took them several years to write. The theme of that novel, as well as of "Chee's Daughter," which first appeared in *Common Ground* magazine, is the Native Americans' struggle to preserve ancient ways amid modern culture.

**Round and Flat Characters**

**Round characters** in stories appear to be fully developed people. They possess a wide and complex range of character traits, or personal qualities, and their actions can be as contradictory or as difficult to predict as those of your friends. **Flat characters** appear to have only one or two superficial character traits. Even though the story centers on Chee's daughter, she is a flat character—always an affectionate child.

**Look For**

As you read "Chee's Daughter," look for the ways in which the characters revere the old ways while trying to live in the modern world.

**Writing**

When someone close to you is no longer near, you may suddenly remember many small things about that person that are dear to you. Freewrite about the small, endearing qualities or habits of a special person that you would remember if that person were far away.

**Vocabulary**

Knowing the following words will help you as you read "Chee's Daughter."

**flicker** (flik' ər) *n.*: A species of woodpecker (p. 73)

**mesas** (mā' səz) *n.*: Flattened hills with steep sides (p. 76)

**queue** (kyōō) *n.*: A braid or pigtail worn down one's back (p. 77)

**indolence** (in' də ləns) *n.*: Idleness; a dislike for work (p. 77)

**jerked** (jʉrkt) *adj.*: Preserved by cutting into strips and drying in the sun (p. 77)

**deference** (def' ər əns) *n.*: Respect and consideration (p. 81)

**surmised** (sər mīzd') *v.*: Guessed; inferred (p. 81)

# Chee's Daughter

## Juanita Platero and Siyowin Miller

**THE CANYON**
*Jack Dudley*

The hat told the story, the big, black, drooping Stetson.[1] It was not at the proper angle, the proper rakish angle for so young a Navaho.[2] There was no song, and that was not in keeping either. There should have been at least a humming, a faint, all-to-himself "he he he heya," for it was a good horse he was riding, a slender-legged, high-stepping buckskin that would race the wind with light knee-urging. This was a day for singing, a warm winter day, when the touch of the sun upon the back belied the snow high on distant mountains.

Wind warmed by the sun touched his high-boned cheeks like flicker feathers, and still he rode on silently, deeper into Little Canyon, until the red rock walls rose straight upward from the stream bed and only a narrow piece of blue sky hung above. Abruptly the sky widened where the canyon walls were pushed back to make a wide place, as though in ancient times an angry stream had tried to go all ways at once.

This was home—this wide place in the

---

1. **Stetson** (stet′ s'n) n.: A man's hat, worn especially by Western cowboys.
2. **Navaho** (nav′ ə hō′) n.: Member of the largest Indian tribe in the U.S., who live in Arizona, New Mexico, and Utah.

canyon—levels of jagged rock and levels of rich red earth. This was home to Chee, the rider of the buckskin, as it had been to many generations before him.

He stopped his horse at the stream and sat looking across the narrow ribbon of water to the bare-branched peach trees. He was seeing them each springtime with their age-gnarled limbs transfigured beneath veils of blossom pink; he was seeing them in autumn laden with their yellow fruit, small and sweet. Then his eyes searched out the indistinct furrows of the fields beside the stream, where each year the corn and beans and squash drank thirstily of the overflow from summer rains. Chee was trying to out-weigh today's bitter betrayal of hope by gathering to himself these reminders of the integrity of the land. Land did not cheat! His mind lingered deliberately on all the days spent here in the sun caring for the young plants, his songs to the earth and to the life springing from it—". . . In the middle of the wide field . . . Yellow Corn Boy . . . He has started both ways . . . ," then the harvest and repayment in full measure. Here was the old feeling of wholeness and of oneness with the sun and earth and growing things.

Chee urged the buckskin toward the family compound where, secure in a recess of overhanging rock, was his mother's dome-shaped hogan,[3] red rock and red adobe like the ground on which it nestled. Not far from the hogan was the half-circle of brush like a dark shadow against the canyon wall—corral for sheep and goats. Farther from the hogan, in full circle, stood the horse corral made of heavy cedar branches sternly interlocked. Chee's long thin lips curved into a smile as he passed his daughter's tiny hogan squatted like a round Pueblo

oven beside the corral. He remembered the summer day when together they sat back on their heels and plastered wet adobe all about the circling wall of rock and the woven dome of piñon twigs. How his family laughed when the Little One herded the bewildered chickens into her tiny hogan as the first snow fell.

Then the smile faded from Chee's lips and his eyes darkened as he tied his horse to a corral post and turned to the strangely empty compound. "Someone has told them," he thought, "and they are inside weeping." He passed his mother's deserted loom on the south side of the hogan and pulled the rude wooden door toward him, bowing his head, hunching his shoulders to get inside.

His mother sat sideways by the center fire, her feet drawn up under her full skirts. Her hands were busy kneading dough in the chipped white basin. With her head down, her voice was muffled when she said, "The meal will soon be ready, son."

Chee passed his father sitting against the wall, hat over his eyes as though asleep. He passed his older sister who sat turning mutton ribs on a crude wire grill over the coals, noticed tears dropping on her hands. "She cared more for my wife than I realized," he thought.

Then because something must be said sometime, he tossed the black Stetson upon a bulging sack of wool and said, "You have heard, then." He could not shut from his mind how confidently he had set the handsome new hat on his head that very morning, slanting the wide brim over one eye: he was going to see his wife and today he would ask the doctors about bringing her home; last week she had looked so much better.

His sister nodded but did not speak. His mother sniffled and passed her velveteen sleeve beneath her nose. Chee sat down, leaning against the wall. "I suppose I was a

---

**3. hogan** (hō′ gôn) *n.*: Traditional Navaho dwelling, built of wood and adobe (ə dō′ bē), unburnt, sun-dried brick.

**CARMEN**
*James Asher*
*Courtesy of the artist*

fool for hoping all the time. I should have expected this. Few of our people get well from the coughing sickness.[4] But *she* seemed to be getting better.''

His mother was crying aloud now and blowing her nose noisily on her skirt. His father sat up, speaking gently to her.

Chee shifted his position and started a cigarette. His mind turned back to the Little One. At least she was too small to understand what had happened, the Little One who had been born three years before in the sanitarium where his wife was being treated for the coughing sickness, the Little One he had brought home to his mother's hogan to be nursed by his sister whose baby was a few months older. As she grew fat-cheeked and sturdy-legged, she followed him about like a shadow; somehow her baby mind had grasped that of all those at the hogan who cared for her and played with her, he—Chee—belonged most to her. She sat cross-legged at his elbow when he worked silver at the forge; she rode before him in the saddle when he drove the horses to water; often she lay wakeful on her sheep-pelts until he stretched out for the night in the darkened hogan and she could snuggle warm against him.

Chee blew smoke slowly and some of the sadness left his dark eyes as he said, ''It is not as bad as it might be. It is not as though we are left with nothing.''

Chee's sister arose, sobs catching in her throat, and rushed past him out the door-

---

**4. coughing sickness:** Tuberculosis.

way. Chee sat upright, a terrible fear possessing him. For a moment his mouth could make no sound. Then: "The Little One! Mother, where is she?"

His mother turned her stricken face to him. "Your wife's people came after her this morning. They heard yesterday of their daughter's death through the trader at Red Sands."

Chee started to protest but his mother shook her head slowly. "I didn't expect they would want the Little One either. But there is nothing you can do. She is a girl child and belongs to her mother's people; it is custom."

Frowning, Chee got to his feet, grinding his cigarette into the dirt floor. "Custom! When did my wife's parents begin thinking about custom? Why, the hogan where they live doesn't even face the East!"[5] He started toward the door. "Perhaps I can overtake them. Perhaps they don't realize how much we want her here with us. I'll ask them to give my daughter back to me. Surely, they won't refuse."

His mother stopped him gently with her outstretched hand. "You couldn't overtake them now. They were in the trader's car. Eat and rest, and think more about this."

"Have you forgotten how things have always been between you and your wife's people?" his father said.

That night, Chee's thoughts were troubled—half-forgotten incidents became disturbingly vivid—but early the next morning he saddled the buckskin and set out for the settlement of Red Sands. Even though his father-in-law, Old Man Fat, might laugh, Chee knew that he must talk to him. There were some things to which Old Man Fat might listen.

Chee rode the first part of the fifteen miles to Red Sands expectantly. The sight of sandstone buttes[6] near Cottonwood Spring reddening in the morning sun brought a song almost to his lips. He twirled his reins in salute to the small boy herding sheep toward many-colored Butterfly Mountain, watched with pleasure the feathers of smoke rising against tree-darkened western mesas from the hogans sheltered there. But as he approached the familiar settlement sprawled in mushroom growth along the highway, he began to feel as though a scene from a bad dream was becoming real.

Several cars were parked around the trading store which was built like two log hogans side by side, with red gas pumps in front and a sign across the tar-paper roofs: *Red Sands Trading Post—Groceries Gasoline Cold Drinks Sandwiches Indian Curios.* Back of the trading post an unpainted frame house and outbuildings squatted on the drab, treeless land. Chee and the Little One's mother had lived there when they stayed with his wife's people. That was according to custom—living with one's wife's people—but Chee had never been convinced that it was custom alone which prompted Old Man Fat and his wife to insist that their daughter bring her husband to live at the trading post.

Beside the post was a large hogan of logs, with brightly painted pseudo-Navaho[7] designs on the roof—a hogan with smoke-smudged windows and a garish blue door which faced north to the highway. Old Man Fat had offered Chee a hogan like this one. The trader would build it if he and his wife would live there and Chee would work at his forge making silver jewelry where tourists

---

**5. East:** By ancient custom, the hogan door is built facing east.

**6. buttes** (byo͞ots) *n.*: Flat-topped rock formations.
**7. pseudo-** (so͞o′ dō) **Navaho** *adj.*: False or imitation Navaho.

could watch him. But Chee had asked instead for a piece of land for a cornfield and help in building a hogan far back from the highway and a corral for the sheep he had brought to this marriage.

A cold wind blowing down from the mountains began to whistle about Chee's ears. It flapped the gaudy Navaho rugs which were hung in one long bright line to attract tourists. It swayed the sign *Navaho Weaver at Work* beside the loom where Old Man Fat's wife sat hunched in her striped blanket, patting the colored thread of a design into place with a wooden comb. Tourists stood watching the weaver. More tourists stood in a knot before the hogan where the sign said: *See Inside a Real Navaho Home 25c.*

Then the knot seemed to unravel as a few people returned to their cars; some had cameras; and there against the blue door Chee saw the Little One standing uncertainly. The wind was plucking at her new purple blouse and wide green skirt; it freed truant strands of soft dark hair from the meager queue into which it had been tied with white yarn.

"Isn't she cunning!" one of the women tourists was saying as she turned away.

Chee's lips tightened as he began to look around for Old Man Fat. Finally he saw him passing among the tourists collecting coins.

Then the Little One saw Chee. The uncertainty left her face and she darted through the crowd as her father swung down from his horse. Chee lifted her in his arms, hugging her tight. While he listened to her breathless chatter, he watched Old Man Fat bearing down on them, scowling.

As his father-in-law walked heavily across the graveled lot, Chee was reminded of a statement his mother sometimes made: "When you see a fat Navaho, you see one who hasn't worked for what he has."

Old Man Fat was fattest in the middle. There was indolence in his walk even though he seemed to hurry, indolence in his cheeks so plump they made his eyes squint, eyes now smoldering with anger.

Some of the tourists were getting into their cars and driving away. The old man said belligerently to Chee, "Why do you come here? To spoil our business? To drive people away?"

"I came to talk with you," Chee answered, trying to keep his voice steady as he faced the old man.

"We have nothing to talk about," Old Man Fat blustered and did not offer to touch Chee's extended hand.

"It's about the Little One." Chee settled his daughter more comfortably against his hip as he weighed carefully all the words he had planned to say. "We are going to miss her very much. It wouldn't be so bad if we knew that *part* of each year she could be with us. That might help you too. You and your wife are no longer young people and you have no young ones here to depend upon." Chee chose his next words remembering the thriftlessness of his wife's parents, and their greed. "Perhaps we could share the care of this little one. Things are good with us. So much snow this year will make lots of grass for the sheep. We have good land for corn and melons."

Chee's words did not have the expected effect. Old Man Fat was enraged. "Farmers, all of you! Long-haired farmers! Do you think everyone must bend his back over the shorthandled hoe in order to have food to eat?" His tone changed as he began to brag a little. "We not only have all the things from cans at the trader's, but when the Pueblos come past here on their way to town we buy their salty jerked mutton, young corn for roasting, dried sweet peaches."

Chee's dark eyes surveyed the land

along the highway as the old man continued to brag about being "progressive." *He* no longer was tied to the land. He and his wife made money easily and could *buy* all the things they wanted. Chee realized too late that he had stumbled into the old argument between himself and his wife's parents. They had never understood his feelings about the land—that a man took care of his land and it in turn took care of him. Old Man Fat and his wife scoffed at him, called him a Pueblo farmer, all during that summer when he planted and weeded and harvested. Yet they ate the green corn in their mutton stews, and the chili paste from the fresh ripe chilis, and the tortillas from the cornmeal his wife ground. None of this working and sweating in the sun for Old Man Fat, who talked proudly of his easy way of living—collecting money from the trader who rented this strip of land beside the highway, collecting money from the tourists.

Yet Chee had once won that argument. His wife had shared his belief in the integrity of the earth, that jobs and people might fail one but the earth never would. After that first year she had turned from her own people and gone with Chee to Little Canyon.

Old Man Fat was reaching for the Little One. "Don't be coming here with plans for my daughter's daughter," he warned. "If you try to make trouble, I'll take the case to the government man in town."

The impulse was strong in Chee to turn and ride off while he still had the Little One in his arms. But he knew his time of victory would be short. His own family would uphold the old custom of children, especially girl children, belonging to the mother's people. He would have to give his daughter up if the case were brought before the Headman of Little Canyon, and certainly he would have no better chance before a strange white man in town.

He handed the bewildered Little One to her grandfather who stood watching every movement suspiciously. Chee asked, "If I brought you a few things for the Little One, would that be making trouble? Some velvet for a blouse, or some of the jerky she likes so well . . . this summer's melon?"

Old Man Fat backed away from him. "Well," he hesitated, as some of the anger disappeared from his face and beads of greed shone in his eyes. "Well," he repeated. Then as the Little One began to squirm in his arms and cry, he said, "No! No! Stay away from here, you and all your family."

The sense of his failure deepened as Chee rode back to Little Canyon. But it was not until he sat with his family that evening in the hogan, while the familiar bustle of meal preparing went on about him, that he began to doubt the wisdom of the things he'd always believed. He smelled the coffee boiling and the oily fragrance of chili powder dusted into the bubbling pot of stew; he watched his mother turning round crusty fried bread in the small black skillet. All around him was plenty—a half of mutton hanging near the door, bright strings of chili drying, corn hanging by the braided husks, cloth bags of dried peaches. Yet in his heart was nothing.

He heard the familiar sounds of the sheep outside the hogan, the splash of water as his father filled the long drinking trough from the water barrel. When his father came in, Chee could not bring himself to tell a second time of the day's happenings. He watched his wiry, soft-spoken father while his mother told the story, saw his father's queue of graying hair quiver as he nodded his head with sympathetic exclamations.

Chee's doubting, acrid thoughts kept forming: Was it wisdom his father had passed on to him or was his inheritance only the stubbornness of a long-haired Navaho resisting change? Take care of the land and it will take care of you. True, the land had always given him food, but now food was not enough. Perhaps if he had gone to school he would have learned a different kind of wisdom, something to help him now. A schoolboy might even be able to speak convincingly to this government man whom Old Man Fat threatened to call, instead of sitting here like a clod of earth itself—Pueblo farmer indeed! What had the land to give that would restore his daughter?

In the days that followed, Chee herded sheep. He got up in the half-light, drank the hot coffee his mother had ready, then started the flock moving. It was necessary to drive the sheep a long way from the hogan to find good winter forage. Sometimes Chee met friends or relatives who were on their way to town or to the road camp where they hoped to get work; then there was friendly banter and an exchange of news. But most of the days seemed endless; he could not walk far enough or fast enough from his memories of the Little One or from his bitter thoughts. Sometimes it seemed his daughter trudged beside him, so real he could almost hear her footsteps—the muffled pad-pad of little feet clad in deerhide. In the glare of a snow bank he would see her vivid face, brown eyes sparkling. Mingling with the tinkle of sheep bells he heard her laughter.

When, weary of following the small sharp hoof marks that crossed and recrossed in the snow, he sat down in the shelter of a rock, it was only to be reminded that in his thoughts he had forsaken his brotherhood with the earth and sun and growing things. If he remembered times when he had flung himself against the earth to rest, to lie there in the sun until he could no longer feel where he left off and the earth began, it was to remember also that now he sat like an alien against the same earth; the belonging-together was gone. The earth was one thing and he was another.

It was during the days when he herded sheep that Chee decided he must leave Little Canyon. Perhaps he would take a job silversmithing for one of the traders in town. Perhaps, even though he spoke little English, he could get a job at the road camp with his cousins; he would ask them about it.

Springtime transformed the mesas. The peach trees in the canyon were shedding fragrance and pink blossoms on the gentled wind. The sheep no longer foraged for the yellow seeds of chamiso[8] but ranged near the hogan with the long-legged new lambs, eating tender young grass.

Chee was near the hogan on the day his cousins rode up with the message for which he waited. He had been watching with mixed emotions while his father and his sister's husband cleared the fields beside the stream.

"The boss at the camp says he needs an extra hand, but he wants to know if you'll be willing to go with the camp when they move it to the other side of the town?" The tall cousin shifted his weight in the saddle.

The other cousin took up the explanation. "The work near here will last only until the new cut-off beyond Red Sands is finished. After that, the work will be too far away for you to get back here often."

That was what Chee had wanted—to get away from Little Canyon—yet he found himself not so interested in the job beyond town as in this new cut-off which was almost finished. He pulled a blade of grass, split it thoughtfully down the center as he

---

**8. chamiso** (chə mē′ sō) n.: Densely growing desert shrub.

asked questions of his cousins. Finally he said: "I need to think more about this. If I decide on this job I'll ride over."

Before his cousins were out of sight down the canyon Chee was walking toward the fields, a bold plan shaping in his mind. As the plan began to flourish, wild and hardy as young tumbleweed, Chee added his own voice softly to the song his father was singing: ". . . In the middle of the wide field . . . Yellow Corn Boy . . . I wish to put in."

Chee walked slowly around the field, the rich red earth yielding to his footsteps. His plan depended upon this land and upon the things he remembered most about his wife's people.

Through planting time Chee worked zealously and tirelessly. He spoke little of the large new field he was planting because he felt so strongly that just now this was something between himself and the land. The first days he was ever stooping, piercing the ground with the pointed stick, placing the corn kernels there, walking around the field and through it, singing, ". . . His track leads into the ground . . . Yellow Corn Boy . . . his track leads into the ground." After that, each day Chee walked through his field watching for the tips of green to break through; first a few spikes in the center and then more and more until the corn in all parts of the field was above ground. Surely, Chee thought, if he sang the proper songs, if he cared for this land faithfully, it would not forsake him now, even though through the lonely days of winter he had betrayed the goodness of the earth in his thoughts.

Through the summer Chee worked long days, the sun hot upon his back, pulling weeds from around young corn plants; he planted squash and pumpkin; he terraced a small piece of land near his mother's hogan and planted carrots and onions and the moisture-loving chili. He was increasingly restless. Finally he told his family what he hoped the harvest from this land would bring him. Then the whole family waited with him, watching the corn: the slender graceful plants that waved green arms and bent to embrace each other as young winds wandered through the field, the maturing plants flaunting their pollen-laden tassels in the sun, the tall and sturdy parent corn with new-formed ears and a froth of purple, red and yellow corn-beards against the dusty emerald of broad leaves.

Summer was almost over when Chee slung the bulging packs across two pack ponies. His mother helped him tie the heavy rolled pack behind the saddle of the buck-skin. Chee knotted the new yellow kerchief about his neck a little tighter, gave the broad black hat brim an extra tug, but these were only gestures of assurance and he knew it. The land had not failed him. That part was done. But this he was riding into? Who could tell?

When Chee arrived at Red Sands, it was as he had expected to find it—no cars on the highway. His cousins had told him that even the Pueblo farmers were using the new cut-off to town. The barren gravel around the Red Sands Trading Post was deserted. A sign banged against the dismantled gas pumps *Closed until further notice.*

Old Fat Man came from the crude summer shelter built beside the log hogan from a few branches of scrub cedar and the sides of wooden crates. He seemed almost friendly when he saw Chee.

"Get down, my son," he said, eyeing the bulging packs. There was no bluster in his voice today and his face sagged, looking somewhat saddened; perhaps because his cheeks were no longer quite full enough to push his eyes upward at the corners. "You are going on a journey?"

Chee shook his head. "Our fields gave us

so much this year, I thought to sell or trade this to the trader. I didn't know he was no longer here.''

Old Man Fat sighed, his voice dropping to an injured tone. ''He says he and his wife are going to rest this winter; then after that he'll build a place up on the new highway.''

Chee moved as though to be traveling on, then jerked his head toward the pack ponies. ''Anything you need?''

''I'll ask my wife,'' Old Man Fat said as he led the way to the shelter. ''Maybe she has a little money. Things have not been too good with us since the trader closed. Only a few tourists come this way.'' He shrugged his shoulders. ''And with the trader gone —no credit.''

Chee was not deceived by his father-in-law's unexpected confidences. He recognized them as a hopeful bid for sympathy and, if possible, something for nothing. Chee made no answer. He was thinking that so far he had been right about his wife's parents: their thriftlessness had left them with no resources to last until Old Man Fat found another easy way of making a living.

Old Man Fat's Wife was in the shelter working at her loom. She turned rather wearily when her husband asked with noticeable deference if she would give him money to buy supplies. Chee surmised that the only income here was from his mother-in-law's weaving.

She peered around the corner of the shelter at the laden ponies, and then she looked at Chee. ''What do you have there, my son?''

Chee smiled to himself as he turned to pull the pack from one of the ponies, dragged it to the shelter where he untied the ropes. Pumpkins and hardshelled squash tumbled out, and the ears of corn —pale yellow husks fitting firmly over plump ripe kernels, blue corn, red corn,

**PRIVATE PERFORMANCE**
*Lois Johnson*
*Courtesy of the artist*

yellow corn, many-colored corn, ears and ears of it—tumbled into every corner of the shelter.

''Yooooh,'' Old Man Fat's Wife exclaimed as she took some of the ears in her hands. Then she glanced up at her son-in-law. ''But we have no money for all this. We have sold almost everything we own—even the brass bed that stood in the hogan.''

Old Man Fat's brass bed. Chee concealed his amusement as he started back for another pack. That must have been a hard parting. Then he stopped, for, coming from the cool darkness of the hogan was the Little One, rubbing her eyes as though she had been asleep. She stood for a moment in the doorway and Chee saw that she was dirty, barefoot, her hair uncombed, her little blouse shorn of all its silver buttons. Then she ran toward Chee, her arms out-stretched. Heedless of Old Man Fat and his wife, her father caught her in his arms, her hair falling in a dark cloud across his face, the sweetness of her laughter warm against his shoulder.

It was the haste within him to get this slow waiting game played through to the finish that made Chee speak unwisely. It was the desire to swing her before him in the saddle and ride fast to Little Canyon that prompted his words. "The money doesn't matter. You still have something. . . ."

Chee knew immediately that he had overspoken. The old woman looked from him to the corn spread before her. Unfriend-liness began to harden in his father-in-law's face. All the old arguments between himself and his wife's people came pushing and crowding in between them now.

Old Man Fat began kicking the ears of corn back onto the canvas as he eyed Chee angrily. "And you rode all the way over here thinking that for a little food we would give up our daughter's daughter?"

Chee did not wait for the old man to reach for the Little One. He walked dazedly to the shelter, rubbing his cheek against her soft dark hair and put her gently into her grandmother's lap. Then he turned back to the horses. He had failed. By his own haste he had failed. He swung into the saddle, his hand touching the roll behind it. Should he ride on into town?

Then he dismounted, scarcely glancing at Old Man Fat, who stood uncertainly at the corner of the shelter, listening to his wife. "Give me a hand with this other pack of corn, Grandfather," Chee said, carefully keeping the small bit of hope from his voice.

Puzzled, but willing, Old Man Fat helped carry the other pack to the shelter, opening it to find more corn as well as carrots and round pale yellow onions. Chee went back for the roll behind the buckskin's saddle

and carried it to the entrance of the shelter where he cut the ropes and gave the canvas a nudge with his toe. Tins of coffee rolled out, small plump cloth bags; jerked meat from several butcherings spilled from a flour sack, and bright red chilis splashed like flames against the dust.

"I will leave all this anyhow," Chee told them. "I would not want my daughter or even you old people to go hungry."

Old Man Fat picked up a shiny tin of coffee, then put it down. With trembling hands he began to untie one of the cloth bags—dried sweet peaches.

The Little One had wriggled from her grandmother's lap, unheeded, and was on her knees, digging her hands into the jerked meat.

"There is almost enough food here to last all winter," Old Man Fat's Wife sought the eyes of her husband.

Chee said, "I meant it to be enough. But that was when I thought you might send the Little One back with me." He looked down at his daughter noisily sucking jerky. Her mouth, both fists were full of it. "I am sorry that you feel you cannot bear to part with her."

Old Man Fat's Wife brushed a straggly wisp of gray hair from her forehead as she turned to look at the Little One. Old Man Fat was looking too. And it was not a thing to see. For in that moment the Little One ceased to be their daughter's daughter and became just another mouth to feed.

"And why not?" the old woman asked wearily.

Chee was settled in the saddle, the bare-footed Little One before him. He urged the buckskin faster, and his daughter clutched his shirtfront. The purpling mesas flung back the echo: ". . . My corn embrace each other. In the middle of the wide field . . . Yellow Corn Boy embrace each other."

## THINKING ABOUT THE SELECTION
### Recalling

1. Why does Chee's family allow Old Man Fat to take away Chee's daughter?
2. What is the "old argument" between Chee and Old Man Fat?
3. How does Chee get his daughter back?

### Interpreting

4. Chee's feeling for the land is strong. Find three passages from the story that show his belief in and relationship with the land.
5. How do Chee's beliefs and way of life differ from Old Man Fat's?
6. Why does losing his daughter make Chee doubt his beliefs and way of life? How does Chee finally resolve the conflict?

### Applying

7. Suppose you had to decide whether Chee or Old Man Fat should have custody of Chee's daughter. What factors would you consider?

## ANALYZING LITERATURE
### Identifying Flat and Round Characters

**Flat characters** have only a few traits. In "Chee's Daughter," for example, Chee's mother is characterized only by her belief in tradition and her grief over her daughter-in-law's death. **Round characters,** on the other hand, have depth and complexity. They are fully formed like real people, and, like real people, they can be unpredictable.

List all of the characters in "Chee's Daughter." Explain whether each is round or flat.

## CRITICAL THINKING AND READING
### Recognizing Stereotypes

A **stereotype** is an oversimplified idea about what a person or group is like. It is a view that does not allow for individual differences. In "Chee's Daughter," for example, the tourists who gather at the trading post likely see the Navahos there as stereotypes of the Navaho Indian, while the Navahos probably view the tourists as stereotypes of tourists. Generally stereotypes are examples of flat characters.

Actual people, however, are not so easily defined, which is why the stereotypical character seems false. A stereotypical character in a book or movie rarely makes us feel that we know human beings better.

Explain how each of these remarks is based on a stereotype.
1. "When you see a fat Navaho, you see one who hasn't worked for what he has."
2. "Farmers, all of you! Long-haired farmers! Do you think everyone must bend his back over the shorthandled hoe in order to have food to eat?"

## UNDERSTANDING LANGUAGE
### Tracing Word Origins

You can learn about the history of a word from a dictionary. In the etymology given there, you can find the language or languages that a word came from as well as its original meaning.

Use a dictionary to find the origin of each of the following words.
1. hogan    3. adobe
2. butte    4. skillet

## THINKING AND WRITING
### Comparing and Contrasting Characters

Suppose you worked at the trading store when Chee and his wife lived there, and you witnessed the growing conflict between Chee and Old Man Fat. Write an essay describing the two men and explaining why they will have trouble getting along together. Before you begin, list the ways the two men are alike and the ways they are different. Use this information to organize your essay. When you have written a draft, revise the essay to be sure that someone who has never met Chee or Old Man Fat will know what they are like.

## The Soldier Ran Away

**Kay Boyle** (1903– ) was born in St. Paul, Minnesota. During her career as a writer, she has produced twelve novels and numerous shorter works. Both before and after World War II, she spent several decades in Europe, and many of her novels and short stories are set there. In the late 1940's, Boyle wrote a number of stories about the Allies' postwar occupation of Germany. One of these is "The Soldier Ran Away," from the collection *Nothing Ever Breaks Except the Heart* (1966).

**Motivation**

**Motivation** is the reason for a character's behavior. Motivation can arise from outside events, a character's inner needs and wants, or a combination of both. As in real life, a character's motivations may change and develop over time.

**Look For**

As you read "The Soldier Ran Away," look for reasons for the characters' behavior. What reasons do Jeff, his father, and the runaway soldier have for what they do—or do *not* do?

**Writing**

Helping is a part of friendship, even when it is difficult to help someone. What would you be willing to do to help a friend? What limits are there to what friends can expect from one another? Freewrite about these questions.

**Vocabulary**

Knowing the following words will help you as you read "The Soldier Ran Away."

**billeted** (bil′ it′d) *v.*: Assigned quarters (p. 85)

**surreptitious** (sur′ əp tish′ əs) *adj.*: Done in a secret way (p. 87)

**beveling** (bev′′l iŋ) *v.*: Cutting to an angle other than a right angle (p. 89)

**rebuke** (ri byo͞ok′) *n.*: Reproof; disapproving statement (p. 90)

**desolation** (des′ ə la′ shən) *n.*: Wretchedness; loneliness (p. 90)

**extenuating** (ik sten′ yo͞o wāt′ iŋ) *adj.*: Serving as excuses (p. 92)

**edelweiss** (ā′ d'l vīs′) *n.*: A small, flowering alpine plant (p. 92)

**chamois** (sham′ ē) *n.*: A small, goatlike antelope (p. 92)

# The Soldier Ran Away

Kay Boyle

The colonel's son was twelve the winter he started to make the pipe rack for his father. He was a handsome, dark-eyed boy, with a voice as high and clear as a choirboy's, and a quickness, a nimbleness, about him that was in his mind as well as in his flesh. He had a skill for carpentry and mechanics in his fingers, and he could shoot game as expertly as any man his father hunted with. In the cellar of the house in which they were billeted in Germany, he and his father had set up a carpenter's bench, and there, underneath the strong stone house, they worked in the evenings or on half days or holidays.

"Look, Jeff, the idea is this," the colonel would say, and, quickly, expertly, he would sketch the plan of the bookshelf, or the oval tray, or the wren house. The boy would come close to study what he drew, and they would talk of the quality of wood and of the forests of home. "Someday we'll build a shack in the wilderness, a real log cabin, with timber we've cut down ourselves," the father would say, speaking of America as if it were a strange, far country that they had still to discover together.

Every morning a staff car would come along under the tall, ancient chestnut trees that lined the avenue, and the boy would stand in the window and watch the man dressed so trimly as a colonel go down the gravel of the path to wait on the sidewalk until the driver had slipped from under the wheel and opened the car door. For he was a doctor, and this was the routine. At a quarter past eight he would leave for the Army hospital, playing the role six days of every week, and two Sundays out of every month. The rest of the time he was a man in a khaki shirt, with the collar open, who worked at the carpenter's bench with his son, or took him hunting in the German hills, or stretched out his legs at leisure while he read of the other, wider forest lands of home.

It was winter, and the mother had taken the boy's sister off for a two-week visit to Swiss and Austrian skiing places, leaving the men with the German maid who came at half past seven and left again at half past three. If the beds were aired and made, the food bought, cooked, the house cleaned, it was accomplished while the men were away. For, in spite of the wisdom in his eyes, the boy was a schoolboy, and after his father had gone off in the morning, he would take his bicycle out and throw one leg in the blue jeans over its saddle, and, his coon cap on his head, speed down the wintry, tree-lined avenue. This was their life, and it might have continued in this coupled intimacy had not the boy thought of making the pipe rack for his father's birthday, which was a week away. He would take the tools he needed,

and the wood, and the diagram, up to the attic, he decided, and work on it there in the evenings in secrecy.

"The attic's so big not even our eight trunks take up any room," he told the two friends who cycled home from school with him, and he took them up to see it. It was a cold, bleak place at this time of year, but the boy believed that if he left the door open at the foot of the stairs, the steam-heated air would move up the stair well. "Here's my Gulf Stream," he said to his friends in his high, musical voice, as they mounted in the current of heat. "We could set the tennis table up in the middle of it," he said, and the friend named Bob Spanner spoke of putting ropes and bars and rings up on the strong wooden beams and making a gymnasium of it.

Two tilted skylights in the solid, sloping roof let in the light of day, and, standing under one of these, the friend called Malcolm Price pointed to a row of carnival masks that hung the length of one great beam. "You'll have company up here," he said, looking at the green poll parrot's face, and the devil's mask, brick red, and crowned with blunt black horns. On the other side of the parrot hung the gray cat's face, with one ear broken and its sharp, white whiskers bent, and then came two great headpieces in papier-mâché. One was a tusked boar and the other a sly, white-breasted fox, to be worn like helmets, with the throat fur molded with artistry.

"I used to collect masks once," Jeff said, as if dismissing the far time of his youth.

"We could have a square dance up

here,'' Bob Spanner said, and he started calling: "The ladies to the center with the right hand around!"

But when Jeff came up to work after supper, the sound of the other boys' voices and the calls of the square dances were there no longer. There was only the sound of his own steps, as he carried a small table up and placed it under one of the two yellow bulbs of light. The wood that he would need, and the tools, he laid on the nearest trunk top, and then he spread open the drawing of the pipe rack, and as he stood studying it there was only his own breathing on the quiet air.

That was the first night, and it could not be said that the suspicion came to him at once, but at the end of the first half hour the beginning of it was there. There was nothing the senses could identify, but every now and then he would lift his eyes from his work and look at the row of masks in uneasiness. "You fox, you devil," he would not say aloud; "you are making me nervous." But on the second night he was so much aware of the undefinable presence that at one instant he swung around from the table, and the wood he was working with fell from his hand. But there was no stir of other life in the cold and silence of the attic.

"When you're ready to start in working in the shop again," said the colonel one evening of that long week, "I had an idea. I thought of making a Lazy Susan for the dining room before the womenfolk get back."

"Sure," said the boy. "Sure, but I've got homework to do," and he saw the eagerness fade quickly from his father's face. Then he turned his head, as if in guilt, and started up the stairs.

He passed the bedroom floor, where the mother so often sat in her own room at her desk in the evening, writing letters home.

But now her room was empty and his sister's room was empty, and he mounted swiftly, softly, in his ancient sneakers, to the floor above. His own room was there, and the extra bathroom, and the spare room; and the attic was even higher in the cold. And when he opened the door at the foot of the stairs, he heard the sound of surreptitious flight above, and he stopped motionless, his heart and blood as quiet as if turned to stone.

It was his hand that first recovered the power of action, and he raised it and turned the electric switch, and instantly the light fell across the steep flight of stairs. But except for this one movement of his hand, all else was halted in him, and he could not put one foot before the other and move up the stair well, and he could not turn and go.

*There is someone up there*, he thought. *There has always been someone. All the time I've been working on the pipe rack, someone's been watching me.* But now there was absolute silence in the attic, and he backed away, hardly knowing that he moved until he came abruptly against the banister rail.

"Dad!" he called out, but from the warm, bright world below came only the far sound of American voices and American laughter from the radio, and he knew that his father was in another country, and that his own voice, calling, could not be heard. *And if I ran and asked him to come up*, he thought, *he would see the pipe rack;* and he held his breath in his teeth, and returned to the open door and mounted into the cold. In the shadows hung the carnival masks, their faces as varied as those of living men and women, but no other sign of flesh and blood was there.

In the morning he questioned his father. "Do you remember the squirrel that used to climb up the vine to the balcony?" the boy asked as his father buttoned his olive-drab tunic over in the hall. "I used to put out nuts for him," he said. "Do you think he might have moved into the attic for the winter?"

"I think he'd be showing a lot of sense if he did," said his father, and he glanced at the time on his wrist before he went out the door.

But when the boy went up to his work in the attic that night, he stopped suddenly beside the table, his eyes held by the masks. Now he knew it was not the squirrel he had heard take flight between the trunks, for the order of the masks had altered. Where the poll parrot's head had hung, the fox grinned slyly now, and the parrot hung between the cat's head and the devil's mask.

The boy looked only for a moment, and then he drew his eyes away and put them on his work, seeking to let no sign betray him. He would keep his attention on the wood, the tools, his hands as active and unshaken as if he worked without the knowledge that a stranger watched him from the obscurity. After a while, he was even able to bring himself to whistle softly, not looking toward the row of masks, but working carefully as he studied the drawing underneath his hand.

Who was it that watched him, he asked the silence. He would be a German, he thought; perhaps one of those Germans who wandered from place to place, as he had seen them wandering in the two years he had been in Germany. He would be a stocky, putty-faced man, with a look of bitterness around his mouth, he thought; and, as he worked, the wood, the tools connived with the shrewdness of the living to foil him, as if knowing this was the first thing he had set out to do alone. In the making of the tray and the wren house and the other jobs of wood and paint, the father, too, had leaned above the table, his patience making more than

the drawing clear. But now the boy's hands stumbled in uncertainty. Time was passing, and the pipe rack was no more than pieces of a puzzle he could not set straight.

He worked for an hour and a half, seeking not to believe that, without his father, he could not do this first thing of his own. Then he went in weariness down the stairs and switched the light off and locked the attic door. He locked it against a wandering German who had no other place to sleep, he thought, before he himself fell asleep; and all the next day, in the big, light classroom, he could see the stranger clearly.

He thought of how the German must climb the vines to the sloping roof at dark. In rain, or snow, or through fog, or in brilliant, icy weather, the man would keep to the chimney sweep's footholds across the roof until he reached the skylight, and then he would pry the window up and drop, soft as a cat, onto the trunk below. The boy could see the German's face, down to the dogged misery of its features, and he did not like the sight of it. But it was the knowledge that the pipe rack was not nearly done, and his father's birthday three days away, that finally took him in the evening up the attic stairs.

This time a shaft of cold cut sharp as a blade across the air, and the boy looked quickly to the roof, and he saw that the skylight window above the carnival masks stood partly open. He knew that he must cross the floor, and step, as if casually, on the trunk top, and reach up and draw it closed. And then he glanced at the wood and the tools lying on his table, and he did not go. For he saw that the pieces of the pipe rack no longer lay undecipherable, as he had left them the night before. The grooves into which the shelves must fit had been expertly cut in the harp-shaped wall piece, and when the boy lifted the delicately turned shelves, he saw that the tedious job of beveling the inner edges had been accomplished. Now they would fit into the wall piece with certainty and logic. There was only the shaping of the open circles of the pipe rests to be done, and one of these had been begun, but not completed; and after that the varnishing. And then the boy looked slowly up from these things he held, knowing, before he saw him, that a man had come out of the shadows of the attic and was standing, silent, there.

He was a young man with a long ruddy face and a light thatch of hair, and he was dressed as any German would have been dressed, his trousers and jacket not matching, his shirt GI khaki; but in his strong, rigid back, his healthy flesh, there was recorded no long and bitter history of misery. He did not speak. He waited, his small, deeply set blue eyes watching the boy with a troubled, concentrated gaze.

"Who are you?" the boy said. "What are you doing here?"

"Trying to get warm," the young man said, the voice hoarse, the speech American. "The night air don't have such a salutary effect on my breathing apparatus." The voice had a sad, vain attempt at humor in it. "You come up the stairs tonight before I could close the French window on the sun terrace." The young man rubbed his upper arms with his open palms. He was big-boned, with a spine and neck straight as a rod, and when he turned to step up on the trunk, the boy could see that the jacket was tight across his back, and tight in the armpits for him. Out of precaution, he wore no shoes, and the socks that had been khaki were washed nearly colorless and were lacy with holes. When he had closed the skylight, he dropped soft as a cat from the trunk and looked at the boy again. "Your folks, they Army or civilian?" he said, and it was important to him, the answer that would come.

"Army," the boy said.

"The brass?" the man said.

"All right, the brass," the boy said quietly.

"You'll laugh, but I picked out these palatial quarters because of the company," the man said, as he jerked his chin at the masks. "That fox! I seen first cousins of his in Pennsylvania." His concentrated gaze was fixed on the boy. "Before you started coming up here at night, I had them heads for company. I had my spiritual communion with them. I'd talk to the poll parrot about my trip to sea. It was O.K., except the boat was going in the wrong direction," he said, and the wind cried suddenly underneath the eaves. "I'd take that cat's head down, and I'd tell it what happened to cats back home if they went around catching songbirds," he said. " 'Keep to field mice,' I'd tell it. But that wild pig there, he belongs to this side of the water, so I just left him be."

"And the devil?" the boy said.

"Oh, that devil!" the man said, and he rubbed one rawboned hand over the short strands of his blond hair. "It used to get me. I couldn't stand it grinning at me, so I moved it so I could get some sleep at night." And now the wind cried louder and sleet lashed across the skylights. "Look, I made a mistake; all right, I made a mistake," he said. "I got out of the Army, and I should have stayed in."

"Well, everybody makes a mistake sometime in his life," the boy said in his clear, high voice of hope. "I was doing everything wrong with this pipe rack, and you straightened it out."

"The evenings was long up here until you started coming up," the man said. "I done something like it in the winter at home, so I thought I'd try my hand. Look,

I'm just like anybody else. I came over here in the Army six months ago. Back home," he said, "my folks got a farm thirty-two miles from Scranton, Pa. Before I came over here, I'd never been farther away from home than Scranton."

"I've heard Pennsylvania's nice. I've heard the country around there's very nice," the boy said courteously.

"It's the prettiest place in the world," the man said. "If I'd of stayed in the Army, I'd of got back there in the end. But now I got a hard time ahead if they catch up with me. I made a bad mistake, and I'll get court-martialed for what I done."

"What is it you've done?" the boy said, and his eyes were filled with adult wisdom as he waited for the man to speak.

"I been AWOL[1] two months now," the man said finally in a low voice, "When I got over here, I got so I couldn't think of nothing but getting out of the Army and getting rid of the uniform, so's I could get back to where I figured I had the right to be. I got friends, German friends, and they help me out. Every day I go and eat with them. But I got to get myself straightened out now. I can't go on like this," he said, and the storm pounded loudly on the roof and the wind cried through the eaves.

"Well, you could go back to the Army and tell them what you just told me."

"I'm afraid to go back," the man said, "and I'm afraid to stay away. I'm nineteen years old, so I figure maybe I got fifty years ahead of me, living like this. Seems like it's getting colder in here, or maybe it's because I got a cold on my chest," and he tried to button the thin jacket over his big bones. "Somebody's got to help me," he said, with no sound of drama or appeal in it. "Somebody's got to help me out of this."

"I'll help you," the boy said. He laid the delicately beveled pipe shelf flat and pushed the other tools aside.

"What's your dad's rank?" the man asked in a low voice, and as the boy began measuring and marking the unpainted wood, the man reached out to hold it steady with his hand.

"Well, he's a colonel," the boy said, not looking up from the thing that he was doing, for the first time speaking of rank as if it required some apology. "I want to cut four holes in each shelf, you know, like the diagram, for the pipes to hang from."

"A colonel," the man repeated. "So I been living in a colonel's quarters!" he said, and he jerked the laughter through his lips. "Officers, they got brass instead of blood in their veins. He'd turn me in, for sure."

"He's not an MP.[2] He's a doctor," the boy said in rebuke. He had picked up the trim electric jigsaw, and now he saw the blade of it was gone.

"That's what I stepped out to tell you," the man said, his face gone sober in apology. "I broke the blade last night, trying to get the first hole done. You'll have to put another one in."

"Only I don't have any more," the boy said, a sense of desolation spreading in him. "We've written home for more, but they haven't come yet."

"I can get you one in a German store tomorrow," the man said.

"The German blades don't fit my jigsaw," said the boy.

"Look!" cried the man, and his voice had come alive with eagerness now. "I got a

<hr>

1. **AWOL:** Absent without leave (permission) from the military.

2. **MP:** Military police.

German friend. He's got a toolshop. He'll let me take a jigsaw out. It won't cost you a cent!'' he said.

"My father's birthday," the boy said then; "it's the day after tomorrow. I got to cut the holes tonight. Tomorrow there'll be the varnishing to do."

"I can get the jigsaw now! You wait!'' said the man. "I'll be back in half an hour."

"There's a gale blowing outside," the boy said, but the inflexible neck, the rigid spine were there before him. "You better put a coat on," he said, watching the man lace up his shoes.

"I done without a coat so far," said the man, with such decision in his voice, his flesh, in the spring of his body to the trunk, that the boy could only stand and watch him go.

He drew himself up on the heels of his hands, his big legs swinging free, and, like a man forcing himself through the hatch of a submarine, he was suddenly released into the current of the streaming, rocking dark.

When he was gone, the boy looked at the watch strapped on his wrist, and saw that it marked half past eight. He jumped up on the trunk to close the skylight, and a spray of sleet struck hard against his hands and mouth. Then he went down the stairs and closed the attic door. He ran down the next flights swiftly. The door to the library stood open, and he could see his father seated, reading, his legs stretched out. The boy stepped softly across the threshold, and he stood hesitant a moment before he spoke.

"I wanted to ask you a question," he said, and his father looked up at the boy from his far, clear island of lamplight. "Did you ever want to leave the Army—I mean, illegally? Did you ever want to go AWOL—I mean, when you were young?"

The father closed his book upon his finger that marked the page. "I wanted to be a doctor in the backwoods," he said. "Perhaps I always wanted to go AWOL for that. But out of cowardice, routine, whatever you call it, I stayed where I was. But, you know, Jeff, on a night like this, with the wind howling outside, I'd like to be the renegade, the timber wolf, with his tail between his haunches. Listen to this," he said, and he opened the book again. "'Picture him with his blond hair and his blue eyes, six-feet-three on his snowshoes or in his moccasins, traveling, over rough country with a hundred pounds of supplies and equipment on his back,'" the father read, his voice quick with excitement. "'He is fifty miles from the nearest settlement and he'll be many miles farther before he swings around south again . . . he finds his way through country no white man has ever seen before, locating his range by a pocket compass, counting his paces, sweeping the forest with his keen blue eyes, sorting out pine from the rest of the timber, studying the soil to judge what lies out of sight (white pine in sandy soil, jack pine and Norway pine in heavier soil), his memory recording this country like a camera. He knows the forest like a Chippewa[3] and he carries whole countries in his mind. Whole countries without a footprint in them, except his own,'" the father read, and then he halted abruptly. "I've got to stop reading stuff like this," he said.

"Well, if a soldier does go—if he takes off—then what do they do to him?" the boy asked quietly.

"A soldier?" said the father. For a moment it seemed to be a strange word to him, and then he came back to reality. "Well, if a

---

**3. Chippewa** (chip′ə wô′): Member of a group of North American tribes living between Michigan and North Dakota.

soldier goes away with the intent to stay away, and is apprehended rather than returning voluntarily to military control, the sentence could be dishonorable discharge after several years of hard labor," the father said. "Is it wartime or peacetime you're thinking of?"

"It's now," said the boy soberly.

"If the offense were one of AWOL only, and not actual desertion," the father said, "the sentence could be of hard labor and time of confinement. But there might be extenuating circumstances."

"But what if he only wanted to go home?" the boy said. "What if that was the reason why he ran away?"

"Well, if you're talking about desertion, and if the soldier is found guilty of desertion, then that's the end of it," said the father, and he gave a yawn. "Whether you do it for murder, or love, or out of loneliness, doesn't matter materially in the end. You might as well rule the motive out, as long as the result is the same."

"That's a bad rule," the boy said.

"What do you mean?"

"Any rule that doesn't consider the reasons for doing a thing must be a bad rule," the boy said, and he stood looking at his father with his grave eyes.

"Well, good or bad, discipline has to be consistent," said the father, but now it was the colonel speaking, and the boy knew there was nothing more to say. "An army couldn't exist on a basis of compromise," the colonel said, and then he went back to the book, and, with the altering look in his face, he escaped into timber country, into conflict that had no concern with man's conflict with man, but with man versus beast and versus element.

The boy crossed the hall to the dining room then, and went through it to the kitchen, switching the lights on as he passed through the doors. He set water in a saucepan on the white-enameled, modern stove. He took a jar of soluble coffee from the dresser shelf and placed it, with a cup and saucer, on the breakfast tray. He filled the sugar bowl and laid the tongs across it, and then he sought the silver spoon he liked the best, with an edelweiss and a chamois head in intricate relief upon it, and put it beside the cup. When the water in the saucepan boiled, he poured it into a metal jug, and set the jug, in its drift of steam, in the middle of the tray.

As he did these things, the boy thought of the man who was out in the storm now, and who had lived two months in the attic over their heads. Any night, he thought, he could have opened the attic door and come down and stolen the things he needed —money and clothes and passports—and gone away. But, instead, the man had talked to the parrot and spoken of song birds to the cat's white-whiskered mask.

The boy picked the tray up carefully, and he came through the dining room with it. From the hall he could see his father reading in his zone of lamplight still, so lost in trailless country that he did not turn his head. But as the boy began to mount the stairs, the father's voice called out suddenly.

"What about getting to bed, Jeff? The women will be coming home tomorrow night, and you don't want to look tired out."

"I'm going to bed," he said. "I've just got some homework to finish first." He was safe now; he had reached the landing, and he kept on climbing toward the attic stairs.

The man came back late. It was half past nine when the boy heard him at the skylight, and he came in as if pounded and discarded by a winter sea. He took out the saw from where he had carried it inside his jacket, and then he pulled off his shoes and peeled the drenched jacket away, but nothing could stop the shaking of his bones. The boy fixed the coffee in the cup, and made him drink it down.

"I'm afraid it's not very hot now," the boy said.

"It seems hot all right to me," the man said, and the boy went down to his own room and took his sheep-lined jacket from the wardrobe, and put it around the man's shoulders, but still the deep, terrible shuddering did not cease. "When I get warm, I'll be O.K.," the man said. "I'll get the pipe rests cut all right; I'll get them done." The boy went down the stairs again and brought up the two wool blankets from his bed. "We got two nights left," the man said. He sat on the edge of the trunk with the blankets held around him, his strong, flat neck and his spine unbending still. "Working together, we'll get it done," he said, the words shaking in his mouth.

The boy did not know at what moment of the night, or the early morning, it may have been, the pipe rack was completed. It was not finished when he went down to bed, but when he went up at eight in the morning, it was already varnished a deep mahogany, and it stood, as if in a gift-shop window, on the work table to dry.

At first the boy believed that the man was out already, and then he heard him murmuring and he moved across the trunks

to where he lay. He was there behind the farthest trunk, bedded down on a mattress of newspapers, with the blankets from the boy's bed that had covered him now tossed away. His eyes were closed as if in sleep, but if this was sleep, it was a state of being so violent that the sleeper himself cried out in protest against it. The boy knelt on the trunk top in his sneakers and blue jeans, and reached down to touch the restless, burning hand.

"A fox'll thieve and kill. I seen him doing it," the man murmured, viewing, it seemed, the endlessly unwinding reel of memory. "A fox'll leave a ring of chicken feathers, and you'll find them in the moonlight. I seen it. Or else you'll find the hind leg of a fawn. Take him!" the man cried out, and from the beam above, the needle-nosed fox smiled slyly, viciously, down on them. "Take him!" the man cried out, his closed eyes fighting for sight. "Take him instead of me! He lied, thieved, killed," he said, his bright, congested face flung wildly from side to side. And then he grew calmer for an instant. "I can swim," he said, with a certain shrewdness in his voice. "I can swim," he whispered. "I can swim," and the boy's heart was stricken in him as he went down the stairs.

Afterward he told himself that he should have squeezed an orange before going to school, and taken the juice up to the man and made him drink. And when he came home from school at lunchtime and found the man's nostrils fanning rapidly for air, he should have done more, far more, than merely get the two aspirin tablets and the glass of water down his throat.

When the boy came home again at half past three, the house was quiet, and he made a pot of tea in the kitchen and carried it, with lemon and sugar, up the stairs. The man slept even more uneasily now, and his flesh was fire to the touch, and the boy's hand trembled as he fed the spoonfuls of liquid into the parched mouth. At five-thirty the staff car brought the colonel down the avenue of chestnut trees, and the boy was there to let him in, and then he stood in silence before him.

"What's up?" said the father, putting his cap on the rack.

"I have a friend," the boy said, forcing the panic out of his voice.

"You mean Bob Spanner, Malcolm Price?" his father said.

"No, it's another friend," the boy said. "He might be going to die."

"Well, I suppose his mother and father have called a doctor in?"

"No," said the boy. "He comes from Pennsylvania. He hasn't anyone in Germany."

"You mean he's over here alone?" the father said, and now he walked toward the library with his arm around his son's thin shoulders.

"Well, he got to be alone," the boy said. "He didn't want to. He didn't start out that way." And then, suddenly, he wheeled and cried out, "Will you give me your word? Will you give me your word about him?"

"My word?" said his father, stopping short in true surprise.

"Your word that you'll be on his side," the boy said, and they faced each other on the threshold of the library.

"But what side is he on?" said the father then. "Don't I have the right to know that?"

"He's my friend, that's all. He's on the same side I'm on," the boy said and he felt the weakness of crying beginning in him.

"All right. I'll give you my word, Jeff," the father said.

The colonel was a strong man, but even for a strong man it was not easy to lift the violent dreamer who fought the poll parrot and the cat and the Pennsylvania fox. The colonel bore him by the shoulders, and the boy took him underneath the knees, and they raised him across the trunks as he cried out in his delirium.

"He'll have to have oxygen," the colonel said, once they had got him on the spare-room bed. The boy fetched the doctor's bag and the night wear from his father's room below, and, having examined the clogged, whistling lungs and listened to the racing heart the colonel gave the penicillin shot. "Pneumonia. We'll have to get him to the hospital," he said.

"The hospital? You mean the Army hospital?" the boy said.

"Well, yes," said the father, his hand already on the door. "I see he hasn't any papers on him, but he's American, isn't he?"

"Yes, he's American," the boy said, and he stood looking at the man whose head tossed on the pillow, fighting for something as commonplace as breath. "But you can't take him to the hospital. If you did that, they'd know."

"Know what?" said the father, with the stethoscope hooked around his neck still.

"That he's a soldier. That he hasn't any right to be here," the boy said.

"So that's it. So he's your soldier," the father said, after a moment, and then he went out of the room, and he did not close the door behind him, but went down the stairs. The boy heard him descend the first flight and cross the bedroom hall, and then go down the second flight. Then he heard him dialing in the entrance hall.

"This is Colonel Wheeler," he heard his father say, the voice not loud. "Give me emergency," he said, and the ill man cried out as if in protest. "Colonel Wheeler," the quiet, authoritative voice said, and it went on, saying: "I want you to get me an ambulance here as quickly as you can." He spelled out the German name of the street, calling it quietly, letter by letter. "I'll need two containers of oxygen, and make it fast," he said.

The boy had come down the stairs, running swiftly, and, as the colonel put the telephone arm back in its place, he stood slender, almost frail-looking, in his cowboy shirt, before him in the hall.

"You can't do that. You can't turn him in. You could put him in a German hospital," he said.

"Look, Jeff," said the colonel. "I've done what I said I'd do. I've taken his side without asking any questions about him. I'm giving him a chance to fight for his life, and maybe that's all he has the right to ask of anyone."

"But he's not asking anything!" the boy cried out, trying to say, and not quite saying: *This is something between me and you!*

"Look, Jeff," the colonel said again. "A pilot fumbles a landing, and he's had it. A fighter miscalculates a punch, and he's down for the count. If you make a mistake—well, somehow you've got to take the rap."

"He's taking the rap!" the boy said, and he tried to keep his voice from trembling. "He's been taking it for two months, and he's taking it upstairs now."

"An army, Jeff—any army—wouldn't get very far on that kind of reasoning" the colonel began saying. "An army—" he said, but he could not find the rest of what he wanted to say because of the look in the boy's strangely adult eyes.

"If that's the kind of army it is, then I don't believe in it," the boy said. "It's not my kind of army," he said in his high, clear, almost-dedicated voice, and the color went out of the colonel's face, and he turned and walked into the library and closed the door.

Going up the stairs, the boy sensed the desolation, as if, in the silence of the library, the forests of their pioneering life together, the long, running trails of their adventuring, were, tree by tall tree, and valley by valley, to be destroyed. If these trees fell, he knew the mysterious horizon which had always lain ahead would dwindle to the horizon of all men's lives. If these valleys were laid waste, there would be no male wilderness to be conquered as men together, sharing the burden and the hardships as they had shared the dream.

*Tomorrow my father will be forty-three,* the boy thought. *He is too old now. He cannot understand.*

It seemed to him that he stood a long time by the ill man's bed, hearing only the throttled rhythm of his drowning, and then the far wail of the siren spiraled, threadlike, coming nearer, ever nearer, the sound of it filled with such grief that the boy put his hands over his ears as the ambulance stopped beneath the chestnut trees. The doorbell did not ring, for the colonel had already known, and opened the door. And then the boy heard their voices—his father's voice and the medical sergeant's voice—and the steps of the others—the stretcher bearers—as they came toward the stairs.

"A pneumonia case," the father was saying. "I've given him penicillin, and I want to get him on oxygen right away. A soldier," he was saying as he and the others crossed the bedroom hall, and the boy stood erect by the soldier's bed, his hands closed into fists. "A young kid who'd been AWOL, and who must have seen my name outside on the door, and came in to give himself up," the father was saying as they started up the second flight.

"How'll we check him in, sir?" the medical sergeant said.

"I don't know his name. We didn't get that far," said the father. "Give him mine. Call him 'Wheeler' until he comes around. I'm responsible for him. I'll ride up with you and take care of the formalities."

"Yes, sir," the medical sergeant said, and now they came through the door together.

"He came here wanting to turn himself in, trying to find the right authority, and I found him suffering from exposure," said the father, and he and the boy might have stood there alone in the lighted room, the trees of their wilderness tall around them, the horizon opening wide and far.

## THINKING ABOUT THE SELECTION

### Recalling

1. What reasons does Jeff have for suspecting that someone is in the attic?
2. Why is the soldier living in the attic?
3. How do Jeff and the soldier help each other?
4. How does the soldier become ill?

### Interpreting

5. Why is Jeff sympathetic to the soldier?
6. Compare Jeff's ideas about the army and its rules with those of his father.
7. Do you think that Jeff is satisfied with the way his father handles the situation with the sick soldier? Explain.
8. In what ways does Jeff act maturely and in what ways does he act immaturely?
9. In what way does Jeff's relationship with his father change during the story?

### Applying

10. Imagine that you are Jeff and have found an AWOL soldier in the attic. What would you do?

## ANALYZING LITERATURE

### Understanding Motivation

**Motivation** is the cause of a character's actions. Wants, needs, or drives may all be motives that determine a character's behavior. Motives can arise from outside events or from a character's internal needs. For example, the soldier's motivation for running away is internal; it springs from his loneliness and longing for home.

1. What is Jeff's motivation for making his father a pipe rack?
2. What is Jeff's motivation for helping the soldier in the attic?
3. What is Jeff's father's motivation for calling the ambulance?
4. What is Jeff's father's motivation for telling a false story to the medical sergeant?

## CRITICAL THINKING AND READING

### Defending a Character

Like real people, characters in stories may act wisely or foolishly; their deeds can cause good or harm. It is clearly against army regulations for a soldier to desert the army. However, the soldier in "The Soldier Ran Away" does not seem unethical when he explains that his motivation was his desperate longing to get back home.

Imagine that you are a lawyer. Prepare a defense for the soldier. Present it to your classmates.

## UNDERSTANDING LANGUAGE

### Appreciating Word Parts

A word may be made up of a number of parts. The **word root** is the base of the word to which prefixes or suffixes can be added. **Prefixes** are syllables joined to the beginnings of words to form new words. **Suffixes** are syllables joined to the ends of words to form new words.

For example, the word *illegally* is made up of the word root *legal* plus the prefix *il-* and the suffix *-ly*. Sometimes the spelling of a word root may change when a suffix is added.

Break each of the following words into its parts. Then define each word.

1. dishonorable      3. miscalculates
2. courteously       4. authoritative

## THINKING AND WRITING

### Writing About Motivation

Imagine that you are either Jeff or his father. First identify all the different motives, both external and internal, you had for your behavior in "The Soldier Ran Away." Then write a diary entry telling what has happened and explaining why you did what you did. Revise it to make sure you have made your actions understandable.

# GUIDE FOR READING

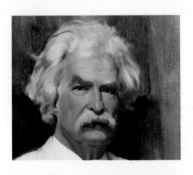

## Luck

**Mark Twain** (1835–1910) is the pen name for Samuel Langhorne Clemens, one of America's greatest writers. He was born in Florida, Missouri, and grew up in nearby Hannibal. Twain worked as a printer and a riverboat pilot, prospected for gold, and gave lectures around the world. His pen name is from the cry of Mississippi riverboatmen: "By the mark, twain!"—assessing the river as two fathoms deep. His two most widely read novels are *The Adventures of Tom Sawyer* (1876) and *The Adventures of Huckleberry Finn* (1885).

### Static and Dynamic Characters

Characters can be classified as either static or dynamic. **Static characters** do not change during the course of the story. They remain the same no matter what happens to them. **Dynamic characters** change and sometimes learn as a result of the events of the story. The changes they undergo affect their personality traits, attitudes, or beliefs.

### Look For

What role does luck play in people's lives? Is a person's reputation determined by what that person is or by sheer luck? As you read "Luck," look for Scoresby's dominant character traits and the role luck plays in shaping his reputation.

### Writing

The character Scoresby in "Luck" is considered a hero and admired by many people. List the character traits you think are necessary to make a person a hero.

### Vocabulary

Knowing the following words will help you as you read "Luck."

**zenith** (zē′ nith) *n*.: The highest point (p. 99)

**countenance** (koun′ tə nəns) *n*.: The expression of a person's face (p. 99)

**veracity** (və ras′ ə tē) *n*.: Truthfulness; honesty (p. 99)

**guileless** (gīl′ lis) *adj*.: Without slyness or cunning; frank (p. 100)

**prodigious** (prə dij′ əs) *adj*.: Enormous (p. 101)

**sublimity** (sə blim′ ə tē) *n*.: A noble or exalted state (p. 101)

# Luck

## Mark Twain

It was at a banquet in London in honor of one of the two or three conspicuously illustrious[1] English military names of this generation. For reasons which will presently appear, I will withhold his real name and titles, and call him Lieutenant-General Lord Arthur Scoresby, V.C., K.C.B., etc., etc., etc. What a fascination there is in a renowned name! There sat the man, in actual flesh, whom I had heard of so many thousands of times since that day, thirty years before, when his name shot suddenly to the zenith from a Crimean battlefield,[2] to remain forever celebrated. It was food and drink to me to look, and look, and look at that demigod; scanning, searching, noting: the quietness, the reserve, the noble gravity of his countenance; the simple honesty that expressed itself all over him; the sweet unconsciousness of his greatness—unconsciousness of the hundreds of admiring eyes fastened upon him, unconsciousness of the deep, loving, sincere worship welling out of the breasts of those people and flowing toward him.

The clergyman at my left was an old acquaintance of mine—clergyman now, but had spent the first half of his life in the camp and field, and as an instructor in the military school at Woolwich. Just at the moment I have been talking about, a veiled and singular light glimmered in his eyes, and he leaned down and muttered confidentially to me—indicating the hero of the banquet with a gesture:

"Privately—he's an absolute fool."

This verdict was a great surprise to me. If its subject had been Napoleon,[3] or Socrates,[4] or Solomon,[5] my astonishment could not have been greater. Two things I was well aware of: that the Reverend was a man of strict veracity, and that his judgment of men was good. Therefore I knew, beyond doubt or question, that the world was mistaken about this hero: he *was* a fool. So I meant to find out, at a convenient moment, how the Reverend, all solitary and alone, had discovered the secret.

Some days later the opportunity came, and this is what the Reverend told me:

About forty years ago I was an instructor in the military academy at Woolwich. I was

---

1. **conspicuously** (kən spik′ yoo wəs lē) **illustrious** (il us′ trē əs): Outstandingly famous.
2. **Crimean** (Krī mē′ən) **battlefield**: A place of battle during the Crimean War (1854–1856), in which Russia was defeated in trying to dominate southeastern Europe.
3. **Napoleon** (nə pō′ lē ən): Napoleon Bonaparte (1769–1821), French military leader and emperor of France from 1804 to 1815.
4. **Socrates** (säk′ rə tēz′): Athenian philosopher and teacher (470?–399 B.C.).
5. **Solomon** (säl′ ə mən): In the Bible, the King of Israel who built the first temple and was noted for his wisdom.

**"HINT TO MODERN SCULPTORS AS
AN ORNAMENT TO A FUTURE SQUARE"**
*Hand-colored etching
by James Gillray*

present in one of the sections when young Scoresby underwent his preliminary examination. I was touched to the quick with pity; for the rest of the class answered up brightly and handsomely, while he—why, dear me, he didn't know *anything,* so to speak. He was evidently good, and sweet, and lovable, and guileless; and so it was exceedingly painful to see him stand there, as serene as a graven image, and deliver himself of answers which were veritably miraculous for stupidity and ignorance. All the compassion in me was aroused in his behalf. I said to myself, when he comes to be examined again, he will be flung over, of course; so it will be simply a harmless act of charity to ease his fall as much as I can. I took him aside, and found that he knew a little of Caesar's history;[6] and as he didn't know anything else, I went to work and drilled him like a galley slave on a certain line of stock questions concerning Caesar which I knew would be used. If you'll believe me, he went through with flying colors on examination day! He went through on that purely superficial "cram," and got compliments too, while others, who knew a thousand times more than he, got plucked. By some strangely lucky accident—an accident not likely to happen twice in a century—he was asked no question outside of the narrow limits of his drill.

It was stupefying. Well, all through his course I stood by him, with something of the sentiment which a mother feels for a crippled child; and he always saved himself —just by miracle, apparently.

Now of course the thing that would expose him and kill him at last was mathematics. I resolved to make his death as easy as I could; so I drilled him and crammed him, and crammed him and drilled him, just on the line of questions which the examiners would be most likely to use, and then launched him on his fate. Well, sir, try to conceive of the result: to my consternation he took the first prize! And with it he got a perfect ovation in the way of compliments.

Sleep? There was no more sleep for me for a week. My conscience tortured me day and night. What I had done I had done purely through charity, and only to ease the poor youth's fall—I never had dreamed of any such preposterous result as the thing that had happened. I felt as guilty and miserable as the creator of Frankenstein. Here

was a woodenhead whom I had put in the way of glittering promotions and prodigious responsibilities, and but one thing could happen: he and his responsibilities would all go to ruin together at the first opportunity.

The Crimean War had just broken out. Of course there had to be a war, I said to myself: we couldn't have peace and give this donkey a chance to die before he is found out. I waited for the earthquake. It came. And it made me reel when it did come. He was actually gazetted[7] to a captaincy in a marching regiment! Better men grow old and gray in the service before they climb to a sublimity like that. And who could ever have foreseen that they would go and put such a load of responsibility on such green and inadequate shoulders? I could just barely have stood it if they had made him a cornet;[8] but a captain—think of it! I thought my hair would turn white.

Consider what I did—I who so loved repose and inaction. I said to myself, I am responsible to the country for this, and I must go along with him and protect the country against him as far as I can. So I took my poor little capital that I had saved up through years of work and grinding economy, and went with a sigh and bought a cornetcy in his regiment, and away we went to the field.

And there—oh dear, it was awful. Blunders?—why, he never did anything *but* blunder. But, you see, nobody was in the fellow's secret—everybody had him focused wrong, and necessarily misinterpreted his performance every time—consequently they took his idiotic blunders for inspirations of genius; they did, honestly! His mildest blunders were enough to make a man in his right mind cry; and they did

---

**6. Caesar's** (sē′ zərz) **history:** The account of Julius Caesar (100?–44 B.C.), Roman emperor from 49 to 44 B.C.

**7. gazetted** (gə zet′ əd) *v.*: Officially promoted.
**8. cornet** (kôr net′) *n.*: A British cavalry officer who carried his troop's flag.

make me cry—and rage and rave too, privately. And the thing that kept me always in a sweat of apprehension was the fact that every fresh blunder he made increased the luster of his reputation! I kept saying to myself, he'll get so high, that when discovery does finally come, it will be like the sun falling out of the sky.

He went right along up, from grade to grade, over the dead bodies of his superiors, until at last, in the hottest moment of the battle of * * * * down went our colonel, and my heart jumped into my mouth, for Scoresby was next in rank! Now for it, said I; we'll all land in Sheol[9] in ten minutes, sure.

The battle was awfully hot; the allies were steadily giving way all over the field. Our regiment occupied a position that was vital; a blunder now must be destruction. At this crucial moment, what does this immortal fool do but detach the regiment from its place and order a charge over a neighboring hill where there wasn't a suggestion of an

---

**9. Sheol** (shē′ ōl) *n.*: In the Bible, a place in the depths of the earth where the dead are thought to dwell.

**SCOTLAND FOREVER**
*Elizabeth Butler*
*Leeds City Art Galleries*

enemy. ''There you go!'' I said to myself; ''this *is* the end at last.''

And away we did go, and were over the shoulder of the hill before the insane movement could be discovered and stopped. And what did we find? An entire and unsuspected Russian army in reserve! And what happened? We were eaten up? That is necessarily what would have happened in ninety-nine cases out of a hundred. But no, those Russians argued that no single regiment would come browsing around there at such a time. It must be the entire English

army, and that the sly Russian game was detected and blocked; so they turned tail, and away they went, pell-mell, over the hill and down into the field, in wild confusion, and we after them; they themselves broke the solid Russian center in the field, and tore through, and in no time there was the most tremendous rout you ever saw, and the defeat of the allies was turned into a sweeping and splendid victory! Marshal Canrobert looked on, dizzy with astonishment, admiration, and delight; and sent right off for Scoresby, and hugged him, and decorated him on the field, in presence of all the armies!

And what was Scoresby's blunder that time? Merely the mistaking his right hand for his left—that was all. An order had come to him to fall back and support our right; and instead, he fell *forward* and went over the hill to the left. But the name he won that day as a marvelous military genius filled the world with his glory, and that glory will never fade while history books last.

He is just as good and sweet and lovable and unpretending as a man can be, but he doesn't know enough to come in when it rains. Now that is absolutely true. He is the supremest fool in the universe; and until half an hour ago nobody knew it but himself and me. He has been pursued, day by day and year by year, by a most phenomenal and astonishing luckiness. He has been a shining soldier in all our wars for a generation; he has littered his whole military life with blunders, and yet has never committed one that didn't make him a knight or a baronet or a lord or something. Look at his breast; why, he is just clothed in domestic and foreign decorations. Well, sir, every one of them is the record of some shouting stupidity or other; and taken together, they are proof that the very best thing in all this world that can befall a man is to be born lucky. I say again, as I said at the banquet, Scoresby's an absolute fool.

## THINKING ABOUT THE SELECTION

### Recalling

1. How does the clergyman describe Scoresby?
2. How does the clergyman feel about Scoresby when he first meets him?
3. Describe two things the clergyman does in order to help Scoresby.
4. Trace the series of lucky events that put Scoresby in a position of leadership.
5. How does Scoresby achieve his "greatest victory"?

### Interpreting

6. How does the narrator's first impression of Scoresby contrast with the view of him given by the clergyman?
7. Compare and contrast Scoresby and the clergyman.
8. Do you agree with the clergyman that Scoresby is a fool? Explain your answer. In what way is the clergyman also a fool?

### Applying

9. The clergyman states that "the very best thing in the world is to be born lucky." In your opinion, to what extent does luck play a role in a person's success? Give examples to support your opinion.

## ANALYZING LITERATURE

### Recognizing Static Characters

Dynamic characters grow and change in response to the events of a story. They are different at the end of the story from the way they were at the beginning of the story. **Static characters,** on the other hand, do not change in any fundamental way. Their personalities, opinions, and attitudes are fixed.

In "Luck," Scoresby is an example of a static character. According to the clergyman, not only is he a fool as a youth and as an older man, but his personality remains the same in other ways.

Find descriptions of Scoresby that indicate he remains the same at each of the following points in his life.

1. while a student in the military academy
2. while a young officer in the Crimean war
3. while an older military hero

## CRITICAL THINKING AND READING

### Recognizing Humor

Some character traits are more likely than others to produce humor. A character such as Scoresby, who is a foolish bungler, may be humorous in a number of ways. For example, his actions may bring unexpected or absurd results, or humorous misunderstandings may arise from his foolishness.

How does Scoresby's character lend humor to each of these situations?

1. the banquet at which hundreds of admirers come to honor Scoresby
2. the major victory Scoresby won in the Crimean war

## THINKING AND WRITING

### Writing About a Person

Think about the traits you wrote about before reading "Luck" and a person that you might nominate for a "Person of the Year" award. List this person's main character traits, and freewrite about them. Use this information to write a description of this person for the nominating committee. Include examples of things the person has said and done to illustrate the traits that you see but that might not be apparent to the committee. When you revise your description, add any anecdotes you can think of that would convince the committee to consider this person as "Person of the Year."

# Point of View

**STAIRWAY, c. 1925**
*Edward Hopper*
Collection of Whitney Museum of American Art

# GUIDE FOR READING

## The Laugher

**Heinrich Böll** (1917–1985) was born in Cologne, Germany. He served in the German Army during World War II, during which he was wounded four times and taken prisoner. After the war, he attended the University of Cologne. Böll, who has written extensively about the social and moral costs of World War II, received the Nobel Prize for literature in 1972. "The Laugher" is about a man who earns his living in an unusual way.

### First-Person Point of View

**Point of view** is the position or perspective from which the events of a story are seen. When an author uses **first-person** point of view, the perspective is that of one of the characters in the story. That character participates in the events and tells the story using the first-person pronoun. What you learn from a first-person narrator is limited to what the narrator thinks and observes. The main character in "The Laugher" tells his own story in the first person.

### Look For

As you read "The Laugher," look for clues to the narrator's personality and background in what he says.

### Writing

The narrator of this story laughs a lot. Try to remember a time when you could not stop laughing. Freewrite about how you felt. Describe specifically how different parts of your body, such as your eyes, facial muscles, stomach, and lungs, felt. If you like, also describe how you probably looked to others.

### Vocabulary

Knowing the following words will help you as you read "The Laugher."

**poise** (pɔiz) *n.*: Self assurance; ease of manner (p. 107)

**avowal** (ə vou′ əl) *n.*: Declaration (p. 107)

**constrained** (kən strānd′) *adj.*: Compelled (p. 107)

**infectious** (in fek′ shəs) *adj.*: Tending to spread; catching (p. 107)

**claque** (klak) *n.*: A group paid to applaud at a performance (p. 107)

**marzipan** (mär′ zi pan′) *n.*: A candy made from almonds, sugar, and egg whites (p. 108)

**taciturn** (tas′ ə turn′) *adj.*: Not talkative (p. 108)

**impassive** (im pas′ iv) *adj.*: Showing no emotion (p. 108)

# The Laugher

Heinrich Böll
translated by Leila Vennewitz

When someone asks me what business I am in, I am seized with embarrassment: I blush and stammer, I who am otherwise known as a man of poise. I envy people who can say: I am a bricklayer. I envy barbers, bookkeepers and writers the simplicity of their avowal, for all these professions speak for themselves and need no lengthy explanation, while I am constrained to reply to such questions: I am a laugher. An admission of this kind demands another, since I have to answer the second question: "Is that how you make your living?" truthfully with "Yes." I actually do make a living at my laughing, and a good one too, for my laughing is—commercially speaking—much in demand. I am a good laugher, experienced, no one else laughs as well as I do, no one else has such command of the fine points of my art. For a long time, in order to avoid tiresome explanations, I called myself an actor, but my talents in the field of mime[1] and elocution[2] are so meager that I felt this designation to be too far from the truth: I love the truth, and the truth is: I am a laugher. I am neither a clown nor a comedian. I do not make people gay, I portray gaiety: I laugh like a Roman emperor, or like a sensitive schoolboy, I am as much at home in the laughter of the seventeenth century as in that of the nineteenth, and when occasion demands I laugh my way through all the centuries, all classes of society, all categories of age: it is simply a skill which I have acquired, like the skill of being able to repair shoes. In my breast I harbor the laughter of America, the laughter of Africa, white, red, yellow laughter—and for the right fee I let it peal out in accordance with the director's requirements.

I have become indispensable; I laugh on records, I laugh on tape, and television directors treat me with respect. I laugh mournfully, moderately, hysterically; I laugh like a streetcar conductor or like a helper in the grocery business; laughter in the morning, laughter in the evening, nocturnal laughter and the laughter of twilight. In short: wherever and however laughter is required—I do it.

It need hardly be pointed out that a profession of this kind is tiring, especially as I have also—this is my specialty—mastered the art of infectious laughter; this has also made me indispensable to third- and fourth-rate comedians, who are scared—and with good reason—that their audiences will miss their punch lines, so I spend most evenings in night clubs as a kind of discreet claque, my job being to laugh infectiously during the weaker parts of the pro-

---

**1. mime** (mīm) *n.*: Pantomime.
**2. elocution** (el′ ə kyü′ s/hən) *n.*: The art of clear and effective public speaking.

gram. It has to be carefully timed: my hearty, boisterous laughter must not come too soon, but neither must it come too late, it must come just at the right spot: at the prearranged moment I burst out laughing, the whole audience roars with me, and the joke is saved.

But as for me, I drag myself exhausted to the checkroom, put on my overcoat, happy that I can go off duty at last. At home I usually find telegrams waiting for me: "Urgently require your laughter. Recording Tuesday," and a few hours later I am sitting in an overheated express train bemoaning my fate.

I need scarcely say that when I am off duty or on vacation I have little inclination to laugh: the cowhand is glad when he can forget the cow, the bricklayer when he can forget the mortar, and carpenters usually have doors at home which don't work or drawers which are hard to open. Confectioners like sour pickles, butchers like marzipan, and the baker prefers sausage to bread; bullfighters raise pigeons for a hobby, boxers turn pale when their children have nosebleeds: I find all this quite natural, for I never laugh off duty. I am a very solemn person, and people consider me—perhaps rightly so—a pessimist.

During the first years of our married life, my wife would often say to me: "Do laugh!" but since then she has come to realize that I cannot grant her this wish. I am happy when I am free to relax my tense face muscles, my frayed spirit, in profound solemnity. Indeed, even other people's laughter gets on my nerves, since it reminds me too much of my profession. So our marriage is a quiet, peaceful one, because my wife has also forgotten how to laugh: now and again I catch her smiling, and I smile too. We converse in low tones, for I detest the noise of the night clubs, the noise that sometimes fills the recording studios. People who do not know me think I am taciturn. Perhaps I am, because I have to open my mouth so often to laugh.

I go through life with an impassive expression, from time to time permitting myself a gentle smile, and I often wonder whether I have ever laughed. I think not. My brothers and sisters have always known me for a serious boy.

So I laugh in many different ways, but my own laughter I have never heard.

## THINKING ABOUT THE SELECTION

### Recalling

1. Identify the laugher's profession. Explain the skills he possesses that qualify him for his job.
2. Describe the atmosphere in which the laugher usually works.
3. Describe the laugher's home life. How has his wife changed over time?

### Interpreting

4. Describe the laugher's personality. Explain how it is at odds with his profession.
5. What does the laugher mean when he says, "I often wonder whether I have ever laughed"?
6. Explain the last line of this selection.

### Applying

7. How do you think people in other occupations might feel about their work when they are away from their work? Supply evidence from life to support your answer.

## ANALYZING LITERATURE

### Interpreting First-Person Point of View

With **first-person point of view,** one of the characters narrates the story, using the pronoun *I.* A first-person narrator, telling only what he or she knows or observes, is likely to convey his or her own attitudes. For example, the narrator of "The Laugher" shows you a world shaded by his own gloom.

The poet Thomas Campbell once wrote,

"'Tis distance lends enchantment to the view, And robes the mountain in its azure hue."

First discuss the meaning of this quotation. Then explain how someone looking at the profession of a laugher from the outside might view it differently from the way the laugher does.

## CRITICAL THINKING AND READING

### Determining the Author's Purpose

Authors can choose to tell their stories from any point of view. The reason that an author uses a particular point of view for a specific story may depend on a number of considerations, such as what the author wants you to know about the characters or how he or she plans to develop the plot. In "The Laugher," Böll goes inside the laugher's mind in order to give his view of the world.

Explain whether or not you think Böll's purpose may have been to show the difference between reality and artifice in modern society. Find evidence from the story that supports your opinion.

## UNDERSTANDING LANGUAGE

### Understanding Synonyms

**Synonyms** are words that have almost the same meaning. The words *serious* and *solemn,* for example, are synonyms.

Rewrite the following sentences substituting a synonym for the italicized word.

1. ". . . my talents in the field of mime and elocution are so *meager* that I felt this designation to be too far from the truth. . . ."
2. "I have become *indispensable;* I laugh on records, I laugh on tape, and television directors treat me with respect."
3. "We *converse* in low tones. . . ."

## THINKING AND WRITING

### Writing in the First Person

Imagine a person in a very unusual profession. Write a journal entry as that person might, using the first-person pronoun *I.* In the entry, describe a day in the life of this person. When you revise the entry, be certain that it is written consistently from that person's viewpoint and have presented events in chronological order.

# GUIDE FOR READING

## Shaving

**Leslie Norris** (1921–    ) was born and brought up in Merthyr Tydfil, Wales—one of the world's first industrial cities. His first book of poems appeared in 1942, and he has been writing poetry and short stories ever since. He studied at the University of Southampton Institute of Education and has always worked as a teacher in addition to writing. In "Shaving" you can detect the poet at work in the vivid words Norris uses for effect.

### Third-Person Point of View

When a writer uses **third-person point of view,** all the characters are referred to by name or by the third-person pronouns *he, she,* or *they.* With **third-person limited** point of view, the perspective is limited to what one character does, observes, and thinks. Even though this character does not narrate the story, you see it through his or her eyes. "Shaving" is told from a third-person limited point of view—that of a sixteen-year-old boy facing an adult crisis.

### Look For

One common theme in literature is acceptance of change and mortality. As you read "Shaving," look for how Barry comes to change and accept the inevitability of his father's death.

### Writing

In this story a routine activity becomes very special. You may have experienced situations when this is true. For example, preparing dinner for a birthday celebration feels different from preparing the same meal on an ordinary day. Freewrite about a real or imagined occasion that might make an everyday activity special.

### Vocabulary

Knowing the following words will help you as you read "Shaving."

**jostling** (jäs' liŋ) *adj.:* Bumping; pushing (p. 111)

**suave** (swäv) *adj.:* Smoothly polite; polished (p. 111)

**libations** (lī bā' shənz) *n.:* The liquids poured as offerings in a religious ritual (p. 113)

**inert** (in ʉrt') *adj.:* Unable to move or act (p. 113)

**arrogantly** (ar' ə gənt lē) *adv.:* Proudly; haughtily (p. 113)

**evocative** (i väk' ə tiv) *adj.:* Having the power to bring forth memories (p. 114)

# Shaving

## Leslie Norris

Earlier, when Barry had left the house to go to the game, an overnight frost had still been thick on the roads, but the brisk April sun had soon dispersed it, and now he could feel the spring warmth on his back through the thick tweed of his coat. His left arm was beginning to stiffen up where he'd jarred it in a tackle, but it was nothing serious. He flexed his shoulders against the tightness of his jacket and was surprised again by the unexpected weight of his muscles, the thickening strength of his body. A few years back, he thought, he had been a small, unimportant boy, one of a swarming gang laughing and jostling to school, hardly aware that he possessed an identity. But time had transformed him. He walked solidly now, and often alone. He was tall, strongly made, his hands and feet were adult and heavy, the rooms in which all his life he'd moved had grown too small for him. Sometimes a devouring restlessness drove him from the house to walk long distances in the dark. He hardly understood how it had happened. Amused and quiet, he walked the High Street among the morning shoppers.

He saw Jackie Bevan across the road and remembered how, when they were both six years old, Jackie had swallowed a pin. The flustered teachers had clucked about Jackie as he stood there, bawling, cheeks awash with tears, his nose wet. But now Jackie was tall and suave, his thick, pale hair sleekly tailored, his gray suit enviable. He was talking to a girl as golden as a daffodil.

"Hey, hey!" called Jackie. "How's the athlete, how's Barry boy?"

He waved a graceful hand at Barry.

"Come and talk to Sue," he said.

Barry shifted his bag to his left hand and walked over, forming in his mind the answers he'd make to Jackie's questions.

"Did we win?" Jackie asked. "Was the old Barry Stanford magic in glittering evidence yet once more this morning? Were the invaders sent hunched and silent back to their hovels in the hills? What was the score? Give us an epic account, Barry, without modesty or delay. This is Sue, by the way."

"I've seen you about," the girl said.

"You could hardly miss him," said Jackie. "Four men, roped together, spent a week climbing him—they thought he was Everest. He ought to carry a warning beacon, he's a danger to aircraft."

"Silly," said the girl, smiling at Jackie. "He's not much taller than you are."

She had a nice voice too.

"We won," Barry said. "Seventeen points to three, and it was a good game. The ground was hard, though."

He could think of nothing else to say.

"Let's all go for a frivolous cup of coffee," Jackie said. "Let's celebrate your safe return from the rough fields of victory. We could pour libations all over the floor for you."

"I don't think so," Barry said. "Thanks. I'll go straight home."

"Okay," said Jackie, rocking on his heels so that the sun could shine on his smile. "How's your father?"

"No better," Barry said. "He's not going to get better."

"Yes, well," said Jackie, serious and uncomfortable, "tell him my mother and father ask about him."

"I will," Barry promised. "He'll be pleased."

Barry dropped the bag in the front hall and moved into the room which had been the dining room until his father's illness. His father lay in the white bed, his long body gaunt, his still head scarcely denting the pillow. He seemed asleep, thin blue lids covering his eyes, but when Barry turned away he spoke.

"Hullo, Son," he said. "Did you win?"

His voice was a dry, light rustling, hardly louder than the breath which carried it. Its sound moved Barry to a compassion that almost unmanned him, but he stepped close to the bed and looked down at the dying man.

"Yes," he said. "We won fairly easily. It was a good game."

His father lay with his eyes closed, inert, his breath irregular and shallow.

"Did you score?" he asked.

"Twice," Barry said. "I had a try in each half."

He thought of the easy certainty with which he'd caught the ball before his second try; casually, almost arrogantly he had taken it on the tips of his fingers, on his full burst for the line, breaking the fullback's tackle. Nobody could have stopped him. But watching his father's weakness he felt humble and ashamed, as if the morning's game, its urgency and effort, was not worth talking about. His father's face, fine-skinned and pallid, carried a dark stubble of beard, almost a week's growth, and his obstinate, strong hair stuck out over his brow.

"Good," said his father, after a long pause. "I'm glad it was a good game."

Barry's mother bustled about the kitchen, a tempest of orderly energy.

"Your father's not well," she said. "He's down today, feels depressed. He's a particular man, your father. He feels dirty with all that beard on him."

She slammed shut the stove door.

"Mr. Cleaver was supposed to come up and shave him," she said, "and that was three days ago. Little things have always worried your father, every detail must be perfect for him."

Barry filled a glass with milk from the refrigerator. He was very thirsty.

"I'll shave him," he said.

His mother stopped, her head on one side.

"Do you think you can?" she asked. "He'd like it if you can."

"I can do it," Barry said.

He washed his hands as carefully as a surgeon. His father's razor was in a blue leather case, hinged at the broad edge and with one hinge broken. Barry unfastened the clasp and took out the razor. It had not been properly cleaned after its last use and lather had stiffened into hard yellow rectangles between the teeth of the guard. There were water-shaped rust stains, brown as chocolate, on the surface of the blade. Barry removed it, throwing it in the wastebin. He washed the razor until it glistened, and dried it on a soft towel, polishing the thin handle, rubbing its metal head to a glittering shine. He took a new blade from its waxed envelope, the paper clinging to the thin metal. The blade was smooth and flexible to the touch, the little angles of its cutting clearly defined. Barry slotted it into the grip of the razor, making it snug and tight in the head.

The shaving soap, hard, white, richly aromatic, was kept in a wooden bowl. Its scent was immediately evocative and Barry could almost see his father in the days of his health, standing before his mirror, thick white lather on his face and neck. As a little boy Barry had loved the generous perfume of the soap, had waited for his father to lift the razor to his face, for one careful stroke to take away the white suds in a clean revelation of the skin. Then his father would renew the lather with a few sweeps of his brush, one with an ivory handle and the bristles worn, which he still used.

His father's shaving mug was a thick cup, plain and serviceable. A gold line ran outside the rim of the cup, another inside, just below the lip. Its handle was large and sturdy, and the face of the mug carried a portrait of the young Queen Elizabeth II, circled by a wreath of leaves, oak perhaps, or laurel. A lion and unicorn balanced precariously on a scroll above her crowned head, and the Union Jack, the Royal Standard, and other flags were furled each side of the portrait. And beneath it all, in small black letters, ran the legend: "Coronation June 2nd 1953." The cup was much older than Barry. A pattern of faint translucent cracks, fine as a web, had worked itself haphazardly, invisibly almost, through the

white glaze. Inside, on the bottom, a few dark bristles were lying, loose and dry. Barry shook them out, then held the cup in his hand, feeling its solidness. Then he washed it ferociously, until it was clinically clean.

Methodically he set everything on a tray, razor, soap, brush, towels. Testing the hot

shoulders, lifting him without effort so that he sat against the high pillows.

"You're strong," his father said. He was as breathless as if he'd been running.

"So are you," said Barry.

"I was," his father said. "I used to be strong once."

He sat exhausted against the pillows.

"We'll wait a bit," Barry said.

"You could have used your electric razor," his father said. "I expected that."

"You wouldn't like it," Barry said. "You'll get a closer shave this way."

He placed the large towel about his father's shoulders.

"Now," he said, smiling down.

The water was hot in the thick cup. Barry wet the brush and worked up the lather. Gently he built up a covering of soft foam on the man's chin, on his cheeks and his stark cheekbones.

"You're using a lot of soap," his father said.

"Not too much," Barry said. "You've got a lot of beard."

His father lay there quietly, his wasted arms at his sides.

"It's comforting," he said. "You'd be surprised how comforting it is."

Barry took up the razor, weighing it in his hand, rehearsing the angle at which he'd use it. He felt confident.

"If you have prayers to say . . ." he said.

"I've said a lot of prayers," his father answered.

Barry leaned over and placed the razor delicately against his father's face, setting the head accurately on the clean line near the ear where the long hair ended. He held the razor in the tips of his fingers and drew the blade sweetly through the lather. The new edge moved light as a touch over the hardness of the upper jaw and down to

water with a finger, he filled the mug and put that, too, on the tray. His care was absorbed, ritualistic. Satisfied that his preparations were complete, he went downstairs, carrying the tray with one hand.

His father was waiting for him. Barry set the tray on a bedside table and bent over his father, sliding an arm under the man's thin

the angle of the chin, sliding away the bristles so easily that Barry could not feel their release. He sighed as he shook the razor in the hot water, washing away the soap.

"How's it going?" his father asked.

"No problem," Barry said. "You needn't worry."

It was as if he had never known what his father really looked like. He was discovering under his hands the clear bones of the face and head; they became sharp and recognizable under his fingers. When he moved his father's face a gentle inch to one side, he touched with his fingers the frail temples, the blue veins of his father's life. With infinite and meticulous care he took away the hair from his father's face.

"Now for your neck," he said. "We might as well do the job properly."

"You've got good hands," his father said. "You can trust those hands, they won't let you down."

Barry cradled his father's head in the crook of his left arm, so that the man could tilt back his head, exposing the throat. He brushed fresh lather under the chin and into the hollows alongside the stretched tendons. His father's throat was fleshless and vulnerable, his head was a hard weight on the boy's arm. Barry was filled with unreasoning protective love. He lifted the razor and began to shave.

"You don't have to worry," he said. "Not at all. Not about anything."

He held his father in the bend of his strong arm and they looked at each other. Their heads were very close.

"How old are you?" his father said.

"Seventeen," Barry said. "Near enough seventeen."

"You're young," his father said, "to have this happen."

"Not too young," Barry said. "I'm bigger than most men."

"I think you are," his father said.

He leaned his head tiredly against the boy's shoulder. He was without strength, his face was cold and smooth. He had let go all his authority, handed it over. He lay back on his pillow, knowing his weakness and his mortality, and looked at his son with wonder, with a curious humble pride.

"I won't worry then," he said. "About anything."

"There's no need," Barry said. "Why should you worry?"

He wiped his father's face clean of all soap with a damp towel. The smell of illness was everywhere, overpowering even the perfumed lather. Barry settled his father down and took away the shaving tools, putting them by with the same ceremonial precision with which he'd prepared them: the cleaned and glittering razor in its broken case; the soap, its bowl wiped and dried, on the shelf between the brush and the coronation mug; all free of taint. He washed his hands and scrubbed his nails. His hands were firm and broad, pink after their scrubbing. The fingers were short and strong, the little fingers slightly crooked, and soft dark hair grew on the backs of his hands and his fingers just above the knuckles. Not long ago they had been small bare hands, not very long ago.

Barry opened wide the bathroom window. Already, although it was not yet two o'clock, the sun was retreating and people were moving briskly, wrapped in their heavy coats against the cold that was to come. But now the window was full in the beam of the dying sunlight, and Barry stood there, illuminated in its golden warmth for a whole minute, knowing it would soon be gone.

## THINKING ABOUT THE SELECTION

### Recalling

1. What do you learn about Barry as he is coming home from his game?
2. Why does Barry shave his father?
3. Summarize the conversation between Barry and his father during the shave.

### Interpreting

4. Why does Barry take such care in preparing to shave his father?
5. What does Barry's handling of the task signify to him and to his father?
6. What message is communicated between Barry and his father during the shave?
7. Explain the change in roles that occurs between Barry and his father during the shave.
8. In what ways does the writer show that Barry has grown up and is now taking adult responsibility?
9. On a literal level, the last sentence of this story refers to the fading warmth of the sun. Explain its greater significance.

### Applying

10. Do you think it is possible to feel two contradictory emotions, such as grief and pride, at the same time? Explain.

## ANALYZING LITERATURE

### Understanding Point of View

In a story told from a **third-person limited point of view,** you see the events through the eyes and mind of one of the characters. That character (as well as others) is referred to in the third person, as *he* or *she* or by name. Seeing the events from one character's point of view can lead to sharing that character's emotions. In "Shaving," you know how Barry feels about what is happening to him, not because he tells you but because you experience his thoughts and feelings with him.

1. What does Barry feel about the changes he observes in himself?
2. What kind of person does Barry seem to be?

## CRITICAL THINKING AND READING

### Appreciating Connotations

A **connotation** of a word is what the word suggests beyond its literal or dictionary definition. The connotations of a given word can be significant to the story in which the word appears. The word *Everest,* for example, connotes great size and ruggedness, remoteness, and invincibility. These suggested meanings are important in "Shaving."

1. Why is Jackie's reference to Barry as "Everest" appropriate?
2. Explain the two connotations of the word *beard* in this story.
3. In preparing to share his father, Barry washes his hands "as carefully as a surgeon." What associations are suggested by the word *surgeon* here. Considering his father's illness, what other associations are brought to mind by the word?

## THINKING AND WRITING

### Writing from a Different Point of View

Retell the shaving incident as Barry's father might have viewed it. From the point of view of the father, describe Barry's appearance and behavior. Include Barry's father's thoughts and feelings and the effect Barry's actions have on him. When you revise, make sure you have included only information that Barry's father would know. Proofread your composition and share it with your classmates.

# GUIDE FOR READING

## Maud Martha Spares the Mouse

**Gwendolyn Brooks** (1917–    ) was born in Topeka, Kansas, and grew up in Chicago, Illinois. Her first book of poems, *A Street in Bronzeville,* is set in the community in Chicago in which she lived. For her second collection of poems, *Annie Allen,* she received the Pulitzer Prize in 1950. She is the first black writer to win this award. The story you are about to read was excerpted from her novel, *Maud Martha,* which was published in 1953. It tells about a young girl growing up in Chicago.

**Third-Person Limited Point of View**

With the **third-person limited point of view,** an outside observer narrates events from the perspective of one character in the story. The narrator uses the pronouns *he* or *she* or the name of the character to refer to this character and presents only what that one character knows and observes. The use of third-person limited point of view in a story with only one character sets up a small, enclosed world that you enter through the character's mind. This is the situation in "Maud Martha Spares the Mouse."

**Look For**

What does Maud Martha think about the mouse? As you read "Maud Martha Spares the Mouse," look not only for what she does but also for the way she feels about it.

**Writing**

Think of an animal that interests you. It might be a pet, a farm animal, or a wild animal. Suppose that you had the ability to know how the animal thinks and feels. Imagine an incident in the animal's life. Then freewrite, relating the incident from the animal's point of view.

**Vocabulary**

Knowing the following words will help you as you read "Maud Martha Spares the Mouse."

**sobriety** (sə brī′ ə tē) *n.:* Seriousness (p. 119)

**avail** (ə vāl′) *n.:* Usefulness; advantage (p. 119)

**reprieve** (ri prēv′) *n.:* Temporary escape from pain or trouble (p. 119)

# Maud Martha
# Spares the Mouse

from *Maud Martha*

### Gwendolyn Brooks

There. She had it at last. The weeks it had devoted to eluding her, the tricks, the clever hide-and-go-seeks, the routes it had in all sobriety devised, together with the delicious moments it had, undoubtedly, laughed up its sleeve—all to no ultimate avail. She had that mouse.

It shook its little self, as best it could, in the trap. Its bright black eyes contained no appeal—the little creature seemed to understand that there was no hope of mercy from the eternal enemy, no hope of reprieve or post-ponement—but a fine small dignity. It waited. It looked at Maud Martha.

She wondered what else it was thinking. Perhaps that there was not enough food in its larder. Perhaps that little Betty, a puny child from the start, would not, now, be getting fed. Perhaps that, now, the family's seasonal house-cleaning, for lack of expert direction, would be left undone. It might be regretting that young Bobby's education was now at an end. It might be nursing personal regrets. No more the mysterious shadows of the kitchenette, the uncharted twists, the unguessed halls. No more the sweet delights of the chase, the charms of being unsuccessfully hounded, thrown at.

Maud Martha could not bear the little look.

"Go home to your children," she urged. "To your wife or husband." She opened the trap. The mouse vanished.

Suddenly, she was conscious of a new cleanness in her. A wide air walked in her. A life had blundered its way into her power and it had been hers to preserve or destroy. She had not destroyed. In the center of that simple restraint was—creation. She had created a piece of life. It was wonderful.

"Why," she thought, as her height doubled, "why, I'm good! I am *good.*"

She ironed her aprons. Her back was straight. Her eyes were mild, and soft with a godlike loving-kindness.

## THINKING ABOUT THE SELECTION

### Recalling

1. Why is Maud Martha pleased at the beginning of the story?
2. What does she imagine the mouse is thinking?
3. Why does Maud Martha let the mouse go?

### Interpreting

4. Describe Maud Martha's emotions throughout the story.
5. Why does Maud Martha think of what she does as "creation"?

### Applying

6. Why would a person feel virtuous after not doing something wrong, rather than as a result of actively doing something right?

## ANALYZING LITERATURE

### Appreciating Point of View

With **third-person limited point of view,** an outside narrator tells the story through the eyes and mind of a character. The narrator refers to the character by name or as "he" or "she." When a story has only one character, third-person limited point of view may take on a special quality. In "Maud Martha Spares the Mouse," for example, the point of view allows you to participate in the action with Maud Martha and share her feelings.

1. How does the point of view in the third paragraph differ from that used in the rest of the story?
2. What do Maud Martha's thoughts about the mouse reveal about her?

## CRITICAL THINKING AND READING

### Determining the Author's Purpose

An author can choose any number of ways to tell a particular story. For example, Brooks might have related the events in "Maud Martha Spares the Mouse" objectively instead of telling them from Maud Martha's point of view. Generally authors decide to tell a story from a particular point of view in order to create a desired effect.

1. How would "Maud Martha Spares the Mouse" change if it were not told from Maud Martha's point of view?
2. What do you think the author was trying to achieve through third-person limited point of view?

## SPEAKING AND LISTENING

### Presenting a Dramatic Reading

Practice reading "Maud Martha Spares the Mouse" aloud. Make your reading dramatic by reflecting Maud Martha's feelings in your voice and facial expressions. When you think your reading captures the flavor of the story, try it out on some friends or relatives. Your teacher may ask you to present the reading in class.

## THINKING AND WRITING

### Responding to Meaning

Rewrite the story from the mouse's point of view. Use a third-person narrator in your story. Remember that your narrator will know what the mouse is thinking and feeling but not what Maud Martha is thinking and feeling. The narrator can comment only on the actions of Maud Martha that can be observed. When you revise, try to replace some verbs with more vivid action verbs. Prepare a final draft and read it aloud to your classmates.

# GUIDE FOR READING

## The Widow and the Parrot

**Virginia Woolf** (1882–1941) was born and spent most of her life in London, England. She was a member of the Bloomsbury group, which included such writers as T. S. Eliot, Robert Graves, and Katherine Mansfield. She and her husband, Leonard Woolf, founded the Hogarth Press to publish the works of experimental writers of her time. Unlike many of Woolf's works, which employ a technique that emphasizes the characters' inner thoughts, "The Widow and the Parrot" has a traditional narrative form.

**Third-Person Omniscient Point of View**

When a writer uses **third-person omniscient point of view,** the events are told from the perspective of an outside observer who knows all and sees all. *Omniscient* means "all-knowing." Such a narrator can get into the mind of any character at any point in the story and can possess information that none of the characters knows. The third-person omniscient narrator's voice is not to be considered the author's voice. When the narrator of "The Widow and the Parrot" mentions that Asheham House was "lately the seat of Mr. Leonard Woolf," Virginia Woolf is making sure you will not confuse her with the voice telling the story.

**Look For**

The widow in this story claims, "It's an ill wind that blows nobody any good." As you read "The Widow and the Parrot," look for whether or not her statement proves to be true.

**Writing**

The widow in this story has a strong connection with animals. Have you ever seen a movie in which an animal trainer or pet owner talks to an animal? Do you think that people and animals can really understand each other? Freewrite about how people and animals might be able to communicate.

**Vocabulary**

Knowing the following words will help you as you read "The Widow and the Parrot."

**ford** (fôrd) *n.*: A shallow place in a stream or river where people can cross (p. 123)

**dilapidated** (di lap' ə dāt' id) *adj.*: Fallen into a shabby and neglected state (p. 125)

**sovereigns** (säv' rənz) *n.*: British gold coins worth one pound each (p. 129)

**sagacity** (sə gas' ə tē) *n.*: Wisdom (p. 129)

# The Widow and the Parrot

## Virginia Woolf

Some fifty years ago Mrs. Gage, an elderly widow, was sitting in her cottage in a village called Spilsby in Yorkshire.[1] Although lame and rather shortsighted she was doing her best to mend a pair of clogs, for she had only a few shillings a week to live on. As she hammered at the clog, the postman opened the door and threw a letter into her lap.

It bore the address "Messrs. Stagg and Beetle, 67 High Street, Lewes, Sussex."

Mrs. Gage opened it and read:

"Dear Madam: We have the honor to inform you of the death of your brother Mr. Joseph Brand."

"Lawk a mussy," said Mrs. Gage. "Old brother Joseph gone at last!"

"He has left you his entire property," the letter went on, "which consists of a dwelling house, stable, cucumber frames, mangles, wheelbarrows, etc., etc., in the village of Rodmell, near Lewes. He also bequeaths to you his entire fortune; Viz: £3,000. (three thousand pounds[2]) sterling."

Mrs. Gage almost fell into the fire with joy. She had not seen her brother for many years, and, as he did not even acknowledge the Christmas card which she sent him every year, she thought that his miserly habits, well known to her from childhood, made him grudge even a penny stamp for a reply.

But now it had all turned out to her advantage. With three thousand pounds, to say nothing of house, etc., etc., she and her family could live in great luxury for ever.

She determined that she must visit Rodmell at once. The village clergyman, the Rev. Samuel Tallboys, lent her two pound ten, to pay her fare, and by next day all preparations for her journey were complete. The most important of these was the care of her dog Shag during her absence, for in spite of her poverty she was devoted to animals, and often went short herself rather than stint her dog of his bone.

She reached Lewes late on Tuesday night. In those days, I must tell you, there was no bridge over the river at Southease, nor had the road to Newhaven yet been made. To reach Rodmell it was necessary to cross the river Ouse by a ford, traces of

---

**1. Yorkshire** (yôrk′ shər): A county of northeastern England.
**2. three thousand pounds:** This amount of British money was worth about $15,000 at the time of the story.

which still exist, but this could only be attempted at low tide, when the stones on the riverbed appeared above the water. Mr. Stacey, the farmer, was going to Rodmell in his cart, and he kindly offered to take Mrs. Gage with him. They reached Rodmell about nine o'clock on a November night and Mr. Stacey obligingly pointed out to Mrs. Gage the house at the end of the village which had been left her by her brother. Mrs. Gage knocked at the door. There was no answer. She knocked again. A very strange high voice shrieked out "Not at home." She was so much taken aback that if she had not heard footsteps coming she would have run away. However, the door was opened by an old village woman, by name Mrs. Ford.

"Who was that shrieking out 'Not at home'?" said Mrs. Gage.

"Drat the bird!" said Mrs. Ford very peevishly, pointing to a large gray parrot. "He almost screams my head off. There he sits all day humped up on his perch like a monument screeching 'Not at home' if ever you go near his perch." He was a very handsome bird, as Mrs. Gage could see; but his feathers were sadly neglected. "Perhaps he is unhappy, or he may be hungry," she said. But Mrs. Ford said it was temper merely; he was a seaman's parrot and had learnt his language in the east. However, she added, Mr. Joseph was very fond of him, had called him James; and, it was said, talked to him as if he were a rational being. Mrs. Ford soon left. Mrs. Gage at once went to her box and fetched some sugar which she had with her and offered it to the parrot, saying in a very kind tone that she meant him no harm, but was his old master's sister, come to take possession of the house, and she would see to it that he was as happy as a bird could be. Taking a lantern she next went round the house to see what sort of property her brother had left her. It was a bitter disappoint-

ment. There were holes in all the carpets. The bottoms of the chairs had fallen out. Rats ran along the mantelpiece. There were large toadstools growing through the kitchen floor. There was not a stick of furniture worth seven pence halfpenny; and Mrs. Gage only cheered herself by thinking of the three thousand pounds that lay safe and snug in Lewes Bank.

She determined to set off to Lewes next day in order to claim her money from Messrs. Stagg and Beetle the solicitors,[3] and then to return home as quick as she could. Mr. Stacey, who was going in to market with some fine Berkshire pigs, again offered to take her with him, and told her some terrible stories of young people who had been drowned through trying to cross the river at high tide, as they drove. A great disappointment was in store for the poor old woman directly she got in to Mr. Stagg's office.

"Pray take a seat, Madam," he said, looking very solemn and grunting slightly. "The fact is," he went on, "that you must prepare to face some very disagreeable news. Since I wrote to you I have gone carefully through Mr. Brand's papers. I regret to say that I can find no trace whatever of the three thousand pounds. Mr. Beetle, my partner, went himself to Rodmell and searched the premises with the utmost care. He found absolutely nothing—no gold, silver, or valuables of any kind—except a fine gray parrot which I advise you to sell for whatever he will fetch. His language, Benjamin Beetle said, is very extreme. But that is neither here nor there. I much fear you have had your journey for nothing. The premises are dilapidated; and of course our expenses are considerable." Here he stopped, and Mrs. Gage well knew that he wished her to go. She was almost crazy with disappointment. Not only had she borrowed two pound ten from the Rev. Samuel Tallboys, but she would return home absolutely empty handed, for the parrot James would have to be sold to pay her fare. It was raining hard, but Mr. Stagg did not press her to stay, and she was too beside herself with sorrow to care what she did. In spite of the rain she started to walk back to Rodmell across the meadows.

Mrs. Gage, as I have already said, was lame in her right leg. At the best of times she walked slowly, and now, what with her disappointment and the mud on the bank, her progress was very slow indeed. As she plodded along, the day grew darker and darker, until it was as much as she could do to keep on the raised path by the river side. You might have heard her grumbling as she walked, and complaining of her crafty brother Joseph, who had put her to all this trouble "Express," she said, "to plague me. He was always a cruel little boy when we were children," she went on. "He liked worrying the poor insects, and I've known him trim a hairy caterpillar with a pair of scissors before my very eyes. He was such a miserly varmint too. He used to hide his pocket money in a tree, and if anyone gave him a piece of iced cake for tea, he cut the sugar off and kept it for his supper. I make no doubt he's all aflame at this very moment in fire, but what's the comfort of that to me?" she asked, and indeed it was very little comfort, for she ran slap into a great cow which was coming along the bank, and rolled over and over in the mud.

She picked herself up as best she could and trudged on again. It seemed to her that she had been walking for hours. It was now

---

**3. solicitors** (sə lis′ it ərz) *n.*: British legal representatives.

pitch dark and she could scarcely see her own hand before her nose. Suddenly she bethought her of Farmer Stacey's words about the ford. "Lawk a mussy," she said, "however shall I find my way across? If the tide's in, I shall step into deep water and be swept out to sea in a jiffy! Many's the couple that been drowned here; to say nothing of horses, carts, herds of cattle, and stacks of hay."

Indeed what with the dark and the mud she had got herself into a pretty pickle. She could hardly see the river itself, let alone tell whether she had reached the ford or not. No lights were visible anywhere, for, as you may be aware, there is no cottage or house on that side of the river nearer than Asheham House, lately the seat of Mr. Leonard Woolf. It seemed that there was nothing for it but to sit down and wait for the morning. But at her age, with the rheumatics in her system, she might well die of cold. On the other hand, if she tried to cross the river it was almost certain that she would be drowned. So miserable was her state that she would gladly have changed places with one of the cows in the field. No more wretched old woman could have been found in the whole county of Sussex; standing on the river bank, not knowing whether to sit or to swim, or merely to roll over in the grass, wet though it was, and sleep or freeze to death, as her fate decided.

At that moment a wonderful thing happened. An enormous light shot up into the sky, like a gigantic torch, lighting up every blade of grass, and showing her the ford not twenty yards away. It was low tide, and the crossing would be an easy matter if only the light did not go out before she had got over.

"It must be a comet or some such wonderful monstrosity," she said as she hobbled across. She could see the village of Rodmell brilliantly lit up in front of her.

"Bless us and save us!" she cried out. "There's a house on fire—thanks be to the Lord"—for she reckoned that it would take some minutes at least to burn a house down, and in that time she would be well on her way to the village.

"It's an ill wind that blows nobody any good," she said as she hobbled along the Roman road. Sure enough, she could see every inch of the way, and was almost in the village street when for the first time it struck her: "Perhaps it's my own house that's blazing to cinders before my very eyes!"

She was perfectly right.

A small boy in his nightgown came capering up to her and cried out, "Come and see old Joseph Brand's house ablaze!"

All the villagers were standing in a ring round the house handing buckets of water which were filled from the well in Monk's house kitchen, and throwing them on the flames. But the fire had got a strong hold, and just as Mrs. Gage arrived, the roof fell in.

"Has anybody saved the parrot?" she cried.

"Be thankful you're not inside yourself, Madam," said the Rev. James Hawkesford, the clergyman. "Do not worry for the dumb creatures. I make no doubt the parrot was mercifully suffocated on his perch."

But Mrs. Gage was determined to see for herself. She had to be held back by the village people, who remarked that she must be crazy to hazard her life for a bird.

"Poor old woman," said Mrs. Ford, "she has lost all her property, save one old wooden box, with her night things in it. No doubt we should be crazed in her place too."

So saying, Mrs. Ford took Mrs. Gage by the hand and led her off to her own cottage, where she was to sleep the night. The fire was now extinguished, and everybody went home to bed. But poor Mrs. Gage could not sleep. She tossed and tumbled thinking of her miserable state, and wondering how she could get back to Yorkshire and pay the Rev. Samuel Tallboys the money she owed him. At the same time she was even more grieved to think of the fate of the poor parrot James. She had taken a liking to the bird, and thought that he must have an affectionate heart to mourn so deeply for the death of old Joseph Brand, who had never done a kindness to any human creature. It was a terrible death for an innocent bird, she thought; and if only she had been in time, she would have risked her own life to save his.

She was lying in bed thinking these thoughts when a slight tap at the window made her start. The tap was repeated three times over. Mrs. Gage got out of bed as quickly as she could and went to the window. There, to her utmost surprise, sitting on the window ledge, was an enormous parrot. The rain had stopped and it was a fine moonlight night. She was greatly alarmed at first, but soon recognized the gray parrot, James, and was overcome with joy at his escape. She opened the window, stroked his head several times, and told him to come in. The parrot replied by gently shaking his head from side to side, then flew to the ground, walked away a few steps, looked back as if to see whether Mrs. Gage were coming, and then returned to the window sill, where she stood in amazement.

"The creature has more meaning in its acts than we humans know," she said to herself. "Very well, James," she said aloud, talking to him as though he were a human being, "I'll take your word for it. Only wait a moment while I make myself decent."

So saying she pinned on a large apron, crept as lightly as possible downstairs, and let herself out without rousing Mrs. Ford.

The parrot James was evidently satisfied. He now hopped briskly a few yards ahead of her in the direction of the burnt house. Mrs. Gage followed as fast as she could. The parrot hopped, as if he knew his way perfectly, round to the back of the house, where the kitchen had originally been. Nothing now remained of it except the brick floor, which was still dripping with the water which had been thrown to put out the fire. Mrs. Gage stood still in amazement while James hopped about, pecking here and there, as if he were testing the bricks with his beak. It was a very uncanny sight, and had not Mrs. Gage been in the habit of living with animals, she would have lost her head, very likely, and hobbled back home. But stranger things yet were to happen. All this time the parrot had not said a word. He suddenly got into a state of the greatest excitement, fluttering his wings, tapping the floor repeatedly with his beak, and crying so shrilly, "Not at home! Not at home!" that Mrs. Gage feared that the whole village would be roused.

"Don't take on so, James; you'll hurt yourself," she said soothingly. But he repeated his attack on the bricks more violently than ever.

"Whatever can be the meaning of it?" said Mrs. Gage, looking carefully at the kitchen floor. The moonlight was bright enough to show her a slight unevenness in the laying of the bricks, as if they had been taken up and then relaid not quite flat with the others. She had fastened her apron with a large safety pin, and she now prized this pin between the bricks and found that they were only loosely laid together. Very soon she had taken one up in her hands. No sooner had she done this than the parrot hopped onto the brick next to it, and, tapping it smartly with his beak, cried, "Not at home!" which Mrs. Gage understood to

mean that she was to move it. So they went on taking up the bricks in the moonlight until they had laid bare a space some six feet by four and a half. This the parrot seemed to think was enough. But what was to be done next?

Mrs. Gage now rested, and determined to be guided entirely by the behavior of the parrot James. She was not allowed to rest for long. After scratching about in the sandy foundations for a few minutes, as you may have seen a hen scratch in the sand with her claws, he unearthed what at first looked like a round lump of yellowish stone. His excitement became so intense that Mrs. Gage now went to his help. To her amazement she found that the whole space which they had uncovered was packed with long rolls of these round yellow stones, so neatly laid together that it was quite a job to move them. But what could they be? And for what purpose had they been hidden here? It was not until they had removed the entire layer on the top, and next a piece of oilcloth which lay beneath them, that a most miraculous sight was displayed before their eyes —there, in row after row, beautifully polished, and shining brightly in the moonlight, were thousands of brand new sovereigns!

This, then, was the miser's hiding place; and he had made sure that no one would detect it by taking two extraordinary precautions. In the first place, as was proved later, he had built a kitchen range over the spot where his treasure lay hid, so that unless the fire had destroyed it, no one could have guessed its existence; and secondly he had coated the top layer of sovereigns with some sticky substance, then rolled them in the earth, so that if by any chance one had been laid bare no one would have suspected that it was anything but a pebble such as you may see for yourself any day in the garden. Thus, it was only by the extraordinary coincidence of the fire and the parrot's sagacity that old Joseph's craft was defeated.

Mrs. Gage and the parrot now worked hard and removed the whole hoard—which numbered three thousand pieces, neither more nor less—placing them in her apron which was spread upon the ground. As the three thousandth coin was placed on the top of the pile, the parrot flew up into the air in triumph and alighted very gently on the top of Mrs. Gage's head. It was in this fashion that they returned to Mrs. Ford's cottage, at a very slow pace, for Mrs. Gage was lame, as I have said, and now she was almost weighted to the ground by the contents of her apron. But she reached her room without anyone knowing of her visit to the ruined house.

Next day she returned to Yorkshire. Mr. Stacey once more drove her into Lewes and was rather surprised to find how heavy Mrs. Gage's wooden box had become. But he was a quiet sort of man, and merely concluded that the kind people at Rodmell had given her a few odds and ends to console her for the dreadful loss of all her property in the fire. Out of sheer goodness of heart Mr. Stacey offered to buy the parrot off her for half a crown; but Mrs. Gage refused his offer with such indignation, saying that she would not sell the bird for all the wealth of the Indies, that he concluded that the old woman had been crazed by her troubles.

It now only remains to be said that Mrs. Gage got back to Spilsby in safety; took her black box to the Bank; and lived with James the parrot and her dog Shag in great comfort and happiness to a very great age.

It was not till she lay on her deathbed that she told the clergyman (the son of the Rev. Samuel Tallboys) the whole story, adding that she was quite sure that the house had been burnt on purpose by the parrot James, who, being aware of her danger on the river bank, flew into the scullery, and upset the oil stove which was keeping some scraps warm for her dinner. By this act, he not only saved her from drowning, but brought to light the three thousand pounds, which could have been found in no other manner. Such, she said is the reward of kindness to animals.

The clergyman thought that she was wandering in her mind. But it is certain that the very moment the breath was out of her body, James the parrot shrieked out, "Not at home! Not at home!" and fell off his perch stone dead. The dog Shag had died some years previously.

Visitors to Rodmell may still see the ruins of the house, which was burnt down fifty years ago, and it is commonly said that if you visit it in the moonlight you may hear a parrot tapping with his beak upon the brick floor, while others have seen an old woman sitting there in a white apron.

# THINKING ABOUT THE SELECTION

## Recalling

1. Why is the news Mrs. Gage receives at the beginning of the story so welcome?
2. What is Mrs. Gage's response to the inhospitable voice of the parrot?
3. In what two ways does the inheritance from her brother prove disappointing?
4. Describe the series of events that reverses Mrs. Gage's fortune.
5. At the end of the story, to what does Mrs. Gage attribute her good fortune?

## Interpreting

6. How does Mrs. Gage show her concern for animals?
7. Compare and contrast Mrs. Gage's ideas about the parrot with Mrs. Ford's.

## Applying

8. Do you think Mrs. Gage's good fortune is a reward, or is it merely a coincidence? Explain your answer.

# ANALYZING LITERATURE

## Understanding Omniscient Point of View

With **third-person omniscient point of view,** an all-knowing observer narrates the events. In "The Widow and the Parrot," the narrator lets you in on the thoughts and feelings of the main character and those of the people she meets.

Find a passage in the story that reveals the thoughts of each of these characters.

1. Mrs. Gage
2. Mrs. Ford
3. Mr. Stacey
4. the clergyman

# CRITICAL THINKING AND READING

## Making Inferences About Character

An **inference** is a conclusion you make based on evidence. For example in "The Widow and the Parrot," you learn that "Mr. Joseph was very fond of [the parrot]." You can infer from this statement that he cared about animals, and no matter how mean he was, he was not entirely heartless.

Make at least one inference about Mrs. Gage based on the evidence of her feelings in each of these statements.

1. When Mrs. Gage learns that there is no fortune, she immediately worries about how she will pay back Rev. Samuel Tallboys.
2. Mrs. Gage thinks her brother left the will in order to cause her trouble.

# UNDERSTANDING LANGUAGE

## Understanding Dialect

When authors write dialogue, they sometimes try to capture the **dialect,** or regional speech pattern, of their characters. Dialect may differ from standard language in vocabulary, sentence structure, or pronunciation. When Mrs. Gage pronounces *Lord have mercy,* "Lawk a mussy," she is using dialect.

Do you think this story would have been more or less effective if the author had not included dialect? Explain your answer.

# THINKING AND WRITING

## Writing About Humor

Humor is hard to define. What makes one person laugh may have little effect on another. Humor is even thought to vary from nation to nation. The English are known for a dry, subtle wit, while Americans are thought to have a broader, more physical sense of what is funny. Select one scene in the story you have just read and freewrite about why you did or did not find it funny. Then use your freewriting as the basis of a first draft of an essay on the use of humor in "The Widow and the Parrot." When you revise, make sure you have supported your thesis with details from the selection.

# Setting

**ROAD WITH CYPRESS AND STAR**
*Vincent van Gogh*
Collection: State Museum, Kröller-Müller Otterlo, The Netherlands

# GUIDE FOR READING

## There Will Come Soft Rains

**Ray Bradbury** (1920–    ) is one of the world's most celebrated science-fiction writers. He was born in Waukegan, Illinois, and grew up along the western shores of Lake Michigan. He began reading the stories of Edgar Allan Poe as a child and also developed a fascination with horror movies and fantasy—especially futuristic fantasy. In many of his stories, including "There Will Come Soft Rains," Bradbury describes a future that reflects the possible outcomes of today's technology.

**Setting**

The **setting** of a story is the time and place of the story's action. In some stories the author may merely establish the setting as a background for the action. In others the setting is vitally important, as important as the characters and plot. A horror story, for example, often needs a setting such as a musty old house with creaking floors to be effective. Bradbury sets "There Will Come Soft Rains" in a house that is anything but musty and old. In fact, the setting is so important that it is actually the central character in the story.

**Look For**

As you read "There Will Come Soft Rains," look for the special qualities of the house that makes it seem a character in the story.

**Writing**

Machines are important in this story. List machines you use regularly and the role they play in your life. Then freewrite about what life would be like without them.

**Vocabulary**

Knowing the following words will help you as you read "There Will Come Soft Rains."

**warrens** (wôr′ ənz) *n.*: Maze-like passages (p. 133)

**titanic** (tī tan′ ik) *adj.*: Having great power (p. 134)

**paranoia** (par′ə noi′ ə) *n.*: A mental disorder characterized by delusions of persecution (p. 134)

**cavorting** (kə vôrt′ iŋ) *v.*: Leaping or prancing about (p. 134)

**spoors** (spŏŏrz) *n.*: Droppings of wild animals (p. 135)

**okapi** (ō kä′ pē) *n.*: An African animal related to the giraffe but with a much shorter neck (p. 135)

**tremulous** (trem′ yŏŏ ləs) *adj.*: Trembling; quivering (p. 135)

**psychopathic** (sī kə pathʹ ik) *adj.*: With a mental disorder (p. 136)

# There Will Come Soft Rains

Ray Bradbury

In the living room the voice-clock sang, *Tick-tock, seven o'clock, time to get up, time to get up, seven o'clock!* as if it were afraid that nobody would. The morning house lay empty. The clock ticked on, repeating and repeating its sounds into the emptiness. *Seven-nine, breakfast time, seven-nine!*

In the kitchen the breakfast stove gave a hissing sigh and ejected from its warm interior eight pieces of perfectly browned toast, eight eggs sunnyside up, sixteen slices of bacon, two coffees, and two cool glasses of milk.

"Today is August 4, 2026," said a second voice from the kitchen ceiling, "in the city of Allendale, California." It repeated the date three times for memory's sake. "Today is Mr. Featherstone's birthday. Today is the anniversary of Tilita's marriage. Insurance is payable, as are the water, gas, and light bills."

Somewhere in the walls, relays clicked, memory tapes glided under electric eyes.

*Eight-one, tick-tock, eight-one o'clock, off to school, off to work, run, run, eight-one!* But no doors slammed, no carpets took the soft tread of rubber heels. It was raining outside. The weather box on the front door sang quietly: "Rain, rain, go away; rubbers, raincoats for today . . ." And the rain tapped on the empty house, echoing.

Outside, the garage chimed and lifted its door to reveal the waiting car. After a long wait the door swung down again.

At eight-thirty the eggs were shriveled and the toast was like stone. An aluminum wedge scraped them into the sink, where hot water whirled them down a metal throat which digested and flushed them away to the distant sea. The dirty dishes were dropped into a hot washer and emerged twinkling dry.

*Nine-fifteen,* sang the clock, *time to clean.*

Out of warrens in the wall, tiny robot mice darted. The rooms were acrawl with the small cleaning animals, all rubber and metal. They thudded against chairs, whirling their mustached runners, kneading the rug nap, sucking gently at hidden dust. Then, like mysterious invaders, they popped into their burrows. Their pink electric eyes faded. The house was clean.

*Ten o'clock.* The sun came out from behind the rain. The house stood alone in a city of rubble and ashes. This was the one house left standing. At night the ruined city gave off a radioactive glow which could be seen for miles.

*Ten-fifteen.* The garden sprinklers whirled up in golden founts, filling the soft morning air with scatterings of brightness. The water pelted windowpanes, running down the charred west side where the house had been burned evenly free of its white paint. The entire west face of the house was black, save for five places. Here the silhouette in paint of a man mowing a lawn. Here, as in a photograph, a woman bent to pick flowers. Still farther over, their images burned on wood in one titanic instant, a small boy, hands flung into the air; higher up, the image of a thrown ball, and opposite him a girl, hands raised to catch a ball which never came down.

The five spots of paint—the man, the woman, the children, the ball—remained. The rest was a thin charcoaled layer.

The gentle-sprinkler rain filled the garden with falling light.

Until this day, how well the house had kept its peace. How carefully it had inquired, "Who goes there? What's the password?" and, getting no answer from lonely foxes and whining cats, it had shut up its windows and drawn shades in an old-maidenly preoccupation with self-protection which bordered on a mechanical paranoia.

It quivered at each sound, the house did. If a sparrow brushed a window, the shade snapped up. The bird, startled, flew off! No, not even a bird must touch the house!

The house was an altar with ten thousand attendants, big, small, servicing, attending, in choirs. But the gods had gone away, and the ritual of the religion continued senselessly, uselessly.

*Twelve noon.*

A dog whined, shivering, on the front porch.

The front door recognized the dog voice and opened. The dog, once huge and fleshy, but now gone to bone and covered with sores, moved in and through the house, tracking mud. Behind it whirred angry mice, angry at having to pick up mud, angry at inconvenience.

For not a leaf fragment blew under the door but what the wall panels flipped open and the copper scrap rats flashed swiftly out. The offending dust, hair, or paper, seized in miniature steel jaws, was raced back to the burrows. There, down tubes which fed into the cellar, it was dropped into the sighing vent of an incinerator which sat like evil Baal[1] in a dark corner.

The dog ran upstairs, hysterically yelping to each door, at last realizing, as the house realized, that only silence was here.

It sniffed the air and scratched the kitchen door. Behind the door, the stove was making pancakes which filled the house with a rich baked odor and the scent of maple syrup.

The dog frothed at the mouth, lying at the door, sniffing, its eyes turned to fire. It ran wildly in circles, biting at its tail, spun in a frenzy, and died. It lay in the parlor for an hour.

*Two o'clock,* sang a voice.

Delicately sensing decay at last, the regiments of mice hummed out as softly as blown gray leaves in an electrical wind.

*Two-fifteen.*

The dog was gone.

In the cellar, the incinerator glowed suddenly and a whirl of sparks leaped up the chimney.

*Two thirty-five.*

Bridge tables sprouted from patio walls. Playing cards fluttered onto pads in a shower of pips. Glasses manifested on an oaken bench with egg-salad sandwiches. Music played.

But the tables were silent and the cards untouched.

At four o'clock the tables folded like great butterflies back through the paneled walls.

*Four-thirty.*

The nursery walls glowed.

Animals took shape: yellow giraffes, blue lions, pink antelopes, lilac panthers cavorting in crystal substance. The walls were glass. They looked out upon color and fantasy. Hidden films clocked through well-oiled sprockets, and the walls lived. The nursery

---

**1. Baal** (bā′ əl): A false god or idol.

floor was woven to resemble a crisp, cereal meadow. Over this ran aluminum roaches and iron crickets, and in the hot still air butterflies of delicate red tissue wavered among the sharp aroma of animal spoors! There was the sound like a great matted yellow hive of bees within a dark bellows, the lazy bumble of a purring lion. And there was the patter of okapi feet and the murmur of a fresh jungle rain, like other hoofs, falling upon the summer-starched grass. Now the walls dissolved into distances of parched weed, mile on mile, and warm endless sky. The animals drew away into thorn brakes and water holes.

It was the children's hour.

*Five o'clock.* The bath filled with clear hot water.

*Six, seven, eight o'clock.* The dinner dishes manipulated like magic tricks, and in the study a *click.* In the hearth a fire now blazed up warmly.

*Nine o'clock.* The beds warmed their hidden circuits, for nights were cool here.

*Nine-five.* A voice spoke from the study ceiling:

"Mrs. McClellan, which poem would you like this evening?"

The house was silent.

The voice said at last, "Since you express no preference, I shall select a poem at random." Quiet music rose to back the voice. "Sara Teasdale. As I recall, your favorite. . . ."

*There will come soft rains and the
  smell of the ground,
And swallows circling with their
  shimmering sound;*

*And frogs in the pools singing at
  night,
And wild plum trees in tremulous
  white;*

*Robins will wear their feathery fire,
Whistling their whims on a low
  fence-wire;*

*And not one will know of the war,
  not one
Will care at last when it is done.*

*Not one would mind, neither bird
  nor tree,
If mankind perished utterly;*

*And Spring herself, when she woke
  at dawn
Would scarcely know that we were
  gone."*

The fire burned on the stone hearth. The empty chairs faced each other between the silent walls, and the music played.

At ten o'clock the house began to die.

The wind blew. A falling tree bough crashed through the kitchen window. Cleaning solvent, bottled, shattered over the stove. The room was ablaze in an instant!

"Fire!" screamed a voice. The house lights flashed, water pumps shot water from the ceilings. But the solvent spread on the linoleum, licking, eating, under the kitchen door, while the voices took it up in chorus: "Fire, fire, fire!"

The house tried to save itself. Doors sprang tightly shut, but the windows were broken by the heat and the wind blew and sucked upon the fire.

The house gave ground as the fire in ten billion angry sparks moved with flaming ease from room to room and then up the stairs. While scurrying water rats squeaked from the walls, pistoled their water, and ran for more. And the wall sprays let down showers of mechanical rain.

But too late. Somewhere, sighing, a pump shrugged to a stop. The quenching rain ceased. The reserve water supply which had filled baths and washed dishes for many quiet days was gone.

The fire crackled up the stairs. It fed upon Picassos and Matisses[2] in the upper halls, like delicacies, baking off the oily flesh, tenderly crisping the canvases into black shavings.

Now the fire lay in beds, stood in windows, changed the colors of drapes!

And then, reinforcements.

From attic trapdoors, blind robot faces peered down with faucet mouths gushing green chemical.

The fire backed off, as even an elephant must at the sight of a dead snake. Now there were twenty snakes whipping over the floor, killing the fire with a clear cold venom of green froth.

But the fire was clever. It had sent flame outside the house, up through the attic to the pumps there. An explosion! The attic brain which directed the pumps was shattered into bronze shrapnel on the beams.

The fire rushed back into every closet and felt of the clothes hung there.

The house shuddered, oak bone on bone, its bared skeleton cringing from the heat, its wire, its nerves revealed as if a surgeon had torn the skin off to let the red veins and capillaries quiver in the scalded air. Help, help! Fire! Run, run! Heat snapped mirrors like the first brittle winter ice. And the voices wailed Fire, fire, run, run, like a tragic nursery rhyme, a dozen voices, high, low, like children dying in a forest, alone, alone. And the voices fading as the wires popped their sheathings like hot chestnuts. One, two, three, four, five voices died.

In the nursery the jungle burned. Blue lions roared, purple giraffes bounded off. The panthers ran in circles, changing color, and ten million animals, running before the fire, vanished off toward a distant steaming river. . . .

Ten more voices died. In the last instant under the fire avalanche, other choruses, oblivious, could be heard announcing the time, playing music, cutting the lawn by remote-control mower, or setting an umbrella frantically out and in the slamming and opening front door, a thousand things happening, like a clock shop when each clock strikes the hour insanely before or after the other, a scene of maniac confusion, yet unity; singing, screaming, a few last cleaning mice darting bravely out to carry the horrid ashes away! And one voice, with sublime disregard for the situation, read poetry aloud in the fiery study, until all the film spools burned, until all the wires withered and the circuits cracked.

The fire burst the house and let it slam flat down, puffing out skirts of spark and smoke.

In the kitchen, an instant before the rain of fire and timber, the stove could be seen making breakfasts at a psychopathic rate, ten dozen eggs, six loaves of toast, twenty dozen bacon strips, which, eaten by fire, started the stove working again, hysterically hissing!

The crash. The attic smashing into kitchen and parlor. The parlor into cellar, cellar into subcellar. Deep freeze, armchair, film tapes, circuits, beds, and all like skeletons thrown in a cluttered mound deep under.

Smoke and silence. A great quantity of smoke.

Dawn showed faintly in the east. Among the ruins, one wall stood alone. Within the wall, a last voice said, over and over again and again, even as the sun rose to shine upon the heaped rubble and steam:

"Today is August 5, 2026, today is August 5, 2026, today is . . ."

---

**2. Picassos** (pi kä′sōz) **and Matisses** (mä tēs′əz): Works by the painters Pablo Picasso and Henri Matisse.

## THINKING ABOUT THE SELECTION
### Recalling

1. List some activities the house performs.
2. Explain what has happened to the occupants of the house.
3. Explain what happens to the dog.
4. Describe the final hours of the house.

### Interpreting

5. Why does the house keep going, even without human occupants?
6. What can you infer about the quality of the lives of the former inhabitants? Explain the evidence that supports your answer.
7. An allusion is a reference to another work. Why do you think Bradbury chose to have the house broadcast the Sara Teasdale poem?
8. Compare the house, both in its normal operation and in its final hours, to a human being.
9. Why do you think the story ends with a voice within one wall repeating the date?

### Applying

10. There have been many books, movies, and television shows about the end of the world. What qualities make this story different from others with which you are familiar?

## ANALYZING LITERATURE
### Understanding Setting

The **setting** is the time and place of a story's action. Some stories contain more information about setting than others. In "There Will Come Soft Rains," the setting is significant, and Bradbury gives you precise information about the time of the events and a detailed description of the place where they occur.

1. When does the story take place?
2. Give two details from the story that reinforce the time period.
3. In what kind of community does it occur?
4. Why does this particular setting make the story effective?

## CRITICAL THINKING AND READING
### Understanding the Effect of Setting

The events in some stories could happen almost anywhere or any time. The events in others could happen only in a particular setting. You can recognize the importance of a setting when you examine whether the events are dependent on this particular setting or if they could happen elsewhere.

1. List three events in the story that could happen only in the future.
2. List three events in the story that could happen in an ordinary house today.
3. Explain whether the events in this story depend on the given setting.

## UNDERSTANDING LANGUAGE
### Appreciating Vivid Verbs

Throughout the story Bradbury uses **vivid verbs** that convey the special character of the actions they represent. For example, he writes that "Water *pelted*" rather than *hit* "the window panes." This single word helps you to see and hear the heavy rainstorm.

1. Use at least four of the following verbs in a paragraph about the weather.

   whirled    fluttered
   burst    crackled
   thudded    crashed

2. Find five other vivid verbs in the story. Use them in sentences of your own.

## THINKING AND WRITING
### Writing About a Place

Suppose that you work for the chamber of commerce of a town or city you know. Write a description of one attraction in the town. The description is for a brochure aimed at getting people to visit. Tell what the place looks like, how people use it, and what makes it special. When you revise the description, replace any dull verbs with vivid ones.

# GUIDE FOR READING

## The Street of the Cañon

**Josephina Niggli** (1910–    ) was born in Monterey, Mexico, where her father, a Texan, was working on the railroad and her mother was a concert violinist. During the Mexican Revolution, the family fled to San Antonio, Texas, where Niggli grew up. Niggli began writing when she was quite young, and her first collection of poems and sketches, *Mexican Silhouettes,* appeared when she was only eighteen. "The Street of the Cañon" is excerpted from *Mexican Village,* which was published in 1945.

**Local Color**

When the setting of a story emphasizes the characteristics of a particular locality, the story has local color. **Local color** refers to the use of details about the customs and way of life in a specific place. "The Street of the Cañon" is so filled with local color that after you read it, you may feel as if you have actually been to the Mexican village in which it is set.

**Look For**

"The Street of the Cañon" takes you into a Mexican village. As you read the story, look for details that reveal the culture and traditions of the people in the village.

**Writing**

This story involves a feud. Sometimes a feud between two groups can go on for years or even generations. Think about why it is so hard to end a feud once it gets started. Then freewrite about how to break the pattern that keeps a feud alive.

**Vocabulary**

Knowing the following words will help you as you read "The Street of the Cañon."

**officious** (ə fish′ əs) *adj.*: Overly ready to serve; obliging (p. 139)
**mottled** (mät′ 'ld) *adj.*: Marked with spots of different shades (p. 141)
**nonchalantly** (nän shə länt′ lē) *adv.*: Casually; indifferently (p. 141)

**audaciously** (ô dā′ shəs lē) *adv.*: In a bold manner (p. 141)
**imperiously** (im pir′ ē əs lē) *adv.*: Arrogantly (p. 141)
**plausibility** (plô′ zə bil′ it ē) *n.*: Believability (p. 142)

# The Street of the Cañon

from *Mexican Village*

## Josephina Niggli

It was May, the flowering thorn was sweet in the air, and the village of San Juan Iglesias in the Valley of the Three Marys was celebrating. The long dark streets were empty because all of the people, from the lowest-paid cowboy to the mayor, were helping Don Roméo Calderón celebrate his daughter's eighteenth birthday.

On the other side of the town, where the Cañon Road led across the mountains to the Sabinas Valley, a tall slender man, a package clutched tightly against his side, slipped from shadow to shadow. Once a dog barked, and the man's black suit merged into the blackness of a wall. But no voice called out, and after a moment he slid into the narrow, dirt-packed street again.

The moonlight touched his shoulder and spilled across his narrow hips. He was young, no more than twenty-five, and his black curly head was bare. He walked swiftly along, heading always for the distant sound of guitar and flute. If he met anyone now, who could say from which direction he had come? He might be a trader from Monterrey, or a buyer of cow's milk from farther north in the Valley of the Three Marys. Who would guess that an Hidalgo[1] man dared to walk alone in the moonlit streets of San Juan Iglesias?

Carefully adjusting his flat package so that it was not too prominent, he squared his shoulders and walked jauntily across the street to the laughter-filled house. Little boys packed in the doorway made way for him, smiling and nodding to him. The long, narrow room with the orchestra at one end was filled with whirling dancers. Rigid-backed chaperones were gossiping together, seated in their straight chairs against the plaster walls. Over the scene was the yellow glow of kerosene lanterns, and the air was hot with the too-sweet perfume of gardenias, tuberoses, and the pungent scent of close-packed humanity.

The man in the doorway, while trying to appear at ease, was carefully examining every smiling face. If just one person recognized him, the room would turn on him like a den of snarling mountain cats, but so far all the laughter-dancing eyes were friendly.

Suddenly a plump, officious little man, his round cheeks glistening with perspiration, pushed his way through the crowd. His voice, many times too large for his small body, boomed at the man in the doorway. "Welcome, stranger, welcome to our house." Thrusting his arm through the stranger's, and almost dislodging the package, he started to lead the way through the maze of dancers. "Come and drink a toast to my daughter—to my beautiful Sarita. She is eighteen this night."

---

**1. Hidalgo** (hi dal'gō) *adj.*: A nearby village.

**EVENING VIEW SAN MIGUEL, 1969**
*Samuel Reindorf*
Collection: Robert Smith

In the square patio the gentle breeze ruffled the pink and white oleander bushes. A long table set up on sawhorses held loaves of flaky crusted French bread, stacks of thin, delicate tortillas, plates of barbecued beef, and long red rolls of spicy sausages. But most of all there were cheeses, for the Three Marys was a cheese-eating valley. There were yellow cheese and white cheese and curded cheese from cow's milk. There was even a flat white cake of goat cheese from distant Linares, a delicacy too expensive for any but feast days.

To set off this feast were bottles of beer floating in ice-filled tin tubs, and another table was covered with bottles of mescal, of tequila, of maguey wine.

Don Roméo Calderón thrust a glass of tequila into the stranger's hand. "Drink, friend, to the prettiest girl in San Juan. As pretty as my fine fighting cocks, she is. On her wedding day she takes to her man, and may she find him soon, the best fighter in my flock. Drink deep, friend. Even the rivers flow with wine."

The Hidalgo man laughed and raised his glass high. "May the earth be always fertile beneath her feet."

Someone called to Don Roméo that more guests were arriving, and with a final delighted pat on the stranger's shoulder, the little man scurried away. As the young fellow smiled after his retreating host, his eyes caught and held another pair of eyes

—laughing black eyes set in a young girl's face. The last time he had seen that face it had been white and tense with rage, and the lips clenched tight to prevent an outgushing stream of angry words. That had been in February, and she had worn a white lace shawl over her hair. Now it was May, and a gardenia was a splash of white in the glossy dark braids. The moonlight had mottled his face that February night, and he knew that she did not recognize him. He grinned impudently back at her, and her eyes widened, then slid sideways to one of the chaperones. The fan in her small hand snapped shut. She tapped its parchment tip against her mouth and slipped away to join the dancing couples in the front room. The gestures of a fan translate into a coded language on the frontier. The stranger raised one eyebrow as he interpreted the signal.

But he did not move toward her at once. Instead, he inched slowly back against the table. No one was behind him, and his hands quickly unfastened the package he had been guarding so long. Then he nonchalantly walked into the front room.

The girl was sitting close to a chaperone. As he came up to her he swerved slightly toward the bushy-browed old lady.

"Your servant, señora. I kiss your hands and feet."

The chaperone stared at him in astonishment. Such fine manners were not common to the town of San Juan Iglesias.

"Eh, you're a stranger," she said. "I thought so."

"But a stranger no longer, señora, now that I have met you." He bent over her, so close she could smell the faint fragrance of talcum on his freshly shaven cheek. "Will you dance the *parada* with me?"

This request startled her eyes into popping open beneath the heavy brows. "So, my young rooster, would you flirt with me, and I old enough to be your grandmother?"

"Can you show me a prettier woman to flirt with in the Valley of the Three Marys?" he asked audaciously.

She grinned at him and turned toward the girl at her side. "This young fool wants to meet you, my child."

The girl blushed to the roots of her hair and shyly lowered her white lids. The old woman laughed aloud.

"Go out and dance, the two of you. A man clever enough to pat the sheep has a right to play with the lamb."

The next moment they had joined the circle of dancers and Sarita was trying to control her laughter.

"She is the worst dragon in San Juan. And how easily you won her!"

"What is a dragon," he asked imperiously, "when I longed to dance with you?"

"Ay," she retorted, "you have a quick tongue. I think you are a dangerous man."

In answer he drew her closer to him, and turned her toward the orchestra. As he reached the chief violinist he called out, "Play the *Virgencita*, 'The Shy Young Maiden.'"

The violinist's mouth opened in soundless surprise. The girl in his arms said sharply, "You heard him, the *Borachita*, 'The Little Drunken Girl.'"

With a relieved grin, the violinist tapped his music stand with his bow, and the music swung into the sad farewell of a man to his sweetheart:

> Farewell, my little drunken one,
> I must go to the capital
> To serve the master
> Who makes me weep for my return.

The stranger frowned down at her. "Is this a joke, señorita?" he asked coldly.

"No," she whispered, looking about her quickly to see if the incident had been observed. "But the *Virgencita* is the favorite song of Hidalgo, a village on the other side of the mountains in the next valley. The people of Hidalgo and San Juan Iglesias do not speak."

"That is a stupid thing," said the man from Hidalgo as he swung her around in a large turn. "Is not music free as air? Why should one town own the rights to a song?"

The girl shuddered slightly. "Those people from Hidalgo—they are wicked monsters. Can you guess what they did not six months since?"

The man started to point out that the space of time from February to May was three months, but he thought it better not to appear too wise. "Did these Hidalgo monsters frighten you, señorita? If they did, I personally will kill them all."

She moved closer against him and tilted her face until her mouth was close to his ear. "They attempted to steal the bones of Don Rómolo Balderas."

"Is it possible?" He made his eyes grow round and his lips purse up in disdain. "Surely not that! Why, all the world knows that Don Rómolo Balderas was the greatest historian in the entire Republic. Every school child reads his books. Wise men from Quintana Roo to the Río Bravo bow their heads in admiration to his name. What a wicked thing to do!" He hoped his virtuous tone was not too virtuous for plausibility, but she did not seem to notice.

"It is true! In the night they came. Three devils!"

"Young devils, I hope."

"Young or old, who cares? They were devils. The blacksmith surprised them even as they were opening the grave. He raised such a shout that all of San Juan rushed to his aid, for they were fighting, I can tell you. Especially one of them—their leader."

"And who was he?"

"You have heard of him doubtless. A proper wild one named Pepe Gonzalez."

"And what happened to them?"

"They had horses and got away, but one, I think, was hurt."

The Hidalgo man twisted his mouth remembering how Rubén the candymaker had ridden across the whitewashed line high on the cañon trail that marked the division between the Three Marys' and the Sabinas' sides of the mountains, and then had fallen in a faint from his saddle because his left arm was broken. There was no candy in Hidalgo for six weeks, and the entire Sabinas Valley resented that broken arm as fiercely as did Rubén.

The stranger tightened his arm in reflexed anger about Sarita's waist as she said, "All the world knows that the men of Hidalgo are sons of the mountain witches."

"But even devils are shy of disturbing the honored dead," he said gravely.

" 'Don Rómolo was born in our village,' Hidalgo says. 'His bones belong to us.' Well, anyone in the valley can tell you he died in San Juan Iglesias, and here his bones will stay! Is that not proper? Is that not right?"

To keep from answering, he guided her through an intricate dance pattern that led them past the patio door. Over her head he could see two men and a woman staring with amazement at the open package on the table.

His eyes on the patio, he asked blandly, "You say the leader was one Pepe Gonzalez? The name seems to have a familiar sound."

"But naturally. He has a talent." She tossed her head and stepped away from him as the music stopped. It was a dance of two *paradas*. He slipped his hand through her arm and guided her into place in the large oval of parading couples. Twice around the room and the orchestra would play again.

"A talent?" he prompted.

"For doing the impossible. When all the world says a thing cannot be done, he does it to prove the world wrong. Why, he climbed to the top of the Prow, and not even the long vanished Joaquín Castillo had ever climbed that mountain before. And this same Pepe caught a mountain lion with nothing to aid him but a rope and his two bare hands.''

"He doesn't sound such a bad friend," protested the stranger, slipping his arm around her waist as the music began to play the merry song of the soap bubbles:

*Pretty bubbles of a thousand colors*
*That ride on the wind*
*And break as swiftly*
*As a lover's heart.*

The events in the patio were claiming his attention. Little by little he edged her closer to the door. The group at the table had considerably enlarged. There was a low murmur of excitement from the crowd.

"What has happened?" asked Sarita, attracted by the noise.

"There seems to be something wrong at the table," he answered, while trying to peer over the heads of the people in front of him. Realizing that this might be the last moment of peace he would have that evening, he bent toward her.

"If I come back on Sunday, will you walk around the plaza with me?"

She was startled into exclaiming, "Ay, no!"

"Please. Just once around."

"And you think I'd walk more than once with you, señor, even if you were no stranger? In San Juan Iglesias, to walk around the plaza with a girl means a wedding."

"Ha, and you think that is common to San Juan alone? Even the devils of Hidalgo respect that law." He added hastily at her puzzled upward glance. "And so they do in all the villages." To cover his lapse he said softly, "I don't even know your name."

A mischievous grin crinkled the corners of her eyes. "Nor do I know yours, señor.

**SEÑORA SABASA GARCIA, 1806–1807**
*Francisco José de Goya*
National Gallery of Art, Washington
Andrew W. Mellon Collection

Strangers do not often walk the streets of San Juan."

Before he could answer, the chattering in the patio swelled to louder proportions. Don Roméo's voice lay on top, like thick cream on milk. "I tell you it is a jewel of a cheese. Such flavor, such texture, such whiteness. It is a jewel of a cheese."

"What has happened?" Sarita asked of a woman at her elbow.

"A fine goat's cheese appeared as if by magic on the table. No one knows where it came from."

"Probably an extra one from Linares," snorted a fat bald man on the right.

"Linares never made such a cheese as this," said the woman decisively.

"Silence!" roared Don Roméo. "Old Tío Daniel would speak a word to us."

A great hand of silence closed down over the mouths of the people. The girl was standing on tiptoe trying vainly to see what was happening. She was hardly aware of the stranger's whispering voice although she remembered the words that he said. "Sunday night—once around the plaza."

She did not realize that he had moved away, leaving a gap that was quickly filled by the blacksmith.

Old Tío Daniel's voice was a shrill squeak, and his thin, stringy neck jutted forth from his body like a turtle's from its shell. "This is no cheese from Linares," he said with authority, his mouth sucking in over his toothless gums between his sentences. "Years ago, when the great Don Rómolo Balderas was still alive, we had such cheese as this—ay, in those days we had it. But after he died and was buried in our own sainted ground, as was right and proper . . ."

"Yes, yes," muttered voices in the crowd. He glared at the interruption. As soon as there was silence again, he continued:

"After he died, we had it no more. Shall I tell you why?"

"Tell us, Tío Daniel," said the voices humbly.

"Because it is made in Hidalgo!"

The sound of a waterfall, the sound of a wind in a narrow cañon, and the sound of an angry crowd are much the same. There were no distinct words, but the sound was enough.

"Are you certain, Tío?" boomed Don Roméo.

"As certain as I am that a donkey has long ears. The people of Hidalgo have been famous for generations for making cheese like this—especially that wicked one, that owner of a cheese factory, Timotéo Gonzalez, father to Pepe, the wild one, whom we have good cause to remember."

"We do, we do," came the sigh of assurance.

"But on the whole northern frontier there are no vats like his to produce so fine a product. Ask the people of Chihuahua, of Sonora. Ask the man on the bridge at Laredo, or the man in his boat at Tampico, 'Hola,[2] friend, who makes the finest goat cheese?' And the answer will always be the same, 'Don Timotéo of Hidalgo.'"

It was the blacksmith who asked the great question. "Then where did that cheese come from, and we haters of Hidalgo these ten long years?"

No voice said, "The stranger," but with one fluid movement every head in the patio turned toward the girl in the doorway. She also turned, her eyes wide with something that she realized to her own amazement was more apprehension than anger.

But the stranger was not in the room. When the angry, muttering men pushed through to the street, the stranger was not on the plaza. He was not anywhere in sight. A few of the more religious crossed themselves for fear that the Devil had walked in their midst. "Who was he?" one voice asked another. But Sarita, who was meekly listening to a lecture from Don Roméo on the propriety of dancing with strangers, did not have to ask. She had a strong suspicion that she had danced that night within the circling arm of Pepe Gonzalez.

---

**2. Hola** (ō´la): Spanish exclamation meaning "Hey there."

## THINKING ABOUT THE SELECTION

### Recalling

1. What kind of welcome does Pepe Gonzalez receive at the party?
2. What two things does Pepe set out to do at the party?
3. What outrageous deed had men from Hidalgo attempted in San Juan Iglesias three months previously?
4. What causes an uproar among the guests?

### Interpreting

5. What does Pepe's caution in arriving in the village suggest about his motives?
6. Describe Pepe's personality.
7. Compare and contrast the villagers' treatment of the stranger with the way they probably would have knowingly treated Pepe.
8. Give three reasons Pepe Gonzalez might have had for leaving the cheese.
9. How does Sarita know who the stranger is?

### Applying

10. What do you think will happen now between Pepe and Sarita and between the two villages? Give your reasons for making those predictions.

## ANALYZING LITERATURE

### Appreciating Local Color

**Local color** includes any descriptions that highlight the special qualities of a place or of a person. By using local color, authors help you feel what a community is like. Readers familiar with the setting can recognize the truth of the local color presented. Readers unfamiliar with the community can get a real feeling of what it is like.

1. From this story, list five details that give the feeling of a small Mexican village.
2. What events in this story depend on the details of local color?

3. List five details of local color about a city, town, or neighborhood with which you are familiar.

## CRITICAL THINKING AND READING

### Making Inferences About Characters

The customs and traditions of the place where a story occurs can be an important aspect of the setting. The rules of the community affect the people who live there. When an author does not directly state how the setting affects a character, you can make inferences about the relationship based on the facts the author does include.

1. What effect do the customs of the village have on Sarita?
2. Why is walking around the plaza so significant to both Sarita and Pepe?

## UNDERSTANDING LANGUAGE

### Recognizing Words from Spanish

Many English words come from the Spanish language. For example, the word *cañon* in the story title is a Spanish word from which the English word *canyon* is derived.

Use a dictionary to find which of the following words have come into English from or through Spanish. Write a sentence for each word derived from Spanish.

1. guitar
2. lanterns
3. chaperone
4. saddle
5. plaza
6. patio

## THINKING AND WRITING

### Describing a Place

Think of a city, town, or neighborhood that you find interesting. Write a letter to a friend recommending that he or she visit the place. Include details of local color that will help your friend understand the special flavor of the location. When you revise, include two more details of local color.

# GUIDE FOR READING

## By the Waters of Babylon

**Stephen Vincent Benét** (1898–1943) was born in Bethlehem, Pennsylvania. He is perhaps best known for his epic poem, *John Brown's Body,* for which he won a Pulitzer Prize in 1929. Although he was also the author of novels and short stories, Benét thought of himself primarily as a poet. The story you are about to read began as a poem, which Benét then transformed into a short story called "The Place of the Gods." He changed the title for its publication in the collection *Thirteen O'Clock* in 1937.

### Time as an Aspect of Setting

The **setting** of a story is both the time and the place of the action. In certain stories the time in which the story takes place is an important aspect, suggesting what has happened or will happen in history. In "By the Waters of Babylon," the time period may at first be unclear, but when you recognize it, you will understand the significance of the story.

### Look For

According to the Bible, the Israelites grieved over their separation from their homeland, Zion, and their captivity by the Babylonians. The following lines come from Psalm 137. "By the waters of Babylon/there we sat now and wept,/when we remembered Zion," As you read "By the Waters of Babylon," look for how these lines relate to the story.

### Writing

In this story objects that you may consider commonplace are unfamiliar to the character. Think of one commonplace object—a frying pan, a pencil, or a hair brush, for example. Try to imagine the impression it would make on someone who had no idea what it was. Freewrite about what possible uses it might suggest to such a person.

### Vocabulary

Knowing the following words will help you as you read "By the Waters of Babylon."

**purified** (pyσσr'ə fīd) *v.:* Cleansed; rid of impurities (p. 147)

**boasted** (bōst'əd) *v.:* Showed too much pride; bragged (p. 147)

**bowels** (bσu' əlz) *n.:* Intestines; guts (p. 150)

**slain** (slān) *adj.:* Killed (p. 150)

# By the Waters of Babylon

Stephen Vincent Benét

The north and the west and the south are good hunting ground, but it is forbidden to go east. It is forbidden to go to any of the Dead Places except to search for metal, and then he who touches the metal must be a priest or the son of a priest. Afterwards, both the man and the metal must be purified! These are the rules and the laws; they are well made. It is forbidden to cross the great river and look upon the place that was the Place of the Gods—this is most strictly forbidden. We do not even say its name though we know its name. It is there that spirits live, and demons—it is there that there are the ashes of the Great Burning. These things are forbidden—they have been forbidden since the beginning of time.

My father is a priest; I am the son of a priest. I have been in the Dead Places near us, with my father—at first, I was afraid. When my father went into the house to search for the metal, I stood by the door and my heart felt small and weak. It was a dead man's house, a spirit house. It did not have the smell of man, though there were old bones in a corner. But it is not fitting that a priest's son should show fear. I looked at the bones in the shadow and kept my voice still.

Then my father came out with the metal —a good, strong piece. He looked at me with both eyes but I had not run away. He gave me the metal to hold—I took it and did not die. So he knew that I was truly his son and would be a priest in my time. That was when I was very young—nevertheless, my brothers would not have done it, though they are good hunters. After that, they gave me the good piece of meat and the warm corner by the fire. My father watched over me—he was glad that I should be a priest. But when I boasted or wept without a reason, he punished me more strictly than my brothers. That was right.

After a time, I myself was allowed to go into the dead houses and search for metal. So I learned the ways of those houses—and if I saw bones, I was no longer afraid. The bones are light and old—sometimes they will fall into dust if you touch them. But that is a great sin.

I was taught the chants and the spells —I was taught how to stop the running of blood from a wound and many secrets. A priest must know many secrets—that was what my father said. If the hunters think we do all things by chants and spells, they may believe so—it does not hurt them. I was taught how to read in the old books and how

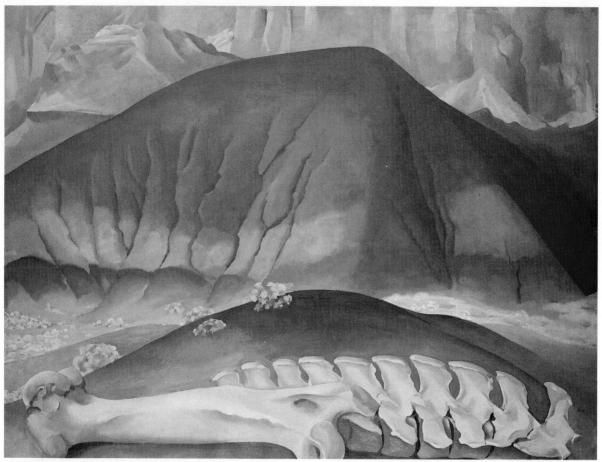

**RED HILLS AND BONES, 1941**
*Georgia O'Keeffe*
*Philadelphia Museum of Art: The Alfred Stieglitz Collection*

to make the old writings—that was hard and took a long time. My knowledge made me happy—it was like a fire in my heart. Most of all, I liked to hear of the Old Days and the stories of the gods. I asked myself many questions that I could not answer, but it was good to ask them. At night, I would lie awake and listen to the wind—it seemed to me that it was the voice of the gods as they flew through the air.

We are not ignorant like the Forest People—our women spin wool on the wheel, our priests wear a white robe. We do not eat grubs from the tree, we have not forgotten the old writings, although they are hard to understand. Nevertheless, my knowledge and my lack of knowledge burned in me—I wished to know more. When I was a man at last, I came to my father and said, "It is time for me to go on my journey. Give me your leave."

He looked at me for a long time, stroking his beard, then he said at last, "Yes. It is time." That night, in the house of the priesthood, I asked for and received purification. My body hurt but my spirit was a cool stone. It was my father himself who questioned me about my dreams.

He bade me look into the smoke of the fire and see—I saw and told what I saw. It was what I have always seen—a river, and, beyond it, a great Dead Place and in it the gods walking. I have always thought about that. His eyes were stern when I told him—he was no longer my father but a priest. He said, "This is a strong dream."

"It is mine," I said, while the smoke waved and my head felt light. They were singing the Star song in the outer chamber and it was like the buzzing of bees in my head.

He asked me how the gods were dressed and I told him how they were dressed. We know how they were dressed from the book, but I saw them as if they were before me. When I had finished, he threw the sticks three times and studied them as they fell.

"This is a very strong dream," he said. "It may eat you up."

"I am not afraid," I said and looked at him with both eyes. My voice sounded thin in my ears but that was because of the smoke.

He touched me on the breast and the forehead. He gave me the bow and the three arrows.

"Take them," he said. "It is forbidden to travel east. It is forbidden to cross the river. It is forbidden to go to the Place of the Gods. All these things are forbidden."

"All these things are forbidden," I said, but it was my voice that spoke and not my spirit. He looked at me again.

"My son," he said. "Once I had young dreams. If your dreams do not eat you up, you may be a great priest. If they eat you, you are still my son. Now go on your journey."

I went fasting, as is the law. My body hurt but not my heart. When the dawn came, I was out of sight of the village. I prayed and purified myself, waiting for a sign. The sign was an eagle. It flew east.

Sometimes signs are sent by bad spirits. I waited again on the flat rock, fasting, taking no food. I was very still—I could feel the sky above me and the earth beneath. I waited till the sun was beginning to sink. Then three deer passed in the valley, going east—they did not wind me or see me. There was a white fawn with them—a very great sign.

I followed them, at a distance, waiting for what would happen. My heart was troubled about going east, yet I knew that I must go. My head hummed with my fasting—I did not even see the panther spring upon the white fawn. But, before I knew it, the bow was in my hand. I shouted and the panther lifted his head from the fawn. It is not easy to kill a panther with one arrow but the arrow went through his eye and into his brain. He died as he tried to spring—he rolled over, tearing at the ground. Then I knew I was meant to go east—I knew that was my journey. When the night came, I made my fire and roasted meat.

It is eight suns' journey to the east and a man passes by many Dead Places. The Forest People are afraid of them but I am not. Once I made my fire on the edge of a Dead Place at night and, next morning, in the dead house, I found a good knife, little rusted. That was small to what came afterward, but it made my heart feel big. Always when I looked for game, it was in front of my arrow, and twice I passed hunting parties of the Forest People without their knowing. So I knew my magic was strong and my journey clean, in spite of the law.

Toward the setting of the eighth sun, I came to the banks of the great river. It was half-a-day's journey after I had left the god-road—we do not use the god-roads now for they are falling apart into great blocks of stone, and the forest is safer going. A long way off, I had seen the water through trees but the trees were thick. At last, I came out upon an open place at the top of a cliff. There was the great river below, like a giant in the sun. It is very long, very wide. It could eat all the streams we know and still be thirsty. Its name is Ou-dis-sun, the Sacred, the Long. No man of my tribe had seen it, not even my father, the priest. It was magic and I prayed.

Then I raised my eyes and looked south. It was there, the Place of the Gods.

How can I tell what it was like—you do not know. It was there, in the red light, and they were too big to be houses. It was there with the red light upon it, mighty and ruined. I knew that in another moment the gods would see me. I covered my eyes with my hands and crept back into the forest.

Surely, that was enough to do, and live. Surely it was enough to spend the night upon the cliff. The Forest People themselves do not come near. Yet, all through the night, I knew that I should have to cross the river and walk in the places of the gods, although the gods ate me up. My magic did not help me at all and yet there was a fire in my bowels, a fire in my mind. When the sun rose, I thought, "My journey has been clean. Now I will go home from my journey." But, even as I thought so, I knew I could not. If I went to the place of the gods, I would surely die, but, if I did not go, I could never be at peace with my spirit again. It is better to lose one's life than one's spirit, if one is a priest and the son of a priest.

Nevertheless, as I made the raft, the tears ran out of my eyes. The Forest People could have killed me without fight, if they had come upon me then, but they did not come. When the raft was made, I said the sayings for the dead and painted myself for death. My heart was cold as a frog and my knees like water, but the burning in my mind would not let me have peace. As I pushed the raft from the shore, I began my death song—I had the right. It was a fine song.

> "I am John, son of John," I sang. "My people are the Hill People. They are the men.
> I go into the Dead Places but I am not slain.
> I take the metal from the Dead Places but I am not blasted.
> I travel upon the god-roads and am not afraid. E-yah! I have killed the panther, I have killed the fawn!
> E-yah! I have come to the great river. No man has come there before.
> It is forbidden to go east, but I have gone, forbidden to go on the great river, but I am there.
> Open your hearts, you spirits, and hear my song.
> Now I go to the Place of the Gods, I shall not return.
> My body is painted for death and my limbs weak, but my heart is big as I go to the Place of the Gods!"

All the same, when I came to the Place of the Gods, I was afraid, afraid. The current of the great river is very strong—it gripped my raft with its hands. That was magic, for the river itself is wide and calm. I could feel evil spirits about me, in the bright morning; I could feel their breath on my neck as I was swept down the stream. Never have I been so much alone—I tried to think of my knowledge, but it was a squirrel's heap of winter nuts. There was no strength in my knowledge any more, and I felt small and naked as a new-hatched bird—alone upon the great river, the servant of the gods.

Yet, after a while, my eyes were opened and I saw. I saw both banks of the river—I saw that once there had been god-roads across it, though now they were broken and fallen like broken vines. Very great they were, and wonderful and broken—broken in the time of the Great Burning when the fire fell out of the sky. And always the current took me nearer to the Place of the Gods, and the huge ruins rose before my eyes.

I do not know the customs of rivers—we are the People of the Hills. I tried to guide my raft with the pole but it spun around. I thought the river meant to take me past the Place of the Gods and out into the Bitter Water of the legends. I grew angry then—my heart felt strong. I said aloud, "I am a priest and the son of a priest!" The gods heard me—they showed me how to paddle with the pole on one side of the raft. The current changed itself—I drew near to the Place of the Gods.

When I was very near, my raft struck and turned over. I can swim in our lakes—I swam to the shore. There was a great spike of rusted metal sticking out into the river—I hauled myself up upon it and sat there, panting. I had saved my bow and two arrows and the knife I found in the Dead Place but that was all. My raft went whirling downstream toward the Bitter Water. I looked after it, and thought if it had trod me under, at least I would be safely dead. Nevertheless, when I had dried my bow-string and restrung it, I walked forward to the Place of the Gods.

It felt like ground underfoot; it did not burn me. It is not true what some of the tales say, that the ground there burns forever, for I have been there. Here and there were the marks and stains of the Great Burning, on the ruins, that is true. But they were old marks and old stains. It is not true either, what some of our priests say, that it is an island covered with fogs and enchantments. It is not. It is a great Dead Place—greater than any Dead Place we know. Everywhere in it there are god-roads, though most are cracked and broken. Everywhere there are the ruins of the high towers of the gods.

How shall I tell what I saw? I went carefully, my strung bow in my hand, my skin ready for danger. There should have been the wailings of spirits and the shrieks of demons, but there were not. It was very silent and sunny where I had landed—the wind and the rain and the birds that drop seeds had done their work—the grass grew in the cracks of the broken stone. It is a fair island—no wonder the gods built there. If I had come there, a god, I also would have built.

How shall I tell what I saw? The towers are not all broken—here and there one still stands, like a great tree in a forest, and the birds nest high. But the towers themselves look blind, for the gods are gone. I saw a fish-hawk, catching fish in the river. I saw a little dance of white butterflies over a great heap of broken stones and columns. I went there and looked about me—there was a carved stone with cut-letters, broken in half. I can read letters but I could not understand these. They said UBTREAS. There was also the shattered image of a man or a god. It had been made of white stone and he wore his hair tied back like a woman's. His name was ASHING, as I read on the cracked half of a stone. I thought it wise to pray to ASHING, though I do not know that god.

How shall I tell what I saw? There was no smell of man left, on stone or metal. Nor were there many trees in that wilderness of stone. There are many pigeons, nesting and dropping in the towers—the gods must have loved them, or, perhaps, they used them for sacrifices. There are wild cats that roam the god-roads, green-eyed, unafraid of man. At night they wail like demons but they are not demons. The wild dogs are more dangerous, for they hunt in a pack, but them I did not meet till later. Everywhere there are the carved stones carved with magical numbers or words.

I went North—I did not try to hide myself. When a god or a demon saw me, then I would die, but meanwhile I was no longer afraid. My hunger for knowledge burned in me—there was so much that I could not understand. After awhile, I knew that my belly was hungry. I could have hunted for my meat, but I did not hunt. It is known that the gods did not hunt as we do—they got their food from enchanted boxes and jars. Sometimes these are still found in the Dead Places—once, when I was a child and foolish, I opened such a jar and tasted it and found the food sweet. But my father found out and punished me for it strictly, for, often, that food is death. Now, though, I had long gone past what was forbidden, and I entered the likeliest towers, looking for the food of the gods.

I found it at last in the ruins of a great temple in the mid-city. A mighty temple it must have been, for the roof was painted like the sky at night with its stars—that much I could see, though the colors were faint and dim. It went down into great caves and tunnels—perhaps they kept their slaves there. But when I started to climb down, I heard the squeaking of rats, so I did not go—rats are unclean, and there must have been many tribes of them, from the squeaking. But near there, I found food, in the heart of a ruin, behind a door that still opened. I ate only the fruits from the jars—they had a

very sweet taste. There was drink, too, in bottles of glass—the drink of the gods was strong and made my head swim. After I had eaten and drunk, I slept on the top of a stone, my bow at my side.

When I woke, the sun was low. Looking down from where I lay, I saw a dog sitting on his haunches. His tongue was hanging out of his mouth; he looked as if he were laughing. He was a big dog, with a gray-brown coat, as big as a wolf. I sprang up and shouted at him but he did not move—he just sat there as if he were laughing. I did not like that. When I reached for a stone to throw, he moved swiftly out of the way of the stone. He was not afraid of me; he looked at me as if I were meat. No doubt I could have killed him with an arrow, but I did not know if there were others. Moreover, night was falling.

I looked about me—not far away there was a great, broken god-road, leading North. The towers were high enough, but not so high, and while many of the dead-houses were wrecked, there were some that stood. I went toward this god-road, keeping to the heights of the ruins, while the dog followed. When I had reached the god-road, I saw that there were others behind him. If I had slept later, they would have come upon me asleep and torn out my throat. As it was, they were sure enough of me; they did not hurry. When I went into the dead-house, they kept watch at the entrance—doubtless they thought they would have a fine hunt. But a dog cannot open a door and I knew, from the books, that the gods did not like to live on the ground but on high.

I had just found a door I could open when the dogs decided to rush. Ha! They were surprised when I shut the door in their faces—it was a good door, of strong metal. I could hear their foolish baying beyond it, but I did not stop to answer them. I was in darkness—I found stairs and climbed. There were many stairs, turning around till my head was dizzy. At the top was another door—I found the knob and opened it. I was in a long small chamber—on one side of it was a bronze door that could not be opened, for it had no handle. Perhaps there was a magic word to open it, but I did not have the word. I turned to the door in the opposite side of the wall. The lock of it was broken and I opened it and went in.

Within, there was a place of great riches. The god who lived there must have been a powerful god. The first room was a small anteroom—I waited there for some time, telling the spirits of the place that I came in peace and not as a robber. When it seemed to me that they had had time to hear me, I went on. Ah, what riches! Few, even, of the windows had been broken—it was all as it had been. The great windows that looked over the city had not been broken at all though they were dusty and streaked with many years. There were coverings on the floors, the colors not greatly faded, and the chairs were soft and deep. There were pictures upon the walls, very strange, very wonderful—I remember one of a bunch of flowers in a jar—if you came close to it, you could see nothing but bits of color, but if you stood away from it, the flowers might have been picked yesterday. It made my heart feel strange to look at this picture—and to look at the figure of a bird, in some hard clay, on a table and see it so like our birds. Everywhere there were books and writings, many in tongues that I could not read. The god who lived there must have been a wise god and full of knowledge. I felt I had right there, as I sought knowledge also.

Nevertheless, it was strange. There was a washing-place but no water—perhaps the gods washed in air. There was a cooking-place but no wood, and though there was a machine to cook food, there was no place to put fire in it. Nor were there candles or lamps—there were things that looked like lamps but they had neither oil nor wick. All these things were magic, but I touched them and lived—the magic had gone out of them. Let me tell one thing to show. In the washing-place, a thing said "Hot" but it was not hot to the touch—another thing said "Cold" but it was not cold. This must have been a strong magic but the magic was gone. I do not understand—they had ways—I wish that I knew.

It was close and dry and dusty in their house of the gods. I have said the magic was gone but that is not true—it had gone from the magic things but it had not gone from the place. I felt the spirits about me, weighing upon me. Nor had I ever slept in a Dead Place before—and yet, tonight, I must sleep there. When I thought of it, my tongue felt dry in my throat, in spite of my wish for knowledge. Almost I would have gone down again and faced the dogs, but I did not.

I had not gone through all the rooms when the darkness fell. When it fell, I went back to the big room looking over the city and made fire. There was a place to make fire and a box with wood in it, though I do not think they cooked there. I wrapped myself in a floor-covering and slept in front of the fire—I was very tired.

Now I tell what is very strong magic. I woke in the midst of the night. When I woke, the fire had gone out and I was cold. It seemed to me that all around me there were whisperings and voices. I closed my eyes to shut them out. Some will say that I slept again, but I do not think that I slept. I could feel the spirits drawing my spirit out of my body as a fish is drawn on a line.

Why should I lie about it? I am a priest and the son of a priest. If there are spirits, as they say, in the small Dead Places near us, what spirits must there not be in that great Place of the Gods? And would not they wish to speak? After such long years? I know that I felt myself drawn as a fish is drawn on a line. I had stepped out of my body—I could see my body asleep in front of the cold fire, but it was not I. I was drawn to look out upon the city of the gods.

It should have been dark, for it was night, but it was not dark. Everywhere there were lights—lines of light—circles and blurs of light—ten thousand torches would not have been the same. The sky itself was alight—you could barely see the stars for the glow in the sky. I thought to myself "This is strong magic" and trembled. There was a roaring in my ears like the rushing of rivers. Then my eyes grew used to the light and my ears to the sound. I knew that I was seeing the city as it had been when the gods were alive.

That was a sight indeed—yes, that was a sight: I could not have seen it in the body—my body would have died. Everywhere went the gods, on foot and in chariots—there were gods beyond number and counting and their chariots blocked the streets. They had turned night to day for their pleasure—they did not sleep with the sun. The noise of their coming and going was the noise of many waters. It was magic what they could do—it was magic what they did.

I looked out of another window—the great vines of their bridges were mended and the god-roads went East and West. Restless, restless, were the gods and always in motion! They burrowed tunnels under rivers—they flew in the air. With unbelievable tools they did giant works—no part of

the earth was safe from them, for, if they wished for a thing, they summoned it from the other side of the world. And always, as they labored and rested, as they feasted and made love, there was a drum in their ears —the pulse of the giant city, beating and beating like a man's heart.

Were they happy? What is happiness to the gods? They were great, they were mighty, they were wonderful and terrible. As I looked upon them and their magic, I felt like a child—but a little more, it seemed to me, and they would pull down the moon from the sky. I saw them with wisdom beyond wisdom and knowledge beyond knowledge. And yet not all they did was well done—even I could see that—and yet their wisdom could not but grow until all was peace.

Then I saw their fate come upon them and that was terrible past speech. It came upon them as they walked the streets of their city. I have been in the fights with the Forest People—I have seen men die. But this was not like that. When gods war with gods, they use weapons we do not know. It was fire falling out of the sky and a mist that poisoned. It was the time of the Great Burning and the Destruction. They ran about like ants in the streets of their city —poor gods, poor gods! Then the towers began to fall. A few escaped—yes, a few. The legends tell it. But, even after the city had become a Dead Place, for many years the poison was still in the ground. I saw it happen, I saw the last of them die. It was darkness over the broken city, and I wept.

All this, I saw. I saw it as I have told it, though not in the body. When I woke in the morning, I was hungry, but I did not think first of my hunger, for my heart was perplexed and confused. I knew the reason for the Dead Places but I did not see why it had

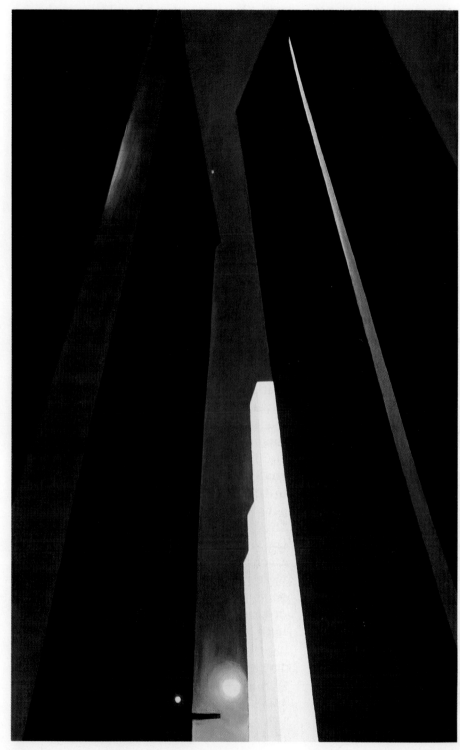

**CITY NIGHT, 1926**
*Georgia O'Keeffe*

happened. It seemed to me it should not have happened, with all the magic they had. I went through the house looking for an answer. There was so much in the house I could not understand—and yet I am a priest and the son of a priest. It was like being on one side of the great river, at night, with no light to show the way.

Then I saw the dead god. He was sitting in his chair, by the window, in a room I had not entered before and, for the first moment, I thought that he was alive. Then I saw the skin on the back of his hand—it was like dry leather. The room was shut, hot and dry—no doubt that had kept him as he was. At first I was afraid to approach him—then the fear left me. He was sitting looking out over the city—he was dressed in the clothes of the gods. His age was neither young nor old—I could not tell his age. But there was wisdom in his face and great sadness. You could see that he would have not run away. He had sat at his window, watching his city die—then he himself had died. But it is better to lose one's life than one's spirit —and you could see from the face that his spirit had not been lost. I knew, that, if I touched him, he would fall into dust—and yet, there was something unconquered in the face.

That is all of my story, for then I knew he was a man—I knew then that they had been men, neither gods nor demons. It is a great knowledge, hard to tell and believe. They were men—they went a dark road, but they were men. I had no fear after that—I had no fear going home, though twice I fought off the dogs and once I was hunted for two days by the Forest People. When I saw my father again, I prayed and was purified. He touched my lips and my breast, he said, "You went away a boy. You come back a man and a priest." I said, "Father, they were men! I have been in the Place of the Gods and seen it! Now slay me, if it is the law—but still I know they were men."

He looked at me out of both eyes. He said, "The law is not always the same shape—you have done what you have done. I could not have done it my time, but you come after me. Tell!"

I told and he listened. After that, I wished to tell all the people but he showed me otherwise. He said, "Truth is a hard deer to hunt. If you eat too much truth at once, you may die of the truth. It was not idly that our fathers forbade the Dead Places." He was right—it is better the truth should come little by little. I have learned that, being a priest. Perhaps, in the old days, they ate knowledge too fast.

Nevertheless, we make a beginning. It is not for the metal alone we go to the Dead Places now—there are the books and the writings. They are hard to learn. And the magic tools are broken—but we can look at them and wonder. At least, we make a beginning. And, when I am chief priest we shall go beyond the great river. We shall go to the Place of the Gods—the place new-york—not one man but a company. We shall look for the images of the gods and find the god ASHING and the others—the gods Licoln and Biltmore[1] and Moses[2]. But they were men who built the city, not gods or demons. They were men. I remember the dead man's face. They were men who were here before us. We must build again.

---

**1. Biltmore:** A hotel in New York City.
**2. Moses:** Robert Moses, New York City municipal official.

# THINKING ABOUT THE SELECTION

## Recalling

1. In what way is John different from his brothers? What are his responsibilities?
2. Why does John set out on his journey? Why is John's journey particularly dangerous?
3. Describe three things John sees in the Place of the Gods.
4. What significant piece of information about the "gods" does John learn on his journey?

## Interpreting

5. What is the significance of the journey to John and his people?
6. Explain why John's father wants to keep secret what John has learned about the Place of the Gods.
7. Near the end of the story, John suggests, "Perhaps, in the old days, they ate knowledge too fast." Explain what this statement might mean. Do you agree that people can eat knowledge too fast? Explain your answer.
8. Explain the title of this story. Why is it appropriate that this story would appear in a collection called, *Thirteen O'Clock*?

## Applying

9. How do you think John's people can best avoid repeating the mistakes that led to the destruction of civilization in the past?

# ANALYZING LITERATURE

## Recognizing Time in Setting

**Setting** has two components: time and place. **Time** can be particularly important in some stories, so important that it can take on the concrete reality of a place. Thus, we often refer to the future or the past as *where*, rather than *when*, the story takes place.

1. When does this story take place?

2. Find at least three facts, incidents, or details that reveal the time period.
3. UBTREAS refers to the Subtreasury Building. To what do the following refer? a. ASHING; b. Ou-dis-sun.
4. What is meant by the Dead Places? Compare and contrast the world of John's people with the world of those who lived in the Place of the Gods.

# UNDERSTANDING LANGUAGE

## Recognizing Multiple Meanings

Many words have more than one meaning. When this is the case, you sometimes know which meaning of the word the author intends from the context, the words and sentences around it. For example, in the statement "He died as he tried to spring," you know spring means "jump," not the "season following winter."

Use each of the following words in two sentences. Each sentence should demonstrate a different meaning of the word.

1. fawn       3. raft
2. current    4. bow

# THINKING AND WRITING

## Writing to Contrast Settings

Imagine that you somehow survived the war that destroyed the Place of the Gods and that the place was where you live. Write a message to leave for future generations telling what the place was like immediately before and immediately after the war. Your purpose is to teach future people about the past and to help them avoid the same fate. When you revise your message, add at least two more visual details so that people who have never seen your city or anything like it will be able to picture it.

# GUIDE FOR READING

## Through the Tunnel

**Doris Lessing** (1919– ) was born in Persia (now Iran) of British parents and raised in a remote area of southern Africa. She left school at fifteen and had a variety of jobs including children's nurse, telephone operator, and typist. She moved to England in 1949 and published her first novel, *The Grass Is Singing,* the following year. Most of Lessing's work centers on social and political questions. "Through the Tunnel," however, focuses on the inner life of a single child.

### Atmosphere

**Atmosphere** is the mood or the overall feeling established by a story. A writer may establish atmosphere by describing specific details of the setting in a way intended to create a desired effect. For example, describing a dark night, the noise of the wind, and the appearance of light and shadows will create an atmosphere of suspense and prepare you to be frightened by the action. Dialogue and action may also contribute to the atmosphere.

### Look For

As you read "Through the Tunnel," look for the details of setting and action that create the atmosphere of the story.

### Writing

In "Through the Tunnel," a boy strives to reach a goal. Think of a difficult goal, such as winning an Olympic event, becoming an astronaut, or being elected to the United States Senate, that would require great effort to achieve. Freewrite about ways to prepare to reach such a goal.

### Vocabulary

Knowing the following words will help you as you read "Through the Tunnel."

**contrition** (kən trish′ ən) *n.:* A feeling of remorse for having done something wrong (p. 159)

**promontories** (präm′ ən tôr′ ēz) *n.:* High places extending out over a body of water (p. 159)

**luminous** (lōō′ mə nəs) *adj.:* Giving off light (p. 159)

**supplication** (sup′ lə kā′ shən) *n.:* The act of asking humbly and earnestly (p. 160)

**frond** (fränd) *n.:* A leaflike shoot of seaweed (p. 162)

**convulsive** (kən vul′ siv) *adj.:* Marked by an involuntary, muscular contraction (p. 164)

**gout** (gout) *n.:* A spurt, splash, or glob (p. 165)

# Through the Tunnel

## Doris Lessing

Going to the shore on the first morning of the vacation, the young English boy stopped at a turning of the path and looked down at a wild and rocky bay, and then over to the crowded beach he knew so well from other years. His mother walked on in front of him, carrying a bright striped bag in one hand. Her other arm, swinging loose, was very white in the sun. The boy watched that white, naked arm, and turned his eyes, which had a frown behind them, toward the bay and back again to his mother. When she felt he was not with her, she swung around. "Oh, there you are, Jerry!" she said. She looked impatient, then smiled. "Why, darling, would you rather not come with me? Would you rather—" She frowned, conscientiously worrying over what amusements he might secretly be longing for, which she had been too busy or too careless to imagine. He was very familiar with that anxious, apologetic smile. Contrition sent him running after her. And yet, as he ran, he looked back over his shoulder at the wild bay; and all morning, as he played on the safe beach, he was thinking of it.

Next morning, when it was time for the routine of swimming and sunbathing, his mother said, "Are you tired of the usual beach, Jerry? Would you like to go somewhere else?"

"Oh, no!" he said quickly, smiling at her out of that unfailing impulse of contrition —a sort of chivalry. Yet, walking down the path with her, he blurted out, "I'd like to go and have a look at those rocks down there."

She gave the idea her attention. It was a wild-looking place, and there was no one there; but she said, "Of course, Jerry. When you've had enough, come to the big beach. Or just go straight back to the villa, if you like." She walked away, that bare arm, now slightly reddened from yesterday's sun, swinging. And he almost ran after her again, feeling it unbearable that she should go by herself, but he did not.

She was thinking, Of course he's old enough to be safe without me. Have I been keeping him too close? He mustn't feel he ought to be with me. I must be careful.

He was an only child, eleven years old. She was a widow. She was determined to be neither possessive nor lacking in devotion. She went worrying off to her beach.

As for Jerry, once he saw that his mother had gained her beach, he began the steep descent to the bay. From where he was, high up among red-brown rocks, it was a scoop of moving bluish green fringed with white. As he went lower, he saw that it spread among small promontories and inlets of rough, sharp rock, and the crisping, lapping surface showed stains of purple and darker blue. Finally, as he ran sliding and scraping down the last few yards, he saw an edge of white surf and the shallow, luminous movement of water over white sand, and, beyond that, a solid, heavy blue.

**THE BEACH TREAT (detail)**
*Suzanne Nagler* *Photograph © Stephen Tucker*
*Collection of Mr. and Mrs. X. Daniel Kafcas*

He ran straight into the water and began swimming. He was a good swimmer. He went out fast over the gleaming sand, over a middle region where rocks lay like discolored monsters under the surface, and then he was in the real sea—a warm sea where irregular cold currents from the deep water shocked his limbs.

When he was so far out that he could look back not only on the little bay but past the promontory that was between it and the big beach, he floated on the buoyant surface and looked for his mother. There she was, a speck of yellow under an umbrella that looked like a slice of orange peel. He swam back to shore, relieved at being sure she was there, but all at once very lonely.

On the edge of a small cape that marked the side of the bay away from the promontory was a loose scatter of rocks. Above them, some boys were stripping off their clothes. They came running, naked, down to the rocks. The English boy swam toward them, but kept his distance at a stone's throw. They were of that coast; all of them were burned smooth dark brown and speaking a language he did not understand. To be with them, of them, was a craving that filled his whole body. He swam a little closer; they turned and watched him with narrowed, alert dark eyes. Then one smiled and waved. It was enough. In a minute, he had swum in and was on the rocks beside them, smiling with a desperate, nervous supplication. They shouted cheerful greetings at him; and then, as he preserved his nervous, uncomprehending smile, they understood that he was a foreigner strayed from his own beach, and they proceeded to forget him. But he was happy. He was with them.

They began diving again and again from a high point into a well of blue sea between rough, pointed rocks. After they had dived and come up, they swam around, hauled themselves up, and waited their turn to dive again. They were big boys—men, to Jerry.

He dived, and they watched him; and when he swam around to take his place, they made way for him. He felt he was accepted and he dived again, carefully, proud of himself.

Soon the biggest of the boys poised himself, shot down into the water, and did not come up. The others stood about, watching. Jerry, after waiting for the sleek brown head to appear, let out a yell of warning; they looked at him idly and turned their eyes back toward the water. After a long time, the boy came up on the other side of a big dark rock, letting the air out of his lungs in a sputtering gasp and a shout of triumph. Immediately the rest of them dived in. One moment, the morning seemed full of chattering boys; the next, the air and the surface of the water were empty. But through the heavy blue, dark shapes could be seen moving and groping.

Jerry dived, shot past the school of underwater swimmers, saw a black wall of rock looming at him, touched it, and bobbed up at once to the surface, where the wall was a low barrier he could see across. There was no one visible; under him, in the water, the dim shapes of the swimmers had disappeared. Then one, and then another of the boys came up on the far side of the barrier of rock, and he understood that they had swum through some gap or hole in it. He plunged down again. He could see nothing through the stinging salt water but the blank rock. When he came up the boys were all on the diving rock, preparing to attempt the feat again. And now, in a panic of failure, he yelled up, in English, "Look at me! Look!" and he began splashing and kicking in the water like a foolish dog.

They looked down gravely, frowning. He knew the frown. At moments of failure, when he clowned to claim his mother's attention, it was with just this grave, embarrassed inspection that she rewarded him.

Through his hot shame, feeling the pleading grin on his face like a scar that he could never remove, he looked up at the group of big brown boys on the rock and shouted, *"Bonjour! Merci! Au revoir! Monsieur, monsieur!"*[1] while he hooked his fingers round his ears and waggled them.

Water surged into his mouth; he choked, sank, came up. The rock, lately weighted with boys, seemed to rear up out of the water as their weight was removed. They were flying down past him, now, into the water; the air was full of falling bodies. Then the rock was empty in the hot sunlight. He counted one, two, three. . . .

At fifty, he was terrified. They must all be drowning beneath him, in the watery caves of the rock! At a hundred, he stared around him at the empty hillside, wondering if he should yell for help. He counted faster, faster, to hurry them up, to bring them to the surface quickly, to drown them quickly—anything rather than the terror of counting on and on into the blue emptiness of the morning. And then, at a hundred and sixty, the water beyond the rock was full of boys blowing like brown whales. They swam back to the shore without a look at him.

He climbed back to the diving rock and sat down, feeling the hot roughness of it under his thighs. The boys were gathering up their bits of clothing and running off along the shore to another promontory. They were leaving to get away from him. He cried openly, fists in his eyes. There was no one to see him, and he cried himself out.

It seemed to him that a long time had passed, and he swam out to where he could see his mother. Yes, she was still there, a yellow spot under an orange umbrella. He swam back to the big rock, climbed up, and

---

**1. *Bonjour! . . . monsieur*** (bôn zhoor′ . . . mə syö′): Babbling of commonly known French words: "Hello! Thank you! Goodbye! Sir, sir!"

dived into the blue pool among the fanged and angry boulders. Down he went, until he touched the wall of rock again. But the salt was so painful in his eyes that he could not see.

He came to the surface, swam to shore and went back to the villa to wait for his mother. Soon she walked slowly up the path, swinging her striped bag, the flushed, naked arm dangling beside her. "I want some swimming goggles," he panted, defiant and beseeching.

She gave him a patient, inquisitive look as she said casually, "Well, of course, darling."

But now, now, now! He must have them this minute, and no other time. He nagged and pestered until she went with him to a shop. As soon as she had bought the goggles, he grabbed them from her hand as if she were going to claim them for herself, and was off, running down the steep path to the bay.

Jerry swam out to the big barrier rock, adjusted the goggles, and dived. The impact of the water broke the rubber-enclosed vacuum, and the goggles came loose. He understood that he must swim down to the base of the rock from the surface of the water. He fixed the goggles tight and firm, filled his lungs, and floated, face down, on the water. Now he could see. It was as if he had eyes of a different kind—fish eyes that showed everything clear and delicate and wavering in the bright water.

Under him, six or seven feet down, was a floor of perfectly clean, shining white sand, rippled firm and hard by the tides. Two grayish shapes steered there, like long, rounded pieces of wood or slate. They were fish. He saw them nose toward each other, poise motionless, make a dart forward, swerve off, and come around again. It was like a water dance. A few inches above them the water sparkled as if sequins were drop-ping through it. Fish again—myriads of minute fish, the length of his fingernail, were drifting through the water, and in a moment he could feel the innumerable tiny touches of them against his limbs. It was like swimming in flaked silver. The great rock the big boys had swum through rose sheer out of the white sand—black, tufted lightly with greenish weed. He could see no gap in it. He swam down to its base.

Again and again he rose, took a big chestful of air, and went down. Again and again he groped over the surface of the rock, feeling it, almost hugging it in the desperate need to find the entrance. And then, once, while he was clinging to the black wall, his knees came up and he shot his feet out forward and they met no obstacle. He had found the hole.

He gained the surface, clambered about the stones that littered the barrier rock until he found a big one, and, with this in his arms, let himself down over the side of the rock. He dropped, with the weight, straight to the sandy floor. Clinging tight to the anchor of stone, he lay on his side and looked in under the dark shelf at the place where his feet had gone. He could see the hole. It was an irregular, dark gap; but he could not see deep into it. He let go of his anchor, clung with his hands to the edges of the hole, and tried to push himself in.

He got his head in, found his shoulders jammed, moved them in sidewise, and was inside as far as his waist. He could see nothing ahead. Something soft and clammy touched his mouth; he saw a dark frond moving against the grayish rock, and panic filled him. He thought of octopuses, of clinging weed. He pushed himself out backward and caught a glimpse, as he retreated, of a harmless tentacle of seaweed drifting in the mouth of the tunnel. But it was enough. He reached the sunlight, swam to shore, and lay on the diving rock. He looked down into the blue well of water. He knew he must find his way through that cave, or hole, or tunnel, and out the other side.

First, he thought, he must learn to control his breathing. He let himself down into the water with another big stone in his arms, so that he could lie effortlessly on the bottom of the sea. He counted. One, two, three. He counted steadily. He could hear the movement of blood in his chest. Fifty-one, fifty-two. . . . His chest was hurting. He let go of the rock and went up into the air. He saw that the sun was low. He rushed to the villa and found his mother at her supper. She said only "Did you enjoy yourself?" and he said "Yes."

All night the boy dreamed of the water-filled cave in the rock, and as soon as breakfast was over he went to the bay.

That night, his nose bled badly. For hours he had been underwater, learning to hold his breath, and now he felt weak and dizzy. His mother said, "I shouldn't overdo things, darling, if I were you."

That day and the next, Jerry exercised his lungs as if everything, the whole of his life, all that he would become, depended upon it. Again his nose bled at night, and his mother insisted on his coming with her the next day. It was a torment to him to waste a day of his careful self-training, but he stayed with her on that other beach, which now seemed a place for small children, a place where his mother might lie safe in the sun. It was not his beach.

He did not ask for permission, on the following day, to go to his beach. He went, before his mother could consider the complicated rights and wrongs of the matter. A day's rest, he discovered, had improved his count by ten. The big boys had made the passage while he counted a hundred and sixty. He had been counting fast, in his fright. Probably now, if he tried, he could get through that long tunnel, but he was not going to try yet. A curious, most unchildlike persistence, a controlled impatience, made him wait. In the meantime, he lay underwater on the white sand, littered now by stones he had brought down from the upper air, and studied the entrance to the tunnel. He knew every jut and corner of it, as far as it was possible to see. It was as if he already felt its sharpness about his shoulders.

He sat by the clock in the villa, when his mother was not near, and checked his time. He was incredulous and then proud to find he could hold his breath without strain for two minutes. The words "two minutes," authorized by the clock, brought close the adventure that was so necessary to him.

In another four days, his mother said casually one morning, they must go home. On the day before they left, he would do it. He would do it if it killed him, he said defiantly to himself. But two days before they were to leave—a day of triumph when he increased his count by fifteen—his nose bled so badly that he turned dizzy and had to lie limply over the big rock like a bit of seaweed, watching the thick red blood flow onto the rock and trickle slowly down to the sea. He was frightened. Supposing he turned dizzy in the tunnel? Supposing he died there, trapped? Supposing—his head went around, in the hot sun, and he almost gave up. He thought he would return to the house and lie down, and next summer, perhaps, when he had another year's growth in him—*then* he would go through the hole.

But even after he had made the decision, or thought he had, he found himself sitting up on the rock and looking down into the water; and he knew that now, this moment, when his nose had only just stopped bleeding, when his head was still sore and throbbing—this was the moment when he would try. If he did not do it now, he never would. He was trembling with fear that he would not go; and he was trembling with horror at that long, long tunnel under the rock, under the sea. Even in the open sunlight, the barrier rock seemed very wide and very heavy; tons of rock pressed down on where he would go. If he died there, he would lie until one day—perhaps not before next year—those big boys would swim into it and find it blocked.

He put on his goggles, fitted them tight, tested the vacuum. His hands were shaking. Then he chose the biggest stone he could carry and slipped over the edge of the rock until half of him was in the cool, enclosing water and half in the hot sun. He looked up once at the empty sky, filled his lungs once, twice, and then sank fast to the bottom with the stone. He let it go and began to count. He took the edges of the hole in his hands and drew himself into it, wriggling his shoulders in sidewise as he remembered he must, kicking himself along with his feet.

Soon he was clear inside. He was in a small rockbound hole filled with yellowish-gray water. The water was pushing him up against the roof. The roof was sharp and pained his back. He pulled himself along with his hands—fast, fast—and used his legs as levers. His head knocked against something; a sharp pain dizzied him. Fifty, fifty-one, fifty-two. . . . He was without light, and the water seemed to press upon him with the weight of rock. Seventy-one, seventy-two. . . . There was no strain on his lungs. He felt like an inflated balloon, his lungs were so light and easy, but his head was pulsing.

He was being continually pressed against the sharp roof, which felt slimy as well as sharp. Again he thought of octopuses, and wondered if the tunnel might be filled with weed that could tangle him. He gave himself a panicky, convulsive kick forward, ducked his head, and swam. His feet and hands moved freely, as if in open water. The hole must have widened out. He thought he must be swimming fast, and he was frightened of banging his head if the tunnel narrowed.

A hundred, a hundred and one . . . The water paled. Victory filled him. His lungs were beginning to hurt. A few more strokes and he would be out. He was counting wildly; he said a hundred and fifteen, and then, a long time later, a hundred and fifteen again. The water was a clear jewel-green all around him. Then he saw, above his head, a crack running up through the rock. Sunlight was falling through it, showing the clean, dark rock of the tunnel, a single mussel shell, and darkness ahead.

He was at the end of what he could do. He looked up at the crack as if it were filled with air and not water, as if he could put his mouth to it to draw in air. A hundred and fifteen, he heard himself say inside his head —but he had said that long ago. He must go on into the blackness ahead, or he would drown. His head was swelling, his lungs cracking. A hundred and fifteen, a hundred and fifteen pounded through his head, and he feebly clutched at rocks in the dark, pulling himself forward, leaving the brief space of sunlit water behind. He felt he was dying. He was no longer quite conscious. He struggled on in the darkness between lapses into unconsciousness. An immense, swelling pain filled his head, and then the darkness cracked with an explosion of green light. His hands, groping forward, met nothing; and his feet, kicking back, propelled him out into the open sea.

He drifted to the surface, his face turned up to the air. He was gasping like a fish. He felt he would sink now and drown; he could not swim the few feet back to the rock. Then he was clutching it and pulling himself up on to it. He lay face down, gasping. He could see nothing but a red-veined, clotted dark. His eyes must have burst, he thought; they were full of blood. He tore off his goggles and

**COAST SCENE, ISLES OF SHOALS, 1901**
*Childe Hassam*
*The Metropolitan Museum of Art*

a gout of blood went into the sea. His nose was bleeding, and the blood had filled the goggles.

He scooped up handfuls of water from the cool, salty sea, to splash on his face, and did not know whether it was blood or salt water he tasted. After a time, his heart quieted, his eyes cleared, and he sat up. He could see the local boys diving and playing half a mile away. He did not want them. He wanted nothing but to get back home and lie down.

In a short while, Jerry swam to shore and climbed slowly up the path to the villa. He flung himself on his bed and slept, waking at the sound of feet on the path outside. His mother was coming back. He rushed to the bathroom, thinking she must not see his face with bloodstains, or tearstains, on it. He came out of the bathroom and met her as she walked into the villa, smiling, her eyes lighting up.

"Have a nice morning?" she asked, laying her hand on his warm brown shoulder a moment.

"Oh, yes, thank you," he said.

"You look a bit pale." And then, sharp and anxious, "How did you bang your head?"

"Oh, just banged it," he told her.

She looked at him closely. He was strained; his eyes were glazed-looking. She was worried. And then she said to herself, Oh, don't fuss! Nothing can happen. He can swim like a fish.

They sat down to lunch together.

"Mummy," he said, "I can stay under water for two minutes—three minutes, at least." It came bursting out of him.

"Can you, darling?" she said. "Well, I shouldn't overdo it. I don't think you ought to swim any more today."

She was ready for a battle of wills, but he gave in at once. It was no longer of the least importance to go to the bay.

## THINKING ABOUT THE SELECTION
### Recalling

1. Describe Jerry's encounter with the local boys. What effect does it have on him?
2. How does Jerry prepare for the task he has set himself?
3. Recount Jerry's passage through the tunnel.

### Interpreting

4. Describe Jerry's relationship with his mother at the beginning of the story. How does it change by the end of the story? Cite specific instances in the story that helped you form your opinions.
5. What must Jerry prove to himself by swimming through the tunnel?
6. Jerry experiences both external and internal conflicts as he swims through the tunnel. Explain both his conflicts.
7. There are both literal and figurative aspects to the title. Explain both.
8. How has Jerry changed in the course of this story? Why does he now feel that it is "no longer of the least importance to go to the bay"?

### Applying

9. Do you think Jerry's victory is worth the pain and risks it entailed? Why or why not?
10. Why do many young people set up situations in which they challenge themselves? Give some examples.

## ANALYZING LITERATURE
### Identifying Atmosphere

**Atmosphere** is the prevalent feeling created by a story or a scene. Descriptions of a story's setting often help establish the atmosphere, but dialogue and action may also play a role in defining a story's mood. The atmosphere developed in a story sets up your expectations about the events and the outcome. In "Through the Tunnel," when Jerry abandons his mother's beach, he leaves behind the carefree atmosphere of a vacation resort, and you expect him to have some sort of adventure.

1. Compare the atmosphere of the two beaches.
2. Describe the atmosphere when Jerry is under water.
3. In what way does the atmosphere affect your expectations when Jerry starts swimming through the tunnel?

## UNDERSTANDING LANGUAGE
### Appreciating Sensory Language

**Sensory language** is language that tells you how things look, smell, feel, sound, and taste. Well-chosen words can almost make you experience the sensation the author describes. For example, saying that a beach umbrella "looked like a slice of orange peel" helps you to see the umbrella as Jerry does.

1. Find at least three examples of sensory language in "Through the Tunnel" that appeal to your sense of sight.
2. Find two examples of sensory language that appeal to your sense of touch.
3. Find two examples of sensory language that appeal to your sense of hearing, taste, or smell.

## THINKING AND WRITING
### Writing About Art

Look at the pieces of fine art used on pages 160 and 165 in this story. For each piece of art, list details that create the atmosphere of the work. Then write a few paragraphs in which you discuss whether you think these pieces appropriately capture the atmospheres of Jerry's world and his mother's world. If you think they do not, explain why. When you revise your work, add sensory details that appeal to more than one sense in your descriptions of the atmospheres in the paintings.

# Symbol

**STREET SCENE IN LOWER NEW YORK, c. 1926**
*Glenn O. Coleman*
Collection of Whitney Museum of American Art

# GUIDE FOR READING

## Abalone, Abalone, Abalone

**Toshio Mori** (1910–1980) was born in Oakland and raised in San Leandro, California. During World War II, he was interned in the Topaz Relocation Center in Utah, where he was camp historian. He began to publish his stories in magazines during the 1940's while he was still in Topaz. After the war Mori returned to San Leandro. *Yokohama, California*, his first collection of short stories, was published in 1949. Mori worked most of his adult life in a small family nursery, as do both characters in "Abalone, Abalone, Abalone."

**Symbols**

A **symbol** is an object, a person, or an event that represents something else. A writer may use a symbol to make a point, to create a mood, or to reinforce a theme. Many common symbols have obvious or universal meanings. Thus a single green leaf can represent springtime and hope, or a gray cloud can represent darkness and despair. Within a given work, a symbol takes its meaning from the work itself. While the object that is a symbol exists as an integral part of the story, it represents something larger or more significant beyond the story, such as an idea or a belief.

**Look For**

As you read "Abalone, Abalone, Abalone," look for hints about the symbolic meaning of the abalone shells.

**Writing**

"Abalone, Abalone, Abalone" is about collectors. Do you collect something, like stamps, coins, baseball cards, or even old jars? If not, think about someone you know who is a collector. Freewrite about the impulses and desires that turn people into collectors.

**Vocabulary**

Knowing the following words will help you as you read "Abalone, Abalone, Abalone."

**abalone** (ab′ ə lō′ nē) *n.*: A shellfish with a flat shell that has a pearly lining (p. 169)

**nursery** (nʉr′ sə rē) *n.*: A place where young trees and plants are grown (p. 169)

**luster** (lus′ tər) *n.*: Soft, reflected light; brilliance (p. 170)

**hues** (hyo͞oz) *n.*: Colors; shades of a given color (p. 170)

**akin** (ə kin′) *adj.*: Having a similar quality or character (p. 170)

# Abalone, Abalone, Abalone

## Toshio Mori

Before Mr. Abe went away I used to see him quite often at his nursery. He was a carnation grower just as I am one today. At noontime I used to go to his front porch and look at his collection of abalone shells.

They were lined up side by side against the side of his house on the front porch. I was curious as to why he bothered to collect them. It was a lot of bother polishing them. I had often seen him sit for hours on Sundays and noon hours polishing each one of the shells with the greatest of care. Of course I knew these abalone shells were pretty. When the sun strikes the insides of these shells it is something beautiful to behold. But I could not understand why he continued collecting them when the front porch was practically full.

He used to watch for me every noon hour. When I approached he would look out of his room and bellow, "Hello, young man!"

"Hello, Abe-*san*,"[1] I said. "I came to see the abalone shells."

Then he came out of the house and we sat on the front porch. But he did not tell me why he collected these shells. I think I have asked him dozens of times but each time he closed his mouth and refused to answer.

"Are you going to pass this collection of abalone shells on to your children?" I said.

"No," he said. "I want my children to collect for themselves. I wouldn't give it to them."

"Why?" I said. "When you die?"

Mr. Abe shook his head. "No. Not even when I die," he said. "I couldn't give the children what I see in these shells. The children must go out for themselves and find their own shells."

"Why, I thought this collecting hobby of abalone shells was a simple affair," I said.

"It is simple. Very simple," he said. But he would not tell me further.

For several years I went steadily to his front porch and looked at the beautiful shells. His collection was getting larger and larger. Mr. Abe sat and talked to me and on each occasion his hands were busy polishing the shells.

"So you are still curious?" he said.

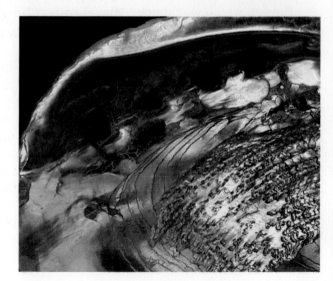

---

**1. Abe-san:** Mister Abe. *San* is a Japanese term of respect often added to a person's name.

"Yes," I said.

One day while I was hauling the old soil from the benches and replacing it with new soil I found an abalone shell half buried in the dust between the benches. So I stopped working. I dropped my wheelbarrow and went to the faucet and washed the abalone shell with soap and water. I had a hard time taking the grime off the surface.

After forty minutes of cleaning and polishing the old shell it became interesting. I began polishing both the outside and the inside of the shell. I found after many minutes of polishing that I could not do very much with the exterior side. It had scabs of the sea which would not come off by scrubbing and the surface itself was rough and hard. And in the crevices the grime stuck so that even with a needle it did not become clean.

But on the other side, the inside of the shell, the more I polished the more luster I found. It had me going.[2] There were colors which I had not seen in the abalone shells before or anywhere else. The different hues, running berserk in all directions, coming together in harmony. I guess I could say they were not unlike a rainbow which men once

---

**2. It had me going:** It had gripped my interest.

symbolized. As soon as I thought of this I thought of Mr. Abe.

I remember running to his place, looking for him. "Abe-*san!*" I said when I found him. "I know why you are collecting the abalone shells!"

He was watering the carnation plants in the greenhouse. He stopped watering and came over to where I stood. He looked me over closely for awhile and then his face beamed.

"All right," he said. "Do not say anything. Nothing, mind you. When you have found the reason why you must collect and preserve them, you do not have to say anything more."

"I want you to see it, Abe-*san*," I said.

"All right. Tonight," he said. "Where did you find it?"

"In my old greenhouse, half buried in the dust," I said.

He chuckled. "That is pretty far from the ocean," he said, "but pretty close to you."

At each noon hour I carried my abalone shell and went over to Mr. Abe's front porch. While I waited for his appearance I kept myself busy polishing the inside of the shell with a rag.

One day I said, "Abe-*san*, now I have three shells."

"Good!" he said. "Keep it up!"

"I have to keep them all," I said. "They are very much alike and very much different."

"Well! Well!" he said and smiled.

That was the last I saw of Abe-*san*. Before the month was over he sold his nursery and went back to Japan. He brought his collection along and thereafter I had no one to talk to at the noon hour. This was before I discovered the fourth abalone shell, and I should like to see Abe-*san* someday and watch his eyes roll as he studies me whose face is now akin to the collectors of shells or otherwise.

# THINKING ABOUT THE SELECTION

## Recalling

1. Why is the narrator drawn to Mr. Abe's nursery day after day?
2. What does the narrator want to know about Mr. Abe?
3. Explain how Mr. Abe responds to the narrator's questions.
4. How does the narrator change after he finds an abalone shell?

## Interpreting

5. Explain why Mr. Abe will not pass his collection on to his children.
6. What is it that Mr. Abe wants his children to discover for themselves?
7. Why does the narrator feel he must save every abalone shell he finds?
8. In what ways is an abalone shell like a rainbow?

## Applying

9. Suppose that you were the narrator and Mr. Abe offered to give you his shell collection. Would you accept it? Why or why not?
10. What is the satisfaction of collecting something yourself rather than acquiring an already assembled collection?

# ANALYZING LITERATURE

## Interpreting Symbols

A **symbol** is anything that represents something outside itself, usually an idea, a belief, or a feeling. A writer may include a symbol to reinforce the point of the story. Sometimes one symbol can represent more than one idea. For example, a rainbow can represent the fulfillment of a dream or wish. It can also represent the return of peace.

1. Describe an abalone shell.
2. Why does Mr. Abe collect them?
3. What is it that Mr. Abe sees in abalone shells?
4. What might the abalone shells symbolize?

5. Name an object that you think of as a symbol and explain the object's symbolic meaning.

# CRITICAL THINKING AND READING

## Interpreting Connotative Meaning

In addition to their literal dictionary definitions, many words also have **connotative meanings,** or ideas and feelings that they suggest. For example, the word *greenhouse* suggests a sheltered environment, damp heat, and lush vegetation. What are some connotations of the following words and phrases?

1. front porch
2. noon
3. shells
4. soap and water

# UNDERSTANDING LANGUAGE

## Finding Word Origins

Many English words are derived from other languages. The word *faucet,* for example, comes from an Old French word that means "to break in." This word, in turn, comes from a Latin word that means "to falsify."

You can use a dictionary to learn the origins of words. Most dictionaries give etymologies, which include the language or languages from which a word came and the form and meaning it had, in brackets either before or after the definitions. Find the origin of these words in your dictionary.

1. crevice
2. berserk
3. scab
4. harmony

# THINKING AND WRITING

## Writing About a Symbol

Suppose that Mr. Abe had not told the narrator that he did "not have to say any more." How might the narrator have explained his discovery and his new-found need to collect abalone shells? Write a letter from the narrator to Mr. Abe explaining what the shells mean to him and expressing his new-found understanding of Mr. Abe and his collection. When you revise, be sure your explanation is logical and clear.

# GUIDE FOR READING

## The Masque of the Red Death

**Edgar Allan Poe** (1809–1849) was born in Boston, Massachusetts. When his parents died, Poe was adopted by Mr. and Mrs. John Allan and raised in Richmond, Virginia. In his short life, Poe wrote a large number of poems and short stories as well as some works of criticism. A masterful craftsman of the short story, his stories usually create a single, horrifying effect. "The Masque of the Red Death," which was first published in 1842, has the eerie and mysterious quality so many of Poe's tales possess.

### Allegory

An **allegory** is a story intended to be read on a symbolic level. In an allegorical story, the characters, settings, and events are intended to have meanings independent of the action in the surface story. For example, the palace in "The Masque of the Red Death" may stand for the entire world. In fact, the entire story can be seen as a symbol representing a truth about a condition of life.

### Look For

As you read "The Masque of the Red Death," try to determine what the events and the people of the story might mean. Then try to interpret the events on an allegorical level.

### Writing

"The Masque of the Red Death" involves a masquerade ball. Suppose that you are invited to a costume party. Write a description of your costume and your reasons for choosing that particular one.

### Vocabulary

Knowing the following words will help you as you read "The Masque of the Red Death."

**masque** (mask) *n.*: A costume ball or masquerade theme (p. 173)

**august** (ô gust′) *adj.*: Imposing and magnificent (p. 173)

**candelabrum** (kan′ də lä′ brəm) *n.*: A large branched candlestick (p. 174)

**piquancy** (pē′ kan sē) *n.*: A pleasantly sharp quality (p. 176)

**arabesque** (ar′ ə besk′) *adj.*: Elaborately designed (p. 176)

**disapprobation** (dis ap′ rə bā′ shən) *n.*: Disapproval (p. 176)

**habiliments** (hə bil′ ə mənts) *n.*: Clothing (p. 177)

**phantasm** (fan′ taz′m) *n.*: Something apparently seen but having no physical reality (p. 176)

**mummer** (mum′ ər) *n.*: A masked and costumed person who acts out pantomimes (p. 178)

# The Masque of the Red Death

Edgar Allan Poe

The "Red Death" had long devastated the country. No pestilence had ever been so fatal, or so hideous. Blood was its Avatar[1] and its seal—the redness and the horror of blood. There were sharp pains, and sudden dizziness, and then profuse bleeding at the pores, with dissolution. The scarlet stains upon the body and especially upon the face of the victim, were the pest ban which shut him out from the aid and from the sympathy of his fellow men. And the whole seizure, progress and termination of the disease, were the incidents of half an hour.

But the Prince Prospero was happy and dauntless and sagacious. When his dominions were half depopulated, he summoned to his presence a thousand hale and light-hearted friends from among the knights and dames of his court, and with these retired to the deep seclusion of one of his castellated abbeys.[2] This was an extensive and magnificent structure, the creation of the prince's own eccentric yet august taste. A strong and lofty wall girdled it in. This wall had gates of iron. The courtiers, having entered, brought furnaces and massy[3] hammers and welded the bolts. They resolved to leave means neither of ingress or egress[4] to the sudden impulses of despair or of frenzy from within. The abbey was amply provisioned. With such precautions the courtiers might bid defiance to contagion. The external world could take care of itself. In the meantime it was folly to grieve, or to think. The prince had provided all the appliances of pleasure. There were buffoons, there were improvisatori,[5] there were ballet dancers, there were musicians, there was Beauty, there was wine. All these and security were within. Without was the "Red Death."

It was toward the close of the fifth or sixth month of his seclusion, and while the pestilence raged most furiously abroad, that the Prince Prospero entertained his thousand friends at a masked ball of the most unusual magnificence.

It was a voluptuous scene, that masquerade. But first let me tell of the rooms in which it was held. There were seven—an imperial suite. In many palaces, however, such suites form a long and straight vista, while the folding doors slide back nearly to the walls on either hand, so that the view of

---

**1. Avatar** (av′ ə tär′) *n*.: A symbol or manifestation of an unseen force.
**2. castellated** (kas′ tə lā′ tid) **abbeys** (ab′ ēz): Monasteries or convents with castle-like towers.
**3. massy** (mas′ ē) *adj*.: Massive or large.

**4. ingress** (in′ gres) **or egress** (ē′ gres): Entering or leaving.
**5. improvisatori** (im′ prə vē zə tôr′ ē) *n*.: Poets who improvise, or create verses without previous thought.

the whole extent is scarcely impeded. Here the case was very different; as might have been expected from the duke's love of the bizarre. The apartments were so irregularly disposed that the vision embraced but little more than one at a time. There was a sharp turn at every twenty or thirty yards, and at each turn a novel effect. To the right and left, in the middle of each wall, a tall and narrow Gothic window looked out upon a closed corridor which pursued the windings of the suite. These windows were of stained glass whose color varied in accordance with the prevailing hue of the decorations of the chamber into which it opened. That at the eastern extremity was hung, for example, in blue—and vividly blue were its windows. The second chamber was purple in its orna-ments and tapestries, and here the panes were purple. The third was green throughout, and so were the casements. The fourth was furnished and lighted with orange—the fifth with white—the sixth with violet. The seventh apartment was closely shrouded in black velvet tapestries that hung all over the ceiling and down the walls, falling in heavy folds upon a carpet of the same material and hue. But in this chamber only, the color of the windows failed to correspond with the decorations. The panes here were scarlet—a deep blood color. Now in no one of the seven apartments was there any lamp or candelabrum amid the profusion of golden ornaments that lay scattered to and fro or depended from the roof. There was no light of any kind emanating from lamp or candle

within the suite of chambers. But in the corridors that followed the suite, there stood, opposite to each window, a heavy tripod, bearing a brazier[6] of fire that projected its rays through the tinted glass and so glaringly illumined the room. And thus were produced a multitude of gaudy and fantastic appearances. But in the western or black chamber the effect of the firelight that streamed upon the dark hangings through the blood-tinted panes, was ghastly in the extreme, and produced so wild a look upon the countenances of those who entered, that there were few of the company bold enough to set foot within its precincts at all.

---

**6. brazier** (brā′ zhər) *n.*: A metal pan or bowl to hold burning coals or charcoal.

It was in this apartment, also, that there stood against the western wall a gigantic clock of ebony. Its pendulum swung to and fro with a dull, heavy, monotonous clang; and when the minute-hand made the circuit of the face, and the hour was to be stricken, there came from the brazen lungs of the clock a sound which was clear and loud and deep and exceedingly musical, but of so peculiar a note and emphasis that, at each lapse of an hour, the musicians of the orchestra were constrained to pause, momentarily, in their performance, to hearken to the sound; and thus the waltzers perforce ceased their evolutions; and there was a brief disconcert of the whole gay company; and, while the chimes of the clock yet rang, it was observed that the giddiest grew pale, and the more aged and sedate passed their hands over their brows as if in confused reverie or meditation. But when the echoes had fully ceased, a light laughter at once pervaded the assembly; the musicians looked at each other and smiled as if at their own nervousness and folly, and made whispering vows, each to the other, that the next chiming of the clock should produce in them no similar emotion; and then, after the lapse of sixty minutes, (which embrace three thousand and six hundred seconds of the Time that flies), there came yet another chiming of the clock, and then were the same disconcert and tremulousness and meditation as before.

But, in spite of these things, it was a gay and magnificent revel. The tastes of the duke were peculiar. He had a fine eye for colors and effects. He disregarded the decora[7] of mere fashion. His plans were bold and fiery, and his conceptions glowed with barbaric luster. There are some who would have thought him mad. His followers felt that he

---

**7. decora** (dā kôr′ ə) *n.*: Requirements of good taste.

was not. It was necessary to hear and see and touch him to be *sure* that he was not.

He had directed, in great part, the movable embellishments of the seven chambers, upon occasion of this great fête; and it was his own guiding taste which had given character to the masqueraders. Be sure they were grotesque. There were much glare and glitter and piquancy and phantasm—much of what has been since seen in *Hernani*.[8] There were arabesque figures with unsuited limbs and appointments. There were delirious fancies such as the madman fashions. There was much of the beautiful, much of the wanton, much of the bizarre, something of the terrible, and not a little of that which might have excited disgust. To and fro in the seven chambers there stalked, in fact, a multitude of dreams. And these—the dreams—writhed in and about, taking hue from the rooms, and causing the wild music of the orchestra to seem as the echo of their steps. And, anon, there strikes the ebony clock which stands in the hall of the velvet. And then, for a moment, all is still, and all is silent save the voice of the clock. The dreams are stiff-frozen as they stand. But the echoes of the chime die away—they have endured but an instant—and a light, half-subdued laughter floats after them as they depart. And now again the music swells, and the dreams live, and writhe to and fro more merrily than ever, taking hue from the many-tinted windows through which stream the rays from the tripods. But to the chamber which lies most westwardly of the seven, there are now none of the maskers who venture; for the night is waning away; and there flows a ruddier light through the blood-colored panes; and the blackness of the sable drapery appalls; and

to him whose foot falls upon the sable carpet, there comes from the near clock of ebony a muffled peal more solemnly emphatic than any which reaches *their* ears who indulge in the more remote gaieties of the other apartments.

But these other apartments were densely crowded, and in them beat feverishly the heart of life. And the revel went whirlingly on, until at length there commenced the sounding of midnight upon the clock. And then the music ceased, as I have told; and the evolutions of the waltzers were quieted; and there was an uneasy cessation of all things as before. But now there were twelve strokes to be sounded by the bell of the clock; and thus it happened, perhaps, that more of thought crept, with more of time, into the meditations of the thoughtful among those who reveled. And thus, too, it happened, perhaps, that before the last echoes of the last chime had utterly sunk into silence, there were many individuals in the crowd who had found leisure to become aware of the presence of a masked figure which had arrested the attention of no single individual before. And the rumor of this new presence having spread itself whisperingly around, there arose at length from the whole company a buzz, or murmur, expressive of disapprobation and surprise—then, finally, of terror, of horror, and of disgust.

In an assembly of phantasms such as I have painted, it may well be supposed that no ordinary appearance could have excited such sensation. In truth the masquerade license of the night was nearly unlimited; but the figure in question had out-Heroded Herod,[9] and gone beyond the bounds of even the prince's indefinite decorum. There are

---

**8. Hernani:** An extravagant drama by the French author Victor Hugo.

**9. out-Heroded Herod:** Behaved excessively, just as King Herod did. In the Bible, Herod slaughtered innocent babies, hoping to kill Jesus.

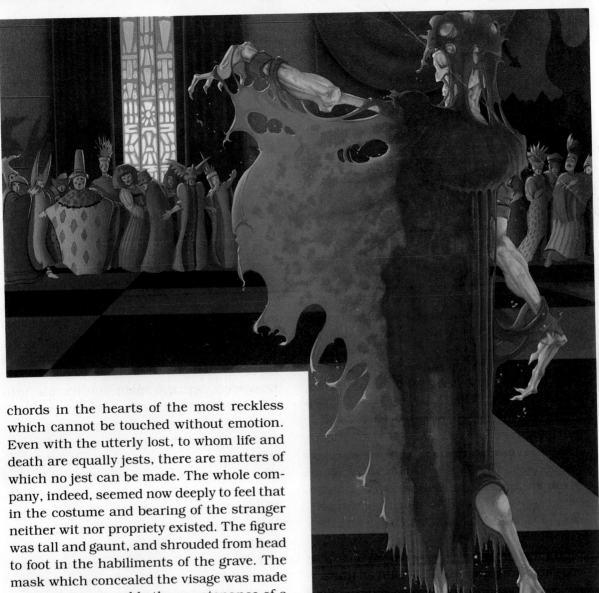

chords in the hearts of the most reckless which cannot be touched without emotion. Even with the utterly lost, to whom life and death are equally jests, there are matters of which no jest can be made. The whole company, indeed, seemed now deeply to feel that in the costume and bearing of the stranger neither wit nor propriety existed. The figure was tall and gaunt, and shrouded from head to foot in the habiliments of the grave. The mask which concealed the visage was made so nearly to resemble the countenance of a stiffened corpse that the closest scrutiny must have had difficulty in detecting the cheat. And yet all this might have been endured, if not approved, by the mad revelers around. But the mummer had gone so far as to assume the type of the Red Death. His vesture was dabbled in *blood*—and his broad brow, with all the features of the face, was besprinkled with the scarlet horror.

When the eyes of Prince Prospero fell upon this spectral image (which with a slow and solemn movement, as if more fully to sustain its role, stalked to and fro among the waltzers) he was seen to be convulsed, in the first moment with a strong shudder either of terror or distaste; but, in the next, his brow reddened with rage.

"Who dares?" he demanded hoarsely of the courtiers who stood near him—"who dares insult us with this blasphemous mockery? Seize him and unmask him —that we may know whom we have to hang at sunrise, from the battlements!"

It was in the eastern or blue chamber in which stood the Prince Prospero as he uttered these words. They rang throughout the seven rooms loudly and clearly—for the prince was a bold and robust man, and the music had become hushed at the waving of his hand.

It was in the blue room where stood the prince, with a group of pale courtiers by his side. At first, as he spoke, there was a slight rushing movement of this group in the direction of the intruder, who at the moment was also near at hand, and now, with deliberate and stately step, made closer approach to the speaker. But from a certain nameless awe with which the mad assumptions of the mummer had inspired the whole party, there were found none who put forth hand to seize him; so that, unimpeded, he passed within a yard of the prince's person; and, while the vast assembly, as if with one impulse, shrank from the centers of the rooms to the walls, he made his way uninterruptedly, but with the same solemn and measured step which had distinguished him from the first, through the blue chamber to the purple—through the purple to the green—through the green to the orange —through this again to the white—and even thence to the violet, ere a decided movement had been made to arrest him. It

was then, however, that the Prince Prospero, maddening with rage and the shame of his own momentary cowardice, rushed hurriedly through the six chambers, while none followed him on account of a deadly terror that had seized upon all. He bore aloft a drawn dagger, and had approached, in rapid impetuosity, to within three or four feet of the retreating figure, when the latter, having attained the extremity of the velvet apartment, turned suddenly and confronted his pursuer. There was a sharp cry—and the dagger dropped gleaming upon the sable carpet, upon which, instantly afterwards, fell prostrate in death the Prince Prospero. Then, summoning the wild courage of despair, a throng of the revelers at once threw themselves into the black apartment, and, seizing the mummer, whose tall figure stood erect and motionless within the shadow of the ebony clock, gasped in unutterable horror at finding the grave cerements[10] and corpselike mask which they handled with so violent a rudeness, untenanted by any tangible form.

And now was acknowledged the presence of the Red Death. He had come like a thief in the night. And one by one dropped the revelers in the blood-bedewed halls of their revel, and died each in the despairing posture of his fall. And the life of the ebony clock went out with that of the last of the gay. And the flames of the tripods expired. And Darkness and Decay and the Red Death held illimitable dominion over all.

---

**10. cerements** (sir′ mənts) *n*.: Wrappings or shroud.

## THINKING ABOUT THE SELECTION

### Recalling

1. Why do Prince Prospero and his followers retreat to his palace?
2. Describe the series of rooms in which the entertainment takes place.
3. Explain how the party is disrupted.

### Interpreting

4. Compare life outside the palace with the life of the people Prospero brought inside.
5. What do you learn about Prince Prospero from his desire and his attempts to keep his household free of the plague?
6. What mood or effect is created by the colors and the lighting in the rooms of the ball?
7. Why does the clock have such a dramatic effect on the dancers?
8. Why does the masked visitor frighten the guests so?
9. Explain how Poe develops the story to build a feeling of terror.

### Applying

10. Ugo Betti has written, "Every tiny part of us cries out against the idea of dying, and hopes to live forever." On the basis of this selection, explain whether you think Poe would agree with this statement. Then explain whether or not you agree.

## ANALYZING LITERATURE

### Understanding Allegory

In an **allegory,** the characters, settings, and events are an interconnected series of symbols. The deeper or symbolic meaning of the story may contain a lesson about life.

1. What might each symbol from "The Masque of the Red Death" respresent?
   a. Prince Prospero    d. the number 7
   b. the masquerade    e. the clock
   c. the masked figure
2. What do you think is the allegorical lesson Poe is presenting in this story?

## CRITICAL THINKING AND READING

### Interpreting Connotative Meaning

The **connotative meaning** of a word is what the word suggests beyond its literal dictionary meaning. Authors can use the connotative meanings of words to help establish symbols. For example, the color red connotes blood and death. Poe uses that connotation in describing the appearance of the masked figure.

1. What are some connotations of the following colors from the story?
   a. green    c. white
   b. orange    d. black
2. Find three words or phrases that suggest the quality of a nightmare.

## UNDERSTANDING LANGUAGE

### Using Context Clues

When you encounter an unfamiliar word in a story, you can use **context clues,** or the words and sentences around the word, to help you figure out its meaning. For example, context clues, which are in italics in the following sentence, tell you that *robust* means "strong and vigorous": Prospero's words *"rang* throughout the seven rooms *loudly* and *clearly—*for the prince was a *bold* and robust man. . . ."

Use context clues to determine the meaning of the following words.

1. dominions (page 173, column 1, line 15)
2. tremulousness (page 175, column 2, line 33)
3. visage (page 177, column 1, line 11)

## THINKING AND WRITING

### Writing About Allegory

Write a key that future readers can use to unlock the meaning of "The Masque of the Red Death." Tell what you believe the various events, characters, and aspects of the setting stand for, giving reasons for your assumptions. Then relate these symbols to the larger lesson Poe is presenting. When you revise your work, be sure your interpretation is clear and makes sense.

# GUIDE FOR READING

## With All Flags Flying

**Anne Tyler** (1941–     ) was born in Minneapolis, Minnesota. During her childhood her family moved frequently, and she lived in many communities in the South and the Midwest. At age sixteen she entered Duke University, where she majored in Russian. Since 1965 Tyler has been writing full time. In 1967 Tyler moved to Baltimore, Maryland, the setting of most of her work, including "With All Flags Flying." Many of her novels including *Dinner at the Homesick Restaurant* and *The Accidental Tourist* have been best-sellers.

**Characters as Symbols**

While symbols in literature are frequently objects, a character may also serve as a symbol, representing various ideas and qualities. In "With All Flags Flying," the main character, Mr. Carpenter, is an important symbol. Other characters serve as symbols for the ideas about life that the main character is weighing.

**Look For**

As you read "With All Flags Flying," look for what the characters look like, do, say, and think that may indicate their symbolic meaning.

**Writing**

"With All Flags Flying" is a story about an independent man. To investigate the meaning of the word *independent,* consider the times in life when people can act alone and the times when they need others for their activities. Write the following headings: "Things That Require Others" and "Things One Should Do for Oneself." Write as many items as you can think of that fall under each heading. You might begin by considering how dependent on others a newborn baby is. When you have finished your lists, examine them to see how the items differ.

**Vocabulary**

Knowing the following words will help you as you read "With All Flags Flying."

**appurtenances** (ə pʉr′ t'n əns əz) *n.*: Accessories (p. 181)
**conspicuous** (kən spik′ yoo wəs) *adj.*: Attracting attention by being unexpected (p. 182)

**lacquering** (lak′ ər iŋ) *v.*: Giving a hard, highly polished finish (p. 187)

# With All Flags Flying

## Anne Tyler

Weakness was what got him in the end. He had been expecting something more definite—chest pains, a stroke, arthritis—but it was only weakness that put a finish to his living alone. A numbness in his head, an airy feeling when he walked. A wateriness in his bones that made it an effort to pick up his coffee cup in the morning. He waited some days for it to go away, but it never did. And meanwhile the dust piled up in corners; the refrigerator wheezed and creaked for want of defrosting. Weeds grew around his rosebushes.

He was awake and dressed at six o'clock on a Saturday morning, with the patchwork quilt pulled up neatly over the mattress. From the kitchen cabinet he took a hunk of bread and two Fig Newtons, which he dropped into a paper bag. He was wearing a brown suit that he had bought on sale in 1944, a white T-shirt and copper-toed work boots. These and his other set of underwear, which he put in the paper bag along with a razor, were all the clothes he took with him. Then he rolled down the top of the bag and stuck it under his arm, and stood in the middle of the kitchen staring around him for a moment.

The house had only two rooms, but he owned it—the last scrap of the farm that he had sold off years ago. It stood in a hollow of dying trees beside a superhighway in Baltimore County. All it held was a few sticks of furniture, a change of clothes, a skillet and a set of dishes. Also odds and ends, which disturbed him. If his inventory were complete, he would have to include six clothespins, a salt and a pepper shaker, a broken-toothed comb, a cheap ballpoint pen—oh, on and on, past logical numbers. Why should he be so cluttered? He was eighty-two years old. He had grown from an infant owning nothing to a family man with a wife, five children, everyday and Sunday china and a thousand appurtenances, down at last to solitary old age and the bare essentials again, but not bare enough to suit him. Only what he needed surrounded him. Was it possible he needed so much?

Now he had the brown paper bag; that was all. It was the one satisfaction in a day he had been dreading for years.

He left the house without another glance, heading up the steep bank toward the superhighway. The bank was covered with small, crawling weeds planted especially by young men with scientific training in how to prevent soil erosion. Twice his knees buckled. He had to sit and rest, bracing himself against the slope of the bank. The scientific weeds, seen from close up, looked straggly and gnarled. He sifted dry earth through his fingers without thinking, concentrating only on steadying his breath and calming the twitching muscles in his legs.

Once on the superhighway, which was fairly level, he could walk for longer stretches of time. He kept his head down and his fingers clenched tight upon the paper bag, which was growing limp and damp now. Sweat rolled down the back of his neck, fell

it swooped from lane to lane. It was a fine way to spend his last free day.

Half an hour later they were on the outskirts of Baltimore, stopped at the first traffic light. The boy turned his head and shouted, "Whereabouts did you plan on going?"

"I'm visiting my daughter, on Belvedere near Charles Street."

"I'll drop you off, then," the boy said. "I'm passing right by there."

The light changed, the motor roared. Now that they were in traffic, he felt more conspicuous, but not in a bad way. People in their automobiles seemed sealed in, overprotected; men in large trucks must envy the way the motorcycle looped in and out, hornetlike, stripped to the bare essentials of a motor and two wheels. By tugs at the boy's shirt and single words shouted into the wind he directed him to his daughter's house, but he was sorry to have the ride over so quickly.

His daughter had married a salesman and lived in a plain, square stone house that the old man approved of. There were sneakers and a football in the front yard, signs of a large, happy family. A bicycle lay in the driveway. The motorcycle stopped just inches from it. "Here we are," the boy said.

"Well, I surely do thank you."

He climbed off, fearing for one second that his legs would give way beneath him and spoil everything that had gone before. But no, they held steady. He took off the helmet and handed it to the boy, who waved and roared off. It was a really magnificent roar, ear-dazzling. He turned toward the house, beaming in spite of himself, with his head feeling cool and light now that the helmet was gone. And there was his daughter on the front porch, laughing. "Daddy, what on *earth?*" she said. "Have you turned into a teeny-bopper?" Whatever that was. She came rushing down the steps to hug

in drops from his temples. When he had been walking maybe half an hour he had to sit down again for a rest. A black motorcycle buzzed up from behind and stopped a few feet away from him. The driver was young and shabby, with hair so long that it drizzled out beneath the back of his helmet.

"Give you a lift, if you like," he said. "You going somewhere?"

"Just into Baltimore."

"Hop on."

He shifted the paper bag to the space beneath his arm, put on the white helmet he was handed and climbed on behind the driver. For safety he took a clutch of the boy's shirt, tightly at first and then more loosely when he saw there was no danger. Except for the helmet, he was perfectly comfortable. He felt his face cooling and stiffening in the wind, his body learning to lean gracefully with the tilt of the motorcycle as

him—a plump, happy-looking woman in an apron. She was getting on toward fifty now. Her hands were like her mother's, swollen and veined. Gray had started dusting her hair.

"You never *told* us," she said. "Did you ride all this way on a motorcycle? Oh, why didn't you find a telephone and call? I would have come. How long can you stay for?"

"Now . . ." he said, starting toward the house. He was thinking of the best way to put it. "I came to a decision. I won't be living alone any more. I want to go to an old folks' home. That's what I *want*," he said, stopping on the grass so she would be sure to get it clear. "I don't want to live with you —I want an old folks' home." Then he was afraid he had worded it too strongly. "It's nice *visiting* you, of course," he said.

"Why, Daddy, you know we always asked you to come and live with us."

"I know that, but I decided on an old folks' home."

"We couldn't do that. We won't even talk about it."

"Clara, my mind is made up."

Then in the doorway a new thought hit her, and she suddenly turned around. "Are you sick?" she said. "You always said you would live alone as long as health allowed."

"I'm not up to that any more," he said.

"What is it? Are you having some kind of pain?"

"I just decided, that's all," he said. "What I *will* rely on you for is the arrangements with the home. I know it's a trouble."

"We'll talk about that later," Clara said. And she firmed the corners of her mouth exactly the way her mother used to do when she hadn't won an argument but wasn't planning to lose it yet either.

In the kitchen he had a glass of milk, good and cold, and the hunk of bread and the two Fig Newtons from his paper bag.

Clara wanted to make him a big breakfast, but there was no sense wasting what he had brought. He munched on the dry bread and washed it down with milk, meanwhile staring at the Fig Newtons, which lay on the smoothed-out bag. They were the worse for their ride—squashed and pathetic-looking, the edges worn down and crumbling. They seemed to have come from somewhere long ago and far away. "Here, now, we've got cookies I baked only yesterday," Clara said; but he said, "No, no," and ate the Fig Newtons, whose warmth on his tongue filled him with a vague, sad feeling deeper than homesickness. "In my house," he said, "I left things a little messy. I hate to ask it of you, but I didn't manage to straighten up any."

"Don't even think about it," Clara said. "I'll take out a suitcase tomorrow and clean everything up. I'll bring it all back."

"I don't want it. Take it to the poor people."

"Don't want any of it? But, Daddy—"

He didn't try explaining it to her. He finished his lunch in silence and then let her lead him upstairs to the guest room.

Clara had five boys and a girl, the oldest twenty. During the morning as they passed one by one through the house on their way to other places, they heard of his arrival and trooped up to see him. They were fine children, all of them, but it was the girl he enjoyed the most. Francie. She was only thirteen, too young yet to know how to hide what she felt. And what she felt was always about love, it seemed: whom she just loved, who she hoped loved her back. Who was just a darling. Had thirteen-year-olds been so aware of love in the old days? He didn't know and didn't care; all he had to do with Francie was sit smiling in an armchair and listen. There was a new boy in the neighborhood who walked his English sheepdog past her yard every morning, looking toward her house. Was it because of her, or did the dog just like to go that way? When he telephoned her brother Donnie, was he hoping for her to answer? And when she did answer, did he want her to talk a minute or hand the receiver straight to Donnie? But what would she say to him, anyway? Oh, all her questions had to do with where she might find love, and everything she said made the old man wince and love her more. She left in the middle of a sentence, knocking against a doorknob as she flew from the room, an unlovable-looking tangle of blond hair and braces and scrapes and Band-Aids. After she was gone the room seemed too empty, as if she had accidentally torn part of it away in her flight.

Getting into an old folks' home was hard. Not only because of lack of good homes, high expenses, waiting lists; it was harder yet to talk his family into letting him go. His son-in-law argued with him every evening, his round, kind face anxious and questioning across the supper table. "Is it that you think you're not welcome here? You are, you know. You were one of the reasons we bought this big house." His grandchildren when they talked to him had a kind of urgency in their voices, as if they were trying to impress him with their acceptance of him. His other daughters called long distance from all across the country and begged him to come to them if he wouldn't stay with Clara. They had room, or they would make room; he had no idea what homes for the aged were like these days. To all of them he gave the same answer: "I've made my decision." He was proud of them for asking, though. All his children had turned out so well, every last one of them. They were good, strong women with happy families, and they had never given him a moment's worry. He was luckier than he had a right to be. He had felt lucky all his

life, dangerously lucky, cursed by luck; it had seemed some disaster must be waiting to even things up. But the luck had held. When his wife died it was at a late age, sparing her the pain she would have had to face, and his life had continued in its steady, reasonable pattern with no more sorrow than any other man's. His final lot was to weaken, to crumble and to die—only a secret disaster, not the one he had been expecting.

He walked two blocks daily, fighting off the weakness. He shelled peas for Clara and mended little household articles, which gave him an excuse to sit. Nobody noticed how he arranged to climb the stairs only once a day, at bedtime. When he had empty time he chose a chair without rockers, one that would not be a symbol of age and weariness and lack of work. He rose every morning at six and stayed in his room a full hour, giving his legs enough warning to face the day ahead. Never once did he disgrace himself by falling down in front of people. He dropped nothing more important than a spoon or a fork.

Meanwhile the wheels were turning; his name was on a waiting list. Not that that meant anything, Clara said. "When it comes right down to driving you out there, I just won't let you go," she told him. "But I'm hoping you won't carry things that far. Daddy, won't you put a stop to this foolishness?"

He hardly listened. He had chosen long ago what kind of old age he would have; everyone does. Most, he thought, were weak, and chose to be loved at any cost. He had seen women turn soft and sad, anxious to please, and had watched with pity and impatience their losing battles. And he had once known a schoolteacher, no weakling at all, who said straight out that when she grew old she would finally eat all she wanted and grow fat without worry. He admired that—a simple plan, dependent upon no one. "I'll sit in an armchair," she had said, "with a lady's magazine in my lap and a box of homemade fudge on the lampstand. I'll get as fat as I like and nobody will give a hang." The schoolteacher was thin and pale, with a kind of stooped, sloping figure that was popular at the time. He had lost track of her long ago, but he liked to think that she had kept her word. He imagined her fifty years later, cozy and fat in a puffy chair, with one hand moving constantly between her mouth and the candy plate. If she had died young or changed her mind or put off her eating till another decade, he didn't want to hear about it.

He had chosen independence. Nothing else had even occurred to him. He had lived to himself, existed on less money than his family would ever guess, raised his own vegetables and refused all gifts but an occasional tin of coffee. And now he would sign himself into the old folks' home and enter on his own two feet, relying only on the impersonal care of nurses and cleaning women. He could have chosen to die alone of neglect, but for his daughters that would have been a burden too—a different kind of burden, much worse. He was sensible enough to see that.

Meanwhile, all he had to do was to look as busy as possible in a chair without rockers and hold fast against his family. Oh, they gave him no peace. Some of their attacks were obvious—the arguments with his son-in-law over the supper table—and some were subtle; you had to be on your guard every minute for those. Francie, for instance, asking him questions about what she called the "olden days." Inviting him to sink unnoticing into doddering reminiscence. "Did I see Granny ever? I don't re-

member her. Did she like me? What kind of person was she?" He stood his ground, gave monosyllabic answers. It was easier than he had expected. For him, middle age tempted up more memories. Nowadays events had telescoped. The separate agonies and worries—the long, hard births of each of his children, the youngest daughter's chronic childhood earaches, his wife's last illness—were smoothed now into a single, summing-up sentence: He was a widowed farmer with five daughters, all married, twenty grandchildren and three great-grandchildren. "Your grandmother was a fine woman," he told Francie; "just fine." Then he shut up.

Francie, not knowing that she had been spared, sulked and peeled a strip of sunburned skin from her nose.

Clara cried all the way to the home. She was the one who was driving; it made him nervous. One of her hands on the steering wheel held a balled-up tissue, which she had stopped using. She let tears run unchecked down her face and drove jerkily with a great deal of brake-slamming and gear-gnashing.

"Clara, I wish you wouldn't take on so," he told her. "There's no need to be sad over *me*."

"I'm not sad so much as mad," Clara said. "I feel like this is something you're doing *to* me, just throwing away what I give. Oh, why do you have to be so stubborn? It's still not too late to change your mind."

The old man kept silent. On his right sat Francie, chewing a thumbnail and scowling out the window, her usual self except for the unexplainable presence of her other hand in his, tight as wire. Periodically she muttered a number; she was counting red convertibles, and had been for days. When she reached a hundred, the next boy she saw would be her true love.

He figured that was probably the reason she had come on this trip—a greater exposure to red convertibles.

Whatever happened to DeSotos?[1] Didn't there use to be a car called a roadster?[2]

They parked in the U-shaped driveway in front of the home, under the shade of a poplar tree. If he had had his way, he would have arrived by motorcycle, but he made the best of it—picked up his underwear sack from between his feet, climbed the front steps ramrod-straight. They were met by a smiling woman in blue who had to check his name on a file and ask more questions. He made sure to give all the answers himself, overriding Clara when necessary. Meanwhile Francie spun on one squeaky sneaker heel and examined the hall, a cavernous, polished square with old-fashioned parlors

---

1. **DeSotos:** Car model of the 1950s.
2. **roadster** (rōd′ stər) *n.:* An early sportscar with an open cab and a "rumble seat" in the rear.

on either side of it. A few old people were on the plush couches, and a nurse sat idle beside a lady in a wheelchair.

They went up a creaking elevator to the second floor and down a long, dark corridor deadened by carpeting. The lady in blue, still carrying a sheaf of files, knocked at number 213. Then she flung the door open on a narrow green room flooded with sunlight.

"Mr. Pond," she said, "this is Mr. Carpenter. I hope you'll get on well together."

Mr. Pond was one of those men who run to fat and baldness in old age. He sat in a rocking chair with a gilt-edged Bible on his knees.

"How-do," he said. "Mighty nice to meet you."

They shook hands cautiously, with the women ringing them like mothers asking their children to play nicely with each other. "Ordinarily I sleep in the bed by the window," said Mr. Pond, "but I don't hold it in much importance. You can take your pick."

"Anything will do," the old man said.

Clara was dry-eyed now. She looked frightened.

"You'd best be getting on back now," he told her. "Don't you worry about me. I'll let you know," he said, suddenly generous now that he had won, "if there is anything I need."

Clara nodded and kissed his cheek. Francie kept her face turned away, but she hugged him tightly, and then she looked up at him as she stepped back. Her eyebrows were tilted as if she were about to ask him one of her questions. Was it her the boy with the sheepdog came for? Did he care when she answered the telephone?

They left, shutting the door with a gentle click. The old man made a great business out of settling his underwear and razor in a bureau drawer, smoothing out the paper bag and folding it, placing it in the next drawer down.

"Didn't bring much," said Mr. Pond, one thumb marking his page in the Bible.

"I don't need much."

"Go on—take the bed by the window. You'll feel better after awhile."

"I *wanted* to come," the old man said.

"That there window is a front one. If you look out, you can see your folks leave."

He slid between the bed and the window and looked out. No reason not to. Clara and Francie were just climbing into the car, the sun lacquering the tops of their heads. Clara was blowing her nose with a dot of tissue.

"*Now* they cry," said Mr. Pond, although he had not risen to look out himself. "Later they'll buy themselves a milkshake to celebrate."

"I wanted to come. I made them bring me."

"And so they did. *I* didn't want to come. My son wanted to put me here—his wife was expecting. And so he did. It all works out the same in the end."

"Well, I could have stayed with one of my daughters," the old man said. "But I'm not like some I have known. Hanging around making burdens of themselves, hoping to be loved. Not me."

"If you don't care about being loved," said Mr. Pond, "how come it would bother you to be a burden?"

Then he opened the Bible again, at the place where his thumb had been all the time and went back to reading.

The old man sat on the edge of the bed, watching the tail of Clara's car flash as sharp and hard as a jewel around the bend of the road. Then, with nobody to watch that mattered, he let his shoulders slump and eased himself out of his suit coat, which he folded over the foot of the bed. He slid his suspenders down and let them dangle at his waist. He took off his copper-toed work boots and set them on the floor neatly side by side. And although it was only noon, he lay down full-length on top of the bedspread. Whiskery lines ran across the plaster of the ceiling high above him. There was a cracking sound in the mattress when he moved; it must be covered with something waterproof.

The tiredness in his head was as vague and restless as anger; the weakness in his knees made him feel as if he had just finished some exhausting exercise. He lay watching the plaster cracks settle themselves into pictures, listening to the silent, neuter voice in his mind form the words he had grown accustomed to hearing now: Let me not give in at the end. Let me continue gracefully till the moment of my defeat. Let Lollie Simpson be alive somewhere even as I lie on my bed; let her be eating homemade fudge in an overstuffed armchair and growing fatter and fatter and fatter.

## THINKING ABOUT THE SELECTION
### Recalling

1. Why does Mr. Carpenter decide not to live alone anymore?
2. How does he plan to live the rest of his life?
3. How does his family feel about his plan?
4. What obstacles does he encounter?
5. Explain whether Mr. Carpenter is able to carry out his plan.

### Interpreting

6. What is Mr. Carpenter's attitude about possessions and unnecessary things? Support your answer with examples from the story.
7. Why is Mr. Carpenter so determined not to move in with his daughter and her family?
8. What does Mr. Pond mean when he says, "It all works out the same in the end"?

### Applying

9. If you had been in Mr. Carpenter's shoes, what would you have done? Explain your answer.

## ANALYZING LITERATURE
### Recognizing Characters as Symbols

Characters can represent ideas, beliefs, and feelings; that is, they can be used as **symbols.** The symbolism of a character comes out of the character's strong traits or pattern of behavior. For example, Florence Nightingale, known for her nursing care, can stand for compassion.

What do you think each of the following characters represents?
1. Mr. Carpenter
2. Lollie Simpson (the teacher)
3. Francie

## CRITICAL THINKING AND READING
### Recognizing Generalizations

A **generalization** is a statement or principle, inferred from a number of specific examples, that has broad general application. "All his children had turned out well" is a generalization. Each of Mr. Carpenter's children has made a good life for herself, so the statement covers five specific instances. If one of his children had turned out badly, the generalization would not be valid.

1. Why is the following statement a generalization: "And what [Francie] felt was always about love"?
2. What generalization does Mr. Carpenter make about old people?

## UNDERSTANDING LANGUAGE
### Using Specific Words

Words can be general or **specific.** *Road* is a general word; *superhighway* is more specific. *Superhighway* names one particular type of road. (Route I-95 is even more specific. It names one single road.) Modifiers can make other words specific. For example, in the phrase "dry bread," the adjective *dry* specifies the type of bread.

Select the specific words in the following list, and use them in a paragraph about a day at Mr. Carpenter's cabin.

| | | |
|---|---|---|
| thumbnail | essentials | lady |
| Fig Newtons | skillet | kitchen |
| rosebushes | patchwork quilt | |

## THINKING AND WRITING
### Writing with a Symbol

Brainstorm with your classmates to come up with possibilities for a character who may be used as a symbol. The character's personality, behavior, or appearance should reflect the idea or feeling the character stands for. Then write about an incident in which the character's behavior or appearance demonstrates the quality or idea for which the character is a symbol. When you revise your paper, try to replace general words with specific ones.

# Tone and Irony

**TELEPHONE BOOTHS (detail), 1967**
*Richard Estes*
Thyssen-Bornemisza Foundation, Lugano, Switzerland

## The Last Unicorns

**Edward D. Hoch** (1930–     ), who was born in Rochester, New York, has worked in publishing, advertising, and library research. He is the author of more than four hundred adventure, mystery, and science-fiction stories, many of which appeared under one of his five pen names. Some of his stories have been adapted for various television series. Although "The Last Unicorns" does not fit into the mystery or adventure category, it does explain a puzzle you may have wondered about.

**Tone in Narration**

The **tone** of a story is the attitude implied by the author toward the subject and audience. The tone of a story may be described as serious or lighthearted, formal or informal, sarcastic or sympathetic, sad, humorous, or as any other attitude or emotion. Tone is conveyed through the writer's choice of words and details. It may also be determined by the writer's intent and comments. "The Last Unicorns" is about a familiar subject, but its tone makes the story unique.

**Look For**

As you read "The Last Unicorns," look for the details and words that determine the tone of the story. What feeling does the story leave you with? With whom are you sympathetic? How does the author convey his attitude and leave you with this feeling?

**Writing**

The character Shem makes an important request in this story. Imagine that you must make an important request of someone who is known to say "no" without listening to reason. Freewrite about how you would plan your approach and how you might respond to a refusal.

**Vocabulary**

Knowing the following words will help you as you read "The Last Unicorns."

**lure** (loor) *v*.: To attract or entice (p. 192)

**wrath** (rath) *n*.: Intense anger, rage, or fury (p. 192)

**scroll** (skrōl) *n*.: A roll of parchment used for writing a document (p. 192)

# The Last Unicorns

## Edward D. Hoch

The rain was still falling by the time he reached the little wooden shack that stood in the center of the green, fertile valley. He opened his cloak for an instant to knock at the door, not really expecting a reply.

But it opened, pulled over the roughness of the rock floor by great hairy hands. "Come in," a voice commanded him. "Hurry! Before this rain floods me out."

"Thank you," the traveler said, removing the soggy garment that covered him and squeezing out some of the water. "It's good to find a dry place. I've come a long way."

"Not many people are about in this weather," the man told him, pulling at his beard with a quick, nervous gesture.

"I came looking for you."

"For me? What is your name?"

"You can call me Shem. I come from beyond the mountains."

The bearded man grunted. "I don't know the name. What do you seek?"

Shem sat down to rest himself on a pale stone seat. "I hear talk that you have two fine unicorns here, recently brought from Africa."

The man smiled proudly. "That is correct. The only such creatures in this part of the world. I intend to breed them and sell them to the farmers as beasts of burden."

"Oh?"

"They can do the work of strong horses and at the same time use their horns to defend themselves against attack."

"True," Shem agreed. "Very true. I . . . I don't suppose you'd want to part with them . . . ?"

"Part with them! Are you mad, man? It cost me money to bring them all the way from Africa!"

"How much would you like for them?"

The bearded man rose from his seat. "No amount, ever! Come back in two years when I've bred some. Until then, begone with you!"

"I *must* have them, sir."

"You *must* have nothing! Begone from here now before I take a club to you!" And with those words he took a menacing step forward.

Shem retreated out the door, back into the rain, skipping lightly over a rushing stream of water from the higher ground. The door closed on him, and he was alone. But he looked out into the fields, where a small barnlike structure stood glistening in the downpour.

They would be in there, he knew.

He made his way across the field, sometimes sinking to his ankles in puddles of muddy water. But finally he reached the outbuilding and went in through a worn, rotten door.

Yes, they were there . . . Two tall and handsome beasts, very much like horses, but with longer tails and with that gleaming, twisted horn shooting straight up from the center of their foreheads. Unicorns —one of the rarest of God's creatures!

**UNICORN**
*Jonathan Meader*

He moved a bit closer, trying now to lure them out of the building without startling them. But there was a noise, and he turned suddenly to see the bearded man standing there, a long staff upraised in his hands.

"You try to steal them," he shouted, lunging forward.

The staff thudded against the wall, inches from Shem's head. "Listen, old man . . ."

"Die! Die, you robber!"

But Shem leaped to one side, around the bearded figure of wrath, and through the open doorway. Behind him, the unicorns gave a fearful snort and trampled the earthen floor with their hoofs.

Shem kept running, away from the shack, away from the man with the staff, away from the fertile valley.

After several hours of plodding over the rain-swept hills, he came at last upon his father's village, and he went down among the houses to the place where the handful of people had gathered.

And he saw his father standing near the base of the great wooden vessel, and he went up to him sadly.

"Yes, my son?" the old man questioned, unrolling a long damp scroll of parchment.

"No unicorns, Father."

"No unicorns," Noah[1] repeated sadly, scratching out the name on his list. "It is too bad. They were handsome beasts . . ."

---

**1. Noah:** In the Bible, Noah gathered two of every kind of animal on his ark, to save them when God flooded the earth as punishment.

# THINKING ABOUT THE SELECTION

## Recalling

1. What does Shem request of the bearded man?
2. What does Shem attempt to do after the bearded man refuses his request?
3. How does the bearded man react to Shem's attempt?
4. What does Shem do after his failure to get the unicorns?

## Interpreting

5. "The Last Unicorns" is based on the Biblical story of Noah and the flood (Genesis 6–8), in which Noah took two of every animal onto his ark before a flood destroyed everything but his ark. What does Shem know that the bearded man does not know?
6. Why doesn't Shem tell the bearded man why he *must* have the unicorns?
7. What is the purpose of the references to the weather?

## Applying

8. How might you have approached the man with your request if you were Shem?

# ANALYZING LITERATURE

## Appreciating Tone

The **tone** of a story is the attitude the author shows toward his subject and audience. Authors establish tone through their style of writing. Aspects of style such as word choice, sentence length and complexity, and rhythm all play a role in establishing tone. For example, in "The Last Unicorns," Hoch uses an informal style and selects words and details that give the story almost a mythical or fairy tale quality. These style elements create a certain effect and leave you with a particular feeling. The feeling the author leaves you with is the best indication of the tone.

1. With what feeling does "The Last Unicorns" leave you?

2. Cite two clues to the tone in Hoch's style and word choice.
3. Cite two details or comments in the story that suggest the tone.

# CRITICAL THINKING AND READING

## Noting Relevant Details

The **relevant details** in a story are those that help establish the situation, advance the plot, or reveal character. A story with a surprise ending often has relevant details throughout it that foreshadow the ending. Find three details in "The Last Unicorns" that help foreshadow the surprise ending. Explain each of your choices.

# UNDERSTANDING LANGUAGE

## Appreciating Allusions

An **allusion** is a reference an author makes to people, places, and events from history or literature outside his or her own work. "The Last Unicorns" is built on an allusion to the Biblical story of Noah and the flood (Genesis 6–8), in which Noah took two of each animal onto his ark before the earth was flooded.

1. What details and situation in "The Last Unicorns" are taken from the Biblical story?
2. How does knowing the Biblical story increase your appreciation of "The Last Unicorns"?

# THINKING AND WRITING

## Writing to Convey a Tone

Imagine that Shem had succeeded in buying the unicorns but had lost them in taking them to Noah. Freewrite about this imagined situation. Then select details from your freewriting to write about this incident. Try to imitate the style and tone that Hoch uses in "The Last Unicorns." Revise your draft, replacing weak words with those that convey a light, sad, slightly humorous tone.

## The Open Window

**Saki** (1870–1916) is the pen name of H. H. Munro. Saki was born in Burma, which was then a British colony, but when his mother died, Saki was sent to England to be raised by two aunts. His earliest works were political satires, which appeared in newspapers. He worked for several newspapers as a foreign correspondent. In 1914 Saki enlisted in the army and was killed in battle during World War I. Saki's stories, including "The Open Window," are noted for their wit and humor.

### Tone in Dialogue

The **tone** of a story is the attitude implied toward the characters, situation, and readers. The characters within a story may also convey a tone toward a situation or toward other characters. A character's tone might be respectful, or sympathetic, or challenging, for example. Characters' attitudes are revealed primarily through their dialogue and actions. You can infer characters' tones from their choice of words and from their intent. Each of the three characters in "The Open Window" who speaks at length has an identifiable tone.

### Look For

As you read "The Open Window," look for details in dialogue that reveal the characters' attitudes toward one another as well as Saki's attitude toward his characters.

### Writing

Framton Nuttel, a nervous young man, pays a formal call on some new acquaintances in "The Open Window." Imagine his thoughts and feelings as he prepares to go to their home. Freewrite about them.

### Vocabulary

Knowing the following words will help you as you read "The Open Window."

**delusion** (di lōō′ zhən) *n.*: A false belief held in spite of evidence to the contrary (p. 197)

**imminent** (im′ ə nənt) *adj.*: Likely to happen presently; threatening (p. 198)

**mackintosh** (mak′ in täsh′) *n.*: A waterproof raincoat (p. 198)

**pariah** (pə rī′ ə) *n.*: A social outcast (p. 198)

# The Open Window

## Saki

"My aunt will be down presently, Mr. Nuttel," said a very self-possessed young lady of fifteen; "in the meantime you must try and put up with me."

Framton Nuttel endeavored to say the correct something that should duly flatter the niece of the moment without unduly discounting the aunt that was to come. Privately he doubted more than ever whether these formal visits on a succession of total strangers would do much towards helping the nerve cure which he was supposed to be undergoing.

"I know how it will be," his sister had said when he was preparing to migrate to this rural retreat; "you will bury yourself down there and not speak to a living soul, and your nerves will be worse than ever from moping. I shall just give you letters of introduction to all the people I know there. Some of them, as far as I can remember, were quite nice."

Framton wondered whether Mrs. Sappleton, the lady to whom he was presenting one of the letters of introduction, came into the nice division.

"Do you know many of the people round here?" asked the niece, when she judged that they had had sufficient silent communion.

"Hardly a soul," said Framton. "My sister was staying here, at the rectory, you know, some four years ago, and she gave me letters of introduction to some of the people here."

He made the last statement in a tone of distinct regret.

"Then you know practically nothing about my aunt?" pursued the self-possessed young lady.

"Only her name and address," admitted the caller. He was wondering whether Mrs. Sappleton was in the married or widowed state. An undefinable something about the room seemed to suggest masculine habitation.

"Her great tragedy happened just three years ago," said the child; "that would be since your sister's time."

"Her tragedy?" asked Framton; somehow in this restful country spot tragedies seemed out of place.

"You may wonder why we keep that window wide open on an October afternoon," said the niece, indicating a large French window that opened on to a lawn.

"It is quite warm for the time of the year," said Framton; "but has that window got anything to do with the tragedy?"

"Out through that window, three years ago to a day, her husband and her two young brothers went off for their day's shooting. They never came back. In crossing the moor to their favorite snipe-shooting ground[1] they were all three engulfed in a treacherous

---

**1. snipe-shooting ground:** Area for hunting snipe, wading birds who live chiefly in marshy places and have long, flexible bills.

piece of bog. It had been that dreadful wet summer, you know, and places that were safe in other years gave way suddenly without warning. Their bodies were never recovered. That was the dreadful part of it.'' Here the child's voice lost its self-possessed note and became falteringly human. ''Poor aunt always thinks that they will come back some day, they and the little brown spaniel that was lost with them, and walk in at that window just as they used to do. That is why the window is kept open every evening till it is quite dusk. Poor dear aunt, she has often told me how they went out, her husband with his white waterproof coat over his arm, and Ronnie, her youngest brother, singing, 'Bertie, why do you bound?' as he always did to tease her, because she said it got on her nerves. Do you know, sometimes on still, quiet evenings like this, I almost get a creepy feeling that they will walk in through that window—''

She broke off with a little shudder. It was a relief to Framton when the aunt bustled into the room with a whirl of apologies for being late in making her appearance.

''I hope Vera has been amusing you?'' she said.

''She has been very interesting,'' said Framton.

''I hope you don't mind the open window,'' said Mrs. Sappleton briskly; ''my husband and brothers will be home directly from shooting, and they always come in this way. They've been out for snipe in the marshes today, so they'll make a fine mess over my poor carpets. So like you menfolk, isn't it?''

She rattled on cheerfully about the shooting and the scarcity of birds, and the prospects for duck in the winter. To Framton, it was all purely horrible. He made a desperate but only partially successful effort to turn the talk on to a less ghastly topic; he was conscious that his hostess was giving him only a fragment of her attention, and her eyes were constantly straying past him to the open window and the lawn beyond. It was certainly an unfortunate coincidence that he should have paid his visit on this tragic anniversary.

''The doctors agree in ordering me complete rest, an absence of mental excitement, and avoidance of anything in the nature of violent physical exercise,'' announced Framton, who labored under the tolerably wide-spread delusion that total strangers and chance acquaintances are hungry for the least detail of one's ailments and infirmities, their cause and cure. ''On the matter of diet they are not so much in agreement,'' he continued.

''No?'' said Mrs. Sappleton, in a voice which only replaced a yawn at the last moment. Then she suddenly brightened into alert attention—but not to what Framton was saying.

''Here they are at last!'' she cried. ''Just in time for tea, and don't they look as if they were muddy up to the eyes!''

Framton shivered slightly and turned towards the niece with a look intended to convey sympathetic comprehension. The child was staring out through the open window with dazed horror in her eyes. In a chill shock of nameless fear Framton swung round in his seat and looked in the same direction.

In the deepening twilight three figures were walking across the lawn towards the window; they all carried guns under their arms, and one of them was additionally burdened with a white coat hung over his shoulders. A tired brown spaniel kept close at their heels. Noiselessly they neared the house, and then a hoarse young voice chanted out of the dusk: ''I said, Bertie, why do you bound?''

Framton grabbed wildly at his stick and hat; the hall door, the gravel drive, and the front gate were dimly noted stages in his headlong retreat. A cyclist coming along the road had to run into the hedge to avoid imminent collision.

"Here we are, my dear," said the bearer of the white mackintosh, coming in through the window; "fairly muddy, but most of it's dry. Who was that who bolted out as we came up?"

"A most extraordinary man, a Mr. Nuttel," said Mrs. Sappleton; "could only talk about his illnesses, and dashed off without a word of goodbye or apology when you arrived. One would think he had seen a ghost."

"I expect it was the spaniel," said the niece calmly; "he told me he had a horror of dogs. He was once hunted into a cemetery somewhere on the banks of the Ganges[2] by a pack of pariah dogs, and had to spend the night in a newly dug grave with the creatures snarling and grinning and foaming just above him. Enough to make anyone lose their nerve."

Romance at short notice was her specialty.

---

**2. Ganges** (gan′ jēz): A river in northern India and Bangladesh.

# THINKING ABOUT THE SELECTION

## Recalling

1. For what reason is Framton Nuttel living in the country? Why is he visiting the Sappletons?
2. How does Vera explain the open window?
3. Explain what causes Framton to rush from the house so suddenly.
4. How does Vera explain Framton's departure?

## Interpreting

5. Contrast the outstanding character traits of Framton and Vera. What qualities or traits of Framton make him susceptible to her story?
6. At what point do you realize that Vera is telling a story? Cite evidence from the story that shows her intent.
7. Saki concludes the story with the statement, "Romance at short notice was her specialty." Explain the meaning of *romance* in this statement.
8. Explain how this story can be thought of as having a double ending.

## Applying

9. Explain how a person's expectations can lead him or her to misunderstand or misinterpret obvious facts.

## ANALYZING LITERATURE
## Recognizing Tone in Dialogue

When you converse with someone, you can recognize that person's **tone** from his or her manner of speaking. The person's tone might be sarcastic or serious, for example. The dialogue in short stories reveals the characters' tone in the same way. In "The Open Window," Framton's tone remains polite throughout the story, showing a respectful attitude toward the Sappletons.

1. What is Vera's tone when speaking to Framton? What evidence indicates this tone?
2. What is Mrs. Sappleton's tone toward Framton before his sudden departure? What words or details reveal her tone?

3. Verbal irony occurs when someone means the opposite of what is said. Find two examples of verbal irony in this story.

## CRITICAL THINKING AND READING
## Making Inferences About Characters

From the characters' dialogue and actions, you can make inferences about the characters themselves. For example, Mrs. Sappleton's suppressed yawn shows her to be bored with Framton's conversation about his condition.

1. What is Framton's social status compared with that of the Sappletons?
2. What kind of person is Framton?
3. What kind of person is Vera? Look up the meaning of her name. What do you think was the author's purpose in choosing the name Vera for this character.

## SPEAKING AND LISTENING
## Reading a Selection Aloud

Read "The Open Window" aloud using different tones of voice. When you read the narrative sections, try to capture the author's tone in your tone of voice. When you read the dialogue, use a tone of voice that reveals each character's attitude toward the topic and the listener. When you have rehearsed a few times, read the selection aloud to the class.

## THINKING AND WRITING
## Writing About Tone

Suppose that you went to tea at the Sappletons' when Framton was there. Write a journal entry describing the experience. Describe each family member and his or her tone of voice in conversing with you. Conclude with the opinion you formed of the family during the tea. Review your entry, adding at least two lines of dialogue that reveal characters' tones.

# GUIDE FOR READING

## The Machine That Won the War

**Isaac Asimov** (1920–    ) was born in the Soviet Union. When he was three, his family emigrated to the United States, and Asimov grew up in Brooklyn, New York. He is the author of some three hundred books on a variety of subjects, including the sciences (astronomy, mathematics, and biochemistry), history, Shakespeare, and the Bible. Asimov remains best known, however, for his works of science fiction including novels like *Fantastic Voyage* and short stories like "The Machine That Won the War."

## Verbal Irony and Irony of Situation

**Irony** is a contrast between what is and what seems to be. There are different kinds of irony. In **verbal irony,** a writer or speaker says one thing but means another, usually the opposite. You use verbal irony when you describe someone you like as "really bad." **Irony of situation** refers to the difference between what you, or a character, expect to happen, and what actually happens. Having a machine turn out to be a war hero might seem ironic, but in "The Machine That Won the War," that is just the beginning.

## Look For

As you read "The Machine That Won the War," look for the contrasts between what the characters think is true and what really is true.

## Writing

Recall a time when you had difficulty operating a machine. How did you respond toward the machine? Freewrite about the experience. Include your thoughts about the relationship between human beings and their machines.

## Vocabulary

Knowing the following words will help you as you read "The Machine That Won the War."

**erratic** (i rat′ ik) *adj.*: Irregular; random (p. 201)

**grisly** (griz′ lē) *adj.*: Horrifying; gruesome (p. 201)

**imperturbable** (im′ pər tʉr′ bə b'l) *adj.*: Unable to be excited or disturbed (p. 201)

**oracle** (ôr′ ə k'l) *n.*: A source of knowledge or wise counsel (p. 201)

**surcease** (sʉr sēs′) *n.*: An end (p. 202)

**subsidiary** (səb sid′ ē er′ ē) *adj.*: Secondary; supporting (p. 202)

**circumvent** (sʉr′ kəm vent′) *v.*: Prevent from happening (p. 203)

# The Machine That Won the War

## Isaac Asimov

The celebration had a long way to go and even in the silent depths of Multivac's underground chambers, it hung in the air.

If nothing else, there was the mere fact of isolation and silence. For the first time in a decade, technicians were not scurrying about the vitals of the giant computer, the soft lights did not wink out their erratic patterns, the flow of information in and out had halted.

It would not be halted long, of course, for the needs of peace would be pressing. Yet now, for a day, perhaps for a week, even Multivac might celebrate the great time, and rest.

Lamar Swift took off the military cap he was wearing and looked down the long and empty main corridor of the enormous computer. He sat down rather wearily in one of the technician's swing-stools, and his uniform, in which he had never been comfortable, took on a heavy and wrinkled appearance.

He said, "I'll miss it all after a grisly fashion. It's hard to remember when we weren't at war with Deneb, and it seems against nature now to be at peace and to look at the stars without anxiety."

The two men with the Executive Director of the Solar Federation were both younger than Swift. Neither was as gray. Neither looked quite as tired.

John Henderson, thin-lipped and finding it hard to control the relief he felt in the midst of triumph, said, "They're destroyed! They're destroyed! It's what I keep saying to myself over and over and I still can't believe it. We all talked so much, over so many years, about the menace hanging over Earth and all its worlds, over every human being, and all the time it was true, every word of it. And now we're alive and it's the Denebians who are shattered and destroyed. They'll be no menace now, ever again."

"Thanks to Multivac," said Swift, with a quiet glance at the imperturbable Jablonsky, who through all the war had been Chief Interpreter of science's oracle. "Right, Max?"

Jablonsky shrugged. He said, "Well, that's what *they* say." His broad thumb moved in the direction of his right shoulder, aiming upward.

"Jealous, Max?"

"Because they're shouting for Multivac? Because Multivac is the big hero of mankind in this war?" Jablonsky's craggy face took on an air of suitable contempt. "What's that to me? Let Multivac be the machine that won the war, if it pleases them."

Henderson looked at the other two out of the corners of his eyes. In this short interlude that the three had instinctively sought out in the one peaceful corner of a metropolis gone mad; in this entr'acte[1] between the dangers of war and the difficulties of peace; when, for one moment, they might all find surcease; he was conscious only of his weight of guilt.

Suddenly, it was as though that weight were too great to be borne longer. It had to be thrown off, along with the war; now!

Henderson said, "Multivac had nothing to do with victory. It's just a machine."

"A big one," said Swift.

"Then just a big machine. No better than the data fed it." For a moment, he stopped, suddenly unnerved at what he was saying.

Jablonsky looked at him. "You should know. You supplied the data. Or is it just that you're taking the credit?"

"No," said Henderson angrily. "There is no credit. What do you know of the data Multivac had to use; predigested from a hundred subsidiary computers here on Earth, on the Moon, on Mars, even on Titan. With Titan always delayed and always feeling that its figures would introduce an unexpected bias."

"It would drive anyone mad," said Swift, with gentle sympathy.

Henderson shook his head. "It wasn't just that. I admit that eight years ago when I replaced Lepont as Chief Programmer, I was nervous. But there was an exhilaration about things in those days. The war was still long range; an adventure without real danger. We hadn't reached the point where manned vessels had had to take over and where interstellar warps could swallow up a planet clean, if aimed correctly. But then, when the real difficulties began—"

Angrily—he could finally permit anger —he said, "You know nothing about it."

"Well," said Swift. "Tell us. The war is over. We've won."

"Yes." Henderson nodded his head. He had to remember that. Earth had won, so all had been for the best. "Well, the data became meaningless."

"Meaningless? You mean that literally?" said Jablonsky.

"Literally. What would you expect? The trouble with you two was that you weren't out in the thick of it. You never left Multivac, Max, and you, Mr. Director, never left the Mansion except on state visits where you saw exactly what they wanted you to see."

"I was not as unaware of that," said Swift, "as you may have thought."

"Do you know," said Henderson, "to what extent data concerning our production capacity, our resource potential, our trained manpower—everything of importance to the war effort, in fact—had become unreliable and untrustworthy during the last half of the war? Group leaders, both civilian and military, were intent on projecting their own improved image, so to speak, so they obscured the bad and magnified the good. Whatever the machines might do, the men who programmed them and interpreted the results had their own skins to think of and competitors to stab. There was no way of stopping that. I tried, and failed."

"Of course," said Swift, in quiet consolation. "I can see that you would."

"Yet I presume you provided Multivac with data in your programming?" Jablonsky said. "You said nothing to us about unreliability."

"How could I tell you? And if I did, how could you afford to believe me?" demanded Henderson, savagely. "Our entire war effort was geared to Multivac. It was the one great weapon on our side, for the Denebians had nothing like it. What else kept up morale in the face of doom but the assurance that Multivac would always predict and circumvent any Denebian move, and would always direct and prevent the circumvention of our moves? Great Space, after our Spy-warp was blasted out of hyperspace we lacked any reliable Denebian data to feed Multivac and we didn't dare make *that* public."

"True enough," said Swift.

"Well, then," said Henderson, "if I told you the data was unreliable, what could you have done but replace me and refuse to believe me? I couldn't allow that."

"What did you do?" said Jablonsky.

"Since the war is won, I'll tell you what I did. I corrected the data."

"How?" asked Swift.

"Intuition, I presume. I juggled them till they looked right. At first, I hardly dared. I changed a bit here and there to correct what were obvious impossibilities. When the sky didn't collapse about us, I got braver. Toward the end, I scarcely cared. I just wrote out the necessary data as it was needed. I even had the Multivac Annex prepare data for me according to a private programming pattern I had devised for the purpose."

"Random figures?" said Jablonsky.

"Not at all. I introduced a number of necessary biases."

Jablonsky smiled, quite unexpectedly, his dark eyes sparkling behind the crinkling of the lower lids. "Three times a report was brought to me about unauthorized uses of the Annex, and I let it go each time. If it had mattered, I would have followed it up and spotted you, John, and found out what you were doing. But, of course, nothing about Multivac mattered in those days, so you got away with it."

"What do you mean, nothing mattered?" asked Henderson, suspiciously.

"Nothing did. I suppose if I had told you

this at the time, it would have spared you your agony, but then if you had told me what you were doing, it would have spared me mine. What made you think Multivac was in working order, whatever the data you supplied it?"

"Not in working order?" said Swift.

"Not really. Not reliably. After all, where were my technicians in the last years of the war? I'll tell you, they were feeding computers on a thousand different space devices. They were gone! I had to make do with kids I couldn't trust and veterans who were out-of-date. Besides, do you think I could trust the solid-state components coming out of Cryogenics[2] in the last years? Cryogenics wasn't any better placed as far as personnel was concerned than I was. To me, it didn't matter whether the data being supplied Multivac were reliable or not. The *results* weren't reliable. That much I knew."

"What did you do?" asked Henderson.

"I did what you did, John. I introduced the bugger factor. I adjusted matters in accordance with intuition—and that's how the machine won the war."

Swift leaned back in the chair and stretched his legs out before him. "Such revelations. It turns out then that the material handed me to guide me in my decision-making capacity was a man-made interpretation of man-made data. Isn't that right?"

"It looks so," said Jablonsky.

"Then I perceive I was correct in not placing too much reliance upon it," said Swift.

"You didn't?" Jablonsky, despite what he had just said, managed to look professionally insulted.

---

**2. Cryogenics** (krī' ə jen' iks): Here, a department concerned with the science of low-temperature phenomena.

"I'm afraid I didn't. Multivac might seem to say, Strike here, not there; do this, not that; wait, don't act. But I could never be certain that what Multivac seemed to say, it really did say; or what it really said, it really meant. I could never be certain."

"But the final report was always plain enough, sir," said Jablonsky.

"To those who did not have to make the decision, perhaps. Not to me. The horror of the responsibility of such decisions was unbearable and not even Multivac was sufficient to remove the weight. But the point is I

was justified in doubting and there is tremendous relief in that."

Caught up in the conspiracy of mutual confession, Jablonsky put titles aside. "What was it you did then, Lamar? After all, you did make decisions. How?"

"Well, it's time to be getting back perhaps, but—I'll tell you first. Why not? I did make use of a computer, Max, but an older one than Multivac, much older."

He groped in his own pocket and brought out a scattering of small change; old-fashioned coins dating to the first years

before the metal
shortage had brought
into being a credit system
tied to a computer-complex.

Swift smiled rather sheepishly.
"I still need these to make money seem
substantial to me. An old man finds it hard
to abandon the habits of youth." He
dropped the coins, one by one, back into
his pocket.

He held the last coin between his fingers,
staring absently at it. "Multivac is not the
first computer, friends, nor the best-known,

nor the one that can most efficiently lift the load of decision from the shoulders of the executive. A machine *did* win the war, John; at least a very simple computing device did; one that I used every time I had a particularly hard decision to make."

With a faint smile of reminiscence, he flipped the coin he held. It glinted in the air as it spun and came down in Swift's outstretched palm. His hand closed over it and brought it down on the back of his left hand. His right hand remained in place, hiding the coin.

"Heads or tails, gentlemen?" said Swift.

---

## THINKING ABOUT THE SELECTION

### Recalling

1. What is the reason for the celebration at the opening of the story? Why is Multivac a hero?
2. What does each man reveal about his wartime activities?
3. What is the primitive computing device that Swift used?

### Interpreting

4. Why do the three men decide to make their confessions?
5. Explain how each character's wartime activities may have affected the victory.
6. In what way was Multivac responsible for winning the war?

### Applying

7. Do you think it is possible that a machine can determine the course of human events? Explain your answer.

## ANALYZING LITERATURE

### Recognizing Irony

In **verbal irony,** what is said is different from, or opposite to, what is meant. Verbal irony often calls more attention to the intended meaning than a direct statement would. In **irony of situation,** there is a contrast between what appears to be true and what really is true. You or the characters are led to expect a certain outcome, but something quite different actually occurs. For example, in this story, it appears to everyone that the Multivac systems succeeded and were responsible for the victory. However, Henderson reveals that data was unusable, and he had to create data to make Multivac work as it should have. This entire story depends on a series of ironic revelations about how the war was won.

1. Explain why the title of this short story is ironic.
2. Explain how each man's confession is ironic.
3. Why is Swift's confession especially ironic?
4. Every day advances are being made in the field of artificial intelligence. What is artificial intelligence? Why is the term itself ironic?

## CRITICAL THINKING AND READING

### Identifying Relevant Details

**Relevant details** in a story give information that is central to the situation, plot, or characters. Some details are relevant because they establish the outcome of the story.

The first hint about the outcome is Swift's saying, "Thanks to Multivac," and Jablonsky's responding, "Well, that's what they say." At this point, you suspect that Multivac may not be responsible for winning the war, after all.

1. Find at least three other details that lead you to the conclusion that Multivac is not responsible for winning the war.
2. At what point were you sure what the ending would reveal? Explain your answer.

## UNDERSTANDING LANGUAGE
### Using the Prefix **un-**

The prefix un- has two meanings: "not, the lack of, or the opposite of" (*unbearable*) and "the reversal or removal of (*unnerve*)."

Use each of the following words in sentences. Then add *un-* to each and use the new words in sentences.

1. expectedly
2. load
3. trustworthy
4. do

## THINKING AND WRITING
### Writing About a Title

Imagine that you are working as an assistant to Isaac Asimov. He has just finished writing this story and he wants your advice about the title he is considering. Write Asimov a memorandum explaining why you think the title he chose is a good one for the story, or suggest another and explain why you think it is better. Include reasons that relate both to the plot of the story and to Asimov's method of developing it. When you revise the memo, include a quotation from the story to support your position.

## The Brothers

**Björnstjerne Björnson** (1832–1910) was born in Bjoergan, Norway. A novelist, poet, and playwright, Björnson also worked as a theater manager and a journalist. In 1903 he won the Nobel Prize for literature. Among his works is the song "Yes, We Love This Land," which became the Norwegian national anthem. His other works range from sagas of ancient Norway to novels about social problems. He also wrote a number of stories about peasants, including "The Brothers," which have the flavor of folk tales.

### Verbal Irony and Dramatic Irony

**Irony** is a contrast between what is and what seems to be. **Verbal irony** involves a speaker's saying something different from what he or she means—usually the opposite. Calling a very tall person "Shorty" is an example of verbal irony. With **dramatic irony** the audience or reader has information that is withheld from the characters. Throughout "The Brothers," you are aware of information that could change the fate of two brothers—if only they knew!

### Look For

As you read "The Brothers," look for the incidents in which you are aware of the true situation but Baard and Anders, the two brothers, are not, because they see only a limited part of it.

### Writing

This story involves two brothers who lose faith in each other. One imagines that the other tricked him into giving up a prized possession. Freewrite about how each brother might react to the situation.

### Vocabulary

Knowing the following words will help you as you read "The Brothers."

**stalwart** (stôl′ wərt) *adj.:* Strong; with unwavering determination (p. 209)

**heirlooms** (er′ lōōmz) *n.:* Treasured possessions handed down from generation to generation (p. 212)

**fagots** (fag′ əts) *n.:* Bundles of sticks used for fuel (p. 212)

**smitten** (smit′n) *v.:* Struck strongly and suddenly (p. 213)

**emaciated** (i mā′ shē āt′ əd) *adj.:* Abnormally thin because of starvation or illness (p. 213)

# The Brothers

## Björnstjerne Björnson
### translated by Anders Orbeck

The schoolmaster's name was Baard, and he had a brother named Anders. They thought a great deal of each other, enlisted together, lived together in town, went through the war together, served in the same company, and both rose to the rank of corporal. When they came home from the war, people said they were two fine stalwart fellows.

Then their father died. He left much personal property, which it was difficult to divide, and therefore they said to each other that they would not let this come between them, but would put the property up at auction, that each might buy what he wanted, and both share the proceeds. And it was so done.

But the father had owned a large gold watch, which had come to be known far and wide, for it was the only gold watch people in those parts had ever seen. When this watch was put up, there were many wealthy men who wanted it, but when both brothers began to bid, all the others desisted. Now Baard expected that Anders would let him have it, and Anders expected the same of Baard. They bid in turn, each trying the other out, and as they bid they looked hard at each other. When the watch had gone up to twenty dollars, Baard began to feel that this was not kind of his brother, and bid over him until he almost reached thirty. When Anders did not withdraw even then,

Baard felt that Anders no longer remembered how good he had often been to him, and that he was furthermore the elder of the two; and the watch went over thirty. Anders still kept on. Baard then raised the price to forty dollars with one bound, and no longer looked at his brother. It grew very still in the auction room; only the bailiff repeated the figures quietly. Anders thought, as he stood there, that if Baard could afford to go to forty dollars, so could he, and if Baard begrudged him the watch, he might as well take it, and bid over him. This to Baard seemed the greatest disgrace that had ever befallen him; he bid fifty dollars in a low voice. There were many people there, and Anders said to himself that he would not let his brother mock him before them all, and again raised the bid. Baard burst out laughing.

"One hundred dollars and my brotherhood into the bargain," he said, and he turned on his heel, and left the room.

A little later, as he stood saddling the horse he had just bought at the auction, a man came out to him.

"The watch is yours; Anders gave in."

The instant Baard heard the news, there welled up in him a sense of remorse; he thought of his brother and not of the watch. The saddle was already in place, but he paused, his hand on his horse, uncertain whether to mount. Many people came out, Anders among them, and when he saw his

**MELANCHOLY**
*Edvard Munch*
Rasmus Meyers Samlinger, Bergen

brother, with horse saddled, ready to leave, he little knew what Baard was turning over in his mind.

"Thanks for the watch, Baard!" he shouted over to him, "You shall never see the day when your brother shall tread on your heels!"

"Nor you the day I shall darken your doors again!" Baard answered, his face pale, as he swung himself on his horse.

After that day neither of them ever set foot in the home where they had both lived with their father.

Anders married into a crofter's[1] family, not long afterwards, but he did not invite Baard to the wedding. Nor did Baard go to the church. The first year he was married,

---

**1. crofter's** (krôft′ ərz) *adj.*: Tenant farmer's.

Anders lost his only cow. It was found dead one morning on the north side of the house, where it had been tethered, and no one could explain what it had died of. Other misfortunes befell him, and he fared from bad to worse. But the heaviest blow came when his hayloft and all it contained burned down one night in the dead of winter. No one knew how the fire had started.

"This has been done by someone who wishes me ill," Anders said, and all that night he wept. He became a poor man, and he lost all inclination to work.

The evening after the fire, Baard appeared at his brother's house. Anders lay on his bed, but sprang up as Baard entered.

"What do you want here?" he asked, then stopped short, and stood staring fixedly at his brother.

Baard waited a little before he answered.

"I want to help you, Anders; you're in a bad way."

"I'm faring no worse than you wished me to fare! Go—else I'm not sure I can master myself."

"You're mistaken, Anders; I regret—"

"Go, Baard, or God have mercy on us both!"

Baard drew back a step.

"If you want the watch," he said in a trembling voice, "you can have it."

"Go, Baard!" shrieked his brother, and Baard, unwilling to stay any longer, left.

In the meanwhile Baard had fared thus. As soon as he heard of his brother's misfortunes, he had suffered a change of heart, but pride held him back. He felt urged to go to church, and there he vowed many a good resolve, but he lacked strength to carry them out. He frequently went so far that he could see the house, but either someone was just coming out, or there were strangers there, or Anders stood chopping wood outside—there was always something in the way.

But one Sunday, late in the winter, he again went to church, and that Sunday Anders too was there. Baard saw him. He had grown pale and thin, and he wore the same clothes he had worn when the brothers were together, although now they were old and patched. All through the service Anders looked steadily at the minister. To Baard it seemed that he was kind and gentle, and he recalled their childhood days, and what a good boy Anders had been. That day Baard even went to communion, and he made a solemn vow that he would make up with his brother, come what might. This resolution swept through his soul, and when he arose he felt an impulse to go over and take a seat beside him, but there was someone in the way, and Anders did not look up. After the service there was still something in the way; there were too many people about; Anders's wife was with him and her he did not know. He decided it would be better to seek Anders in his home and have a quiet talk with him.

When evening came, he set out. He went right up to the door. Then he paused, and as he stood there listening, he heard his name mentioned; it was the wife speaking.

"He went to communion this morning," she was saying. "I am sure he was thinking of you."

"No, it wasn't of me he was thinking," Anders replied. "I know him; he thinks only of himself."

For a long time nothing was said, and Baard sweat, as he stood there, although it was a cold night. The wife inside was busy with a kettle; the fire on the hearth crackled and hissed; a child cried now and then, and Anders rocked it. At length the wife spoke again.

"I believe you are both thinking of each other though you won't admit it."

"Let us talk of something else," Anders answered.

After a little he got up to go out. Baard had to hide in the woodshed; but then Anders, too, came to the shed to get an armful of wood. From where he stood in the corner Baard could see him clearly. He had taken off his threadbare Sunday clothes, and put on his uniform, just like Baard's own. These they had promised each other never to wear, but to pass on as heirlooms to their children. Anders's was now patched and worn out, so that his strong well-built frame seemed bundled in rags, while at the same time Baard could hear the gold watch ticking in his own pocket. Anders went over to the brush wood, but instead of bending down immediately to gather up his load, he leaned back against a pile of wood, and looked up at the sky glimmering brightly with stars. Then he sighed heavily and muttered to himself, "Well—well—well—oh Lord, oh Lord!"

As long as he lived, Baard never forgot those words. He wanted to step forward then, but the brother coughed, and it seemed so difficult. No more was needed to hold him back. Anders took his armful of fagots, and as he went out, brushed past Baard so close that the twigs struck him in the face.

For fully ten minutes more he stood rooted to the spot, and it is doubtful how much longer he might have stayed, had not a chill, on top of the emotional stress, seized him, and set him shivering through and through. Then he went out. He frankly confessed to himself that he was too cowardly to enter now; wherefore he conceived another plan. From an ash barrel, which stood in the corner he had just left, he selected some bits

of charcoal, found a pitch pine splinter, went up into the hayloft, closed the door, and struck a light. When he had lit the torch he searched about for the peg on which Anders hung his lantern when he came out early in the morning to thresh. Baard then took his gold watch and hung it on the peg, put out his light, and left. He felt so relieved in his mind that he raced over the snow like a youngster.

The day following he heard that the hayloft had burned down during the night. Presumably sparks had flown from the torch he had used while hanging up the watch.

This so overwhelmed Baard that all that day he kept to himself as though he were ill, brought out his hymn book, and sang until the people in the house thought something was wrong with him. But in the evening he went out. It was bright moonlight. He went over to his brother's place, dug around in the charred ruins of the fire, and found, sure enough, a little lump of melted gold—all that remained of the watch.

It was with this in his hand that he went in to his brother, anxious to explain everything, and to sue for peace. But how he fared that evening has already been told.

A little girl had seen him digging in the ashes; some boys, on their way to a dance, had observed him go down toward his brother's the Sunday evening in question; and the people where he lived explained how strangely he had acted on the Monday following. And inasmuch as every one knew that he and his brother were bitter enemies, these details were reported to the authorities, and an inquiry instituted. No one could prove anything against him, yet suspicion hovered around him. He could now less than ever approach his brother.

Anders had thought of Baard when the hayloft burned, but had said nothing. When he had seen him enter his house, the following evening, pale and strange, he had forthwith thought: He is smitten with remorse, but for such a terrible outrage against his brother there can be no forgiveness. Since then he heard how people had seen Baard go down towards his home the evening of the fire, and although nothing was brought to light at the inquiry, he felt convinced that his brother was the guilty one.

They met at the hearing, Baard in his good clothes, Anders in his worn-out rags. Baard looked at his brother as he entered, and Anders was conscious, in his inmost heart, of an anxious pleading in his eyes. He doesn't want me to say anything, thought Anders; and when he was asked whether he suspected his brother of the deed he answered loudly and decisively, "No!"

After that day, it was not long before Anders was in a bad way. Even worse, however, fared Baard; he was so changed that people hardly knew him.

Then late one evening a poor woman entered the little room Baard rented and asked him to come with her. He recognized her; it was his brother's wife. Baard understood at once what her errand was, turned deathly pale, dressed himself, and followed her without a word. A pale glimmer shone from Anders's window, now flickering, now vanishing, and this light they followed, for there was no path across the snow. When Baard again stood in the doorway, he was met with a strange odor which almost made him ill. They went in. A little child sat eating charcoal over by the hearth, its face all black, but it looked up and laughed and showed its white teeth. It was his brother's child.

Over on the bed, with all sorts of clothes over him, lay Anders, pale, emaciated, his forehead high and smooth, and stared at his brother with hollow eyes. Baard's knees trembled. He sat down at the foot of the bed and burst into uncontrollable weeping. The sick man looked at him intently and said nothing. At length he asked his wife to go out, but Baard motioned for her to remain. And then the two brothers began to talk to each other. They explained everything, from the day they bid for the watch down through the years to this day when they finally met again. Baard ended by taking out the lump of gold, which he always carried about him, and it came to light in the course of their talk that never for one single day in all these years had they been really happy.

Anders did not say much, for he had little strength, but Baard watched by the bedside as long as Anders was ill.

"Now I am perfectly well," Anders said one morning, on awakening. "Now, brother, we shall live together always, just as in the old days, and never leave each other."

But that day he died.

The widow and the child Baard took home with him, and they were henceforth well taken care of. But what the brothers had talked of at the bedside came out through the walls and the night, and became generally known to all the people in the valley. Baard grew to be the most highly respected man among them. They all honored him as one who had a great sorrow and had found peace again, or as one who had returned after a long absence. And Baard grew in strength of mind by reason of all their friendliness. He became a pious man, and wishing to be of some use, as he said, the old corporal turned schoolmaster. What he impressed upon the children, first and last, was love, and himself he practiced it till the children came to love him as a playmate and a father.

## THINKING ABOUT THE SELECTION
### Recalling

1. What causes Baard and Anders to become estranged?
2. Describe Anders's life after the estrangement.
3. Although Baard wants to visit his brother sooner, what keeps him from doing so?
4. How do the brothers become reconciled?
5. How does Baard change after his brother's death?

### Interpreting

6. Compare and contrast the behavior of the two brothers, pointing out the characteristics that lead to their estrangement.
7. Despite their estrangement, the brothers remain loyal to each other. Find three examples of their concern during their estrangement.
8. Before dying, Anders tells Baard, "Now, brother, we shall live together always, just as in the old days, and never leave each other." In what way do his words prove to be true?

### Applying

9. What advice would you like to have given the two brothers immediately after the auction?

## ANALYZING LITERATURE
### Recognizing Irony

**Verbal irony** involves a contrast between what is said and what is meant. The speaker might not intend irony, but you are able to perceive it. **Dramatic irony** occurs when the audience or reader knows or is able to perceive what the characters cannot. In "The Brothers," for example, you know that Baard is hiding in the woodshed, while Anders does not. Dramatic irony heightens your feelings of suspense as you wait for the character to realize the truth.

Find at least two examples of dramatic irony in the story and two examples of verbal irony.

## CRITICAL THINKING AND READING
### Predicting Possible Outcomes

As you read a story, you usually make predictions about how it will end. You may revise your predictions from time to time as you acquire more information. When you reach the end, you may have the satisfaction of knowing you were right—or the thrill of a surprise.

1. How did you think "The Brothers" would end? What made you think so?
2. Compare your prediction or predictions with the actual ending.

## UNDERSTANDING LANGUAGE
### Interpreting Synonyms

**Synonyms** are words that have the same or nearly the same meanings. However, sometimes the shades of difference between synonyms can be quite significant.

Explain the difference between each of the following synonyms.
a. irony   b. wit   c. sarcasm

## THINKING AND WRITING
### Writing About Irony

Björnson could have written a story with the same plot but without the dramatic irony. It would have been a very different story. Write an essay for a classmate who does not understand the irony. Tell what the author achieves by the use of irony and how the reader is affected. Develop your ideas in a logical way by first defining dramatic irony and giving examples of it from the story. Then you can explain what the author achieves by the use of irony and how the reader is affected. When you revise, eliminate any unnecessary words.

# Theme

**GIRL LOOKING AT LANDSCAPE, 1957**
*Richard Diebenkorn*
Collection of Whitney Museum of American Art

# GUIDE FOR READING

## The Apple Tree

**Katherine Mansfield** (1888–1923), whose real name was Katherine Mansfield Beauchamp, was born in Wellington, New Zealand. She moved to London when she was twenty, and she began writing while in Germany recovering from tuberculosis. Because she continued to suffer from the disease, Mansfield spent much of her life in France and Italy, where the climate was thought to be beneficial. Many of Mansfield's stories, including "The Apple Tree," are set in the New Zealand she had known as a child and had left behind.

**Theme**

The **theme** of a story is its general idea or the insight into life that is revealed through the story. While this idea is developed through specific events and characters, it is an idea that applies generally to situations in human life. Sometimes authors state the theme directly, but more often they do not. The theme of "The Apple Tree" is unstated. Mansfield reveals her theme through what the characters learn.

**Look For**

As you read "The Apple Tree," look for the lesson about life that the characters learn from their experience.

**Writing**

The characters in this story wait a whole season to taste a special apple. Think of something that you spent a long time waiting for, perhaps a vacation planned months in advance or an object that you had to save your money to buy. Freewrite about your anticipation while you waited for the event or object.

**Vocabulary**

Knowing the following words will help you as you read "The Apple Tree."

**damsons** (dam' z'nz) *n.*: Small purple plums (p. 217)
**paddocks** (pad' əks) *n.*: Small enclosed fields (p. 217)
**wattles** (wät' 'lz) *n.*: Small flowering trees (p. 217)
**quinces** (kwins' iz) *n.*: Hard, green-yellow, apple-shaped fruit (p. 217)

**syringa** (sə riŋ' gə) *n.*: A hardy shrub with tiny fragrant flowers, also known as lilac (p. 219)
**exquisite** (eks' kwi zit) *adj.*: Delicately beautiful (p. 219)

# The Apple Tree

## Katherine Mansfield

There were two orchards belonging to the old house. One, that we called the "wild" orchard, lay beyond the vegetable garden; it was planted with bitter cherries and damsons and transparent yellow plums. For some reason it lay under a cloud; we never played there, we did not even trouble to pick up the fallen fruit; and there, every Monday morning, to the round open space in the middle, the servant girl and the washerwoman carried the wet linen —Grandmother's nightdresses, Father's striped shirts, the hired man's cotton trousers and the servant girl's "dreadfully vulgar" salmon-pink flannelette drawers jigged and slapped in horrid familiarity.

But the other orchard, far away and hidden from the house, lay at the foot of a little hill and stretched right over to the edge of the paddocks—to the clumps of wattles bobbing yellow in the bright sun and the blue gums with their streaming sickle-shaped leaves. There, under the fruit trees, the grass grew so thick and coarse that it tangled and knotted in your shoes as you walked, and even on the hottest day it was damp to touch when you stopped and parted it this way and that, looking for windfalls[1]—the apples marked with a bird's beak, the big bruised pears, the quinces, so good to eat with a pinch of salt, but so delicious to smell that you could not bite for sniffing. . . .

One year the orchard had its Forbidden Tree.[2] It was an apple tree discovered by Father and a friend during an after-dinner prowl one Sunday afternoon.

"Great Scott!" said the friend, lighting upon it with every appearance of admiring astonishment: "Isn't that a—?" And a rich, splendid name settled like an unknown bird on the tree.

"Yes, I believe it is," said Father lightly. He knew nothing whatever about the names of fruit trees.

"Great Scott!" said the friend again: "They're wonderful apples. Nothing like 'em—and you're going to have a tiptop crop. Marvelous apples! You can't beat 'em!"

---

1. **windfalls** (wind' fôlz') *n.*: Fruits blown down from the trees by the wind.
2. **Forbidden Tree:** Reference, from the Bible, to the apple tree in Paradise that Adam and Eve, the first man and woman, were forbidden to touch.

**ORCHARD WITH FLOWERING FRUIT TREES, SPRINGTIME, PONTOISE, 1877**
*Camille Pissaro*
Paris, Musée d'Orsay

"No, they're very fine—very fine," said Father carelessly, but looking upon the tree with new and lively interest.

"They're rare—they're very rare. Hardly ever see 'em in England nowadays," said the visitor and set a seal on Father's delight. For Father was a self-made man and the price he had to pay for everything was so huge and so painful that nothing rang so sweet to him as to hear his purchase praised. He was young and sensitive still. He still wondered whether in the deepest sense he got his money's worth. He still had hours when he walked up and down in the moonlight half deciding to "chuck this confounded rushing to the office every day—and clear out—clear out once and for all." And now to discover that he'd a valuable apple tree thrown in with the orchard—an apple tree that this Johnny from England positively envied!

Don't touch that tree! Do you hear me, children!" said he, bland and firm; and when the guest had gone, with quite another voice and manner:

"If I catch either of you touching those apples you shall not only go to bed—you shall each have a good sound whipping." Which merely added to its magnificence.

Every Sunday morning after church Father, with Bogey and me tailing after, walked through the flower garden, down the violet path, past the lace-bark tree, past the white rose and syringa bushes, and down the hill to the orchard. The apple tree seemed to have been miraculously warned of its high honor, standing apart from its fellows, bending a little under its rich clusters, fluttering its polished leaves, important and exquisite before Father's awful eye. His heart swelled to the sight—we knew his heart swelled. He put his hands behind his back and screwed up his eyes in the way he had. There it stood—the accidental thing —the thing that no one had been aware of when the hard bargain was driven. It hadn't been counted in, hadn't in a way been paid for. If the house had been burned to the ground at that time it would have meant less to him than the destruction of his tree. And how we played up to him, Bogey and I, —Bogey with his scratched knees pressed together, his hands behind his back, too, and a round cap on his head with "H.M.S. Thunderbolt" printed across it.

The apples turned from pale green to yellow; then they had deep pink stripes painted on them, and then the pink melted all over the yellow, reddened, and spread into a fine clear crimson.

At last the day came when Father took out of his waistcoat pocket a little pearl penknife. He reached up. Very slowly and very carefully he picked two apples growing on a bough.

"Why, they're warm," cried Father in amazement. "They're wonderful apples! Tiptop! Marvelous!" he echoed. He rolled them over in his hands.

"Look at that!" he said. "Not a spot —not a blemish!" And he walked through the orchard with Bogey and me stumbling after, to a tree stump under the wattles. We sat, one on either side of Father. He laid one apple down, opened the penknife and neatly and beautifully cut the other in half.

"Look at that!" he exclaimed.

"Father!" we cried, dutiful but really enthusiastic, too. For the lovely red color had bitten right through the white flesh of the apple; it was pink to the shiny black pips lying so justly in their scaly pods. It looked as though the apple had been dipped in wine.

"Never seen *that* before," said Father. "You won't find an apple like that in a hurry!" He put it to his nose and pronounced an unfamiliar word. "Bouquet.[3] What a bouquet!" And then he handed to Bogey one half, to me the other.

"Don't *bolt* it!" said he. It was agony to give even so much away. I knew it, while I took mine humbly and humbly Bogey took his.

Then he divided the second with the same neat beautiful little cut of the pearl knife.

I kept my eyes on Bogey. Together we took a bite. Our mouths were full of a floury stuff, a hard, faintly bitter skin—a horrible taste of something dry. . . .

"Well?" asked Father, very jovial. He

---

**3. bouquet** (bō kā') *n.*: Fragrance.

had cut his two halves into quarters and was taking out the little pods. "Well?"

Bogey and I stared at each other, chewing desperately. In that second of chewing and swallowing a long silent conversation passed between us—and a strange meaning smile. We swallowed. We edged near Father, just touching him.

"Perfect," we lied. "Perfect—Father! Simply lovely!"

But it was no use. Father spat his out and never went near the apple tree again.

**APPLE PLENTY, 1970**
*Herbert Shuptrine*
Private Collection. Courtesy New York Graphic Society

# THINKING ABOUT THE SELECTION
## Recalling

1. What does the guest tell Father about one of the apple trees?
2. How does Father treat the tree after the guest's revelation?
3. Describe the apples' appearance.
4. Explain how their taste does not live up to everyone's expectation.

## Interpreting

5. Point out some of the facts that cause the tree to take on so much value in the eyes of the children.
6. What did the two children communicate during their "long silent conversation" when they tasted the apples?
7. At the end of the story, why does Father spit out the apple and never go near the tree again?

## Applying

8. Explain how image and public opinion play a role in determining the worth of some of the things you value.

# ANALYZING LITERATURE
## Understanding Theme

The **theme** of a story is the general insight about life, revealed through the events. In "The Apple Tree," how do the characters in the story learn a significant lesson.

1. What standards does Father use in determining value at the opening of the story?
2. What standards do you think he may use in the future?
3. What lesson do he and his children learn?
4. How would you express the theme of this story?

# CRITICAL THINKING AND READING
## Interpreting Connotative Meaning

The **connotative meanings** of words are not found in a dictionary but reflect the associations or overtones that the words carry. For example, the word *pearl* usually connotes wealth and luster.

What are some of the associations brought to mind by the following words?

1. apple     2. orchard     3. plum

# UNDERSTANDING LANGUAGE
## Appreciating Allusions

**Allusions** are references to people, places, ideas, and events from history, literature, or the Bible. In "The Apple Tree," Mansfield makes an allusion to the Biblical story of Eve eating the fruit of the forbidden tree (Genesis 3–4).

1. Point out two references in "The Apple Tree" to the Biblical story.
2. How does "The Apple Tree" parallel the Biblical story?
3. How does knowing the Biblical story increase your appreciation of "The Apple Tree"?

# THINKING AND WRITING
## Writing a Summary

Write a summary of "The Apple Tree" to appear in *Short Story Digest* magazine. Keep the summary as brief as possible, but be sure to include the most important developments. End the summary with a statement of the story's theme. When you revise your summary, eliminate any unimportant details. Then proofread it and prepare a final draft.

# GUIDE FOR READING

## White Gardens

**Mark Helprin** (1947–    ) was born in New York City. He studied Middle Eastern culture at Harvard College and Renaissance history at Oxford University. He has published two novels, *Refiner's Fire* and *Winter's Tale*. His stories, many of which first appeared in *The New Yorker*, are collected in *A Dove of the East* and *Ellis Island*. Helprin's best stories, including "White Gardens," seem suspended in an almost magical realm, somewhere between reality and the imaginary.

### Symbol as a Key to Theme

The **theme** of a story is a general idea about life that the story conveys. Sometimes authors express the theme through **symbols** —objects, ideas, or actions that represent something other than themselves. Interpreting such symbols can help you identify the theme. In "White Gardens," for example, which contains several symbols, the "consuming firestorm" in which six firemen perish represents the suddenness with which life can end.

### Look For

As you read "White Gardens," look for objects and images to which the author calls your attention. They may be symbols that help you discover the theme.

### Writing

"White Gardens" involves a very moving moment during a ceremony. Think about a ritual, such as a wedding, graduation, or funeral, that marks a special moment. Freewrite about its meaning.

### Vocabulary

Knowing the following words will help you as you read "White Gardens."

**eulogy** (yōō′ lə jē) *n.*: A formal speech in praise of someone who has recently died (p. 223)
**billowing** (bil′ ō iŋ) *v.*: Surging, swelling (p. 223)

**temporal** (tem′ pər əl) *adj.*: Lasting only for a time, not eternal; worldly, not spiritual (p. 224)

# White Gardens

## Mark Helprin

It was August. In the middle of his eulogy the priest said, "Now they must leave us, to repose in white gardens," and then halted in confusion, for he had certainly meant green gardens. But he was not sure. No one in the overcrowded church knew what he meant by white gardens instead of green, but they felt that the mistake was in some way appropriate, and most of them would remember for the rest of their lives the moment afterward, when he had glanced at them in alarm and puzzlement.

The stone church in Brooklyn, on one of the long avenues stretching to the sea, was full of firefighters, the press, uncharacteristically quiet city politicians in tropical suits, and the wives and eighteen children of the six men who, in the blink of an eye, had dropped together through the collapsing roof of a burning building, deep into an all-consuming firestorm.

Everyone noticed that the wives of the firemen who had died looked exceptionally beautiful. The young women—with the golden hair of summer, in dark print dresses —several of whom carried flowers, and the older, more matronly women who were less restrained because they understood better what was to become of them, all had a frightening, elevated quality which seemed to rule the parishioners and silence the politicians.

The priest was tumbling over his own words, perhaps because he was young and too moved to be eloquent according to convention. He looked up after a long silence and said, simply, "repose of rivers . . ." They strained to understand, but couldn't, and forgave him immediately. His voice was breaking—not because so many were in the church, for in the raw shadow of the event itself, their numbers were unimpressive. It wasn't that the Mayor was in the crowd: the Mayor had become just a man, and no one felt the power of his office. It may have been the heat. The city had been under siege for a week. Key West humidity and rains had swept across Brooklyn, never-ending, trying to cover it with the sea. The sun was shining now, through a powerful white haze, and the heat inside the church was phenomenal and frightening, ninety-five degrees—like a boiler room. All the seasons have their mystery, and perhaps the mystery of summer is that it overwhelms with easy life, and makes one feel improperly immortal.

One of the wives glanced out a high window and saw white smoke billowing from a chimney. Even in this kind of weather, she thought, they have to turn on the furnaces to make hot water. The smoke rushed past the masonry as if the chimney were the stack of a ship. She had been to a fireman's funeral before, and she knew what it was going to be like when the flag-draped coffin was borne from the church and placed on the bed of a shiny new engine. Hundreds of uniformed men would snap to

attention, their blue hats aligning suddenly. Then the procession would flow away like a blue river, and she, the widow (for she was now the widow), would stagger into a waiting black car to follow after it.

She was one of the younger wives, one of those who were filled with restrained motion, one of the ones in a dark print dress with flowers. She was looking to the priest for direction, but he was coming apart, and as he did she could not keep out of her mind the million things she was thinking, the things which came to her for no reason, just the way the priest had said "white gardens," and "repose of rivers." She thought of the barges moving slowly up the Hudson in a tunnel of silver and white haze, and of the wind-polished bridges standing in the summer sun. She thought of the men in the church. She knew them. They were firefighters; they were rough, and they carried with them in the church more ambition, sadness, power, courage, greed, and anger than she cared to think about on this day. But despite their battalion's worth of liveliness and strength, they were drawn to the frail priest whose voice broke every now and then in the presence of the wives and the children and the six coffins.

She thought of Brooklyn, of its vastness, and of the things that were happening in Brooklyn, right then. Even as the men were buried, traffic on the streets and parkways would be thick as blood; a hundred million emotions would pass from soul to soul, into the air, into walls in dark hot rooms, into thin groves of trees in the parks. Even as the men were buried in an emerald field dazzling with row upon row of bone-white gravestones, there would be something of resurrection and life all over Brooklyn. But now it was still, and the priest was lost in a moment during which everyone was brought together, and the suited children and lovely wives learned that there are quiet times when the world is touched, and when that which is truly important arises to claim all allegiances.

"It is bitter," said the priest, finally in control of himself, "bitter that only through windows like these do we see clearly into past and future, that in such scenes we burn through our temporal concerns to see that everything that was, is; and that everything that is, will always be." She looked at him, bending her head slightly and pursing her lips in an expression of love and sadness, and he continued. "For we shall always have green gardens, and we shall always have white gardens, too."

Now they knew what he meant, and it shot like electricity through the six wives, the eighteen children, and the blue river of men.

## THINKING ABOUT THE SELECTION
### Recalling

1. On what occasion does the story take place?
2. What mistake does the priest make at the beginning of the story?
3. What does the young woman expect from the priest?
4. How does the priest end his eulogy?

### Interpreting

5. What do the woman's thoughts about Brooklyn during the eulogy suggest?
6. The participants in this ceremony "learned that there are quiet times when the world is touched, and when that which is truly important arises to claim all allegiances." What does this statement mean?
7. Why do you think the priest finds the moment especially "bitter"?
8. Do you think that, in the end, the priest is able to give the woman what she seeks?

### Applying

9. What words and ideas do you think are of most comfort to people who have just experienced a significant loss? Explain your answer.

## ANALYZING LITERATURE
### Recognizing Symbols

A **symbol** is an object, idea, or action that represents something other than itself. Helprin uses several symbols in "White Gardens." For example, the rivers mentioned in this story symbolize life, flowing on. Writers may use symbols to express important ideas, and, therefore, to reinforce the **theme,** or central idea, of a story. The gardens mentioned in this story are symbols that point to the theme.

1. What do green gardens symbolize?
2. What do white gardens symbolize?
3. What does the priest mean when he says, "For we shall always have green gardens, and we shall always have white gardens, too"?

## CRITICAL THINKING AND READING
### Recognizing Emotive Language

Sometimes authors use **emotive language** —words, phrases, and images intended to evoke a strong emotional response.

1. What emotions does the following passage arouse? "Even as the men were buried, traffic on the streets and parkways would be thick as blood; a hundred million emotions would pass from soul to soul, into the air, into walls in dark hot rooms, into thin groves of trees in the parks."
2. Find another example of emotive language and describe the feelings it evokes.

## UNDERSTANDING LANGUAGE
### Building Words from Latin Roots

Many English words have Latin **roots** from which other words can be built. For example, the English word *avenue* comes from the Latin word *venire,* which means "to come." The root *ven* appears in other English words, like *adventure.*

For each of the following words from "White Gardens," use a dictionary to find the Latin root, the meaning of the root, and the meaning of the English word. Then think of another English word that comes from the same root.

1. matronly
2. repose
3. despite
4. resurrection

## THINKING AND WRITING
### Writing About Symbols

Imagine that your class is constructing an exhibit entitled "Gardens, Rivers, and Fire as Symbols in Art and Literature." Write an introduction to the exhibit. First list the ideas, beliefs, and feelings each of these symbols often represents. Then use this information to draft an introduction to the exhibit. In it, explain why gardens, rivers, and fire make good symbols. Revise your introduction to use vivid language that clearly expresses the force of the symbols.

## The Hiltons' Holiday

**Sarah Orne Jewett** (1849–1909) was born and lived her entire life in South Berwick, Maine, where her father was a country doctor. This small coastal village, under the fictional name Deephaven, and the neighboring towns and farms provide the settings for many of her stories of rural New England. Jewett had her first literary success at age nineteen when the *Atlantic Monthly* magazine accepted one of her stories. "The Hiltons' Holiday" is a sympathic portrayal of the people of rural New England.

### Characters as a Key to Theme

The **theme** of a story is its central idea, or the insight into life the story presents through the characters and action. This insight may be about problems, conditions, or situations in human life. Often an author will use characters to point to the theme. An outstanding character trait, a character's view of life, or the relationship among characters may be a clue to the theme. The family in "The Hiltons' Holiday" is close-knit and hard-working, and its members want to do what is best for the others. The writer obviously is pointing out these qualities.

### Look For

What has value? As you read "The Hiltons' Holiday," look for the things that matter most to Mr. Hilton. What do these things suggest about a theme?

### Writing

The Hiltons of this story take a special trip. Think of a place you have visited that is special to you. Freewrite about the place, describing what aspects of it make it so appealing to you.

### Vocabulary

Knowing the following words will help you as you read "The Hiltons' Holiday."

**unkempt** (un kempt') *adj.*: Untidy; rough (p. 227)

**wistfully** (wist' fəl ē) *adv.*: Longingly (p. 228)

**plaintive** (plān' tiv) *adj.*: Mournful, sad (p. 229)

**incessant** (in ses' 'nt) *adj.*: Never ceasing (p. 229)

**ominously** (äm' ə nəs lē) *adv.*: Threateningly (p. 229)

**inevitable** (in ev' ə tə b'l) *adj.*: Certain to occur (p. 231)

**sedate** (si dāt') *adj.*: Quiet; composed; serious (p. 233)

**dowered** (dou' ərd) *v.*: Endowed (p. 238)

# The Hiltons' Holiday

## Sara Orne Jewett

### I

There was a bright, full moon in the clear sky, and the sunset was still shining faintly in the west. Dark woods stood all about the old Hilton farmhouse, save down the hill, westward, where lay the shadowy fields which John Hilton, and his father before him, had cleared and tilled with much toil,—the small fields to which they had given the industry and even affection of their honest lives.

John Hilton was sitting on the doorstep of his house. As he moved his head in and out of the shadows, turning now and then to speak to his wife, who sat just within the doorway, one could see his good face, rough and somewhat unkempt, as if he were indeed a creature of the shady woods and brown earth, instead of the noisy town. It was late in the long spring evening, and he had just come from the lower field as cheerful as a boy, proud of having finished the planting of his potatoes.

"I had to do my last row mostly by feelin'," he said to his wife. "I'm proper glad I pushed through, an' went back an' ended off after supper. 'Twould have taken me a good part o' tomorrow mornin', an' broke my day."

"'Tain't no use for ye to work yourself all to pieces, John," answered the woman quickly. "I declare it does seem harder than ever that we couldn't have kep' our boy; he'd been comin' fourteen years old this fall, most a grown man, and he'd work right 'longside of ye now the whole time."

"'Twas hard to lose him; I do seem to miss little John," said the father sadly. "I expect there was reasons why 'twas best. I feel able an' smart to work; my father was a girt[1] strong man, an' a monstrous worker afore me. 'Tain't that; but I was thinkin' by myself today what a sight o' company the boy would ha' been. You know, small's he was, how I could trust to leave him anywheres with the team, and how he'd beseech to go with me wherever I was goin'; always right in my tracks I used to tell 'em. Poor little John, for all he was so young he had a great deal o' judgment; he'd ha' made a likely man."

The mother sighed heavily as she sat within the shadow.

"But then there's the little girls, a sight o' help an' company," urged the father eagerly, as if it were wrong to dwell upon sorrow and loss. "Katy, she's most as good as a boy, except that she ain't very rugged. She's a real little farmer, she's helped me a sight this spring; an' you've got Susan Ellen, that makes a complete little housekeeper for ye as far as she's learnt. I don't see but we're better off than most folks, each on us having a workmate."

---

1. **girt:** Dialect expression meaning "great."

**SIMONE IN A WHITE BONNET,** *c.* **1903**
*Mary Cassatt*
Collection, Dale F. Dorn, San Antonio, Texas

"That's so, John," acknowledged Mrs. Hilton wistfully, beginning to rock steadily in her straight, splint-bottomed chair. It was always a good sign when she rocked.

"Where be the little girls so late?" asked their father. "'Tis gettin' long past eight o'clock. I don't know when we've all set up so late, but it's so kind o' summer-like an' pleasant. Why, where be they gone?"

"I've told ye; only over to Becker's folks," answered the mother. "I don't see myself what keeps 'em so late; they beseeched me after supper till I let 'em go. They're all in a dazzle with the new teacher; she asked 'em to come over. They say she's unusual smart with 'rethmetic, but she has a kind of a gorpen look to me. She's goin' to give Katy some pieces for her doll, but I told Katy she ought to be ashamed wantin' dolls' pieces, big as she's gettin' to be. I don't know's she ought, though; she ain't but nine this summer."

"Let her take her comfort," said the kind-hearted man. "Them things draws her to the teacher, an' makes them acquainted. Katy's shy with new folks, more so'n Susan Ellen, who's of the business kind. Katy's shy-feelin' and wishful."

"I don't know but she is," agreed the mother slowly. "Ain't it sing'lar how well acquainted you be with that one, an' I with Susan Ellen? 'Twas always so from the first. I'm doubtful sometimes our Katy ain't one that'll be like to get married—anyways not about here. She lives right with herself, but Susan Ellen ain't nothin' when she's alone, she's always after company; all the boys is waitin' on her a'ready. I ain't afraid but she'll take her pick when the time comes. I expect to see Susan Ellen well settled,—she feels grown up now,—but Katy don't care one mite 'bout none o' them things. She wants to be rovin' out o' doors. I do believe she'd stand an' hark to a bird the whole forenoon."

"Perhaps she'll grow up to be a teacher," suggested John Hilton. "She takes to her book more 'n the other one. I should like one on 'em to be a teacher same's my mother was. They're good girls as anybody's got."

"So they be," said the mother, with unusual gentleness, and the creak of her rocking chair was heard, regular as the ticking of a clock. The night breeze stirred in the great woods, and the sound of a brook that went falling down the hillside grew louder and louder. Now and then one could hear the plaintive chirp of a bird. The moon glittered with whiteness like a winter moon, and shone upon the low-roofed house until its small windowpanes gleamed like silver, and one could almost see the colors of a blooming bush of lilac that grew in a sheltered angle of the kitchen door. There was an incessant sound of frogs in the lowlands.

"Be you sound asleep, John?" asked the wife presently.

"I don't know but what I was a'most," said the tired man, starting a little. "I should laugh if I was to fall sound asleep right here on the step; 'tis the bright night, I expect, makes my eyes feel heavy, an' 'tis so peaceful. I was up an' dressed a little past four an' out to work. Well, well!" and he laughed sleepily and rubbed his eyes. "Where's the little girls? I'd better step along an' meet 'em."

"I wouldn't just yet; they'll get home all right, but 'tis late for 'em certain. I don't want 'em keepin' Mis' Becker's folks up neither. There, le's wait a few minutes," urged Mrs. Hilton.

"I've be'n a-thinkin' all day I'd like to give the child'n some kind of a treat," said the father, wide awake now. "I hurried up my work 'cause I had it so in mind. They don't have the opportunities some do, an' I want 'em to know the world, an' not stay right here on the farm like a couple o' bushes."

"They're a sight better off not to be so full o' notions as some is," protested the mother suspiciously.

"Certain," answered the farmer; "but they're good, bright child'n, an' commencin' to take a sight o' notice. I want 'em to have all we can give 'em. I want 'em to see how other folks does things."

"Why, so do I,"—here the rocking chair stopped ominously,—"but so long's they're contented"—

"Contented ain't all in this world; hopper-toads may have that quality an' spend all their time a-blinkin'. I don't know's bein' contented is all there is to look for in a child. Ambition's somethin' to me."

"Now you've got your mind on to some plot or other." (The rocking chair began to move again.) "Why can't you talk right out?"

"'Tain't nothin' special," answered the good man, a little ruffled; he was never prepared for his wife's mysterious powers of divination.[2] "Well there, you do find things out the master! I only thought perhaps I'd take 'em tomorrow, an' go off somewhere if 'twas a good day. I've been promisin' for a good while I'd take 'em to Topham Corners; they've never been there since they was very small."

"I believe you want a good time yourself. You ain't never got over bein' a boy." Mrs. Hilton seemed much amused. "There, go if you want to an' take 'em; they've got their summer hats an' new dresses. I don't know o' nothin' that stands in the way. I should sense it better if there was a circus or anythin' to go to. Why don't you wait an' let the girls pick 'em some strawberries or nice ros'berries, and then they could take an' sell 'em to the stores?"

John Hilton reflected deeply. "I should like to get me some good yellow-turnip seed to plant late. I ain't more 'n satisfied with what I've been gettin' o' late years o' Ira Speed. An' I'm goin' to provide me with a good hoe; mine's gettin' wore out an' all shackly.[3] I can't seem to fix it good."

"Them's excuses," observed Mrs. Hilton, with friendly tolerance. "You just cover

---

**2. divination** (div′ ə nā′ shən) *n.*: Guessing correctly.
**3. shackly** (shak′ lē) *adj.*: Dialect expression meaning "ramshackle," or falling apart.

up the hoe with somethin', if you get it—I would. Ira Speed's so jealous he'll remember it of you this twenty year, your goin' an' buyin' a new hoe o' anybody but him.''

"I've always thought 't was a free country," said John Hilton soberly. "I don't want to vex Ira neither; he favors us all he can in trade. 'Tis difficult for him to spare a cent, but he's as honest as daylight.''

At this moment there was a sudden sound of young voices, and a pair of young figures came out from the shadow of the woods into the moonlighted open space. An old cock crowed loudly from his perch in the shed, as if he were a herald of royalty. The little girls were hand in hand, and a brisk young dog capered about them as they came.

"Wa'n't it dark gittin' home through the woods this time o' night?'' asked the mother hastily, and not without reproach.

"I don't love to have you gone so late; mother an' me was timid about ye, and you've kep' Mis' Becker's folks up, I expect," said their father regretfully. "I don't want to have it said that my little girls ain't got good manners.''

"The teacher had a party," chirped Susan Ellen, the elder of the two children. "Goin' home from school she asked the Grover boys, an' Mary an' Sarah Speed. An' Mis' Becker was real pleasant to us: she passed round some cake, an' handed us sap sugar on one of her best plates, an' we played games an' sung some pieces too. Mis' Becker thought we did real well. I can pick out most of a tune on the cabinet organ; teacher says she'll give me lessons.''

"I want to know, dear!" exclaimed John Hilton.

"Yes, an' we played Copenhagen,[4] an'

---

**4. Copenhagen:** Game in which players join hands in a circle.

took sides spellin', an' Katy beat everybody spellin' there was there.''

Katy had not spoken; she was not so strong as her sister, and while Susan Ellen stood a step or two away addressing her eager little audience, Katy had seated herself close to her father on the doorstep. He put his arm around her shoulders, and drew her close to his side, where she stayed.

"Ain't you got nothin' to tell, daughter?'' he asked, looking down fondly; and Katy gave a pleased little sigh for answer.

"Tell 'em what 's goin' to be the last day o' school, and about our trimmin' the schoolhouse,'' she said; and Susan Ellen gave the program in most spirited fashion.

"'T will be a great time," said the mother, when she had finished. "I don't see why folks wants to go trapesin' off to strange places when such things is happenin' right about 'em." But the children did not observe her mysterious air. "Come, you must step yourselves right to bed!''

They all went into the dark, warm house; the bright moon shone upon it steadily all night, and the lilac flowers were shaken by no breath of wind until the early dawn.

## II

The Hiltons always waked early. So did their neighbors, the crows and song-sparrows and robins, the light-footed foxes and squirrels in the woods. When John Hilton waked, before five o'clock, an hour later than usual because he had sat up so late, he opened the house door and came out into the yard, crossing the short green turf hurriedly as if the day were too far spent for any loitering. The magnitude of the plan for taking a whole day of pleasure confronted him seriously, but the weather was fair, and his wife, whose disapproval could not have been set aside, had accepted and even smiled upon the great project. It was inevitable now, that he and the children should go to Topham Corners. Mrs. Hilton had the pleasure of waking them, and telling the news.

In a few minutes they came frisking out to talk over the great plans. The cattle were already fed, and their father was milking. The only sign of high festivity was the wagon pulled out into the yard, with both seats put in as if it were Sunday; but Mr. Hilton still wore his everyday clothes, and Susan Ellen suffered instantly from disappointment.

"Ain't we goin', father?" she asked complainingly; but he nodded and smiled at her, even though the cow, impatient to get to pasture, kept whisking her rough tail across his face. He held his head down and spoke cheerfully, in spite of this vexation.

"Yes, sister, we 're goin' certain', an' goin' to have a great time too." Susan Ellen thought that he seemed like a boy at that delightful moment, and felt new sympathy and pleasure at once. "You go an' help mother about breakfast an' them things; we want to get off quick 's we can. You coax mother now, both on ye, an' see if she won't go with us."

"She said she wouldn't be hired to," responded Susan Ellen. "She says it's goin' to be hot, an' she's laid out to go over an' see how her aunt Tamsen Brooks is this afternoon."

The father gave a little sigh; then he took heart again. The truth was that his wife made light of the contemplated pleasure, and, much as he usually valued her companionship and approval, he was sure that they should have a better time without her. It was impossible, however, not to feel guilty of disloyalty at the thought. Even though she might be completely unconscious of his best ideals, he only loved her and the ideals the more, and bent his energies to satisfying her indefinite expectations. His wife still kept much of that youthful beauty which Susan Ellen seemed likely to reproduce.

An hour later the best wagon was ready, and the great expedition set forth. The little dog sat apart, and barked as if it fell entirely upon him to voice the general excitement. Both seats were in the wagon, but the empty place testified to Mrs. Hilton's unyielding disposition. She had wondered why one broad seat would not do, but John Hilton meekly suggested that the wagon looked better with both. The little girls sat on the back seat dressed alike in their Sunday hats of straw with blue ribbons, and their little plaid shawls pinned neatly about their small shoulders. They wore gray thread gloves, and sat very straight. Susan Ellen was half a head the taller, but otherwise, from behind, they looked much alike. As for their father, he was in his Sunday best,—a plain black coat, and a winter hat of felt, which was heavy and rusty-looking for that warm early summer day. He had it in mind to buy a new straw hat at Topham, so that this with the turnip seed and the hoe made three important reasons for going.

"Remember an' lay off your shawls when you get there, an' carry them over your arms," said the mother, clucking like an excited hen to her chickens. "They'll do to keep the dust off your new dresses goin' an' comin'. An' when you eat your dinners don't get spots on you, an' don't point at folks as you ride by, an' stare, or they'll know you come from the country. An' John, you call into Cousin Ad'line Marlow's an' see how they all be, an' tell her I expect her over certain to stop awhile before hayin'. It always eases her phthisic[5] to git up here on the highland, an' I've got a new notion about doin' over her best-room carpet sence I see her that'll save rippin' one breadth. An' don't come home all wore out; an', John, don't you go an' buy me no kickshaws[6] to fetch home. I ain't a child, an' you ain't got no money to waste. I expect you'll go, like's not, an' buy you some kind of a foolish boy's hat; do look an' see if it's reasonable good straw, an' won't splinter all off round the edge. An' you mind, John''—

"Yes, yes, hold on!" cried John impatiently; then he cast a last affectionate, reassuring look at her face, flushed with the hurry and responsibility of starting them off in proper shape. "I wish you was goin' too," he said, smiling. "I do so!" Then the old horse started, and they went out at the bars, and began the careful long descent of the hill. The young dog, tethered to the lilac bush, was frantic with piteous appeals; the little girls piped their eager goodbys again and again, and their father turned many times to look back and wave his hand. As for their mother, she stood alone and watched them out of sight.

There was one place far out on the high road where she could catch a last glimpse of the wagon, and she waited what seemed a very long time until it appeared and then was lost to sight again behind a low hill. "They're nothin' but a pack o' child'n together," she said aloud; and then felt lonelier than she expected. She even stooped and patted the unresigned little dog as she passed him, going into the house.

The occasion was so much more important than any one had foreseen that both the little girls were speechless. It seemed at first like going to church in new clothes, or to a funeral; they hardly knew how to behave at the beginning of a whole day of pleasure. They made grave bows at such persons of their acquaintance as happened to be straying in the road. Once or twice they stopped before a farmhouse, while their father talked an inconsiderately long time with someone about the crops and the weather, and even dwelt upon town business and the doings of the selectmen,[7] which might be talked of at any time. The explanations that he gave of their excursion[8] seemed quite unnecessary. It was made entirely clear that he had a little business to do at Topham Corners, and thought he had better give the little girls a ride; they had been very steady at school, and he had finished planting, and could take the day as well as not. Soon, however, they all felt as if such an excursion were an everyday affair, and Susan Ellen began to ask eager questions, while Katy silently sat apart enjoying herself as she never had done before. She liked to see the strange houses, and the children who belonged to them; it was delightful to find flowers that she knew growing all along the road, no matter how far she went from home. Each small homestead looked its best and pleasantest, and shared the exquisite beauty that early summer made,—shared the luxury of greenness and floweriness that decked the rural world. There was an early peony or a late lilac in almost every dooryard.

It was seventeen miles to Topham. After a while they seemed very far from home, having left the hills far behind, and descended to a great level country with fewer tracts of woodland, and wider fields where the crops were much more forward. The

---

**5. phthisic** (tiz′ ik) *n.*: Asthma.
**6. kickshaws:** Trinkets or trifles.

**7. selectmen** (sə lekt′ mən) *n.*: Board of officials who manage local affairs in many New England towns.
**8. excursion** (ik skʉr′ zhən) *n.*: A short trip.

houses were all painted, and the roads were smoother and wider. It had been so pleasant driving along that Katy dreaded going into the strange town when she first caught sight of it, though Susan Ellen kept asking with bold fretfulness if they were not almost there. They counted the steeples of four churches, and their father presently showed them the Topham Academy, where their grandmother once went to school, and told them that perhaps some day they would go there too. Katy's heart gave a strange leap; it was such a tremendous thing to think of, but instantly the suggestion was transformed for her into one of the certainties of life. She looked with solemn awe at the tall belfry, and the long rows of windows in the front of the academy, there where it stood high and white among the clustering trees. She hoped that they were going to drive by, but something forbade her taking the responsibility of saying so.

Soon the children found themselves among the crowded village houses. Their father turned to look at them with affectionate solicitude.[9]

"Now sit up straight and appear pretty," he whispered to them. "We 're among the best people now, an' I want folks to think well of you."

"I guess we're as good as they be," remarked Susan Ellen, looking at some innocent passers-by with dark suspicion, but Katy tried indeed to sit straight, and folded her hands prettily in her lap, and wished with all her heart to be pleasing for her father's sake. Just then an elderly woman saw the wagon and the sedate party it carried, and smiled so kindly that it seemed to Katy as if Topham Corners had welcomed and received them. She smiled back again as if this hospitable person were an old

friend, and entirely forgot that the eyes of all Topham had been upon her.

"There, now we're coming to an elegant house that I want you to see; you'll never forget it," said John Hilton. "It's where Judge Masterson lives, the great lawyer; the handsomest house in the county, everybody says."

"Do you know him, father?" asked Susan Ellen.

"I do," answered John Hilton proudly. "Him and my mother went to school together in their young days, and were always called the two best scholars of their time. The judge called to see her once; he stopped to our house to see her when I was a boy. An' then, some years ago—you've heard me tell how I was on the jury, an' when he heard my name spoken he looked at me sharp, and asked if I wa'n't the son of Catharine Winn, an' spoke most beautiful of your grandmother, an' how well he remembered their young days together."

"I like to hear about that," said Katy.

"She had it pretty hard, I'm afraid, up on the old farm. She was keepin' school in our district when father married her—that's the main reason I backed 'em down when they wanted to tear the old schoolhouse all to pieces," confided John Hilton, turning eagerly. "They all say she lived longer up here on the hill than she could anywhere, but she never had her health. I wa'n't but a boy when she died. Father an' me lived alone afterward till the time your mother come; 'twas a good while, too; I wa'n't married so young as some. 'Twas lonesome, I tell you; father was plumb discouraged losin' of his wife, an' her long sickness an' all set him back, an' we 'd work all day on the land an' never say a word. I s'pose 'tis bein' so lonesome early in life that makes me so pleased to have some nice girls growin' up round me now."

---

9. **solicitude** (sə lis′ ə tōod′), *n.*: Caring or concern.

**BENNINGTON**
*Grandma Moses*
Copyright ©1988, Grandma Moses Properties Co., NY
The Bennington Museum, Bennington, Vermont

There was a tone in her father's voice that drew Katy's heart toward him with new affection. She dimly understood, but Susan Ellen was less interested. They had often heard this story before, but to one child it was always new and to the other old. Susan Ellen was apt to think it tiresome to hear about her grandmother, who, being dead, was hardly worth talking about.

"There's Judge Masterson's place," said their father in an everyday manner, as they turned a corner, and came into full view of the beautiful old white house standing be-hind its green trees and terraces and lawns. The children had never imagined anything so stately and fine, and even Susan Ellen exclaimed with pleasure. At that moment they saw an old gentleman, who carried himself with great dignity, coming slowly down the wide box-bordered path toward the gate.

"There he is now, there's the judge!" whispered John Hilton excitedly, reining his horse quickly to the green roadside. "He's goin' downtown to his office; we can wait right here an' see him. I can't expect

---

*Anna Mary Robertson Moses (1860–1961) began painting in old age and became known as "Grandma" Moses. She painted country landscapes and scenes remembered from her childhood.

him to remember me; it's been a good many years. Now you are goin' to see the great Judge Masterson!"

There was a quiver of expectation in their hearts. The judge stopped at his gate, hesitating a moment before he lifted the latch, and glanced up the street at the country wagon with its two prim little girls on the back seat, and the eager man who drove. They seemed to be waiting for something; the old horse was nibbling at the fresh roadside grass. The judge was used to being looked at with interest, and responded now with a smile as he came out to the sidewalk, and unexpectedly turned their way. Then he suddenly lifted his hat with grave politeness, and came directly toward them.

"Good morning, Mr. Hilton," he said. "I am very glad to see you, sir," and Mr. Hilton, the little girls' own father, took off his hat with equal courtesy, and bent forward to shake hands.

Susan Ellen cowered and wished herself away, but little Katy sat straighter than ever, with joy in her father's pride and pleasure shining in her pale, flower-like little face.

"These are your daughters, I am sure," said the old gentleman kindly, taking Susan Ellen's limp and reluctant hand; but when he looked at Katy, his face brightened. "How she recalls your mother!" he said with great feeling. "I am glad to see this dear child. You must come to see me with your father, my dear," he added, still looking at her. "Bring both the little girls, and let them run about the old garden; the cherries are just getting ripe," said Judge Masterson hospitably. "Perhaps you will have time to stop this afternoon as you go home?"

"I should call it a great pleasure if you would come and see us again some time. You may be driving our way, sir," said John Hilton.

"Not very often in these days," answered the old judge. "I thank you for the kind invitation. I should like to see the fine view again from your hill westward. Can I serve you in any way while you are in town? Goodby, my little friends!"

Then they parted, but not before Katy, the shy Katy, whose hand the judge still held unconsciously while he spoke, had reached forward as he said goodby, and lifted her face to kiss him. She could not have told why, except that she felt drawn to something in the serious, worn face. For the first time in her life the child had felt the charm of manners; perhaps she owned a kinship[10] between that which made him what he was, and the spark of nobleness and purity in her own simple soul. She turned again and again to look back at him as they drove away.

"Now you have seen one of the first gentlemen in the country," said their father. "It was worth comin' twice as far"—but he did not say any more, nor turn as usual to look in the children's faces.

In the chief business street of Topham a great many country wagons like the Hiltons' were fastened to the posts, and there seemed to our holiday-makers to be a great deal of noise and excitement.

"Now I've got to do my errands, and we can let the horse rest and feed," said John Hilton. "I'll slip his headstall[11] right off, an' put on his halter. I'm goin' to buy him a real good treat o' oats. First we'll go an' buy me my straw hat; I feel as if this one looked a little past to wear in Topham. We'll buy the things we want, an' then we'll walk all along the street, so you can look in the win-

---

**10. kinship:** Relationship or close connection.
**11. headstall** (hed′ stôl′) *n.*: The part of a bridle that fits over a horse's head.

dows an' see the han'some things, same's your mother likes to. What was it mother told you about your shawls?''

"To take 'em off an' carry 'em over our arms,'' piped Susan Ellen, without comment, but in the interest of alighting and finding themselves afoot upon the pavement the shawls were forgotten. The children stood at the doorway of a shop while their father went inside, and they tried to see what the Topham shapes of bonnets were like, as their mother had advised them; but everything was exciting and confusing, and they could arrive at no decision. When Mr. Hilton came out with a hat in his hand to be seen in a better light, Katy whispered that she wished he would buy a shiny one like Judge Masterson's; but her father only smiled and shook his head, and said that they were plain folks, he and Katy. There were dry goods for sale in the same shop, and a young clerk who was measuring linen kindly pulled off some pretty labels with gilded edges and gay pictures, and gave them to the little girls, to their exceeding joy. He may have had small sisters at home, this friendly lad, for he took pains to find two pretty blue boxes besides, and was rewarded by their beaming gratitude.

It was a famous day; they even became used to seeing so many people pass. The village was full of its morning activity, and Susan Ellen gained a new respect for her father, and an increased sense of her own consequence, because even in Topham several persons knew him and called him familiarly by name. The meeting with an old man who had once been a neighbor seemed to give Mr. Hilton the greatest pleasure. The old man called to them from a house doorway as they were passing, and they all went in. The children seated themselves wearily on the wooden step, but their father shook his old friend eagerly by the hand, and declared that he was delighted to see him so well and enjoying the fine weather.

"Oh, yes,'' said the old man, in a feeble, quavering voice, "I'm astonishin' well for my age. I don't complain, John, I don't complain.''

They talked long together of people whom they had known in the past, and Katy, being a little tired, was glad to rest, and sat still with her hands folded, looking about the front yard. There was some kinds of flowers that she never had seen before.

"This is the one that looks like my mother,'' her father said, and touched Katy's shoulder to remind her to stand up and let herself be seen. "Judge Masterson saw the resemblance; we met him at his gate this morning.''

"Yes, she certain does look like your mother, John,'' said the old man, looking pleasantly at Katy, who found that she liked him better than at first. "She does, certain; the best of young folks is, they remind us of the old ones. 'Tis nateral to cling to life, folks say, but for me, I git impatient at times. Most everybody's gone now, an' I want to be goin'. 'Tis somethin' before me, an' I want to have it over with. I want to be there 'long o' the rest o' the folks. I expect to last quite a while though; I may see ye couple o' times more, John.''

John Hilton responded cheerfully, and the children were urged to pick some flowers. The old man awed them with his impatience to be gone. There was such a townful of people about him, and he seemed as lonely as if he were the last survivor of a former world. Until that moment they had felt as if everything were just beginning.

"Now I want to buy somethin' pretty for your mother,'' said Mr. Hilton, as they went soberly away down the street, the children keeping fast hold of his hands. "By now the old horse will have eat his dinner and had a good rest, so pretty soon we can jog along home. I'm goin' to take you round by the academy, and the old North Meetinghouse where Dr. Barstow used to preach. Can't you think o' somethin' that your mother'd want?" he asked suddenly, confronted by a difficulty of choice.

"She was talkin' about wantin' a new pepper box, one day; the top o' the old one won't stay on," suggested Susan Ellen, with delightful readiness. "Can't we have some candy, father?"

"Yes, ma'am," said John Hilton, smiling and swinging her hand to and fro as they walked. "I feel as if some would be good myself. What's all this?" They were passing a photographer's doorway with its enticing array of portraits. "I do declare!" he exclaimed excitedly, "I'm goin' to have our pictures taken; 'twill please your mother more 'n a little."

This was, perhaps, the greatest triumph of the day, except the delightful meeting with the judge; they sat in a row, with the father in the middle, and there was no doubt as to the excellence of the likeness. The best hats had to be taken off because they cast a shadow, but they were not missed, as their

**HENRY LOOK UNHITCHING**
*Thomas Hart Benton*
*Indianapolis Museum of Art*

owners had feared. Both Susan Ellen and Katy looked their brightest and best; their eager young faces would forever shine there; the joy of the holiday was mirrored in the little picture. They did not know why their father was so pleased with it; they would not know until age had dowered them with the riches of association and remembrance.

Just at nightfall the Hiltons reached home again, tired out and happy. Katy had climbed over into the front seat beside her father, because that was always her place when they went to church on Sundays. It was a cool evening, there was a fresh sea wind that brought a light mist with it, and the sky was fast growing cloudy. Somehow the children looked different; it seemed to their mother as if they had grown older and taller since they went away in the morning, and as if they belonged to the town now as much as to the country. The greatness of their day's experience had left her far behind; the day had been silent and lonely without them, and she had had their supper ready, and been watching anxiously, ever since five o'clock. As for the children themselves they had little to say at first—they had eaten their luncheon early on the way to Topham. Susan Ellen was childishly cross, but Katy was pathetic and wan. They could hardly wait to show the picture, and their mother was as much pleased as everybody had expected.

"There, what did make you wear your shawls?" she exclaimed a moment afterward, reproachfully. "You ain't been an' wore 'em all day long? I wanted folks to see how pretty your new dresses was, if I did make 'em. Well, well! I wish more 'n ever now I'd gone an' seen to ye!"

"An' here's the pepper box!" said Katy, in a pleased, unconscious tone.

"That really is what I call beautiful," said Mrs. Hilton, after a long and doubtful look. "Our other one was only tin. I never did look so high as a chiny[12] one with flowers, but I can get us another any time for every day. That's a proper hat, as good as you could have got, John. Where's your new hoe?" she asked as he came toward her from the barn, smiling with satisfaction.

"I declare to Moses if I didn't forget all about it," meekly acknowledged the leader of the great excursion. "That an' my yellow turnip seed, too; they went clean out o' my head, there was so many other things to think of. But 'tain't no sort o' matter; I can get a hoe just as well to Ira Speed's."

His wife could not help laughing. "You an' the girls have had a great time. They was full o' wonder to me about everything, and I expect they'll talk about it for a week. I guess we was right about havin' 'em' see somethin' more o' the world."

"Yes," answered John Hilton, with humility, "yes, we did have a beautiful day. I didn't expect so much. They looked as nice as anybody, and appeared so modest an' pretty. The little girls will remember it perhaps by an' by. I guess they won't never forget this day they had 'long 'o father."

It was evening again, the frogs were piping in the lower meadows, and in the woods, higher up the great hill, a little owl began to hoot. The sea air, salt and heavy, was blowing in over the country at the end of the hot, bright day. A lamp was lighted in the house, the happy children were talking together, and supper was waiting. The father and mother lingered for a moment outside and looked down over the shadowy fields; then they went in, without speaking. The great day was over, and they shut the door.

---

**12. chiny** (chī′ nē) *adj.*: China.

## THINKING ABOUT THE SELECTION

### Recalling

1. What reason does John Hilton give for wanting to take his daughters on a holiday?
2. What are the highlights of the holiday?
3. What does John bring home to his wife?

### Interpreting

4. Describe the relationship between Mr. and Mrs. Hilton.
5. John Hilton's mother is an important figure in his life. Cite two references in the story that indicate his feelings for her.
6. What do the girls learn on their holiday?
7. In what way does the day fulfill John's hopes for it?
8. When the family arrives home, it seems to Mrs. Hilton that the children "had grown older and taller since they went away in the morning." Explain how their holiday might seem to have such an effect on them.

### Applying

9. Mr. Hilton values his family background. Why do you think many people are interested in learning about their ancestors' lives and in saving family momentos?

## ANALYZING LITERATURE

### Understanding Theme

The **theme** of a story is its central idea or the insight into life that it presents beyond the specific circumstances in which the characters find themselves. The characters the author creates can help you understand the theme of a story.

1. What particular people and places does John point out to his daughters? Why does he point out these people and places?
2. Why is the photograph particularly important to John?
3. Using your answers, form a statement of the theme of this story.

## CRITICAL THINKING AND READING

### Comparing and Contrasting Characters

When you **compare** characters, you point out the similarities between them. When you **contrast** characters, you point out the differences between them.

1. Compare and contrast Mr. and Mrs. Hilton.
2. Compare and contrast Katy and Susan Ellen, showing how each reflects one of their parents.

## UNDERSTANDING LANGUAGE

### Appreciating Dialect

**Dialect** is the regional speech pattern of a particular group of people. The dialogue in "The Hiltons' Holiday" shows the dialect of northern New England. For example, John says "afore me" and "mornin'" instead of "before me" and "morning."

Rewrite the following sentences from the story in standard English.

1. "I'm proper glad I pushed through, an' went back an' ended off after supper."
2. "'Tain't that; but I was thinkin' by myself today what a sight o' company the boy would ha' been."
3. "They're all in a dazzle with the new teacher."

## THINKING AND WRITING

### Writing About Character and Theme

Imagine that you are Judge Masterson. Write a journal entry for the day "The Hiltons' Holiday" takes place. Begin your entry, "I ran into John Hilton today. I think his mother would be pleased if she could see him now." Go on to describe what John is like, what he expects of himself, and what he wants for his children. End by telling *why* John's mother would be pleased. Revise the entry, adding two quotations about John that accurately portray John's character. Share your entry with your classmates.

## Old Pipes and the Dryad

**Frank R. Stockton** (1834–1902) worked as a wood engraver and as a journalist on newspapers in Philadelphia, where he was born, and in New York. His earliest literary works were children's stories. In addition to writing, Stockton served on the editorial staffs of *Scribner's* and *St. Nicholas* magazines. Stockton's stories are full of comic invention. In the fairy tale "Old Pipes and the Dryad," he allows a dryad from Greek mythology to cross paths with a dwarf from Western European folklore.

**Key Statements as a Clue to Theme**

The **theme** of a story is the central idea or insight about life that the story reveals. Often an author will include key statements that point to the theme. **Key statements** are those that make points that go beyond the events of the story. Identifying and understanding these key statements can lead you to a story's theme.

**Look For**

As you read "Old Pipes and the Dryad," look for statements that have meaning beyond the story. Use these key statements to help you understand the story's theme.

**Writing**

Old Pipes, a character in this story, receives a reward for helping someone in distress. Think of a time when you or someone you know helped somebody else and saw immediate results of the kindness. Freewrite about this experience.

**Vocabulary**

Knowing the following words will help you as you read "Old Pipes and the Dryad."

**traverse** (tra vʉrs') *v.*: Travel over, across, or through (p. 241)

**doleful** (dōl' fəl) *adj.*: Full of sadness (p. 244)

**rueful** (roo' fəl) *adj.*: Causing sorrow or pity (p. 244)

**hale** (hāl) *adj.*: Vigorous; healthy (p. 245)

**avenge** (ə venj') *v.*: To get revenge for an injury (p. 248)

**decrepit** (di krep' it) *adj.*: Worn out by old age (p. 249)

**vile** (vīl) *adj.*: Evil; wicked (p. 250)

**perceived** (pər sēvd') *v.*: Became aware of (p. 250)

# Old Pipes and the Dryad[1]

## Frank R. Stockton

A mountain brook ran through a little village. Over the brook there was a narrow bridge, and from the bridge a footpath led out from the village and up the hillside, to the cottage of Old Pipes and his mother. For many, many years, Old Pipes had been employed by the villagers to pipe the cattle down from the hills. Every afternoon, an hour before sunset, he would sit on a rock in front of his cottage and play on his pipes. Then all the flocks and herds that were grazing on the mountains would hear him, wherever they might happen to be, and would come down to the village—the cows by the easiest paths, the sheep by those not quite so easy, and the goats by the steep and rocky ways that were hardest of all.

But now, for a year or more, Old Pipes had not piped the cattle home. It is true that every afternoon he sat upon the rock and played upon his familiar instrument; but the cattle did not hear him. He had grown old, and his breath was feeble. The echoes of his cheerful notes, which used to come from the rocky hill on the other side of the valley, were heard no more; and twenty yards from Old Pipes one could scarcely tell what tune he was playing. He had become somewhat deaf, and did not know that the sound of his pipes was so thin and weak, and that the

cattle did not hear him. The cows, the sheep, and the goats came down every afternoon as before, but this was because two boys and a girl were sent up after them. The villagers did not wish the good old man to know that his piping was no longer of any use, so they paid him his little salary every month, and said nothing about the two boys and the girl.

Old Pipe's mother was, of course, a great deal older than he was, and was as deaf as a gate,—posts, latch, hinges, and all,—and she never knew that the sound of her son's pipe did not spread over all the mountainside, and echo back strong and clear from the opposite hills. She was very fond of Old Pipes, and proud of his piping; and as he was so much younger than she was, she never thought of him as being very old. She cooked for him, and made his bed, and mended his clothes; and they lived very comfortably on his little salary.

One afternoon, at the end of the month, when Old Pipes had finished his piping, he took his stout staff and went down the hill to the village to receive the money for his month's work. The path seemed a great deal steeper and more difficult than it used to be; and Old Pipes thought that it must have been washed by the rains and greatly damaged. He remembered it as a path that was quite easy to traverse either up or down. But Old Pipes had been a very active man, and as his mother was so much older than he

---

1. **Dryad** (drī′ əd) *n.*: A nature goddess who lives in a tree.

**ETRUSCAN FLUTE PLAYER**
*Fresco, Tomb of the Leopards*
Scala/Art Resource

was, he never thought of himself as aged and infirm.

When the Chief Villager had paid him, and he had talked a little with some of his friends, Old Pipes started to go home. But when he had crossed the bridge over the brook, and gone a short distance up the hillside, he became very tired, and sat down upon a stone. He had not been sitting there half a minute, when along came two boys and a girl.

"Children," said Old Pipes, "I'm very tired tonight, and I don't believe I can climb up this steep path to my home. I think I shall have to ask you to help me."

"We will do that," said the boys and the

girl, quite cheerfully; and one boy took him by the right hand, and the other by the left, while the girl pushed him in the back. In this way he went up the hill quite easily, and soon reached his cottage door. Old Pipes gave each of the three children a copper coin, and then they sat down for a few minutes' rest before starting back to the village.

"I'm sorry that I tired you so much," said Old Pipes.

"Oh, that would not have tired us," said one of the boys, "if we had not been so far today after the cows, the sheep, and the goats. They rambled high up on the mountain, and we never before had such a time in finding them."

"Had to go after the cows, the sheep, and the goats!" exclaimed Old Pipes. "What do you mean by that?"

The girl, who stood behind the old man, shook her head, put her hands on her mouth, and made all sorts of signs to the boy to stop talking on this subject; but he did not notice her, and promptly answered Old Pipes.

"Why, you see, good sir," said he, "that as the cattle can't hear your pipes now, somebody has to go after them every evening to drive them down from the mountain, and the Chief Villager has hired us three to do it. Generally it is not very hard work, but tonight the cattle had wandered far."

"How long have you been doing this?" asked the old man.

The girl shook her head and clapped her hand on her mouth more vigorously than before, but the boy went on.

"I think it is about a year now," he said, "since the people first felt sure that the cattle could not hear your pipes; and from that time we've been driving them down. But we are rested now and will go home. Good night, sir."

The three children then went down the hill, the girl scolding the boy all the way home. Old Pipes stood silent a few moments, and then he went into his cottage.

"Mother," he shouted; "did you hear what those children said?"

"Children!" exclaimed the old woman; "I did not hear them. I did not know there were any children here."

Then Old Pipes told his mother, shouting very loudly to make her hear, how the two boys and the girl had helped him up the hill, and what he had heard about his piping and the cattle.

"They can't hear you?" cried his mother. "Why, what's the matter with the cattle?"

"Ah, me!" said Old Pipes; "I don't believe there's anything the matter with the cattle. It must be with me and my pipes that there is something the matter. But one thing is certain, if I do not earn the wages the Chief Villager pays me, I shall not take them. I shall go straight down to the village and give back the money I received today."

"Nonsense!" cried his mother. "I'm sure you've piped as well as you could, and no more can be expected. And what are we to do without the money?"

"I don't know," said Old Pipes; "but I'm going down to the village to pay it back."

The sun had now set; but the moon was shining very brightly on the hillside, and Old Pipes could see his way very well. He did not take the same path by which he had gone before, but followed another, which led among the trees upon the hillside, and, though longer, was not so steep.

When he had gone about halfway, the old man sat down to rest, leaning his back against a great oak tree. As he did so, he heard a sound like knocking inside the tree, and then a voice distinctly said:

"Let me out! let me out!"

Old Pipes instantly forgot that he was tired, and sprang to his feet. "This must be a

Dryad tree!'' he exclaimed. ''If it is, I'll let her out.''

Old Pipes had never, to his knowledge, seen a Dryad tree, but he knew there were such trees on the hillsides and the mountains, and that Dryads lived in them. He knew, too, that in the summertime, on those days when the moon rose before the sun went down, a Dryad could come out of her tree if anyone could find the key which locked her in, and turn it. Old Pipes closely examined the trunk of the tree, which stood in the full moonlight. ''If I see that key,'' he said, ''I shall surely turn it.'' Before long he perceived a piece of bark standing out from the tree, which appeared to him very much like the handle of a key. He took hold of it, and found he could turn it quite around. As he did so, a large part of the side of the tree was pushed open, and a beautiful Dryad stepped quickly out.

For a moment she stood motionless, gazing on the scene before her,—the tranquil valley, the hills, the forest, and the mountainside, all lying in the soft clear light of the moon. ''Oh, lovely! lovely!'' she exclaimed. ''How long it is since I have seen anything like this!'' And then, turning to Old Pipes, she said: ''How good of you to let me out! I am so happy and so thankful, that I must kiss you, you dear old man!'' And she threw her arms around the neck of Old Pipes and kissed him on both cheeks. ''You don't know,'' she then went on to say, ''how doleful it is to be shut up so long in a tree. I don't mind it in the winter, for then I am glad to be sheltered, but in summer it is a rueful thing not to be able to see all the beauties of the world. And it's ever so long since I've been let out. People so seldom come this way; and when they do come at the right time they either don't hear me, or they are frightened, and run away. But you, you dear old man, you were not frightened, and you looked and looked for the key, and you let me out, and

now I shall not have to go back till winter has come, and the air grows cold. Oh, it is glorious! What can I do for you, to show you how grateful I am?''

''I am very glad,'' said Old Pipes, ''that I let you out, since I see that it makes you so happy; but I must admit that I tried to find the key because I had a great desire to see a Dryad. But if you wish to do something for me, you can, if you happen to be going down toward the village.''

''To the village!'' exclaimed the Dryad. ''I will go anywhere for you, my kind old benefactor.''

''Well, then,'' said Old Pipes, ''I wish you would take this little bag of money to the Chief Villager and tell him that Old Pipes cannot receive pay for the services which he does not perform. It is now more than a year that I have not been able to make the cattle hear me, when I piped to call them home. I did not know this until tonight; but now that I know it, I cannot keep the money, and so I send it back.'' And, handing the little bag to the Dryad, he bade her good night, and turned toward his cottage.

''Good night,'' said the Dryad. ''And I thank you over and over and over again, you good old man!''

Old Pipes walked toward his home, very glad to be saved the fatigue of going all the way down to the village and back again. ''To be sure,'' he said to himself, ''this path does not seem at all steep, and I can walk along it very easily; but it would have tired me dreadfully to come up all the way from the village, especially as I could not have expected those children to help me again.'' When he reached home, his mother was surprised to see him returning so soon.

''What!'' she exclaimed; ''have you already come back? What did the Chief Villager say? Did he take the money?''

Old Pipes was just about to tell her that he had sent the money to the village by a

Dryad, when he suddenly reflected that his mother would be sure to disapprove such a proceeding, and so he merely said he had sent it by a person whom he had met.

"And how do you know that the person will ever take it to the Chief Villager?" cried his mother. "You will lose it, and the villagers will never get it. Oh, Pipes! Pipes! when will you be old enough to have ordinary common sense?"

Old Pipes considered that as he was already seventy years of age he could scarcely expect to grow any wiser, but he made no remark on this subject; and, saying that he doubted not that the money would go safely to its destination, he sat down to his supper. His mother scolded him roundly, but he did not mind it; and after supper he went out and sat on a rustic chair in front of the cottage to look at the moonlit village, and to wonder whether or not the Chief Villager really received the money. While he was doing these two things, he went fast asleep.

When Old Pipes left the Dryad, she did not go down to the village with the little bag of money. She held it in her hand, and thought about what she had heard. "This is a good and honest old man," she said; "and it is a shame that he should lose this money. He looked as if he needed it, and I don't believe the people in the village will take it from one who has served them so long. Often, when in my tree, have I heard the sweet notes of his pipes. I am going to take the money back to him." She did not start immediately, because there were so many beautiful things to look at; but after a while she went up to the cottage, and, finding Old Pipes asleep in his chair, she slipped the little bag into his coat pocket, and silently sped away.

The next day, Old Pipes told his mother that he would go up the mountain and cut some wood. He had a right to get wood from the mountain, but for a long time he had

been content to pick up the dead branches which lay about his cottage. Today, however, he felt so strong and vigorous that he thought he would go and cut some fuel that would be better than this. He worked all the morning, and when he came back he did not feel at all tired, and he had a very good appetite for his dinner.

Now, Old Pipes knew a good deal about Dryads, but there was one thing which, although he had heard, he had forgotten. This was that a kiss from a Dryad made a person ten years younger. The people of the village knew this, and they were very careful not to let any child of ten years or younger go into the woods where the Dryads were supposed to be; for, if they should chance to be kissed by one of these tree nymphs, they would be set back so far that they would cease to exist. A story was told in the village that a very bad boy of eleven once ran away into the woods, and had an adventure of this kind; and when his mother found him he was a little baby of one year old. Taking advantage of her opportunity, she brought him up more carefully than she had done before; and he grew to be a very good boy indeed.

Now, Old Pipes had been kissed twice by the Dryad, once on each cheek, and he therefore felt as vigorous and active as when he was a hale man of fifty. His mother noticed how much work he was doing, and told him that he need not try in that way to make up for the loss of his piping wages; for he would only tire himself out and get sick. But her son answered that he had not felt so well for years, and that he was quite able to work. In the course of the afternoon, Old Pipes, for the first time that day, put his hand in his coat pocket, and there, to his amazement, he found the little bag of money. "Well, well!" he exclaimed, "I am stupid, indeed! I really thought that I had seen a Dryad; but when I sat down by that big oak tree I must have gone to sleep and dreamed it all; and then I came home thinking I had given the money to a Dryad, when it was in my pocket all the time. But the Chief Villager shall have the money. I shall not take it to him today, but tomorrow I wish to go to the village to see some of my old friends; and then I shall give up the money.''

Toward the close of the afternoon, Old Pipes, as had been his custom for so many years, took his pipes from the shelf on which they lay, and went out to the rock in front of the cottage.

''What are you going to do?'' cried his mother. ''If you will not consent to be paid, why do you pipe?''

''I am going to pipe for my own pleasure,'' said her son. ''I am used to it, and I do not wish to give it up. It does not matter now whether the cattle hear me or not, and I am sure that my piping will injure no one.''

When the good man began to play upon his favorite instrument he was astounded at the sound that came from it. The beautiful notes of the pipes sounded clear and strong down into the valley, and spread over the hills, and up the sides of the mountain beyond, while, after a little interval, an echo came back from the rocky hill on the other side of the valley.

''Ha! ha!'' he cried, ''what has happened to my pipes? They must have been stopped up of late, but now they are as clear and good as ever.''

Again the merry notes went sounding far and wide. The cattle on the mountain heard them, and those that were old enough remembered how these notes had called them from their pastures every evening, and so they started down the mountainside, the others following.

The merry notes were heard in the village below, and the people were much astonished thereby. ''Why, who can be blowing the pipes of Old Pipes?'' they said. But,

as they were all very busy, no one went up to see. One thing, however, was plain enough: the cattle were coming down the mountain. And so the two boys and the girl did not have to go after them, and had an hour for play, for which they were very glad.

The next morning Old Pipes started down to the village with his money, and on the way he met the Dryad. ''Oh, ho!'' he cried. ''is that you? Why, I thought my letting you out of the tree was nothing but a dream.''

''A dream!'' cried the Dryad; ''if you only knew how happy you have made me, you would not think it merely a dream. And has it not benefited you? Do you not feel happier? Yesterday I heard you playing beautifully on your pipes.''

''Yes, yes,'' cried he. ''I did not understand it before, but I see it all now. I have really grown younger. I thank you, I thank you, good Dryad, from the bottom of my heart. It was the finding of the money in my pocket that made me think it was a dream.''

''Oh, I put it in when you were asleep,'' she said, laughing, ''because I thought you ought to keep it. Goodbye, kind, honest man. May you live long, and be as happy as I am now.''

Old Pipes was greatly delighted when he understood that he was really a younger man; but that made no difference about the money, and he kept on his way to the village. As soon as he reached it, he was eagerly questioned as to who had been playing his pipes the evening before, and when the people heard that it was himself, they were very much surprised. Thereupon, Old Pipes told what had happened to him, and then there was greater wonder, with hearty congratulations and handshakes; for Old Pipes was liked by everyone. The Chief Villager refused to take his money, and, although Old Pipes said that he had not earned it, everyone present insisted that, as he would now

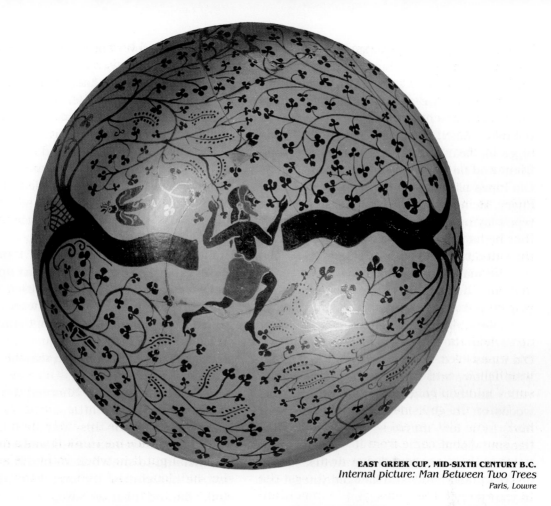

**EAST GREEK CUP, MID-SIXTH CENTURY B.C.**
*Internal picture: Man Between Two Trees*
Paris, Louvre

play on his pipes as before, he should lose nothing, because, for a time, he was unable to perform his duty.

So Old Pipes was obliged to keep his money, and after an hour or two spent in conversation with his friends, he returned to his cottage.

There was one individual, however, who was not at all pleased with what had happened to Old Pipes. This was an Echo-dwarf, who lived on the hills on the other side of the valley, and whose duty it was to echo back the notes of the pipes whenever they could be heard. There were a great many other Echo-dwarfs on these hills, some of whom echoed back the songs of maidens, some the shouts of children, and others the music that was often heard in the village.

But there was only one who could send back the strong notes of the pipes of Old Pipes, and this had been his sole duty for many years. But when the old man grew feeble, and the notes of his pipes could not be heard on the opposite hills, this Echo-dwarf had nothing to do, and he spent his time in delightful idleness; and he slept so much and grew so fat that it made his companions laugh to see him walk.

On the afternoon on which, after so long an interval, the sound of the pipes was heard on the echo hills, this dwarf was fast asleep behind a rock. As soon as the first notes reached them, some of his companions ran to wake him. Rolling to his feet, he echoed back the merry tune of Old Pipes. Naturally, he was very much annoyed and indignant at being thus obliged to give up his life of comfortable leisure, and he hoped very much that this pipe-playing would not occur again. The next afternoon he was awake and listening, and, sure enough, at the usual hour, along came the notes of the pipes as clear and strong as they ever had been; and he was obliged to work as long as Old Pipes played. The Echo-dwarf was very angry. He had supposed, of course, that the pipe-playing had ceased forever, and he felt that he had a right to be indignant at being thus deceived. He was so much disturbed that he made up his mind to go and try to find out whether this was to be a temporary matter or not. He had plenty of time, as the pipes were played but once a day, and he set off early in the morning for the hill on which Old Pipes lived. It was hard work for the fat little fellow, and when he had crossed the valley and had gone some distance into the woods on the hillside, he stopped to rest, and, in a few minutes, the Dryad came tripping along.

"Ho, ho!" exclaimed the dwarf; "what are you doing here? and how did you get out of your tree?"

"Doing!" cried the Dryad; "I am being happy; that's what I am doing. And I was let out of my tree by the good old man who plays the pipes to call the cattle down from the mountain. And it makes me happier to think that I have been of service to him. I gave him two kisses of gratitude, and now he is young enough to play his pipes as well as ever."

The Echo-dwarf stepped forward, his face pale with passion. "Am I to believe," he said, "that you are the cause of this great evil that has come upon me? and that you are the wicked creature who has again started this old man upon his career of pipe-playing? What have I ever done to you that you should have condemned me for years

and years to echo back the notes of those wretched pipes?"

At this the Dryad laughed loudly.

"What a funny little fellow you are!" she said. "Anyone would think you had been condemned to toil from morning till night; while what you really have to do is merely to imitate for half an hour every day the merry notes of Old Pipes's piping. Fie upon you, Echo-dwarf! You are lazy and selfish; and that is what is the matter with you. Instead of grumbling at being obliged to do a little wholesome work, which is less, I am sure, than that of any other echo-dwarf upon the rocky hillside, you should rejoice at the good fortune of the old man who has regained so much of his strength and vigor. Go home and learn to be just and generous; and then, perhaps, you may be happy. Goodbye."

"Insolent creature!" shouted the dwarf, as he shook his fat little fist at her. "I'll make you suffer for this. You shall find out what it is to heap injury and insult upon one like me, and to snatch from him the repose that he has earned by long years of toil." And, shaking his head savagely, he hurried back to the rocky hillside.

Every afternoon the merry notes of the pipes of Old Pipes sounded down into the valley and over the hills and up the mountainside; and every afternoon when he had echoed them back, the little dwarf grew more and more angry with the Dryad. Each day, from early morning till it was time for him to go back to his duties upon the rocky hillside, he searched the woods for her. He intended, if he met her, to pretend to be very sorry for what he had said, and he thought he might be able to play a trick upon her which would avenge him well. One day, while thus wandering among the trees, he met Old Pipes. The Echo-dwarf did not generally care to see or speak to ordinary people; but now he was so anxious to find the subject of his search, that he stopped and asked Old Pipes if he had seen the Dryad. The piper had not noticed the little fellow, and he looked down on him with some surprise.

"No," he said; "I have not seen her, and I have been looking everywhere for her."

"You!" cried the dwarf, "what do you wish with her?"

Old Pipes then sat down on a stone, so that he should be nearer the ear of his small companion, and he told what the Dryad had done for him.

When the Echo-dwarf heard that this was the man whose pipes he was obliged to echo back every day, he would have slain him on the spot had he been able; but, as he was not able, he merely ground his teeth and listened to the rest of the story.

"I am looking for the Dryad now," Old Pipes continued, "on account of my aged mother. When I was old myself, I did not notice how very old my mother was; but now it shocks me to see how feeble and decrepit her years have caused her to become; and I am looking for the Dryad to ask her to make my mother younger, as she made me."

The eyes of the Echo-dwarf glistened. Here was a man who might help him in his plans.

"Your idea is a good one," he said to Old Pipes, "and it does you honor. But you should know that a Dryad can make no person younger but one who lets her out of her tree. However, you can manage the affair very easily. All you need do is to find the Dryad, tell her what you want, and request her to step into her tree and be shut up for a short time. Then you will go and bring your mother to the tree; she will open it, and everything will be as you wish. Is not this a good plan?"

"Excellent!" cried Old Pipes; "and I will go instantly and search more diligently for the Dryad."

"Take me with you," said the Echo-dwarf. "You can easily carry me on your strong shoulders; and I shall be glad to help you in any way that I can."

"Now, then," said the little fellow to himself, as Old Pipes carried him rapidly along, "if he persuades the Dryad to get into a tree,—and she is quite foolish enough to do it,—and then goes away to bring his mother, I shall take a stone or a club and I will break off the key of that tree, so that nobody can ever turn it again. Then Mistress Dryad will see what she has brought upon herself by her behavior to me."

Before long they came to the great oak tree in which the Dryad had lived, and, at a distance, they saw that beautiful creature herself coming toward them.

"How excellently well everything happens!" said the dwarf. "Put me down, and I will go. Your business with the Dryad is more important than mine; and you need not say anything about my having suggested your plan to you. I am willing that you should have all the credit of it yourself."

Old Pipes put the Echo-dwarf upon the ground, but the little rogue did not go away. He concealed himself between some low, mossy rocks, and he was so much of their color that you would not have noticed him if you had been looking straight at him.

When the Dryad came up, Old Pipes lost no time in telling her about his mother, and what he wished her to do. At first, the Dryad answered nothing, but stood looking very sadly at Old Pipes.

"Do you really wish me to go into my tree again?" she said. "I should dreadfully dislike to do it, for I don't know what might happen. It is not at all necessary, for I could make your mother younger at any time if she would give me the opportunity. I had already

**FLORA DE STABIA**
*Museo Archeologico Nazionale, Naples*

"I think he has gone away," said Old Pipes.

"No he has not," said the Dryad, whose quick eyes perceived the Echo-dwarf among the rocks. "There he is. Seize him and drag him out, I beg of you."

Old Pipes perceived the dwarf as soon as he was pointed out to him, and, running to the rocks, he caught the little fellow by the arm and pulled him out.

"Now, then," cried the Dryad, who had opened the door of the great oak, "just stick him in there, and we will shut him up. Then I shall be safe from his mischief for the rest of the time I am free."

Old Pipes thrust the Echo-dwarf into the tree; the Dryad pushed the door shut; there was a clicking sound of bark and wood, and no one would have noticed that the big oak had ever had an opening in it.

"There!" said the Dryad; "now we need not be afraid of him. And I assure you, my good piper, that I shall be very glad to make your mother younger as soon as I can. Will you not ask her to come out and meet me?"

"Of course I will," cried Old Pipes; "and I will do it without delay."

And then, the Dryad by his side, he hurried to his cottage. But when he mentioned the matter to his mother, the old woman became very angry indeed. She did not believe in Dryads; and, if they really did exist, she knew they must be witches and sorceresses, and she would have nothing to do with them. If her son had ever allowed himself to be kissed by one of them, he ought to be ashamed of himself. As to its doing him the least bit of good, she did not believe a word of it. He felt better than he used to feel, but that was very common; she had sometimes felt that way herself. And she forbade him ever to mention a Dryad to her again.

That afternoon, Old Pipes, feeling very sad that his plan in regard to his mother had

thought of making you still happier in this way, and several times I have waited about your cottage, hoping to meet your aged mother, but she never comes outside, and you know a Dryad cannot enter a house. I cannot imagine what put this idea into your head. Did you think of it yourself?"

"No, I cannot say that I did," answered Old Pipes. "A little dwarf whom I met in the woods proposed it to me."

"Oh!" cried the Dryad; "now I see through it all. It is the scheme of that vile Echo-dwarf—your enemy and mine. Where is he? I should like to see him."

failed, sat down upon the rock and played upon his pipes. The pleasant sounds went down the valley and up the hills and mountain, but, to the great surprise of some persons who happened to notice the fact, the notes were not echoed back from the rocky hillside, but from the woods on the side of the valley on which Old Pipes lived. The next day many of the villagers stopped in their work to listen to the echo of the pipes coming from the woods. The sound was not as clear and strong as it used to be when it was sent back from the rocky hillside, but it certainly came from among the trees. Such a thing as an echo changing its place in this way had never been heard of before, and nobody was able to explain how it could have happened. Old Pipes, however, knew very well that the sound came from the Echo-dwarf shut up in the great oak tree. The sides of the tree were thin, and the sound of the pipes could be heard through them, and the dwarf was obliged by the laws of his being to echo back those notes whenever they came to him. But Old Pipes thought he might get the Dryad in trouble if he let anyone know that the Echo-dwarf was shut up in the tree, and so he wisely said nothing about it.

One day the two boys and the girl who had helped Old Pipes up the hill were playing in the woods. Stopping near the great oak tree, they heard a sound of knocking within it, and then a voice plainly said:

"Let me out! let me out!"

For a moment the children stood still in astonishment, and then one of the boys exclaimed:

"Oh, it is a Dryad, like the one Old Pipes found! Let's let her out!"

"What are you thinking of?" cried the girl. "I am the oldest of all, and I am only thirteen. Do you wish to be turned into crawling babies? Run! run! run!"

And the two boys and the girl dashed down into the valley as fast as their legs could carry them. There was no desire in their youthful hearts to be made younger than they were. And for fear that their parents might think it well that they should commence their careers anew, they never said a word about finding the Dryad tree.

As the summer days went on, Old Pipes's mother grew feebler and feebler. One day when her son was away, for he now frequently went into the woods to hunt or fish, or down into the valley to work, she arose from her knitting to prepare the simple dinner. But she felt so weak and tired that she was not able to do the work to which she had been so long accustomed. "Alas! alas!" she said, "the time has come when I am too old to work. My son will have to hire someone to come here and cook his meals, make his bed, and mend his clothes. Alas! alas! I had hoped that as long as I lived I should be able to do these things. But it is not so. I have grown utterly worthless, and someone else must prepare the dinner for my son. I wonder where he is." And tottering to the door, she went outside to look for him. She did not feel able to stand, and reaching the rustic chair, she sank into it, quite exhausted, and soon fell asleep.

The Dryad, who had often come to the cottage to see if she could find an opportunity of carrying out Old Pipes's affectionate design, now happened by; and seeing that the much-desired occasion had come, she stepped up quietly behind the old woman and gently kissed her on each cheek, and then as quietly disappeared.

In a few minutes the mother of Old Pipes awoke, and looking up at the sun, she exclaimed, "Why, it is almost dinner-time! My son will be here directly, and I am not ready for him." And rising to her feet, she hurried into the house, made the fire, set the meat and vegetables to cook, laid the cloth, and by the time her son arrived the meal was on the table.

"How a little sleep does refresh one," she said to herself, as she was bustling about. She was a woman of very vigorous constitution, and at seventy had been a great deal stronger and more active than her son was at that age. The moment Old Pipes saw his mother, he knew that the Dryad had been there; but, while he felt as happy as a king, he was too wise to say anything about her.

"It is astonishing how well I feel today," said his mother; "and either my hearing has improved or you speak much more plainly than you have done of late."

The summer days went on and passed away, the leaves were falling from the trees, and the air was becoming cold.

"Nature has ceased to be lovely," said the Dryad, "and the night winds chill me. It is time for me to go back into my comfortable quarters in the great oak. But first I must pay another visit to the cottage of Old Pipes."

She found the piper and his mother sitting side by side on the rock in front of the door. The cattle were not to go to the mountain any more that season, and he was piping them down for the last time. Loud and merrily sounded the pipes of Old Pipes, and down the mountainside came the cattle, the cows by the easiest paths, the sheep by those not quite so easy, and the goats by the most difficult ones among the rocks; while from the great oak tree were heard the echoes of the cheerful music.

"How happy they look, sitting there together!" said the Dryad; "and I don't believe it will do them a bit of harm to be still younger." And moving quietly up behind them, she first kissed Old Pipes on his cheek and then his mother.

Old Pipes, who had stopped playing, knew what it was, but he did not move, and said nothing. His mother, thinking that her son had kissed her, turned to him with a smile and kissed him in return. And then she arose and went into the cottage, a vigorous woman of sixty, followed by her son, erect and happy, and twenty years younger than herself.

The Dryad sped away to the woods, shrugging her shoulders as she felt the cool evening wind.

When she reached the great oak, she turned the key and opened the door. "Come out," she said to the Echo-dwarf, who sat blinking within. "Winter is coming on, and I want the comfortable shelter of my tree for myself. The cattle have come down from the mountain for the last time this year, the pipes will no longer sound, and you can go to your rocks and have a holiday until next spring."

Upon hearing these words the dwarf skipped quickly out, and the Dryad entered the tree and pulled the door shut after her. "Now, then," she said to herself, "he can break off the key if he likes. It does not matter to me. Another will grow out next spring. And although the good piper made me no promise, I know that when the warm days arrive next year, he will come and let me out again."

The Echo-dwarf did not stop to break the key of the tree. He was too happy to be released to think of anything else, and he hastened as fast as he could to his home on the rocky hillside.

The Dryad was not mistaken when she trusted in the piper. When the warm days came again he went to the oak tree to let her out. But, to his sorrow and surprise, he found the great tree lying upon the ground. A winter storm had blown it down, and it lay with its trunk shattered and split. And what became of the Dryad no one ever knew.

## THINKING ABOUT THE SELECTION
### Recalling

1. Describe the situation at the beginning of the story.
2. Why does Old Pipes decide to return his salary?
3. Describe the encounter Old Pipes has on the way to the village. How does it change his life?
4. What does Old Pipes find when he comes the following spring to let the Dryad out of the tree?

### Interpreting

5. What is the attitude of the villagers toward Old Pipes?
6. What kind of person is Old Pipes? Give examples to support your answer.
7. Explain the role of the Echo-dwarf in this story.

### Applying

8. If you had the opportunity to be made younger by a dryad, what would you do? Explain your answer.

## ANALYZING LITERATURE
### Understanding Key Statements

**Key statements** are those that make a point about life in general and therefore help you infer a story's theme. For example, Old Pipes makes a key statement when he says to his mother, "But one thing is certain, if I do not earn the wages the Chief Villager pays me, I shall not take them." This key statement tells you that Old Pipes is a person of honesty and integrity.
1. Find key statements made by the following characters.
   a. the Dryad to Old Pipes
   b. the Echo-dwarf to the Dryad
   c. the Dryad to the Echo-dwarf
2. State the theme, and explain how these statements point to that theme.

## CRITICAL THINKING AND READING
### Summarizing a Story

When you **summarize** a story, you state the main events in your own words. A good summary can help you see the structure of a story and better understand its meaning.

Write a paragraph summarizing "Old Pipes and the Dryad." Be sure to add all the pertinent events.

## UNDERSTANDING LANGUAGE
### Appreciating Words from Myths

In Greek mythology, the Dryads were one group of *nymphs*, or nature goddesses. The Dryads were the tree nymphs. Each Dryad was linked with her own tree and died when the tree died.

Other nymphs were associated with other aspects of nature. Use a dictionary or book of mythology to find out what types of nymphs the following nymphs were. Prepare an oral report on one of them. Rehearse your presentation. Then present your report to your classmates. You may want to use some visual aids such as charts and diagrams to enliven your report.
1. Nereids     3. Naiads
2. Oceanides   4. Oreads

## THINKING AND WRITING
### Writing About Music

Imagine that your class is performing a play version of "Old Pipes and the Dryad," and that you are responsible for selecting the background music. List the music you would choose for a few key moments in the play. Then use this list in writing a memo to the director about your choices. Describe the music, explaining why you believe it is appropriate for that moment. Revise your memo, adding comments about the music that explain why it is appropriate. Proofread your work and prepare a final draft.

# The Short Story

To increase your enjoyment of a short story, look at the interplay of elements in the story and ask yourself questions about these elements.

**Plot**

Make sure you follow the sequence of events. Do you know the order in which the events occur? Do you understand how they are related to each other? Can you identify the conflict, or central problem? Can you anticipate the way in which the conflict will be resolved? Do you see how the actions affect the characters?

**Characters**

Make sure you can identify the characters in the story. Who is the main character? Who are the minor characters? Are the characters believable? Do you see them as real people—people you know now or might someday know?

**Point of View**

Notice how the story is being narrated. Is it being told in the first person or in the third person? Is it being told by a main character, a minor character, or an outside observer? Would the story be different if another character were telling it?

**Setting**

Put yourself in the story and visualize the setting. Where does the story take place? Do the events occur in the present, the past, or the future? How much detail does the author give you about the setting? Is it enough or not enough? Can you visualize the place? Does the setting play an important role in the story?

**Symbols**

Some stories contain symbols. Does this short story contain an object that seems to stand for something larger than itself? If so, what does it represent?

**Tone and Irony**

Tone is the writer's attitude toward what he has written. What is the tone of this short story? Is it ironic?

**Theme**

Some stories reveal an important insight into life. Does this story have a theme? Not all stories do. Does it leave you feeling a bit wiser about the human condition?

As you read the following model short story, keep these questions in mind. Pay attention to the annotations in the side column.

# The Sentimentality of William Tavener

### Willa Cather

**Character:** What could the title mean?

It takes a strong woman to make any sort of success of living in the West, and Hester undoubtedly was that. When people spoke of William Tavener as the most prosperous farmer in McPherson County, they usually added that his wife was a "good manager." She was an executive woman, quick of tongue and something of an imperatrix.[1] The only reason her husband did not consult her about his business was that she did not wait to be consulted.

**Setting:** Where does the story take place?

**Point of View:** Is the story being told in the first person or in the third person?

It would have been quite impossible for one man, within the limited sphere of human action, to follow all Hester's advice, but in the end William usually acted upon some of her suggestions. When she incessantly denounced the "shiftlessness" of letting a new threshing machine[2] stand unprotected in the open, he eventually built a shed for it. When she sniffed contemptuously at his notion of fencing a hog corral with sod walls, he made a spiritless beginning on the structure —merely to "show his temper," as she put it—but bought enough barbed wire to complete the fence. When the first heavy rains came on, and the pigs rooted down the sod wall and made little paths all over it to facilitate their ascent, he heard his wife relate with relish the story of the little pig that built a mud house, to the minister at the dinner table, and William's gravity never relaxed for an instant. Silence, indeed, was William's refuge and his strength.

**Plot:** How does William's usual response to his wife's suggestions foreshadow, or hint at, the events of the story?

**Setting:** How does the setting affect the characters' decisions?

**Character:** What type of impression of Hester and William do you form based on their actions?

William set his boys a wholesome example to respect their mother. People who knew him very well suspected that he even admired her. He was a hard man towards his neighbors, and even towards his sons: grasping, determined and ambitious.

**Tone:** What is the author's attitude toward the characters?

There was an occasional blue day about the house when William went over the store bills, but he never objected to

**Character:** What inference can you make about William's

---

**1. imperatrix** (im′ pə rā′ triks) *n.*: A woman emperor.
**2. threshing machine:** A machine for beating out grain from its husk.

relationship to his wife from his reaction to her spending habits?

**Plot:** When does the rising action begin?

**Plot:** What is the conflict?

**Character:** What does Billy's behavior suggest?

**Point of View:** Can the narrator see into all of the characters' minds or into the mind of only one character?

**Character:** What does Hester's request suggest about the nature of her relationship with her sons?

**Character:** What do you learn about the family and its situation from Hester?

items relating to his wife's gowns or bonnets. So it came about that many of the foolish, unnecessary little things that Hester bought for the boys, she had charged to her personal account.

One spring night Hester sat in a rocking chair by the sitting room window, darning socks. She rocked violently and sent her long needle vigorously back and forth over her gourd,[3] and it took only a very casual glance to see that she was wrought up over something. William sat on the other side of the table reading his farm paper. If he had noticed his wife's agitation, his calm, clean-shaven face betrayed no sign of concern. He must have noticed the sarcastic turn of her remarks at the supper table, and he must have noticed the moody silence of the older boys as they ate. When supper was but half over little Billy, the youngest, had suddenly pushed back his plate and slipped away from the table, manfully trying to swallow a sob. But William Tavener never heeded ominous forecasts in the domestic horizon, and he never looked for a storm until it broke.

After supper the boys had gone to the pond under the willows in the big cattle corral, to get rid of the dust of plowing. Hester could hear an occasional splash and a laugh ringing clear through the stillness of the night, as she sat by the open window. She sat silent for almost an hour reviewing in her mind many plans of attack. But she was too vigorous a woman to be much of a strategist, and she usually came to her point with directness. At last she cut her thread and suddenly put her darning down, saying emphatically:

"William, I don't think it would hurt you to let the boys go to that circus in town tomorrow."

William continued to read his farm paper, but it was not Hester's custom to wait for an answer. She usually divined his arguments and assailed them one by one before he uttered them.

"You've been short of hands all summer, and you've worked the boys hard, and a man ought use his own flesh and blood as well as he does his hired hands. We're plenty able to afford it, and it's little enough our boys ever spend. I don't see how you can expect 'em to be steady and hard workin',

---

**3. gourd** (gôrd) *n.*: The dried, hollowed-out shell of a squash used to hold the shape of the sock.

unless you encourage 'em a little. I never could see much harm in circuses, and our boys have never been to one. Oh, I know Jim Howley's boys get drunk an' carry on when they go, but our boys ain't that sort, an' you know it, William. The animals are real instructive, an' our boys don't get to see much out here on the prairie. It was different where we were raised, but the boys have got no advantages here, an' if you don't take care, they'll grow up to be greenhorns."

Is this direct characterization or indirect characterization?

**Setting:** What effect does the setting have on the boys' development?

Hester paused a moment, and William folded up his paper, but vouchsafed[4] no remark. His sisters in Virginia had often said that only a quiet man like William could ever have lived with Hester Perkins. Secretly, William was rather proud of his wife's "gift of speech," and of the fact that she could talk in prayer meeting fluently. He confined his own efforts in that line to a brief prayer at Covenant meetings.

**Character:** What does the fact that William keeps his pride in his wife's talents a secret tell you about his character?

Hester shook out another sock and went on.

"Nobody was ever hurt by goin' to a circus. Why, law me! I remember I went to one myself once, when I was little. I had most forgot about it. It was over at Pewtown, an' I remember how I had set my heart on going. I don't think I'd ever forgiven my father if he hadn't taken me, though that red clay road was in a frightful way after the rain. I mind they had an elephant and six poll parrots, an' a Rocky Mountain lion, an' a cage of monkeys, an' two camels. My! but they were a sight to me then!"

**Setting:** What does the name Pewtown suggest to you?

**Plot:** Why are Hester's recollections important to the story?

Hester dropped the black sock and shook her head and smiled at the recollection. She was not expecting anything from William yet, and she was fairly startled when he said gravely, in much the same tone in which he announced the hymns in prayer meeting:

"No, there was only one camel. The other was a dromedary."

She peered around the lamp and looked at him keenly.

"Why, William, how come you to know?"

William folded his paper and answered with some hesitation, "I was there, too."

Hester's interest flashed up—"Well, I never, William! To think of my finding it out after all these years! Why, you couldn't have been much bigger'n our Billy then. It seems queer I never saw you when you was little, to remember

**Character:** Why is Hester startled when William speaks? How does the author suggest that William's comment brings about a change in Hester's attitude?

**Plot:** What is the climax of the story?

**Character:** Why does William answer with hesitation?

---

**4. vouchsafed** (vouch′ sāft) *v*.: Granted a reply.

**THE CIRCUS, 1874**
*A. Logan*
*Collection of the Whitney Museum of American Art*

**Setting:** What do the names Back Creek and Gap suggest?

**Character:** How is William's relationship with his sons similar to his relationship with his own father?

**Character:** What does the fact that William still remembers the clown's jokes tell you about the impact that the circus had on him?

**Setting:** What can you infer about the time of the

about you. But then you Back Creek folks never have anything to do with us Gap people. But how come you to go? Your father was stricter with you than you are with your boys."

"I reckon I shouldn't 'a gone," he said slowly, "but boys will do foolish things. I had done a good deal of fox hunting the winter before, and father let me keep the bounty money. I hired Tom Smith's Tap to weed the corn for me, an' I slipped off unbeknownst to father an' went to the show."

Hester spoke up warmly: "Nonsense, William! It didn't do you no harm, I guess. You was always worked hard enough. It must have been a big sight for a little fellow. That clown must have just tickled you to death."

William crossed his knees and leaned back in his chair.

"I reckon I could tell all that fool's jokes now. Sometimes I can't help thinkin' about 'em in meetin' when the sermon's long. I mind I had on a pair of new boots that hurt me like the mischief, but I forgot all about 'em when that fellow rode the donkey. I recall I had to take them boots off as soon as I got out of sight o' town, and walked home in the mud barefoot."

"O poor little fellow!" Hester ejaculated, drawing her chair nearer and leaning her elbows on the table. "What cruel shoes they did use to make for children. I remember I went up to Back Creek to see the circus wagons go by. They came down from Romney, you know. The circus men stopped at the creek to water the animals, an' the elephant got stubborn an' broke a big limb off the yellow willow tree that grew there by the tollhouse porch, an' the Scribners were 'fraid as death he'd pull the house down. But this much I saw him do; he waded in the creek an' filled his trunk with water and squirted it in at the window and nearly ruined Ellen Scribner's pink lawn dress that she had just ironed an' laid out on the bed ready to wear to the circus.''

''I reckon that must have been a trial to Ellen,'' chuckled William, ''for she was mighty prim in them days.''

Hester drew her chair still nearer William's. Since the children had begun growing up, her conversation with her husband had been almost wholly confined to questions of economy and expense. Their relationship had become purely a business one, like that between landlord and tenant. In her desire to indulge her boys she had unconsciously assumed a defensive and almost hostile attitude towards her husband. No debtor ever haggled with his usurer[5] more doggedly than did Hester with her husband in behalf of her sons. The strategic contest had gone on so long that it had almost crowded out the memory of a closer relationship. This exchange of confidences tonight, when common recollections took them unawares and opened their hearts, had all the miracle of romance. They talked on and on; of old neighbors, of old familiar faces in the valley where they had grown up, of long-forgotten incidents of their youth—weddings, picnics, sleighing parties and baptizings. For years they had talked of nothing else but butter and eggs and the prices of things, and now they had as much to say to each other as people who meet after a long separation.

When the clock struck ten, William rose and went over to his walnut secretary and unlocked it. From his red leather wallet he took out a ten dollar bill and laid it on the table beside Hester.

''Tell the boys not to stay late, an' not to drive the horses hard,'' he said quietly, and went off to bed.

Hester blew out the lamp and sat still in the dark a long time. She left the bill lying on the table where William had placed it. She had a painful sense of having missed some-

setting from Hester's comments?

**Symbol:** What does Hester's movement toward William suggest to you?

**Character:** What caused Hester and William to grow apart?

**Character:** Are Hester and William static characters or dynamic characters?

**Plot:** How is the conflict resolved?

**Theme:** What might Hester's thoughts suggest

---

**5. usurer** (yoo' zhoo rər) *n.*: A person who lends money at a high rate of interest.

about the theme of the story?

**Symbol:** What do the white blossoms suggest to you about Hester and William's relationship?

**Character:** Why does Hester recall a night long ago?

**Symbol:** What does Hester's gesture suggest to you?

**Character:** What change has taken place in Hester's relationship with her sons?

thing, or lost something; she felt that somehow the years had cheated her.

The little locust trees that grew by the fence were white with blossoms. Their heavy odor floated in to her on the night wind and recalled a night long ago, when the first whippoorwill of the spring was heard, and the rough buxom girls of Hawkins Gap had held her laughing and struggling under the locust trees, and searched in her bosom for a lock of her sweetheart's hair, which is supposed to be on every girl's breast when the first whippoorwill sings. Two of those same girls had been her bridesmaids. Hester had been a very happy bride. She rose and went softly into the room where William lay. He was sleeping heavily, but occasionally moved his hand before his face to ward off the flies. Hester went into the parlor and took the piece of mosquito net from the basket of wax apples and pears that her sister had made before she died. One of the boys had brought it all the way from Virginia, packed in a tin pail, since Hester would not risk shipping so precious an ornament by freight. She went back to the bedroom and spread the net over William's head. Then she sat down by the bed and listened to his deep, regular breathing until she heard the boys returning. She went out to meet them and warn them not to waken their father.

"I'll be up early to get your breakfast, boys. Your father says you can go to the show." As she handed the money to the eldest, she felt a sudden throb of allegiance to her husband and said sharply, "And you be careful of that, an' don't waste it. Your father works hard for his money."

The boys looked at each other in astonishment and felt that they had lost a powerful ally.

**Willa Cather** (1873–1947) was born in Virginia. Her experiences growing up on the frontier of Nebraska inspired some of her most famous work. She was graduated from the University of Nebraska and left her job as managing editor of *McClure's Magazine* in 1912 to write full time. Cather won the Pulitzer Prize for fiction in 1922. Her best-known novels are *My Antonia* and *Death Comes for the Archbishop*.

## THINKING ABOUT THE SELECTION

### Recalling

1. How do people refer to Hester Tavener?
2. How does the author characterize Hester and William's relationship?
3. What reasons does Hester give for allowing the boys to go to the circus?
4. What does William say in the middle of her argument that surprises Hester?

### Interpreting

5. Why does Hester feel "a painful sense of having missed something"?
6. Which details indicate that Hester and William's relationship has changed at the end of the story?
7. Why do the boys feel they have lost an ally?

### Applying

8. Hester and William have been married for most of their adult lives, but they barely know each other. Do you think it believable that their conversation about the circus should have changed their feelings toward one another? Why or why not?
9. Do you think it possible for people to lose that part of themselves that they value most? Why or why not?

## ANALYZING LITERATURE

### Identifying the Total Effect

The **total effect** is the impression you form about a piece of literature after examining each of the elements individually and then putting them together.

1. Around what conflict does the plot of the story revolve?
2. How are Hester and William different from one another?
3. In what way are they very much alike?
4. How does the setting help shape them?
5. How does the title suggest the theme?
6. How would you describe the total effect of the story?

## CRITICAL THINKING AND READING

### Drawing Valid Conclusions

A **valid conclusion** is a judgment or decision based on evidence. For example, Hester forms a valid conclusion when she concludes that it would not hurt the boys to allow them to go to the circus. She then gives several reasons that support this conclusion.

Find the evidence in the story that supports each of the conclusions below.

1. Hester is a good manager.
2. William is a strong, silent man.
3. William admires Hester.

## UNDERSTANDING LANGUAGE

### Using the Glossary

At the back of this book you will find a glossary—a brief dictionary of the words you may not know in the selections that follow. These words are listed in alphabetical order. Each entry contains the part of speech, the pronunciation, and its definitions.

Look up the following words in your glossary. Write the part of speech, pronunciation, and meaning of each word.

1. executive
2. prosperous
3. contemptuously
4. incessantly
5. refuge
6. vigorously

## THINKING AND WRITING

### Writing About Art

Hester and William are two of the "common" people we think of as making our country great. Many American artists have tried to capture the dignity and strength of these everyday people who form the backbone of this nation. Thumb through a collection of paintings by American regionalist artists. Find a painting you would use as an illustration for this story. Then write an essay defending your choice. When you revise your essay, make sure you have provided adequate support for your choice. Proofread your essay and share it with your classmates.

# Understanding Relationships

Relationships are connections. You can increase your understanding of what you read by noting the connections between events, people, and ideas. Three common relationship patterns are cause and effect, comparison and contrast, and order of importance.

## Cause and Effect

A **cause-and-effect** relationship shows why something happened and the results or effects of the causes. A **cause** is what makes something happen. An **effect** is that result or what happens. For example, in "Contents of the Dead Man's Pocket" Tom Benecke stays home and works because he hopes to obtain a promotion. The underlying assumption is that hard work will lead to a promotion. The cause is hard work; the effect, promotion.

People sometimes find incorrect causes for actions. For example, someone might say, "I got an *A* on the test because I was carrying my lucky rabbit's foot." Carrying a rabbit's foot does not lead to getting an *A* on a test. Studying and paying attention in class do. This person has not found the right cause for the effect. If he fails to study for the next test and does not pay attention in class, there is a good chance he will not get an *A*, even if he carries his lucky rabbit's foot. Most superstitions are based on identifying incorrect causes for effects.

## Activity

Which of the items below show a logical relationship between cause and effect? For each item that does not, rewrite, providing a logical cause.
1. An athlete wins the All-State Championship because she has practiced daily and maintained a good diet.
2. It rained today because we planned to go on a picnic.
3. It rained today because I just washed my car.
4. The fuse blew because we had overloaded the circuit.
5. The fan belt broke because it had been improperly installed.

## Comparison and Contrast

A **comparison-and-contrast** relationship shows similarities and differences. When you **compare** you show how things are alike. When you **contrast** you show how they are different. Seeing similarities and differences helps us better understand things.

**Activity**

Answer the question that follows each of the quotations below.

1. "There is a great deal of difference between an eager man [or woman] who wants to read a book and the tired man [or woman] who wants to read a book." —G. K. Chesterton
   What is this difference?
2. "In a very real sense, people who have read good literature have lived more than people who cannot or will not read . . . It is not true that we have only one life to live; if we can read, we can live as many lives and as many kinds of lives as we wish." —S. I. Hayakawa
   How are people who read good literature different from people who cannot or will not read?
3. "The man [or woman] who does not read good books has no advantage over the man [or woman] who cannot." —Mark Twain
   How are both alike?
4. "Some read to think—these are rare; some to write, these are common; and some to talk, and these form the great majority." —Charles Caleb Colton
   How are these three groups different?

## Order of Importance

**Order-of-importance** arranges ideas according to how important they are. For example, you might make a list of ten things to do today, starting with the least important and ending with the most important. Arranging ideas according to order of importance is a powerful tool for persuasive writing. By ending with the most important idea, you let your thoughts build to a climax.

**Activity**

John Ruskin divided books into two classes—"The books of the hour, and the books of all time." "Books of the hour" consist of books that seem important to read now, but probably will not seem important in a few years, or even a few months. Many best sellers would fall into this category. "Books of all time" consist of books that seem important now and probably will seem as important, if not more so, throughout our lifetimes. Classics fall into this category. Choose one of these categories. Prepare a reading list for a friend. Arrange your list according to order of importance, starting the list with the least important book and ending with the most important.

# YOU THE WRITER

**Assignment**

**1.** Short stories involve careful planning. Make a story chart for a short story. Include setting (time and place), plot, and characters.

**Prewriting.** Freewrite about what you want to happen in the story. Jot down ideas for characters, setting, and plot. Then, choose two characters, one setting, and one plot.

**Writing.** Draw a chart on which to put the elements of the story. Write the elements in their proper places and, under each, write a list of descriptive details about that element. If possible, write a sentence underneath the chart that tells the theme.

**Revising.** Check the chart carefully for errors in spelling and grammar. Be certain that all of the elements are in place and that there are several details describing each one.

**Assignment**

**2.** Some short stories are written in the form of a journal. Write a journal entry for a character in one of the short stories you have read.

**Prewriting.** Make a list of words that describe the character you have chosen from your reading.

**Writing.** Write the journal entry, relating one of the events in the short story. Include specific details that reveal what the character is like.

**Revising.** Make certain you have maintained a consistent point of view.

**Assignment**

**3.** Some short stories are written through the exchange of letters. Choose two characters from two different short stories and write a series of letters they might exchange.

**Prewriting.** Think of the characters you have encountered and select two. Freewrite, exploring what would happen if these two characters ever met. Then outline the plot of your short story.

**Writing.** Write a series of at least three letters from one character to another. Make sure the letters reveal the plot of your short story and provide insight into the characters.

**Revising.** Make sure each character's voice rings clearly through his or her letters.

# YOU THE CRITIC

**Assignment**

**1.** A diagram is a graphic representation of something. Diagram the elements that contribute to a short-story theme.

**Prewriting.** Choose one of the short stories you have read. Freewrite about any themes in the story, and about the parts of the story that help the author to convey these themes.

**Writing.** Select the theme you think is best supported in the story. Write the theme within a circle in the center of your diagram. Then draw lines out from the circle to outer circles. In the outer circles, write the specific elements that create the theme.

**Revising.** Check the diagram to make certain that all the necessary elements have been included.

**Assignment**

**2.** An exposition sets up a story by providing enough information to readers so that they can understand what is going on from the beginning. Write a short essay discussing the effectiveness of a short-story exposition.

**Prewriting.** List the events, places, people, and dialogue used in the exposition, or setting up, of the story.

**Writing.** Decide if the exposition of the story you have chosen effectively sets up the story. Write an essay to support your conclusions.

**Revising.** Make sure you have provided adequate support for your opinion.

**Assignment**

**3.** Point of view is the way in which an author controls the information the reader receives. Write an essay analyzing the use of first-person point of view in two stories you have read.

**Prewriting.** List each narrator's attitudes and any characteristics that might play a part in how he or she tells the story.

**Writing.** Write a carefully constructed essay in which you compare and contrast the use of first-person point of view by the two narrators. First show the similarities of the narrators, and then the differences. Then compare the effectiveness of the first-person point of view in each story. Explore the impact each narrator has on the reader's ability to understand what is going on.

**Revising.** Make certain that your comparisons and contrasts are well supported with examples. Proofread the essay to eliminate any errors in spelling, grammar, and punctuation.

**RAISED STAGE WITH MASKS, NARRATOR, AND AUDITORIUM, 1981**
*David Hockney*
© David Hockney, 1981

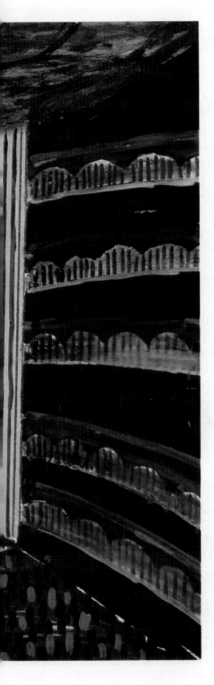

# DRAMA

One of our earliest literary forms, drama evolved from man's tribal past. Early people would act out great triumphs, deep fears, or heartfelt wishes in early religious rites. Still a religious ritual, drama became an art form in fifth century B.C. Greece, where ancient myths were retold in dramatic form at religious festivals. These ancient playwrights shaped drama into its modern form, with acts and scenes performed by a large cast. The Greek philosopher Aristotle divided all drama into tragedy, which tells of the fall of an individual, and comedy, which describes the regeneration or reformation of a group or society. Even with the rise of Christianity, drama remained connected to religion through much of its history. During the medieval period, drama was reborn in the mystery and morality plays of the Catholic Church. Eventually old Greek and Roman manuscripts were discovered, translated, and produced on stage. By the end of the sixteenth century, English drama entered a golden age with William Shakespeare. Currently drama throughout the world has taken many and varied forms, from musicals to biting satires.

The word *drama* comes from the Greek word *dran,* meaning "to do" or "to act." It is this doing or acting quality that makes drama unique in literature. While plays share many elements with prose fiction and poetry—plot, character, point of view, setting, tone, symbolism, and theme—the greatest difference is that drama is designed to be presented by actors on a stage before an audience. Actors speak to one another or to the audience, bringing life to their characters through tone of voice, expressions, and movement. On the stage, sets and props help to create a specific place and underscore ideas the playwright is trying to convey. Costumes, lighting, music, and sound effects add to the total effect of the drama. Even the audience plays a part, for its reactions provide feedback to the actors.

In this unit you will read a play by William Shakespeare as well as works by more modern authors.

# Drama

Let us examine the elements of drama. First, as a story, a play shows a character in conflict—facing a problem that gets progressively worse until it reaches a crisis, the climax. At this point a decisive action solves the problem. This action speedily brings about the end of the story. Second, a play is told through dialogue and action. Because the audience cannot look directly into the minds of the characters to see what they are thinking and feeling, the audience must infer those thoughts or feelings by "reading" the actions. A character who pounds his fist on a table is angry. One who bites her nails is nervous.

Plays are meant to be performed. When you read a play, you are reading a script. The stage directions, printed in italics and in brackets, are intended to show the actors when and how to move and speak. They suggest to the director what kinds of sound effects and lighting are needed and what the stage should look like. Stage directions use a particular vocabulary. *Right, left, up, down,* and *center* refer to areas of the stage as the actors see it. To help you visualize what is meant when a stage direction tells an actor to move up center, for example, picture the stage like this:

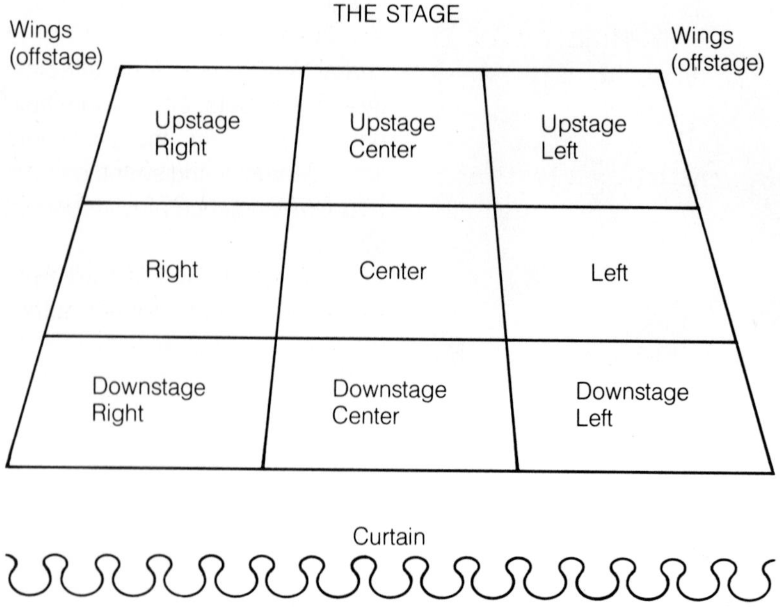

THE STAGE

Wings (offstage)

Wings (offstage)

| Upstage Right | Upstage Center | Upstage Left |
|---|---|---|
| Right | Center | Left |
| Downstage Right | Downstage Center | Downstage Left |

Curtain

Being an active reader of drama will increase your appreciation of drama. An active reader sees the play in his or her mind while questioning the meaning of the actors' words and actions.

The following strategies will help you read drama actively.

**Visualize**

Picture the stage and the characters in action. Use the directions and information supplied by the playwright to create the scene in your mind. See the characters move; hear them speak. Let them reveal to you what is happening.

**Question**

Ask yourself what each character wants. What motives are revealed through a character's words or actions? What is the conflict?

**Predict**

Once you recognize the conflict and understand the characters' motives, predict what you think will happen. How will the conflict be resolved? What will become of each character?

**Clarify**

If a character's words or actions are not clear to you, stop to make sense of them. You may find clarification in earlier words or actions. Look for answers to your questions, and check your predictions.

**Summarize**

Occasionally pause to review what has happened. What is the conflict? What is happening toward its resolution? Put the characters' actions and words together as you summarize.

**Pull It Together**

Finally pull together all the elements of the play. What does the play mean? What has it revealed about life? What does it say to you?

You will be a more effective reader of drama if you use these strategies. You will be better able to understand the conflict and resolution of a play and apply your understanding to your own world.

## Tevya and the First Daughter

**Sholom Aleichem** (1859–1916) was born Solomon Rabinovitch in the Ukraine. In 1883 he adopted as his pen name the Hebrew greeting that means "Peace be with you." His sketches of *Tevya,* from which this play is adapted, were written between 1895 and 1899 and were the basis of the 1964 Broadway musical *Fiddler on the Roof.*

　　**Arnold Perl** (1914–1971) was the theatrical producer for *The World of Sholom Aleichem,* based on Aleichem's stories.

**The One-Act Play**

The **one-act play** is a form of drama that consists of a single act, although it may contain more than one scene. The plot of a one-act play centers on a single incident and develops quickly to a climax. It depends for its effect on dynamic characters and lively dialogue. In *Tevya and the First Daughter,* Tevya's character and his comments on life not only move the play along but also provide the humor of the play.

**Look For**

As you read *Tevya and the First Daughter,* look for the way that Tevya behaves in different situations. What does he say and do that keeps you interested in his situation?

**Writing**

Tevya, a poor man, encounters some unexpected good fortune. Think of a time when you had some unexpected good luck. Freewrite about this experience, describing your response.

**Vocabulary**

Knowing the following words will help you as you read *Tevya and the First Daughter.*

**subtleties** (sut′ 'l tēz) *n.*: Fine qualities that are not immediately obvious (p. 280)
**dowry** (dou′ rē) *n.*: Money or property brought by a bride to her husband at marriage (p. 281)
**paraphernalia** (par′ ə fər nāl′ yə) *n.*: Personal belongings (p. 283)

# Tevya and
# the First Daughter

## Arnold Perl

### Based on the Tevya stories of Sholom Aleichem

---

**CHARACTERS**

**Tevya,** a drayman[1]
**Golde,** his wife
**Tzeitl,** his oldest daughter
**Hodel,** his second daughter
**Chava,** his third daughter

**Older Woman**
**Young Woman**
**Rich Merchant**
**Lazar Wolf**
**Mottel Kamzoil**

*Time: The latter part of the nineteenth century*
*Place: Czarist Russia*

---

## Scene 1

[TEVYA *crosses the darkened stage, carrying an armful of food in packages. He is fifty, a drayman and wearing his Sabbath "best," which is to say his weekday "best," that is, his work clothes. Now he stands, at midnight, just outside his house, arms laden, in a state of exultation. A miracle has happened.*]

**TEVYA.** Lord, with all the troubles of the universe on your back, accept thanks for the blessings of this night. It's me, Tevya the drayman, with the mud on his wagon, his horse, and himself. A man. But as is written, a man may be in the mud, but he's never of the mud; he may be down, but he's never extinguished; as long as your teeth are chattering, dear Lord, you're alive. And this night Thou has performed a miracle; and as the Bible tells us, let there be light. [*Lights slowly come on.*] Let there also be celebration. Golde, children, everyone! Arise, awake, a mazel tov[2] and a holiday! Everybody come.

[*Lights reveal the interior of* TEVYA'S *mansion: a poor Jewish hut in Russia, in the latter part of the nineteenth century. The furniture is rough, bare, and well used.*

---

**1. drayman** (drā′ mən) *n*.: The driver of a horse-drawn cart with detachable sides for carrying heavy loads.

**2. mazel tov** (mä′ z'l tōv′): A Hebrew expression of congratulations; good luck.

GOLDE, *his wife, and his three eldest daughters,* TZEITL, HODEL, *and* CHAVA, *enter sleepily.*]

As King David[3] said, "Prepare, for there came a day. . . ." That day has come.

[*The girls rush into his arms in happy anticipation.*]

**GOLDE.** Do you know what time it is?

**TEVYA.** Get the white tablecloth; set the table.

**GOLDE.** Have you gone out of your mind?

**TEVYA.** Mazel tov, my darlings; mazel tov, Golde.

[*He kisses all the girls and tries to kiss* GOLDE.]

**GOLDE.** An endless mazel tov to you!

**TEVYA.** Get the dishes; more candles!

**GOLDE.** What are we celebrating, my beloved breadwinner in rags?

[TEVYA *reveals the food he has been carrying.*]

**TEVYA.** Behold soup with noodles, behold roast beef, stuffed goose's neck, kishka,[4] herring, sturgeon![5] Why are you standing around? Get the platters and the forks. My jaws have been aching for an hour to get at

---

**3. King David:** A King of Israel and thought to be the writer of the Psalms.

**4. kishka** (kish′ kə) *n.*: Beef casing stuffed with bread crumbs and seasonings and roasted.
**5. sturgeon** (stur′ jən) *n.*: A large fish.

it. [*He draws a bottle from inside his shirt.*] Plus wine, fit for King Solomon[6] himself.

**GOLDE.** [*Looking and smelling, but not believing her eyes*] Tell me, my helpmate, what insane benefactor has decided to feed the countryside, including Tevya and his seven daughters?

**TEVYA.** I'll tell everything. Only first, Hodel, heat up the samovar! Get the glasses for tea. And we will celebrate our Independence; because, Golde— Hold out your nightgown!

[GOLDE *has grown silent.* TEVYA *scatters a pile of bills into her apron.*]

Look. One's, two's, even three-ruble[7] notes! Count . . .

[GOLDE *cries, and counts to herself.*]

**HODEL.** Mother, why are you crying? Mama!

**TEVYA.** I'll explain. When your heart is full, your eyes run over. It relieves the pressure. Your mother is thinking as follows. Tevya is a drayman, she is thinking, with a wagon and half a horse. What does he do all day? Hauls wood from the forest to the railroad station for, I'm ashamed to admit it, half a ruble a day. And not every day; right, Golde?

[GOLDE *cries louder.*]

I'm on the right track. So, asks your mother, my Golde, where would Tevya get such a fortune? (A little glass, please, Tzeitl.) Where? He turned into a highway robber and held up one of the rich merchants who is in our neck of the woods? Wrong. No, Golde, listen! Dry your eyes and listen to your schlimazl[8] of a husband. This is food and drink and money that has come to Tevya honestly because of his labor, and on account of his wits.

**GOLDE.** Thirty-seven rubles! [*She wails.*]

**HODEL.** Oh, Mama, that's no reason to carry on.

**TEVYA.** Let her cry. She has, your blessed mother, something to worry about. A house that leaks, a kitchen forever empty, a husband that is not the First Provider on earth, and seven [*He counts them off*]. One, two, three—where are the little ones? Ah, don't wake them; we'll save theirs for the morning. So with seven daughters, seven to marry off, she is entitled to her tears. As King Solomon tells us in the Prophets[9]—

**GOLDE.** Never mind the quotation; what happened?

**TEVYA.** Sit down, eat, satisfy your hunger, wash it down with a little tea, and I will tell you how Tevya made his fortune. Oh, I forgot . . . [*He leaps up.*] We have a cow. And better than a cow, a cow that, perhaps, gives milk.

**GOLDE.** Begin at the beginning!

[*During the following re-enactment,* TEVYA *has moved to stage left.* GOLDE *and the* GIRLS *are all at stage right, and remain there throughout the following story.* TEVYA *is in the room with them, telling the story as it happened. As other people enter the story, they relate to* TEVYA *at left. But* TEVYA *can, and does, turn from the people of the story and speak to his wife and children. Light on* GOLDE *and the* CHILDREN *diminishes.*]

**TEVYA.** This afternoon, there is, as usual, no work. The horse and I are walking, both in the dust, for why should I tax the poor animal and make him carry me?

**GOLDE.** Tevya!

---

**6. King Solomon:** A king of Israel noted for his wisdom.
**7. ruble** (roo′ b'l) *n.*: The monetary unit of Russia.
**8. schlimazl** (shli mä′ z'l) *n.*: Yiddish for a person who is constantly the victim of bad luck; an inept person.

**9. Prophets** (präf′ its) *n.*: One of the three major divisions of the Jewish Holy Scripture.

**TEVYA.** As I said, we're walking and thinking. That is, I'm thinking; the horse is only walking. I'm thinking: eight mouths, eight, that is, not including the horse, who, after all, can't be satisfied with a quotation from the Talmud.[10]

**GOLDE.** Tevya!

**TEVYA.** It's time for the afternoon prayers. . . . Just as I finish the last blessing, I see them.

**GOLDE.** Who?

**TEVYA.** Them! Two mysterious creatures are approaching stealthily, and I remember the thieves that are all over the forest, and I think I'll say a prayer. What's the good? I ask myself. I just finished a prayer, and here they are. So I jump into the wagon. I crack the whip and I holler, "Giddyap!"

**GOLDE.** And?

**TEVYA.** The horse is nibbling. He doesn't notice me. And the two terrors are upon me.

[TEVYA *covers his head as* TWO WOMEN *approach him, an elderly woman and her young daughter. His eyes close tight.*]

If it's gold you're after, you've got the wrong man.

**OLDER WOMAN.** Calm yourself, my good man, and open your eyes. We are two women, visitors from Kiev.[11] We are staying in Boiberik.[12] We went for a walk and got lost.

**YOUNG WOMAN.** Can you tell us the way to Boiberik?

**TEVYA.** Of course, I can tell you the way to Boiberik. I am Tevya, the drayman, and the way to Boiberik is the road I travel every day.

---

10. **Talmud** (täl′ mood) *n.*: The collection of writings that make up the Jewish civil and religious law.
11. **Kiev** (kē′ ef): A city in southwest Russia.
12. **Boiberik** (boi′ ber ik): A village in Russia.

**YOUNG WOMAN.** Is it far?

**TEVYA.** Far, to some, is near. If, to give an instance, it is a load of wood to haul from here to Boiberik, for me it's far. If you're paying for the load, for you it's near.

**OLDER WOMAN.** How far, my good man?

**TEVYA.** Now there's a fair question. A few miles, maybe eight.

[THE WOMEN *are alarmed at the distance.*]

**YOUNG WOMAN.** That's terrible.

**TEVYA.** I'm sorry it's so far. If it was up to me, I'd bring it closer. But the Lord in Heaven who planted Boiberik didn't consult Tevya.

**OLDER WOMAN.** Now listen, my good man, we are tired and cannot take another step. All day long we have had only a glass of coffee, a little fish, some rolls and butter . . .

**TEVYA.** On such a diet, you cannot expect a person to dance.

**YOUNG WOMAN.** [*Winningly*] Couldn't you take us to Boiberik?

**OLDER WOMAN.** That's exactly the idea.

**TEVYA.** It is a fine idea, with this exception. I am coming from Boiberik, and you are going to Boiberik. As the Talmud states, you can't go in two directions at the same time.

**YOUNG WOMAN.** A wise and learned man like yourself, who can quote scripture, can surely figure that out. Turn your wagon around, move over so we can get in, and there's your answer.

**TEVYA.** That's one answer. Another is "Giddyap" and I'm gone.

**OLDER WOMAN.** My good man, we shall see to it that your kindness is rewarded.

**TEVYA.** Rewarded is an excellent word. Perhaps it means, thank you very much? [*He turns toward* GOLDE *and the* GIRLS.] And before I know it, they interpret that question as an invitation, and they are crowding in the wagon with me.

[*The* TWO WOMEN *have come around until they are sitting on either side of* TEVYA. *He turns back to them.*]

**OLDER WOMAN.** Let us not dally here all day, Reb[13] Tevya.

**TEVYA.** I'm sorry, but the horse doesn't want to play.

**YOUNG WOMAN.** The whip, Tevya; use the whip!

**TEVYA.** Thanks for the suggestion, but my friend, the horse, is as used to the whip as I am to poverty. Whup! There he goes.

[*They jog along with the horse.*]

**OLDER WOMAN.** Is this as fast as he goes?

**TEVYA.** To answer you directly, you're lucky he started. This is Tevya's horse, and he knows this is not the way home. For him, this is the way to work. So be content he's moving. [*To* GOLDE] We jog along—up, down, around. Finally I ask: [*He turns back to the women.*] Tell me, since we're nearby, where do you wish to be dropped off?

**OLDER WOMAN.** My dear man, what kind of language is that? We don't wish to be dropped off anywhere.

**TEVYA.** I beg your pardon. Dropped off is an expression among logs. Among genteel folks we say: where do you wish to be transported, dear ladies, when, with God's help and the blessings of providence, we finally arrive at our destination? Where in Boiberik?

**OLDER WOMAN.** Why didn't you say so in the first place?

**TEVYA.** As the saying goes, it is better to ask twice than to go wrong.

**YOUNG WOMAN.** Are you familiar with the green dacha[14] with the black trim?

**TEVYA.** Oh, the millionaire's! Do me a favor, please. If you are connected with anyone living there, tell the master of the house that Tevya with the wagon is something of a pauper.

**YOUNG WOMAN.** Mother, we're here!

[*A babble of offstage* VOICES *is heard, as the* TWO WOMEN *rush into the arms of their family.*]

**VOICES.** Grandma! Mother! Auntie! We thought: wolves! We were so worried. What happened? Mazel tov!

[*And* TEVYA *is left alone. From his position in the wagon, he turns and addresses* GOLDE.]

**TEVYA.** They rush onto the porch, hugging and kissing and blessing God; and there I see such a spread—everything in the world there is to eat. And I am standing at a distance, listening to all the mazel tovs, and smelling all the smells, and saying: Tevya, you are forgotten. Tevya, you're a fool, a schlimazl . . .

[*A* MERCHANT, *the head of the house, comes out, as* TEVYA *is saying this to* GOLDE.]

**MERCHANT.** Where's the schlimazl? Where is he? Oh, there you are.

**TEVYA.** Yes, sir, it's me. Here, in the dark.

**MERCHANT.** Let's have a look at you. Come on in. Maybe you'd like a little drink?

**TEVYA.** A little drink?

[TEVYA *and the* MERCHANT *are joined by the* TWO WOMEN. *A festive table is seen.* TEVYA *is handed his drink.*]

---

**13. Reb** (reb) *n.*: A Jewish title of respect equivalent to *Mister*, used with a given name.

**14. dacha** (dä′ chə) *n.*: A country house or cottage.

L'chaim.[15]

**MERCHANT.** Long life! Tell us about yourself. Do you have children?

**TEVYA.** [*His drink finished*] To answer you truthfully, sir, do I have children? If it is true each child is worth a million, then I am richer by several millions than the richest in Boiberik. The only trouble is: with all my wealth we still go to bed hungry. But as the saying goes: "If you have enough girls, the whole world whirls." And I have enough. Seven. However, I am not complaining. For God is the Father; He has his way. He sits on high; I struggle below. My grandmother, may she rest in peace, used to say: "If we didn't have to eat, we'd all be rich." I'll take another drop.

**MERCHANT.** [*Nodding and laughing*] All right, give the man what he deserves. Help yourself, Reb Tevya. Take what you like—fowl, giblets, fish—take what you want.

**TEVYA.** You mean me?

**MERCHANT.** Of course, of course. Won't you take something?

**TEVYA.** A sick person you ask, a healthy one you give . . .

**MERCHANT.** [*Expansively*] Go ahead; why wait?

**TEVYA.** Excuse me, but don't expect me to sit down and start packing away such a spread, when my wife and my seven are in bed without supper.

**MERCHANT.** You're a fine man, Reb Tevya. Mother, fix a bundle of food for Reb Tevya and his wife and his seven daughters. Enough for all of them. [*He turns to* TEVYA.] Now tell me, what do you want for yourself?

**TEVYA.** What you're doing—that's fine.

**MERCHANT.** Now, now, don't be shy! What do you want for *yourself*? You know what I'm talking about.

**TEVYA.** Well, how do I know what what I did is worth?

**MERCHANT.** Whatever you think. You tell me how much. It's yours.

[TEVYA *turns from the* MERCHANT *in his dilemma, and speaks to* GOLDE.]

**TEVYA.** Now this is the worst moment. If I said one ruble, when he might have been ready to give me two, what will I do? On the other hand, suppose I said two rubles and he thinks I'm greedy, and throws me out. So, I take a deep breath and . . . [TEVYA *takes a deep breath and . . . in a small voice*] Three rubles, please. [*The* MERCHANT *and the* OTHERS *laugh.*] Too much? Too little? Excuse me if I said the wrong thing. After all, a horse who has four legs stumbles once in a while. Why shouldn't a man who has only one tongue?

**MERCHANT.** [*Laughing*] Put that food in his wagon! Here, Reb Tevya, take this! Count it when you get home. It's more than three rubles, I can tell you.

**OLDER WOMAN.** [*Approaches*] My good man, I want to give you something else. I have a cow. A milk cow. She used to be a wonderful milker—twenty-four glasses a day—until someone cast an evil eye on her, and you can't milk her any more.

**TEVYA.** That's all right.

**OLDER WOMAN.** You can milk her, but what I mean is, nothing comes.

**TEVYA.** Don't worry. We'll not only milk her; we'll get cream. My Golde knows how to make noodles out of nothing. To this she adds water and produces noodle soup. Every week she performs a miracle: we have food on the table for the Sabbath. So we'll take the cow. Thank you; bless you.

[*The* MERCHANT *and the* OTHERS *fade out, and* TEVYA *turns, finishing his story, toward* GOLDE. *By the end of his next speech,* GOLDE *and the* GIRLS *are in the room with him, fully lit.*]

I thanked them. I blessed them. I raced back, and I can't eat another bite.

**TZEITL.** It's wonderful, Papa.

**HODEL.** Mama, you're still crying.

**GOLDE.** I had a dream about Grandmother Tzeitl, for whom you, my oldest, are named. Just before your father came, I dreamed my grandmother—may she rest in peace —carried toward me a milk pail, filled to the brim.

**TZEITL.** You see, Mama, it's a sign . . .

**GOLDE.** Only she carried the pail under her apron to shield it from the evil eye.

**HODEL.** Oh, Mama, you don't believe that . . .

**TEVYA.** Exactly. Superstition. Bubbemeise.[16] An old woman's story. Not tonight. Let Grandmother Tzeitl be happy in the true world, in paradise. We all have this, plus a cow.

**GOLDE.** I can't get the sight out of my eyes.

**TEVYA.** [*Who well knows how to distract her*] Tell me, my darling, what shall we do with our fortune? First, what shall we do with the cow? What is your opinion?

**GOLDE.** The cow is simple. We'll drink the milk; we'll make the butter. What we don't eat, we'll sell.

**TEVYA.** And the money?

**GOLDE.** The money is something else. Thirty-seven rubles is a responsibility.

**TEVYA.** I've been thinking. Maybe if we bought a pair of horses . . .

**GOLDE.** Horses get lame, my thinker.

**TEVYA.** How about a grocery store near Boiberik?

**GOLDE.** There are eleven groceries in Boiberik. Eight are starving, and two just went bankrupt.

**TEVYA.** I'll go to the grain market in Odessa.[17] Do you know what's going on in Odessa these days?

**GOLDE.** In Odessa they have the plague.[18]

**TEVYA.** Your second-cousin-once-removed, Menachem Mendel, told me how in Kiev, on mortgage[19] alone—

**GOLDE.** My second-cousin-once-removed is a luftmensch[20] who lives on air and pipe dreams. Since he has been in business —forty-one years—he has amassed one thing: old age.

**TEVYA.** So what will we do with our wealth, if you're so intelligent?

**GOLDE.** First, girls, to bed! Put away the celebration, and to bed!

[*The* GIRLS *protest, then go.*]

Take a look around you, Tevya: the mansion we live in, the chair, what we use for a table. And peek into the other room. For one night, your seven daughters have been fed. Congratulations! But you still have seven daughters. Seven arrangements to be arranged;

---

16. **bubbemeise** (bu bə mī′ sə) *n.*: Yiddish for a fairy tale.

17. **Odessa** (ō des′ə): A seaport in southwest Russia.
18. **plague** (plāg) *n.*: A contagious epidemic disease.
19. **mortgage** (môr′ gij) *n.*: The pledging of property for money.
20. **luftmensch** (lŏŏft′ mensh′) *n.*: Yiddish for an impractical person.

seven dowries to be dowered; seven still, in one word, to get married. So therefore we'll take the cow—if it is a cow—and buy us another cow. With the two, we will have milk and cream and butter and cheese. And with the girls and me to make it, and you to sell it, we'll try to make a living from the rich who come to spend the summer in Boiberik.

**TEVYA.** Such a head! [*He kisses her.*] You're right. As is written, "Man is wise, but the ways of a woman . . ." So Tevya the dray-man is now Tevya the dairyman. And he will work and work and, the Lord willing, take care of his girls and his wife and himself.

**GOLDE.** Already he's a dairyman.

**TEVYA.** I mean it. For the first time in my life, I think I'm beginning to see a little light.

**GOLDE.** Look yonder, you'll see light. Real light. It's dawn.

**TEVYA.** Already?

**GOLDE.** If I hadn't cut you off with the tracts and the citations,[21] it would have been noon. All right, dairyman, the day of labor has begun.

**TEVYA.** All right. Such excitement, I'm dead on my feet. Let me lie down for an hour and, God willing, get back some strength.

**GOLDE.** It'll be daylight in half an hour.

**TEVYA.** That's what I said. Half an hour. Then Tevya the dairyman begins a new life.

## Scene 2

[TEVYA *is seen driving his horse along the road. The music is spirited.*]

**TEVYA.** So, horse, we ride; that is to say we move. Your head is in the air, you pick your

---

21. **tracts and citations:** Religious quotations.

feet off the ground. No longer the nag of Tevya the drayman, but the horse of Tevya the dairyman. Aye, people: formerly when I was a pauper—that is to say two weeks ago—everyone wished me well. Now they see me milking my two skinny cows, they haven't got a decent word to say. Where did Tevya get them? He stole them; he's making illegal schnapps on the side. Will you ever get a word of praise from your own kind? It's admitted I make the best butter you can buy. Do you think a single Jewish customer would ever say so? Never. On the other hand, only yesterday the rich Gentile[22] banker from the North tasted my Golde's cheese. Do you know what he said? Tevya, says he, you serve a decent product. Where can you get such praise from your own? [*He pulls the reins of the horse.*] Today we're seeing Lazar Wolf, the butcher. I'm opposed to the whole idea, but when Golde makes up her mind to something, it's done. Go see the butcher, she says. He's anxious to speak to you. Why, I answer. He's already got an eye on our little milch[23] cow? Never mind, she tells me: you'll see him. If he offers a good price, you'll sell her. She's not such a great milker. No, I reply. It's written . . . She interrupts the quotation and tells me, "Every Thursday when our Tzeitl is in his shop, he tells her, 'Send your Papa to my house! I want to see him!'" I say; no. She says, Tevya! I repeat the no, and here I am. As the Midrash[24] tells us, man proposes, but who makes up his mind for him? Golde.

[TEVYA *leaves the wagon and enters* LAZAR WOLF'S. *The butcher's is a substantial dwelling for a Russian Jew. The furniture is solid.* TEVYA *wanders about, alone, looking, touching, testing, peeking.*]

---

22. **Gentile** (jen' tīl) *n.*: Any person not a Jew.
23. **milch** *adj.*: Kept for milking.
24. **Midrash** (mid' räsh) *n.*: Explanatory notes and comments on the Scriptures written between the sixth century B.C. and about 1200 A.D.

Lazar Wolf? You're here? You're not here? It's me, Tevya.

LAZAR. [*Off*] I'll be right there. Make yourself at home, Reb Tevya.

TEVYA. Make myself at home. All right. It is a home. In my house, you sit on a chair, so. [*He sits on the edge.*] Here. [*He sits solidly.*] That's a chair. [*Examines the table. Bangs it*] Mine would have come down with such a blow. [*Sees a samovar*] A brass samovar. A butcher, as is written, is a man of substance. What I wouldn't give to see my daughters the mistress of such a house. [*He sees a goblet near the samovar.*] Mm, a fine cup to drink from! A cup? A goblet! To make a toast with. Nu. L'chaim.

[*He pretends to drain it.* LAZAR WOLF *stomps in: a big man, drying beefy hands on a white, stained apron.*]

LAZAR. L'chaim to you, Reb Tevya. You like it? It's yours. A present.

TEVYA. I couldn't.

LAZAR. What do you mean, you couldn't? Do it; it's done. I'm sorry you had to wait. I was just butchering an ox.

TEVYA. [*Puts the cup down*] It's no good, Lazar Wolf; I won't do it. Golde insisted I come, so I came, but the answer is no.

LAZAR. Sit down, take a glass of tea; let's talk like sensible people. First listen, then say no.

TEVYA. I'll listen, but no is no.

LAZAR. Let's begin at the beginning. How are things with you? [*He hands* TEVYA *the tea.*]

TEVYA. How are things? I go and go and I go, and I get nowhere. As the Torah says, "Money is round. It rolls away."

LAZAR. Yes, but compared with the way things were . . .

TEVYA. You heard?

LAZAR. Of course, I heard. A butcher hears about things.

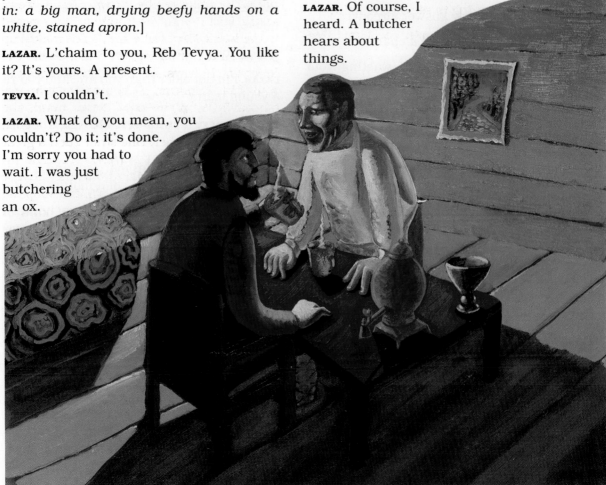

**TEVYA.** I told you no.

**LAZAR.** All right, no. But let's talk. A piece of hard sugar?

**TEVYA.** Thank you.

**LAZAR.** Compared with yesterday, Reb Tevya, you're a rich man.

**TEVYA.** As the Talmud says, "May we both have what I still need to make a rich man."

**LAZAR.** It's a wonderful thing to be a learned man, Reb Tevya, and have a line of Talmud for every occasion.

**TEVYA.** There's a quotation for that too, Lazar Wolf.

**LAZAR.** I'm sure. I'm sure. However, business is business, so let's begin . . .

**TEVYA.** You heard my answer already.

**LAZAR.** Listen, give a man a chance.

**TEVYA.** There's no sense in wasting your breath. A no from Tevya means no.

**LAZAR.** Why not?

**TEVYA.** I'm in no hurry. My house isn't on fire—and besides, I feel sorry for the poor thing.

**LAZAR.** Listen to him! He feels sorry. You talk as if she's the only one you've got.

**TEVYA.** She's my first. There's none like her.

**LAZAR.** I know. I know how you feel. Everyone is special—each one. But we are men of the world. There'd be a little something in it for you. Lazar Wolf is not a stingy man.

**TEVYA.** I heard last year, in the dead of winter, you gave away ice . . .

**LAZAR.** Maybe I'm a little rough in business. But this is a family matter.

**TEVYA.** What are you talking about—a family matter—what family?

**LAZAR.** Wait a minute, Tevya. What have *you* been talking about?

**TEVYA.** My cow, what else?

**LAZAR.** [*Laughing*] His cow; that's a great one.

**TEVYA.** So what are *you* talking about? Tell me, please, so I can laugh, too. Tevya also enjoys a joke.

**LAZAR.** I'm talking about your daughter, what else? Tzeitl, your eldest.

**TEVYA.** You want my Tzeitl? No. Impossible. Absolutely no. No, and again no.

**LAZAR.** I gather you don't like the idea. Why?

**TEVYA.** Why, he asks. You're a butcher.

**LAZAR.** A butcher always has meat in the house.

**TEVYA.** You're an old man, twice her age.

**LAZAR.** I'm not older than you are, and you're a young man.

**TEVYA.** You're a widower with grown children.

**LAZAR.** My children are married, and a widower has the experience of a mature man.

**TEVYA.** Nah, you haven't the right kind of feelings for a delicate girl like Tzeitl. Her singing, her sewing, her cooking—could you appreciate her subtleties?

**LAZAR.** When it comes to eating, Lazar Wolf is not backward.

**TEVYA.** No, no, and again, no!

**LAZAR.** Now let me talk.

[TEVYA *turns his back.*]

I'm pretty well off, Reb Tevya. I have, heaven will forgive my boasting, my own house. Try the table.

**TEVYA.** I tried.

**LAZAR.** I have two shops, here and in Boiberik. In my attic there are hides. In my chest, a little money.

**TEVYA.** Money is not everything.

**LAZAR.** If, worse luck, your Tzeitl found herself a man of solid substance, a good provider, with a mature head on his shoulders and a Sabbath chicken for her father every week —plus no dowry—and a little something for all the other daughters as well, is that a calamity? . . . Why are you silent?

**TEVYA.** I'm thinking. And thoughts are private, if you don't mind. I'm thinking, as it says in Rashi, from the heart. Good looking you're not. Still, good looks is on the surface.

**LAZAR.** Exactly.

**TEVYA.** Further, you're not a scholar. You can just about manage to say your prayers, but after all, everybody can't be a scholar, and Tevya can quote for two, at least. As the saying goes, "If it's your luck to have a little money, well, there's learning in a bank account." But I'm still thinking no.

**LAZAR.** We don't have to bargain with each other, Reb Tevya, and beat around the bush. Let's shake hands and call it a match. What do you say? Speak up!

**TEVYA.** What do you want me to do: yell? This is not something a person drives into, like a wagon. This is my oldest daughter.

**LAZAR.** Exactly. Once she's out of the way, you'll have a chance to concentrate on your second oldest, and your third . . .

**TEVYA.** To marry a daughter is no trick. When God, at His own pace, decides to send for each child her predestined[25] one . . .

---

**25. predestined** (prē des′ tin'd) *adj.*: Decreed beforehand; foreordained.

**LAZAR.** Naturally, but does it hurt, Reb Tevya, to help our destiny a little? This one you can get rid of without a dowry. That'll leave a little something for the second one. Clothes, I told you I'd take care of, and if you yourself would consider something . . .

**TEVYA.** A daughter is not a piece of meat to bargain over. You think you're still in the butcher store.

**LAZAR.** I'm sorry if I offended. I'll say no more. Only where is it written that Lazar Wolf is not destined to be her predestined one?

**TEVYA.** That's a sensible answer. If it's meant to be that my Tzeitl will have a nice and comfortable life with Lazar Wolf, the butcher, with meat each day in the week . . .

**LAZAR.** Every day.

**TEVYA.** Then it's written. But remember; it's also written that a woman is not a dishrag. Therefore Golde must be consulted. Also the girl herself.

**LAZAR.** Of course. Give them the pros and cons. I know your Golde is a practical woman. Meanwhile, take the goblet I gave you, and have a drink.

**TEVYA.** Well, why not? As the saying goes, "A drink is a"—not so much.

**LAZAR.** A real l'chaim this time.

**TEVYA.** Maybe a mazel tov.

**LAZAR.** Drink hearty!

**TEVYA.** [*Drinks*] Do you know what a treasure she is?

**LAZAR.** I know.

**TEVYA.** A jewel! A pearl! A diamond!

**LAZAR.** What she'll eat in my house on weekdays, she never eats in your house on holidays. Another drink?

**TEVYA.** [*Takes it*] Don't think feeding a woman is everything. You can't eat five-ruble pieces; and frankly, Reb Lazar Wolf —that's nice schnapps—you're a coarse fellow, something of a bull yourself.

**LAZAR.** Agreed. Everything is agreed.

**TEVYA.** If you had a million rubles on one side of the scales, and my Tzeitl on the other . . .

**LAZAR.** Believe me, my father-in-law-to-be, I understand. Even if you are older than I am, Tevya, you're a bigger fool. I understand.

[*In great good humor, they embrace, as the scene fades.* TEVYA *makes his way home, singing a Rosh Hashana*[26] *song, suggestive of the forthcoming wedding. He carries the goblet before him. Then he realizes where he is—home—and enters cautiously.* GOLDE *is waiting for him, face to face.*]

**GOLDE.** Oh, that's a shining example for a father of seven girls, to come home so late!

**TEVYA.** Golde, if I'm a little late, believe me I have cause. Behold—a silver goblet.

**GOLDE.** I know all about it. Quick, go wash your face; there's a thousand things to do. I've already got the pencil and paper.

**TEVYA.** What are you talking about? I only just walked in the door. I haven't even told you the good news and—

**GOLDE.** I know. I know.

**TEVYA.** What do you know?

**GOLDE.** Tzeitl is engaged. To Lazar Wolf. I know. Without a dowry. I know. He'll buy the clothes. I know everything.

**TEVYA.** [*Drying his face*] How do you know?

**GOLDE.** If you think a butcher hears about a cow quickly, let me tell you a mother hears about the engagement of her daughter be-fore that. Besides, my Tevya, from Lazar Wolf's you went to the Rabbi's house, about the marriage contract. Then you managed to arrive at your wagon, and there stood Pessie, the wife of the cantor,[27] and Pessie has a tongue from here to Yehupetz. Besides, I knew it even before you left.

**TEVYA.** What?

**GOLDE.** Grandmother Tzeitl—may she rest in peace—for whom our Tzeitl is named, came to me in a vision, a dream. She stood in the doorway, holding by her hand our Tzeitl, and she was dressed as a bride.

**TEVYA.** Grandma Tzeitl was dressed as a bride?

**GOLDE.** Our Tzeitl was the bride. Grandma was dressed in her Sabbath best, the blue dress, and with the gray shawl over her head, that Poppa gave her on their fifteenth anniversary. She led our Tzeitl into the room. And there, standing under the canopy, was Reb Yozivel, the Rabbi, waiting to start the ceremony.

**TEVYA.** And the bridegroom?

**GOLDE.** To tell you the truth, I didn't get a good look at his face. But now I realize it was Lazar Wolf. So sit down; there's a million things to do. Take the pencil . . .

**TEVYA.** It is written that a woman is like a melon; who knows what's inside?

**GOLDE.** For one night, spare me the quotations, and listen what you have to tell Lazar Wolf our Tzeitl needs. First of all, she doesn't have a thing to wear, not a pair of stockings. She'll need a silk dress for the wedding—blue is her best color—write . . .

**TEVYA.** Blue.

**GOLDE.** A cotton dress for summer, a wool

---

**26. Rosh Hashana** (rōsh' hə shô'nə) *n.*: The Jewish New Year.

**27. cantor** (kan' tər) *n.*: A singer of solos in a synagogue, who leads the congregation in prayer.

dress for winter. Three petticoats, three shawls. Then there's handkerchiefs, a silk parasol, nightgowns and at least two pairs of other things.

**TEVYA.** You're going too fast. Other things? What's that?

**GOLDE.** Just put it down. Other things. Two pairs.

**TEVYA.** [*Writing*] Tell me, my darling, where did you become acquainted with all this paraphernalia for fancy ladies?

**GOLDE.** I'm not a lady of fashion? I'm not used to silks and satins? Besides, I haven't got eyes when a train comes through? Listen, give *me* the list. I'll take it to Lazar Wolf, myself. You wouldn't even know how to *pronounce* half of them.

**TEVYA.** [*Thinking the whole thing over. Pleased*] We made a good match, Golde!

**GOLDE.** Our Tzeitl will be a happy girl.

**TEVYA.** We thank Thee, Heavenly Father, that Thou has moved Lazar Wolf to take our daughter, Tzeitl, without even a dowry. May she grow old with him in contentment and honor, not like Fruma-Sarah, his first wife, may she rest in peace. May we know the joy of seeing her the mistress of a fine house, filled to overflowing—in the backyard, chicken coops and goose coops and duck coops. Amen.

**GOLDE.** [*Affectionately*] Sometimes, Tevya, you are not such a fool. Amen.

**TEVYA.** Now, where's the bride-to-be? TZEITL! Tzeitl!

[*The three* GIRLS *walk through, stiffly.* TZEITL *is crying.*]

She's crying for joy. [*To* TZEITL] You heard?

**TZEITL.** [*Crying*] Papa . . .

**HODEL.** Tzeitl, we agreed.

[*And the three* GIRLS *stand stonily, in silence.*]

**TEVYA.** What's the matter?

**TZEITL.** [*Running off*] Oh, Papa, I . . .

**TEVYA.** Go with her! Find out . . .

[GOLDE *leaves.* TEVYA *speaks to* HODEL.]

What's the matter with your sister? I did something?

**HODEL.** Look at me, Papa.

**TEVYA.** [*He looks.*] I see. I committed a crime. What crime?

**HODEL.** Did it ever occur to you that Tzeitl has some feelings in the matter?

**TEVYA.** It occurred to me that Tzeitl likes to eat every day.

**HODEL.** What does she want, Papa? That's the important question.

**TEVYA.** She doesn't want to be warm, winter as well as summer?

**HODEL.** Did the question ever come into your mind: does she love this man?

**TEVYA.** The novels of Paris and St. Petersburg[28] are with us. Waltzes is not something to live on, my darling.

**HODEL.** You're not listening to what I'm saying.

**TEVYA.** Give me a quotation; maybe then I'll understand.

**HODEL.** Your head is so full of quotations, you don't see what's going on under your nose.

**TEVYA.** Enlighten your papa. He's listening.

**HODEL.** The world is changing, Papa. People are changing. Tzeitl has a right to her own life.

---

**28. St. Petersburg:** Former name of the city of Leningrad in Russia.

**TEVYA.** Rights, this is what you're talking about?

**HODEL.** Today is not yesterday, Papa.

**TEVYA.** Now it's clear to me. Yesterday they ate bread; today they chew on rights.

**HODEL.** You don't marry off a daughter. You *ask* a daughter . . .

**TEVYA.** This I intended all along. I said it even to Lazar Wolf. The girl herself, I said, is not a dishrag. Ask him if I didn't say that!

**HODEL.** [*Walks to the table and picks up the goblet*] You made your arrangements. You had a drink on it. You signed a marriage contract. You set a date with the Rabbi. Did you or didn't you?

**TEVYA.** I did. Sentence me to prison for life. Only put down the goblet before you break it.

**HODEL.** You think because a thing has been done for a thousand years, it has to be that way forever. Talk to Tzeitl! Listen to her! With both your ears! Go, Papa! Ask her.

**TEVYA.** The mother takes the words out of your mouth before you get a chance to speak. The daughter puts new ones in before you can draw a second breath. It is written truly—

**HODEL.** Papa!

**TEVYA.** I'm going. [*He starts walking, speaks to no one in particular.*] Modern children! [TEVYA *joins* GOLDE *and* TZEITL, *right. This is the wagon shed.*] So, my Tzeitl, come to your Papa's arms, and tell me . . . [*He takes* TZEITL *from* GOLDE'S *arms and, as he embraces her, speaks to* GOLDE *over her shoulder.*] What is it?

**GOLDE.** Tears. All I hear is tears. No, and tears.

**TEVYA.** I'll talk to her. I'm the father.

**GOLDE.** Talk, but don't say too much! Don't say anything you'll be sorry for.

**TEVYA.** Tevya, the dairyman, doesn't talk out of both sides of his mouth.

**GOLDE.** [*Going*] Lazar Wolfs don't grow on trees.

**TEVYA.** So, my biggest girl, my silliest, biggest girl, tell me . . .

**TZEITL.** Papa, I'm so unhappy.

**TEVYA.** Why? Your father is asking why.

**TZEITL.** I don't want to marry him.

**TEVYA.** And the reason?

**TZEITL.** I don't love him, Papa.

**TEVYA.** Love, I'll tell you about. Love doesn't always happen in the morning. Sometimes it takes all afternoon and part of the evening.

**TZEITL.** I'll carry stones. I'll dig holes. I'll be a servant for the Gentiles.

**TEVYA.** What terrible life am I sending you to? I'm rescuing you. No more three-in-a-bed. No more without supper. Look at the dress you're wearing!

**TZEITL.** I couldn't, Papa. Never.

**TEVYA.** You enjoy it so much, being the daughter in a house where the wind runs through everything?

**TZEITL.** How can I tell you? I'd be fed and warm—but in that house, Papa, I would die.

**TEVYA.** So much you don't want to?

**TZEITL.** Please, Papa, have pity on me.

**TEVYA.** Tevya's daughters will never be unhappy. Hungry, maybe; but never unhappy. You don't want to marry him, that's all there is to it. After all, today is not yesterday.

**TZEITL.** Thank you, Papa.

**TEVYA.** Not me; thank the Lord in heaven, who opened my eyes. Did you think I was going to force you? Never. Even if in some circles a rich man is not a calamity.

**TZEITL.** Papa, you're wonderful.

**TEVYA.** Listen, what Tevya thought was preordained was not ordained. So be it. Done and done. Wipe your eyes; you've done enough crying for one day. [*He helps her blow her nose.*] So—I'll return his goblet in the morning. I'll make my explanations to the Rabbi. As the good book tells us. Period.

**TZEITL.** Papa, could I talk to you?

**TEVYA.** Something else?

**TZEITL.** I think this is the best time. [*Calling offstage*] Psst. It's all right. Come out!

**TEVYA.** What's going on?

[MOTTEL *enters from under the wagon. He is a small, threadbare but ingratiating young tailor.*]

**TZEITL.** Papa, you know Mottel Kamzoil.

**TEVYA.** The tailor from Anatevka. What brings you here?

**MOTTEL.** I walked, Reb Tevya.

**TEVYA.** That I didn't ask you. What I asked was: what is Mottel Kamzoil, all the way from Anatevka, doing in Tevya's barn?

**MOTTEL.** I came because I have a match for Tzeitl.

**TEVYA.** Since when did a tailor become a matchmaker? Is it a good match?

**MOTTEL.** Like a glove fits a hand.

**TEVYA.** In whose behalf are you here? If he smells from a butcher shop—no!

**MOTTEL.** This is a match that was made—as we say in the shop—
to the measure.

**TEVYA.** Who, please?

**MOTTEL.** Who else? We love each other.

**TZEITL.** We gave each other our pledge over a year ago.

**TEVYA.** You gave yourself your pledge? And where was I? What about my rights? Or is this also part of today, that a father is treated like dust?

**MOTTEL.** Nothing like that, Reb Tevya. I've been working in the shop, to get a little ahead, so that when I came to ask you I would have a little something to start in life with.

**TEVYA.** What's the matter? A father doesn't give a dowry any more?

**MOTTEL.** Up until just recently, Reb Tevya —no offense meant—you weren't exactly in a position to . . .

**TEVYA.** That's not the point. Now let me ask some questions. A father asks questions. How do you expect to support my Tzeitl, a tailor with one shirt to his name . . .

**MOTTEL.** When you married your Golde, did you have a large mansion?

**TEVYA.** All right—passed. What kind of a family do you come from?

**MOTTEL.** My family is my family. I have a trade. That no one can take from me. The name, I haven't made yet.

**TEVYA.** You know something: that's a good answer. My own pedigree isn't exactly aristocratic, so why am I giving myself airs?

**TZEITL.** Oh, Papa, Papa . . .

**TEVYA.** Still, to deny to an old man the pleasure of his rights . . . "to go and pledge" —such a word—without giving a father the joy of a drink and a mazel tov and a little arguing back and forth . . .

**MOTTEL.** We're having it right now, Reb Tevya, aren't we?

**TEVYA.** Maybe he is only a tailor, but he's a good man. He'll make a living by the sweat of his brow—like your father. So let's give thanks to God. You won't change your mind tomorrow?

**MOTTEL.** May I become a stone, a bone, and sink into earth right here if I ever change my mind.

**TEVYA.** Tzeitl?

**TZEITL.** I love him, Papa.

**TEVYA.** Thy will be done. We thank Thee, O Heavenly Father, who in his infinite wisdom has sent forth Mottel, the tailor, for Tzeitl, the daughter of Tevya, the daughter of Golde. [*He stops.*] Your mama! What will I tell your mama?

**MOTTEL.** We'll tell her ourselves, Reb Tevya.

**TZEITL.** You've done enough already, Papa.

**TEVYA.** No. And when Tevya says "No" regarding Golde, it's "No."

**TZEITL.** What will you tell her?

**TEVYA.** The truth. The truth, as is written, can be stated in several ways. If a little something is left out, it can still be the truth. Or if a drop is added, that doesn't make it a lie. Like the time the Czar's[29] general came to my father to take me into the army. My father replied: "The boy is crazy, your honor: look in his eyes; he wouldn't make a good soldier." Crazy, I wasn't; but a good soldier I wouldn't have been. My father helped the Czar. Right? So go, my children, and be happy. The problem of Golde is between Tevya and his Maker.

[*The lights fade slowly out.*]

---

**29. Czar** (zär) *n.*: The emperor of Russia.

## THINKING ABOUT THE SELECTION

### Recalling

1. How does Tevya's situation in life improve?
2. Describe Tevya's meeting with Lazar Wolf. What agreement do they make?
3. What sign does Golde have that Tzeitl is meant to marry Lazar Wolf?
4. Explain why Tzeitl is unhappy about the news of her planned marriage.
5. What is Tevya's response to Tzeitl's choice of a husband?

### Interpreting

6. How do Tzeitl's sisters feel about her arranged marriage?
7. Describe Tevya's character. Discuss his motivation, his strengths, and his attitude toward life.
8. What makes this play humorous? Cite examples to support your answer.

### Applying

9. Hodel tells Tevya, "The world is changing, Papa. . . . Tzeitl has a right to her own life." How do you think that Tevya will adjust to a changing world?

## ANALYZING LITERATURE

### Understanding the One-Act Play

The **one-act play** is a brief drama with few characters and a simple plot. Because of its condensed form, its plot develops quickly, sometimes from actions that took place before the play begins. Also some events are not shown on the stage but are told to you in dialogue.

1. Summarize the plot of the play. Point out two scenes that are important to the action but are not shown on stage. You learn about them through the dialogue.
2. What event necessary to the plot occurred before the start of the play?
3. What characteristics of Tevya's speech provide humor?

## CRITICAL THINKING AND READING

### Making Inferences About Characters

An **inference** is a reasonable conclusion that you can draw based on evidence. Because a play consists mainly of dialogue, you can make inferences about the characters' traits and personalities based on what they say and how they say it. For example, Tevya says, "I say, no. She says, Tevya! I repeat the no, and here I am. As the Midrash tells us, man proposes, but who makes up his mind for him? Golde." From this statement you can infer that Tevya knows that his wife determines most of what he does, regardless of his opinion, but he is amused and philosophical about it.

What inferences can you make about characters from the following lines?

1. Golde: "But you still have seven daughters . . . to get married. So therefore we'll take the cow—if it is a cow—and buy us another cow. With the two, we will have milk and cream and butter and cheese. And with the girls and me to make it, and you to sell it, we'll try to make a living from the rich who come to spend the summer in Boiberik."
2. Lazar Wolf: "This one you can get rid of without a dowry. That'll leave a little something for the second one. Clothes, I told you I'd take care of, and if you yourself would consider something . . ."

## THINKING AND WRITING

### Writing About Characters in a Play

Imagine that you are the director for *Tevya and the First Daughter*. Write an essay directed toward the producer stating which actors you would like to play each role. First make a list of the actors you want, matching the actor's traits to the character's traits. Then use this information in your essay, including an explanation for each of your choices. Revise your essay to be persuasive about your choice of actors.

# GUIDE FOR READING

## Invasion from Mars

**Howard Koch** (1902–    ), born in New York, has lived much of his life there and in Hollywood. He has written for the stage, screen, and radio. Koch won an Oscar for his screenplay for the movie *Casablanca*. He said his goal was to "dramatize as honestly as I can any aspect of the human condition in its social framework, with an emphasis on life-supporting values." When his radio play *Invasion from Mars,* based on the novel *War of the Worlds* by H. G. Wells, was broadcast, many listeners believed it to be real.

### Radio Play

A **radio play** is a play that is read by actors for a radio broadcast rather than performed on a stage. Since the play is heard and not seen, you must rely on the dialogue, sound effects, and music to create the images in your mind, to develop the characters and plot, and to indicate the passage of time. You also must imagine the characters' appearance and actions.

### Look For

On Halloween night, 1938, *Invasion from Mars* was broadcast. Many listeners who did not know it was a play panicked, thinking an invasion from Mars was happening. As you read this play, imagine that you are hearing it over the radio. Look for the techniques that make it seem like an actual radio news broadcast.

### Writing

Imagine that you are present during an invasion of Earth by aliens from Mars. You hear about it on the news. How would you react? Freewrite about what you would do.

### Vocabulary

Knowing the following words will help you as you read *Invasion from Mars.*

**mortal** (môr′ t'l) *adj.*: That which must eventually die (p. 289)

**scrutinized** (skr<del>oo</del>t′ 'n īzd′) *v.*: Examined closely (p. 289)

**complacence** (kəm plās′ 'ns) *n.*: Self-satisfaction (p. 289)

**serene** (sə rēn′) *adj.*: Undisturbed (p. 289)

**conjecture** (kən jek′ chər) *n.*: An inference based on incomplete or inconclusive evidence (p. 291)

**silhouettes** (sil′ ∞ wetz′) *n.*: Outlines of things that appear dark against a light background (p. 293)

# Invasion from Mars

### Howard Koch

## CHARACTERS

**Three Announcers**
**Orson Welles**
**Carl Phillips,** radio commentator
**Professor Richard Pierson,** astronomer
**A Policeman**
**Mr. Wilmuth,** a farmer
**Brigadier General Montgomery Smith**
**Harry McDonald**

**Captain Lansing**
**Secretary of the Interior**
**Soldiers of the 22nd Field Artillery:**
  An officer, a gunner, and an observer
**Lieutenant Voght,** commander of an
  Army bomber plane
**Five Radio Operators**
**A Stranger**

COLUMBIA BROADCASTING SYSTEM
ORSON WELLES AND MERCURY THEATRE
ON THE AIR
SUNDAY, OCTOBER 30, 1938
8:00 TO 9:00 P.M.

**ANNOUNCER.** The Columbia Broadcasting System and its affiliated[1] stations present Orson Welles and the Mercury Theatre on the Air in a radio play by Howard Koch suggested by the H. G. Wells novel *The War of the Worlds.*

[*Mercury Theatre Musical Theme*]

**ANNOUNCER.** Ladies and gentlemen: the director of the Mercury Theatre and star of these broadcasts, Orson Welles . . .

**ORSON WELLES.** We know now that in the early years of the twentieth century this world was being watched closely by intelligences greater than man's and yet as mortal as his own. We know now that as human beings busied themselves about their various concerns they were scrutinized and studied, perhaps almost as narrowly as a man with a microscope might scrutinize the transient[2] creatures that swarm and multiply in a drop of water. With infinite complacence people went to and fro over the earth about their little affairs, serene in the assurance of their dominion[3] over this small spinning fragment of solar driftwood which by chance or design man has inherited out of the dark mystery of Time and Space. Yet across an immense ethereal[4] gulf, minds that are to our minds as ours are to the beasts in the jungle, intellects vast, cool and unsympathetic, regarded this earth with envious eyes and slowly and surely drew their plans

---

**2. transient** (tran′ s·hənt) *adj.*: Not permanent; passing quickly.
**3. dominion** (də min′ yən) *n.*: Power to rule.
**4. ethereal** (i thir′ ē əl) *adj.*: Of the upper regions of space.

---

**1. affiliated** (ə fil′ē āt əd) *adj.*: Associated.

against us. In the thirty-eighth year of the twentieth century came the great disillusionment.[5]

It was near the end of October. Business was better. The war was over. More men were back at work. Sales were picking up. On this particular evening, October 30, the Crossley service[6] estimated that thirty-two million people were listening in on radios.

**ANNOUNCER.** . . . for the next twenty-four hours not much change in temperature. A slight atmospheric disturbance of undetermined origin is reported over Nova Scotia,[7] causing a low pressure area to move down rather rapidly over the northeastern states, bringing a forecast of rain, accompanied by winds of light gale force. Maximum temperature 66; minimum 48. This weather report comes to you from the Government Weather Bureau.

. . . We now take you to the Meridian Room in the Hotel Park Plaza in downtown New York, where you will be entertained by the music of Ramón Raquello and his orchestra.

[*Spanish theme song . . . fades.*]

**ANNOUNCER THREE.** Good evening, ladies and gentlemen. From the Meridian Room in the Park Plaza in New York City, we bring you the music of Ramón Raquello and his orchestra. With a touch of the Spanish, Ramón Raquello leads off with "La Cumparsita."

[*Piece starts playing.*]

**ANNOUNCER TWO.** Ladies and gentlemen, we interrupt our program of dance music to bring you a special bulletin from the Inter-

continental Radio News. At twenty minutes before eight, central time, Professor Farrell of the Mount Jennings Observatory, Chicago, Illinois, reports observing several explosions of incandescent gas, occurring at regular intervals on the planet Mars.

The spectroscope[8] indicates the gas to be hydrogen and moving toward the earth with enormous velocity. Professor Pierson of the observatory at Princeton[9] confirms Farrell's observation, and describes the phenomenon as (quote) like a jet of blue flame shot from a gun (unquote). We now return you to the music of Ramón Raquello, playing for you in the Meridian Room of the Park Plaza Hotel, situated in downtown New York.

[*Music plays for a few moments until piece ends . . . sound of applause*]

Now a tune that never loses favor, the ever-popular "Star Dust." Ramón Raquello and his orchestra . . .

[*Music*]

**ANNOUNCER TWO.** Ladies and gentlemen, following on the news given in our bulletin a moment ago, the Government Meteorological Bureau has requested the large observatories of the country to keep an astronomical watch on any further disturbances occurring on the planet Mars. Due to the unusual nature of this occurrence, we have arranged an interview with the noted astronomer, Professor Pierson, who will give us his views on this event. In a few moments we will take you to the Princeton Observatory at Princeton, New Jersey. We return you until then to the music of Ramón Raquello and his orchestra.

---

**5. disillusionment** (dis′ i l oo′ zhən mənt) *n.*: Disappointment.
**6. Crossley service:** A service that estimated the size of radio audiences as the Nielsen rating service estimates the size of television audiences today.
**7. Nova Scotia** (nō′və skō′ shə): A southeastern province of Canada.

**8. spectroscope** (spek′ trə skōp′) *n.*: A scientific instrument used to identify substances.
**9. Princeton:** A university in Princeton, New Jersey.

[*Music . . .*]

ANNOUNCER TWO. We are ready now to take you to the Princeton Observatory at Princeton where Carl Phillips, our commentator, will interview Professor Richard Pierson, famous astronomer. We take you now to Princeton, New Jersey.

[*Echo chamber*]

PHILLIPS. Good evening, ladies and gentlemen. This is Carl Phillips, speaking to you from the observatory at Princeton. I am standing in a large semi-circular room, pitch black except for an oblong split in the ceiling. Through this opening I can see a sprinkling of stars that cast a kind of frosty glow over the intricate mechanism of the huge telescope. The ticking sound you hear is the vibration of the clockwork. Professor Pierson stands directly above me on a small platform, peering through the giant lens. I ask you to be patient, ladies and gentlemen, during any delay that may arise during our interview. Beside his ceaseless watch of the heavens, Professor Pierson may be interrupted by telephone or other communications. During this period he is in constant touch with the astronomical centers of the world . . . Professor, may I begin our questions?

PIERSON. At any time, Mr. Phillips.

PHILLIPS. Professor, would you please tell our radio audience exactly what you see as you observe the planet Mars through your telescope?

PIERSON. Nothing unusual at the moment, Mr. Phillips. A red disk swimming in a blue sea. Transverse[10] stripes across the disk. Quite distinct now because Mars happens to be at the point nearest the earth . . . in opposition, as we call it.

PHILLIPS. In your opinion, what do these transverse stripes signify, Professor Pierson?

PIERSON. Not canals, I can assure you, Mr. Phillips, although that's the popular conjecture of those who imagine Mars to be inhabited. From a scientific viewpoint the stripes are merely the result of atmospheric conditions peculiar to the planet.

PHILLIPS. Then you're quite convinced as a scientist that living intelligence as we know it does not exist on Mars?

PIERSON. I should say the chances against it are a thousand to one.

PHILLIPS. And yet how do you account for these gas eruptions occurring on the surface of the planet at regular intervals?

PIERSON. Mr. Phillips, I cannot account for it.

PHILLIPS. By the way, Professor, for the benefit of our listeners, how far is Mars from the earth?

PIERSON. Approximately forty million miles.

PHILLIPS. Well, that seems a safe enough distance.

PHILLIPS. Just a moment, ladies and gentlemen, someone has just handed Professor Pierson a message. While he reads it, let me remind you that we are speaking to you from the observatory in Princeton, New Jersey, where we are interviewing the world-famous astronomer, Professor Pierson . . . One moment, please. Professor Pierson has passed me a message which he has just received . . . Professor, may I read the message to the listening audience?

PIERSON. Certainly, Mr. Phillips.

PHILLIPS. Ladies and gentlemen, I shall read

---

10. **transverse** (trans vurs') *adj.*: Crossing from side to side.

you a wire addressed to Professor Pierson from Dr. Gray of the National History Museum, New York. "9:15 P.M. eastern standard time. Seismograph[11] registered shock of almost earthquake intensity occurring within a radius of twenty miles of Princeton. Please investigate. Signed, Lloyd Gray, Chief of Astronomical Division." . . . Professor Pierson, could this occurrence possibly have something to do with the disturbances observed on the planet Mars?

**PIERSON.** Hardly, Mr. Phillips. This is probably a meteorite[12] of unusual size and its arrival at this particular time is merely a coincidence. However, we shall conduct a search, as soon as daylight permits.

**PHILLIPS.** Thank you, Professor. Ladies and gentlemen, for the past ten minutes we've been speaking to you from the observatory at Princeton, bringing you a special interview with Professor Pierson, noted astronomer. This is Carl Phillips speaking. We now return you to our New York studio.

[*Fade in piano playing*]

**ANNOUNCER TWO.** Ladies and gentlemen, here is the latest bulletin from the Intercontinental Radio News. Montreal, Canada: Professor Morse of McGill University reports observing a total of three explosions on the planet Mars, between the hours of 7:45 P.M. and 9:20 P.M., eastern standard time. This confirms earlier reports received from American observatories. Now, nearer home, comes a special announcement from Trenton,[13] New Jersey. It is reported that at 8:50 P.M. a huge, flaming object, believed to be a meteorite, fell on a farm in the neighborhood of Grovers Mill, New Jersey, twenty-two miles from Trenton. The flash in the sky was visible within a radius of several hundred miles and the noise of the impact was heard as far north as Elizabeth.

We have dispatched a special mobile unit to the scene, and will have our commentator, Mr. Phillips, give you a word description as soon as he can reach there from Princeton. In the meantime, we take you to the Hotel Martinet in Brooklyn, where Bobby Millette and his orchestra are offering a program of dance music.

[*Swing band for twenty seconds . . . then cut*]

**ANNOUNCER TWO.** We take you now to Grovers Mill, New Jersey.

[*Crowd noises . . . police sirens*]

**PHILLIPS.** Ladies and gentlemen, this is Carl Phillips again, at the Wilmuth farm, Grovers Mill, New Jersey. Professor Pierson and myself made the eleven miles from Princeton in ten minutes. Well, I . . . I hardly know where to begin, to paint for you a word picture of the strange scene before my eyes, like something out of a modern *Arabian Nights*.[14] Well, I just got here. I haven't had a chance to look around yet. I guess that's it. Yes, I guess that's the . . . thing, directly in front of me, half buried in a vast pit. Must have struck with terrific force. The ground is covered with splinters of a tree it must have struck on its way down. What I can see of the . . . object itself doesn't look very much like a meteor, at least not the meteors I've seen. It looks more like a huge cylinder. It has a diameter of . . . what would you say, Professor Pierson?

**PIERSON.** [*Off*] About thirty yards.

---

**11. seismograph** (sīz' mə graf') *n*.: An instrument that records the intensity and duration of earthquakes.
**12. meteorite** (mēt' ē ə rīt') *n*.: Part of a heavenly body that passes through the atmosphere and falls to the earth's surface as a piece of matter.
**13. Trenton** (tren' tən): The capital of New Jersey.

**14. *Arabian Nights*:** A collection of tales from Arabia, India, and Persia.

**PHILLIPS.** About thirty yards . . . The metal on the sheath[15] is . . . well, I've never seen anything like it. The color is sort of yellowish-white. Curious spectators now are pressing close to the object in spite of the efforts of the police to keep them back. They're getting in front of my line of vision. Would you mind standing on one side, please?

**POLICEMAN.** One side, there, one side.

**PHILLIPS.** While the policemen are pushing the crowd back, here's Mr. Wilmuth, owner of the farm here. He may have some interesting facts to add. . . . Mr. Wilmuth, would you please tell the radio audience as much as you remember of this rather unusual visitor that dropped in your backyard? Step closer, please. Ladies and gentlemen, this is Mr. Wilmuth.

**WILMUTH.** I was listenin' to the radio.

**PHILLIPS.** Closer and louder, please.

**WILMUTH.** Pardon me!

**PHILLIPS.** Louder, please, and closer.

**WILMUTH.** Yes, sir—while I was listening to the radio and kinda drowsin', that Professor fellow was talkin' about Mars, so I was half dozin' and half . . .

**PHILLIPS.** Yes, Mr. Wilmuth. Then what happened?

**WILMUTH.** As I was sayin', I was listenin' to the radio kinda halfways . . .

**PHILLIPS.** Yes, Mr. Wilmuth, and then you saw something?

**WILMUTH.** Not first off. I heard something.

**PHILLIPS.** And what did you hear?

**WILMUTH.** A hissing sound. Like this: sssssss . . . kinda like a fourt' of July rocket.

**PHILLIPS.** Then what?

**WILMUTH.** Turned my head out the window and would have swore I was to sleep and dreamin'.

**PHILLIPS.** Yes?

**WILMUTH.** I seen a kinda greenish streak and then zingo! Somethin' smacked the ground. Knocked me clear out of my chair!

**PHILLIPS.** Well, were you frightened, Mr. Wilmuth?

**WILMUTH.** Well, I—I ain't quite sure. I reckon I—I was kinda riled.[16]

**PHILLIPS.** Thank you, Mr. Wilmuth. Thank you.

**WILMUTH.** Want me to tell you some more?

**PHILLIPS.** No . . . That's quite all right, that's plenty.

**PHILLIPS.** Ladies and gentlemen, you've just heard Mr. Wilmuth, owner of the farm where this thing has fallen. I wish I could convey the atmosphere . . . the background of this . . . fantastic scene. Hundreds of cars are parked in a field in back of us. Police are trying to rope off the roadway leading into the farm. But it's no use. They're breaking right through. Their headlights throw an enormous spot on the pit where the object's half buried. Some of the more daring souls are venturing near the edge. Their silhouettes stand out against the metal sheen.

[*Faint humming sound*]

One man wants to touch the thing . . . he's having an argument with a policeman. The policeman wins. . . . Now, ladies and gentlemen, there's something I haven't mentioned in all this excitement, but it's becoming more distinct. Perhaps you've caught it already on your radio. Listen:

---

**15. sheath** (shēth) *n.*: A case or covering.

**16. riled** (rīl'd) *v.*: Irritated; angered.

[*Long pause*] . . . Do you hear it? It's a curious humming sound that seems to come from inside the object. I'll move the microphone nearer. Here. [*Pause*] Now we're not more than twenty-five feet away. Can you hear it now? Oh, Professor Pierson!

**PIERSON.** Yes, Mr. Phillips?

**PHILLIPS.** Can you tell us the meaning of that scraping noise inside the thing?

**PIERSON.** Possibly the unequal cooling of its surface.

**PHILLIPS.** Do you still think it's a meteor, Professor?

**PIERSON.** I don't know what to think. The metal casing is definitely extraterrestrial . . . not found on this earth. Friction[17] with the earth's atmosphere usually tears holes in a meteorite. This thing is smooth and, as you can see, of cylindrical shape.

**PHILLIPS.** Just a minute! Something's happening! Ladies and gentlemen, this is terrific! This end of the thing is beginning to flake off! The top is beginning to rotate like a screw! The thing must be hollow!

**VOICES.**
She's a movin'!
Look, the darn thing's unscrewing!
Keep back, there! Keep back, I tell you!
Maybe there's men in it trying to escape!
It's red hot, they'll burn to a cinder!
Keep back there. Keep those idiots back!

[*Suddenly the clanking sound of a huge piece of falling metal*]

**VOICES.**
She's off! The top's loose!
Look out there! Stand back!

**PHILLIPS.** Ladies and gentlemen, this is the most terrifying thing I have ever witnessed . . . Wait a minute! *Someone's crawling out of the hollow top.* Someone or . . . something. I can see peering out of that black hole two luminous disks . . . are they eyes? It might be a face. It might be . . .

[*Shout of awe from the crowd*]

**PHILLIPS.** Good heavens, something's wriggling out of the shadow like a gray snake. Now it's another one, and another. They look like tentacles to me. There, I can see the thing's body. It's large as a bear and it glistens like wet leather. But that face. It . . . it's indescribable. I can hardly force myself to keep looking at it. The eyes are black and gleam like a serpent. The mouth is V-shaped with saliva dripping from its rimless lips that seem to quiver and pulsate. The monster or whatever it is can hardly move. It seems weighed down by . . . possibly gravity or something. The thing's raising up. The crowd falls back. They've seen enough. This is the most extraordinary experience. I can't find words . . . I'm pulling this microphone with me as I talk. I'll have to stop the description until I've taken a new position. Hold on, will you please, I'll be back in a minute.

[*Fade into piano*]

**ANNOUNCER TWO.** We are bringing you an eyewitness account of what's happening on the Wilmuth farm, Grovers Mill, New Jersey. [*More piano*] We now return you to Carl Phillips at Grovers Mill.

**PHILLIPS.** Ladies and gentlemen (Am I on?). Ladies and gentlemen, here I am, back of a stone wall that adjoins Mr. Wilmuth's garden. From here I get a sweep of the whole scene. I'll give you every detail as long as I can talk. As long as I can see. More state police have arrived. They're drawing up a cordon[18] in front of the pit, about thirty of

---

**17. friction** (frik′ shən) *n.:* Resistance.

**18. cordon** (kôr′ d'n) *n.:* A line or circle of police stationed around an area to guard it.

them. No need to push the crowd back now. They're willing to keep their distance. The captain is conferring with someone. We can't quite see who. Oh yes, I believe it's Professor Pierson. Yes, it is. Now they've parted. The professor moves around one side, studying the object, while the captain and two policemen advance with something in their hands. I can see it now. It's a white handkerchief tied to a pole . . . a flag of truce. If those creatures know what that means . . . what anything means! . . . *Wait!* Something's happening!

[*Hissing sound followed by a humming that increases in intensity*]

A humped shape is rising out of the pit. I can make out a small beam of light against a mirror. What's that? There's a jet of flame springing from that mirror, and it leaps right at the advancing men. It strikes them head on! Good Lord, they're turning into flame!

[*Screams and unearthly shrieks*]

Now the whole field's caught fire. [*Explosion*] The woods . . . the barns . . . the gas tanks of automobiles . . . it's spreading everywhere. It's coming this way. About twenty yards to my right . . .

[*Crash of microphone . . . then dead silence*]

ANNOUNCER TWO. Ladies and gentlemen, due to circumstances beyond our control, we are unable to continue the broadcast from Grovers Mill. Evidently there's some difficulty with our field transmission. However, we will return to that point at the earliest opportunity. In the meantime, we have a late bulletin from San Diego, California. Professor Indellkoffer, speaking at a dinner of the

California Astronomical Society, expressed the opinion that the explosions on Mars are undoubtedly nothing more than severe volcanic disturbances on the surface of the planet. We continue now with our piano interlude.

[*Piano . . . then cut*]

Ladies and gentlemen, I have just been handed a message that came in from Grovers Mill by telephone. Just a moment. At least forty people, including six state troopers lie dead in a field east of the village of Grovers Mill, their bodies burned and distorted beyond all possible recognition. The next voice you hear will be that of Brigadier General Montgomery Smith, commander of the state militia[19] at Trenton, New Jersey.

**SMITH.** I have been requested by the governor of New Jersey to place the counties of Mercer and Middlesex as far west as Princeton, and east to Jamesburg, under martial law.[20] No one will be permitted to enter this area except by special pass issued by state or military authorities. Four companies of state militia are proceeding from Trenton to Grovers Mill, and will aid in the evacuation of homes within the range of military operations. Thank you.

**ANNOUNCER.** You have just been listening to General Montgomery Smith, commanding the state militia at Trenton. In the meantime, further details of the catastrophe at Grovers Mill are coming in. The strange creatures after unleashing their deadly assault, crawled back in their pit and made no attempt to prevent the efforts of the firemen to recover the bodies and extinguish the fire. Combined fire departments of Mercer County are fighting the flames which menace the entire countryside.

We have been unable to establish any contact with our mobile unit at Grovers Mill, but we hope to be able to return you there at the earliest possible moment. In the meantime we take you—uh, just one moment please.

[*Long pause*]

[*Whisper*] Ladies and gentlemen, I have just been informed that we have finally established communication with an eyewitness of the tragedy. Professor Pierson has been located at a farmhouse near Grovers Mill where he has established an emergency observation post. As a scientist, he will give you his explanation of the calamity. The next voice you hear will be that of Professor Pierson, brought to you by direct wire. Professor Pierson.

**PIERSON.** Of the creatures in the rocket cylinder at Grovers Mill, I can give you no authoritative information—either as to their nature, their origin, or their purposes here on earth. Of their destructive instrument I might venture some conjectural explanation. For want of a better term, I shall refer to the mysterious weapon as a heat ray. It's all too evident that these creatures have scientific knowledge far in advance of our own. It is my guess that in some way they are able to generate an intense heat in a chamber of practically absolute nonconductivity.[21] This intense heat they project in a parallel beam against any object they choose, by means of a polished parabolic[22] mirror of unknown composition, much as the mirror of a lighthouse projects a beam of light. That is my conjecture of the origin of the heat ray . . .

---

**19. militia** (mə lish′ ə) *n.*: An army of citizens rather than professional soldiers, called out in time of emergency.
**20. martial law** (mär′ shəl lô′) *n.*: Temporary rule by the military authorities.

**21. nonconductivity** (nän′ kən duk tiv′ə tē) *n.*: The ability to contain and not transmit heat.
**22. parabolic** (par′ ə bäl′ ik) *adj.*: Bowl-shaped.

**ANNOUNCER TWO.** Thank you, Professor Pierson. Ladies and gentlemen, here is a bulletin from Trenton. It is a brief statement informing us that the charred body of Carl Phillips has been identified in a Trenton hospital. Now here's another bulletin from Washington, D.C.

Office of the director of the National Red Cross reports ten units of Red Cross emergency workers have been assigned to the headquarters of the state militia stationed outside of Grovers Mill, New Jersey. Here's a bulletin from state police, Princeton Junction: The fires at Grovers Mill and vicinity now under control. Scouts report all quiet in the pit, and no sign of life appearing from the mouth of the cylinder . . . And now, ladies and gentlemen, we have a special statement from Mr. Harry McDonald, vice-president in charge of operations.

**McDONALD.** We have received a request from the militia at Trenton to place at their disposal our entire broadcasting facilities. In view of the gravity of the situation, and believing that radio has a definite responsibility to serve in the public interest at all times, we are turning over our facilities to the state militia at Trenton.

**ANNOUNCER.** We take you now to the field headquarters of the state militia near Grovers Mill, New Jersey.

**CAPTAIN.** This is Captain Lansing of the signal corps,[23] attached to the state militia now engaged in military operations in the vicinity of Grovers Mill. Situation arising from the reported presence of certain individuals of unidentified nature is now under complete control.

The cylindrical object which lies in a pit directly below our position is surrounded on all sides by eight battalions of infantry, without heavy fieldpieces,[24] but adequately armed with rifles and machine guns. All cause for alarm, if such cause ever existed, is now entirely unjustified. The things, whatever they are, do not even venture to poke their heads above the pit. I can see their hiding place plainly in the glare of the searchlights here. With all their reported resources, these creatures can scarcely stand up against heavy machine-gun fire. Anyway, it's an interesting outing for the troops. I can make out their khaki uniforms, crossing back and forth in front of the lights. It looks almost like a real war. There appears to be some slight smoke in the woods bordering the Millstone River. Probably fire started by campers. Well, we ought to see some action soon. One of the companies is deploying[25] on the left flank.[26] A quick thrust and it will all be over. Now wait a minute! I see something on top of the cylinder. No, it's nothing but a shadow. Now the troops are on the edge of the Wilmuth farm. Seven thousand armed men closing in on an old metal tube. Wait, that wasn't a shadow! It's something moving . . . solid metal . . . kind of a shieldlike affair rising up out of the cylinder . . . It's going higher and higher. Why, it's standing on legs . . . actually rearing up on a sort of metal framework. Now it's reaching above the trees and the searchlights are on it! Hold on!

**ANNOUNCER TWO.** Ladies and gentlemen, I have a grave announcement to make. Incredible as it may seem, both the observations of science and the evidence of our eyes lead to the inescapable assumption[27] that those strange beings who landed in the Jer-

---

**23. signal corps:** The part of the army in charge of communications.

**24. fieldpieces** (fēld′ pēs əz) *n.*: Mobile artillery.
**25. deploying** (dē ploi′ iŋ) *v.*: Spreading out.
**26. flank** (flaŋk) *n.*: Side.
**27. assumption** (ə sump′ shən) *n.*: Idea accepted as true without proof.

sey farmlands tonight are the vanguard[28] of an invading army from the planet Mars. The battle which took place tonight at Grovers Mill has ended in one of the most startling defeats ever suffered by an army in modern times; seven thousand men armed with rifles and machine guns pitted against a single fighting machine of the invaders from Mars. One hundred and twenty known survivors. The rest strewn over the battle area from Grovers Mill to Plainsboro crushed and trampled to death under the metal feet of the monster, or burned to cinders by its heat ray. The monster is now in control of the middle section of New Jersey and has effectively cut the state through its center. Communication lines are down from Pennsylvania to the Atlantic Ocean. Railroad tracks are torn and service from New York to Philadelphia discontinued except routing some of the trains through Allentown and Phoenixville.[29] Highways to the north, south, and west are clogged with frantic human traffic. Police and army reserves are unable to control the mad flight. By morning the fugitives will have swelled Philadelphia, Camden and Trenton, it is estimated, to twice their normal population.

At this time martial law prevails throughout New Jersey and eastern Pennsylvania. We take you now to Washington for a special broadcast on the National Emergency . . . the Secretary of the Interior . . .

**SECRETARY.** Citizens of the nation: I shall not try to conceal the gravity of the situation that confronts the country, nor the concern of your government in protecting the lives and property of its people. However, I wish to impress upon you—private citizens and public officials, all of you—the urgent need of calm and resourceful action. Fortunately, this formidable enemy is still confined to a comparatively small area, and we may place our faith in the military forces to keep them there. In the meantime placing our faith in God we must continue the performance of our duties each and every one of us, so that we may confront this destructive adversary with a nation united, courageous, and consecrated[30] to the preservation of human supremacy on this earth. I thank you.

**ANNOUNCER.** You have just heard the Secretary of the Interior speaking from Washington. Bulletins too numerous to read are piling up in the studio here. We are informed that the central portion of New Jersey is blacked out from radio communication due to the effect of the heat ray upon power lines and electrical equipment. Here is a special bulletin from New York. Cables received from English, French, German scientific bodies offering assistance. Astronomers report continued gas outbursts at regular intervals on planet Mars. Majority voice opinion that enemy will be reinforced by additional rocket machines. Attempts made to locate Professor Pierson of Princeton, who has observed Martians at close range. It is feared he was lost in recent battle. Langham Field, Virginia: Scouting planes report three Martian machines visible above treetops, moving north toward Somerville with population fleeing ahead of them. Heat ray not in use; although advancing at express-train speed, invaders pick their way carefully. They seem to be making conscious effort to avoid destruction of cities and countryside. However, they stop to uproot power lines, bridges, and railroad tracks. Their apparent objective is to crush resistance, paralyze

---

**28. vanguard** (van' gärd) *n.*: The part of an army that goes ahead of the main body in an advance.
**29. Allentown and Phoenixville:** Cities in eastern Pennsylvania.

**30. consecrated** (kän' sə krāt' əd) *adj.*: Dedicated.

communication, and disorganize human society.

❧ Here is a bulletin from Basking Ridge, New Jersey: Raccoon hunters have stumbled on a second cylinder similar to the first embedded in the great swamp twenty miles south of Morristown. U.S. army field-pieces are proceeding from Newark to blow up second invading unit before cylinder can be opened and the fighting machine rigged. They are taking up position in the— foothills of Watchung Mountains.[31] Another bulletin from Langham Field, Virginia: Scouting planes report enemy machines, now three in number, increasing speed northward kicking over houses and trees in their evident haste to form a conjunction[32] with their allies south of Morristown. Machines also sighted by telephone operator east of Middlesex within ten miles of Plainfield. Here's a bulletin from Winston Field, Long Island. Fleet of army bombers carrying heavy explosives flying north in pursuit of enemy. Scouting planes act as guides. They keep speeding enemy in sight. Just a moment please. Ladies and gentlemen, we've run special wires to the artillery line in adjacent villages to give you direct reports in the zone of the advancing enemy. First we take you to the battery of the 22nd Field Artillery, located in the Watchung Mountains.

OFFICER. Range, thirty-two meters.

GUNNER. Thirty-two meters.

OFFICER. Projection, thirty-nine degrees.

GUNNER. Thirty-nine degrees.

OFFICER. Fire! [*Boom of heavy gun . . . pause*]

OBSERVER. One hundred and forty yards to the right, sir.

OFFICER. Shift range . . . thirty-one meters.

GUNNER. Thirty-one meters.

OFFICER. Projection . . . thirty-seven degrees.

GUNNER. Thirty-seven degrees.

OFFICER. Fire! [*Boom of heavy gun . . . pause*]

OBSERVER. A hit, sir! We got the tripod[33] of one of them. They've stopped. The others are trying to repair it.

OFFICER. Quick, get the range! Shift thirty meters.

GUNNER. Thirty meters.

OFFICER. Projection . . . twenty-seven degrees.

GUNNER. Twenty-seven degrees.

OFFICER. Fire! [*Boom of heavy gun . . . pause*]

OBSERVER. Can't see the shell land, sir. They're letting off a smoke.

OFFICER. What is it?

OBSERVER. A black smoke, sir. Moving this way. Lying close to the ground. It's moving fast.

OFFICER. Put on gas masks. [*Pause*] Get ready to fire. Shift to twenty-four meters.

GUNNER. Twenty-four meters.

OFFICER. Projection, twenty-four degrees.

GUNNER. Twenty-four degrees.

OFFICER. Fire! [*Boom*]

OBSERVER. Still can't see, sir. The smoke's coming nearer.

31. **Watchung** (wăch′ uŋ) **Mountains:** A range of low mountains in New Jersey.
32. **conjunction** (kən juŋk′ sʰən) *n.:* Union.

33. **tripod** (trī′ păd) *n.:* Three-legged support.

**OFFICER.** Get the range. [*Coughs*]

**OBSERVER.** Twenty-three meters. [*Coughs*]

**OFFICER.** Twenty-three meters. [*Coughs*]

**GUNNER.** Twenty-three meters. [*Coughs*]

**OBSERVER.** Projection, twenty-two degrees. [*Coughing*]

**OFFICER.** Twenty-two degrees. [*Fade in coughing*]

[*Fading in . . . sound of airplane motor*]

**COMMANDER.** Army bombing plane, V-8-43, off Bayonne, New Jersey, Lieutenant Voght, commanding eight bombers. Reporting to Commander Fairfax, Langham Field . . . This is Voght, reporting to Commander Fairfax, Langham Field . . . Enemy tripod machines now in sight. Reinforced by three machines from the Morristown cylinder . . . Six altogether. One machine partially crippled. Believed hit by shell from army gun in Watchung Mountains. Guns now appear silent. A heavy black fog hanging close to the earth . . . of extreme density,[34] nature unknown. No sign of heat ray. Enemy now turns east, crossing Passaic River into the Jersey marshes. Another straddles the Pulaski Skyway.[35] Evident objective is New York City. They're pushing down a high tension power station. The machines are close together now, and we're ready to attack. Planes circling, ready to strike. A thousand yards and we'll be over the first —eight hundred yards . . . six hundred . . . four hundred . . . two hundred . . . There they go! The giant arm raised . . . Green flash! They're spraying us with flame! Two thousand feet. Engines are giving out. No chance to release bombs. Only one thing

left . . . drop on them, plane and all. We're diving on the first one. Now the engine's gone! Eight . . .

**OPERATOR ONE.** This is Bayonne, New Jersey, calling Langham Field . . .

This is Bayonne, New Jersey, calling Langham Field . . .

Come in, please . . . Come in, please . . .

**OPERATOR TWO.** This is Langham Field . . . go ahead . . .

---

**34. density** (den′ sə tē) *n.*: Thickness.
**35. Pulaski** (pѹ las′ kē) **Skyway:** An elevated highway in eastern New Jersey.

**OPERATOR ONE.** Eight army bombers in engagement with enemy tripod machines over Jersey flats.[36] Engines incapacitated[37] by heat ray. All crashed. One enemy machine destroyed. Enemy now discharging heavy black smoke in direction of—

**OPERATOR THREE.** This is Newark, New Jersey . . .

---

36. **flats** *n.*: Low-lying marshlands.
37. **incapacitated** (in′ kə pas′ ə tāt əd) *adj.*: Disabled.

This is Newark, New Jersey . . .

Warning! Poisonous black smoke pouring in from Jersey marshes. Reaches South Street. Gas masks useless. Urge population to move into open spaces . . . automobiles use Routes 7, 23, 24 . . . Avoid congested areas. Smoke now spreading over Raymond Boulevard . . .

**OPERATOR FOUR.** 2X2L . . . calling CQ . . .
2X2L . . . calling CQ . . .
2X2L . . . calling 8X3R . . .
Come in, please . . .

**OPERATOR FIVE.** This is 8X3R . . . coming back at 2X2L.

**OPERATOR FOUR.** How's reception? How's reception? K, please. Where are you, 8X3R?
What's the matter? Where are you?

[*Bells ringing over city gradually diminishing*]

**ANNOUNCER.** I'm speaking from the roof of Broadcasting Building, New York City. The bells you hear are ringing to warn the people to evacuate the city as the Martians approach. Estimated in last two hours three million people have moved out along the roads to the north, Hutchison River Parkway still kept open for motor traffic. Avoid bridges to Long Island . . . hopelessly jammed. All communication with Jersey shore closed ten minutes ago. No more defenses. Our army wiped out . . . artillery, air force, everything wiped out. This may be the last broadcast. We'll stay here to the end . . . People are holding service below us . . . in the cathedral.

[*Voices singing hymn*]

Now I look down the harbor. All manner of boats, overloaded with fleeing population, pulling out from docks.

[*Sound of boat whistles*]

Streets are all jammed. Noise in crowds like New Year's Eve in city. Wait a minute . . . Enemy now in sight above the Palisades.[38] Five great machines. First one is crossing river. I can see it from here, wading the Hudson like a man wading through a brook . . . A bulletin's handed me . . . Martian cylinders are falling all over the country. One outside Buffalo, one in Chicago, St. Louis . . . seem to be timed and spaced. . . . Now the first machine reaches the shore. He stands watching, looking over the city. His steel, cowlish[39] head is even with the skyscrapers. He waits for the others. They rise like a line of new towers on the city's west side . . . Now they're lifting their metal hands. This is the end now. Smoke comes out . . . black smoke, drifting over the city. People in the streets see it now. They're running toward the East River . . . thousands of them, dropping in like rats. Now the smoke's spreading faster. It's reached Times Square. People trying to run away from it, but it's no use. They're falling like flies. Now the smoke's crossing Sixth Avenue . . . Fifth Avenue . . . one hundred yards away . . . it's fifty feet . . .

**OPERATOR FOUR.** 2X2L calling CQ . . .
2X2L calling CQ . . .
2X2L calling CQ . . . New York.
Isn't there anyone on the air?
Isn't there anyone . . .
2X2L—

**ANNOUNCER.** You are listening to a CBS presentation of Orson Welles and the Mercury Theatre on the Air in an original dramatization of *The War of the Worlds* by H. G. Wells. The performance will continue after a brief intermission.

---

**38. Palisades** (pal′ ə sādz′): The line of steep cliffs in northeastern New Jersey and southeastern New York on the west shore of the Hudson River.
**39. cowlish** (koul ish) *adj.*: Hood-shaped.

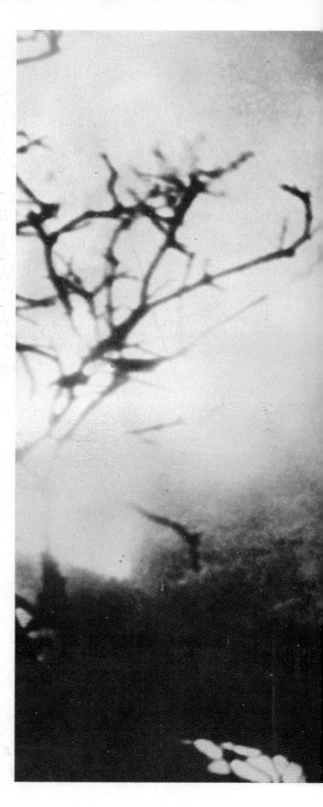

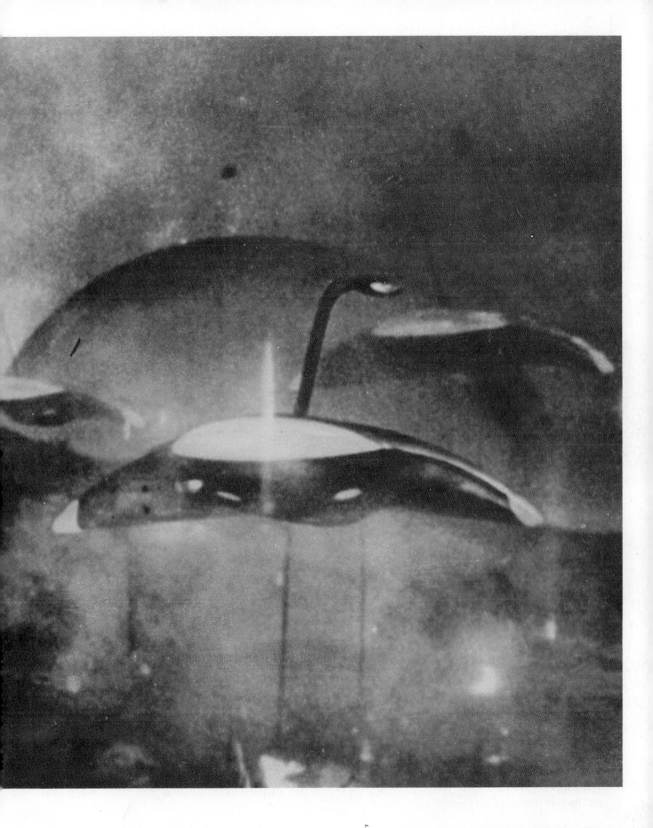

This is the Columbia . . . Broadcasting System.

[*Music*]

**PIERSON.** As I set down these notes on paper, I'm obsessed by the thought that I may be the last living man on earth. I have been hiding in this empty house near Grovers Mill—a small island of daylight cut off by the black smoke from the rest of the world. All that happened before the arrival of these monstrous creatures in the world now seems part of another life . . . a life that has no continuity with the present, furtive[40] existence of the lonely derelict who pencils these words on the back of some astronomical notes bearing the signature of Richard Pierson. I look down, at my blackened hands, my torn shoes, my tattered clothes, and I try to connect them with a professor who lives at Princeton, and who on the night of October 30, glimpsed through his telescope an orange splash of light on a distant planet. My wife, my colleagues, my students, my books, my observatory, my . . . my world . . . where are they? Did they ever exist? Am I Richard Pierson? What day is it? Do days exist without calendars? Does time pass when there are no human hands left to wind the clocks? . . . In writing down my daily life I tell myself I shall preserve human history between the dark covers of this little book that was meant to record the movements of the stars . . . But to write I must live, and to live I must eat . . . I find moldy bread in the kitchen, and an orange not too spoiled to swallow. I keep watch at the window. From time to time I catch sight of a Martian above the black smoke.

The smoke still holds the house in its black coil . . . But at length there is a hissing sound and suddenly I see a Martian mounted on his machine, spraying the air with a jet of steam, as if to dissipate[41] the smoke. I watch in a corner as his huge metal legs nearly brush against the house. Exhausted by terror, I fall asleep . . . It's morning. Sun streams in the window. The black cloud of gas has lifted, and the scorched meadows to the north look as though a black snowstorm has passed over them. I venture from the house. I make my way to a road. No traffic. Here and there a wrecked car, baggage overturned, a blackened skeleton. I push on north. For some reason I feel safer trailing these monsters than running away from them. And I keep a careful watch. I have seen the Martians feed. Should one of their machines appear over the top of trees, I am ready to fling myself flat on the earth. I come to a chestnut tree. October, chestnuts are ripe. I fill my pockets. I must keep alive. Two days I wander in a vague northerly direction through a desolate world. Finally I notice a living creature . . . a small red squirrel in a beech tree. I stare at him, and wonder. He stares back at me. I believe at that moment the animal and I shared the same emotion . . . the joy of finding another living being . . . I push on north. I find dead cows in a brackish[42] field. Beyond, the charred ruins of a dairy. The silo remains standing guard over the waste land like a lighthouse deserted by the sea. Astride the silo perches a weathercock. The arrow points north.

Next day I came to a city vaguely familiar in its contours, yet its buildings strangely dwarfed and leveled off, as if a giant had sliced off its highest towers with a capricious[43] sweep of his hand. I reached the

---

**40. furtive** (fur′ tiv) *adj.*: Sneaky; secretive.

**41. dissipate** (dis′ ə pāt′) *v.*: Scatter.
**42. brackish** (brak′ ish) *adj.*: Salty and marshy.
**43. capricious** (ka prish′əs) *adj.*: Without apparent reason.

outskirts. I found Newark, undemolished, but humbled by some whim of the advancing Martians. Presently, with an odd feeling of being watched, I caught sight of something crouching in a doorway. I made a step toward it, and it rose up and became a man—a man, armed with a large knife.

**STRANGER.** Stop . . . Where did you come from?

**PIERSON.** I come from . . . many places. A long time ago from Princeton.

**STRANGER.** Princeton, huh? That's near Grovers Mill!

**PIERSON.** Yes.

**STRANGER.** Grovers Mill . . . [*Laughs as at a great joke*] There's no food here. This is my country . . . all this end of town down to the river. There's only food for one . . . Which way are you going?

**PIERSON.** I don't know. I guess I'm looking for—for people.

**STRANGER.** [*Nervously*] What was that? Did you hear something just then?

**PIERSON.** Only a bird [*Marvels*] . . . A live bird!

**STRANGER.** You get to know that birds have shadows these days . . . Say, we're in the open here. Let's crawl into this doorway and talk.

**PIERSON.** Have you seen any Martians?

**STRANGER.** They've gone over to New York. At night the sky is alive with their lights. Just as if people were still living in it. By daylight you can't see them. Five days ago a couple of them carried something big across the flats from the airport. I believe they're learning how to fly.

**PIERSON.** Fly!

**STRANGER.** Yeah, fly.

**PIERSON.** Then it's all over with humanity. Stranger, there's still you and I. Two of us left.

**STRANGER.** They got themselves in solid; they wrecked the greatest country in the world. Those green stars, they're probably falling somewhere every night. They've only lost one machine. There isn't anything to do. We're done. We're licked.

**PIERSON.** Where were you? You're in a uniform.

**STRANGER.** What's left of it. I was in the militia—national guard . . . That's good! Wasn't any war any more than there's war between men and ants.

**PIERSON.** And we're edible ants. I found that out . . . What will they do to us?

**STRANGER.** I've thought it all out. Right now we're caught as we're wanted. The Martian only has to go a few miles to get a crowd on the run. But they won't keep doing that. They'll begin catching us systematic like —keeping the best and storing us in cages and things. They haven't begun on us yet!

**PIERSON.** Not begun!

**STRANGER.** Not begun. All that's happened so far is because we don't have sense enough to keep quiet . . . bothering them with guns and such stuff and losing our heads and rushing off in crowds. Now instead of our rushing around blind we've got to fix ourselves up according to the way things are now. Cities, nations, civilization, progress . . . done.

**PIERSON.** But if that's so, what is there to live for?

**STRANGER.** There won't be any more concerts for a million years or so, and no nice little dinners at restaurants. If it's amusement you're after, I guess the game's up.

**PIERSON.** And what is there left?

**STRANGER.** Life . . . that's what! I want to live. And so do you! We're not going to be exterminated. And I don't mean to be caught, either, and tamed, and fattened like an ox.

**PIERSON.** What are you going to do?

**STRANGER.** I'm going on . . . right under their feet. I gotta plan. We humans as humans are finished. We don't know enough. We gotta learn plenty before we've got a chance. And we've got to live and keep free while we learn. I've thought it all out, see.

**PIERSON.** Tell me the rest.

**STRANGER.** Well, it isn't all of us that are made for wild beasts, and that's what it's got to be. That's why I watched you. All these little office workers that used to live in these houses—they'd be no good. They haven't any stuff to 'em. They just used to run off to work. I've seen hundreds of 'em, running wild to catch their commuters' train in the morning for fear that they'd get canned if they didn't; running back at night afraid they won't be in time for dinner. Lives insured and a little invested in case of accidents. And on Sundays, worried about the hereafter. The Martians will be a godsend for those guys. Nice roomy cages, good food, no worries. After a week or so chasing about the fields on empty stomachs they'll come and be glad to be caught.

**PIERSON.** You've thought it all out, haven't you?

**STRANGER.** You bet I have! And that isn't all. These Martians will make pets of some of them, train 'em to do tricks. Who knows? Get sentimental over the pet boy who grew up and had to be killed. And some, maybe, they'll train to hunt us.

**PIERSON.** No, that's impossible. No human being . . .

**STRANGER.** Yes, they will. There's people who'll do it gladly. If one of them ever comes after me . . .

**PIERSON.** In the meantime, you and I and others like us . . . where are we to live when the Martians own the earth?

**STRANGER.** I've got it all figured out. We'll live underground. I've been thinking about the sewers. Under New York are miles and miles of 'em. The main ones are big enough for anybody. Then there's cellars, vaults, underground storerooms, railway tunnels, subways. You begin to see, eh? And we'll get a bunch of strong people together. No weak ones, that rubbish, out.

**PIERSON.** And you meant me to go?

**STRANGER.** Well, I gave you a chance, didn't I?

**PIERSON.** We won't quarrel about that. Go on.

**STRANGER.** And we've got to make safe places for us to stay in, see, and get all the books we can—science books. That's where people like you come in, see? We'll raid the museums, we'll even spy on the Martians. It may not be so much we have to learn before —just imagine this: four or five of their own fighting machines suddenly start off—heat rays right and left and not a Martian in 'em. Not a Martian in 'em! But humans —humans who have learned the way how. It may even be in our time. Gee! Imagine having one of them lovely things with its heat ray wide and free! We'd turn it on Martians, we'd turn it on people. We'd bring everybody down to their knees.

**PIERSON.** That's your plan?

**STRANGER.** You and me and a few more of us we'd own the world.

**PIERSON.** I see.

**STRANGER.** Say, what's the matter? Where are you going?

**PIERSON.** Not to your world . . . Good-bye, stranger . . .

**PIERSON.** After parting with the artilleryman, I came at last to the Holland Tunnel.[44] I entered that silent tube anxious to know the fate of the great city on the other side of the Hudson. Cautiously I came out of the tunnel and made my way up Canal Street.

I reached Fourteenth Street, and there again were black powder and several bodies, and an evil ominous[45] smell from the gratings of the cellars of some of the houses. I wandered up through the Thirties and Forties;[46] I stood alone on Times Square.[47] I caught sight of a lean dog running down Seventh Avenue with a piece of dark brown meat in his jaws, and a pack of starving mongrels at his heels. He made a wide circle around me, as though he feared I might prove a fresh competitor. I walked up Broadway in the direction of that strange powder —past silent shopwindows, displaying their mute wares to empty sidewalks—past the Capitol Theatre, silent, dark—past a shooting gallery, where a row of empty guns faced an arrested line of wooden ducks. Near Columbus Circle I noticed models of 1939 motorcars in the showrooms facing empty streets. From over the top of the General Motors Building, I watched a flock of black birds circling in the sky. I hurried on. Sud-denly I caught sight of the hood of a Martian machine, standing somewhere in Central Park, gleaming in the late afternoon sun. An insane idea! I rushed recklessly across Columbus Circle and into the Park. I climbed a small hill above the pond at Sixtieth Street. From there I could see, standing in a silent row along the mall, nineteen of those great metal Titans,[48] their cowls empty, their steel arms hanging listlessly by their sides. I looked in vain for the monsters that inhabit those machines.

Suddenly, my eyes were attracted to the immense flock of black birds that hovered directly below me. They circled to the ground, and there before my eyes, stark and silent, lay the Martians, with the hungry birds pecking and tearing brown shreds of flesh from their dead bodies. Later when their bodies were examined in laboratories, it was found that they were killed by the putrefactive[49] and disease bacteria against which their systems were unprepared . . . slain, after all man's defenses had failed, by the humblest thing that God in His wisdom put upon this earth.

Before the cylinder fell there was a general persuasion that through all the deep of space no life existed beyond the petty surface of our minute sphere. Now we see further. Dim and wonderful is the vision I have conjured up in my mind of life spreading slowly from this little seedbed of the solar system throughout the inanimate vastness of sidereal[50] space. But that is a remote dream. It may be that the destruction of the Martians is only a reprieve.[51] To them, and not to us, is the future ordained perhaps.

---

**44. Holland Tunnel:** A tunnel under the Hudson River between New York and New Jersey.
**45. ominous** (äm′ ə nəs) *adj.*: Threatening; sinister.
**46. Thirties and Forties:** Numbered streets across Manhattan.
**47. Times Square:** The center of the theater district in New York City.

**48. Titans** (tī′ tənz) *n.*: Giants.
**49. putrefactive** (pyōō′ trə fak′ tiv) *adj.*: Rotting; decomposing.
**50. sidereal** (sī dir′ ē əl) *adj.*: Of the stars.
**51. reprieve** (ri prēv′) *n.*: Postponement.

Strange it now seems to sit in my peaceful study at Princeton writing down this last chapter of the record begun at a deserted farm in Grovers Mill. Strange to see from my window the university spires dim and blue through an April haze. Strange to watch children playing in the streets. Strange to see young people strolling on the green, where the new spring grass heals the last black scars of a bruised earth. Strange to watch the sightseers enter the museum where the disassembled parts of a Martian machine are kept on public view. Strange when I recall the time when I first saw it, bright and clean-cut, hard and silent, under the dawn of that last great day.

[*Music*]

This is Orson Welles, ladies and gentlemen, out of character to assure you that The War of the Worlds has no further significance than as the holiday offering it was intended to be. The Mercury Theatre's own radio version of dressing up in a sheet and jumping out of a bush and saying Boo! Starting now, we couldn't soap all your windows and steal all your garden gates, by tomorrow night . . . so we did the next best thing. We annihilated the world before your very ears, and utterly destroyed the Columbia Broadcasting System. You will be relieved, I hope, to learn that we didn't mean it, and that both institutions are still open for business. So good-bye everybody, and remember, please, for the next day or so, the terrible lesson you learned tonight. That grinning, glowing, globular invader of your living room is an inhabitant of the pumpkin patch, and if your doorbell rings and nobody's there, that was no Martian . . . it's Hallowe'en.

## THINKING ABOUT THE SELECTION

### Recalling

1. What are the first signs of an unusual occurrence?
2. Describe the sight at the landing as seen by the people of Grovers Mill.
3. What is the first reaction of the people at Grovers Mill to the "thing"? How does their reaction change?
4. What methods are used to try to thwart the invaders? What are the results of these attempts?
5. What finally destroys the invaders?

### Interpreting

6. In what ways does the invaders' takeover seem to show intelligent planning?

7. Explain why Pierson rejects the Stranger's plan for resistance. How does his attitude contrast with that of the Stranger?

### Applying

8. This radio play was broadcast on Halloween in 1938. How would an audience today react to such a broadcast? Explain your answer.

## ANALYZING LITERATURE

### Understanding the Radio Play

A **radio play,** which is read by actors for a radio broadcast rather than performed on a stage, relies on dialogue, sound effects, and music to create the scenes in your mind. There are no visual cues. The dialogue reveals characters and carries the plot along. The sound effects and music may indicate the passage of time or create mood.

1. Describe how you envision Grovers Mill when the aliens first land.
2. Give three examples of the use of music to indicate passage of time. Discuss the different lengths of time.
3. With what kind of expression do you think the last paragraph spoken by Pierson should be read? Why?
4. Explain whether or not you think a radio broadcast is an especially effective format for this play. Would the play be as successful produced as a television broadcast or as a movie? Explain your answer.

## CRITICAL THINKING AND READING
### Evaluating Technique

When *Invasion from Mars* was first broadcast, many people believed it was a report of an actual invasion. The playwright presents the play in a newscast format, which creates realism and suspense. Within this format he uses four techniques that make the play seem like an authentic broadcast. Give examples of each of the following techniques used in the play, and explain how each example contributes to the apparent authenticity of it.

1. news bulletin
2. interview
3. eyewitness account
4. official statement

## SPEAKING AND LISTENING
### Producing a Radio Play

With your classmates, plan your own production of *Invasion from Mars*. Begin by listing the music and sound effects you need. Keep in mind that reading with expression is important, since the audience will hear, and not see, the play. Practice reading the lines aloud, interpreting them appropriately. When you have rehearsed and are prepared, you might tape your performance.

## THINKING AND WRITING
### Writing a Drama Review

Imagine that you were in New York City when *Invasion from Mars* was first broadcast. You observed hundreds of people panicking in the streets as a result of the broadcast. Make notes describing this reaction. Then use your notes in writing a review of the radio play for a New York City newspaper. Explain the relationship between the play and the panic. Comment on the effectiveness of the play. Discuss the authentic sound of the play's broadcast and what elements of the play contribute to this authenticity. Revise your review by adding quotations from the play.

## Twelve Angry Men, Act I

**Reginald Rose** (1920–    ) was born in New York City, where he attended City College and worked as a publicity writer and advertising copywriter. Rose wrote many television plays and created the courtroom television series *The Defenders.* His television drama *Twelve Angry Men,* which he wrote after he sat on a jury, won an Emmy award in 1954. A movie version of the drama appeared in 1957, and a stage version was produced in London in 1964. His interest in courtroom law is apparent in *Twelve Angry Men.*

**Staging**

**Staging** is the art of bringing a play to life on the stage or screen. Staging involves all that is necessary to transform a play from a written work to a theatrical production—actors, scenery, lighting, props, and sound effects—everything that is seen or heard in a performance. An important guide to the staging is the stage directions, which often provide clues to the characters' feelings and attitudes that dialogue alone may not convey.

**Look For**

The characters in this play are confined to a single room, a jury room. As you read Act I, look for the stage directions and the clues they provide to the meaning of a scene. How do the actors convey their messages?

**Writing**

Think of a time when you had to convince someone to see your point of view. List the reasons you gave that they should consider changing their view and the facts that you presented to support your view.

**Vocabulary**

Knowing the following words will help you as you read Act I of *Twelve Angry Men.*

**dogged** (dôg′ id) *adj.*: Persistent, stubborn (p. 311)

**naive** (nä ēv′) *adj.*: Unsophisticated; lacking in worldly wisdom (p. 311)

**subservient** (səb sʉr′ vē ənt) *adj.*: Submissive (p. 312)

**defendant** (di fen′dənt) *n.*: In law, the person accused (p. 312)

**unanimous** (yoo nan′ ə məs) *adj.*: Showing complete agreement (p. 312)

**monopoly** (mə näp′ ə lē) *n.*: Exclusive control (p. 315)

**counsel** (koun′ s'l) *n.*: Lawyer (p. 318)

**abstain** (əb stān′) *v.*: Voluntarily refrain from (p. 320)

# Twelve Angry Men

## Reginald Rose

## CHARACTERS

**Foreman**  A small, petty man who is impressed with the authority he has and handles himself quite formally. Not overly bright, but dogged.

**Juror Number Two**  A meek, hesitant man who finds it difficult to maintain any opinions of his own. Easily swayed and usually adopts the opinion of the last person to whom he has spoken.

**Juror Number Three**  A very strong, very forceful, extremely opinionated man within whom can be detected a streak of sadism. A humorless man who is intolerant of opinions other than his own and accustomed to forcing his wishes and views upon others.

**Juror Number Four**  Seems to be a man of wealth and position. A practiced speaker who presents himself well at all times. Seems to feel a little bit above the rest of the jurors. His only concern is with the facts in this case, and he is appalled at the behavior of the others.

**Juror Number Five**  A naive, very frightened young man who takes his obligations in this case very seriously, but who finds it difficult to speak up when his elders have the floor.

**Juror Number Six**  An honest but dull-witted man who comes upon his decisions slowly and carefully. A man who finds it difficult to create positive opinions, but who must listen to and digest and accept those opinions offered by others which appeal to him most.

**Juror Number Seven**  A loud, flashy, glad-handed salesman type who has more important things to do than to sit on a jury. He is quick to show temper, quick to form opinions on things about which he knows nothing. Is a bully and, of course, a coward.

**Juror Number Eight**  A quiet, thoughtful, gentle man. A man who sees all sides of every question and constantly seeks the truth. A man of strength tempered with compassion. Above all, a man who wants justice to be done and will fight to see that it is.

**Juror Number Nine**  A mild, gentle old man, long since defeated by life and now merely waiting to die. A man who recognizes himself for what he is and mourns the days when it would have been possible to be courageous without shielding himself behind his many years.

**Juror Number Ten** An angry, bitter man. A man who antagonizes almost at sight. A bigot[1] who places no values on any human life save his own. A man who has been nowhere and is going nowhere and knows it deep within him.

**Juror Number Eleven** A refugee from Europe who had come to this country in 1941. A man who speaks with an accent and who is ashamed, humble, almost subservient to the people around him, but who will honestly seek justice because he has suffered through so much injustice.

**Juror Number Twelve** A slick, bright advertising man who thinks of human beings in terms of percentages, graphs, and polls and has no real understanding of people. A superficial snob, but trying to be a good fellow.

---

**1. bigot** (big′ ət) *n.*: A narrow-minded person; one who holds blindly and intolerantly to a particular opinion.

From *Six Television Plays* by Reginald Rose. Reprinted by permission of International Creative Management. Copyright © 1956 by Reginald Rose.

## ACT I

[*Fade in on a jury box. Twelve men are seated in it, listening intently to the voice of the* JUDGE *as he charges them.*[2] *We do not see the* JUDGE. *He speaks in slow, measured tones and his voice is grave. The camera drifts over the faces of the* JURYMEN *as the* JUDGE *speaks and we see that most of their heads are turned to camera's left.* SEVEN *looks down at his hands.* THREE *looks off in another direction, the direction in which the defendant would be sitting.* TEN *keeps moving his head back and forth nervously. The* JUDGE *drones on.*]

**JUDGE.** Murder in the first degree— premeditated homicide[3]—is the most serious charge tried in our criminal courts. You've heard a long and complex case, gentlemen, and it is now your duty to sit down to try and separate the facts from the fancy. One man is dead. The life of another is at stake. If there is a reasonable doubt[4] in your minds as to the guilt of the accused . . . then you must declare him not guilty. If, however, there is no reasonable doubt, then he must be found guilty. Whichever way you decide, the verdict must be unanimous. I urge you to deliberate honestly and thoughtfully. You are faced with a grave responsibility. Thank you, gentlemen.

[*There is a long pause.*]

**CLERK.** [*Droning*] The jury will retire.

[*And now, slowly, almost hesitantly, the members of the jury begin to rise. Awkwardly, they file out of the jury box and off camera to the left. Camera holds on jury box, then fades out.*

*Fade in on a large, bare, unpleasant-looking room. This is the jury room in the county criminal court of a large Eastern city. It is about 4:00 P.M. The room is furnished with a long conference table and a dozen chairs. The walls are bare, drab, and badly in need of a fresh coat of paint. Along*

---

**2. charges them:** Gives the jurors instruction in points of law they need to know in order to carry out their duties.

**3. premeditated homicide** (pri med′ ə tāt′ id häm′ ə síd): Murder that is planned in advance.

**4. reasonable doubt:** Uncertainty because of lack of conclusive evidence.

one wall is a row of windows which look out on the skyline of the city's financial district. High on another wall is an electric clock. A washroom opens off the jury room. In one corner of the room is a water fountain. On the table are pads, pencils, ashtrays. One of the windows is open. Papers blow across the table and onto the floor as the door opens. Lettered on the outside of the door are the words "Jury Room." A uniformed GUARD holds the door open. Slowly, almost self-consciously, the twelve JURORS file in. The GUARD counts them as they enter the door, his lips moving, but no sound coming forth. Four or five of the JURORS light cigarettes as they enter the room. FIVE lights his pipe, which he smokes constantly throughout the play. TWO and TWELVE go to the water fountain, NINE goes into the washroom, the door of which is lettered "Men." Several of the JURORS take seats at the table. Others stand awkwardly around the room. Several look out the windows. These are men who are ill at ease, who do not really know each other to talk to, and who wish they were anywhere but here. SEVEN, standing at window, takes out a pack of gum, takes a piece, and offers it around. There are no takers. He mops his brow.]

SEVEN. [To SIX] Y'know something? It's hot. [SIX nods.] You'd think they'd at least air-condition the place. I almost dropped dead in court.

[SEVEN opens the window a bit wider. The GUARD looks them over and checks his count. Then, satisfied, he makes ready to leave.]

GUARD. Okay, gentlemen. Everybody's here. If there's anything you want, I'm right outside. Just knock.

[He exits, closing the door. Silently they all look at the door. We hear the lock clicking.]

FIVE. I never knew they locked the door.

TEN. [Blowing nose] Sure, they lock the door. What did you think?

FIVE. I don't know. It just never occurred to me.

[Some of the JURORS are taking off their jackets. Others are sitting down at the table. They still are reluctant to talk to each other. FOREMAN is at head of table, tearing slips of paper for ballots. Now we get a close shot of EIGHT. He looks out the window. We hear THREE talking to TWO.]

THREE. Six days. They should have finished it in two. Talk, talk, talk. Did you ever hear so much talk about nothing?

TWO. [Nervously laughing] Well . . . I guess . . . they're entitled.

THREE. Everybody gets a fair trial. [He shakes his head.] That's the system. Well, I suppose you can't say anything against it.

[TWO looks at him nervously, nods, and goes over to water cooler. Cut to shot of EIGHT staring out window. Cut to table. SEVEN stands at the table, putting out a cigarette.]

SEVEN. [To TEN] How did you like that business about the knife? Did you ever hear a phonier story?

TEN. [Wisely] Well, look, you've gotta expect that. You know what you're dealing with.

SEVEN. Yeah, I suppose. What's the matter, you got a cold?

TEN. [Blowing] A lulu. These hot-weather colds can kill you.

[SEVEN nods sympathetically.]

FOREMAN. [Briskly] All right, gentlemen. Let's take seats.

SEVEN. Right. This better be fast. I've got

tickets to *The Seven Year Itch*[5] tonight. I must be the only guy in the whole world who hasn't seen it yet. [*He laughs and sits down.*] Okay, your honor, start the show.

[*They all begin to sit down. The* FOREMAN *is seated at the head of the table.* EIGHT *continues to look out the window.*]

**FOREMAN.** [*To* EIGHT] How about sitting down?

[EIGHT *doesn't hear him.*] The gentleman at the window.

[EIGHT *turns, startled.*]

**FOREMAN.** How about sitting down?

**EIGHT.** Oh, I'm sorry. [*He heads for a seat.*]

**TEN.** [*To* SIX] It's tough to figure, isn't it? A kid kills his father. Bing! Just like that. Well, it's the element. They let the kids run wild. Maybe it serves 'em right.

**FOREMAN.** Is everybody here?

**TWELVE.** The old man's inside.

[*The* FOREMAN *turns to the washroom just as the door opens.* NINE *comes out, embarrassed.*]

**FOREMAN.** We'd like to get started.

**NINE.** Forgive me, gentlemen. I didn't mean to keep you waiting.

**FOREMAN.** It's all right. Find a seat.

[NINE *heads for a seat and sits down. They look at the* FOREMAN *expectantly.*]

**FOREMAN.** All right. Now, you gentlemen can handle this any way you want to. I mean, I'm not going to make any rules. If we want to discuss it first and then vote, that's one way. Or we can vote right now to see how we stand.

**SEVEN.** Let's vote now. Who knows, maybe we can all go home.

**TEN.** Yeah. Let's see who's where.

**THREE.** Right. Let's vote now.

**FOREMAN.** Anybody doesn't want to vote? [*He looks around the table. There is no answer.*] Okay, all those voting guilty raise your hands.

[*Seven or eight hands go up immediately. Several others go up more slowly. Everyone looks around the table. There are two hands not raised,* NINE*'s and* EIGHT*'s.* NINE*'s hand goes up slowly now as the* FOREMAN *counts.*]

**FOREMAN.**     . . . Nine . . . ten . . . eleven . . . That's eleven for guilty. Okay. Not guilty? [EIGHT*'s hand is raised.*] One. Right. Okay. Eleven to one, guilty. Now we know where we are.

**THREE.** Somebody's in left field. [*To* EIGHT] You think he's not guilty?

**EIGHT.** [*Quietly*] I don't know.

**THREE.** I never saw a guiltier man in my life. You sat right in court and heard the same thing I did. The man's a dangerous killer. You could see it.

**EIGHT.** He's nineteen years old.

**THREE.** That's old enough. He knifed his own father. Four inches into the chest. An innocent little nineteen-year-old kid. They proved it a dozen different ways. Do you want me to list them?

**EIGHT.** No.

**TEN.** [*To* EIGHT] Well, do you believe his story?

**EIGHT.** I don't know whether I believe it or not. Maybe I don't.

**SEVEN.** So what'd you vote not guilty for?

**EIGHT.** There were eleven votes for guilty. It's

---

**5. *The Seven Year Itch:*** A popular Broadway comedy during the 1950's.

not so easy for me to raise my hand and send a boy off to die without talking about it first.

**SEVEN.** Who says it's easy for me?

**EIGHT.** No one.

**SEVEN.** What, just because I voted fast? I think the guy's guilty. You couldn't change my mind if you talked for a hundred years.

**EIGHT.** I don't want to change your mind. I just want to talk for a while. Look, this boy's been kicked around all his life. You know, living in a slum, his mother dead since he was nine. That's not a very good head start. He's a tough, angry kid. You know why slum kids get that way? Because we knock 'em on the head once a day, every day. I think maybe we owe him a few words. That's all.

[*He looks around the table. Some of them look back coldly. Some cannot look at him. Only* NINE *nods slowly.* TWELVE *doodles steadily.* FOUR *begins to comb his hair.*]

**TEN.** I don't mind telling you this, mister. We don't owe him a thing. He got a fair trial, didn't he? You know what that trial cost? He's lucky he got it. Look, we're all grown-ups here. You're not going to tell us that we're supposed to believe him, knowing what he is. I've lived among 'em all my life. You can't believe a word they say. You know that.

**NINE.** [*To* TEN *very slowly*] I don't know that. What a terrible thing for a man to believe! Since when is dishonesty a group characteristic? You have no monopoly on the truth—

**THREE.** [*Interrupting*] All right. It's not Sunday. We don't need a sermon.

**NINE.** What this man says is very dangerous—

[EIGHT *puts his hand on* NINE's *arm and stops him. Somehow his touch and his gentle expression calm the old man. He draws a deep breath and relaxes.*]

**FOUR.** I don't see any need for arguing like this. I think we ought to be able to behave like gentlemen.

**SEVEN.** Right!

**FOUR.** If we're going to discuss this case, let's discuss the facts.

**FOREMAN.** I think that's a good point. We have a job to do. Let's do it.

**ELEVEN.** [*With accent*] If you gentlemen don't mind, I'm going to close the window. [*He gets up and does so.*] [*Apologetically*] It was blowing on my neck.

[TEN *blows his nose fiercely.*]

**TWELVE.** I may have an idea here. I'm just thinking out loud now, but it seems to me that it's up to us to convince this gentleman —[*Indicating* EIGHT]—that we're right and he's wrong. Maybe if we each took a minute or two, you know, if we sort of try it on for size—

**FOREMAN.** That sounds fair enough. Supposing we go once around the table.

**SEVEN.** Okay, let's start it off.

**FOREMAN.** Right. [*To* TWO] I guess you're first.

**TWO.** [*Timidly*] Oh. Well . . .[*Long pause*] I just think he's guilty. I thought it was obvious. I mean nobody proved otherwise.

**EIGHT.** [*Quietly*] Nobody has to prove otherwise. The burden of proof is on the prosecu-

tion.[6] The defendant doesn't have to open his mouth. That's in the Constitution. The Fifth Amendment.[7] You've heard of it.

**TWO.** [*Flustered*] Well, sure, I've heard of it. I know what it is. I . . . what I meant . . . well, anyway, I think he was guilty.

**THREE.** Okay, let's get to the facts. Number one, let's take the old man who lived on the second floor right underneath the room where the murder took place. At ten minutes after twelve on the night of the killing he heard loud noises in the upstairs apartment. He said it sounded like a fight. Then he heard the kid say to his father, "I'm gonna kill you." A second later he heard a body falling, and he ran to the door of his apartment, looked out, and saw the kid running down the stairs and out of the house. Then he called the police. They found the father with a knife in his chest.

**FOREMAN.** And the coroner[8] fixed the time of death at around midnight.

**THREE.** Right. Now what else do you want?

**FOUR.** The boy's entire story is flimsy. He claimed he was at the movies. That's a little ridiculous, isn't it? He couldn't even remember what pictures he saw.

**THREE.** That's right. Did you hear that? [*To* FOUR] You're absolutely right.

**TEN.** Look, what about the woman across the street? If her testimony don't prove it, then nothing does.

**TWELVE.** That's right. She saw the killing, didn't she?

**FOREMAN.** Let's go in order.

**6. prosecution** (präs′ ə kyoō′ shən) *n.*: The conducting of criminal proceedings in court against a person.
**7. Fifth Amendment:** In the U.S. Constitution, the amendment that says no person "shall be compelled in any criminal case to be a witness against himself."
**8. coroner** (kôr′ ə nər) *n.*: A public official whose chief duty is to determine the cause of a death.

**TEN.** [*Loud*] Just a minute. Here's a woman who's lying in bed and can't sleep. It's hot, you know. [*He gets up and begins to walk around, blowing his nose and talking.*] Anyway, she looks out the window, and right across the street she sees the kid stick the knife into his father. She's known the kid all his life. His window is right opposite hers, across the el[9] tracks, and she swore she saw him do it.

**EIGHT.** Through the windows of a passing elevated train.

**TEN.** Okay. And they proved in court that you can look through the windows of a passing el train at night and see what's happening on the other side. They proved it.

**EIGHT.** I'd like to ask you something. How come you believed her? She's one of "them," too, isn't she?

[TEN *walks over to* EIGHT.]

**TEN.** You're a pretty smart fellow, aren't you?

**FOREMAN.** [*Rising*] Now take it easy.

[THREE *gets up and goes to* TEN.]

**THREE.** Come on. Sit down. [*He leads* TEN *back to his seat.*] What're you letting him get you all upset for? Relax.

[TEN *and* THREE *sit down.*]

**FOREMAN.** Let's calm down now. [*To* FIVE] It's your turn.

**FIVE.** I'll pass it.

**FOREMAN.** That's your privilege. [*To* SIX] How about you?

**SIX.** [*Slowly*] I don't know. I started to be convinced, you know, with the testimony from those people across the hall. Didn't they say something about an argument between the father and the boy around seven o'clock that night? I mean, I can be wrong.

***

**9. el:** An elevated railway.

**ELEVEN.** I think it was eight o'clock. Not seven.

**EIGHT.** That's right. Eight o'clock. They heard the father hit the boy twice and then saw the boy walk angrily out of the house. What does that prove?

**SIX.** Well, it doesn't exactly prove anything. It's just part of the picture. I didn't say it proved anything.

**FOREMAN.** Anything else?

**SIX.** No.

[SIX *goes to the water fountain.*]

**FOREMAN.** [*To* SEVEN] All right. How about you?

**SEVEN.** I don't know, most of it's been said already. We can talk all day about this thing, but I think we're wasting our time. Look at the kid's record. At fifteen he was in reform school. He stole a car. He's been arrested for mugging. He was picked up for knife-fighting. I think they said he stabbed somebody in the arm. This is a very fine boy.

**EIGHT.** Ever since he was five years old his father beat him up regularly. He used his fists.

**SEVEN.** So would I! A kid like that.

**THREE.** You're right. It's the kids. The way they are—you know? They don't listen. [*Bitter*] I've got a kid. When he was eight years old he ran away from a fight. I saw him. I was so ashamed, I told him right out, "I'm gonna make a man out of you or I'm gonna bust you up into little pieces trying." When he was fifteen he hit me in the face. He's big, you know. I haven't seen him in three years. Rotten kid! You work your heart out. . . . [*Pause*] All right. Let's get on with it. [*Looks away embarrassed*]

**FOUR.** We're missing the point here. This boy—let's say he's a product of a filthy neighborhood and a broken home. We can't help that. We're not here to go into reasons why slums are breeding grounds for criminals. They are. I know it. So do you. The children who come out of slum backgrounds are potential menaces to society.

**TEN.** You said it there. I don't want any part of them, believe me.

[*There is a dead silence for a moment, and then* FIVE *speaks haltingly.*]

**FIVE.** I've lived in a slum all my life—

**TEN.** Oh, now wait a second!

**FIVE.** I used to play in a backyard that was filled with garbage. Maybe it still smells on me.

**FOREMAN.** Now let's be reasonable. There's nothing personal—[FIVE *stands up.*]

**FIVE.** There is something personal!

[*Then he catches himself and, seeing everyone looking at him, sits down, fists clenched.*]

**THREE.** [*Persuasively*] Come on, now. He didn't mean you, feller. Let's not be so sensitive.

[*There is a long pause.*]

**ELEVEN.** I can understand this sensitivity.

**FOREMAN.** Now let's stop the bickering. We're wasting time. [*To* EIGHT] It's your turn.

**EIGHT.** All right. I had a peculiar feeling about this trial. Somehow I felt that the defense counsel never really conducted a thorough cross-examination.[10] I mean, he was appointed by the court to defend the boy. He hardly seemed interested. Too many questions were left unasked.

**THREE.** [*Annoyed*] What about the ones that were asked? For instance, let's talk about

that cute little switch-knife.[11] You know, the one that fine upright kid admitted buying.

**EIGHT.** All right. Let's talk about it. Let's get it in here and look at it. I'd like to see it again, Mr. Foreman.

[*The* FOREMAN *looks at him questioningly and then gets up and goes to the door. During the following dialogue the* FOREMAN *knocks, the* GUARD *comes in, the* FOREMAN *whispers to him, the* GUARD *nods and leaves, locking the door.*]

**THREE.** We all know what it looks like. I don't see why we have to look at it again. [*To* FOUR] What do you think?

**FOUR.** The gentleman has a right to see exhibits in evidence.[12]

**THREE.** [*Shrugging*] Okay with me.

**FOUR.** [*To* EIGHT] This knife is a pretty strong piece of evidence, don't you agree?

**EIGHT.** I do.

**FOUR.** The boy admits going out of his house at eight o'clock after being slapped by his father.

**EIGHT.** Or punched.

**FOUR.** Or punched. He went to a neighborhood store and bought a switch-knife. The storekeeper was arrested the following day when he admitted selling it to the boy. It's a very unusual knife. The storekeeper identified it and said it was the only one of its kind he had in stock. Why did the boy get it? [*Sarcastically*] As a present for a friend of his, he says. Am I right so far?

**EIGHT.** Right.

**THREE.** You bet he's right. [*To all*] Now listen

---

**10. cross examination** *n.*: The questioning of a witness who has already been questioned by the opposing side.

**11. switch-knife:** A large jackknife that snaps open when a release button on the handle is pressed.
**12. exhibits in evidence** *n.*: Documents or objects officially presented as evidence in a trial.

to this man. He knows what he's talking about.

**FOUR.** Next, the boy claims that on the way home the knife must have fallen through a hole in his coat pocket, that he never saw it again. Now there's a story, gentlemen. You know what actually happened. The boy took the knife home and a few hours later stabbed his father with it and even remembered to wipe off the fingerprints.

[*The door opens and the* GUARD *walks in with an oddly designed knife with a tag on it.* FOUR *gets up and takes it from him. The* GUARD *exits.*]

**FOUR.** Everyone connected with the case identified this knife. Now are you trying to tell me that someone picked it up off the street and went up to the boy's house and stabbed his father with it just to be amusing?

**EIGHT.** No, I'm saying that it's possible that the boy lost the knife and that someone else stabbed his father with a similar knife. It's possible.

[FOUR *flips open the knife and jams it into the table.*]

**FOUR.** Take a look at that knife. It's a very strange knife. I've never seen one like it before in my life. Neither had the storekeeper who sold it to him.

[EIGHT *reaches casually into his pocket and withdraws an object. No one notices this. He stands up quietly.*]

**FOUR.** Aren't you trying to make us accept a pretty incredible coincidence?

**EIGHT.** I'm not trying to make anyone accept it. I'm just saying it's possible.

**THREE.** [*Shouting*] And I'm saying it's not possible.

[EIGHT *swiftly flicks open the blade of a switch-knife and jams it into the table next to the first one. They are exactly alike. There are several gasps and everyone stares at the knife. There is a long silence.*]

**THREE.** [*Slowly, amazed*] What are you trying to do?

**TEN.** [*Loud*] Yeah, what is this? Who do you think you are?

**FIVE.** Look at it! It's the same knife!

**FOREMAN.** Quiet! Let's be quiet.

[*They quiet down.*]

**FOUR.** Where did you get it?

**EIGHT.** I got it last night in a little junk shop around the corner from the boy's house. It cost two dollars.

**THREE.** Now listen to me! You pulled a real smart trick here, but you proved absolutely zero. Maybe there are ten knives like that, so what?

**EIGHT.** Maybe there are.

**THREE.** The boy lied and you know it.

**EIGHT.** He may have lied. [*To* TEN] Do you think he lied?

**TEN.** [*Violently*] Now that's a stupid question. Sure he lied!

**EIGHT.** [*To* FOUR] Do you?

**FOUR.** You don't have to ask me that. You know my answer. He lied.

**EIGHT.** [*To* FIVE] Do you think he lied?

[FIVE *can't answer immediately. He looks around nervously.*]

**FIVE.** I . . . I don't know.

**SEVEN.** Now wait a second. What are you, the guy's lawyer? Listen, there are still eleven of us who think he's guilty. You're alone. What do you think you're gonna accomplish? If you want to be stubborn and hang this jury,[13] he'll be tried again and found guilty, sure as he's born.

**EIGHT.** You're probably right.

**SEVEN.** So what are you gonna do about it? We can be here all night.

**NINE.** It's only one night. A man may die.

[SEVEN *glares at* NINE *for a long while, but has no answer.* EIGHT *looks closely at* NINE *and we can begin to sense a rapport between them. There is a long silence. Then suddenly everyone begins to talk at once.*]

**THREE.** Well, whose fault is that?

**SIX.** Do you think maybe if we went over it again? What I mean is—

**TEN.** Did anyone force him to kill his father? [*To* THREE] How do you like him? Like someone forced him!

**ELEVEN.** Perhaps this is not the point.

---

**13. hang this jury:** Prevent this jury from reaching a verdict.

**FIVE.** No one forced anyone. But listen—

**TWELVE.** Look, gentlemen, we can spitball all night here.

**TWO.** Well, I was going to say—

**SEVEN.** Just a minute. Some of us've got better things to do than sit around a jury room.

**FOUR.** I can't understand a word in here. Why do we all have to talk at once?

**FOREMAN.** He's right. I think we ought to get on with it.

[EIGHT *has been listening to this exchange closely.*]

**THREE.** [*To* EIGHT] Well, what do you say? You're the one holding up the show.

**EIGHT.** [*Standing*] I've got a proposition to make.

[*We catch a close shot of* FIVE *looking steadily at him as he talks.* FIVE, *seemingly puzzled, listens closely.*]

**EIGHT.** I want to call for a vote. I want you eleven men to vote by secret ballot. I'll abstain. If there are still eleven votes for guilty, I won't stand alone. We'll take in a guilty verdict right now.

**SEVEN.** Okay. Let's do it.

**FOREMAN.** That sounds fair. Is everyone agreed?

[*They all nod their heads.* EIGHT *walks over to the window, looks out for a moment, and then faces them.*]

**FOREMAN.** Pass these along.

[*The* FOREMAN *passes ballot slips to all of them, and now* EIGHT *watches them tensely as they begin to write.*]

[*Fade out*]

# THINKING ABOUT THE SELECTION

## Recalling

1. What are the basic facts of the case, including the testimony of two witnesses, against the nineteen-year-old boy?
2. What are some of Juror Eight's reasons for his uncertainty about the defendant's guilt?
3. Which two jurors seem to show prejudice against the defendant? What are their prejudices?
4. What is known to the jurors of the defendant's past behavior and police record?
5. What does the knife that Juror Eight supplies contribute to the discussion?
6. What conditions are set for voting at the end of Act I?

## Interpreting

7. Juror Two thinks the defendant is guilty because "nobody proved otherwise." In what way is his thinking in conflict with the legal system?
8. Juror Eight believes that the court-appointed defense attorney did not thoroughly cross-examine witnesses for the prosecution. If Juror Eight is right, how might this situation affect the defendant's chances? Explain your answer.
9. What are some of the problems the jurors must resolve before they can reach a verdict?

## Applying

10. How would criminal trials be different if defendants were considered guilty until proven innocent?

# ANALYZING LITERATURE

## Understanding Staging

Staging a play means producing it on the stage or screen, with actors, scenery, lighting, props, and sound effects. Stage directions, which indicate the actors' movements and expressions, may suggest the meaning or emotions to be conveyed.

Reread the stage directions and dialogue for the courtroom scene at the beginning of Act I. Imagine that the nineteen-year-old defendant is present in the courtroom and that he interrupts the judge to protest his innocence. The defendant, the judge, and the jurors are visible on camera. Describe the stage directions for this scene, noting the reactions of the defendant, the judge, and some of the jurors.

# CRITICAL THINKING AND READING

## Making Inferences from Stage Directions

An **inference** is a reasonable conclusion that you can draw from evidence. The stage directions of a play often provide clues from which you may draw inferences.

Read the speech on page 315 by Juror Eight beginning "I don't want to change your mind" and the stage directions that follow it. From the stage directions, make inferences about the differing attitudes of the jurors. Describe the reactions of the jurors and the attitudes they suggest.

# THINKING AND WRITING

## Writing About Staging

Imagine that you are directing a movie version of *Twelve Angry Men*. Write your plan describing in detail the staging that you would use. First list the props, lighting, sound effects, and scenery that you need. Then use this information in your written plan. When you revise, refer to your lists and add any items you might still need.

# GUIDE FOR READING

## Twelve Angry Men, Act II

Most dramas have a central conflict that involves a **protagonist,** who is the hero or central character, and one or more **antagonists,** opponents who struggle against the protagonist. In Act I it becomes clear that Juror Eight is the protagonist. It is he alone who votes "not guilty" against the other jurors, and who persuades the others to consider the possibility that the defendant may not be guilty. A single antagonist does not emerge clearly until Act II.

### Look For

As you read Act II, look for the character who is Juror Eight's major antagonist. Which character seems the most determined to find the defendant guilty?

### Writing

The protagonist in this play takes a stand against eleven others. Freewrite about the obstacles he faces and the opposition he feels from other characters.

### Vocabulary

Knowing the meaning of the following words will help you as you read Act II of *Twelve Angry Men.*

**motives** (mōt′ivz) *n.*: The emotions or impulses that cause a person to act in a certain way (p. 324)

**insignificant** (in′sig nif′ə kənt) *adj.*: Having little or no importance (p. 324)

**simulated** (sim′yoo lāt′id) *adj.*: Taking on the appearance of (p. 329)

# ACT II

[*Fade in on same scene, no time lapse.* EIGHT *stands tensely watching as the* JURORS *write on their ballots. He stays perfectly still as one by one they fold the ballots and pass them along to the* FOREMAN. *The* FOREMAN *takes them, riffles through the folded ballots, counts eleven, and now begins to open them. He reads each one out loud and lays it aside. They watch him quietly, and all we hear is his voice and the sound of* TWO *sucking on a cough drop.*]

**FOREMAN.** Guilty. Guilty. Guilty. Guilty. Guilty. Guilty. Guilty. Guilty. Guilty. [*He pauses at the tenth ballot and then reads it.*] Not Guilty.

[THREE *slams down hard on the table. The* FOREMAN *opens the last ballot.*]

Guilty.

**TEN.** [*Angry*] How do you like that!

**SEVEN.** Who was it? I think we have a right to know.

**ELEVEN.** Excuse me. This was a secret ballot. We agreed on this point, no? If the gentleman wants it to remain secret—

**THREE.** [*Standing up angrily*] What do you mean? There are no secrets in here! I know who it was. [*He turns to* FIVE.] What's the matter with you? You come in here and you vote guilty and then this slick preacher starts to tear your heart out with stories about a poor little kid who just couldn't help becoming a murderer. So you change your vote. If that isn't the most sickening—

[FIVE *stares at* THREE. *frightened at this outburst.*]

**FOREMAN.** Now hold it.

**THREE.** Hold it? We're trying to put a guilty man into the chair where he belongs—and

all of a sudden we're paying attention to fairy tales.

**FIVE.** Now just a minute—

**ELEVEN.** Please. I would like to say something here. I have always thought that a man was entitled to have unpopular opinions in this country. This is the reason I came here. I wanted to have the right to disagree. In my own country, I am ashamed to say—

**TEN.** What do we have to listen to now—the whole history of your country?

**SEVEN.** Yeah, let's stick to the subject. [*To* FIVE] I want to ask you what made you change your vote.

[*There is a long pause as* SEVEN *and* FIVE *eye each other angrily.*]

**NINE.** [*Quietly*] There's nothing for him to tell you. He didn't change his vote. I did. [*There is a pause.*] Maybe you'd like to know why.

**THREE.** No, we wouldn't like to know why.

**FOREMAN.** The man wants to talk.

**NINE.** Thank you. [*Pointing at* EIGHT] This gentleman chose to stand alone against us. That's his right. It takes a great deal of courage to stand alone even if you believe in something very strongly. He left the verdict up to us. He gambled for support and I gave it to him. I want to hear more. The vote is ten to two.

**TEN.** That's fine. If the speech is over, let's go on.

[FOREMAN *gets up, goes to door, knocks, hands* GUARD *the tagged switch-knife and sits down again.*]

**THREE.** [*To* FIVE] Look, buddy, I was a little excited. Well, you know how it is. I . . . I didn't mean to get nasty. Nothing personal.

[FIVE *looks at him.*]

**SEVEN.** [*To* EIGHT] Look, supposing you answer me this. If the kid didn't kill him, who did?

**EIGHT.** As far as I know, we're supposed to decide whether or not the boy on trial is guilty. We're not concerned with anyone else's motives here.

**NINE.** Guilty beyond a reasonable doubt. This is an important thing to remember.

**THREE.** [*To* TEN] Everyone's a lawyer. [*To* NINE] Supposing you explain what your reasonable doubts are.

**NINE.** This is not easy. So far, it's only a feeling I have. A feeling. Perhaps you don't understand.

**TEN.** A feeling! What are we gonna do, spend the night talking about your feelings? What about the facts?

**THREE.** You said a mouthful. [*To* NINE] Look, the old man heard the kid yell, "I'm gonna kill you." A second later he heard the father's body falling, and he saw the boy running out of the house fifteen seconds after that.

**TWELVE.** That's right. And let's not forget the woman across the street. She looked into the open window and saw the boy stab his father. She saw it. Now if that's not enough for you . . .

**EIGHT.** It's not enough for me.

**SEVEN.** How do you like him? It's like talking into a dead phone.

**FOUR.** The woman saw the killing through the windows of a moving elevated train. The train had five cars, and she saw it through the windows of the last two. She remembers the most insignificant details.

[*Cut to close shot of* TWELVE, *who doodles a picture of an el train on a scrap of paper.*]

**THREE.** Well, what have you got to say about that?

**EIGHT.** I don't know. It doesn't sound right to me.

**THREE.** Well, supposing you think about it. [*To* TWELVE] Lend me your pencil.

[TWELVE *gives it to him. He draws a tick-tack-toe square on the same sheet of paper on which* TWELVE *has drawn the train. He fills in an X, hands the pencil to* TWELVE.]

**THREE.** Your turn. We might as well pass the time.

[TWELVE *takes the pencil.* EIGHT *stands up and snatches the paper away.* THREE *leaps up.*]

**THREE.** Wait a minute!

**EIGHT.** [*Hard*] This isn't a game.

**THREE.** [*Angry*] Who do you think you are?

**SEVEN.** [*Rising*] All right, let's take it easy.

**THREE.** I've got a good mind to walk around this table and belt him one!

**FOREMAN.** Now, please. I don't want any fights in here.

**THREE.** Did ya see him? The nerve! The absolute nerve!

**TEN.** All right. Forget it. It don't mean anything.

**SIX.** How about sitting down.

**THREE.** This isn't a game. Who does he think he is?

[*He lets them sit him down.* EIGHT *remains standing, holding the scrap of paper. He looks at it closely now and seems to be suddenly interested in it. Then he throws it back toward* THREE. *It lands in center of table.* THREE *is angered again at this, but*

FOUR *puts his hand on his arm.* EIGHT *speaks now and his voice is more intense.*]

EIGHT. [*To* FOUR] Take a look at that sketch. How long does it take an elevated train going at top speed to pass a given point?

FOUR. What has that got to do with anything?

EIGHT. How long? Guess.

FOUR. I wouldn't have the slightest idea.

EIGHT. [*To* FIVE] What do you think?

FIVE. About ten or twelve seconds, maybe.

EIGHT. I'd say that was a fair guess. Anyone else?

ELEVEN. I would think about ten seconds, perhaps.

TWO. About ten seconds.

FOUR. All right. Say ten seconds. What are you getting at?

EIGHT. This. An el train passes a given point in ten seconds. That given point is the window of the room in which the killing took place. You can almost reach out of the window of that room and touch the el. Right? [*Several of them nod.*] All right. Now let me ask you this. Did anyone here ever live right next to the el tracks? I have. When your window is open and the train goes by, the noise is almost unbearable. You can't hear yourself think.

TEN. Okay. You can't hear yourself think. Will you get to the point?

EIGHT. The old man heard the boy say, "I'm going to kill you," and one second later he heard a body fall. One second. That's the testimony, right?

TWO. Right.

EIGHT. The woman across the street looked through the windows of the last two cars of the el and saw the body fall. Right? The *last two* cars.

TEN. What are you giving us here?

EIGHT. An el takes ten seconds to pass a given point or two seconds per car. That el had been going by the old man's window for at least six seconds, and maybe more, before the body fell, according to the woman. The old man would have had to hear the boy say, "I'm going to kill you," while the front of the el was roaring past his nose. It's not possible that he could have heard it.

THREE. What d'ya mean! Sure he could have heard it.

EIGHT. Could he?

THREE. He said the boy yelled it out. That's enough for me.

NINE. I don't think he could have heard it.

TWO. Maybe he didn't hear it. I mean with the el noise—

THREE. What are you people talking about? Are you calling the old man a liar?

FIVE. Well, it stands to reason.

THREE. You're crazy. Why would he lie? What's he got to gain?

NINE. Attention, maybe.

THREE. You keep coming up with these bright sayings. Why don't you send one in to a newspaper? They pay two dollars.

[EIGHT *looks hard at* THREE *and then turns to* NINE.]

EIGHT. [*Softly*] Why might the old man have lied? You have a right to be heard.

NINE. It's just that I looked at him for a very long time. The seam of his jacket was split under the arm. Did you notice that? He was a very old man with a torn jacket, and he carried two canes. I think I know him better than anyone here. This is a quiet, frightened, insignificant man who has been nothing all his life, who has never had recognition—his name in the newspapers. Nobody knows him after seventy-five years. That's a very sad thing. A man like this needs to be recognized. To be questioned, and listened to, and quoted just once. This is very important.

**TWELVE.** And you're trying to tell us he lied about a thing like this just so that he could be important?

**NINE.** No, he wouldn't really lie. But perhaps he'd make himself believe that he heard those words and recognized the boy's face.

**THREE.** [*Loud*] Well, that's the most fantastic story I've ever heard. How can you make up a thing like that? What do you know about it?

**NINE.** [*Low*] I speak from experience.

[*There is a long pause. Then the* FOREMAN *clears his throat.*]

**FOREMAN.** [*To* EIGHT] All right. Is there anything else?

[EIGHT *is looking at* NINE. TWO *offers the* FOREMAN *a box of cough drops. The* FOREMAN *pushes it away.*]

**TWO.** [*Hesitantly*] Anybody . . . want a cough . . . drop?

**FOREMAN.** [*Sharply*] Come on. Let's get on with it.

**EIGHT.** I'll take one.

[TWO *almost gratefully slides him one along the table.*]

Thanks.

[TWO *nods and* EIGHT *puts the cough drop into his mouth.*]

**EIGHT.** Now. There's something else I'd like to point out here. I think we proved that the old man couldn't have heard the boy say, "I'm going to kill you," but supposing he really did hear it? This phrase: how many times has each of you used it? Probably hundreds. "If you do that once more, Junior, I'm going to murder you." "Come on, Rocky, kill him!" We say it every day. This doesn't mean that we're going to kill someone.

**THREE.** Wait a minute. The phrase was "I'm going to kill you," and the kid screamed it out at the top of his lungs. Don't try and tell me he didn't mean it. Anybody says a thing like that the way he said it—they mean it.

**TEN.** And how they mean it!

**EIGHT.** Well, let me ask you this. Do you really think the boy would shout out a thing like that so the whole neighborhood would hear it? I don't think so. He's much too bright for that.

**TEN.** [*Exploding*] Bright! He's a common, ignorant slob. He don't even speak good English!

**ELEVEN.** [*Slowly*] He *doesn't* even speak good English.

[TEN *stares angrily at* ELEVEN, *and there is silence for a moment. Then* FIVE *looks around the table nervously.*]

**FIVE.** I'd like to change my vote to not guilty.

[THREE *gets up and walks to the window, furious, but trying to control himself.*]

**FOREMAN.** Are you sure?

**FIVE.** Yes. I'm sure.

**FOREMAN.** The vote is nine to three in favor of guilty.

**SEVEN.** Well, if that isn't the end. [*To* FIVE] What are you basing it on? Stories this guy—[*Indicating* EIGHT]—made up! He oughta write for *Amazing Detective Monthly.* He'd make a fortune. Listen, the kid had a lawyer, didn't he? Why didn't his lawyer bring up all these points?

**FIVE.** Lawyers can't think of everything.

**SEVEN.** Oh, brother! [*To* EIGHT] You sit in here and pull stories out of thin air. Now we're supposed to believe that the old man didn't get up out of bed, run to the door, and see the kid beat it downstairs fifteen seconds after the killing. He's only saying he did to be important.

**FIVE.** Did the old man say he ran to the door?

**SEVEN.** Ran. Walked. What's the difference? He got there.

**FIVE.** I don't remember what he said. But I don't see how he could run.

**FOUR.** He said he went from his bedroom to the front door. That's enough, isn't it?

**EIGHT.** Where was his bedroom again?

**TEN.** Down the hall somewhere. I thought you remembered everything. Don't you remember that?

**EIGHT.** No. Mr. Foreman, I'd like to take a look at the diagram of the apartment.

**SEVEN.** Why don't we have them run the trial over just so you can get everything straight?

**EIGHT.** Mr. Foreman—

**FOREMAN.** [*Rising*] I heard you.

[*The* FOREMAN *gets up, goes to door during following dialogue. He knocks on door,* GUARD *opens it, he whispers to* GUARD, GUARD *nods and closes door.*]

**THREE.** [*To* EIGHT] All right. What's this for? How come you're the only one in the room who wants to see exhibits all the time?

**FIVE.** I want to see this one, too.

**THREE.** And I want to stop wasting time.

**FOUR.** If we're going to start wading through all that nonsense about where the body was found . . .

**EIGHT.** We're not. We're going to find out how a man who's had two strokes in the past three years, and who walks with a pair of canes, could get to his front door in fifteen seconds.

**THREE.** He said twenty seconds.

**TWO.** He said fifteen.

**THREE.** How does he know how long fifteen seconds is? You can't judge that kind of a thing.

**NINE.** He said fifteen. He was positive about it.

**THREE.** [*Angry*] He's an old man. You saw him. Half the time he was confused. How could he be positive about . . . anything?

[THREE *looks around sheepishly, unable to cover up his blunder. The door opens and the* GUARD *walks in, carrying a large pen-and-ink diagram of the apartment. It is a railroad flat.[1] A bedroom faces the el tracks. Behind it is a series of rooms off a long hall. In the front bedroom is a diagram of the spot where the body was found. At the back of the apartment we see the entrance into the apartment hall from the building hall. We see a flight of stairs in the building hall. The diagram is clearly labeled and included in the information on it*

---

**1. railroad flat:** An apartment whose rooms are in a straight line.

*are the dimensions of the various rooms. The* GUARD *gives the diagram to the* FOREMAN.]

**GUARD.** This what you wanted?

**FOREMAN.** That's right. Thank you.

[*The* GUARD *nods and exits.* EIGHT *goes to* FOREMAN *and reaches for it.*]

**EIGHT.** May I?

[*The* FOREMAN *nods.* EIGHT *takes the diagram and sets it up on a chair so that all can see it.* EIGHT *looks it over. Several of the* JURORS *get up to see it better.* THREE, TEN, *and* SEVEN, *however, barely bother to look at it.*]

**SEVEN.** [*To* TEN] Do me a favor. Wake me up when this is over.

**EIGHT.** [*Ignoring him*] All right. This is the apartment in which the killing took place. The old man's apartment is directly beneath it and exactly the same. [*Pointing*] Here are the el tracks. The bedroom. Another bedroom. Living room. Bathroom. Kitchen. And this is the hall. Here's the front door to the apartment. And here are the steps. [*Pointing to front bedroom and then front door*] Now the old man was in bed in this room. He says he got up, went out into the hall, down the hall to the front door, opened it, and looked out just in time to see the boy racing down the stairs. Am I right?

**THREE.** That's the story.

**EIGHT.** Fifteen seconds after he heard the body fall.

**ELEVEN.** Correct.

**EIGHT.** His bed was at the window. It's —[*Looking closer*]—twelve feet from his bed to the bedroom door. The length of the hall is forty-three feet, six inches. He had to get up out of bed, get his canes, walk twelve feet, open the bedroom door, walk forty-three feet, and open the front door—all in fifteen seconds. Do you think this possible?

**TEN.** You know it's possible.

**ELEVEN.** He can only walk very slowly. They had to help him into the witness chair.

**THREE.** You make it sound like a long walk. It's not.

[EIGHT *gets up, goes to the end of the room, and takes two chairs. He puts them together to indicate a bed.*]

**NINE.** For an old man who uses canes, it's a long walk.

*The layout of the apartment*

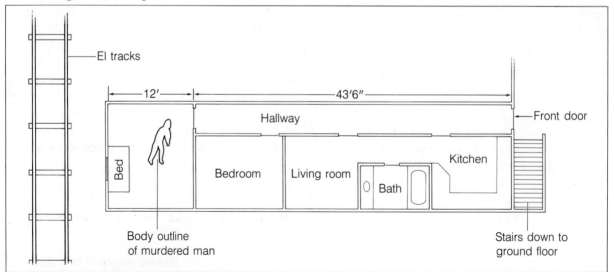

**THREE.** [*To* EIGHT] What are you doing?

**EIGHT.** I want to try this thing. Let's see how long it took him. I'm going to pace off twelve feet—the length of the bedroom. [*He begins to do so.*]

**THREE.** You're crazy. You can't re-create a thing like that.

**ELEVEN.** Perhaps if we could see it . . . this is an important point.

**THREE.** [*Mad*] It's a ridiculous waste of time.

**SIX.** Let him do it.

**EIGHT.** Hand me a chair. [*Someone pushes a chair to him.*] All right. This is the bedroom door. Now how far would you say it is from here to the door of this room?

**SIX.** I'd say it was twenty feet.

**TWO.** Just about.

**EIGHT.** Twenty feet is close enough. All right, from here to the door and back is about forty feet. It's shorter than the length of the hall, wouldn't you say that?

**NINE.** A few feet, maybe.

**TEN.** Look, this is absolutely insane. What makes you think you can—

**EIGHT.** Do you mind if I try it? According to you, it'll only take fifteen seconds. We can spare that. [*He walks over to the two chairs now and lies down on them.*] Who's got a watch with a second hand?

**TWO.** I have.

**EIGHT.** When you want me to start, stamp your foot. That'll be the body falling. Time me from there. [*He lies down on the chairs.*] Let's say he keeps his canes right at his bedside. Right?

**TWO.** Right!

**EIGHT.** Okay. I'm ready.

[*They all watch carefully.* TWO *stares at his watch, waiting for the second hand to reach sixty. Then, as it does, he stamps his foot loudly.* EIGHT *begins to get up. Slowly he swings his legs over the edges of the chairs, reaches for imaginary canes, and struggles to his feet.* TWO *stares at the watch.* EIGHT *walks as a crippled old man would walk, toward the chair which is serving as the bedroom door. He gets to it and pretends to open it.*]

**TEN.** [*Shouting*] Speed it up. He walked twice as fast as that.

[EIGHT, *not having stopped for this outburst, begins to walk the simulated forty-foot hallway.*]

**ELEVEN.** This is, I think, even more quickly than the old man walked in the courtroom.

**EIGHT.** If you think I should go faster, I will.

[*He speeds up his pace slightly. He reaches the door and turns now, heading back, hobbling as an old man would hobble, bent over his imaginary canes. They watch him tensely. He hobbles back to the chair, which also serves as the front door. He stops there and pretends to unlock the door. Then he pretends to push it open.*]

**EIGHT.** [*Loud*] Stop.

**TWO.** Right.

**EIGHT.** What's the time?

**TWO.** Fifteen . . . twenty . . . thirty . . . thirty-one seconds exactly.

**ELEVEN.** Thirty-one seconds.

[*Some of the* JURORS *ad-lib[2] their surprise to each other.*]

---

2. **ad-lib** (ad′ lib′) *v.*: To add words not in the script.

**EIGHT.** It's my guess that the old man was trying to get to the door, heard someone racing down the stairs, and assumed that it was the boy.

**SIX.** I think that's possible.

**THREE.** [*Infuriated*] Assumed? Now, listen to me, you people. I've seen all kinds of dishonesty in my day . . . but this little display takes the cake. [*To* FOUR] Tell him, will you?

[FOUR *sits silently.* THREE *looks at him and then he strides over to* EIGHT.]

**THREE.** You come in here with your heart bleeding all over the floor about slum kids and injustice and you make up these wild stories, and you've got some soft-hearted old ladies listening to you. Well I'm not. I'm getting real sick of it. [*To all*] What's the matter with you people? This kid is guilty! He's got to burn! We're letting him slip through our fingers here.

**EIGHT.** [*Calmly*] Our fingers. Are you his executioner?

**THREE.** [*Raging*] I'm one of 'em.

**EIGHT.** Perhaps you'd like to pull the switch.

**THREE.** [*Shouting*] For this kid? You bet I'd like to pull the switch!

**EIGHT.** I'm sorry for you.

**THREE.** [*Shouting*] Don't start with me.

**EIGHT.** What it must feel like to want to pull the switch!

**THREE.** Shut up!

**EIGHT.** You're a sadist.[3]

**THREE.** [*Louder*] Shut up!

**EIGHT.** [*Strong*] You want to see this boy die because you personally want it—not because of the facts.

**THREE.** [*Shouting*] Shut up!

[*He lunges at* EIGHT, *but is caught by two of the* JURORS *and held. He struggles as* EIGHT *watches calmly.*]

**THREE.** [*Screaming*] Let me go! I'll kill him. I'll kill him!

**EIGHT.** [*Softly*] You don't really mean you'll kill me, do you?

[THREE *stops struggling now and stares at* EIGHT. *All the* JURORS *watch in silence as we fade out.*]

---

**3. sadist** (sad′ ist) *n*.: One who gets pleasure from inflicting physical or psychological pain on others.

## THINKING ABOUT THE SELECTION

### Recalling

1. What is the result of the secret ballot at the beginning of Act II?
2. Identify the juror who seems particularly angry that everyone does not agree on the defendant's guilt. Explain why.
3. How does Juror Eight explain the old man's testimony of what he *saw?*

### Interpreting

4. Explain the connection between the *noise* of the elevated train and the testimony of what the old man *heard.*
5. What does the timed reenactment performed by Juror Eight show?
6. At the end of Act II, Juror Three shouts, "I'll kill him!" What is the significance of this statement at this point in the play?

### Applying

7. Suppose the defendant had had a first-rate defense attorney. What objective might that attorney have tried to achieve in cross-examining each of these witnesses?
   a. the storekeeper who sold the knife
   b. the old man who lived downstairs
   c. the woman who lived across the street

## ANALYZING LITERATURE

### Recognizing Protagonist and Antagonist

Juror Eight is clearly the **protagonist,** the principal character, of *Twelve Angry Men.* At first it seems that all the other jurors may be antagonists of Juror Eight, since they all disagree with him. However, in Act II, one juror clearly and consistently emerges as the **antagonist,** the character who struggles to defeat the aims of the protagonist.

Identify the major antagonist and explain his position. Cite several speeches that reveal his opposition to Juror Eight, the protagonist.

## CRITICAL THINKING AND READING

### Evaluating Arguments

A **sound argument** involves a conclusion derived from plausible reasons that truly support the conclusion. For example, Juror Nine argues that the old man's testimony about the defendant may not be valid. Juror Nine supports this statement by saying that the old man may have made himself believe his own testimony because he needs to be recognized for once in his life. Juror Nine, an old man who is unrecognized himself, says he knows from experience that the need for recognition could provoke such action.

An **unsound argument** involves a conclusion derived from reasons that are false or prove something that is beside the point. For example, in Act I Juror Ten argues that the jurors do not owe the defendant any words beyond finding him guilty. He supports this statement by saying that the defendant, who has a slum background, should not be believed because "I've lived among 'em all my life. You can't believe a word they [people with slum backgrounds] say." These reasons are not necessarily true, and they do not support his argument.

Find one sound argument and one unsound argument in Act Two. Explain why you judge each sound or unsound.

## THINKING AND WRITING

### Writing About a Play

Write an essay to be read aloud at a formal student debate on what can be learned about the legal system from this play. First review the play, taking note of how the system works. Then draft an essay in which you summarize what you learned. Include examples and details from the play to back up your findings. Finally revise your essay, adding details that would make the system clear to someone who had no knowledge of it. Proofread your essay and share it with your classmates.

# GUIDE FOR READING

**Plot Structure in Drama**

## Twelve Angry Men, Act III

**Plot** is the sequence of related events or incidents that make up a play or a story. The events are interrelated in such a way that one action causes another. A plot revolves around the development and resolution of a conflict. The exposition, which goes on through Act I, presents the information that will be important in the development of the play. Juror Eight, the protagonist, struggles to resolve the conflict throughout the second and third acts. His actions and his interrelationships with other characters bring about events that finally lead to a climax—the point of maximum conflict, after which the action turns. The resolution, or outcome, brings the play to its conclusion.

**Look For**

By Act III, the tension among the jurors has built. As you read, look for signs that the action of the play is reaching a critical stage that will spell victory or defeat for the protagonist.

**Writing**

In Act III of *Twelve Angry Men,* Juror Five draws on his own experience and background to make a judgment and persuade the other jurors. Think of a time when you drew on your own experience and background to make a judgment and persuade others. Free-write about this experience, including details of the situation.

**Vocabulary**

Knowing the following words will help you as you read Act III of *Twelve Angry Men.*

**arrogance** (ar′ ə gəns) *n.*: Pride; self-importance (p. 334)

**acquittal** (ə kwit′ 'l) *n.*: The judgment of a judge or jury that a person is not guilty of a crime as charged (p. 336)

**intimidate** (in tim′ə dāt′) *v.*: To discourage or inhibit by making threats (p. 339)

## ACT III

[*Fade in on same scene. No time lapse.* THREE *glares angrily at* EIGHT. *He is still held by two* JURORS. *After a long pause, he shakes himself loose and turns away. He walks to the windows. The other* JURORS *stand around the room now, shocked by this display of anger. There is silence. Then the door opens and the* GUARD *enters. He looks around the room.*]

**GUARD.** Is there anything wrong, gentlemen? I heard some noise.

**FOREMAN.** No. There's nothing wrong.

[*He points to the large diagram of the apartment.*]

You can take that back. We're finished with it.

[*The* GUARD *nods and takes the diagram. He looks curiously at some of the* JURORS *and exits. The* JURORS *still are silent. Some of them slowly begin to sit down.* THREE *still stands at the window. He turns around now. The* JURORS *look at him.*]

**THREE.** [*Loud*] Well, what are you looking at?

[*They turn away. He goes back to his seat now. Silently the rest of the* JURORS *take their seats.* TWELVE *begins to doodle.* TEN *blows his nose, but no one speaks. Then, finally—*]

**FOUR.** I don't see why we have to behave like children here.

**ELEVEN.** Nor do I. We have a responsibility. This is a remarkable thing about democracy. That we are . . . what is the word? . . . Ah, notified! That we are notified by mail to come down to this place and decide on the guilt or innocence of a man we have not known before. We have nothing to gain or lose by our verdict. This is one of the rea-

sons why we are strong. We should not make it a personal thing.

[*There is a long, awkward pause.*]

**TWELVE.** Well—we're still nowhere. Who's got an idea?

**SIX.** I think maybe we should try another vote. Mr. Foreman?

**FOREMAN.** It's all right with me. Anybody doesn't want to vote?

[*He looks around the table.*]

**SEVEN.** All right, let's do it.

**THREE.** I want an open ballot. Let's call out our votes. I want to know who stands where.

**FOREMAN.** That sounds fair. Anyone object?

[*No one does.*]

All right. I'll call off your jury numbers. [*He takes a pencil and paper and makes marks now in one of two columns after each vote.*]

**FOREMAN.** I vote guilty. Number Two?

**TWO.** Not guilty.

**FOREMAN.** Number Three?

**THREE.** Guilty.

**FOREMAN.** Number Four?

**FOUR.** Guilty.

**FOREMAN.** Number Five?

**FIVE.** Not guilty.

**FOREMAN.** Number Six?

**SIX.** Not guilty.

**FOREMAN.** Number Seven?

**SEVEN.** Guilty.

**FOREMAN.** Number Eight?

**EIGHT.** Not guilty.

**FOREMAN.** Number Nine?

**NINE.** Not guilty.

**FOREMAN.** Number Ten?

**TEN.** Guilty.

**FOREMAN.** Number Eleven?

**ELEVEN.** Not guilty.

**FOREMAN.** Number Twelve?

**TWELVE.** Guilty.

**FOUR.** Six to six.

**TEN.** [*Mad*] I'll tell you something. The crime is being committed right in this room.

**FOREMAN.** The vote is six to six.

**THREE.** I'm ready to walk into court right now and declare a hung jury. There's no point in this going on anymore.

**SEVEN.** I go for that, too. Let's take it in to the judge and let the kid take his chances with twelve other guys.

**FIVE.** [*To* SEVEN] You mean you still don't think there's room for reasonable doubt?

**SEVEN.** No, I don't.

**ELEVEN.** I beg your pardon. Maybe you don't understand the term ''reasonable doubt.''

**SEVEN.** [*Angry*] What do you mean I don't understand it? Who do you think you are to talk to me like that? [*To all*] How do you like this guy? He comes over here running for his life, and before he can even take a big breath he's telling us how to run the show. The arrogance of him!

**FIVE.** [*To* SEVEN] Wait a second. Nobody around here's asking where you came from.

**SEVEN.** I was born right here.

**FIVE.** Or where your father came from. . . .

[*He looks at* SEVEN, *who doesn't answer but looks away.*]

Maybe it wouldn't hurt us to take a few tips from people who come running here! Maybe they learned something we don't know. We're not so perfect!

**ELEVEN.** Please—I am used to this. It's all right. Thank you.

**FIVE.** It's not all right!

**SEVEN.** Okay, okay, I apologize. Is that what you want?

**FIVE.** That's what I want.

**FOREMAN.** All right. Let's stop the arguing. Who's got something constructive to say?

**TWO.** [*Hesitantly*] Well, something's been bothering me a little . . . this whole business about the stab wound and how it was made, the downward angle of it, you know?

**THREE.** Don't tell me we're gonna start that. They went over it and over it in court.

**TWO.** I know they did—but I don't go along with it. The boy is five feet eight inches tall. His father was six two. That's a difference of six inches. It's a very awkward thing to stab *down* into the chest of someone who's half a foot taller than you are.

[THREE *jumps up, holding the knife.*]

**THREE.** Look, you're not going to be satisfied till you see it again. I'm going to give you a demonstration. Somebody get up.

[*He looks around the table.* EIGHT *stands up and walks toward him.* THREE *closes the knife and puts it in his pocket. They stand face to face and look at each other for a moment.*]

**THREE.** Okay. [*To* TWO] Now watch this. I don't want to have to do it again. [*He crouches down now until he is quite a bit shorter than* EIGHT.] Is that six inches?

**TWELVE.** That's more than six inches.

**THREE.** Okay, let it be more.

[*He reaches into his pocket and takes out the knife. He flicks it open, changes its position in his hand, and holds the knife aloft, ready to stab. He and* EIGHT *look steadily into each other's eyes. Then he stabs downward, hard.*]

**TWO.** [*Shouting*] Look out!

[*He stops short just as the blade reaches* EIGHT*'s chest.* THREE *laughs.*]

**SIX.** That's not funny.

**FIVE.** What's the matter with you?

**THREE.** Now just calm down. Nobody's hurt, are they?

**EIGHT.** [*Low*] No. Nobody's hurt.

**THREE.** All right. There's your angle. Take a look at it. Down and in. That's how I'd stab a taller man in the chest, and that's how it was done. Take a look at it and tell me I'm wrong.

[TWO *doesn't answer.* THREE *looks at him for a moment, then jams the knife into the table, and sits down. They all look at the knife.*]

**SIX.** Down and in. I guess there's no argument.

[EIGHT *picks the knife out of the table and closes it. He flicks it open and, changing its position in his hand, stabs downward with it.*]

**EIGHT.** [*To* SIX] Did you ever stab a man?

**SIX.** Of course not.

**EIGHT.** [*To* THREE] Did you?

**THREE.** All right, let's not be silly.

**EIGHT.** Did you?

**THREE.** [*Loud*] No, I didn't!

**EIGHT.** Where do you get all your information about how it's done?

**THREE.** What do you mean? It's just common sense.

**EIGHT.** Have you ever seen a man stabbed?

**THREE.** [*Pauses and looks around the room nervously*] No.

**EIGHT.** All right. I want to ask you something. The boy was an experienced knife fighter. He was even sent to reform school for knifing someone, isn't that so?

**TWELVE.** That's right.

**EIGHT.** Look at this. [EIGHT *closes the knife, flicks it open, and changes the position of the knife so that he can stab overhanded.*] Doesn't it seem like an awkward way to handle a knife?

**THREE.** What are you asking me for?

[EIGHT *closes the blade and flicks it open, holds it ready to slash underhanded.*]

**FIVE.** Wait a minute! What's the matter with me? Give me that. [*He reaches out for the knife.*]

**EIGHT.** Have you ever seen a knife fight?

**FIVE.** Yes, I have.

**EIGHT.** In the movies?

**FIVE.** In my backyard. On my stoop. In the vacant lot across the street. Too many of them. Switch-knives came with the neighborhood where I lived. Funny I didn't think of it before. I guess you try to forget those things. [*Flicking the knife open*] Anyone who's ever used a switch-knife would never have stabbed downward. You don't handle a switch-knife that way. You use it under-handed.

**EIGHT.** Then he couldn't have made the kind of wound which killed his father.

**FIVE.** No. He couldn't have. Not if he'd ever had any experience with switch-knives.

**THREE.** I don't believe it.

**TEN.** Neither do I. You're giving us a lot of mumbo jumbo.

**EIGHT.** [*To* TWELVE] What do you think?

**TWELVE.** [*Hesitantly*] Well . . . I don't know.

**EIGHT.** [*To* SEVEN] What about you?

**SEVEN.** Listen, I'll tell you something. I'm a little sick of this whole thing already. We're getting nowhere fast. Let's break it up and go home. I'm changing my vote to not guilty.

**THREE.** You're what?

**SEVEN.** You heard me. I've had enough.

**THREE.** What do you mean, you've had enough? That's no answer.

**ELEVEN.** [*Angry*] I think perhaps you're right. This is not an answer. [*To* SEVEN] What kind of a man are you? You have sat here and voted guilty with everyone else because there are some theater tickets burning a hole in your pocket. Now you have changed your vote for the same reason. I do not think you have the right to play like this with a man's life. This is an ugly and terrible thing to do.

**SEVEN.** Now wait a minute . . . you can't talk like that to me.

**ELEVEN.** [*Strong*] I can talk like that to you! If you want to vote not guilty, then do it be-cause you are convinced the man is not guilty. If you believe he is guilty, then vote that way. Or don't you have the . . . the . . . guts—the guts to do what you think is right?

**SEVEN.** Now listen . . .

**ELEVEN.** Is it guilty or not guilty?

**SEVEN.** [*Hesitantly*] I told you. Not . . . guilty.

**ELEVEN.** [*Hard*] Why?

**SEVEN.** I don't have to—

**ELEVEN.** You have to! Say it! Why?

[*They stare at each other for a long while.*]

**SEVEN.** [*Low*] I . . . don't think . . . he's guilty.

**EIGHT.** [*Fast*] I want another vote.

**FOREMAN.** Okay, there's another vote called for. I guess the quickest way is a show of hands. Anybody object? [*No one does.*] All right. All those voting not guilty, raise your hands.

[TWO, FIVE, SIX, SEVEN, EIGHT, NINE, *and* ELEVEN *raise their hands immediately. Then, slow-ly,* TWELVE *raises his hand. The* FOREMAN *looks around the table carefully and then he too raises his hand. He looks around the table, counting silently.*]

**FOREMAN.** Nine. [*The hands go down.*] All those voting guilty.

[THREE, FOUR, *and* TEN *raise their hands.*]

**FOREMAN.** Three. [*They lower their hands.*] The vote is nine to three in favor of acquittal.

**TEN.** I don't understand you people. How can you believe this kid is innocent? Look, you know how those people lie. I don't have to tell you. They don't know what the truth is. And lemme tell you, they—[FIVE *gets up*

*from table, turns his back to it, and goes to window.*]—don't need any real big reason to kill someone either. You know, they get drunk, and *bang*, someone's lying in the gutter. Nobody's blaming them. That's how they are. You know what I mean? Violent!

[NINE *gets up and does the same. He is followed by* ELEVEN.]

**TEN.** Human life don't mean as much to them as it does to us. Hey, where are you going? Look, these people are drinking and fighting all the time, and if somebody gets killed, so somebody gets killed. They don't care. Oh, sure, there are some good things about them, too. Look, I'm the first to say that.

[EIGHT *gets up, and then* TWO *and* SIX *follow him to the window.*]

**TEN.** I've known a few who were pretty de-

cent, but that's the exception. Most of them, it's like they have no feelings. They can do anything. What's going on here?

[*The* FOREMAN *gets up and goes to the window, followed by* SEVEN *and* TWELVE.]

**TEN.** I'm speaking my piece, and you —Listen to me! They're no good. There's not a one of 'em who's any good. We better watch out. Take it from me. This kid on trial . . .

[THREE *sits at table toying with the knife and* FOUR *gets up and starts for the window. All have their backs to* TEN.]

**TEN.** Well, don't you know about them? Listen to me! What are you doing? I'm trying to tell you something. . . .

[FOUR *stands over him as he trails off. There is a dead silence. Then* FOUR *speaks softly.*]

**FOUR.** I've had enough. If you open your mouth again, I'm going to split your skull.

[FOUR *stands there and looks at him. No one moves or speaks.* TEN *looks at him, then looks down at the table.*]

**TEN.** [*Softly*] I'm only trying to tell you. . . .

[*There is a long pause as* FOUR *stares down at* TEN.]

**FOUR.** [*To all*] All right. Sit down, everybody.

[*They all move back to their seats. When they are all seated,* FOUR *then sits down.*]

**FOUR.** [*Quietly*] I still believe the boy is guilty of murder. I'll tell you why. To me, the most damning evidence was given by the woman across the street who claimed she actually saw the murder committed.

**THREE.** That's right. As far as I'm concerned, that's the most important testimony.

**EIGHT.** All right. Let's go over her testimony. What exactly did she say?

**FOUR.** I believe I can recount it accurately. She said that she went to bed at about eleven o'clock that night. Her bed was next to the open window, and she could look out of the window while lying down and see directly into the window across the street. She tossed and turned for over an hour, unable to fall asleep. Finally she turned toward the window at about twelve-ten and, as she looked out, she saw the boy stab his father. As far as I can see, this is unshakable testimony.

**THREE.** That's what I mean. That's the whole case.

[TWO *takes off his eyeglasses and begins to polish them, as they all sit silently watching him.*]

**FOUR.** [*To the* JURY] Frankly, I don't see how you can vote for acquittal. [*To* TWELVE] What do you think about it?

**TWELVE.** Well . . . maybe . . . there's so much evidence to sift.

**THREE.** What do you mean, maybe? He's absolutely right. You can throw out all the other evidence.

**FOUR.** That was my feeling.

[TWO, *polishing his glasses, squints at clock, can't see it.* SIX *watches him closely.*]

**TWO.** What time is it?

**ELEVEN.** Ten minutes of six.

**TWO.** It's late. You don't suppose they'd let us go home and finish it in the morning. I've got a kid with mumps.

**FIVE.** Not a chance.

**SIX.** [*To* TWO]. Pardon me. Can't you see the clock without your glasses?

**TWO.** Not clearly. Why?

**SIX.** Oh, I don't know. Look, this may be a dumb thought, but what do you do when you wake up at night and want to know what time it is?

**TWO.** What do you mean? I put on my glasses and look at the clock.

**SIX.** You don't wear them to bed.

**TWO.** Of course not. No one wears eyeglasses to bed.

**TWELVE.** What's all this for?

**SIX.** Well, I was thinking. You know the woman who testified that she saw the killing wears glasses.

**THREE.** So does my grandmother. So what?

**EIGHT.** Your grandmother isn't a murder witness.

**SIX.** Look, stop me if I'm wrong. This woman wouldn't wear her eyeglasses to bed, would she?

**FOREMAN.** Wait a minute! Did she wear glasses at all? I don't remember.

**ELEVEN.** [*Excited*] Of course she did. The woman wore bifocals.[1] I remember this very clearly. They looked quite strong.

**NINE.** That's right. Bifocals. She never took them off.

**FOUR.** She did wear glasses. Funny. I never thought of it.

**EIGHT.** Listen, she wasn't wearing them in bed. That's for sure. She testified that in the midst of her tossing and turning she rolled over and looked casually out the window. The murder was taking place as she looked out, and the lights went out a split second later. She couldn't have had time to put on her glasses. Now maybe she honestly thought she saw the boy kill his father. I say that she saw only a blur.

**THREE.** How do you know what she saw? Maybe she's farsighted. [*He looks around. No one answers.*]

**THREE.** [*Loud*] How does he know all these things?

[*There is silence.*]

**EIGHT.** Does anyone think there still is not a reasonable doubt?

[*He looks around the room, then squarely at* TEN. TEN *looks down and shakes his head no.*]

**THREE.** [*Loud*] I think he's guilty.

_____
**1. bifocals** (bī′ fō′ k'lz) *n.:* A pair of glasses with one part of each lens for close focus and the other part of each lens for distant focus.

**EIGHT.** [*Calmly*] Does anyone else?

**FOUR.** [*Quietly*] No. I'm convinced.

**EIGHT.** [*To* THREE] You're alone.

**THREE.** I don't care whether I'm alone or not! I have a right.

**EIGHT.** You have a right.

[*There is a pause. They all look at* THREE.]

**THREE.** Well, I told you I think the kid's guilty. What else do you want?

**EIGHT.** Your arguments.

[*They all look at* THREE.]

**THREE.** I gave you my arguments.

**EIGHT.** We're not convinced. We're waiting to hear them again. We have time.

[THREE *runs to* FOUR *and grabs his arm.*]

**THREE.** [*Pleading*] Listen. What's the matter with you? You're the guy. You made all the arguments. You can't turn now. A guilty man's gonna be walking the streets. A murderer. He's got to die! Stay with me.

**FOUR.** I'm sorry. There's a reasonable doubt in my mind.

**EIGHT.** We're waiting.

[THREE *turns violently on him.*]

**THREE.** [*Shouting*] Well, you're not going to intimidate me! [*They all look at* THREE.] I'm entitled to my opinion! [*No one answers him.*] It's gonna be a hung jury! That's it!

**EIGHT.** There's nothing we can do about that, except hope that some night, maybe in a few months, you'll get some sleep.

**FIVE.** You're all alone.

**NINE.** It takes a great deal of courage to stand alone.

[THREE *looks around at all of them for a long time. They sit silently, waiting for him to speak, and all of them despise him for his stubbornness. Then, suddenly, his face contorts as if he is about to cry, and he slams his fist down on the table.*]

**THREE.** [*Thundering*] All right!

[THREE *turns his back on them. There is silence for a moment and then the* FOREMAN *goes to the door and knocks on it. It opens. The* GUARD *looks in and sees them all standing. The* GUARD *holds the door for them as they begin slowly to file out.* EIGHT *waits at the door as the others file past him. Finally he and* THREE *are the only ones left.* THREE *turns around and sees that they are alone.* Slowly he moves toward the door. Then he stops at the table. He pulls the switch-knife out of the table and walks over to* EIGHT *with it. He holds it in the approved knife-fighter fashion and looks long and hard at* EIGHT, *pointing the knife at his belly.* EIGHT *stares back. Then* THREE *turns the knife around.* EIGHT *takes it by the handle.* THREE *exits.* EIGHT *closes the knife, puts it away, and, taking a last look around the room, exits, closing the door. The camera moves in close on the littered table in the empty room, and we clearly see a slip of crumpled paper on which are scribbled the words "Not guilty."*]

[*Fade out*]

## THINKING ABOUT THE SELECTION

### Recalling

1. What is the result of the vote taken at the beginning of Act III?
2. What information does Juror Five provide that shows a piece of evidence to be false?
3. How does Juror Six prove that the evidence provided by the woman is invalid?
4. What question do the jurors ask themselves in voting "guilty" or "not guilty"?
5. What is the final outcome of the jurors' deliberations?

### Interpreting

6. State in your own words the argument that Juror Ten makes for the guilt of the defendant in his monologue on pages 336–37.
7. Explain why most of the other jurors turn their backs on Juror Ten during his monologue.
8. Juror Four changes his vote to "not guilty" after the evidence he believes is most damning is shown to be doubtful. What does this tell you about Juror Four?
9. Explain in detail the character traits that make Juror Three give in at the end.

### Applying

10. Near the end of Act III, Juror Three is sticking to his vote of "guilty" out of stubbornness. Describe a situation in which stubbornness can be harmful and one in which it can be helpful.
11. In your opinion, has the jury proven the defendant not guilty? Discuss your answer.

## ANALYZING LITERATURE

### Understanding Plot Structure

**Plot structure,** the sequence and relationship of events that make up a play or story, includes exposition, conflict, climax, and resolution.

Summarize the events in *Twelve Angry Men* that make up each of the following elements of the plot structure.

    a. exposition    c. climax
    b. conflict     d. resolution

## CRITICAL THINKING AND READING

### Recognizing Hasty Generalization

A **hasty generalization,** an example of faulty reasoning, is a conclusion based on insufficient evidence. For example, to conclude, after observing two or three students being driven to a particular school in expensive cars, that all the students at the school come from wealthy families is a hasty generalization.

1. Reread the speech of Juror Four in Act I (pp. 317–18) beginning "We're missing the point here." State whether you consider Four's argument an example of a hasty generalization. Give reasons for your opinion.
2. Reread the monologue of Juror Ten in Act III (pp. 336–37) beginning "I don't understand you people" and ending "I'm trying to tell you something." Show how this speech exhibits faulty reasoning, resulting in a hasty generalization.

## THINKING AND WRITING

### Writing a Different Ending

First summarize the plot of *Twelve Angry Men.* How else might the trial have turned out? Freewrite, exploring your answer. Using your freewriting as a base, write a different ending for the play. For instance, the accused may be found not guilty, but a different character might provide key evidence. You may write your revised ending in dialogue form, or you may write a prose explanation. Share your outcome with your classmates.

# THE SHAKESPEAREAN THEATER

## Julius Caesar

*The Tragedy of Julius Caesar* is based on historical facts of the first century B.C. Julius Caesar (100?–44 B.C.), a brilliant military and political strategist, won a number of high offices. He was popular with the people but unpopular with his former political allies, who were jealous of him. William Shakespeare took the facts, which he found in a translation of *Plutarch's Lives of the Noble Greeks and Romans,* and developed them into a play. At the beginning of the play, the Roman Republic is at peace. In the course of the play, one man is assassinated and many others die. In *Julius Caesar* Shakespeare was less concerned with the interplay of these events than he was in the motives of the protagonists. The play, therefore, is not so much about the life and death of the dictator Caesar but about the minds and motives of Caesar's murderers. It is about Brutus and Cassius rather than about Caesar.

### The Theater in Shakespeare's Day

*Julius Caesar,* like most of Shakespeare's plays, was produced in a public theater. Public theaters were built around roofless courtyards without artificial light. Performances, therefore, were given only during daylight hours. Surrounding the courtyard were three levels of galleries with benches where wealthier playgoers sat. Poorer spectators, called groundlings, stood and watched a play from the courtyard, which was called the pit.

The stage was a platform that extended into the pit. Actors entered and left the stage from doors located behind the platform. The portion of the galleries behind and above the stage was used primarily as dressing and storage rooms. The second-level gallery right above the stage, however, was used as an upper stage. There was no scenery in the theaters of Shakespeare's day. Settings were indicated by references in the dialogue. As a result, one scene could follow another in rapid succession. There were, however, elaborate costumes and plenty of props. Thus, the plays produced in Shakespeare's day were fast-paced, colorful productions. Usually a play lasted two hours.

**SWAN THEATRE, LONDON, c. 1596**
*Drawing by Johannes DeWitt*
The Granger Collection

An important difference between Shakespeare's theater and today's is that acting companies of the sixteenth century were made up only of men and boys. Women did not perform on the stage. Young boys performed female roles.

## Some Common Elizabethan Words

The English language was somewhat different during Shakespeare's time. As you read *Julius Caesar,* most of the unfamiliar words and phrases you will encounter are explained in footnotes. The following, however, appear so frequently that learning them now will make your reading of the play easier.

| | |
|---|---|
| anon: Soon | hither: Here |
| aye: Yes | marry: Indeed |
| betimes: Right now | prithee: Pray thee |
| e'en: Even | sooth: Truly |
| e'er: Ever | withal: In addition |
| hence: Away, from here | wont: Accustomed |
| hie: Hurry | |

## The Tragedy of Julius Caesar, Act I

**William Shakespeare** (1564–1616) was born in Stratford-on-Avon, England. Little is known about his personal life, except that he married Anne Hathaway, became the father of four, and went to London to work as an actor, playwright, and poet. Despite the majesty of his poetry, Shakespeare was above all a playwright. His knowledge of acting and audiences gave him a great insight into what was dramatically workable. Shakespeare based *The Tragedy of Julius Caesar* on actual events that occurred in Rome in 44 B.C.

**Blank Verse**

**Blank verse** is a poetic form written in the metrical pattern of iambic pentameter. *Iambic* means that an unaccented or unstressed syllable is followed by an accented or stressed one. *Pentameter* means that there are five iambs per line. In the following lines, / labels a stressed syllable and ∪ an unstressed one.

> ∪ / ∪ / ∪ / ∪ / ∪ /
> What tributaries follow him to Rome
>
> ∪ / ∪ / ∪ / ∪ / ∪ /
> To grace in captive bonds his chariot-wheels?
> (Act I, scene i, lines 34–35)

**Look For**

Can someone be too ambitious? As you read Act I, look for reactions to Caesar's military conquests and his ambitions.

**Writing**

In Scene ii, Cassius says, "The fault, dear Brutus, is not in our stars,/ but in ourselves . . . " Freewrite, exploring the meaning of this quotation.

**Vocabulary**

Knowing the following words will help you as you read Act I of *The Tragedy of Julius Caesar.*

**replication** (rep′lə kā′shən) *n.*: Echo or reverberation (p. 347)

**mettle** (met′'l) *n.*: Basic character; (p. 347)

**spare** (sper) *adj.*: Lean or thin (p. 354)

**infirmity** (in fur′mə tē) *n.*: Bodily weakness (p. 356)

**tempest** (tem′pist) *n.*: Violent windstorm often with rain, snow, or hail (p. 358)

**surly** (sur′lē) *adv.*: In a proud, commanding way (p. 358)

**portentous** (pôr ten′ təs) *adj.*: Foreboding; full of unspecified meaning (p. 358)

**prodigious** (prə dij′əs) *adj.*: Impressively forceful (p. 360)

# The Tragedy of Julius Caesar

## William Shakespeare

### CHARACTERS

**Julius Caesar**

**Octavius Caesar** ⎫
**Marcus Antonius** ⎬ triumvirs* after
**M. Aemilius Lepidus** ⎭ the death of Julius Caesar

**Cicero** ⎫
**Publius** ⎬ senators
**Popilius Lena** ⎭

**Marcus Brutus**
**Cassius**
**Casca**
**Trebonius** ⎫ conspirators against
**Ligarius** ⎬ Julius Caesar
**Decius Brutus**
**Metellus Cimber** ⎭

**Cinna** ⎫
**Flavius** ⎬ tribunes
**Marullus** ⎭

**Artemidorus of Cnidos,** a teacher of rhetoric

**A Soothsayer**
**Cinna,** a poet
**Another Poet**

**Lucilius** ⎫
**Titinius** ⎪ friends
**Messala** ⎬ to Brutus
**Young Cato** ⎪ and Cassius
**Volumnius** ⎭

**Varro**
**Clitus**
**Claudius** ⎫ servants
**Strato** ⎬ to Brutus
**Lucius**
**Dardanius** ⎭

**Pindarus,** servant to Cassius
**Calpurnia,** wife to Caesar
**Portia,** wife to Brutus
**Senators, Citizens, Guards, Attendants, and so on**

*Scene:* During most of the play, at Rome; afterward near Sardis, and near Philippi.

*__triumvirs__ (trī um′ vərz) *n.*: In ancient Rome, a group of three rulers who share authority equally.

# Act I

**Scene i.** *Rome. A street.*

[*Enter Flavius, Marullus, and certain Commoners[1] over the stage.*]

**FLAVIUS.** Hence! Home, you idle creatures, get you home!
Is this a holiday? What, know you not,
Being mechanical,[2] you ought not walk
Upon a laboring day without the sign
5    Of your profession?[3] Speak, what trade art thou?

**CARPENTER.** Why, sir, a carpenter.

**MARULLUS.** Where is thy leather apron and thy rule?
What dost thou with thy best apparel on?
You, sir, what trade are you?

10    **COBBLER.** Truly, sir, in respect of a fine workman,[4] I am
but, as you would say, a cobbler.[5]

**4. in respect of a fine workman:** In relation to a skilled worker.

**5. cobbler:** Mender of shoes or a clumsy, bungling worker.

**MARULLUS.** But what trade art thou? Answer me directly.

**COBBLER.** A trade, sir, that, I hope, I may use with a safe
conscience, which is indeed, sir, a mender of bad
15    soles.

**FLAVIUS.** What trade, thou knave?[6] Thou naughty knave,
what trade?

**6. knave** (nāv) *n.*: A tricky rascal; a rogue.

**7. be not out . . . if you be out:** Be not angry . . . if you have worn-out shoes.

**8. mend you:** Mend your shoes or improve your disposition.

**COBBLER.** Nay, I beseech you, sir, be not out with me: yet,
if you be out,[7] sir, I can mend you.[8]

**MARULLUS.** What mean'st thou by that? Mend me, thou
saucy fellow?

20    **COBBLER.** Why, sir, cobble you.

**FLAVIUS.** Thou art a cobbler, art thou?

**COBBLER.** Truly, sir, all that I live by is with the awl:[9] I
meddle with no tradesman's matters, nor women's
matters; but withal, I am indeed, sir, a surgeon to old
25    shoes: when they are in great danger, I recover them.
As proper men as ever trod upon neat's leather[10]
have gone upon my handiwork.

**9. awl** (ôl) *n.*: A small, pointed tool for making holes in leather.

**10. neat's leather:** Leather made from the hides of cattle.

**FLAVIUS.** But wherefore art not in thy shop today?
Why dost thou lead these men about the streets?

**COBBLER.** Truly, sir, to wear out their shoes, to get 30
myself into more work. But indeed, sir, we make
holiday to see Caesar and to rejoice in his triumph.[11]

**MARULLUS.** Wherefore rejoice? What conquest brings he
home?

What tributaries[12] follow him to Rome,
To grace in captive bonds his chariot wheels? 35
You blocks, you stones, you worse than senseless
things!
O you hard hearts, you cruel men of Rome,
Knew you not Pompey?[13] Many a time and oft
Have you climbed up to walls and battlements,
To tow'rs and windows, yea, to chimney tops, 40
Your infants in your arms, and there have sat
The livelong day, with patient expectation,
To see great Pompey pass the streets of Rome.
And when you saw his chariot but appear,
Have you not made an universal shout, 45
That Tiber[14] trembled underneath her banks
To hear the replication of your sounds
Made in her concave shores?[15]
And do you now put on your best attire?
And do you now cull out[16] a holiday? 50
And do you now strew flowers in his way
That comes in triumph over Pompey's blood?[17]
Be gone!
Run to your houses, fall upon your knees,
Pray to the gods to intermit the plague[18] 55
That needs must light on this ingratitude.

**FLAVIUS.** Go, go, good countrymen, and, for this fault,
Assemble all the poor men of your sort;
Draw them to Tiber banks and weep your tears
Into the channel, till the lowest stream 60
Do kiss the most exalted shores of all.[19]

*[All the Commoners exit.]*

See, whe'r their basest mettle[20] be not moved,
They vanish tongue-tied in their guiltiness.
Go you down that way toward the Capitol;
This way will I. Disrobe the images, 65
If you do find them decked with ceremonies.[21]

**MARULLUS.** May we do so?
You know it is the feast of Lupercal.[22]

**11. triumph** (trī əmf) *n.*:
In ancient Rome, a
procession celebrating the
return of a victorious
general and his army.

**12. tributaries** (trib′yoo
ter′ ēs) *n.*: Captives.

**13. Pompey** (päm′ pē): A
Roman general and
triumvir defeated by Caesar
in 48 B.C. and later
murdered.

**14. Tiber** (tī′ bər): River
that flows through Rome.
**15. concave shores:**
hollowed-out banks;
overhanging banks.
**16. cull out:** Pick out;
select.

**17. Pompey's blood:**
Pompey's sons, whom
Caesar has just defeated.
**18. intermit the plague**
(plāg): Stop the calamity or
trouble.

**19. the most exalted
shores of all:** The highest
banks.
**20. whe'r their basest
mettle:** Whether the most
inferior material of which
they are made.
**21. Disrobe the
images . . . decked with
ceremonies:** Strip the
statues . . . covered with
decorations.
**22. feast of Lupercal**
(loo′ pər kal): An ancient
Roman festival celebrated
on February 15.

**FLAVIUS.** It is no matter; let no images
70    Be hung with Caesar's trophies. I'll about
      And drive away the vulgar²³ from the streets;
      So do you too, where you perceive them thick.
      These growing feathers plucked from Caesar's wing
      Will make him fly an ordinary pitch,²⁴
75    Who else would soar above the view of men
      And keep us all in servile fearfulness.          [*Exit.*]

### Scene ii. *A public place.*

[*Enter Caesar, Antony (for the course),¹ Calpurnia, Portia,
Decius, Cicero, Brutus, Cassius, Casca, a Soothsayer; after
them, Marullus and Flavius.*]

**CAESAR.** Calpurnia!

**CASCA.**                          Peace, ho! Caesar speaks.

**CAESAR.**                                        Calpurnia!

**CALPURNIA.** Here, my lord.

**CAESAR.** Stand you directly in Antonius' way
      When he doth run his course. Antonius!

5    **ANTONY.** Caesar, my lord?

**CAESAR.** Forget not in your speed, Antonius,
      To touch Calpurnia; for our elders say
      The barren, touchèd in this holy chase,
      Shake off their sterile curse.²

**ANTONY.**                          I shall remember:
10    When Caesar says "Do this," it is performed.

**CAESAR.** Set on, and leave no ceremony out.

**SOOTHSAYER.** Caesar!

**CAESAR.** Ha! Who calls?

**CASCA.** Bid every noise be still; peace yet again!

15    **CAESAR.** Who is it in the press³ that calls on me?
      I hear a tongue, shriller than all the music,
      Cry "Caesar." Speak; Caesar is turned to hear.

**SOOTHSAYER.** Beware the ides of March.⁴

**CAESAR.**                          What man is that?

**BRUTUS.** A soothsayer bids you beware the ides of March.

**23. vulgar** (vul′ gər) *n.*:
The common people.

**24. pitch:** The upward
flight of a hawk.

**1. for the course:** Ready
for the footrace that was
part of the Lupercal
festivities.

**2. barren . . . sterile
curse:** It was believed that
women who were unable to
bear children (such as
Calpurnia), if touched by a
runner during this race,
would then be able to bear
children.

**3. press** *n.*: Crowd.

**4. ides** (īdz) **of March:**
March 15.

20    **CAESAR.** Set him before me; let me see his face.

    **CASSIUS.** Fellow, come from the throng; look upon
      Caesar.

    **CAESAR.** What say'st thou to me now? Speak once again.

    **SOOTHSAYER.** Beware the ides of March.

    **CAESAR.** He is a dreamer, let us leave him. Pass.
    [*A trumpet sounds. Exit all but Brutus and Cassius.*]

25   **CASSIUS.** Will you go see the order of the course?[5]

    **BRUTUS.** Not I.

    **CASSIUS.** I pray you do.

    **BRUTUS.** I am not gamesome:[6] I do lack some part
      Of that quick spirit[7] that is in Antony.
30     Let me not hinder, Cassius, your desires;
      I'll leave you.

**5. order of the course:**
The race.

**6. gamesome** (gām′ səm)
*adj.*: Having a liking for
sports.
**7. quick spirit:** Lively
disposition.

**CASSIUS.** Brutus, I do observe you now of late;
    I have not from your eyes that gentleness
    And show of love as I was wont[8] to have;
35    You bear too stubborn and too strange a hand[9]
    Over your friend that loves you.

**BRUTUS.**                      Cassius,
    Be not deceived: if I have veiled my look,
    I turn the trouble of my countenance
    Merely upon myself.[10] Vexèd I am
40    Of late with passions[11] of some difference,[12]
    Conceptions only proper to myself,[13]
    Which give some soil,[14] perhaps, to my behaviors;
    But let not therefore my good friends be grieved
    (Among which number, Cassius, be you one)
45    Nor construe any further my neglect
    Than that poor Brutus, with himself at war,
    Forgets the shows of love to other men.

**CASSIUS.** Then, Brutus, I have much mistook your passion;
    By means whereof this breast of mine hath buried[15]
50    Thoughts of great value, worthy cogitations.[16]
    Tell me, good Brutus, can you see your face?

**BRUTUS.** No, Cassius; for the eye sees not itself
    But by reflection, by some other things.

**CASSIUS.** 'Tis just.[17]
55    And it is very much lamented,[18] Brutus,
    That you have no such mirrors as will turn
    Your hidden worthiness into your eye,
    That you might see your shadow.[19] I have heard
    Where many of the best respect[20] in Rome
60    (Except immortal Caesar), speaking of Brutus,
    And groaning underneath this age's yoke,[21]
    Have wished that noble Brutus had his eyes.

**BRUTUS.** Into what dangers would you lead me, Cassius,
    That you would have me seek into myself
65    For that which is not in me?

**CASSIUS.** Therefore, good Brutus, be prepared to hear;
    And since you know you cannot see yourself
    So well as by reflection, I, your glass
    Will modestly discover to yourself
70    That of yourself which you yet know not of.[22]
    And be not jealous on[23] me, gentle Brutus:

**8. wont** (wōnt): Accustomed.

**9. bear . . . hand:** Treat too harshly and too like a stranger.

**10. If I . . . upon myself:** If I have been less open, my troubled face is due entirely to personal matters.

**11. passions:** Feelings; emotions.

**12. of some difference:** In conflict.

**13. Conceptions . . . myself:** Thoughts that concern only me.

**14. soil:** Blemish.

**15. By means . . . buried:** Because of which I have kept to myself.

**16. cogitations** (käj′ ə tā′ shəns) *n.*: Thoughts.

**17. 'Tis just:** It is true.

**18. lamented** (lə men′ t'd) *v.*: Regretted.

**19. turn . . . shadow:** Reflect your hidden noble qualities so you could see their image.

**20. the best respect:** Most respected people.

**21. this age's yoke:** The tyranny of Caesar.

**22. Will modestly . . . know not of:** Will without exaggeration make known to you the qualities you have that you are unaware of.

**23. be not jealous on:** Do not be suspicious of.

Were I a common laughter,[24] or did use
To stale with ordinary oaths my love
To every new protester;[25] if you know
That I do fawn on men and hug them hard,
And after scandal[26] them; or if you know
That I profess myself in banqueting
To all the rout,[27] then hold me dangerous.

[*Flourish of trumpets and shout.*]

**BRUTUS.** What means this shouting? I do fear the people
Choose Caesar for their king.

**CASSIUS.**                              Ay, do you fear it?
Then must I think you would not have it so.

**BRUTUS.** I would not, Cassius, yet I love him well.
But wherefore do you hold me here so long?
What is it that you would impart to me?
If it be aught toward the general good,[28]
Set honor in one eye and death i' th' other,
And I will look on both indifferently;[29]
For let the gods so speed me,[30] as I love
The name of honor more than I fear death.

**CASSIUS.** I know that virtue to be in you, Brutus,
As well as I do know your outward favor.[31]
Well, honor is the subject of my story.
I cannot tell what you and other men
Think of this life, but for my single self,
I had as lief not be,[32] as live to be
In awe of such a thing as I myself.[33]
I was born free as Caesar; so were you:
We both have fed as well, and we can both
Endure the winter's cold as well as he:
For once, upon a raw and gusty day,
The troubled Tiber chafing with[34] her shores,
Caesar said to me "Darest thou, Cassius, now
Leap in with me into this angry flood,
And swim to yonder point?" Upon the word,
Accout'red[35] as I was, I plungèd in
And bade him follow: so indeed he did.
The torrent roared, and we did buffet[36] it
With lusty sinews,[37] throwing it aside
And stemming it with hearts of controversy.[38]
But ere we could arrive the point proposed,
Caesar cried "Help me, Cassius, or I sink!"
I, as Aeneas,[39] our great ancestor,

75
80
85
90
95
100
105
110

**24. common laughter:**
Object of ridicule.
**25. To stale . . . new
protester:** To make cheap
my friendship to anyone
who promises to be my
friend.
**26. scandal:** Slander;
gossip about.
**27. profess myself . . .
rout:** Declare my
friendship to the common
crowd.

**28. aught . . . good:**
Anything to do with the
public welfare.
**29. indifferently:** Without
preference or concern.
**30. speed:** Give good
fortune to.

**31. favor:** Face;
appearance.

**32. as lief not be:** Just as
soon not exist.
**33. such a thing as
myself:** Another human
being (Caesar).

**34. chafing with:** Raging
against.
**35. Accout'red:** Dressed
in armor.
**36. buffet** (buf' it) *v.*:
Struggle against.
**37. lusty sinews** (sin'
yo͞os): Strong muscles.
**38. stemming
it . . . controversy:**
Making progress against it
with our intense rivalry.
**39. Aeneas** (i nē' əs):
Trojan hero of the poet
Virgil's epic poem *Aeneid*,
who carried his old father
Anchises from the burning
city of Troy and later
founded Rome.

Did from the flames of Troy upon his shoulder
The old Anchises bear, so from the waves of Tiber
115  Did I the tired Caesar. And this man
Is now become a god, and Cassius is
A wretched creature, and must bend his body
If Caesar carelessly but nod on him.
He had a fever when he was in Spain,
120  And when the fit was on him, I did mark
How he did shake: 'tis true, this god did shake.
His coward lips did from their color fly,[40]
And that same eye whose bend[41] doth awe the world
Did lose his[42] luster: I did hear him groan;
125  Ay, and that tongue of his, that bade the Romans
Mark him and write his speeches in their books,
Alas, it cried, "Give me some drink, Titinius,"
As a sick girl. Ye gods! It doth amaze me,
A man of such a feeble temper[43] should
130  So get the start of[44] the majestic world,
And bear the palm[45] alone.

[Shout. Flourish of trumpets.]

BRUTUS. Another general shout?
I do believe that these applauses are
For some new honors that are heaped on Caesar.

135  CASSIUS. Why, man, he doth bestride the narrow world
Like a Colossus,[46] and we petty men
Walk under his huge legs and peep about
To find ourselves dishonorable[47] graves.
Men at some time are masters of their fates:
140  The fault, dear Brutus, is not in our stars,[48]
But in ourselves, that we are underlings.[49]
Brutus and Caesar: what should be in that "Cae-
sar"?
Why should that name be sounded[50] more than
yours?
Write them together, yours is as fair a name;
145  Sound them, it doth become the mouth as well;
Weigh them, it is as heavy; conjure[51] with 'em,
"Brutus" will start[52] a spirit as soon as "Caesar."
Now, in the names of all the gods at once,
Upon what meat doth this our Caesar feed,
150  That he is grown so great? Age, thou art shamed!
Rome, thou hast lost the breed of noble bloods!
When went there by an age, since the great flood,[53]
But it was famed with[54] more than with one man?

**40. His coward
lips . . . fly:** The color fled
from his lips, which were
like cowardly soldiers
fleeing from a battle.
**41. bend** n.: Glance.
**42. his:** Its.
**43. feeble temper:** Weak
physical constitution.
**44. get the start of:**
Become the leader of.
**45. palm:** Symbol of
victory; victor's prize.

**46. Colossus** (kə läs' əs)
n.: A gigantic statue of
Apollo, a god of Greek and
Roman mythology, which
was set at the entrance to
the harbor of Rhodes about
280 B.C. and included
among the seven wonders
of the ancient world.
**47. dishonorable** (dis än'
ər ə b'l) adj.: Shameful
(because they will not be of
free men).
**48. stars:** Destinies. The
stars were thought to
control people's lives.
**49. underlings:** Inferior
people.
**50. sounded:** Spoken or
announced by trumpets.
**51. conjure** (kän jər) v.:
Summon a spirit by a
magic spell.
**52. start:** Raise.
**53. great flood:** In Greek
mythology a flood that
drowned everyone except
Deucalion and his wife
Pyrrha, saved by the god
Zeus because of their
virtue.
**54. But it was famed
with:** Without the age
being made famous by.

When could they say (till now) that talked of Rome,
155  That her wide walks encompassed but one man?
Now is it Rome indeed, and room enough,
When there is in it but one only man.
O, you and I have heard our fathers say,
There was a Brutus[55] once that would have brooked[56]
160  Th' eternal devil to keep his state in Rome
As easily as a king.

BRUTUS. That you do love me, I am nothing jealous;[57]
What you would work me to,[58] I have some aim;[59]
How I have thought of this, and of these times,
165  I shall recount hereafter. For this present,
I would not so (with love I might entreat you)
Be any further moved. What you have said
I will consider; what you have to say
I will with patience hear, and find a time
170  Both meet to hear and answer such high things.
Till then, my noble friend, chew[60] upon this:
Brutus had rather be a villager
Than to repute himself a son of Rome
Under these hard conditions as this time
Is like to lay upon us.

175  CASSIUS.                    I am glad
That my weak words have struck but thus much
show
Of fire from Brutus.

[Enter Caesar and his Train.]

BRUTUS. The games are done, and Caesar is returning.

CASSIUS. As they pass by, pluck Casca by the sleeve,
180  And he will (after his sour fashion) tell you
What hath proceeded worthy note today.

BRUTUS. I will do so. But look you, Cassius,
The angry spot doth glow on Caesar's brow,
And all the rest look like a chidden train:[61]
185  Calpurnia's cheek is pale, and Cicero
Looks with such ferret[62] and such fiery eyes
As we have seen him in the Capitol,
Being crossed in conference[63] by some senators.

CASSIUS. Casca will tell us what the matter is.

190  CAESAR. Antonius.

ANTONY. Caesar?

**55. Brutus:** Lucius Junius Brutus had helped expel the last King of Rome and had helped found the Republic in 509 B.C.
**56. brooked:** Put up with.
**57. nothing jealous:** not at all doubting.
**58. work me to:** Persuade me of.
**59. aim:** Idea.

**60. chew upon:** Think about.

**61. chidden train:** Scolded attendants.
**62. ferret** (fer' it) n.: A small animal like a weasel with reddish eyes.
**63. crossed in conference:** Opposed in debate.

**CAESAR.** Let me have men about me that are fat,
Sleek-headed men, and such as sleep a-nights.
Yond Cassius has a lean and hungry look;
195  He thinks too much: such men are dangerous.

**ANTONY.** Fear him not, Caesar, he's not dangerous;
He is a noble Roman, and well given.[64]

**CAESAR.** Would he were fatter! But I fear him not.
Yet if my name were liable to fear,
200  I do not know the man I should avoid
So soon as that spare Cassius. He reads much,
He is a great observer, and he looks
Quite through the deeds[65] of men. He loves no plays,
As thou dost, Antony; he hears no music;
205  Seldom he smiles, and smiles in such a sort[66]
As if he mocked himself, and scorned his spirit
That could be moved to smile at anything.

**64. well given:** Well disposed.

**65. looks . . . deeds of men:** Sees through people's actions to their motives.
**66. sort:** Way.

Such men as he be never at heart's ease
Whiles they behold a greater than themselves,
210 And therefore are they very dangerous.
I rather tell thee what is to be feared
Than what I fear; for always I am Caesar.
Come on my right hand, for this ear is deaf,
And tell me truly what thou think'st of him.

[*A trumpet sounds. Caesar and his Train exit.*]

CASCA. You pulled me by the cloak; would you speak
215 with me?

BRUTUS. Ay, Casca; tell us what hath chanced[67] today,
That Caesar looks so sad.

**67. hath chanced:** Has happened.

CASCA. Why, you were with him, were you not?

BRUTUS. I should not then ask Casca what had chanced.

220 CASCA. Why, there was a crown offered him; and being
offered him, he put it by[68] with the back of his hand,
thus; and then the people fell a-shouting.

**68. put it by:** Pushed it away.

BRUTUS. What was the second noise for?

CASCA. Why, for that too.

225 CASSIUS. They shouted thrice; what was the last cry for?

CASCA. Why, for that too.

BRUTUS. Was the crown offered him thrice?

CASCA. Ay, marry, was't, and he put it by thrice, every
time gentler than other; and at every putting-by
230 mine honest neighbors shouted.

CASSIUS. Who offered him the crown?

CASCA. Why, Antony.

BRUTUS. Tell us the manner of it, gentle Casca.

CASCA. I can as well be hanged as tell the manner of it: it
235 was mere foolery; I did not mark it. I saw Mark
Antony offer him a crown—yet 'twas not a crown
neither, 'twas one of these coronets[69]—and, as I told
you, he put it by once; but for all that, to my thinking,
he would fain[70] have had it. Then he offered it to him
240 again; then he put it by again; but to my thinking, he
was very loath to lay his fingers off it. And then he
offered it the third time. He put it the third time by;

**69. coronets** (kôr′ ə nets′) *n.*: Ornamental bands used as crowns.
**70. fain** (fān) *adv.*: Gladly.

245 and still as he refused it, the rabblement[71] hooted, and clapped their chopt[72] hands, and threw up their sweaty nightcaps,[73] and uttered such a deal of stinking breath because Caesar refused the crown, that it had, almost, choked Caesar; for he swounded[74] and fell down at it. And for mine own part, I durst not laugh, for fear of opening my lips and receiving the
250 bad air.

CASSIUS. But, soft,[75] I pray you; what, did Caesar swound?

CASCA. He fell down in the market place, and foamed at mouth, and was speechless.

BRUTUS. 'Tis very like he hath the falling-sickness.[76]

255 CASSIUS. No, Caesar hath it not; but you, and I,
And honest Casca, we have the falling-sickness.[77]

CASCA. I know not what you mean by that, but I am sure Caesar fell down. If the tag-rag people[78] did not clap him and hiss him, according as he pleased and
260 displeased them, as they use[79] to do the players in the theater, I am no true man.

BRUTUS. What said he when he came unto himself?

CASCA. Marry, before he fell down, when he perceived the common herd was glad he refused the crown, he
265 plucked me ope his doublet[80] and offered them his throat to cut. An I had been a man of any occupation,[81] if I would not have taken him at a word, I would I might go to hell among the rogues. And so he fell. When he came to himself again, he said,
270 if he had done or said anything amiss, he desired their worships to think it was his infirmity.[82] Three or four wenches,[83] where I stood, cried "Alas, good soul!" and forgave him with all their hearts; but there's no heed to be taken of them; if Caesar had stabbed their
275 mothers, they would have done no less.

BRUTUS. And after that, he came thus sad away?

CASCA. Ay.

CASSIUS. Did Cicero say anything?

CASCA. Ay, he spoke Greek.

280 CASSIUS. To what effect?

**71. rabblement** (rab' 'l mənt) *n.*: Mob.
**72. chopt** (chäpt) *adj.*: Chapped.
**73. nightcaps:** Workers' caps.
**74. swounded:** Swooned; fainted.

**75. soft:** Slowly.

**76. falling-sickness:** Epilepsy.
**77. We have the falling sickness:** We are becoming helpless under Caesar's rule.

**78. tag-rag people:** The rabble.
**79. use:** Are accustomed.

**80. doublet** (dub' lit) *n.*: Closefitting jacket.
**81. An I . . . occupation:** If I had been a workingman (or a man of action).

**82. infirmity** (in fur' mə tē) *n.*: Weakness; ailment.
**83. wenches** (wench əs) *n.*: Young women.

**CASCA.** Nay, an I tell you that, I'll ne'er look you i' th' face again. But those that understood him smiled at one another and shook their heads; but for mine own part, it was Greek to me. I could tell you more news too: Marullus and Flavius, for pulling scarfs off Caesar's images, are put to silence.[84] Fare you well. There was more foolery yet, if I could remember it.

**CASSIUS.** Will you sup with me tonight, Casca?

**CASCA.** No, I am promised forth.[85]

**CASSIUS.** Will you dine with me tomorrow?

**CASCA.** Ay, if I be alive, and your mind hold,[86] and your dinner worth the eating.

**CASSIUS.** Good; I will expect you.

**CASCA.** Do so. Farewell, both.         [*Exit.*]

285

290

**BRUTUS.** What a blunt[87] fellow is this grown to be!
He was quick mettle[88] when he went to school.

295

**CASSIUS.** So is he now in execution[89]
Of any bold or noble enterprise,
However he puts on this tardy form.[90]
This rudeness is a sauce to his good wit,[91]
Which gives men stomach to disgest[92] his words
With better appetite.

300

**BRUTUS.** And so it is. For this time I will leave you.
Tomorrow, if you please to speak with me,
I will come home to you; or if you will,
Come home to me, and I will wait for you.

305

**CASSIUS.** I will do so. Till then, think of the world.[93]
        [*Exit Brutus.*]

Well, Brutus, thou art noble; yet I see
Thy honorable mettle may be wrought
From that it is disposed;[94] therefore it is meet
That noble minds keep ever with their likes;
For who so firm that cannot be seduced?
Caesar doth bear me hard,[95] but he loves Brutus.
If I were Brutus now, and he were Cassius,
He should not humor[96] me. I will this night,
In several hands,[97] in at his windows throw,
As if they came from several citizens,
Writings, all tending to the great opinion[98]

310

315

**84. for pulling . . . silence:** For taking decorations off statues of Caesar, have been silenced (by being forbidden to take part in public affairs, exiled, or perhaps even executed).

**85. am promised forth:** Have a previous engagement.

**86. hold:** Does not change.

**87. blunt:** Dull; not sharp.

**88. quick mettle:** Of a lively disposition.

**89. execution** (ek′ sə kyoo′ shən) *n*.: A carrying out; doing.

**90. tardy form:** Sluggish appearance.

**91. wit:** Intelligence.

**92. disgest:** Digest.

**93. the world:** The present state of affairs.

**94. wrought . . . is disposed:** Shaped (like iron) in a way different from its usual form.

**95. bear me hard:** Dislikes me.

**96. humor me:** Win me over.

**97. several hands:** Different handwritings.

**98. tending to the great opinion:** Pointing out the great respect.

That Rome holds of his name; wherein obscurely
320 Caesar's ambition shall be glancèd at.[99]
And after this, let Caesar seat him sure;[100]
For we will shake him, or worse days endure. [*Exit.*]

**99. glancèd at:** Hinted at.
**100. seat him sure:** Establish himself securely.

## Scene iii. *A street.*

[*Thunder and lightning. Enter from opposite sides, Casca and Cicero.*]

CICERO. Good even, Casca; brought you Caesar home?
Why are you breathless? And why stare you so?

CASCA. Are not you moved, when all the sway of earth[1]
Shakes like a thing unfirm? O Cicero,
5 I have seen tempests, when the scolding winds
Have rived[2] the knotty oaks, and I have seen
Th' ambitious ocean swell and rage and foam,
To be exalted with[3] the threat'ning clouds;
But never till tonight, never till now,
10 Did I go through a tempest dropping fire.
Either there is a civil strife in heaven,
Or else the world, too saucy[4] with the gods,
Incenses[5] them to send destruction.

**1. all the sway of earth:** The stable order of earth.

**2. have rived:** Have split.

**3. exalted with:** Lifted up to.

**4. saucy:** Rude; impudent.
**5. Incenses:** Enrages.

CICERO. Why, saw you anything more wonderful?

15 CASCA. A common slave—you know him well by sight—
Held up his left hand, which did flame and burn
Like twenty torches joined, and yet his hand,
Not sensible of[6] fire, remained unscorched.
Besides—I ha' not since put up my sword—
20 Against[7] the Capitol I met a lion,
Who glazed[8] upon me and went surly by
Without annoying me. And there were drawn
Upon a heap[9] a hundred ghastly[10] women,
Transformèd with their fear, who swore they saw
25 Men, all in fire, walk up and down the streets.
And yesterday the bird of night[11] did sit
Even at noonday upon the market place,
Hooting and shrieking. When these prodigies[12]
Do so conjointly meet,[13] let not men say,
30 "These are their reasons, they are natural,"
For I believe they are portentous things
Unto the climate that they point upon.[14]

**6. sensible of:** Sensitive to.
**7. Against:** Opposite or near.
**8. glazed:** Stared.
**9. were drawn . . . heap:** Huddled together.
**10. ghastly** (gast' lē) *adj.*: Ghostlike; pale.
**11. bird of night:** Owl.
**12. prodigies** (präd'ə jēs) *n.*: Extraordinary happenings.
**13. conjointly meet:** Occur at the same time and place.
**14. portentous** (pôr ten' təs) **. . . upon:** Bad omens for the country they point to.

**CICERO.** Indeed, it is a strange-disposèd[15] time:
　　But men may construe things after their fashion,[16]
35　Clean from the purpose[17] of the things themselves.
　　Comes Caesar to the Capitol tomorrow?

**CASCA.** He doth; for he did bid Antonius
　　Send word to you he would be there tomorrow.

**CICERO.** Good night then, Casca; this disturbèd sky
　　Is not to walk in.

40　**CASCA.**　　　　　　Farewell, Cicero.　　[*Exit Cicero.*]

[*Enter Cassius.*]

**CASSIUS.** Who's there?

**CASCA.**　　　　　A Roman.

**CASSIUS.**　　　　　　　　Casca, by your voice.

**CASCA.** Your ear is good. Cassius, what night is this?

**CASSIUS.** A very pleasing night to honest men.

**CASCA.** Who ever knew the heavens menace so?

**CASSIUS.** Those that have known the earth so full of
45　　　faults.
　　For my part, I have walked about the streets,
　　Submitting me unto the perilous night,
　　And thus unbracèd,[18] Casca, as you see,
　　Have bared my bosom to the thunder-stone;[19]
50　And when the cross[20] blue lightning seemed to open
　　The breast of heaven, I did present myself
　　Even in the aim and very flash of it.

**CASCA.** But wherefore did you so much tempt the
　　　heavens?
　　It is the part[21] of men to fear and tremble
55　When the most mighty gods by tokens send
　　Such dreadful heralds to astonish[22] us.

**CASSIUS.** You are dull, Casca, and those sparks of life
　　That should be in a Roman you do want,[23]
　　Or else you use not. You look pale, and gaze,
60　And put on fear, and cast yourself in wonder,[24]
　　To see the strange impatience of the heavens;
　　But if you would consider the true cause
　　Why all these fires, why all these gliding ghosts,
　　Why birds and beasts from quality and kind,[25]

**15. strange-disposèd:**
Abnormal.
**16. construe . . . fashion:**
Explain in their own way.
**17. Clean from the
purpose:** Different from
the real meaning.

**18. unbracèd:** With jacket
open.
**19. thunder-stone:**
Thunderbolt.
**20. cross:** Zigzag.

**21. part:** Role.

**22. by tokens . . . to
astonish:** By portentous
signs send such awful
announcements to frighten
and stun.
**23. want:** Lack.
**24. put on . . . in wonder:**
Show fear and are amazed.

**25. from quality and
kind:** Acting contrary to
their nature.

| | |
|---|---|
| 65 | Why old men, fools, and children calculate,[26] |
| | Why all these things change from their ordinance,[27] |
| | Their natures and preformèd faculties, |
| | To monstrous quality,[28] why, you shall find |
| | That heaven hath infused them with these spirits[29] |
| 70 | To make them instruments of fear and warning |
| | Unto some monstrous state.[30] |
| | Now could I, Casca, name to thee a man |
| | Most like this dreadful night, |
| | That thunders, lightens, opens graves, and roars |
| 75 | As doth the lion in the Capitol; |
| | A man no mightier than thyself, or me, |
| | In personal action, yet prodigious grown |
| | And fearful,[31] as these strange eruptions are. |

**CASCA.** 'Tis Caesar that you mean, is it not, Cassius?

80 **CASSIUS.** Let it be who it is; for Romans now
Have thews[32] and limbs like to their ancestors;
But, woe the while![33] Our fathers' minds are dead,
And we are governed with our mothers' spirits;
Our yoke and sufferance[34] show us womanish.

85 **CASCA.** Indeed, they say the senators tomorrow
Mean to establish Caesar as a king;
And he shall wear his crown by sea and land,
In every place save here in Italy.

**CASSIUS.** I know where I will wear this dagger then;
90 Cassius from bondage will deliver[35] Cassius.
Therein,[36] ye gods, you make the weak most strong;
Therein, ye gods, you tyrants do defeat.
Nor stony tower, nor walls of beaten brass,
Nor airless dungeon, nor strong links of iron,
95 Can be retentive to[37] the strength of spirit;
But life, being weary of these worldly bars,
Never lacks power to dismiss itself.
If I know this, know all the world besides,
That part of tyranny that I do bear
I can shake off at pleasure.        [*Thunder still.*]

100 **CASCA.**                    So can I;
So every bondman in his own hand bears
The power to cancel his captivity.

**CASSIUS.** And why should Caesar be a tyrant then?
Poor man, I know he would not be a wolf
105 But that he sees the Romans are but sheep;

**26. calculate:** Make predictions.
**27. ordinance:** Regular behavior.
**28. preformèd . . . quality:** Established function to unnatural behavior.
**29. infused . . . spirits:** Filled them with supernatural powers.
**30. monstrous state:** Abnormal condition of government.

**31. fearful:** Causing fear.

**32. thews** (thyo͞oz) *n.*: Muscles or sinews; strength.
**33. woe the while!:** Alas for the times.
**34. yoke and sufferance:** Slavery and meek acceptance of it.

**35. will deliver:** Will set free.
**36. Therein:** In that way (by using his dagger on himself).

**37. be retentive to:** Confine.

He were no lion, were not Romans hinds.[38]
Those that with haste will make a mighty fire
Begin it with weak straws. What trash is Rome,
What rubbish and what offal,[39] when it serves
110     For the base matter[40] to illuminate
So vile a thing as Caesar! But, O grief,
Where hast thou led me? I, perhaps, speak this
Before a willing bondman; then I know
My answer must be made.[41] But I am armed,
115     And dangers are to me indifferent.

CASCA. You speak to Casca, and to such a man
That is no fleering tell-tale.[42] Hold, my hand.
Be factious[43] for redress of all these griefs,[44]
And I will set this foot of mine as far
As who goes farthest.           [*They clasp hands.*]

120 CASSIUS.                There's a bargain made.
Now know you, Casca, I have moved already
Some certain of the noblest-minded Romans
To undergo[45] with me an enterprise
Of honorable dangerous consequence;[46]
125     And I do know, by this[47] they stay for me
In Pompey's porch;[48] for now, this fearful night,
There is no stir or walking in the streets,
And the complexion of the element[49]
In favor's like[50] the work we have in hand,
130     Most bloody, fiery, and most terrible.

[*Enter Cinna.*]

CASCA. Stand close[51] awhile, for here comes one in haste.

CASSIUS. 'Tis Cinna; I do know him by his gait;[52]
He is a friend. Cinna, where haste you so?

CINNA. To find out you. Who's that? Metellus Cimber?

135 CASSIUS. No, it is Casca, one incorporate[53]
To our attempts. Am I not stayed[54] for, Cinna?

CINNA. I am glad on't.[55] What a fearful night is this!
There's two or three of us have seen strange sights.

CASSIUS. Am I not stayed for? Tell me.

CINNA.                   Yes, you are.
140     O Cassius, if you could
But win the noble Brutus to our party—

**38. hinds** (hīndz) *n.*: Female deer; peasants; servants.
**39. offal** (ôf′ʼl) *n.*: Garbage.
**40. base matter:** Inferior or low material; foundation materials.

**41. speak this . . . answer must be made:** Say this before a willing servant of Caesar's; then I know I will have to answer for my words.
**42. fleering tell-tale:** Sneering tattletale.
**43. factious** (fak′ shəs) *adj.*: Active in forming a faction or a political party.
**44. redress** (rē′ dres) **of all these griefs:** Setting right all these grievances.

**45. undergo:** Undertake.
**46. consequence** (kän′ sə kwens′) *n.*: Importance.
**47. by this:** By this time.
**48. Pompey's porch:** Portico of Pompey's Theater.
**49. complexion of the element:** Condition of the sky; weather.
**50. In favor's like:** In appearance is like.

**51. close:** Hidden.

**52. gait** (gāt) *n.*: Way of moving.

**53. incorporate** (in kôr′ pər it) *adj.*: United.
**54. stayed:** Waited.
**55. on't:** Of it.

**CASSIUS.** Be you content. Good Cinna, take this paper,
And look you lay it in the praetor's chair,[56]
Where Brutus may but find it;[57] and throw this

145     In at his window; set this up with wax
Upon old Brutus'[58] statue. All this done,
Repair to Pompey's porch, where you shall find us.
Is Decius Brutus and Trebonius there?

**CINNA.** All but Metellus Cimber, and he's gone

150     To seek you at your house. Well, I will hie,
And so bestow these papers as you bade me.

**CASSIUS.** That done, repair to Pompey's Theater.

                               *[Exit Cinna.]*

Come, Casca, you and I will yet ere day
See Brutus at his house; three parts of him

155     Is ours already, and the man entire
Upon the next encounter yields him ours.

**CASCA.** O, he sits high in all the people's hearts;
And that which would appear offense[59] in us,
His countenance,[60] like richest alchemy,[61]

160     Will change to virtue and to worthiness.

**CASSIUS.** Him, and his worth, and our great need of him,
You have right well conceited.[62] Let us go,
For it is after midnight, and ere day
We will awake him and be sure of him.         *[Exit.]*

**56. praetor's** (prēt′ ərs) **chair:** Roman magistrate's (or judge's) chair.

**57. Where . . . find it:** Where only Brutus (as the chief magistrate) will find it.

**58. old Brutus:** Lucius Junius Brutus, the founder of Rome.

**59. offense** (ə fens′) *n.*: Crime.

**60. countenance** (koun′ tə nəns) *n.*: Support.

**61. alchemy** (al′ kə mē) *n.*: An early form of chemistry in which the goal was to change baser metals into gold.

**62. conceited** (kən sēt′ id): Understood.

---

## THINKING ABOUT THE SELECTION
### Recalling

1. Explain why the tribunes have nothing but contempt for the common people of Rome.
2. What warning does the soothsayer give? What is Caesar's reaction to this warning?
3. Summarize Casca's report of what happened at the games.
4. Whom does Cassius say the night of unnatural events is like.

### Interpreting

5. How does Cassius feel about Caesar? Why does Caesar fear Cassius?
6. Why is Brutus's participation essential to Cassius? In what essential way is he different from Cassius?
7. How does Cassius try to win Brutus over? What is it in Brutus that allows this technique to be effective?
8. Why do you think Caesar refused the crown?

9. Compare and contrast the reactions of Cicero and Casca to the violent storm. What do their reactions tell you about each man? How does the storm itself help advance the plot?

## Applying

10. The philosopher Jeremy Bentham has written, "Tyranny and anarchy are never far asunder." First discuss the meaning of this quotation. Then explain how it relates to this play.

## ANALYZING LITERATURE

### Understanding Blank Verse

The metrical pattern of blank verse is *iambic pentameter*—five sets of an accented syllable following an unaccented one. It is the natural rhythm of English speech. This line, for instance, could occur in dialogue of any kind:

U / U / U / U / U /
"Set him before me; let me see his face." (Act I, scene ii, line 20)

Within this pattern, however, some variation allows for natural speech rhythms. This line, for example, ends with an extra unaccented syllable and is said to have a feminine ending:

U / U / U / U / U
"I know that virtue to be in you, Brutus." (Act I, scene ii, line 90)

The following line contains examples of two other variations: (1) an accented syllable followed by an unaccented one at the beginning of the line and (2) *elision,* a sliding over of one syllable to fit the meter:

/ U U / U / U / U /
"Caesar cried, 'Help me, Cassius, or I sink!'" (Act I, scene ii, line 111).

1. Analyze Marullus's speech in Act I, scene i, lines 34–43. Mark stressed syllables with /. Mark unstressed syllables with U.
2. Which characters in Act I speak in blank verse? Which speak in prose? What do you think is the reason for this difference?

## CRITICAL THINKING AND READING

### Interpreting the Effect of Imagery

In this act, the impression the audience forms of Caesar comes mainly from the way in which other characters describe him, often with imagery rather than in direct terms. For example, look at Flavius's speech in Act I, scene i, lines 73–76. Flavius compares Caesar to a menacing bird of prey circling above the Romans to keep them in their place. The image portrays Caesar as a tyrant and threat to Roman liberty.

Analyze the imagery in the following speeches of Cassius and discuss what they contribute to the audience's idea of Caesar.
1. Act I, scene ii, lines 135–138
2. Act I, scene iii, lines 103–111

## SPEAKING AND LISTENING

### Speaking Blank Verse

When you speak blank verse, use natural speech patterns with appropriate pauses at punctuation marks. If you can, listen to a recording or videotape of a Shakespeare play to hear how the blank verse is spoken. Then choose any speech of more than twenty lines from Act I to practice reading aloud. When you are satisfied with your reading, ask a classmate to listen and criticize your reading of it.

## THINKING AND WRITING

### Writing Blank Verse

Using Shakespeare's blank verse as a model, write at least eight lines of blank verse. Describe the character traits of a real or imagined historical figure. When you have revised, mark the metrical patterns of your blank verse with / and U. Read your verse aloud.

# GUIDE FOR READING

## The Tragedy of Julius Caesar, Act II

**Dramatic Irony**

**Dramatic irony** occurs when a character fails to recognize realities that are clear to the audience. For example, Brutus is swayed by the letters he has been receiving because he believes that they were written by ordinary Roman citizens. The audience, however, knows they were written by Cassius.

**Look For**

As you read Act II, look for examples of dramatic irony. Try to foresee the consequences of the characters' misconceptions or lack of knowledge.

**Writing**

People have always wished they could foretell the future. In Act I you read a prediction made by a soothsayer foretelling the future. Freewrite about ways in which people today still attempt to foretell the future. Why do you think some people feel such a great need to do this?

**Vocabulary**

Knowing the following words will help you as you read Act II of *The Tragedy of Julius Caesar.*

**augmented** (ôg ment' id) v.: Made greater (p. 365)

**entreated** (in trēt' id) v.: Begged, pleaded with (p. 366)

**conspiracy** (kən spir'ə sē) n.: (1) A group of people plotting an illegal or evil act (2) Such a plot itself (p. 367)

**resolution** (rez'ə loo'shən) n.: Strong determination (p. 368)

**exploit** (eks'ploit) n.: Act or deed, especially a heroic achievement (p. 374)

**imminent** (im' ə nənt) adj.: About to happen (p. 377)

**emulation** (em'yə lā'shən) n.: Old word for envy, jealousy (p. 379)

# Act II

**Scene i.** *Rome.*

[*Enter Brutus in his orchard.*]

**BRUTUS.** What, Lucius, ho!
 I cannot, by the progress of the stars,
 Give guess how near to day. Lucius, I say!
 I would it were my fault to sleep so soundly.
5 When, Lucius, when? Awake, I say! What, Lucius!

[*Enter Lucius.*]

**LUCIUS.** Called you, my lord?

**BRUTUS.** Get me a taper in my study, Lucius.
 When it is lighted, come and call me here.

**LUCIUS.** I will, my lord.       [*Exit.*]

10 **BRUTUS.** It must be by his death; and for my part,
 I know no personal cause to spurn at[1] him,
 But for the general.[2] He would be crowned.
 How that might change his nature, there's the question.
 It is the bright day that brings forth the adder,[3]
15 And that craves[4] wary walking. Crown him that,
 And then I grant we put a sting in him
 That at his will he may do danger with.
 Th' abuse of greatness is when it disjoins
 Remorse from power;[5] and, to speak truth of Caesar,
20 I have not known when his affections swayed[6]
 More than his reason. But 'tis a common proof[7]
 That lowliness[8] is young ambition's ladder,
 Whereto the climber upward turns his face;
 But when he once attains the upmost round,
25 He then unto the ladder turns his back,
 Looks in the clouds, scorning the base degrees[9]
 By which he did ascend. So Caesar may;
 Then lest he may, prevent.[10] And, since the quarrel
 Will bear no color for the thing he is,[11]
30 Fashion it[12] thus: that what he is, augmented
 Would run to these and these extremities;[13]
 And therefore think him as a serpent's egg
 Which hatched, would as his kind grow mischievous,
 And kill him in the shell.

**1. spurn at:** Kick against; rebel.
**2. the general:** The public good.

**3. adder** (ad' ər) *n.*: A poisonous snake.
**4. craves:** Requires.

**5. disjoins . . . power:** Separates mercy from power.
**6. affections swayed:** Emotions ruled.
**7. proof:** Experience.
**8. lowliness:** Humility.
**9. base degrees:** Low steps or people in lower positions.
**10. lest . . . prevent:** In case he may, we must stop him.
**11. the quarrel . . . no color:** Our complaint cannot be justified in view of what he now is.
**12. Fashion it:** State the case.
**13. extremities** (ik strem' ə tēs) *n.*: Extremes (of tyranny).

*[Enter Lucius.]*

35 **LUCIUS.** The taper burneth in your closet,[14] sir.
  Searching the window for a flint,[15] I found
  This paper thus sealed up, and I am sure
  It did not lie there when I went to bed.

  *[Gives him the letter.]*

**BRUTUS.** Get you to bed again; it is not day.
40 Is not tomorrow, boy, the ides of March?

**LUCIUS.** I know not, sir.

**BRUTUS.** Look in the calendar and bring me word.

**LUCIUS.** I will, sir.                      *[Exit.]*

**BRUTUS.** The exhalations[16] whizzing in the air
45 Give so much light that I may read by them.

  *[Opens the letter and reads.]*

  "Brutus, thou sleep'st; awake, and see thyself.
  Shall Rome, &c.[17] Speak, strike, redress.
  Brutus, thou sleep'st; awake."

  Such instigations[18] have been often dropped
50 Where I have took them up.
  "Shall Rome, &c." Thus must I piece it out:[19]
  Shall Rome stand under one man's awe?[20] What,
    Rome?
  My ancestors did from the streets of Rome
  The Tarquin[21] drive, when he was called a king.
55 "Speak, strike, redress." Am I entreated
  To speak and strike? O Rome, I make thee promise,
  If the redress will follow, thou receivest
  Thy full petition at the hand of[22] Brutus!

*[Enter Lucius.]*

  **LUCIUS.** Sir, March is wasted fifteen days. *[Knock within.]*

60 **BRUTUS.** 'Tis good. Go to the gate; somebody knocks.
                      *[Exit Lucius.]*

  Since Cassius first did whet[23] me against Caesar,
  I have not slept.
  Between the acting of a dreadful thing
  And the first motion,[24] all the interim is
65 Like a phantasma,[25] or a hideous dream.
  The genius and the mortal instruments[26]
  Are then in council, and the state of a man,

**14. closet:** Study.
**15. flint:** Stone used to start a fire.

**16. exhalations** (eks' hə lā' shəns) *n.*: Meteors.

**17. & c.:** et cetera (Latin for *and so forth*).

**18. instigations** (in' stə gā' shəns) *n.*: Urgings, incitements, or spurs to act.
**19. piece it out:** Figure out the meaning.
**20. under one man's awe:** In fearful reverence of one man.
**21. Tarquin** (tär' kwin): King of Rome driven out by Lucius Junius Brutus, Brutus's ancestor.

**22. Thy full . . . hand of:** All you ask from.

**23. whet** (hwet) *v.*: Sharpen; incite.
**24. motion:** Idea; suggestion.
**25. all the . . . a phantasma:** All the time between seems like a nightmare.
**26. mortal instruments:** Bodily powers.

Like to a little kingdom, suffers then
The nature of an insurrection.[27]

[Enter Lucius.]

70 LUCIUS. Sir, 'tis your brother[28] Cassius at the door,
Who doth desire to see you.

BRUTUS.                              Is he alone?

LUCIUS. No, sir, there are moe[29] with him.

BRUTUS.                              Do you know them?

LUCIUS. No, sir; their hats are plucked about their ears,
And half their faces buried in their cloaks,
75 That by no means I may discover them
By any mark of favor.[30]

BRUTUS.                    Let 'em enter.  [Exit Lucius.]
They are the faction. O conspiracy,
Sham'st thou to show thy dang'rous brow by night,
When evils are most free? O, then by day
80 Where wilt thou find a cavern dark enough
To mask thy monstrous visage? Seek none, con-
    spiracy;
Hide it in smiles and affability:
For if thou path, thy native semblance on,[31]
Not Erebus[32] itself were dim enough
85 To hide thee from prevention.[33]

[Enter the conspirators, Cassius, Casca, Decius, Cinna, Metellus Cimber, and Trebonius.]

CASSIUS. I think we are too bold upon[34] your rest.
Good morrow, Brutus; do we trouble you?

BRUTUS. I have been up this hour, awake all night.
Know I these men that come along with you?

90 CASSIUS. Yes, every man of them; and no man here
But honors you; and every one doth wish
You had but that opinion of yourself
Which every noble Roman bears of you.
This is Trebonius.

BRUTUS.                    He is welcome hither.

CASSIUS. This, Decius Brutus.

95 BRUTUS.                    He is welcome too.

**27. insurrection** (in′ sə
rek′ shən) n.: Revolt.

**28. brother:**
Brother-in-law (Cassius
was married to Brutus's
sister).

**29. moe:** More.

**30. discover . . . favor:**
Identify them by their
appearance.

**31. path . . . semblance
on:** Walk looking as you
normally do.
**32. Erebus** (er′ ə bəs):
The dark place between
earth and Hades.
**33. prevention:** Being
discovered and stopped.
**34. upon:** In interfering
with.

**CASSIUS.** This, Casca; this, Cinna; and this, Metellus
    Cimber.

**BRUTUS.** They are all welcome.
    What watchful cares do interpose themselves
    Betwixt your eyes and night?[35]

100   **CASSIUS.** Shall I entreat[36] a word?     *[They whisper.]*

**DECIUS.** Here lies the east; doth not the day break here?

**CASCA.** No.

**CINNA.** O, pardon, sir, it doth; and yon gray lines
    That fret[37] the clouds are messengers of day.

105   **CASCA.** You shall confess that you are both deceived.
    Here, as I point my sword, the sun arises,
    Which is a great way growing on[38] the south,
    Weighing[39] the youthful season of the year.
    Some two months hence, up higher toward the north
110     He first presents his fire; and the high[40] east
    Stands as the Capitol, directly here.

**BRUTUS.** Give me your hands all over, one by one.

**CASSIUS.** And let us swear our resolution.

**BRUTUS.** No, not an oath. If not the face of men,
115     The sufferance of our souls, the time's abuse[41]—
    If these be motives weak, break off betimes,[42]
    And every man hence to his idle bed.
    So let high-sighted[43] tyranny range on
    Till each man drop by lottery.[44] But if these
120     (As I am sure they do) bear fire enough
    To kindle cowards and to steel with valor
    The melting spirits of women, then, countrymen,
    What need we any spur but our own cause
    To prick us to redress?[45] What other bond
125     Than secret Romans, that have spoke the word,
    And will not palter?[46] And what other oath
    Than honesty to honesty engaged[47]
    That this shall be, or we will fall for it?
    Swear priests and cowards and men cautelous,[48]
130     Old feeble carrions[49] and such suffering souls
    That welcome wrongs; unto bad causes swear
    Such creatures as men doubt; but do not stain
    The even[50] virtue of our enterprise,
    Nor th' insuppressive mettle[51] of our spirits,
135     To think that or our cause or[52] our performance

**35. watchful . . . night:** Worries that keep you from sleep.
**36. entreat** (in trēt') *v.:* Speak.

**37. fret** (fret) *v.:* Decorate with a pattern.

**38. growing on:** Tending toward.
**39. Weighing:** Considering.
**40. high:** Due.

**41. the face . . . time's abuse:** The sadness on men's faces, the suffering of our souls, the present abuses.
**42. betimes:** Quickly.
**43. high-sighted:** Arrogant (as a hawk about to swoop down on its prey).
**44. by lottery:** By chance or in his turn.

**45. prick us to redress:** Goad or spur us on to correct these evils.
**46. palter** (pôl' tər) *v.:* Talk insincerely.
**47. honesty engaged:** Personal honor pledged.
**48. cautelous:** Cautious.
**49. carrions** (kar' ē əns) *n.:* Decaying flesh.

**50. even:** Constant.
**51. insuppressive mettle:** Uncrushable courage.
**52. or . . . or:** Either our cause or.

Did need an oath; when every drop of blood
That every Roman bears, and nobly bears,
Is guilty of a several bastardy[53]
If he do break the smallest particle
140     Of any promise that hath passed from him.

**CASSIUS.** But what of Cicero? Shall we sound[54] him?
I think he will stand very strong with us.

**CASCA.** Let us not leave him out.

**CINNA.**                          No, by no means.

**METELLUS.** O, let us have him, for his silver hairs
145     Will purchase us a good opinion,
And buy men's voices to commend our deeds.
It shall be said his judgment ruled our hands;
Our youths and wildness shall no whit[55] appear,
But all be buried in his gravity.

150  **BRUTUS.** O, name him not! Let us not break with him;[56]
For he will never follow anything
That other men begin.

**CASSIUS.**                     Then leave him out.

**CASCA.** Indeed, he is not fit.

**DECIUS.** Shall no man else be touched but only Caesar?

**53. guilty . . . bastardy:**
Is no true Roman.

**54. sound him:** Find out
his opinion.

**55. no whit** (hwit) *n.*: Not
the least bit.

**56. break with him:**
Confide in him.

155 **CASSIUS.** Decius, well urged. I think it is not meet
Mark Antony, so well beloved of Caesar,
Should outlive Caesar; we shall find of[57] him
A shrewd contriver;[58] and you know, his means;
If he improve[59] them, may well stretch so far
160 As to annoy[60] us all; which to prevent,
Let Antony and Caesar fall together.

**BRUTUS.** Our course will seem too bloody, Caius Cassius,
To cut the head off and then hack the limbs,
Like wrath in death and envy afterwards;[61]
165 For Antony is but a limb of Caesar.
Let's be sacrificers, but not butchers, Caius.
We all stand up against the spirit of Caesar,
And in the spirit of men there is no blood.
O, that we then could come by Caesar's spirit,[62]
170 And not dismember Caesar! But, alas,
Caesar must bleed for it. And, gentle[63] friends,
Let's kill him boldly, but not wrathfully;
Let's carve him as a dish fit for the gods,
Not hew him as a carcass fit for hounds.
175 And let our hearts, as subtle masters do,
Stir up their servants[64] to an act of rage,
And after seem to chide 'em.[65] This shall make
Our purpose necessary, and not envious;
Which so appearing to the common eyes,
180 We shall be called purgers,[66] not murderers.
And for Mark Antony, think not of him;
For he can do no more than Caesar's arm
When Caesar's head is off.

**CASSIUS.**                    Yet I fear him;
For in the ingrafted[67] love he bears to Caesar—

185 **BRUTUS.** Alas, good Cassius, do not think of him.
If he love Caesar, all that he can do
Is to himself—take thought[68] and die for Caesar.
And that were much he should,[69] for he is given
To sports, to wildness, and much company.

190 **TREBONIUS.** There is no fear in him; let him not die,
For he will live and laugh at this hereafter.

[*Clock strikes.*]

**BRUTUS.** Peace! Count the clock.

**CASSIUS.**                    The clock hath stricken three.

**TREBONIUS.** 'Tis time to part.

**57. of:** In.
**58. contriver** (kən trīv′ ər)
*n.*: Schemer.
**59. improve:** Increase.
**60. annoy:** Harm.

**61. Like . . . envy:** As if
we were killing in anger
with hatred afterwards.

**62. come by Caesar's
spirit:** Get hold of the
principles of tyranny for
which Caesar stands.
**63. gentle:** Honorable;
noble.

**64. servants:** Their
hands.
**65. chide 'em:** Scold
them.

**66. purgers:** Healers.

**67. ingrafted:** Deeply
rooted.

**68. take thought:** Become
melancholy.
**69. that were much he
should:** It is unlikely he
would do that.

CASSIUS.                     But it is doubtful yet
                    Whether Caesar will come forth today or no;
195              For he is superstitious grown of late,
                    Quite from the main[70] opinion he held once
                    Of fantasy, of dreams, and ceremonies.[71]
                    It may be these apparent prodigies,
                    The unaccustomed terror of this night,
200              And the persuasion of his augurers[72]
                    May hold him from the Capitol today.

DECIUS. Never fear that. If he be so resolved,
                    I can o'ersway him;[73] for he loves to hear
                    That unicorns may be betrayed with trees,[74]
205              And bears with glasses,[75] elephants with holes,[76]
                    Lions with toils,[77] and men with flatterers;
                    But when I tell him he hates flatterers;
                    He says he does, being then most flatterèd.
                    Let me work;
210              For I can give his humor the true bent,[78]
                    And I will bring him to the Capitol.

CASSIUS. Nay, we will all of us be there to fetch him.

BRUTUS. By the eighth hour; is that the uttermost?[79]

CINNA. Be that the uttermost, and fail not then.

215    METELLUS. Caius Ligarius doth bear Caesar hard,[80]
                    Who rated[81] him for speaking well of Pompey.
                    I wonder none of you have thought of him.

BRUTUS. Now, good Metellus, go along by him.
                    He loves me well, and I have given him reasons;
220              Send him but hither, and I'll fashion[82] him.

CASSIUS. The morning comes upon 's; we'll leave you,
                    Brutus.
                    And, friends, disperse yourselves; but all remember
                    What you have said, and show yourselves true
                    Romans.

BRUTUS. Good gentlemen, look fresh and merrily.
225              Let not our looks put on[83] our purposes,
                    But bear it[84] as our Roman actors do,
                    With untired spirits and formal constancy.[85]
                    And so good morrow to you every one.
                                        [*Exit all but Brutus.*]
                    Boy! Lucius! Fast asleep? It is no matter;
230              Enjoy the honey-heavy dew of slumber.
                    Thou hast no figures nor no fantasies

**70. Quite from the main:** Quite changed from the strong.

**71. ceremonies:** Omens.

**72. augurers** (ô gər ərz) *n.*: Officials who interpreted omens to decide if they were favorable or unfavorable for an undertaking.

**73. I can o'ersway him:** I can change his mind.

**74. unicorns . . . trees:** The story that tells how standing in front of a tree and stepping aside at the last moment causes a charging unicorn to bury his horn in the tree and be caught.

**75. glasses:** Mirrors.

**76. holes:** Pitfalls.

**77. toils:** Nets; snares.

**78. give his humor the true bent:** Bend his feelings in the right direction.

**79. uttermost:** Latest.

**80. doth bear Caesar hard:** Has a grudge against Caesar.

**81. rated:** Berated.

**82. fashion:** Mold.

**83. put on:** Show.

**84. bear it:** Carry it off.

**85. formal constancy:** Consistent dignity.

Which busy care draws in the brains of men;
Therefore thou sleep'st so sound.

[*Enter Portia.*]

**PORTIA.**                                    Brutus, my lord.

**BRUTUS.** Portia, what mean you? Wherefore rise you now
235     It is not for your health thus to commit
        Your weak condition to the raw cold morning.

**PORTIA.** Nor for yours neither. Y'have ungently, Brutus
        Stole from my bed; and yesternight at supper
        You suddenly arose and walked about,
240     Musing and sighing, with your arms across;
        And when I asked you what the matter was,
        You stared upon me with ungentle looks.
        I urged you further; then you scratched your head,
        And too impatiently stamped with your foot.
245     Yet I insisted, yet you answered not,
        But with an angry wafter[86] of your hand
        Gave sign for me to leave you. So I did,
        Fearing to strengthen that impatience
        Which seemed too much enkindled, and withal
250     Hoping it was but an effect of humor,
        Which sometime hath his[87] hour with every man.
        It will not let you eat, nor talk, nor sleep,
        And could it work so much upon your shape
        As it hath much prevailed on your condition,[88]
255     I should not know you[89] Brutus. Dear my lord,
        Make me acquainted with your cause of grief.

**BRUTUS.** I am not well in health, and that is all.

**PORTIA.** Brutus is wise and, were he not in health,
        He would embrace the means to come by it.

260     **BRUTUS.** Why, so I do. Good Portia, go to bed.

**PORTIA.** Is Brutus sick, and is it physical[90]
        To walk unbracèd and suck up the humors[91]
        Of the dank morning? What, is Brutus sick,
        And will he steal out of his wholesome bed,
265     To dare the vile contagion of the night,
        And tempt the rheumy and unpurgèd air[92]
        To add unto his sickness? No, my Brutus;
        You have some sick offense[93] within your mind,
        Which by the right and virtue of my place
270     I ought to know of; and upon my knees
        I charm[94] you, by my once commended[95] beauty,

**86. wafter:** Waving.

**87. his:** Its.

**88. condition:**
Disposition.
**89. I should not know
you:** I would not recognize
you as.

**90. physical:** Healthy.
**91. humors:** Dampness.

**92. Tempt . . . air:** Risk
the air that is likely to
cause rheumatism and air
that has not been purified
by the sun.
**93. sick offense:** Harmful
sickness.
**94. charm:** Beg.
**95. commended:** Praised.

By all your vows of love, and that great vow[96]
Which did incorporate and make us one,
That you unfold to me, your self, your half,
275  Why you are heavy,[97] and what men tonight
Have had resort to you; for here have been
Some six or seven, who did hide their faces
Even from darkness.

**BRUTUS.**                    Kneel not, gentle Portia.

**PORTIA.** I should not need, if you were gentle Brutus.
280  Within the bond of marriage, tell me, Brutus,
Is it excepted[98] I should know no secrets
That appertain[99] to you? Am I your self
But, as it were, in sort or limitation,[100]
To keep with you at meals, comfort your bed,
And talk to you sometimes? Dwell I but in the
285      suburbs[101]
Of your good pleasure? If it be no more,
Portia is Brutus' harlot, not his wife.

**BRUTUS.** You are my true and honorable wife,
As dear to me as are the ruddy drops[102]
290  That visit my sad heart.

**PORTIA.** If this were true, then should I know this secret.
I grant I am a woman; but withal
A woman that Lord Brutus took to wife.
I grant I am a woman; but withal
295  A woman well reputed, Cato's daughter.[103]
Think you I am no stronger than my sex,
Being so fathered and so husbanded?
Tell me your counsels,[104] I will not disclose 'em.
I have made strong proof of my constancy,
300  Giving myself a voluntary wound
Here in the thigh; can I bear that with patience,
And not my husband's secrets?

**BRUTUS.**                    O ye gods,
Render[105] me worthy of this noble wife!      [Knock.]
Hark, hark! One knocks. Portia, go in a while,
305  And by and by thy bosom shall partake
The secrets of my heart.
All my engagements[106] I will construe to thee,
All the charactery of my sad brows.[107]
Leave me with haste.                    [Exit Portia.]

[Enter Lucius and Caius Ligarius.]

Lucius, who's that knocks?

---

**96. great vow:** Marriage vow.

**97. heavy:** Sorrowful.

**98. excepted:** Made an exception.
**99. appertain** (ap′ ər tān′) v.: Belong.
**100. in sort or limitation:** Within a limited way.
**101. suburbs:** Outskirts.

**102. ruddy drops:** Blood.

**103. Cato's daughter:** Marcus Porcius Cato had been an ally of Pompey and enemy of Caesar. He killed himself rather than be captured by Caesar.
**104. counsels:** Secrets.

**105. Render** (ren′ dər) v.: Make.

**106. engagements:** Commitments.
**107. All the charactery of my sad brows:** All that is written on my face.

310     **LUCIUS.** Here is a sick man that would speak with you.

    **BRUTUS.** Caius Ligarius, that Metellus spake of.
        Boy, stand aside. Caius Ligarius! How?

    **CAIUS.** Vouchsafe good morrow from a feeble tongue.

    **BRUTUS.** O, what a time have you chose out,[108] brave
        Caius,
315       To wear a kerchief![109] Would you were not sick!

    **CAIUS.** I am not sick, if Brutus have in hand
        Any exploit worthy the name of honor.

    **BRUTUS.** Such an exploit have I in hand, Ligarius,
        Had you a healthful ear to hear of it.

320     **CAIUS.** By all the gods that Romans bow before,
        I here discard my sickness! Soul of Rome,
        Brave son, derived from honorable loins,[110]
        Thou, like an exorcist,[111] hast conjured up
        My mortifièd spirit.[112] Now bid me run,
325       And I will strive with things impossible.
        Yea, get the better of them. What's to do?

    **BRUTUS.** A piece of work that will make sick men whole.

    **CAIUS.** But are not some whole that we must make sick?

    **BRUTUS.** That must we also. What it is, my Caius,
330       I shall unfold[113] to thee, as we are going
        To whom it must be done.

    **CAIUS.**                   Set on[114] your foot,
        And with a heart new-fired I follow you,
        To do I know not what; but it sufficeth[115]
        That Brutus leads me on.         *[Thunder.]*

    **BRUTUS.**            Follow me, then.     *[Exit.]*

### Scene ii. *Caesar's house.*

*[Thunder and lightning. Enter Julius Caesar in his nightgown.]*

    **CAESAR.** Nor heaven nor earth have been at peace tonight:
        Thrice hath Calpurnia in her sleep cried out,
        "Help, ho! They murder Caesar!" Who's within?

*[Enter a Servant.]*

    **SERVANT.** My lord?

---

**108. chose out:** Picked out.

**109. To wear a kerchief:** Caius wears a scarf to protect him from drafts because he is sick.

**110. derived from honorable loins:** Descended from Lucius Junius Brutus, founder of Rome.

**111. exorcist** (ek′ sôr sist) *n.:* One who calls up spirits.

**112. mortifièd spirit:** Paralyzed, as if dead, spirit.

**113. unfold:** Disclose.

**114. Set on:** Advance.

**115. sufficeth** (sə fis′ eth) *v.:* Is enough.

5  CAESAR. Go bid the priests do present[1] sacrifice,
       And bring me their opinions of success.

    SERVANT. I will, my lord.                    [*Exit.*]

[*Enter Calpurnia.*]

    CALPURNIA. What mean you, Caesar? Think you to walk
       forth?
       You shall not stir out of your house today.

    CAESAR. Caesar shall forth. The things that threatened
10      me
       Ne'er looked but on my back; when they shall see
       The face of Caesar, they are vanishèd.

    CALPURNIA. Caesar, I never stood on ceremonies,[2]
       Yet now they fright me. There is one within,
15     Besides the things that we have heard and seen,
       Recounts most horrid sights seen by the watch.[3]
       A lioness hath whelpèd[4] in the streets,
       And graves have yawned, and yielded up their dead;
       Fierce fiery warriors fought upon the clouds
20     In ranks and squadrons and right form of war,[5]
       Which drizzled blood upon the Capitol;
       The noise of battle hurtled[6] in the air,
       Horses did neigh and dying men did groan,
       And ghosts did shriek and squeal about the streets.
25     O Caesar, these things are beyond all use,[7]
       And I do fear them.

    CAESAR.                 What can be avoided
       Whose end is purposed[8] by the mighty gods?
       Yet Caesar shall go forth; for these predictions
       Are to the world in general as to Caesar.[9]

30  CALPURNIA. When beggars die, there are no comets seen;
       The heavens themselves blaze forth[10] the death of
          princes.

    CAESAR. Cowards die many times before their deaths;
       The valiant never taste of death but once.
       Of all the wonders that I yet have heard,
35     It seems to me most strange that men should fear,
       Seeing that death, a necessary end,
       Will come when it will come.

[*Enter a Servant.*]

                    What say the augurers?

**1. present:** Immediate.

**2. stood on ceremonies:** Paid attention to omens.

**3. Recounts . . . watch:** Tells about the awful sights seen by the watchman.
**4. whelpèd:** Given birth.

**5. right form of war:** Proper military formation of war.
**6. hurtled** (hurt' 'ld) *v.*: Clashed together.

**7. beyond all use:** Contrary to all experience.

**8. is purposed:** Is intended.

**9. For these . . . as to Caesar:** Because these predictions apply to the rest of the world as much as they apply to Caesar.
**10. blaze forth:** Proclaim with meteors and comets.

**SERVANT.** They would not have you to stir forth today.
Plucking the entrails of an offering forth,[11]

40 They could not find a heart within the beast.

**CAESAR.** The gods do this in shame of[12] cowardice:
Caesar should be a beast without a heart
If he should stay at home today for fear.
No, Caesar shall not; Danger knows full well

45 That Caesar is more dangerous than he.
We are two lions littered[13] in one day,
And I the elder and more terrible,
And Caesar shall go forth.

**CALPURNIA.**                              Alas, my lord,
Your wisdom is consumed in confidence.[14]

50 Do not go forth today. Call it my fear
That keeps you in the house and not your own.
We'll send Mark Antony to the Senate House,
And he shall say you are not well today.
Let me, upon my knee, prevail in this.

55 **CAESAR.** Mark Antony shall say I am not well,
And for thy humor,[15] I will stay at home.

[*Enter Decius.*]

Here's Decius Brutus, he shall tell them so.

**DECIUS.** Caesar, all hail! Good morrow, worthy Caesar;
I come to fetch you to the Senate House.

60 **CAESAR.** And you are come in very happy time[16]
To bear my greeting to the senators,
And tell them that I will not come today.
Cannot, is false; and that I dare not, falser:
I will not come today. Tell them so, Decius.

**CALPURNIA.** Say he is sick.

65 **CAESAR.**                              Shall Caesar send a lie?
Have I in conquest stretched mine arm so far
To be afeard to tell graybeards[17] the truth?
Decius, go tell them Caesar will not come.

**DECIUS.** Most mighty Caesar, let me know some cause,

70 Lest I be laughed at when I tell them so.

**CAESAR.** The cause is in my will: I will not come.
That is enough to satisfy the Senate.
But for your private satisfaction,
Because I love you, I will let you know.

**11. Plucking . . . forth:** Pulling out the insides of a sacrificed animal.

**12. in shame of:** In order to shame.

**13. littered:** Born.

**14. confidence:** Overconfidence.

**15. humor:** Whim.

**16. in very happy time:** At just the right moment.

**17. afeard to tell graybeards:** Afraid to tell old men (the senators).

75    Calpurnia here, my wife, stays me at home.
She dreamt tonight she saw my statue,
Which, like a fountain with an hundred spouts,
Did run pure blood, and many lusty Romans
Came smiling and did bathe their hands in it.
80    And these does she apply for[18] warnings and
      portents
And evils imminent, and on her knee
Hath begged that I will stay at home today.

**DECIUS.** This dream is all amiss interpreted;
It was a vision fair and fortunate:
85    Your statue spouting blood in many pipes,
In which so many smiling Romans bathed,
Signifies that from you great Rome shall suck
Reviving blood, and that great men shall press
For tinctures, stains, relics, and cognizance.[19]
90    This by Calpurnia's dream is signified.

**CAESAR.** And this way have you well expounded[20] it.

**DECIUS.** I have, when you have heard what I can say;
And know it now, the Senate have concluded
To give this day a crown to mighty Caesar.
95    If you shall send them word you will not come,
Their minds may change. Besides, it were a mock
Apt to be rendered,[21] for someone to say
"Break up the Senate till another time,
When Caesar's wife shall meet with better dreams."
100    If Caesar hide himself, shall they not whisper
"Lo, Caesar is afraid"?
Pardon me, Caesar, for my dear dear love
To your proceeding[22] bids me tell you this,
And reason to my love is liable.[23]

105    **CAESAR.** How foolish do your fears seem now, Calpurnia!
I am ashamèd I did yield to them.
Give me my robe,[24] for I will go.

[*Enter Brutus, Ligarius, Metellus Cimber, Casca, Trebonius,
Cinna, and Publius.*]

    And look where Publius is come to fetch me.

**PUBLIUS.** Good morrow, Caesar.

**CAESAR.**                   Welcome, Publius.
110    What, Brutus, are you stirred so early too?
Good morrow, Casca. Caius Ligarius,

**18. apply for:** Consider to be.

**19. shall press . . . cognizance:** Decius interprets Calpurnia's dream with a double meaning. To Caesar he suggests that people will beg for badges to show they are Caesar's servants. To the audience, that people will seek remembrances of his death.

**20. expounded** (ik spound′ əd) *v.*: Interpreted; explained.

**21. mock . . . rendered:** Jeering comment likely to be made.

**22. proceeding:** Advancing in your career.

**23. reason . . . liable:** My judgment is not as strong as my affection for you is.

**24. robe:** Toga.

Caesar was ne'er so much your enemy[25]
As that same ague[26] which hath made you lean.
What is't o'clock?

    **BRUTUS.**               Caesar, 'tis strucken eight.

115    **CAESAR.** I thank you for your pains and courtesy.

[*Enter Antony.*]

    See! Antony, that revels[27] long a-nights,
    Is notwithstanding up. Good morrow, Antony.

    **ANTONY.** So to most noble Caesar.

    **CAESAR.**             Bid them prepare[28]
                    within.

120    I am to blame to be thus waited for.
    Now, Cinna; now, Metellus; what, Trebonius,
    I have an hour's talk in store for you;
    Remember that you call on me today;
    Be near me, that I may remember you.

125    **TREBONIUS.** Caesar, I will [*aside*] and so near will I be,
    That your best friends shall wish I had been further.

    **CAESAR.** Good friends, go in and taste some wine with
      me,
    And we (like friends) will straightway go together.

**25. Caius Ligarius . . . your enemy:** Caesar had recently pardoned Ligarius for supporting Pompey during the civil war.
**26. ague** (ā' gyoo) *n.*: Fever.

**27. revels** (rev' 'ls) *v.*: Makes merry.

**28. prepare:** Set out refreshments.

**BRUTUS.** [*Aside*] That every like is not the same,[29] O Caesar,
    The heart of Brutus earns[30] to think upon.    [*Exit.*]

**29. That every like . . . the same:** That everyone who seems to be a friend may actually be an enemy.
**30. earns:** Sorrows.

**Scene iii.** *A street near the Capitol, close to Brutus' house.*

[*Enter Artemidorus, reading a paper.*]

**ARTEMIDORUS.** "Caesar, beware of Brutus; take heed of
    Cassius; come not near Casca; have an eye to Cinna;
    trust not Trebonius; mark well Metellus Cimber;
    Decius Brutus loves thee not; thou hast wronged
5    Caius Ligarius. There is but one mind in all these
    men, and it is bent against Caesar. If thou beest not
    immortal, look about you: security gives way to con-
    spiracy.[1] The mighty gods defend thee!
                     Thy lover,[2] ARTEMIDORUS."
10    Here will I stand till Caesar pass along,
    And as a suitor[3] will I give him this.
    My heart laments that virtue cannot live
    Out of the teeth of emulation.
    If thou read this, O Caesar, thou mayest live;
15    If not, the Fates with traitors do contrive.[4]    [*Exit.*]

**1. security . . . conspiracy:** Overconfident carelessness allows the conspiracy to proceed.
**2. lover:** Devoted friend.
**3. suitor** (sōōt′ər) *n.*: A person who requests, petitions, or entreats.

**4. contrive:** Conspire.

**Scene iv.** *Another part of the street.*

[*Enter Portia and Lucius.*]

**PORTIA.** I prithee, boy, run to the Senate House;
    Stay not to answer me, but get thee gone.
    Why dost thou stay?

**LUCIUS.**               To know my errand, madam.

**PORTIA.** I would have had thee there and here again
5    Ere I can tell thee what thou shouldst do there.
    O constancy,[1] be strong upon my side;
    Set a huge mountain 'tween my heart and tongue!
    I have a man's mind, but a woman's might.[2]
    How hard it is for women to keep counsel![3]
    Art thou here yet?

10    **LUCIUS.**            Madam, what should I do?
    Run to the Capitol, and nothing else?
    And so return to you, and nothing else?

**PORTIA.** Yes, bring me word, boy, if thy lord look well,
    For he went sickly forth; and take good note

**1. constancy** (kän′ stən sē) *n.*: Firmness of mind or purpose; resoluteness.
**2. might:** Strength.
**3. counsel:** Secret.

15     What Caesar doth, what suitors press to him.
    Hark, boy, what noise is that?

**LUCIUS.** I hear none, madam.

**PORTIA.**                 Prithee, listen well.
    I heard a bustling rumor like a fray,[4]
    And the wind brings it from the Capitol.

**4. fray** (frā) *n.*: Fight or brawl.

20   **LUCIUS.** Sooth, madam, I hear nothing.

[*Enter the Soothsayer.*]

**PORTIA.** Come hither, fellow. Which way hast thou been?

**SOOTHSAYER.** At mine own house, good lady.

**PORTIA.** What is't o'clock?

**SOOTHSAYER.**             About the ninth hour, lady.

**PORTIA.** Is Caesar yet gone to the Capitol?

25   **SOOTHSAYER.** Madam, not yet; I go to take my stand,
    To see him pass on to the Capitol.

**PORTIA.** Thou hast some suit[5] to Caesar, hast thou not?

**5. suit** (so͞ot) *n.*: Petition.

**SOOTHSAYER.** That I have, lady; if it will please Caesar
    To be so good to Caesar as to hear me,
30     I shall beseech him to befriend himself.

**PORTIA.** Why, know'st thou any harm's intended to-
    wards him?

**SOOTHSAYER.** None that I know will be, much that I fear
    may chance.
    Good morrow to you. Here the street is narrow;
    The throng that follows Caesar at the heels,
35     Of senators, of praetors, common suitors,
    Will crowd a feeble man almost to death.
    I'll get me to a place more void,[6] and there
    Speak to great Caesar as he comes along.     [*Exit.*]

**6. void:** Empty.

**PORTIA.** I must go in. Ay me, how weak a thing
40     The heart of woman is! O Brutus,
    The heavens speed[7] thee in thine enterprise![8]
    Sure, the boy heard me—Brutus hath a suit
    That Caesar will not grant—O, I grow faint.
    Run, Lucius, and commend me[9] to my lord;
45     Say I am merry; come to me again,
    And bring me word what he doth say to thee.
                         [*Exit separately.*]

**7. speed:** Prosper.
**8. enterprise** (en' tər prīz') *n.*: Undertaking; project.
**9. commend** (kə mend') *v.*: Give the kind regards of.

## THINKING ABOUT THE SELECTION
### Recalling

1. In his soliloquy, what reasons does Brutus give for killing Caesar?
2. Why is a meeting held at Brutus's house, and who attends the meeting?
3. Explain the two changes Brutus recommends in the assassination plan.
4. What reasons does Calpurnia, Caesar's wife, give for wanting him to stay home?
5. How is Caesar convinced to go to the Capitol and by whom?

### Interpreting

6. Why do you think the writer left gaps in the letter that Lucius finds? What inferences do you draw from the way Brutus fills in these gaps?
7. Brutus justifies his actions by comparing Caesar to a serpent's egg in Act II, scene i, lines 32–34. Explain how this is an example of a false analogy, or a comparison that is not logical.
8. Why does Brutus decide to go along with the conspirators? Explain whether or not you think his decision proves him honorable.

### Applying

9. How might unwillingness to seem weak lead people to take unnecessary risks?

## ANALYZING LITERATURE
### Recognizing Irony

In addition to dramatic **irony,** in which the audience knows something a character does not, this act also contains ironic situations in which one character intentionally says something with a meaning that another character is not aware of. For example, Trebonius speaks ironically in Act II, scene ii, lines 124–125. Caesar is unaware of the meaning, but the audience and Trebonius know the meaning.

1. First find and explain an example of dramatic irony in Act I or II.

2. Then find and explain an example of irony spoken by Decius in Act II, scene ii.
3. Find and explain an example of irony spoken by Portia in Act II, scene iv.

## CRITICAL THINKING AND READING
### Predicting Outcomes

An **outcome** is the natural result of what has gone before. To predict an outcome, you must consider both the action that has taken place and what has been said by and about the characters. For example, given what we have learned about Caesar in this act—his pride and his unwillingness to appear weak and fearful—it is reasonable to predict that he will go to the Capitol even if he is warned.

Predict outcomes to these questions and support them with evidence from Acts I and II.
1. Who will assume power after Caesar's death?
2. How will the people react to Caesar's death?

## UNDERSTANDING LANGUAGE
### Understanding Archaic Words

**Archaic words** are words that are no longer used. An archaic word may be a word form (for example, *art* or *doth*) that is no longer used or a meaning that is no longer used, as in the example: "Good morrow, Brutus; do we trouble you?"

Define the italicized archaic words.
1. "If these be motives weak, break off *betimes.*" (Act II, scene i, line 116)
2. "I *prithee,* boy, run to the Senate House." (Act II, scene iv, line 1)

## THINKING AND WRITING
### Writing with Dramatic Irony

Write a short scene in which Calpurnia explains her dream and her fears to Portia. Portia must respond in a way that is truthful but that does not reveal what she knows about Brutus's intentions. The scene should follow Act II, scene iv. You may write it in prose, rather than blank verse, if you prefer.

# GUIDE FOR READING

## The Tragedy of Julius Caesar, Act III

In drama characters often make special kinds of speeches. One of these is the aside. An **aside** is a brief comment a character makes that is not heard by anyone else onstage and that reveals the character's thoughts or feelings. An example is Brutus's last two lines in Act II, scene ii, lines 129–130.

Another special kind of speech is the soliloquy. A **soliloquy** is a speech made by a character alone onstage. Cassius's speech in Act I, scene ii, lines 308–322 is an example of a soliloquy.

A type of speech similar to the soliloquy is the monologue. A **monologue** is a very long speech by one person without interruption from others onstage. Cassius's speech in Act I, scene ii, lines 90–131 is an example of a monologue.

### Look For

As you read Act III, look for asides, soliloquies, and monologues. In particular notice what they reveal about the characters who speak them.

### Writing

Imagine a situation in which someone in a group seems to be concealing his or her true thoughts or feelings. Jot down some brief notes describing the general situation. Then freewrite a speech the person could make after everyone else had left that would reveal his or her true thoughts or feelings.

### Vocabulary

Knowing the following words will help you as you read Act III of *The Tragedy of Julius Caesar.*

**suit** (soot) *n.*: Old word for "petition" (p. 383)

**spurn** (spurn) *v.*: Old word for "to kick disdainfully" (p. 384)

**repealing** (ri pēl' iŋ) *n.*: Old word for "recalling," especially from exile (p. 384)

**confounded** (kən found' id) *adj.*: Confused (p. 385)

**mutiny** (myoot' 'n ē) *n.*: Open rebellion against authority (p. 385); *v.*: To commit mutiny (p. 396)

**malice** (mal'is) *n.*: A desire to harm or see harm done to others (p. 389)

**oration** (ô rā'shən) *n.*: A formal speech, especially one given at a state occasion, ceremony, or funeral (p. 392)

**discourse** (dis' kôrs) *v.*: To speak formally and at length (p. 392)

**vile** (vīl) *adj.*: Depraved; ignoble (p. 393)

# Act III

**Scene i.** *Rome. Before the Capitol.*

[*Flourish of trumpets. Enter Caesar, Brutus, Cassius, Casca, Decius, Metellus Cimber, Trebonius, Cinna, Antony, Lepidus, Artemidorus, Publius, Popilius, and the Soothsayer.*]

**CAESAR.** The ides of March are come.

**SOOTHSAYER.** Ay, Caesar, but not gone.

**ARTEMIDORUS.** Hail, Caesar! Read this schedule.[1]

**DECIUS.** Trebonius doth desire you to o'er-read,
5 At your best leisure, this his humble suit.

**ARTEMIDORUS.** O Caesar, read mine first; for mine's a suit
 That touches Caesar nearer. Read it, great Caesar.

**CAESAR.** What touches us ourself shall be last served.

**ARTEMIDORUS.** Delay not, Caesar; read it instantly.

**CAESAR.** What, is the fellow mad?

10 **PUBLIUS.**        Sirrah, give place.[2]

**CASSIUS.** What, urge you your petitions in the street?
 Come to the Capitol.

[*Caesar goes to the Capitol, the rest following.*]

**POPILIUS.** I wish your enterprise today may thrive.

**CASSIUS.** What enterprise, Popilius?

**POPILIUS.**        Fare you well.
        [*Advances to Caesar.*]

15 **BRUTUS.** What said Popilius Lena?

**CASSIUS.** He wished today our enterprise might thrive.
 I fear our purpose is discoverèd.

**BRUTUS.** Look how he makes to[3] Caesar; mark him.

**CASSIUS.** Casca, be sudden,[4] for we fear prevention.
20 Brutus, what shall be done? If this be known,
 Cassius or Caesar never shall turn back,[5]
 For I will slay myself.

**1. schedule** (skej' ool) *n.*: Paper.

**2. give place:** Get out of the way.

**3. makes to:** Approaches.

**4. be sudden:** Be quick.

**5. Cassius . . . back:** Either Cassius or Caesar will not return alive.

**BRUTUS.** Cassius, be constant.[6]
Popilius Lena speaks not of our purposes;
For look, he smiles, and Caesar doth not change.[7]

25 **CASSIUS.** Trebonius knows his time; for look you,
Brutus,
He draws Mark Antony out of the way.

[*Exit Antony and Trebonius.*]

**DECIUS.** Where is Metellus Cimber? Let him go
And presently prefer his suit[8] to Caesar.

**BRUTUS.** He is addressed.[9] Press near and second[10] him.

30 **CINNA.** Casca, you are the first that rears your hand.

**CAESAR.** Are we all ready? What is now amiss
That Caesar and his Senate must redress?[11]

**METELLUS.** Most high, most mighty, and most puissant[12]
Caesar,
Metellus Cimber throws before thy seat
An humble heart. [*Kneeling.*]

35 **CAESAR.** I must prevent thee, Cimber.
These couchings and these lowly courtesies[13]
Might fire the blood of ordinary men,
And turn preordinance and first decree
Into the law of children.[14] Be not fond[15]
40 To think that Caesar bears such rebel blood
That will be thawed from the true quality[16]
With that which melteth fools—I mean sweet words,
Low-crookèd curtsies, and base spaniel fawning.[17]
Thy brother by decree is banishèd.
45 If thou dost bend and pray and fawn for him,
I spurn thee like a cur out of my way.
Know, Caesar doth not wrong, nor without cause
Will he be satisfied.

**METELLUS.** Is there no voice more worthy than my own,
50 To sound more sweetly in great Caesar's ear
For the repealing of my banished brother?

**BRUTUS.** I kiss thy hand, but not in flattery, Caesar,
Desiring thee that Publius Cimber may
Have an immediate freedom of repeal.

**CAESAR.** What, Brutus?

55 **CASSIUS.** Pardon, Caesar; Caesar, pardon!

**6. constant:** Firm; calm.

**7. change:** Change the expression on his face.

**8. presently prefer his suit:** Immediately present his petition.
**9. addressed:** Ready.
**10. second:** Support.

**11. amiss . . . redress:** Wrong that Caesar and his Senate must correct.
**12. puissant** (pyo͞o′ i sənt) *adj.*: Powerful.

**13. couchings . . . courtesies:** Low bowings and humble gestures of reverence.

**14. And turn . . . law of children:** And change what has already been decided as children might change their minds.
**15. fond** *adj.*: Foolish.
**16. rebel . . . quality:** Unstable disposition that will be changed from firmness.
**17. base spaniel fawning:** Low doglike cringing.

As low as to thy foot doth Cassius fall
To beg enfranchisement[18] for Publius Cimber.

**CAESAR.** I could be well moved, if I were as you;
If I could pray to move,[19] prayers would move me;
60 But I am constant as the Northern Star,
Of whose true-fixed and resting[20] quality
There is no fellow[21] in the firmament.[22]
The skies are painted with unnumb'red sparks,
They are all fire and every one doth shine;
65 But there's but one in all doth hold his[23] place.
So in the world; 'tis furnished well with men,
And men are flesh and blood, and apprehensive;[24]
Yet in the number I do know but one
That unassailable holds on his rank,[25]
70 Unshaked of motion;[26] and that I am he,
Let me a little show it, even in this—
That I was constant. Cimber should be banished,
And constant do remain to keep him so.

**CINNA.** O Caesar—

**CAESAR.**                Hence! Wilt thou lift up Olympus?[27]

**DECIUS.** Great Caesar—

75 **CAESAR.**                Doth not Brutus bootless[28] kneel?

**CASCA.** Speak hands for me!        [*They stab Caesar.*]

**CAESAR.** *Et tu, Brutè?*[29] Then fall Caesar.        [*Dies.*]

**CINNA.** Liberty! Freedom! Tyranny is dead!
Run hence, proclaim, cry it about the streets.

80 **CASSIUS.** Some to the common pulpits,[30] and cry out
"Liberty, freedom, and enfranchisement!"

**BRUTUS.** People, and senators, be not affrighted.
Fly not; stand still; ambition's debt is paid.[31]

**CASCA.** Go to the pulpit, Brutus.

**DECIUS.**                And Cassius too.

85 **BRUTUS.** Where's Publius?

**CINNA.** Here, quite confounded with this mutiny.

**METELLUS.** Stand fast together, lest some friend of
Caesar's
Should chance—

**18. enfranchisement** (in fran' chíz mənt) *n.*: Freedom.
**19. pray to move:** Beg others to change their minds.
**20. resting:** Immovable.
**21. fellow:** Equal.
**22. firmament** (fŭr' mə mənt) *n.*: Sky.

**23. his:** Its.

**24. apprehensive** (ap' rə hen' siv) *adj.*: Able to understand.
**25. unassailable . . . rank:** Unattackable maintains his position.
**26. Unshaked of motion:** Unmoved by his own or others' impulses.

**27. Olympus** (ō lim' pəs): Mountain in northern Greece that was, in Greek mythology, the home of the gods.
**28. bootless:** Uselessly.

**29. *Et tu, Brutè?*:** In Latin, *And you, Brutus?*

**30. pulpits** (pŏŏl' pits) *n.*: Speakers' platforms.

**31. ambition's . . . paid:** Ambition received what it deserved.

**BRUTUS.** Talk not of standing. Publius, good cheer;
90   There is no harm intended to your person,
    Nor to no Roman else. So tell them, Publius.

**CASSIUS.** And leave us, Publius, lest that the people
    Rushing on us should do your age some mischief.

**BRUTUS.** Do so; and let no man abide³² this deed
95   But we the doers.

[*Enter Trebonius.*]

**32. let no man abide:** Let no man take responsibility for.

**CASSIUS.** Where is Antony?

**TREBONIUS.**                    Fled to his house amazed.[33]
Men, wives, and children stare, cry out and run,
As[34] it were doomsday.

**BRUTUS.**                    Fates, we will know your pleasures.
That we shall die, we know; 'tis but the time,
100    And drawing days out, that men stand upon.[35]

**CASCA.** Why, he that cuts off twenty years of life
Cuts off so many years of fearing death.

**BRUTUS.** Grant that, and then is death a benefit.
So are we Caesar's friends, that have abridged
105    His time of fearing death. Stoop, Romans, stoop,
And let us bathe our hands in Caesar's blood
Up to the elbows, and besmear our swords.
Then walk we forth, even to the market place,
And waving our red weapons o'er our heads,
110    Let's all cry "Peace, freedom, and liberty!"

**CASSIUS.** Stoop then, and wash. How many ages hence
Shall this our lofty scene be acted over
In states unborn and accents yet unknown!

**BRUTUS.** How many times shall Caesar bleed in sport,[36]
115    That now on Pompey's basis lies along[37]
No worthier than the dust!

**CASSIUS.**                    So oft as that shall be,
So often shall the knot[38] of us be called
The men that gave their country liberty.

**DECIUS.** What, shall we forth?

**CASSIUS.**                    Ay, every man away.
120    Brutus shall lead, and we will grace his heels[39]
With the most boldest and best hearts of Rome.

[*Enter a Servant.*]

**BRUTUS.** Soft, who comes here? A friend of Antony's.
**SERVANT.** Thus, Brutus, did my master bid me kneel;
Thus did Mark Antony bid me fall down;
125    And, being prostrate, thus he bade me say:
Brutus is noble, wise, valiant, and honest;
Caesar was mighty, bold, royal, and loving.
Say I love Brutus and I honor him;
Say I feared Caesar, honored him, and loved him.

**33. amazed:** Astounded.

**34. As:** As if.

**35. drawing . . . upon:**
Prolonging life that people
care about.

**36. in sport:** In plays.
**37. on Pompey's basis
lies along:** By the pedestal
of Pompey's statue lies
stretched out.

**38. Knot:** Group.

**39. grace his heels:**
Honor him by following
him.

130 If Brutus will vouchsafe that Antony
May safely come to him and be resolved[40]
How Caesar hath deserved to lie in death,
Mark Antony shall not love Caesar dead
So well as Brutus living; but will follow
135 The fortunes and affairs of noble Brutus
Thorough the hazards of this untrod state[41]
With all true faith. So says my master Antony.

**BRUTUS.** Thy master is a wise and valiant Roman;
I never thought him worse.
140 Tell him, so[42] please him come unto this place,
He shall be satisfied and, by my honor,
Depart untouched.

**SERVANT.** I'll fetch him presently.
[*Exit Servant.*]

**BRUTUS.** I know that we shall have him well to friend.[43]

**CASSIUS.** I wish we may. But yet have I a mind
145 That fears him much; and my misgiving still
Falls shrewdly to the purpose.[44]

[*Enter Antony.*]

**BRUTUS.** But here comes Antony. Welcome, Mark
Antony.

**ANTONY.** O mighty Caesar! Dost thou lie so low?
Are all thy conquests, glories, triumphs, spoils,
150 Shrunk to this little measure? Fare thee well.
I know not, gentlemen, what you intend,
Who else must be let blood,[45] who else is rank.[46]
If I myself, there is no hour so fit
As Caesar's death's hour, nor no instrument
155 Of half that worth as those your swords, made rich
With the most noble blood of all this world.
I do beseech ye, if you bear me hard,[47]
Now, whilst your purpled hands[48] do reek and smoke,
Fulfill your pleasure. Live[49] a thousand years,
160 I shall not find myself so apt[50] to die;
No place will please me so, no mean of death,[51]
As here by Caesar, and by you cut off,
The choice and master spirits of this age.

**BRUTUS.** O Antony, beg not your death of us!
165 Though now we must appear bloody and cruel,
As by our hands and this our present act

**40. be resolved:** Have it explained.

**41. Thorough . . . state:** Through the dangers of this new state of affairs.

**42. so:** If it should.

**43. to friend:** As a friend.

**44. my misgiving . . . to the purpose:** My doubts always turn out to be justified.

**45. be let blood:** Be killed.
**46. rank:** Too powerful; in need of bloodletting.

**47. bear me hard:** Have a grudge against me.
**48. purpled hands:** Bloody hands.
**49. Live:** If I live.
**50. apt:** Ready.
**51. mean of death:** Way of dying.

You see we do, yet see you but our hands
And this the bleeding business they have done.
170 Our hearts you see not; they are pitiful;[52]
And pity to the general wrong of Rome—
As fire drives out fire, so pity pity[53]—
Hath done this deed on Caesar. For your part,
To you our swords have leaden[54] points, Mark
   Antony:
Our arms in strength of malice, and our hearts
175 Of brothers' temper,[55] do receive you in
With all kind love, good thoughts, and reverence.

CASSIUS. Your voice[56] shall be as strong as any man's
In the disposing of new dignities.[57]

BRUTUS. Only be patient till we have appeased
180 The multitude, beside themselves with fear,
And then we will deliver[58] you the cause
Why I, that did love Caesar when I struck him,
Have thus proceeded.

ANTONY.                    I doubt not of your wisdom.
Let each man render me his bloody hand.
185 First, Marcus Brutus, will I shake with you;
Next, Caius Cassius, do I take your hand;
Now, Decius Brutus, yours; now yours, Metellus;
Yours, Cinna; and, my valiant Casca, yours;
Though last, not least in love, yours, good Trebonius.
190 Gentlemen all—alas, what shall I say?
My credit[59] now stands on such slippery ground
That one of two bad ways you must conceit[60] me,
Either a coward or a flatterer.
That I did love thee, Caesar, O, 'tis true!
195 If then thy spirit look upon us now,
Shall it not grieve thee dearer[61] than thy death
To see thy Antony making his peace,
Shaking the bloody fingers of thy foes,
Most noble, in the presence of thy corse?[62]
200 Had I as many eyes as thou hast wounds,
Weeping as fast as they stream forth thy blood,
It would become me better than to close[63]
In terms of friendship with thine enemies.
Pardon me, Julius! Here wast thou bayed,[64] brave
   hart;[65]
205 Here didst thou fall, and here thy hunters stand,
Signed in thy spoil[66] and crimsoned in thy lethe.[67]

**52. pitiful:** Full of pity.

**53. pity pity:** Pity for Rome drove out pity for Caesar.

**54. leaden:** Dull; blunt.

**55. of brothers' temper:** Filled with brotherly feelings.

**56. voice:** Vote.

**57. dignities:** Offices.

**58. deliver:** Tell to.

**59. credit:** Reputation.

**60. conceit** (kən sēt′) *v.*: Think of.

**61. dearer:** More deeply.

**62. corse:** Corpse.

**63. close** (clōz) *v.*: To reach an agreement.

**64. bayed:** Cornered.

**65. hart** (härt) *n.*: Deer.

**66. Signed in thy spoil:** Marked by signs of your decaying parts.

**67. lethe:** A river in Hades, but in this case a river of blood.

O world, thou wast the forest to this hart;
And this indeed, O world, the heart of thee.
How like a deer, stroken[68] by many princes,
210 Dost thou here lie!

CASSIUS. Mark Antony—

ANTONY.                    Pardon me, Caius Cassius.
The enemies of Caesar shall say this;
Then, in a friend, it is cold modesty.[69]

CASSIUS. I blame you not for praising Caesar so;
215 But what compact[70] mean you to have with us?
Will you be pricked[71] in number of our friends,
Or shall we on,[72] and not depend on you?

ANTONY. Therefore I took your hands, but was indeed
Swayed from the point by looking down on Caesar.
220 Friends am I with you all, and love you all,
Upon this hope, that you shall give me reasons
Why, and wherein, Caesar was dangerous.

BRUTUS. Or else were this a savage spectacle.
Our reasons are so full of good regard[73]
225 That were you, Antony, the son of Caesar,
You should be satisfied.

ANTONY.                    That's all I seek;
And am moreover suitor that I may
Produce[74] his body to the market place,
And in the pulpit, as becomes a friend,
230 Speak in the order[75] of his funeral.

BRUTUS. You shall, Mark Antony.

CASSIUS.                    Brutus, a word with you.
[*Aside to Brutus*] You know not what you do; do not
    consent
That Antony speak in his funeral.
Know you how much the people may be moved
By that which he will utter?

235 BRUTUS.                    By your pardon:
I will myself into the pulpit first,
And show the reason of our Caesar's death.
What Antony shall speak, I will protest[76]
He speaks by leave and by permission,
240 And that we are contented Caesar shall
Have all true rites and lawful ceremonies.
It shall advantage more than do us wrong.[77]

**68. stroken:** Struck down.

**69. cold modesty:** Calm, moderate speech.

**70. compact** (käm′ pakt) *n.:* Agreement.
**71. pricked:** Marked.
**72. on:** Proceed.

**73. so full of good regard:** So carefully considered.

**74. Produce:** Bring forth.

**75. order:** Course of the ceremonies.

**76. protest:** Declare.

**77. advantage . . . wrong:** Benefit us more than hurt us.

**CASSIUS.** I know not what may fall;[78] I like it not.

**BRUTUS.** Mark Antony, here, take you Caesar's body.
245     You shall not in your funeral speech blame us,
    But speak all good you can devise of Caesar,
    And say you do't by our permission;
    Else shall you not have any hand at all
    About his funeral. And you shall speak
250     In the same pulpit whereto I am going,
    After my speech is ended.

**ANTONY.**                   Be it so;
    I do desire no more.

**BRUTUS.** Prepare the body then, and follow us.

                            [*Exit all but Antony.*]

**ANTONY.** O pardon me, thou bleeding piece of earth,
255     That I am meek and gentle with these butchers!
    Thou art the ruins of the noblest man
    That ever livèd in the tide of times.[79]
    Woe to the hand that shed this costly blood!
    Over thy wounds now do I prophesy
260     (Which like dumb mouths do ope their ruby lips
    To beg the voice and utterance of my tongue),
    A curse shall light upon the limbs of men;
    Domestic fury and fierce civil strife
    Shall cumber[80] all the parts of Italy;
265     Blood and destruction shall be so in use,[81]
    And dreadful objects so familiar,
    That mothers shall but smile when they behold
    Their infants quartered with the hands of war,
    All pity choked with custom of fell deeds;[82]
270     And Caesar's spirit, ranging[83] for revenge,
    With Ate[84] by his side come hot from hell,
    Shall in these confines[85] with a monarch's voice
    Cry "Havoc,"[86] and let slip[87] the dogs of war,
    That this foul deed shall smell above the earth
275     With carrion[88] men, groaning for burial.

[*Enter Octavius' Servant.*]

    You serve Octavius Caesar, do you not?

**SERVANT.** I do, Mark Antony.

**ANTONY.** Caesar did write for him to come to Rome.

**SERVANT.** He did receive his letters and is coming,
280     And bid me say to you by word of mouth—
    O Caesar!                [*Seeing the body.*]

**78. what may fall:** What may happen.

**79. tide of times:** Course of all history.

**80. cumber** (kum' bər) *v.*: Distress; burden.
**81. in use:** Customary.

**82. fell deeds:** Cruel acts.
**83. ranging:** Roaming like a wild beast in search of prey.
**84. Ate** (ā' tē): Greek goddess personifying reckless ambition in man.
**85. confines** (kän' fīns) *n.*: Boundaries.
**86. Havoc:** Latin for *no quarter*, a signal for general slaughter.
**87. slip:** Loose.
**88. carrion** (kar' ē ən) *adj.*: Dead and rotting.

**ANTONY.** Thy heart is big;[89] get thee apart and weep.
    Passion, I see, is catching, for mine eyes,
    Seeing those beads of sorrow stand in thine,
285    Began to water. Is thy master coming?

**SERVANT.** He lies tonight within seven leagues[90] of Rome.

**ANTONY.** Post[91] back with speed, and tell him what hath
    chanced.[92]
    Here is a mourning Rome, a dangerous Rome,
    No Rome of safety for Octavius yet.
290    Hie hence and tell him so. Yet stay awhile;
    Thou shalt not back till I have borne this corse
    Into the market place; there shall I try[93]
    In my oration how the people take
    The cruel issue[94] of these bloody men;
295    According to the which, thou shalt discourse
    To young Octavius of the state of things.
    Lend me your hand.                 [*Exit.*]

**89. big:** Swollen with grief.

**90. lies . . . seven leagues:** Is camped tonight within twenty-one miles.
**91. Post:** Hasten.
**92. hath chanced:** Has happened.

**93. try:** Test.

**94. cruel issue:** Outcome of the cruelty.

## Scene ii. *The Forum*

[*Enter Brutus and goes into the pulpit, and Cassius, with the Plebeians.[1]*]

**PLEBEIANS.** We will be satisfied![2] Let us be satisfied!

**BRUTUS.** Then follow me, and give me audience, friends.
    Cassius, go you into the other street
    And part the numbers.[3]
5    Those that will hear me speak, let 'em stay here;
    Those that will follow Cassius, go with him;
    And public reasons shall be renderèd
    Of Caesar's death.

**FIRST PLEBEIAN.**        I will hear Brutus speak.

**SECOND PLEBEIAN.** I will hear Cassius, and compare their
    reasons,
10    When severally[4] we hear them renderèd.
         [*Exit Cassius, with some of the Plebeians.*]
**THIRD PLEBEIAN.** The noble Brutus is ascended. Silence!

**BRUTUS.** Be patient till the last.
    Romans, countrymen, and lovers,[5] hear me for my
    cause, and be silent, that you may hear. Believe me
15    for mine honor, and have respect to mine honor, that
    you may believe. Censure[6] me in your wisdom, and

**1. Plebeians** (pli bē′ əns) *n.*: Commoners; members of the lower class.
**2. be satisfied:** Get an explanation.

**3. part the numbers:** Divide the crowd.

**4. severally** (sev′ ər əl ē) *adv.*: Separately.

**5. lovers:** Dear friends.

**6. Censure** (sen′ shər) *v.*: Condemn as wrong; criticize.

awake your senses,[7] that you may the better judge. If there be any in this assembly, any dear friend of Caesar's, to him I say that Brutus' love to Caesar was no less than his. If then that friend demand why Brutus rose against Caesar, this is my answer: Not that I loved Caesar less, but that I loved Rome more. Had you rather Caesar were living, and die all slaves, than that Caesar were dead, to live all free men? As Caesar loved me, I weep for him; as he was fortunate, I rejoice at it; as he was valiant, I honor him; but, as he was ambitious, I slew him. There is tears, for his love; joy, for his fortune; honor, for his valor; and death, for his ambition. Who is here so base,[8] that would be a bondman?[9] If any, speak; for him have I offended. Who is here so rude,[10] that would not be a Roman? If any, speak; for him have I offended. Who is here so vile, that will not love his country? If any, speak; for him have I offended. I pause for a reply.

**ALL.** None, Brutus, none!

**BRUTUS.** Then none have I offended. I have done no more to Caesar than you shall do to Brutus. The question of his death is enrolled[11] in the Capitol; his glory not extenuated,[12] wherein he was worthy, nor his offenses enforced,[13] for which he suffered death.

[*Enter Mark Antony, with Caesar's body.*]

Here comes his body, mourned by Mark Antony, who, though he had no hand in his death, shall receive the benefit of his dying, a place in the commonwealth, as which of you shall not? With this I depart, that, as I slew my best lover for the good of Rome, I have the same dagger for myself, when it shall please my country to need my death.

**ALL.** Live, Brutus! Live, live!

**FIRST PLEBEIAN.** Bring him with triumph home unto his house.

**SECOND PLEBEIAN.** Give him a statue with his ancestors.

**THIRD PLEBEIAN.** Let him be Caesar.

**FOURTH PLEBEIAN.** Caesar's better parts[14]
Shall be crowned in Brutus.

**7. senses:** Powers of reason.

**8. base:** Low.

**9. bondman:** Slave.

**10. rude:** Ignorant.

**11. The question . . . in the Capitol:** The whole matter of his death is on record in the Capitol.
**12. extenuated** (ik sten′ yōō wāt id) *v.*: Underrated.
**13. enforced** (in fôrs′d′) *v.*: Given force to.

**14. parts:** Qualities.

**FIRST PLEBEIAN.** We'll bring him to his house with shouts and clamors.

**BRUTUS.** My countrymen—

**SECOND PLEBEIAN.**                    Peace! Silence! Brutus speaks.

55   **FIRST PLEBEIAN.** Peace, ho!

**BRUTUS.** Good countrymen, let me depart alone,
And, for my sake, stay here with Antony.
Do grace to Caesar's corpse, and grace his speech
Tending to Caesar's glories,[15] which Mark Antony
60   By our permission, is allowed to make.
I do entreat you, not a man depart,
Save I alone, till Antony have spoke.            [*Exit.*]

**FIRST PLEBEIAN.** Stay, ho! And let us hear Mark Antony.

**THIRD PLEBEIAN.** Let him go up into the public chair;
65   We'll hear him. Noble Antony, go up.

**ANTONY.** For Brutus' sake, I am beholding[16] to you.

**FOURTH PLEBEIAN.** What does he say of Brutus?

**THIRD PLEBEIAN.**                    He says, for Brutus' sake,
He finds himself beholding to us all.

**FOURTH PLEBEIAN.** 'Twere best he speak no harm of Brutus here!

**FIRST PLEBEIAN.** This Caesar was a tyrant.

70   **THIRD PLEBEIAN.**                    Nay, that's certain.
We are blest that Rome is rid of him.

**SECOND PLEBEIAN.** Peace! Let us hear what Antony can say.

**ANTONY.** You gentle Romans—

**ALL.**                    Peace, ho! Let us hear him.

**ANTONY.** Friends, Romans, countrymen, lend me your ears;
75   I come to bury Caesar, not to praise him.
The evil that men do lives after them,
The good is oft interrèd with their bones;
So let it be with Caesar. The noble Brutus
Hath told you Caesar was ambitious.
80   If it were so, it was a grievous fault,
And grievously hath Caesar answered[17] it.

**15. Do grace . . . glories:** Honor Caesar's body and the speech telling of Caesar's achievements.

**16. beholding:** Indebted.

**17. answered:** Paid the penalty for.

Here, under leave of Brutus and the rest
(For Brutus is an honorable man,
So are they all, all honorable men),
85    Come I to speak in Caesar's funeral.
He was my friend, faithful and just to me;
But Brutus says he was ambitious,
And Brutus is an honorable man.
He hath brought many captives home to Rome,
90    Whose ransoms did the general coffers fill;
Did this in Caesar seem ambitious?
When that the poor have cried, Caesar hath wept;
Ambition should be made of sterner stuff.
Yet Brutus says he was ambitious;
95    And Brutus is an honorable man.

You all did see that on the Lupercal
I thrice presented him a kingly crown,
Which he did thrice refuse. Was this ambition?
Yet Brutus says he was ambitious;
100 And sure he is an honorable man.
I speak not to disprove what Brutus spoke,
But here I am to speak what I do know.
You all did love him once, not without cause;
What cause withholds you then to mourn for him?
105 O judgment, thou art fled to brutish beasts,
And men have lost their reason! Bear with me;
My heart is in the coffin there with Caesar,
And I must pause till it come back to me.

**FIRST PLEBEIAN.** Methinks there is much reason in his
　　　sayings.

110 **SECOND PLEBEIAN.** If thou consider rightly of the matter,
　　　Caesar has had great wrong.

**THIRD PLEBEIAN.** 　　　　　　Has he, masters?
　　　I fear there will a worse come in his place.

**FOURTH PLEBEIAN.** Marked ye his words? He would not
　　　take the crown,
　　　Therefore 'tis certain he was not ambitious.

115 **FIRST PLEBEIAN.** If it be found so, some will dear abide
　　　it.[18]

**SECOND PLEBEIAN.** Poor soul, his eyes are red as fire with
　　　weeping.

**THIRD PLEBEIAN.** There's not a nobler man in Rome than
　　　Antony.

**FOURTH PLEBEIAN.** Now mark him, he begins again to
　　　speak.

**ANTONY.** But yesterday the word of Caesar might
120 Have stood against the world; now lies he there,
And none so poor to[19] do him reverence.
O masters! If I were disposed to stir
Your hearts and minds to mutiny and rage,
I should do Brutus wrong and Cassius wrong,
125 Who, you all know, are honorable men.
I will not do them wrong; I rather choose
To wrong the dead, to wrong myself and you,
Than I will wrong such honorable men.

**18. dear abide it:** Pay
dearly for it.

**19. to:** As to.

But here's a parchment with the seal of Caesar;
130  I found it in his closet; 'tis his will.
Let but the commons[20] hear this testament,
Which, pardon me, I do not mean to read,
And they would go and kiss dead Caesar's wounds,
And dip their napkins[21] in his sacred blood;
135  Yea, beg a hair of him for memory,
And dying, mention it within their wills,
Bequeathing it as a rich legacy
Unto their issue.[22]

**FOURTH PLEBEIAN.** We'll hear the will; read it, Mark
Antony.

140  **ALL.** The will, the will! We will hear Caesar's will!

**ANTONY.** Have patience, gentle friends, I must not read
it.
It is not meet you know how Caesar loved you.
You are not wood, you are not stones, but men;
And being men, hearing the will of Caesar,
145  It will inflame you, it will make you mad.
'Tis good you know not that you are his heirs;
For if you should, O, what would come of it?

**FOURTH PLEBEIAN.** Read the will! We'll hear it, Antony!
You shall read us the will, Caesar's will!

150  **ANTONY.** Will you be patient? Will you stay awhile?
I have o'ershot myself[23] to tell you of it.
I fear I wrong the honorable men
Whose daggers have stabbed Caesar; I do fear it.

**FOURTH PLEBEIAN.** They were traitors. Honorable men!

155  **ALL.** The will! The testament!

**SECOND PLEBEIAN.** They were villains, murderers! The
will! Read the will!

**ANTONY.** You will compel me then to read the will?
Then make a ring about the corpse of Caesar,
160  And let me show you him that made the will.
Shall I descend? And will you give me leave?

**ALL.** Come down.

**SECOND PLEBEIAN.** Descend.       [*Antony comes down.*]

**THIRD PLEBEIAN.** You shall have leave.

165  **FOURTH PLEBEIAN.** A ring! Stand round.

**20. commons:** Plebeians;
commoners.

**21. napkins:**
Handkerchiefs.

**22. issue:** Heirs.

**23. o'ershot myself:** Gone
too far.

**FIRST PLEBEIAN.** Stand from the hearse,[24] stand from the body!

**SECOND PLEBEIAN.** Room for Antony, most noble Antony!

**ANTONY.** Nay, press not so upon me; stand far off.

**ALL.** Stand back! Room! Bear back.

170 **ANTONY.** If you have tears, prepare to shed them now.
You all do know this mantle;[25] I remember
The first time ever Caesar put it on:
'Twas on a summer's evening, in his tent,
That day he overcame the Nervii.

175 Look, in this place ran Cassius' dagger through;
See what a rent[26] the envious[27] Casca made;
Through this the well-belovèd Brutus stabbed,
And as he plucked his cursèd steel away,

**24. hearse** (hʉrs) *n.*: Coffin.

**25. mantle** (man' t'l) *n.*: Cloak; toga.

**26. rent** (rent) *n.*: Torn place.
**27. envious** (en' vē əs) *adj.*: Spiteful.

Mark how the blood of Caesar followed it,
180 As[28] rushing out of doors, to be resolved[29]
If Brutus so unkindly knocked, or no;
For Brutus, as you know, was Caesar's angel.
Judge, O you gods, how dearly Caesar loved him!
This was the most unkindest cut of all;
185 For when the noble Caesar saw him stab,
Ingratitude, more strong than traitors' arms,
Quite vanquished him. Then burst his mighty heart;
And, in his mantle muffling up his face,
Even at the base of Pompey's statue
190 (Which all the while ran blood) great Caesar fell.
O, what a fall was there, my countrymen!
Then I, and you, and all of us fell down,
Whilst bloody treason flourished[30] over us.
O, now you weep, and I perceive you feel
195 The dint[31] of pity; these are gracious drops.
Kind souls, what[32] weep you when you but behold
Our Caesar's vesture[33] wounded? Look you here,
Here is himself, marred as you see with[34] traitors.

**FIRST PLEBEIAN.** O piteous spectacle!

200 **SECOND PLEBEIAN.** O noble Caesar!

**THIRD PLEBEIAN.** O woeful day!

**FOURTH PLEBEIAN.** O traitors, villains!

**FIRST PLEBEIAN.** O most bloody sight!

**SECOND PLEBEIAN.** We will be revenged.

205 **ALL.** Revenge! About![35] Seek! Burn! Fire! Kill! Slay!
Let not a traitor live!

**ANTONY.** Stay, countrymen.

**FIRST PLEBEIAN.** Peace there! Hear the noble Antony.

**SECOND PLEBEIAN.** We'll hear him, we'll follow him, we'll
210 die with him!

**ANTONY.** Good friends, sweet friends, let me not stir you
up
To such a sudden flood of mutiny.
They that have done this deed are honorable.
What private griefs[36] they have, alas, I know not,
215 That made them do it. They are wise and honorable,
And will, no doubt, with reasons answer you.

**28. As:** As if.
**29. to be resolved:** To learn for certain.

**30. flourished** (flŭr′ ish'd) *v.*: Grew; triumphed.

**31. dint** (dint) *n.*: Force.
**32. what:** Why.
**33. vesture** (ves′ chər) *n.*: Clothing.
**34. with:** By.

**35. About:** Let's go.

**36. griefs** (grēfs) *n.*: Grievances.

I come not, friends, to steal away your hearts;
I am no orator, as Brutus is;
But (as you know me all) a plain blunt man
220 That love my friend, and that they know full well
That gave me public leave[37] to speak of him.
For I have neither writ, nor words, nor worth,
Action, nor utterance,[38] nor the power of speech
To stir men's blood; I only speak right on.[39]
225 I tell you that which you yourselves do know,
Show you sweet Caesar's wounds, poor poor dumb
  mouths,
And bid them speak for me. But were I Brutus,
And Brutus Antony, there were an Antony
Would ruffle up your spirits, and put a tongue
230 In every wound of Caesar's that should move
The stones of Rome to rise and mutiny.

**ALL.** We'll mutiny.

**FIRST PLEBEIAN.** We'll burn the house of Brutus.

**THIRD PLEBEIAN.** Away, then! Come, seek the conspirators.

**ANTONY.** Yet hear me, countrymen. Yet hear me speak.

235 **ALL.** Peace, ho! Hear Antony, most noble Antony!

**ANTONY.** Why, friends, you go to do you know not what:
Wherein hath Caesar thus deserved your loves?
Alas, you know not; I must tell you then:
You have forgot the will I told you of.

240 **ALL.** Most true, the will! Let's stay and hear the will.

**ANTONY.** Here is the will, and under Caesar's seal.
To every Roman citizen he gives,
To every several man, seventy-five drachmas.

**SECOND PLEBEIAN.** Most noble Caesar! We'll revenge his
death!

245 **THIRD PLEBEIAN.** O royal Caesar!

**ANTONY.** Hear me with patience.

**ALL.** Peace, ho!

**ANTONY.** Moreover, he hath left you all his walks,
His private arbors, and new-planted orchards,[40]
250 On this side Tiber; he hath left them you,

**37. leave:** Permission.

**38. neither writ . . .
utterance** (ut' ər əns):
Neither written speech, nor
fluency, nor reputation, nor
gestures, nor style of
speaking.
**39. right on:** Directly.

**40. walks . . . orchards:**
Parks, his private trees,
and newly planted gardens.

And to your heirs forever: common pleasures,[41]
To walk abroad and recreate yourselves.
Here was a Caesar! When comes such another?

FIRST PLEBEIAN. Never, never! Come, away, away!
255   We'll burn his body in the holy place,
And with the brands[42] fire the traitors' houses.
Take up the body.

SECOND PLEBEIAN. Go fetch fire.

THIRD PLEBEIAN. Pluck down benches.

260   FOURTH PLEBEIAN. Pluck down forms, windows, anything!

[Exit Plebeians with the body.]

ANTONY. Now let it work: Mischief, thou art afoot,
Take thou what course thou wilt.

[Enter Servant.]

How now, fellow?

SERVANT. Sir, Octavius is already come to Rome.

ANTONY. Where is he?

265   SERVANT. He and Lepidus are at Caesar's house.

ANTONY. And thither[43] will I straight to visit him;
He comes upon a wish. Fortune is merry,
And in this mood will give us anything.

SERVANT. I heard him say, Brutus and Cassius
270   Are rid[44] like madmen through the gates of Rome.

ANTONY. Belike[45] they had some notice of the people,[46]
How I had moved them. Bring me to Octavius. [Exit.]

Scene iii. _A street._

[Enter Cinna the Poet, and after him the Plebeians.]

CINNA. I dreamt tonight that I did feast with Caesar,
And things unluckily charge my fantasy.[1]
I have no will to wander forth of doors,[2]
Yet something leads me forth.

5   FIRST PLEBEIAN. What is your name?

SECOND PLEBEIAN. Whither are you going?

**41. common pleasures:**
Public places of recreation.

**42. brands:** Torches.

**43. thither:** There.

**44. are rid:** Have ridden.
**45. Belike:** Probably.
**46. notice of the people:**
Word about the mood of
the people.

**1. things . . . fantasy:**
The events that have
happened weigh heavily on
my imagination.
**2. of doors:** Outdoors.

**THIRD PLEBEIAN.** Where do you dwell?

**FOURTH PLEBEIAN.** Are you a married man or a bachelor?

**SECOND PLEBEIAN.** Answer every man directly.

10 **FIRST PLEBEIAN.** Ay, and briefly.

**FOURTH PLEBEIAN.** Ay, and wisely.

**THIRD PLEBEIAN.** Ay, and truly, you were best.

**CINNA.** What is my name? Whither am I going? Where do
I dwell? Am I a married man or a bachelor? Then, to
15 answer every man directly and briefly, wisely and
truly: wisely I say, I am a bachelor.

**SECOND PLEBEIAN.** That's as much as to say, they are
fools that marry; you'll bear me a bang³ for that, I
fear. Proceed directly.

20 **CINNA.** Directly, I am going to Caesar's funeral.

**FIRST PLEBEIAN.** As a friend or an enemy?

**CINNA.** As a friend.

**SECOND PLEBEIAN.** That matter is answered directly.

**FOURTH PLEBEIAN.** For your dwelling, briefly.

25 **CINNA.** Briefly, I dwell by the Capitol.

**THIRD PLEBEIAN.** Your name, sir, truly.

**CINNA.** Truly, my name is Cinna.

**FIRST PLEBEIAN.** Tear him to pieces! He's a conspirator.

**CINNA.** I am Cinna the poet! I am Cinna the poet!

30 **FOURTH PLEBEIAN.** Tear him for his bad verses! Tear him
for his bad verses!

**CINNA.** I am not Cinna the conspirator.

**FOURTH PLEBEIAN.** It is no matter, his name's Cinna;
pluck but his name out of his heart, and turn him
35 going.⁴

**THIRD PLEBEIAN.** Tear him, tear him! [*They attack him.*]
Come, brands, ho! Firebrands!⁵ To Brutus', to Cas-
sius'! Burn all! Some to Decius' house, and some to
Casca's; some to Ligarius'! Away, go!
                    [*Exit all the Plebeians with Cinna.*]

**3. bear me a bang:** Get a
blow from me.

**4. turn him going:** Send
him on his way.

**5. Firebrands:** People who
stir up others to revolt.

## THINKING ABOUT THE SELECTION

### Recalling

1. What petition is presented to Caesar, and how does he respond to it?
2. What reason does Brutus give the people for the assassination?
3. How does Antony repeatedly refer to Brutus during the funeral oration?
4. What effect does Antony's speech have on the plebeians?

### Interpreting

5. Why does Antony befriend the conspirators immediately after the assassination?
6. Why does Brutus allow Antony to speak at Caesar's funeral?
7. How does Caesar's will affect the people?

### Applying

8. Antony convinces the crowd to accept his opinion of Caesar and the conspirators. Think of a modern example of a leader trying to convince an audience to adopt a certain opinion. Discuss the techniques used to influence the people.

## ANALYZING LITERATURE

### Examining Types of Speeches by Actors

Usually an **aside** is spoken by a character as if speaking to himself or herself. In this act, however, two characters speak asides not overheard by the others, and they reveal their true feelings. In a **soliloquy,** a character alone onstage reveals and examines his or her thoughts and feelings. A **monologue** is a long speech spoken without interruption by one character in the presence of others. It may or may not reveal what the speaker really thinks or feels.

1. Compare what Cassius says to Antony in Act III, scene i, line 177 with what he says to Brutus in the aside beginning in line 232.
2. Compare what Antony says in Act III, scene i,

lines 218–222 with his soliloquy from line 254 on.
3. Examine Brutus's speech (Act III, scene ii, line 12 on). Give examples to support your opinion about the extent to which Brutus is speaking his true feelings.

## CRITICAL THINKING AND READING

### Understanding Tone

**Tone** shows the speaker's attitude toward the subject and toward the audience. The tone of Antony's soliloquy over Caesar's body (Act III, scene i, line 254 on) is that of sincere grief and rage, as you can infer from details of language and sentence structure. Brutus's speech at the beginning of scene ii begins with a reasonable tone and shifts to one urging the crowd's acceptance of the assassination.

1. Examine Antony's funeral oration, actually all four long sections of the oration.
2. Identify the tone and shifts in tone within the oration.
3. Give an example from the text to support each of your inferences about the tone.

## SPEAKING AND LISTENING

### Giving a Funeral Oration

Choose one section of Antony's funeral oration. Practice reading it aloud, using an appropriate tone. Have a classmate critique your reading.

## THINKING AND WRITING

### Writing About Background Music

Select a piece of music that would be an appropriate background for the assassination scene. Write a brief explanation of why the selection is appropriate. When you revise, make sure you have given at least three reasons for your choice of music.

# GUIDE FOR READING

## The Tragedy of Julius Caesar, Act IV

**Conflict**

**Conflict** is a struggle between opposing forces. The forces involved in a conflict may be a person and nature, two people or two groups of people, or a person struggling to decide between two opposing ideas or values within himself or herself upon which the action in fiction or drama depends. In earlier acts we have seen conflict between Caesar and the conspirators, within Brutus over what his course of action should be, and between Cassius and Brutus over how to deal with Antony. Cassius and Brutus disagreed over whether Antony should be killed along with Caesar and whether he should be allowed to speak at Caesar's funeral. These conflicts have arisen because the two characters have differing attitudes toward people and situations.

**Look For**

As you read Act IV, look for new conflicts that develop between Cassius and Brutus. Notice how the character of each contributes to the conflict, and think about how each person's arguments reveal his character.

**Writing**

Lord Acton once wrote, "Power tends to corrupt and absolute power corrupts absolutely." An anonymous wit responded, "Power can corrupt, but absolute power is absolutely delightful." Freewrite, exploring the meaning of these quotations and their relation to *The Tragedy of Julius Caesar*.

**Vocabulary**

Knowing the following words will help you as you read Act IV of *The Tragedy of Julius Caesar*.

**legacies** (leg′ə sēz) *n*.: Money, property, or position left in a will to someone (p. 405)

**slanderous** (slan′dər əs) *adj*.: Damaging to a person's reputation (p. 405)

**covert** (kuv′ərt) *adj*.: Hidden; secret (p. 406)

**chastisement** (chas tīz′mənt) *n*.: Punishment; severe criticism (p. 409)

**philosophy** (fil äs′ə fē) *n*.: System of values (p. 413)

# Act IV

**Scene i.** *A house in Rome.*

[*Enter Antony, Octavius, and Lepidus.*]

**ANTONY.** These many then shall die; their names are
   pricked.

**OCTAVIUS.** Your brother too must die; consent you, Lepidus?

**LEPIDUS.** I do consent—

**OCTAVIUS.**                    Prick him down, Antony.

**LEPIDUS.** Upon condition Publius shall not live,
5    Who is your sister's son, Mark Antony.

**ANTONY.** He shall not live; look, with a spot I damn him.[1]
   But, Lepidus, go you to Caesar's house;
   Fetch the will hither, and we shall determine
   How to cut off some charge in legacies.

10   **LEPIDUS.** What, shall I find you here?

**OCTAVIUS.** Or[2] here or at the Capitol.        [*Exit Lepidus.*]

**ANTONY.** This is a slight unmeritable[3] man,
   Meet to be sent on errands; is it fit,
   The threefold world[4] divided, he should stand
   One of the three to share it?

15   **OCTAVIUS.**                         So you thought him,
   And took his voice[5] who should be pricked to die
   In our black sentence and proscription.[6]

**ANTONY.** Octavius, I have seen more days[7] than you;
   And though we lay these honors on this man.
20   To ease ourselves of divers sland'rous loads,[8]
   He shall but bear them as the ass bears gold,
   To groan and sweat under the business,
   Either led or driven, as we point the way;
   And having brought our treasure where we will,
25   Then take we down his load, and turn him off,
   (Like to the empty ass) to shake his ears
   And graze in commons.[9]

**OCTAVIUS.**                    You may do your will;
   But he's a tried and valiant soldier.

**1. with a spot . . . him:**
With a mark on the tablet,
I condemn him.

**2. Or:** Either.

**3. slight unmeritable:**
Insignificant and without
merit.
**4. threefold world:** Three
areas of the Roman
Empire—Europe, Asia, and
Africa.

**5. voice:** Vote; opinion.
**6. proscription:** List of
those sentenced to death or
exile.
**7. have seen more days:** I
am older.
**8. divers sland'rous
loads:** Various burdens of
blame.

**9. in commons:** On public
pasture.

**ANTONY.** So is my horse, Octavius, and for that
30  I do appoint him store of provender.[10]
It is a creature that I teach to fight,
To wind,[11] to stop, to run directly on,
His corporal motion governed by my spirit.[12]
And, in some taste,[13] is Lepidus but so.
35  He must be taught, and trained, and bid go forth.
A barren-spirited[14] fellow; one that feeds
On objects, arts, and imitations,[15]
Which, out of use and staled[16] by other men,
Begin his fashion.[17] Do not talk of him
40  But as a property. And now, Octavius,
Listen great things. Brutus and Cassius
Are levying powers;[18] we must straight make head.[19]
Therefore let our alliance be combined,
Our best friends made, our means stretched;[20]
45  And let us presently go sit in council
How covert matters may be best disclosed,
And open perils surest answerèd.[21]

**OCTAVIUS.** Let us do so; for we are at the stake,[22]
And bayed about with many enemies;
50  And some that smile have in their hearts, I fear,
Millions of mischiefs.[23]                    [*Exit.*]

**10. appoint . . . provender:** Allot him a supply of food.
**11. wind** (wīnd) *v.*: Turn.
**12. His . . . spirit:** His body movements governed by my mind.
**13. taste:** Degree.
**14. barren-spirited:** Without ideas of his own.
**15. feeds on objects, arts, and imitations:** Enjoys curiosities, arts, and styles.
**16. staled:** Cheapened.
**17. Begin his fashion:** He begins to use. (He is hopelessly behind the times.)
**18. levying powers:** Enlisting troops.
**19. straight make head:** Quickly gather soldiers.
**20. stretched:** Used to the fullest advantage.
**21. How . . . answerèd:** How secrets may be discovered and dangers met.
**22. at the stake:** Like a bear tied to a stake and set upon by many dogs.
**23. mischiefs:** Plans to injure us.

**Scene ii.** *Camp near Sardis.*
[*Drum. Enter Brutus, Lucilius, Lucius, and the Army. Titinius and Pindarus meet them.*]

**BRUTUS.** Stand ho!

**LUCILIUS.** Give the word, ho! and stand.

**BRUTUS.** What now, Lucilius, is Cassius near?

**LUCILIUS.** He is at hand, and Pindarus is come
5     To do you salutation[1] from his master.

**BRUTUS.** He greets me well. Your master, Pindarus,
    In his own change, or by ill officers,
    Hath given me some worthy cause to wish
    Things done undone;[2] but if he be at hand,
    I shall be satisfied.

10 **PINDARUS.**             I do not doubt
    But that my noble master will appear
    Such as he is, full of regard and honor.

**BRUTUS.** He is not doubted. A word, Lucilius,
    How he received you; let me be resolved.[3]

15 **LUCILIUS.** With courtesy and with respect enough,
    But not with such familiar instances,[4]
    Nor with such free and friendly conference[5]
    As he hath used of old.

**BRUTUS.**            Thou hast described
    A hot friend cooling. Ever note, Lucilius,
20     When love begins to sicken and decay
    It useth an enforcèd ceremony.[6]
    There are no tricks in plain and simple faith;
    But hollow[7] men, like horses hot at hand,[8]
    Make gallant show and promise of their mettle;
                 [*Low march within.*]
25     But when they should endure the bloody spur,
    They fall their crests, and like deceitful jades
    Sink in the trial.[9] Comes his army on?

**LUCILIUS.** They mean this night in Sardis to be quar-
    tered;
    The greater part, the horse in general,[10]
    Are come with Cassius.

[*Enter Cassius and his Powers.*]

30 **BRUTUS.**            Hark! He is arrived.
    March gently[11] on to meet him.

**1. To do you salutation:**
To bring you greetings.

**2. In his own . . . done
undone:** Has changed in
his feelings toward me or
has received bad advice
from subordinates and has
made me wish we had not
done what we did.

**3. resolved:** Fully
informed.

**4. familiar instances:**
Marks of friendship.
**5. conference:**
Conversation.

**6. enforcèd ceremony:**
Forced formality.
**7. hollow:** Insincere.
**8. hot at hand:** Full of
spirit when reined in.

**9. They fall . . . the
trial:** They drop their
necks, and like worn-out
worthless horses fail the
test.
**10. horse in general:**
Cavalry.

**11. gently:** Slowly.

**CASSIUS.** Stand, ho!

**BRUTUS.** Stand, ho! Speak the word along.

**FIRST SOLDIER.** Stand!

35   **SECOND SOLDIER.** Stand!

**THIRD SOLDIER.** Stand!

**CASSIUS.** Most noble brother, you have done me wrong.

**BRUTUS.** Judge me, you gods! Wrong I mine enemies?
    And if not so, how should I wrong a brother.

40   **CASSIUS.** Brutus, this sober form[12] of yours hides
      wrongs;
    And when you do them—

**12. sober form:** Serious manner.

**BRUTUS.**                Cassius, be content.[13]
    Speak your griefs softly; I do know you well.
    Before the eyes of both our armies here
    (Which should perceive nothing but love from us)
45     Let us not wrangle. Bid them move away;
    Then in my tent, Cassius, enlarge[14] your griefs,
    And I will give you audience.

**13. be content:** Be patient.

**14. enlarge:** Freely express.

**CASSIUS.**                Pindarus,
    Bid our commanders lead their charges[15] off
    A little from this ground.

**15. charges:** Troops.

50   **BRUTUS.** Lucilius, do you the like, and let no man
    Come to our tent till we have done our conference.
    Let Lucius and Titinius guard our door.
               *[Exit all but Brutus and Cassius.]*

**Scene iii.** *Brutus' tent.*

**CASSIUS.** That you have wronged me doth appear in this:
    You have condemned and noted[1] Lucius Pella
    For taking bribes here of the Sardians;
    Wherein my letters, praying on his side,[2]
5     Because I knew the man, was slighted off.[3]

**1. noted:** Publicly denounced.
**2. praying on his side:** Pleading on his behalf.
**3. slighted off:** Disregarded.

**BRUTUS.** You wronged yourself to write in such a case.

**CASSIUS.** In such a time as this it is not meet
    That every nice offense should bear his comment.[4]

**4. every . . . comment:** Every petty fault should receive its criticism.

**BRUTUS.** Let me tell you, Cassius, you yourself
10     Are much condemned to have an itching palm,[5]
    To sell and mart[6] your offices for gold
    To undeservers.

**5. condemned . . . palm:** Accused of having a hand eager to accept bribes.
**6. mart:** trade.

**CASSIUS.** I an itching palm?
You know that you are Brutus that speaks this,
Or, by the gods, this speech were else your last.

15 **BRUTUS.** The name of Cassius honors[7] this corruption,
And chastisement doth therefore hide his head.

**7. honors:** Give respectability to.

**CASSIUS.** Chastisement!

**BRUTUS.** Remember March, the ides of March remember.
Did not great Julius bleed for justice' sake?

20 What villain touched his body, that did stab,
And not[8] for justice? What, shall one of us,
That struck the foremost man of all this world
But for supporting robbers,[9] shall we now
Contaminate our fingers with base bribes,

25 And sell the mighty space of our large honors[10]
For so much trash[11] as may be graspèd thus?
I had rather be a dog, and bay[12] the moon,
Than such a Roman.

**8. And not:** Except.
**9. But . . . robbers:** Here Brutus says, for the first time, that Caesar's officials were also involved in taking bribes and that this was a motive in his assassination.
**10. honors:** Offices.
**11. trash:** Dirty money.
**12. bay:** Howl at.

**CASSIUS.** Brutus, bait[13] not me;
I'll not endure it. You forget yourself

30 To hedge me in.[14] I am a soldier, I,
Older in practice, abler than yourself
To make conditions.[15]

**13. bait:** Harass (as a bear tied to a stake is harassed by dogs).
**14. hedge me in:** Restrict my actions.
**15. conditions:** Decisions.

**BRUTUS.** Go to! You are not, Cassius.

**CASSIUS.** I am.

**BRUTUS.** I say you are not.

35 **CASSIUS.** Urge[16] me no more, I shall forget myself;
Have mind upon your health;[17] tempt me no farther.

**16. Urge:** Drive.
**17. health:** Safety.

**BRUTUS.** Away, slight[18] man!

**18. slight:** Insignificant.

**CASSIUS.** Is't possible?
**BRUTUS.** Hear me, for I will speak.
Must I give way and room to your rash choler?[19]

40 Shall I be frighted when a madman stares?

**19. choler** (käl′ ər) *n.*: Anger.
**20. choleric** (käl′ər ik) *adj.*: Quick-tempered.
**21. budge:** Flinch away from you.
**22. observe you:** Show reverence toward you.
**23. testy humor:** Irritability.
**24. digest . . . spleen:** Eat the poison of your spleen. (The spleen was thought to be the source of anger.)

**CASSIUS.** O ye gods, ye gods! Must I endure all this?

**BRUTUS.** All this? Ay, more: fret till your proud heart
   break.
Go show your slaves how choleric[20] you are,
And make your bondmen tremble. Must I budge?[21]

45 Must I observe[22] you? Must I stand and crouch
Under your testy humor?[23] By the gods,
You shall digest the venom of your spleen,[24]

Though it do split you; for, from this day forth,
I'll use you for my mirth,[25] yea, for my laughter,
When you are waspish.[26]

**25. mirth:** Amusement.
**26. waspish:**
Bad-tempered.

50 **CASSIUS.** Is it come to this?

**BRUTUS.** You say you are a better soldier:
Let it appear so; make your vaunting[27] true,
And it shall please me well. For mine own part,
I shall be glad to learn of[28] noble men.

**27. vaunting** (vônt' iŋ) *n.*:
Boasting.
**28. learn of:** Hear about;
learn from.

**CASSIUS.** You wrong me every way; you wrong me,
55     Brutus;
I said, an elder soldier, not a better.
Did I say, better?

**BRUTUS.** If you did, I care not.

**CASSIUS.** When Caesar lived, he durst not thus have
moved[29] me.

**29. moved:** Irritated.

**BRUTUS.** Peace, peace, you durst not so have tempted
him.

60 **CASSIUS.** I durst not?

**BRUTUS.** No.

**CASSIUS.** What? Durst not tempt him?

**BRUTUS.** For your life you durst not.

**CASSIUS.** Do not presume too much upon my love;
I may do that I shall be sorry for.

65 **BRUTUS.** You have done that you should be sorry for.
There is no terror, Cassius, in your threats;
For I am armed so strong in honesty
That they pass by me as the idle wind,
Which I respect not. I did send to you
70 For certain sums of gold, which you denied me;
For I can raise no money by vile means.
By heaven, I had rather coin my heart
And drop my blood for drachmas than to wring
From the hard hands of peasants their vile trash
75 By any indirection.[30] I did send
To you for gold to pay my legions,
Which you denied me. Was that done like Cassius?
Should I have answered Caius Cassius so?
When Marcus Brutus grows so covetous[31]

**30. indirection:** Irregular
methods.

**31. covetous** (kuv' it əs)
*adj.*: Greedy.

80      To lock such rascal counters[32] from his friends,
        Be ready, gods, with all your thunderbolts,
        Dash him to pieces!

**32. rascal counters:**
Worthless coins.

CASSIUS.                    I denied you not.

BRUTUS. You did.

CASSIUS.            I did not. He was but a fool
        That brought my answer back. Brutus hath rived[33]
            my heart.

**33. rived** (rīv'd) *v.*:
Broken.

85      A friend should bear his friend's infirmities;
        But Brutus makes mine greater than they are.

BRUTUS. I do not, till you practice them on me.

CASSIUS. You love me not.

BRUTUS.                    I do not like your faults.

CASSIUS. A friendly eye could never see such faults.

90      BRUTUS. A flatterer's would not, though they do appear
        As huge as high Olympus.

CASSIUS. Come, Antony, and young Octavius, come,
        Revenge yourselves alone[34] on Cassius,
        For Cassius is aweary of the world:

**34. alone:** Only.
**35. braved:** Bullied.
**36. Checked like a bondman:** Scolded like a slave.

95      Hated by one he loves; braved[35] by his brother;
        Checked like a bondman;[36] all his faults observed,
        Set in a notebook, learned and conned by rote[37]
        To cast into my teeth. O, I could weep
        My spirit from mine eyes! There is my dagger,

**37. conned by rote:**
Memorized.

100     And here my naked breast; within, a heart
        Dearer than Pluto's mine,[38] richer than gold;
        If that thou be'st a Roman, take it forth.
        I, that denied thee gold, will give my heart.
        Strike as thou didst at Caesar; for I know,
        When thou didst hate him worst, thou lovedst him

**38. Pluto's mine:** The mythological Roman god of the underworld and of riches symbolized by his mine.

105         better
        Than ever thou lovedst Cassius.

BRUTUS.                    Sheathe your dagger.
        Be angry when you will, it shall have scope.[39]
        Do what you will, dishonor shall be humor.[40]
        O Cassius, you are yokèd[41] with a lamb

**39. scope:** Free play.
**40. dishonor . . . humor:**
Any dishonorable acts will be considered just your irritable disposition.
**41. yokèd:** In partnership.
**42. enforcèd:** Provoked.

110     That carries anger as the flint bears fire,
        Who, much enforcèd,[42] shows a hasty spark,
        And straight is cold again.

CASSIUS.                       Hath Cassius lived
    To be but mirth and laughter to his Brutus
    When grief and blood ill-tempered vexeth him?

115   BRUTUS. When I spoke that, I was ill-tempered too.

CASSIUS. Do you confess so much? Give me your hand.

BRUTUS. And my heart too.

CASSIUS.                 O Brutus!

BRUTUS.                       What's the matter?

CASSIUS. Have not you love enough to bear with me
    When that rash humor which my mother gave me
    Makes me forgetful?

120   BRUTUS.            Yes, Cassius, and from henceforth,
    When you are over-earnest with your Brutus,
    He'll think your mother chides, and leave you so.[43]

[*Enter a Poet, followed by Lucilius, Titinius, and Lucius.*]

POET. Let me go in to see the generals;

**43. your mother . . . so:**
It is just your inherited
disposition and let it go at
that.

There is some grudge between 'em; 'tis not meet
125        They be alone.

**LUCILIUS.** You shall not come to them.

**POET.** Nothing but death shall stay me.

**CASSIUS.** How now. What's the matter?

**POET.** For shame, you generals! What do you mean?
130        Love, and be friends, as two such men should be;
       For I have seen more years, I'm sure, than ye.

**CASSIUS.** Ha, ha! How vilely doth this cynic[44] rhyme!

**44. cynic:** Rude fellow.

**BRUTUS.** Get you hence, sirrah! Saucy fellow, hence!

**CASSIUS.** Bear with him, Brutus, 'tis his fashion.

135  **BRUTUS.** I'll know his humor when he knows his time.[45]
       What should the wars do with these jigging[46] fools?
       Companion,[47] hence!

**45. I'll know . . . time:** I'll accept his eccentricity when he chooses a proper time to exhibit it.
**46. jigging:** Rhyming.
**47. Companion:** Fellow (used to show contempt).

**CASSIUS.**              Away, away, be gone! [*Exit Poet.*]

**BRUTUS.** Lucilius and Titinius, bid the commanders
       Prepare to lodge their companies tonight.

**CASSIUS.** And come yourselves, and bring Messala with
140        you
       Immediately to us.        [*Exit Lucilius and Titinius.*]

**BRUTUS.**              Lucius, a bowl of wine. [*Exit Lucius.*]

**CASSIUS.** I did not think you could have been so angry.

**BRUTUS.** O Cassius, I am sick of many griefs.

**CASSIUS.** Of your philosophy you make no use,
145        If you give place to accidental evils.[48]

**48. Of your philosophy . . . accidental evils:** Brutus's philosophy was Stoicism. As a Stoic he believed that nothing evil would happen to a good man.

**BRUTUS.** No man bears sorrow better. Portia is dead.

**CASSIUS.** Ha? Portia?

**BRUTUS.** She is dead.

**CASSIUS.** How scaped I killing when I crossed you so?[49]
150        O insupportable and touching loss!
       Upon[50] what sickness?

**49. How scaped . . . you so?:** How did I escape being killed when I opposed you so?
**50. Upon:** As a result of.

**BRUTUS.**                    Impatient of my absence,
       And grief that young Octavius with Mark Antony
       Have made themselves so strong—for with her death
       That tidings came[51]—with this she fell distract,[52]
155        And (her attendants absent) swallowed fire.

**51. tidings:** News.
**52. fell distract:** Became distraught.

CASSIUS. And died so?

BRUTUS.                    Even so.

CASSIUS.                                        O ye immortal gods!

[*Enter Lucius, with wine and tapers.*]

BRUTUS. Speak no more of her. Give me a bowl of wine.
In this I bury all unkindness, Cassius.        [*Drinks.*]

CASSIUS. My heart is thirsty for that noble pledge.
160        Fill, Lucius, till the wine o'erswell the cup;
I cannot drink too much of Brutus' love.
                              [*Drinks. Exit Lucius.*]

[*Enter Titinius and Messala.*]

BRUTUS. Come in, Titinius! Welcome, good Messala.
Now sit we close about this taper here,
And call in question[53] our necessities.

CASSIUS. Portia, art thou gone?

165    BRUTUS.                          No more, I pray you.
Messala, I have here receivèd letters
That young Octavius and Mark Antony
Come down upon us with a mighty power,[54]
Bending their expedition toward Philippi.[55]

170    MESSALA. Myself have letters of the selfsame tenure.[56]

BRUTUS. With what addition?

MESSALA. That by proscription and bills of outlawry
Octavius, Antony, and Lepidus
Have put to death an hundred senators.

175    BRUTUS. Therein our letters do not well agree.
Mine speak of seventy senators that died
By their proscriptions, Cicero being one.

CASSIUS. Cicero one?

MESSALA.                Cicero is dead,
And by that order of proscription.
180        Had you your letters from your wife, my lord?

BRUTUS. No, Messala.

MESSALA. Nor nothing in your letters writ of her?

BRUTUS. Nothing, Messala.

MESSALA.                    That methinks is strange.

**53. call in question:**
Examine.

**54. power:** Army.
**55. Bending . . . Philippi**
(fi lip′ ī): Directing their
rapid march toward
Philippi.
**56. selfsame tenure:**
Same message.

**BRUTUS.** Why ask you? Hear you aught[57] of her in yours?

185   **MESSALA.** No, my lord.

**BRUTUS.** Now as you are a Roman, tell me true.

**MESSALA.** Then like a Roman bear the truth I tell,
For certain she is dead, and by strange manner.

**BRUTUS.** Why, farewell, Portia. We must die, Messala.
190   With meditating that she must die once,
I have the patience to endure it now.

**MESSALA.** Even so great men great losses should endure.

**CASSIUS.** I have as much of this in art[58] as you,
But yet my nature could not bear it so.

195   **BRUTUS.** Well, to our work alive.[59] What do you think
Of marching to Philippi presently?

**CASSIUS.** I do not think it good.

**BRUTUS.**                 Your reason?

**CASSIUS.**                     This it is:
'Tis better that the enemy seek us;
So shall he waste his means, weary his soldiers,
200   Doing himself offense,[60] whilst we, lying still,
Are full of rest, defense, and nimbleness.

**BRUTUS.** Good reasons must of force[61] give place to
    better.
The people 'twixt Philippi and this ground
Do stand but in a forced affection;[62]
205   For they have grudged us contribution.[63]
The enemy, marching along by them,
By them shall make a fuller number up,[64]
Come on refreshed, new-added[65] and encouraged;
From which advantage shall we cut him off
210   If at Philippi we do face him there,
These people at our back.

**CASSIUS.**               Hear me, good brother.

**BRUTUS.** Under your pardon.[66] You must note beside
That we have tried the utmost of our friends,
Our legions are brimful, our cause is ripe.
215   The enemy increaseth every day;
We, at the height, are ready to decline.
There is a tide in the affairs of men
Which, taken at the flood, leads on to fortune;
Omitted,[67] all the voyage of their life

**57. aught** (ôt) *n.*:
Anything at all.

**58. have . . . art:** Have as
much Stoicism in theory.
**59. to our work alive:** Let
us go about the work we
have to do as living men.

**60. offense:** Harm.

**61. of force:** Of necessity.

**62. Do stand . . .
affection:** Support us only
by fear of force.
**63. grudged us
contribution:** Given us aid
and supplies grudgingly.
**64. shall make . . . up:**
Will add more to their
numbers.
**65. new-added:**
Reinforced.

**66. Under your pardon:**
Excuse me.

**67. Omitted:** Neglected.

220    Is bound[68] in shallows and in miseries.
       On such a full sea are we now afloat,
       And we must take the current when it serves,
       Or lose our ventures.

       CASSIUS.            Then, with your will,[69] go on;
       We'll along ourselves and meet them at Philippi.

225    BRUTUS. The deep of night is crept upon our talk,
       And nature must obey necessity,
       Which we will niggard with a little rest.[70]
       There is no more to say?

       CASSIUS.            No more. Good night.
       Early tomorrow will we rise and hence.[71]

[*Enter Lucius.*]

       BRUTUS. Lucius, my gown.[72]            [*Exit Lucius.*]
230                     Farewell, good Messala.
       Good night, Titinius. Noble, noble Cassius,
       Good night, and good repose.

       CASSIUS.            O my dear brother,
       This was an ill beginning of the night.
       Never come[73] such division 'tween our souls!
       Let it not, Brutus.

[*Enter Lucius, with the gown.*]

235    BRUTUS.            Everything is well.

       CASSIUS. Good night, my lord.

       BRUTUS.            Good night, good brother.

       TITINIUS, MESSALA. Good night, Lord Brutus.

       BRUTUS.                 Farewell, every one.
                              [*Exit.*]
       Give me the gown. Where is thy instrument?[74]

       LUCIUS. Here in the tent.

       BRUTUS.            What, thou speak'st drowsily?
       Poor knave,[75] I blame thee not; thou art
240       o'erwatched.[76]
       Call Claudius and some other of my men;
       I'll have them sleep on cushions in my tent.

       LUCIUS. Varro and Claudius!

[*Enter Varro and Claudius.*]

       VARRO. Calls my lord?

**68. bound:** Confined.

**69. with your will:** As you wish.

**70. niggard . . . rest:** Satisfy stingily with a short sleep.

**71. hence:** Leave.

**72. gown:** Nightgown.

**73. Never come:** May there never come.

**74. instrument:** Lute (probably).

**75. knave** (nāv) *n.*: Servant.
**76. o'erwatched:** Weary with too much watchfulness.

**BRUTUS.** I pray you, sirs, lie in my tent and sleep.
It may be I shall raise[77] you by and by
On business to my brother Cassius.

**VARRO.** So please you, we will stand and watch your
pleasure.

**BRUTUS.** I will not have it so; lie down, good sirs;
It may be I shall otherwise bethink me.[78]

[*Varro and Claudius lie down.*]

Look. Lucius, here's the book I sought for so;
I put it in the pocket of my gown.

**LUCIUS.** I was sure your lordship did not give it me.

**BRUTUS.** Bear with me, good boy, I am much forgetful.
Canst thou hold up thy heavy eyes awhile,
And touch[79] thy instrument a strain or two?

**LUCIUS.** Ay, my lord, an't[80] please you.

**BRUTUS.**                                    It does, my boy.
I trouble thee too much, but thou art willing.

**LUCIUS.** It is my duty, sir.

**BRUTUS.** I should not urge thy duty past thy might;
I know young bloods[81] look for a time of rest.

**LUCIUS.** I have slept, my lord, already.

**BRUTUS.** It was well done, and thou shalt sleep again;
I will not hold thee long. If I do live,
I will be good to thee.

[*Music, and a song.*]

This is a sleepy tune. O murd'rous[82] slumber!
Layest thou thy leaden mace[83] upon my boy,
That plays thee music? Gentle knave, good night;
I will not do thee so much wrong to wake thee.
If thou dost nod, thou break'st thy instrument;
I'll take it from thee; and, good boy, good night.
Let me see, let me see; is not the leaf[84] turned down
Where I left reading? Here it is, I think.

[*Enter the Ghost of Caesar.*]

How ill this taper burns. Ha! Who comes here?
I think it is the weakness of mine eyes
That shapes this monstrous apparition.[85]
It comes upon[86] me. Art thou anything?
Art thou some god, some angel, or some devil,

**77. raise:** Wake.

**78. otherwise bethink
me:** Change my mind.

**79. touch:** Play.

**80. an't:** If it.

**81. bloods:** Constitutions.

**82. murd'rous:** Deathlike.
**83. mace** (mās) *n.*: Staff of
office (an allusion to the
practice of tapping a
person on the shoulder
with a mace when
arresting him).

**84. leaf:** Page.

**85. monstrous
apparition:** Ominous
ghost.
**86. upon:** Toward.

That mak'st my blood cold, and my hair to stare?[87]

280 Speak to me what thou art.

**GHOST.** Thy evil spirit, Brutus.

**BRUTUS.**                                    Why com'st thou?

**GHOST.** To tell thee thou shalt see me at Philippi.

**BRUTUS.** Well; then I shall see thee again?

**GHOST.** Ay, at Philippi.

285 **BRUTUS.** Why, I will see thee at Philippi then.

                                    [*Exit Ghost.*]
Now I have taken heart thou vanishest.
Ill spirit, I would hold more talk with thee.
Boy! Lucius! Varro! Claudius! Sirs, awake!
Claudius!

290 **LUCIUS.** The strings, my lord, are false.[88]

**BRUTUS.** He thinks he still is at his instrument.
Lucius, awake!

**LUCIUS.** My lord?

**BRUTUS.** Didst thou dream, Lucius, that thou so criedst
out?

295 **LUCIUS.** My lord, I do not know that I did cry.

**BRUTUS.** Yes, that thou didst. Didst thou see anything?

**LUCIUS.** Nothing, my lord.

**BRUTUS.** Sleep again, Lucius. Sirrah Claudius!
[*To Varro*] Fellow thou, awake!

300 **VARRO.** My lord?

**CLAUDIUS.** My lord?

**BRUTUS.** Why did you so cry out, sirs, in your sleep?

**BOTH.** Did we, my lord?

**BRUTUS.**                                    Ay. Saw you anything?

**VARRO.** No, my lord, I saw nothing.

**CLAUDIUS.**                                    Nor I, my lord.

305 **BRUTUS.** Go and commend me[89] to my brother Cassius;
Bid him set on his pow'rs betimes before,[90]
And we will follow.

**BOTH.**                                    It shall be done, my lord.   [*Exit.*]

**87. stare:** Stand on end.

**88. false:** Out of tune.

**89. commend:** Carry my greetings.
**90. set on ... before:** Advance his troops.

## THINKING ABOUT THE SELECTION

### Recalling

1. What three men rule Rome after Caesar's death? Describe each of them.
2. What is the immediate cause of the quarrel between Brutus and Cassius? How does Cassius defend himself?
3. How does Portia die? Describe Brutus's reaction and Cassius's reaction to the death.
4. What supernatural event occurs at the end of the act? Describe Brutus's reaction to the event.

### Interpreting

5. How is the argument between Brutus and Cassius different from the one between Octavius and Antony in scene i?
6. What does the ghost mean when he says to Brutus, "Thou shalt see me at Philippi"?

### Applying

7. Charles Dickens once wrote, "An idea, like a ghost, according to the common notion of ghosts, must be spoken to a little before it will explain itself." First discuss the meaning of this quotation. Then provide an explanation for Caesar's ghost.

## ANALYZING LITERATURE

### Understanding Conflict

This act contains the bitter quarrel between the two old friends Brutus and Cassius, a conflict that does much to reveal the characters' natures.

1. Discuss the argument: How does it begin? How does it build? How is it resolved?
2. What does the argument show us about the characters' natures? Use examples from the play to support your inferences.

## CRITICAL THINKING AND READING

### Analyzing Arguments

An **argument** is a course of reasoning intended to prove a point. For example, Brutus's speech to the Roman crowd in Act III was an argument suggesting that Caesar's assassination was necessary to preserve the freedom of Roman citizens.

Contrast Cassius's and Brutus's arguments about going to Philippi in Act IV, scene iii, lines 196–230. Whose arguments are stronger and more reasonable? Explain why.

## UNDERSTANDING LANGUAGE

### Understanding Figurative Language

A **metaphor** compares two things by identifying one with the other. The purpose of a metaphor is to suggest an insight into the nature of the two things compared. This metaphor, for example, suggests the desperation Octavius feels: ". . . for we are at the stake, / And bayed about with many enemies." (Act IV, scene i, lines 48–49) Octavius transfers to the triumvirate the qualities of a bear tied to the stake about to be attacked by dogs. The image conveys the rage of the Roman people and the seriousness of the triumvirate's position.

Explain briefly each of the metaphors that can be found where indicated.

1. Act IV, scene iii, lines 67–69
2. Act IV, scene iii, line 160
3. Act IV, scene iii, lines 217–220

## THINKING AND WRITING

### Rewriting in Contemporary Language

Rewrite in contemporary language the discussion between Brutus and Cassius in Act IV, scene iii, lines 196–230. As you work, try to make the dialogue in keeping with each man's character. When you have finished revising and proofreading your work, team up with a classmate to perform first one and then the other's version.

# GUIDE FOR READING

## The Tragedy of Julius Caesar, Act V

**Tragedy**

**Tragedy** is a dramatic form in which the main character is involved in a struggle of great significance that ends in disaster. This main character is a noble person whose ruin is caused by a **tragic flaw,** or weakness. The tragic flaw may be excessive ambition, pride, jealousy, and so on. Despite the character's nobility and worth, the character flaw leads to his or her eventual downfall.

**Look For**

As you read this final act, keep the definition of a tragedy in mind. Think about which of these elements of tragedy the play contains and watch for the way in which all these elements of tragedy come together here. Who is the noble hero? What is his character flaw? How does this weakness of character lead inevitably to his downfall?

**Writing**

Think of what you would consider a real-life, modern tragedy. It might involve a political leader, a sports hero, an explorer, a scientist, or someone else who was known and admired by many people and who was overcome by disaster. Remember that the disaster must have overcome the noble person because of a character flaw that he or she had. Describe that character flaw, what brought the tragedy about, and what its consequences were.

**Vocabulary**

Knowing the following words will help you as you read Act V of *The Tragedy of Julius Caesar.*

**Epicurus** (ep′ə kyoor′əs) *n.*: A Greek philosopher who tried to find freedom from physical pain and emotional disturbance (p. 423)

**ensign** (en′s'n) *n.*: Old word for a standard bearer; one who carries a flag (p. 423)

**envy** (en′vē) *n.*: Feeling of desire for another's possessions or qualities and jealousy at not having them (p. 432)

# Act V

**Scene i.** *The plains of Philippi.*

*[Enter Octavius, Antony, and their Army.]*

**OCTAVIUS.** Now, Antony, our hopes are answerèd;
    You said the enemy would not come down,
    But keep the hills and upper regions.
    It proves not so; their battles[1] are at hand;
5  They mean to warn[2] us at Philippi here,
    Answering before we do demand of them.[3]

**ANTONY.** Tut, I am in their bosoms,[4] and I know
    Wherefore[5] they do it. They could be content
    To visit other places, and come down
10  With fearful bravery,[6] thinking by this face[7]
    To fasten in our thoughts[8] that they have courage;
    But 'tis not so.

*[Enter a Messenger.]*

**MESSENGER.**           Prepare you, generals,
    The enemy comes on in gallant show;
    Their bloody sign[9] of battle is hung out,
15  And something to be done immediately.

**ANTONY.** Octavius, lead your battle softly[10] on
    Upon the left hand of the even[11] field.

**OCTAVIUS.** Upon the right hand I; keep thou the left.

**ANTONY.** Why do you cross me in this exigent?[12]

20  **OCTAVIUS.** I do not cross you; but I will do so.    *[March.]*

*[Drum. Enter Brutus, Cassius, and their Army; Lucilius, Titinius, Messala, and others.]*

**BRUTUS.** They stand, and would have parley.[13]

**CASSIUS.** Stand fast, Titinius, we must out and talk.

**OCTAVIUS.** Mark Antony, shall we give sign of battle?

**ANTONY.** No, Caesar, we will answer on their charge.[14]
25      Make forth;[15] the generals would have some words.

**OCTAVIUS.** Stir not until the signal.

**BRUTUS.** Words before blows; is it so, countrymen?

**1. battles:** Armies.
**2. warn:** Challenge.
**3. Answering . . . of them:** Appearing in opposition to us before we challenged them.
**4. am in their bosoms:** Know what they are thinking.
**5. Wherefore:** Why.
**6. fearful bravery:** Awesome show of bravery covering up their fear.
**7. face:** Appearance.
**8. fasten in our thoughts:** Convince us.

**9. bloody sign:** Red flag.

**10. softly:** Slowly.
**11. even:** Level.

**12. exigent:** Critical situation.

**13. parley:** Conference between enemies.

**14. answer their charge:** Meet their advance.
**15. Make forth:** Go forward.

**OCTAVIUS.** Not that we love words better, as you do.

**BRUTUS.** Good words are better than bad strokes, Octavius.

30 **ANTONY.** In your bad strokes, Brutus, you give good words;
Witness the hole you made in Caesar's heart,
Crying "Long live! Hail, Caesar!"

**CASSIUS.**                                    Antony,
The posture[16] of your blows are yet unknown;
But for your words, they rob the Hybla bees,[17]
And leave them honeyless.

35 **ANTONY.**                          Not stingless too.

**BRUTUS.** O, yes, and soundless too;
For you have stol'n their buzzing, Antony,
And very wisely threat before you sting.

**ANTONY.** Villains! You did not so, when your vile daggers
40 Hacked one another in the sides of Caesar.
You showed your teeth[18] like apes, and fawned like hounds,
And bowed like bondmen, kissing Caesar's feet;
Whilst damnèd Casca, like a cur, behind
Struck Caesar on the neck. O you flatterers!

45 **CASSIUS.** Flatterers! Now, Brutus, thank yourself;
This tongue had not offended so today,
If Cassius might have ruled.[19]

**OCTAVIUS.** Come, come, the cause.[20] If arguing make us sweat,
The proof[21] of it will turn to redder drops.
50 Look,
I draw a sword against conspirators.
When think you that the sword goes up[22] again?
Never, till Caesar's three and thirty wounds
Be well avenged; or till another Caesar
55 Have added slaughter to the sword of traitors.[23]

**BRUTUS.** Caesar, thou canst not die by traitors' hands,
Unless thou bring'st them with thee.

**OCTAVIUS.**                                    So I hope.
I was not born to die on Brutus' sword.

**16. posture:** Quality.
**17. Hybla bees:** Bees, from the town of Hybla in Sicily, noted for their sweet honey.

**18. showed your teeth:** Grinned.

**19. If Cassius might have ruled:** If Cassius had had his way when he urged that Antony be killed.
**20. cause:** Business at hand.
**21. proof:** Test.

**22. goes up:** Goes into its scabbard.

**23. till another Caesar . . . traitors:** Until I, another Caesar, have also been killed by you.

**BRUTUS.** O, if thou wert the noblest of thy strain,[24]
60  Young man, thou couldst not die more honorable.

**CASSIUS.** A peevish[25] schoolboy, worthless of such honor,
Joined with a masker and a reveler.[26]

**ANTONY.** Old Cassius still!

**OCTAVIUS.**                    Come, Antony; away!
Defiance, traitors, hurl we in your teeth.
65  If you dare fight today, come to the field;
If not, when you have stomachs.[27]
                    [*Exit Octavius, Antony, and Army.*]

**CASSIUS.** Why, now blow wind, swell billow, and swim bark![28]
The storm is up, and all is on the hazard.[29]

**BRUTUS.** Ho, Lucilius, hark, a word with you.
                    [*Lucilius and Messala stand forth.*]

**LUCILIUS.**                    My lord?
                [*Brutus and Lucilius converse apart.*]

**CASSIUS.** Messala.

**MESSALA.**                    What says my general?

70  **CASSIUS.**                    Messala,
This is my birthday; as this very day
Was Cassius born. Give me thy hand, Messala:
Be thou my witness that against my will
(As Pompey was)[30] am I compelled to set[31]
75  Upon one battle all our liberties.
You know that I held Epicurus strong,[32]
And his opinion; now I change my mind.
And partly credit things that do presage.[33]
Coming from Sardis, on our former[34] ensign
80  Two mighty eagles fell,[35] and there they perched,
Gorging and feeding from our soldiers' hands,
Who to Philippi here consorted[36] us.
This morning are they fled away and gone,
And in their steads do ravens, crows, and kites[37]
85  Fly o'er our heads and downward look on us
As we were sickly prey; their shadows seem
A canopy most fatal,[38] under which
Our army lies, ready to give up the ghost.

**MESSALA.** Believe not so.

**24. noblest of thy strain:** Best of your family.

**25. peevish:** Silly.

**26. a masker and a reveler:** One who takes part in masquerades and festivities.

**27. stomachs:** Appetites for battle.

**28. bark:** Ship.

**29. on the hazard:** At stake.

**30. As Pompey was:** Against his own judgment, Pompey was urged to do battle against Caesar. The battle resulted in Pompey's defeat and murder.

**31. set:** Stake.

**32. held Epicurus strong:** Believed in Epicurus's philosophy that the gods do not interest themselves in human affairs and that omens are merely superstitions.

**33. presage:** Foretell.

**34. former:** Foremost.

**35. fell:** Swooped down.

**36. consorted:** Accompanied.

**37. ravens . . . kites:** Birds that are bad omens.

**38. a canopy most fatal:** A rooflike covering foretelling death.

**CASSIUS.**                    I but believe it partly,
90      For I am fresh of spirit and resolved
        To meet all perils very constantly.[39]

**BRUTUS.** Even so, Lucilius.

**CASSIUS.**                    Now, most noble Brutus,
        The gods today stand friendly, that we may,
        Lovers in peace, lead on our days to age!
95      But since the affairs of men rests still incertain,[40]
        Let's reason with the worst that may befall.[41]
        If we do lose this battle, then is this
        The very last time we shall speak together.
        What are you then determinèd to do?

100     **BRUTUS.** Even by the rule of that philosophy
        By which I did blame Cato for the death
        Which he did give himself; I know not how,
        But I do find it cowardly and vile,
        For fear of what might fall, so to prevent
105     The time of life,[42] arming myself with patience
        To stay the providence[43] of some high powers
        That govern us below.

**CASSIUS.**                    Then, if we lose this battle,
        You are contented to be led in triumph[44]
        Thorough the streets of Rome?

110     **BRUTUS.** No, Cassius, no; think not, thou noble Roman,
        That ever Brutus will go bound to Rome;
        He bears too great a mind. But this same day
        Must end that work the ides of March begun;
        And whether we shall meet again I know not.
115     Therefore our everlasting farewell take.
        Forever, and forever, farewell, Cassius!
        If we do meet again, why, we shall smile;
        If not, why then this parting was well made.

**CASSIUS.** Forever, and forever, farewell, Brutus!
120     If we do meet again, we'll smile indeed;
        If not, 'tis true this parting was well made.

**BRUTUS.** Why then, lead on. O, that a man might know
        The end of this day's business ere it come!
        But it sufficeth that the day will end,
125     And then the end is known. Come, ho! Away! [*Exit.*]

**39. very constantly:** Most resolutely.

**40. rests still incertain:** Always remain uncertain.
**41. befall:** Happen.

**42. so to prevent . . . life:** Thus to anticipate the natural end of life.
**43. stay the providence:** Await the ordained fate.

**44. in triumph:** As a captive in the victor's procession.

**Scene ii.** *The field of battle.*

[*Call to arms sounds. Enter Brutus and Messala.*]

BRUTUS. Ride, ride, Messala, ride, and give these bills[1]
    Unto the legions on the other side.[2]

                        [*Loud call to arms.*]

    Let them set on at once; for I perceive
    But cold demeanor[3] in Octavius' wing,
5    And sudden push gives them the overthrow,[4]
    Ride, ride, Messala! Let them all come down.[5] [*Exit.*]

**Scene iii.** *The field of battle.*

[*Calls to arms sound. Enter Cassius and Titinius.*]

CASSIUS. O, look, Titinius, look, the villains[1] fly!
    Myself have to mine own turned enemy.[2]
    This ensign here of mine was turning back;
    I slew the coward, and did take it[3] from him.

5  TITINIUS. O Cassius, Brutus gave the word too early,
    Who, having some advantage on Octavius,
    Took it too eagerly; his soldiers fell to spoil,[4]
    Whilst we by Antony are all enclosed.

[*Enter Pindarus.*]

PINDARUS. Fly further off, my lord, fly further off!
10  Mark Antony is in your tents, my lord.
    Fly, therefore, noble Cassius, fly far off!

CASSIUS. This hill is far enough. Look, look, Titinius!
    Are those my tents where I perceive the fire?

TITINIUS. They are, my lord.

CASSIUS.                 Titinius, if thou lovest me,
15  Mount thou my horse and hide[5] thy spurs in him
    Till he have brought thee up to yonder troops
    And here again, that I may rest assured
    Whether yond troops are friend or enemy.

TITINIUS. I will be here again even with a thought.[6] [*Exit.*]

20  CASSIUS. Go, Pindarus, get higher on that hill;
    My sight was ever thick.[7] Regard[8] Titinius,
    And tell me what thou not'st about the field.

                       [*Exit Pindarus.*]

1. **bills:** Written orders.
2. **other side:** The wing of the army commanded by Cassius.
3. **cold demeanor** (di měn′ ər): Lack of spirit in their conduct.
4. **sudden push . . . overthrow:** Sudden attack will defeat them.
5. **Let . . . down:** Attack all at once.

1. **villains:** His own men.
2. **Myself . . . enemy:** I have become an enemy to my own soldiers.
3. **it:** The banner or standard.

4. **fell to spoil:** Began to loot.

5. **hide:** Sink.

6. **even with a thought:** As quick as a thought.

7. **thick:** Dim.
8. **Regard:** Observe.

This day I breathèd first. Time is come round,
And where I did begin, there shall I end.
25 My life is run his compass.⁹ Sirrah, what news?

PINDARUS. [*Above*] O my lord!

CASSIUS. What news?

PINDARUS. [*Above*] Titinius is enclosèd round about
With horsemen that make to him on the spur;¹⁰
30 Yet he spurs on. Now they are almost on him.
Now, Titinius! Now some light.¹¹ O, he lights too!
He's ta'en!¹² [*Shout.*] And, hark! They shout for joy.

CASSIUS. Come down; behold no more.
O, coward that I am, to live so long,
35 To see my best friend ta'en before my face!

[*Enter Pindarus.*]

Come hither, sirrah.
In Parthia did I take thee prisoner;
And then I swore thee, saving of thy life,
That whatsoever I did bid thee do,
40 Thou shouldst attempt it. Come now, keep thine
oath.
Now be a freeman, and with this good sword,
That ran through Caesar's bowels, search¹³ this
bosom.
Stand not¹⁴ to answer. Here, take thou the hilts,
And when my face is covered, as 'tis now,
45 Guide thou the sword—Caesar, thou art revenged,
Even with the sword that killed thee.         [*Dies.*]

PINDARUS. So, I am free; yet would not so have been,
Durst I have done my will. O Cassius!
Far from this country Pindarus shall run,
50 Where never Roman shall take note of him.   [*Exit.*]

[*Enter Titinius and Messala.*]

MESSALA. It is but change,¹⁵ Titinius; for Octavius
Is overthrown by noble Brutus' power,
As Cassius' legions are by Antony.

TITINIUS. These tidings will well comfort Cassius.

MESSALA. Where did you leave him?

55 TITINIUS.                              All disconsolate,
With Pindarus his bondman, on this hill.

**9. his compass:** Its full
course.

**10. make . . . spur:** Ride
toward him at top speed.

**11. light:** Dismount from
their horses.
**12. ta'en:** Taken;
captured.

**13. search:** Penetrate.

**14. Stand not:** Do not
wait.

**15. change:** An exchange.

**MESSALA.** Is not that he that lies upon the ground?

**TITINIUS.** He lies not like the living. O my heart!

**MESSALA.** Is not that he?

**TITINIUS.**                        No, this was he, Messala,
60    But Cassius is no more. O setting sun,
      As in thy red rays thou dost sink to night,
      So in his red blood Cassius' day is set.
      The sun of Rome is set. Our day is gone;
      Clouds, dews, and dangers come; our deeds are done!
65    Mistrust of my success[16] hath done this deed.

**16. Mistrust . . . success:**
Fear that I would not
succeed.

**MESSALA.** Mistrust of good success hath done this deed.
    O hateful Error, Melancholy's child,[17]
    Why dost thou show to the apt thoughts of men
    The things that are not?[18] O Error, soon conceived,[19]
70    Thou never com'st unto a happy birth,
    But kill'st the mother that engend'red thee![20]

**TITINIUS.** What, Pindarus! Where art thou, Pindarus?

**MESSALA.** Seek him, Titinius, whilst I go to meet
    The noble Brutus, thrusting this report
75    Into his ears. I may say "thrusting" it;
    For piercing steel and darts envenomèd[21]
    Shall be as welcome to the ears of Brutus
    As tidings of this sight.

**TITINIUS.**                Hie you, Messala,
    And I will seek for Pindarus the while. [*Exit Messala.*]

80    Why didst thou send me forth, brave[22] Cassius?
    Did I not meet thy friends, and did not they
    Put on my brows this wreath of victory,
    And bid me give it thee? Didst thou not hear their
        shouts?
    Alas, thou hast misconstrued everything!
85    But hold thee,[23] take this garland on thy brow;
    Thy Brutus bid me give it thee, and I
    Will do his bidding. Brutus, come apace,[24]
    And see how I regarded[25] Caius Cassius.
    By your leave,[26] gods. This is a Roman's part:[27]
90    Come, Cassius' sword, and find Titinius' heart. [*Dies.*]

[*Call to arms sounds. Enter Brutus, Messala, young Cato,
Strato, Volumnius, and Lucilius.*]

**BRUTUS.** Where, where, Messala, doth his body lie?

**MESSALA.** Lo, yonder, and Titinius mourning it.

**BRUTUS.** Titinius' face is upward.

**CATO.**                He is slain.

**BRUTUS.** O Julius Caesar, thou art mighty yet!
95    Thy spirit walks abroad, and turns our swords
    In our own proper entrails.[28]        [*Low calls to arms.*]

**CATO.**                Brave Titinius!
    Look, whe'r[29] he have not crowned dead Cassius.

---

**17. Melancholy's child:** One of despondent temperament.

**18. Why dost . . . are not?:** Why do you (despondent temperament) fill easily impressed men's thoughts with imagined fears?

**19. conceived:** Created.

**20. mother . . . thee:** Cassius (in this case) that conceived the error.

**21. envenomèd:** Poisoned.

**22. brave:** Noble.

**23. hold thee:** Wait a moment.

**24. apace:** Quickly.

**25. regarded:** Honored.

**26. By your leave:** With your permission.

**27. part:** Role; duty.

**28. own proper entrails:** Very own inner organs.

**29. whe'r:** Whether.

**BRUTUS.** Are yet two Romans living such as these?
　　　The last of all the Romans, fare thee well!
100　　It is impossible that ever Rome
　　　Should breed thy fellow.[30] Friends, I owe moe tears
　　　To this dead man than you shall see me pay.
　　　I shall find time, Cassius; I shall find time.
　　　Come, therefore, and to Thasos[31] send his body;
105　　His funerals shall not be in our camp,
　　　Lest it discomfort us.[32] Lucilius, come,
　　　And come, young Cato; let us to the field.
　　　Labeo and Flavius set our battles[33] on.
　　　'Tis three o'clock; and, Romans, yet ere night
110　　We shall try fortune in a second fight.　　　*[Exit.]*

**30. fellow:** Equal.

**31. Thasos:** An island not far from Philippi.

**32. discomfort us:** Discourage our soldiers.

**33. battles:** Armies.

---

**Scene iv.** *The field of battle.*

*[Call to arms sounds. Enter Brutus, Messala, young Cato, Lucilius, and Flavius.]*

　　**BRUTUS.** Yet, countrymen, O, yet hold up your heads!
　　　　　　　　*[Exit, with followers.]*

　　**CATO.** What bastard[1] doth not? Who will go with me?
　　　I will proclaim my name about the field.
　　　I am the son of Marcus Cato,[2] ho!
5　　　A foe to tyrants, and my country's friend.
　　　I am the son of Marcus Cato, ho!

*[Enter Soldiers and fight.]*

　　**LUCILIUS.** And I am Brutus, Marcus Brutus, I;
　　　Brutus, my country's friend; know me for Brutus![3]
　　　　　　　　　　　*[Young Cato falls.]*
　　　O young and noble Cato, art thou down?
10　　Why, now thou diest as bravely as Titinius,
　　　And mayst be honored, being Cato's son.

　　**FIRST SOLDIER.** Yield, or thou diest.

　　**LUCILIUS.**　　　　　　　　Only I yield to die.[4]
　　　There is so much that thou wilt kill me straight;[5]
　　　Kill Brutus, and be honored in his death.

15　　**FIRST SOLDIER.** We must not. A noble prisoner!

*[Enter Antony.]*

　　**SECOND SOLDIER.** Room, ho! Tell Antony, Brutus is ta'en.

**1. bastard:** Person who is not a true Roman.

**2. Marcus Cato:** Brutus's wife's father.

**3. And I am . . . Brutus:** Lucilius impersonates Brutus in order to protect him and confuse the enemy.

**4. Only . . . die:** I will surrender only to die.
**5. much . . . straight:** Much honor in it that you will kill me immediately.

**FIRST SOLDIER.** I'll tell thee news. Here comes the
    general.
    Brutus is ta'en, Brutus is ta'en, my lord.

**ANTONY.** Where is he?

20 **LUCILIUS.** Safe, Antony; Brutus is safe enough.
    I dare assure thee that no enemy
    Shall ever take alive the noble Brutus.
    The gods defend him from so great a shame!
    When you do find him, or alive or dead,
25    He will be found like Brutus, like himself.[6]

**ANTONY.** This is not Brutus, friend, but, I assure you,
    A prize no less in worth. Keep this man safe;
    Give him all kindness. I had rather have
    Such men my friends than enemies. Go on,
30    And see whe'r Brutus be alive or dead,
    And bring us word unto[7] Octavius' tent
    How everything is chanced.[8]                    [*Exit.*]

**Scene v.** *The field of battle.*

[*Enter Brutus, Dardanius, Clitus, Strato, and Volumnius.*]

**BRUTUS.** Come, poor remains[1] of friends, rest on this
    rock.

**CLITUS.** Statilius showed the torchlight,[2] but, my lord,
    He came not back; he is or ta'en or slain.

**BRUTUS.** Sit thee down, Clitus. Slaying is the word;
5    It is a deed in fashion. Hark thee, Clitus.[*Whispers.*]

**CLITUS.** What, I, my lord? No, not for all the world!

**BRUTUS.** Peace then, no words.

**CLITUS.**                          I'll rather kill myself.

**BRUTUS.** Hark thee, Dardanius.             [*Whispers.*]

**DARDANIUS.**                          Shall I do such a deed?

**CLITUS.** O Dardanius!

10 **DARDANIUS.** O Clitus!

**CLITUS.** What ill request did Brutus make to thee?

**DARDANIUS.** To kill him, Clitus. Look, he meditates.

**CLITUS.** Now is that noble vessel[3] full of grief,
    That it runs over even at his eyes.

---

**6. like himself:** Behaving
in a noble way.

**7. unto:** In.
**8. is chanced:** Has
happened.

**1. poor remains:** Pitiful
survivors.

**2. showed the torchlight:**
Signaled with a torch.

**3. vessel:** Human being.

15    **BRUTUS.** Come hither, good Volumnius; list[4] a word.

   **VOLUMNIUS.** What says my lord?

   **BRUTUS.**                     Why, this, Volumnius:
     The ghost of Caesar hath appeared to me
     Two several[5] times by night; at Sardis once,
     And this last night here in Philippi fields.
     I know my hour is come.

20    **VOLUMNIUS.**                Not so, my lord.

   **BRUTUS.** Nay, I am sure it is, Volumnius.
     Thou seest the world, Volumnius, how it goes;
     Our enemies have beat us to the pit.[6]

                       [*Low calls to arms.*]
It is more worthy to leap in ourselves
25     Than tarry till they push us.[7] Good Volumnius,
     Thou know'st that we two went to school together;
     Even for that our love of old, I prithee
     Hold thou my sword-hilts whilst I run on it.

   **VOLUMNIUS.** That's not an office[8] for a friend, my lord.

                    [*Call to arms still.*]

30    **CLITUS.** Fly, fly, my lord, there is no tarrying here.

   **BRUTUS.** Farewell to you; and you; and you, Volumnius.
     Strato, thou hast been all this while asleep;
     Farewell to thee too, Strato. Countrymen,
     My heart doth joy that yet in all my life
35     I found no man but he was true to me.
     I shall have glory by this losing day
     More than Octavius and Mark Antony
     By this vile conquest shall attain unto.[9]
     So fare you well at once, for Brutus' tongue
40     Hath almost ended his life's history.
     Night hangs upon mine eyes; my bones would rest,
     That have but labored to attain this hour.[10]

       [*Call to arms sounds. Cry within,* "*Fly, fly, fly!*"]

   **CLITUS.** Fly, my lord, fly!

   **BRUTUS.**            Hence! I will follow.
        [*Exit Clitus, Dardanius, and Volumnius.*]
     I prithee, Strato, stay thou by thy lord,
45     Thou art a fellow of a good respect.[11]
     Thy life hath had some smatch[12] of honor in it;
     Hold then my sword, and turn away thy face,
     While I do run upon it. Wilt thou, Strato?

**4. list:** Hear.

**5. several:** Separate.

**6. pit:** Trap or grave.

**7. tarry . . . us:** Wait until they kill us.

**8. office:** Task.

**9. By this . . . unto:** By this evil victory shall gain. (Brutus sees the victory of Octavius and Antony as causing the downfall of Roman freedom.)
**10. this hour:** Time of death.

**11. respect:** Reputation.
**12. smatch:** Smack or taste.

**STRATO.** Give me your hand first. Fare you well, my lord.

50 **BRUTUS.** Farewell, good Strato—Caesar, now be still;
  I killed not thee with half so good a will.          [*Dies.*]

[*Call to arms sounds. Retreat sounds. Enter Antony,
Octavius, Messala, Lucilius, and the Army.*]

**OCTAVIUS.** What man is that?

**MESSALA.** My master's man.[13] Strato, where is thy master?

**STRATO.** Free from the bondage you are in, Messala;
55  The conquerors can but make a fire of him.
  For Brutus only overcame himself,
  And no man else hath honor[14] by his death.

**LUCILIUS.** So Brutus should be found. I thank thee, Brutus,
  That thou hast proved Lucilius' saying[15] true.

60 **OCTAVIUS.** All that served Brutus, I will entertain them.[16]
  Fellow, wilt thou bestow[17] thy time with me?

**STRATO.** Ay, if Messala will prefer[18] me to you.

**OCTAVIUS.** Do so, good Messala.

**MESSALA.** How died my master, Strato?

65 **STRATO.** I held the sword, and he did run on it.

**MESSALA.** Octavius, then take him to follow thee,
  That did the latest service to my master.

**ANTONY.** This was the noblest Roman of them all.
  All the conspirators save[19] only he
70  Did that[20] they did in envy of great Caesar;
  He, only in a general honest thought
  And common good to all, made one of them.[21]
  His life was gentle,[22] and the elements
  So mixed[23] in him that Nature might stand up
75  And say to all the world, "This was a man!"

**OCTAVIUS.** According to his virtue,[24] let us use[25] him
  With all respect and rites of burial.
  Within my tent his bones tonight shall lie,
  Most like a soldier ordered honorably.[26]
80  So call the field[27] to rest, and let's away
  To part[28] the glories of this happy day.          [*Exit all.*]

---

**13. man:** Servant.

**14. no man else hath honor:** No other man gains honor.

**15. Lucilius' saying:** See Act V, Scene iv, line 25.
**16. entertain them:** Take them into my service.
**17. bestow:** Spend.
**18. prefer:** Recommend.

**19. save:** Except.
**20. that:** What.

**21. made one of them:** Became one of the conspirators.
**22. gentle:** Noble.
**23. so mixed:** Well-balanced.
**24. Virtue:** Excellence.
**25. use:** Treat.

**26. ordered honorably:** Treated with honor.
**27. field:** Army.
**28. part:** Share.

## THINKING ABOUT THE SELECTION

### Recalling

1. On whose birthday does the battle take place, and how does he feel about the battle?
2. Explain the misunderstanding that led to Cassius's death.
3. Why does Brutus think it is time to die?

### Interpreting

4. What does Cassius mean in Act V, scene i, lines 45–47?
5. What does Brutus mean by his final words: "Caesar, now be still; / I killed not thee with half so good a will"?
6. How and why does Antony's attitude toward Brutus change from the beginning of the act to the end?

### Applying

7. Who was the tragic hero of this play—Julius Caesar or Brutus? Form a team of three classmates to argue each side of a debate. Use evidence from the play to support your side's argument.

## ANALYZING LITERATURE

### Understanding Tragedy

The Greek philosopher Aristotle defined tragedy: "Tragedy, then, is an imitation of an action that is serious, complete, and of a certain magnitude." He explained that although the main character is noble, a tragedy must focus on action rather than on character development. The action should arouse feelings of pity and fear in the audience. The theme of a tragedy is the meaning of the central action and the main character's recognition of that meaning and its consequences.

1. What is the central action of this play?
2. What does Brutus see as the meaning of the central action and its consequences?
3. Explain the theme of this tragedy.

## CRITICAL THINKING AND READING

### Understanding Metaphorical Language

**Metaphorical language** describes one thing in terms of another. In Act V, scene i, line 87, for example, Cassius says the shadow of the birds of prey is a canopy, suggesting how dark and dense the shadow is.

Explain the metaphors that can be found where indicated.

1. Act V, scene iii, line 15;
2. Act V, scene v, line 13;
3. Act V, scene v, line 23;
4. Act V, scene v, line 41.

## UNDERSTANDING LANGUAGE

### Choosing Precise Words

Choosing a word with the precise meaning for a situation heightens the meaning of the entire sentence. For example, the word *hacked* in Antony's lines "your vile daggers / Hacked one another in the sides of Caesar." (Act V, scene i, lines 39–40) suggests the idea of mutilation, which the words, *cut* and *stabbed* do not.

Tell how the meaning of each underlined word differs slightly from the related words in parentheses.

1. peevish (Act V, scene i, line 61) (bothersome, fretful)
2. slew (Act V, scene iii, line 4) (killed, stabbed)
3. meditates (Act V, scene v, line 12) (thinks, reflects)

## THINKING AND WRITING

### Preparing an Argument

In Act V, scene i, lines 39–44, Antony launches a bitter verbal attack against Brutus and Cassius. Brutus, however, makes no attempt to respond. Write a short speech in which Brutus *does* respond to Antony's criticism. Keep your tone consistent both with the situation and with what you know of Brutus's character.

# Mapping

A **map** is a graphic representation of the parts of something. A **semantic map** is a graphic representation using language. Preparing a semantic map is an uncomplicated method of organizing the information you read. It is also a valuable study technique, since it provides a picture of how ideas are related.

**Steps**

Follow these steps to prepare a semantic map. First decide on the topic of your map. For example, for a play you might want to prepare a map that shows the connection between the plot, the characters, and the setting. Or you might want to make a map that shows the character traits of several characters. Then jot down the main ideas. Note the supporting details that back up your main ideas.

Once you have this information jotted down, you are ready to prepare a map. Determine what sort of diagram is best suited to organizing your information. The shape of the map should be functional; that is, it should make it easy to see the relationship between ideas.

When the skeleton of your map is completed, fill in the information you had jotted down and also the information you recall from memory. Then skim to find the information you can't remember and to check your facts.

You have probably noticed that a map is similar to an outline. However, it is a lot more flexible. Feel free to change the shape of your map as seems appropriate. In addition, expand it if you want by adding branches.

**Guidelines**

- Select the main ideas or concepts
- Identify supporting details
- Determine the best shape to show the relationships among the pieces of information
- Construct the map
- Fill in the map from your notes and from memory
- Fill in gaps by skimming
- Review your map to recall information

**Activity**   Use the following map skeleton to show the relationship between the parts of *Twelve Angry Men*. When filling it in, feel free to change the format slightly and to add and delete branches.

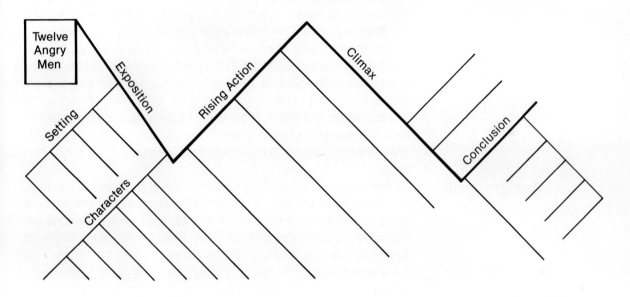

**Activity**   Make your own map to show similarities and differences between Julius Caesar, Brutus, and Mark Anthony in *The Tragedy of Julius Caesar*. Follow the previous guidelines in making your map.

# YOU THE WRITER

**Assignment**

**1.** A soliloquy is a lengthy speech in which a character speaks in great detail on a subject. Select one character from the plays you have just read who you think is especially well drawn. Write a soliloquy for this character in which he or she turns toward the audience and tells about another character.

**Prewriting.** List as many details about the character you have selected as you can.

**Writing.** Write the first draft of a soliloquy for the character you selected telling about another character in the play. Try to capture the voice of your character. Make sure the character uses persuasive techniques to persuade the audience of his or her opinion.

**Revising.** Revise your soliloquy, making sure it clearly conveys the narrator's opinion of another character. Is the supporting information organized in the most effective manner?

**Assignment**

**2.** Ask yourself, "What if?" in regard to one of the plays in this unit. For example, you might ask, "What if the defendant had been found guilty in *Twelve Angry Men,* or "What if the Martians had conquered the world in *Invasion from Mars?*" Then write a scene providing your ending to the play.

**Prewriting.** First select a play. Then freewrite, exploring your answer to the question, "What if?"

**Writing.** Write the first draft of your scene. Use the characters who already appear in the play you have chosen. Tell your new ending through dialogue.

**Revising.** When you revise, make sure you have followed the conventions of drama. Have you begun each speech by naming the speaker? Have you related events through dialogue? Have you included stage directions?

**Assignment**

**3.** *Julius Caesar* is based on an actual event from history. Write a short play dramatizing a historical incident.

**Prewriting.** First select your event. For example, you might select the Boston Tea Party or Amundsen's reaching the South Pole. List all the characters who would appear in your play. Use the clustering technique to generate as many ideas about your topic as you can.

**Writing.** Write the first draft of your play. Reveal what the characters are like through the use of dialogue.

**Revising.** When you revise, add any details that will make your event more dramatic. Proofread your play and prepare a final draft.

# YOU THE CRITIC

**Assignment**

**1.** Setting is the time and place of a play. It is also the political climate of the period. In drama the setting may play a very important role. It can affect what happens to the characters and what they learn from life. Choose a character from one of the plays you have read. Write an essay on how the setting affected his or her life.

**Prewriting.** Choose a play in which you think setting plays an important role. Brainstorm to develop a list of ideas of how settings affected characters.

**Writing.** Begin your essay with an introductory paragraph stating your thesis. Then go on to discuss how the specific setting of the drama affected the character. In the last paragraph, reach a conclusion about how the setting changed or affected the character's life.

**Revising.** Read over your essay. Edit for order, style, tone, vocabulary, and focus. Check to see that you have presented your points clearly and arranged them in a logical order.

**Assignment**

**2.** Making choices is a common theme in drama. Write an essay explaining how one character makes a choice and the result of this choice.

**Prewriting.** First select a play in which a character makes a choice. Freewrite, exploring this character's choice.

**Writing.** Write the first draft of an essay showing how the theme of making choices is developed in one of the plays in this unit. Support your thesis with details from the play.

**Revising.** When you revise, make sure you have provided adequate support for your thesis.

**Assignment**

**3.** Amy Lowell wrote, "Poetry and history are the textbooks to the heart of man. . . ." Write an essay revealing how Shakespeare reveals the heart of man in *Julius Caesar*.

**Prewriting.** First discuss the meaning of this quotation with your classmates. Make notes about how the meaning relates to *Julius Caesar*.

**Writing.** Begin your essay with a thesis statement. Include quotations from the play to support your thesis. End by restating your thesis.

**Revising.** Make sure you have supported your thesis with quotations from the play. Should you include additional quotations? Have you related your thesis to Amy Lowell's words? Have you arranged your support in an effective order? Proofread your essay and prepare a final draft.

**UNTITLED, 1968**
*Robert Rauschenberg*
*Collection of Whitney Museum of American Art*

438

# NONFICTION

Nonfiction is simply literature that is true, that is based on facts—real people, actual places, and true incidents. Writers of nonfiction concern themselves with reality, not with the world of the imagination. This area of literature includes biographies, autobiographies, and essays.

Autobiographies and biographies try to create a portrait of an individual with words instead of paint. While some autobiographies and biographies are written about famous people, many are stories of individuals who have lived interesting lives or have lived ordinary lives in an interesting way. An autobiography tells of the events, experiences, and impressions in the life of the writer. It reveals the qualities and character of its subject. Since an autobiography is written by the individual, it will be a subjective work. A biography also reveals the character of the subject, but it is written by another person. Some biographers try to present the facts objectively and let the reader interpret the character and life of their subject, but most make subjective interpretations for the reader. These two forms of nonfiction can be considered types of history with a point of view and information about a way of life.

The word *essay* comes from the French *essais,* meaning "attempts" or "tries." One of the most flexible forms of literature, essays literally try out ideas about a subject on the reader. This literary form can be formal or informal; entertaining, persuasive, explanatory, or instructive; and can be written in any of the four major forms of discourse—description, exposition, narration, or persuasion. The subject matter can range from serious to silly.

Although nonfiction by definition must be based on fact, it shares many elements with fiction. Character can be developed, settings established, suspense built, and theme or purpose presented. Nonfiction can entertain just as fiction can present serious concerns and ideas about life.

As you read the selections in this unit, be aware of the elements that nonfiction shares with fiction. Notice the great variety within the nonfiction form—its ability to instruct, inform, amuse, and entertain. Note how the writers blend creative details with factual information.

# Nonfiction

Active readers are those who keep in mind their own experiences while they read, interpreting the literary work according to what they know. As they read, they take an active role: they ask themselves questions about the information presented and try to predict where this information will lead. Through such active involvement, they enhance their own understanding of what they read.

You, too, can become an active reader through use of the following strategies.

**Question**  Ask yourself questions about the information presented. What does the author reveal about the subject? What conclusions does he or she reach? Are these conclusions based on the information provided? Furthermore, ask yourself what the author's purpose is in writing. Does the author want to persuade you to think or act in a particular way?

**Predict**  Think about your own experience in or knowledge about this subject. Based on this information, try to predict what conclusions the author might make. As you continue reading, you will see how accurate your predictions are.

**Clarify**  As you read, search for the answers to the questions you ask yourself, and check how accurate your predictions are. This will help you monitor your own reading and will enhance your understanding of the information the author presents. Check in a dictionary any words that are unfamiliar to you, and check in a reference book any information that seems inaccurate.

**Summarize**  Pause occasionally while you read to summarize the information that has been presented. What points has the author made? What statements support these points?

**Pull It Together**  Determine and state the main idea of the selection as a whole. What information did you gain about the subject? How do you react to the information that has been presented?

On the following page is a model of how to read an essay actively.

# The Dog That Bit People

James Thurber

**Questions:** The meaning of the title seems clear, but whose dog is this? Does it belong to the writer or to someone else? Is it a famous dog?

Probaby no one man should have as many dogs in his life as I have had, but there was more pleasure than distress in them for me except in the case of an Airedale named Muggs. He gave me more trouble than all the other fifty-four or -five put together, although my moment of keenest embarrassment was the time a Scotch terrier named Jeannie, who had just had six puppies in the clothes closet of a fourth floor apartment in New York, had the unexpected seventh and last at the corner of Eleventh Street and Fifth Avenue during a walk she had insisted on taking. Then, too, there was the prize winning French poodle, a great big black poodle—none of your little, untroublesome white miniatures—who got sick riding in the rumble seat[1] of a car with me on her way to the Greenwich Dog Show. She had a red rubber bib tucked around her throat and, since a rain storm came up when we were halfway through the Bronx, I had to hold over her a small green umbrella, really more of a parasol. The rain beat down fearfully and suddenly the driver of the car drove into a big garage, filled with mechanics. It happened so quickly that I forgot to put the umbrella down and I will always remember, with sickening distress, the look of incredulity mixed with hatred that came over the face of the particular hardened garage man that came over to see what we wanted, when he took a look at me and the poodle. All garage men, and people of that intolerant stripe, hate poodles with their curious hair cut, especially the pom-poms that you got to leave on their hips if you expect the dogs to win a prize.

**Prediction:** Perhaps the writer will discuss how Muggs gave him distress.

**Clarification:** First the writer is describing other dogs who gave him distress.

---

**1. rumble seat:** In some earlier automobiles, an open seat in the rear, behind the roofed seat, which could be folded shut when not in use.

But the Airedale, as I have said, was the worst of all my dogs. He really wasn't my dog, as a matter of fact: I came home from a vacation one summer to find that my brother Roy had bought him while I was away. A big, burly, choleric[2] dog, he always acted as if he thought I wasn't one of the family. There was a slight advantage in being one of the family, for he didn't bite the family as often as he bit strangers. Still, in the years that we had him he bit everybody but mother, and he made a pass at her once but missed. That was during the month when we suddenly had mice, and Muggs refused to do anything about them. Nobody ever had mice exactly like the mice we had that month. They acted like pet mice, almost like mice somebody had trained. They were so friendly that one night when mother entertained at dinner the Friraliras, a club she and my father had belonged to for twenty years, she put down a lot of little dishes with food in them on the pantry floor so that the mice would be satisfied with that and wouldn't come into the dining room. Muggs stayed out in the pantry with the mice, lying on the floor, growling to himself—not at the mice, but about all the people in the next room that he would have liked to get at. Mother slipped out into the pantry once to see how everything was going. Everything was going fine. It made her so mad to see Muggs lying there, oblivious of the mice—they came running up to her—that she slapped him and he slashed at her, but didn't make it. He was sorry immediately, mother said. He was always sorry, she said, after he bit someone, but we could not understand how she figured this out. He didn't act sorry.

Mother used to send a box of candy every Christmas to the people the Airedale bit. The list finally contained forty or more names. Nobody could understand why we didn't get rid of the dog. I didn't understand it very well myself, but we didn't get rid of him. I think that one or two people tried to poison Muggs—he acted poisoned once in a while—and old Major Moberly fired at him once with his service revolver near the Seneca Hotel in East Broad Street—but Muggs lived to be almost eleven years old and even when he could hardly get around he bit a Congressman who had called to see my father on business. My mother had never liked the Congressman

---

**2. choleric** (käl′ ər ik) *adj.*: Quick-tempered.

Nobody Knew Exactly What Was the Matter with Him

—she said the signs of his horoscope[3] showed he couldn't be trusted (he was Saturn with the moon in Virgo)—but she sent him a box of candy that Christmas. He sent it right back, probably because he suspected it was trick candy. Mother persuaded herself it was all for the best that the dog had bitten him, even though father lost an important business association because of it. "I wouldn't be associated with such a man," mother said, "Muggs could read him like a book."

**Question:** Why does Mother take this attitude about Muggs biting the Congressman?

We used to take turns feeding Muggs to be on his good side, but that didn't always work. He was never in a very good humor, even after a meal. Nobody knew exactly what was the matter with him, but whatever it was it made him irascible, especially in the mornings. Roy never felt very well in the morning, either, especially before breakfast, and once when he came downstairs and found that Muggs had moodily chewed up the morning paper he hit him in the face with a

**Clarification:** The entire family goes out of its way to deal with Muggs.

---

**3. horoscope** (hôr′ ə skōp′) *n.*: The position of the planets and stars with relation to one another at a given time, especially at the time of a person's birth.

grapefruit and then jumped up on the dining room table, scattering dishes and silverware and spilling the coffee. Muggs' first free leap carried him all the way across the table and into a brass fire screen in front of the gas grate but he was back on his feet in a moment and in the end he got Roy and gave him a pretty vicious bite in the leg. Then he was all over it; he never bit anyone more than once at a time. Mother always mentioned that as an argument in his favor; she said he had a quick temper but that he didn't hold a grudge. She was forever defending him. I think she liked him because he wasn't well. "He's not strong," she would say, pityingly, but that was inaccurate; he may not have been well but he was terribly strong.

Question: Why does Mother defend Muggs's outrageous behavior?

One time my mother went to the Chittenden Hotel to call on a woman mental healer who was lecturing in Columbus on the subject of "Harmonious Vibrations." She wanted to find out if it was possible to get harmonious vibrations into a dog. "He's a large tan-colored Airedale," mother explained. The woman said that she had never treated a dog but she advised my mother to hold the thought that he did not bite and would not bite. Mother was holding the thought the very next morning when Muggs got the iceman but she blamed that slip-up on the iceman. "If you didn't think he would bite you, he wouldn't," mother told him. He stomped out of the house in a terrible jangle of vibrations.

Prediction: Maybe this will affect Muggs's behavior.

One morning when Muggs bit me slightly, more or less in passing, I reached down and grabbed his short stumpy tail and hoisted him into the air. It was a foolhardy thing to do and the last time I saw my mother, about six months ago, she said she didn't know what possessed me. I don't either, except that I was pretty mad. As long as I held the dog off the floor by his tail he couldn't get at me, but he twisted and jerked so, snarling all the time, that I realized I couldn't hold him that way very long. I carried him to the kitchen and flung him onto the floor and shut the door on him just as he crashed against it. But I forgot about the backstairs. Muggs went up the backstairs and down the frontstairs and had me cornered in the living room. I managed to get up onto the mantelpiece above the fireplace, but it gave way and came down with a tremendous crash throwing a large marble clock, several vases, and myself heavily to the floor. Muggs was so alarmed by the racket that when I picked myself up he had disappeared. We couldn't find him anywhere, although we whistled and shouted, until old Mrs. Detweiler called after dinner that night. Muggs had bitten her once, in the leg, and she came into the living room only after we assured her that Muggs had run away. She had just seated herself when, with a great growling and scratching of claws, Muggs emerged from under a davenport[4] where he had been quietly hiding all the time, and bit her again. Mother examined the bite and put arnica[5] on it and told Mrs. Detweiler that it was only a bruise. "He just bumped you," she said. But Mrs. Detweiler left the house in a nasty state of mind.

**Clarification:** No, Muggs's behavior remains the same.

Lots of people reported our Airedale to the police but my father held a municipal office at the time and was on friendly terms with the police. Even so, the cops had been out a couple of times—once when Muggs bit Mrs. Rufus Sturtevant and again when he bit Lieutenant-Governor Malloy—but mother told them that it hadn't been Muggs' fault but the fault of the people who were bitten. "When he starts for them, they scream," she explained, "and that excites him." The cops

**Clarification:** This is another example of Mother's defending Muggs's behavior.

---

4. **davenport** (dav′ ən pôrt′) *n.*: A large couch or sofa.
5. **arnica** (är′ ni kə) *n.*: A preparation made from certain plants, once used for treating sprains, bruises, and so forth.

Lots of People Reported Our Dog to the Police

suggested that it might be a good idea to tie the dog up, but mother said that it mortified him to be tied up and that he wouldn't eat when he was tied up.

**Clarification:** This is another way Muggs distressed people.

Muggs at his meals was an unusual sight. Because of the fact that if you reached toward the floor he would bite you, we usually put his food plate on top of an old kitchen table with a bench alongside the table. Muggs would stand on the bench and eat. I remember that my mother's Uncle Horatio, who boasted that he was the third man up Missionary Ridge,[6] was splutteringly indignant when he found out that we fed the dog on a table because we were afraid to put his plate on the floor. He said he wasn't afraid of any dog that ever lived and that he would put the dog's plate on the floor if we would give it to

**Clarification:** Roy is implying that Muggs would have been so terrifying that Uncle Horatio would have had to run to the front of the battle line.

him. Roy said that if Uncle Horatio had fed Muggs on the ground just before the battle he would have been the first man up Missionary Ridge. Uncle Horatio was furious. "Bring him in! Bring him in now!" he shouted. "I'll feed the—on the floor!" Roy was all for giving him a chance, but my father wouldn't hear of it. He said that Muggs had already been fed. "I'll feed him again!" bawled Uncle Horatio. We had quite a time quieting him.

**Question:** Muggs upsets the household's routine. Will they continue to put up with him?

In his last year Muggs used to spend practically all of his time outdoors. He didn't like to stay in the house for some reason or other—perhaps it held too many unpleasant memories for him. Anyway, it was hard to get him to come in and as a result the garbage man, the iceman, and the laundryman wouldn't come near the house. We had to haul the garbage down to the corner, take the laundry out and bring it back, and meet the iceman a block from home. After this had gone on for some time we hit on an ingenious arrangement for getting the dog in the house so that we could lock him up while the gas meter was read, and so on. Muggs was afraid of only one thing, an electrical storm. Thunder and lightning frightened him out of his senses (I think he thought a storm had broken the day the mantelpiece fell). He would rush into the house and hide under a bed or in a clothes closet. So we fixed up a thunder machine out of a long narrow piece of sheet iron with a wooden handle on one end. Mother would shake this vigorously when she wanted to get Muggs into the

**Clarification:** The family adapts itself—no matter how oddly—to Muggs's habits.

**6. Missionary Ridge:** A height south of Chattanooga, Tennessee, that was the site of a Civil War battle.

house. It made an excellent imitation of thunder, but I suppose it was the most roundabout system for running a household that was ever devised. It took a lot out of mother.

A few months before Muggs died, he got to "seeing things." He would rise slowly from the floor, growling low, and stalk stiff-legged and menacing toward nothing at all. Sometimes the Thing would be just a little to the right or left of a visitor. Once a Fuller Brush salesman got hysterics. Muggs came wandering into the room like Hamlet[7] following his father's ghost. His eyes were fixed on a spot just to the left of the Fuller Brush man, who stood it until Muggs was about three slow, creeping paces from him. Then he shouted. Muggs wavered on past him into the hallway grumbling to himself but the Fuller man went on shouting. I think mother had to throw a pan of cold water on him before he stopped. That was the way she used to stop us boys when we got into fights.

Muggs died quite suddenly one night. Mother wanted to bury him in the family lot under a marble stone with some such inscription as "Flights of angels sing thee to thy rest" but we persuaded her it was against the law. In the end we just put up a smooth board above his grave along a lonely road. On the board I wrote with an indelible pencil "Cave Canem."[8] Mother was quite pleased with the simple classic dignity of the old Latin epitaph.

**Summarize:** Muggs's outrageous behavior progressively grows worse till the end of his life, and the family always adjusts to it.

**Pulling It Together:** In spite of Muggs's distressing habits, Mother was fond of him, and the family humored her in her attitude toward Muggs.

---

**7. Hamlet:** The tragic hero of the play *Hamlet* by William Shakespeare. Hamlet follows his father's ghost and learns that his father, a Danish king, had been murdered by Hamlet's uncle Claudius.
**8. Cave canem** (kä′ vä kä′ nəm): Latin for *Beware the dog.*

---

**James Thurber** (1894–1961) was a celebrated American humorist. Born in Columbus, Ohio, Thurber worked as a code clerk in the U.S. State Department and as a journalist. Much of his work first appeared in *The New Yorker* magazine. Thurber's works often humorously describe the anxieties of the average individual in modern society. Many of his works include cartoons of frightened men, menacing women, wicked children, and sad dogs. "The Dog That Bit People" is an example of Thurber's hilarious style.

## THINKING ABOUT THE SELECTION

### Recalling

1. What is Muggs's most troublesome quality?
2. In dealing with Muggs, what is the advantage in being one of the family?
3. Describe Thurber's "foolhardy" experience with Muggs.
4. How does Mother explain that Muggs's reaction is the fault of other people?
5. How does Muggs eat his meals? Why does he eat this way?
6. How does Mother get Muggs into the house? Why does this method work?

### Interpreting

7. How does Thurber feel about Muggs? Find evidence in the selection to support your answer.
8. Describe Mother. Find evidence in the selection to support your answer.

### Applying

9. Thurber describes an aspect of his home life in a humorous way. What other aspects of daily life could be the subject of a humorous essay?

## ANALYZING LITERATURE

### Understanding the Humorous Essay

A **humorous essay** is a nonfiction composition that presents the author's thoughts on a subject in an amusing way. This lighthearted approach is intended to make the reader laugh.

A writer may create humor in an essay by describing a ridiculous situation in a serious way, or by using exaggeration. Some writers may use anecdotes to enhance the humor of the essay, as Thurber does by describing Muggs trying to bite Roy.

1. Give an example of a ridiculous situation that Thurber describes in a serious way.
2. Give two examples of anecdotes that Thurber uses to enhance the humor of the essay.

## CRITICAL THINKING AND READING

### Supporting the Main Idea

A writer uses details to support the main idea of a literary work. Such details may include descriptions, phrases, examples, or anecdotes that provide evidence for the main idea. In "The Dog That Bit People," the main idea is that Muggs gave Thurber more distress than pleasure.

Give two examples of details from the essay that support this main idea.

## UNDERSTANDING LANGUAGE

### Appreciating Synonyms

A **synonym** is a word that has the same or almost the same meaning as another word. For example, *fury* is a synonym for *rage*.

Choose the word that is nearest in meaning to the following italicized words.

1. *mortified*
   - a. amused
   - b. humiliated
   - c. strengthened
   - d. hungry
2. *indelible*
   - a. eliminated
   - b. chalky
   - c. permanent
   - d. inky

## THINKING AND WRITING

### Describing a Pet

Pets sometimes seem more human than humans, with personalities that make their relationship with their owners seem outrageously funny to outsiders. Select an irascible, or irritable, pet that you have owned, have read about, or have seen in a television show or movie. (If you like, you may make up a pet.) List all the traits that make up this pet's peculiar personality. Using this list as your starting point, write an essay describing the animal. You may want to use exaggeration to make the pet's personality seem even more outrageous. When you revise, make sure you have included enough details to create a vivid picture of the pet. Proofread your essay and share it with your classmates.

# Biographies and
# Personal Accounts

**DIEGO MARTELLI**
*Edgar Degas*
National Gallery of Scotland, Edinburgh

## Emily Dickinson

**Van Wyck Brooks** (1886–1963) was born in Plainfield, New Jersey. After graduating from Harvard University, he lived in Europe for several years and then taught at Stanford University. Shortly after his first book was published in 1909, he became well known as a writer of biography, criticism, and the history of American literature. *The Flowering of New England,* which was the first volume of that history, was a best seller and won Brooks the Pulitzer Prize in 1937. In this essay he explores Emily Dickinson's life.

### Characterization in Biography

The facts about a person's life can be obtained in an encyclopedia or other reference book. A biography attempts to go beyond the facts and portray the subject as a real person. By knowing the subject's joys, sorrows, problems, and influences, you gain a better understanding of the character of the subject. In this essay, Brooks presents the character of Emily Dickinson in great detail.

### Look For

Brooks wants you to understand what kind of person Emily Dickinson was. As you read "Emily Dickinson," look for the passages where Brooks interprets the factual evidence, suggesting what Dickinson might have been thinking or feeling about certain events in her life. How does this increase your understanding of her actions?

### Writing

Brooks's presentation of Emily Dickinson's character helps you understand her unique style of poetry. Think about someone you admire, such as a professional athlete, a singer, or a writer. Write down the character traits that would have contributed to the person's success and give your reasons for admiring the person.

### Vocabulary

Knowing the following words will help you as you read "Emily Dickinson."

**propriety** (prə prī'ə tē) *n.*: The quality of being proper, fitting, or suitable (p. 451)

**punctilious** (puŋk til'ē əs) *adj.*: Very careful about every detail of behavior (p. 451)

**abated** (ə bāt''d) *v.*: Lessened; ended (p. 451)

**malign** (mə līn') *adj.*: Evil; harmful (p. 452)

**cryptic** (krip' tik) *adj.*: Having a hidden meaning (p. 452)

**transcendental** (tran sen den'tl) *adj.*: Supernatural; not concrete (p. 453)

# Emily Dickinson

## Van Wyck Brooks

The Dickinsons lived in the principal house in Amherst. A large, square, red-brick mansion that stood behind a hemlock hedge, with three gates accurately closed, it was a symbol of rural propriety and all the substantialities of western New England. Edward Dickinson, the lawyer, had always had his office in the village and four times a day, in his broadcloth coat and beaver hat, with a gold-headed cane in his hand, he had passed through one of the gates, going or coming. A thin, severe punctilious man who had once been a member of Congress, a friend of Daniel Webster[1] in his youth, a Calvinist[2] of the strictest persuasion, he was a pillar of Amherst College until his death in 1874. The college had been founded, largely by his father, to check the sort of errors that were spreading from Harvard, and he never abated his rigor in the interests of pleasure. He was said to have laughed on one occasion, but usually he was as cold and still as the white marble mantel in his parlor. The story was told in Amherst, however, that once he had rung the church bell, as if to summon the people to a fire. The whole town came running, for he rang the bell excitedly. He wished to call attention to the sunset.

*Tintype of Emily Dickinson*

Next door, behind the hemlock hedge, another ample dwelling stood, suggesting in its style an Italian villa. Here lived the Squire's son Austin, once his partner, who kept open house for the college. While the Dickinson mansion was somewhat forbidding, with the stamp of the Squire's grim ways and his invalid wife, the villa was a

---

**1. Daniel Webster** (1782–1852): U. S. statesman and orator.
**2. Calvinist** (kal′ vin ist) *n.*: Follower of the theology of John Calvin (1509–1564), which emphasized the doctrine of predestination, salvation solely by God's grace, and a strict moral code.

center of Hampshire hospitality that shared its rolling lawns and charming garden. Olmsted[3] had visited there, when he was planning Central Park, to examine the shrubs and trees, the plants and flowers; and distinguished guests at the college commencements and lecturers during the winter season were received and welcomed there as nowhere else. Emerson, Phillips, Beecher and Curtis[4] had stayed in this house next door, and Samuel Bowles of the *Springfield Republican* was an intimate friend of all the Dickinsons. The *Republican* was a school for journalists, known far and wide, and travelers,—Dickens and Kingsley[5] among them,—constantly stopped at Springfield in order to have a chat with Samuel Bowles. His paper was a sovereign authority in Amherst, and he often drove over for a call at the villa or the mansion, sometimes bringing manuscripts by well-known authors to show the Dickinson daughters before they were published. His favorite was Emily, who was older than Lavinia, but Emily usually "elfed it" when visitors came. She was always in the act of disappearing. Through the blinds of her western windows, overlooking the garden, she observed the hospitalities of the villa, and snatches of whatever was current in the books and talk of a college town, in the politics and thought of the moment, reached her when the guests had gone away. But even her oldest friends seldom saw her. While sometimes, in the evening, she flitted across the garden, she never left the place by day or night. To have

caught a fleeting glimpse of her was something to boast of, and a young girl across the way who watched at night for a light at her window was thrilled if Miss Emily's shadow appeared for a moment. There were nursemaids who thought she was a witch. They frightened the children by uttering her name, as if there were something malign in Miss Dickinson's queerness.

While her friends seldom saw her, and almost never face to face,—for she spoke from the shadows of the hallway, as they sat in the parlor, or sometimes down the stairs, —they were used to receiving little letters from her. These letters were also peculiar. Miss Dickinson rarely addressed the envelopes. Some other hand, perhaps her sister's, performed this office for her. More often the names of the person and town had been clipped from a printed paper and pasted together, as if it were a sort of violation to expose the strokes of her pen to the touch of the postman. The letters themselves were brief and cryptic, usually only a line or two: "Do you look out tonight?" for example. "The moon rides like a girl through a topaz town." Or "The frogs sing sweet today —they have such pretty, lazy times—how nice to be a frog." Or "Tonight the crimson children are playing in the West." Or "The lawn is full of south and the odors tangle, and I hear today for the first the river in the tree." Now and again, some fine phrase emerged from the silvery spray of words, —"Not what the stars have done, but what they are to do, is what detains the sky." Sometimes her notes had a humorous touch: "Father steps like Cromwell[6] when he gets the kindlings," or "Mrs. S. gets bigger, and rolls down the lane to church like a reverend marble." But her messages

---

**3. Olmsted:** Frederick Law Olmsted (1822–1903): The landscape architect who designed New York City's Central Park.

**4. Emerson . . . Curtis:** Men active in the intellectual life of the United States.

**5. Dickens and Kingsley:** Charles Dickens (1812–1870) and Charles Kingsley (1819–1875), English novelists.

---

**6. Cromwell:** Oliver Cromwell (1599–1658), English revolutionary leader.

often contained no words at all. She would lower baskets of goodies out of the window to children waiting below. At times, instead of a letter, she sent a poem, an odd little fragment of three or four lines, with a box of chocolate caramels or frosted cakes and a flower or a sprig of pine on top, heliotrope, perhaps, or an oleander blossom or a dandelion tied with a scarlet ribbon. Her letters were rhythmical, they scanned like the poems, and they were congested with images,—every phrase was an image; and the poems themselves suggested nursery rhymes or Dr. Watts's hymns, broken up and filled with a strange new content. They might have struck unsympathetic readers as a sort of transcendental baby talk. It was evident that Miss Dickinson had lost the art of communication, as the circle of her school friends understood it. She vibrated towards them, she put forth shy, impalpable[7] tentacles, she instantly signalized with a verse or a note every event in their lives. But she did not speak the language of the world outside her, and one gathered that she did not wish to touch it. She was rapt in a private world of sensations and thoughts. It was even observed that her handwriting went through three distinct phases and that towards the end the letters never touched. Each character, separately formed, stood quite alone.

She had been a recluse since the early sixties, and her family surmised the reason. She had fallen in love with a married man, a Philadelphia clergyman, and had buried herself at home by way of refuge. When her supposed lover supposedly pursued her there, her sister dashed across to the house next door and exclaimed to their brother Austin's wife, "Sue, come! That man is here. Father and mother are away, and I am

afraid Emily will go away with him." Such was the family legend, which may have been apocryphal.[8] Undoubtedly, the clergyman came to see her, but probably only to call. Was he in love with Emily? Probably not. In any case, she did not go away. She withdrew from all activities outside the household, and her mind turned in upon itself. She had hitherto been eminently social, or as much so as her little world permitted. Born in 1830, in the red-brick mansion, she had grown up a lively girl who was always a center of attention. She was a capital[9] mimic. She travestied[10] the young-lady pieces, the "Battle of Prague" and others, which she played on the mahogany piano, and her old and funny stories enthralled her friends. Later they remembered that she placed bouquets of flowers in the pews of those she liked best, at church. Helen Hunt Jackson, now a well-known writer, had been her favorite playmate in early childhood. Dancing and card playing were not allowed in Amherst, but Noah Webster's granddaughter, who lived there, evaded the prohibition on behalf of her circle. She held "P.O.M." meetings for the Poetry of Motion, and Emily Dickinson excelled in this branch of learning. She joined in picnics and walks over the Amherst hills with groups of boys and girls from the town and the college. They had "sugaring-off" parties and valentine parties, and they often climbed Mount Norwottuck where they found ferns and lady-slippers; and sometimes they met at a brookside in the woods, where the boys went fishing and the girls made chowder. Emily was an ardent botanist. She knew the haunts of all the wild flowers in the region,

---

**7. impalpable** (im pal' pə b'l) *adj.*: That which cannot be felt by touching.

**8. apocryphal** (ə pä' krə f'l) *adj.*: Fictitious; false.
**9. capital** (kap' ə t'l) *adj.*: Excellent.
**10. travestied** (trav' is tēd) *v.*: Ridiculed; represented in a crude, distorted, or ridiculous way.

and sometimes she scrambled alone through the forest, perhaps with her big dog Carlo. She was an expert cook. At home she baked the bread and boiled her father's puddings, but her father was difficult to please. He read "lonely and rigorous books," she said, on Sunday afternoons, fearing that anything else might "joggle the mind;" and Shakespeare, the Bible, and Dr. Watts's hymns were the reading that he chose for his daughter. He did not like her to work in the garden, or to make visits without him, and when she was too witty he left the table. At fifteen she could not tell the time: her father supposed he had taught her, but she had not understood him, and she did not dare to ask him again or ask anyone else who might have told him. Now and again, she rebelled. She smashed a plate or a tea-cup, and her friends and her brother found ways to provide her with books, hiding them in the box-bush that stood beside the front door or on the parlor piano, under the cover. In one way or another, she contrived to read most of the current authors, especially the Brontës and the Brownings, with Hawthorne, Coleridge, Irving, Keats and Ruskin. One of her special favorites was Sir Thomas Browne, and she loved the drollery[11] of Dickens. For the rest, she read Heine in German

---

**11. drollery** (drōl' ər ē) *n.*: Wry humor.

*Emily Dickinson's bedroom with a tintype of her on the table*

and Emerson's poems, and Frank B. Sanborn's letters in the *Springfield Republican* kept her in the literary current. She was by no means passive in this house of duty. Once, at a funeral in Hadley, whither she had gone with her father in the family barouche,[12] she ran away for several hours with a young cousin from Worcester and drove back to Amherst in his buggy. At school, she declared her independence. She had been sent as a boarding pupil to Mary Lyon's seminary, where she had written her themes on the nature of sin. She had listened to lectures on total depravity[13] as if, like most of the other girls, she had meant to be a missionary's wife; but when, one day, Miss Lyon asked all the girls to rise, all who wished to be Christians, Emily alone refused to do so. She had found that she could not share the orthodox[14] faith. Otherwise her life went on, with a few journeys here and there, like that of any country lawyer's daughter. As a young girl, she had visited Boston. She remembered the concerts and Bunker Hill, the Chinese Museum and Mount Auburn; and later, on two occasions, she stayed in Cambridge, to receive some treatment for her eyes. When her father was serving his term in Congress, in 1854, she spent seven weeks in Washington with him. Her father's friends were struck by her charm and her wit. It was on her way home that she stopped at Philadelphia and received the sudden shock that had changed her life.

This was the whole of Miss Dickinson's story, so far as outward events were concerned, when Thomas Wentworth Higginson entered the picture. Higginson had written an appeal in *The Atlantic*, addressed to the rising generation. Remembering the days of *The Dial*, when the hazel wand, waved over New England, had indicated hidden springs of talent in many a country town, he said that to find a "new genius" was an editor's greatest privilege. If any such existed who read *The Atlantic*, let him court the editor,—"draw near him with soft approaches and mild persuasions." Higginson added a number of admonitions: "Charge your style with life . . . Tolerate no superfluities[15] . . . There may be years of crowded passion in a word, and half a life in a sentence." This appeal was anonymous, but many of the Amherst people knew who wrote the articles in *The Atlantic*, for Sanborn's literary gossip kept them posted; and presently Colonel Higginson, who was living in Worcester, received an odd little letter. The letter was unsigned, but the writer sent four poems, and she placed in a separate envelope the signature "Emily Dickinson." She begged this distant friend to be her "master." The poems puzzled Higginson. While he felt a curious power in them, he was not prepared for a "new genius" who broke so many rules as this lady in Amherst, who punctuated with dashes only and seemed to have small use for rhyme and merely wished to know if she was "clear." She did not ask him to publish the poems, and he did not pass them on to the editor, but he wrote her a sympathetic letter that was followed by a long correspondence. She continued to send him poems at intervals, signing her notes "your gnome" and "your scholar," but, although she asked him again if he would be her "preceptor,"[16] and he offered her a number of suggestions, she never changed a line or a word to please

---

12. **barouche** (bə roo̅sh') *n.*: A horse-drawn carriage.
13. **depravity** (di prav' ə tē) *n.*: Wickedness.
14. **orthodox** (ôr' thə däks') *adj.*: Conforming to the usual beliefs.

15. **superfluities** (soo̅' pər floo̅' ə tēs) *n.*: Excesses.
16. **preceptor** (pri sep' tər) *n.*: Teacher.

him. In one note she said, "If I read a book and it makes my whole body so cold no fire can ever warm me, I know that is poetry. If I feel physically as if the top of my head were taken off, I know that is poetry. These are the only ways I know it. Is there any other way?" And once she replied, when he asked her for a photograph, "I had no portrait now, but am small, like the wren; and my hair is bold, like the chestnut burr; and my eyes like the sherry in the glass that the guest leaves." This feminine mystification piqued[17] the colonel. He wrote, "You enshroud yourself in this fiery mist and I cannot reach you, but only rejoice in the rare sparkles of light." When she told him that her companions were the hills and the sundown, he replied that she ought to come to Boston: she would find herself at home at Mrs. Sargent's. At last, in 1870, he went to Amherst. After a brief delay, while he waited in the parlor, he heard a faint footstep in the hallway and a shy, little childlike creature glided in. She carried two day-lilies, which she placed in his hand, saying, in a soft, breathless voice, "These are my introduction," adding in a whisper, "Forgive me if I am frightened. I never see strangers and hardly know what to say." She spoke of her household occupations and said that "people must have puddings," and she added a few detached, enigmatic[18] remarks. She seemed to the amiable Higginson as unique and remote as Undine or Mignon or Thekla.[19] But he was disturbed by the tension in the air and was glad he did not live too near this lady. There was something abnormal about her, he felt. He had never met anyone before who drained his nerve power so much.

At that time, Miss Dickinson was forty years old and had long since withdrawn from the world; and the friends who came to see her sister were used to the "hurrying whiteness" that was always just going through a door. She sometimes swept into the parlor, bowed and touched a hand or two, poised over the flowered Brussels carpet, and vanished like a ghost or an exhalation; but even these appearances had grown rarer and rarer. Only the neighbors' children really saw her. She had given up wearing colors and was always dressed in diaphanous[20] white, with a cameo pin that held the ruching[21] together. She was decisive in manner, anything but frail. Her complexion was velvety white, her lips were red. Her hair was bound with a chestnut-colored snood,[22] and when it was chilly she wore a little shoulder cape crocheted of soft white worsted run through with a ribbon. She often had a flower in her hand. She moved about in a sort of revery, flitting "as quick as a trout" when she was disturbed. This was one of her sister Lavinia's phrases. The children knew her "high, surprised voice." They knew her dramatic way of throwing up her hands as she ended one of the stories she liked to tell them. She made them her fellow conspirators. They followed her upstairs and heard her comments on the guests she had left in the parlor. She would say, with finger on lip, as feminine callers left, "Listen! Hear them kiss, the traitors!" Or, peeping down the stairs, she would say of some man. "Look, dear, his face is as

---

**17. piqued** (pēk'd) v.: Provoked.
**18. enigmatic** (en' ig mat' ik) adj.: Baffling.
**19. Undine or Mignon or Thekla:** Mysterious women.

**20. diaphanous** (dī af' ə nəs) adj.: Fine; gauzy.
**21. ruching** (rōō' shiŋ) n.: Pleats of lace at the neck of a dress.
**22. snood** (snōōd) n.: A baglike net worn at the back of the head to hold the hair.

pretty as a cloth pink," or "His face is as handsome and meaningless as the full moon." She remarked, apropos[23] of some scholarly person, "He has the facts, but not the phosphorescence[24] of learning." She said that her own ideal caller was always just going out of sight, and that it made her shiver to hear people talk as if they were "taking all the clothes off their souls." She called herself the "cow lily," because of the orange lights in her hair and her eyes, and she observed that the housemaid moved about "in a calico sarcophagus."[25] Once she said to her little niece, who was puzzled by her shy ways, "No one could ever punish a Dickinson by shutting her up alone." Meanwhile, her life went on with her flowers and her sister. She had a small conservatory, opening out of the dining room, a diminutive glass chamber with shelves around it; and there she grouped the ferns and the jasmine, the lilies and the heliotrope and the oxalis plants in their hanging baskets. She had a little watering pot, with a long, slender spout that was like the antenna of an insect, and she sat up all night at times in winter to keep her flowers from freezing. The garden was her special care, and occasionally one saw her at dusk through the gate fluttering about the porch like a moth in the moonlight. When it was damp, she knelt on an old red army blanket that she had thrown on the ground, to reach the flowers. Usually, on summer evenings, she sat for a while with Lavinia on the side piazza, overlooking the flagged path that led to the villa. There stood the giant daphne odora, moved out from the conservatory, and the two small oleanders in their tubs.

Meanwhile, since 1862, Miss Dickinson had been writing poems, although there were very few of her friends who knew it. They all knew the little rhymes she sent them with arbutus buds, but they did not know how seriously she pursued her writing, at night, beside the Franklin stove, in the upstairs corner bedroom, in the light that often glimmered over the snow. From her window she had caught suggestions that gave her a picture, a fancy, an image. Perhaps a boy passed whistling, or a neighbor on her way to church, or a dog with feet "like intermittent plush;" or perhaps she knew that a traveling circus was going to pass in the early morning, and she sat up to watch the "Algerian procession." A dead fly on the windowpane stirred her imagination, and once in the glare of a fire at night she saw a caterpillar measuring a leaf far down in the orchard. She saw the bluebirds darting round "with little dodging feet,"

> The motions of the dipping birds,
> The lightning's jointed road;

and all these observations went into her verses. She wrote on sheets of notepaper, which she sewed together, rolling and tying the bundles with a thread or a ribbon and tucking them away in the drawers of her bureau; although sometimes the back of an envelope served her as well, or a scrap of the *Springfield Republican*. But, casual in this, she was anything but casual,—she was a cunning workman,—in her composition. Poetry was her solitaire[26] and, so to speak, her journal, for, like Thoreau[27] in Concord, she watched the motions of her mind, re-

---

23. **apropos** (ap′ rə pō′) *adv.*: Aptly; fittingly for the occasion.
24. **phosphorescence** (fäs′ fə res′ 'ns) *n.*: Light.
25. **sarcophagus** (sär käf′ ə gəs) *n.*: A stone coffin.

26. **solitaire** (säl′ ə tar′) *n.*: A card game played by one person.
27. **Thoreau:** Henry David Thoreau (1817–1862), U.S. naturalist and writer.

cording its ebbs and flows and the gleams that shot through it; and she labored over her phrases to make them right. Were they all her own? Were there echoes in them, or anything of the conventional, the rhetorical,[28] the fat? Were they clear, were they exact, were they compact? She liked the common hymn meters, and the meters of nursery jingles, which had been deeply ingrained in her mind as a child, and she seemed to take a rebellious joy in violating all their rules, fulfilling the traditional patterns while she also broke them. She was always experimenting with her rhymes and her rhythms, sometimes adding extra syllables to break up their monotony, sometimes deliberately twisting a rhyme, as Emerson did, for the sake of harshness, to escape the mellifluous[29] effect of conventional poems. Many of her pieces were like parodies of hymns, whose gentle glow in her mind had become heat lightning. For Emily Dickinson's light was quick. It was sudden, sharp and evanescent;[30] and this light was the dry light that is closest to the fire.

The visible setting of these poems was the New England countryside, the village, the garden, the household that she knew so well, a scene, the only scene she knew, that she invested with magic, so that the familiar objects became portents and symbols. Here were the hills, the changing seasons, the winter light, the light of spring, the bee, the mouse, the hummingbird, the cricket, the lonely houses off the road, the village inn, the lamppost that became, in the play of her fancy, sublime[31] or droll; and with what gifts

of observation she caught the traits of her birds and insects, of everything that crept or ran or flew,—the snake "unbraiding in the sun," the robin's eyes, "like frightened beads," the umbrella of the bat that was "quaintly halved." She often seemed a little girl, amusing herself with childish whimsies, and, in fact, as the ward of her father, she remained in some ways adolescent; and, as she dressed to the end in the fashion of her early youth, so she retained the imagery of the child in the household. But her whimsies sometimes turned into bold ideas that expressed an all but fathomless[32] insight or wisdom. She saw the mountain, like her father, sitting "in his eternal chair;" her ocean had a "basement," like the house in Amherst, and her wind and snow swept the road like the brooms that she had been taught to use,—the brooms of the breeze swept vale and tree and hill. A journey to the Day of Judgment struck her as a "buggy ride," and she saw a "schoolroom" in the sky. She domesticated the universe and read her own experience into the motions of nature and the world she observed. The sun rose in the East for her "a ribbon at a time," and the "housewife in the evening West" came back to "dust the pond." Clouds for her were "millinery,"[33] mountains wore bonnets, shawls and sandals, eternity "rambled" with her, like her dog Carlo; the wind had fingers and combed the sky, and March walked boldly up and knocked like a neighbor. Volcanoes purred for her like cats, and she saw the planets "frisking about," and her Providence[34] kept a store on the village street, and she thought of death as

---

**28. rhetorical** (ri tôr′ i k'l) *adj.*: Elaborate in style.
**29. mellifluous** (mə lif′ loo wəs) *adj.*: Sweet and smooth.
**30. evanescent** (ev′ ə nes′ 'nt) *adj.*: Tending to fade from sight.
**31. sublime** (sə blīm′) *adj.*: Noble; exalted; majestic.

**32. fathomless** (faṯh′ əm lis) *adj.*: Too deep to be measured.
**33. millinery** (mil′ ə ner′ ē) *n.*: Women's hats.
**34. Providence:** God.

*Emily Dickinson's house in Amherst, Massachusetts*

coming with a broom and a dustpan. The moon slid down the stairs for her "to see who's there," and the grave for her was a little cottage where she could "lay the marble tea." One could not "fold a flood," she said, and "put it in a drawer," but she rolled up the months in mothballs and laid them away, as she had swept up the heart and put away love; and she saw hope, fear, time, future and past as persons to rally, tease, flee, welcome, mock or play with.

The turns of fancy that marked these poems were sharp and unpredictable, and yet they were singularly natural,—nothing was forced. Miss Dickinson lived in a world of paradox, for, while her eye was microscopic, her imagination dwelt with mysteries and grandeurs. Ribbons and immortality were mingled in her mind, which passed from one to the other with the speed of lightning, though she sometimes took a mischievous pleasure in extravagant combinations of thought, uniting the droll and the sublime, the trivial and the grand. There was in this an element of the characteristic American humor that liked to play with incongruities,[35] and Miss Dickinson maintained in the poems of her later years the fun-loving spirit she had shown as a school-

---

**35. incongruities** (in′ kən grō͞o′ ə tēs) *n.*: Things lacking harmony or agreement; inconsistencies.

girl. To juxtapose[36] the great and the small, in unexpected ways, had been one of her prime amusements as the wit of her circle, and this, like the laconic[37] speech that also marked the Yankee, had remained an essential note of her style as a poet. "Shorter than a snake's delay," her poems were packed with meaning; and, swiftly as her images changed, they were scarcely able to keep the pace with which her mind veered from mood to mood, from faith to mockery, from mysticism to rationalism, through ecstasy, disillusion, anguish, joy. These poems were fairylike in their shimmer and lightness, they moved like bees upon a raft of air; and yet one felt behind them an energy of mind and spirit that only the rarest poets ever possessed. Was not Emily Dickinson's idiom[38] the final proof that she possessed it? Her style, her stamp, her form were completely her own.

Such were the games of solitaire that Miss Dickinson played in the silent room, as lonely as Jane Eyre,[39] in her red-curtained alcove, dreaming over the book with its pictures of the arctic wastes and the rock that stood up in the sea of billow and spray. Miss Dickinson had only this "acre of a rock," and yet what a harvest it yielded of grape and maize. Having but a crumb, she was sovereign of them all, as she said quite truly; for her constant theme was deprivation, the "banquet of abstemiousness,"[40] and this sharpened as nothing else her perception of values. When the well's dry, we know the worth of water, and she felt that she knew victory because she knew defeat, she felt that she knew love because she had lost it; and certainly for all she missed she made up in intensity. Where others merely glowed, she was incandescent.

---

36. **juxtapose** (juk′ stə pōz′) v.: Put side by side to show contrast.
37. **laconic** (lə kän′ ik) adj.: Using few words; terse.
38. **idiom** (id′ ē əm) n.: Language different from the literal; the style of artistic expression characteristic of an individual.

39. **Jane Eyre** (air): Heroine of the novel *Jane Eyre* by Charlotte Brontë.
40. **abstemiousness** (əb stē′ mē əs nes) n.: Moderation.

---

## THINKING ABOUT THE SELECTION

### Recalling

1. Describe Emily's father, Edward Dickinson.
2. Explain the event that caused Emily to withdraw socially.
3. How did Emily declare her independence when she was attending boarding school?
4. What was Colonel Higginson's reaction to the first poems that Emily sent to him?

### Interpreting

5. What in Emily's childhood and adolescence influenced the development of her character?
6. How did her neighbors feel about Emily?
7. What is the author's attitude toward Emily Dickinson's unique style of poetry?
8. ". . . while her eye was microscopic, her imagination dwelt with mysteries and grandeurs." How does this statement relate to Dickinson's poetry?

## Applying

9. How do you think that someone with a personality like Emily Dickinson's would be treated today?

her poetry based on Higginson's suggestions?

2. Give evidence to support this inference by Brooks, ". . . she did not speak the language of the world outside her, and one gathered that she did not wish to touch it."

## ANALYZING LITERATURE
### Understanding Characterization

One of the purposes of a biography is to present the subject as a person. To accomplish this, the **character** is revealed to help in understanding the motives behind the events of the subject's life. By understanding Dickinson's character, you are better able to understand her poetry.

> The Soul selects her own Society—
> Then—shuts the Door—
> To her divine Majority—
> Present no more—

1. To what aspect of Dickinson's character could this stanza of her poetry be referring?
2. Is your understanding of this stanza enhanced by the information in the essay? Support your answer.

## UNDERSTANDING LANGUAGE
### Using Context Clues

You often come across unfamiliar words as you are reading. Many times you can figure out the meaning of the word by examining the meaning of the words around it, its **context.** For example, "They frightened the children by uttering her name, as if there were something malign in Miss Dickinson's queerness." By knowing the meaning of *frightened*, you can guess the correct meaning of *malign*, which is something evil, or harmful.

Use this sentence to answer the questions that follow it. ". . . she sat for a while with Lavinia on the side piazza, overlooking the flagged path that led to the villa. There stood . . . the two small oleanders in their tubs."

1. Which word names a part of a house?
2. Which word names a kind of paving?
3. Which word names a plant?

## CRITICAL THINKING AND READING
### Drawing Conclusions About Characters

The author of a biography presents facts about a person's character and the events in his or her life. From this information you can **draw conclusions** that help you understand the character. For example, Dickinson had turned inward and become a recluse in her adult life. From these facts you could conclude that she was eccentric.

1. What inference can you make based on her character and her refusal to change any of

## THINKING AND WRITING
### Writing About Emily Dickinson's Poetry

Choose two poems by Emily Dickinson and write a paragraph on each one. Include what the poem means to you and how Dickinson's character and life might have influenced its content.

Be sure to support your judgment with evidence from the poems and from this biographical sketch. When you revise, make sure you have included adequate support from your judgment. Proofread your paper and prepare a final draft.

# GUIDE FOR READING

## Marian Anderson: Famous Concert Singer

**Langston Hughes** (1902–1967) was a poet, novelist, dramatist, and songwriter who first came to prominence as a leading artist of the Harlem Renaissance, an important literary movement of the 1920's. His life was similar in some ways to that of Marian Anderson. They were born in 1902 and became nationally and internationally recognized during their lifetimes. This essay first appeared in Hughes's 1954 collection of biographies of famous black Americans.

### Biography

A **biography** is an account of a person's life written by another individual. In many biographies the major events and accomplishments in the subject's life are covered from birth to death in chronological order. The biographer gathers these facts from firsthand documents such as letters and diaries, from interviews with people who knew the subject, or from other research done on the subject. These facts are then interwoven with the biographer's impressions or interpretation.

### Look For

What does Langston Hughes emphasize in the life of Marian Anderson? Look for the facts about her life and Hughes's impressions and interpretation. How does he feel about his subject? What about her does he want you to know?

### Writing

Suppose you wanted to write a short biography about someone you know and admire. What would you emphasize about that person in order to get the reader to share your opinion? Write a list of the attributes and experiences that would best convey your feelings.

### Vocabulary

Knowing the following words will help you as you read "Marian Anderson: Famous Concert Singer."

**arias** (är'ē əz) n.: Melodies in an opera, especially for solo voice with instrumental accompaniment (p. 463)

**staunch** (stônch) adj.: Steadfast; loyal (p. 463)

**repertoire** (rep'ər twär) n.: The stock of songs that a singer is familiar with and is ready to perform (p. 466)

# Marian Anderson: Famous Concert Singer

### Langston Hughes

When Marian Anderson was born in a little red brick house in Philadelphia, a famous group of Negro singers, the Fisk Jubilee Singers, had already carried the spirituals all over Europe. And a colored woman billed as "Black Patti" had become famous on variety programs as a singer of both folk songs and the classics. Both Negro and white minstrels had popularized American songs. The all-Negro musical comedies of Bert Williams and George Walker had been successful on Broadway. But no well-trained colored singers performing the great songs of Schubert, Handel, and the other masters, or the arias from famous operas, had become successful on the concert stage. And most people thought of Negro vocalists only in connection with spirituals. Roland Hayes[1] and Marian Anderson were the first to become famous enough to break this stereotype.

Marian Anderson's mother was a staunch church worker who loved to croon the hymns of her faith about the house, as did the aunt who came to live with them when Marian's father died. Both parents were from Virginia. Marian's mother had been a school teacher there, and her father a farm boy. Shortly after they moved to Philadelphia where three daughters were born, the father died, and the mother went to work at Wanamaker's department store. But she saw to it that her children attended school and church regularly. The father had been an usher in the Union Baptist Church, so the congregation took an interest in his three little girls. Marian was the oldest and, before she was eight, singing in the Sunday school choir, she had already learned a great many hymns and spirituals by heart.

One day Marian saw an old violin in a pawnshop window marked $3.45. She set her mind on that violin, and began to save the nickels and dimes neighbors would give her for scrubbing their white front steps —the kind of stone steps so characteristic of Philadelphia and Baltimore houses —until she had $3.00. The pawnshop man let her take the violin at a reduced price. Marian never became very good on the violin. A few years later her mother bought a piano, so the child forgot all about it in favor of their newer instrument. By that time, too, her unusual singing voice had attracted the attention of her choir master, and at the age of fourteen she was promoted to a place in the main church choir. There she learned all four parts of all the hymns and anthems and could easily fill in anywhere from bass to soprano.

---

1. **Roland Hayes** (1887–1977): Famous black U.S. tenor.

*Marian Anderson with her accompanist Franz Rupp, 1949*

Sensing that she had exceptional musical talent, some of the church members began to raise money so that she might have singing lessons. But her first teacher, a colored woman, refused to accept any pay for instructing so talented a child. So the church folks put their money into a trust fund called "Marian Anderson's Future," banking it until the time came for her to have advanced training. Meanwhile, Marian attended South Philadelphia High School for Girls and took part in various group concerts, usually doing the solo parts. When she was fifteen she sang a group of songs alone at a Sunday School Convention in Harrisburg and word of her talent began to spread about the state. When she was graduated from high school, the Philadelphia Choral Society, a Negro group, sponsored her further study and secured for her one of the best local teachers. Then in 1925 she journeyed to New York to take part, with three hundred other young singers, in the New York Philharmonic Competitions, where she won first place, and appeared with the orchestra at Lewisohn Stadium.

This appearance was given wide publicity, but very few lucrative engagements came in, so Marian continued to study. A Town Hall concert was arranged for her in New

York, but it was unsuccessful. Meanwhile, she kept on singing with various choral groups, and herself gave concerts in churches and at some of the Negro colleges until, in 1930, a Rosenald Fellowship made European study possible. During her first year abroad she made her debut in Berlin. A prominent Scandinavian concert manager read of this concert, but was attracted more by the name, *Anderson*, than by what the critics said about her voice. "Ah," he said, "a Negro singer with a Swedish name! She is bound to be a success in Scandinavia." He sent two of his friends to Germany to hear her, one of them being Kosti Vehanen who shortly became her accompanist and remained with her for many years.

Sure enough, Marian Anderson did become a great success in the Scandinavian countries, where she learned to sing in both Finnish and Swedish, and her first concert tour of Europe became a critical triumph. When she came back home to America, she gave several programs and appeared as soloist with the famous Hall Johnson Choir, but without financial success. However, the Scandinavian people, who had fallen in love with her, kept asking her to come back there. So, in 1933, she went again to Europe for 142 concerts in Norway, Sweden, Denmark, and Finland. She was decorated by the King of Denmark and the King of Sweden. Sibelius[2] dedicated a song to her. And the following spring she made her debut in Paris where she was so well received that she had to give three concerts that season at the Salle Gaveau.[3] Great successes followed in all the European capitals. In 1935 the famous conductor, Arturo Toscanini, listened to her sing at Salzburg.[4] He said,

"What I heard today one is privileged to hear only once in a hundred years." It was in Europe that Marian Anderson began to be acclaimed by critics as "the greatest singer in the world."

When Marian Anderson again returned to America, she was a seasoned artist. News of her tremendous European successes had preceded her, so a big New York concert was planned. But a few days before she arrived at New York, in a storm on the liner crossing the Atlantic, Marian fell and broke her ankle. She refused to allow this to interfere with her concert, however, nor did she even want people to know about it. She wore a very long evening gown that night so that no one could see the plaster cast on her leg. She propped herself in a curve of the piano before the curtains parted, and gave her New York concert standing on one foot! The next day Howard Taubman wrote enthusiastically in *The New York Times:*

> Marian Anderson has returned to her native land one of the great singers of our time. . . . There is no doubt of it, she was mistress of all she surveyed. . . . It was music making that proved too deep for words.

A coast-to-coast American tour followed. And, from that season on, Marian Anderson has been one of our country's favorite singers, rated, according to *Variety*,[5] among the top ten of the concert stage who earn over $100,000 a year. Miss Anderson has sung with the great symphony orchestras, and appeared on all the major radio and television networks many times, being a particular favorite with the millions of listeners to the Ford Hour. During the years she has returned often to Europe for concerts, and among the numerous honors accorded her

---

**2. Sibelius:** (si bā′ lē oos) Jean Sibelius (1865–1957), a Finnish composer.
**3. Salle Gaveau:** (sal′ ga vō′) A concert hall in Paris, France.
**4. Salzburg:** A city in Austria, noted for its music festivals.

**5. *Variety:*** A show business newspaper.

abroad was a request for a command performance before the King and Queen of England, and a decoration from the government of Finland. Her concerts in South America and Asia have been as successful as those elsewhere. Since 1935 she has averaged over one hundred programs a year in cities as far apart as Vienna, Buenos Aires, Moscow, and Tokyo. Her recordings have sold millions of copies around the world. She has been invited more than once to sing at the White House. She has appeared in concert at the Paris Opera and at the Metropolitan Opera House in New York. Several colleges have granted her honorary degrees, and in 1944 Smith College made her a Doctor of Music.

In spite of all this, as a Negro, Marian Anderson has not been immune from those aspects of racial segregation which affect most traveling artists of color in the United States. In his book, *Marian Anderson,* her longtime accompanist, Vehanen, tells of hotel accommodations being denied her, and service in dining rooms often refused. Once after a concert in a Southern city, Vehanen writes that some white friends drove Marian to the railroad station and took her into the main waiting room. But a policeman ran them out, since Negroes were not allowed in that part of the station. Then they went into the smaller waiting room marked, COLORED. But again they were ejected, because *white* people were not permitted in the cubby hole allotted to Negroes. So they all had to stand on the platform until the train arrived.

The most dramatic incident of prejudice in all Marian Anderson's career occurred in 1939 when the Daughters of the American Revolution, who own Constitution Hall in Washington, refused to allow her to sing there. The newspapers headlined this and many Americans were outraged. In protest a committee of prominent people, including a number of great artists and distinguished figures in the government, was formed. Through the efforts of this committee, Marian Anderson sang in Washington, anyway —before the statue of Abraham Lincoln —to one of the largest crowds ever to hear a singer at one time in the history of the world. Seventy-five thousand people stood in the open air on a cold clear Easter Sunday afternoon to hear her. And millions more listened to Marian Anderson that day over the radio or heard her in the newsreels that recorded the event. Harold Ickes, then Secretary of the Interior, presented Miss Anderson to that enormous audience standing in the plaza to pay honor, as he said, not only to a great singer, but to the basic ideals of democracy and equality.

In 1943 Marian Anderson married Orpheus H. Fisher, an architect, and settled down—between tours—in a beautiful country house in Connecticut where she rehearses new songs to add to her already vast repertoire. Sometimes her neighbors across the fields can hear the rich warm voice that covers three octaves singing in English, French, Finnish, or German. And sometimes they hear in the New England air that old Negro spiritual, "Honor, honor unto the dying Lamb. . . ."

Friends say that Marian Anderson has invested her money in real estate and in government bonds. Certainly, throughout her career, she has lived very simply, traveled without a maid or secretary, and carried her own sewing machine along by train, ship, or plane to mend her gowns. When in 1941 in Philadelphia she was awarded the coveted Bok Award for outstanding public service, the $10,000 that came with the medallion she used to establish a trust fund for "talented American artists without regard to race or creed." Now, each year from this fund promising young musicians receive scholarships.

# THINKING ABOUT THE SELECTION

## Recalling

1. How did Marian Anderson's congregation help her?
2. Where did she first become a success?
3. What difficulties did Anderson face traveling in the United States?

## Interpreting

4. Why was it so difficult for Anderson to gain success in the United States?
5. What does the incident involving her broken ankle reveal about Anderson's personality?
6. What was the significance of Anderson's concert in front of the Lincoln Memorial?

## Applying

7. What young artists would you recommend for the award established by Marion Anderson?

# ANALYZING LITERATURE

## Understanding Biography

The account of a person's life written by another individual is a **biography.** Like most biographers, Langston Hughes provides factual information about Marian Anderson's life, while emphasizing certain aspects of her character. In this way you get to know not only the events in Marian Anderson's life, but also the strengths of her personality.

1. What incidents in the essay reveal Anderson's personality?
2. What aspects of Anderson's life has the author emphasized?

# CRITICAL THINKING AND READING

## Understanding a Biographer's Purpose

The **biographer's purpose** is the point he wants to make. A biographer will emphasize certain qualities or aspects of the subject in order to achieve that purpose. Two biographers, who have the same subject, may interpret factual information differently. For example, one might present certain facts to inform you of the difficulties Anderson faced as a black opera singer. Another might present different information to try to persuade you that she was the best American soprano in the twentieth century.

1. What is Hughes's purpose in this biography?
2. How might the purpose change if the essay were in a book about people from Philadelphia?

# UNDERSTANDING LANGUAGE

## Completing Sentences

Many aptitude tests include sentence completion sections that test your vocabulary skills. The following sentences are incomplete, with four choices for completing the sentence. Choose the word that best completes the meaning of the sentence.

1. Because of her obvious talent, Marian's first voice teacher considered it (a)_____to teach her.
   a. chore            c. privilege
   b. easy             d. no cost
2. Despite the fact that she was a famous singer, Marian Anderson_____racial predjudice.
   a. encountered      c. avoided
   b. favored          d. victimized
3. Marian Anderson sang to 75,000 people in Washington, one of the_____crowds ever to hear a singer at one time.
   a. quietest         c. largest
   b. rowdiest         d. most appreciative

# THINKING AND WRITING

## Writing a Biography

Write a short biography of a friend or a family member. Your purpose is to present those characteristics of your subject that you admire. As you plan your biography, use the list you made for the Writing section of this Guide for Reading. Pick one incident in your subject's life that is interesting and best presents your purpose. As you revise, be sure you have presented only the facts that fit your purpose.

# GUIDE FOR READING

## A Child's Christmas in Wales

**Dylan Thomas** (1914–1953) grew up in a seaport in Wales, a country on the western coast of Great Britain. Although his education lasted only through grammar school, Thomas's brilliance as a poet was recognized with the publication of his first book, when he was only twenty. He also wrote the radio play *Under Milk Wood,* which has been adapted for stage, movie, and television productions. "A Child's Christmas in Wales" presents memories of several Christmas seasons of his youth, poetically blended together.

**Autobiography**

An **autobiography** is the story of a person's life written by that person. The writer of an autobiography can share personal thoughts and feelings and may comment on the effect of certain events on his or her life. As a result, you share in the life of the subject more intimately than in a biography. However, you must also be aware that all autobiographers present their lives subjectively; they do not reveal everything about themselves.

**Look For**

What does Dylan Thomas share about his Christmases? As you read "A Child's Christmas in Wales," look for the details that only Thomas could have known.

**Writing**

In this autobiographical sketch, Dylan Thomas writes affectionately about what his Christmas holidays were like. Freewrite to record some impressions, emotions, and events of a vacation or holiday that you especially enjoyed.

**Vocabulary**

Knowing the following words will help you as you read, "A Child's Christmas in Wales."

**bundling** (bun′ d'liŋ) *v.*: Moving quickly; bustling (p. 469)

**sidle** (sī′d'l) *v.*: To move sideways in a sneaky manner (p. 469)

**prey** (prā) *n.*: An animal hunted or killed for food (p. 469)

**wallowed** (wäl′ō'd) *v.*: Enjoyed completely; took great pleasure (p. 470)

**crocheted** (krō shā′'d) *v.*: Made with thread or yarn woven together with hooked needles (p. 472)

**brittle** (brit′'l) *adj.*: Stiff and unbending; easily broken or shattered (p. 473)

**trod** (träd) *v.*: Walked (p. 473)

**forlorn** (fər lôrn′) *adj.*: Abandoned; deserted (p. 473)

# A Child's Christmas in Wales

## Dylan Thomas

One Christmas was so much like another, in those years around the sea-town corner now and out of all sound except the distant speaking of the voices I sometimes hear a moment before sleep, that I can never remember whether it snowed for six days and six nights when I was twelve or whether it snowed for twelve days and twelve nights when I was six. All the Christmases roll down toward the two-tongued sea, like a cold and headlong moon bundling down the sky that was our street; and they stop at the rim of the ice-edged, fish-freezing waves, and I plunge my hands in the snow and bring out whatever I can find. In goes my hand into that wool-white bell-tongued ball of holidays resting at the rim of the carol-singing seas, and out come Mrs. Prothero and the firemen.

It was on the afternoon of the day of Christmas Eve, and I was in Mrs. Prothero's garden, waiting for cats, with her son Jim. It was snowing. It was always snowing at Christmas. December, in my memory, is white as Lapland, though there were no reindeers. But there were cats. Patient, cold and callous, our hands wrapped in socks, we waited to snowball the cats. Sleek and long as jaguars and horrible-whiskered, spitting and snarling, they would slink and

sidle over the white back-garden walls, and the lynx-eyed hunters, Jim and I, fur-capped and moccasined trappers from Hudson Bay,[1] off Mumbles Road, would hurl our deadly snowballs at the green of their eyes. The wise cats never appeared. We were so still, Eskimo-footed arctic marksmen in the muffling silence of the eternal snows —eternal, ever since Wednesday—that we never heard Mrs. Prothero's first cry from her igloo at the bottom of the garden. Or, if we heard it at all, it was, to us, like the far-off challenge of our enemy and prey, the neighbor's polar cat. But soon the voice grew louder. "Fire!" cried Mrs. Prothero, and she beat the dinner-gong.

And we ran down the garden, with the snowballs in our arms, toward the house; and smoke, indeed, was pouring out of the dining room, and the gong was bombilating,[2] and Mrs. Prothero was annoucing ruin like a town crier in Pompeii.[3] This was

---

**1. Hudson Bay:** Inland sea in northeastern Canada.
**2. bombilating** (bäm′ bə lāt iŋ) *v.*: Making a buzzing, droning sound as though a bomb was approaching.
**3. Pompeii** (päm pā′ ē): City in Italy that was destroyed by the eruption of Mount Vesuvius in 79 A.D.

better than all the cats in Wales standing on the wall in a row. We bounded into the house, laden with snowballs, and stopped at the open door of the smoke-filled room.

Something was burning all right; perhaps it was Mr. Prothero, who always slept there after midday dinner with a newspaper over his face. But he was standing in the middle of the room, saying "A fine Christmas!" and smacking at the smoke with a slipper.

"Call the fire brigade," cried Mrs. Prothero as she beat the gong.

"They won't be there," said Mr. Prothero, "it's Christmas."

There was no fire to be seen, only clouds of smoke and Mr. Prothero standing in the middle of them, waving his slipper as though he were conducting.

"Do something," he said.

And we threw all our snowballs into the smoke—I think we missed Mr. Prothero —and ran out of the house to the telephone box.

"Let's call the police as well," Jim said.

"And the ambulance."

"And Ernie Jenkins, he likes fires."

But we only called the fire brigade, and soon the fire engine came and three tall men in helmets brought a hose into the house and Mr. Prothero got out just in time before they turned it on. Nobody could have had a noisier Christmas Eve. And when the firemen turned off the hose and were standing in the wet, smoky room, Jim's aunt, Miss Prothero, came downstairs and peered in at them. Jim and I waited, very quietly, to hear what she would say to them. She said the right thing, always. She looked at the three tall firemen in their shining helmets, standing among the smoke and cinders and dissolving snowballs, and she said: "Would you like anything to read?"

Years and years and years ago, when I was a boy, when there were wolves in Wales, and birds the color of red-flannel petticoats whisked past the harp-shaped hills, when we sang and wallowed all night and day in caves that smelt like Sunday afternoons in damp front farmhouse parlors, and we chased, with the jawbones of deacons, the English and the bears, before the motor car, before the wheel, before the duchess-faced horse, when we rode the daft[4] and happy hills bareback, it snowed and it snowed. But here a small boy says: "It snowed last year, too. I made a snowman and my brother knocked it down and I knocked my brother down and then we had tea."

"But that was not the same snow," I say. "Our snow was not only shaken from white-wash buckets down the sky, it came shawling[5] out of the ground and swam and drifted out of the arms and hands and bodies of the trees; snow grew overnight on the roofs of the houses like a pure and grandfather moss, minutely white-ivied the walls and settled on the postman, opening the gate, like a dumb, numb thunderstorm of white, torn Christmas cards."

"Were there postmen then, too?"

"With sprinkling eyes and wind-cherried noses, on spread, frozen feet they crunched up to the doors and mittened on them manfully. But all that the children could hear was a ringing of bells."

"You mean that the postman went rat-a-tat-tat and the doors rang?"

"I mean that the bells that the children could hear were inside them."

"I only hear thunder sometimes, never bells."

---

**4. daft:** Silly; foolish.
**5. shawling:** Draping like a shawl.

*Fritz Eichenberg etching*

"There were church bells, too."

"Inside them?"

"No, no, no, in the bat-black, snow-white belfries, tugged by bishops and storks. And they rang their tidings over the bandaged town, over the frozen foam of the powder and ice-cream hills, over the crackling sea. It seemed that all the churches boomed for joy under my window; and the weathercocks crew for Christmas, on our fence."

"Get back to the postmen."

"They were just ordinary postmen, fond of walking and dogs and Christmas and the snow. They knocked on the doors with blue knuckles. . . ."

"Ours has got a black knocker. . . ."

"And then they stood on the white Welcome mat in the little, drifted porches and huffed and puffed, making ghosts with their breath, and jogged from foot to foot like small boys wanting to go out."

"And then the presents?"

"And then the Presents, after the Christmas box. And the cold postman, with a rose on his button-nose, tingled down the tea-tray-slithered run of the chilly glinting hill. He went in his ice-bound boots like a man on fish-monger's slabs.[6] He wagged his bag like a frozen camel's hump, dizzily turned the corner on one foot, and was gone."

"Get back to the Presents."

"There were the Useful Presents: engulfing mufflers of the old coach days, and mittens made for giant sloths;[7] zebra scarfs of a substance like silky gum that could be tug-o'-warred down to the galoshes;[8] blinding tam-o'-shanters[9] like patchwork tea cozies[10] and bunny-suited busbies[11] and balaclavas[12] for victims of head-shrinking tribes; from aunts who always wore wool next to the skin there were mustached and rasping vests that made you wonder why the aunts had any skin left at all; and once I had a little crocheted nose bag from an aunt now, alas, no longer whinnying with us. And picture-less books in which small boys, though warned with quotations not to, *would* skate on Farmer Giles' pond and did and drowned; and books that told me everything about the wasp, except why."

"Go on to the Useless Presents."

"Bags of moist and many-colored jelly babies[13] and a folded flag and a false nose and a tram-conductor's cap[14] and a machine that punched tickets and rang a bell; never a catapult;[15] once, by mistake that no one could explain, a little hatchet; and a celluloid duck that made, when you pressed it, a most unducklike sound, a mewing moo that an ambitious cat might make who wished to be a cow; and a painting book in which I could make the grass, the trees, the sea and the animals any color I pleased, and still the dazzling sky-blue sheep are grazing in the red field under the rainbow-billed and pea-green birds. Hard-boileds, toffee, fudge and allsorts, crunches, cracknels, humbugs, glaciers, marzipan, and butterwelsh[16] for the Welsh. And troops of bright tin soldiers who, if they could not fight, could always run. And Snakes-and-Families and Happy Ladders.[17] And Easy Hobbi-Games for Little Engineers, complete with instructions. Oh, easy for Leonardo![18] And a whistle to make the dogs bark to wake up the old man next door to make him beat on the wall with his stick to shake our picture off the wall. And a packet of cigarettes: you put one in your mouth and you stood at the corner of the street and you waited for hours, in vain, for an old lady to scold you for smoking a cigarette, and then with a smirk you ate it. And then it was breakfast under the balloons."

"Were there Uncles, like in our house?"

---

**6. fishmonger's slabs:** Flat, slimy surface on which fish are displayed for sale.

**7. sloths:** (slôths) Two-toed mammals that hang from trees.

**8. galoshes:** (gə läsh′ əz) Rubber overshoes or boots.

**9. tam-o'-shanters:** Scottish caps.

**10. tea cozies:** Knitted or padded covers placed over a teapot to keep the contents warm.

**11. busbies** (buz′ bēz): Tall fur hats worn as part of the full-dress uniforms of guardsmen in the British army.

**12. balaclavas** (bäl′ ə klä′ vəz): Knitted helmets with an opening for the nose and eyes.

**13. jelly babies:** Candies in the shape of babies.

**14. tram conductor's cap:** Streetcar or trolley car operator's cap.

**15. catapult** (kat′ ə pult′): An ancient military machine for throwing or shooting stones or spears; a slingshot.

**16. hard-boileds, . . . butterwelsh:** Various kinds of candy.

**17. Snakes-and-Families and Happy Ladders:** Games, the names of which Dylan Thomas mixes up on purpose. The games are actually Snakes-and-Ladders and Happy Families.

**18. Leonardo:** Leonardo da Vinci (1452–1519), an Italian painter, sculptor, architect, engineer, and scientist.

"There are always Uncles at Christmas. The same Uncles. And on Christmas mornings, with dog-disturbing whistle and sugar fags,[19] I would scour the swatched town for the news of the little world, and find always a dead bird by the white Post Office or by the deserted swings; perhaps a robin, all but one of his fires out. Men and women wading or scooping back from chapel, with taproom noses and wind-bussed cheeks, all albinos,[20] huddled their stiff black jarring feathers against the irreligious snow. Mistletoe hung from the gas brackets[21] in all the front parlors; there was sherry and walnuts and bottled beer and crackers by the dessert-spoons; and cats in their fur-abouts watched the fires; and the high-heaped fire spat, all ready for the chestnuts and the mulling pokers. Some few large men sat in the front parlors, without their collars, Uncles almost certainly, trying their new cigars, holding them out judiciously at arms' length, returning them to their mouths, coughing, then holding them out again as though waiting for the explosion; and some few small aunts, not wanted in the kitchen, nor anywhere else for that matter, sat on the very edges of their chairs, poised and brittle, afraid to break, like faded cups and saucers."

Not many those mornings trod the piling streets: an old man always, fawn-bowlered,[22] yellow-gloved and, at this time of year, with spats[23] of snow, would take his constitutional[24] to the white bowling green and back, as he would take it wet or fine on Christmas Day or Doomsday; sometimes two hale young men, with big pipes blazing, no overcoats and wind-blown scarfs, would trudge, unspeaking, down to the forlorn sea, to work up an appetite, to blow away the fumes, who knows, to walk into the waves until nothing of them was left but the two curling smoke clouds of their inextinguishable briars.[25] Then I would be slap-dashing home, the gravy smell of the dinners of others, the bird smell, the brandy, the pudding and mince, coiling up to my nostrils, when out of a snow-clogged side lane would come a boy the spit of myself, with a pink-tipped cigarette and the violet past of a black eye, cocky as a bullfinch, leering all to himself. i hated him on sight and sound, and would be about to put my dog whistle to my lips and blow him off the face of Christmas when suddenly he, with a violet wink, put *his* whistle to *his* lips and blew so stridently, so high, so exquisitely loud, that gobbling faces, their cheeks bulged with goose, would press against their tinseled windows, the whole length of the white echoing street. For dinner we had turkey and blazing pudding, and after dinner the Uncles sat in front of the fire, loosened all buttons, put their large moist hands over their watch chains, groaned a little and slept. Mothers, aunts and sisters scuttled to and fro, bearing tureens.[26] Auntie Bessie, who had already been frightened, twice, by a clock-work mouse, whimpered at the sideboard and had some elderberry wine. The dog was sick. Auntie Dosie had to have three aspirins, but Auntie Hannah, who liked port, stood in the

---

**19. sugar fags:** Candy cigarettes.
**20. albinos** (al bī′ nō): People who because of a genetic factor have unusually pale skin and white hair.
**21. gas brackets:** Wall fixtures for gas lights.
**22. fawn-bowlered:** Tan-hatted.
**23. spats:** Coverings for the instep and ankle.
**24. constitutional:** A walk taken for one's health.

**25. briars:** Pipes.
**26. tureens** (too rēnz′): Deep dishes with covers.

*Fritz Eichenberg etching*

middle of the snowbound back yard, singing like a big-bosomed thrush. I would blow up balloons to see how big they would blow up to; and, when they burst, which they all did, the Uncles jumped and rumbled. In the rich and heavy afternoon, the Uncles breathing like dolphins and the snow descending, I would sit among festoons[27] and Chinese lanterns and nibble dates and try to make a model man-o'-war,[28] following the Instructions for Little Engineers, and produce what might be mistaken for a sea-going tramcar.

Or I would go out, my bright new boots squeaking, into the white world, on to the seaward hill, to call on Jim and Dan and Jack and to pad through the still streets, leaving huge deep footprints on the hidden pavements.

---

**27. festoons:** Wreaths and garlands.

**28. man-o'-war:** A warship.

"I bet people will think there's been hippos."

"What would you do if you saw a hippo coming down our street?"

"I'd go like this, bang! I'd throw him over the railings and roll him down the hill and then I'd tickle him under the ear and he'd wag his tail."

"What would you do if you saw *two* hippos?"

Iron-flanked and bellowing he-hippos clanked and battered through the scudding snow toward us as we passed Mr. Daniel's house.

"Let's post Mr. Daniel a snowball through his letter box."

"Let's write things in the snow."

"Let's write, 'Mr. Daniel looks like a spaniel' all over his lawn."

Or we walked on the white shore. "Can the fishes see it's snowing?"

The silent one-clouded heavens drifted on to the sea. Now we were snow-blind travelers lost on the north hills, and vast dewlapped[29] dogs, with flasks round their necks, ambled and shambled up to us, baying "Excelsior."[30] We returned home through the poor streets where only a few children fumbled with bare red fingers in the wheel-rutted snow and cat-called after us, their voices fading away, as we trudged uphill, into the cries of the dock birds and the hooting of ships out in the whirling bay. And then, at tea the recovered Uncles would be jolly; and the ice cake loomed in the center of the table like a marble grave. Auntie Hannah laced her tea with rum, because it was only once a year.

---

**29. dewlapped:** Having loose folds of skin hanging from the throat.

**30. Excelsior** (ek sel′ sē ôr′): Latin phrase meaning *onward and upward.*

Bring out the tall tales now that we told by the fire as the gaslight bubbled like a diver. Ghosts whooed like owls in the long nights when I dared not look over my shoulder; animals lurked in the cubbyhole under the stairs where the gas meter ticked. And I remember that we went singing carols once, when there wasn't the shaving of a moon to light the flying streets. At the end of a long road was a drive that led to a large house, and we stumbled up the darkness of the drive that night, each one of us afraid, each one holding a stone in his hand in case, and all of us too brave to say a word. The wind through the trees made noises as of old and unpleasant and maybe webfooted men wheezing in caves. We reached the black bulk of the house.

"What shall we give them? Hark the Herald?"

"No," Jack said, "Good King Wenceslas. I'll count three."

One, two, three, and we began to sing, our voices high and seemingly distant in the snow-felted darkness round the house that was occupied by nobody we knew. We stood close together, near the dark door.

*Good King Wenceslas looked out*
*On the Feast of Stephen . . .*

And then a small, dry voice, like the voice of someone who has not spoken for a long time, joined our singing: a small, dry, eggshell voice from the other side of the door: a small dry voice through the keyhole. And when we stopped running we were outside *our* house; the front room was lovely; balloons floated under the hot-water-bottle-gulping gas; everything was good again and shone over the town.

"Perhaps it was a ghost," Jim said.

*Fritz Eichenberg etching*

"Perhaps it was trolls,"[31] Dan said, who was always reading.

"Let's go in and see if there's any jelly left," Jack said. And we did that.

Always on Christmas night there was music. An uncle played the fiddle, a cousin sang "Cherry Ripe," and another uncle sang "Drake's Drum." It was very warm in the little house. Auntie Hannah, who had got on to the parsnip wine, sang a song about Bleeding Hearts and Death, and then another in which she said her heart was like a Bird's Nest; and then everybody laughed again; and then I went to bed. Looking through my bedroom window, out into the moonlight and the unending smoke-colored snow, I could see the lights in the windows of all the other houses on our hill and hear the music rising from them up the long, steadily falling night. I turned the gas down, I got into bed. I said some words to the close and holy darkness, and then I slept.

---

**31. trolls:** Mythical Scandinavian beings.

## THINKING ABOUT THE SELECTION

### Recalling

1. What does the opening passage indicate about the effects of time on Thomas's Christmas memory?
2. Describe the events concerning the fire in the Protheros' kitchen.
3. Describe at least four of the "Useful Presents."
4. How are the Uncles and Aunts described?
5. Explain what happened when the boys went caroling.

### Interpreting

6. How does answering questions from a young boy affect the telling of the story?
7. In what ways was Christmas for the children different from Christmas for the adults?
8. What does the final sentence add to Thomas's memory of childhood?

### Analyzing

9. Why do people's memories tend to blend together and exaggerate the past?

## ANALYZING LITERATURE

### Understanding Autobiography

A person writing an autobiography can reveal details and thoughts about certain events that would never be known through research.
1. Why do you think Dylan Thomas tells this memory of his childhood?
2. What details in the essay support your opinion?

## CRITICAL THINKING AND READING

### Recognizing Subjective Details

**Objective** details are impersonal. Details that are based on personal opinions and feelings are **subjective.** Dylan Thomas is not interested in providing an objective picture of his childhood. Instead, he wants to re-create the feelings, thoughts, and impressions of a young person at Christmas. His essay is therefore filled with subjective details. "It was snowing. It was always snowing at Christmas. December, in my memory, is white as Lapland, though there were no reindeers. But there were cats."
1. Find three examples of subjective information.
2. How does Dylan Thomas's use of subjective information reinforce the childlike quality of the essay?

## UNDERSTANDING VOCABULARY

### Understanding Simile and Metaphor

**Similes** and **metaphors** are used by writers to compare two seemingly unlike things. A simile uses the words *like* or *as*. A metaphor presents one thing in terms of another. Thomas uses a simile when he says that the postmen, ". . . jogged from foot to foot *like* small boys wanting to go out." He could have made a direct comparison in a metaphor: The postmen were small boys wanting to go out, jogging from foot to foot.

Identify as metaphor or simile the following examples from the essay.
1. "Sleek and long as jaguars . . ."
2. "Jim and I, fur-capped and moccasined trappers from Hudson Bay . . ."
3. ". . . snow grew overnight on the roofs of the houses like a pure and grandfather moss . . ."

## THINKING AND WRITING

### Writing an Autobiographical Sketch

Write a short, autobiographical sketch about a time in your life that has left an impression on your memory. Use the ideas generated in the Writing section on page 468 or freewrite about your impressions and memories from another time. Try to re-create, as closely as possible, your feelings and thoughts as you are writing. As you revise, make sure you have included subjective as well as objective information.

# GUIDE FOR READING

## A Christmas Memory

**Truman Capote** (1924–1984) was born in New Orleans, Louisiana, and spent most of his childhood in the care of relatives in the South. One of these relatives, an elderly cousin named Sook Faulk, was the inspiration for "A Christmas Memory." Capote also wrote short stories, novels, plays, screenplays, and travel sketches. His most successful work, *In Cold Blood,* is a "nonfiction novel," which combines factual reporting with imagination. He adapted a number of his works, including "A Christmas Memory," for television.

### Reminiscence

A **reminiscence** is an autobiographical account of an experience from the past. Unlike a full-length autobiography, which usually recounts most, if not all, of the writer's life, a reminiscence focuses on an experience of particular significance. It presents the events and the characters, as well as the special quality or meaning that keeps the memory alive and fresh in the writer's mind.

### Look For

What emotions does Capote evoke in this essay? What special quality or meaning is he presenting through these emotions?

### Writing

Truman Capote portrays a special relationship he had with one of his relatives in "A Christmas Memory." Write a brief description of people or even animals who share or have shared an especially close relationship.

### Vocabulary

Knowing the following words will help you as you read "A Christmas Memory."

**calico** (kal'ə kō) *adj.*: Made of cotton cloth, usually printed (p. 479)

**inaugurating** (in ô'gyə rāt'iŋ) *v.*: Making a formal beginning; celebrating the opening of (p. 480)

**exhilarates** (ig zil'ə rāts) *v.*: Makes cheerful, lively, stimulates (p. 480)

**dilapidated** (dil lap'ə dāt id) *adj.*: Broken down; shabby and neglected (p. 480)

**paraphernalia** (par'ə fər nāl'yə) *n.*: Collection of articles, gear necessary for some activity (p. 480)

**prosaic** (prō zā'ik) *adj.*: Commonplace; dull; ordinary (p. 482)

**chastising** (chas tīz'iŋ) *adj.*: Punishing; scolding (p. 484)

# A Christmas Memory

## Truman Capote

Imagine a morning in late November. A coming of winter morning more than twenty years ago. Consider the kitchen of a spreading old house in a country town. A great black stove is its main feature; but there is also a big round table and a fireplace with two rocking chairs placed in front of it. Just today the fireplace commenced its seasonal roar.

A woman with shorn white hair is standing at the kitchen window. She is wearing tennis shoes and a shapeless gray sweater over a summery calico dress. She is small and sprightly, like a bantam hen; but, due to a long youthful illness, her shoulders are pitifully hunched. Her face is remarkable—not unlike Lincoln's, craggy like that, and tinted by sun and wind; but it is delicate too, finely boned, and her eyes are sherry-colored and timid. "Oh my," she exclaims, her breath smoking the windowpane, "it's fruitcake weather!"

The person to whom she is speaking is myself. I am seven; she is sixty-something.

We are cousins, very distant ones, and we have lived together—well, as long as I can remember. Other people inhabit the house, relatives; and though they have power over us, and frequently make us cry, we are not, on the whole, too much aware of them. We are each other's best friend. She calls me Buddy, in memory of a boy who was formerly her best friend. The other Buddy died in the 1880's, when she was still a child. She is still a child.

"I knew it before I got out of bed," she says, turning away from the window with a purposeful excitement in her eyes. "The courthouse bell sounded so cold and clear. And there were no birds singing; they've gone to warmer country, yes indeed. Oh, Buddy, stop stuffing biscuit and fetch our buggy. Help me find my hat. We've thirty cakes to bake."

It's always the same: a morning arrives in November, and my friend, as though officially inaugurating the Christmas time of year that exhilarates her imagination and fuels the blaze of her heart, announces: "It's fruitcake weather! Fetch our buggy. Help me find my hat."

The hat is found, a straw cartwheel corsaged with velvet roses out-of-doors has faded: it once belonged to a more fashionable relative. Together, we guide our buggy, a dilapidated baby carriage, out to the garden and into a grove of pecan trees. The buggy is mine; that is, it was bought for me when I was born. It is made of wicker, rather unraveled, and the wheels wobble like a drunkard's legs. But it is a faithful object; springtimes, we take it to the woods and fill it with flowers, herbs, wild fern for our porch pots; in the summer, we pile it with picnic paraphernalia and sugar-cane fishing poles and roll it down to the edge of a creek; it has its winter uses, too: as a truck for hauling firewood from the yard to the kitchen, as a

warm bed for Queenie, our tough little orange and white rat terrier who has survived distemper[1] and two rattlesnake bites. Queenie is trotting beside it now.

Three hours later we are back in the kitchen hulling[2] a heaping buggyload of windfall pecans. Our backs hurt from gathering them: how hard they were to find (the main crop having been shaken off the trees and sold by the orchard's owners, who are not us) among the concealing leaves, the frosted, deceiving grass. Caarackle! A cheery crunch, scraps of miniature thunder sound as the shells collapse and the golden mound of sweet oily ivory meat mounts in the milk-glass bowl. Queenie begs to taste, and now and again my friend sneaks her a mite, though insisting we deprive ourselves. "We mustn't, Buddy. If we start, we won't stop. And there's scarcely enough as there is. For thirty cakes." The kitchen is growing dark. Dusk turns the window into a mirror: our reflections mingle with the rising moon as we work by the fireside in the firelight. At last, when the moon is quite high, we toss the final hull into the fire and, with joined sighs, watch it catch flame. The buggy is empty, the bowl is brimful.

We eat our supper (cold biscuits, bacon, blackberry jam) and discuss tomorrow. Tomorrow the kind of work I like best begins: buying. Cherries and citron,[3] ginger and vanilla and canned Hawaiian pineapple, rinds[4] and raisins and walnuts and whiskey and oh, so much flour, butter, so many eggs, spices, flavorings: why, we'll need a pony to pull the buggy home.

---

**1. distemper** (dis tem' pər) n.: An infectious virus disease of young dogs.
**2. hulling:** (hul' iŋ) v.: Taking the shells off nuts.
**3. citron** (si' trən) n.: A yellow, thick-skinned, lemonlike fruit.
**4. rinds** (rīnds) n.: The skins of oranges and lemons.

But before these purchases can be made, there is the question of money. Neither of us has any. Except for skinflint[5] sums persons in the house occasionally provide (a dime is considered very big money); or what we earn ourselves from various activities: holding rummage sales, selling buckets of hand-picked blackberries, jars of homemade jam and apple jelly and peach preserves, rounding up flowers for funerals and weddings. Once we won seventy-ninth prize, five dollars, in a national football contest. Not that we know a fool thing about football. It's just that we enter any contest we hear about: at the moment our hopes are centered on the fifty-thousand-dollar Grand Prize being offered to name a new brand of coffee (we suggested "A.M."; and, after some hesitation, for my friend thought it perhaps sacrilegious,[6] the slogan "A.M.! Amen!"). To tell the truth, our only *really* profitable enterprise was the Fun and Freak Museum we conducted in a back-yard woodshed two summers ago. The Fun was a stereopticon[7] with slide views of Washington and New York lent us by a relative who had been to those places (she was furious when she discovered why we'd borrowed it); the Freak was a three-legged biddy chicken hatched by one of our own hens. Everybody hereabouts wanted to see that biddy: we charged grownups a nickel, kids two cents. And took in a good twenty dollars before the museum shut down due to the decease of the main attraction.

But one way and another we do each year accumulate Christmas savings, a Fruit-cake Fund. These moneys we keep hidden in an ancient bead purse under a loose board under the floor under a chamber pot under my friend's bed. The purse is seldom removed from this safe location except to make a deposit, or, as happens every Saturday, a withdrawal; for on Saturdays I am allowed ten cents to go to the picture show. My friend has never been to a picture show, nor does she intend to: "I'd rather hear you tell the story, Buddy. That way I can imagine it more. Besides, a person my age shouldn't squander their eyes. When the Lord comes, let me see Him clear." In addition to never having seen a movie, she has never: eaten in a restaurant, traveled more than five miles from home, received or sent a telegram, read anything except funny papers and the Bible, worn cosmetics, cursed, wished someone harm, told a lie on purpose, let a hungry dog go hungry. Here are a few things she has done, does do: killed with a hoe the biggest rattlesnake ever seen in this county (sixteen rattles), dip snuff (secretly), tame hummingbirds (just try it) till they balance on her finger, tell ghost stories (we both believe in ghosts) so tingling they chill you in July, talk to herself, take walks in the rain, grow the prettiest japonicas[8] in town, know the recipe for every sort of old-time Indian cure, including a magical wart-remover.

Now, with supper finished, we retire to the room in a faraway part of the house where my friend sleeps in a scrap-quilt-covered iron bed painted rose pink, her favorite color. Silently, wallowing in the pleasures of conspiracy, we take the bead purse from its secret place and spill its contents on the scrap quilt. Dollar bills, tightly rolled and green as May buds. Somber fifty-cent pieces, heavy enough to weight a dead

---

**5. skinflint** (skin' flint') *adj.*: Miserly.
**6. sacrilegious** (sak' rə lij' əs) *adj.*: Disrespectful or irreverent toward anything regarded as sacred.
**7. stereopticon** (ster' ē äp' ti kən) *n.*: An instrument with two eyepieces through which a pair of photographs of the same scene taken at slightly different angles are viewed to give a three-dimensional effect.

---

**8. japonicas** (jə pän' i kəs) *n.*: Flowers such as camellias or Japanese quince.

man's eyes. Lovely dimes, the liveliest coin, the one that really jingles. Nickels and quarters, worn smooth as creek pebbles. But mostly a hateful heap of bitter-odored pennies. Last summer others in the house contracted to pay us a penny for every twenty-five flies we killed. Oh, the carnage[9] of August: the flies that flew to heaven! Yet it was not work in which we took pride. And, as we sit counting pennies, it is as though we were back tabulating dead flies. Neither of us has a head for figures; we count slowly, lose track, start again. According to her calculations, we have $12.73. According to mine, exactly $13. "I do hope you're wrong, Buddy. We can't mess around with thirteen. The cakes will fall. Or put somebody in the cemetery. Why, I wouldn't dream of getting out of bed on the thirteenth." This is true: she always spends thirteenths in bed. So, to be on the safe side, we subtract a penny and toss it out the window.

Of the ingredients that go into our fruitcakes, whiskey is the most expensive, as well as the hardest to obtain: State laws forbid its sale. But everybody knows you can buy a bottle from Mr. Haha Jones. And the next day, having completed our more prosaic shopping, we set out for Mr. Haha's business address, a "sinful " (to quote public opinion) fish-fry and dancing café down by the river. We've been there before, and on the same errand; but in previous years our dealings have been with Haha's wife, an iodine-dark Indian woman with brassy peroxided hair and a dead-tired disposition. Actually, we've never laid eyes on her husband, though we've heard that he's an Indian too. A giant with razor scars across his cheeks. They call him Haha because he's so gloomy, a man who never laughs. As we approach his café (a large log cabin festooned inside and out with chains of garish-gay naked light bulbs and standing by the river's muddy edge under the shade of river trees where moss drifts through the branches like gray mist) our steps slow down. Even Queenie stops prancing and sticks close by. People have been murdered in Haha's café. Cut to pieces. Hit on the head. There's a case coming up in court next month. Naturally these goings-on happen at night when the colored lights cast crazy patterns and the victrola[10] wails. In the daytime Haha's is shabby and deserted. I knock at the door, Queenie barks, my friend calls: "Mrs. Haha, ma'am? Anyone to home?"

Footsteps. The door opens. Our hearts overturn. It's Mr. Haha Jones himself! And he *is* a giant; he *does* have scars; he *doesn't* smile. No, he glowers at us through Satan-tilted eyes and demands to know: "What you want with Haha?"

For a moment we are too paralyzed to tell. Presently my friend half-finds her voice, a whispery voice at best: "If you please, Mr. Haha, we'd like a quart of your finest whiskey."

His eyes tilt more. "Would you believe it? Haha is smiling! Laughing, too. "Which one of you is a drinkin' man?"

"It's for making fruitcakes, Mr. Haha. Cooking."

This sobers him. He frowns. "That's no way to waste good whiskey." Nevertheless, he retreats into the shadowed café and seconds later appears carrying a bottle of daisy-yellow unlabeled liquor. He demonstrates its sparkle in the sunlight and says: "Two dollars."

We pay him with nickels and dimes and pennies. Suddenly, as he jangles the coins in his hand like a fistful of dice, his face softens. "Tell you what," he proposes, pour-

---

**9. carnage** (kär′ nij) *n.*: Slaughter; massacre.

**10. victrola** (vic trōl′ ə) *n.*: A record player.

ing the money back into our bead purse, "just send me one of them fruitcakes instead."

"Well," my friend remarks on our way home, "there's a lovely man. We'll put an extra cup of raisins in *his* cake."

The black stove, stoked with coal and firewood, glows like a lighted pumpkin. Eggbeaters whirl, spoons spin round in bowls of butter and sugar, vanilla sweetens the air, ginger spices it; melting, nose-tingling odors saturate the kitchen, suffuse the house, drift out to the world on puffs of chimney smoke. In four days our work is done. Thirty-one cakes, dampened with whiskey, bask on window sills and shelves.

Who are they for?

Friends. Not necessarily neighbor friends: indeed, the larger share is intended for persons we've met maybe once, perhaps not at all. People who've struck our fancy. Like President Roosevelt.[11] Like the Reverend and Mrs. J. C. Lucey, Baptist missionaries to Borneo who lectured here last winter. Or the little knife grinder who comes through town twice a year. Or Abner Packer, the driver of the six o'clock bus from Mobile,[12] who exchanges waves with us every day as he passes in a dust-cloud whoosh. Or the young Wistons, a California couple whose car one afternoon broke down outside the house and who spent a pleasant hour chatting with us on the porch (young Mr. Wiston snapped our picture, the only one we've ever had taken). Is it because my friend is shy with everyone *except* strangers that these strangers, and merest acquaintances, seem to us our truest friends? I think yes. Also, the scrapbooks we keep of thank-you's on White House stationery, time-to-time communications from California and Borneo, the knife grinder's penny post cards, make us feel connected to eventful worlds beyond the kitchen with its view of a sky that stops.

Now a nude December fig branch grates against the window. The kitchen is empty, the cakes are gone; yesterday we carted the last of them to the post office, where the cost of stamps turned our purse inside out. We're broke. That rather depresses me, but my friend insists on celebrating—with two inches of whiskey left in Haha's bottle. Queenie has a spoonful in a bowl of coffee (she likes her coffee chicory-flavored and strong). The rest we divide between a pair of jelly glasses. We're both quite awed at the prospect of drinking straight whiskey; the taste of it brings screwed-up expressions and sour shudders. But by and by we begin to sing, the two of us singing different songs simultaneously. I don't know the words to mine, just: *Come on along, come on along, to the dark-town strutters' ball.* But I can dance: that's what I mean to be, a tap dancer in the movies. My dancing shadow rollicks on the walls; our voices rock the chinaware; we giggle: as if unseen hands were tickling us. Queenie rolls on her back, her paws plow the air, something like a grin stretches her black lips. Inside myself, I feel warm and sparky as those crumbling logs, carefree as the wind in the chimney. My friend waltzes round the stove, the hem of her poor calico skirt pinched between her fingers as though it were a party dress: *Show me the way to go home*

Enter: two relatives. Very angry. Potent[13] with eyes that scold, tongues that scald.

**11. President Roosevelt:** Franklin Delano Roosevelt (1882–1945), thirty-second President of the United States (1933–1945).
**12. Mobile** (mō bēl′): City in Alabama.
**13. potent** (pōt′ 'nt) *adj.*: Powerful.

Listen to what they have to say, the words tumbling together into a wrathful tune: "A child of seven! whiskey on his breath! are you out of your mind? feeding a child of seven! must be loony! road to ruination! remember Cousin Kate? Uncle Charlie? Uncle Charlie's brother-in-law? shame! scandal! humiliation! kneel, pray beg the Lord!"

Queenie sneaks under the stove. My friend gazes at her shoes, her chin quivers, she lifts her skirt and blows her nose and runs to her room. Long after the town has gone to sleep and the house is silent except for the chimings of clocks and sputter of fading fires, she is weeping into a pillow already as wet as a widow's handkerchief.

"Don't cry," I say, sitting at the bottom of her bed and shivering despite my flannel nightgown that smells of last winter's cough syrup, "don't cry," I beg, teasing her toes, tickling her feet, "you're too old for that."

"It's because," she hiccups, "I *am* too old. Old and funny."

"Not funny. Fun. More fun than anybody. Listen. If you don't stop crying you'll be so tired tomorrow we can't go cut a tree."

She straightens up. Queenie jumps on the bed (where Queenie is not allowed) to lick her cheeks. "I know where we'll find real pretty trees, Buddy. And holly, too. With berries big as your eyes. It's way off in the woods. Farther than we've ever been. Papa used to bring us Christmas trees from there: carry them on his shoulder. That's fifty years ago. Well, now: I can't wait for morning."

Morning. Frozen rime[14] lusters the grass; the sun, round as an orange and orange as hot-weather moons, balances on the horizon, burnishes the silvered winter woods. A wild turkey calls. A renegade hog

grunts in the undergrowth. Soon, by the edge of knee-deep, rapid-running water, we have to abandon the buggy. Queenie wades the stream first, paddles across barking complaints at the swiftness of the current, the pneumonia-making coldness of it. We follow, holding our shoes and equipment (a hatchet, a burlap sack) above our heads. A mile more: of chastising thorns, burs and briers that catch at our clothes; of rusty pine needles brilliant with gaudy fungus and molted feathers. Here, there, a flash, a flutter, an ecstasy of shrillings remind us that not all the birds have flown south. Always, the path unwinds through lemony sun pools and pitch-black vine tunnels. Another creek

---

**14. rime** (rīm) *n.*: Frost.

to cross: a disturbed armada[15] of speckled trout froths the water round us, and frogs the size of plates practice belly flops; beaver workmen are building a dam. On the farther shore, Queenie shakes herself and trembles. My friend shivers, too: not with cold but enthusiasm. One of her hat's ragged roses sheds a petal as she lifts her head and inhales the pine-heavy air. "We're almost there; can you smell it, Buddy?" she says, as though we were approaching an ocean.

---

**15. armada** (är mä′ də) *n.*: A fleet of warships.

And, indeed, it is a kind of ocean. Scented acres of holiday trees, prickly-leafed holly. Red berries shiny as Chinese bells: black crows swoop upon them screaming. Having stuffed our burlap sacks with enough greenery and crimson to garland a dozen windows, we set about choosing a tree. "It should be," muses my friend, "twice as tall as a boy. So a boy can't steal the star." The one we pick is twice as tall as me. A brave handsome brute that survives thirty hatchet strokes before it keels with a creaking rending cry. Lugging it like a kill, we commence the long trek out. Every few yards we abandon the struggle, sit down

and pant. But we have the strength of triumphant huntsmen; that and the tree's virile, icy perfume revive us, goad us on. Many compliments accompany our sunset return along the red clay road to town; but my friend is sly and noncommittal when passers-by praise the treasure perched in our buggy: what a fine tree and where did it come from? "Yonderways," she murmurs vaguely. Once a car stops and the rich mill owner's lazy wife leans out and whines: "Giveya two-bits cash for that ol tree." Ordinarily my friend is afraid of saying no; but on this occasion she promptly shakes her head: "We wouldn't take a dollar." The mill owner's wife persists. "A dollar, my foot! Fifty cents. That's my last offer. Goodness, woman, you can get another one." In answer, my friend gently reflects: "I doubt it. There's never two of anything."

Home: Queenie slumps by the fire and sleeps till tomorrow, snoring loud as a human.

A trunk in the attic contains: a shoebox of ermine[16] tails (off the opera cape of a curious lady who once rented a room in the house), coils of frazzled tinsel gone gold with age, one silver star, a brief rope of dilapidated, undoubtedly dangerous candy-like light bulbs. Excellent decorations, as far as they go, which isn't far enough: my friend wants our tree to blaze "like a Baptist window," droop with weighty snows of ornament. But we can't afford the made-in-Japan splendors at the five-and-dime. So we do what we've always done: sit for days at the kitchen table with scissors and crayons and stacks of colored paper. I make sketches and my friend cuts them out: lots of cats, fish too

(because they're easy to draw), some apples, some watermelons, a few winged angels devised from saved-up sheets of candy-bar tin foil. We use safety pins to attach these creations to the tree; as a final touch, we sprinkle the branches with shredded cotton (picked in August for this purpose). My friend, surveying the effect, clasps her hands together. "Now honest, Buddy. Doesn't it look good enough to eat?" Queenie tries to eat an angel.

After weaving and ribboning holly wreaths for all the front windows, our next project is the fashioning of family gifts. Tie-dye scarves for the ladies, for the men a home-brewed lemon and licorice and aspirin syrup to be taken "at the first Symptoms of a Cold and after Hunting." But when it comes time for making each other's gift, my friend and I separate to work secretly. I would like to buy her a pearl-handled knife, a radio, a whole pound of chocolate-covered cherries (we tasted some once, and she always swears: "I could live on them, Buddy, Lord yes I could—and that's not taking His name in vain"). Instead, I am building her a kite. She would like to give me a bicycle (she's said so on several million occasions: "If only I could, Buddy. It's bad enough in life to do without something *you* want; but confound it, what gets my goat is not being able to give somebody something you want *them* to have. Only one of these days I will, Buddy. Locate you a bike. Don't ask how. Steal it, maybe"). Instead, I'm fairly certain that she is building me a kite—the same as last year, and the year before: the year before that we exchanged slingshots. All of which is fine by me. For we are champion kite-fliers who study the wind like sailors; my friend, more accomplished than I, can get a kite aloft when there isn't enough breeze to carry clouds.

---

**16. ermine** (ᴜr′ mən) *adj.*: Of the soft white fur with black tips of a weasel.

Christmas Eve afternoon we scrape together a nickel and go to the butcher's to buy Queenie's traditional gift, a good gnawable beef bone. The bone, wrapped in funny paper, is placed high in the tree near the silver star. Queenie knows it's there. She squats at the foot of the tree staring up in a trance of greed: when bedtime arrives she refuses to budge. Her excitement is equaled by my own. I kick the covers and turn my pillow as though it were a scorching summer's night. Somewhere a rooster crows: falsely, for the sun is still on the other side of the world.

"Buddy, are you awake?" It is my friend, calling from her room, which is next to mine; and an instant later she is sitting on my bed holding a candle. "Well, I can't sleep a hoot," she declares. "My mind's jumping like a jack rabbit. Buddy, do you think Mrs. Roosevelt will serve our cake at dinner?" We huddle in the bed, and she squeezes my hand I-love-you. "Seems like your hand used to be so much smaller. I guess I hate to see you grow up. When you're grown up, will we still be friends?" I say always. "But I feel so bad, Buddy. I wanted so bad to give you a bike. I tried to sell my cameo[17] Papa gave me. Buddy"—she hesitates, as though embarrassed—"I made you another kite." Then I confess that I made her one, too; and we laugh. The candle burns too short to hold. Out it goes, exposing the starlight, the stars spinning at the window like a visible caroling that slowly, slowly daybreak silences. Possibly we doze; but the beginnings of dawn splash us like cold water: we're up, wide-eyed and wandering while we wait for others to waken. Quite deliberately my friend drops a kettle on the kitchen floor. I tap-dance in front of closed doors. One by one the household emerges, looking as though they'd like to kill us both; but it's Christmas, so they can't. First, a gorgeous breakfast: just everything you can imagine —from flapjacks and fried squirrel to hominy grits and honey-in-the-comb. Which puts everyone in a good humor except my friend and me. Frankly, we're so impatient to get at the presents we can't eat a mouthful.

Well, I'm disappointed. Who wouldn't be? With socks, a Sunday school shirt, some handkerchiefs, a hand-me-down sweater and a year's subscription to a religious magazine for children. *The Little Shepherd.* It makes me boil. It really does.

My friend has a better haul. A sack of Satsumas,[18] that's her best present. She is proudest, however, of a white wool shawl knitted by her married sister. But she *says* her favorite gift is the kite I built her. And it *is* very beautiful; though not as beautiful as the one she made me, which is blue and scattered with gold and green Good Conduct stars; moreover, my name is painted on it, "Buddy."

"Buddy, the wind is blowing."

The wind is blowing, and nothing will do till we've run to a pasture below the house where Queenie has scooted to bury her bone (and where, a winter hence, Queenie will be buried, too). There, plunging through the healthy waist-high grass, we unreel our kites, feel them twitching at the string like sky fish as they swim into the wind. Satisfied, sun-warmed, we sprawl in the grass and peel Satsumas and watch our kites cavort. Soon I forget the socks and hand-me-down sweater. I'm as happy as if we'd al-

---

**17. cameo** (kam′ ē ō′) *n.*: A shell or stone carved with a head in profile and used as jewelry.

**18. Satsumas** (sat′ soo məs) *n.*: Small, loose-skinned oranges.

ready won the fifty-thousand-dollar Grand Prize in that coffee-naming contest.

"My, how foolish I am!" my friend cries, suddenly alert, like a woman remembering too late she has biscuits in the oven. "You know what I've always thought?" she asks in a tone of discovery, and not smiling at me but a point beyond. "I've always thought a body would have to be sick and dying before they saw the Lord. And I imagined that when He came it would be like looking at the Baptist window: pretty as colored glass with the sun pouring through, such a shine you don't know it's getting dark. And it's been a comfort: to think of that shine taking away all the spooky feeling. But I'll wager it never happens. I'll wager at the very end a body realizes the Lord has already shown Himself. That things as they are"—her hand circles in a gesture that gathers clouds and kites and grass and Queenie pawing earth over her bone—"just what they've always seen, was seeing Him. As for me, I could leave the world with today in my eyes."

This is our last Christmas together.

Life separates us. Those who Know Best decide that I belong in a military school. And so follows a miserable succession of bugle-blowing prisons, grim reveille-ridden summer camps. I have a new home too. But it doesn't count. Home is where my friend is, and there I never go.

And there she remains, puttering around the kitchen. Alone with Queenie. Then alone. ("Buddy dear," she writes in her wild hard-to-read script, "yesterday Jim Macy's horse kicked Queenie bad. Be thankful she didn't feel much. I wrapped her in a Fine Linen sheet and rode her in the buggy down to Simpson's pasture where she can be with all her Bones . . .".) For a few Novembers she continues to bake her fruit-

cakes single-handed; not as many, but some: and, of course, she always sends me "the best of the batch." Also, in every letter she encloses a dime wadded in toilet paper: "See a picture show and write me the story." But gradually in her letters she tends to confuse me with her other friend,

the Buddy who died in the 1880's; more and more thirteenths are not the only days she stays in bed: a morning arrives in November, a leafless birdless coming of winter morning, when she cannot rouse herself to exclaim: "Oh my, it's fruitcake weather!"

And when that happens, I know it. A message saying so merely confirms a piece of news some secret vein had already received, severing from me an irreplaceable part of myself, letting it loose like a kite on a broken string. That is why, walking across a school campus on this particular December morning, I keep searching the sky. As if I expected to see, rather like hearts, a lost pair of kites hurrying toward heaven.

## THINKING ABOUT THE SELECTION
### Recalling

1. Briefly describe Capote's cousin.
2. What are some of the ways that the two earn money?
3. What three tasks, in preparation for Christmas, do Capote and his cousin accomplish?
4. What gifts do Capote and his cousin exchange?

### Interpreting

5. How does Capote feel about the other members of the household?
6. Why do Capote and his cousin send the fruitcakes to people they hardly know?
7. What are Capote's feelings about leaving and being apart from his cousin?
8. Reread the final paragraph. What does Capote mean by "a lost pair of kites hurrying toward heaven"?

### Applying

9. What is the true meaning of gift giving?

## ANALYZING LITERATURE
### Understanding Reminiscense

A **reminiscense** is an autobiographical account of an experience in the writer's life. The most important aspect of a reminiscense is the special quality of memory that can impart a hazy, dreamlike character to remembered events.
1. Why does Capote use the present tense to describe events twenty years old?
2. Explain how "A Christmas Memory" is a reminiscense.

## CRITICAL THINKING AND READING
### Recognizing Emotive Language

**Emotive language** consists of words and phrases that produce a specific emotional response from the reader. Writers often spend a great deal of time searching for the word or phrase that conveys a meaning or feeling exactly. This was especially true of Truman Capote, who claimed that he sometimes worked for days on a single sentence. Think of the feelings Capote evokes at the beginning of the story. The following are some of the words and phrases he uses to create these feelings: *sprightly; remarkable; purposeful excitement; exhilarates her imagination; fuels the blaze of her heart.* This language evokes warm, happy, positive feelings.
1. What emotion do you feel as the two approach the house of Haha Jones (page 482)? What words and phrases evoke this emotion?
2. What emotion do you feel at the end of the story? What words and phrases evoke this emotion?

## UNDERSTANDING VOCABULARY
### Understanding Compound Adjectives

Throughout the essay, Capote uses **compound adjectives** to create vivid and original descriptions. For example, instead of describing the pennies as *pennies with a bitter odor,* he describes them as "bitter-odored pennies."
1. Locate five other compound adjectives in the story and write their meaning.
2. Create three of your own compound adjectives. Write the adjectives and their meanings.

## THINKING AND WRITING
### Comparing and Contrasting Memories

Write an essay comparing and contrasting "A Child's Christmas in Wales," and "A Christmas Memory." Consider the subject, setting, tone, and special meaning that each author sought to convey as you plan your essay. As you write a draft, include specific examples from each story. Present ideas along corresponding points of comparison or contrast. Finally, revise your essay, replacing general words with more specific ones.

# Types of Essays

**A YOUNG GIRL READING, 1776**
*Jean-Honoré Fragonard*
*National Gallery of Art, Washington*

# GUIDE FOR READING

## The Hawk Is Flying

**Harry Crews** (1935–    ) was born in Alma, Georgia, and grew up on a sharecropper's farm. After serving in the Marine Corps, Crews earned his Bachelor's and Master's degrees at the University of Florida, where he now teaches writing. Crews also writes articles for magazines and has published eight novels, including *The Hawk Is Dying*. This novel centers, as the essay does, on the care and training of hawks.

### Narrative Essay

An essay is a brief composition in which the author offers an opinion or point of view on the subject. A **narrative essay** tells a factual story from the author's point of view. The events have a definite beginning, middle, and end and are arranged in chronological order. They also take place over a limited period of time. In this essay, the author relates the story of how he cared for a wounded hawk.

### Look For

Pay attention as you read "The Hawk Is Flying" to the way the author relates an actual event in the form of a story. How does this enhance your enjoyment of the essay?

### Writing

Think of a time when you thought of an animal as though it were human. If you have never had that experience, imagine what it might be like. Spend a few minutes freewriting about the topic.

### Vocabulary

Knowing the following words will help you as you read "The Hawk Is Flying."

**falconry** (fal′kən rē) *n*.: The training of falcons to hunt game (p. 495)

**docile** (däs′′l) *adj*.: Easy to teach or manage (p. 495)

**perverse** (pər vʉrs′) *adj*.: Wicked, wrong, improper (p. 495)

**aberration** (ab′ər ā′shən) *n*.: Something that differs from the norm (p. 495)

**abhorrently** (əb hôr′ənt lē) *adv*.: Frighteningly; disgustingly; hatefully (p. 496)

**exertion** (ig zʉr′shən) *n*.: The active use of strength or power (p. 496)

**averted** (ə vur′tid) *v*.: Turned away (p. 496)

# The Hawk Is Flying

## Harry Crews

**ONE WING ABOVE DREAM OR HUNGER**
*Richard Casey*
© 1985 Mill Pond Press Inc.

I was jogging between Lake Swan and Lake Rosa[1] on a ridge full of blackjack oak when I saw the hawk, tail feathers fanned and wings half spread, beside a clump of palmetto[2] about twenty yards off the dim path. From the attitude of her wings and tail

I first thought she was sitting on a kill, maybe a rabbit or a rat, but then she turned her wild dandelion eyes toward me and I knew that she was there in the sand not because of something she had killed but because she herself had almost been killed. Blood was dark and clotted oj the trailing edge of her right wing. Some hunter had brought her down with a gun and then not had the decency to find where she fell.

I stood there in the path for a long time,

---

**1. Lake Swan and Lake Rosa:** Lakes in southeastern Georgia.
**2. palmetto** (pal met′ ō) *n.*: Palm tree with fan-shaped leaves.

deciding whether or not to kill her. I knew the chances of keeping her alive were slim after she'd been hurt. But leaving her wing-shot in the dirt like that would take more meanness than I thought I could manage. At the same time, though, I knew the right thing to do would be to step quickly across the sand and kick her to death. I watched her where she sat quietly, feathers ruffled now and unafraid, and I knew I was not going to find it in myself either to leave her or kill her. There was nothing to do but take her up and try to save her.

Because the direct stare of a man is terrifying to a hawk, I kept my eyes averted and slowly circled to the edge of the palmetto, where I knelt in the sand. Her sharp, hooked beak was open from heat and exhaustion, and her peach-colored tongue beat like a pulse with her rapid breathing. From her size and plumage she was obviously a red-tailed hawk, less than two years old and in her prime, but even so, she would have a nervous system as fine and as delicate as a Swiss watch and be subject to death by heart attack or apoplexy[3] if she was not handled carefully. I would need not only whatever skill I might have but also enormous luck, since she would rather die than submit to me. Moving very slowly so as not to disturb her any more than was absolutely necessary, I took off one of my shoes and rolled down a long one-size-fits-all sweat sock I was wearing. Then, moving the hand that held the sock out in front of her so that she would follow it with her eyes, I eased my other hand over her back and pinned her wings down so she could not beat them against the ground. Her shallow, rapid heart trembled under the fine bright feathers of her breast. I tore the toe out of the sock and put it around her neck like a collar and rolled it down until she was encased in a tight tube of elastic cotton. All that was visible was her head at one end of the sock and talons at the other.

On the long slow walk back home, the only sound she made was a soft clucking very much like that of a chicken. I held her as loosely as I could because I was worried about the heat of my hands and the way she was wrapped. I really expected her to die, but apparently she was not hurt as badly as I thought. By the time I put her on my bed her breathing had slowed and she had grown calm under the tight sock.

I sat down and opened my desk, and there, nearly filling the bottom drawer, was leather from all the years I had kept and trained and flown hawks. On top was a pair of leather welder's gloves, the right one bloodstained between the thumb and fore-finger. And under the gloves were several pairs of eighteen-inch jesses[4] and two four-foot leashes and fifteen hoods, each one with the size and date it was made cut into the top of it, and finally four tiny brass falcon bells and as many shark swivels,[5] used to join the jesses to the leashes.

I took the hoods out of the drawer and arbitrarily selected Number 7 to fit to the hawk's head to see if it was lighttight. It was too big, so I tried the next one down, Number 6, which was nearly right. When I went to Number 5, the fit was perfect, so I drew the leather hood strings, and the hawk, in total darkness now, lay utterly still. With a pair of scissors I carefully cut away the sock. I put

---

**3. apoplexy** (ap′ ə plek′ sē) *n*.: A stroke.

**4. jesses** (jes′ əs) *n*.: Straps for fastening around a hawk's legs with a ring at one end for attaching a leash.

**5. shark swivels** (shärk swiv′ 'ls) *n*.: A link that permits the attached parts to turn freely.

on the leather gloves and with my right hand under her breast lifted her to stand on the floor. In the darkness and confusion of the lighttight hood, she stood without moving while I looped the leather jesses around her legs and attached one of the bells to a tail feather. I then attached the ends of the two jesses to the shark swivel and hooked the other end of the swivel to a leash. Her blood-clotted wing hung half spread from her body. I ran my fingers gently along the leading edge to see whether or not the bone was broken. It was not. The flesh was torn, but not badly, and I was able to remove four tiny bird shot from the wound with a pair of tweezers without cutting away any of her feathers. With the leather glove covering my wrist, I touched her legs from behind, and as all hawks will do, she immediately stepped up and back, her talons gripping my arm tightly enough to hurt through the quarter-inch leather.

It has always seemed an awesome mystery to me that any hooded hawk anywhere in the world will step in precisely the same way if the backs of its legs are touched. It was true when Attila the Hun[6] carried hawks on his wrist, and it is still true. Presumably it is something that will be true forever. It is part of the reason men have been fascinated with the art of falconry through all the centuries of recorded history.

The hood was the only way I could possibly keep her while her wing healed because without the hood she would beat herself to death at the end of the jesses. A hood makes a hawk's movements and reactions predictable, but there is something about it that is

disgusting, too. To make a hawk as docile as a kitten, to reduce even the biggest and most magnificent raptor in the world to something any child can carry, has always caused a sour ball of shame to settle solid as bone inside me.

I made a perch for her out of a broomstick attached to the top of a ladder-back chair and put her on it. She gripped the perch and sat as still as if she had been killed and stuffed. Eventually she would move, but only a little. She would lower her head and rake at the hood with her talons, but not for long, and the period of quietness would give her some chance of staying alive until she healed. I drew the blinds on the windows and stood watching her in the darkened room, thinking again of the perverse pleasure and unreasonable joy, dating all the way back to my childhood, that I have found in meat-eating birds.

One of my most vivid memories is of riding bareback on a mule in the pinewoods of South Georgia and seeing a buzzard walk out of the stomach of a dead and bloated cow, a piece of putrid flesh caught in its stinking beak. And right behind that memory is a hawk swinging into our farmyard and driving its talons into the back of a screaming chicken and flying toward the darkened tree line on the horizon. And necessarily linked to that memory is my grandmother immediately cooping up all the chickens except one puny biddy[7] left unprotected in the yard with arsenic[8] on its head for the same hawk to come back later and take away toward the same dark tree line, never to be seen again. A bird that drinks blood and eats flesh seemed to me then, and seems to me now, an aberration of nature, and I have

---

**6. Attila the Hun:** King of a group of Asiatic people who invaded eastern and central Europe in the fourth and fifth centuries A.D.

**7. puny biddy:** Weak, little chicken.
**8. arsenic** (är′ s′n ik′) *n.*: A poison.

always thought it must be for this very reason that I have been driven to capture, train, and fly hawks, to participate in the thing that I find so abhorrently and consistently beautiful.

I left the room and let the hawk sit in silence for the rest of the day and that night. I knew there was some danger she might die of shock or thirst. But unless she was kept still so the damaged wing could start to heal, she would surely die from exertion.

Toward the end of the next day I went down to a feedstore and bought a biddy and carried it dead into the room where the hawk sat on her perch, more alert now, shaking the bell with her tail feathers and holding the damaged wing closer to her body and turning her hooded head toward me as I came to the perch. The blinds were still drawn, and I knew after the long blind night of the hood she would not be afraid of me if I did not look directly at her and made no sudden movements. I held the biddy between the thumb and forefinger of my right hand while I slipped the strings at the back of the hood and drew it away from her head.

I held the biddy about six inches away from the perch and stood very still while the hawk raised the feathers on her head and looked from the glove to my averted face and back again. She had to be hungry, perhaps dangerously so, but I was not going to feed her unless she stepped to my hand. I was not surprised when she had not taken that step after I had held the food in front of her for nearly an hour.

Finally, I backed quietly to the door and left her sitting unhooded in the darkened room. I didn't know how long it would take before she stepped to my glove to eat. But she had to do it or I could never release her and let her fly free again. The problem was simple enough and even easy to solve if she would just cooperate. If she did not lose her

fear of me and step to my glove to eat, I would not be able to work her to a lure. And if I could not work her to a lure, I'd never be able to strengthen her wing enough so she could hunt for herself again, because it would take from three weeks to a month of inactivity for her wing to heal, and after she sat on a perch for a month, she wouldn't even be able to fly to the top of a tree, much less catch a darting rabbit. The choice was brutally necessary: either she lost her fear of me and ate off my glove or I would starve her to death.

Fortunately, most birds of prey—except owls, which are too dumb to do much with —react favorably to patience and calm persistence. After two days on the perch without food, half the time wearing the hood I put on her to accustom her to it, the hawk stepped to my glove and ate the biddy right down to the feet. The next day I gave her strips of beef heart and began taking her outside and fastening her leash to a block of wood where she could weather in the sun and bathe from time to time in a shallow pan of water. There are few things in the world more beautiful to me than a hawk rising from the water and slowly turning in the sun, wings stretched and fanning on the air.

There was no infection, and even though the red-tailed hawk did finally lose two of her flight feathers, she was soon flying the length of her leash to my glove. But her eyes and feathers were dull, and she was extremely weak. With no work, her appetite had gotten smaller and smaller until she was eating barely enough to stay alive.

Twenty days after I brought her home, I decided to start flying her to a lure. I didn't think she was ready for it, but I was afraid she was going to die if she didn't start taking more food, and the only way she was going to do that was if I worked her.

The lure is a pillow-shaped piece of

leather with a freshly killed chicken's head tied to it along with a nice bit of bloody meat. I introduced her to the lure in the room where I kept her, letting her fly to it and eat with it caught between the thumb and forefinger of my glove. When she had become thoroughly accustomed to it, I let her go entirely without food for thirty hours and then took her to a wide, empty field and set her on a portable perch. I fastened her jesses to a twenty-foot length of light but very strong nylon cord. From a distance of about seven feet, I showed her the lure, swung it round and round before finally offering it to her on the glove. Her bobbing head followed the bloody meat, and then, giving a short, startled cry, she flew to it, her talons stretched and ready.

By the end of two weeks I had lengthened the nylon cord to sixty yards. At first there were a few lapses when she swerved away from the lure and headed straight up. But she didn't have to be jerked out of the air many times by the cord before she was convinced she was somehow irrevocably joined to me and the lure.

**SOARING**
*Andrew Wyeth*
Shelburne Museum, Shelburne Vermont

Five weeks after I took her crippled and bleeding out of the sand, she was flying free, diving at the lure as I swung it in long arcs over my head, finally catching it high in the air and powering to the ground with it. As she sat on the lure eating, I would quietly walk to her and touch the backs of her legs with the glove and she would step up and back, finishing her meal on my arm.

I kept her longer than I needed to because I had come to love her, probably because she did not love me, and never would. She was as wild the day I flew her free as she was the day I found her. Hawks are not your friend and do not want to be. They are incapable of love, and I have for a long time thought that was precisely why I so much loved them.

One Sunday morning, trying to do it mechanically and without thought, I drove sixty miles to the Okefenokee Swamp[9] with the hawk hooded so she would stay quiet. When I had taken the canoe five hours deep in the black-water cypress,[10] I unclipped the falconer's bell, slipped her jesses, removed the hood, and threw her from my wrist toward the bright blue sky. I had taken her as deep into the swamp as I could because she had lost her fear of man and at least here she would have some chance of survival. But given the number of fools with guns, I did not think that chance very good, even though she had been freed in the middle of a national preserve.

For a long time I heard her high trailing cry above me. But I never looked up. I felt bad enough as it was.

---

**9. Okefenokee Swamp** (ō′ kē fa nō′ kē): A large swamp in southeastern Georgia and northeastern Florida.
**10. black-water cypress** (sī′ pris) *n.*: A type of evergreen tree that grows in swamps.

---

## THINKING ABOUT THE SELECTION

### Recalling

1. What does the author have to decide when he finds the hawk?
2. Describe some of the techniques Crews uses in handling and caring for the hawk.
3. How long had Crews been interested in hawks?
4. What happens to the hawk at the end of the essay?

### Interpreting

5. Describe Crews's attitude toward birds of prey.

6. What aspects of Crews's character are revealed in this essay?
7. Why does Crews feel badly at the end?

### Applying

8. Why do you think humans are so interested in capturing and training wild animals?
9. Name three other creatures you would consider "abhorently beautiful." Explain the reason for each of your choices.

## ANALYZING LITERATURE

### Understanding a Narrative Essay

Think of a narrative essay as a story that happens to be true. The events take place over a distinct period of time and are related by cause and effect. In addition, a narrative essay may relate many facts about its subject.

1. Who is the author of this essay? Who is the narrator? How is the relationship between author and narrator in a narrative essay different from the relationship in a short story?
2. How much time elapses between the beginning and the end of the essay?
3. List at least three facts Crews includes about hawks.
4. What is the topic of this essay? What conclusion does Crews reach about his topic?

## CRITICAL THINKING AND READING
### Sequencing Events in a Narrative Essay

Because a narrative essay relates a true story, it is important to follow the sequence of events correctly. Rewrite the following list of events from the essay, putting them into the correct order.

    a. Crews attempts to feed the hawk.
    b. Crews brings the hawk to a national preserve.
    c. Crews leaves the hawk in darkness and silence for a day and a night.
    d. Crews lets the bird sit outside in the sun.
    e. Crews begins to fly the bird to a lure.
    f. Crews puts a hood over the hawk's head.

## UNDERSTANDING LANGUAGE
### Understanding Jargon

Jargon is the specialized vocabulary used by the members of an occupation or some other specific group. For example, in popular music, a successful, popular song is called a *hit*. If the song's success is immediate and rapid, it is called a *bullet*. "The Hawk Is Flying" contains examples of the jargon used in falconry.

1. Find three examples of jargon in this essay and write down the meaning of each term.
2. Use a dictionary to find the meaning of the following words as they are used as jargon.
    a. *bridge,* as used by songwriters and musicians
    b. *angel,* as used by play producers
    c. *eagle,* as used by golfers

## THINKING AND WRITING
### Writing a Narrative Essay

Write a narrative essay about an experience that you had training an animal or helping a friend accomplish something. Plan your essay by writing a list of the major events in chronological order. Be sure you present only the events that are related to your experience and that are related by cause and effect. To maintain your reader's interest, include descriptive details to make events as vivid and precise as possible. Proofread your essay and prepare a final draft.

# GUIDE FOR READING

## The Way to Rainy Mountain

**Navarre Scott Momaday** (1934–     ), a Kiowa Indian, spent his youth on several Indian reservations where his parents taught. This contributed to his interest in Native American culture and history. Momaday earned a doctoral degree from Stanford University, where he now teaches English. His first novel, *House Made of Dawn,* was awarded a Pulitzer Prize. *The Way to Rainy Mountain* includes his impressions of contemporary Kiowa culture and world view, as well as their history and legends.

### Imagery in a Narrative Essay

**Imagery** is the use of words and phrases to create pictures or images in the reader's mind. The most common image is visual, but writers also use images appealing to the senses of sound, taste, touch, and smell. The subject in a narrative essay is often an experience from the author's memory. Because memories include a great deal of information recorded through the senses, writers often rely on the use of imagery to convey their experiences graphically and accurately.

### Look For

As you read "The Way to Rainy Mountain," look for Momaday's use of imagery to make incidents and details come alive.

### Writing

Think about an especially memorable place that you have visited. Spend time freewriting about some impressions and thoughts you had as you were traveling to and when you arrived at your destination. Concentrate on images—at least one for each of the five senses.

### Vocabulary

Knowing the following words will help you as you read "The Way to Rainy Mountain."

**writhe** (rīth) *v.*: To twist in pain and agony (p. 501)

**infirm** (in fʉrm') *adj.*: Weak; feeble (p. 501)

**disposition** (dis pə zish'ən) *n.*: Inclination; tendency; choice (p. 501)

**pillage** (pil'ij) *n.*: The act of robbing and destroying, especially during wartime (p. 501)

**engender** (in jen'dər) *v.*: To bring about; cause; produce (p. 503)

**tenuous** (ten'yoo wəs) *adj.*: Slight; flimsy; not substantial or strong (p. 504)

**wariness** (wer'ē nis) *n.*: Caution (p. 504)

**opaque** (ō pāk') *adj.*: Not letting light pass through (p. 505)

*from* # The Way to Rainy Mountain

## N. Scott Momaday

A single knoll rises out of the plain in Oklahoma, north and west of the Wichita Range.[1] For my people, the Kiowas, it is an old landmark, and they gave it the name Rainy Mountain. The hardest weather in the world is there. Winter brings blizzards, hot tornadic winds arise in the spring, and in summer the prairie is an anvil's edge.[2] The grass turns brittle and brown, and it cracks beneath your feet. There are green belts along the rivers and creeks, linear groves of hickory and pecan, willow and witch hazel. At a distance in July or August the steaming foliage seems almost to writhe in fire. Great green and yellow grasshoppers are everywhere in the tall grass, popping up like corn to sting the flesh, and tortoises crawl about on the red earth, going nowhere in the plenty of time. Loneliness is an aspect of the land. All things in the plain are isolate; there is no confusion of objects in the eye, but *one* hill or *one* tree or *one* man. To look upon that landscape in the early morning, with the sun at your back, is to lose the sense of proportion. Your imagination comes to life, and this, you think, is where Creation was begun.

I returned to Rainy Mountain in July. My grandmother had died in the spring, and I wanted to be at her grave. She had lived to be very old and at last infirm. Her only living daughter was with her when she died, and I was told that in death her face was that of a child.

I like to think of her as a child. When she was born, the Kiowas were living the last great moment of their history. For more than a hundred years they had controlled the open range from the Smoky Hill River to the Red, from the headwaters of the Canadian to the fork of the Arkansas and Cimarron. In alliance with the Comanches, they had ruled the whole of the southern Plains. War was their sacred business, and they were among the finest horsemen the world has ever known. But warfare for the Kiowas was preeminently a matter of disposition rather than of survival, and they never understood the grim, unrelenting advance of the U.S. Cavalry. When at last, divided and ill-provisioned, they were driven onto the Staked Plains in the cold rains of autumn, they fell into panic. In Palo Duro Canyon they abandoned their crucial stores to pillage and had nothing then but their lives. In order to save themselves, they surrendered to the soldiers at Fort Sill and were imprisoned in the old stone corral that now stands as a military museum. My grandmother was spared the humiliation of those high gray walls by eight or ten years, but she must have known from birth the affliction of defeat, the dark brooding of old warriors.

Her name was Aho, and she belonged to the last culture to evolve in North America.

---

**1. Wichita** (wic*h* ə tô′) **Range:** A mountain range in southwestern Oklahoma.
**2. anvil's edge:** The edge of the iron or steel block on which metal objects are hammered into shape.

Her forebears came down from the high country in western Montana nearly three centuries ago. They were a mountain people, a mysterious tribe of hunters whose language has never been positively classified in any major group. In the late seventeenth century they began a long migration to the south and east. It was a journey toward the dawn, and it led to a golden age. Along the way the Kiowas were befriended by the Crows, who gave them the culture and religion of the Plains. They acquired horses, and their ancient nomadic spirit was suddenly free of the ground. They acquired Tai-me, the sacred Sun Dance doll, from that moment the object and symbol of their worship, and so shared in the divinity of the sun. Not least, they acquired the sense of destiny, therefore courage and pride. When they entered upon the southern Plains they had been transformed. No longer were they slaves to the simple necessity of survival; they were a lordly and dangerous society of fighters and thieves, hunters and priests of the sun. According to their origin myth, they entered the world through a hollow log. From one point of view, their migration was the fruit of an old prophecy, for indeed they emerged from a sunless world.

Although my grandmother lived out her long life in the shadow of Rainy Mountain, the immense landscape of the continental interior lay like memory in her blood. She could tell of the Crows, whom she had never seen, and of the Black Hills, where she had never been. I wanted to see in reality what she had seen more perfectly in the mind's eye, and traveled fifteen hundred miles to begin my pilgrimage.

Yellowstone,[3] it seemed to me, was the top of the world, a region of deep lakes and dark timber, canyons and waterfalls. But, beautiful as it is, one might have the sense of confinement there. The skyline in all directions is close at hand, the high wall of the woods and deep cleavages of shade. There is a perfect freedom in the mountains, but it belongs to the eagle and the elk, the badger and the bear. The Kiowas reckoned their stature by the distance they could see, and they were bent and blind in the wilderness.

Descending eastward, the highland meadows are a stairway to the plain. In July the inland slope of the Rockies is luxuriant with flax and buckwheat, stonecrop and larkspur. The earth unfolds and the limit of the land recedes. Clusters of trees, and animals grazing far in the distance, cause the vision to reach away and wonder to build upon the mind. The sun follows a longer course in the day, and the sky is immense beyond all comparison. The great billowing clouds that sail upon it are shadows that move upon the brain like water, dividing light. Farther down, in the land of the Crows and Blackfeet, the plain is yellow. Sweet clover takes hold of the hills and bends upon itself to cover and seal the soil. There the Kiowas paused on their way; they had come to the place where they must change their lives. The sun is at home on the plains. Precisely there does it have the certain character of a god. When the Kiowas came to the land of the Crows, they could see the dark lees of the hills at dawn across the Bighorn River, the profusion of light on the grain shelves, the oldest deity ranging after the solstices. Not yet would they veer southward to the caldron[4] of the land that lay below; they must wean their blood from the northern winter and hold the mountains a while longer in their view. They bore Tai-me in procession to the east.

---

**3. Yellowstone**: Yellowstone National Park, mostly in northwestern Wyoming but including narrow strips in southern Montana and eastern Idaho.

---

**4. caldron** (kôl′ drən) *n.*: Heat like that of a boiling kettle.

*This map shows the area through which Momaday traveled as he retraced the route followed by the Kiowas nearly three centuries ago. The route stretched from the high country of what is today western Montana to the southern plains of what is now Kansas and Oklahoma.*

A dark mist lay over the Black Hills, and the land was like iron. At the top of a ridge I caught sight of Devil's Tower upthrust against the gray sky as if in the birth of time the core of the earth had broken through its crust and the motion of the world was begun. There are things in nature that engender an awful quiet in the heart of man; Devil's Tower is one of them. Two centuries ago, because they could not do otherwise, the Kiowas made a legend at the base of the rock. My grandmother said:

*Eight children were there at play, seven sisters and their brother.*
*Suddenly the boy was struck dumb; he trembled and began to run*
*upon his hands and feet. His fingers became claws, and his body*
*was covered with fur. Directly there was a bear where the boy had*
*been. The sisters were terrified; they ran, and the bear after them.*
*They came to the stump of a great tree, and the tree spoke to*
*them. It bade them climb upon it, and as they did so it began to*
*rise into the air. The bear came to kill them, but they were just*
*beyond its reach. It reared against the tree and scored the bark*

from *The Way to Rainy Mountain*  503

*all around with its claws. The seven sisters were borne into the*
*sky, and they became the stars of the Big Dipper.*

From that moment, and so long as the legend lives, the Kiowas have kinsmen in the night sky. Whatever they were in the mountains, they could be no more. However tenuous their well-being, however much they had suffered and would suffer again, they had found a way out of the wilderness.

My grandmother had a reverence for the sun, a holy regard that now is all but gone out of mankind. There was a wariness in her, and an ancient awe. She was a Christian in her later years, but she had come a long way about, and she never forgot her birthright. As a child she had been to the Sun Dances; she had taken part in those annual rites, and by them she had learned the restoration of her people in the presence of Tai-me. She was about seven when the last Kiowa Sun Dance was held in 1887 on the Washita River above Rainy Mountain Creek. The buffalo were gone. In order to consummate the ancient sacrifice—to impale the head of a buffalo bull upon the medicine tree—a delegation of old men journeyed into Texas, there to beg and barter for an animal from the Goodnight herd. She was ten when the Kiowas came together for the last time as a living Sun Dance culture. They could find no buffalo; they had to hang an old hide from the sacred tree. Before the dance could begin, a company of soldiers rode out from Fort Sill under orders to disperse the tribe. Forbidden without cause the essential act of their faith, having seen the wild herds slaughtered and left to rot upon the ground, the Kiowas backed away forever

ANNIE OLD CROW
*James Bama*
Courtesy of the artist

from the medicine tree. That was July 20, 1890, at the great bend of the Washita. My grandmother was there. Without bitterness, and for as long as she lived, she bore a vision of deicide.[5]

Now that I can have her only in memory, I see my grandmother in the several postures that were peculiar to her: standing at the wood stove on a winter morning and turning meat in a great iron skillet; sitting at the south window, bent above her beadwork, and afterwards, when her vision failed, looking down for a long time into the fold of her hands; going out upon a cane, very slowly as she did when the weight of age came upon her; praying. I remember her most often at prayer. She made long, ram-

---

**5. deicide** (dē′ ə sīd′) *n*.: The killing of a god.

bling prayers out of suffering and hope, having seen many things. I was never sure that I had the right to hear, so exclusive were they of all mere custom and company. The last time I saw her she prayed standing by the side of her bed at night, naked to the waist, the light of a kerosene lamp moving upon her dark skin. Her long, black hair, always drawn and braided in the day, lay upon her shoulders and against her breasts like a shawl. I do not speak Kiowa, and I never understood her prayers, but there was something inherently sad in the sound, some merest hesitation upon the syllables of sorrow. She began in a high and descending pitch, exhausting her breath to silence; then again and again—and always the same intensity of effort, of something that is, and is not, like urgency in the human voice. Transported so in the dancing light among the shadows of her room, she seemed beyond the reach of time. But that was illusion; I think I knew then that I should not see her again.

Houses are like sentinels in the plain, old keepers of the weather watch. There, in a very little while, wood takes on the appearance of great age. All colors wear soon away in the wind and rain, and then the wood is burned gray and the grain appears and the nails turn red with rust. The windowpanes are black and opaque; you imagine there is nothing within, and indeed there are many ghosts, bones given up to the land. They stand here and there against the sky, and you approach them for a longer time than you expect. They belong in the distance; it is their domain.

Once there was a lot of sound in my grandmother's house, a lot of coming and going, feasting and talk. The summers there were full of excitement and reunion. The Kiowas are a summer people; they abide the cold and keep to themselves, but when the season turns and the land becomes warm and vital they cannot hold still; an old love of going returns upon them. The aged visitors who came to my grandmother's house when I was a child were made of lean and leather, and they bore themselves upright. They wore great black hats and bright ample shirts that shook in the wind. They rubbed fat upon their hair and wound their braids with strips of colored cloth. Some of them painted their faces and carried the scars of old and cherished enmities. They were an old council of warlords, come to remind and be reminded of who they were. Their wives and daughters served them well. The women might indulge themselves; gossip was at once the mark and compensation of their servitude. They made loud and elaborate talk among themselves, full of jest and gesture, fright and false alarm. They went abroad in fringed and flowered shawls, bright beadwork and German silver. They were at home in the kitchen, and they prepared meals that were banquets.

There were frequent prayer meetings, and great nocturnal feasts. When I was a child I played with my cousins outside, where the lamplight fell upon the ground and the singing of the old people rose up around us and carried away into the darkness. There were a lot of good things to eat, a lot of laughter and surprise. And afterwards, when the quiet returned, I lay down with my grandmother and could hear the frogs away by the river and feel the motion of the air.

Now there is a funeral silence in the rooms, the endless wake of some final word. The walls have closed in upon my grandmother's house. When I returned to it in mourning, I saw for the first time in my life how small it was. It was late at night, and there was a white moon, nearly full. I sat for a long time on the stone steps by the kitchen

**OLD ONES TALKING**
*R. Brownell McGrew*
*Courtesy of the artist*

door. From there I could see out across the land; I could see the long row of trees by the creek, the low light upon the rolling plains, and the stars of the Big Dipper. Once I looked at the moon and caught sight of a strange thing. A cricket had perched upon the handrail, only a few inches away from me. My line of vision was such that the creature filled the moon like a fossil. It had gone there, I thought, to live and die, for there, of all places, was its small definition made whole and eternal. A warm wind rose up and purled[6] like the longing within me.

The next morning I awoke at dawn and went out on the dirt road to Rainy Mountain. It was already hot, and the grasshoppers began to fill the air. Still, it was early in the morning, and the birds sang out of the shadows. The long yellow grass on the mountain shone in the bright light, and a scissortail[7] hied above the land. There, where it ought to be, at the end of a long and legendary way, was my grandmother's grave. Here and there on the dark stones were ancestral names. Looking back once, I saw the mountain and came away.

---

**6. purled** (purl'd) *v.*: Moved in ripples or with a murmuring sound; swirled.

**7. scissortail** (siz' ər tāl') *n.*: A pale gray and pink variety of flycatcher.

## THINKING ABOUT THE SELECTION

### Recalling

1. Why does Momaday prefer to remember his grandmother as a child?
2. What did the Kiowas acquire that transformed their culture on their journey south?
3. What legend was inspired by Devil's Tower?
4. What happened when the Kiowas last came together as a living Sun Dance culture?
5. Describe the summer activities that Momaday remembers at his grandmother's house.

### Interpreting

6. To what two people or things is Momaday paying respect on his visit to Rainy Mountain?
7. What aspects of her culture does Momaday believe his grandmother never lost?
8. What does seeing the Big Dipper and the image of the cricket at the end suggest about Momaday and the spirit of his people?

### Applying

9. Frederick Douglass has written, "We have to do with the past only as we can make it useful to the present and the future." First discuss the meaning of this quotation. Do you agree with it? Do you think Momaday would agree with it? Explain your answers.

## ANALYZING LITERATURE

### Understanding Imagery in Essays

**Imagery** is the use of words and phrases to create pictures in the mind of the reader. Create a chart with a column for each of the five senses. List details from the selection under each column. For example, under *Hearing,* you might list "cracks beneath your feet."

## CRITICAL THINKING AND READING

### Reading a Map

The Kiowa Indians traveled a great distance when they migrated from western Montana to the southern plains. Look at the map on page 503 and answer the following questions.

1. What direction did the Kiowas travel in their journey from the Yellowstone Park area to the Black Hills?
2. What was the distance of the journey from the Black Hills to the Wichita mountain range?
3. Approximately how many square miles was the Kiowas' territory (page 501)?

## UNDERSTANDING LANGUAGE

### Using Prefixes and Suffixes

By adding prefixes before words and suffixes after words, you can form new words with related meanings. For example, if you add the suffix *-ful,* to the verb *help,* you form the adjective *helpful.* Adding the prefix *un-*creates another adjective, *unhelpful.* Use the following words from Momaday's essay to form new words.

1. war (add a suffix)
2. understood (add a prefix)
3. talk (add a prefix and a suffix)

## THINKING AND WRITING

### Writing About a Journey

Imagine that you are writing an advertisement for a travel agent to convince people to visit there. Use the ideas and impressions generated from the writing assignment on page 500. Then write an essay about a trip or visit to some memorable place. As you write, focus as much as possible on using images that will enable the reader to create a picture in his or her mind. Make sure that all of your descriptions are vivid and appeal to as many of the five senses as possible.

# GUIDE FOR READING

## Flood

**Annie Dillard** (1945–    ) grew up in Tinker Creek, Virginia. "Flood" is set in Tinker Creek and presents, as much of her writing does, the natural world as its subject. The essay is an excerpt from Annie Dillard's Pulitzer Prize-winning first book, *Pilgrim at Tinker Creek,* and recalls the effects of Hurricane Agnes. This storm struck the eastern United States in 1972 and transformed the creek into a destructive force.

**Descriptive Essay**

A **descriptive essay,** through the use of imagery and other sensory language, creates a picture in the reader's mind. Dillard's essay is filled with sights, sounds, and smells intended to help you experience the flood and its impressions on her imagination as vividly as she did.

**Look For**

As you read, imagine that you are going to make a film based on "Flood." Which visual details would you try to include in the film in order to re-create the events as Dillard experienced them?

**Writing**

Annie Dillard uses descriptions in this essay that appeal to the five senses. Think about a natural occurrence that can be described using sensory language. Write about it briefly and try to evoke its exact sight, sound, smell, and so forth.

**Vocabulary**

Knowing the following words will help you as you read "Flood."
**obliterates** (ə blit'ə rāts) *v.:* Destroys; erases without a trace (p. 511)
**opacity** (ō pas'ə tē) *n.:* The quality of not letting light pass through (p. 511)
**usurped** (yōō sʉrpt') *v.:* Taken power over; held by force (p. 511)
**mauled** (môld) *v.:* Roughly or clumsily handled (p. 512)

**predator** (pred'ə tər) *n.:* An animal that eats other animals (p. 513)
**malevolent** (mə lev'ə lənt) *adj.:* Intended as evil or harmful (p. 513)
**repressed** (ri prest') *v.:* Held back; restrained (p. 513)

# Flood

## Annie Dillard

It's summer. We had some deep spring sunshine about a month ago, in a drought; the nights were cold. It's been gray sporadically, but not oppressively, and rainy for a week, and I would think: When is the real hot stuff coming, the mind-melting weeding weather? It was rainy again this morning, the same spring rain, and then this afternoon a different rain came: a pounding, three-minute shower. And when it was over, the cloud dissolved to haze. I can't see Tinker Mountain.[1] It's summer now: the heat is on. It's summer now all summer long.

The season changed two hours ago. Will my life change as well? This is a time for resolutions, revolutions. The animals are going wild. I must have seen ten rabbits in as many minutes. Baltimore orioles are here; brown thrashers seem to be nesting down by Tinker Creek across the road. The coot[2] is still around, big as a Thanksgiving turkey, and as careless; it doesn't even glance at a barking dog.

The creek's up. When the rain stopped today I walked across the road to the downed log by the steer crossing. The steers were across the creek, a black clot on a distant hill. High water had touched my log, the log I sit on, and dumped a smooth slope of muck in its lee. The water itself was an opaque pale green, like pulverized jade,[3] still high and very fast, lightless, like no earthly water. A dog I've never seen before, thin as death, was flushing rabbits.

A knot of yellow, fleshy somethings had grown up by the log. They didn't seem to have either proper stems or proper flowers, but instead only blind, featureless growth, like etiolated[4] potato sprouts in a root cellar. I tried to dig one up from the crumbly soil, but they all apparently grew from a single, well-rooted corm,[5] so I let them go.

Still, the day had an air of menace. A broken whiskey bottle by the log, the brown tip of a snake's tail disappearing between two rocks on the hill at my back, the rabbit the dog nearly caught, the rabies I knew was in the county, the bees who kept unaccountably fumbling at my forehead with their furred feet . . .

I headed over to the new woods by the creek, the motorbike woods. They were strangely empty. The air was so steamy I could barely see. The ravine separating the woods from the field had filled during high water, and a dead tan mud clogged it now. The horny orange roots of one tree on the ravine's jagged bank had been stripped of

---

**1. Tinker Mountain**: Mountain in Virginia.
**2. coot** (ko͞ot) *n.*: A ducklike, freshwater bird.

**3. pulverized jade** (pul′ və rīz′′d jād′): Crushed green stone.
**4. etiolated** (ēt′ē ə lāt′əd) *adj.*: Pale and stunted.
**5. corm** (kôrm) *n.*: An underground stem similar to a bulb.

soil; now the roots hung, an empty net in the air, clutching an incongruous light bulb stranded by receding waters. For the entire time that I walked in the woods, four jays flew around me very slowly, acting generally odd, and screaming on two held notes. There wasn't a breath of wind.

Coming out of the woods, I heard loud shots; they reverberated ominously in the damp air. But when I walked up the road, I saw what it was, and the dread quality of the whole afternoon vanished at once. It was a couple of garbage trucks, huge trash compacters humped like armadillos, and they were making their engines backfire to impress my neighbors' pretty daughters, high school girls who had just been let off the school bus. The long-haired girls strayed into giggling clumps at the corner of the road; the garbage trucks sped away glorious-ly, as if they had been the Tarleton twins on thoroughbreds cantering away from the gates of Tara.[6] In the distance a white vapor was rising from the waters of Carvin's Cove and catching in trailing tufts in the mountains' sides. I stood on my own porch, exhilarated, unwilling to go indoors.

It was just this time last year that we had the flood. It was Hurricane Agnes, really, but by the time it got here, the weather bureau had demoted it to a tropical storm. I see by a clipping I saved that the date was June twenty-first, the solstice, midsummer's night, the longest daylight of the year; but I didn't notice it at the time. Everything was so exciting, and so very dark.

---

**6. Tarleton twins . . . of Tara:** Characters in the novel *Gone with the Wind*.

All it did was rain. It rained, and the creek started to rise. The creek, naturally, rises every time it rains; this didn't seem any different. But it kept raining, and, that morning of the twenty-first, the creek kept rising.

That morning I'm standing at my kitchen window. Tinker Creek is out of its four-foot banks, way out, and it's still coming. The high creek doesn't look like our creek. Our creek splashes transparently over a jumble of rocks; the high creek obliterates everything in flat opacity. It looks like somebody else's creek that has usurped or eaten our creek and is roving frantically to escape, big and ugly, like a blacksnake caught in a kitchen drawer. The color is foul, a rusty cream. Water that has picked up clay soils looks worse than other muddy waters, because the particles of clay are so fine; they spread out and cloud the water so that you can't see light through even an inch of it in a drinking glass.

Everything looks different. Where my eye is used to depth, I see the flat water, near, too near. I see trees I never noticed before, the black verticals of their rain-soaked trunks standing out of the pale water like pilings for a rotted dock. The stillness of grassy banks and stony ledges is gone; I see rushing, a wild sweep and hurry in one direction, as swift and compelling as a waterfall. The Atkins kids are out in their tiny rain gear, staring at the monster creek. It's risen up to their gates; the neighbors are gathering; I go out.

I hear a roar, a high windy sound more like air than like water, like the run-together whaps of a helicopter's propeller after the engine is off, a high million rushings. The air smells damp and acrid, like fuel oil, or insecticide. It's raining.

I'm in no danger; my house is high. I hurry down the road to the bridge. Neighbors who have barely seen each other all winter are there, shaking their heads. Few have ever seen it before: the water is *over* the bridge. Even when I see the bridge now, which I do every day, I still can't believe it: the water was *over* the bridge, a foot or two over the bridge, which at normal times is eleven feet above the surface of the creek.

Now the water is receding slightly; someone has produced empty metal drums, which we roll to the bridge and set up in a square to keep cars from trying to cross. It takes a bit of nerve even to stand on the bridge; the flood has ripped away a wedge of concrete that buttressed the bridge on the bank. Now one corner of the bridge hangs apparently unsupported while water hurls in an arch just inches below.

It's hard to take it all in, it's all so new. I look at the creek at my feet. It smashes under the bridge like a fist, but there is no end to its force; it hurtles down as far as I can see till it lurches round the bend, filling the valley, flattening, mashing, pushed, wider and faster, till it fills my brain.

It's like a dragon. Maybe it's because the bridge we are on is chancy, but I notice that no one can help imagining himself washed overboard, and gauging his chances for survival. You couldn't live. Mark Spitz[7] couldn't live. The water arches where the bridge's supports at the banks prevent its enormous volume from going wide, forcing it to go high; that arch drives down like a diving whale, and would butt you on the bottom. "You'd never know what hit you," one of the men says. But if you survived that part and managed to surface . . .? How fast can you live? You'd need a windshield. You couldn't keep your head up; the water under the surface is

---

7. **Mark Spitz:** Winner of seven gold medals in swimming in the 1972 Olympic Games.

fastest. You'd spin around like a sock in a clothes dryer. You couldn't grab onto a tree trunk without leaving that arm behind. No, you couldn't live. And if they ever found you, your gut would be solid red clay.

It's all I can do to stand. I feel dizzy, drawn, mauled. Below me the floodwater roils to a violent froth that looks like dirty lace, a lace that continuously explodes before my eyes. If I look away, the earth moves backwards, rises and swells, from the fixing of my eyes at one spot against the motion of the flood. All the familiar land looks as though it were not solid and real at all, but painted on a scroll like a backdrop, and that unrolled scroll has been shaken, so the earth sways and the air roars.

Everything imaginable is zipping by, almost too fast to see. If I stand on the bridge and look downstream, I get dizzy; but if I look upstream, I feel as though I am looking up the business end of an avalanche. There are dolls, split wood and kindling, dead fledgling songbirds, bottles, whole bushes and trees, rakes and garden gloves. Wooden, rough-hewn railroad ties charge by faster than any express. Lattice fencing bobs along, and a wooden picket gate. There are so many white plastic gallon milk jugs that when the flood ultimately recedes, they are left on the grassy banks looking from a distance like a flock of white geese.

I expect to see anything at all. In this one way, the creek is more like itself when it floods than at any other time: mediating, bringing things down. I wouldn't be at all surprised to see John Paul Jones coming round the bend, standing on the deck of the *Bon Homme Richard*,[8] or Amelia Earhart[9]

waving gaily from the cockpit of her floating Lockheed. Why not a cello, a basket of breadfruit, a casket of antique coins? Here comes the Franklin expedition on snowshoes, and the three magi,[10] plus camels, afloat on a canopied barge!

The whole world is in flood, the land as well as the water. Water streams down the trunks of trees, drips from hat-brims, courses across roads. The whole earth seems to slide like sand down a chute; water pouring over the least slope leaves the grass flattened, silver side up, pointing downstream. Everywhere windfall and flotsam twigs and leafy boughs, wood from woodpiles, bottles, and saturated straw spatter the ground or streak it in curving windrows.[11] Tomatoes in flat gardens are literally floating in mud; they look as though they have been dropped whole into a boiling, brown-gravy stew. The level of the water table is at the top of the toe of my shoes. Pale muddy water lies on the flat so that it all but drowns the grass; it looks like a hideous parody[12] of a light snow on the field, with only the dark tips of the grass blades visible.

When I look across the street, I can't believe my eyes. Right behind the road's shoulder are waves, waves whipped in rhythmically peaking scallops, racing downstream. The hill where I watched the praying mantis lay her eggs is a waterfall that splashes into a brown ocean. I can't even remember where the creek usually runs—it is everywhere now. My log is gone for sure, I think—but in fact, I discover later, it holds, rammed between growing trees. Only the cable suspending the steers' fence is visible, and not the fence itself; the steers' pasture

---

**8. John Paul Jones . . . the *Bon Homme Richard*:** American naval officer and his ship. Both were involved in the Revolutionary War.
**9. Amelia Earhart** (1898–1937): U.S. pioneer aviator lost at sea.

**10. three magi** (mā′ jī): Three wise men from the East who brought gifts to the infant Jesus.
**11. windrows** (wind′ rōs′) *n*.: Rows as of raked hay or windblown leaves.
**12. parody** (par′ ə dē) *n*.: Poor imitation.

is entirely in flood, a brown river. The river leaps its banks and smashes into the woods where the motorbikes go, devastating all but the sturdiest trees. The water is so deep and wide it seems as though you could navigate the *Queen Mary*[13] in it, clear to Tinker Mountain.

What do animals do in these floods? I see a drowned muskrat go by like he's flying, but they all couldn't die; the water rises after every hard rain, and the creek is still full of muskrats. This flood is higher than their raised sleeping platforms in the banks; they must just race for high ground and hold on. Where do the fish go, and what do they do? Presumably their gills can filter oxygen out of this muck, but I don't know how. They must hide from the current behind any barriers they can find, and fast for a few days. They must: otherwise we'd have no fish; they'd all be in the Atlantic Ocean. What about herons and kingfishers,[14] say? They can't see to eat. It usually seems to me that when I see any animal, its business is urgent enough that it couldn't easily be suspended for forty-eight hours. Crayfish, frogs, snails, rotifers?[15] Most things must simply die. They couldn't live. Then I suppose that when the water goes down and clears, the survivors have a field day with no competition. But you'd think the bottom would be knocked out of the food chain—the whole pyramid would have no base plankton,[16] and it would crumble, or crash with a thud. Maybe enough spores[17] and

larvae and eggs are constantly being borne down from slower upstream waters to repopulate . . . I don't know.

Some little children have discovered a snapping turtle as big as a tray. It's hard to believe that this creek could support a predator that size: its shell is a foot and a half across, and its head extends a good seven inches beyond the shell. When the children —in the company of a shrunken terrier —approach it on the bank, the snapper rears up on its thick front legs and hisses very impressively. I had read earlier that since turtles' shells are rigid, they don't have bellows lungs; they have to gulp for air. And, also since their shells are rigid, there's only room for so much inside, so when they are frightened and planning a retreat, they have to expel air from their lungs to make room for head and feet—hence the malevolent hiss.

The next time I look, I see that the children have somehow maneuvered the snapper into a washtub. They're waving a broom handle at it in hopes that it will snap the wood like a matchstick, but the creature will not deign[18] to oblige. The kids are crushed; all their lives they've heard that this is the one thing you do with a snapping turtle—you shove a broom handle near it, and it "snaps it like a matchstick." It's nature's way; it's sure-fire. But the turtle is having none of it. It avoids the broom handle with an air of patiently repressed rage. They let it go, and it beelines down the bank, dives unhesitatingly into the swirling floodwater, and that's the last we see of it.

A cheer comes up from the crowd on the bridge. The truck is here with a pump for the Bowerys' basement, hooray! We roll away the metal drums, the truck makes it

---

**13. Queen Mary:** A large ocean-going liner.
**14. herons and kingfishers:** Birds that catch fish to eat.
**15. rotifers** (rōt′ ə fers) *n.*: Microscopic invertebrates.
**16. base plankton:** Microscopic animal and plant life that is the first stage of the food chain.
**17. spores:** Small, usually one-celled reproductive bodies produced by bacteria, algae, mosses, ferns, and so forth.

**18. deign** (dān) *v.*: Do something regarded as beneath one's dignity.

over the bridge, to my amazement—the crowd cheers again. State police cruise by; everything's fine here; downstream people are in trouble. The bridge over by the Bings' on Tinker Creek looks like it's about to go. There's a tree trunk wedged against its railing, and a section of concrete is out. The Bings are away, and a young couple is living there, "taking care of the house." What can they do? The husband drove to work that morning as usual; a few hours later, his wife was evacuated from the front door in a *motorboat*.

I walk to the Bings'. Most of the people who are on our bridge eventually end up over there; it's just down the road. We straggle along in the rain, gathering a crowd. The men who work away from home are here, too; their wives have telephoned them at work this morning to say that the creek is rising fast, and they'd better get home while the gettin's good.

There's a big crowd already there; everybody knows that the Bings' is low. The creek is coming in the recreation-room windows; it's halfway up the garage door. Later that day people will haul out everything salvageable and try to dry it: books, rugs, furniture —the lower level was filled from floor to ceiling. Now on this bridge a road crew is trying to chop away the wedged tree trunk with a long-handled ax. The handle isn't so long that they don't have to stand on the bridge, in Tinker Creek. I walk along a low brick wall that was built to retain the creek away from the house at high water. The wall holds just fine, but now that the creek's receding, it's retaining water around the house. On the wall I can walk right out into the flood and stand in the middle of it. Now on the return trip I meet a young man who's going in the opposite direction. The wall is one brick wide; we can't pass. So we clasp hands and lean out backwards over the turbulent water; our feet interlace like teeth on a zipper, we pull together, stand, and continue on our ways. The kids have spotted a rattlesnake draping itself out of harm's way in a bush; now they all want to walk over the brick wall to the bush, to get bitten by the snake.

The little Atkins kids are here, and they are hopping up and down. I wonder if I hopped up and down, would the bridge go? I could stand at the railing as at the railing of a steamboat, shouting deliriously, "Mark three! Quarter-less-three! Half twain! Quarter twain![19] . . ." as the current bore the broken bridge out of sight around the bend before she sank. . . .

Everyone else is standing around. Some of the women are carrying curious plastic umbrellas that look like diving bells —umbrellas they don't put up, but on; they don't get under, but in. They can see out dimly, like goldfish in bowls. Their voices from within sound distant, but with an underlying cheerfulness that plainly acknowledges, "Isn't this ridiculous?" Some of the men are wearing their fishing hats. Others duck their heads under folded newspapers held not very high in an effort to compromise between keeping their heads dry and letting rain run up their sleeves. Following some form of courtesy, I guess, they lower these newspapers when they speak with you, and squint politely into the rain.

Women are bringing coffee in mugs to the road crew. They've barely made a dent in the tree trunk, and they're giving up. It's a job for power tools; the water's going down anyway, and the danger is past. Some kid starts doing tricks on a skateboard; I head home.

---

**19. "Mark three! . . . Quarter twain!":** Announcements of the depth in fathoms of the water as measured by marks on a lead line.

## THINKING ABOUT THE SELECTION
### Recalling

1. How was the creek's appearance changed?
2. What was fascinating about the bridge near Dillard's home?
3. What are some of the things that rush by in the water?
4. Why does Dillard eventually head home?

### Interpreting

5. How does the flood bring the neighbors together?
6. What is the effect on your imagination of the paragraph on page 512 describing the whole world as being in flood?
7. Why are the people attracted to the Bings' house?
8. How does the use of flashback and present tense affect your impression of the events?

### Applying

9. Why do many people find extreme weather such as floods, blizzards, hurricanes and even lightning storms so fascinating?

## ANALYZING LITERATURE
### Understanding Descriptive Essay

A **descriptive essay** contains words and phrases that appeal to the senses. Sensory language appeals most often to the sense of sight; however, most writers use language appealing to the other senses as well. This language is used to create pictures of people, places, or scenes in your imagination. For example, ". . . four jays flew around me very slowly, acting generally odd, and screaming on two held notes. There wasn't a breath of wind." These two sentences from the essay appeal to three senses: sight, sound, and feel.

1. Find three examples of language appealing to each of the five senses.

2. What is Dillard's purpose in describing her impression of the flood?

## CRITICAL THINKING AND READING
### Separating Fact from Opinion

A **fact** is information that can be proven true or false. An **opinion** is information that cannot be proven true or false because it is based on someone's judgment or feelings. A fact concerning this essay is that it is a description of a flooded creek. An opinion is that the essay beautifully recreates the sights, sounds, and feelings of Dillard's experience.

Identify each of the following quotations from "Flood" as a statement of fact or opinion.

1. "I see by a clipping I saved that the date was June twenty-first . . . the longest daylight of the year."
2. "[The fish] must hide from the current behind any barriers they can find, and fast for a few days."
3. "I had read earlier that since turtles' shells are rigid, they don't have bellows lungs; they have to gulp for air."

## THINKING AND WRITING
### Writing About a Descriptive Essay

The following comment is from a review of *Pilgrim at Tinker Creek*.

> "While readers and reviewers . . . appreciate Dillard's poetic descriptions of her natural world, they generally question how she is able to celebrate an existence which is often senseless and chaotic to her."

Do you agree or disagree with any or all of this statement? Write a short essay, supporting your opinion with examples from "Flood." Revise your essay, making sure you have included adequate support for your ideas.

## The White Lantern

**Evan S. Connell** (1924–     ) is an American novelist and essayist. Born in Kansas City, Missouri, Connell attended Dartmouth College, the University of Kansas, and did graduate work at Stanford and Columbia. He served as a Navy pilot during World War II. His collection of essays entitled *The White Lantern* recount the "irrational, marvelous passion of history's adventurers."

**Expository Essay**

An **expository essay** explains, defines, or interprets an idea, event, or process. This type of essay uses concrete, objective information to develop the author's purpose, the reason for writing the essay. The purpose can be directly stated in a thesis statement or implied from the facts and arguments presented. This essay explains and interprets the characters of two arctic explorers and the events of their expeditions to the South Pole.

**Look For**

As you read "The White Lantern," try to determine the author's purpose. What do you think is his opinion of the two explorers?

**Writing**

Some people believe that luck has an important impact on their lives while others do not believe in luck at all. Freewrite about your feelings on luck and its importance in life.

**Vocabulary**

Knowing the following words will help you read "The White Lantern."

**subsequently** (sub'si kwənt lē) *adv.*: following (p. 517)

**terse** (tʉrs) *adj.*: Concise; polished (p. 517)

**obligatory** (ə blig'ə tôr'ē) *adj.*: Required; necessary (p. 517)

**rigorously** (rig'ər əs lē) *adv.*: Strictly; harshly (p. 518)

**logistics** (lō jis'tiks) *n.*: The providing and transporting of people and equipment (p. 519)

**idyllic** (ī dil'ik) *adj.*: Pleasing and simple (p. 521)

**disdain** (dis dān') *n.*: Scorn; lofty contempt (p. 522)

**lethargic** (li t͟här'jik) *adj.*: Abnormally drowsy or dull; sluggish (p. 522)

**predilection** (pred'l ek'shən) *n.*: An inclination to like something; a special fondness (p. 523)

**scrupulously** (skrōō'pyə ləs lē) *adv.*: Conscientiously; painstakingly (p. 524)

# from The White Lantern

## Evan S. Connell

Amundsen and Scott are the illustrious names. They got to the Pole[1] within five weeks of each other, which suggests nothing more than good luck and bad luck; but there was such a difference in what happened subsequently that luck cannot explain it. The explanation must be found in the characters of the two men.

Roald Amundsen's opinion of luck is terse and revealing:

"Victory awaits those who have everything in order. People call this luck. Defeat awaits those who fail to take the necessary precautions. This is known as bad luck."

There we have it. To be lucky you must know what you are doing.

At the age of fifteen, after reading about Sir John Franklin's disastrous attempt to find a northwest passage, Amundsen began to get ready. He trained his body to endure hardship. He detested football, but forced himself to play it. He went skiing in the mountains whenever possible. He slept with his bedroom windows open all winter. He looked forward to the obligatory term of military service "both because I wanted to be a good citizen and because I felt that military training would be of great benefit to me as further preparation for my life."

When he was twenty-two he persuaded a friend to go with him on a miniature polar passage. West of Oslo[2] is a mile-high plateau extending nearly to the coast. In summer it is used by Lapp[3] herdsmen pasturing reindeer, but when winter arrives the Lapps descend to the valley and the plateau is deserted. There is no record of anyone ever having crossed it during winter. Amundsen resolved to cross it.

In the middle of their third night on the plateau he woke up because of a temperature change. Instead of sleeping on top of the snow he had burrowed into it, hoping to escape the wind, and while he lay snugly in the hole he had been pleased with himself for such a clever idea. He woke up lying on his back, feeling cramped. Without opening his eyes he tried to roll over but was unable to move. The damp snow of early evening had filled the entrance to his burrow, sifted over his sleeping bag, and then had frozen into a solid block of ice. He began struggling and shouting, but he was helpless—absolutely unable to move—and his voice probably was inaudible at the surface. He very soon quit shouting, he says, because it was hard to breathe, and he realized that if he did not keep quiet he would suffocate. Presumably his friend also had burrowed into the snow, which meant he must be trapped in the same way. Unless there

---

**1. Pole:** the South Pole.

**2. Oslo** (äs' lō): Capital of Norway.
**3. Lapp** (lap) *adj.*: Of Lapland, an area in northern Norway, Sweden, and Finland.

*Captain Amundsen*

digging. His friend had slept on the surface, too exhausted to do anything else, and was astonished when he woke up to find himself alone. The only trace of Amundsen was a tuft of hair at one corner of his sleeping bag. Another snow flurry would have hidden him until the Lapps returned.

They got back in such poor shape that people who had seen them eight days earlier did not recognize them.

Commenting on this experience years later, Amundsen remarks that an "adventure" is merely an interruption of an explorer's serious work and indicates bad planning.

This trip across the Norwegian plateau seems to have been rigorously educational. What he learned from it, beyond the danger of burrowing, cannot even be estimated; but it is obvious that, like most extraordinary people, he knew how to distinguish the shape of the world from a grain of sand. Again and again he talks about preparation. Planning. Attention to detail.

He chose the site of his South Polar base only after studying every existing description of the Ross Ice Shelf[4] from the day it was discovered in 1841. Each member of his expedition was judiciously selected. Every bit of equipment, right down to the tent pegs and buttons, was inspected for weakness or inadequacy. He ordered the boots ripped apart and rebuilt according to his own ideas of comfort and safety. He insisted that a new dog whip be designed.

Aboard the *Fram,*[5] in addition to nineteen men, were almost 100 huskies. Amundsen was convinced that dogs were

should be a quick thaw they both would die in these ice coffins.

Amundsen does not know whether he fell asleep or fainted, but the next time he became conscious he heard the sound of

**4. Ross Ice Shelf:** Frozen section of the Ross Sea along the coast of Antarctica.
**5. Fram:** The ship Amundsen's expedition used to get to Antarctica.

essential to success and he had a false deck constructed on the ship to protect them from the tropic sun. He watched their health as closely as he watched the health of his men. He had calculated the day-by-day weight of the sledges that must be hauled to the Pole, and he knew how much weight each animal could pull. As the journey progressed the sledges would become lighter, which meant that fewer dogs would be required. Logistics demanded, therefore, that at a certain point a certain number of dogs be slaughtered. Yet even in death they must contribute. He had calculated that the average dog carried fifty pounds of edible meat. He worked out the precise day on which he intended to kill each dog, and he adhered to this schedule almost exactly.

Amundsen says nothing about the liver, but Arctic Eskimos had known for a long time that you should not eat a husky's liver and he probably was aware of this. He would not have known just why the liver was dangerous, but it would be characteristic of him to credit the Eskimos with some valid reason for their belief.

On the central plateau twenty-four huskies were killed.

"We had agreed to shrink from nothing," he wrote. "The pemmican[6] was cooked remarkably quickly that evening and I was unusually industrious in stirring it. I am not a nervous man, but at the sound of the first shot I found myself trembling. Shot now followed shot in quick succession, echoing uncannily over the great white plain. Each time a trusty servant lost his life."

The Norwegians afterward referred to this campground as the Butcher's Shop.

At first they were reluctant to devour their trusty servants, but the cook Wisting knew his trade. He selected a young animal named Rex.

"I could not take my eyes off his work," says Amundsen.

The delicate little cutlets had an absolutely hypnotizing effect as they were spread out one by one over the snow. They recalled memories of old days, when no doubt a dog cutlet would have been less tempting than now—memories of dishes on which the cutlets were elegantly arranged side by side, with paper frills on the bones, and a neat pile of petits pois[7] in the middle. Ah, my thoughts wandered still farther afield—but that does not concern us now, nor has it anything to do with the South Pole. . . . The meat was excellent, quite excellent, and one cutlet after another disappeared with lightninglike rapidity. I must admit that they would have lost nothing by being a little more tender, but one must not expect too much of a dog. At this first meal I finished five cutlets myself, and looked in vain in the pot for more. Wisting appeared not to have reckoned on such a brisk demand.

About three o'clock on the afternoon of December 14, 1911, Amundsen's men calculated that they had reached the end of the trail.

There were no cheers, no orations. All together the five men grasped a Norwegian flag and thrust it into the snow: Amundsen, Sverre Hassel, Oskar Wisting, Helmer Hansen, Olav Bjaaland.

---

6. **pemmican** (pem′ i kən) *n.*: Dried meat.

7. **petits pois** (pə tē pwa′): French for "small green peas".

"Thus we plant thee, beloved flag, at the South Pole, and give to the plain on which it lies the name of King Haakon VII's plateau.[8]"

That brief speech was the only concession to ritual. One gets out of the way of protracted ceremonies in these regions, says Amundsen. The shorter they are, the better.

The Norwegians were in no hurry to leave. The trip had not been difficult, the weather was mild, and they had more than enough food. They stayed several days, taking measurements, circling the area on skis to be sure they truly had encompassed the Pole, and otherwise enjoyed themselves.

They were camped in the middle of a continent almost as large as Australia and Europe combined. The Ross Ice Shelf, over which they had traveled at the beginning, appears to be only a deep indentation on the map of Antarctica, although it is about the size of France. Ice has buried the entire continent—all of its mountains, plains, and valleys, with very few exceptions—in some places to a depth of two miles. Astronauts say that it is the earth's most noticeable feature and that it radiates light from the bottom of the world like a great white lantern.

Once upon a time Antarctica was different. There were pine forests, swamps, and fern jungles. Shackleton's party[9] found a seam of coal eight feet thick near the top of Beardmore Glacier. Scott, following the same route, came across fossilized twigs and leaves:

"The best leaf impressions and the most obvious were in the rotten clumps of weathered coal which split up easily to sheath-knife and hammer. Every layer of these gave abundant vegetable remains. Most of the bigger leaves were like beech leaves in shape and venation, in size a little smaller than British beech."

On the Palmer Peninsula are traces of fig leaves, sequoia, and an evergreen called araucaria that reached a height of 150 feet and still grows in South America. At Mount Weaver, close to the Pole, is a petrified log eighteen inches in diameter; it dates from the Jurassic period, the age of dinosaurs. What reptiles, animals, and birds lived in prehistoric Antarctica is not known—except for some ancestral families of the penguin, one of which grew as tall as a man.

Nor does anybody know what changed the climate. There are theories, but not much agreement.

At present more than a million people live within a radius of 2,000 miles of the North Pole, yet within that radius of the South Pole—excluding the men at weather stations—there is no human life. There are no land animals or birds, only the indestructible aquatic penguin. There is not a single living tree. There are lichens clinging to exposed rocks, a little moss, some coarse grass, a few spiders and flies. The spiders do not spin webs because of the wind and the flies have no wings. These tiny creatures, as obstinate as Sir Douglas Mawson,[10] spend most of their lives frozen stiff, but thaw out several days a year and hurriedly go about their business in order to maintain the species. Such is life today in Antarctica, which may explain why King Haakon's real estate has never been developed.

Before starting the return journey Amundsen lashed a small Norwegian flag to a tent pole. Inside the tent he left a bag containing a letter to the king, just in case

---

**8. King Haakon's** (hô kŏŏns) **plateau:** They named the high, level area after King Haakon VII (1872–1957), King of Norway from 1905 to 1957.
**9. Shackleton's party:** A group of Antarctic explorers from Great Britain.

**10. Sir Douglas Mawson:** An Antarctic explorer.

*The Five at the Pole*

they should not make it back to their ship. He discarded some items: reindeerskin foot bags, mitts, a sextant, a hypsometer case— which is an instrument for measuring heights above sea level. And he addressed a letter to Scott.

"He will be here sooner or later," Amundsen told a member of the party. "I hope for his sake it will be sooner."

What Amundsen meant was that the weather could only get worse.

Their trip home sounds idyllic. They had marked the route, and the wind and sun were at their backs. They planned to travel eighteen miles a day, which they did without effort in less than five hours. There was so much food that sometimes they threw away biscuits and pemmican, and fed chocolate to the dogs. The dogs had such an easy time pulling the sledges that they began to get fat.

"We were in high spirits and bowled along at a cracking pace. . . ."

They reached their base on January 25, the date Amundsen had selected two years earlier in Norway. A week later the *Fram* sailed with all aboard in perfect health.

Scott at this time was hundreds of miles away, writing in his diary: "February 2. Three out of five of us injured. We shall be lucky if we get through. . . ."

On March 18 he wrote: "Ill fortune presses. . . ."

March 19: "The weather doesn't give us a chance. . . ."

Earlier he had told a Melbourne journalist:[11] "We may get through, we may not. We may lose our lives. We may be wiped out. It is all a matter of providence and luck."

Shortly after that while en route to the Antarctic: ". . . fortune has determined to put every difficulty in our path."

Again, the following week: "I begin to wonder if fortune will ever turn her wheel."

At the start of the final journey: "The future is in the lap of the gods. . . ."

While struggling up Beardmore Glacier, unaware that Amundsen had just reached the Pole: "Our luck is very bad."

Eight days later: "I trust this may prove the turning point in our fortunes. . . ."

Near the end of March as he lay dying he wrote to the mother of one of his dead companions: "The ways of Providence are inscrutable. . . ."

And in his *Message to the Public,* found beside his body, he begins: "The causes of the disaster are not due to faulty organization, but to misfortune. . . ."

Perhaps. Perhaps he was right. Maybe all things rest in the lap of the gods. Maybe "faulty organization" was not the cause, though it is hard to forget something he had said ten years before:

"To my mind no journey ever made with dogs can approach the height of the fine conception which is realized when a party of men go forth to face hardships, dangers, and difficulties with their own unaided efforts, and by days and weeks of hard physical labor succeed in solving some problem of the great unknown. Surely in this case the conquest is more nobly and splendidly won."

It's arguable, of course, whether one should extract particular phrases from a man's life to offer as proof of anything. On the subject of luck, for example, Amundsen himself occasionally referred to it without disdain, in a rather idle fashion, as something to be hoped for.

Still, there's a difference. And the difference becomes more significant when you learn what others thought about Scott. As a child he was so lethargic and preoccupied that he was called "Old Moony." He seems to have been the storybook sissy: emotional, horrified at the sight of blood, physically weak, pampered by his mother and an older sister. A doctor who examined him before he joined the navy advised him to choose a different career.

Scott himself recognized his languid[12] disposition and tried to do something about it; and considering how rapidly he was promoted in the navy he must have changed. Yet in every photograph he looks bemused, tentative, almost doubtful. His stance, his expression—he lives far away from the frigid brutal world of Roald Amundsen. Biographer Peter Brent speaks of a brooding, melancholy air. "His mouth, with its full rounded lips, suggests a leaning toward sensuality and pleasure. . . ."

Scott's resemblance to his romantic kinsman, Sir Walter Scott, is startling; they look like brothers. And his written "impressions" of the Antarctic are what you might expect from a mystic poet, not an explorer:

The small green tent and the great white road.

The drift snow like finest flour penetrating every hole and corner—flickering up beneath one's head cov-

---

11. **Melbourne** (mel' bərn) **journalist:** A news writer from a city in Australia.

12. **languid** (laŋ' gwid) *adj.:* Weak; listless.

ering, pricking sharply as a sand blast.

The sun with blurred image peeping shyly through the wreathing drift giving pale shadowless light.

The eternal silence of the great white desert. Cloudy columns of snow drift advancing from the south, pale yellow wraiths, heralding the coming storm, blotting out one by one the sharp-cut lines of the land.

Given such a temperament, why was he chosen to lead an expedition? The answer seems to be that as a midshipman he won a whaleboat race. This sounds like a petty triumph, but among the excited spectators was Sir Clements Markham, president of the Royal Geographical Society. He invited Scott to supper and later commented: "I was much struck with his intelligence, information, and the charm of his manner."

Because of Markham's patronage, when a British exploratory party sailed for the Antarctic in 1901 its commander was Scott. Even then he admits he is out of place: "I may as well confess that I have no predilection for polar exploration. . . ."

Subsequently he married an actress, Kathleen Bruce, and began to associate with actors, authors, painters, and musicians—a doubtful lot. How much these people unsettled him can only be imagined. Once he wrote to Kathleen: "I seem to hold in reserve something that makes for success and yet to see no worthy field for it and so there is this consciousness of a truly deep unrest."

Now listen to Roald Amundsen on the same subject: "Success is a woman who has to be won, not courted. You've got to seize her and carry her off, not stand under her window with a mandolin."

In 1910 when the South Polar expedition departed Scott once more was put in charge. And it is a little strange—or perhaps not—that the London *Evening Standard* should remark: "We may never see them again."

Scott's wife also had premonitions, confiding to her diary:

"I had rather a horrid day today. I woke up having a bad dream about you, and then Peter came very close to me and said emphatically, 'Daddy won't come back,' as though in answer to my silly thoughts."

"I was very taken up with you all evening. I wonder if anything special is happening to you. Something odd happened to the clocks and watches between nine and ten P.M."

"I was still rather taken up by you and a wee bit depressed. As you ought about now to be returning to ship I see no reason for depression. I wonder."

Ernest Shackleton wrote to a New Zealand friend: "I suppose that we shall soon hear of Scott. I am inclined to think that we will hear from Amundsen first."

Today, from this distance, as one reads about the expedition, a feeling of doom soars overhead like an albatross.[13] Aboard ship—even before they reach Antarctica—things do not go well. Icebergs appear farther north than expected. Then a storm threatens the *Terra Nova*[14] and ten precious bags of coal which had not been lashed down must be jettisoned. At four in the morning the pumps become choked, water rises in the engine room, the men start bailing with buckets. A dog drowns. Two ponies die.

Upon reaching Antarctica they were unable to establish winter quarters on Cape

---

**13. albatross** (al′ bə trôs′) *n*.: A large sea bird often used as a symbol of a burden or source of distress.
**14. *Terra Nova*:** The ship Scott's expedition used to get to Antarctica.

Crozier as they had planned. Three motor sledges were brought along for heavy work but one sledge broke through the ice and sank, so that in order to get the ponies' fodder ashore the men harnessed themselves to bales of hay. And the expedition's photographer, standing quite literally on thin ice, was almost knocked into the water by a scheming killer whale.

About this time they got news of Amundsen, who had set up camp on an indentation sixty miles nearer the Pole. Scott wrote in his diary: "I never thought he could have got so many dogs safely to the ice. His plan for running them seems excellent. . . ."

Three more ponies died while the first depot was being stocked. Two more drowned when the ice disintegrated beneath them. And Scott writes: "I could not rid myself of the fear that misfortune was in the air. . . ."

Despite every problem he scrupulously kept his journal.

January 15: "We left our depot today with nine days' provisions, so that it ought to be a certain thing now, and the only appalling possibility the sight of the Norwegian flag forestalling ours."

January 16: "The worst has happened. . . . Bowers's sharp eyes detected what he thought was a cairn;[15] he was uneasy about it, but argued that it might be sastrugus.[16] Half an hour later he detected a black speck ahead. Soon we knew that this could not be a natural snow feature. We marched on, found that it was a black flag tied to a sledge bearer; nearby the remains of a camp; sledge tracks and ski tracks coming and going and the clear trace of dogs' paws —many dogs."

---

**15. cairn** (kern) *n.*: A cone-shaped heap of stones used as a marker or monument.
**16. sastrugus** (sas′ trʊ gəs) *n.*: A wavelike ridge of hard snow formed by the wind and common in polar regions.

Next day Scott reached the Pole: "Great God! this is an awful place. . . ."

Inside the tent was Amundsen's message.

Poleheim
15 December 1911

Dear Captain Scott:

As you are probably the first to reach this area after us, I will ask you kindly to forward this letter to King Haakon VII. If you can use any of the articles left in this tent, please do not hesitate to do so. The sledge left outside may be of use to you. With best regards, I wish you a safe return.

Roald Amundsen

The British party stayed just long enough to verify the location. By their measurements, Amundsen's tent was only a few hundred yards from the geographical center.

It is hard to understand why they loitered on the way back. They did not have much food, the weather was savage, and they had 900 miles to go. But here is Scott's journal entry on February 8: "I decided to camp and spend the rest of the day geologizing. It has been extremely interesting. We found ourselves under perpendicular cliffs of Beacon sandstone, weathering rapidly and carrying veritable coal seams. From the last Wilson, with his sharp eyes, has picked several plant impressions, the last a piece of coal with beautifully traced leaves in layers, also some excellently preserved impressions of thick stems, showing cellular structure. In one place we saw the cast of small waves in the sand."

Why did they do this? Two explanations have been proposed. If they could bring back some scientific information that the Norwe-

*Amundsen Taking a Sight*

gians had overlooked their defeat would not be total. Certainly they knew that. The other explanation, which seeps through Scott's journal like a stain, is that they sensed they could never make it. By now they were crippled and suffering from the cold. Wilson had pulled a tendon in his leg. Evans's hands were so badly frozen that his fingernails had begun to drop off. Oates's feet were turning black. Scott had injured his shoulder. Bowers seems to be the only one in good shape.

Yet the next day they again stopped to collect geological specimens. Scott remarks on "the delight of setting foot on rock after 14 weeks of snow and ice."

A few days later Evans died.

Temperatures dropped so low that in the mornings it took them an hour to put on their footgear. The cooking oil was almost gone. Food rations were cut. Scott meditates: "I wonder what is in store for us. . . ."

On the fifteenth of March while they waited in the tent for a blizzard to let up

Oates said, "I am just going outside and maybe some time." His feet had become so painful that he could hardly walk, and he did not want to delay the other men.

The bodies of Scott, Bowers, and Wilson were discovered eleven miles from a food depot. Their tent was almost buried by snow. The men lay in their sleeping bags, Wilson with his hands folded on his chest. Bowers also appeared to have died without anguish. Between them lay Scott, the flaps of his sleeping bag open. His diaries were in a green wallet underneath the bag, the last letters on a groundsheet beside him. His left arm was extended, his hand resting on Wilson's shoulder. The interior of the tent had been kept neat. There was an improvised lamp, a bag of tea, a bag of tobacco, and their scientific notes.

Outside stood the sledge. Along with the necessities, it carried thirty-five pounds of rock.

Scott's wife was aboard ship en route to New Zealand to meet him when she learned of his death—five days after the captain got the news by radio. The captain had been so distressed that he could not approach her. She reports in her diary that his hands trembled when he finally showed her the message. After reading it she said to him: "Oh, well, never mind! I expected that. Thanks very much. I will go and think about it."

Then, as she usually did each morning on the ship, she took a Spanish lesson. Then she ate lunch and discussed American politics and in the afternoon spent a while reading about the *Titanic*,[17] determined to avoid thinking of her husband's death until she was sure she could control herself.

Just as curious—perhaps more so—is the fact that Amundsen, the victor, is not as renowned as the loser. Quite a few people think Scott was the first man to reach the South Pole. There is no logical explanation for this belief, though his dramatic death may account for it, together with the fact that he and his companions are still there—frozen like insects or splinters on the side of the great white lantern. However, they won't stay there indefinitely. Calculations by scientists at McMurdo Sound indicate that the bodies now lie fifty feet beneath the surface and fifteen miles closer to the edge of the ice shelf. What this means is that sometime in the future Scott and his companions will be carried out to sea on an iceberg.

As for Roald Amundsen, who knows what became of him? Almost no one. He died on a gallant but useless errand, searching for General Umberto Nobile whose dirigible crash-landed in the Arctic. Amundsen's plane may have developed engine trouble; pieces of it were found off the Norwegian coast. The plane had been lent by the French government, which had at that time two modern seaplanes: one with a water-cooled engine, the other with an air-cooled engine. The French, exhibiting that singular wisdom we have come to associate with all federal government, provided Amundsen with the water-cooled engine for his long flight through subzero temperatures.

A Swedish pilot later rescued the Italian general.

Scott is now remembered and honored throughout the English-speaking world while Amundsen is not. One might say this is folly, because Amundsen has more to teach us. But in the end, of course, they are equally instructive.

---

**17. Titanic** (tī tan′ ik) *n.*: A ship considered unsinkable that hit an iceberg and sank in 1912 on its first voyage.

## THINKING ABOUT THE SELECTION

### Recalling

1. In what ways did Amundsen prepare for arctic exploration during his youth?
2. Why does Connell refer to Antarctica as a "white lantern"?
3. Which group reached the South Pole first?
4. What were some of the difficulties that Scott's party encountered?

### Interpreting

5. What do Scott's and Amundsen's differing views of fortune or luck indicate about the differences in their personalities?
6. In what ways was Amundsen better prepared for the journey?
7. Whom does Connell admire more, Amundsen or Scott? Support your answer. Whom do you admire more?

### Applying

8. Reread the final paragraph of the essay. How are both explorers "equally instructive"?

## ANALYZING LITERATURE

### Understanding Expository Essay

The author of an **expository essay** presents facts in a manner that fits the purpose. The purpose of "The White Lantern" is not directly stated. You can, however, infer the author's purpose based on the statements and the facts that he chooses to present.

1. What was Connell's purpose in comparing and contrasting Amundsen and Scott?
2. Find at least three facts about each man's life that Connell uses to support his purpose.

## CRITICAL THINKING AND READING

### Using Comparison and Contrast

**Comparison** points out similarities between people or things; **contrast** points out differences. For example, on page 517, Connell describes Amundsen's attempts to toughen himself as a youngster. In contrast, he concludes that, as a child, Scott, "seems to have been the storybook sissy: emotional, . . . physically weak, pampered by his mother . . ."

Contrast the attitudes of Amundsen and Scott toward each of the following: luck, success, adventure. Support your answers.

## UNDERSTANDING LANGUAGE

### Understanding Verbal Analogies

A **verbal analogy** consists of two pairs of words in which the members of each pair have the same relation to each other. For example: *Kind* is to *cruel* as *generous* is to *stingy*.

Kind and cruel are antonyms—words of opposite meaning. Generous and stingy have the same relationship.

Complete each of the following analogies.
1. *Unknown* is to *obscure* as *illustrious* is to
   - a. shiny
   - b. famous
   - c. wealthy
   - d. notorious
2. *Lively* is to *animated* as *lethargic* is to
   - a. sluggish
   - b. inanimate
   - c. active
   - d. athletic
3. *Legal* is to *illegal* as *obligatory* is to
   - a. compulsory
   - b. duty bound
   - c. optional
   - d. required
4. *Admiration* is to *approval* as *disdain* is to
   - a. envy
   - b. anger
   - c. regard
   - d. scorn

## THINKING AND WRITING

### Writing About an Expository Essay

Write a brief essay, summarizing the characteristics of each explorer as Connell has presented them. Then evaluate the writer's attitudes toward Amundsen and Scott and decide whether his conclusions are fair or unfair.

# GUIDE FOR READING

## On Summer

**Lorraine Hansberry** (1930–1965) was born and brought up in Chicago, Illinois. After high school, Hansberry studied art for two years before moving to New York City. While working at several jobs, she wrote *A Raisin in the Sun.* In 1959 this play became the first by a black woman to be produced on Broadway. This essay is from *To Be Young, Gifted, and Black,* a collection of writings that was published after her death.

**Persuasive Essay**

A **persuasive essay** attempts to persuade the reader to accept an opinion. Although the opinion is usually subjective, the writer defends it by presenting facts and reasons in a reasonable and compelling manner. Persuasive essays are written to shed new light on the subject, to create interest in the subject, or to persuade the reader to act. In this essay Lorraine Hansberry attempts to convince the reader of the virtues of summer.

**Look For**

As you read "On Summer," pay attention to the reasons for the author's initial dislike of summer, and then compare them to the reasons that she eventually comes to appreciate the season.

**Writing**

In this essay the author presents summer as the best season of the year. What is your favorite season? List reasons why your favorite season is superior to the other three.

**Vocabulary**

Knowing the following words will help you as you read "On Summer."

**aloofness** (ə lōōf′nəs) *n.*: The state of being distant, removed, or uninvolved (p. 529)

**melancholy** (mel′ən käl′ ē) *adj.*: Sadness, gloominess, depression (p. 529)

**relief** (ri lēf′) *n.*: The projection of shapes from a flat surface, so that they stand out (p. 529)

**negotiate** (ni gō′shē āt) *v.*: To master or successfully move through a situation (p. 531)

**palpable** (pal′pə b'l) *adj.*: Able to be perceived by the senses (p. 531)

**ribald** (rib′əld) *adj.*: Characterized by coarse or vulgar joking (p. 531)

# On Summer

## Lorraine Hansberry

It has taken me a good number of years to come to any measure of respect for summer. I was, being May-born, literally an "infant of the spring" and, during the later childhood years, tended, for some reason or other, to rather worship the cold aloofness of winter. The adolescence, admittedly lingering still, brought the traditional passionate commitment to melancholy autumn —and all that. For the longest kind of time I simply thought that *summer* was a mistake.

In fact, my earliest memory of anything at all is of waking up in a darkened room where I had been put to bed for a nap on a summer's afternoon, and feeling very, very hot. I acutely disliked the feeling then and retained the bias for years. It had originally been a matter of the heat but, over the years, I came actively to associate displeasure with most of the usually celebrated natural features and social by-products of the season: the too-grainy texture of sand; the too-cold coldness of the various waters we constantly try to escape into, and the icky-perspiry feeling of bathing caps.

It also seemed to me, esthetically[1] speaking, that nature had got inexcusably carried away on the summer question and let the whole thing get to be rather much. By duration alone, for instance, a summer's day seemed maddeningly excessive; an utter overstatement. Except for those few hours at either end of it, objects always appeared in too sharp a relief against backgrounds; shadows too pronounced and light too blinding. It always gave me the feeling of walking around in a motion picture which had been too artsily-craftsily exposed. Sound also had a way of coming to the ear without that muting influence, marvelously common to winter, across patios or beaches or through the woods. I suppose I found it too stark and yet too intimate a season.

My childhood Southside[2] summers were the ordinary city kind, full of the street games which the other rememberers have turned into fine ballets these days and rhymes that anticipated what some people insist on calling modern poetry:

*Oh, Mary Mack, Mack, Mack*
*With the silver buttons, buttons, buttons*
*All down her back, back, back*
*She asked her mother, mother, mother*
*For fifteen cents, cents, cents*
*To see the elephant, elephant, elephant*
*Jump the fence, fence, fence*
*Well, he jumped so high, high, high*
*'Til he touched the sky, sky, sky*
*And he didn't come back, back, back*
*'Til the Fourth of Ju-ly, ly, ly!*

---

1. **esthetically** (es thet' ik lē) *adv.*: Artistically.

2. **Southside:** A section of Chicago, Illinois.

Evenings were spent mainly on the back porches where screen doors slammed in the darkness with those really very special summertime sounds. And, sometimes, when Chicago nights got too steamy, the whole family got into the car and went to the park and slept out in the open on blankets. Those were, of course, the best times of all because the grownups were invariably reminded of having been children in rural parts of the country and told the best stories then. And it was also cool and sweet to be on the grass and there was usually the scent of freshly cut lemons or melons in the air. And Daddy would lie on his back, as fathers must, and explain about how men thought the stars above us came to be and how far away they were. I never did learn to believe that anything could be as far away as *that*. Especially the stars.

My mother first took us south to visit her Tennessee birthplace one summer when I was seven or eight, I think. I woke up on the back seat of the car while we were still driving through some place called Kentucky and my mother was pointing out to the beautiful hills on both sides of the highway and telling my brothers and my sister about how her father had run away and hidden

from his master in those very hills when he was a little boy. She said that his mother had wandered among the wooded slopes in the moonlight and left food for him in secret places. They were very beautiful hills and I looked out at them for miles and miles after that wondering who and what a *master* might be.

I remember being startled when I first saw my grandmother rocking away on her porch. All my life I had heard that she was a great beauty and no one had ever remarked that they meant a half century before. The woman that I met was as wrinkled as a prune and could hardly hear and barely see and always seemed to be thinking of other times. But she could still rock and talk and even make wonderful cupcakes which were like cornbread, only sweet. She was captivated by automobiles and, even though it was well into the Thirties,[3] I don't think she had ever been in one before we came down and took her driving. She was a little afraid of them and could not seem to negotiate the windows, but she loved driving. She died the next summer and that is all that I remember about her, except that she was born in slavery and had memories of it and they didn't sound anything like *Gone with the Wind.*[4]

Like everyone else, I have spent whole or bits of summers in many different kinds of places since then: camps and resorts in the Middle West and New York State; on an island; in a tiny Mexican village; Cape Cod, perched atop the Truro bluffs at Longnook Beach that Millay[5] wrote about; or simply strolling the streets of Provincetown[6] before the hours when the parties begin.

And, lastly, I do not think that I will forget days spent, a few summers ago, at a beautiful lodge built right into the rocky cliffs of a bay on the Maine coast. We met a woman there who had lived a purposeful and courageous life and who was then dying of cancer. She had, characteristically, just written a book and taken up painting. She had also been of radical viewpoint all her life; one of those people who energetically believe that the world *can* be changed for the better and spend their lives trying to do just that. And that was the way she thought of cancer; she absolutely refused to award it the stature of tragedy, a devastating instance of the brooding doom and inexplicability[7] of the absurdity of human destiny, etc., etc. The kind of characterization given, lately, as we all know, to far less formidable foes in life than cancer.

But for this remarkable woman it was a matter of nature in imperfection, implying, as always, work for man to do. It was an *enemy,* but a palpable one with shape and effect and source; and if it existed, it could be destroyed. She saluted it accordingly, without despondency, but with a lively, beautiful and delightfully ribald anger. There was one thing, she felt, which would prove equal to its relentless ravages and that was the genius of man. Not his mysticism, but man with tubes and slides and the stubborn human notion that the stars are very much within our reach.

The last time I saw her she was sitting

---

**3. Thirties:** The 1930's.
**4. Gone with the Wind:** A novel set in the South during the Civil War period.
**5. Millay:** Edna St. Vincent Millay (1892–1950), U.S. poet.

**6. Provincetown:** Resort town at the northern tip of Cape Cod, Massachusetts.
**7. inexplicability** (in eks′ pli kə bil′ ə tē) *n.*: A condition that cannot be explained.

surrounded by her paintings with her manuscript laid out for me to read, because, she said, she wanted to know what a *young person* would think of her thinking; one must always keep up with what *young people* thought about things because, after all, they were *change*.

Every now and then her jaw set in anger as we spoke of things people should be angry about. And then, for relief, she would look out at the lovely bay at a mellow sunset settling on the water. Her face softened with love of all that beauty and, watching her, I wished with all my power what I knew that she was wishing: that she might live to see

at least one more *summer*. Through her eyes I finally gained the sense of what it might mean; more than the coming autumn with its pretentious melancholy; more than an austere and silent winter which must shut dying people in for precious months; more even than the frivolous spring, too full of too many false promises, would be the gift of another summer with its stark and intimate assertion of neither birth nor death but life at the apex; with the gentlest nights and, above all, the longest days.

I heard later that she did live to see another summer. And I have retained my respect for the noblest of the seasons.

## THINKING ABOUT THE SELECTION
### Recalling

1. What were Hansberry's feelings about summer before she met the lady in Maine?
2. Describe some of Hansberry's memories of her childhood summers.
3. Explain what was wrong with the woman Hansberry met in Maine.
4. What was the woman in Maine's "radical viewpoint" of life?

### Interpreting

5. What is Hansberry implying about adolescents when she refers to "the traditional passionate commitment to melancholy autumn"?
6. How do her childhood memories contrast with her statement that "For the longest kind of time I simply thought that *summer* was a mistake?"
7. Why was the woman from Maine finally able to change Hansberry's mind about summer?

### Applying

8. Why do people associate certain feelings and emotions, such as melancholy with fall, with each season?
9. In his journal André Gide wrote, "I should like to enjoy this summer flower by flower, as if it were to be the last one for me." How can you enjoy summer "flower by flower"?

## ANALYZING LITERATURE
### Understanding Persuasive Essay

The goal of a **persuasive essay** is to convince the reader of the validity of an opinion. Facts and reasons that support the writer's viewpoint are presented in a forceful, convincing way.

1. What are some of the facts and reasons that the author presents to persuade you?
2. Was Lorraine Hansberry successful in convincing you that summer is the "noblest of the seasons"? Explain your answer.

## CRITICAL THINKING AND READING
### Identifying Persuasive Techniques

Writers of persuasive essays use several techniques to present their opinions as convincingly as possible. One of these techniques, an appeal to your emotions, is used in "On Summer." By retelling memories of her childhood and her experience with the woman who had cancer, Hansberry is attempting to evoke an emotional response that will lead you to agree with her that summer is the best season.

1. What specific emotions does Hansberry's essay appeal to?
2. Select two sentences that are especially effective in their appeal. Explain why each is effective.

## SPEAKING AND LISTENING
### Debating the Premise

A **debate** is a public discussion in which two groups take opposite sides of a statement, or **premise,** and use reasoned argument to support their side.

Debate the premise of this essay: Summer is the noblest of seasons. The class will be divided into two groups, one of which will defend the premise and the other of which will argue against it. Brainstorm with your group for five minutes to generate ideas in support of your side of the debate. Next choose a spokesperson from your group to argue your ideas. The teacher will be the judge and will decide which group presented a better argument.

## THINKING AND WRITING
### Summarizing an Essay

In a short essay, summarize the main points the author made in "On Summer" that support her premise. Start by writing a brief outline of the essay to be sure you include all of the important points. Then prepare your first draft. As you are writing, be sure to link each of the main points to the conclusion.

## Some Remarks on Humor

**E. B. (Elwyn Brooks) White** (1899–1985) was born and brought up in Mount Vernon, New York. He wrote for *The New Yorker* magazine from the time it began in 1925, until his death. *The Second Tree from the Corner* and *The Points of My Compass* are two collections of his magazine writings. He also wrote three best-selling children's books—*Stuart Little, Charlotte's Web,* and *The Trumpet of the Swan.* His work as an essayist combines humor, honesty, insight, and a remarkable sense for the correct word.

**Understanding an Extended Definition**

In a dictionary, a definition is an explanation of the meaning of a word. An **extended definition** is an essay in which a writer goes beyond the literal meaning of the word and explores the ideas the word represents. It also attempts to show how the ideas affect people and how people affect the ideas. The writer of an extended definition usually assumes that you already know the literal, dictionary definition. This essay is meant for you to think about the ideas behind the literal meaning of the word *humor.*

**Look For**

As you read "Some Remarks on Humor," take note of how White's use of metaphors and analogies—comparisons of things that are basically unlike—help to define his subject.

**Writing**

Think of a simple word, such as *friendship* or *work,* that people use to mean many different things. First, look up its dictionary definition. Then freewrite for five minutes about ideas and feelings represented by the word that someone would not find in the dictionary.

**Vocabulary**

Knowing the following words will help you as you read "Some Remarks on Humor."

**dissected** (di sekt′id) *v.*: Cut up into parts (p. 535)

**lather** (lath′ər) *n.*: An excited or disturbed state (Slang) (p. 535)

**repulsive** (ri pul′siv) *adj.*: Disgusting or offensive (p. 535)

**fragility** (frə jil′ə tē) *n.*: State of being easily broken (p. 535)

**evasiveness** (i vā′siv nis) *n.*: The tendency to avoid or escape something (p. 535)

**throes** (thrōz) *n.*: Spasms or pangs of pain (p. 535)

**sensible** (sen′ sə b′l) *adj.*: Emotionally or intellectually aware (p. 535)

# from Some Remarks on Humor

## E. B. White

Analysts have had their go at humor, and I have read some of this interpretative literature, but without being greatly instructed. Humor can be dissected, as a frog can, but the thing dies in the process and the innards are discouraging to any but the pure scientific mind.

In a newsreel theater the other day I saw a picture of a man who had developed the soap bubble to a higher point than it had ever before reached. He had become the ace soap bubble blower of America, had perfected the business of blowing bubbles, refined it, doubled it, squared it, and had even worked himself up into a convenient lather. The effect was not pretty. Some of the bubbles were too big to be beautiful, and the blower was always jumping into them or out of them, or playing some sort of unattractive trick with them. It was, if anything, a rather repulsive sight. Humor is a little like that: it won't stand much blowing up, and it won't stand much poking. It has a certain fragility, an evasiveness, which one had best respect. Essentially, it is a complete mystery. A human frame convulsed with laughter, and the laughter becoming hysterical and uncontrollable, is as far out of balance as one shaken with the hiccoughs or in the throes of a sneezing fit.

One of the things commonly said about humorists is that they are really very sad people—clowns with a breaking heart.

There is some truth in it, but it is badly stated. It would be more accurate, I think, to say that there is a deep vein of melancholy running through everyone's life and that the humorist, perhaps more sensible of it than some others, compensates for it actively and positively. Humorists fatten on trouble. They have always made trouble pay. They struggle along with a good will and endure pain cheerfully, knowing how well it will serve them in the sweet by and by. You find

them wrestling with foreign languages, fighting folding ironing boards and swollen drainpipes, suffering the terrible discomfort of tight boots (or as Josh Billings[1] wittily called them, "tite" boots). They pour out their sorrows profitably, in a form that is not quite fiction nor quite fact either. Beneath the sparkling surface of these dilemmas flows the strong tide of human woe.

Practically everyone is a manic-depressive[2] of sorts, with his up moments and his down moments, and you certainly don't have to be a humorist to taste the sadness of situation and mood. But there is often a rather fine line between laughing and crying, and if a humorous piece of writing brings a person to the point where his emotional responses are untrustworthy and seem likely to break over into the opposite realm, it is because humor, like poetry, has an extra content. It plays close to the big hot fire which is Truth, and sometimes the reader feels the heat.

The world likes humor, but it treats it patronizingly. It decorates its serious artists with laurel, and its wags[3] with Brussels sprouts. It feels that if a thing is funny it can be presumed to be something less than great, because if it were truly great it would be wholly serious. Writers know this, and those who take their literary selves with great seriousness are at considerable pains never to associate their name with anything funny or flippant or nonsensical or "light." They suspect it would hurt their reputation, and they are right. Many a poet writing today signs his real name to his serious verse and a pseudonym to his comical verse, being unwilling to have the public discover him in any but a pensive and heavy moment. It is a wise precaution. (It is often a bad policy too.)

When I was reading over some of the parody diaries of Franklin P. Adams,[4] I came across this entry for April 28, 1926:

> Read H. Canby's book, *Better Writing,* very excellent. But when he says, "A sense of humor is worth gold to any writer," I disagree with him vehemently. For the writers who amass the greatest gold have, it seems to me, no sense of humor; and I think also that if they had, it would be a terrible thing for them, for it would paralyze them so that they would not write at all. For in writing, emotion is more to be treasured than a sense of humor, and the two are often in conflict.

That is a sound observation. The conflict is fundamental. There constantly exists, for a certain sort of person of high emotional content, at work creatively, the danger of coming to a point where something cracks within himself or within the paragraph under construction—cracks and turns into a snicker. Here, then, is the very nub of the conflict: the careful form of art, and the careless shape of life itself. What a man does with this uninvited snicker (which may closely resemble a sob, at that) decides his destiny. If he resists it, conceals it, destroys it, he may keep his architectural scheme intact and save his building, and the world will never know. If he gives in to it, he becomes a humorist, and the sharp brim of the fool's cap leaves a mark forever on his brow.

---

**1. Josh Billings:** Pseudonym of Henry Wheeler Shaw (1818–1885), U.S. humorist.
**2. manic-depressive:** A person who alternates between wildly excited and deeply despondent moods.
**3. wags:** comical or humorous persons.

**4. Franklin P. Adams** (1881–1960): U.S. journalist and humorist.

# THINKING ABOUT THE SELECTION

## Recalling

1. In what way, according to White, is humor like a soap bubble?
2. How do humorists react to trouble?
3. What is the difference between the way the world treats serious and comedic artists?

## Interpreting

4. What does White mean by the "fine line between laughing and crying"?
5. What is White's attitude towards humorists?
6. Explain why the "nub of the conflict" is the "careful form of art, and the careless shape of life itself."

## Applying

7. What are some examples of humor that show a humorist to be "more sensible" of the sadness in life?

# ANALYZING LITERATURE

## Understanding an Extended Definition

An **extended definition** attempts to explain ideas associated with words. The definition of the word humor could be "the quality that makes something seem funny." White goes beyond this definition and explores the part humor plays in human affairs.

1. What does White state about the attempts to define humor?
2. Why is humor similar to poetry?

# CRITICAL THINKING AND READING

## Evaluating Reasons

A **reason** explains or justifies a decision or conclusion. It might be either a fact or an opinion, but it must be clearly linked to the conclusion. For example, in the following statement the reason for the conclusion is printed in italics.

The effect of the man who blew soap bubbles was not pretty *because some bubbles were too big to be beautiful and he kept playing unattractive tricks with them.*

Some of E. B. White's comments may become clearer if you understand the reasons for making them.

1. What are the reasons that humorists are different from other people?
2. Why do people feel that anything humorous cannot be taken as serious art?

# UNDERSTANDING LANGUAGE

## Understanding Antonyms

**Antonyms** are words that have opposite or nearly opposite meanings. Sometimes a writer will emphasize a word by using its antonym in the same sentence or paragraph. White does this in his second paragraph: The effect was not pretty . . . It was . . . a *repulsive* sight.

When you wish to use an antonym in your writing and cannot think of one, use a thesaurus. A thesaurus is a reference book that gives one or more synonyms for each entry word. Many entry words also include antonyms.

Use a thesaurus to find one or more antonyms for these words from the essay.

1. discouraging
2. commonly
3. actively
4. positively

# THINKING AND WRITING

## Writing an Extended Definition

Write an extended definition of a word that is important to you. You might choose a technical subject, such as government or science, or a personal subject such as friendship, love, or hate. If you think it is necessary, begin with the dictionary definition of the word when you write. As you revise, be sure that you have supported any conclusions with sound, properly linked reasons.

## Rural Literalism

**Calvin Trillin** (1935–    ) was born and brought up in Kansas City, Missouri. After graduating from Yale, he worked as a staff writer for *Time* magazine for several years before moving to *The New Yorker,* which has published most of his writings since 1963. Trillin's books include collections of humorous essays about food and humorous essays concerning politics. Trillin often writes about the difficulty of dealing with people who do not share his eccentric attitudes. "Rural Literalism" is an example of this kind of humor.

**Tone**

The **tone** is the attitude of the author toward the subject and the audience. It should be consistent throughout the selection and express an emotion or emotions appropriate to the subject. Tone is conveyed through all of the elements in literature.

**Look For**

As you read "Rural Literalism," watch for the way the author's attitude is presented. Does the tone match the mood of the story?

**Writing**

In this essay you will read several aphorisms, short statements expressing a wise or clever observation or general truth. "An apple a day keeps the doctor away," or "That was the straw that broke the camel's back" are examples. Think of some aphorisms that you are familiar with and freewrite about their figurative meanings and the literal images they evoke.

**Vocabulary**

Knowing the following words will help you as you read "Rural Literalism."

**rural** (rŏŏr′əl) *adj*.: Having to do with country, farming (p. 539)

**literalism** (lit′ ər əl iz′m) *n*.: Tendency to take things according to their dictionary definitions, instead of figuratively (p. 539)

**priming** (prī′miŋ) *v*.: 1. Preparing a water pump for operation by pouring in water  2. pre-

paring a person or thing for work or action (p. 539)

**fluke** (flōōk) *n*.: 1. A flounder or other flatfish  2. Successful result brought about by accident; stroke of luck (p. 539)

**windfalls** (wind′fôlz) *n*.: 1. Things blown down by the wind  2. Unexpected profits or gains (p. 539)

# Rural Literalism

## Calvin Trillin

My problem with country living began innocently enough when our well ran dry and a neighbor said some pump priming would be necessary.

"I didn't come up here to discuss economics," I said. Actually, I don't discuss economics in the city either. As it happens, I don't understand economics. There's no use revealing that, though, to every Tom, Dick and Harry who interrupts his dinner to try to get your water running, so I said, "I come up here to get away from that sort of thing." My neighbor gave me a puzzled look.

"He's talking about the water pump," my wife told me. "It needs priming."

I thought that experience might have been just a fluke—until, on a fishing trip with the same neighbor, I proudly pulled in a fish with what I thought was a major display of deep-sea angling skill, only to hear a voice behind me say, "It's just a fluke."

"This is dangerous," I said to my wife, while helping her weed the vegetable garden the next day. I had thought our problem was limited to the pump-priming ichthyologist[1] down the road, but that morning at the post office I had overheard a farmer say that since we seemed to be in for a few days of good weather he intended to make his hay while the sun was shining. "These people are robbing me of aphorisms," I said, taking advantage of the discussion to rest for a while on my hoe. "How can I encourage the children to take advantage of opportunities by telling them to make hay while the sun shines if they think that means making hay while the sun shines?"

"Could you please keep weeding those peas while you talk," she said. "You've got a long row to hoe."

I began to look at my wife with new eyes. By that, of course, I don't mean that I actually went to a discount eye outlet, acquired two new eyes (20/20 this time), replaced my old eyes with the new ones and looked at my wife. Having to make that explanation is just the sort of thing I found troubling. What I mean is that I was worried about the possibility of my wife falling into the habit of rural literalism herself. My concern was deepened a few days later by a conversation that took place while I was in one of our apple trees, looking for an apple that was not used as a *dacha*[2] by the local worms. "I just talked to the Murrays, and they say that the secret is picking up windfalls," my wife said.

"Windfalls?" I said. "Could it be that the Murrays have a natural-gas operation in the back forty I didn't know about?"

"Not those kinds of windfalls," my wife said. "The apples that fall from the tree

---

1. **ichthyologist** (ik′ thē äl′ ə jist) *n.*: One who studies fish.

2. **dacha** (dä′ chə): In Russia, a country house or cottage.

**AROUND THE FISH**
*Paul Klee*
*The Museum of Modern Art, New York*

because of the wind. They're a breeding place for worms.''

"There's nothing wrong with our apples," I said, reaching for a particularly plump one.

"Be careful," she said. "You may be getting yourself too far out on a limb."

"You may be getting yourself out on a limb yourself," I said to my wife at breakfast the next morning.

She looked around the room. "I'm sitting at the kitchen table," she said.

"I meant it symbolically," I said. "The way it was meant to be meant. This has got to stop. I won't have you coming in from the garden with small potatoes in your basket and saying that what you found was just small potatoes. 'Small potatoes' doesn't mean small potatoes."

"Small potatoes doesn't mean small potatoes?"

"I refuse to discuss it," I said. "The tide's in, so I'm going fishing, and I don't want to hear any encouraging talk about that fluke not being the only fish in the ocean."

"I was just going to ask why you have to leave before you finish your breakfast," she said.

"Because time and tide wait for no man," I said. "And I mean it."

Had she trapped me into saying that? Or was it possible that I was falling into the habit myself? Was I, as I waited for a bite, thinking that there were plenty of other fish in the sea? Then I had a bite—then another. I forgot about the problem until after I had returned to the dock and done my most skillful job of filleting.[3]

_____
**3. filleting** (fǐ lā′ iŋ) *n.*: Boning and slicing fish.

"Look!" I said, holding up the carcass of one fish proudly, as my wife approached the dock. "It's nothing but skin and bones."

The shock of realizing what I had said caused me to stumble against my fish-cleaning table and knock the fillets off the dock. "Now we won't have anything for dinner," I said.

"Don't worry," my wife said. "I have other fish to fry."

"That's not right!" I shouted. "That's not what that means. It means you have something better to do."

"It can also mean that I have other fish to fry," she said. "And I do. I'll just get that other fish you caught out of the freezer. Even though it was just a fluke."

I tried to calm myself. I apologized to my wife for shouting and offered to help her pick vegetables from the garden for dinner.

"I'll try to watch my language," she said, as we stood among the peas.

"It's all right, really," I said.

"I was just going to say that tonight it seems rather slim pickings," she said. "Just about everything has gone to seed."

"Perfectly all right," I said, wandering over toward the garden shed, where some mud seemed to be caked in the eaves. I pushed at the mud with a rake, and a swarm of wasps burst out at me. I ran for the house, swatting at wasps with my hat. Inside, I suddenly had the feeling that some of them had managed to crawl up the legs of my jeans, and I tore the jeans off. My wife found me there in the kitchen, standing quietly in what the English call their smalls.

"That does it," I said. "We're going back to the city."

"Just because of a few stings?"

"Can't you see what happened?" I said. "They scared the pants off me."

## THINKING ABOUT THE SELECTION
### Recalling

1. What did the author think his neighbor was referring to when he mentioned pump priming?
2. What did his wife mean when she talked to him about windfalls?
3. What did the author tell his wife after he was chased inside by the wasps?

### Interpreting

4. How does the author seem to see himself in relation to other people?
5. Why is the author upset at the literal use of aphorisms?
6. How does the author's attitude toward "rural literalism" gradually change?

### Applying

7. How can aphorisms be a useful way to communicate and how can they be confusing?

## ANALYZING LITERATURE
### Understanding Tone

Whether the author approaches the subject lightly or seriously, enthusiastically or coolly, is revealed by the tone. Tone also reflects purpose; a flat, unemotional tone would be inappropriate for someone writing a love letter. In this essay the author's tone of mock-concern heightens the humorous effect and purpose.

1. Sometimes the way a writer says something is as important as what the writer says. Do you think this is the case with "Rural Literalism"? Explain your answer.
2. How would the tone change if the purpose of the essay were to persuade the audience to avoid using aphorisms?

## CRITICAL THINKING AND READING
### Understanding Figurative Meaning

**Figurative language** is language used descriptively, beyond the actual meaning of the individual words. Literal language is language that means exactly what is stated. If you are not sure whether a statement is meant literally or figuratively, look at its context. The context of the statement is the meaning of the words, phrases, and sentences around it.

Decide whether the following words in italics are being used literally or figuratively.

1. The heat and humidity in the *steaming* jungle made travel exhausting.
2. The Concorde *flew* into town last night.
3. The sprinter *flew* across the finish line.

## UNDERSTANDING LANGUAGE
### Understanding Aphorisms

An **aphorism** is a short sentence expressing a sentiment, a wise or clever observation, or a general truth. In this essay the author uses the term aphorism loosely, applying it to words that have more than one meaning, such as *fluke,* as well as to genuine aphorisms such as "Make hay while the sun shines."

The following are aphorisms from "Rural Literalism." Write down their figurative and literal meanings and then try to decide from where the expressions were derived.

1. "You've got a long row to hoe."
2. "You may be . . . too far out on a limb."
3. "Time and tide wait for no man."
4. "I have other fish to fry."

## THINKING AND WRITING
### Continuing the Selection

Write another paragraph continuing the essay in the same pattern and style. Use one or two of the sayings or aphorisms you wrote down earlier and continue the plot, or action, from where it concluded in the essay. Try to match the tone and style of the author as much as possible when you write the paragraph. As you are revising, be sure that you have shown both the literal and figurative meanings of the expression you have chosen.

# Essays in the Arts and Sciences

SONG, 1950
*Ben Shahn*
*Hirshhorn Museum and Sculpture Gallery,*
*Smithsonian Institution*

## Notes on Punctuation

**Lewis Thomas** (1913–    ) is an American physician, scientist, and teacher who is also a gifted writer. In his brief essays, often published in the *New England Journal of Medicine,* Thomas offers his insights and opinions on a variety of topics. In his essay "Notes on Punctuation" from *The Medusa and the Snail: More Notes of a Biology Watcher* (1979), Thomas expresses his opinions about the useful but sometimes annoying marks that help writers convey structure and meaning.

### Classification

**Classification** is an arrangement according to a systematic division into classes or groups. For example, a short-story writer can be grouped with his or her counterparts and then classified according to categories such as style, subject, and popularity. A classification essay divides the subject into major categories, arranges the categories in a sequence, and defines the categories. In "Notes on Punctuation" the writer classifies different types of punctuation as useful or not, and as those he likes and those he doesn't.

### Look For

Look at a page of a book. Imagine all the words on the page without any punctuation marks. How difficult the page would be to read! As you read "Notes on Punctuation," look for the uses the writer finds for these essential marks.

### Writing

Make a list of the punctuation marks that you find helpful in your own writing and of those that you dislike or rarely use.

### Vocabulary

Knowing the following words will help you as you read "Notes on Punctuation."

**deploying** (dē ploi′iŋ) *v.*: Using (p. 545)

**ambiguity** (am′bə gyoo′ə tē) *n.*: Uncertainty (p. 545)

**implication** (im′plə kā′shən) *n.*: Suggestion (p. 545)

**banal** (bā′n'l) *adj.*: Without originality or freshness (p. 546)

**unethical** (un eth′i k'l) *adj.*: Not moral; not conforming to cer-

tain rules (p. 546)

**disown** (dis ōn′) *v.*: To deny ownership of or responsibility for (p. 546)

**clichés** (klē sħāz′) *n.*: Overused phrases or expressions (p. 546)

**parsimonious** (pär′sə mō′nē əs) *adj.*: Stingy (p. 546)

# Notes on Punctuation

## Lewis Thomas

There are no precise rules about punctuation (Fowler[1] lays out some general advice (as best he can under the complex circumstances of English prose (he points out, for example, that we possess only four stops (the comma, the semicolon, the colon and the period (the question mark and exclamation point are not, strictly speaking, stops; they are indicators of tone (oddly enough, the Greeks employed the semicolon for their question mark (it produces a strange sensation to read a Greek sentence which is a straightforward question: Why weepest thou; (instead of Why weepest thou? (and, of course, there are parentheses (which are surely a kind of punctuation making this whole matter much more complicated by having to count up the left-handed parentheses in order to be sure of closing with the right number (but if the parentheses were left out, with nothing to work with but the stops, we would have considerably more flexibility in the deploying of layers of meaning than if we tried to separate all the clauses by physical barriers (and in the latter case, while we might have more precision and exactitude for our meaning, we would lose the essential flavor of language, which is its wonderful ambiguity)))))))))))).

The commas are the most useful and usable of all the stops. It is highly important to put them in place as you go along. If you try to come back after doing a paragraph and stick them in the various spots that tempt you you will discover that they tend to swarm like minnows into all sorts of crevices whose existence you hadn't realized and before you know it the whole long sentence becomes immobilized and lashed up squirming in commas. Better to use them sparingly, and with affection, precisely when the need for each one arises, nicely, by itself.

I have grown fond of semicolons in recent years. The semicolon tells you that there is still some question about the preceding full sentence; something needs to be added; it reminds you sometimes of the Greek usage. It is almost always a greater pleasure to come across a semicolon than a period. The period tells you that that is that; if you didn't get all the meaning you wanted or expected, anyway you got all the writer intended to parcel out and now you have to move along. But with a semicolon there you get a pleasant little feeling of expectancy; there is more to come; read on; it will get clearer.

Colons are a lot less attractive, for several reasons: firstly, they give you the feeling of being rather ordered around, or at least having your nose pointed in a direction you might not be inclined to take if left to yourself, and, secondly, you suspect you're in for one of those sentences that will be labeling the points to be made: firstly, secondly and so forth, with the implication that you haven't sense enough to keep track of a sequence of notions without having them numbered. Also, many writers use this system loosely and incompletely, starting out

---

**1. Fowler:** Henry Watson Fowler (1858–1933), an expert on the English language and author of *A Dictionary of Modern English Usage*.

with number one and number two as though counting off on their fingers and then going on and on without the succession of labels you've been led to expect, leaving you floundering about searching for the ninethly or seventeenthly that ought to be there but isn't.

Exclamation points are the most irritating of all. Look! they say, look at what I just said! How amazing is my thought! It is like being forced to watch someone else's small child jumping up and down crazily in the center of the living room shouting to attract attention. If a sentence really has something of importance to say, something quite remarkable, it doesn't need a mark to point it out. And if it is really, after all, a banal sentence needing more zing, the exclamation point simply emphasizes its banality!

Quotation marks should be used honestly and sparingly, when there is a genuine quotation at hand, and it is necessary to be very rigorous about the words enclosed by the marks. If something is to be quoted, the *exact* words must be used. If part of it must be left out because of space limitations, it is good manners to insert three dots to indicate the omission, but it is unethical to do this if it means connecting two thoughts which the original author did not intend to have tied together. Above all, quotation marks should not be used for ideas that you'd like to disown, things in the air so to speak. Nor should they be put in place around clichés; if you want to use a cliché you must take full responsibility for it yourself and not try to job it off on anon.,[2] or on society. The most objectionable misuse of quotation marks, but one which illustrates the dangers of misuse in ordinary prose, is seen in advertising, especially in advertisements for small restaurants, for example "just around the corner," or "a good place to eat." No single, identifiable, citable[3] person ever really said, for the record, "just around the corner," much less "a good place to eat," least likely of all for restaurants of the type that use this type of prose.

The dash is a handy device, informal and essentially playful, telling you that you're about to take off on a different tack but still in some way connected with the present course—only you have to remember that the dash is there, and either put a second dash at the end of the notion to let the reader know that he's back on course, or else end the sentence, as here, with a period.

The greatest danger in punctuation is for poetry. Here it is necessary to be as economical and parsimonious with commas and periods as with the words themselves, and any marks that seem to carry their own subtle meanings, like dashes and little rows of periods, even semicolons and question marks, should be left out altogether rather than inserted to clog up the thing with ambiguity. A single exclamation point in a poem, no matter what else the poem has to say, is enough to destroy the whole work.

The things I like best in T. S. Eliot's poetry, especially in the *Four Quartets,* are the semicolons. You cannot hear them, but they are there, laying out the connections between the images and the ideas. Sometimes you get a glimpse of a semicolon coming, a few lines farther on, and it is like climbing a steep path through woods and seeing a wooden bench just at a bend in the road ahead, a place where you can expect to sit for a moment, catching your breath.

Commas can't do this sort of thing; they can only tell you how the different parts of a complicated thought are to be fitted together, but you can't sit, not even take a breath, just because of a comma,

---

**2. anon.:** Abbreviation of *anonymous.*

**3. citable** (sīt′ ə b'l) *adj.*: Able to be named.

## THINKING ABOUT THE SELECTION

### Recalling

1. What four stops and two indicators of tone does the English language include?
2. According to Thomas, what are the three most useful stops?
3. In the writer's opinion, which three punctuation marks present problems for writers? Give his reasons.
4. What is the writer's suggestion for punctuating poetry?

### Interpreting

5. Do you think the purpose of this essay is to explain, entertain, or persuade?
6. What does the writer assume about the knowledge and needs of the audience?

### Applying

7. Suppose that you used no punctuation marks in your writing. How would that affect your ability to write and your readers' ability to understand what you have written?

## READING IN THE ARTS AND SCIENCES

### Understanding Classification

**Classification** is an arrangement according to some systematic division into classes or groups. In "Notes on Punctuation" the classification of different types of punctuation as useful or not, and as those the writer likes and those he doesn't, depends largely on the writer's point of view.

For example, the writer says that exclamation points are irritating and unnecessary. However, the playwright of an emotional drama might feel that they are helpful in showing the actors where to infuse more emotion into their speech; an effusive person might feel that exclamation points are helpful in expressing his or her feelings.

1. The writer feels that dashes are "informal and essentially playful." How might a poet known for her quick wit feel about dashes?
2. The writer feels that quotation marks should be used "honestly and sparingly, when there is a genuine quotation at hand." How might a novelist known for his use of convincing dialogue feel about the use of quotation marks?

## CRITICAL THINKING AND READING

### Finding the Main Idea

The **main idea** is the most important idea expressed. Sometimes the main idea of a paragraph is stated directly in one sentence, called the topic sentence. When the main idea is not stated directly but is implied, you must infer it.

1. Reread the first paragraph in column 1 on page 546. What is the main idea?
2. Reread the second paragraph in column 2 on page 546. What is the main idea.

## THINKING AND WRITING

### Writing About Language Arts

Select a punctuation mark that either helps you or irritates you when you read or write. Write a brief persuasive essay in which you try to convince other students to agree with your opinion. If you wish, use humor to make your point.

First state the main idea you want your essay to convey. Then list the reasons or supporting details and examples for your main idea. List the best argument last in order to leave your readers with the strongest point. End your essay with a statement that summarizes or clinches your argument. Revise your essay to make sure it is persuasive. Proofread for errors in spelling, grammar, and punctuation.

## The American Idea

**Theodore H. White** (1915–1986), born in Boston, Massachusetts, spent most of his life as a foreign correspondent and political writer. He is best known for his Pulitzer Prize-winning book, *The Making of the President: 1960,* a report on the 1960 presidential campaign. White's adaptation of this book as a television documentary won an Emmy award in 1964. In "The American Idea," published in *The New York Times Magazine* (July 6, 1986), White celebrates the anniversary of American independence.

**Definition**

A **definition** describes the special qualities that identify a person, place, object, process, or concept and distinguishes it from others that may be similar. Writers may use definitions to explain, to entertain, to persuade, or to instruct.

**Look For**

As you read "The American Idea," look for the writer's definition of the American idea and his explanation of what it means to different people.

**Writing**

Suppose that you met a student from a foreign country, such as the Soviet Union or China. How would you explain what it is like to be an American and to live in an independent, democratic nation? Free-write about your thoughts and feelings on the subject.

**Vocabulary**

Knowing the following words will help you as you read "The American Idea."

**feisty** (fīst′ē) *adj.*: Spunky; touchy and quarrelsome (p. 550)

**pragmatic** (prag mat′ ik) *adj.*: Practical (p. 550)

**subversion** (səb vʉr′zhən) *n.*: A systematic attempt to overthrow a government from within (p. 550)

**ministration** (min′is trā′shən) *n.*: The act of serving as a minister or clergyman (p. 551)

# The American Idea

## Theodore H. White

The idea was there at the very beginning, well before Thomas Jefferson put it into words—and the idea rang the call.

Jefferson himself could not have imagined the reach of his call across the world in time to come when he wrote:

"We hold these truths to be self-evident, that all men are created equal, that they are endowed by their Creator with certain unalienable rights,[1] that among these are life, liberty, and the pursuit of happiness."

But over the next two centuries the call would reach the potato patches of Ireland, the ghettoes of Europe, the paddyfields of China, stirring farmers to leave their lands and townsmen their trades and thus unsettling all traditional civilizations.

It is the call from Thomas Jefferson, embodied in the great statue that looks down the Narrows of New York Harbor,[2] and in the immigrants who answered the call, that we now celebrate.

Some of the first European Americans had come to the new continent to worship God in their own way, others to seek their fortunes. But, over a century-and-a-half, the new world changed those Europeans, above all the Englishmen who had come to North America. Neither King nor Court nor Church could stretch over the ocean to the wild continent. To survive, the first emigrants had to learn to govern themselves. But the freedom of the wilderness whetted their appetites for more freedoms. By the time Jefferson drafted his call, men were in the field fighting for those new-learned freedoms, killing and being killed by English soldiers, the best-trained troops in the world, supplied by the world's greatest navy. Only something worth dying for could unite American volunteers and keep them in the field—a stated cause, a flag, a nation they could call their own.

When, on the Fourth of July, 1776, the colonial leaders who had been meeting as a Continental Congress in Philadelphia voted to approve Jefferson's Declaration of Independence, it was not puffed-up rhetoric for them to pledge to each other "our lives, our fortunes and our sacred honor." Unless

---

**1. unalienable** (un āl′ yən ə b'l) **rights**: Rights that cannot be taken away. This quote is from the beginning of the Declaration of Independence, written by Thomas Jefferson and adopted July 4, 1776, by the Second Continental Congress.

**2. Narrows of New York Harbor:** The strait, or narrow channel of water, that connects Upper New York Bay with Lower New York Bay.

their new "United States of America" won the war, the Congressmen would be judged traitors as relentlessly as would the irregulars-under-arms[3] in the field.

The new Americans were tough men fighting for a very tough idea. How they won their battles is a story for the schoolbooks, studied by scholars, wrapped in myths by historians and poets. But what is most important is the story of the idea that made them into a nation, the idea that had an explosive power undreamed of in 1776.

All other nations had come into being among people whose families had lived for time out of mind on the same land where they were born. Englishmen are English, Frenchmen are French, Chinese are Chinese, while their governments come and go; their national states can be torn apart and remade without losing their nationhood. But Americans are a nation born of an idea; not the place, but the idea, created the United States Government.

The story we celebrate is the story of how this idea worked itself out, how it stretched and changed and how the call for "life, liberty and the pursuit of happiness" does still, as it did in the beginning, mean different things to different people.

The debate began with the drafting of the Declaration of Independence. That task was left to Jefferson of Virginia, who spent two weeks in an upstairs room in a Philadelphia boarding house penning a draft, while John Adams and Benjamin Franklin questioned, edited, hardened its phrases. By the end of that hot and muggy June, the three had reached agreement: the Declaration contained the ringing universal theme Jefferson strove for and, at the same time, voiced American grievances toughly enough

to please the feisty Adams and the pragmatic Franklin. After brief debate, Congress passed it.

As the years wore on, the great debate expanded between Jefferson and Adams. The young nation flourished and Jefferson chose to think of America's promise as a call to all the world, its promises universal. A few weeks before he died, he wrote, "May it be to the world, what I believe it will be (to some parts sooner, to others later, but finally to all), the signal of arousing men to burst their chains." To Adams, the call meant something else—it was the call for *American* independence, the cornerstone of an *American* state.

Their argument ran through their successive Administrations. Adams, the second President, suspected the French Revolutionaries;[4] Alien and Sedition Acts[5] were passed during his term of office to protect the American state and its liberties against French subversion. But Jefferson, the third President, welcomed the French. The two men, once close friends, became archrivals. Still, as they grew old, their rivalry faded; there was glory enough to share in what they had made; in 1812, they began a correspondence that has since become classic, remembering and taking comfort in the triumphs of their youth.

Adams and Jefferson lived long lives and died on the same day—the Fourth of July, 1826, 50 years to the day from the Continental Congress's approval of the Declaration. Legend has it that Adams breathed on his death bed, "Thomas Jefferson still survives." As couriers set out from Braintree[6] carrying the news of Adams's death, couri-

---

**3. irregulars-under-arms:** Fighters who do not belong to a regularly established army.

**4. French Revolutionaries:** People who revolted against the French king from 1789 to 1799.
**5. Alien and Sedition Acts:** A series of laws passed by the U.S. Congress in 1798 that restricted immigration and criticism of the government.
**6. Braintree:** The town in Massachusetts (now called Quincy) where John Adams lived and died.

ers were riding north from Virginia with the news of Jefferson's death. The couriers met in Philadelphia. Horace Greeley,[7] then a youth in Vermont, later remembered: ". . . When we learned . . . that Thomas Jefferson and John Adams, the author and the great champion, respectively, of the Declaration, had both died on that day, and that the messengers bearing South and North, respectively, the tidings of their decease, had met in Philadelphia, under the shadow of that Hall in which our independence was declared, it seemed that a Divine attestation[8] had solemnly hallowed and sanctified the great anniversary by the impressive ministration of Death."

---

7. **Horace Greeley:** A famous American newspaper publisher (1811–1872).

8. **attestation** (aʹ tes tāʹ shən) n.: Testimony or evidence.

---

## THINKING ABOUT THE SELECTION
### Recalling

1. What is "the American idea"?
2. Why were the people in America ready to make the idea a reality?
3. What distinction does the writer make between the American nation and other nations?
4. Why did archrivals Jefferson and Adams finally become friends again?

### Interpreting

5. According to legend, John Adams said these words on his deathbed: "Thomas Jefferson still survives." What do you think John Adams meant by that?

### Applying

6. Do you agree with Jefferson or with Adams about how broadly the American idea should be interpreted? Explain your answer.

## READING IN THE ARTS AND SCIENCES
### Understanding Definition

A **definition** describes the qualities that identify and distinguish one element from others that may be similar. Definitions may explain, entertain, persuade, or instruct, One technique for defining is using examples.

1. What definition does Jefferson give the American idea?
2. What definition does Adams give the American idea?
3. Do you think the writer uses definition to explain, to entertain, to persuade, or to instruct?
4. What examples does the writer give of people who responded to the American idea?

## THINKING AND WRITING
### Writing a Journal Entry About History

Imagine that you are living in America on July 4, 1776, when American independence is declared. Write a journal entry describing your thoughts and feelings about this new freedom and the inalienable rights to "life, liberty, and the pursuit of happiness." How will this event affect your way of life—as a farmer, blacksmith, or statesman? Describe, too, how you celebrated this good news. Draw on what you know of American life at that time. Revise your journal entry to be as historically accurate as possible. Proofread for errors in spelling, grammar, and punctuation.

## The Creative Process in Music

**Aaron Copland** (1900–      ), born in Brooklyn, New York, is one of the greatest composers of music for the symphony orchestra, ballet, stage, films, and voice. His best-known works are based on American themes. Also a teacher and a writer, Copland has said, "The more I live the life of music the more I am convinced that it is the freely imaginative mind that is at the core of all vital music making and music listening." In "The Creative Process in Music," he discusses how good music is created.

**Process Analysis**

**Process analysis** is the examination of the steps involved in a particular operation performed to bring about a desired result. The purposes of a process analysis essay may be to give directions and to provide information. In "The Creative Process in Music" the writer examines the elements involved in composing music.

**Look For**

As you read "The Creative Process in Music," look for the writer's description of the different steps in the process of composing music.

**Writing**

Suppose that you could interview one of your favorite artists for an hour. What questions would you ask about his or her way of working? List five or more questions to ask the artist about the creative process.

**Vocabulary**

Knowing the following words will help you as you read "The Creative Process in Music."

**shrouded** (shroud'id) v.: Clothed or wrapped to conceal (p. 553)

**perspective** (pər spek'tiv) n.: Point of view (p. 553)

**dilettante** (dil'ə tänt') n.: An amateur or dabbler in the arts (p. 553)

**poignancy** (poin'yən sē) n.: The quality of being deeply affecting (p. 555)

**metamorphoses** (met'ə môr'fə sēz) n.: Changes in form, structure, or substance (p. 555)

**criterion** (krī tir'ē ən) n.: A standard or rule for making a judgment (p. 555)

**coherent** (kō hir'ənt) adj.: Logically connected or ordered (p. 558)

# The Creative Process in Music

## Aaron Copland

Most people want to know how things are made. They frankly admit, however, that they feel completely at sea when it comes to understanding how a piece of music is made. Where a composer begins, how he manages to keep going—in fact, how and where he learns his trade—all are shrouded in impenetrable darkness. The composer, in short, is a man of mystery to most people, and the composer's workshop an unapproachable ivory tower.[1]

One of the first things most people want to hear discussed in relation to composing is the question of inspiration. They find it difficult to believe that composers are not as preoccupied with that question as they had supposed. The layman[2] always finds it hard to realize how natural it is for the composer to compose. He has a tendency to put himself into the position of the composer and to visualize the problems involved, including that of inspiration, from the perspective of the layman. He forgets that composing to a composer is like fulfilling a natural function. It is like eating or sleeping. It is something that the composer happens to have been born to do; and, because of that, it loses the character of a special virtue in the composer's eyes.

The composer, therefore, confronted with the question of inspiration, does not say to himself: "Do I feel inspired?" He says to himself: "Do I feel like composing today?" And if he feels like composing, he does. It is more or less like saying to yourself: "Do I feel sleepy?" If you feel sleepy, you go to sleep. If you don't feel sleepy, you stay up. If the composer doesn't feel like composing, he doesn't compose. It's as simple as that.

Of course, after you have finished composing, you hope that everyone, including yourself, will recognize the thing you have written as having been inspired. But that is really an idea tacked on at the end.

Someone once asked me, in a public forum, whether I waited for inspiration. My answer was: "Every day!" But that does not, by any means, imply a passive waiting around for the divine afflatus.[3] That is exactly what separates the professional from the dilettante. The professional composer can sit down day after day and turn out some kind of music. On some days it will undoubt-

---

**1. ivory** (i′ vər ē) **tower:** A place to which someone withdraws from daily life in order to think and create.
**2. layman** (lā′ mən) *n.*: A person not belonging to or skilled in a given profession.

**3. divine afflatus** (ə flāt′ əs): Inspiration from heaven.

edly be better than on others; but the primary fact is the ability to compose. Inspiration is often only a by-product.

The second question that most people find intriguing is generally worded thus: "Do you or don't you write your music at the piano?" A current idea exists that there is something shameful about writing a piece of music at the piano. Along with that goes a mental picture of Beethoven[4] composing out in the fields. Think about it a moment and you will realize that writing away from the piano nowadays is not nearly so simple a matter as it was in Mozart[5] or Beethoven's day. For one thing, harmony[6] is so much more complex than it was then. Few composers are capable of writing down entire compositions without at least a passing reference to the piano. In fact, Stravinsky[7] in his *Autobiography* has even gone so far as to say that it is a bad thing to write music away from the piano because the composer should always be in contact with sound. That's a violent taking of the opposite side. But, in the end, the way in which a composer writes is a personal matter. The method is unimportant. It is the result that counts.

The really important question is: "What does the composer start with; where does he begin?" The answer to that is, Every composer begins with a musical idea—a *musical* idea, you understand, not a mental, literary, or extramusical idea.[8] Suddenly a theme comes to him. (Theme is used as synonymous with musical idea.) The composer starts with his theme; and the theme is a gift from Heaven. He doesn't know where it comes from—has no control over it. It comes almost like automatic writing.[9] That's why he keeps a book very often and writes themes down whenever they come. He collects musical ideas. You can't do anything about that element of composing.

The idea itself may come in various forms. It may come as a melody—just a one-line simple melody which you might hum to yourself. Or it may come to the composer as a melody with an accompaniment.[10] At times he may not even hear a melody; he may simply conceive an accompanimental figure to which a melody will probably be added later. Or, on the other hand, the theme may take the form of a purely rhythmic idea. He hears a particular kind of drumbeat, and that will be enough to start him off. Over it he will soon begin hearing an accompaniment and melody. The original conception, however, was a mere rhythm. Or, a different type of composer may possibly begin with a contrapuntal[11] web of two or three melodies which are heard at the same instant. That, however, is a less usual species of thematic inspiration.

All these are different ways in which the musical idea may present itself to the composer.

Now, the composer has the idea. He has a number of them in his book, and he examines them in more or less the way that you,

---

**4. Beethoven** (bā′ tō vən): Ludwig van (lōōt′ vig vän) Beethoven (1770–1827), a German composer whose work is known throughout the world.
**5. Mozart** (mō′ tsärt): Wolfgang Amadeus (Vôlf′ gäŋk′ ä′mä dä′ oos) Mozart (1756–1791), a famous Austrian composer.
**6. harmony** (här′ mə nē) *n*.: The study of chords in music; chords are combinations of tones sounded together.
**7. Stravinsky** (strə vin′ skē): Igor (ē′ gôr) Stravinsky (1882–1971), a United States composer and conductor who was born in Russia.
**8. extramusical idea:** An idea that is not from the field of music.

**9. automatic writing:** Writing a person does so quickly that he or she does not seem to know where the ideas come from.
**10. accompaniment** (ə kump′ ni mənt) *n*.: A part, usually instrumental, performed together with the main part for richer effect.
**11. contrapuntal** (kän′ trə pun′t'l) *adj*.: Using one melody in contrast to or interaction with another.

the listener, would examine them if you looked at them. He wants to know what he has. He examines the musical line for its purely formal beauty. He likes to see the way it rises and falls, as if it were a drawn line instead of a musical one. He may even try to retouch it, just as you might in drawing a line, so that the rise and fall of the melodic contour might be improved.

But he also wants to know the emotional significance of his theme. If all music has expressive value, then the composer must become conscious of the expressive values of his theme. He may be unable to put it into so many words, but he feels it! He instinctively knows whether he has a gay or a sad theme, a noble or diabolic one. Sometimes he may be mystified himself as to its exact quality. But sooner or later he will probably instinctively decide what the emotional nature of his theme is, because that's the thing he is about to work with.

Always remember that a theme is, after all, only a succession of notes. Merely by changing the dynamics, that is, by playing it loudly and bravely or softly and timidly, one can transform the emotional feeling of the very same succession of notes. By a change of harmony a new poignancy may be given the theme; or by a different rhythmic treatment the same notes may result in a war dance instead of a lullaby. Every composer keeps in mind the possible metamorphoses of his succession of notes. First he tries to find its essential nature, and then he tries to find what might be done with it—how that essential nature may momentarily be changed.

As a matter of fact, the experience of most composers has been that the more complete a theme is the less possibility there is of seeing it in various aspects. If the theme itself, in its original form, is long enough and complete enough, the composer may have difficulty in seeing it in any other way. It already exists in its definitive form. That is why great music can be written on themes that in themselves are insignificant. One might very well say that the less complete, the less important, the theme the more likely it is to be open to new connotations. Some of Bach's[12] greatest organ fugues[13] are constructed on themes that are comparatively uninteresting in themselves.

The current notion that all music is beautiful according to whether the theme is beautiful or not doesn't hold true in many cases. Certainly the composer does not judge his theme by that criterion alone.

Having looked at his thematic material, the composer must now decide what sound medium will best fit it. Is it a theme that belongs in a symphony, or does it seem more intimate in character and therefore better fitted for a string quartet? Is it a lyrical theme that would be used to best advantage in a song; or had it better be saved, because of its dramatic quality, for operatic treatment? A composer sometimes has a work half finished before he understands the medium for which it is best fitted.

Thus far I have been presupposing[14] an abstract[15] composer before an abstract theme. But actually I can see three different types of composers in musical history, each of whom conceives music in a somewhat different fashion.

The type that has fired public imagina-

---

**12. Bach** (bäк̇h): Johann Sebastian (yō′hän si bas′ сhən) Bach (1685–1750), a famous German composer.
**13. fugues** (fyo͞ogs) *n.*: Musical compositions designed for a definite number of instruments or voices in which a theme is presented in one voice and then developed contrapuntally by each of the other voices.
**14. presupposing** (prē′ sə pōz′ iŋ) *v.*: Assuming beforehand.
**15. abstract** (ab strakt′) *adj.*: Apart from any particular example; theoretical.

tion most is that of the spontaneously inspired composer—the Franz Schubert[16] type, in other words. All composers are inspired of course, but this type is more spontaneously inspired. Music simply wells out of him. He can't get it down on paper fast enough. You can almost always tell this type of composer by his prolific output. In certain months, Schubert wrote a song a day. Hugo Wolf[17] did the same.

In a sense, men of this kind begin not so much with a musical theme as with a completed composition. They invariably work best in the shorter forms. It is much easier to improvise a song than it is to improvise a symphony. It isn't easy to be inspired in that spontaneous way for long periods at a stretch. Even Schubert was more successful in handling the shorter forms of music. The spontaneously inspired man is only one type of composer, with his own limitations.

Beethoven symbolizes the second type —the constructive type, one might call it. This type exemplifies my theory of the creative process in music better than any other, because in this case the composer really does begin with a musical theme. In Beethoven's case there is no doubt about it, for we have the notebooks in which he put the themes down. We can see from his notebooks how he worked over his themes —how he would not let them be until they were as perfect as he could make them. Beethoven was not a spontaneously inspired composer in the Schubert sense at all. He was the type that begins with a theme; makes it a germinal[18] idea; and upon that constructs a musical work, day after day, in painstaking fashion. Most compos-

ers since Beethoven's day belong to this second type.

The third type of creator I can only call, for lack of a better name, the traditionalist type. Men like Palestrina[19] and Bach belong in this category. They both exemplify the kind of composer who is born in a particular period of musical history, when a certain musical style is about to reach its fullest development. It is a question at such a time of creating music in a well-known and accepted style and doing it in a way that is better than anyone has done it before you.

Beethoven and Schubert started from a different premise. They both had serious pretensions[20] to originality! After all, Schubert practically created the song form singlehanded; and the whole face of music changed after Beethoven lived. But Bach and Palestrina simply improved on what had gone before them.

The traditionalist type of composer begins with a pattern rather than with a theme. The creative act with Palestrina is not the thematic conception so much as the personal treatment of a well-established pattern. And even Bach, who conceived forty-eight of the most varied and inspired themes in his *Well Tempered Clavichord*, knew in advance the general formal mold that they were to fill. It goes without saying that we are not living in a traditionalist period nowadays.

One might add, for the sake of completeness, a fourth type of composer—the pioneer type: men like Gesualdo[21] in the seventeenth century, Moussorgsky[22] and Berlioz[23]

---

**16. Franz Schubert** (sho͞o′ bərt): A famous Austrian composer (1797–1828).
**17. Hugo Wolf:** A famous Austrian composer (1860–1903).
**18. germinal** (jʉr′ mə n'l) *adj.*: Serving as a basis for further development.

**19. Palestrina** (pä′ les trē′ nä): Giovanni (jô vän′ ē) Palestrina (1525?–1594), a famous Italian composer.
**20. pretensions** (pri ten′ shəns) *n.*: Claims.
**21. Gesualdo** (jə swäl′ dō): Carlo Gesualdo (1560–1613), an Italian composer.
**22. Moussorgsky** (mus org′ skē): Modeste (mō des′ tə) Moussorgsky (1839–1881), a Russian composer.
**23. Berlioz** (ber lyōz′): Louis Hector Berlioz (1803–1869), a famous French composer.

**BEETHOVEN'S STERBEZIMMER IM SCHWARZPANIERHAUS, 1827**
*Johann Nepomuk Hoechle*
Historisches Museum der Stadt Wien

in the nineteenth, Debussy[24] and Edgar Varèse[25] in the twentieth. It is difficult to summarize the composing methods of so variegated a group. One can safely say that their approach to composition is the opposite of the traditionalist type. They clearly oppose conventional solutions of musical problems. In many ways, their attitude is experimental—they seek to add new harmonies, new sonorities,[26] new formal principles. The pioneer type was the characteristic one at the turn of the seventeenth century and also at the beginning of the twentieth century, but it is much less evident today.

But let's return to our theoretical composer. We have him with his idea—his musical idea—with some conception of its expressive nature, with a sense of what can be done with it, and with a preconceived notion of what medium is best fitted for it. Still he hasn't a piece. A musical idea is not the same as a piece of music. It only induces a piece of music. The composer knows very well that something else is needed in order to create the finished composition.

He tries, first of all, to find other ideas

---

**24. Debussy** (də bü sē′): Claude Debussy (1862–1918), a famous French composer.
**25. Edgar Varèse** (va räz′): A French composer (1883–1965).
**26. sonorities** (sə nôr′ ə tēs) *n.*: Qualities of sound.

that seem to go with the original one. They may be ideas of a similar character, or they may be contrasting ones. These additional ideas will probably not be so important as the one that came first—usually they play a subsidiary role. Yet they definitely seem necessary in order to complete the first one. Still that's not enough! Some way must be found for getting from one idea to the next, and it is generally achieved through use of so-called bridge material.

There are also two other important ways in which the composer can add to his original material. One is the elongation process.[27] Often the composer finds that a particular theme needs elongating so that its character may be more clearly defined. Wagner[28] was a master at elongation. I referred to the other way when I visualized the composer's examining the possible metamorphoses of his theme. That is the much written-about development of his material, which is a very important part of his job.

All these things are necessary for the creation of a full-sized piece—the germinal idea, the addition of other lesser ideas, the elongation of the ideas, the bridge material for the connection of the ideas, and their full development.

Now comes the most difficult task of all—the welding together of all that material so that it makes a coherent whole. In the finished product, everything must be in its place. The listener must be able to find his way around in the piece. There should be no possible chance of his confusing the principal theme with the bridge material, or vice versa. The composition must have a beginning, a middle, and an end; and it is up to the composer to see to it that the listener always has some sense of where he is in relation to beginning, middle, and end. Moreover, the whole thing should be managed artfully so that none can say where the soldering[29] began—where the composer's spontaneous invention left off and the hard work began.

Of course, I do not mean to suggest that in putting his materials together the composer necessarily begins from scratch. On the contrary, every well-trained composer, has, as his stock in trade, certain formal structural molds on which to lean for the basic framework of his compositions. These formal molds I speak of have all been gradually evolved over hundreds of years as the combined efforts of numberless composers seeking a way to ensure the coherence of their compositions.

But whatever the form the composer chooses to adopt, there is always one great desideratum:[30] The form must have what in my student days we used to call "the long line." It is difficult adequately to explain the meaning of that phrase to the layman. To be properly understood in relation to a piece of music, it must be felt. In mere words, it simply means that every good piece of music must give us a sense of flow—a sense of continuity from first note to last. Every elementary music student knows the principle, but to put it into practice has challenged the greatest minds in music! A great symphony is a man-made Mississippi down which we irresistibly flow from the instant of our leave-taking to a long foreseen destination. Music must always flow, for that is part of its very essence, but the creation of that continuity and flow—that long line— constitutes the be-all and end-all of every composer's existence.

---

**27. elongation** (i lôŋ′ gā′ shən) **process**: The method by which the material is extended or lengthened.
**28. Wagner** (väg′ nər): Richard Wagner (1813—1883), a German composer.

**29. soldering** (säd′ ər iŋ) n.: Piecing together; uniting.
**30. desideratum** (di sid′ ə rät′ əm) n.: Something needed or wanted.

## THINKING ABOUT THE SELECTION
### Recalling

1. How does the writer respond to the question people ask about inspiration?
2. How does the writer respond to the question people ask about composing at the piano?
3. Which four types of composers does the writer describe? Give an example of each one.

### Interpreting

4. Why do you think the writer gives such a detailed account of the creative process of composing?
5. What does the writer's care in explaining the creative process tell you about him?

### Applying

6. How does the creative process of composing music compare with or contrast to your own process of writing a composition? Name at least two similarities and two differences.

## READING IN THE ARTS AND SCIENCES
### Understanding Process Analysis

**Process analysis,** the examination of the steps involved in a particular operation performed to bring about a desired result, is used in "The Creative Process in Music" to examine the elements involved in composing music.

1. In what form do ideas enter the composer's mind?
2. What three things does a composer think about before developing a musical idea?
3. What are four ways in which a composer may develop a musical idea into a full composition?
4. Which is the most difficult part of the process?

5. What advice does the writer give for assessing the results of the process?

## CRITICAL THINKING AND READING
### Finding Supporting Details

The **main idea** of each paragraph of a piece of literature is its most important idea. The main idea may be stated directly or it may be implied. A writer includes **supporting details** that back up the main idea.

In "The Creative Process in Music," for example, the main idea could be stated as: *A composer creates a piece of fully developed music by using a particular creative process.* The writer develops this main point through the use of specific details, such as descriptions of the distinct parts of the music-making process.

Which of the following details support the main idea of the essay? Give reasons for your choices.

1. "Of course, after you have finished composing, you hope that everyone, including yourself, will recognize the thing you have written as having been inspired."
2. "Every composer begins with a musical idea."
3. "Having looked at his thematic material, the composer must now decide what sound medium will best fit it."

## THINKING AND WRITING
### Writing an Essay About Music

Choose a musical experience—whether that of a listener, a performer, or a musical composer —and write an essay explaining this process to students your age. First list the steps involved, in the order in which they occur in the process. Then use this information to write your essay, describing each step. Revise your essay to include an example, such as an anecdote or a comparison. Proofread for errors in spelling, grammar, and punctuation.

# GUIDE FOR READING

## Alex Katz's *The Table*

**Ann Beattie** (1947–    ) writes novels and short stories concerned with young people who came of age in the 1960's and became disillusioned in the following years. Her writing—particularly her description of people and objects—is characterized by attention to detail. This aspect of Beattie's writing suggests a reason for her interest in the painter Alex Katz, whose work invites you to look at a commonplace object "in its own right, instead of the way we usually look at it."

### Critical Writing

**Critical writing** is that concerned with judgments and evaluations of books, plays, movies, paintings, and other works of art. Critical writing usually describes a particular work of art and gives an opinion about it and reasons to support that opinion. An example of critical writing is a review of a ballet or a concert. In "Alex Katz's *The Table*," the writer evaluates a painting by Alex Katz.

### Look For

As you read "Alex Katz's *The Table*," look for indications of the writer's opinion of the painting and the reasons she uses to support that opinion.

### Writing

Look at the reproduction of *The Table* on page 562. Then freewrite about your impressions of the painting, describing your thoughts and feelings.

### Vocabulary

Knowing the meaning of the following words will help you as you read "Alex Katz's *The Table*."

**perplexing** (pər pleks'iŋ) *adj.*: Puzzling; difficult to understand (p. 561)

**conventional** (kən ven' shən 'l) *adj.*: Of the usual kind; customary (p. 561)

**particularization** (pər tik'yə lə rīz ā' shən) *n.*: Presentation in minute detail (p. 561)

**utilitarian** (yoo til'ə ter'ē ən) *adj.*: Meant to be useful (p. 561)

**provocativeness** (prə väk'ə tiv nis) *n.*: Stimulation; incitement (p. 561)

**repository** (ri päz'ə tôr'ē) *n.*: A place where things are stored and saved (p. 561)

**inherently** (in hir'ənt lē) *adv.*: Basically; by its very nature (p. 561)

# Alex Katz's *The Table*

## Ann Beattie

Although Alex Katz is most often associated with painting people, he has painted everything from the branch of a tree to a picnic table. While it is difficult to say that the picnic table seen here is remarkable in and of itself, it is nevertheless a perplexing painting. If the painter can make us stare at it—if the table seems large and obvious and conventional but we are still drawn to it—we may have been given a clue about Katz's vision as well as a lesson in how to look and why.

As such, a picnic table is not very detailed. Detail is usually included so that something becomes more believable or unique in a way we may not have expected. Yet we would be foolish to look for particularization of a humble picnic table; we do not have the interest in detail the way we do when, say, we look at a bowl of fruit painted by Bonnard.[1] This is just a picnic table—yet what associations we all have with it: it is a symbol of summer and all that the season connotes; it is a timeless thing, something that will not likely be refined, improved and recycled into something *au courant*.[2] Its

form is a composite of horizontals, an assemblage that is a little more complex when seen at this angle than straight on, an object that is revealed to us as potentially less simple than we probably first thought. It is a nice painting. Easy to look at. The table is composed of dark and light, a representation of what a picnic table *essentially* looks like, rather than a very defined, scarred, splintery table affected by the elements. We associate this table with its utilitarian function, but since we do not see it functioning that way, it becomes mysterious, the way an empty movie house seems strange. What about this *thing,* this thing in its own right, instead of the way we usually think of it, defined by function? It forces us to admit that we rely on context—that context is linked in our minds with function—and that there is a provocativeness akin to nakedness when we must look at something in isolation. The table becomes a repository for our imaginings, a thing inherently useful, simple, and neutral. It is recognizable, though we may not have taken the time to stop and study it before. It also functions symbolically, and since we know what it represents, nothing needs to be done to interpret it. But we cannot be fooled into thinking that because it is inconspicuous, it is not important. At the very least, we are

---

**1. Bonnard** (bô när'): Pierre Bonnard (1864–1947), a French impressionist painter.
**2. *au courant*** (ō kōō rän'): French for "up-to-date."

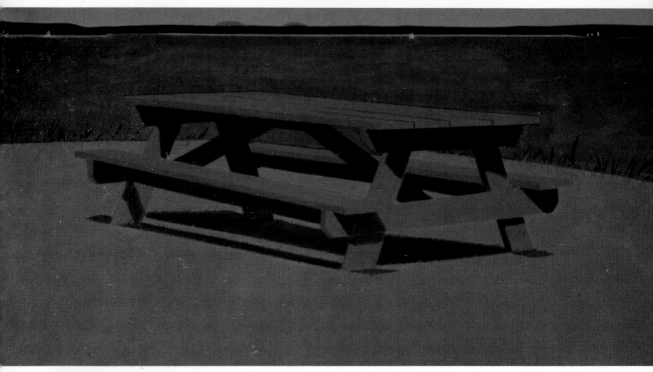

**THE TABLE**
*Alex Katz*
Courtesy of Marlborough Gallery

told something about the artist's sensibility. This painting tells us what he finds worth presenting; that simple things have inherent beauty, even if it is a taken-for-granted beauty; and it suggests that things have an inherent quality. Though the table does not confound us or awaken us to some complexity we would never have imagined, having it presented this way still puzzles and attracts us. The picnic table is, if not of our dreams, of the painter's dreams, because his world is a dream, told to him and to us through symbols. This painting is a dream of color, of form, of the way light falls on the world. It also has enough openness, enough emptiness that is merely tinged with specificity that we at once believe in it, yet don't see it as so particular that we can only relate to it in some predetermined way. Given a symbol and a context, we may project a life upon it.

## THINKING ABOUT THE SELECTION
### Recalling

1. What kind of table is depicted in the painting *The Table*?
2. What kind of subject is Alex Katz best known for—landscapes, people, or objects?
3. How, according to the writer, does the painter make the table become mysterious and interesting in its own right?

### Interpreting

4. What does the writer mean by saying the table is "a symbol of summer and all that the season connotes"?

### Applying

5. Familiar objects or places may seem strange when viewed apart from their usual function. The writer mentions an empty movie house as one example. Think of an object or place that has seemed strange or mysterious to you because you suddenly saw it in a new way.

## READING IN THE ARTS AND SCIENCES
### Understanding Critical Writing

**Critical writing** makes a direct or an implied judgment of a work of art. Good critical writing helps you to perceive features of the work that you might fail to notice and to form insights about the meaning of the work.

1. What is the writer's judgment about the painting *The Table*?
2. How does the essay enhance your first impression and appreciation of the painting?

## CRITICAL THINKING AND READING
### Making a Judgment About a Work of Art

Critical writing makes a judgment about a work of art. It also helps you to make your own judgment about it. In *The Table,* the writer comments on details of the work and the artist's craft that support her view of the artist's achievement. For instance, she says that *The Table* does not invite the viewer to take an interest in minute detail, as does a still life painting by Pierre Bonnard, whose attention to detail was remarkable. If you agree with the writer's comments, you are likely to share her overall estimate of the work. If you disagree with one or more of her observations, you may disagree with her overall judgment.

Reread the essay and answer the following questions.

1. Find two specific statements about the painting or the artist's craft that support the writer's view of the work and summarize each statement.
2. Write a short statement expressing your own judgment of *The Table*.

## UNDERSTANDING LANGUAGE
### Appreciating Art Terms

Art is a field that has some of its own terminology. In Beattie's essay, for example, the table is described as being "a composite of horizontals." Used as a noun in this context, *horizontal* is an art term that refers to the horizontal lines and surfaces the painter has used to present the table.

Use a dictionary to find the meaning of each of the following art terms. Then use each term in a sentence.

1. still life     2. perspective     3. primitives

## THINKING AND WRITING
### Writing About Art

Think of a painting or a photograph that you particularly like. First jot down some features of the work that you consider noteworthy. Then use this information to write a critical paragraph about the picture that will help other students who are unfamiliar with it to share your appreciation. Revise the paragraph to be persuasive. Proofread for errors in spelling, grammar, and punctuation.

## The Marginal World

**Rachel Carson** (1907–1964), born in Springfield, Pennsylvania, was a naturalist who specialized in marine biology—the study of sea life. Carson spent several summers during college at the Marine Biological Laboratory in Woods Hole, Massachusetts. She later observed, "I am sure that the genesis of *The Sea Around Us* belongs to that first year at Woods Hole, when I began storing away facts about the sea—facts discovered in scientific literature or by personal observation and experience . . ."

### Observation and Inference

**Observation** is the act of carefully noting facts and events. Observation focuses on what you see, rather than on what you think or feel. More precise and systematic than the way you usually look at people and events, observation is often used by scientists in research.

**Inference** is a reasonable conclusion that you can draw based on evidence. Often you can make inferences based on factual information you have observed. In "The Marginal World" the writer's descriptions of sea life show her skill as an observer and allows her to make some inferences.

### Look For

As you read "The Marginal World," look for the factual descriptions of what the writer experiences and the way she interprets these descriptions to find another meaning.

### Writing

Freewrite about a place in nature that has had special meaning for you. Focus on the specific details that describe what you saw, heard, tasted, smelled, and felt in the place you recall.

### Vocabulary

Knowing the following words will help you as you read "The Marginal World."

**marginal** (mär′jən ′l) *adj.*: Occupying the borderland of a stable area (p. 565)

**mutable** (myoōt′ə b′l) *adj.*: Capable of change (p. 565)

**ephemeral** (i fem′ə rəl) *adj.*: Passing quickly (p. 567)

**primeval** (prī mē′v′l) *adj.*: Ancient or primitive (p. 568)

**essence** (es′′ns) *n.*: Real nature of something (p. 568)

**subjectively** (səb jek′tiv lē) *adv.*: Personally (p. 570)

**manifestations** (man′ə fes tā′shənz) *n.*: Appearances or evidence (p. 570)

**cosmic** (käz′mik) *adj.*: Relating to the universe (p. 570)

# The Marginal World

## Rachel Carson

The edge of the sea is a strange and beautiful place. All through the long history of Earth it has been an area of unrest where waves have broken heavily against the land, where the tides have pressed forward over the continents, receded, and then returned. For no two successive days is the shoreline precisely the same. Not only do the tides advance and retreat in their eternal rhythms, but the level of the sea itself is never at rest. It rises or falls as the glaciers melt or grow, as the floor of the deep ocean basins shifts under its increasing load of sediments, or as the earth's crust along the continental margins warps up or down in adjustment to strain and tension. Today a little more land may belong to the sea, tomorrow a little less. Always the edge of the sea remains an elusive and indefinable boundary.

The shore has a dual nature, changing with the swing of the tides, belonging now to the land, now to the sea. On the ebb tide it knows the harsh extremes of the land world, being exposed to heat and cold, to wind, to rain and drying sun. On the flood tide it is a water world, returning briefly to the relative stability of the open sea.

Only the most hardy and adaptable can survive in a region so mutable, yet the area between the tide lines is crowded with plants and animals. In this difficult world of the shore, life displays its enormous toughness and vitality by occupying almost every conceivable niche. Visibly, it carpets the intertidal rocks; or half hidden, it descends into fissures and crevices, or hides under boulders, or lurks in the wet gloom of sea caves. Invisibly, where the casual observer would say there is no life, it lies deep in the sand, in burrows and tubes and passageways. It tunnels into solid rock and bores into peat and clay. It encrusts weeds or drifting spars[1] or the hard, chitinous[2] shell

---

**1. spars** (spärs) *n.*: Masts, booms, or other supports for sails.
**2. chitinous** (kī′ tən əs) *adj.*: Of a material which forms the tough outer covering of insects, crustaceans, and so on.

of a lobster. It exists minutely, as the film of bacteria that spreads over a rock surface or a wharf piling; as spheres of protozoa, small as pinpricks, sparkling at the surface of the sea; and as Lilliputian[3] beings swimming through dark pools that lie between the grains of sand.

The shore is an ancient world, for as long as there has been an earth and sea there has been this place of the meeting of land and water. Yet it is a world that keeps alive the sense of continuing creation and of the relentless drive of life. Each time that I enter it, I gain some new awareness of its beauty and its deeper meanings, sensing that intricate fabric of life by which one creature is linked with another, and each with its surroundings.

In my thoughts of the shore, one place stands apart for its revelation of exquisite beauty. It is a pool hidden within a cave that one can visit only rarely and briefly when the lowest of the year's low tides fall below it, and perhaps from that very fact it acquires some of its special beauty. Choosing such a tide, I hoped for a glimpse of the pool. The ebb was to fall early in the morning. I knew that if the wind held from the northwest and no interfering swell ran in from a distant storm the level of the sea should drop below the entrance to the pool. There had been sudden ominous showers in the night, with rain like handfuls of gravel flung on the roof. When I looked out into the early morning the sky was full of a gray dawn light but the sun had not yet risen. Water and air were pallid. Across the bay the moon was a luminous disc in the western sky, suspended above the dim line of distant shore—the full August moon, drawing the tide to the low, low levels of the threshold of the alien sea world. As I watched, a gull flew by, above the spruces. Its breast was rosy with the light of the unrisen sun. The day was, after all, to be fair.

Later, as I stood above the tide near the entrance to the pool, the promise of that rosy light was sustained. From the base of the steep wall of rock on which I stood, a moss-covered ledge jutted seaward into deep water. In the surge at the rim of the ledge the dark fronds[4] of oarweeds swayed, smooth and gleaming as leather. The projecting ledge was the path to the small hidden cave and its pool. Occasionally a swell, stronger than the rest, rolled smoothly over the rim and broke in foam against the cliff. But the intervals between such swells were long enough to admit me to the ledge and long enough for a glimpse of that fairy pool, so seldom and so briefly exposed.

And so I knelt on the wet carpet of sea moss and looked back into the dark cavern that held the pool in a shallow basin. The floor of the cave was only a few inches below the roof, and a mirror had been created in which all that grew on the ceiling was reflected in the still water below.

Under water that was clear as glass the pool was carpeted with green sponge. Gray patches of sea squirts[5] glistened on the ceiling and colonies of soft coral[6] were a pale apricot color. In the moment when I looked into the cave a little elfin starfish hung down, suspended by the merest thread, perhaps by only a single tube foot. It reached down to touch its own reflection, so perfectly delineated that there might have been, not

---

**3. Lilliputian** (lil'ə pyoo' shən) *adj.*: Tiny and thus like the tiny people about six inches tall who inhabit Lilliput in the book *Gulliver's Travels* by Jonathan Swift.

**4. fronds** (fränds) *n.*: Leaves.
**5. sea squirts:** Sac-shaped water animals with tough outer coverings.
**6. coral** (kôr'əl) *n.*: Animals with tentacles at the top of tubelike bodies.

one starfish, but two. The beauty of the reflected images and of the limpid[7] pool itself was the poignant[8] beauty of things that are ephemeral, existing only until the sea should return to fill the little cave.

Whenever I go down into this magical zone of the low water of the spring tides, I look for the most delicately beautiful of all the shore's inhabitants—flowers that are not plant but animal, blooming on the threshold of the deeper sea. In that fairy cave I was not disappointed. Hanging from its roof were the pendent[9] flowers of the hydroid Tubularia, pale pink, fringed and delicate as the wind flower. Here were creatures so exquisitely fashioned that they seemed unreal, their beauty too fragile to exist in a world of crushing force. Yet every detail was functionally useful, every stalk and hydranth[10] and petallike tentacle fashioned for dealing with the realities of existence. I knew that they were merely waiting, in that moment of the tide's ebbing, for the return of the sea. Then in the rush of water, in the surge of surf and the pressure of the incoming tide, the delicate flower heads would stir with life. They would sway on their slender stalks, and their long tentacles would sweep the returning water, finding in it all that they needed for life.

And so in that enchanted place on the threshold of the sea the realities that possessed my mind were far from those of the land world I had left an hour before. In a different way the same sense of remoteness and of a world apart came to me in a twilight hour on a great beach on the coast of Georgia. I had come down after sunset and walked far out over sands that lay wet and gleaming, to the very edge of the retreating sea. Looking back across that immense flat, crossed by winding, waterfilled gullies and here and there holding shallow pools left by the tide, I was filled with awareness that this intertidal area, although abandoned briefly and rhythmically by the sea, is always reclaimed by the rising tide. There at the edge of low water the beach with its reminders of the land seemed far away. The only sounds were those of the wind and the sea and the birds. There was one sound of wind moving over water, and another of water sliding over the sand and tumbling down the faces of its own wave forms. The flats were astir with birds, and the voice of the willet[11] rang insistently. One of them stood at the edge of the water and gave its loud, urgent cry; an answer came from far up the beach and the two birds flew to join each other.

The flats took on a mysterious quality as dusk approached and the last evening light was reflected from the scattered pools and creeks. Then birds became only dark shadows, with no color discernible. Sanderlings[12] scurried across the beach like little ghosts, and here and there the darker forms of the willets stood out. Often I could come very close to them before they would start up in alarm—the sanderlings running, the willets flying up, crying. Black skimmers[13] flew along the ocean's edge silhouetted against the dull, metallic gleam, or they went flitting above the sand like large, dimly seen moths. Sometimes they "skimmed" the winding creeks of tidal water, where little spreading surface ripples marked the presence of small fish.

The shore at night is a different world, in

---

7. **limpid** (lim′ pid) *adj.*: Clear.
8. **poignant** (poin′ yənt) *adj.*: Emotionally moving.
9. **pendent** (pen′ dənt) *adj.*: Hanging.
10. **hydranth** (hi′ drantʌ) *n.*: Feeding individual.

11. **willet** (wil′ it) *n.*: Large, gray and white, long-legged wading bird.
12. **sanderlings**: Small, gray and white birds found on sandy beaches.
13. **skimmers**: Long-winged sea birds.

which the very darkness that hides the distractions of daylight brings into sharper focus the elemental realities. Once, exploring the night beach, I surprised a small ghost crab in the searching beam of my torch. He was lying in a pit he had dug just above the surf, as though watching the sea and waiting. The blackness of the night possessed water, air, and beach. It was the darkness of an older world, before Man. There was no sound but the all-enveloping, primeval sounds of wind blowing over water and sand, and of waves crashing on the beach. There was no other visible life—just one small crab near the sea. I have seen hundreds of ghost crabs in other settings, but suddenly I was filled with the odd sensation that for the first time I knew the creature in its own world—that I understood, as never before, the essence of its being. In that moment time was suspended; the world to which I belonged did not exist and I might have been an onlooker from outer space. The little crab alone with the sea became a symbol that stood for life itself—for the delicate, destructible, yet incredibly vital force that somehow holds its place amid the harsh realities of the inorganic world.

The sense of creation comes with memories of a southern coast, where the sea and the mangroves,[14] working together, are building a wilderness of thousands of small islands off the southwestern coast of Florida, separated from each other by a tortuous[15] pattern of bays, lagoons, and narrow waterways, I remember a winter day when the sky was blue and drenched with sunlight; though there was no wind one was

conscious of flowing air like cold clear crystal. I had landed on the surf-washed tip of one of those islands, and then worked my way around to the sheltered bay side. There I found the tide far out, exposing the broad mud flat of a cove bordered by the mangroves with their twisted branches, their glossy leaves, and their long prop roots reaching down, grasping and holding the mud, building the land out a little more, then again a little more.

The mud flats were strewn with the shells of that small, exquisitely colored mollusk,[16] the rose tellin, looking like scattered

**16. mollusk** (mäl′ əsk) *n.*: One of a large group of soft-bodied animals with shells that include clams, oysters, mussels, snails, and so on.

---

**14. mangroves** (maŋ′ grōvs) *n.*: Tropical trees that grow in swampy ground with spreading branches that send down roots and thus form more trunks.
**15. tortuous** (tôr′ choo wəs) *adj.*: Full of twists and turns.

petals of pink roses. There must have been a colony nearby, living buried just under the surface of the mud. At first the only creature visible was a small heron[17] in gray and rusty plumage—a reddish egret that waded across the flat with the stealthy, hesitant movements of its kind. But other land creatures had been there, for a line of fresh tracks wound in and out among the mangrove roots, marking the path of a raccoon feeding on the oysters that gripped the supporting roots with projections from their shells. Soon I found the tracks of a shore bird, probably a sanderling, and followed

---

**17. heron** (her′ ən) *n.*: A wading bird with long legs and a long, tapered bill.

them a little; then they turned toward the water and were lost, for the tide had erased them and made them as though they had never been.

Looking out over the cove I felt a strong sense of the interchangeability of land and sea in this marginal world of the shore, and of the links between the life of the two. There was also an awareness of the past and of the continuing flow of time, obliterating much that had gone before, as the sea had that morning washed away the tracks of the bird.

The sequence and meaning of the drift of time were quietly summarized in the existence of hundreds of small snails—the mangrove periwinkles—browsing on the branches and roots of the trees. Once their ancestors had been sea dwellers, bound to the salt waters by every tie of their life processes. Little by little over the thousands and millions of years the ties had been broken, the snails had adjusted themselves to life out of water, and now today they were living many feet above the tide to which they only occasionally returned. And perhaps, who could say how many ages hence, there would be in their descendants not even this gesture of remembrance for the sea.

The spiral shells of other snails—these quite minute[18]—left winding tracks on the mud as they moved about in search of food. They were horn shells, and when I saw them I had a nostalgic moment when I wished I might see what Audubon[19] saw, a century and more ago. For such little horn shells were the food of the flamingo, once so numerous on this coast, and when I half closed my eyes I could almost imagine a flock of

---

**18. minute** (mī nōōt′) *adj.*: Tiny.
**19. Audubon** (ôd′ə bän′): John James Audubon (1785–1851), a famous ornithologist, naturalist, and painter, famed for his paintings of North American birds.

these magnificent flame birds feeding in that cove, filling it with their color. It was a mere yesterday in the life of the earth that they were there; in nature, time and space are relative matters, perhaps most truly perceived subjectively in occasional flashes of insight, sparked by such a magical hour and place.

There is a common thread that links these scenes and memories—the spectacle of life in all its varied manifestations as it has appeared, evolved, and sometimes died out. Underlying the beauty of the spectacle there is meaning and significance. It is the elusiveness of that meaning that haunts us, that sends us again and again into the natural world where the key to the riddle is hidden. It sends us back to the edge of the sea, where the drama of life played its first scene on earth and perhaps even its prelude;[20] where the forces of evolution are at work today, as they have been since the appearance of what we know as life; and where the spectacle of living creatures faced by the cosmic realities of their world is crystal clear.

---

**20. prelude** (prel′ yōōd) *n*.: Introduction.

# THINKING ABOUT THE SELECTION

## Recalling

1. In "The Marginal World," what time and special place does the writer describe first?
2. Why is this place rare and remote?
3. What special beauty does the writer find in this first place?
4. What second time, place, and experience does the writer describe?
5. What is the third time, place, and discovery the writer describes?

## Interpreting

6. What broader meaning about life does this marginal world help you see?
7. Think of another title for this essay—one that states the meaning of the essay for you.

## Applying

8. Besides the seashore, what other places could help you experience the interconnectedness of life?

# READING IN THE ARTS AND SCIENCES

## Seeing Observation and Inference

**Observation,** the act of carefully reporting facts and events, focuses on what you see, rather than on what you think or feel. **Inference,** a reasonable conclusion that you can draw based on evidence, often can be made based on factual information you have observed. For example, a journalist may report on the events he or she observes in a foreign country's government, while a political analyst can make inferences based on these observations.

1. The writer makes observations about the sky when she visits the pool hidden within a cave at low tide. What inference does she make about the day?
2. The writer makes observations about the hundreds of snails browsing in trees. What inferences does she make about the snails?

# CRITICAL THINKING AND READING

## Recognizing Cause-and-Effect

**Cause-and-effect relationships** describe the connection between a cause, or reason, and its effects, or results. A cause makes something occur; an effect is the outcome of the cause.

1. What causes the following events?
   a. The shore is littered with mollusks and other shells.
   b. The level of the sea itself changes.
2. What are the effects of the following events?
   a. The snails move about in search of food.
   b. A flood tide comes in.

# UNDERSTANDING LANGUAGE

## Appreciating Science Terms

Science has its own terminology that helps you define and clearly discuss this subject area.

Use a dictionary to find the meaning of the following science terms from the essay.

1. bacteria          4. intertidal
2. ebb tide          5. mollusk
3. glacier           6. tentacles (plant)

# THINKING AND WRITING

## Writing About Science

Choose one element of the marginal world of the seashore that you know about, such as the ebb tide, an animal, or a plant that lives in the intertidal world. First list any scientific observation about this element that you can think of. Then use this information to write a vivid description of your subject that is both scientifically accurate and personally expressive. Revise your description to be a first-person observation of your subject in its natural world.

# PUTTING IT TOGETHER

# Nonfiction

Nonfiction presents factual information that is based on real people and real events. A writer of nonfiction often has a specific purpose for writing and a specific audience to whom the writing is directed. An active reader examines the techniques a writer uses to accomplish his or her purpose. An active reader also pays close attention to the kind of information the writer uses to support or to clarify the main idea and to the way the writer arranges this supporting information.

**Purpose**

The **purpose** is the writer's reason for writing. Usually, the writer has a general purpose, such as to give information about a topic, to persuade readers to do something, to give directions for doing something, or to entertain readers. The writer usually will have a specific point to make about the topic as well. In an essay this point, or main idea, is often stated in a thesis statement.

**Techniques**

Writers use **techniques,** or certain methods, to accomplish their purposes. These techniques include describing people or a scene with vivid adjectives and using strong active verbs to present actions or events. Effective writers choose words with appropriate connotations, create humorous effects with exaggeration, or use figurative language to present unusual or startling images.

**Support**

**Support** for the thesis statement of an essay is the information used to back up or clarify the main point. Support can include examples, details, facts, opinions, reasons, and incidents.

**Arrangement**

A writer arranges support to best suit his or her purpose for writing. In describing how to do something, for example, a writer might present steps arranged in chronological order. In describing a scene, a writer might present information in a spatial order—from left to right, for instance. A writer may write about the cause of an event and then describe the result or effect that was produced.

On the following pages is a model of an essay. As you read, pay close attention to the annotations in the side column. They show how an active reader might put together what he or she has learned about reading essays.

# Glove's Labor Lost

## Thomas Boswell

Each spring, when the ground loses its threadbare look, I wonder if I should buy a baseball glove. It is a quick, fleeting thought, "And what would you do with it?" I ask myself, and that is that.

For so many years the five-finger, Warren Spahn 300[1] with the trapper's web came up out of the wintry basement with a string tied around it and an old ball clamped inside the pocket. Pulling that string was a truer sign of spring than any robin.

My first glove, a parental gift at age eight, is now only a blurry memory, less vivid than the cowboy guns and garbage cans that I cherished at an earlier period. It was a very dark infielder model and it lived a hard life.

It was once soaked in linseed oil, because in the first stages of my growing addiction I confused linseed with neat's-foot oil, the proper glove preservative.

My rather academic parents thought linseed sounded foolish enough to be correct, so into the oil bath went the new glove. The linseeded glove quickly dried up, cracked like a stoned windshield, and literally flaked away.

During its years of disintegration, I laid plans for a real glove, one that would last a millennium, or at least until high school.

While the first glove was just another toy to be misused, the second, bought with money I saved for over a year, fell somewhere between the last toy and the first personal possession.

Once the money was saved, the shopping began. It took almost as long as the saving. For weeks I was late coming

---

**Purpose:** The title may be a clue to the author's purpose. What does the title mean?

**Arrangement:** This paragraph seems to be written in the present tense. Will the essay be written about today?

**Arrangement:** Now the author is discussing a past time. Will the rest of the essay be a reminiscence of a previous time?

**Support:** The author presents several facts about his first glove here. What are they?

**Technique:** The author uses figurative language in this incident. What type of figurative language is used?

---

1. **Warren Spahn 300:** A baseball mitt named for Warren Spahn who won 363 games in his twenty-one years as a pitcher.

home from school since, after getting off my bus downtown, I would be buffeted by the price tags, models, and signatures available at Irvings, Atlas, and Woodie's. My mother accused me of knowing every glove in the city personally. My father predicted, dourly, that I would grow up and marry a ball.

With a mixture of elation and sadness I settled on the Spahn 300. Before I handed over my thirty dollars to Atlas, I had owned every glove in town, and none of them. Now I had just one. I felt the same paradoxical emotion next when I picked a college.

The new, properly neat's-footed glove slept on my bed at night like a summer puppy and traveled back and forth to school every day, wrist strap looped through belt.

In the alley, beside my house, I saved many a home run from going over a hypothetical outfield fence, and before breakfast and after dinner fielded many a lazy bouncer off the garage wall.

The glove, a ball, and the brick wall of my house, covered with ivy, were my stadium and my major league. When the ball would stick in the ivy, I would dislodge it by throwing sticks and rocks, but only once, my glove. The Spahnie stuck thirty feet up in the ivy, barely peeking out, and my heart hung there, too.

In a still vivid instant, I saw it in my mind's eye lodged there for years, rotting, a testimony to my split-second insanity.

Once retrieved, the glove was never endangered again. I knew, because everyone told me, that it was much too good a glove for a young boy, and I kept it from the careless and uncaring hands of what seemed like hundreds of would-be borrowers. It taught me lessons in saying, "No."

In fact, when my junior high principal, Dick Babyak, sees me now, he still asks, sometimes, "Hey, Tom, can I borrow your glove?"

He still remembers that twenty years ago, when he was my principal, math teacher, and summer camp director rolled into one, I would not let him use it. He wasn't going to get me out in those Sunday camp softball games with my own glove.

The Spahnie stayed with me nearly ten years. I used it in practice in both high school and college, though I used the schools' big first baseman's mitts in games.

Eventually, I lent the glove to Babyak in the summer (to his endless amusement), and by high school I was playing on the same camp counselors' team with him. By my college days he had stepped out of most of the games, unable to hit the ball to the Mattaponi River[2] every time up, as he had once. I inherited his old position.

When I left college, I apparently left the Spahnie behind somewhere. Its role had dwindled considerably. Perhaps I left it on the Theta Delta[3] lawn the week of graduation.

Though service in Vietnam, graduate school, or a job were the uncertain possibilities in my near future, I spent one last summer working in the humid, but still idyllic world of scrapping children and hot macaroni in July.

When the first Sunday softball game came, I had no glove. From the pitcher's mound I watched the twelve-, thirteen-, and fourteen-year-olds running up to bat, tossing down their gloves. I looked for a mitt that seemed familiar, too big for its owner, and almost too well loved.

"Excuse me," I called to a new camper. "May I borrow your glove?"

He looked down, hesitated, then said, "Okay, sir. But take care of it."

"I'm not going to hurt it," I said.

---

**2. Mattaponi River:** A river in eastern Virginia.
**3. Theta Delta:** A college fraternity.

**Thomas Boswell** (1947–    ) was born in Washington and graduated from Amherst College in Massachusetts. He is a sports reporter for the *Washington Post*. Boswell won the Best Sportswriting award from the American Society of Newspaper Editors in 1981 and is a three-time winner in the *Best Sports Stories* competition. "Glove's Labor Lost" appears in his book *How Life Imitates the World Series*.

# THINKING ABOUT THE SELECTION

## Recalling

1. What was a truer sign of spring to the author than any robin?
2. Describe when and how the author acquired his first baseball glove.
3. Describe the steps involved in acquiring the second glove.
4. Name three ways the author kept his glove safe from harm.
5. What finally became of the glove?

## Interpreting

6. In writing about a beloved baseball glove, the author tells us about himself. What do you learn about the kind of person the author is from the essay?
7. Why do you think the author included the last incident in the essay? What other incident does the last one resemble?

## Applying

8. A personal narrative essay often appeals to a wide audience because it discusses an experience that is recognized by people in many different circumstances. Why might someone uninterested in baseball still enjoy this essay? If that person were to write an essay about his or her youth, what might that person write about in the essay instead of a baseball glove?

# ANALYZING LITERATURE

## Understanding a Narrative Essay

In a personal narrative essay like "Glove's Labor Lost," the author's purpose is to write about an aspect of his life that readers can relate to their own experiences.

1. Find three vivid adjectives in the essay. Explain why each is effective.
2. Give examples from the essay of two types of support—facts, opinions, reasons, details, examples, or incidents.
3. How is the essay arranged?

4. Do you think Boswell accomplished his purpose? Explain your answer.

# CRITICAL THINKING AND READING

## Making Inferences About an Author

In a personal narrative essay, you can make **inferences,** or judgments based on evidence presented, about the author. What inferences can you draw from the following pieces of evidence?

1. "Each spring, . . . I wonder if I should buy a baseball glove."
2. ". . . the second, bought with money I saved for over a year, fell somewhere between the last toy and the first personal possession."

# UNDERSTANDING LANGUAGE

## Identifying Similes

Authors use similes to create vivid and unusual images for readers. A **simile** is a comparison of unlike things using the words *like* or *as.* For example, in "The sun was like a giant red balloon," the word *like* is used to compare the sun to a balloon.

1. Find a simile that describes the effect of using the wrong oil on the author's first glove. What is being compared? Is the image effective? Why or why not?
2. Find a simile that describes where the new glove was kept. What is being compared? Is the image effective? Why or why not?

# THINKING AND WRITING

## Writing a Personal Narrative Essay

Think of an object that you or someone you know might remember fondly. List pieces of supporting information that indicate the importance of the object. Write a first draft of an essay about the object's significance in the life of its owner. Try to include at least one simile in your essay. When you have finished, make sure you have organized your essay chronologically. Finally, proofread the essay and share it with your classmates.

# Reading Charts and Tables

Since nonfiction is the type of literature that presents information, when you read nonfiction you may come across charts and tables. Each provides a visual representation of information.

**Charts**

A chart presents a series of facts in the form of a diagram or graph. For example, imagine that James Thurber wanted to show the number of people Muggs bit each day over the course of one week. He might prepare a graph that looks like this.

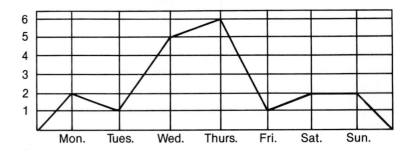

Suppose he wanted to show the relationship between the front door, the mail box, Muggs's doghouse, and Muggs's favorite tree. He might prepare a diagram that looks like this.

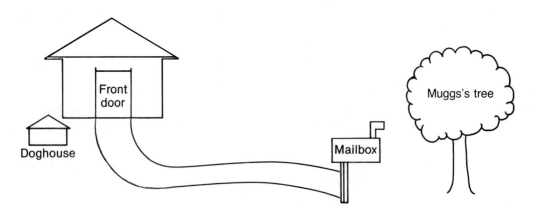

**Activity**

Imagine that you are writing an essay on the popularity of a particular music group. To provide support for your ideas, you have asked a local record store to give you daily sales figures on the group's latest record album. Prepare a graph you might use in your essay.

**Activity**     Imagine that you are writing an essay explaining how to play a popular sport such as baseball or football. Prepare a diagram that you might use in your report.

**Tables**      A table presents statistical information—facts, figures, and other data—in list form. For example, in an essay on the metric system, you might find a table showing metric conversions.

---

**METRIC EQUIVALENTS**

**Linear Measure**

| | |
|---|---|
| 1 centimeter . . . . . . . . . 0.393 in. | 1 in. . . . . . . . . . . 2.54 centimeters |
| 1 decimeter . . . . 3.937 in.-0.328 ft. | 1 ft. . . . . . . . . . . . 3.048 decimeters |
| 1 meter. . . . . 39.37 in.-1.0936 yds. | 1 yd. . . . . . . . . . . . 0.9144 meter |
| 1 dekameter . . . . . . . 1.9844 rods | 1 rod. . . . . . . . . 0.5029 dekameter |
| 1 kilometer . . . . . . . . 0.62137 mile | 1 mile . . . . . . . . 1.6093 kilometers |

**Square Measure**

| | |
|---|---|
| 1 sq. centimeter . . . . 0.1550 sq. in. | 1 sq. in. . . . . 6.452 sq. centimeters |
| 1 sq. decimeter . . . . 0.1076 sq. ft. | 1 sq. ft. . . . . 9.2903 sq. decimeter |
| 1 sq. meter . . . . . . . 1.196 sq. yds. | 1 sq. yd. . . . . . . . 0.8361 sq. meter |
| 1 are . . . . . . . . . 3.954 sq. rods | 1 sq. rod . . . . . . . . . . 0.2529 are |
| 1 hectare . . . . . . . . . . 2.47 acre | 1 acre . . . . . . . . . 0.4047 hectare |
| 1 sq. kilometer . . . . 0.386 sq. mile | 1 sq. mi. . . . . . . 2.59 sq. kilometer |

**Weights**

| | |
|---|---|
| 1 gram . . . . . . . . . . 0.03527 oz. | 1 oz. . . . . . . . . . . . . 28.35 grams |
| 1 kilogram . . . . . . . . . 2.2046 lbs. | 1 lb. . . . . . . . . . . . 0.4536 kilogram |
| 1 metric ton . . . 1.1023 English ton | 1 English ton . . . 0.9072 metric ton |

**Approximate Metric Equivalents**

| | |
|---|---|
| 1 decimeter. . . . . . . . . . 4 inches | 1 liter . . . . 1.06 qts. liq.-0.9 qt. dry |
| 1 meter . . . . . . . . . . . . . 1.1 yds. | 1 hektoliter . . . . . . . . . 2⅘ bushels |
| 1 kilometer. . . . . . . . . . . . ⅝ mile | 1 kilogram. . . . . . . . . . . . 2⅕ lbs. |
| 1 hectare . . . . . . . . . . . 2½ acres | 1 metric ton . . . . . . . . . 2,200 lbs. |
| 1 stere or cu. meter . . . . . . ¼ cord | |

---

**Activity**     Prepare a table that you might include in an essay on a popular sport such as baseball or football. For example, you might prepare a table of batting averages.

# YOU THE WRITER

### Assignment

**1.** Write introductory sentences for three different essays about the following: a person whom you have met, an important event that happened to you, and a topic related to the arts or sciences.

**Prewriting.** Brainstorm about possible essay topics in each category. You might want to look at the opening sentences to "Emily Dickinson," "A Christmas Memory," and "Notes on Punctuation."

**Writing.** Write three introductory sentences. Make certain that each sentence clearly states the topic of each essay. Try to write sentences that will make a reader want to continue.

**Revising.** Check the sentences for errors in spelling, grammar, and punctuation. Make certain that each sentence clearly expresses the topic of the essay.

### Assignment

**2.** Write a personal narrative relating a humorous event. Describe details about the experience, and explain your thoughts about what happened.

**Prewriting.** Freewrite, exploring your topic. Then jot down notes, including answers to *why, where, when, who, what,* and *how.* You might want to look at "A Child's Christmas in Wales" and "A Christmas Memory."

**Writing.** Write the first draft of your narrative. Include details about the experience. Arrange events in chronological order.

**Revising.** Be certain that the narrative conveys your experience in an interesting, coherent way. Check for errors in spelling, grammar, and punctuation.

### Assignment

**3.** Write an essay on a topic currently in the news. Be certain to include a strong introduction and conclusion, and give the essay a title.

**Prewriting.** Brainstorm about essay topics. Then prepare an outline of information you already have about the topic. Do library research to fill in information you need.

**Writing.** Write your essay, keeping in mind these important elements as you write: voice, style, structure, and thought. Make certain to include an introduction, a conclusion, and a title.

**Revising.** Make certain the essay is organized in a clear, logical way. Check the essay for errors in spelling, grammar, and punctuation.

# YOU THE CRITIC

**Assignment**

**1.** Compare essays with short stories. List three points that explain how essays are similar to short stories, and three points that explain how the two forms are different. Label the points *Similarities* and *Differences.*

   **Prewriting.** Look at a short story selection and at an essay. Jot down notes on the important elements in each type of writing.

   **Writing.** Write the two lists on the similarities and differences of essays and short stories. Use the prewriting notes as a basis.

   **Revising.** Make certain that each list includes three differences or similarities between the two forms.

**Assignment**

**2.** Imagine that you are creating an advertising campaign to "sell" a type of essay. Write a description of your favorite type of essay, which will serve as advertising copy. Include reasons why you like this type, and reasons why consumers of the written word also will like this type of essay when they read it.

   **Prewriting.** Review the types of essays you have read, and choose your favorite. List reasons why you like this type of essay.

   **Writing.** Write the description of the type of essay you like, using the kinds of persuasive techniques you might read in an advertisement. Give reasons and examples to support your opinion.

   **Revising.** Make certain that you have given reasons and examples to support your opinion. You might want to create an advertising slogan to accompany your description. Check your ad copy for errors in spelling, grammar, and punctuation.

**Assignment**

**3.** Is the essay literature? Why or why not? Your analysis should include a clear statement of the question, your position on the argument, and reasons to support your opinion.

   **Prewriting.** Jot down the question on a sheet of paper. Then create two columns in which you list reasons arguing for or against.

   **Writing.** Write your analysis of the question. Include an introduction that states your position. Give reasons and examples from essays you have read that support your opinion. Finish with a strong conclusion.

   **Revising.** Make certain that you state an opinion and include reasons for supporting it. Check for spelling, grammatical, and compositional errors.

**RED POPPIES**
*Georgia O'Keeffe*

# POETRY

Voltaire called poetry "the music of the soul," while Carl Sandburg defined it as "the synthesis of hyacinths and biscuits." Although there are almost as many definitions of poetry as there are poets, there is no neat, simple way to define poetry. Poems can be written in too many different forms and styles, on too many different subjects and emotions, and with too many different motives to describe in a single definition. Likewise, poetry cannot be defined by the way it looks. We think that poetry is a work with short lines, rhythm, perhaps some rhyme, and a lot of white space, yet some of the poems in this section are not written with short lines, have no rhythm or rhyme, and are not made of neat little stanzas. Poetry can look like prose or can actually form a picture with the placement of words. Poetry escapes definition by word or appearance.

If poetry defies definition, then how can it be studied? There are some common elements to poetry that can be stated: Poetry is an imaginative statement expressed with economy and resonance. It presents a compressed moment of thought, feeling, and experience. Poetry can tell a story, express an idea, define a character, convey an emotion, describe a setting, examine a situation singly or all at once. A poem may even contain a wish, as in one poem in this section where a poet would like her admirer to send her a limousine every once in a while. Ideally, good poetry evokes an intellectual and emotional response from you, the reader.

Although on the surface poetry seems very different from other fiction, it actually shares a great deal. Elements such as speaker or narrator, point of view, tone, style, and theme are common to all. However, there are significant ways in which poetry differs from prose. Poems have economy, meaning that they are more condensed and compressed than prose so that each word contributes to a poem's total impact and meaning. Poems depend more on imagery, references to sensory impressions that create immediacy and vividness, often through comparison, allusion, or suggestion. Because poetry is compact, its rhythm can be as important as the words, images, and ideas. Finally, the sound of a poem as it is read aloud or as it is heard in the mind can contribute to its impact.

# Poetry

The poet Dylan Thomas has written, "Poetry is what in a poem makes you laugh, cry, prickle, be silent, makes your toenails twinkle, makes you want to do this or that or nothing, makes you know that you are alone in the unknown world, that your bliss and suffering is forever shared and forever your own." How do you find the poetry in a poem? You find it by interacting with the poem and reading it with a questioning mind.

Use the following strategies to help you read a poem actively.

**Question**
Have a dialogue with the poem. If a poem has characters and a plot, question why the characters act as they do and how the events will turn out. What does the poet seem to be saying to you? Question the meaning of the language and the impact of the images. What effect does the poem have on you?

**Clarify**
Seek out answers. Stop to clarify meaning and clear up any questions you may have. Allow your mind to be playful. Perhaps the poet has not intended the words to mean exactly what they say, but has used them figuratively with a more imaginative meaning.

**Listen**
Listen to the music of the language. What effect is created by the use of rhythm and rhyme? What effect is created by other sound devices such as repetition and alliteration?

**Summarize**
Pause to summarize whenever this seems appropriate. Review everything that has happened in the poem up to this point.

**Paraphrase**
Put the poem in your own words. Make sure you understand it by restating its meaning.

**Pull It Together**
John Ciardi has said, "The success of a poem is determined not by how much the poet felt in writing it, but by how much the reader feels in reading it." Let the poem speak to you. Pull all the details together and think about its meaning.

On the following page is a model with annotations in the side column showing how an active reader might read a poem.

# The Centaur

## May Swenson

The summer that I was ten—
Can it be there was only one
summer that I was ten? It must

have been a long one then—
5   each day I'd go out to choose
a fresh horse from my stable

which was a willow grove
down by the old canal.
I'd go on my two bare feet.

10   But when, with my brother's jack-knife,
I had cut me a long limber horse
with a good thick knob for a head,

and peeled him slick and clean
except a few leaves for the tail,
15   and cinched my brother's belt

around his head for a rein,
I'd straddle and canter him fast
up the grass bank to the path,

trot along in the lovely dust
20   that talcumed[1] over his hoofs,
hiding my toes, and turning

his feet to swift half-moons.
The willow knob with the strap
jouncing between my thighs

**Question:** What is a centaur?

**Question:** Why does the speaker express amazement at there being only one summer when she was ten?

**Clarification:** She expresses amazement because that summer occupies such a long period of time in her memory.

**Clarification:** This is not a real horse but a pretend one.

**Listen:** Notice the repetition of the *t* sound here. The lines almost sound like a horse trotting.

---

**1. talcumed** (tal′ kəmd) *v*.: Powdered.

**Clarification:** In Greek mythology, a centaur was a creature with a horse's body and legs and a man's head, trunk, and arms. This is where the centaur of the title comes in. In her imagination the speaker is a centaur.

25  was the pommel[2] and yet the poll[3]
of my nickering pony's head.
My head and my neck were mine,

yet they were shaped like a horse.
My hair flopped to the side
30  like the mane of a horse in the wind.

My forelock swung in my eyes,
my neck arched and I snorted.
I shied and skittered and reared,

stopped and raised my knees,
35  pawed at the ground and quivered.
My teeth bared as we wheeled

and swished through the dust again.
I was the horse and the rider,
and the leather I slapped to his rump

**Paraphrase:** The speaker feels at one with her make-believe horse.

40  spanked my own behind.
Doubled, my two hoofs beat
a gallop along the bank,

---

**2. pommel** (pum′ əl) *n.:* The part of a saddle that sticks up at the front.
**3. poll** (pōl) *n.:* The head.

the wind twanged in my mane,
my mouth squared to the bit.

45 And yet I sat on my steed

quiet, negligent riding,
my toes standing the stirrups,
my thighs hugging his ribs.

At a walk we drew up to the porch.
50 I tethered him to a paling.
Dismounting, I smoothed my skirt

**Summarize:** When the speaker was ten, each day she would go out to the willow grove, cut a branch from a tree, and ride it as if it were a horse.

and entered the dusky hall.
My feet on the clean linoleum
left ghostly toes in the hall.

55 *Where have you been?* said my mother.
*Been riding,* I said from the sink,
and filled me a glass of water.

*What's that in your pocket?* she said.
*Just my knife.* It weighted my pocket
60 and stretched my dress awry.

*Go tie back your hair,* said my mother,
and *Why is your mouth all green?*
*Rob Roy, he pulled some clover
as we crossed the field,* I told her.

**Pulling It Together:** The speaker contrasts her real world with her world of make-believe.

**May Swenson** (1919–   ) was born in Logan, Utah, but now resides in New York City. Her poems have appeared in many magazines, including *Poetry* and *The New Yorker.* As a poet, she likes to get behind the appearance of things and wonder at their true nature. Notice the sense of wonder conveyed in "The Centaur."

## THINKING ABOUT THE SELECTION
### Recalling

1. When did the events in this poem take place?
2. Explain how the speaker would make her horse.
3. Describe where she would ride her horse.

### Interpreting

4. How does riding the horse make the speaker feel? Find details that support your answer.
5. What are the "ghostly toes" the speaker's feet leave in the hall?
6. At the end of the poem, why is the speaker's mouth all green?

### Applying

7. The poet John Milton wrote, "The childhood shows the man as morning shows the night." The speaker in the poem is an adult looking back on one summer of her childhood. Based on this glimpse of her childhood, describe the person you think the speaker grew up to be.

## ANALYZING LITERATURE
### Understanding Allusion

An **allusion** is a reference in one work of literature to something that is well known in another work of literature, of art, of music, or to history or current affairs. By using an allusion, a writer calls to mind all the associations and feelings aroused by the original source.

1. What associations are called to mind by the allusion to centaurs?
2. Why is "The Centaur" an appropriate title for this poem?
3. Would the title "The Summer I Was Ten" have been as effective? Explain your answer.

## CRITICAL THINKING AND READING
### Reading Sentences in Poetry

In poetry the end of a line does not always signal the end of a sentence. Sometimes the sentence consists of more than one line, and sometimes it ends in the middle of a line. When you read poetry, look for end marks—periods, question marks, and exclamation marks—to tell you that a sentence is completed.

1. In this poem, the poet uses dashes to tell you that she is ending a sentence with an uncompleted thought. What effect is created by ending the first line with a dash?
2. Look at line 10. Where does the sentence end that begins with this line? What effect is created by using a sentence this long?

## UNDERSTANDING LANGUAGE
### Appreciating Specific Verbs

**Specific verbs** give you a vivid picture of the way an action is performed. For example, when a writer writes, "The man slouched in the chair," you see not only a man sitting in a chair, but a man sitting in a tired fashion.

Find the meaning of each of the following specific verbs from "The Centaur." Then use each verb in a sentence.

1. cinch 2. straddle 3. canter 4. trot 5. snort

## THINKING AND WRITING
### Writing a Poem

Make-believe is a very important part of childhood. Recall a time from your childhood when in your play you made believe you were a pirate, a king, a princess, or any other fantastic creature. (If you prefer, make up a time.) Free-write about this experience. Then write a poem relating the events of your make-believe. As May Swenson does in "The Centaur," make sure you capture the feelings and associations of the experience. When you revise, make sure you have made your experience come alive for your readers. Proofread your poem and read it aloud to your classmates.

# Narrative Poetry

**CENTRAL PARK, 1901**
*Maurice Prendergast*
*Collection of Whitney Museum of American Art*

# GUIDE FOR READING

## La Belle Dame sans Merci

**John Keats** (1795–1821) was born in England. Both of his parents died while he was still a boy, and his guardian sent Keats to school in London. Later, Keats studied surgery. He decided, however, to devote his life to writing poetry. He emphasized feeling and imagination over reason and logic in his poetry. Because he died young, Keats left only a small body of work. His poems, including the narrative poem "La Belle Dame sans Merci," communicate an appreciation of beauty and a sadness at its impermanence.

**Narrative Poetry**

A **narrative poem** tells a story and is usually longer than other types of poems. Narrative poems may be the oldest form of poetry. Because few people could read many years ago, story tellers traveled from place to place telling about real and imagined events and people. These wanderers told stories to entertain listeners, but they were also the newscasters and historians of their time. The story tellers used rhymes and rhythms to help them remember the stories.

Like any story, a narrative poem has one or more characters, a setting, a conflict, and a series of events that come to a conclusion. Most narrative poems are divided into stanzas, or groups of lines that have the same rhyme pattern. In "La Belle Dame sans Merci," the second and fourth lines of each stanza rhyme.

**Look For**

In this poem the knight falls under the spell of "the beautiful lady without pity." As you read, look for the effects of her enchantment.

**Writing**

What is the difference between loving someone and being in love with someone? Freewrite, exploring your answer.

**Vocabulary**

Knowing the following words will help you as you read "La Belle Dame Sans Merci."

**sedge** (sej) *n.*: A grassy plant that grows in wet areas (l. 3)
**thrall** (thrôl) *n.*: Complete control; slavery (l. 40)

**sojourn** (sō'jʉrn) *n.*: Stay temporarily (l. 45)

LA BELLE DAME SANS MERCI
*T. W. Waterhouse*
*Hessiches Landes Museum, Darmstadt*

# La Belle Dame sans Merci[1]

**John Keats**

O what can ail thee, knight-at-arms,
    Alone and palely loitering?
The sedge has withered from the lake,
    And no birds sing.

5  O what can ail thee, knight-at-arms,
    So haggard and so woe-begone?
The squirrel's granary is full,
    And the harvest's done.

---

**1. La Belle Dame sans Merci:** French for "The
Beautiful Lady Without Pity."

I see a lily on thy brow,
10  With anguish moist and fever dew,
And on thy cheeks a fading rose
  Fast withereth too.

I met a lady in the meads,[2]
  Full beautiful—a faery's child,
15 Her hair was long, her foot was light,
  And her eyes were wild.

I made a garland for her head,
  And bracelets too, and fragrant zone;[3]
She looked at me as she did love,
20  And made sweet moan.

I set her on my pacing steed,
  And nothing else saw all day long,
For sidelong would she bend, and sing
  A faery's song.

25 She found me roots of relish sweet,
  And honey wild, and manna dew,[4]
And sure in language strange she said—
  'I love thee true.'

She took me to her elfin grot,[5]
30  And there she wept, and sighed full sore,
And there I shut her wild wild eyes
  With kisses four.

And there she lullèd me asleep,
  And there I dreamed—Ah! woe betide!
35 The latest dream I ever dreamed
  On the cold hill's side.

I saw pale kings and princes too,
  Pale warriors, death-pale were they all;
They cried—'La Belle Dame sans Merci
40  Hath thee in thrall!'

---

**2. meads** (mēdz) *n.*: Old-fashioned form of *meadow*.
**3. fragrant** (frā′ grənt) **zone** (zōn): A sweet-smelling plant.
**4. manna** (man′ ə) **dew** (dü): A sweet substance obtained from the bark of certain ash trees.
**5. elfin** (el′ fən) **grot:** A cave belonging to a fairy.

I saw their starved lips in the gloam,
     With horrid warning gapèd wide,
And I awoke and found me here,
     On the cold hill's side.

45  And this is why I sojourn here,
     Alone and palely loitering,
Though the sedge has withered from the lake,
     And no birds sing.

---

## THINKING ABOUT THE SELECTION

### Recalling

1. What is the setting of the poem?
2. Describe the lady the knight meets.
3. Describe the knight's dream.

### Interpreting

4. Explain how the people in the knight's dream relate to his present condition.
5. Why is the knight "alone and palely loitering"?

### Applying

6. In ancient myths, the fertility of the land is tied to the health of a heroic figure such as a king or a knight. The land can be bountiful again only when a spell put on the heroic figure is broken. Explain how "La Belle Dame sans Merci" is similar to such a myth. Then explain why the fertility of the land would be of such vital importance to ancient peoples.

## ANALYZING LITERATURE

### Understanding Narrative Poetry

Because a narrative poem tells a story, some of its elements are the same as those in a short story. These elements include setting, characters, plot, conflict, and theme.

1. Which stanzas describe the setting and introduce the main character?
2. The subject of the sentences in stanzas 4–6 is different from the subject in stanzas 7–9. How does this shift help communicate what is happening in the story?
3. How does the last stanza tie everything together?

## THINKING AND WRITING

### Writing a Narrative Poem

Write a short narrative poem with or without rhyming lines. First think of an interesting real or imagined event. Then list three or four pieces of information needed for the event to make sense to a reader. Plan a stanza of as many lines as you need for each piece of information. Use the first stanza to ask the question and the other stanzas to answer it. The last stanza should bring it to a close. When you revise your poem make sure you have related the events in a logical order. Proofread your poem for errors in spelling.

## Two Tramps in Mud Time

**Robert Frost** (1874–1963) was one of the most popular American poets of the twentieth century. He was born in San Francisco, but his family moved to Massachusetts when he was eleven years old. As a young man, he worked as a farmer, a teacher, and an editor. Frost's first book of poetry was published in 1913. He later won four Pulitzer Prizes for poetry and a Congressional gold medal. In much of his poetry, Frost uses his experiences as a New England farmer to present his feelings about life.

### The Speaker in Narrative Poetry

The **speaker** in a poem may actually be the voice of the poet, or the speaker may be the voice of a character in the poem invented by the poet. Even when a poet uses the pronoun *I* in a poem, the speaker may be fictional and not the poet himself or herself. Like other fictional characters, the speaker in a narrative poem may reveal information about himself or herself directly, through forthright statements, or indirectly, through hints and implications.

### Look For

As you read "Two Tramps in Mud Time," look for pieces of information the speaker reveals about himself. You can expect to find both direct statements and indirect hints about the kind of person the speaker is.

### Writing

In "Two Tramps in Mud Time," Frost writes about the relationship of work and play. Freewrite for five minutes about your own idea of the relationship between work and play.

### Vocabulary

Knowing the following words and expressions will help you as you read "Two Tramps in Mud Time."

**put me off my aim:** Made me miss what I was aiming at (l. 3)

**playing possum:** Pretending to be asleep or dead (l. 30)

**hulking** (hul'kiŋ) *adj*.: Large; heavy; clumsy (l. 49)

**in twain** (in twān): Together; side-by-side; as a pair (l. 63)

# Two Tramps in Mud Time

**Robert Frost**

Out of the mud two strangers came
And caught me splitting wood in the yard.
And one of them put me off my aim
By hailing cheerily "Hit them hard!"
5  I knew pretty well why he dropped behind
And let the other go on a way.
I knew pretty well what he had in mind:
He wanted to take my job for pay.

Good blocks of oak it was I split,
10  As large around as the chopping block;
And every piece I squarely hit
Fell splinterless as a cloven[1] rock.
The blows that a life of self-control
Spares to strike[2] for the common good,
15  That day, giving a loose to my soul,
I spent on the unimportant wood.

The sun was warm but the wind was chill.
You know how it is with an April day
When the sun is out and the wind is still,
20  You're one month on in the middle of May.
But if you so much as dare to speak,
A cloud comes over the sunlit arch,
A wind comes off a frozen peak,
And you're two months back in the middle of March.

25  A bluebird comes tenderly up to alight
And turns to the wind to unruffle a plume,
His song so pitched as not to excite
A single flower as yet to bloom.

---

1. **cloven** (klō′ vən) *adj.*: Split.
2. **Spares to strike:** Refrains from striking.

It is snowing a flake: and he half knew
30  Winter was only playing possum.
Except in color he isn't blue,
But he wouldn't advise a thing to blossom.

The water for which we may have to look
In summertime with a witching wand,[3]
35  In every wheelrut's now a brook,
In every print of a hoof a pond.
Be glad of water, but don't forget
The lurking frost in the earth beneath
That will steal forth after the sun is set
40  And show on the water its crystal teeth.

The time when most I loved my task
These two must make me love it more
By coming with what they came to ask.
You'd think I never had felt before
45  The weight of an ax-head poised aloft,
The grip on earth of outspread feet,
The life of muscles rocking soft
And smooth and moist in vernal[4] heat.

Out of the woods two hulking tramps
50  (From sleeping God knows where last night,
But not long since in the lumber camps).
They thought all chopping was theirs of right.
Men of the woods and lumberjacks,
They judged me by their appropriate tool.
55  Except as a fellow handled an ax
They had no way of knowing a fool.

Nothing on either side was said.
They knew they had but to stay their stay
And all their logic would fill my head:
60  As that I had no right to play
With what was another man's work for gain.
My right might be love but theirs was need.
And where the two exist in twain
Theirs was the better right—agreed.

---

**3. witching wand:** A twig that some people believe will
lead the holder to underground water.
**4. vernal** (vʉr′ nəl) *adj.*: Spring.

65 But yield who will to their separation,
My object in living is to unite
My avocation[5] and my vocation[6]
As my two eyes make one in sight.
Only where love and need are one,
70 And the work is play for mortal stakes,
Is the deed ever really done
For Heaven and the future's sakes.

---

**5. avocation** (a və kā′ s/hən) *n.*: Hobby.
**6. vocation** (vō kā′ s/hən) *n.*: Occupation.

## THINKING ABOUT THE SELECTION
### Recalling

1. How, according to the speaker, does chopping wood give "a loose to my soul"?
2. How do the tramps probably earn a living?
3. How might the two tramps judge other men?
4. What does the speaker think the tramps want?
5. Does the speaker give them what they want? Explain your answer.

### Interpreting

6. Explain lines 13–16. How does the speaker give "a loose to [his] soul"? What is the "unimportant wood"?
7. Why do the two tramps make the speaker love his work more?
8. How do you know that the speaker does or does not enjoy the outdoors? Find evidence in the poem to support your answer.

### Applying

9. Do you agree with the speaker that the tramp's right was "the better right"? Explain your answer.
10. Explain why you do or do not agree with the speaker that only work that is both hobby and occupation is ever properly done.

## ANALYZING LITERATURE
### Understanding the Speaker

The **speaker** in a narrative poem is the voice in the poem. Even if the speaker uses the pronoun *I*, you cannot assume the speaker is the voice of the poet. He or she may still be a fictional character. "Two Tramps in Mud Time" reveals several traits of an interesting speaker.

1. Of the nine stanzas, only the first two and the last three actually narrate the event. What are stanzas 3–5 about and what does that topic reveal about the speaker?
2. The speaker is ambivalent—that is, he has conflicting feelings—about the two tramps. What are these conflicting feelings?

## CRITICAL THINKING AND READING
### Making Inferences About Characters

You make inferences about a character's personality as you do with people you meet. You look for clues in their words and actions.

1. Write the number of the line or lines that support each of the following inferences.
   a. The speaker is suspicious of strangers.
   b. He does not normally express his emotions.
   c. Chopping wood is a pleasure for him.
   d. He is sensitive to seasonal changes.
   e. He is aware of nature in its tiniest details.
   f. He is proud of his wood-chopping ability.
   g. He feels he should hire the two tramps.
   h. He has a clear understanding of what he wants his life to be like.
2. Based on your answers to the above questions, describe the speaker.

## UNDERSTANDING LANGUAGE
### Investigating Words' Multiple Meanings

Many common words have more than one meaning. Look at the various meanings of the following words from "Two Tramps in Mud Time." Then write the meaning that Frost was using.
1. loose (l. 15)
   a. irresponsible   b. not packaged   c. free

2. pitched (1. 27)
   a. erected   b. set the key of   c. thrown
3. right (l. 52)
   a. virtuous   b. the side toward the east when facing north   c. by reason of law, justice, or morality

## THINKING AND WRITING
### Writing About the Speaker

The following comment about Frost's poems was written by Reginald L. Cook in *Robert Frost, A Living Voice.*

"To a mid-twentieth-century [reader], Frost's . . . poems . . . strike the legendary note of 'once upon a time.' . . . What was once common in Frost's experience has now become memory to an older generation."

Suppose you are writing a short review of Cook's book for the school paper. Write an explanation of how the speaker in "Two Tramps in Mud Time" is an example of what Cook meant. When you revise, make sure you have supported your explanation. Proofread for errors in spelling, grammar, and punctuation.

## The Wreck of the Hesperus

**Henry Wadsworth Longfellow** (1807–1882) was born and lived in what is now Portland, Maine. During the nineteenth century, he became one of America's most popular poets. Some of his best-known poems are "Evangeline," "The Song of Hiawatha," "Paul Revere's Ride," and "The Village Blacksmith." Besides poetry, Longfellow wrote travel books and textbooks on foreign languages. He is best remembered, however for his narrative poems such as "The Wreck of the Hesperus."

### Suspense and Foreshadowing in Narrative Poetry

Suspense is as important in a narrative poem as in any other form of storytelling. **Suspense** is the building of curiosity so that readers want to find out what will happen next. One technique for maintaining suspense is **foreshadowing**, or giving hints of what is to come. A good writer plants hints in such a way that they do not interfere with the story. A good reader picks up the hints and watches for the events that have been foreshadowed. The title of the poem you are about to read foreshadows an event that will happen in the poem to the sailing ship *Hesperus*. What do you think that event will be?

### Look For

As you read "The Wreck of the Hesperus," look for hints and clues about what is about to happen next in the poem's story. Notice the different kinds of hints Longfellow uses to foreshadow later events.

### Writing

Imagine that you are putting together a collection of short stories and poems entitled *Tales to Keep You Awake at Night*. Freewrite describing the type of illustration you would put on the cover of the book.

### Vocabulary

Knowing the following words will help you as you read "The Wreck of the Hesperus."

**schooner** (skoo'nər) *n.*: A ship with two or more masts, or supports for sails (l. 1)

**spar** (spär) *n.*: A pole that supports a sail (l. 35)

**shrouds** (shroudz) *n.*: A set of ropes used to tie a mast to the side of a ship (l. 73)

THE WRECK OF
A TRANSPORT SHIP,
1810
*Joseph Mallord
William Turner*
*Calouste Gulbenkian
Foundation Museum*

# The Wreck of the Hesperus

## Henry Wadsworth Longfellow

It was the schooner Hesperus,
    That sailed the wintry sea;
And the skipper had taken his little daughtèr,
    To bear him company.

5  Blue were her eyes as the fairy-flax,[1]
    Her cheeks like the dawn of day,
And her bosom white as the hawthorn buds,
    That ope[2] in the month of May.

The skipper he stood beside the helm,
10    His pipe was in his mouth,
And he watched how the veering flaw[3] did blow
    The smoke now West, now South.

---

**1. fairy-flax** (fer′ ē flaks) *n*.: The blue flowers of the
flax plant of fairies, or supernatural beings with magic powers.
**2. ope** (ōp) *v*.: Old-fashioned form of *open*.
**3. veering** (vir′ iŋ) **flaw:** Gust of wind that changes direction.

Then up and spake[4] an old sailòr,
    Had sailed to the Spanish Main,
15 "I pray thee, put into yonder port,
    For I fear a hurricane.

"Last night, the moon had a golden ring,
    And tonight no moon we see!"
The skipper, he blew a whiff from his pipe,
20     And a scornful laugh laughed he.

Colder and louder blew the wind,
    A gale from the Northeast,
The snow fell hissing in the brine,
    And the billows frothed like yeast.

25 Down came the storm, and smote amain,[5]
    The vessel in its strength;
She shuddered and paused, like a frighted[6] steed,
    Then leaped her cable's length.

"Come hither! come hither! my little daughtèr,
30     And do not tremble so;
For I can weather the roughest gale,
    That ever wind did blow."

He wrapped her warm in his seaman's coat
    Against the stinging blast;
35 He cut a rope from a broken spar,
    And bound her to the mast.

"O father! I hear the church-bells ring,
    O say, what may it be?"
"'Tis a fog-bell on a rock-bound coast!"—
40     And he steered for the open sea.

"O father! I hear the sound of guns,
    O say, what may it be?"
"Some ship in distress, that cannot live
    In such an angry sea!"

---

**4. spake** (spāk) *v.*: Old-fashioned form of *spoke*.
**5. smote** (smōt) **amain** (ə mān'): To strike violently.
**6. frighted** (frī' tid) *adj.*: Terrified.

45   "O father! I see a gleaming light,
      O say, what may it be?"
  But the father answered never a word,
      A frozen corpse was he.

  Lashed to the helm, all stiff and stark,
50      With his face turned to the skies,
  The lantern gleamed through the gleaming snow
      On his fixed and glassy eyes.

  Then the maiden clasped her hands and prayed
      That savèd she might be;
55   And she thought of Christ, who stilled the wave,
      On the Lake of Galilee.

  And fast through the midnight dark and drear
      Through the whistling sleet and snow,
  Like a sheeted ghost, the vessel swept
60      Towards the reef of Norman's Woe.

  And ever the fitful gusts between
      A sound came from the land;
  It was the sound of the trampling surf,
      On the rocks and the hard sea-sand.

65   The breakers were right beneath her bows,
      She drifted a dreary wreck,
  And a whooping billow swept the crew
      Like icicles from her deck.

  She struck where the white and fleecy waves
70      Looked soft as carded wool,
  But the cruel rocks, they gored her side
      Like the horns of an angry bull.

  Her rattling shrouds, all sheathed in ice,
      With the masts went by the board;
75   Like a vessel of glass, she stove and sank,
      Ho! ho! the breakers roared!

  At daybreak, on the bleak sea-beach,
      A fisherman stood aghast,
  To see the form of a maiden fair,
80      Lashed close to a drifting mast.

The salt sea was frozen on her breast,
    The salt tears in her eyes;
And he saw her hair, like the brown sea-weed,
    On the billows fall and rise.

85  Such was the wreck of the Hesperus,
    In the midnight and the snow!
Christ save us all from a death like this,
    On the reef of Norman's Woe!

---

## THINKING ABOUT THE SELECTION

### Recalling

1. Describe the setting of the poem.
2. Describe the two main characters.
3. Explain how the skipper is warned of an approaching hurricane. How does the skipper react to the warning?
4. What does he do to protect his daughter from the storm?
5. Explain what happens to the ship and its people.

### Interpreting

6. Why does the skipper ignore the old sailor's warning?
7. Explain how the skipper's attitude toward the old sailor is consistent with his reaction to the storm.
8. Longfellow often wrote poems that contained moral lessons. What lesson do you think this poem presents? Find evidence in the poem to support your answer.

### Applying

9. Put yourself in the skipper's shoes. What measures might you have taken to protect your daughter?
10. Taking pride in one's abilities can be considered a positive quality. Explain how it can also be a negative quality. Use examples from life to support your answer.

## ANALYZING LITERATURE

### Understanding Foreshadowing

    **Foreshadowing** is hinting at what is to come. Foreshadowing serves a double purpose. It allows an author to prepare the reader for what is about to happen, and it gives the reader a chance to take part in the story by predicting what will happen without actually having been told about it. "The Wreck of the Hesperus" includes several examples of foreshadowing of later events.

1. How is the sea described in the first stanza?
2. What detail in the third stanza hints at what is to come?
3. How do lines 29–32 foreshadow the skipper's actions during the storm?
4. What detail in lines 57–60 suggests that there will be no survivors of the wreck?

## THINKING AND WRITING

### Writing About Suspense

    Write a review of "The Wreck of the Hesperus." First jot down notes explaining the poet's use of foreshadowing to heighten the suspense in the story. When you write your first draft, include specific details to illustrate the use of foreshadowing. When you revise, make sure you have explained the use of foreshadowing clearly. Proofread for errors in spelling, grammar, and punctuation.

# Dramatic Poetry

**PORTRAIT OF KITTY JAGGER, THE ARTIST'S WIFE**
*David Jagger*
The Bridgeman Art Library/Art Resource

## Danny Deever

**Rudyard Kipling** (1865–1936) in 1907 was the first English author to win the Nobel Prize for literature. He produced a vast body of work including poems, stories, and novels. Born in Bombay, India, Kipling was sent at an early age to England for a formal education. Returning to India at about eighteen, Kipling worked as a journalist. Many of his early poems and stories first appeared in newspapers. "Danny Deever" was included in a collection of Kipling's poems called *Barracks Room Ballads*.

**Dramatic Poetry**

**Dramatic poetry** is poetry in which one or more characters speak. By using the words of one or more speakers to tell directly what is happening, dramatic poetry creates the illusion that the reader is actually witnessing a dramatic event. The words of each speaker are often, but not always, enclosed in quotation marks.

**Look For**

As you read "Danny Deever," look for the speakers in the poem. Who are they? How does their conversation about the execution help you feel as if you are actually witnessing the event?

**Writing**

"Danny Deever" deals with one aspect of life in a military regiment. Freewrite about how life in the military would be different from civilian life.

**Vocabulary**

Knowing the following words will help you as you read "Danny Deever."

**whimpers** (hwim′pərs) *v.*: Makes a low, whining sound, as in crying or in fear (l. 27)

**quickstep** (kwik′step′) *n.*: The pace used in normal military marching, as contrasted with the slower pace of the dead march (l. 29)

# Danny Deever

## Rudyard Kipling

"What are the bugles blowin' for?" said Files-on-Parade.[1]
"To turn you out, to turn you out," the Color-Sergeant[2] said.
"What makes you look so white, so white?" said Files-on-Parade.
"I'm dreadin' what I've got to watch," the Color-Sergeant said.
5      For they're hangin' Danny Deever, you can hear the Dead March play,
        The regiment's in 'ollow square[3]—they're hangin' him today;

---

**1. Files-on-Parade:** The soldier who directs marching formation.
**2. Color-Sergeant:** The flag-bearer.
**3. 'ollow square:** For a hanging, soldiers' ranks form three sides of a square; the fourth side is the gallows.

THE BATTLE OF BUNKER HILL
*Howard Pyle*
*Delaware Art Museum*

They've taken of his buttons off an' cut his stripes away,
An' they're hangin' Danny Deever in the mornin'.

10 "What makes the rear-rank breathe so 'ard?" said Files-on-Parade.
"It's bitter cold, it's bitter cold," the Color-Sergeant said.
"What makes that front-rank man fall down?" says Files-on-Parade.
"A touch o' sun, a touch o' sun," the Color-Sergeant said.
    They are hangin' Danny Deever, they are marchin' of 'im round,
    They 'ave 'alted Danny Deever by 'is coffin on the ground;
15     An' 'e'll swing in 'arf a minute for a sneakin' shootin' hound—
    O they're hangin' Danny Deever in the mornin'!

"'Is cot was right-'and cot to mine," said Files-on-Parade.
"'E's sleepin' out an' far tonight," the Color-Sergeant said.
"I've drunk 'is beer a score o' times," said Files-on-Parade.
20 "'E's drinkin' bitter beer alone," the Color-Sergeant said.
    They are hangin' Danny Deever, you must mark 'im to 'is place,
    For 'e shot a comrade sleepin'—you must look 'im in the face;
    Nine 'undred of 'is county an' the regiment's disgrace,
    While they're hangin' Danny Deever in the mornin'.

25 "What's that so black agin the sun?" said Files-on-Parade.
"It's Danny fightin' 'ard for life," the Color-Sergeant said.
"What's that that whimpers over'ead?" said Files-on-Parade.
"It's Danny's soul that's passin' now," the Color-Sergeant said.
    For they're done with Danny Deever, you can 'ear the quickstep play,
30     The regiment's in column, an' they're marchin' us away;
    Ho! the young recruits are shakin', an' they'll want their beer to-day,
    After hangin' Danny Deever in the mornin'.

## THINKING ABOUT THE SELECTION

### Recalling

1. Describe the setting of "Danny Deever."
2. Of the two speakers in the poem, which has some prior experience with military executions?
3. For what crime is Danny Deever being executed?

### Interpreting

4. In the second stanza, the Color-Sergeant explains one soldier's hard breathing by saying it is "bitter cold." He explains another soldier's fainting as the result of "a touch of sun." Are these conflicting explanations believable? What really accounts for the physical problems of the men?
5. What does Files-on-Parade mean when he says, "I've drunk 'is beer a score o' times"?
6. Compare and contrast Files-on-Parade and the Color-Sergeant.

### Applying

7. The poem gives few facts about Danny Deever or his crime. Explain whether this lack of information makes you more or less sympathetic to him.

## ANALYZING LITERATURE

### Understanding Dramatic Poetry

The actual words of speakers play an important part in **dramatic poetry**—poetry that makes you feel that you are present witnessing dramatic events. In dramatic poetry, as in a play, the main action is conveyed through the words of speakers.

1. What effect is created by having Files-on-Parade and the Color-Sergeant speak in dialect?
2. The last half of each stanza of "Danny Deever" employs the same distinctive speech patterns used by Files-on-Parade and the Color-Sergeant. These lines, however are not enclosed in quotation marks. Who do you think is speaking these words—another soldier, the poet, or some other observer?
3. Tell whether you think the poem would have been more effective if all the action had been revealed through the words of Files-on-Parade and the Color-Sergeant. Explain your answer.

## SPEAKING AND LISTENING

### Reading Dramatic Poetry Aloud

Dramatic poetry cries out to be read aloud. Actually hearing a poem will make you more aware of its rhyme scheme and its rhythms. To get still more out of reading dramatic poetry aloud, try making each speaker's voice sound a little different by capturing the flavor of the particular character. In addition, give questions and statements the proper inflection.

Practice reading "Danny Deever" aloud, experimenting with ways of making each speaker sound natural but different from the other. Decide whether you want the last four lines of each stanza to sound like the voices of the two soldiers or to contrast with them.

# GUIDE FOR READING

## O What Is That Sound

**Wystan Hugh Auden** (1907–1973) was born in England. He first attracted attention as a poet while a student at Oxford University in England and was recognized as a leading poet of his time while he was still a young man. In 1935 Auden married Erika Mann, daughter of the novelist Thomas Mann, to provide the British passport she needed to escape from Hitler's Germany. The poem "O What Is That Sound" suggests the predicament of someone less fortunate than Erika Mann.

**Rhythm and Rhyme**

**Rhythm** is the pattern of stressed and unstressed syllables in language. **Rhyme** refers to the repeated ending sounds in words —usually the final words in their lines. In "O What Is That Sound," two kinds of rhyme are found. The first is **masculine rhyme** in which the last word in a line rhymes with the last word in another line. The other is **feminine rhyme** in which the last accented syllable rhymes and is followed by an identical unaccented syllable.

In the following stanza from "O What Is That Sound," the stressed syllables are marked / and the unstressed syllables are marked ∪. Notice the masculine (ear/dear) and feminine (drumming/coming) rhymes.

> /　∪ ∪　　/　　∪ ∪　/　∪ /
> O what is that sound which so thrills the ear
> 　/　∪ ∪ /　∪　　/　　∪　　/　∪
> Down in the valley drumming, drumming?
> 　/ ∪ ∪　/　∪　/　∪　/
> Only the scarlet soldiers, dear,
> 　∪　/　∪　/　∪
> The soldiers coming.

**Look For**

As you read "O What Is That Sound," listen for its rhyme and rhythm. Notice the change in rhythm in each stanza.

**Writing**

You will read about a dishonorable act in "O What Is That Sound." Friedrich Nietzsche, the German philosopher, observed that fear is the cause of most dishonorable acts people commit. Freewrite for five minutes exploring this idea.

**Vocabulary**

Knowing the following word will help you as you read the poem.
**wheeling** (hwēl'iŋ) *adj.:* Changing direction suddenly (l. 14)

# O What
# Is That Sound

W. H. Auden

O what is that sound which so thrills the ear
    Down in the valley drumming, drumming?
Only the scarlet soldiers, dear,
    The soldiers coming.

5    O what is that light I see flashing so clear
    Over the distance brightly, brightly?
Only the sun on their weapons, dear,
    As they step lightly.

O what are they doing with all that gear,
10    What are they doing this morning, this morning?
Only their usual maneuvers, dear,
    Or perhaps a warning.

O why have they left the road down there,
    Why are they suddenly wheeling, wheeling?
15  Perhaps a change in their orders, dear.
    Why are you kneeling?

O haven't they stopped for the doctor's care,
    Haven't they reined their horses, their horses?
Why, they are none of them wounded, dear,
20    None of these forces.

O is it the parson they want, with white hair,
    Is it the parson, is it, is it?
No, they are passing his gateway, dear,
    Without a visit.

25    O it must be the farmer who lives so near.
    It must be the farmer so cunning, so cunning?
They have passed the farmyard already, dear,
    And now they are running.

O where are you going? Stay with me here!
      Were the vows you swore deceiving, deceiving?
No, I promised to love you, dear,
      But I must be leaving.

O it's broken the lock and splintered the door,
      O it's the gate where they're turning, turning;
Their boots are heavy on the floor
      And their eyes are burning.

30 (line number at left of "Were the vows...")
35 (line number at left of "Their boots...")

---

## THINKING ABOUT THE SELECTION

### Recalling

1. What sound signals the soldiers' approach?
2. How can you tell if the soldiers are armed?
3. For what reasons does one speaker hope that the soldiers have arrived?
4. For what reason have the soldiers arrived?
5. What dishonorable act occurs?

### Interpreting

6. How many speakers are there in the poem?
7. What is the probable relation between the speakers—relatives, business associates, sweethearts, friends, or what? Find evidence in the poem to support your answer.
8. Who do you think speaks the final two lines of the poem? Find evidence in the poem to support your answer.

### Applying

9. How do the speakers' attitudes toward their neighbors and toward each other help explain their fear?
10. Newspapers teem with stories of civilians in other countries who are taken prisoner by soldiers for political crimes—real or imagined—against the State. Discuss a current political situation that might be an appropriate backdrop for this poem.

## ANALYZING LITERATURE

### Understanding Rhythm and Rhyme

**Meter** is the rhythmical pattern of a poem —the systematic way in which accented and unaccented syllables are arranged. Meter is usually described as consisting of units called feet. A **metrical foot** consists of one accented syllable and one or more unaccented ones. The common kinds of feet in English poetry follow.

**iamb** an unaccented syllable followed by an accented one

    ⏑ /
(before)

**anapest** two unaccented syllables followed by an accented one

    ⏑  ⏑  /
('Twas the night . . .)

**trochee** one accented syllable followed by one unaccented syllable

    /  ⏑
(drumming)

**dactyl** one accented syllable followed by two unaccented syllables

    / ∪ ∪
(tenderly).

Note that accented and unaccented syllables are marked by the symbols / and ∪.

**Rhyme,** or the matching of sounds at the ends of lines, may be masculine or feminine. In masculine rhyme, the last syllables of the final words in two or more lines rhyme (ear/dear, away/today).

In **feminine rhyme**, the accented syllables are followed by identical unaccented syllables

    /    ∪ / ∪
(brightly/lightly).

1. Each of the following words makes up a metrical foot in "O What Is That Sound." Use the symbols / and ∪ to indicate the accented and unaccented syllables. Then label each according to the kind of metrical foot it is.

   a. drumming     c. flashing
   b. indicate      d. suddenly

2. Analyze the metrical pattern of the first stanza of this poem.

3. Auden makes consistent use of feminine rhymes in this poem. Which lines in which stanzas rhyme in this way?

## THINKING AND WRITING
### Patterning the Style of the Poem

In "O What Is That Sound" the soldiers pass by the houses of a doctor, a parson, and a farmer. Imagine some other character whose house the soldiers might pass by. Then write a stanza about your character. Pattern your stanza after the rhythm and rhyme scheme of a stanza in "O What Is That Sound." When you revise, make sure the first two lines have been spoken by one speaker, the last two lines by the other.

# GUIDE FOR READING

## Eldorado

**Edgar Allan Poe** (1809–1849) was born in Boston, Massachusetts. Orphaned at an early age, Poe went to live with his godfather, John Allan, a wealthy Richmond, Virginia, merchant. Poe attended the University of Virginia for a year. After an unsuccessful try at a military career, Poe turned to journalism, a career to which he was far better suited. Although he achieved fame in his short lifetime, happiness and financial security eluded him. In "Eldorado" Poe writes of a search for a legendary city of gold.

**Dialogue**

**Dialogue** is talking between characters, or conversation. It is the direct representation of a character's words in a play, story, or poem. In dramatic poetry, dialogue is the main way in which the story of the poem is told. Dialogue in a poem may be set off by enclosing the speaker's words in quotation marks, or the beginning and end of a speaker's words may be suggested in some other way.

**Look For**

As you read "Eldorado," look for the use of dialogue. Notice where each speaker's words begin and end. What does the dialogue tell you about the reasons for the knight's quest?

**Writing**

In "Eldorado" a knight seeks the legendary city of riches and gold that was said to exist somewhere in South America. Poe wrote the poem after gold had been discovered in California in 1849. Thousands of people were rushing to California to try to make their fortunes. "Eldorado" expresses Poe's feelings about such a quest.

Imagine that you are one of those planning to take part in the Gold Rush. Write a letter to a friend or relative explaining your reasons for leaving family and friends and setting off on such a dangerous adventure.

**THE BATTLE OF LIFE (THE GOLDEN KNIGHT)**
*Gustav Klimt*
Collection, Courtesy Galerie St. Etienne, New York

# Eldorado¹

### Edgar Allan Poe

Gaily bedight,²
  A gallant knight,
In sunshine and in shadow,
  Had journeyed long,
5  Singing a song,
In search of Eldorado.

  But he grew old—
  This knight so bold—

And o'er his heart a shadow
10  Fell as he found
  No spot of ground
That looked like Eldorado.

  And, as his strength
  Failed him at length,
15  He met a pilgrim³ shadow—
  "Shadow," said he,
  "Where can it be—
This land of Eldorado?"

  "Over the Mountains
20  Of the Moon,
Down the Valley of the Shadow,
  Ride, boldly ride,"
  The shade⁴ replied,—
"If you seek for Eldorado!"

---

**1. Eldorado** (el də rä′ dō): A legendary kingdom in
South America, supposed to be rich in gold and
precious stones and sought by sixteenth-century
explorers.
**2. bedight** (bi dīt′) *adj.*: Adorned.

**3. pilgrim** *adj.*: Wanderer.
**4. shade** *n.*: Ghost.

## THINKING ABOUT THE SELECTION

### Recalling

1. Explain what the knight has been doing for a long time.
2. Does he feel he has been successful? Find evidence to support your answer.
3. What pair of rhyming words is repeated in each stanza of "Eldorado"?

### Interpreting

4. Explain what is about to happen to the knight at the end of the poem. Find evidence in the poem to support your answer.

### Applying

5. Eldorado is a symbol for an unattainable ideal. In this poem, does Poe seem to suggest that striving for unreachable goals is good or bad? Do you agree or disagree with him? Give reasons to support your opinion.

## ANALYZING LITERATURE

### Understanding Dialogue

**Dialogue** represents the exact words of characters in a play, story, or poem. Dialogue is an important feature of dramatic poetry. When characters speak directly to one another about what is going on, the reader feels present at the scene. In "Eldorado" the dialogue provides a dramatic climax to the poem. Remember that a speaker's exact words in a poem are usually, but not always, enclosed in quotation marks.

1. Who are the speakers in this dramatic poem?
2. Why do they speak to one another at this particular time?
3. Explain how the conversation provides a dramatic climax to the poem.

## UNDERSTANDING LANGUAGE

### Choosing the Right Meaning

Although some words, like *carbon dioxide* and *tweezers,* have only one meaning, most English words have more than one. Some of these meanings may be general; others may be specialized. To find the right meaning, you must consider the context in which the word appears. If the meanings you are familiar with do not fit, consult a dictionary for help.

1. In "Eldorado" Poe uses the word *shadow* in every stanza, each time with a different meaning. Examine the context for each use of the word. Then write the number of the stanza after the letter of the definition that fits that use of *shadow* best.
   a. sadness; something that causes sadness
   b. dominant influence of something; as, to live in the *shadow* of fear
   c. ghostly figure; apparition
   d. area of shade
2. Explain "the Valley of the Shadow" in the last stanza.

# The Speaker and Tone

**COUPLE**
*Kees Van Dongen*
Galleria d'Arte Moderna-Parigi/Servizio

# GUIDE FOR READING

## The Sonnet-Ballad

**Gwendolyn Brooks** (1917–     ) was born in Topeka, Kansas, but lived most of her life in Chicago, Illinois. She wrote her first poems at age seven and was regularly submitting her poetry to a Chicago newspaper by age sixteen. In 1950 she won the Pulitzer Prize for poetry. "The Sonnet-Ballad" exemplifies Brooks's attempt in her writing to "feature people and their concerns—their troubles as well as their joys."

## One Perfect Rose

**Dorothy Parker** (1893–1967) grew up in New York City. Beginning as a fashion writer and drama critic, she later wrote short stories, verse, and book reviews for *The New Yorker* and other magazines. Parker published several volumes of short stories and poetry, including *Enough Rope* (1926) and *Death and Taxes* (1931). She was famous for her wit and sarcasm. For example, when told that President Calvin Coolidge, known for his poker face and rigid manner, had died, she replied, "How can they tell?" "One Perfect Rose" exemplifies her sarcastic wit.

## To Satch

**Samuel Allen** (1917–     ), who also writes under the name of Paul Vesey, was born in Columbus, Ohio. After receiving a law degree from Harvard University, he practiced law for many years and wrote poetry and essays for publication. Eventually he chose to concentrate on his writing and a second career as a college professor of African and Afro-American literature. Among his many published works are *Ivory Tusks and Other Poems* (1968) and *Poems from Africa* (1973). "To Satch" glorifies the black baseball pitcher Satchel Paige.

## Speaker and Tone

The **speaker** of a poem is the voice of the poem. The speaker and the poet are not necessarily the same, although the speaker can be the poet. The speaker can also be a character that the poet creates, as in "The Sonnet-Ballad." To identify the speaker, ask yourself whose point of view the poem expresses and whom the poem addresses.

Each speaker also uses a certain **tone**—the attitude the speaker takes toward the poem's subject. A speaker may use a serious tone, as in "The Sonnet-Ballad." Or the speaker may take a humorous attitude, as in "One Perfect Rose." Speaker and tone cannot be separated. Understanding the speaker's tone can help you understand the poem's meaning.

In ordinary conversation, a speaker conveys a certain attitude, mainly through tone of voice. The word *yes,* for example, takes on a different meaning when said eagerly or angrily or laughingly. Poets must impart the same attitude using only the written word, by choosing precise words and arranging the lines with care.

## Look For

As you read the following three poems, look for the way in which identifying the character of the speaker helps you recognize tone and meaning.

## Writing

Loss, deceit, undying love—think of a situation like these that would stir the reader's imagination and emotions. Freewrite about this situation, describing your thoughts and reactions.

## Vocabulary

Knowing the following words will help you as you read these poems.

**lamenting** (lə men'tiŋ) *v.:* Feeling or expressing great sorrow (p. 620)

**coquettish** (kō ket'ish) *adj.:* Flirtatious (p. 621)

**impudent** (im'pyoo dənt) *adj.:* Shamelessly bold or disrespectful (p. 621)

**floweret** (flou'ər it) *n.:* A small flower (p. 622)

**amulet** (am'yə lit) *n.a:* A charm worn to protect against evil (p. 622)

# The Sonnet-Ballad

Gwendolyn Brooks

Oh mother, mother, where is happiness?
They took my lover's tallness off to war,
Left me lamenting. Now I cannot guess
What I can use an empty heart-cup for.
5  He won't be coming back here any more.
Some day the war will end, but, oh, I knew
When he went walking grandly out that door
That my sweet love would have to be untrue.

Would have to be untrue. Would have to court
10  Coquettish death, whose impudent and strange
Possessive arms and beauty (of a sort)
Can make a hard man hesitate—and change.
And he will be the one to stammer, "Yes."
Oh mother, mother, where is happiness?

## THINKING ABOUT THE SELECTION
### Recalling

1. What situation is the subject of this poem?
2. What does the speaker expect to happen to her lover?
3. What four adjectives describe death's characteristics?

### Interpreting

4. To what do you think "my lover's tallness" refers in line 2? Explain your answer.
5. The speaker personifies death—talks about death as a person. Describe the kind of person death is in this poem.
6. How is death a rival? What is death's beauty?

### Applying

7. What other situations might cause one to ask "Where is happiness?"

## ANALYZING LITERATURE
### Understanding Speaker and Tone

The **speaker** is the poem's voice. It may be the voice of the poet, of a character, or even of an object. The speaker in "The Sonnet-Ballad" is a young woman speaking to her mother.

The speaker's words communicate to the reader the **tone**—the speaker's attitude toward the poem's subject. The speaker's tone helps convey a poem's meaning and create its effect on its audience. For example, the speaker in "The Sonnet-Ballad" uses a serious, sad, somewhat bitter tone about the subject of a lover going off to war. But suppose the speaker laughed at this subject and made light of it. Changing the tone not only would change the poem's meaning but also would alter the audience's view and response.

1. What key verb used in line 3 helps set the poem's tone? Explain how it does so.
2. Describe the speaker of this poem. Why is she bitter?
3. Where does the speaker first state the poem's subject?
4. How does the speaker convey her attitude toward the poem's subject?
5. How might the tone of this poem be different if the speaker's true love were returning home from war instead of leaving?

# One Perfect Rose

Dorothy Parker

A single flow'r he sent me, since we met.
    All tenderly his messenger he chose;
Deep-hearted, pure, with scented dew still wet—
    One perfect rose.

5  I knew the language of the floweret;
    "My fragile leaves," it said, "his heart enclose."
Love long has taken for his amulet
    One perfect rose.

Why is it no one ever sent me yet
10    One perfect limousine, do you suppose?
Ah no, it's always just my luck to get
    One perfect rose.

---

## THINKING ABOUT THE SELECTION
### Recalling

1. What event is described in the first line of this poem?
2. What would the speaker prefer to "one perfect rose"?

### Interpreting

3. Describe the speaker of the poem.

### Applying

4. Imagine that a similar poem about receiving "one perfect rose" was written by a teen-age girl who had never before received flowers as a token of affection. How might this change in speaker affect the tone of the poem?

## ANALYZING LITERATURE
### Understanding Irony and Sarcasm

In verbal **irony,** the apparent meaning of the words is the opposite of the intended meaning. For example, when you say to a friend after everything has gone wrong, "Great day, isn't it?" you are using verbal irony.

1. What attitude does the speaker seem to take toward the perfect rose in the first two stanzas?
2. What attitude is apparent in the last stanza?
3. How does the tone of this poem border on sarcasm, which is a biting form of irony?

# To Satch[1]

## Samuel Allen (Paul Vesey)

Sometimes I feel like I will *never* stop
Just go forever
Till one fine mornin'
I'm gonna up and grab me a handfulla stars
Swing out my long lean leg
And whip three hot strikes burnin' down the heavens
And look over at God and say
How about that!

---

**1. Satch**: Nickname (Satchel) for LeRoy Robert Paige
(1905–1982), legendary black baseball pitcher who,
after more than 20 years in the Negro leagues, entered
the major leagues in 1948.

## THINKING ABOUT THE SELECTION

### Recalling

1. How does the speaker say he feels?
2. What does the speaker say he will do?

### Interpreting

3. What is the speaker's feeling about himself? What shows this feeling about himself?
4. The poem presents a picture in words to help convey the tone. What are the three parts of the image the speaker uses? What tone do the three parts of the image express?
5. Do you think this poem is a fitting tribute to the indomitable spirit of this legendary ball player? Explain your answer.
6. In the poem, the poet exaggerates the character of Satchel Paige. What does this exaggeration add to the poem and its impact?

### Applying

7. The baseball star Roy Campanella said, "You gotta be a man to play baseball for a living, but you gotta have a lot of little boy in you, too." Discuss the meaning of this quotation.

## THINKING AND WRITING

### Comparing and Contrasting Tones

Choose two of the poems in the poetry unit and compare and contrast their tone. First, re-read the poems and list how they are alike and different in tone. Include specific details that contribute to the tone. Then use this information to write a paragraph of comparison and one of contrast. Begin with a general statement of the paragraph's topic. Revise each paragraph to make it persuasive. Proofread for errors in spelling, grammar, and punctuation.

# Lyric Poetry

**VIOLINIST AT THE WINDOW, 1917/18**
*Henri Matisse*
Paris, Musée Nationale d'Art Moderne

## Music I Heard

**Conrad Aiken** (1889–1973) was born in Savannah, Georgia, and grew up in Massachusetts in a family that encouraged self-expression. His parents taught him to love poetry, and his maternal grandfather—a free-thinking founder of a religious group—greatly influenced his work. He received a Pulitzer Prize for his *Selected Poems* (1930) and a National Book Award for his *Collected Poems* (1954). He once commented about poetry, "The feelings come first, the rationalization comes afterward." "Music I Heard" expresses this relationship between poetry and emotion.

## Making a Fist

**Naomi Shihab Nye** (1952–    ) was born in St. Louis, Missouri. A poet, songwriter, and story writer, she lives in San Antonio, Texas. She has twice traveled abroad—to the Middle East and to the Far East—as a participant in the Arts America program. Her poetry has been published internationally and has won several literary prizes. Among her works are collections of her poems, *Hugging the Jukebox* (1982) and *Yellow Glove* (1986). Her perception, imaginative sense of language, and ability to keep you close to experience is evident in "Making a Fist."

## Generations

**Amy Lowell** (1874–1925) was born in Brookline, Massachusetts, and lived in the family mansion, Sevenels, all her life. She spent years reading, studying, and writing poetry before joining a group of radical poets called "Imagists," led by Ezra Pound. She became an energetic leader of the movement, which used precise, concrete images, free verse, and suggestion. She published several volumes of poetry and was posthumously awarded the 1926 Pulitzer Prize for *What's O'Clock*. The Imagist poets' vivid pictorial style that Lowell adopted and later refined is evident in "Generations."

## Lyric Poetry

**Lyric poetry** is poetry that expresses a speaker's personal thoughts and feelings. In ancient Greece, such poems were sung to the music of a harplike instrument called a *lyre*. Lyric poems take their name and songlike quality from that stringed instrument.

Lyric poems express thoughts and feelings about a topic. For example, Conrad Aiken writes about a lost love, Naomi Nye about dealing with fear, and Amy Lowell about the old compared with the young. Often, too, the lyric poet uses vivid images to express these emotions.

## Look For

As you read these three lyric poems, look for the poets' thoughts and feelings and the fresh, lively images the poets use to express them.

## Writing

Imagine that you are planning to write a lyric poem to express emotion about someone you know. Write a brief description of that person. Use vivid words and images—including a description of the person's actions—that appeal to the senses and that will recall the person. Then circle the words and images that you might use in your poem.

## Vocabulary

Knowing the following words will help you as you read these poems.
**desolate** (des′ə lit) *adj.*: Deserted, gloomy, lifeless (p. 629)

**stripling** (strip′liŋ) *adj.*: Young or youthful (p. 632)

**GROUND HOG DAY**
*Andrew Wyeth*
*Philadelphia Museum of Art*

# Music I Heard

## Conrad Aiken

Music I heard with you was more than music,
And bread I broke with you was more than bread;
Now that I am without you, all is desolate;
All that was once so beautiful is dead.

5    Your hands once touched this table and this silver,
And I have seen your fingers hold this glass.
These things do not remember you, belovèd,—
And yet your touch upon them will not pass.

For it was in my heart you moved among them,
10   And blessed them with your hands and with your eyes;
And in my heart they will remember always,—
They knew you once, O beautiful and wise.

---

## THINKING ABOUT THE SELECTION
### Recalling

1. Which line first tells you how the poet feels and why?

### Interpreting

2. Which adjectives in the first stanza most strongly convey the poet's feeling of loss? Explain your answer.
3. Which adjectives in the poem most strongly convey the poet's praise for his love? Explain your answer.
4. What mixture of feelings is the poet expressing in this poem?

### Applying

5. Think of someone you love. What objects do you associate with this person? Why might you say these objects "remember" this person?

## ANALYZING LITERATURE
### Appreciating the Lyric Poem

   **Lyric poetry** expresses the poet's thoughts and feelings through vivid words and images that help you picture and share the experience. Vivid words and images appeal to your senses. For example, Aiken appeals to your sense of hearing when he says, "Music I heard with you was more than music."

1. What other senses does the poem appeal to?
2. The poet also appeals to your senses by referring to parts of the human body. What physical parts does the poet name?
3. What is the significance of each of the words "heart" and "hands," which are mentioned twice?

# Making a Fist

Naomi Shihab Nye

For the first time, on the road north of Tampico,[1]
I felt the life sliding out of me,
a drum in the desert, harder and harder to hear.
I was seven, I lay in the car
5  watching palm trees swirl a sickening pattern
    past the glass.
My stomach was a melon split wide inside my skin.

"How do you know if you are going to die?"
I begged my mother.
We had been traveling for days.

---

**1. Tampico** (tam pē′ kō): Seaport in eastern Mexico.

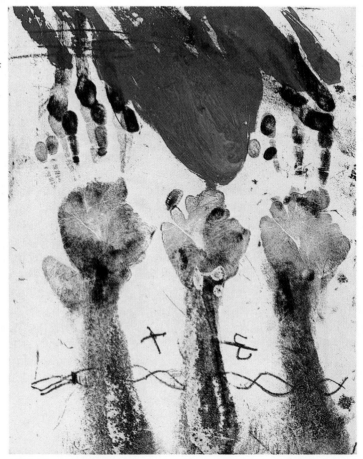

**IMPRESSIONS OF HANDS**
*Antoni Tapies*
The Museum of Modern Art, New York

10    With strange confidence she answered,
      "When you can no longer make a fist."

      Years later I smile to think of that journey,
      the borders we must cross separately,
      stamped with our unanswerable woes.
15    I who did not die, who am still living,
      still lying in the backseat behind all my questions,
      clenching and opening one small hand.

---

## THINKING ABOUT THE SELECTION
### Recalling

1. What fear does the speaker express in line 2?
2. Which line first tells you what the speaker is feeling?
3. According to the speaker's mother, what happens "when you can no longer make a fist"?

### Interpreting

4. In line 3, the speaker uses this powerful image: "a drum in the desert, harder and harder to hear." What is she describing with these words? Why is this description appropriate?
5. The images in the first two stanzas are clear, concrete pictures from the speaker's childhood. How does the last stanza contrast with the first two?
6. State in your own words the mother's response.
7. What is the significance of the title?

### Applying

8. Explain one common method people use to deal with fear. Share this method with your classmates.

## CRITICAL THINKING AND READING
### Inferring Theme in Lyric Poetry

An **inference** is a reasonable conclusion that you draw from given facts or clues. You can infer the theme of a poem, when it is not evident, from specific details and images. The **theme** of a poem is its central meaning—the comment the poet is making about human life and values. In "Making a Fist" the poet comments on human life as a continuing journey and a test of survival. Her image of "life sliding out" of her early in the poem suggests that she has something to say about living and dying.

1. Dialogue in this poem is a clue to the theme. How does the dialogue between the child and her mother help you understand the poet's theme of survival?
2. The poet uses a fist as a symbol of life, yet it is not a fist that remains closed but one that is continually "clenching and opening." How does this detail in the poem relate to the poet's theme?

# Generations

Amy Lowell

You are like the stem
Of a young beech-tree,
Straight and swaying,
Breaking out in golden leaves.
5   Your walk is like the blowing of a beech-tree
On a hill.
Your voice is like leaves
Softly struck upon by a South wind.
Your shadow is no shadow, but a scattered sunshine;
10   And at night you pull the sky down to you
And hood yourself in stars.

But I am like a great oak under a cloudy sky,
Watching a stripling beech grow up at my feet.

## THINKING ABOUT THE SELECTION

### Recalling

1. To what three attributes of the beech-tree does the speaker compare the listener?

### Interpreting

2. When the poet speaks of the "young beech-tree," whom do you think the poet might be describing?
3. Using the poet's comparison to the beech-tree, how would you describe this person's physical appearance and movements?
4. Why is this poem called "Generations"?

### Applying

5. This poem is written from the point of view of an older person speaking to a younger one. Explain how the feelings in the poem might change if the younger person were speaking.

## THINKING AND WRITING

### Writing About Lyric Poetry

Choose one of the lyric poems you have read in this book. Then, using the definition of lyric poetry you have learned, write a brief essay explaining why the poem you selected is a lyric. First list specific words and images from the poem that exemplify lyric poetry. Then use this information to write your essay for someone who is being introduced to lyric poetry for the first time. Revise your essay, making sure you have presented your information in a logical order. Proofread for errors in spelling, grammar, and punctuation.

# GUIDE FOR READING

## A Blessing

**James Wright** (1927–    ) was born in Martins Ferry, Ohio, and graduated from Kenyon College and the University of Washington. A poet and a college English instructor, he has translated the works of Chilean writer Pablo Neruda and German writer Hermann Hesse. Among Wright's published works are *The Branch Will Not Break* (1963) and *Two Citizens* (1973). He received the Pulitzer Prize for poetry in 1972. In "A Blessing," from *Collected Poems* (1971), he uses an image to generate, as a critic has described, "powerful emotions beyond the reach of logic or analysis."

## The Street

**Octavio Paz** (1914–    ) was born in Mexico City, Mexico, and attended the National University there. He began his literary career at the age of seventeen and has since achieved international acclaim as a poet, critic, and social philosopher. *The Green Wave* (1948) and *Sun Stone* (1963) have been translated into English and published in the United States. According to one critic, Octavio Paz sees his poems, such as "The Street," as "journeys" or "bridges of words" across which the poet travels from one side to another.

## A Letter from Home

**Mary Oliver** (1935–    ) was born in Cleveland, Ohio, and attended Ohio State University and Vassar College. She traveled to England to live and work at Steepletop, the estate of deceased poet Edna St. Vincent Millay. Oliver now lives in Massachusetts and contributes poetry to periodicals in England and the United States. Her published works include *No Voyage and Other Poems* (1965) and *The River Styx, Ohio, and Other Poems* (1972). "A Letter from Home" expresses feelings Oliver may have felt while living in England.

## Free Verse

**Free verse** is more open than poetry that uses conventional patterns of rhythm and rhyme. A poem written in free verse has no regular rhythm or line length and rarely has rhyme. Instead, poets who write in free verse usually try to imitate the rhythms of natural speech and invent new, individual arrangements of words and sounds that fit what they are saying and sound natural.

## Look For

As you read these free-verse poems, look for the line arrangements and listen for the sounds and rhythms that the poets use to express their ideas and feelings.

## Writing

Imagine that you want to write a poem in free verse about a brief experience with something in nature—perhaps an animal or a sunset or a violent storm. List specific details and images of the setting and action of that encounter.

## Vocabulary

Knowing the following words will help you as you read these poems.

**caress** (kə res') v.: To touch or stroke lightly or lovingly (p. 637)

**stricken** (strik' 'n) adj.: Hit or wounded, as if by a missile (p. 639)

# A Blessing

James Wright

Just off the highway to Rochester, Minnesota,
Twilight bounds softly forth on the grass.
And the eyes of those two Indian ponies
Darken with kindness.
5  They have come gladly out of the willows
To welcome my friend and me.
We step over the barbed wire into the pasture
Where they have been grazing all day, alone.
They ripple tensely, they can hardly contain their
    happiness

10   That we have come.
    They bow shyly as wet swans. They love each other.
    There is no loneliness like theirs.
    At home once more,
    They begin munching the young tufts of spring in the
        darkness.
15   I would like to hold the slenderer one in my arms,
    For she has walked over to me
    And nuzzled my left hand.
    She is black and white,
    Her mane falls wild on her forehead,
20   And the light breeze moves me to caress her long ear
    That is delicate as the skin over a girl's wrist.
    Suddenly I realize
    That if I stepped out of my body I would break
    Into blossom.

---

## THINKING ABOUT THE SELECTION
### Recalling

1. What incident is the poet describing?
2. Describe what happens between the speaker and the slender, black-and-white pony.

### Interpreting

3. A blessing may be defined as "anything that gives happiness." With that definition in mind, what significance does the poem's title have?
4. How does the speaker feel about his experience with the ponies?
5. What is the poet saying in the last three lines?

### Applying

6. In a free-verse poem, pauses at the ends of lines are important to the poem's rhythm and meaning. Read the poem twice more, once *without* pauses at the end of each line and one *with* pauses. How did the different readings of the poem change your response to and understanding of it?

## ANALYZING LITERATURE
### Understanding Free Verse

**Free verse** is poetry that has no regular patterns of rhythm and rhyme. Free verse may sound more like prose than poetry because the verse lines are closely related to sentences. Yet the free-verse poet's use of line breaks indicates that the composition is, indeed, poetry.

1. Reread lines 5 and 6 of "A Blessing." What are the two parts of this complete thought? Explain why you think the poet divided these lines as he did.
2. Suppose the poet wrote the last three lines of his poem in one long line: "Suddenly I realize that if I stepped out of my body I would break into blossom." What would be lost as a result?
3. The rhythm of the poem is conversational until the last three lines. How does the poet emphasize the significance of the last three lines?
4. Read the poem aloud. Do you find the poem musical? Explain your answer.

# The Street

Octavio Paz
translated by Muriel Rukeyser

A long and silent street.
I walk in blackness and I stumble and fall
and rise, and I walk blind, my feet
stepping on silent stones and dry leaves.
5   Someone behind me also stepping on stones, leaves:
if I slow down, he slows;
if I run, he runs. I turn: nobody.
Everything dark and doorless.
Turning and turning among these corners
10  which lead forever to the street
where nobody waits for, nobody follows me,
where I pursue a man who stumbles
and rises and says when he sees me: nobody.

---

## THINKING ABOUT THE SELECTION
### Recalling

1. What is the setting for this poem?
2. Describe the speaker's actions.

### Interpreting

3. Reread the poem thinking of what it is like to be followed or to follow someone. The poet tries to suggest this idea in the pattern of the poem. Explain what this pattern might mean —for example, a bad dream or circumstances from which one can't escape.

### Applying

4. Why is the mood of anxiety created by this poem especially appropriate for the modern world?
5. Julius Caesar once wrote, "As a rule, what is out of sight disturbs men's minds more seriously than what they see." Do you agree? Explain your answer.

## CRITICAL THINKING AND READING
### Recognizing Details That Create Mood

Most literary works have a **mood,** or dominant emotional atmosphere, that the writer seeks to establish. The mood sometimes can be described in a single word, such as *hopeful* or *sad;* other cases may require more involved descriptions. The details a poet uses can help you recognize the mood of a poem.

In free verse, poets may reinforce mood by using patterns of sound and rhythm. In "The Street," Octavio Paz supports a mood of anxiety through repeated words and rhythms. For example, the phrase "where nobody waits for, nobody follows me" enhances the anxious mood of flight.

1. Find another example of words, phrases, or details that add to the poem's mood. Explain your choice.
2. Which words in the poem are repeated? Give at least two reasons why the poet may have repeated these particular words.

# A Letter from Home

## Mary Oliver

She sends me news of bluejays, frost,
Of stars, and now the harvest moon
That rides above the stricken hills.
Lightly, she speaks of cold, of pain,
5   And lists what is already lost.
Here where my life seems hard and slow,
I read of glowing melons piled
Beside the door, and baskets filled
With fennel, rosemary and dill,[1]
10  While all she could not gather in
Or hide in leaves, grows black and falls.
Here where my life seems hard and strange,
I read her wild excitements when
Stars climb, frost comes, and bluejays sing.
15  The broken year will make no change
Upon her wise and whirling heart;—
She knows how people always plan
To live their lives, and never do.
She will not tell me if she cries.

20  I touch the crosses[2] by her name;
I fold the pages as I rise,
And tip the envelope, from which
Drift scraps of borage, woodbine, rue.[3]

---

**1. fennel** (fen′ əl), **rosemary** (rōz′ mer′ ē), **and dill**
(dil): Herbs used in cooking. Rosemary symbolizes
fidelity and remembrance.
**2. crosses**: Xs, symbols for kisses.
**3. borage** (bôr′ ij) **and rue** (rü): Herbs used in
cooking. Borage symbolizes courage and is thought to
drive away sadness. Rue symbolizes bitterness, grief,
and forgiveness.

## THINKING ABOUT THE SELECTION

### Recalling

1. What are some of the topics the letter writer writes about?
2. Unlike many free-verse poems, this poem contains some scattered rhyming words, such as *frost* and *lost*. What other rhymes are used?

### Interpreting

3. At what time of year does the action of the poem take place? Identify at least two clues from which you inferred the season.
4. How does the speaker react to the letter?
5. What comparison is implied between the letter writer's life and the speaker's life?
6. What do you know about the letter writer?
7. With a few exceptions, each line in the poem begins with an unaccented syllable followed by an accented one: "She sends," "Of stars," "That rides." How does this rhythm contribute to the mood of the poem?

### Applying

8. Describe another situation in which one might have similar feelings to those of the speaker in this poem.

## THINKING AND WRITING

### Writing About Meaning in Free Verse

Choose one of the three free-verse poems in this book or another free-verse poem you like. Study the poem and list vivid words, phrases, sounds, and rhythms through which the poet expresses his or her ideas and feelings. Then use this information to write a paragraph explaining *what* the poem means and *how,* through the use of language and poetic devices, the poet communicates the meaning to you. Revise your paragraph to include examples that support your statements. Proofread for errors in spelling, grammar, and punctuation.

# Figurative Language

**MEDITERRANEAN LANDSCAPE**
*Pablo Picasso*
Giraudon/Private Collection

# GUIDE FOR READING

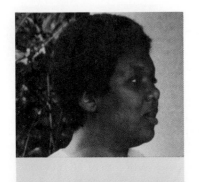

## Miss Rosie

**Lucille Clifton** (1936–    ), born in Depew, New York, has written books for children, as well as poetry for adults. The author of *The Black ABC's* and *Good News About the Earth,* Clifton won a National Endowment for the Arts award in 1970 and 1972. She lives in Baltimore, Maryland, where she is poet-in-residence at Coppin State College. Her book of poetry *An Ordinary Woman* and the poem "Miss Rosie" reflect Clifton's compassionate concern for the people and events of everyday life.

## July Storm

**Elizabeth Coatsworth** (1893–1986), born in Buffalo, New York, attended Vassar College. She wrote for audiences ranging from four-year-olds to adults. Coatsworth's published works include nine volumes of poetry, novels, nature sketches, and many children's books. In 1930 she was awarded the Newbery Award for *The Cat Who Went to Heaven.* Coatsworth traveled widely, but she most often wrote about New England, which is the setting for "July Storm."

## Metaphor

**Eve Merriam** (1916–    ) has been a poet, biographer, radio writer, fashion-magazine editor, and teacher. Merriam finds poetry "the most immediate and richest form of communication." She lives in New York City, where she expects to be the "last living inhabitant . . . when everyone else has quit for sub- or exurbia." Merriam's optimistic anticipation of what each new day has to offer is reflected in "Metaphor."

## First Lesson

**Philip Booth** (1925–    ), born in Hanover, New Hampshire, is a poet, a critic, and an English professor at Syracuse University in New York. Among the many awards Booth has won is the Bess Hokin prize, awarded by *Poetry* magazine, for his long poem "Letter from a Distant Land." Booth, a water-sports enthusiast, often writes about topics such as swimming in tidal streams and in the ocean, as is evident in "First Lesson."

## Simile and Metaphor

Many literary works and even ordinary conversations use figurative language—language that is not literal but represents one thing in terms of another. Such language includes specific figures of speech that enhance its meaning and imaginative quality. Two common figures of speech are simile and metaphor.

A **simile** is a direct comparison between items that are unlike in most ways but similar in one respect. The comparison in a simile is usually made through the use of the words *like* and *as*.

A **metaphor** is an implied comparison that, like a simile, compares two items that are alike in one respect but unlike in others. However, instead of saying A is like B, a metaphor states that A *is* B—it equates the two items.

The following stanza from "The Day Is Done" by Henry Wadsworth Longfellow contains both simile and metaphor.

> The day is done, and the darkness
>     Falls from the wings of night,
> As a feather is wafted downward
>     From an eagle in his flight.

In this stanza, Longfellow uses the simile "*as* a feather is wafted downward" to describe the gentle approach of darkness. He uses the metaphor "wings of night" to depict the evening.

## Look For

As you read these four poems, look for similes and metaphors. In what ways do these figures of speech make the ideas in the poems more vivid?

## Writing

Think of an object or an image—for example, a cold damp wind or a smile on a friend's face. Describe the object using a simile or a metaphor.

## Vocabulary

Knowing the following words will help you as you read these poems.

**serenely** (sə rēn′lē) *adv.*: In a calm, untroubled way (p. 645)

**assurance** (ə shoor′əns) *n.*: Sureness; confidence (p. 645)

# Miss Rosie

## Lucille Clifton

When I watch you
wrapped up like garbage
sitting, surrounded by the smell
of too old potato peels
5  or
when I watch you
in your old man's shoes
with the little toe cut out
sitting, waiting for your mind
10  like next week's grocery
I say
when I watch you
you wet brown bag of a woman
who used to be the best looking gal in Georgia
15  used to be called the Georgia Rose
I stand up
through your destruction
I stand up

---

## THINKING ABOUT THE SELECTION

### Recalling

1. Describe Miss Rosie.
2. What was Miss Rosie known as when she was young and beautiful?
3. What reaction does the speaker say she has when she views Miss Rosie's destruction?

### Interpreting

4. Reread the simile in lines 9 and 10. What comparison is being made? What effect does this simile have? Explain your answer.

5. What has happened to Miss Rosie over the years?
6. What does the speaker mean in the last three lines?

### Applying

7. The speaker in the poem gains determination to "stand up" from seeing the "destruction" of Rosie. Can you think of instances in which a person gained strength or determination from witnessing the defeat of another?

# July Storm

Elizabeth Coatsworth

Like a tall woman walking across the hayfield,
The rain came slowly, dressed in crystal and the sun,
Rustling along the ground. She stopped at our apple tree
Only a whispering moment, then swept darkening
5    skirts over the lake
And so serenely climbed the wooded hills.
Was the rainbow a ribbon that she wore?
We never wondered. It seemed a part of her brightness
And the way she moved lightly but with assurance over the
earth.

## THINKING ABOUT THE SELECTION

### Recalling

1. Describe the movement of the rain across the hayfield.
2. To what is the rain compared?
3. Give three details that make this comparison.
4. What places does the rain touch?

### Interpreting

5. Why does it appear that the rain is "dressed in crystal"?
6. What are the "darkening skirts" that sweep over the lake?

### Applying

7. By comparing the rain to a tall, gracefully moving woman, the poet is able to create a vivid impression of a gentle summer storm. To what image could you compare one of the following—a tornado, a blizzard, or a hurricane—to create a vivid impression? Explain your answer.

## THINKING AND WRITING

### Writing About Simile

Write a sentence describing an item through simile and write another sentence describing the same item in a similar way *without* the use of simile. Then write a paragraph of advice to a creative writer focusing on the advantages and disadvantages of using a simile. Revise your paragraph to include examples. Proofread for errors in spelling, grammar, and punctuation.

# Metaphor

### Eve Merriam

Morning is
a new sheet of paper
for you to write on.

Whatever you want to say,
all day,
until night
folds it up
and files it away.

The bright words and the dark words
are gone
until dawn
and a new day
to write on.

---

## THINKING ABOUT THE SELECTION

### Recalling

1. To what is morning compared?
2. What does night do at the end of the day?
3. What happens to words at night?

### Interpreting

4. What does "files it away" in line 8 suggest?
5. What do you think the poet means by "bright words and dark words" in line 9?

### Applying

6. The poet says that morning is a new sheet of paper that you write on all day. Would the metaphor be more or less effective, in your opinion, if it said, "Each *day* is a new sheet of paper"? Give reasons for your opinion.

## ANALYZING LITERATURE

### Understanding Metaphor

A **metaphor** compares two different items, usually by equating them. As with a simile, a good metaphor is more than mere description. Its purpose is, through only a few words, to present something familiar in a new light, giving you a new insight into its nature. In "Metaphor," morning is presented in terms of "a new sheet of paper."

1. What qualities do morning and a new sheet of paper share?
2. Why is this metaphor effective?

# First Lesson

## Philip Booth

Lie back, daughter, let your head
be tipped back in the cup of my hand.
Gently, and I will hold you. Spread
your arms wide, lie out on the stream
5   and look high at the gulls. A dead-
man's-float is face down. You will dive
and swim soon enough where this tidewater
ebbs to the sea. Daughter, believe
me, when you tire on the long thrash
10  to your island, lie up, and survive.
As you float now, where I held you
and let go, remember when fear
cramps your heart what I told you:
lie gently and wide to the light-year
15  stars, lie back, and the sea will hold you.

**MELANIE AND ME SWIMMING**
*Michael Andrews*
*The Tate Gallery, London*

## THINKING ABOUT THE SELECTION
### Recalling

1. Who is the speaker of "First Lesson"?
2. What is the speaker teaching his daughter?
3. What specific instructions does he give her?

### Interpreting

4. What does the poet mean by "you will dive and swim soon enough" (lines 6 and 7)?
5. What experience in life is being compared to floating face up in the water?
6. How does the father feel toward his daughter? Find evidence in the poem to support your answer.

### Applying

7. Mark Van Doren has written, "The art of teaching is the art of assisting discovery." First discuss the meaning of this quotation. Then explain how it relates to "First Lesson."

## THINKING AND WRITING
### Writing About Metaphors

Create a metaphor for life that appeals to you—such as a journey, a game, or a race. Then write a brief essay for students being introduced to metaphors explaining or showing how you can express what life is like by using only the metaphor you have chosen. Revise your essay to include examples to support your statements. Proofread for errors in spelling, grammar, and punctuation.

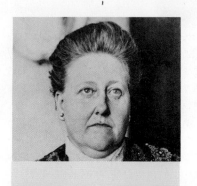

## Night Clouds

**Amy Lowell** (1874–1925) was famous for her readings and lectures, as well as for her poetry. She was awarded the Pulitzer Prize after her death for her volume entitled *What's O'Clock?* Lowell was a pioneer of the Imagist movement. Influenced by Japanese haiku poets, the Imagists focused on a single, precisely presented image. "Night Clouds" typifies Imagist poetry, with its strong central image and its rhythmic but irregular lines.

## A Jelly-Fish

**Marianne Moore** (1887–1972) was remarkable both for her poetic skill and for her wide range of interests. An avid baseball fan and an admirer of Muhammed Ali, the heavyweight boxer, her other interests included zoology, motion pictures, popular magazines, and Oriental art. Moore was awarded the Pulitzer Prize for poetry in 1952. "A Jelly-Fish" shows Moore's interest in animals and her gift for precise observation.

## Fueled

**Marcie Hans** (1928–1975), born in Chicago, was an advertising copywriter and the author of several humorous books. Her works include *There's an Elephant in My Sandwich* and *Serve Me a Slice of Moon.* "Fueled" shows her whimsical approach to life.

## The Wind—tapped like a tired Man

**Emily Dickinson** (1830–1886) spent most of her life in the small New England town of Amherst, Massachusetts. Lively and sociable as a young girl, she gradually became withdrawn and avoided all contact with strangers. Only seven of her poems were published during her lifetime. Dickinson is now recognized as a major writer of striking originality. The poem that follows displays one feature of her poetry—highly individualistic punctuation.

## Figurative Language

**Figurative language** includes extended metaphor, symbol, and personification. An extended metaphor is a comparison made by equating two different items throughout the entire work. An example is "Night Clouds," in which clouds are equated with mares not only in one line, but throughout the entire poem.

A symbol is an object, idea, or action that represents something other than itself. While many common symbols have fixed meanings, like a dove as a symbol of peace, poetry often makes up its own symbols. A symbol suggests meanings beyond those stated.

Personification is a figure of speech in which an object, animal, or idea is given the characteristics of a human being. For example, in the line by A. E. Housman "And then the clock collected in the tower / Its strength, and struck," the clock is given the characteristics of a person with strength.

## Look For

As you read these poems, look for the figurative language. What vivid pictures do the poets create through extended metaphor, symbols, or personification?

## Writing

Think of an aspect of nature that has special appeal for you. List your ideas for an extended metaphor, a symbol, or personification that you could use to describe it.

## Vocabulary

Knowing the following words will help you as you read these four poems.

**vermilion** (vər mil'yən) *adj.*: Bright red or reddish orange in color (p. 650)

**fluctuating** (fluk'chōō wāt'iŋ) *adj.*: Moving in a wavelike manner (p. 651)

**countenance** (koun'tə nəns) *n.*: The face; facial features (p. 654)

**tremulous** (trem'yōō ləs) *adj.*: Trembling; quivering (p. 654)

**flurriedly** (flur'əd lē) *adv.*: In a flustered, agitated way (p. 654)

# Night Clouds

## Amy Lowell

The white mares of the moon rush along the sky
Beating their golden hoofs upon the glass Heavens;
The white mares of the moon are all standing on their hind legs
Pawing at the green porcelain doors of the remote Heavens.
Fly, Mares!
Strain your utmost.
Scatter the milky dust of stars,
Or the tiger sun will leap upon you and destroy you
With one lick of his vermilion tongue.

---

## THINKING ABOUT THE SELECTION

### Recalling

1. Describe the appearance of the clouds.

### Interpreting

2. Lowell uses an extended metaphor. List all the details that compare clouds to mares.
3. Why are the horses' hoofs "golden"?

4. To what does the "milky dust of stars" refer?
5. What is the effect of the phrase "tiger sun"?

### Applying

6. The speaker in the poem urges the white mares of the moon to exert themselves to the utmost. What do you think is the implied message for the reader?

# A Jelly-Fish

## Marianne Moore

Visible, invisible,
    a fluctuating charm
an amber-tinctured amethyst[1]
    inhabits it, your arm
approaches and it opens
    and it closes; you had meant
to catch it and it quivers;
    you abandon your intent.

---

**1. an amber-tinctured** (tink′ c⁄hərd) **amethyst** (am′ ə
thist): A purple variety of quartz with a yellowish color.

## THINKING ABOUT THE SELECTION
### Recalling

1. To what is the jelly-fish compared?
2. What does the jelly-fish do when your arm approaches?
3. What does the jelly-fish do when you try to catch it?
4. Because of its behavior, what happens to your intent to capture the jelly-fish?

### Interpreting

5. Why is *fluctuating* a good word to describe the motion of a jelly-fish?
6. What feeling about the jelly-fish does the speaker describe?

### Applying

7. What other creatures might arouse a feeling similar to the one described in this poem?

## THINKING AND WRITING
### Writing a Poem with a Metaphor

Brainstorm to list subjects about which you could write a short poem. Once you have selected a topic, decide on an appropriate metaphor to describe it. Then write the poem for your classmates using an extended metaphor. Revise your poem to use irregular, unrhymed lines, as in "Night Clouds," if you wish. Proofread for spelling errors.

# Fueled

## Marcie Hans

Fueled
by a million
man-made
wings of fire—
5   the rocket tore a tunnel
through the sky—
and everybody cheered.
Fueled
only by a thought from God—
10   the seedling

urged its way
through the thicknesses of black—
and as it pierced
the heavy ceiling of the soil—
15   and launched itself
up into outer space—
no
one
even
20   clapped.

**APOLLO 13 LAUNCH**
*Fletcher Martin*
*NASA*

**CHRISTMAS ROSE**
*Engraving from Hortus Floridus by Crispin de Passe*
*New York Public Library*

## THINKING ABOUT THE SELECTION

### Recalling

1. What is fueled by "a million man-made wings of fire"?
2. What reaction does this event bring?
3. What is fueled by "a thought from God"?
4. What reaction does this event bring?

### Interpreting

5. What does "a million man-made wings of fire" mean?
6. What do you think the phrase "Fueled only by a thought from God" means?
7. What does "outer space" refer to in line 16?
8. Compare what fuels the rocket to what fuels the seedling.
9. What does the rocket tear through compared to what the seedling tears through?
10. What is people's reaction to the rocket in contrast to their reaction to the seedling?

### Applying

11. The poet seems to suggest that people make much of human achievements but take natural wonders for granted. Do you agree or disagree? State your reasons.

## ANALYZING LITERATURE

### Understanding a Symbol

A **symbol** is an object, action, or idea that represents something other than itself. In "Fueled," the seedling pushing up from the earth is a symbol of life and birth. The poet helps you see this symbolic meaning by juxtaposing the seed, which is fueled "by a thought from God," next to the rocket, which is fueled by man-made means. Both seed and rocket tear through one thing into another.

1. What feelings does this symbol of life—the seedling—arouse in you?
2. What does the title of the poem have to do with a symbol of life?

# The Wind— tapped like a tired Man

## Emily Dickinson

The Wind—tapped like a tired Man—
And like a Host—"Come in"
I boldly answered—entered then
My Residence within

5   A Rapid—footless Guest—
To offer whom a Chair
Were as impossible as hand
A Sofa to the Air—

No Bone had He to bind Him—
10  His Speech was like the Push
Of numerous Humming Birds at once
From a superior Bush—

His Countenance—a Billow—
His Fingers, as He passed
15  Let go a music—as of tunes
Blown tremulous in Glass—

He visited—still flitting—
Then like a timid Man
Again, He tapped—'twas flurriedly—
20  And I became alone—

## THINKING ABOUT THE SELECTION
### Recalling

1. Who or what is the "Guest" who enters the speaker's residence? Who is the "Host"?
2. What does the poet say the "Guest's" speech is like?

### Interpreting

3. Why can't the "Host" offer the "Guest" a chair?
4. Look up the meanings of *flurry* in the dictionary. What related meaning of *flurry* makes *flurriedly* a good adverb to apply to the "Guest" in this poem?

### Applying

5. Emily Dickinson makes the dash stand for many things—a comma, a period, a semicolon, and even missing words that must be understood. However, not understanding her intent, the early publishers of her poems replaced the dashes with conventional punctuation. How do you think you would respond to this poem if it were punctuated in the regular way? Explain your answer.

## ANALYZING LITERATURE
### Understanding Personification

    **Personification** is a figure of speech in which an object or idea is represented as a person. In "The Wind—tapped like a tired Man," the wind is personified as a weary man.

1. The wind is described as tapping like a tired man. How might a tired man tap on a window or a door?
2. The wind is described as a rapid, footless guest. What sounds might such a guest make when moving?
3. What offer might one make to a guest that is impossible to offer to the wind?
4. What impression of the wind does Emily Dickinson present through this poem?

# Imagery

**MEMORY, 1870**
*Elihu Vedder*
*Los Angeles County Museum of Art*

## Big Wind

**Theodore H. Roethke** (1908–1963), who was born in Michigan, is the author of more than a dozen books of poetry, as well as the author of children's books and essays. He has been recognized with numerous awards and degrees, including the Pulitzer Prize in poetry and two National Book Awards. In "Big Wind," Roethke draws on the scenes of his childhood as the son of a greenhouse owner.

## Loss

**A. R. Ammons** (1926–    ) began writing when he was a boy growing up in North Carolina. He published his first poems in 1955 while he was executive vice-president of a firm in Atlantic City, New Jersey. Since 1964 he has taught creative writing at Cornell University in Ithaca, New York, and has published nine additional books of poems. In 1973 Ammons won the National Book award for a collection of his poetry. "Loss" is typical of his work in the way that it transforms a small, ordinary moment into a vivid, memorable event.

## One Morning

**John Ciardi** (1916–1986), who was born in Boston, was not only a poet but also an educator, editor, translator, critic, and lecturer. His career as a poet began while he was still in college when he won the Avery Hopkins Major Award in poetry. He published four volumes of poetry for adults and four others for children, in addition to textbooks, essays, and a translation of Dante's *The Divine Comedy*. As in many of his other poems, in "One Morning" Ciardi addresses the audience in the first person by using the pronouns *I* and *my*.

## Imagery

**Imagery** is the use of vivid descriptions or figures of speech to create a mental image. In the poem "Night Clouds," the phrase "the milky dust of stars" paints a picture of a night sky that makes a reader or listener really see it.

Imagery involves not only descriptions that appeal to the senses but also nonliteral uses of language. Nonliteral uses of language include similes, metaphors, personification, and other figures of speech. No one believes, for example, that flowers really *dance* in the sunlight or that autumn leaves *scamper* in the wind. Such expressions are figures of speech used to create a mental image of movement.

Often a vivid image can be achieved by joining ideas or words in unexpected combinations. In a poem about spring, for instance, E. E. Cummings used the words *mud-luscious* and *puddle-wonderful*. Such unexpected combinations take the reader by surprise and bring the image into sharper focus.

## Look For

As you read the three poems, look for words and phrases that make you see, hear, or feel what the poet is talking about. Also look for nonliteral uses of language or for words or ideas that have been combined in unexpected ways.

## Writing

Think of the fiercest storm (wind, rain, or snow) you can remember. Using the five senses as cues, write words or phrases you could use to describe the storm vividly.

## Vocabulary

Knowing the following words will help you as you read the poems.

**pith** (pith) *n.*: Force or strength (p. 658)

**flailing** (flāl'iŋ) *adj.*: Beating or striking with a thrashing movement (p. 658)

**sumac** (shoo'mak) *n.*: Small tree or shrub with compound flowers and clusters of small greenish flowers followed by hairy fruits. Some varieties cause an itching rash (p. 659)

**diffuse** (di fyoos') *adj.*: Widely spread or scattered (p. 659)

**rigorous** (rig'ər əs) *adj.*: Precisely accurate; strict (p. 659)

# Big Wind

### Theodore Roethke

Where were the greenhouses going,
Lunging into the lashing
Wind driving water
So far down the river
5   All the faucets stopped?—
So we drained the manure-machine
For the steam plant,
Pumping the stale mixture
Into the rusty boilers,
10   Watching the pressure gauge
Waver over to red,
As the seams hissed
And the live steam
Drove to the far
15   End of the rose-house,
Where the worst wind was,
Creaking the cypress window-frames,
Cracking so much thin glass
We stayed all night,
20   Stuffing the holes with burlap;
But she rode it out,
That old rose-house,
She hove into the teeth of it,
The core and pith of that ugly storm,
25   Ploughing with her stiff prow,
Bucking into the wind-waves
That broke over the whole of her,
Flailing her sides with spray,
Flinging long strings of wet across the
    roof-top,
30   Finally veering, wearing themselves out,
    merely
Whistling thinly under the wind-vents;
She sailed until the calm morning,
Carrying her full cargo of roses.

## THINKING ABOUT THE SELECTION
### Recalling

1. What is happening to the greenhouse?
2. What measures are taken to protect the plants from the storm?

### Interpreting

3. To what does the poet compare the greenhouse throughout the poem?
4. Why does the poet use the pronoun *she*, rather than *it*, to refer to the greenhouse?
5. What change in tone and mood occurs in the last two lines?

### Applying

6. Several times the poet refers to *we* without identifying who the people are. Without even speaking, the people seem to think and act as one person. Describe a situation in which you have seen two or more people function in such a way. What common goals did they have that made them cooperate so well?

## ANALYZING LITERATURE
### Understanding Imagery

Sensory images appeal to the senses and enable the reader to experience the fury of the storm. The word *lunging*, for example, conveys the feeling of the violent, irregular movement, and *whistling* enables us to hear the wind.

1. List two words or phrases from the poem containing sensory images that appeal to your sense of sight.
2. List two words or phrases containing sensory images that appeal to your sense of hearing.

# Loss

## A. R. Ammons

When the sun
falls behind the sumac
thicket the
wild
5    yellow daisies
in diffuse evening shade
lose their
rigorous attention
and
10   half-wild with loss
turn
any way the wind does
and lift their
petals up
15   to float
off their stems
and go

## THINKING ABOUT LITERATURE

### Recalling

1. What two forces of nature are at work in the poem?
2. How do the daisies react to each of the natural forces?

### Interpreting

3. What change occurs at lines 5–17?
4. What kinds of words (parts of speech) create the contrast in imagery between the two parts of the poem?
5. What is the effect of having no punctuation, not even at the end?
6. Explain how the title relates to the poem. What do you think the loss is and why?

### Applying

7. Describe how feelings and behavior can change as a result of a change in the weather.

# One Morning

## John Ciardi

I remember my littlest one in a field
running so hard at the morning in him
he kicked the heads off daisies. Oh, wild
and windy and spilling over the brim
5    of his sun-up juices he ran
in the dew of himself. My son.

And the white flower heads
shot like sparks where his knees
pumped, and his hot-shod
10   feet took off from time, as who knows
when ever again a running morning will be
so light-struck, flower-sparked-full between him and me.

---

## THINKING ABOUT THE SELECTION

### Recalling

1. What is the child doing?
2. Describe the setting of the poem.

### Interpreting

3. What is the meaning of "the morning in him"?
4. What is the poet describing as "the dew of himself"?
5. In the second stanza, to what animal is the poet comparing the boy? How can you tell?

### Applying

6. Describe what you think are the emotions of the parent watching the scene.

## ANALYZING LITERATURE

### Investigating Unexpected Combinations

Part of the effect of the imagery in this poem is achieved by unexpected combinations of words and ideas. One unexpected image is referring to the boy's youth as "the morning in him."

1. Give at least three other examples of such combinations in the poem.
2. Explain whether or not you find these unexpected combinations effective.

## THINKING AND WRITING
### Writing About Imagery

When you read a poem, the imagery in it appeals to your senses and affects your emotions. Suppose you have been asked to decide whether or not this poem or one of the others you have read should be included in an anthology, a collection of poems. Write a recommendation to the people compiling the anthology in which you explain the various types of imagery in the poem and the way that each appeals to your senses and affects your emotions. When you revise be sure you have given your opinion about whether or not the poem should be included in the anthology. Proofread your recommendation carefully.

## Reapers

**Jean Toomer** (1894–1967) was born in Washington, D.C., of French, Dutch, Welsh, German, Jewish, black, and Indian descent. He once said that "Because of these, my position in America has been a curious one. I have lived equally amid the two race groups." Toomer became famous at a young age with the publication of his book *Cane* (1923), which contained short stories, poems, and a short novel. In "Reapers" Toomer writes of a crew of farm workers mowing a field.

## The Fish

**Elizabeth Bishop** (1911–1979) was born and raised in Massachusetts, but she loved to travel and spent many years living in Brazil. In 1945 Bishop entered a poetry contest along with 800 other contestants, and she won. As a result, her first book, *North and South* (1946), was published. "The Fish" was included in that book. Bishop was always a close observer of nature. She said in an interview, "I think geography comes first in my work, and then animals. But I like people, too."

## Pitcher

**Robert Francis** (1901–    ) was born in Pennsylvania but now lives by himself in rural Massachusetts. He has written many books, including fiction such as *We Fly Away* (1948) and poetry such as *Come Out into the Sun: Poems New and Selected* (1965). Francis has said, "By reducing my needs and doing all my own work, I am able to live on a very small income and have most of my time free for writing, reading, music, and gardening." "Pitcher" is one of many poems Francis has written about sports.

## Cargoes

**John Masefield** (1878–1967) was born in England. When he was about sixteen, he agreed to work on a sailing ship and sailed around Cape Horn to Chile. A few years later Masefield was in New York, where he worked in a bakery, in a stable, on the waterfront, and in a carpet factory. He returned to England in 1897 to work for a newspaper, the *Manchester Guardian*. In 1930 King George V appointed him Poet Laureate of England. Masefield is best known for his poems about the sea, such as the poem "Cargoes."

## Mood

**Mood** is the atmosphere or tone a poem conveys. A poet uses specific words, phrases, and images to convey the mood of a poem. In "The Fish," the poet says, "I looked into his eyes / which were far larger than mine / but shallower, and yellowed, / the irises backed and packed / with tarnished tinfoil. . . ." With specific words and phrases, she conveys the speaker's longing to understand the fish by looking into its eyes.

A poem can change moods from beginning to end. In "Cargoes," John Masefield conveys a feeling of warmth, sensuousness, wealth, and happiness in the first two stanzas. This feeling contrasts with one that is cold, industrial, and poor in the last stanza.

## Look For

As you read these four poems, be aware of the mood or atmosphere they convey: Are they sad, happy, thoughtful, relieved? Then look for specific words, phrases, and images that help the poet create the mood of the poem.

## Writing

Choose a feeling that you might like to express in a poem, such as joy, anxiety, loneliness, fatigue, anger, or excitement. Then list specific words, phrases, and images that help you create that mood.

## Vocabulary

Knowing the following words will help you as you read these poems.

**scythes** (sīthz) *n.*: Tools with long curving blades, used for mowing grass or grain (p. 664)

**hones** (hōnz) *n.*: Stones used for sharpening cutting tools (p. 664)

**venerable** (ven'ər ə b'l) *adj.*: Worthy of respect because of age and character (p. 665)

**errant** (er'ənt) *adj.*: Straying outside the proper path or bounds (p. 668)

**arrant** (ar'ənt) *adj.*: Extreme (p. 668)

**aberration** (ab'ər ā'shən) *n.*: Something that goes astray (p. 668)

# Reapers

## Jean Toomer

Black reapers with the sound of steel on stones
Are sharpening scythes. I see them place the hones
In their hip-pockets as a thing that's done,
And start their silent swinging, one by one.
Black horses drive a mower through the weeds,
And there, a field rat, startled, squealing bleeds,
His belly close to ground. I see the blade,
Blood-stained, continue cutting weeds and shade.

## THINKING ABOUT THE SELECTION

### Recalling

1. What are the reapers doing?
2. What happens to the field rat?

### Interpreting

3. What does Toomer mean when he says, "I see the blade, / Blood-stained, continue cutting weeds and shade"?
4. What effect is created by the repetition of the sound s in the first two lines?
5. What do you think is the theme of this poem?

### Applying

6. If the mower were to stop after the rat was hit, how would the mood of the poem change?

## ANALYZING LITERATURE

### Understanding Mood

**Mood** is the atmosphere or tone conveyed by a poem. Mood makes us feel a certain way after we have read a poem. A poet uses specific words, phrases, and images to create the mood of a poem. In "Reapers," Toomer uses sharp sounds—"the sound of steel on stones" and the squealing rat—to convey a feeling of harshness.

1. How do the colors black (of the reapers and the horses) and red (the bleeding rat, the blood-stained mower blade) contribute to the mood of the poem?
2. How does the reapers' "silent swinging" contribute to the mood of the poem?
3. What is the atmosphere at the end of the poem, when the mower keeps going after hitting the rat?

# The Fish

**Elizabeth Bishop**

I caught a tremendous fish
and held him beside the boat
half out of water, with my hook
fast in a corner of his mouth.
5  He didn't fight.
He hadn't fought at all.
He hung a grunting weight,
battered and venerable
and homely. Here and there
10  his brown skin hung in strips
like ancient wallpaper,
and its pattern of darker brown
was like wallpaper:
shapes like full-blown roses
15  stained and lost through age.
He was speckled with barnacles,
fine rosettes[1] of lime,
and infested
with tiny white sea-lice,
20  and underneath two or three
rags of green weed hung down.
While his gills were breathing in
the terrible oxygen
—the frightening gills,

---

**1. rosettes** (rō zets′) *n.*: Patterns suggesting a rose.

25   fresh and crisp with blood,
      that can cut so badly—
      I thought of the coarse white flesh
      packed in like feathers,
      the big bones and the little bones,
30   the dramatic reds and blacks
      of his shiny entrails,²
      and the pink swim-bladder³
      like a big peony.⁴
      I looked into his eyes
35   which were far larger than mine
      but shallower, and yellowed,
      the irises⁵ backed and packed
      with tarnished tinfoil
      seen through the lenses
40   of old scratched isinglass.⁶
      They shifted a little, but not
      to return my stare.
      —It was more like the tipping
      of an object toward the light.
45   I admired his sullen face,
      the mechanism of his jaw,
      and then I saw
      that from his lower lip
      —if you could call it a lip—

50   grim, wet, and weaponlike,
      hung five old pieces of fish-line,
      or four and a wire leader
      with the swivel still attached,
      with all their five big hooks
55   grown firmly in his mouth.
      A green line, frayed at the end
      where he broke it, two heavier lines,
      and a fine black thread
      still crimped from the strain and snap
60   when it broke and he got away.
      Like medals with their ribbons
      frayed and wavering,
      a five-haired beard of wisdom
      trailing from his aching jaw.
65   I stared and stared
      and victory filled up
      the little rented boat,
      from the pool of bilge⁷
      where oil had spread a rainbow
70   around the rusted engine
      to the bailer⁸ rusted orange,
      the sun-cracked thwarts,⁹
      the oarlocks on their strings,
      the gunnels¹⁰—until everything
75   was rainbow, rainbow, rainbow!
      And I let the fish go.

---

**2. entrails** (en′ trālz) *n.*: Intestines, guts.
**3. swim-bladder:** The gas-filled sac that gives buoyancy to a fish.
**4. peony** (pē′ ə nē) *n.*: A plant with large, showy flowers often red or pink in color.
**5. irises** (ī′ ris əz) *n.*: The iris is the round, colored part of an eye.
**6. isinglass** (ī′ z′n glas′) *n.*: A semitransparent substance obtained from fish bladders and sometimes used for windows.

---

**7. bilge** (bilj) *n.*: Dirty water in the bottom of a boat.
**8. bailer** (bā′ lər) *n.*: A scoop for removing water from a boat.
**9. thwarts** (th wôrts) *n.*: Rowers' seats lying across a boat.
**10. gunnels** (gun′ ′lz) *n.*: The upper edges of the sides of a boat.

## THINKING ABOUT THE SELECTION

### Recalling

1. Describe the fish the speaker has caught.
2. What does the speaker find in the lower lip of the fish?
3. Explain what the speaker does with the fish.

### Interpreting

4. Interpret line 74–75: "—until everything/was rainbow, rainbow, rainbow!"
5. Why does the speaker let the fish go?

### Applying

6. In this poem the speaker looks into the eyes of the fish and becomes a respecter of life—she throws the fish back. In what other small ways do people show that they are respecters of life?

## THINKING AND WRITING

### Writing About Mood

A critic has said about "The Fish" that it is one "of the most calmly beautiful, deeply sympathetic poems of our time." Expand on this statement by writing a review of the poem for a newspaper. Include the specific words, phrases, and images Bishop uses to create a mood that is "calmly beautiful" and "deeply sympathetic" in her poem. When you revise your review, include two more specific examples from the poem. Proofread for errors in spelling, grammar, and punctuation.

# Pitcher

## Robert Francis

His art is eccentricity, his aim
How not to hit the mark he seems to aim at,

His passion how to avoid the obvious,
His technique how to vary the avoidance.

The others throw to be comprehended. He
Throws to be a moment misunderstood.

Yet not too much. Not errant, arrant, wild,
But every seeming aberration willed.

Not to, yet still, still to communicate
Making the batter understand too late.

## THINKING ABOUT THE SELECTION
### Recalling

1. Explain what the poet is describing.

### Interpreting

2. Why do you think the poet uses only pronouns to name the speaker in the poem?
3. What does the poet mean by the phrase, "His art is eccentricity"?
4. Why is it important to "communicate / Making the batter understand too late?"

### Applying

5. The poet never describes the physical appearance of the character in the poem, but he does use specific phrases to describe the character's passion and purpose, and this conveys the mood of the poem. What is the mood of "Pitcher," and what phrases does Francis use to convey it?

## THINKING AND WRITING
### Writing Couplets

A **couplet** is a set of two lines in a poem, one right after the other, that expresses an idea and has a set rhythm. A set rhythm, or meter, helps the language of a poem move along smoothly. "Pitcher" is written in couplets. Notice that each couplet expresses an idea, and each has a set rhythm. When you say each line out loud, it has four stresses.

Write a short poem of your own using couplets. Choose for your subject an athlete, such as a figure skater, race-car driver, football quarterback, or a gymnast. Have the title of your poem name the athlete, but use only pronouns within the poem. Each of your couplets should express an idea and each should have a set rhythm. Check the rhythm by saying each line out loud. After you have proofread your poem carefully, read it to your classmates and see if they can determine the title without being told.

# Cargoes

## John Masefield

Quinquireme[1] of Nineveh[2] from distant Ophir,[3]
Rowing home to haven in sunny Palestine,
With a cargo of ivory,
And apes and peacocks,
5 Sandalwood, cedarwood, and sweet white wine.

Stately Spanish galleon[4] coming from the Isthmus,[5]
Dipping through the Tropics by the palm-green shores,
With a cargo of diamonds,
Emeralds, amethysts,
10 Topazes, and cinnamon, and gold moidores.[6]

Dirty British coaster[7] with a salt-caked smoke stack,
Butting through the Channel in the mad March days,
With a cargo of Tyne coal,[8]
Road-rails, pig-lead,[9]
15 Firewood, iron-ware, and cheap tin trays.

---

**1. quinquireme** (kwin′ kwī rēm) *n.*: An ancient ship propelled by sails and oars.
**2. Nineveh** (nin′ ə və) *n.*: A city of ancient Assyria.
**3. Ophir** (ō′ fər) *n.*: A biblical land rich in gold.
**4. galleon** (gal′ yən) *n.*: A large Spanish ship of the fifteenth and sixteenth centuries.
**5. Isthmus** (is′ məs) *n.*: Isthmus of Panama.
**6. moidores** (moi′ dorz) *n.*: Gold coins of Portugal and Brazil.
**7. coaster** (kōs′ tər) *n.*: A ship that carries cargo or passengers from port to port along a coast.
**8. Tyne coal:** Coal from Newcastle-upon-Tyne, a shipping and trade center in northeast England.
**9. pig-lead:** Lead that has been poured from a furnace into a mold.

## THINKING ABOUT THE SELECTION

### Recalling

1. What is the source of power for each of the three ships?
2. What cargo does each ship carry?
3. What kind of weather does the British coaster sail through?

### Interpreting

4. Cargo ships carry things that are valuable to people. What do the three different cargoes tell you about the people for whom they are destined?

### Applying

5. Which of the three ships would you rather be on? Why?

## UNDERSTANDING LANGUAGE

### Appreciating Specific Words

**Specific words** appeal to our senses. They help us see, hear, taste, touch, and smell what is happening in a poem. They help the poem come alive for us. They also help the poet convey the mood. In "Cargoes" Masefield uses specific words to paint a picture of the cargo that Quinquireme carries: "a cargo of ivory, / and apes and peacocks / Sandalwood, cedarwood, and sweet white wine." We can see, hear, smell, and taste the richness of this cargo.

1. In contrast with Quinquireme, the British coaster carries a very different cargo. What specific words and phrases does Masefield use to describe the cargo of the British coaster?
2. What specific words does Masefield use to describe the ships themselves?
3. What specific words and phrases does Masefield use to describe the three climates in which the ships sail?
4. How do Masefield's descriptions of the cargoes, ships, and weather affect the moods of the poem?

## THINKING AND WRITING

### Writing a Poem with Imagery

Choose an object with which you are familiar. You might choose an ordinary household object or one that occurs in nature. Write a poem about the object you have chosen using imagery that will be meaningful to your classmates. Write at least four lines. If you wish, you may include rhyming words. Try to include both sensory images and nonliteral uses of language in your poem. When you revise your poem, make sure your images will be clear to your classmates. Be prepared to read your poem aloud.

# Musical Devices

SWING LANDSCAPE (detail), 1938
*Stuart Davis*
*Indiana University Art Museum*

## My Heart's in the Highlands

**Robert Burns** (1759–1796) was thought by many to be the greatest of Scottish poets. Known as the "Ayrshire ploughman," he was born in a small cottage in rural Alloway. Though the family was poor, Burns's father often bought books for the children with his scanty earnings. Burns learned to love the traditional songs and ballads of Scotland, and he began to write his own songs, including "My Heart's in the Highlands." Burns, however, could not sing the songs himself because he was tone deaf.

## The Splendor Falls

**Alfred, Lord Tennyson** (1809–1892) was born in England. He wrote a great deal as a teenager and published his first book with his brother in 1827, called *Poems by Two Brothers*. His greatest poem "In Memoriam" was published in 1850, the same year in which he was named Poet Laureate of England. He continued to write throughout his life, including collections of poetry such as *Charge of the Light Brigade and Other Poems* (1855). "The Splendor Falls" is set in the country Tennyson loved.

## Nursery Rhymes for the Tender-Hearted

**Christopher Morley** (1890–1957) was a famous novelist and essayist, but he preferred to think of himself as a poet. He was born in Haverford, Pennsylvania, and had a long career writing for magazines and newspapers, including *Ladies Home Journal, New York Post,* and *Saturday Review of Literature.* He also wrote plays and helped found a group called the Hoboken Theatrical Company. "Nursery Rhymes for the Tender-Hearted" is a good example of the light verse for which Morley was also well-known.

## Jazz Fantasia

**Carl Sandburg** (1878–1967) was born in Galesburg, Illinois. After first working for several Milwaukee newspapers, Sandburg went to the *Chicago Daily News.* While there, from 1917 to 1932, he worked as a reporter, an editorial writer, a motion picture editor, and a columnist. Sandburg won the Pulitzer Prize in history in 1939 for his book *Abraham Lincoln: The War Years.* He won the Pulitzer Prize for poetry in 1951. The poem "Jazz Fantasia" is set in the city, about which Sandburg wrote many of his poems.

# In Flanders Fields

**John McCrae** (1872–1918) was born in Guelph, Ontario, Canada. He became a physician, and in World War I he served as a medical officer in France. McCrae wrote poems during and about the war and is best remembered for his poem "In Flanders Fields," which was published by the British magazine *Punch* in 1915. The poem was reprinted in the United States to boost the morale of soldiers and encourage others to join the service. McCrae died of pneumonia in 1918.

## Musical Devices

Sound devices are the tools of language that a poet uses to make a poem sound a certain way. Different devices achieve different effects. **Repetition** gives a poem the sound of a song. **Alliteration** is the repetition of the first sound of several words in a line. **Meter** is the formal organization of rhythms in a poem. Each line in the poem has a specific number of stresses if the poem is said out loud. **Assonance,** the repetition of vowel sounds, is still another sound device. **Onomatopoeia** is the use of words to imitate actual sounds.

## Look For

As you read this group of poems, be aware of their sounds. Look for the devices the poets use to create certain effects with sounds.

## Writing

Imagine that you are a poet getting ready to write a poem that creates an image. You want to create your image with sounds. Try using several methods. Write a line containing alliteration. Then write a line containing assonance. Write two lines together using repetition and meter.

## Vocabulary

Knowing the following words will help you as you read these poems.

**summits** (sum'its) *n.*: The highest points of mountains (p. 676)

**glens** (glenz) *n.*: Secluded, narrow valleys between mountains (p. 676)

**vermin** (vʉr'min) *n.*: Small animals that are offensive to humans (p. 678)

**trekked** (trek'd) *v.*: Journeyed (p. 678)

**abandonment** (ə ban'dən mənt) *n.*: Freedom from restraint (p. 678)

# My Heart's in the Highlands

Robert Burns

My heart's in the Highlands,[1] my heart is not here,
My heart's in the Highlands a-chasing the deer,
A-chasing the wild deer and following the roe—[2]
My heart's in the Highlands, wherever I go!

5  Farewell to the Highlands, farewell to the North,
The birthplace of valor, the country of worth!
Wherever I wander, wherever I rove,
The hills of the Highlands forever I love.

Farewell to the mountains high cover'd with snow,
10  Farewell to the straths[3] and green valleys below,
Farewell to the forests and wild-hanging woods,
Farewell to the torrents and loud-pouring floods!

My heart's in the Highlands, my heart is not here,
My heart's in the Highlands a-chasing the deer,
15  A-chasing the wild deer and following the roe—
My heart's in the Highlands, wherever I go!

---

**1. Highlands:** Hilly areas in Scotland.
**2. roe** (rō) *n.*: A small, graceful European or Asiatic deer.
**3. straths** (stra*th*z) *n.*: Wide river valleys.

## THINKING ABOUT THE SELECTION

### Recalling

1. Which two stanzas are repeated entirely?
2. To what does Burns say farewell in the second stanza? What two words in the second stanza characterize this place?
3. In the third stanza, what specific aspects of the place Burns loves does he mention?

### Interpreting

4. What does Burns mean when he says, "My heart's in the Highlands, wherever I go"?
5. How does Burns feel about the Highlands?

### Applying

6. Burns says, "my heart is not here." What kind of place do you imagine "here" to be?
7. William Shakespeare once wrote, "Praising what is lost/Makes the remembrance dear." Discuss the meaning of this quotation. Then explain how its meaning relates to "My Heart's in the Highlands."

## ANALYZING LITERATURE

### Understanding Repetition

**Repetition** is the repeating of words and phrases. It is a device that a poet uses to make a poem sound a certain way. By using repetition, Burns makes "My Heart's in the Highlands" sound like a song; he also emphasizes his idea. Burns not only repeats one entire stanza, he also repeats certain words, phrases, and rhymes throughout the poem. For instance, he uses the word *Highlands* eight times in the poem.

**Parallelism** refers to the repetition of the same grammatical form or structure. For example, notice that lines 1 and 2 both begin with the same grammatical structure—a possessive pronoun followed by a possessive noun followed by a preposition, an article, and a noun.

1. Which words and phrases are repeated in this poem? What effect is created by this repetition?
2. Which phrase is repeated most often in the poem? Why do you think the poet chose to repeat this phrase so often?
3. Which lines begin with a parallel structure? How does the use of parallel structure give the poem a musical quality?

# The Splendor Falls

### Alfred, Lord Tennyson

The splendor falls on castle walls
    And snowy summits old in story:
    The long light shakes across the lakes,
    And the wild cataract[1] leaps in glory.
5  Blow, bugle, blow, set the wild echoes flying,
Blow, bugle; answer, echoes, dying, dying, dying.

    O hark, O hear! how thin and clear,
      And thinner, clearer, farther going!
    O sweet and far from cliff and scar[2]
10      The horns of Elfland[3] faintly blowing!
Blow, let us hear the purple glens replying:
Blow, bugle; answer, echoes, dying, dying, dying.

    O love, they die in yon rich sky,
      They faint on hill or field or river:
15    Our echoes roll from soul to soul,
      And grow for ever and for ever.
Blow, bugle, blow, set the wild echoes flying,
And answer, echoes, answer, dying, dying, dying.

---

**1. cataract** (kat′ ə rakt) *n.*: Waterfall.
**2. scar** (skär) *n.*: Steep, rocky place.
**3. Elfland** (elf′ land′): Fairyland.

## THINKING ABOUT THE SELECTION

### Recalling

1. Describe the setting for this poem.
2. To whom is the speaker in this poem speaking and to what are the people listening?
3. Explain what happens to what they hear.

### Interpreting

4. What effect is created by the images in this poem?
5. Who are "they" in lines 13 and 14?
6. A refrain is a group of words repeated throughout the poem, usually at the end of stanzas. What is the refrain in this poem? What effect is created by the refrain?
7. What does the word *splendor* mean in the title of this poem? How can splendor fall? Interpret the meaning of the title.
8. This poem is sometimes called "The Bugle Song." Which title do you consider more effective? Why?

### Applying

9. Explain why you do or do not think this is a love poem.

## ANALYZING LITERATURE

### Understanding Alliteration and Rhyme

**Alliteration** is the repetition of the first sound of several words in a line. In line 3 of "The Splendor Falls," Tennyson says, "The *l*ong *l*ight shakes across the *l*akes." He repeats the *l* in *long, light,* and *lakes*. He also uses internal rhyme to enhance the sound. **Internal rhyme** is created when two words with the same sound are used in one line of verse. In line 3 the words are *shakes* and *lakes*. By using these sounds the poet creates an image of light rippling on the water of the lakes.

1. Name a line and the words in it that illustrate Tennyson's use of alliteration. How does alliteration help create the image?
2. Name another line and the words Tennyson used to create alliteration. How does alliteration help create the image?
3. Give two examples of internal rhyme (other than *shakes* and *lakes*) from the poem.
4. Read the poem aloud. How does the use of alliteration contribute to its musical quality? How does the use of internal rhyme contribute to this quality?

# Nursery Rhymes for the Tender-Hearted

Christopher Morley

Scuttle, scuttle, little roach—
How you run when I approach:
Up above the pantry shelf,
Hastening to secrete yourself.

5   Most adventurous of vermin,
How I wish I could determine
How you spend your hours of ease,
Perhaps reclining on the cheese.

Cook has gone, and all is dark—
10  Then the kitchen is your park:
In the garbage heap that she leaves
Do you browse among the tea leaves?

How delightful to suspect
All the places you have trekked:
15  Does your long antenna whisk its
Gentle tip across the biscuits?

Do you linger, little soul,
Drowsing in our sugar bowl?
Or, abandonment most utter,
20  Shake a shimmy[1] on the butter?

Do you chant your simple tunes
Swimming in the baby's prunes?
Then, when dawn comes, do you slink
Homeward to the kitchen sink?

25  Timid roach, why be so shy?
We are brothers, thou and I.
In the midnight, like yourself,
I explore the pantry shelf!

---

**1. shimmy** (shim′ ē) *n.*: A jazz dance popular in the
early 1920s involving shaking the body.

## THINKING ABOUT THE SELECTION
### Recalling

1. In what ways does the speaker of the poem suggest that the roach may spend its time?
2. How does the kitchen become the roach's park?
3. Morley says that he and the roach are brothers. How are they alike?

### Interpreting

4. An **apostrophe** is a poem that addresses an animal or an inanimate object as if it could respond. In this poem Morley gives the roach human emotions and asks it a question as if it might answer. Name three things Morley says about the roach that make it seem more human than roachlike.
5. Why do you think the poet considers this poem for "the tender-hearted"?

### Applying

6. What other creatures would make good subjects for nursery rhymes for the tender-hearted? Explain your choices.

## ANALYZING LITERATURE
### Understanding Assonance

**Assonance** is a sound device in which vowel sounds within a word are repeated. The line "In the garbage heap that she leaves" contains assonance.

1. Find two more lines of this poem that contain assonance. Identify the repeated vowel sounds.
2. Find two lines of other poems that contain assonance and identify the repeated vowel sounds.

## CRITICAL THINKING AND READING
### Responding to Parody

**Parody** is the imitation of one poem by another. A parody is usually meant to be funny. If you read "Nursery Rhymes for the Tender-Hearted" out loud, you probably discovered that it sounds like "Twinkle, Twinkle, Little Star." Morley's poem has the same metrical pattern as "Twinkle, Twinkle, Little Star": trochiac tetrameter. A **trochee** is the opposite of an iamb; it begins with a stressed syllable and ends with an unstressed syllable. For example, in line 25 the word "Timid" is a trochee. **Tetrameter** means that there are four stresses in a line.

Morley also parodies "Twinkle, Twinkle, Little Star" by repeating or replacing words that appear in "Twinkle, Twinkle, Little Star."

1. In line 1, which repeated word parodies "Twinkle, Twinkle, Little Star"?
2. In lines 2 and 3, which two words or phrases are the same in both poems?
3. Is "Nursery Rhymes for the Tender-Hearted" meant to be serious? How can you tell?

## THINKING AND WRITING
### Parodying a Nursery Rhyme

"Nursery Rhymes for the Tender-Hearted" parodies the nursery rhyme "Twinkle, Twinkle, Little Star" by imitating its meter and repeating or replacing certain words.

Write your own parody of "Mary Had a Little Lamb." Make your parody at least one stanza long. In your parody, use the same meter as that of "Mary Had a Little Lamb," and repeat or replace words and phrases that appear in "Mary Had a Little Lamb." Revise by repeating at least one more word from "Mary Had a Little Lamb" in your parody. Proofread for errors in punctuation and spelling.

# Jazz Fantasia

## Carl Sandburg

Drum on your drums, batter on your banjoes,
sob on the long cool winding saxophones.
Go to it, O jazzmen.

Sling your knuckles on the bottoms of the happy
tin pans, let your trombones ooze, and go husha-
husha-hush with the slippery sand-paper.

Moan like an autumn wind high in the lonesome treetops,
moan soft like you wanted somebody terrible, cry like a
racing car slipping away from a motorcycle cop,
bang-bang! you jazzmen, bang altogether drums, traps,
banjoes, horns, tin cans—make two people fight on the
top of a stairway and scratch each other's eyes in a
clinch[1] tumbling down the stairs.

Can[2] the rough stuff . . . now a Mississippi steamboat
pushes up the night river with a hoo-hoo-hoo-oo . . . and
the green lanterns calling to the high soft stars . . . a red
moon rides on the humps of the low river hills . . .go to it,
O jazzmen.

---

**1. clinch** (klinch) *n.*: Slang for *embrace.*
**2. can:** Slang for *stop.*

## THINKING ABOUT THE SELECTION

### Recalling

1. What six instruments does Sandburg name in stanzas 1 and 2?
2. In stanza 3, what does the speaker say the music should make happen?
3. The mood of the poem changes in the last stanza. Name two images that indicate that the sound of the music has also changed.

### Interpreting

4. In stanza 4, Sandburg writes, "Can the rough stuff." To what may he be referring?

### Applying

5. Which kind of jazz would you rather hear—the kind described in stanzas 2 and 3 or the kind described in stanza 4? Why?

## ANALYZING LITERATURE

### Understanding Onomatopoeia

**Onomatopoeia** is the creation of words that imitate actual sounds. In "Jazz Fantasia" Sandburg says that the musicians go "husha-husha-hush with the slippery sandpaper." "Husha-husha-hush" imitates the sound of the sandpaper.

A poet can also use real words to suggest a sound. In "Jazz Fantasia" Sandburg says "batter on your banjoes." "Batter" suggests the sound the musicians make on their banjoes.

1. Name three examples of onomatopoeia in "Jazz Fantasia" other than those listed above.
2. In addition to the sounds made by the musicians with their instruments, what other sounds do you hear in "Jazz Fantasia"?

# In Flanders Fields

### John McCrae

In Flanders fields the poppies blow
Between the crosses, row on row,
    That mark our place; and in the sky
    The larks, still bravely singing, fly
5  Scarce heard amid the guns below.

We are the Dead. Short days ago
We lived, felt dawn, saw sunset glow,
    Loved and were loved, and now we lie
    In Flanders fields.

10  Take up our quarrel with the foe:
To you from failing hands we throw
    The torch; be yours to hold it high.
    If ye break faith with us who die
We shall not sleep, though poppies grow
    In Flanders fields.

## THINKING ABOUT THE SELECTION
### Recalling

1. Who is the speaker of this poem and to whom is the poem addressed?

### Interpreting

2. What message is the speaker giving?
3. What does McCrae mean when he says, "If ye break faith with us who die / We shall not sleep, though poppies grow / In Flanders fields"?

### Applying

4. Describe ways in which we keep faith with the dead in everyday life.

## ANALYZING LITERATURE
### Understanding Meter

**Meter** is the organized pattern of rhythm in a poem. A poet may use many different kinds of metrical patterns, or combinations of stressed and unstressed syllables. Meter is usually described as consisting of units called feet. A metrical foot consists of one stressed or accented syllable and one or more unstressed or unaccented ones. Stressed syllables are marked / and unstressed syllables are marked ∪.

An iamb consists of two syllables, the first unstressed and the second stressed. Tetrameter means that there are four feet, or four stresses, per line. "In Flanders fields the poppies grow" is a line of iambic tetrameter.

To find the meter of a poem, use scansion, which is the analysis of the meter of a poem. You may need to use scansion for several lines of a poem to determine its meter. Sometimes a poet may change the pattern of lines, as in line 9 of "In Flanders Fields."

1. Copy line 14 of the poem. Place the mark / over stressed syllables and the mark ∪ over unstressed syllables.
2. Do lines 3 and 4, 12 and 13, follow the iambic tetrameter pattern? What line (other than line 9) does not follow the pattern?

# Forms

**STILL LIFE WITH MAGNOLIA, 1941**
*Henri Matisse*
Paris Musée Nationale d'Art Moderne

# GUIDE FOR READING

## Shall I Compare Thee to a Summer's Day?

**William Shakespeare** (1564–1616) was an actor, theater owner, and a renowned playwright and poet. Among the best known of his thirty-eight plays, written over about twenty years, are *Hamlet, Macbeth, King Lear, Romeo and Juliet, A Midsummer Night's Dream,* and *The Merchant of Venice.* As early as 1591, Shakespeare began writing sonnets, the most popular poetic form in the England of his day. So well did he master this form, shown in "Shall I Compare Thee to a Summer's Day?" that the terms *Shakespearean sonnet* and *English sonnet* are interchangeable today.

## Puritan Sonnet

**Elinor Wylie** (1885–1928) grew up in Washington, D.C., where her father served in the McKinley and Theodore Roosevelt administrations. She studied painting at the Corcoran Museum and wrote poetry, first as a hobby, then as a vocation. After one unhappy marriage, Wylie eloped with her second husband to England, where she spent several years writing. She returned in 1916 to the United States. "Puritan Sonnet" reveals her intense, vivid poetic style.

## Sonnet

A **sonnet** is a fourteen-line lyric poem written in iambic pentameter (ten syllables, with each unaccented syllable followed by an accented one), with a particular rhyme scheme. An example is the first line

$$\underset{\smile}{} \underset{/}{} \underset{\smile}{} \underset{/}{} \underset{\smile}{} \underset{/}{} \underset{\smile}{} \underset{/}{} \underset{\smile}{} \underset{/}{}$$

of Shakespeare's poem: "Shall I compare thee to a summer's day?" Robert Frost has said of the sonnet, "A true sonnet goes eight lines and then takes a turn for better or worse and goes six . . . lines more?"

## Look For

As you read these sonnets, notice how they fit or depart from the form described above.

## Writing

Love is a popular theme in poetry. Freewrite, exploring the meaning of this much-used word.

## Vocabulary

Knowing the following words will help you as you read these sonnets.

**temperate** (tem′pər it) *adj.:* Moderate in degree or quality (p. 686)

**sheaves** (shēvz) *n.:* Bunches of cut stalks of grain bound up in a bundle (p. 688)

# Shall I Compare Thee to a Summer's Day?

## William Shakespeare

Shall I compare thee to a summer's day?
Thou art more lovely and more temperate:
Rough winds do shake the darling buds of May,
And summer's lease hath all too short a date:
5   Sometime too hot the eye of heaven shines,
And often is his gold complexion dimmed;
And every fair from fair sometime declines,

By chance or nature's changing course untrimmed;[1]
But thy eternal summer shall not fade,
10 Nor lose possession of that fair thou owest;[2]
Nor shall Death brag thou wander'st in his shade,
When in eternal lines to time thou grow'st:
    So long as men can breathe, or eyes can see,
    So long lives this, and this gives life to thee.

---

**1. untrimmed** (un trimd') *adj.*: Shorn (of its beauty).
**2. owest** (ō' ist) *v.*: Own.

## THINKING ABOUT THE SELECTION

### Recalling

1. To what is the speaker comparing the subject of the poem?
2. What does the speaker say shall not fade?
3. What does the speaker say Death shall not do?

### Interpreting

4. To whom is the poet speaking?
5. To what does "the eye of heaven" refer?
6. To what does the word *this* in the last line refer?
7. In the comparison, does the beloved fare better or worse than a summer's day? Give details to support your opinion.
8. What makes the beloved immortal?

### Applying

9. Do you agree with the statement made in the last two lines? What are some examples of this sentiment today?

## ANALYZING LITERATURE

### Understanding Shakespearean Sonnets

All sonnets have fourteen lines of iambic pentameter—a line of five unaccented syllables each followed by an accented syllable. An example is the following line from the poem.

  U   /  U  /  U  /  U  /  U  /
Rough winds do shake the darling buds of May

A **Shakespearean sonnet,** also known as an English sonnet, consists of three quatrains (four-line groups) and a couplet (a two-line group). Each quatrain has alternating rhymes at the end of its lines *(ababcdcdefef)*. The two lines of the couplet rhyme at the end *(gg)*. Usually each quatrain explores a different aspect of the poem's central idea. The couplet sums up the poem or comments on what was said in the quatrains.

Discuss how the sonnet you just read fits the typical structure of an English, or Shakespearean, sonnet. How is it different from Frost's description on page 685?

# Puritan Sonnet

Elinor Wylie

Down to the Puritan marrow of my bones
There's something in this richness that I hate.
I love the look, austere, immaculate,
Of landscapes drawn in pearly monotones.
5   There's something in my very blood that owns
Bare hills, cold silver on a sky of slate,
A thread of water, churned to milky spate[1]
Streaming through slanted pastures fenced with stones.

I love those skies, thin blue or snowy gray,
10  Those fields sparse-planted, rendering meager sheaves;
That spring, briefer than apple-blossom's breath,
Summer, so much too beautiful to stay,
Swift autumn, like a bonfire of leaves,
And sleepy winter, like the sleep of death.

---

**1. spate:** sudden downpour.

## THINKING ABOUT THE SELECTION

### Recalling

1. What does the speaker of "Puritan Sonnet" says she loves in the first stanza?
2. What does the speaker of the poem hate?
3. What does the speaker say her very blood owns?
4. How does the speaker describe spring, summer, autumn, and winter?

### Interpreting

5. Look up the word *Puritan* in a dictionary. How would you characterize someone who is a Puritan? Why is it appropriate that this word has the same root as the word *pure*?
6. How do the colors mentioned in the poem reflect a Puritan view? In what way is winter appropriate to a Puritan soul?

### Applying

7. What kind of landscape, in your opinion, would be the opposite of a Puritan landscape?

## ANALYZING LITERATURE

### Understanding the Petrarchan Sonnet

The **Petrarchan sonnet,** also called the Italian sonnet, is a form of lyric poetry that was developed in thirteenth-century Italy. It is named after the famous Italian poet Francesco Petrarch (1304–1374).

The Petrarchan sonnet is usually divided into two stanzas. The first stanza, called the octave, is eight lines long; its rhyme scheme is *abbaabba*. The second stanza, called the sestet, is six lines long; its rhyme scheme is usually *cdecde*. The octave often presents a situation, and the sestet usually resolves or comments on it.

The Petrarchan sonnet usually is fourteen lines of iambic pentameter—a line of five unaccented syllables each followed by an accented syllable. An example is the following line:

$$\cup \quad / \quad \cup \quad / \quad \cup \quad / \quad \cup \quad / \quad \cup$$
"There's something in this richness that I

$$/$$
hate."

In "Puritan Sonnet," iambic pentameter is not followed exactly.

1. Find an example in "Puritan Sonnet" in which iambic pentameter is not followed exactly. Why has the poet varied the rhythm?
2. Explain what situation is presented in the octave in "Puritan Sonnet" and what, if any, solution is provided in the sestet.

## THINKING AND WRITING

### Comparing and Contrasting Sonnets

Write a brief essay for a literary magazine in which you compare and contrast the two sonnets in this section. First, list the similarities and differences in structure (rhyme and meter), subject, and images. Then use this information to write your essay. Revise your essay to include examples to support your statements. Proofread for errors in spelling, grammar, and punctuation.

# GUIDE FOR READING

**Hyakuchi** was a Japanese haiku poet about whose life little is known. The following haiku reveals a spirit of quiet reflection.

**Chiyojo** (1703–1775) was another Japanese haiku poet about whom little is known. When her husband, a servant of a samurai, died, she became a nun and studied poetry with a well-known teacher of haiku. The following haiku reflects her lightness of spirit.

**Matsuo Bashō** (1644-1694), the most famous of the Japanese haiku poets, was not known for haiku in his own day. He was a master of a type of long, linked poem called a *regna* and traveled around the country teaching people how to write regna. A regna could consist of one hundred stanzas or more and was usually the work of two, three, or more poets in collaboration. The haiku evolved from the "starting verse" of a regna. Bashō believed that a poet must express the essential nature of an object.

**Kobayashi Issa** (1762–1826), probably the favorite haiku poet of the Japanese, led a life marked by hardship and personal loss. Banished from his rural home as a teen-ager, Issa lived most of his life in urban poverty. All of his children died in infancy, and the young wives who bore them died before Issa. Through all his adversity, Issa seemed to draw strength from small creatures like insects, sparrows, and the rat in the following haiku—creatures whose lives are fleeting and that appear overwhelmed by the elements.

**Haiku**

**Haiku** (hī′kōō) is a lyric form of poetry from Japan consisting of seventeen syllables arranged in unrhymed lines of five, seven, and five syllables. Traditionally, haiku have as their subjects images from the natural world. Through the haiku's simple images, the poet tries to elicit the same sudden, intense response in the reader that he or she experienced. Haiku remains the most popular of Japanese poetic forms.

**Look For**

As you read the following haiku, look for the ways the four poets express the essential nature of an image or moment of their experience.

**Writing**

Brainstorm and write down your ideas about objects or experiences about which you could write a haiku.

**Vocabulary**

Knowing the following word will help you as you read these haiku.
**muses** (myōōz′ əz) v.: Thinks
deeply; meditates (p. 691)

# Haiku

思うほど
物言わぬ人
と涼みけり

### Hyakuchi

With one who muses
But says not a single word
I enjoy the cool.

### Chiyojo

Having viewed the moon
I say farewell to this world
With heartfelt blessing.

月を見て
我はこの世を
かしくかな

落ちざまに
水こぼしけり
花椿

### Bashō

Falling upon earth,
Pure water spills from the cup
Of the camellia.

**SNOW-LADEN CAMELLIA AND SPARROW**
*Ando Hiroshige*
*Metropolitan Museum of Art*

**A SUDDEN SHOWER AT OHASHI**
*Ando Hiroshige*
*Metropolitan Museum of Art*

春
雨
や
鼠
の
な
め
る
隅
田
川

## Issa

A gentle spring rain.
Look, a rat is lapping
Sumida River.

## THINKING ABOUT THE SELECTION

### Recalling

1. What does Bashō describe in his haiku?
2. What small creature does Issa write about in his haiku?
3. What natural object is central to the haiku by Chiyojo?
4. Who is with the speaker in the Hyakuchi haiku?

### Interpreting

5. A haiku can make us see two things at the same time. What two things do we see in Issa's haiku?
6. Is the silence in the Hyakuchi haiku a comfortable or an uncomfortable one? Explain your answer.
7. How does Hyakuchi appeal to our senses of hearing and touch?
8. Which adjective best describes the attitude of the speaker in the Chiyojo haiku—bitter, kind, or remorseful? Give reasons for your answer.

### Applying

9. The haiku by Hyakuchi deals with a moment of experience, not with a natural object. What other moments of experience can you think of that might be good subjects for haiku? Give reasons for your answer.

## ANALYZING LITERATURE

### Understanding Haiku

A **haiku** is a poem which, when written in Japanese, consists of three unrhymed lines of five syllables, seven syllables, and five syllables.

The subject is usually an image from nature or an intense moment of personal experience, which the haiku poet tries to put into words for the reader to share. Haiku have influenced many modern poets, including Ezra Pound and Amy Lowell.

In many haiku, the poet brings together seemingly unrelated images in startling and delightful ways. The poet also tries to appeal to more than one sense at the same time. The poet furthermore tries to condense in concentrated form a sequence of events.

1. To which of our senses does Bashō appeal?
2. To which of our senses does Issa appeal?
3. What emotions does Hyakuchi express?
4. What sequence of events occurs in Chiyojo's haiku?
5. Why do you suppose prepositions (such as *on, in,* and *over*) and articles *(a, an,* and *the)* are used so sparingly in English haiku and translations of haiku?

## THINKING AND WRITING

### Writing Haiku

Try your hand at writing a haiku. Choose as your subject one of your ideas from the Guide for Reading page. First freewrite about it describing the subject and your thoughts about it. Then use this information to write your haiku. Your haiku does not have to form a complete sentence but can present an image or suggest a feeling. Revise your haiku to make sure it has five syllables in the first line, seven syllables in the second, and five in the last. Proofread for spelling errors.

## Letter Slot

**John Updike** (1932–      ) is an American novelist, short-story writer, and poet. He was born in Shillington, Pennsylvania, where many of his early stories and novels are set. He attended Harvard College and was a staff member of *The New Yorker* magazine. Updike's work shows a deep concern for the pain and striving that are a part of human relationships. His novel *Rabbit Is Rich* won the 1982 Pulitzer Prize for fiction. "Letter Slot" is his comment on a daily occurrence.

## Constantly Risking Absurdity

**Lawrence Ferlinghetti** (1919–      ) was a leader in the American poetry revival in San Francisco in the 1950's. A founder of the first all-paperback bookstore, he later became a publisher of new poetry. Much of Ferlinghetti's poetry is political in focus, and its main theme is the opposition to violence, both in life and in art. Ferlinghetti has said that the function of the poet is "to uncover the secret meaning of things."

## Concrete Poetry

**Concrete poetry** is poetry in which the lines form pictures. Concrete poetry uses the arrangement of words or lines of poetry on the page to convey meaning by forming a picture or an image of the poem's subject. Sometimes even the letters of words are used to create a picture. For example, a poem about sorrow might be written in the form of a teardrop. Although this visual approach to poetry became popular in the middle decades of this century, its history is much older. Poems whose shape matched their sense were written in the seventeenth century by English poets such as George Herbert.

## Look For

As you read these poems, look for the pictures or images that the poet forms by the arrangement of the lines of poetry. Think about why the poet formed that picture or image.

## Writing

Brainstorm and write down your ideas for subjects about which you might write a concrete poem. Some examples are snowflakes falling, ocean waves, or the path of a ball thrown through the air.

## Vocabulary

Knowing the following words will help you as you read these poems.
**spews** (spyo͞oz) *v.*: Throws up from, or as from, the stomach (p. 696)

**rime** (rīm) *n.*: Another spelling for rhyme; poetry or verse in general (p. 697)

# Letter Slot

## John Updike

Once each day this broad mouth spews

Apologies,

bills,

rags,[1]

and news.

---

**1. rags:** Slang for newspapers.

---

## THINKING ABOUT THE SELECTION

### Recalling

1. How often does the event occur?
2. What comes out of the "broad mouth"?

### Interpreting

3. What is the "broad mouth"? Is the image of a "broad mouth" spewing a pleasant or an unpleasant one? Explain your answer.
4. What does this spewing suggest that the poet feels about this typical occurrence?

### Applying

5. What kind of shape might you create for a concrete poem about a present?

## ANALYZING LITERATURE

### Understanding Concrete Poetry

An example of a concrete poem would be a poem about sorrow written in the shape of a teardrop. Although this visual approach to poetry became popular in the middle decades of this century, its history is much older. Poems whose shape matched their sense were written in the seventeenth century by English poets such as George Herbert.

1. What is the central idea of "Letter Slot"?
2. Explain how the arrangement of words in "Letter Slot" helps convey the central idea.

## THINKING AND WRITING

### Writing Concrete Poetry

**Concrete poetry** is poetry whose shape shows its meaning. The arrangement of its lines and words give the poem a shape that matches or enhances its meaning.

Choose one of the subjects from the list you brainstormed. Choose a shape for the subject that matches the meaning of your subject. Freewrite about the subject, describing it and your thoughts. Then use this material to write a concrete poem to fit the shape. A concrete poem may consist of one or more complete sentences, several phrases, or even individual words or letters. Revise your poem to make sure it fits the shape you chose. Proofread for spelling errors.

# Constantly Risking Absurdity

### Lawrence Ferlinghetti

          Constantly risking absurdity
                        and death
                whenever he performs
                        above the heads
5                       of his audience
        the poet like an acrobat
                climbs on rime
                        to a high wire of his own making
        and balancing on eyebeams
10                        above a sea of faces
                paces his way
                        to the other side of day
        performing entrechats[1]
                and sleight-of-foot tricks
15      and other high theatrics
                and all without mistaking
                any thing
                        for what it may not be

                For he's the super realist
20                      who must perforce[2] perceive
                taut truth
                        before the taking of each stance or step
        in his supposed advance
                        toward that still higher perch
25      where Beauty stands and waits
                        with gravity
                        to start her death-defying leap

---

**1. entrechats** (on' trə cha'), *n.*: Leaps in which a
ballet dancer's legs crisscross several times.
**2. perforce** (pər fôrs'), *adv.*: Necessarily.

And he
    a little charley chaplin[3] man
30             who may or may not catch
    her fair eternal form
           spreadeagled in the empty air
    of existence

---

**3. Charley Chaplin:** Charles Chaplin (1889–1977), British actor and producer, who worked in the U.S. from 1913 to 1952.

---

## THINKING ABOUT THE SELECTION

### Recalling

1. About whom is the poem written?
2. To what is the subject of the poem compared?
3. What must the "super realist" perceive?
4. Who stands on "that still higher perch" and "waits with gravity"?
5. What might or might not the "little charley chaplin man" do?

### Interpreting

6. What common expression is "sleight-of-foot" in line 14 a play on?
7. What effect does this variation of the expression achieve?
8. The phrase "with gravity" in line 26 has at least two meanings. State and explain these meanings.
9. What does the description "a little charley chaplin man" suggest about the poet/ acrobat?
10. What is the significance of the title?

### Applying

11. A circus acrobat takes obvious risks. In what ways does a poet (or other artist) take risks? Explain your answer.

## THINKING AND WRITING

### Writing a Paraphrase of a Poem

To **paraphrase** is to restate the meaning of a written work in your own words. Paraphrasing can help you understand the theme of a written work. First list the most important points in the order in which the poet uses them in "Constantly Risking Absurdity." Then use this information to write a paraphrase of the poem. Discuss how the poet develops the comparison of the poet to the acrobat. Revise your paraphrase, making sure you include a statement of the poem's theme. Proofread for errors in spelling, grammar, and punctuation.

# Themes

**GIRL WITH CAT**
*Franz Marc*
Three Lions

## To James

**Frank Horne** (1899–1974) had a varied career as a college president, an optometrist, a race relations administrator, and a poet. As a student at the College of the City of New York, Horne distinguished himself as a track star. In "To James," Horne uses a race as a metaphor for life.

## Auto Wreck

**Karl Shapiro** (1913–      ) has been a college professor, a critic, and an editor of *Poetry* and *Prairie Schooner,* as well as a distinguished American poet. He won the Pulitzer Prize in 1945 for *V-Letter and Other Poems,* which draws on his experience as a Jewish soldier in the United States Army during World War II. Shapiro has said that he would like to see the elimination "of the line between poetry and prose." The harsh realism of "Auto Wreck" reflects Shapiro's preferred poetic style.

## The Oxen

**Thomas Hardy** (1840–1928), born in Dorset, England, regarded poetry as superior to fiction, although he is more famous for his novels, such as *Tess of the d'Urbervilles* (1891). Both his novels and his poems deal with the struggle of human beings who suffer and sometimes seem to be the victims of cruel jokes in an indifferent world. As a young man, Hardy considered taking Holy Orders, but he lost his religious faith. "The Oxen" nostalgically recalls a time when he shared the simple faith of villagers.

## Ebb

**Edna St. Vincent Millay** (1892–1950) was born in Rockland, Maine, and attended Vassar College. She achieved fame as a poet by age twenty with *Renascence and Other Poems.* Her early poems expressed the disillusionment of the post-World War I generation and a reckless disdain for traditions and conventions. Dorothy Parker, a famous contemporary of Millay's, said of her, "[She] made poetry seem so easy that we could all do it. But, of course, we couldn't."

## Theme

**Theme** is the central idea of a story or poem, or the general idea or insight about life that the work reveals. Sometimes the writer states the theme directly, but more often only implies, or suggests, it. You can identify the theme through careful reading, analysis, and thought.

## Look For

As you read these poems, look for the events or objects the poets use to suggest theme or underlying meanings.

## Writing

Brainstorm and write down your ideas for themes about which you could write a poem. Include experiences, people, or places that have special meaning for you.

## Vocabulary

Knowing the following words will help you as you read these poems.

**sinews** (sin′yo͞oz) *n.*: Tendons —the fibrous cords attaching muscle to bone (p. 702)

**deranged** (di rānjd′) *adj.*: Disturbed out of the normal way of acting (p. 704)

**douches** (do͞osh′əz) *v.*: Washes or flushes away (p. 704)

**banal** (bā′n′l) *adj.*: Stale from overuse; commonplace (p. 704)

**occult** (ə kult′) *adj.*: Having to do with so-called mystic arts such as alchemy and astrology (p. 705)

**expedient** (ik spē′dē ənt) *adj.*: Useful; convenient (p. 705)

**tepid** (tep′id) *adj.*: Barely warm; lukewarm (p. 707)

# To James

### Frank Horne

Do you remember
how you won
that last race . . .?
how you flung your body
5   at the start . . .
how your spikes
ripped the cinders
in the stretch . . .
how you catapulted
10   through the tape . . .
do you remember . . .?
Don't you think
I lurched with you
out of those starting holes . . .?
15   Don't you think
my sinews tightened
at those first
few strides . . .
and when you flew into the stretch
20   was not all my thrill
of a thousand races
in your blood . . .?
At your final drive
through the finish line
25   did not my shout
tell of the
triumphant ecstasy
of victory . . .?

    Live
30   as I have taught you
to run, Boy—
it's a short dash.
Dig your starting holes
deep and firm
35   lurch out of them

into the straightaway[1]
with all the power
that is in you
look straight ahead
40  to the finish line
think only of the goal
run straight
run high
run hard
45  save nothing
and finish
with an ecstatic burst
that carries you
hurtling
50  through the tape
to victory . . .

_____

**1. straightaway** (strāt′ ə wā′),
*n.*: A straight course.

## THINKING ABOUT THE SELECTION
### Recalling

1. What is the outcome for James in the race described in the first part of the poem?
2. What does the speaker do at the end of James's final drive through the finish line?
3. What does the speaker tell James to do?

### Interpreting

4. Does the speaker seem to be older, younger, or about the same age as James? Give reasons for your answer.
5. How does the speaker feel about James?
6. Find examples in the poem in which living one's life is compared to running a race. Explain the comparison.
7. What feeling about life does the speaker want James to have?

### Applying

8. What other games, sports, or events could be used as a metaphor for life? Explain your choices.

## ANALYZING LITERATURE
### Understanding Theme

**Theme,** or the general idea or insight about life that the work reveals, often is only implied, or suggested. You can identify the theme of a poem through careful reading, analysis, and thought.

In "To James," the poet uses a race as a metaphor for life: "Live / as I have taught you / to run, Boy— / it's a short dash." Throughout the poem the speaker uses descriptions of a race to advise James about how to live.

State in your own words the theme of the poem.

# Auto Wreck

## Karl Shapiro

Its quick soft silver bell beating, beating,
And down the dark one ruby flare
Pulsing out red light like an artery,
The ambulance at top speed floating down
5   Past beacons and illuminated clocks
Wings in a heavy curve, dips down,
And brakes speed, entering the crowd.
The doors leap open, emptying light;
Stretchers are laid out, the mangled lifted
10  And stowed into the little hospital.
Then the bell, breaking the hush, tolls once,
And the ambulance with its terrible cargo
Rocking, slightly rocking, moves away,
As the doors, an afterthought, are closed.

15  We are deranged, walking among the cops
Who sweep glass and are large and composed.
One is still making notes under the light.
One with a bucket douches ponds of blood
Into the street and gutter.
20  One hangs lanterns on the wrecks that cling,
Empty husks of locusts, to iron poles.

Our throats were tight as tourniquets,[1]
Our feet were bound with splints, but now,
Like convalescents intimate and gauche,[2]
25  We speak through sickly smiles and warn
With the stubborn saw of common sense,
The grim joke and the banal resolution.
The traffic moves around with care,
But we remain, touching a wound
30  That opens to our richest horror.
Already old, the question Who shall die?
Becomes unspoken Who is innocent?

---

**1. tourniquets** (tŭr′ nə ketz). *n.*: Bandages to stop bleeding by compressing a blood vessel.
**2. gauche** (gōsh) *adj.*: Awkward.

For death in war is done by hands;
Suicide has cause and stillbirth, logic;
35 And cancer, simple as a flower, blooms.
But this invites the occult mind,
Cancels our physics with a sneer,
And spatters all we knew of denouement[3]
Across the expedient and wicked stones.

---

**3. denouement** (dā' nü män'), *n.*: Outcome or the end.

## THINKING ABOUT THE SELECTION

### Recalling

1. What do the first fourteen lines of the poem describe?
2. To what does the speaker compare himself and other onlookers?
3. What question does the speaker ask?
4. How does the speaker describe other forms of death?

### Interpreting

5. What is it that pulses "out red light" like an artery? Explain your answer.

6. What does the tolling of the bell in line 11 suggest?
7. What is the *wound* in line 29? Give reasons for your answer.
8. To whom does *we* in the poem refer? Give reasons for your answer.
9. What does the image "empty husks of locusts" in line 21 suggest?

### Applying

10. "Auto Wreck" describes a sudden death, beyond human understanding, which shocks observers out of their usual way of responding. Think of another human experience that could have such an effect.

# The Oxen

## Thomas Hardy

Christmas Eve, and twelve of the clock,
    "Now they are all on their knees,"
An elder said as we sat in a flock
    By the embers in hearthside ease.

5  We pictured the meek mild creatures where
    They dwelt in their strawy[1] pen,
Nor did it occur to one of us there
    To doubt they were kneeling then.

So fair a fancy few would weave
10    In these years! Yet, I feel,
If someone said on Christmas Eve,
    "Come; see the oxen kneel

"In the lonely barton[2] by yonder coomb[3]
    Our childhood used to know,"
15  I should go with him in the gloom,
    Hoping it might be so.

---

**1. strawy:** The adjectival form of *straw.*
**2. barton** (bär′ t'n) *n.*: An enclosure or pen for animals.
**3. coomb** (kōōm) *n.*: A deep, narrow valley.

---

## THINKING ABOUT THE SELECTION

### Recalling

1. Which lines in each stanza rhyme?
2. What time of day does the speaker describe?
3. How does the speaker react to the elder's statement that the oxen are kneeling?
4. How would the speaker react now to being invited to look at the oxen?

### Interpreting

5. Is the Christmas Eve the speaker is recalling in his recent past or in the fairly distant past?

6. The speaker refers to a folk superstition that farm animals kneel down on Christmas Eve to honor Jesus. How does the speaker think adults would view this superstition?
7. What hope does the speaker express in the last line?

### Applying

8. John J. Plomp has written: "You know children are growing up when they start asking questions that have answers." Explain the meaning of this quotation. How does it relate to "The Oxen"?

# Ebb

Edna St. Vincent Millay

I know what my heart is like
    Since your love died:
It is like a hollow ledge
Holding a little pool
    Left there by the tide,
    A little tepid pool,
Drying inward from the edge.

## THINKING ABOUT THE SELECTION
### Recalling

1. To what does the speaker compare her heart?

### Interpreting

2. What does "Drying inward from the edge" suggest about what the speaker's feelings will be in the future?

### Applying

3. Create another simile that suggests a feeling of loss?

## THINKING AND WRITING
### Patterning a Poem

    Choose an image to which you could compare a person's life after a loss. Freewrite about this loss. Use this information to write a poem for a friend following the pattern of "Ebb." Revise your poem. Proofread for spelling errors.

# Poetry

Poetry is difficult to define but easy to recognize. It is known by its musicality and compactness. Fully appreciating a poem takes active involvement. As you read, examine the elements that make up the poem and see how they work together.

**Types of Poetry**

Poetry may be narrative, dramatic, or lyric. Narrative poetry tells a story, while dramatic poetry dramatizes the action. Lyric poetry expresses strong feelings about the subject of the poem.

**The Speaker and Tone**

The speaker is the person, animal, or even object the poet uses to tell the poem. Tone is the attitude of the poet that comes through the poem.

**Figurative Language**

Figurative language consists of words used to represent one thing in terms of another. Three common types of figurative language are simile, metaphor, and personification.

**Imagery**

Imagery is the use of vivid language to form word pictures. These pictures may arouse sensory memories by appealing to the senses.

**Musical Devices**

Musical devices are the techniques the poet uses to create the music of the poem. Some common musical devices are rhythm, rhyme, alliteration, repetition, and onomatopoeia.

**Forms**

Poetry can take a variety of forms. Some common forms are the sonnet, the haiku, and concrete poetry.

**Theme**

Much poetry carries a general idea, or insight into life. This insight is its theme.

On the following pages is a model with annotations in the margin showing how an active reader might pull together the elements of the poem.

# Ex-Basketball Player

## John Updike

Pearl Avenue runs past the high-school lot,
Bends with the trolley tracks, and stops, cut off
Before it has a chance to go two blocks,
At Colonel McComsky Plaza. Berth's Garage
5  Is on the corner facing west, and there,
Most days, you'll find Flick Webb, who helps Berth out.

Flick stands tall among the idiot pumps—
Five on a side, the old bubble-head style,
Their rubber elbows hanging loose and low.
One's nostrils are two S's, and his eyes
An E and O. And one is squat, without
A head at all—more of a football type.

Once Flick played for the high-school team, the Wizards.
He was good: in fact, the best. In '46
He bucketed[1] three hundred ninety points,
A county record still. The ball loved Flick.
I saw him rack up[2] thirty-eight or forty
In one home game. His hands were like wild birds.

He never learned a trade, he just sells gas,
Checks oil, and changes flats. Once in a while,
As a gag, he dribbles an inner tube,
But most of us remember anyway.
His hands are fine and nervous on the lug wrench.
It makes no difference to the lug wrench, though.

Off work, he hangs around Mae's luncheonette.
Grease-gray and kind of coiled, he plays pinball,
Smokes those thin cigars, nurses lemon phosphates.[3]
Flick seldom says a word to Mae, just nods
Beyond her face toward bright applauding tiers
Of Necco Wafers, Nibs, and Juju Beads.[4]

1. **bucketed** (buk′ it əd), *v*.: Scored.
2. **rack up:** Accumulate.
3. **lemon phosphates** (fos′ fātz): Carbonated water flavored with lemon syrup.
4. **Necco . . . Beads:** Packaged candy.

John Updike (1932–  ) is one of the foremost contemporary writers in the United States. Born in the small town of Shillington, Pennsylvania, Updike often uses this location as the setting of his writing. Updike brings to his short stories, novels, essays, and poems the eyes and ears of a keen observer. A recurring character in much of his work is the former high-school athlete who missed his chance for success.

## THINKING ABOUT THE SELECTION

### Recalling

1. How does Flick Webb earn his living?
2. What had Flick done in the past? Why did the speaker consider him "the best"?

### Interpreting

3. How do you think Flick got his nickname? Support your answer with details from the poem.
4. Explain the speaker's changing attitude toward Flick.
5. How do you think the speaker would prefer for Flick to behave today? Support your answer with details from the poem.
6. High-school athletes are often the heroes of our youth. F. Scott Fitzgerald has written, "Show me a hero and I will write you a tragedy." In what way is Flick's life a tragedy?

### Applying

7. Why do you think it is difficult for people to live up to their early successes?
8. The poet Dylan Thomas wrote, "A good poem helps to change the shape and significance of the universe, helps to extend everyone's knowledge of himself and the world around him." How does "Ex-Basketball Player" do this?

## ANALYZING LITERATURE

### Understanding Free Verse

**Free verse** is poetry that does not follow any regular pattern of rhythm. Instead, it gains its musical quality from the sounds of the language and the use of punctuation to indicate pauses and stops. Poets sometimes use free verse to give their poems a natural feeling.

Explain why the use of free verse is especially appropriate to the topic of "Ex-Basketball Player."

## CRITICAL THINKING AND READING

### Classifying

**Classifying** means grouping items according to a common element. For example, if you took an inventory of the clothes in your closet, you might group them into two categories: casual clothes and formal clothes.

1. Find all the verbs in this poem that could be classified as basketball terms.
2. Find the nouns that could be classified as gas-station terms.

## UNDERSTANDING LANGUAGE

### Recognizing Colloquial Language

**Colloquial language** sounds like everyday conversation. It contains phrases and idioms commonly used in informal speech. For example, the speaker says that Flick "hangs around Mae's luncheonette." "Hangs around" is an informal way of saying *loiters about.*

Find the meaning of each of the following colloquial phrases based on the verb *hang.*

1. hanging loose
2. hang back
3. hang together
4. get the hang of

## THINKING AND WRITING

### Writing Free Verse

Choose a sport you like to play or watch. Brainstorm to list all the details of the sport that seem especially vivid. Then, using free verse and colloquial language, write a brief poem describing an athlete playing this sport. When you revise, make sure your description is vivid. Proofread your poem and share it with your classmates.

# Making Inferences

An **inference** is a conclusion or intelligent guess. You make an inference after examining the evidence. In other words, you arrive at your opinion or judgment after reasoning from known facts. The word *infer* is based on the Latin root *fer* and carries the meaning of "to bring into." When you infer, you bring information in so that you may reach a logical conclusion.

**Character**

When you read poetry, you often make inferences about characters. You reach decisions about what they are like and what they are thinking and feelings based on the details in the poem. For example, when you read "The Wreck of the Hesperus," you probably made the inference that the girl is terrified. You based your inference on evidence: She shudders and trembles while speaking to her father.

**Past and Present Events**

When you read you make inferences about past and present events. For example, when you read "Music I Heard," you probably inferred that the speaker had once spent many beautiful moments with his beloved. You based this inference on evidence: He says, "Now that I am without you, all is desolate; / All that was once so beautiful is dead." When you read "Making a Fist," you probably inferred that the speaker would continue facing the future with courage. You based your inference on evidence: She says, "I who did not die, who am still living, / still lying in the backseat behind all my questions, / clenching and opening one small hand."

**Tone**

Tone is the attitude toward the subject that the poet conveys through the poem. Since tone is rarely stated directly, when you read you must make inferences based on not only what the poet says but also on how the poet says it. For example, when you read "Miss Rosie," you probably inferred that the speaker's tone was defiant. You based your inference on evidence: The speaker refuses to accept Miss Rosie's fate as her own. She says, "I stand up / through your destruction / I stand up."

## Activity

Read the following poem. Then use your inference-making skills to answer the questions that follow it.

**Woman with Flower**

Naomi Long Madgett

I wouldn't coax the plant if I were you.
Such watchful nurturing may do it harm.
Let the soil rest from so much digging
And wait until it's dry before you water it.
5  The leaf's inclined to find its own direction;
Give it a chance to seek the sunlight for itself.

Much growth is stunted by too careful prodding.
Too eager tenderness.
The things we love we have to learn to leave alone.

1. What do you think has happened to the speaker in the past? Find evidence to support your answer.
2. What lesson has the speaker learned for the future?
3. How would you characterize the speaker?
4. What is the tone of this poem? What evidence supports your answer?

# YOU THE WRITER

**Assignment**

**1.** Write a poem describing a friend, a family member, or a famous person, using figurative language and imagery.

**Prewriting.** Freewrite, describing the subject of your poem. Explore this person's appearance, personality traits, and effect on other people.

**Writing.** Write a short poem using figurative language and imagery to describe your subject. Try to give your poem a musical quality.

**Revising.** Make certain that you have created a vivid portrait of the person. Read the poem aloud to check its musical quality.

**Assignment**

**2.** Write a narrative poem relating a current event. Use a newspaper article about the event as your source.

**Prewriting.** Select an event that interests you. List the events you will cover in your poem. Arrange the events in chronological order.

**Writing.** Write the first draft of your narrative poem. Use rhythm and rhyme to relate events in a lively fashion.

**Revising.** Check that the narrative is told in chronological order. Have you shown why this event has captured your imagination? Does the poem contain both rhythm and rhyme?

**Assignment**

**3.** Imagine you are the state's poet laureate. You are to write a poem extolling the virtues of a place in your state.

**Prewriting.** To get ideas for your poem, look again at poems such as "Eldorado," "The Street," and "My Heart's in the Highlands." Freewrite about places you would like to write about. Then, choose the place you want to write about, and list as many specific images—sights, sounds, smells, and so forth—as you can.

**Writing.** Write the poem, using the figurative language and imagery from the list you have created. Try to help the reader feel as if he or she must visit this place some day.

**Revising:** Make sure your poem accomplishes its purpose—to make readers want to visit this place.

**Assignment**

**1.** You are a visitor to a planet where imagery and figurative language do not exist. In order to make the literature from your planet understood, you have to rewrite a poem without either of these two poetic devices.

**Prewriting.** Choose your poem. Jot down the language that would be missing or altered if figurative language and imagery did not exist.

**Writing.** Rewrite your poem, eliminating all figurative language and imagery. Make certain the poem still delivers the message the poet intended.

**Revising.** Check that no figurative language or imagery remains and that the poet's message has been maintained.

**Assignment**

**2.** You have been asked to read a poem as part of the program for a banquet. The banquet is being held to honor someone who is retiring after long years of service. You want to choose a poem that has the proper tone. Write a letter to the chairperson of the event explaining your reasons for choosing the poem.

**Prewriting.** Ask yourself whether the poem should be humorous or serious. Freewrite about the reasons for your choice.

**Writing.** Write the letter of explanation. State your choice clearly, and support your choice with logical reasons based on your study of poetry.

**Revising.** Make certain that the letter clearly presents the reasons for your choice. Check your paragraph for errors in spelling, grammar, punctuation, and mechanics.

**Assignment**

**3.** Write an analysis of the similarities and differences between lyric and narrative poetry. Determine why a poet would choose one form over the other.

**Prewriting.** Look at one of the narrative poems and one of the lyric poems you have read. Freewrite about each type, noting their differences and similarities.

**Writing.** Write the analysis, comparing the similarities in one paragraph and contrasting the differences in another. Give evidence from the poems you have read that illustrates these similarities and differences. Include introductory and concluding statements that explain the reasons why a poet would choose one form over the other.

**Revising.** Check that you have supported your conclusions and have organized your ideas in a logical manner. Check the analysis for errors in spelling, grammar, and punctuation.

**MINIATURE OF THE ROUND TABLE FROM *LE ROMAN DE LANCELOT DU LAC***
*14th Century French Manuscript*
Bibliothèque Nationale, Paris

# THE LEGEND OF KING ARTHUR

In the ruins of Glastonbury Abbey, which is identified as the original Isle of Avalon, can be seen an ancient grave. A marker on it reads:

> SITE OF KING ARTHUR'S TOMB
> In the year 1191 the bodies of
> King Arthur and his queen were
> said to have been found on the
> south side of the Lady Chapel.
> On 19th April 1278 their remains were
> removed in the presence of
> King Edward I and Queen Eleanor
> to a black marble tomb on this site.

Why, after all these years, was this marker saved even though the abbey that once held it was dissolved in 1539? Why are people today concerned about a sixth-century leader of a small band of Britons who fought against the invading Anglo-Saxons?

The body of tales surrounding King Arthur and his Round Table was the supreme expression of romantic chivalry. The real Arthur most probably was a primitive Welsh battle leader of the sixth century, but his exploits were embellished by legend until he and his court became the very symbols of medieval knighthood.

The best-known English compilation of the legends is *Morte d'Arthur* (1485), written by Sir Thomas Malory, himself a knight. In Malory's time, feudalism was dying and a wealthy middle class was replacing the knights in power and influence. His tale lacks historical perspective, for Malory gave Arthur and his knights the chivalry, Christianity, and idealized courtly love that he regretfully saw dying in his own era. Since Malory's time, many versions of Arthurian legends have been created to entertain readers and present ideas about the ideal society. One of the most enduring was *Idylls of the King* by Alfred, Lord Tennyson, which retells in poetry several of the most popular Arthurian adventures and stresses Arthur's great moral leadership. In the twentieth century, T. H. White has modernized and combined the Arthur stories into *The Once and Future King,* a four-volume novel that suggests hope in our tumultuous times.

# The Legend of King Arthur

**Background**

The King Arthur legend has been written about in poetry and prose for more than a thousand years. A legend is a kind of folktale that exaggerates the achievements of a real-life individual. A sixth-century account of the invasion of Britain by Saxon warriors tells of a heroic British general named Arturius. He led the Britons to a decisive victory over the Saxons and is believed to have been killed in battle. His remains were excavated six centuries later, in 1190, and his coffin bore an inscription that read, "Here lies buried the renowned King Arthur in the Isle of Avalon."

From these scant beginnings, the legend of King Arthur, the gloriously heroic king of the Britons, emerged. The legend was greatly enhanced by French writers who contributed the idea of the Round Table as well as several love stories involving Arthur, Guenevere, and Launcelot. But it was not until the late fifteenth century that the first unified English version of the Arthurian legend was produced in *Le Morte d'Arthur,* or *The Death of Arthur,* by Sir Thomas Malory. Malory's version is the basis for most subsequent versions of the legend of King Arthur.

**Reading Strategy**

You may have some difficulty understanding the language that the characters use in the legends of King Arthur. It is meant to convey a sense of a courtly love and distant time and place. King Arthur, Merlin, and the knights and ladies all speak a very formal and rather stilted form of English to recall the sound of the language spoken in medieval Britain. A strategy for overcoming this difficulty is to remember the overall theme of each legend and to use context clues to determine what each character is saying.

Finally, interact with the literature by using the active reading strategies: question, predict, clarify, summarize, and pull together. Stop to clarify each character's dialogue that you do not immediately understand. By going back and reading the dialogue slowly and by putting it in its proper context, you can unravel the meaning of the most seemingly complicated dialogue.

## Themes

You will encounter the following themes in the legend of King Arthur.

- bravery
- loyalty and devotion
- virtue
- chivalry and the heroic tradition
- wars, jousts, and contests

## Characters

Become familiar with the following characters from the legend of King Arthur before you start reading.

King Pellinore—the king who breaks the news of the death of Arthur's father and predecessor, King Uther the Conqueror.

Sir Ector—father of Sir Kay and guardian of Wart, the future King Arthur

Sir Kay—a young man who wants to go to London to try to remove the sword from the stone and become King of England

Wart—squire to Sir Kay but really Arthur, the future King of England

King Arthur—the son of King Uther. Arthur is the King of England by birth and by his act of removing the sword from the stone

Merlin—a magician and chief councellor to King Arthur

Guenevere—King Arthur's wife

King Leodegrance—Guenevere's father and keeper of the Round Table, which he gives to Arthur as a wedding present

Sir Launcelot du Lake—the best knight at King Arthur's Round Table

Queen Morgan le Fay—King Arthur's sister and an enchantress

Sir Turquine—an enemy of the knights of the Round Table

Sir Brandel, Sir Marhaus, Sir Galind, Sir Brian de Listnois, Sir Sliduke, Sir Mador de la Porte, Sir Mordred—all knights of the Round Table

# GUIDE FOR READING

## Arthur Becomes King of Britain

**T(erence) H(anbury) White** (1906–1964) was born in Bombay, India. At the age of thirty, he resigned a teaching position to research flying, filmmaking, falconry, and the Arthurian legends. His most famous work is the four-part novel *The Once and Future King* (1958), which took nearly twenty years to complete and became the basis for Lerner and Loewe's musical *Camelot* (1960). The following excerpt shows the parodylike style of this retelling of Sir Thomas Malory's fifteenth-century romance *Morte d'Arthur.*

**Legend**

A **legend** is an imaginative story handed down for generations and believed to have an historical basis. With retelling, variations in the story may occur. Legends also give you information about the values and lifestyles of the culture that originated them. For example, the King Arthur legends are replete with incidents of wars, jousts, and chivalry.

**Look For**

What is it about the Arthurian legend that fascinates people of all ages? As you read the following excerpt, look for what the legend tells you about life in King Arthur's time. How does White's humor in retelling the legend contribute to your enjoyment?

**Writing**

Young Arthur, known as "Wart," is surprised to discover an ability he didn't know he had. Imagine surprising everyone with a particular ability that they didn't know you had. Freewrite about this experience, describing your reactions and those of others.

**Vocabulary**

Knowing the following words will help you as you read "Arthur Becomes King of Britain."

**stickler** (stik′lər) *n.:* A person who insists uncompromisingly on the observance of something specified (p. 722)

**pommel** (pum′′l) *n.:* The round knob on the end of the hilt of some swords (p. 723)

**surmise** (sər mīz′) *n.:* Guess (p. 724)

**dematerialize** (dē′ mə tir′ē ə līz′) *v.:* To lose or cause to lose physical form (p. 725)

**sumptuous** (sump′ choo wəs) *adj.:* Magnificent (p. 725)

**palfrey** (pôl′frē) *n.:* A saddle horse, especially one for a woman (p. 726)

**impregnable** (im preg′nə b'l) *adj.:* Not capable of being entered by force (p. 727)

# Arthur Becomes King of Britain

## T. H. White

King Pellinore arrived for the important weekend in a high state of flurry.

"I say," he exclaimed, "do you know? Have you heard? Is it a secret, what?"

"Is what a secret, what?" they asked him.

"Why, the King," cried his majesty. "You know, about the King?"

"What's the matter with the King?" inquired Sir Ector. "You don't say he's comin' down to hunt with those darned hounds of his or anythin' like that?"

CROWNING OF ARTHUR
*The British Library Royal MS*

"He's dead," cried King Pellinore tragically. "He's dead, poor fellah, and can't hunt any more."

Sir Grummore stood up respectfully and took off his cap.

"The King is dead," he said. "Long live the King."

Everybody else felt they ought to stand up too, and the boys' nurse burst into tears.

"There, there," she sobbed. "His loyal highness dead and gone, and him such a respectful gentleman. Many's the illuminated picture I've cut out of him, from the Illustrated Missals, aye, and stuck up over the mantel. From the time when he was in swaddling bands,[1] right through them world towers till he was a-visiting the dispersed areas as the world's Prince Charming, there wasn't a picture of 'im but I had it out, aye, and give 'im a last thought o' nights."

"Compose yourself, Nannie," said Sir Ector.

"It is solemn, isn't it?" said King Pellinore, "what? Uther the Conqueror, 1066 to 1216."

"A solemn moment," said Sir Grummore. "The King is dead. Long live the King."

"We ought to pull down the curtains," said Kay, who was always a stickler for good form, "or half-mast[2] the banners."

"That's right," said Sir Ector. "Somebody go and tell the sergeant-at-arms."

It was obviously the Wart's duty to execute this command, for he was now the junior nobleman present, so he ran out cheerfully to find the sergeant. Soon those who were left in the solar[3] could hear a voice crying out, "Nah then, one-two, special mourning fer 'is lite majesty, lower awai on the command Two!" and then the flapping of all the standards, banners, pennons, pennoncells, banderolls, guidons, streamers and cognizances[4] which made gay the snowy turrets of the Forest Sauvage.

"How did you hear?" asked Sir Ector.

"I was pricking through the purlieus[5] of the forest after that Beast, you know, when I met with a solemn friar of orders gray, and he told me. It's the very latest news."

"Poor old Pendragon," said Sir Ector.

"The King is dead," said Sir Grummore solemnly. "Long live the King."

"It is all very well for you to keep on mentioning that, my dear Grummore," exclaimed King Pellinore petulantly, "but who is this King, what, that is to live so long, what, accordin' to you?"

"Well, his heir," said Sir Grummore, rather taken aback.

"Our blessed monarch," said the Nurse tearfully, "never had no hair. Anybody that studied the loyal family knowed that."

"Good gracious!" exclaimed Sir Ector. "But he must have had a next-of-kin?"

"That's just it," cried King Pellinore in high excitement. "That's the excitin' part of it, what? No hair and no next of skin, and who's to succeed to the throne? That's what my friar was so excited about, what, and why he was asking who could succeed to what, what? What?"

"Do you mean to tell me," exclaimed Sir Grummore indignantly, "that there ain't no King of Gramarye?"

"Not a scrap of one," cried King Pellinore, feeling important. "And there have been signs and wonders of no mean might."

"I think it's a scandal," said Sir Grummore. "God knows what the dear old country is comin' to."

---

**1. swaddling bands:** Long, narrows bands of cloths wrapped around a newborn baby in former times.

**2. half-mast** (haf mast′) v.: Hang a flag at half-mast.

**3. solar** (sō′ lər) n.: Here, sun room. *Solar* is often used as an adjective.

---

**4. standards . . . cognizances** (käg′ nə zən′ səz) n.: Banners or flags.

**5. purlieus** (pur′ lo͞oz) n.: An outlying part of a forest, exempted from forest laws.

"What sort of signs and wonders?" asked Sir Ector.

"Well, there has appeared a sort of sword in a stone, what, in a sort of a church. Not in the church, if you see what I mean, and not in the stone, but that sort of thing, what, like you might say."

"I don't know what the Church is coming to," said Sir Grummore.

"It's in an anvil,"[6] explained the King.

"The Church?"

"No, the sword."

"But I thought you said the sword was in the stone?"

"No," said King Pellinore. "The stone is outside the Church."

"Look here, Pellinore," said Sir Ector. "You have a bit of a rest, old boy, and start again. Here, drink up this horn of mead[7] and take it easy."

"The sword," said King Pellinore, "is stuck through an anvil which stands on a stone. It goes right through the anvil and into the stone. The anvil is stuck to the stone. The stone stands outside a church. Give me some more mead."

"I don't think that's much of a wonder," remarked Sir Grummore. "What I wonder at is that they should allow such things to happen. But you can't tell nowadays, what with all these Saxon agitators."[8]

"My dear fellah," cried Pellinore, getting excited again, "it's not where the stone is, what, that I'm trying to tell you, but what is written on it, what, where it is."

"What?"

"Why, on its pommel."

"Come on, Pellinore," said Sir Ector. "You just sit quite still with your face to the wall for a minute, and then tell us what you are talkin' about. Take it easy, old boy. No need for hurryin'. You sit still and look at the wall, there's a good chap, and talk as slow as you can."

"There are words written on this sword in this stone outside this church," cried King Pellinore piteously, "and these words are as follows. Oh, do try to listen to me, you two, instead of interruptin' all the time about nothin', for it makes a man's head go ever so."

"What are these words?" asked Kay.

"These words say this," said King Pellinore, "so far as I can understand from that old friar of orders gray."

"Go on, do," said Kay, for the King had come to a halt.

"Go on," said Sir Ector, "what do these words on this sword in this anvil in this stone outside this church, say?"

King Pellinore closed his eyes tight, extended his arms in both directions, and announced in capital letters, "Whoso Pulleth Out This Sword of this Stone and Anvil, is Rightwise King Born of All England."

"Who said that?" asked Sir Grummore.

"But the sword said it, like I tell you."

"Talkative weapon," remarked Sir Grummore skeptically.

"It was written on it," cried the King angrily. "Written on it in letters of gold."

"Why didn't you pull it out then?" asked Sir Grummore.

"But I tell you that I wasn't there. All this that I am telling you was told to me by that friar I was telling you of, like I tell you."

"Has this sword with this inscription been pulled out?" inquired Sir Ector.

"No," whispered King Pellinore dramatically. "That's where the whole excitement comes in. They can't pull this sword out at all, although they have all been tryin' like fun, and so they have had to proclaim a tournament all over England, for New Year's

---

**6. anvil** (an'vəl) *n.*: An iron or steel block.

**7. mead** (mēd) *n.*: A drink made of fermented honey and water, often with spices or fruit added.

**8. Saxon** (sak's'n) **agitators:** Members of an ancient Germanic people who invaded and conquered parts of England in the fifth and sixth centuries A.D.

Day, so that the man who comes to the tournament and pulls out the sword can be King of all England forever, what, I say?"

"Oh, father," cried Kay. "The man who pulls that sword out of the stone will be the King of England. Can't we go to the tournament, father, and have a shot?"

"Couldn't think of it," said Sir Ector.

"Long way to London," said Sir Grummore, shaking his head.

"My father went there once," said King Pellinore.

Kay said, "Oh, surely we could go? When I am knighted I shall have to go to a tournament somewhere, and this one happens at just the right date. All the best people will be there, and we should see the famous knights and great kings. It does not matter about the sword, of course, but think of the tournament, probably the greatest there has ever been in Gramarye, and all the things we should see and do. Dear father, let me go to this tourney, if you love me, so that I may bear away the prize of all, in my maiden fight."

"But, Kay," said Sir Ector, "I have never been to London."

"All the more reason to go. I believe that anybody who does not go for a tournament like this will be proving that he has no noble blood in his veins. Think what people will say about us, if we do not go and have a shot at that sword. They will say that Sir Ector's family was too vulgar and knew it had no chance."

"We all know the family has no chance," said Sir Ector, "that is, for the sword."

"Lot of people in London," remarked Sir Grummore, with a wild surmise. "So they say."

He took a deep breath and goggled at his host with eyes like marbles.

"And shops," added King Pellinore suddenly, also beginning to breathe heavily.

"Dang it!" cried Sir Ector, bumping his horn mug on the table so that it spilled. "Let's all go to London, then, and see the new King!"

They rose up as one man.

"Why shouldn't I be as good a man as my father?" exclaimed King Pellinore.

"Dash it all," cried Sir Grummore. "After all, it is the capital!"

"Hurray!" shouted Kay.

"Lord have mercy," said the nurse.

At this moment the Wart came in with Merlyn, and everybody was too excited to notice that, if he had not been grown up now, he would have been on the verge of tears.

"Oh, Wart," cried Kay, forgetting for the moment that he was only addressing his squire, and slipping back into the familiarity of their boyhood. "What do you think? We are all going to London for a great tournament on New Year's Day!"

"Are we?"

"Yes, and you will carry my shield and spears for the jousts, and I shall win the palm[9] of everybody and be a great knight!"

"Well, I am glad we are going," said the Wart, "for Merlyn is leaving us too."

"Oh, we shan't need Merlyn."

"He is leaving us," repeated the Wart.

"Leavin' us?" asked Sir Ector. "I thought it was we that were leavin'?"

"He is going away from the Forest Sauvage."

Sir Ector said, "Come now, Merlyn, what's all this about? I don't understand all this a bit."

"I have come to say Goodbye, Sir Ector," said the old magician. "Tomorrow my pupil Kay will be knighted, and the next week my other pupil will go away as his squire. I have outlived my usefulness here, and it is time to go."

---

**9. win the palm:** Be the winner. A palm leaf is a symbol of victory.

"Now, now, don't say that," said Sir Ector. "I think you're a jolly useful chap whatever happens. You just stay and teach me, or be the librarian or something. Don't you leave an old man alone, after the children have flown."

"We shall all meet again," said Merlyn. "There is no cause to be sad."

"Don't go," said Kay.

"I must go," replied their tutor. "We have had a good time while we were young, but it is in the nature of Time to fly. There are many things in other parts of the kingdom which I ought to be attending to just now, and it is a specially busy time for me. Come, Archimedes, say Goodbye to the company."

"Goodbye," said Archimedes tenderly to the Wart.

"Goodbye," said the Wart without looking up at all.

"But you can't go," cried Sir Ector, "not without a month's notice."

"Can't I?" replied Merlyn, taking up the position always used by philosophers who propose to dematerialize. He stood on his toes, while Archimedes held tight to his shoulder—began to spin on them slowly like a top—spun faster and faster till he was only a blur of grayish light—and in a few seconds there was no one there at all.

"Goodbye, Wart," cried two faint voices outside the solar window.

"Goodbye," said the Wart for the last time—and the poor fellow went quickly out of the room.

The knighting took place in a whirl of preparations. Kay's sumptuous bath had to be set up in the box room, between two towel-horses and an old box of selected games which contained a worn-out straw dart-board—it was called fléchette in those days—because all the other rooms were full of packing. The nurse spent the whole time constructing new warm pants for everybody, on the principle that the climate of any place outside the Forest Sauvage must be treacherous to the extreme, and, as for the sergeant, he polished all the armor till it was quite brittle and sharpened the swords till they were almost worn away.

At last it was time to set out.

Perhaps, if you happen not to have lived in the Old England of the twelfth century, or whenever it was, and in a remote castle on the borders of the Marshes at that, you will find it difficult to imagine the wonders of their journey.

The road, or track, ran most of the time along the high ridges of the hills or downs, and they could look down on either side of them upon the desolate marshes where the snowy reeds sighed, and the ice crackled, and the duck in the red sunsets quacked loud on the winter air. The whole country was like that. Perhaps there would be a moory marsh on one side of the ridge, and a forest of a hundred thousand acres on the other, with all the great branches weighted in white. They could sometimes see a wisp of smoke among the trees, or a huddle of buildings far out among the impassable reeds, and twice they came to quite respectable towns which had several inns to boast of, but on the whole it was an England without civilization. The better roads were cleared of cover for a bow-shot on either side of them, lest the traveler should be slain by hidden thieves.

They slept where they could, sometimes in the hut of some cottager who was prepared to welcome them, sometimes in the castle of a brother knight who invited them to refresh themselves, sometimes in the firelight and fleas of a dirty little hovel with a bush tied to a pole outside it—this was the signboard used at that time by inns—and once or twice on the open ground, all huddled together for warmth between their grazing chargers. Wherever they went and wherever they slept, the east wind whistled in the reeds, and the geese went over high in the starlight, honking at the stars.

London was full to the brim. If Sir Ector had not been lucky enough to own a little land in Pie Street, on which there stood a respectable inn, they would have been hard put to it to find a lodging. But he did own it, and as a matter of fact drew most of his dividends from that source, so they were able to get three beds between the five of them. They thought themselves fortunate.

On the first day of the tournament, Sir Kay managed to get them on the way to the lists at least an hour before the jousts could possibly begin. He had lain awake all night, imagining how he was going to beat the best barons in England, and he had not been able to eat his breakfast. Now he rode at the front of the cavalcade, with pale cheeks, and Wart wished there was something he could do to calm him down.

For country people, who only knew the dismantled tilting ground[10] of Sir Ector's castle, the scene which met their eyes was ravishing. It was a huge green pit in the earth, about as big as the arena of a football match. It lay ten feet lower than the surrounding country, with sloping banks, and the snow had been swept off it. It had been kept warm with straw, which had been cleared off that morning, and now the close-worn grass sparkled green in the white landscape. Round the arena there was a world of color so dazzling and moving and twinkling as to make one blink one's eyes. The wooden grandstands were painted in scarlet and white. The silk pavilions of famous people, pitched on every side, were azure and green and saffron and checkered.

The pennons and pennoncells which floated everywhere in the sharp wind were flapping with every color of the rainbow, as they strained and slapped at their flagpoles, and the barrier down the middle of the arena itself was done in chessboard squares of black and white. Most of the combatants and their friends had not yet arrived, but one could see from those few who had come how the very people would turn the scene into a bank of flowers, and how the armor would flash, and the scalloped sleeves of the heralds jig in the wind, as they raised their brazen trumpets to their lips to shake the fleecy clouds of winter with joyances[11] and fanfares.

"Good heavens!" cried Sir Kay. "I have left my sword at home."

"Can't joust without a sword," said Sir Grummore. "Quite irregular."

"Better go and fetch it," said Sir Ector. "You have time."

"My squire will do," said Sir Kay. "What an awful mistake to make! Here, squire, ride hard back to the inn and fetch my sword. You shall have a shilling[12] if you fetch it in time."

The Wart went as pale as Sir Kay was, and looked as if he were going to strike him. Then he said, "It shall be done, master," and turned his ambling palfrey against the stream of newcomers. He began to push his way toward their hostelry[13] as best he might.

"To offer me money!" cried the Wart to himself. "To look down at this beastly little donkey-affair off his great charger and to call me Squire! Oh, Merlyn, give me patience with the brute, and stop me from throwing his filthy shilling in his face."

When he got to the inn it was closed. Everybody had thronged to see the famous

---

**10. tilting ground:** Ground on which a joust takes place.

**11. joyances** (joi'əns əz) *n*.: Old word for *rejoicing*.
**12. shilling** (shil' iŋ) *n*.: British silver coin.
**13. hostelry** (häs' t'l rē) *n*.: Inn.

tournament, and the entire household had followed after the mob. Those were lawless days and it was not safe to leave your house —or even to go to sleep in it—unless you were certain that it was impregnable. The wooden shutters bolted over the downstairs windows were two inches thick, and the doors were double-barred.

"Now what do I do," asked the Wart, "to earn my shilling?"

He looked ruefully at the blind little inn, and began to laugh.

"Poor Kay," he said. "All that shilling stuff was only because he was scared and miserable, and now he has good cause to be. Well, he shall have a sword of some sort if I have to break into the Tower of London.

"How does one get hold of a sword?" he continued. "Where can I steal one? Could I waylay some knight even if I am mounted on an ambling pad, and take his weapons by force? There must be some swordsmith or armorer in a great town like this, whose shop would be still open."

He turned his mount and cantered off along the street. There was a quiet church-yard at the end of it, with a kind of square in front of the church door. In the middle of the square there was a heavy stone with an anvil on it, and a fine new sword was stuck through the anvil.

"Well," said the Wart, "I suppose it is some sort of war memorial, but it will have to do. I am sure nobody would grudge Kay a war memorial, if they knew his desperate straits."

He tied his reins round a post of the lych gate,[14] strode up the gravel path, and took hold of the sword.

"Come, sword," he said. "I must cry your mercy and take you for a better cause.

"This is extraordinary," said the Wart.

"I feel strange when I have hold of this sword, and I notice everything much more clearly. Look at the beautiful gargoyles[15] of the church, and of the monastery which it belongs to. See how splendidly all the famous banners in the aisle are waving. How nobly that yew[16] holds up the red flakes of its timbers to worship God. How clean the snow is. I can smell something like sweet briar—and is it music that I hear?"

It was music, whether of pan-pipes or of recorders, and the light in the churchyard was so clear, without being dazzling, that one could have picked a pin out twenty yards away.

"There is something in this place," said the Wart. "There are people. Oh, people, what do you want?"

Nobody answered him, but the music was loud and the light beautiful.

"People," cried the Wart, "I must take this sword. It is not for me, but for Kay. I will bring it back."

There was still no answer, and Wart turned back to the anvil. He saw the golden letters, which he did not read, and the jewels on the pommel, flashing in the lovely light.

"Come, sword," said the Wart.

He took hold of the handles with both hands, and strained against the stone. There was a melodious consort[17] on the recorders, but nothing moved.

The Wart let go of the handles, when they were beginning to bite into the palms of his hands, and stepped back, seeing stars.

"It is well fixed," he said.

He took hold of it again and pulled with all his might. The music played more strongly, and the light all about the churchyard

---

**14. lych** (*lich'*) **gate**: A roofed gate at the entrance to a churchyard.

**15. gargoyles** (gär' goilz) *n.*: Projecting ornaments, usually grotesquely carved animals or fantastic creatures, on a building.
**16. yew** (yōō) *n.*: Evergreen shrubs and trees of the yew family.
**17. consort** (kän' sôrt) *n.*: Harmony of sounds.

glowed like amethysts; but the sword still stuck.

"Oh, Merlyn," cried the Wart, "help me to get this weapon."

There was a kind of rushing noise, and a long chord played along with it. All round the churchyard there were hundreds of old friends. They rose over the church wall all together, like the Punch-and-Judy[18] ghosts of remembered days, and there were badgers and nightingales and vulgar crows and hares and wild geese and falcons and fishes and dogs and dainty unicorns and solitary wasps and hedgehogs and griffins and the thousand other animals he had met. They loomed round the church wall, the lovers and helpers of the Wart, and they all spoke solemnly in turn. Some of them had come from the banners in the church, where they were painted in heraldry, some from the waters and the sky and the fields about —but all, down to the smallest shrew mouse, had come to help on account of love. Wart felt his power grow.

"Put your back into it," said a luce (or pike) off one of the heraldic banners, "as you once did when I was going to snap you up. Remember that power springs from the nape of the neck."

"What about those forearms," asked a badger gravely, "that are held together by a chest? Come along, my dear embryo,[19] and find your tool."

A merlin sitting at the top of the yew tree cried out, "Now then, Captain Wart, what is the first law of the foot? I thought I once heard something about never letting go?"

"Don't work like a stalling woodpecker," urged a tawny owl affectionately. "Keep up a steady effort, my duck, and you will have it yet."

A white-front said, "Now, Wart, if you were once able to fly the great North Sea, surely you can coordinate a few little wing-muscles here and there? Fold your powers together, with the spirit of your mind, and it will come out like butter. Come along, Homo sapiens,[20] for all we humble friends of yours are waiting here to cheer."

The Wart walked up to the great sword for the third time. He put out his right hand softly and drew it out as gently as from a scabbard.

There was a lot of cheering, a noise like a hurdy-gurdy[21] which went on and on. In the middle of this noise, after a long time, he saw Kay and gave him the sword. The people at the tournament were making a frightful row.

"But this is not my sword," said Sir Kay.

"It was the only one I could get," said the Wart. "The inn was locked."

"It is a nice-looking sword. Where did you get it?"

"I found it stuck in a stone, outside a church."

Sir Kay had been watching the tilting nervously, waiting for his turn. He had not paid much attention to his squire.

"That is a funny place to find one," he said.

"Yes, it was stuck through an anvil."

"What?" cried Sir Kay, suddenly rounding upon him. "Did you just say this sword was stuck in a stone?"

"It was," said the Wart. "It was a sort of war memorial."

---

**18. Punch-and-Judy:** Puppets of the quarrelsome Punch and his wife Judy, who constantly fight in a comical way.
**19. embryo** (em′ brē ō) *n.:* Anything in an early stage of development.

**20. Homo sapiens** (hō′ mō sā′ pē ənz′): Human being.
**21. hurdy-gurdy** (hur′ dē gur′ dē) *n.:* A musical instrument, like a barrel organ, played by turning a crank.

**GALLAHAD AND SWORD IN STONE**
*The British Library Royal MS*

Sir Kay stared at him for several seconds in amazement, opened his mouth, shut it again, licked his lips, then turned his back and plunged through the crowd. He was looking for Sir Ector, and the Wart followed after him.

"Father," cried Sir Kay, "come here a moment."

"Yes, my boy," said Sir Ector. "Splendid falls these professional chaps do manage. Why, what's the matter, Kay? You look as white as a sheet."

"Do you remember that sword which the King of England would pull out?"

"Yes."

"Well, here it is. I have it. It is in my hand. I pulled it out."

Sir Ector did not say anything silly. He looked at Kay and he looked at the Wart. Then he stared at Kay again, long and lovingly, and said, "We will go back to the church."

"Now then, Kay," he said, when they were at the church door. He looked at his firstborn kindly, but straight between the eyes. "Here is the stone, and you have the sword. It will make you the King of England. You are my son that I am proud of, and always will be, whatever you do. Will you promise me that you took it out by your own might?"

Kay looked at his father. He also looked at the Wart and at the sword.

Then he handed the sword to the Wart quite quietly.

He said, "I am a liar. Wart pulled it out."

As far as the Wart was concerned, there was a time after this in which Sir Ector kept telling him to put the sword back into the stone—which he did—and in which Sir Ector and Kay then vainly tried to take it out. The Wart took it out for them, and stuck it back again once or twice. After this, there was another time which was more painful.

He saw that his dear guardian was looking quite old and powerless, and that he was kneeling down with difficulty on a gouty[22] knee.

"Sir," said Sir Ector, without looking up, although he was speaking to his own boy.

"Please do not do this, father," said the Wart, kneeling down also. "Let me help you up, Sir Ector, because you are making me unhappy."

"Nay, nay, my lord," said Sir Ector, with some very feeble old tears. "I was never your father nor of your blood, but I wote[23] well ye are of an higher blood than I wend[24] ye were."

"Plenty of people have told me you are not my father," said the Wart, "but it does not matter a bit."

"Sir," said Sir Ector humbly, "will ye be my good and gracious lord when ye are King?"

"Don't!" said the Wart.

"Sir," said Sir Ector, "I will ask no more of you but that you will make my son, your foster-brother, Sir Kay, seneschal[25] of all your lands?"

Kay was kneeling down too, and it was more than the Wart could bear.

"Oh, do stop," he cried. "Of course he can be seneschal, if I have got to be this King, and, oh, father, don't kneel down like that, because it breaks my heart. Please get up, Sir Ector, and don't make everything so horrible. Oh, dear, oh, dear, I wish I had never seen that filthy sword at all."

And the Wart also burst into tears.

---

**22. gouty** (gout′ ē) *adj*: Having gout, a disease causing swelling and severe pain in the joints.

**23. wote** (wōt) *v*.: Old word meaning *know*.
**24. wend** (wend) *v*.: Here, old word meaning *thought*.
**25. seneschal** (sen′ ə shəl) *n*.: A steward in the house of a medieval noble.

# THINKING ABOUT THE SELECTION

## Recalling

1. What news does King Pellinore bring? What is significant about this news?
2. Explain how the new King of England is to be chosen.
3. At the end of this selection, why do Sir Kay and Sir Ector kneel? Explain the effect their kneeling has on the Wart.

## Interpreting

4. In what ways is the Wart's drawing the sword from the stone a moment of magic and mystery?
5. What do Sir Kay's explanations to Sir Ector about pulling the sword reveal about Sir Kay's character?
6. How does the Wart feel about becoming King?

## Applying

7. Reread the words of encouragement given by the luce, the badger, the merlin, the tawny owl, and the white-front. How might their advice be useful to the future king and pertinent to life in general?

# ANALYZING LITERATURE

## Understanding the Legend

A **legend** is an imaginative story handed down for generations and believed, but not proved, to have an historical basis. A King Arthur may actually have existed in the sixth century. A legend provides information about the culture that created it. For instance, the idea of chivalry in King Arthur legends tells you that brave and courteous behavior in knights was valued by people of that time.

1. On the basis of this legend, what conclusions do you draw about loyalty to the king?
2. Do you think warfare was a common occurence during this period? What evidence leads you to this opinion?

# CRITICAL THINKING AND READING

## Recognizing Tone

**Tone** is the attitude a writer takes toward his or her subject. You can recognize the tone of a literary work based on the attitude the writer shows through certain words and phrases. The tone of "Arthur Becomes King of Britain" is light and humorous.

1. Find three examples in this selection that provide evidence from which you can infer a light and humorous tone.
2. Find at least two examples in which the author seems to parody, or poke gentle fun at, the King Arthur legend.

# UNDERSTANDING LANGUAGE

## Finding Word Origins

The word *brazen* derives from Old English. Originally it meant "made of brass." Today, *brazen* also means "bold, impudent, or shameless." This meaning developed from the idea that the sound of brass clashing is loud, piercing, and harsh.

Use a dictionary to find the origins and definitions of the following words. Then use each word correctly in a sentence.

1. purlieus
2. cavalcade
3. dismantled
4. scalloped

# GUIDE FOR READING

## The Marriage of King Arthur

**Sir Thomas Malory** (c. 1400–1471) is believed to have been born in Warwickshire, England, where he was charged with various crimes that he may not have committed. He may have spent as many as twenty-one years in prison, where he wrote *Le Morte d'Arthur* (French for "The Death of Arthur"), based on the legend of King Arthur. Malory lived during a troubled time; he may have written this work—from which "The Marriage of King Arthur" is taken —to recapture the chivalric ideals that his age had lost.

### Chivalry

**Chivalry** was a code of brave and courteous conduct for knights in the Middle Ages. According to this system of morals and manners honored by King Arthur's Knights of the Round Table, a knight vowed to remain faithful to God, loyal to his king, and true to his lady-love. He used his strength and skills to aid ladies in distress; to defend and protect the weak and underprivileged; and to champion right against evil, injustice, and cruelty. He was generous to all, courageous in the face of the enemy, and prepared to die for his country.

### Look For

Chivalry prevails in the Arthurian stories. As you read "The Marriage of King Arthur," look for the basic tenets of the code of chivalry.

### Writing

What standards of behavior do you think are important? Think of a code of conduct for daily living. List the main points of this code.

### Vocabulary

Knowing the following words will help you as you read "The Marriage of King Arthur."

**grace** (grās) *n.*: Seemingly effortless beauty or charm of movement, form, or proportion (p. 733)

**damsel** (dam′z'l) *n.*: A young woman or girl; maiden (p. 733)

**worthy** (wʉr′*th*ē) *adj.*: Honorable; admirable (p. 733)

**prowess** (prou′is) *n.*: Skill; bravery (p. 733)

**homage** (häm′ij) *n.*: Public show of honor and allegiance (p. 734)

**void** (void) *adj.*: Containing no matter; empty (p. 734)

**treason** (trē′z'n) *n.*: Betrayal of trust or confidence; treachery (p. 734)

**forfeiture** (fôr′fə chər) *n.*: The act of giving up something as punishment for a crime (p. 734)

# The Marriage of King Arthur

## Sir Thomas Malory

*How King Arthur took a wife, and wedded Guenevere, daughter to Leodegrance, King of the Land of Cameliard, who had the Round Table*

In the beginning of Arthur, after he was chosen king by adventure and by grace, most of the barons knew not that he was Uther Pendragon's son, unless Merlin told them. But yet many kings and lords made war against him for that cause, but well Arthur overcame them all. For most of the days of his life Arthur was ruled much by the counsel of Merlin. So it fell on a time King Arthur said unto Merlin, "My barons will let me have no rest, unless I take a wife, and I will none take but by thy counsel and by thine advice."

"It is well done," said Merlin, "that ye take a wife, for a man of your bounty[1] and noblesse[2] should not be without a wife. Now is there any that ye love more than another?"

"Yea," said King Arthur, "I love Guenevere, the daughter of King Leodegrance of the land of Cameliard, who holdeth in his house the Table Round that ye told me had been given to him by my father Uther. And this damsel is the most valiant and fairest lady that I know living, or yet that ever I could find."

"Sir," said Merlin, "as of her beauty and fairness she is one of the fairest alive, but if ye loved her not so well as ye do, I should find you a damsel of beauty and of goodness that should like you and please you, if your heart were not set; but as a man's heart is set, he will be loath to return."[3]

"That is truth," said King Arthur.

Then Merlin asked the king for men to go with him to enquire of Guenevere, and so the king granted him, and Merlin went forth unto King Leodegrance of Cameliard, and told him of the desire of the king that he would have for his wife Guenevere, his daughter.

"That is to me," said King Leodegrance, "the best tidings that ever I heard, that so worthy a king of prowess and noblesse will wed my daughter. And I would give him lands if I thought it would please him, but he has lands enough; instead I shall send him a gift that shall please him much more, for I shall give him the Table Round, which Uther Pendragon gave me, and when it is full complete, there is a hundred knights and fifty. A hundred good knights I have

---

**1. bounty** (boun′ tē) *n.*: Generosity.
**2. noblesse** (nō bles′) *n.*: Nobility.

**3. loath** (lōth) **to return:** Reluctant to change his mind.

myself, but I faute[4] fifty, for so many have been slain in my days."

And so Leodegrance delivered his daughter Guenevere unto Merlin, and the Table Round with the hundred knights, and so they rode freshly, with great royalty, part of the way by water and part of the way by land, till they came nigh unto London.

*How the Knights of the Round Table were ordained[5] and their sieges[6] blessed by the Bishop of Canterbury*

When King Arthur heard of the coming of Guenevere and the hundred knights with the Table Round, then King Arthur made great joy for her coming and for that rich present and said openly, "This fair lady is welcome, for I have loved her long, and therefore there is nothing so lief to me. And these knights with the Round Table please me more than right great riches." And in all haste the king arranged for the marriage and the coronation in the most honorable way that could be devised.

"Now, Merlin," said King Arthur, "go thou and espy me in all this land fifty knights which be of most prowess and worship."

Within a short time Merlin had found twenty and eight knights, but no more could he find. Then the Bishop of Canterbury was fetched, and he blessed the sieges with great royalty and devotion, and there set the eight and twenty knights in their sieges. And when this was done Merlin said, "Fair sirs, ye must all arise and come to King Arthur to do him homage; then he will have the better will to maintain you."[7]

And so they arose and did their homage, and when they were gone Merlin found in every siege letters of gold that told the knight's name that had been sitting therein. But two sieges were void.

And so anon came young Gawain and asked the king a gift. "Ask," said the king, "and I shall grant it you."

"Sir, I ask that ye will make me knight on the same day ye shall wed fair Guenevere."

"I will do it with a good will," said King Arthur, "and do unto you all the worship that I may, for I must because ye are my nephew, my sister's son.". . .

Then was the high feast made ready, and the king was wedded at Camelot unto Dame Guenevere, in the church of Saint Stephen's, with great solemnity. And as every man was set according to his degree,[8] Merlin went to all the knights of the Round Table, and bade them sit still, that none of them remove. . . .

Then the king established all his knights, and he gave lands to those that had no lands, and charged them never to do anything outrageous nor to commit murder, and always to flee treason; also, by no means to be cruel, but to give mercy unto him that asketh mercy, upon pain of forfeiture of their worship and lordship of King Arthur forevermore; and always to do ladies, damsels, and gentlewomen succor,[9] upon pain of death. Also, that no man do battle in a wrongful quarrel against the law or for world's goods. Unto this were all the knights sworn of the Table Round, both old and young. And every year were they sworn at the high feast of Pentecost.[10]

---

**4. faute** (fōt) *v.*: Lack.
**5. ordained** (ôr dānd') *v.*: Established.
**6. sieges** (sēj' əs) *n.*: Seats.
**7. better will to maintain you:** A stronger desire to provide for and to protect you.

**8. degree:** Rank.
**9. succor** (suk' ər) *n.*: Aid; help.
**10. Pentecost** (pen' tə kôst') *n.*: A Christian religious celebration.

## THINKING ABOUT THE SELECTION

### Recalling

1. Why does Arthur value Guenevere above other women?
2. What is King Leodegrance's response to Arthur's request to marry his daughter?
3. What else occurs on the day Arthur weds Guenevere?
4. To what does King Arthur swear his knights?

### Interpreting

5. Explain the significance of Leodegrance's gift to Arthur?
6. The King Arthur legends tell of a time in the early history of England when a belief in magic was supplanted by Christianity. What elements do you find of both magic and religion in this legend?

### Applying

7. King Leodegrance gave Arthur the Round Table upon agreeing that Arthur would marry his daughter. How does this compare with customs today when two people marry?

## ANALYZING LITERATURE

### Understanding Chivalry

**Chivalry,** a knightly code of morals and manners in the Middle Ages, was more an ideal than a reality. Many of our modern ideas about heroism come in part from this vision of knighthood. The stirring idea of a brave and honorable knight who lives according to a high personal moral code has endured through the ages.

1. In your own words, summarize the code of conduct that Arthur establishes for his knights.
2. How does Merlin's response to King Arthur about marrying Guenevere fit in with the idea of chivalry?
3. Is chivalry alive in the modern world? Use examples from life to support your answer.

## CRITICAL THINKING AND READING

### Understanding Inversion

**Inversion** is a reversal of standard word order. An example of standard word order is "I went into the town to see the zebras in the zoo." An example of inverted word order is "Into the town to see the zebras in the zoo went I."

Inverted word order sounds somewhat artificial today, but was commonly used in literature long ago. For example, King Arthur in "The Marriage of King Arthur" says that Guenevere is the "fairest lady . . . that ever I could find."

Find two other examples of inverted word order in this selection, and rewrite the sentence or phrase in standard word order.

## UNDERSTANDING LANGUAGE

### Appreciating Changes in Language

As cultures mix and change, so does language. One way in which language changes is through its vocabulary. Words that have fallen out of use altogether are called **archaic.** For example, the archaic word *faute,* meaning "lack," derives, or comes originally, from a French word meaning "fault."

Find three other examples of archaic words in this selection. Look in a dictionary to find their meaning.

## THINKING AND WRITING

### Writing About a Code of Conduct

Write an essay for a self-help magazine explaining a code of conduct appropriate for today. Use the list you developed earlier as the basis for your essay. First freewrite about why you think a code of conduct is valuable in life. Then use this information in writing your essay. Revise your essay to make sure you have included examples that support your opinion. Proofread for errors in spelling, grammar, and punctuation.

# GUIDE FOR READING

## The Adventures of Sir Launcelot

**The Hero and the Heroic Tradition**

In the legends of King Arthur, the **hero** is usually a knight whose heroism takes a special form. A true knight is, above all, chivalrous. He fights to overcome evil, to honor promises he has made, and to serve his king and his lady, to whom he has sworn everlasting loyalty. In "The Adventures of Sir Launcelot" Sir Launcelot is an ideal knight who performs his duties with bravado and ease.

Through the centuries, the **heroic tradition** of the King Arthur legends has come to include the ideas of glory, nobility, justice, adventure, and loyalty.

**Look For**

As you read "The Adventures of Sir Launcelot," look for the ways in which Sir Launcelot upholds the ideals of chivalry and the heroic tradition.

**Writing**

The novelist Nathaniel Hawthorne has written; "A hero cannot be a hero unless in a heroic world." Freewrite about the meaning of this quotation. React to it. Do you agree with it or disagree?

**Vocabulary**

Knowing the following words will help you as you read "The Adventures of Sir Launcelot."

**sundry** (sun'drē) *adj.*: Various; several; miscellaneous (p. 737)

**wroth** (rôth) *adj.*: Archaic form of wrathful; angry (p. 738)

**manor** (man'ər) *n.*: The district over which a lord had domain in medieval western Europe (p. 738)

**ford** (fôrd) *n.*: A shallow place in a body of water, such as a river, where a crossing can be made (p. 738)

**buffet** (buf'it) *n.*: A blow or cuff with, or as if with, the hand (p. 738)

**enchantment** (in chant'mənt) *n.*: An act of casting under a spell (p. 738)

**proffered** (präf'ərd) *v.*: Offered or tendered (p. 742)

**repast** (ri past') *n.*: A meal, or the food eaten or provided at a meal (p. 746)

# The Adventures of Sir Launcelot

## Sir Thomas Malory

*How Sir Launcelot and Sir Lionel departed from the court, and how Sir Lionel left him sleeping and was taken*

Soon all the knights of the Table Round arrived to take part in jousts and tournaments, and some of the knights increased so in arms and worship that they passed all their fellows in prowess and noble deeds. That was true of many; but especially it was true of Sir Launcelot du Lake, for in all tournaments and jousts and deeds of arms, both for life and death, he passed all other knights, and at no time was he overcome except by treason or enchantment. Wherefore Queen Guenevere held him in great favor, and for her he did many deeds of arms.

Thus Sir Launcelot rested himself for a long time with play and game. And then he thought to prove himself in strange adventures, so he bade his nephew, Sir Lionel, to make ready to seek adventures. They mounted on their horses, armed at all rights,[1] and rode into a deep forest and so into a deep plain.

The weather was hot about noon, and Sir Launcelot had a great desire to sleep. Sir Lionel espied a great apple tree that stood by a hedge, and said, "Brother, yonder is a fair shadow; there may we rest."

"It is well said, fair brother," said Sir Launcelot, so they alighted there and tied their horses unto sundry trees. Sir Launcelot lay down under an apple tree, and his helm[2] he laid under his head. And Sir Lionel waked while he slept. So Sir Launcelot was asleep passing fast.

In the meanwhile there came three knights riding, as fast fleeing as ever they might ride. And following them was one knight. When Sir Lionel saw him, he thought he had never seen so great a knight, nor so well faring a man, neither so well appareled unto all rights. In a while this strong knight overtook one of the three knights, and he smote him to the cold earth so that he lay still. And then he rode unto the second knight, and smote him so that man and horse fell down. And then straight to the third knight he rode, and smote him. Then he alighted and reined his horse on the bridle, and bound all three knights fast with the reins of their own bridles.

When Sir Lionel saw the knight do this, he decided to assay[3] him, and made ready, and quietly took his horse, so as not to awake Sir Launcelot. And when he was mounted upon his horse, he overtook this strong knight, and bade him turn, and the other smote Sir Lionel so hard that horse and man fell to the earth. The knight alight-

---

1. **armed at all rights:** Well-armed.

2. **helm:** Helmet.
3. **to assay** (as′ ā) *v.*: To test.

ed and bound Sir Lionel fast and threw him over his own horse. Thus the knight captured all four and rode away with them to his own castle. And when he came there he disarmed them, and put them in a deep prison where were many more knights, that made great dolor.[4]

*How Sir Ector followed to seek Sir Launcelot, and how he was taken by Sir Turquine*

When Sir Ector de Maris found out that Sir Launcelot had left the court to seek adventures, he was wroth with himself, and made ready to seek Sir Launcelot. He had ridden long in a great forest when he met a man who was a forester.

"Fair fellow," said Sir Ector, "knowest thou in this country any adventures that be here nigh hand?"

"Sir," said the forester, "this country know I well, and hereby, within this mile, is a strong manor, and well dyked, and by that manor, on the left hand, there is a fair ford for horses to drink of, and over that ford there groweth a fair tree, and thereon hang many fair shields that were wielded at one time by good knights, and at the hole of the tree hangeth a basin of copper. Strike upon that basin with the butt of thy spear thrice, and soon after thou shalt hear new tidings."

"Gramercy," said Sir Ector, and departed and came to the tree, and saw many fair shields. And among them he saw his brother's shield, Sir Lionel, and many more that he knew that were his fellows of the Round Table, which grieved his heart, and he promised to revenge his brother.

Then anon Sir Ector beat on the basin and gave his horse a drink at the ford, and there came a knight behind him and bade him come out of the water and make ready; and Sir Ector cast his spear, and smote the other knight a great buffet so that his horse turned twice about.

"This was well done," said the strong knight, "and knightly thou hast stricken me"; and therewith he rushed his horse on Sir Ector, and caught him under his right arm, and bore him clean out of the saddle, and rode with him away into his own hall, and threw him down in the midst of the floor. The name of this knight was Sir Turquine.

Then he said unto Sir Ector, "For thou hast done this day more to me than any knight has done in the last twelve years. Now I will grant thee thy life, if thou will swear to be my prisoner all thy life days."

"Nay," said Sir Ector, "that will I never promise thee."

Sir Turquine then disarmed him and put him down in a deep dungeon, where he knew many of his fellows. But when Sir Ector saw Sir Lionel, then made he great sorrow. "Alas, brother," said Sir Ector, "where is my brother Sir Launcelot?"

"Fair brother, I left him asleep under an apple tree, and what is become of him I cannot tell you."

"Alas," said the knights, "unless Sir Launcelot helps us we may never be delivered, for we know no knight that is able to match our master Turquine."

*How four queens found Launcelot sleeping, and how by enchantment he was taken and led into a castle*

Now leave we these knights prisoners to speak of Sir Launcelot du Lake, who lieth under the apple tree sleeping. About noon there came by him four queens of great estate;[5] and so the heat would not annoy them, four knights rode about them, carrying a cloth of green silk on four spears

---

**4. dolor** (dō′ lər) *n*.: Sorrow; grief.

**5. estate** (ə stāt′) *n*.: Status; wealth.

between them and the sun, and the queens rode on four white mules.

Thus as they rode they heard a great horse grimly neigh, then they became aware of a sleeping knight, who lay all armed under an apple tree; anon as these queens looked on his face, they knew it was Sir Launcelot. Then each queen said she wanted him to be her own.

"We shall not argue," said Morgan le Fay, King Arthur's sister. "I shall put an enchantment upon him so he will not wake for six hours, and then I will lead him away to my castle. When he is my prisoner, I shall take the enchantment from him, and then let him choose which of us he will have.''

So this enchantment was cast upon Sir Launcelot, and then they laid him upon his shield, and carried him so on horseback between two knights, and brought him to the castle Chariot. There they laid him in a chamber cold, and at night they sent unto him a fair damsel with his supper. By that time the enchantment was past, and when she came she saluted him, and asked him what cheer.

''I cannot say, fair damsel,'' said Sir Launcelot, for I know not how I came into this castle unless it was by enchantment.

''Sir,'' said she, ''ye must make good cheer, and if ye be such a knight as it is said ye be, I shall tell you more tomorrow morning.''

''Gramercy, fair damsel,'' said Sir Launcelot. And so she departed. And there he lay all that night without comfort.

And on the morn early came these four queens, all bidding him good morn, and he them again. ''Sir knight,'' the four queens said, ''thou must understand thou art our prisoner, and we here know that thou art Sir Launcelot du Lake, King Ban's son, and because we understand your worthiness, that thou art the noblest knight living, thou must now choose one of us four. I am the Queen Morgan le Fay, queen of the land of Gore, and here is the queen of Northgalis, and the queen of Eastland, and the queen of the Out Isles; now choose one of us which thou wilt have to be thy love, or else you will die in this prison.''

''This is a hard case,'' said Sir Launcelot, ''that either I must die or else choose one of you, yet had I liefer[6] to die in this prison

with worship, than to have one of you for my love maugre my head.[7] And therefore ye be answered, I will have none of you, for ye be false enchantresses.''

''Well,'' said the queens, ''is this your answer, that ye will refuse us?''

''Yea, on my life,'' said Sir Launcelot, ''I have refused you.'' So they departed and left him there alone in great sorrow.

### How Sir Launcelot was delivered by the mean of a damsel

At noon the damsel came to him with his dinner, and asked him what cheer.

''Truly, fair damsel,'' said Sir Launcelot, ''in my life days never so ill.''

''Sir,'' she said, ''I am sorry for you, but I shall help you out of this distress if you will make me a promise.''

''Fair damsel, I will promise you because sore I am afraid of these queen-sorceresses, for they have destroyed many a good knight.''

''Sir,'' said she, ''The queens say that your name is Sir Launcelot du Lake, the flower of knights, and they are wroth with you because ye have refused them. But Sir, if you would promise to help my father next Tuesday in a tournament between him and the King of Northgalis—for last Tuesday past my father lost the field through three knights of Arthur's court—if ye will be there on Tuesday next coming and help my father, tomorrow morning I shall deliver you clean.''

''Fair maiden,'' said Sir Launcelot, ''tell me what is your father's name, and then shall I give you an answer.''

''Sir knight,'' she said, ''my father is King Bagdemagus, that was beaten at the last tournament.''

---

**6. liefer** (lēf′ ər) *adv.*: Willingly; gladly.

**7. maugre** (mô′ gər) **my head:** In spite of my wishes.

"I know your father well," said Sir Launcelot, "for a noble king and a good knight, and I shall be ready to do your father and you service at that day."

"Sir," she said, "gramercy, and tomorrow be ready and I shall bring you your armor and your horse, shield and spear. Within ten miles, is an abbey of white monks, there I pray you that ye wait, and I shall bring my father to you."

"All this shall be done," said Sir Launcelot, "as I am a true knight."

And so she departed, and came on the morn early, and found him ready; then she brought him out of twelve locks, and brought him his armor, and when he was clean armed, she brought him his own horse, and he saddled him and took a great spear in his hand, and so rode forth, and said, "Fair damsel, I shall not fail you, by the grace of God." . . .


*How Sir Launcelot was received of King Bagdemagus' daughter, and how he made his complaint to her father*

As soon as Sir Launcelot came within the abbey yard, the daughter of King Bagdemagus had him led into a fair chamber, and unarmed him, and the lady sent him a long gown, and anon she came herself. She made Launcelot passing good cheer, and she said he was most welcome.

Then in all haste she sent for her father Bagdemagus, who came with a fair fellowship of knights. And when the king was alighted off his horse he went straight to Sir Launcelot's chamber, and there he found his daughter, and the king embraced Sir Launcelot in his arms, and either made other good cheer.

Anon Sir Launcelot made his complaint to the king about how he was betrayed, and how his brother Sir Lionel was departed from him he knew not where. Sir Launcelot told the king how his daughter had delivered him out of prison; "Therefore while I live I shall do her service and all her kindred."

"Then I am sure of your help," said the king, "on next Tuesday."

"Yea, sire," said Sir Launcelot, "I shall not fail you, for so I have promised my lady, your daughter. But, sir, what knights be they of my lord Arthur's that were with the King of Northgalis?"

And the king said, "It was Sir Mador de la Porte, and Sir Mordred, and Sir Gahalantine. Against them neither I nor my knights had enough strength."

"Sir," said Sir Launcelot, "as I hear that the tournament shall be within three miles of this abbey, send to me three knights of yours that you trust, and see that the three knights have all white shields with no painting on them, and I also. We four will come out of a little wood in the midst of both parties, and we shall fall in the front of our enemies and grieve them if we can; and thus no one shall know who I am."

So they took their rest that night, and this was on Sunday, and then the king departed, and sent unto Sir Launcelot three knights with the four white shields.

On Tuesday they stayed in a little wood beside the place where the tournament was to be held. And there were scaffolds and holes from which lords and ladies might watch and from which prizes could be given.

Then came into the field the King of Northgalis with eight score[8] helms. And then the three knights of Arthur's stood by themselves. Then came into the field King Bagdemagus with four score of helms. They feutred[9] their spears, and came together with a great dash. Twelve of King Bagdema-

---

**8. score** (skôr) *n.*: Twenty people or things. In this case 160 knights in armor.
**9. feutred** (fyoo′ trəd) *v.*: Fit into the special rest on a saddle for a spear or lance.

gus' party, and six of the King of Northgalis' party were slain at the first encounter, and King Bagdemagus' party was set far back.

*How Sir Launcelot behaved him in a tournament, and how he met with Sir Turquine leading Sir Gaheris*

With that came Sir Launcelot du Lake, and he thrust in with his spear in the thickest of the press. He smote down five knights with one spear, and he broke the backs of four of them. And in that throng he smote down the King of Northgalis and broke his thigh in that fall. The three knights of Arthur saw Sir Launcelot do these things.

"Yonder is a shrewd guest," said Sir Mador de la Porte. "Therefore let us have at him." So they encountered, and Sir Launcelot bare him down horse and man so that his shoulder went out of lith.[10]

"Now befalleth it to me to joust," said Mordred, "for Sir Mador hath a sore fall."

Sir Launcelot was aware of him, and gat a great spear in his hand, and met him. Sir Mordred broke a spear upon him, and Sir Launcelot gave him such a buffet that the arson[11] of his saddle broke, and he flew over his horse's tail. His helm butted into the earth a foot and more so that he almost broke his neck, and there he lay long in a swoon.[12]

Then came in Sir Gahalantine with a great spear and Launcelot against him. They drove with all their strength so that both their spears broke in their hands, and then they flung out with their swords and gave many a grim stroke. Sir Launcelot was very angry, and he smote Sir Gahalantine on the helm so that he bled from his nose, ears, and mouth, and therewith his head hung low, and his horse ran away with him, and he fell down to the earth.

Anon therewithal Sir Launcelot gat a great spear in his hand, and before that great spear broke, he bore down to the earth sixteen knights, some horse and man, and some the man and not the horse. Everyone that he hit surely bore no arms again that day.

And then he gat another great spear and smote down twelve knights, and most of them never throve after.

And then the knights of the King of Northgalis would joust no more. Therefore, the gree[13] was given to King Bagdemagus.

So each party departed to its own place, and Sir Launcelot rode forth with King Bagdemagus to his castle. There he had passing good cheer both with the king and with his daughter, and they proffered him great gifts.

And on the morn he took his leave, and told the king that he would go and seek his brother Sir Lionel, who had disappeared while he slept. He took his horse, and betaught them all to God. And there he said unto the king's daughter, "If ye have need any time of my service, I pray you let me know, and I shall not fail you as I am a true knight."

And so Sir Launcelot departed, and by adventure he came into the same forest where he had been captured as he was sleeping. And in the midst of a highway he met a damsel riding on a white palfrey,[14] and each saluted the other.

"Fair damsel," said Sir Launcelot, "know ye in this country any adventures?"

"Sir knight," said that damsel, "there are adventures near at hand, if thou dare try them."

---

**10. lith** (lith) *n.*: Joint.
**11. arson** (är′ sən) *n.*: Curved piece of wood or metal at the front or rear of a saddle.
**12. swoon** (swoon) *n.*: Fainting spell; unconscious state.

**13. gree** (grē) *n.*: Victory.
**14. palfrey** (pôl′ frē) *n.*: A saddle horse, especially a gentle one.

"Why should I not try adventures?" said Sir Launcelot, "That is why I came here."

"Well," said she, "thou seem to be a good knight. I shall bring thee where the best knight lives and the mightiest that ever thou could find if thou tell me what thy name is and what knight thou art."

"Damsel, to get me to tell thee my name will take no great force; truly my name is Sir Launcelot du Lake."

"Sir, there are suitable adventures for you here, for nearby dwelleth a knight that will not be overmatched by anyone I know unless ye overmatch him, and his name is Sir Turquine. And, as I understand, he hath in his prison, of Arthur's court, good knights three score and four, that he hath won with his own hands. But when ye have done that journey ye shall promise me as ye are a true knight for to go with me, and to help me and other damsels that are distressed daily with a false knight."

"All you want, damsel, I will fulfil, if ye will bring me unto this knight."

"Now, fair knight, come on your way"; and so she brought him unto the ford and the tree where hung the basin.

So Sir Launcelot let his horse drink, and then he beat on the basin with the butt of his spear so hard with all his might till the bottom fell out, and long he did so, but he saw nothing. Then he rode up back and forth in front of the gates of that manor for half an hour. Finally, he saw a great knight that drove a horse before him, and over the horse there lay an armed knight bound. As they came nearer and nearer, Sir Launcelot thought he should know him. Then Sir Launcelot realized that it was Sir Gaheris, Gawain's brother, a knight of the Table Round.

"Now, fair damsel," said Sir Launcelot, "I see yonder cometh a knight fast bounden that is a fellow of mine, and brother he is unto Sir Gawain. And at the first beginning I promise you, by the leave of God, to rescue that knight; if his master does not sit better in the saddle, I shall deliver all the prisoners that he hath out of danger, for I am sure he hath two brethren of mine prisoners with him."

When each knight had seen the other, they gripped their spears unto them. "Now, fair knight," said Sir Launcelot, "put that wounded knight off the horse, and let him rest awhile, and let us two prove our strengths; for I have been told that thou hast done great despite[15] and shame unto knights of the Round Table, and therefore now defend thee."

"And thou be of the Table Round," said Turquine. "I defy thee and all thy fellowship."

"That is overmuch said," said Sir Launcelot.

### How Sir Launcelot and Sir Turquine fought together

And then they put their spears in the rests, and came together with their horses as fast as they might run, and either smote other in the middle of their shields, so that both their horses' backs broke under them, and the knights were both stonied.[16] And as soon as they might avoid their horses, they held their shields before them, and drew out their swords, and came together eagerly, and either gave the other many strong strokes, for neither shields nor armor could protect them. And so within a while they both had grim wounds and bled grievously. Thus they spent two hours or more wounding each other, whenever they could hit any bare place.

Then at the last they were breathless both, and stood leaning on their swords.

---

**15. despite** (di spīt′) *n.*: insult; injury.
**16. stonied** (stŏn′ ēd) *v.*: Stunned.

**SIR MADOR'S SPEAR BRAKE ALL TO PIECES**
*N. C. Wyeth/Illustration for* The Boy's King Authur
*Delaware Art Museum*

"Now fellow," said Sir Turquine, "hold thy hand a while, and tell me what I shall ask thee.

"Say on."

Then Turquine said, "Thou are the biggest man that ever I met, and the best breathed, and like one knight that I hate above all other knights; but if thou are not the knight I hate, I will treat thee lightly, and I will deliver all the prisoners that I have to you, that is three score and four. So tell me thy name. And thou and I we will be fellows together, and I will never fail thee as long as I live.''

''It is well said,'' said Sir Launcelot. ''But to see if I may have thy friendship, what knight is he that thou so hatest above all others?''

''Faithfully,'' said Sir Turquine, ''his name is Sir Launcelot du Lake, for he slew my brother, Sir Carados, who was one of the best knights alive; therefore, him I except of all knights. If I ever meet him, I vow that one of us shall make an end of the other. And for Sir Launcelot's sake I have slain a hundred good knights, and as many I have maimed all utterly that they might never after help themselves, and many have died in prison. Yet I still have three score and four, and all shall be delivered if thou wilt tell me thy name, and if thou be not Sir Launcelot.''

''Now, see I well,'' said Sir Launcelot, ''if I were one man I might have peace, and if I were another man, there would be war between us. And now, sir knight, at thy request I will tell thee that I am Launcelot du Lake, King Ban's son of Benwick and knight of the Table Round. And now I defy thee, and do thy best.''

''Ah,'' said Turquine, ''Launcelot, thou art unto me most welcome that ever was knight, for we shall never depart till one of us is dead.''

Then they hurtled together as two wild bulls rushing and lashing with their shields and swords, so that sometimes they fell over their own noses. Thus they fought still two hours and more, and never would have rest, and Sir Turquine gave Sir Launcelot many wounds that all the ground where they fought was all bespeckled with blood.

*How Sir Turquine was slain, and how Sir Launcelot bade Sir Gaheris deliver all the prisoners*

Then at the last Sir Turquine waxed faint, and gave somewhat aback, and bore his shield low for weariness. Sir Launcelot saw that and leapt upon him fiercely and gat him by the beaver[17] of his helmet and plucked him down on his knees. Then he tore off his helm, and smote his neck in sunder.[18]

And when Sir Launcelot had done this, he went to the damsel and said, ''Damsel, I am ready to go with you where ye will have me, but I have no horse.''

''Fair sir,'' said she, ''take this wounded knight's horse and send him into this manor, and command him to deliver all the prisoners.''

So Sir Launcelot went to Gaheris, and asked him to lend him his horse. ''Nay, fair lord,'' said Gaheris. ''I want ye to take my horse for your own, for ye have saved both me and my horse, and this day I say ye are the best knight in the world, for ye have slain this day in my sight the mightiest man and the best knight except you that ever I saw, and fair sir,'' said Gaheris, ''I pray you tell me your name.''

''Sir, my name is Sir Launcelot du Lake, who helped you for King Arthur's sake, and especially for my lord Sir Gawain's sake, your own dear brother; and when ye go into yonder manor, I am sure ye shall find there many knights of the Round Table, for I have seen many of their shields that I know on yonder tree. There is Kay's shield, and Sir Brandel's shield, and Sir Marhaus's shield, and Sir Galind's shield, and Sir Brian de Listnois's shield, and Sir Sliduke's shield, with many more that I do not recognize, and also my two brethren's shields, Sir Ector de Maris and Sir Lionel; wherefore I pray you

---

**17. beaver** (bē′ vər) *n*.: A movable piece of armor on the lower part of a knight's helmet for protecting the mouth and chin.
**18. in sunder** (sun′ dər): Apart.

greet them all for me, and say that I bid them take such stuff there as they find, and tell my brethren to go to the court and wait there till I come. I promise to be there by the feast of Pentecost,[19] but now I must ride with this damsel to keep my promise to her."

And so he departed from Gaheris, and Gaheris went into the manor, and there he found a yeoman porter[20] keeping many keys. Sir Gaheris threw the porter on the ground and took the keys from him. Hastily he opened the prison door and let out all the prisoners, and every man loosed others of their bonds. And when they saw Sir Gaheris, they all thanked him for saving them, for they saw that he was wounded.

"Not so," said Gaheris, "it was Launcelot that slew Turquine with his own hands. I saw it with mine own eyes. And he greeteth you all well and prayeth you to haste you to the court; and as for Sir Lionel and Ector de Maris he prayeth you to wait for him at the court.

"That we shall not do," said his brethren. "We will find him."

"So shall I," said Sir Kay, "find him before I go to the court, as I am a true knight."

Then all those knights sought the house where their armor was, and then they armed themselves, and every knight found his own horse, and everything that belonged to him. And when this was done, there came a forester with four horses laden with fat venison.[21]

"Anon," Sir Kay said, "Here is good meat for us for one meal, for we have gone many a day with no good repast."

And so the venison was roasted, baked, and boiled. After supper some of the knights stayed there all night, but Sir Lionel and Ector de Maris and Sir Kay rode after Sir Launcelot to find him if they could. . . .

*How Sir Launcelot came to King Arthur's Court, and how there were recounted all his noble feats and acts*

Now turn we to Sir Launcelot du Lake, who came home two days before the Feast of Pentecost; and the king and all the court were glad to see him. And there was laughing and smiling among them. And soon all the knights that Sir Turquine had as prisoners came home, and they all honored and worshiped Sir Launcelot.

When Sir Gaheris heard them speak, he said, "I saw all the battle from the beginning to the ending," and then he told King Arthur what had happened and how Sir Turquine was the strongest knight that ever he saw except Sir Launcelot: there were many knights agreed with him, nigh three score.

And all his deeds were known, how four queens, sorceresses, had him in prison, and how he was delivered by King Bagdemagus' daughter. Also all the great deeds of arms that Sir Launcelot did between the two kings, the King of Northgalis and King Bagdemagus, were told. All the truth Sir Gahalantine did tell, and Sir Mador de la Porte and Sir Mordred. . . . And so at that time Sir Launcelot had the greatest name of any knight of the world, and he was honored most by high and low.

---

**19. Pentecost** (pen′ tə kôst′) *n.*: A Christian religious celebration.
**20. yeoman porter** (yō′ mən pôr′ tər) *n.*: A servant or attendant who is a doorman or gatekeeper.
**21. venison** (ven′ i s′n) *n.*: The flesh of a game animal, now especially the deer, used as food.

## THINKING ABOUT THE SELECTION
### Recalling

1. What important facts about Sir Launcelot are given in the opening paragraph?
2. How may a knight seeking adventure meet with Sir Turquine?
3. What offer does Sir Turquine make to Sir Ector after he has beaten him?
4. How does Sir Launcelot earn his freedom from Morgan le Fay and the other queens?
5. What service does Sir Launcelot perform in return?
6. Why has Sir Turquine killed and wounded hundreds of knights?

### Interpreting

7. How does Sir Launcelot prove his honor after he is captured by the four queens?
8. How does Sir Launcelot prove his honor to the daughter of King Bagdemagus?
9. Although Sir Turquine is motivated by a desire for revenge, he too lives and acts honorably. On what two occasions does he exhibit his own form of honor?

### Applying

10. What contemporary hero can you think of who carries on the heroic tradition?

## ANALYZING LITERATURE
### Understanding the Heroic Tradition

In "The Adventures of Sir Launcelot," Sir Launcelot portrays the ideal hero: a chivalrous knight who is courageous, trustworthy, and successful in battle. Down through generations the King Arthur legends have undergone different versions but have preserved the ideals of the **heroic tradition:** glory, nobility, justice, adventure, and loyalty. Find examples in "The Adventures of Sir Launcelot" that show the importance of glory, nobility, justice, adventure, and loyalty.

## UNDERSTANDING LANGUAGE
### Appreciating Vivid Writing

**Vivid writing** appeals to your imagination and senses, catches your attention, and compels you to read on. A skillful writer chooses words carefully and creates images that are clear, fresh, and strong. Sir Thomas Malory uses vivid language in his descriptions of knights in combat:

"Sir Mordred broke a spear upon him, and Sir Launcelot gave him such a buffet that the arson of his saddle broke, and he flew over his horse's tail. His helm butted into the earth a foot and more so that he almost broke his neck, and there he lay long in a swoon."

Find another vivid description in the story. Point out particular word choices and images that make the passage memorable.

## THINKING AND WRITING
### Writing About the Heroic Tradition

The heroic tradition includes the concepts of glory, nobility, justice, adventure, and loyalty. Choose one of these aspects and write an essay for your school magazine, discussing how the heroic tradition does or does not continue today. First choose an example from "The Adventures of Sir Launcelot" that illustrates this aspect of the heroic tradition. Then think of an example in contemporary life that illustrates the presence or lack of the same aspect. Use this information in writing your essay. Revise your essay to be persuasive. Proofread for errors in spelling, grammar, and punctuation.

## Morte d'Arthur

**Alfred, Lord Tennyson** (1809–1892) was born in Somersby, Lincolnshire, England. Tennyson prepared for college at home. He attended Cambridge but never received a degree. He strove to perfect his craft as a poet, experimenting with different poetic forms. He wrote exquisite short lyrics as well as powerful longer works. The following excerpt from the epic *Idylls of the King,* twelve narrative poems based on the Arthurian legends, describes the aftermath of Arthur's last great battle and his death.

**Epic Poetry**

**Epic poetry** is long narrative poetry that celebrates the life of a hero who embodies the values of a particular society. Epics, which can be traced to prehistoric times, were improvised and performed by poet-musicians and passed down through generations. The most famous epics in Western culture are the *Iliad* and the *Odyssey* by the Greek poet Homer.

Epic poems, like "Morte d'Arthur," relate larger-than-life events, generally of heroes and heroines. Often the background of epics is a great war or love. Epics are composed in dignified, sometimes lofty language. "Morte d'Arthur" is from the epic *Idylls of the King.*

**Look For**

What makes Arthur an epic hero? In what ways does his life demonstrate heroic behavior? As you read, look for the heroic and larger-than-life elements that make this story an epic for all time.

**Writing**

Brainstorm to list the qualities that would make an ideal—or, at least, better—society.

**Vocabulary**

Knowing the following words will help you as you read "Morte d'Arthur."

**giddy** (gid′ē) *adj.*: Mad or foolish (p. 754)

**brandished** (bran′disht) *v.*: Waved or flourished menacingly (p. 755)

**stately** (stāt′lē) *adj.*: Majestic (p. 757)

**lamentation** (lam′ən tā′ shən) *n.*: Mourning (p. 757)

**withered** (with′ərd) *adj.*: Weakened; dried up (p. 757)

**swarthy** (swôr′thē) *adj.*: Having a dark complexion (p. 760)

**redeemed** (ri dēmd′) *v.*: Rescued or saved (p. 760)

# Morte d'Arthur

### Alfred, Lord Tennyson

*The Epic*

    At Francis Allen's on the Christmas eve—
The game of forfeits[1] done—the girls all kissed
Beneath the sacred bush[2] and passed away—
The parson Holmes, the poet Everard Hall,

5    The host, and I sat round the wassail bowl,[3]
Then halfway ebbed; and there we held a talk,
How all the old honor had from Christmas gone,
Or gone or dwindled down to some odd games
In some odd nooks like this; till I, tired out

10    With cutting eights[4] that day upon the pond,
Where, three times slipping from the outer edge,
I bumped the ice into three several stars,
Fell in a doze; and half-awake I heard
The parson taking wide and wider sweeps,

15    Now harping on the church commissioners,
Now hawking at geology and schism;[5]
Until I woke, and found him settled down
Upon the general decay of faith
Right through the world: "at home was little left,

20    And none abroad; there was no anchor, none,
To hold by." Francis, laughing, clapped his hand
On Everard's shoulder, with "I hold by him."
"And I," quoth Everard, "by the wassail-bowl."
"Why yes," I said, "we knew your gift that way

25    At college; but another which you had—
I mean of verse (for so we held it then),

---

**1. forfeits** (fôr′ fits) *n.*: A game in which something is taken away as a penalty for making a mistake.
**2. sacred bush:** Mistletoe.
**3. wassail bowl** (wäs′ 'l bōl′) *n.*: Punch bowl.
**4. cutting eights:** Ice-skating so the skates cut figure eights in the ice.
**5. schism** (siz′ 'm) *n.*: A division within an organization, especially a church, because of a difference of opinion.

What came of that?'' "You know," said Frank, "he burnt
His epic, his King Arthur, some twelve books"—
And then to me demanding why: "O, sir,
30  He thought that nothing new was said, or else
Something so said 'twas nothing—that a truth
Looks freshest in the fashion of the day;
God knows; he has a mint of reasons; ask.
It pleased *me* well enough." "Nay, nay," said Hall,
35  "Why take the style of those heroic times?
For nature brings not back the mastodon,[6]
Nor we those times; and why should any man
Remodel models? these twelve books of mine
Were faint Homeric echoes,[7] nothing-worth,
40  Mere chaff and draff,[8] much better burnt." "But I,"
Said Francis, "picked the eleventh from this hearth,
And have it; keep a thing, its use will come.
I hoard it as a sugarplum for Holmes."
He laughed, and I, though sleepy, like a horse
45  That hears the corn-bin open, pricked my ears;
For I remembered Everard's college fame
When we were Freshmen. Then at my request
He brought it; and the poet, little urged,
But with some prelude of disparagement,
50  Read, mouthing out his hollow o's and a's,
Deep-chested music, and to this result.


*Morte d'Arthur*

So all day long the noise of battle rolled
Among the mountains by the winter sea,
Until King Arthur's table, man by man,
Had fallen in Lyonnesse[9] about their lord,
55  King Arthur; then, because his wound was deep,
The bold Sir Bedivere uplifted him,
Sir Bedivere, the last of all his knights,
And bore him to a chapel nigh the field,
60  A broken chancel[10] with a broken cross,
That stood on a dark strait of barren land.

---

**6. mastodon** (mas′ tə dän′) *n.*: An extinct animal resembling the
elephant but larger.
**7. Homeric echoes** (hō mer′ ik ek′ ōs): Imitations of the poems of the
Greek poet Homer (of about the eighth century B.C.).
**8. chaff and draff:** Anything worthless; dregs.
**9. Lyonnesse** (lī′ ə nes′): A legendary country of the southwestern
coast of England, supposed to have sunk beneath the sea.
**10. chancel** (chan′ s'l) *n.*: The part of a church around the altar.

On one side lay the ocean, and on one
Lay a great water, and the moon was full.
    Then spake King Arthur to Sir Bedivere:
65    "The sequel of today unsolders[11] all
The goodliest fellowship of famous knights
Whereof this world holds record. Such a sleep
They sleep—the men I loved. I think that we
Shall never more, at any future time,
70    Delight our souls with talk of knightly deeds,
Walking about the gardens and the halls
Of Camelot, as in the days that were.
I perish by this people which I made—
Though Merlin sware that I should come again

---

**11. unsolders** (un säd' ərs) *v.*: Separates.

75  To rule once more—but let what will be be,
I am so deeply smitten through the helm[12]
That without help I cannot last till morn.
Thou therefore take my brand[13] Excalibur,
Which was my pride; for thou rememberest how
80  In those old days, one summer noon, an arm
Rose up from out the bosom of the lake,
Clothed in white samite,[14] mystic, wonderful,
Holding the sword—and how I rowed across
And took it, and have worn it, like a king;
85  And, wheresoever I am sung or told
In aftertime, this also shall be known.
But now delay not; take Excalibur,
And fling him far into the middle mere;[15]
Watch what thou seest, and lightly[16] bring me word."
90      To him replied the bold Sir Bedivere:
"It is not meet,[17] Sir King, to leave thee thus,
Aidless, alone, and smitten through the helm.
A little thing may harm a wounded man.
Yet I thy hest will all perform at full,[18]
95  Watch what I see, and lightly bring thee word."
        So saying, from the ruined shrine he stepped
And in the moon athwart the place of tombs,
Where lay the mighty bones of ancient men,
Old knights, and over them the sea wind sang
100  Shrill, chill, with flakes of foam. He, stepping down
By zigzag paths and juts of pointed rock,
Came on the shining levels of the lake.
        There drew he forth the brand Excalibur,
And o'er him, drawing it, the winter moon,
105  Brightening the skirts of a long cloud, ran forth
And sparkled keen with frost against the hilt;
For all the haft[19] twinkled with diamond sparks,
Myriads[20] of topaz lights, and jacinth work[21]
Of subtlest jewelry. He gazed so long

---

**12. helm:** Helmet.
**13. brand:** Sword.
**14. samite** (sam' īt) *n.*: A heavy silk fabric.
**15. mere** (mir) *n.*: Lake.
**16. lightly** *adv.*: Quickly.
**17. meet** *adj.*: proper.
**18. I thy hest will all perform at full:** I will carry out your order completely.
**19. haft** *n.*: Handle or hilt of a sword.
**20. myriads** (mir' ē ədz) *n.*: Large numbers.
**21. topaz** (tō' paz) **... jacinth** (jā' sinth): Yellow and reddish-orange jewels.

110 That both his eyes were dazzled, as he stood,
This way and that dividing the swift mind,
In act to throw; but at the last it seemed
Better to leave Excalibur concealed
There in the many-knotted water flags,[22]
115 That whistled still and dry about the marge.[23]
So strode he back slow to the wounded king.
    Then spake King Arthur to Sir Bedivere:
"Hast thou performed my mission which I gave?
What is it thou hast seen, or what hast heard?"
120     And answer made the bold Sir Bedivere:
"I heard the ripple washing in the reeds,
And the wild water lapping on the crag."
    To whom replied King Arthur, faint and pale:
"Thou hast betrayed thy nature and thy name,
125 Not rendering[24] true answer, as beseemed[25]
Thy fealty, nor like a noble knight;
For surer sign had followed, either hand,
Or voice, or else a motion of the mere.
This is a shameful thing for men to lie.
130 Yet now, I charge thee, quickly go again
As thou art lief and dear, and do the thing
I bade thee, watch, and lightly bring me word."
    Then went Sir Bedivere the second time
Across the ridge, and paced beside the mere,
135 Counting the dewy pebbles, fixed in thought;
But when he saw the wonder of the hilt,
How curiously and strangely chased,[26] he smote
His palms together, and he cried aloud:
    "And if indeed I cast the brand away;
140 Surely a precious thing, one worthy note,
Should thus be lost forever from the earth,
Which might have pleased the eyes of many men.
What good should follow this, if this were done?
What harm, undone? deep harm to disobey,
145 Seeing obedience is the bond of rule.
Were it well to obey then, if a king demand
An act unprofitable, against himself?
The king is sick, and knows not what he does.
What record, or what relic of my lord

---

**22. water flags:** Marsh plants.
**23. marge** (märj) *n.*: Edge.
**24. rendering** (ren' dər iŋ) *v.*: Giving.
**25. beseemed** (bi sēm'd') *v.*: Was suitable to.
**26. chased** *v.*: Decorated by engraving or embossing.

150 Should be to aftertime, but empty breath
And rumors of a doubt? but were this kept,
Stored in some treasure-house of mighty kings,
Some one might show it at a joust of arms,
Saying, 'King Arthur's sword, Excalibur,
155 Wrought by the lonely maiden of the lake;
Nine years she wrought it, sitting in the deeps
Upon the hidden bases of the hills.'
So might some old man speak in the aftertime
To all the people, winning reverence;
160 But now much honor and much fame were lost."
    So spake he, clouded with his own conceit,
And hid Excalibur the second time,
And so strode back slow to the wounded king.
    Then spoke King Arthur, breathing heavily:
165 "What is it thou hast seen, or what hast heard?"
    And answer made the bold Sir Bedivere:
"I heard the water lapping on the crag,
And the long ripple washing in the reeds."
    To whom replied King Arthur, much in wrath:
170 "Ah, miserable and unkind, untrue,
Unknightly, traitor-hearted! Woe is me!
Authority forgets a dying king,
Laid widowed of the power in his eye
That bowed the will. I see thee what thou art,
175 For thou, the latest-left of all my knights,
In whom should meet the offices[27] of all,
Thou wouldst betray me for the precious hilt;
Either from lust of gold, or like a girl
Valuing the giddy pleasure of the eyes.
180 Yet, for a man may fail in duty twice,
And the third time may prosper, get thee hence;
But, if thou spare to fling Excalibur,
I will arise and slay thee with my hands."
    Then quickly rose Sir Bedivere, and ran,
185 And, leaping down the ridges lightly, plunged
Among the bulrush beds,[28] and clutched the sword,
And strongly wheeled and threw it. The great brand
Made lightnings in the splendor of the moon,
And flashing round and round, and whirled in an arch,
190 Shot like a streamer of the northern morn,[29]

---

**27. offices** *n.*: Duties.
**28. bulrush** (bŏŏl' rush) **beds:** Growth of marsh plants.
**29. a streamer of the northern morn:** The northern lights; the aurora borealis.

Seen where the moving isles of winter shock[30]
By night, with noises of the northern sea.
So flashed and fell the brand Excalibur;
But ere he dipped the surface, rose an arm

195    Clothed in white samite, mystic, wonderful,
And caught him by the hilt, and brandished him
Three times, and drew him under in the mere.
And lightly went the other to the king.

        Then spoke King Arthur, drawing thicker breath:

200    "Now see I by thine eyes that this is done.
Speak out; what is it thou hast heard, or seen?"

        And answer made the bold Sir Bedivere:
"Sir King, I closed mine eyelids, lest the gems
Should blind my purpose, for I never saw,

205    Nor shall see, here or elsewhere, till I die,
Not though I live three lives of mortal men,
So great a miracle as yonder hilt.
Then with both hands I flung him, wheeling him;
But when I looked again, behold an arm,

210    Clothed in white samite, mystic, wonderful,
That caught him by the hilt, and brandished him
Three times, and drew him under in the mere."

        And answer made King Arthur, breathing hard:
"My end draws nigh; 'tis time that I were gone.

215    Make broad thy shoulders to receive my weight,
And bear me to the margin,[31] yet I fear
My wound hath taken cold, and I shall die."

        So saying, from the pavement he half rose,
Slowly, with pain, reclining on his arm,

220    And looking wistfully with wide blue eyes
As in a picture. Him Sir Bedivere
Remorsefully regarded through his tears,
And would have spoken, but he found not words,
Then took with care, and kneeling on one knee,

225    O'er both his shoulders drew the languid hands,
And rising bore him through the place of tombs.

        But, as he walked, King Arthur panted hard,
Like one that feels a nightmare on his bed
When all the house is mute. So sighed the king,

230    Muttering and murmuring at his ear, "Quick, quick!
I fear it is too late, and I shall die."

---

**30. the moving isles of winter shock:** The icebergs crash.
**31. margin** (mär′ jən) *n.*: Edge.

**HOW SIR BEDIVERE CAST THE SWORD EXCALIBER INTO THE WATER**
*Aubrey Beardsley*
*Houghton Library, Harvard University*

But the other swiftly strode from ridge to ridge,
Clothed with his breath, and looking, as he walked,
Larger than human on the frozen hills.
235 He heard the deep behind him, and a cry
Before. His own thought drove him like a goad.[32]
Dry clashed his harness[33] in the icy caves
And barren chasms, and all to left and right
The bare black cliff clanged round him, as he based
240 His feet on juts of slippery crag that rang
Sharp-smitten with the dint of armèd heels—
And on a sudden, lo! the level lake,
And the long glories of the winter moon.

Then saw they how there hove a dusky barge,
245 Dark as a funeral scarf from stem to stern,
Beneath them; and descending they were ware
That all the decks were dense with stately forms
Black-stoled,[34] black-hooded, like a dream—by these
Three queens with crowns of gold—and from them rose
250 A cry that shivered to the tingling stars,
And, as it were one voice, an agony
Of lamentation, like a wind that shrills
All night in a waste land, where no one comes,
Or hath come, since the making of the world.
255 Then murmured Arthur, "Place me in the barge,"
And to the barge they came. There those three queens
Put forth their hands, and took the king, and wept.
But she that rose the tallest of them all
And fairest laid his head upon her lap,
260 And loosed the shattered casque,[35] and chafed his hands,
And called him by his name, complaining loud,
And dropping bitter tears against his brow
Striped with dark blood; for all his face was white
And colorless, and like the withered moon
265 Smote by the fresh beam of the springing east;
And all his greaves and cuisses dashed with drops
Of onset;[36] and the light and lustrous curls—

---

**32. goad** (gōd) *n.*: A sharp-pointed stick used to drive oxen.
**33. harness** (här′ nis) *n.*: Armor.
**34. black-stoled:** Wearing long black scarves around their shoulders.
**35. casque** (kask) *n.*: Helmet.
**36. greaves** (grēvz) **and cuisses** (kwis′ əs) **. . . onset:** Armor for the legs below the knee and for the thigh spattered with blood from the battle.

**ARTHUR IN AVALON**
*T. Archer R.S.A.*
Culver Pictures

That made his forehead like a rising sun
High from the dais-throne—were parched with dust;
270   Or, clotted into points and hanging loose,
Mixed with the knightly growth that fringed his lips.
So like a shattered column lay the king;
Not like that Arthur who, with lance in rest,
From spur to plume a star of tournament,
275   Shot through the lists at Camelot, and charged
Before the eyes of ladies and of kings.

      Then loudly cried the bold Sir Bedivere:
"Ah! my Lord Arthur, whither shall I go?

Where shall I hide my forehead and my eyes?
280　For now I see the true old times are dead,
When every morning brought a noble chance,
And every chance brought out a noble knight.
Such times have been not since the light that led
The holy Elders with the gift of myrrh.[37]
285　But now the whole ROUND TABLE is dissolved
Which was an image of the mighty world;
And I, the last, go forth companionless,
And the days darken round me, and the years,
Among new men, strange faces, other minds."
290　　　And slowly answered Arthur from the barge:
"The old order changeth, yielding place to new,
And God fulfills himself in many ways,
Lest one good custom should corrupt the world.
Comfort thyself: what comfort is in me?
295　I have lived my life, and that which I have done
May He within himself make pure! but thou,
If thou shouldst never see my face again,
Pray for my soul. More things are wrought by prayer
Than this world dreams of. Wherefore, let thy voice
300　Rise like a fountain for me night and day.
For what are men better than sheep or goats
That nourish a blind life within the brain,
If, knowing God, they lift not hands of prayer
Both for themselves and those who call them friend?
305　For so the whole round earth is every way
Bound by gold chains about the feet of God.
But now farewell. I am going a long way
With these thou seest—if indeed I go—
For all my mind is clouded with a doubt—
310　To the island-valley of Avilion;[38]
Where falls not hail, or rain, or any snow,
Nor ever wind blows loudly, but it lies
Deep-meadowed, happy, fair with orchard lawns
And bowery[39] hollows crowned with summer sea,

---

**37. the light . . . of myrrh** (mur): The star that guided the three Kings (the holy Elders) with their gift of incense (myrrh) to Bethlehem at the time of the birth of Jesus.
**38. island-valley of Avilion:** The island paradise of Avalon where heroes were taken after death, according to Celtic mythology and medieval romances.
**39. bowery** (bou′ ər ē) *adj.*: Enclosed by overhanging boughs of trees or by vines.

315 Where I will heal me of my grievous wound."
    So said he, and the barge with oar and sail
Moved from the brink, like some full-breasted swan
That, fluting a wild carol ere her death,
Ruffles her pure cold plume, and takes the flood
320 With swarthy webs. Long stood Sir Bedivere
Revolving many memories, till the hull
Looked one black dot against the verge of dawn,
And on the mere the wailing died away.

    Here ended Hall, and our last light, that long
325 Had winked and threatened darkness, flared and fell;
At which the parson, sent to sleep with sound,
And waked with silence, grunted "Good!" but we
Sat rapt:[40] it was the tone with which he read—
Perhaps some modern touches here and there
330 Redeemed it from the charge of nothingness—
Or else we loved the man, and prized his work;
I know not; but we sitting, as I said,
The cock crew loud, as at that time of year
The lusty bird takes every hour for dawn.
335 Then Francis, muttering, like a man ill-used,
"There now—that's nothing!" drew a little back,
And drove his heel into the smoldered log,
That sent a blast of sparkles up the flue.
And so to bed, where yet in sleep I seemed
340 To sail with Arthur under looming shores,
Point after point; till on to dawn, when dreams
Begin to feel the truth and stir of day,
To me, methought, who waited with the crowd,
There came a bark that, blowing forward, bore
345 King Arthur; like a modern gentleman
Of stateliest port;[41] and all the people cried,
"Arthur is come again: he cannot die."
Then those that stood upon the hills behind
Repeated—"Come again, and thrice as fair";
350 And, further inland, voices echoed—"Come
With all good things, and war shall be no more."
At this a hundred bells began to peal,
That with the sound I woke, and heard indeed
The clear church bells ring in the Christmas morn.

---

**40. rapt** *adj.*: Completely absorbed; engrossed.
**41. of stateliest port:** Who carried himself in a most majestic or dignified manner.

## THINKING ABOUT THE SELECTION

### Recalling

1. What occasion is being celebrated at the start of the poem?
2. Who is said to be the "author" of the poem within the poem?
3. In the poem within the poem, what has happened to King Arthur?
4. Explain the responsibility that Arthur has given to Sir Bedivere. Explain how Sir Bedivere executes Arthur's command.
5. Describe Arthur's departure.

### Interpreting

6. What does Arthur say will soon be lost forever? How, in lines 277–289, does Sir Bedivere echo Arthur's feelings?
7. What are Sir Bedivere's arguments for not throwing Excalibur into the lake?
8. Interpret Arthur's final words to Sir Bedivere.
9. How does the speaker's vision at the very end of the poem relate to Arthur's words in lines 73–75?

### Applying

10. The modern novelist F. Scott Fitzgerald has written "Show me a hero and I will write you a tragedy." Do you think that the Arthurian legend is a tragedy? Explain your answer. In which way is Fitzgerald expressing a particular modern view of the hero?

## ANALYZING LITERATURE

### Understanding Epic Poetry

**Epic poetry** is long narrative poetry that centers on the deeds of a single heroic individual who stands for and upholds the values of a particular society. Tennyson's version of the Arthurian legends focuses on Arthur's own high moral character. Arthur's creation of Camelot represents an ideal of community and brotherhood founded on courage, faith, honor, love, and loyalty. But Arthur cannot change human nature.

Human weakness and the world's evil eventually bring about the downfall of Camelot. What makes the legend poignant is that Arthur must die, and his high ideals must pass with him.

1. How is Arthur's decision to return Excalibur to the lake a final act of generosity and honor?
2. How do Sir Bedivere's actions relate to the theme of chivalry?

## CRITICAL THINKING AND READING

### Interpreting Metaphorical Meaning

The legend of King Arthur and Camelot continues to exert a powerful hold on our imagination. One reason is that the legend involves larger concerns that hover over this story of a boy growing up to be a king, and of knights and their adventures. When Arthur dies, his kingdom lies in ruins. Far more important and far sadder than the physical destruction of a kingdom is the loss of the *spirit* of Camelot. A glorious and beautiful vision has come and gone; this is the metaphorical significance of King Arthur's great story.

1. What metaphorical meaning do you find in the story of the lady of the lake?
2. What metaphorical meaning do you find in Arthur's description of "the island-valley of Avilion" (lines 310–315)?

## THINKING AND WRITING

### Writing About Epic Poetry

Write an essay for a literary magazine analyzing what qualities of *Morte d'Arthur* make it an epic. First list the values and attitudes that are embodied and expressed in this selection, what makes Arthur a hero, and in what ways the events and actions are larger than life. Develop this information in a draft of your essay. Revise your essay, making sure that your points are clear and that you have supported them with examples. Proofread for errors in spelling, grammar, and punctuation.

# GUIDE FOR READING

## Merlin

**Geoffrey Hill** (1932–   ) was born in Bromsgrove, Worcestershire, England. Educated at Oxford University, he serves as senior lecturer and professor of English at the University of Leeds. Hill writes poetry with a controlled and formal style. One critic has noted that Hill "feels a deep responsibility to address the reality of history." His preoccupation with the past and with legend can be seen in "Merlin."

**Edwin Muir** (1887–1959) was born in Devoness, Orkney, Scotland. In 1919 he moved to London, where he wrote literary reviews. His verse collections include *The Voyage* (1946), *The Labyrinth* (1949), and *Collected Poems* (1960). Muir is perhaps best remembered as the principal English translator (with his wife Willa) of the great German writer Franz Kafka. His poem "Merlin" addresses the famous wizard from the legend of King Arthur.

## Theme in Poetry

**Theme** is the central idea, or the general idea or insight about life, that a literary work reveals. When a theme is not stated directly, but is implied, you must infer it from evidence in the selection.

## Look For

What point does each of these poems make about Merlin? As you read them, look for the words, phrases, and ideas the poets use to make a point or reveal a theme.

## Writing

Imagine that, like Merlin, you have the power to see into the past and the future. Freewrite, exploring how you would use your power.

## Vocabulary

Knowing the following words will help you as you read these two poems about Merlin.

**outstrip** (out strip') v.: Move ahead of (p. 764)

**raftered** (raf'tərd) adj.: Supported by horizontal beams (p. 764)

**barrows** (bar'ōz) n.: Ancient graves (p. 764)

**pinnacled** (pin'ə k'ld) adj.: Decorated with turrets, like a high tower (p. 764)

**furrow** (fur'ō) n.: Narrow groove or rut (p. 766)

**bower** (bou'ər) n.: Private chamber (p. 766)

**THE ASTROLOGER**
*N. C. Wyeth*
*Diamond M Museum of Fine Art, Texas*

# Merlin

## Geoffrey Hill

I will consider the outnumbering dead:
For they are the husks of what was rich seed.
Now, should they come together to be fed,
They would outstrip the locusts' covering tide.

5   Arthur, Elaine, Mordred;[1] they are all gone
Among the raftered galleries of bone.
By the long barrows of Logres[2] they are made one,
And over their city stands the pinnacled corn.

---

**1. Arthur, Elaine, Mordred:** King Arthur, the mother
of Sir Galahad, treacherous nephew of King Arthur.
**2. Logres:** England.

## THINKING ABOUT THE SELECTION

### Recalling

1. Whom will the speaker consider?
2. What would happen if the dead came together?
3. Who is mentioned in the second stanza?
4. What now stands over their fabled former city?

### Interpreting

5. What does "outnumbering dead" mean in line 1?

6. In what ways were the dead "rich seed"?
7. What qualities, both positive and negative, possessed by the people named in line 5 "are all gone"?
8. Why do you think the poet made Merlin the speaker of this poem?

### Applying

9. The poet seems to feel that certain heroic qualities are missing from our time. Do you agree or disagree? Explain your answer.

# Merlin

## Edwin Muir

O Merlin in your crystal cave
Deep in the diamond of the day,
Will there ever be a singer
Whose music will smooth away
5    The furrow drawn by Adam's[1] finger
Across the meadow and the wave?
Or a runner who'll outrun
Man's long shadow driving on,
Break through the gate of memory
10   And hang the apple on the tree?[2]
Will your magic ever show
The sleeping bride shut in her bower,
The day wreathed in its mound of snow
And Time locked in his tower?

---

**1. Adam's:** In the Bible (Genesis 1–5), Adam was the first man.
**2. hang . . . tree:** In the Bible, when Eve, the first woman, ate the forbidden apple from the tree, she and Adam were cast out of Paradise and forced to live on Earth.

## THINKING ABOUT THE SELECTION

### Recalling

1. What might the "singer" do?
2. What might the "runner" do?
3. What three things might Merlin's sorcery show?

### Interpreting

4. Considering the biblical allusion to Adam, the first man, in line 5, how would you interpret the speaker's first question?
5. What does the phrase "Man's long shadow" signify?
6. What would happen if one could "hang the apple on the tree"?
7. What do the three images in lines 12–14 have in common?
8. State each of the speaker's questions in your own words.
9. Why does the speaker pose these questions to Merlin?

### Applying

10. The poet is asking whether there will ever be another Camelot—a time of peace, prosper-ity, and virtue. What is your opinion? Explain your answer.

## ANALYZING LITERATURE

### Understanding Theme in Poetry

The **theme** of a poem is an insight into life. In the poem by Geoffrey Hill, the theme is that certain heroic qualities are missing from our time. In the poem by Edwin Muir, the theme is whether there will ever be another Camelot. Find evidence in each of these poems that supports the themes?

## THINKING AND WRITING

### Comparing and Contrasting Poems

Write an essay for your classmates compar-ing and contrasting these two poems about Merlin. First list the similarities and differences in the images contained in each poem, the vision presented by each poem, and the tone commu-nicated by each speaker. Then use this informa-tion to write your essay. Revise your essay to include examples to support your statements. Proofread for errors in spelling, grammar, and punctuation.

# Reading a Map

Maps help us visualize important locations in literature. Maps make locations come alive if you know how to read them. A map can tell you a lot about the terrain of a place and can explain the reason for characters' actions.

**Information**

There are different kinds of maps that provide different types of information. For example, a road map shows major roads and highways as well as the locations of towns, cities, and points of interest. A topographical map shows the surface features of a region in relief, including rivers, lakes, and mountains. A population map shows population densities. The map of Great Britain that you will be using is basically a political map. It shows cities and towns as well as administrative, or national, borders or boundaries. It also shows such features as rivers and other bodies of water.

**Lay Out**

It is essential that you view a map with the correct directional orientation. The top area of the map is the north, and the bottom is the south. The area to the right is the east, and the area to the left is the west. Maps often contain a symbol, such as an arrow pointing up and the word *North,* to indicate direction.

**Symbols**

You also need to know how to identify the features on the map you are using. Dots indicate cities and towns, and a circled star indicates the capital city. A dashed line indicates a national boundary. Much of this information is given to you in the map's key.

**Keys**

Most maps include keys, or legends, which are located in a corner of the map. The key enables you to interpret the map. In addition to explaining the symbols used on the map, the key usually provides a scale of distance in miles or kilometers.

**Guidelines**

- Understand what type of map you are looking at.
- Understand how the map is laid out in terms of direction.
- Identify the features on the map by recognizing the symbols.
- Study the information provided in the key and apply it to interpreting the map.

One unit equals approx. 60 miles

**Activity**

Use the map of Great Britain to answer the following questions.

1. Locate London on the map. Based on evidence in one of the legends, how can you tell that London has always been an important center of events?

2. After studying England's natural boundaries on the map, explain why King Arthur would have found England a difficult country to defend against foreign invaders?

3. What role does the Archbishop of Canterbury play in the Arthurian legend? Where is Canterbury in relation to London?

4. King Arthur's magician Merlin was born in Wales. Describe the location of Wales in terms of direction from London.

# YOU THE WRITER

**Assignment**

**1.** Create a new knight for the Round Table. Write a character sketch of a knight renowned for his bravery.

**Prewriting.** Prepare a chart with the following headings: Physical Description, Character Traits, Exploits. List details for your knight under each of these headings.

**Writing.** Write the first draft of your character sketch. Include details from your chart that help create a vivid portrait of your knight.

**Revising.** Make sure you have created a unified impression of your knight. Proofread to correct any grammar, usage, or mechanics errors.

**Assignment**

**2.** You are a reporter for the *Town Crier,* the first newspaper published in medieval England. You have just received a tip that King Arthur is involved in a newsworthy exploit. Write a short news story about the event.

**Prewriting.** Before you begin to write, review the selections about King Arthur. Select one incident that you consider appropriate for your news story. Freewrite about the incident.

**Writing.** Structure your story by answering the questions *who, what, why, when, where,* and *how.* Use only those details that state facts or add specific information related to the incident. Write an appropriate and interesting headline.

**Revising.** Before you write your final draft, make certain that you give the most important information first. Proofread to correct any grammar, usage, or mechanics errors.

**Assignment**

**3.** Create your own legend. Write a new adventure that might have happened to King Arthur, Sir Launcelot, or Merlin.

**Prewriting.** Prepare a semantic map for the new adventure. Work out the characters, the conflict, and the resolution.

**Writing.** Write your legend, including an introduction that will catch your readers' interest and a conclusion that summarizes the outcome of the legend. Also include vivid imagery, precise descriptions, and suspense to create the feel of legend.

**Revising.** Make sure events are related in chronological order. Have you made the resolution of the conflict logical?

# YOU THE CRITIC

**Assignment**

**1.** Choose one character from the King Arthur legend and write a sketch describing him or her.

**Prewriting.** As you review the selections about King Arthur and the knights and ladies, select one and jot down important characteristics. Make note of which are positive and which are negative.

**Writing.** Write the first draft of your sketch. Include details that create a life-like portrait.

**Revising.** Have you made the character come alive for your readers? If not, include additional details.

**Assignment**

**2.** Write an analysis of King Arthur's rise to the throne. Include in your analysis a discussion of the role of Excalibur.

**Prewriting.** Scan the selections for important points that explain how and why Arthur became king. Make a list of those points.

**Writing.** Write your analysis, answering the question, How and why did Arthur become king? Include an introductory sentence that clearly states your opinion, ideas and details from your list to support your explanation, and a concluding statement.

**Revising.** Be certain that your opinion is written with a clear introductory sentence and that your conclusion is complete. Write a title for your analysis and correct any errors.

**Assignment**

**3.** Evaluate the evidence in the selections and write an essay answering the question, Do you think King Arthur was a living person?

**Prewriting.** Write King Arthur's name on a sheet of paper and draw lines radiating out from it. On the lines, write any associations and impressions about his name that come to mind. Also list facts and details.

**Writing.** Write the first draft of your essay on the validity of the King Arthur legend. Weigh the evidence; be certain to use details and information that support your opinion. Begin with your conclusion about the King Arthur legend and logically organize the information. End your explanation with a concluding statement.

**Revising.** Be certain that you state your opinion clearly and give reasons and examples to support that opinion.

**HYDE PARK, 1905–06**
*André Derain*
Paris, Musée Nationale d'Art Moderne

# THE NOVEL

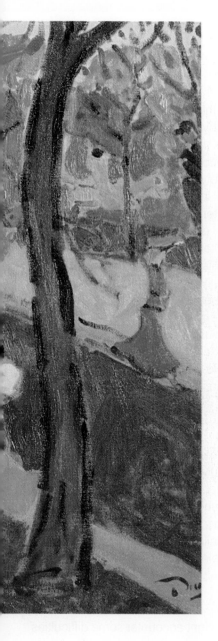

Our word *novel,* meaning a long work of prose fiction, comes from the French word for "new." The first true works of fiction as we know it were the lengthy romances written in France and Spain during the sixteenth and seventeenth centuries. In fact, the French word for novel is still *roman.* The English used the Old French word *novel* to describe these stories and to differentiate them from medieval and classical romances, thus indicating they were something that was new. A distinct literary form was born.

Because of the increased levels of general education and literacy in the eighteenth century, growth of fiction in general and of the novel especially developed rapidly. Reading a novel even became a social event: In an age without television, people read to one another as a means of entertainment. A writer could write a novel and have it printed by a publisher. The publisher, in turn, could sell the story to this expanded audience and pay the author a percentage of the sales. With this wider audience and greater demand, novelists could earn a living with their words. The novel had arrived as a major genre of literature.

The novel has a plot as short stories do, but it is usually longer and more complex in its development and resolution. The creation of characters is important in a novel, for the writer has time to allow the reader to examine the innermost thoughts of the characters. Like most literature, novels have themes or the ideas about life that the story reveals. A novelist, like a writer of short stories or a poet, writes from a point of view that could be first person or third person, limited or omniscient. Certainly tone and style are part of a novel as they are a part of other fiction.

Gothic romances, exciting espionage adventures, science-fiction thrillers, and biting social commentaries are but a few of the forms novels can take. In this unit you will read two novels, one a parable that presents a moral lesson and the other a perceptive commentary about life.

# The Novel

## Background
*The Pearl*

Two novels are presented in this section: *The Pearl* by John Steinbeck and *A Separate Peace* by John Knowles. They are very different in tone, subject matter, and style. The settings and characters in each could not be more dissimilar. Become familiar with the following information before you read them. On a sailing trip with his friend Ed Ricketts in 1940, John Steinbeck heard a folk tale about a fisherman's misfortunes after his discovery of a great pearl. Inspired by the legend, Steinbeck published *The Pearl* four years later. In his preface to *The Pearl* Steinbeck wrote: "If the story is a parable, perhaps everyone takes his own meaning from it. . . ." An important novel like *The Pearl* usually can be interpreted on several levels. To present his multilevel theme, John Steinbeck chose to write this novel as a parable or allegory. A parable or allegory is a short work, usually fictitious, that illustrates a lesson, usually about good and evil. Many lessons in the New Testament, such as the story of the Good Samaritan, are told in parables. Some readers see *The Pearl* as an allegory about human greed, while others find it a parable about social oppression.

Steinbeck often writes of the struggle between the wealthy and the poor, between the strong and the weak, and between different cultures. To understand *The Pearl,* it will help you to understand that Indians of Mexico had been under the domination of people of Spanish descent for over three hundred years at the time of the legend (1900). In many cases the Indians were not allowed to attend school or own the land. While Spanish culture was forced upon the Indians, many retained elements of their tribal customs, just as Juana does when she combines Catholic Hail Marys with ancient prayers.

## Reading Strategies
*The Pearl*

When you read *The Pearl,* you might encounter some difficulties understanding the significance of the culture in the story, the style in which it is written, and the many scientific figures of speech the author uses. Read the background and biographical information carefully for clues to understanding. Also, it might help you to understand the concept of *mi tierra,* or my land. To the Indians, the place of their birth is especially important. Many Mexican Indians believe that they were meant to remain in their birthplace. Therefore you can understand why Kino's leaving La Paz was such an enormous step. In terms of style, *The Pearl* contains little dialogue, and you know very little about the characters. You need to understand that Steinbeck intentionally wrote in this style to reflect the biblical elements of his parable, and he imitated the spoken quality of the New Testament to do so. Also, Steinbeck was fascinated by science, especially marine biology. He used his knowledge of science to create analogies about the human condition. For instance, Kino's village is compared to the habitat of a colonial animal. You might want to ask a science teacher for help in understanding these comparisons. Finally, interact with the literature, using the active reading strategies for questioning, predicting, clarifying, summarizing, and pulling together.

## Themes
## *The Pearl*

You will encounter the following themes in *The Pearl*.
- The struggle for survival
- Free will versus determinism
- Oppression and social class
- Corruption by material wealth and possessions
- The relationship of human beings to nature

## Background
## *A Separate Peace*

John Knowles was only thirty-three when *A Separate Peace* was first published in England in 1959. (It was published in the United States a year later.) The novel was an immediate success, winning the William Faulkner Foundation Award and the Rosenthal Award of the National Institute of Arts and Letters.

Knowles based the book on experiences he had as a fifteen-year-old boarding student at Phillips Exeter Academy in New Hampshire during World War II. World War II caused enormous changes in American society. On the home front, families were faced with separation, frequent relocation, and worry about members fighting overseas. People grew "victory gardens" in their back yards to supplement the food supply. Rubber and metals, which were scarce at the time, were collected in drives. Americans used coupons and stood in lengthy lines to buy rationed gasoline, tires, coffee, canned food, and meat. Instead of advertising to encourage purchases, industries mounted campaigns to promote conservation or to suggest waiting to buy. As the demand for workers to produce wartime material rose, women entered the work force in industries previously closed to them. The double pressures of adolescence in this wartime environment and the conflicting surrounding of a protected yet competitive boarding school served as the foundation of *A Separate Peace.*

**Reading Strategies**
***A Separate Peace***

You will probably have little difficulty reading *A Separate Peace.* There are no tricks and no attempts to catch you off guard. You do need to be aware that Gene, the narrator, is an adult relating events from his school days, and his insights are those of a person in his mid-thirties. As you read, be aware that you will find young people speaking and acting appropriately to their time and age, as well as the voice of a more mature person looking back on those actions. Notice that the point of view is first person. As a reader, you know only Gene's thoughts and impressions. When you read his "confessions," consider what the other characters might have felt. Read to discover whether Gene perhaps judges himself too harshly. Because this novel takes place at a school, there are some references to foreign language and works of literature. You do not need to understand all the references, but do read to understand the reason why they are mentioned. Likewise, there are some references to political and military leaders of World War II. If you are unsure about who they are, you might refer to a history text for clarification. Finally, interact with the literature by using the active reading strategies: question, predict, clarify, summarize, pull together.

**Themes**
***A Separate Peace***

You will encounter the following themes in *A Separate Peace.*
• Friendship in all its complexity
• Conformity and rebellion
• Truth and falsehood
• The nature and extent of maturity; growing up and responsibility
• The stress of war

# The Pearl

LA MOLENDERA, 1924
*Diego Rivera*
Museo de Art Moderno

# GUIDE FOR READING

## The Pearl, Chapters 1–3

**John Steinbeck** (1902–1968) grew up in Salinas in southern California. He loved the outdoors and once worked as a ranch hand and a laborer on a canal. Steinbeck began writing at an early age, and even joined a hobo camp to learn about its people and their life. Steinbeck wrote novels, short stories, newspaper articles, plays, and film scripts. He won the Pulitzer Prize in 1940 for *The Grapes of Wrath* and the Nobel Prize in 1962. His belief that life can be filled with tragedy is evident in *The Pearl* (1947).

**Characters in a Parable**

A **parable** is a short tale that illustrates a universal truth. In a parable, characters are seldom three-dimensional; instead, they tend to be flat, representing qualities rather than real-life people.

**Look For**

As you read the first three chapters of *The Pearl,* look for what Kino learns in this parable. What universal truth does the parable reveal?

**Writing**

Can an object of value bring nothing but misery? Imagine that you suddenly found a priceless treasure. How would your life change? Freewrite about this imagined experience, describing your thoughts and feelings.

**Vocabulary**

Knowing the following words will help you as you read the first three chapters of *The Pearl.*

**parable** (par′ə b′l) *n.*: A short story that illustrates a spiritual truth (p. 779)

**feinted** (fānt′id) *v.*: Made a pretense of attack (p. 781)

**scorpion** (skôr′pē ən) *n.*: Any of a group of arachnids found in warm regions, with a long tail ending in a curved, poisonous sting (p. 781)

**avarice** (av′ər is) *n.*: Greediness (p. 784)

**indigent** (in′di jənt) *adj.*: Needy; poor (p. 784)

**undulating** (un′joo lāt′ iŋ) *v.*: Rising and falling (p. 788)

**dissembling** (di sem′b′liŋ) *v.*: Concealing the real feelings by a pretense (p. 795)

# The Pearl

## John Steinbeck

"In the town they tell the story of the great pearl—how it was found and how it was lost again. They tell of Kino, the fisherman, and of his wife, Juana, and of the baby, Coyotito. And because the story has been told so often, it has taken root in every man's mind. And, as with all retold tales that are in people's hearts, there are only good and bad things and black and white things and good and evil things and no in-between anywhere.

"If this story is a parable, perhaps everyone takes his own meaning from it and reads his own life into it. In any case, they say in the town that . . . ."

### Chapter 1

Kino awakened in the near dark. The stars still shone and the day had drawn only a pale wash of light in the lower sky to the east. The roosters had been crowing for some time, and the early pigs were already beginning their ceaseless turning of twigs and bits of wood to see whether anything to eat had been overlooked. Outside the brush house in the tuna[1] clump, a covey of little birds chittered and flurried with their wings.

Kino's eyes opened, and he looked first at the lightening square which was the door and then he looked at the hanging box where Coyotito slept. And last he turned his head to Juana, his wife, who lay beside him on the mat, her blue head shawl over her nose and over her breasts and around the small of her back. Juana's eyes were open too. Kino could never remember seeing them closed when he awakened. Her dark eyes made little reflected stars. She was looking at him as she was always looking at him when he awakened.

Kino heard the little splash of morning waves on the beach. It was very good—Kino closed his eyes again to listen to his music. Perhaps he alone did this and perhaps all of his people did it. His people had once been great makers of songs so that everything they saw or thought or did or heard became a song. That was very long ago. The songs remained; Kino knew them, but no new songs were added. That does not mean that there were no personal songs. In Kino's head there was a song now, clear and soft, and if he had been able to speak of it, he would have called it the Song of the Family.

His blanket was over his nose to protect him from the dank air. His eyes flicked to a rustle beside him. It was Juana arising, almost soundlessly. On her hard bare feet she went to the hanging box where Coyotito slept, and she leaned over and said a little reassuring word. Coyotito looked up for a moment and closed his eyes and slept again.

Juana went to the fire pit and uncovered a coal and fanned it alive while she broke little pieces of brush over it.

---

1. **tuna** (to͞o′ nə) *adj.*: Prickly-pear cactus.

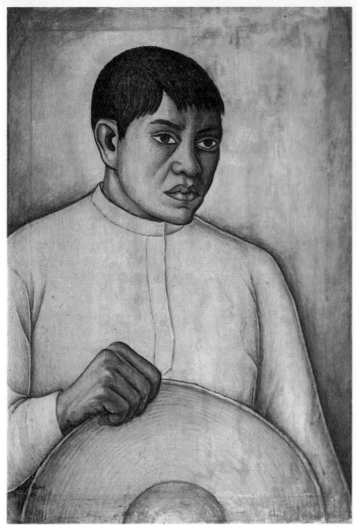

**PEASANT WITH SOMBRERO (PEON), 1926**
*Diego Rivera*
Galería Arvil, Mexico City

Now Kino got up and wrapped his blanket about his head and nose and shoulders. He slipped his feet into his sandals and went outside to watch the dawn.

Outside the door he squatted down and gathered the blanket ends about his knees. He saw the specks of Gulf[2] clouds flame high in the air. And a goat came near and sniffed at him and stared with its cold yellow eyes. Behind him Juana's fire leaped into flame and threw spears of light through the chinks of the brush-house wall and threw a wavering square of light out the door. A late moth blustered in to find the fire. The Song of the Family came now from behind Kino. And the rhythm of the family song was the grinding stone where Juana worked the corn for the morning cakes.

The dawn came quickly now, a wash, a glow, a lightness, and then an explosion of fire as the sun arose out of the Gulf. Kino looked down to cover his eyes from the glare. He could hear the pat of the corncakes in the house and the rich smell of them on the

---

**2. Gulf:** The Gulf of California, a body of water between Baja California—a Mexican peninsula—and the main part of Mexico.

cooking plate. The ants were busy on the ground, big black ones with shiny bodies, and little dusty quick ants. Kino watched with the detachment of God while a dusty ant frantically tried to escape the sand trap an ant lion had dug for him. A thin, timid dog came close and, at a soft word from Kino, curled up, arranged its tail neatly over its feet, and laid its chin delicately on the pile. It was a black dog with yellow-gold spots where its eyebrows should have been. It was a morning like other mornings and yet perfect among mornings.

Kino heard the creak of the rope when Juana took Coyotito out of his hanging box and cleaned him and hammocked him in her shawl in a loop that placed him close to her breast. Kino could see these things without looking at them. Juana sang softly an ancient song that had only three notes and yet endless variety of interval. And this was part of the family song too. It was all part. Sometimes it rose to an aching chord that caught the throat, saying this is safety, this is warmth, this is the *Whole.*

Across the brush fence were other brush houses, and the smoke came from them too, and the sound of breakfast, but those were other songs, their pigs were other pigs, their wives were not Juana. Kino was young and strong and his black hair hung over his brown forehead. His eyes were warm and fierce and bright and his mustache was thin and coarse. He lowered his blanket from his nose now, for the dark poisonous air was gone and the yellow sunlight fell on the house. Near the brush fence two roosters bowed and feinted at each other with squared wings and neck feathers ruffed out. It would be a clumsy fight. They were not game chickens. Kino watched them for a moment, and then his eyes went up to a flight of wild doves twinkling inland to the hills. The world was awake now, and Kino arose and went into his brush house.

As he came through the door Juana stood up from the glowing fire pit. She put Coyotito back in his hanging box and then she combed her black hair and braided it in two braids and tied the ends with thin green ribbon. Kino squatted by the fire pit and rolled a hot corncake and dipped it in sauce and ate it. And he drank a little pulque[3] and that was breakfast. That was the only breakfast he had ever known outside of feast days and one incredible fiesta on cookies that had nearly killed him. When Kino had finished, Juana came back to the fire and ate her breakfast. They had spoken once, but there is not need for speech if it is only a habit anyway. Kino sighed with satisfaction—and that was conversation.

The sun was warming the brush house, breaking through its crevices in long streaks. And one of the streaks fell on the hanging box where Coyotito lay, and on the ropes that held it.

It was a tiny movement that drew their eyes to the hanging box. Kino and Juana froze in their positions. Down the rope that hung the baby's box from the roof support a scorpion moved slowly. His stinging tail was straight out behind him, but he could whip it up in a flash of time.

Kino's breath whistled in his nostrils and he opened his mouth to stop it. And then the startled look was gone from him and the rigidity from his body. In his mind a new song had come, the Song of Evil, the music of the enemy, of any foe of the family, a savage, secret, dangerous melody, and underneath, the Song of the Family cried plaintively.

The scorpion moved delicately down the rope toward the box. Under her breath Juana repeated an ancient magic to guard against such evil, and on top of that she

---

**3. pulque** (pōōl' kā) *n.*: A milky drink made from the juice of the agave, a family of Mexican desert plant.

muttered a Hail Mary[4] between clenched teeth. But Kino was in motion. His body glided quietly across the room, noiselessly and smoothly. His hands were in front of him, palms down, and his eyes were on the scorpion. Beneath it in the hanging box Coyotito laughed and reached up his hand toward it. It sensed danger when Kino was almost within reach of it. It stopped, and its tail rose up over its back in little jerks and the curved thorn on the tail's end glistened.

Kino stood perfectly still. He could hear Juana whispering the old magic again, and he could hear the evil music of the enemy. He could not move until the scorpion moved, and it felt for the source of the death that was coming to it. Kino's hand went forward very slowly, very smoothly. The thorned tail jerked upright. And at that moment the laughing Coyotito shook the rope and the scorpion fell.

Kino's hand leaped to catch it, but it fell past his fingers, fell on the baby's shoulder, landed and struck. Then, snarling, Kino had it, had it in his fingers, rubbing it to a paste in his hands. He threw it down and beat it into the earth floor with his fist, and Coyotito screamed with pain in his box. But Kino beat and stamped the enemy until it was only a fragment and a moist place in the dirt. His teeth were bared and fury flared in his eyes and the Song of the Enemy roared in his ears.

But Juana had the baby in her arms now. She found the puncture with redness starting from it already. She put her lips down over the puncture and sucked hard and spat and sucked again while Coyotito screamed.

Kino hovered; he was helpless, he was in the way.

The screams of the baby brought the neighbors. Out of their brush houses they poured—Kino's brother Juan Tomás and his fat wife Apolonia and their four children crowded in the door and blocked the entrance, while behind them others tried to look in, and one small boy crawled among legs to have a look. And those in front passed the word back to those behind —"Scorpion. The baby has been stung."

Juana stopped sucking the puncture for a moment. The little hole was slightly enlarged and its edges whitened from the sucking, but the red swelling extended farther around it in a hard lymphatic mound. And all of these people knew about the scorpion. An adult might be very ill from the sting, but a baby could easily die from the poison. First, they knew, would come swelling and fever and tightened throat, and then cramps in the stomach, and then Coyotito might die if enough of the poison had gone in. But the stinging pain of the bite was going away. Coyotito's screams turned to moans.

Kino had wondered often at the iron in his patient, fragile wife. She, who was obedient and respectful and cheerful and patient, she could arch her back in child pain with hardly a cry. She could stand fatigue and hunger almost better than Kino himself. In the canoe she was like a strong man. And now she did a most surprising thing.

"The doctor," she said. "Go to get the doctor."

The word was passed out among the neighbors where they stood close packed in the little yard behind the brush fence. And they repeated among themselves, "Juana wants the doctor." A wonderful thing, a memorable thing, to want the doctor. To get him would be a remarkable thing. The doctor never came to the cluster of brush houses. Why should he, when he had more than

---

**4. Hail Mary:** A prayer to the Virgin Mary, the mother of Jesus, used in the Roman Catholic Church.

**DELFINA AND DIMAS**
*Diego Rivera*
*Private Collection*

he could do to take care of the rich people who lived in the stone and plaster houses of the town.

"He would not come," the people in the yard said.

"He would not come," the people in the door said, and the thought got into Kino.

"The doctor would not come," Kino said to Juana.

She looked up at him, her eyes as cold as the eyes of a lioness. This was Juana's first baby—this was nearly everything there was in Juana's world. And Kino saw her determination and the music of the family sounded in his head with a steely tone.

"Then we will go to him," Juana said, and with one hand she arranged her dark blue shawl over her head and made of one end of it a sling to hold the moaning baby and made of the other end of it a shade over his eyes to protect him from the light. The people in the door pushed against those behind to let her through. Kino followed her. They went out of the gate to the rutted path and the neighbors followed them.

The thing had become a neighborhood affair. They made a quick soft-footed procession into the center of the town, first Juana and Kino, and behind them Juan Tomás and Apolonia, her big stomach jiggling with the strenuous pace, then all the neighbors with the children trotting on the flanks. And the yellow sun threw their black shadows ahead of them so that they walked on their own shadows.

They came to the place where the brush houses stopped and the city of stone and plaster began, the city of harsh outer walls and inner cool gardens where a little water played and the bougainvillaea[5] crusted the walls with purple and brick-red and white. They heard from the secret gardens the singing of caged birds and heard the splash of cooling water on hot flagstones. The procession crossed the blinding plaza and passed in front of the church. It had grown now, and on the outskirts the hurrying newcomers were being softly informed how the baby had been stung by a scorpion, how the father and mother were taking it to the doctor.

And the newcomers, particularly the beggars from the front of the church who were great experts in financial analysis, looked quickly at Juana's old blue skirt, saw the tears in her shawl, appraised the green ribbon on her braids, read the age of Kino's blanket and the thousand washings of his clothes, and set them down as poverty people and went along to see what kind of drama might develop. The four beggars in front of the church knew everything in the town. They were students of the expressions of young women as they went in to confession, and they saw them as they came out and read the nature of the sin. They knew every little scandal and some very big crimes. They slept at their posts in the shadow of the church so that no one crept in for consolation without their knowledge. And they knew the doctor. They knew his ignor-

ance, his cruelty, his avarice, his appetites, his sins. They knew his clumsy operations and the little brown pennies he gave sparingly for alms. They had seen his corpses go into the church. And, since early Mass was over and business was slow, they followed the procession, these endless searchers after perfect knowledge of their fellow men, to see what the fat lazy doctor would do about an indigent baby with a scorpion bite.

The scurrying procession came at last to the big gate in the wall of the doctor's house. They could hear the splashing water and the singing of caged birds and the sweep of the long brooms on the flagstones. And they could smell the frying of good bacon from the doctor's house.

Kino hesitated a moment. This doctor was not of his people. This doctor was of a race which for nearly four hundred years had beaten and starved and robbed and despised Kino's race, and frightened it too, so that the indigene[6] came humbly to the door. And as always when he came near to one of this race, Kino felt weak and afraid and angry at the same time. Rage and terror went together. He could kill the doctor more easily than he could talk to him, for all of the doctor's race spoke to all of Kino's race as though they were simple animals. And as Kino raised his right hand to the iron ring knocker in the gate, rage swelled in him, and the pounding music of the enemy beat in his ears, and his lips drew tight against his teeth—but with his left hand he reached to take off his hat. The iron ring pounded against the gate. Kino took off his hat and stood waiting. Coyotito moaned a little in Juana's arms, and she spoke softly to him. The procession crowded close the better to see and hear.

---

**5. bougainvillaea** (bōo′ gən vil′ ē ə) *n.*: A tropical vine with large, colorful flowers.

**6. indigene** (in′ di jēn′) *n.*: A native.

After a moment the big gate opened a few inches. Kino could see the green coolness of the garden and little splashing fountain through the opening. The man who looked out at him was one of his own race. Kino spoke to him in the old language. "The little one—the firstborn—has been poisoned by the scorpion," Kino said. "He requires the skill of the healer."

The gate closed a little, and the servant refused to speak in the old language. "A little moment," he said. "I go to inform myself," and he closed the gate and slid the bolt home. The glaring sun threw the bunched shadows of the people blackly on the white wall.

In his chamber the doctor sat up in his high bed. He had on his dressing gown of red watered silk that had come from Paris, a little tight over the chest now if it was buttoned. On his lap was a silver tray with a silver chocolate pot and a tiny cup of eggshell china, so delicate that it looked silly when he lifted it with his big hand, lifted it with the tips of thumb and forefinger and spread the other three fingers wide to get them out of the way. His eyes rested in puffy little hammocks of flesh and his mouth drooped with discontent. He was growing very stout, and his voice was hoarse with the fat that pressed on his throat. Beside him on a table was a small Oriental gong and a bowl of cigarettes. The furnishings of the room were heavy and dark and gloomy. The pictures were religious, even the large tinted photograph of his dead wife, who, if Masses willed and paid for out of her own estate could do it, was in Heaven. The doctor had once for a short time been a part of the great world and his whole subsequent life was memory and longing for France. "That," he said, "was civilized living"—by which he meant that on a small income he had been able to keep a mistress and eat in restaurants. He poured his second cup of chocolate and crumbled a sweet biscuit in his fingers. The servant from the gate came to the open door and stood waiting to be noticed.

"Yes?" the doctor asked.

"It is a little Indian with a baby. He says a scorpion stung it."

The doctor put his cup down gently before he let his anger rise.

"Have I nothing better to do than cure insect bites for 'little Indians'? I am a doctor, not a veterinary."

"Yes, *Patron*,"[7] said the servant.

"Has he any money?" the doctor demanded. "No, they never have any money. I, I alone in the world am supposed to work for nothing—and I am tired of it. See if he has any money!"

At the gate the servant opened the door a trifle and looked out at the waiting people. And this time he spoke in the old language.

"Have you money to pay for the treatment?"

Now Kino reached into a secret place somewhere under his blanket. He brought out a paper folded many times. Crease by crease he unfolded it, until at last there came to view eight small misshapen seed pearls,[8] as ugly and gray as little ulcers, flattened and almost valueless. The servant took the paper and closed the gate again, but this time he was not gone long. He opened the gate just wide enough to pass the paper back.

"The doctor has gone out," he said. "He was called to a serious case." And he shut the gate quickly out of shame.

And now a wave of shame went over the whole procession. They melted away. The

---

7. **Patron** (pä trōn'): Spanish for "master."
8. **seed pearls:** Very small pearls, often imperfect.

beggars went back to the church steps, the stragglers moved off, and the neighbors departed so that the public shaming of Kino would not be in their eyes.

For a long time Kino stood in front of the gate with Juana beside him. Slowly he put his suppliant hat on his head. Then, without warning, he struck the gate a crushing blow with his fist. He looked down in wonder at his split knuckles and at the blood that flowed down between his fingers.

## Chapter 2

The town lay on a broad estuary,[1] its old yellow plastered buildings hugging the beach. And on the beach the white and blue canoes that came from Nayarit[2] were drawn up, canoes preserved for generations by a hard shell-like waterproof plaster whose making was a secret of the fishing people. They were high and graceful canoes with curving bow and stern and a braced section midships where a mast could be stepped to carry a small lateen sail.[3]

The beach was yellow sand, but at the water's edge a rubble of shell and algae took its place. Fiddler crabs bubbled and sputtered in their holes in the sand, and in the shallows little lobsters popped in and out of their tiny homes in the rubble and sand. The sea bottom was rich with crawling and swimming and growing things. The brown algae waved in the gentle currents and the green eel grass swayed and little sea horses clung to its stems. Spotted botete, the poison fish, lay on the bottom in the eel-grass beds, and the bright-colored swimming crabs scampered over them.

On the beach the hungry dogs and the hungry pigs of the town searched endlessly for any dead fish or sea bird that might have floated in on a rising tide.

Although the morning was young, the hazy mirage was up. The uncertain air that magnified some things and blotted out others hung over the whole Gulf so that all sights were unreal and vision could not be trusted; so that sea and land had the sharp clarities and the vagueness of a dream. Thus it might be that the people of the Gulf trust things of the spirit and things of the imagination, but they do not trust their eyes to show them distance or clear outline or any optical exactness. Across the estuary from the town one section of mangroves stood clear and telescopically defined, while another mangrove clump was a hazy black-green blob. Part of the far shore disappeared into a shimmer that looked like water. There was no certainty in seeing, no proof that what you saw was there or was not there. And the people of the Gulf expected all places were that way, and it was not strange to them. A copper haze hung over the water, and the hot morning sun beat on it and made it vibrate blindingly.

The brush houses of the fishing people were back from the beach on the right-hand side of the town, and the canoes were drawn up in front of this area.

Kino and Juana came slowly down to the beach and to Kino's canoe, which was the one thing of value he owned in the world. It was very old. Kino's grandfather had brought it from Nayarit, and he had given it to Kino's father, and so it had come to Kino. It was at once property and source of food, for a man with a boat can guarantee a woman that she will eat something. It is

---

**1. estuary** (es' choo wer' ē) *n.*: An inlet formed where a river enters the ocean.
**2. Nayarit** (nä' yä rēt'): A state of western Mexico across the Gulf of California from Baja California.
**3. stepped . . . lateen** (la tēn') **sail:** Raised and fixed in place to carry a triangular sail attached to a long rod.

the bulwark against starvation. And every year Kino refinished his canoe with the hard shell-like plaster by the secret method that had also come to him from his father. Now he came to the canoe and touched the bow tenderly as he always did. He laid his diving rock and his basket and the two ropes in the sand by the canoe. And he folded his blanket and laid it in the bow.

Juana laid Coyotito on the blanket, and she placed her shawl over him so that the hot sun could not shine on him. He was quiet now, but the swelling on his shoulder had continued up his neck and under his ear and his face was puffed and feverish. Juana went to the water and waded in. She gathered some brown seaweed and made a flat damp poultice[4] of it, and this she applied to the baby's swollen shoulder, which was as good a remedy as any and probably better than the doctor could have done. But the remedy lacked his authority because it was simple and didn't cost anything. The stomach cramps had not come to Coyotito. Perhaps Juana had sucked out the poison in time, but she had not sucked out her worry over her firstborn. She had not prayed directly for the recovery of the baby—she had prayed that they might find a pearl with which to hire the doctor to cure the baby, for the minds of people are as unsubstantial as the mirage of the Gulf.

Now Kino and Juana slid the canoe down the beach to the water, and when the bow floated, Juana climbed in, while Kino pushed the stern in and waded beside it until it floated lightly and trembled on the little breaking waves. Then in coordination Juana and Kino drove their double-bladed paddles into the sea, and the canoe creased the water and hissed with speed. The other pearlers were gone out long since. In a few moments Kino could see them clustered in the haze, riding over the oyster bed.

Light filtered down through the water to the bed where the frilly pearl oysters lay fastened to the rubbly bottom, a bottom strewn with shells of broken, opened oysters. This was the bed that had raised the King of Spain to be a great power in Europe in past years, had helped to pay for his wars, and had decorated the churches for his soul's sake. The gray oysters with ruffles like skirts on the shells, the barnacle-crusted oysters with little bits of weed clinging to the skirts and small crabs climbing over them. An accident could happen to these oysters, a grain of sand could lie in the folds of muscle and irritate the flesh until in self-protection the flesh coated the grain with a layer of smooth cement. But once started, the flesh continued to coat the foreign body until it fell free in some tidal flurry or until the oyster was destroyed. For centuries men had dived down and torn the oysters from the beds and ripped them open, looking for the coated grains of sand. Swarms of fish lived near the bed to live near the oysters thrown back by the searching men and to nibble at the shining inner shells. But the pearls were accidents, and the finding of one was luck, a little pat on the back by God or the gods or both.

Kino had two ropes, one tied to a heavy stone and one to a basket. He stripped off his shirt and trousers and laid his hat in the bottom of the canoe. The water was oily smooth. He took his rock in one hand and his basket in the other, and he slipped feet first over the side and the rock carried him to the bottom. The bubbles rose behind him until the water cleared and he could see. Above, the surface of the water was an

---

**4. poultice** (pōl′ tis) *n.*: An absorbent mass applied to a sore or inflamed part of the body.

undulating mirror of brightness, and he could see the bottoms of the canoes sticking through it.

Kino moved cautiously so that the water would not be obscured with mud or sand. He hooked his foot in the loop on his rock and his hands worked quickly, tearing the oysters loose, some singly, others in clusters. He laid them in his basket. In some places the oysters clung to one another so that they came free in lumps.

Now, Kino's people had sung of everything that happened or existed. They had made songs to the fishes, to the sea in anger and to the sea in calm, to the light and the dark and the sun and the moon, and the songs were all in Kino and in his people —every song that had ever been made, even the ones forgotten. And as he filled his basket the song was in Kino, and the beat of the song was his pounding heart as it ate the oxygen from his held breath, and the melody of the song was the gray-green water and the little scuttling animals and the clouds of fish that flitted by and were gone. But in the song there was a secret little inner song, hardly perceptible, but always there, sweet and secret and clinging, almost hiding in the countermelody, and this was the Song of the Pearl That Might Be, for every shell thrown in the basket might contain a pearl. Chance was against it, but luck and the gods might be for it. And in the canoe above him Kino knew that Juana was making the magic of prayer, her face set rigid and her muscles hard to force the luck, to tear the luck out of the gods' hands, for she needed the luck for the swollen shoulder of Coyotito. And because the need was great and the desire was great, the little secret melody of the pearl that might be was stronger this morning. Whole phrases of it came clearly and softly into the Song of the Undersea.

Kino, in his pride and youth and strength, could remain down over two minutes without strain, so that he worked deliberately, selecting the largest shells. Because they were disturbed, the oyster shells were tightly closed. A little to his right a hummock[5] of rubbly rock stuck up, covered with young oysters not ready to take. Kino moved next to the hummock, and then, beside it, under a little overhang, he saw a very large oyster lying by itself, not covered with its clinging brothers. The shell was partly open, for the overhang protected this ancient oyster, and in the liplike muscle Kino saw a ghostly gleam, and then the shell closed down. His heart beat out a heavy rhythm and the melody of the maybe pearl shrilled in his ears. Slowly he forced the oyster loose and held it tightly against his breast. He kicked his foot free from the rock loop, and his body rose to the surface and his black hair gleamed in the sunlight. He reached over the side of the canoe and laid the oyster in the bottom.

Then Juana steadied the boat while he climbed in. His eyes were shining with excitement, but in decency he pulled up his rock, and then he pulled up his basket of oysters and lifted them in. Juana sensed his excitement, and she pretended to look away. It is not good to want a thing too much. It sometimes drives the luck away. You must want it just enough, and you must be very tactful with God or the gods. But Juana stopped breathing. Very deliberately Kino opened his short strong knife. He looked speculatively at the basket. Perhaps it would be better to open *the* oyster last. He took a small oyster from the basket, cut the muscle, searched the folds of flesh, and threw it in the water. Then he seemed to see the great oyster for the first time. He squatted in the bottom of the canoe, picked up the shell

---

**5. hummock** (hum′ ək) *n.*: A low, rounded hill.

and examined it. The flutes were shining black to brown, and only a few small barnacles adhered to the shell. Now Kino was reluctant to open it. What he had seen, he knew, might be a reflection, a piece of flat shell accidentally drifted in or a complete illusion. In this Gulf of uncertain light there were more illusions than realities.

But Juana's eyes were on him and she could not wait. She put her hand on Coyotito's covered head. "Open it," she said softly.

Kino deftly slipped his knife into the edge of the shell. Through the knife he could feel the muscle tighten hard. He worked the blade leverwise and the closing muscle parted and the shell fell apart. The liplike flesh writhed up and then subsided. Kino lifted the flesh, and there it lay, the great pearl, perfect as the moon. It captured the light and refined it and gave it back in silver incandescence. It was as large as a sea gull's egg. It was the greatest pearl in the world.

Juana caught her breath and moaned a little. And to Kino the secret melody of the maybe pearl broke clear and beautiful, rich and warm and lovely, glowing and gloating and triumphant. In the surface of the great pearl he could see dream forms. He picked the pearl from the dying flesh and held it in his palm, and he turned it over and saw that its curve was perfect. Juana came near to stare at it in his hand, and it was the hand he had smashed against the doctor's gate, and the torn flesh of the knuckles was turned grayish white by the sea water.

Instinctively Juana went to Coyotito where he lay on his father's blanket. She lifted the poultice of seaweed and looked at the shoulder. "Kino," she cried shrilly.

He looked past his pearl, and he saw that the swelling was going out of the baby's shoulder, the poison was receding from its body. Then Kino's fist closed over the pearl and his emotion broke over him. He put back his head and howled. His eyes rolled up and he screamed and his body was rigid. The men in the other canoes looked up, startled, and then they dug their paddles into the sea and raced toward Kino's canoe.

## Chapter 3

A town is a thing like a colonial animal. A town has a nervous system and a head and shoulders and feet. A town is a thing separate from all other towns, so that there are no two towns alike. And a town has a whole emotion. How news travels through a town is a mystery not easily to be solved. News seems to move faster than small boys can scramble and dart to tell it, faster than women can call it over the fences.

Before Kino and Juana and the other fishers had come to Kino's brush house, the nerves of the town were pulsing and vibrating with the news—Kino had found the Pearl of the World. Before panting little boys could strangle out the words, their mothers knew it. The news swept on past the brush houses, and it washed in a foaming wave into the town of stone and plaster. It came to the priest walking in his garden, and it put a thoughtful look in his eyes and a memory of certain repairs necessary to the church. He wondered what the pearl would be worth. And he wondered whether he had baptized Kino's baby, or married him for that matter. The news came to the shopkeepers, and they looked at men's clothes that had not sold so well.

The news came to the doctor where he sat with a woman whose illness was age, though neither she nor the doctor would admit it. And when it was made plain who Kino was, the doctor grew stern and judicious at the same time. "He is a client of mine," the doctor said. "I am treating his child for a scorpion sting." And the doctor's

eyes rolled up a little in their fat hammocks and he thought of Paris. He remembered the room he had lived in there as a great and luxurious place, and he remembered the hard-faced woman who had lived with him as a beautiful and kind girl, although she had been none of these three. The doctor looked past his aged patient and saw himself sitting in a restaurant in Paris and a waiter was just opening a bottle of wine.

The news came early to the beggars in front of the church, and it made them giggle a little with pleasure, for they knew that there is no almsgiver in the world like a poor man who is suddenly lucky.

Kino had found the Pearl of the World. In the town, in little offices, sat the men who bought pearls from the fishers. They waited in their chairs until the pearls came in, and then they cackled and fought and shouted and threatened until they reached the lowest price the fisherman would stand. But there was a price below which they dared not go, for it had happened that a fisherman in despair had given his pearls to the church. And when the buying was over, these buyers sat alone and their fingers played restlessly with the pearls, and they wished they owned the pearls. For there were not many buyers really—there was only one, and he kept these agents in separate offices to give a semblance of competition. The news came to these men, and their eyes squinted and their fingertips burned a little, and each one thought how the patron could not live forever and someone had to take his place. And each one thought how with some capital he could get a new start.

All manner of people grew interested in Kino—people with things to sell and people with favors to ask. Kino had found the Pearl of the World. The essence of pearl mixed with essence of men and a curious dark residue was precipitated. Every man suddenly became related to Kino's pearl, and Kino's pearl went into the dreams, the speculations, the schemes, the plans, the futures, the wishes, the needs, the lusts, the hungers, of everyone, and only one person stood in the way and that was Kino, so that he became curiously every man's enemy. The news stirred up something infinitely black and evil in the town; the black distillate was like the scorpion, or like hunger in the smell of food, or like loneliness when love is withheld. The poison sacs of the town began to manufacture venom, and the town swelled and puffed with the pressure of it.

But Kino and Juana did not know these things. Because they were happy and excited they thought everyone shared their joy. Juan Tomás and Apolonia did, and they were the world too. In the afternoon, when the sun had gone over the mountains of the Peninsula to sink in the outward sea, Kino squatted in his house with Juana beside him. And the brush house was crowded with neighbors. Kino held the great pearl in his hand, and it was warm and alive in his hand. And the music of the pearl had merged with the music of the family so that one beautified the other. The neighbors looked at the pearl in Kino's hand and they wondered how such luck could come to any man.

And Juan Tomás, who squatted on Kino's right hand because he was his brother, asked, "What will you do now that you have become a rich man?"

Kino looked into his pearl, and Juana cast her eyelashes down and arranged her shawl to cover her face so that her excite-ment could not be seen. And in the incandescence of the pearl the pictures formed of the things Kino's mind had considered in the past and had given up as impossible. In the pearl he saw Juana and Coyotito and himself standing and kneeling at the high altar, and they were being married now that they could pay. He spoke softly, "We will be married—in the church."

In the pearl he saw how they were dressed—Juana in a shawl stiff with new-ness and a new skirt, and from under the long skirt Kino could see that she wore shoes. It was in the pearl—the picture glowing there. He himself was dressed in new white clothes, and he carried a new hat —not of straw but of fine black felt—and he too wore shoes—not sandals but shoes that laced. But Coyotito—he was the one—he wore a blue sailor suit from the United States and a little yachting cap such as Kino had seen once when a pleasure boat put into the estuary. All of these things Kino saw in the lucent[1] pearl and he said, "We will have new clothes."

And the music of the pearl rose like a chorus of trumpets in his ears.

Then to the lovely gray surface of the pearl came the little things Kino wanted: a harpoon to take the place of one lost a year ago, a new harpoon of iron with a ring in the end of the shaft; and—his mind could hard-ly make the leap—a rifle—but why not, since he was so rich. And Kino saw Kino in the pearl, Kino holding a Winchester car-bine. It was the wildest day-dreaming and very pleasant. His lips moved hesitantly over this—"A rifle," he said. "Perhaps a rifle."

It was the rifle that broke down the barriers. This was an impossibility, and if he could think of having a rifle whole hori-

---

**1. lucent** ($\overline{loo}'$ sənt) *adj.*: Shining.

zons were burst and he could rush on. For it is said that humans are never satisfied, that you give them one thing and they want something more. And this is said in disparagement, whereas it is one of the greatest talents the species has and one that has made it superior to animals that are satisfied with what they have.

The neighbors, close pressed and silent in the house, nodded their heads at his wild imaginings. And a man in the rear murmured, "A rifle. He will have a rifle."

But the music of the pearl was shrilling with triumph in Kino. Juana looked up, and her eyes were wide at Kino's courage and at his imagination. And electric strength had come to him now the horizons were kicked out. In the pearl he saw Coyotito sitting at a little desk in a school, just as Kino had once seen it through an open door. And Coyotito was dressed in a jacket, and he had on a white collar and a broad silken tie. Moreover, Coyotito was writing on a big piece of paper. Kino looked at his neighbors fiercely. "My son will go to school," he said, and the neighbors were hushed. Juana caught her breath sharply. Her eyes were bright as she watched him, and she looked quickly down at Coyotito in her arms to see whether this might be possible.

But Kino's face shone with prophecy. "My son will read and open the books, and my son will write and will know writing. And my son will make numbers, and these things will make us free because he will know—he will know and through him we will know." And in the pearl Kino saw himself and Juana squatting by the little fire in the brush hut while Coyotito read from a great book. "This is what the pearl will do," said Kino. And he had never said so many words together in his life. And suddenly he was afraid of his talking. His hand closed down over the pearl and cut the light away

from it. Kino was afraid as a man is afraid who says, "I will," without knowing.

Now the neighbors knew they had witnessed a great marvel. They knew that time would now date from Kino's pearl, and that they would discuss this moment for many years to come. If these things came to pass, they would recount how Kino looked and what he said and how his eyes shone, and they would say, "He was a man transfigured. Some power was given to him, and there it started. You see what a great man he has become, starting from that moment. And I myself saw it."

And if Kino's planning came to nothing, those same neighbors would say, "There it started. A foolish madness came over him so that he spoke foolish words. God keep us from such things. Yes, God punished Kino because he rebelled against the way things are. You see what has become of him. And I myself saw the moment when his reason left him."

Kino looked down at his closed hand and the knuckles were scabbed over and tight where he had struck the gate.

Now the dusk was coming. And Juana looped her shawl under the baby so that he hung against her hip, and she went to the fire hole and dug a coal from the ashes and broke a few twigs over it and fanned a flame alive. The little flames danced on the faces of the neighbors. They knew they should go to their own dinners, but they were reluctant to leave.

The dark was almost in, and Juana's fire threw shadows on the brush walls when the whisper came in, passed from mouth to mouth. "The Father is coming—the priest is coming." The men uncovered their heads and stepped back from the door, and the women gathered their shawls about their faces and cast down their eyes. Kino and Juan Tomás, his brother, stood up. The priest came in—a graying, aging man with an old skin and a young sharp eye. Children, he considered these people, and he treated them like children.

"Kino," he said softly, "thou art named after a great man—and a great Father of the Church."[2] He made it sound like a benediction. "Thy namesake tamed the desert and sweetened the minds of thy people, didst thou know that? It is in the books."

Kino looked quickly down at Coyotito's head, where he hung on Juana's hip. Some day, his mind said, that boy would know what things were in the books and what things were not. The music had gone out of Kino's head, but now, thinly, slowly, the melody of the morning, the music of evil, of the enemy sounded, but it was faint and weak. And Kino looked at his neighbors to see who might have brought this song in.

But the priest was speaking again. "It has come to me that thou hast found a great fortune, a great pearl."

Kino opened his hand and held it out, and the priest gasped a little at the size and beauty of the pearl. And then he said, "I hope thou wilt remember to give thanks, my son, to Him who has given thee this treasure, and to pray for guidance in the future."

Kino nodded dumbly, and it was Juana who spoke softly. "We will, Father. And we will be married now. Kino has said so." She looked at the neighbors for confirmation, and they nodded their heads solemnly.

The priest said, "It is pleasant to see that your first thoughts are good thoughts. God bless you, my children." He turned and left quietly, and the people let him through.

But Kino's hand had closed tightly on the pearl again, and he was glancing about suspiciously, for the evil song was in his

---

**2. Father of the Church:** Eusebius Kino, a Spanish missionary and explorer in the seventeenth century.

ear

pear

T

houses

set her

flame. K

looked out

smoke from

hazy stars an

so that he cove

dog came to him

ing like a windbl

down at it and did          oken

through the horizon          and lonely

outside. He felt alone         unprotected, and scraping crickets and shrilling tree frogs and croaking toads seemed to be carrying the melody of evil. Kino shivered a little and drew his blanket more tightly against his nose. He carried the pearl still in his hand, tightly closed in his palm, and it was warm and smooth against his skin.

Behind him he heard Juana patting the cakes before she put them down on the clay cooking sheet. Kino felt all the warmth and security of his family behind him, and the Song of the Family came from behind him like the purring of a kitten. But now, by saying what his future was going to be like, he had created it. A plan is a real thing, and things projected are experienced. A plan once made and visualized becomes a reality along with other realities—never to be destroyed but easily to be attacked. Thus Kino's future was real, but having set it up, other forces were set up to destroy it, and this he knew, so that he had to prepare to meet the attack. And this Kino knew also —that the gods do not love men's plans, and the gods do not love success unless it comes by accident. He knew that the gods take their revenge on a man if he be successful through his own efforts. Consequently Kino was afraid of plans, but having made

And to meet
... making a hard
... the world. His eyes
...bed for danger before it
...ing in the door, he saw two men
...ach; and one of them carried a lantern
...hich lighted the ground and the legs of the
men. They turned in through the opening of
Kino's brush fence and came to his door.
And Kino saw that one was the doctor and
the other the servant who had opened the
gate in the morning. The split knuckles on
Kino's right hand burned when he saw who
they were.

The doctor said, "I was not in when you
came this morning. But now, at the first
chance, I have come to see the baby."

Kino stood in the door, filling it, and
hatred raged and flamed in back of his eyes,
and fear too, for the hundreds of years of
subjugation were cut deep in him.

"The baby is nearly well now," he said
curtly.

The doctor smiled, but his eyes in their
little lymph-lined hammocks did not smile.

He said, "Sometimes, my friend, the
scorpion sting has a curious effect. There
will be apparent improvement, and then
without warning—pouf!" He pursed his lips
and made a little explosion to show how
quick it could be, and he shifted his small
black doctor's bag about so that the light of
the lamp fell upon it, for he knew that Kino's
race love the tools of any craft and trust
them. "Sometimes," the doctor went on in a
liquid tone, "sometimes there will be a withered leg or a blind eye or a crumpled back.
Oh, I know the sting of the scorpion, my
friend, and I can cure it."

Kino felt the rage and hatred melting
toward fear. He did not know, and perhaps
this doctor did. And he could not take the
chance of pitting his certain ignorance
against this man's possible knowledge. He
was trapped as his people were always
trapped, and would be until, as he had said,
they could be sure that the things in the
books were really in the books. He could not
take a chance—not with the life or with the
straightness of Coyotito. He stood aside
and let the doctor and his man enter the
brush hut.

Juana stood up from the fire and backed
away as he entered, and she covered the
baby's face with the fringe of her shawl. And
when the doctor went to her and held out his
hand, she clutched the baby tight and
looked at Kino where he stood with the fire
shadows leaping on his face.

Kino nodded, and only then did she let
the doctor take the baby.

"Hold the light," the doctor said, and
when the servant held the lantern high,
the doctor looked for a moment at the wound
on the baby's shoulder. He was thoughtful
for a moment and then he rolled back the
baby's eyelid and looked at the eyeball. He
nodded his head while Coyotito struggled
against him.

"It is as I thought," he said. "The poison
has gone inward and it will strike soon.
Come look!" He held the eyelid down.
"See—it is blue." And Kino, looking anxiously, saw that indeed it was a little blue.
And he didn't know whether or not it was
always a little blue. But the trap was set. He
couldn't take the chance.

The doctor's eyes watered in their little
hammocks. "I will give him something to try
to turn the poison aside," he said. And he
handed the baby to Kino.

Then from his bag he took a little bottle
of white powder and a capsule of gelatine.
He filled the capsule with the powder and
closed it, and then around the first capsule
he fitted a second capsule and closed it.
Then he worked very deftly. He took the

baby and pinched its lower lip until it opened its mouth. His fat fingers placed the capsule far back on the baby's tongue, back of the point where he could spit it out, and then from the floor he picked up the little pitcher of pulque and gave Coyotito a drink, and it was done. He looked again at the baby's eyeball and he pursed his lips and seemed to think.

At last he handed the baby back to Juana, and he turned to Kino. "I think the poison will attack within the hour," he said. "The medicine may save the baby from hurt, but I will come back in an hour. Perhaps I am in time to save him." He took a deep breath and went out of the hut, and his servant followed him with the lantern.

Now Juana had the baby under her shawl, and she stared at it with anxiety and fear. Kino came to her, and he lifted the shawl and stared at the baby. He moved his hand to look under the eyelid, and only then saw that the pearl was still in his hand. Then he went to a box by the wall, and from it he brought a piece of rag. He wrapped the pearl in the rag, then went to the corner of the brush house and dug a little hole with his fingers in the dirt floor, and he put the pearl in the hole and covered it up and concealed the place. And then he went to the fire where Juana was squatting, watching the baby's face.

The doctor, back in his house, settled into his chair and looked at his watch. His people brought him a little supper of chocolate and sweet cakes and fruit, and he stared at the food discontentedly.

In the houses of the neighbors the subject that would lead all conversations for a long time to come was aired for the first time to see how it would go. The neighbors showed one another with their thumbs how big the pearl was, and they made little caressing gestures to show how lovely it was.

From now on they would watch Kino and Juana very closely to see whether riches turned their heads, as riches turn all people's heads. Everyone knew why the doctor had come. He was not good at dissembling and he was very well understood.

Out in the estuary a tight woven school of small fishes glittered and broke water to escape a school of great fishes that drove in to eat them. And in the houses the people could hear the swish of the small ones and the bouncing splash of the great ones as the slaughter went on. The dampness arose out of the Gulf and was deposited on bushes and cacti and on little trees in salty drops. And the night mice crept about on the ground and the little night hawks hunted them silently.

The skinny black puppy with flame spots over his eyes came to Kino's door and looked in. He nearly shook his hind quarters loose when Kino glanced up at him, and he subsided when Kino looked away. The puppy did not enter the house, but he watched with frantic interest while Kino ate his beans from the little pottery dish and wiped it clean with a corncake and ate the cake and washed the whole down with a drink of pulque.

Kino was finished and was rolling a cigarette when Juana spoke sharply. "Kino." He glanced at her and then got up and went quickly to her for he saw fright in her eyes. He stood over her, looking down, but the light was very dim. He kicked a pile of twigs into the fire hole to make a blaze, and then he could see the face of Coyotito. The baby's face was flushed and his throat was working and a little thick drool of saliva issued from his lips. The spasm of the stomach muscles began, and the baby was very sick.

Kino knelt beside his wife. "So the doctor knew," he said, but he said it for himself as well as for his wife, for his mind was hard and suspicious and he was remembering the white powder. Juana rocked from side to side and moaned out the little Song of the Family as though it could ward off the danger, and the baby vomited and writhed in her arms. Now uncertainty was in Kino, and the music of evil throbbed in his head and nearly drove out Juana's song.

The doctor finished his chocolate and nibbled the little fallen pieces of sweet cake. He brushed his fingers on a napkin, looked at his watch, arose, and took up his little bag.

The news of the baby's illness traveled quickly among the brush houses, for sickness is second only to hunger as the enemy of poor people. And some said softly, "Luck, you see, brings bitter friends." And they nodded and got up to go to Kino's house. The neighbors scuttled with covered noses through the dark until they crowded into Kino's house again. They stood and gazed, and they made little comments on the sadness that this should happen at a time of joy, and they said, "All things are in God's hands." The old women squatted down beside Juana to try to give her aid if they could and comfort if they could not.

Then the doctor hurried in, followed by his man. He scattered the old women like chickens. He took the baby and examined it and felt its head. "The poison it has worked," he said. "I think I can defeat it. I will try my best." He asked for water, and in the cup of it he put three drops of ammonia, and he pried open the baby's mouth and poured it down. The baby spluttered and screeched under the treatment, and Juana watched him with haunted eyes. The doctor spoke a little as he worked. "It is lucky that I know about the poison of the scorpion, otherwise—" and he shrugged to show what could have happened.

But Kino was suspicious, and he could not take his eyes from the doctor's open bag, and from the bottle of white powder there. Gradually the spasms subsided and the baby relaxed under the doctor's hands. And then Coyotito sighed deeply and went to sleep, for he was very tired with vomiting.

The doctor put the baby in Juana's arms. "He will get well now," he said. "I have won the fight." And Juana looked at him with adoration.

The doctor was closing his bag now. He said, "When do you think you can pay this bill?" He said it even kindly.

"When I have sold my pearl I will pay you," Kino said.

"You have a pearl? A good pearl?" the doctor asked with interest.

And then the chorus of the neighbors broke in. "He has found the Pearl of the World," they cried, and they joined forefinger with thumb to show how great the pearl was.

"Kino will be a rich man," they clamored. "It is a pearl such as one has never seen."

The doctor looked surprised. "I had not heard of it. Do you keep this pearl in a safe place? Perhaps you would like me to put it in my safe?"

Kino's eyes were hooded now, his cheeks were drawn taut. "I have it secure," he said. "Tomorrow I will sell it and then I will pay you."

The doctor shrugged, and his wet eyes never left Kino's eyes. He knew the pearl would be buried in the house, and he thought Kino might look toward the place where it was buried. "It would be a shame to have it stolen before you could sell it," the doctor said, and he saw Kino's eyes flick involuntarily to the floor near the side post of the brush house.

When the doctor had gone and all the neighbors had reluctantly returned to their houses, Kino squatted beside the little glowing coals in the fire hole and listened to the night sound, the soft sweep of the little waves on the shore and the distant barking of dogs, the creeping of the breeze through the brush house roof and the soft speech of his neighbors in their houses in the village. For these people do not sleep soundly all night; they awaken at intervals and talk a little and then go to sleep again. And after a while Kino got up and went to the door of his house.

He smelled the breeze and he listened for any foreign sound of secrecy or creeping, and his eyes searched the darkness, for the music of evil was sounding in his head and he was fierce and afraid. After he had probed the night with his senses he went to the place by the side post where the pearl was buried, and he dug it up and brought it to his sleeping mat, and under his sleeping mat he dug another little hole in the dirt floor and buried the pearl and covered it up again.

And Juana, sitting by the fire hole, watched him with questioning eyes, and when he had buried his pearl she asked, "Who do you fear?"

Kino searched for a true answer, and at last he said, "Everyone." And he could feel a shell of hardness drawing over him.

After a while they lay down together on the sleeping mat, and Juana did not put the baby in his box tonight, but cradled him in her arms and covered his face with her head shawl. And the last light went out of the embers in the fire hole.

But Kino's brain burned, even during his sleep, and he dreamed that Coyotito could read, that one of his own people could tell him the truth of things. And in his dream, Coyotito was reading from a book as large as a house, with letters as big as dogs, and the words galloped and played on the

book. And then darkness spread over the page, and with the darkness came the music of evil again, and Kino stirred in his sleep; and when he stirred, Juana's eyes opened in the darkness. And then Kino awakened, with the evil music pulsing in him, and he lay in the darkness with his ears alert.

Then from the corner of the house came a sound so soft that it might have been simply a thought, a little furtive movement, a touch of a foot on earth, the almost inaudible purr of controlled breathing. Kino held his breath to listen, and he knew that whatever dark thing was in his house was holding its breath too, to listen. For a time no sound at all came from the corner of the brush house. Then Kino might have thought he had imagined the sound. But Juana's hand came creeping over to him in warning, and then the sound came again! the whisper of a foot on dry earth and the scratch of fingers in the soil.

And now a wild fear surged in Kino's breast, and on the fear came rage, as it always did. Kino's hand crept into his breast where his knife hung on a string, and then he sprang like an angry cat, leaped striking and spitting for the dark thing he knew was in the corner of the house. He felt cloth, struck at it with his knife and missed, and struck again and felt his knife go through cloth, and then his head crashed with lightning and exploded with pain. There was a soft scurry in the doorway, and running steps for a moment, and then silence.

Kino could feel warm blood running from his forehead, and he could hear Juana calling to him. "Kino! Kino!" And there was terror in her voice. Then coldness came over him as quickly as the rage had, and he said, "I am all right. The thing has gone."

He groped his way back to the sleeping mat. Already Juana was working at the fire.

She uncovered an ember from the ashes and shredded little pieces of cornhusk over it and blew a little flame into the cornhusks so that a tiny light danced through the hut. And then from a secret place Juana brought a little piece of consecrated candle and lighted it at the flame and set it upright on a fireplace stone. She worked quickly, crooning as she moved about. She dipped the end of her head shawl in water and swabbed the blood from Kino's bruised forehead. "It is nothing," Kino said, but his eyes and his voice were hard and cold and a brooding hate was growing in him.

Now the tension which had been growing in Juana boiled up to the surface and her lips were thin. "This thing is evil," she cried harshly. "This pearl is like a sin! It will destroy us," and her voice rose shrilly. "Throw it away, Kino. Let us break it between stones. Let us bury it and forget the place. Let us throw it back into the sea. It has brought evil. Kino, my husband, it will destroy us." And in the firelight her lips and her eyes were alive with her fear.

But Kino's face was set, and his mind and his will were set. "This is our one chance," he said. "Our son must go to school. He must break out of the pot that holds us in."

"It will destroy us all," Juana cried. "Even our son."

"Hush," said Kino. "Do not speak any more. In the morning we will sell the pearl, and then the evil will be gone, and only the good remain. Now hush, my wife." His dark eyes scowled into the little fire, and for the first time he knew that his knife was still in his hands, and he raised the blade and looked at it and saw a little line of blood on the steel. For a moment he seemed about to wipe the blade on his trousers but then he plunged the knife into the earth and so cleansed it.

The distant roosters began to crow and the air changed and the dawn was coming. The wind of the morning ruffled the water of the estuary and whispered through the mangroves, and the little waves beat on the rubbly beach with an increased tempo. Kino raised the sleeping mat and dug up his pearl and put it in front of him and stared at it.

And the beauty of the pearl, winking and glimmering in the light of the little candle, cozened[3] his brain with its beauty. So lovely it was, so soft, and its own music came from it—its music of promise and delight, its guarantee of the future, of comfort, of security. Its warm lucence promised a poultice against illness and a wall against insult. It closed a door on hunger. And as he stared at it Kino's eyes softened and his face relaxed. He could see the little image of the consecrated candle reflected in the soft surface of the pearl, and he heard again in his ears the lovely music of the undersea, the tone of the diffused green light of the sea bottom. Juana, glancing secretly at him, saw him smile. And because they were in some way one thing and one purpose, she smiled with him.

And they began this day with hope.

---

**3. cozened** (kuz' ənd) v.: Deceived.

## THINKING ABOUT THE SELECTION

### Recalling

1. What is Kino's Song of the Family? Explain the Song of Evil.
2. What harm comes to Coyotito?
3. Why does Juana wish for a great pearl? Why does she feel that it is "not good to want a thing too much"?
4. How does the attitude of people toward Kino change after he finds "the Pearl of the World"?

### Interpreting

5. Why does the doctor turn Kino away? What is the doctor's attitude toward Kino and his people?
6. Explain how the news of Kino's find stirs up something "infinitely black and evil in the town"?
7. In what ways does luck bring Kino and Juana "bitter friends"?
8. By the end of Chapter 3, what changes have come about in Kino?

### Applying

9. The narrator writes, "For it is said that humans are never satisfied, that you give them one thing and they want something more." Do you agree that this is a universal trait in human beings. Explain your answer.

## ANALYZING LITERATURE

### Understanding Characters

A **parable** is a short tale told to illustrate a universal truth. In parables, characters tend to be flat, representing certain traits.

1. Explain what traits are represented by Kino, Juana, and Coyotito.
2. Do you agree with the narrator that in tales that are in people's hearts, "there are only good and bad things and black and white things and good and evil things and no in-between anywhere"? Explain your answer.

## UNDERSTANDING LANGUAGE

### Appreciating Words from Spanish

The English language has many words that come from Spanish. For example, *coyote*, meaning "a small animal related to the wolf," comes from the Mexican Nahuatl (Indian) language.

Look in a dictionary for the definition and the language of origin for each of the following words. Then use each word correctly in a sentence.

1. pulque
2. plaza
3. hammocks
4. fiesta

## THINKING AND WRITING

### Writing from Juana's Point of View

Choose an incident in the story and rewrite it from Juana's point of view. First imagine that you are Juana and freewrite about the incident, describing your thoughts, feelings, and actions. Then use this information in rewriting the incident from her point of view for your classmates. Revise your description to make sure that it suits Juana's character in *The Pearl*. Proofread for errors in spelling, grammar, and punctuation.

# GUIDE FOR READING

## The Pearl, Chapters 4–6

**Plot and Theme**

**Plot** is the sequence of related events or incidents that make up a story or literary work. Plot usually involves conflict, climax, and resolution. Conflict, a struggle between opposing sides or forces, can occur between people, people and nature, or within a person. Climax is the story's highest point of interest, after which the action turns and begins to resolve. The resolution is the outcome or ending of the conflict or plot.

 **Theme** is the central idea of a story, or the general idea or insight about life that a story reveals. In a parable a writer uses plot to help express theme. What happens in a parable can help you understand the meaning of the story.

**Look For**

As you read Chapters 4–6 of *The Pearl,* look for the major events of the story. Notice the sequence in which they occur and what clues they give you to the theme.

**Writing**

Do you agree that wisdom can be gained from tragedy? Freewrite, exploring your answer.

**Vocabulary**

Knowing the following words will help you as you read Chapters 4–6 of *The Pearl.*

**spurned** (spurnd) *v.*: Kicked; rejected (p. 805)

**lethargy** (leth'ər jē) *n.*: Laziness or indifference (p. 808)

**waning** (wān'iŋ) *adj.:* A full moon shrinking to a new moon (p. 814)

**covert** (kuv'ərt) *n.*: A hiding place (p. 815)

**goading** (gōd'iŋ) *n.*: Urging (p. 817)

**monolithic** (män'ə lith'ik) *adj.*: Formed from a single block (p. 819)

**escarpment** (e skärp'mənt) *n.*: A long cliff (p. 820)

**intercession** (in'tər sesh'ən) *n.*: A prayer said on behalf of another person (p. 823)

## Chapter 4

It is wonderful the way a little town keeps track of itself and of all its units. If every single man and woman, child and baby, acts and conducts itself in a known pattern and breaks no walls and differs with no one and experiments in no way and is not sick and does not endanger the ease and peace of mind or steady unbroken flow of the town, then that unit can disappear and never be heard of. But let one man step out of the regular thought or the known and trusted pattern, and the nerves of the townspeople ring with nervousness and communication travels over the nerve lines of the town. Then every unit communicates to the whole.

Thus, in La Paz,[1] it was known in the early morning through the whole town that Kino was going to sell his pearl that day. It was known among the neighbors in the brush huts, among the pearl fishermen; it was known among the Chinese grocery-store owners; it was known in the church, for the altar boys whispered about it. Word of it crept in among the nuns; the beggars in front of the church spoke of it, for they would be there to take the tithe[2] of the first fruits of the luck. The little boys knew about it with excitement, but most of all the pearl buyers knew about it, and when the day had come, in the offices of the pearl buyers, each man sat alone with his little black velvet tray, and each man rolled the pearls about with his fingertips and considered his part in the picture.

It was supposed that the pearl buyers were individuals acting alone, bidding against one another for the pearls the fishermen brought in. And once it had been so. But this was a wasteful method, for often, in the excitement of bidding for a fine pearl, too great a price had been paid to the fishermen. This was extravagant and not to be countenanced. Now there was only one pearl buyer with many hands, and the men who sat in their offices and waited for Kino knew what price they would offer, how high they would bid, and what method each one would use. And although these men would not profit beyond their salaries, there was excitement among the pearl buyers, for there was excitement in the hunt, and if it be a man's function to break down a price, then he must take joy and satisfaction in breaking it as far down as possible. For every man in the world functions to the best of his ability, and no one does less than his best, no matter what he may think about it. Quite apart from any reward they might get, from any word of praise, from any promotion, a pearl buyer was a pearl buyer, and the best and happiest pearl buyer was he who bought for the lowest prices.

The sun was hot yellow that morning, and it drew the moisture from the estuary and from the Gulf and hung it in shimmering scarves in the air so that the air vibrated and vision was insubstantial. A vision hung in the air to the north of the city—the vision of a mountain that was over two hundred miles away, and the high slopes of this mountain were swaddled with pines and a great stone peak arose above the timber line.

And the morning of this day the canoes lay lined up on the beach; the fishermen did not go out to dive for pearls, for there would be too much happening, too many things to see when Kino went to sell the great pearl.

In the brush houses by the shore Kino's neighbors sat long over their breakfasts, and they spoke of what they would do if they had found the pearl. And one man said that he would give it as a present to the Holy Father in Rome. Another said that he would buy Masses for the souls of his family for a

---

**1. La Paz:** City in southern Baja California.
**2. tithe** (tī th) *n.*: One tenth of one's income; here, a small amount given to charity.

**GROUP**
*Jesus Guerrero Galván*
Collection IBM Corporation, Armonk, New York

thousand years. Another thought he might take the money and distribute it among the poor of La Paz; and a fourth thought of all the good things one could do with the money from the pearl, of all the charities, benefits, of all the rescues one could perform if one had money. All of the neighbors hoped that sudden wealth would not turn Kino's head, would not make a rich man of him, would not graft onto him the evil limbs of greed and hatred and coldness. For Kino was a well-liked man; it would be a shame if the pearl destroyed him. "That good wife Juana," they said, "and the beautiful baby Coyotito, and the others to come. What a

pity it would be if the pearl should destroy them all."

For Kino and Juana this was the morning of mornings of their lives, comparable only to the day when the baby had been born. This was to be the day from which all other days would take their arrangement. Thus they would say, "It was two years before we sold the pearl," or, "It was six weeks after we sold the pearl." Juana, considering the matter, threw caution to the winds, and she dressed Coyotito in the clothes she had prepared for his baptism, when there would be money for his baptism. And Juana combed and braided her hair and tied the ends with two little bows of red ribbon, and she put on her marriage skirt and waist.[3] The sun was quarter high when they were ready. Kino's ragged white clothes were clean at least, and this was the last day of his raggedness. For tomorrow, or even this afternoon, he would have new clothes.

The neighbors, watching Kino's door through the crevices in their brush houses, were dressed and ready too. There was no self-consciousness about their joining Kino and Juana to go pearl selling. It was expected, it was an historic moment, they would be crazy if they didn't go. It would be almost a sign of unfriendship.

Juana put on her head shawl carefully, and she draped one long end under her right elbow and gathered it with her right hand so that a hammock hung under her arm, and in this little hammock she placed Coyotito, propped up against the head shawl so that he could see everything and perhaps remember. Kino put on his large straw hat and felt it with his hand to see that it was properly placed, not on the back or side of his head, like a rash, unmarried, irresponsible man, and not flat as an elder would wear it, but tilted a little forward to show aggressiveness and seriousness and vigor. There is a great deal to be seen in the tilt of a hat on a man. Kino slipped his feet into his sandals and pulled the thongs up over his heels. The great pearl was wrapped in an old soft piece of deerskin and placed in a little leather bag, and the leather bag was in a pocket in Kino's shirt. He folded his blanket carefully and draped it in a narrow strip over his left shoulder, and now they were ready.

Kino stepped with dignity out of the house, and Juana followed him, carrying Coyotito. And as they marched up the freshet-washed[4] alley toward the town, the neighbors joined them. The houses belched people; the doorways spewed out children. But because of the seriousness of the occasion, only one man walked with Kino, and that was his brother, Juan Tomás.

Juan Tomás cautioned his brother. "You must be careful to see they do not cheat you," he said.

And, "Very careful," Kino agreed.

"We do not know what prices are paid in other places," said Juan Tomás. "How can we know what is a fair price, if we do not know what the pearl buyer gets for the pearl in another place?"

"That is true," said Kino, "but how can we know? We are here, we are not there."

As they walked up toward the city the crowd grew behind them, and Juan Tomás, in pure nervousness, went on speaking.

"Before you were born, Kino," he said, "the old ones thought of a way to get more money for their pearls. They thought it would be better if they had an agent who took all the pearls to the capital and sold them there and kept only his share of the profit."

Kino nodded his head. "I know," he said. "It was a good thought."

"And so they got such a man," said Juan Tomás, "and they pooled their pearls, and they started him off. And he was never heard of again and the pearls were lost. Then they got another man, and they started him off, and he was never heard of again. And so they gave the whole thing up and went back to the old way."

"I know," said Kino. "I have heard our father tell of it. It was a good idea, but it was against religion, and the Father made that very clear. The loss of the pearl was a pun-

---

**3. waist** (wāst) *n.*: Blouse.

**4. freshet** (fresh' it) -**washed** *adj.*: Washed by a stream.

ishment visited on those who tried to leave their station. And the Father made it clear that each man and woman is like a soldier sent by God to guard some part of the castle of the Universe. And some are in the ramparts and some far deep in the darkness of the walls. But each one must remain faithful to his post and must not go running about, else the castle is in danger from the assaults of Hell."

"I have heard him make that sermon," said Juan Tomás. "He makes it every year."

The brothers, as they walked along, squinted their eyes a little, as they and their grandfathers and their great-grandfathers had done for four hundred years, since first the strangers came with argument and authority and gunpowder to back up both. And in the four hundred years Kino's people had learned only one defense—a slight slitting of the eyes and a slight tightening of the lips and a retirement. Nothing could break down this wall, and they could remain whole within the wall.

The gathering procession was solemn, for they sensed the importance of this day, and any children who showed a tendency to scuffle, to scream, to cry out, to steal hats and rumple hair, were hissed to silence by their elders. So important was this day that an old man came to see, riding on the stalwart shoulders of his nephew. The procession left the brush huts and entered the stone and plaster city where the streets were a little wider and there were narrow pavements beside the buildings. And as before, the beggars joined them as they passed the church; the grocers looked out at them as they went by; the little saloons lost their customers and the owners closed up shop and went along. And the sun beat down on the streets of the city and even tiny stones threw shadows on the ground.

The news of the approach of the procession ran ahead of it, and in their little dark offices the pearl buyers stiffened and grew alert. They got out papers so that they could be at work when Kino appeared, and they put their pearls in the desks, for it is not good to let an inferior pearl be seen beside a beauty. And word of the loveliness of Kino's pearl had come to them. The pearl buyers' offices were clustered together in one narrow street, and they were barred at the windows, and wooden slats cut out the light so that only a soft gloom entered the offices.

A stout slow man sat in an office waiting. His face was fatherly and benign, and his eyes twinkled with friendship. He was a caller of good mornings, a ceremonious shaker of hands, a jolly man who knew all jokes and yet who hovered close to sadness, for in the midst of a laugh he could remember the death of your aunt, and his eyes could become wet with sorrow for your loss. This morning he had placed a flower in a vase on his desk, a single scarlet hibiscus, and the vase sat beside the black velvet-lined pearl tray in front of him. He was shaved close to the blue roots of his beard, and his hands were clean and his nails polished. His door stood open to the morning, and he hummed under his breath while his right hand practiced legerdemain.[5] He rolled a coin back and forth over his knuckles and made it appear and disappear, made it spin and sparkle. The coin winked into sight and as quickly slipped out of sight, and the man did not even watch his own performance. The fingers did it all mechanically, precisely, while the man hummed to himself and peered out the door. Then he heard the tramp of feet of the approaching crowd, and the fingers of his right hand worked faster

---

**5. legerdemain** (lej′ ər də mān′) *n.*: Trickery; tricks with the hand.

and faster until, as the figure of Kino filled the doorway, the coin flashed and disappeared.

"Good morning, my friend," the stout man said. "What can I do for you?"

Kino stared into the dimness of the little office, for his eyes were squeezed from the outside glare. But the buyer's eyes had become as steady and cruel and unwinking as a hawk's eyes, while the rest of his face smiled in greeting. And secretly, behind his desk, his right hand practiced with the coin.

"I have a pearl," said Kino. And Juan Tomás stood beside him and snorted a little at the understatement. The neighbors peered around the doorway, and a line of little boys clambered on the window bars and looked through. Several little boys, on their hands and knees, watched the scene around Kino's legs.

"You have a pearl," the dealer said. "Sometimes a man brings in a dozen. Well, let us see your pearl. We will value it and give you the best price." And his fingers worked furiously with the coin.

Now Kino instinctively knew his own dramatic effects. Slowly he brought out the leather bag, slowly took from it the soft and dirty piece of deerskin, and then he let the great pearl roll into the black velvet tray, and instantly his eyes went to the buyer's face. But there was no sign, no movement, the face did not change, but the secret hand behind the desk missed in its precision. The coin stumbled over a knuckle and slipped silently into the dealer's lap. And the fingers behind the desk curled into a fist. When the right hand came out of hiding, the forefinger touched the great pearl, rolled it on the black velvet; thumb and forefinger picked it up and brought it near to the dealer's eyes and twirled it in the air.

Kino held his breath, and the neighbors held their breath, and the whispering went back through the crowd. "He is inspecting it—No price has been mentioned yet —They have not come to a price."

Now the dealer's hand had become a personality. The hand tossed the great pearl back in the tray, the forefinger poked and insulted it, and on the dealer's face there came a sad and contemptuous smile.

"I am sorry, my friend," he said, and his shoulders rose a little to indicate that the misfortune was no fault of his.

"It is a pearl of great value," Kino said.

The dealer's fingers spurned the pearl so that it bounced and rebounded softly from the side of the velvet tray.

"You have heard of fool's gold," the dealer said. "This pearl is like fool's gold. It is too large. Who would buy it? There is no market for such things. It is a curiosity only. I am sorry. You thought it was a thing of value, and it is only a curiosity."

Now Kino's face was perplexed and worried. "It is the Pearl of the World," he cried. "No one has ever seen such a pearl."

"On the contrary," said the dealer, "it is large and clumsy. As a curiosity it has interest; some museum might perhaps take it to place in a collection of seashells. I can give you, say, a thousand pesos."[6]

Kino's face grew dark and dangerous. "It is worth fifty thousand," he said. "You know it. You want to cheat me."

And the dealer heard a little grumble go through the crowd as they heard his price. And the dealer felt a little tremor of fear.

"Do not blame me," he said quickly. "I am only an appraiser. Ask the others. Go to their offices and show your pearl—or better let them come here, so that you can see there is no collusion.[7] Boy," he called. And

---

**6. pesos** (pā′ sōz) *n.:* Mexican unit of money.
**7. collusion** (kə loō′ zhən) *n.:* A secret agreement for an illegal purpose.

when his servant looked through the rear door, "Boy, go to such a one, and such another one and such a third one. Ask them to step in here and do not tell them why. Just say that I will be pleased to see them." And his right hand went behind the desk and pulled another coin from his pocket, and the coin rolled back and forth over the knuckles.

Kino's neighbors whispered together. They had been afraid of something like this. The pearl was large, but it had a strange color. They had been suspicious of it from the first. And after all, a thousand pesos was not to be thrown away. It was comparative wealth to a man who was not wealthy. And suppose Kino took a thousand pesos. Only yesterday he had nothing.

But Kino had grown tight and hard. He felt the creeping of fate, the circling of wolves, the hover of vultures. He felt the evil coagulating about him, and he was helpless to protect himself. He heard in his ears the evil music. And on the black velvet the great pearl glistened, so that the dealer could not keep his eyes from it.

The crowd in the doorway wavered and broke and let the three pearl dealers through. The crowd was silent now, fearing to miss a word, to fail to see a gesture or an expression. Kino was silent and watchful. He felt a little tugging at his back, and he turned and looked in Juana's eyes, and when he looked away he had renewed strength.

The dealers did not glance at one another nor at the pearl. The man behind the desk said, "I have put a value on this pearl. The owner here does not think it fair. I will ask you to examine this—this thing and make an offer. Notice," he said to Kino, "I have not mentioned what I have offered."

The first dealer, dry and stringy, seemed now to see the pearl for the first time. He took it up, rolled it quickly between thumb and forefinger, and then cast it contemptuously back into the tray.

"Do not include me in the discussion," he said dryly. "I will make no offer at all. I do not want it. This is not a pearl—it is a monstrosity." His thin lips curled.

Now the second dealer, a little man with a shy soft voice, took up the pearl, and he examined it carefully. He took a glass from his pocket and inspected it under magnification. Then he laughed softly.

"Better pearls are made of paste," he said. "I know these things. This is soft and chalky, it will lose its color and die in a few months. Look—." He offered the glass to Kino, showed him how to use it, and Kino, who had never seen a pearl's surface magnified, was shocked at the strange-looking surface.

The third dealer took the pearl from Kino's hands. "One of my clients likes such things," he said. "I will offer five hundred pesos, and perhaps I can sell it to my client for six hundred."

Kino reached quickly and snatched the pearl from his hand. He wrapped it in the deerskin and thrust it inside his shirt.

The man behind the desk said, "I'm a fool, I know, but my first offer stands. I still offer one thousand. What are you doing?" he asked, as Kino thrust the pearl out of sight.

"I am cheated," Kino cried fiercely. "My pearl is not for sale here. I will go, perhaps even to the capital."

Now the dealers glanced quickly at one another. They knew they had played too hard; they knew they would be disciplined for their failure, and the man at the desk said quickly, "I might go to fifteen hundred."

But Kino was pushing his way through the crowd. The hum of talk came to him dimly, his rage blood pounded in his ears, and he burst through and strode away. Juana followed, trotting after him.

When the evening came, the neighbors in the brush houses sat eating their corncakes and beans, and they discussed the great theme of the morning. They did not know, it seemed a fine pearl to them, but they had never seen such a pearl before, and surely the dealers knew more about the value of pearls than they. "And mark this," they said. "Those dealers did not discuss these things. Each of the three knew the pearl was valueless."

"But suppose they had arranged it before?"

"If that is so, then all of us have been cheated all of our lives."

Perhaps, some argued, perhaps it would have been better if Kino took the one thousand five hundred pesos. That is a great deal of money, more than he has ever seen. Maybe Kino is being a pigheaded fool. Suppose he should really go to the capital and find no buyer for his pearl. He would never live that down.

And now, said other fearful ones, now that he had defied them, those buyers will not want to deal with him at all. Maybe Kino has cut off his own head and destroyed himself.

And others said, Kino is a brave man, and a fierce man; he is right. From his courage we may all profit. These were proud of Kino.

In his house Kino squatted on his sleeping mat, brooding. He had buried his pearl under a stone of the fire hole in his house, and he stared at the woven tules[8] of his sleeping mat until the crossed design danced in his head. He had lost one world and had not gained another. And Kino was afraid. Never in his life had he been far from home. He was afraid of strangers and of strange places. He was terrified of that monster of strangeness they called the capital. It lay over the water and through the mountains, over a thousand miles, and every strange terrible mile was frightening. But Kino had lost his old world and he must clamber on to a new one. For his dream of the future was real and never to be destroyed, and he had said "I will go," and that made a real thing too. To determine to go and to say it was to be halfway there.

Juana watched him while he buried his pearl, and she watched him while she cleaned Coyotito and nursed him, and Juana made the corncakes for supper.

Juan Tomás came in and squatted down beside Kino and remained silent for a long time, until at last Kino demanded, "What else could I do? They are cheats."

Juan Tomás nodded gravely. He was the elder, and Kino looked to him for wisdom. "It is hard to know," he said. "We do know that we are cheated from birth to the overcharge on our coffins. But we survive. You have defied not the pearl buyers, but the whole structure, the whole way of life, and I am afraid for you."

"What have I to fear but starvation?" Kino asked.

But Juan Tomás shook his head slowly. "That we must all fear. But suppose you are correct—suppose your pearl is of great value—do you think then the game is over?"

"What do you mean?"

"I don't know," said Juan Tomás, "but I am afraid for you. It is new ground you are walking on, you do not know the way."

"I will go. I will go soon," said Kino.

"Yes," Juan Tomás agreed. "That you must do. But I wonder if you will find it any different in the capital. Here, you have friends and me, your brother. There, you will have no one."

"What can I do?" Kino cried. "Some deep outrage is here. My son must have a

---

**8. tules** (tōō′ lēz) n.: Grasslike plants.

chance. That is what they are striking at. My friends will protect me.''

''Only so long as they are not in danger or discomfort from it,'' said Juan Tomás. He arose, saying, ''Go with God.''

And Kino said, ''Go with God,'' and did not even look up, for the words had a strange chill in them.

Long after Juan Tomás had gone Kino sat brooding on his sleeping mat. A lethargy had settled on him, and a little gray hopelessness. Every road seemed blocked against him. In his head he heard only the dark music of the enemy. His senses were burningly alive, but his mind went back to the deep participation with all things, the gift he had from his people. He heard every little sound of the gathering night, the sleepy complaint of settling birds, the love agony of cats, the strike and withdrawal of little waves on the beach, and the simple hiss of distance. And he could smell the sharp odor of exposed kelp[9] from the receding tide. The little flare of the twig fire made the design on his sleeping mat jump before his entranced eyes.

Juana watched him with worry, but she knew him and she knew she could help him best by being silent and by being near. And as though she too could hear the Song of Evil, she fought it, singing softly the melody of the family, of the safety and warmth and wholeness of the family. She held Coyotito in her arms and sang the song to him, to keep the evil out, and her voice was brave against the threat of the dark music.

Kino did not move nor ask for his supper. She knew he would ask when he wanted it. His eyes were entranced, and he could sense the wary, watchful evil outside the brush house; he could feel the dark creeping things waiting for him to go out into the night. It was shadowy and dreadful, and yet it called to him and threatened him and challenged him. His right hand went into his shirt and felt his knife; his eyes were wide; he stood up and walked to the doorway.

Juana willed to stop him; she raised her hand to stop him, and her mouth opened with terror. For a long moment Kino looked out into the darkness and then he stepped outside. Juana heard the little rush, the grunting struggle, the blow. She froze with terror for a moment, and then her lips drew back from her teeth like a cat's lips. She set Coyotito down on the ground. She seized a stone from the fireplace and rushed outside, but it was over by then. Kino lay on the ground, struggling to rise, and there was no one near him. Only the shadows and the strike and rush of waves and the hiss of distance. But the evil was all about, hidden behind the brush fence, crouched beside the house in the shadow, hovering in the air.

Juana dropped her stone, and she put her arms around Kino and helped him to his feet and supported him into the house. Blood oozed down from his scalp and there was a long deep cut in his cheek from ear to chin, a deep, bleeding slash. And Kino was only half conscious. He shook his head from side to side. His shirt was torn open and his clothes half pulled off. Juana sat him down on his sleeping mat and she wiped the thickening blood from his face with her skirt. She brought him pulque to drink in a little pitcher, and still he shook his head to clear out the darkness.

''Who?'' Juana asked.

''I don't know,'' Kino said. ''I didn't see.''

Now Juana brought her clay pot of water and she washed the cut on his face while he stared dazed ahead of him.

''Kino, my husband,'' she cried, and his

---

**9. kelp** *n.*: Seaweed.

**MEXICAN PEASANT WITH SOMBRERO AND SERAPE**
*Diego Rivera*
Harry Ransom Humanities Research Center
The University of Texas at Austin

eyes stared past her. "Kino, can you hear me?"

"I hear you," he said dully.

"Kino, this pearl is evil. Let us destroy it before it destroys us. Let us crush it between two stones. Let us—let us throw it back in the sea where it belongs. Kino, it is evil, it is evil!"

And as she spoke the light came back in Kino's eyes so that they glowed fiercely and his muscles hardened and his will hardened.

"No," he said. "I will fight this thing. I will win over it. We will have our chance." His fist pounded the sleeping mat. "No one shall take our good fortune from us," he said. His eyes softened then and he raised a gentle hand to Juana's shoulder. "Believe me," he said. "I am a man." And his face grew crafty.

"In the morning we will take our canoe and we will go over the sea and over the mountains to the capital, you and I. We will not be cheated. I am a man."

"Kino," she said huskily, "I am afraid. A man can be killed. Let us throw the pearl back into the sea."

"Hush," he said fiercely. "I am a man. Hush." And she was silent, for his voice was command. "Let us sleep a little," he said. "In the first light we will start. You are not afraid to go with me?"

"No, my husband."

His eyes were soft and warm on her then, his hand touched her cheek. "Let us sleep a little," he said.

## Chapter 5

The late moon arose before the first rooster crowed. Kino opened his eyes in the darkness, for he sensed movement near him, but he did not move. Only his eyes searched the darkness, and in the pale light of the moon that crept through the holes in the brush house Kino saw Juana arise silently from beside him. He saw her move toward the fireplace. So carefully did she work that he heard only the lightest sound when she moved the fireplace stone. And then like a shadow she glided toward the door. She paused for a moment beside the hanging box where Coyotito lay, then for a second she was black in the doorway, and then she was gone.

And rage surged in Kino. He rolled up to his feet and followed her as silently as she had gone, and he could hear her quick footsteps going toward the shore. Quietly he tracked her, and his brain was red with anger. She burst clear out of the brush line and stumbled over the little boulders toward the water, and then she heard him coming and she broke into a run. Her arm was up to throw when he leaped at her and caught her arm and wrenched the pearl from her. He struck her in the face with his clenched fist and she fell among the boulders, and he kicked her in the side. In the pale light he could see the little waves break over her, and her skirt floated about and clung to her legs as the water receded.

Kino looked down at her and his teeth were bared. He hissed at her like a snake, and Juana stared at him with wide unfrightened eyes, like a sheep before the butcher. She knew there was murder in him, and it was all right; she had accepted it, and she would not resist or even protest. And then the rage left him and a sick disgust took its place. He turned away from her and walked up the beach and through the brush line. His senses were dulled by his emotion.

He heard the rush, got his knife out and lunged at one dark figure and felt his knife go home, and then he was swept to his knees and swept again to the ground. Greedy fingers went through his clothes, frantic figures searched him, and the pearl, knocked from his hand, lay winking behind a little stone in the pathway. It glinted in the soft moonlight.

Juana dragged herself up from the rocks on the edge of the water. Her face was a dull pain and her side ached. She steadied herself on her knees for a while and her wet skirt clung to her. There was no anger in her for Kino. He had said, "I am a man," and that meant certain things to Juana. It meant that he was half insane and half god. It meant that Kino would drive his strength against a mountain and plunge his strength against the sea. Juana, in her woman's soul, knew that the mountain would stand while the man broke himself; that the sea would surge while the man drowned in it. And yet it was this thing that made him a man, half insane and half god, and Juana had need of a man; she could not live without a man. Although she might be puzzled by these differences between man and woman, she knew them and accepted them and needed them. Of course she would follow him, there was no question of that. Sometimes the quality of woman, the reason, the caution, the sense of preservation, could cut through Kino's manness and save them all. She climbed painfully to her feet, and she dipped her cupped palms in the little waves and washed her bruised face with the stinging salt water, and then she went creeping up the beach after Kino.

A flight of herring clouds had moved over the sky from the south. The pale moon dipped in and out of the strands of clouds so that Juana walked in darkness for a moment and in light the next. Her back was bent with pain and her head was low. She went through the line of brush when the moon was covered, and when it looked through she saw the glimmer of the great pearl in the path behind the rock. She sank to her knees and picked it up, and the moon went into the darkness of the clouds again. Juana remained on her knees while she considered whether to go back to the sea and finish her job, and as she considered, the light came again, and she saw two dark figures lying in the path ahead of her. She leaped forward and saw that one was Kino and the other a stranger with dark shiny fluid leaking from his throat.

Kino moved sluggishly, arms and legs stirred like those of a crushed bug, and a thick muttering came from his mouth. Now, in an instant, Juana knew that the old life was gone forever. A dead man in the path and Kino's knife, dark bladed beside him, convinced her. All of the time Juana had been trying to rescue something of the old peace, of the time before the pearl. But now it was gone, and there was no retrieving it. And knowing this, she abandoned the past instantly. There was nothing to do but to save themselves.

Her pain was gone now, her slowness. Quickly she dragged the dead man from the pathway into the shelter of the brush. She went to Kino and sponged his face with her wet skirt. His senses were coming back and he moaned.

"They have taken the pearl. I have lost it. Now it is over," he said. "The pearl is gone."

Juana quieted him as she would quiet a sick child. "Hush," she said. "Here is your pearl. I found it in the path. Can you hear me now? Here is your pearl. Can you understand? You have killed a man. We must go away. They will come for us, can you understand? We must be gone before the daylight comes."

"I was attacked," Kino said uneasily. "I struck to save my life."

"Do you remember yesterday?" Juana asked. "Do you think that will matter? Do you remember the men of the city? Do you think your explanation will help?"

Kino drew a great breath and fought off his weakness. "No," he said. "You are right." And his will hardened and he was a man again.

"Go to our house and bring Coyotito," he said, "and bring all the corn we have. I will drag the canoe into the water and we will go."

He took his knife and left her. He stumbled toward the beach and he came to his canoe. And when the light broke through again he saw that a great hole had been knocked in the bottom. And a searing rage came to him and gave him strength. Now the darkness was closing in on his family; now the evil music filled the night, hung over the mangroves, skirled[1] in the wave beat. The canoe of his grandfather, plastered over and over, and a splintered hole broken in it. This was an evil beyond thinking. The killing of a man was not so evil as the killing of a boat. For a boat does not have sons, and a boat cannot protect itself, and a wounded boat does not heal. There was sorrow in Kino's rage, but this last thing had tightened him beyond breaking. He was an animal now, for hiding, for attacking, and he lived only to preserve himself and his family. He was not conscious of the pain in his head. He leaped up the beach, through the brush line toward his brush house, and it did not occur to him to take one of the canoes of his neighbors. Never once did the

---

**1. skirled** (skŭrld) *v.*: Made a shrill, piercing sound.

thought enter his head, any more than he could have conceived breaking a boat.

The roosters were crowing and the dawn was not far off. Smoke of the first fires seeped out through the walls of the brush houses, and the first smell of cooking corn-cakes was in the air. Already the dawn birds were scampering in the bushes. The weak moon was losing its light and the clouds thickened and curdled to the southward. The wind blew freshly into the estuary, a nervous, restless wind with the smell of storm on its breath, and there was change and uneasiness in the air.

Kino, hurrying toward his house, felt a surge of exhilaration. Now he was not confused, for there was only one thing to do, and Kino's hand went first to the great pearl in his shirt and then to his knife hanging under his shirt.

He saw a little glow ahead of him, and then without interval a tall flame leaped up in the dark with a crackling roar, and a tall edifice of fire lighted the pathway. Kino broke into a run; it was his brush house, he knew. And he knew that these houses could burn down in a very few moments. And as he ran a scuttling figure ran toward him —Juana, with Coyotito in her arms and Kino's shoulder blanket clutched in her hand. The baby moaned with fright, and Juana's eyes were wide and terrified. Kino could see the house was gone, and he did not question Juana. He knew, but she said, "It was torn up and the floor dug—even the baby's box turned out, and as I looked they put the fire to the outside."

The fierce light of the burning house lighted Kino's face strongly. "Who?" he demanded.

"I don't know," she said. "The dark ones."

The neighbors were tumbling from their houses now, and they watched the falling sparks and stamped them out to save their own houses. Suddenly Kino was afraid. The light made him afraid. He remembered the man lying dead in the brush beside the path, and he took Juana by the arm and drew her into the shadow of a house away from the light, for light was danger to him. For a moment he considered and then he worked among the shadows until he came to the house of Juan Tomás, his brother, and he slipped into the doorway and drew Juana after him. Outside, he could hear the squeal of children and the shouts of the neighbors, for his friends thought he might be inside the burning house.

The house of Juan Tomás was almost exactly like Kino's house; nearly all the brush houses were alike, and all leaked light and air, so that Juana and Kino, sitting in the corner of the brother's house, could see the leaping flames through the wall. They saw the flames tall and furious, they saw the roof fall and watched the fire die down as quickly as a twig fire dies. They heard the cries of warning of their friends, and the shrill, keening[2] cry of Apolonia, wife of Juan Tomás. She, being the nearest woman relative, raised a formal lament for the dead of the family.

Apolonia realized that she was wearing her second-best head shawl and she rushed to her house to get her fine new one. As she rummaged in a box by the wall, Kino's voice said quietly, "Apolonia, do not cry out. We are not hurt."

"How do you come here?" she demanded.

"Do not question," he said. "Go now to Juan Tomás and bring him here and tell no one else. This is important to us, Apolonia."

She paused, her hands helpless in front

---

**2. keening** (kēn' iŋ) *adj.*: Wailing for the dead.

of her, and then, "Yes, my brother-in-law," she said.

In a few moments Juan Tomás came back with her. He lighted a candle and came to them where they crouched in a corner and he said, "Apolonia, see to the door, and do not let anyone enter." He was older, Juan Tomás, and he assumed the authority. "Now, my brother," he said.

"I was attacked in the dark," said Kino. "And in the fight I have killed a man."

"Who?" asked Juan Tomás quickly.

"I do not know. It is all darkness—all darkness and shape of darkness."

"It is the pearl," said Juan Tomás. "There is a devil in this pearl. You should have sold it and passed on the devil. Perhaps you can still sell it and buy peace for yourself."

And Kino said, "Oh, my brother, an insult has been put on me that is deeper than my life. For on the beach my canoe is broken, my house is burned, and in the brush a dead man lies. Every escape is cut off. You must hide us, my brother."

And Kino, looking closely, saw deep worry come into his brother's eyes and he forestalled him in a possible refusal. "Not for long," he said quickly. "Only until a day has passed and the new night has come. Then we will go."

"I will hide you," said Juan Tomás.

"I do not want to bring danger to you," Kino said. "I know I am like a leprosy. I will go tonight and then you will be safe."

"I will protect you," said Juan Tomás, and he called, "Apolonia, close up the door. Do not even whisper that Kino is here."

They sat silently all day in the darkness of the house, and they could hear the neighbors speaking of them. Through the walls of the house they could watch their neighbors raking through the ashes to find the bones. Crouching in the house of Juan Tomás, they heard the shock go into their neighbors' minds at the news of the broken boat. Juan Tomás went out among the neighbors to divert their suspicions, and he gave them theories and ideas of what had happened to Kino and to Juana and to the baby. To one he said, "I think they have gone south along the coast to escape the evil that was on them." And to another, "Kino would never leave the sea. Perhaps he found another boat." And he said, "Apolonia is ill with grief."

And in that day the wind rose up to beat the Gulf and tore the kelps and weeds that lined the shore, and the wind cried through the brush houses and no boat was safe on the water. Then Juan Tomás told among the neighbors, "Kino is gone. If he went to the sea, he is drowned by now." And after each trip among the neighbors Juan Tomás came back with something borrowed. He brought a little woven straw bag of red beans and a gourd full of rice. He borrowed a cup of dried peppers and a block of salt, and he brought in a long working knife, eighteen inches long and heavy, as a small ax, a tool and a weapon. And when Kino saw this knife his eyes lighted up, and he fondled the blade and his thumb tested the edge.

The wind screamed over the Gulf and turned the water white, and the mangroves plunged like frightened cattle, and a fine sandy dust arose from the land and hung in a stifling cloud over the sea. The wind drove off the clouds and skimmed the sky clean and drifted the sand of the country like snow.

Then Juan Tomás, when the evening approached, talked long with his brother. "Where will you go?"

"To the north," said Kino. "I have heard that there are cities in the north."

"Avoid the shore," said Juan Tomás. "They are making a party to search the shore. The men in the city will look for you. Do you still have the pearl?"

"I have it," said Kino. "And I will keep it. I might have given it as a gift, but now it is my misfortune and my life and I will keep it." His eyes were hard and cruel and bitter.

Coyotito whimpered and Juana muttered little magics over him to make him silent.

"The wind is good," said Juan Tomás. "There will be no tracks."

They left quietly in the dark before the moon had risen. The family stood formally in the house of Juan Tomás. Juana carried Coyotito on her back, covered and held in by her head shawl, and the baby slept, cheek turned sideways against her shoulder. The head shawl covered the baby, and one end of it came across Juana's nose to protect her from the evil night air. Juan Tomás embraced his brother with the double embrace and kissed him on both cheeks. "Go with God," he said, and it was like a death. "You will not give up the pearl?"

"This pearl has become my soul," said Kino. "If I give it up I shall lose my soul. Go thou also with God."

## Chapter 6

The wind blew fierce and strong, and it pelted them with bits of sticks, sand, and little rocks. Juana and Kino gathered their clothing tighter about them, and covered their noses and went out into the world. The sky was brushed clean by the wind and the stars were cold in a black sky. The two walked carefully, and they avoided the center of the town where some sleeper in a doorway might see them pass. For the town closed itself in against the night, and anyone who moved about in the darkness would be noticeable. Kino threaded his way around the edge of the city and turned north, north

by the stars, and found the rutted sandy road that led through the brushy country toward Loreto[1] where the miraculous Virgin has her station.[2]

Kino could feel the blown sand against his ankles and he was glad, for he knew there would be no tracks. The little light from the stars made out for him the narrow road through the brushy country. And Kino could hear the pad of Juana's feet behind him. He went quickly and quietly, and Juana trotted behind him to keep up.

Some ancient thing stirred in Kino. Through his fear of dark and the devils that haunt the night, there came a rush of exhilaration; some animal thing was moving in him so that he was cautious and wary and dangerous; some ancient thing out of the past of his people was alive in him. The wind was at his back and the stars guided him. The wind cried and whisked in the brush, and the family went on monotonously, hour after hour. They passed no one and saw no one. At last, to their right, the waning moon arose, and when it came up the wind died down, and the land was still.

Now they could see the little road ahead of them, deep cut with sand-drifted wheel tracks. With the wind gone there would be footprints, but they were a good distance from the town and perhaps their tracks might not be noticed. Kino walked carefully in a wheel rut, and Juana followed in his path. One big cart, going to the town in the morning, could wipe out every trace of their passage.

All night they walked and never changed their pace. Once Coyotito awakened, and Juana shifted him in front of her and soothed him until he went to sleep again.

---

**1. Loreto** (lō rā′ tō): A town on the western coast of Baja California.
**2. station:** Religious shrine.

And the evils of the night were about them. The coyotes cried and laughed in the brush, and the owls screeched and hissed over their heads. And once some large animal lumbered away, crackling the undergrowth as it went. And Kino gripped the handle of the big working knife and took a sense of protection from it.

The music of the pearl was triumphant in Kino's head, and the quiet melody of the family underlay it, and they wove themselves into the soft padding of sandaled feet in the dust. All night they walked, and in the first dawn Kino searched the roadside for a covert to lie in during the day. He found his place near to the road, a little clearing where deer might have lain, and it was curtained thickly with the dry brittle trees that lined the road. And when Juana had seated herself and had settled to nurse the baby, Kino went back to the road. He broke a branch and carefully swept the footprints where they had turned from the roadway. And then, in the first light, he heard the creak of a wagon, and he crouched beside the road and watched a heavy two-wheeled cart go by, drawn by slouching oxen. And when it had passed out of sight, he went back to the roadway and looked at the rut and found that the footprints were gone. And again he swept out his traces and went back to Juana.

She gave him the soft corncakes Apolonia had packed for them, and after a while she slept a little. But Kino sat on the ground and stared at the earth in front of him. He watched the ants moving, a little column of them near to his foot, and he put his foot in their path. Then the column climbed over his instep and continued on its way, and Kino left his foot there and watched them move over it.

The sun arose hotly. They were not near the Gulf now, and the air was dry and hot so that the brush cricked[3] with heat and a good resinous smell[4] came from it. And when Juana awakened, when the sun was high, Kino told her things she knew already.

"Beware of that kind of tree there," he said, pointing. "Do not touch it, for if you do and then touch your eyes, it will blind you. And beware of the tree that bleeds. See, that one over there. For if you break it the red blood will flow from it, and it is evil luck." And she nodded and smiled a little at him, for she knew these things.

"Will they follow us?" she asked. "Do you think they will try to find us?"

"They will try," said Kino. "Whoever finds us will take the pearl. Oh, they will try."

And Juana said, "Perhaps the dealers were right and the pearl has no value. Perhaps this has all been an illusion."

Kino reached into his clothes and brought out the pearl. He let the sun play on it until it burned in his eyes. "No," he said, "they would not have tried to steal it if it had been valueless."

"Do you know who attacked you? Was it the dealers?"

"I do not know," he said. "I didn't see them."

He looked into his pearl to find his vision. "When we sell it at last, I will have a rifle," he said, and he looked into the shining surface for his rifle, but he saw only a huddled dark body on the ground with shining blood dripping from its throat. And he said quickly, "We will be married in a great church." And in the pearl he saw Juana with her beaten face crawling home through the night. "Our son must learn to read," he

---

**3. cricked** (krikt) *v.*: Twisted.
**4. resinous** (rez' 'n əs) **smell:** Odor of the pitchy substance that is discharged from some trees, such as evergreens.

said frantically. And there in the pearl Coyotito's face, thick and feverish from the medicine.

And Kino thrust the pearl back into his clothing, and the music of the pearl had become sinister in his ears, and it was interwoven with the music of evil.

The hot sun beat on the earth so that Kino and Juana moved into the lacy shade of the brush, and small gray birds scampered on the ground in the shade. In the heat of the day Kino relaxed and covered his eyes with his hat and wrapped his blanket about his face to keep the flies off, and he slept.

But Juana did not sleep. She sat quiet as a stone and her face was quiet. Her mouth was still swollen where Kino had struck her, and big flies buzzed around the cut on her chin. But she sat as still as a sentinel, and when Coyotito awakened she placed him on the ground in front of her and watched him wave his arms and kick his feet, and he smiled and gurgled at her until she smiled too. She picked up a little twig from the ground and tickled him, and she gave him water from the gourd she carried in her bundle.

Kino stirred in a dream, and he cried out in a guttural voice, and his hand moved in symbolic fighting. And then he moaned and sat up suddenly, his eyes wide and his nostrils flaring. He listened and heard only the cricking heat and the hiss of distance.

"What is it?" Juana asked.

"Hush," he said.

"You were dreaming."

"Perhaps." But he was restless, and when she gave him a corncake from her store he paused in his chewing to listen. He was uneasy and nervous; he glanced over his shoulder; he lifted the big knife and felt its edge. When Coyotito gurgled on the ground Kino said, "Keep him quiet."

"What is the matter?" Juana asked.

"I don't know."

He listened again, an animal light in his eyes. He stood up then, silently; and crouched low, he threaded his way through the brush toward the road. But he did not step into the road; he crept into the cover of a thorny tree and peered out along the way he had come.

And then he saw them moving along. His body stiffened and he drew down his head and peeked out from under a fallen branch. In the distance he could see three figures, two on foot and one on horseback. But he knew what they were, and a chill of fear went through him. Even in the distance he could see the two on foot moving slowly along, bent low to the ground. Here, one would pause and look at the earth, while the other joined him. They were the trackers, they could follow the trail of a bighorn sheep in the stone mountains. They were as sensitive as hounds. Here, he and Juana might have stepped out of the wheel rut, and these people from the inland, these hunters, could follow, could read a broken straw or a little tumbled pile of dust. Behind them, on a horse, was a dark man, his nose covered with a blanket, and across his saddle a rifle gleamed in the sun.

Kino lay as rigid as the tree limb. He barely breathed, and his eyes went to the place where he had swept out the track. Even the sweeping might be a message to the trackers. He knew these inland hunters. In a country where there was little game they managed to live because of their ability to hunt, and they were hunting him. They scuttled over the ground like animals and found a sign and crouched over it while the horseman waited.

The trackers whined a little, like excited dogs on a warming trail. Kino slowly drew his big knife to his hand and made it ready. He knew what he must do. If the trackers found the swept place, he must leap for the horseman, kill him quickly and take the rifle. That was his only chance in the world. And as the three drew nearer on the road, Kino dug little pits with his sandaled toes so that he could leap without warning, so that his feet would not slip. He had only a little vision under the fallen limb.

Now Juana, back in her hidden place, heard the pad of the horse's hoofs, and Coyotito gurgled. She took him up quickly and put him under her shawl and gave him her breast and he was silent.

When the trackers came near, Kino could see only their legs and only the legs of the horse from under the fallen branch. He saw the dark horny feet of the men and their ragged white clothes, and he heard the creak of leather of the saddle and the clink of spurs. The trackers stopped at the swept place and studied it, and the horseman stopped. The horse flung his head up against the bit and the bit-roller clicked under his tongue and the horse snorted. Then the dark trackers turned and studied the horse and watched his ears.

Kino was not breathing, but his back arched a little and the muscles of his arms and legs stood out with tension and a line of sweat formed on his upper lip. For a long moment the trackers bent over the road, and then they moved on slowly, studying the ground ahead of them, and the horseman moved after them. The trackers scuttled along, stopping, looking, and hurrying on. They would be back, Kino knew. They would be circling and searching, peeping, stooping, and they would come back sooner or later to his covered track.

He slid backward and did not bother to cover his tracks. He could not; too many

little signs were there, too many broken twigs and scuffed places and displaced stones. And there was a panic in Kino now, a panic of flight. The trackers would find his trail, he knew it. There was no escape, except in flight. He edged away from the road and went quickly and silently to the hidden place where Juana was. She looked up at him in question.

"Trackers," he said. "Come!"

And then a helplessness and a hopelessness swept over him, and his face went black and his eyes were sad. "Perhaps I should let them take me."

Instantly Juana was on her feet and her hand lay on his arm. "You have the pearl," she cried hoarsely. "Do you think they would take you back alive to say they had stolen it?"

His hand strayed limply to the place where the pearl was hidden under his clothes. "They will find it," he said weakly.

"Come," she said. "Come!"

And when he did not respond, "Do you think they would let me live? Do you think they would let the little one here live?"

Her goading struck into his brain; his lips snarled and his eyes were fierce again. "Come," he said. "We will go into the mountains. Maybe we can lose them in the mountains."

Frantically he gathered the gourds and the little bags that were their property. Kino carried a bundle in his left hand, but the big knife swung free in his right hand. He parted the brush for Juana and they hurried to the west, toward the high stone mountains. They trotted quickly through the tangle of the undergrowth. This was panic flight. Kino did not try to conceal his passage as he trotted, kicking the stones, knocking the telltale leaves from the little trees. The high sun streamed down on the dry creaking

**CACTUS ON THE PLAINS (HANDS), 1931**
*Diego Rivera*
Edsel and Eleanor Ford House
Grosse Pointe Shores, Michigan

earth so that even the vegetation ticked in protest. But ahead were the naked granite mountains, rising out of erosion rubble and standing monolithic against the sky. And Kino ran for the high place, as nearly all animals do when they are pursued.

This land was waterless, furred with the cacti which could store water and with the great-rooted brush which could reach deep into the earth for a little moisture and get along on very little. And underfoot was not soil but broken rock, split into small cubes, great slabs, but none of it water-rounded. Little tufts of sad dry grass grew between the stones, grass that had sprouted with one single rain and headed,[5] dropped its seed, and died. Horned toads watched the family go by and turned their little pivoting dragon heads. And now and then a great jackrabbit, disturbed in his shade, bumped away and hid behind the nearest rock. The singing heat lay over this desert country, and ahead the stone mountains looked cool and welcoming.

And Kino fled. He knew what would happen. A little way along the road the trackers would become aware that they had missed the path, and they would come back, searching and judging, and in a little while they would find the place where Kino and Juana had rested. From there it would be easy for them—these little stones, the fallen leaves and the whipped branches, the scuffed places where a foot had slipped. Kino could see them in his mind, slipping along the track, whining a little with eagerness, and behind them, dark and half disinterested, the horseman with the rifle. His work would come last, for he would not take them back. Oh, the music of evil sang loud in Kino's head now, it sang with the whine of heat and with the dry ringing of snake rattles. It was not large and overwhelming now, but secret and poisonous, and the pounding of his heart gave it undertone and rhythm.

The way began to rise, and as it did the rocks grew larger. But now Kino had put a little distance between his family and the trackers. Now, on the first rise, he rested. He climbed a great boulder and looked back over the shimmering country, but he could not see his enemies, not even the tall horseman riding through the brush. Juana had squatted in the shade of the boulder. She raised her bottle of water to Coyotito's lips; his little dried tongue sucked greedily at it. She looked up at Kino when he came back; she saw him examine her ankles, cut and scratched from the stones and brush, and she covered them quickly with her skirt. Then she handed the bottle to him, but he shook his head. Her eyes were bright in her tired face. Kino moistened his cracked lips with his tongue.

"Juana," he said, "I will go on and you will hide. I will lead them into the mountains, and when they have gone past, you will go north to Loreto or to Santa Rosalia.[6] Then, if I can escape them, I will come to you. It is the only safe way."

She looked full into his eyes for a moment. "No," she said. "We go with you."

"I can go faster alone," he said harshly. "You will put the little one in more danger if you go with me."

"No," said Juana.

"You must. It is the wise thing and it is my wish," he said.

"No," said Juana.

He looked then for weakness in her face,

---

**5. headed** (hed′ əd) v.: Grew to maturity.

**6. Santa Rosalia** (san′ tə  rō za′ lē ə): A town on the western coast of Baja California.

for fear or irresolution, and there was none. Her eyes were very bright. He shrugged his shoulders helplessly then, but he had taken strength from her. When they moved on it was no longer panic flight.

The country, as it rose toward the mountains, changed rapidly. Now there were long outcroppings of granite with deep crevices between, and Kino walked on bare unmarkable stone when he could and leaped from ledge to ledge. He knew that wherever the trackers lost his path they must circle and lose time before they found it again. And so he did not go straight for the mountains any more; he moved in zigzags, and sometimes he cut back to the south and left a sign and then went toward the mountains over bare stone again. And the path rose steeply now, so that he panted a little as he went.

The sun moved downward toward the bare stone teeth of the mountains, and Kino set his direction for a dark and shadowy cleft in the range. If there were any water at all, it would be there where he could see, even in the distance, a hint of foliage. And if there were any passage through the smooth stone range, it would be by this same deep cleft. It had its danger, for the trackers would think of it too, but the empty water bottle did not let that consideration enter. And as the sun lowered, Kino and Juana struggled wearily up the steep slope toward the cleft.

High in the gray stone mountains, under a frowning peak, a little spring bubbled out of a rupture in the stone. It was fed by shade-preserved snow in the summer, and now and then it died completely and bare rocks and dry algae were on its bottom. But nearly always it gushed out, cold and clean and lovely. In the times when the quick rains fell, it might become a freshet and send its column of white water crashing down the mountain cleft, but nearly always it was a lean little spring. It bubbled out into a pool and then fell a hundred feet to another pool, and this one, overflowing, dropped again, so that it continued, down and down, until it came to the rubble of the upland, and there it disappeared altogether. There wasn't much left of it then anyway, for every time it fell over an escarpment the thirsty air drank it, and it splashed from the pools to the dry vegetation. The animals from miles around came to drink from the little pools, and the wild sheep and the deer, the pumas and raccoons, and the mice—all came to drink. And the birds which spent the day in the brushland came at night to the little pools that were like steps in the mountain cleft. Beside this tiny stream, wherever enough earth collected for roothold, colonies of plants grew, wild grape and little palms, maidenhair fern, hibiscus, and tall pampas grass[7] with feathery rods raised above the spike leaves. And in the pool lived frogs and water-skaters, and waterworms crawled on the bottom of the pool. Everything that loved water came to these few shallow places. The cats took their prey there, and strewed feathers and lapped water through their bloody teeth. The little pools were places of life because of the water, and places of killing because of the water, too.

The lowest step, where the stream collected before it tumbled down a hundred feet and disappeared into the rubbly desert, was a little platform of stone and sand. Only a pencil of water fell into the pool, but it was enough to keep the pool full and to keep the ferns green in the underhang of the cliff, and wild grape climbed the stone mountain

---

**7. pampas** (pam′ pǝs) **grass:** Grass that grows on treeless plains in certain areas of the south.

and all manner of little plants found comfort here. The freshets had made a small sandy beach through which the pool flowed, and bright green watercress grew in the damp sand. The beach was cut and scarred and padded by the feet of animals that had come to drink and to hunt.

The sun had passed over the stone mountains when Kino and Juana struggled up the steep broken slope and came at last to the water. From this step they could look out over the sunbeaten desert to the blue Gulf in the distance. They came utterly weary to the pool, and Juana slumped to her knees and first washed Coyotito's face and then filled her bottle and gave him a drink. And the baby was weary and petulant, and he cried softly until Juana gave him her breast, and then he gurgled and clucked against her. Kino drank long and thirstily at the pool. For a moment, then, he stretched out beside the water and relaxed all his muscles and watched Juana feeding the baby, and then he got to his feet and went to the edge of the step where the water slipped over, and he searched the distance carefully. His eyes set on a point and he became rigid. Far down the slope he could see the two trackers; they were little more than dots or scurrying ants and behind them a larger ant.

Juana had turned to look at him and she saw his back stiffen.

"How far?" she asked quietly.

"They will be here by evening," said Kino. He looked up the long steep chimney of the cleft where the water came down. "We must go west," he said, and his eyes searched the stone shoulder behind the cleft. And thirty feet up on the gray shoulder he saw a series of little erosion caves. He slipped off his sandals and clambered up to them, gripping the bare stone with his toes,

and he looked into the shallow caves. They were only a few feet deep, wind-hollowed scoops, but they sloped slightly downward and back. Kino crawled into the largest one and lay down and knew that he could not be seen from the outside. Quickly he went back to Juana.

"You must go up there. Perhaps they will not find us there," he said.

Without question she filled her water bottle to the top, and then Kino helped her up to the shallow cave and brought up the packages of food and passed them to her. And Juana sat in the cave entrance and watched him. She saw that he did not try to erase their tracks in the sand. Instead, he climbed up the brush cliff beside the water, clawing and tearing at the ferns and wild grape as he went. And when he had climbed a hundred feet to the next bench, he came down again. He looked carefully at the smooth rock shoulder toward the cave to see that there was no trace of passage, and last he climbed up and crept into the cave beside Juana.

"When they go up," he said, "we will slip away, down to the lowlands again. I am afraid only that the baby may cry. You must see that he does not cry."

"He will not cry," she said, and she raised the baby's face to her own and looked into his eyes and he stared solemnly back at her.

"He knows," said Juana.

Now Kino lay in the cave entrance, his chin braced on his crossed arms, and he watched the blue shadow of the mountain move out across the brushy desert below until it reached the Gulf, and the long twilight of the shadow was over the land.

The trackers were long in coming, as though they had trouble with the trail Kino had left. It was dusk when they came at last to the little pool. And all three were on foot now, for a horse could not climb the last steep slope. From above they were thin figures in the evening. The two trackers scurried about on the little beach, and they saw Kino's progress up the cliff before they drank. The man with the rifle sat down and rested himself, and the trackers squatted near him, and in the evening the points of their cigarettes glowed and receded. And then Kino could see that they were eating, and the soft murmur of their voices came to him.

Then darkness fell, deep and black in the mountain cleft. The animals that used the pool came near and smelled men there and drifted away again into the darkness.

He heard a murmur behind him. Juana was whispering, "Coyotito." She was begging him to be quiet. Kino heard the baby whimper, and he knew from the muffled sounds that Juana had covered his head with her shawl.

Down on the beach a match flared, and in its momentary light Kino saw that two of the men were sleeping, curled up like dogs, while the third watched, and he saw the glint of the rifle in the match light. And then the match died, but it left a picture on Kino's eyes. He could see it, just how each man was, two sleeping curled up and the third squatting in the sand with the rifle between his knees.

Kino moved silently back into the cave. Juana's eyes were two sparks reflecting a low star. Kino crawled quietly close to her and he put his lips near to her cheek.

"There is a way," he said.

"But they will kill you."

"If I get first to the one with the rifle," Kino said, "I must get to him first, then I will be all right. Two are sleeping."

Her hand crept out from under her shawl and gripped his arm. "They will see your white clothes in the starlight."

"No," he said. "And I must go before moonrise."

He searched for a soft word and then gave it up. "If they kill me," he said, "lie quietly. And when they are gone away, go to Loreto."

Her hand shook a little, holding his wrist.

"There is no choice," he said. "It is the only way. They will find us in the morning."

Her voice trembled a little. "Go with God," she said.

He peered closely at her and he could see her large eyes. His hand fumbled out and found the baby, and for a moment his palm lay on Coyotito's head. And then Kino raised his hand and touched Juana's cheek, and she held her breath.

Against the sky in the cave entrance Juana could see that Kino was taking off his white clothes, for dirty and ragged though they were, they would show up against the dark night. His own brown skin was a better protection for him. And then she saw how he hooked his amulet[8] neck-string about the horn handle of his great knife, so that it hung down in front of him and left both hands free. He did not come back to her. For a moment his body was black in the cave entrance, crouched and silent, and then he was gone.

Juana moved to the entrance and looked out. She peered like an owl from the hole in the mountain, and the baby slept under the blanket on her back, his face turned sideways against her neck and shoulder. She could feel his warm breath against her skin, and Juana whispered her combination of

---

**8. amulet** (am′ yə lit) *adj.*: Charm worn to protect against evil.

prayer and magic, her Hail Marys and her ancient intercession, against the black unhuman things.

The night seemed a little less dark when she looked out, and to the east there was a lightning in the sky, down near the horizon where the moon would show. And, looking down, she could see the cigarette of the man on watch.

Kino edged like a slow lizard down the smooth rock shoulder. He had turned his neck-string so that the great knife hung down from his back and could not clash against the stone. His spread fingers gripped the mountain, and his bare toes found support through contact, and even his chest lay against the stone so that he would not slip. For any sound, a rolling pebble or a sigh, a little slip of flesh on rock, would rouse the watchers below. Any sound that was not germane[9] to the night would make them alert. But the night was not silent; the little tree frogs that lived near the stream twittered like birds, and the high metallic ringing of the cicadas filled the mountain cleft. And Kino's own music was in his head, the music of the enemy, low and pulsing, nearly asleep. But the Song of the Family had become as fierce and sharp and feline as the snarl of a female puma. The family song was alive now and driving him down on the dark enemy. The harsh cicada seemed to take up its melody, and the twittering tree frogs called little phrases of it.

And Kino crept silently as a shadow down the smooth mountain face. One bare foot moved a few inches and the toes touched the stone and gripped, and the other foot a few inches, and then the palm of one hand a little downward, and then the

---

**9. germane** (jər mān') *adj.*: Truly related.

other hand, until the whole body, without seeming to move, had moved. Kino's mouth was open so that even his breath would make no sound, for he knew that he was not invisible. If the watcher, sensing movement, looked at the dark place against the stone which was his body, he could see him. Kino must move so slowly he would not draw the watcher's eyes. It took him a long time to reach the bottom and to crouch behind a little dwarf palm. His heart thundered in his chest and his hands and face were wet with sweat. He crouched and took great slow long breaths to calm himself.

Only twenty feet separated him from the enemy now, and he tried to remember the ground between. Was there any stone which might trip him in his rush? He kneaded his legs against cramp and found that his muscles were jerking after their long tension. And then he looked apprehensively to the east. The moon would rise in a few moments now, and he must attack before it rose. He could see the outline of the watcher, but the sleeping men were below his vision. It was the watcher Kino must find—must find quickly and without hesitation. Silently he drew the amulet string over his shoulder and loosened the loop from the horn handle of his great knife.

He was too late, for as he rose from his crouch the silver edge of the moon slipped above the eastern horizon, and Kino sank back behind his bush.

It was an old and ragged moon, but it threw hard light and hard shadow into the mountain cleft, and now Kino could see the seated figure of the watcher on the little beach beside the pool. The watcher gazed full at the moon, and then he lighted another cigarette, and the match illumined his dark face for a moment. There could be no waiting now; when the watcher turned his head, Kino must leap. His legs were as tight as wound springs.

And then from above came a little murmuring cry. The watcher turned his head to listen and then he stood up, and one of the sleepers stirred on the ground and awakened and asked quietly, "What is it?"

"I don't know," said the watcher. "It sounded like a cry, almost like a human —like a baby."

The man who had been sleeping said, "You can't tell. Some coyote bitch with a litter. I've heard a coyote pup cry like a baby."

The sweat rolled in drops down Kino's forehead and fell into his eyes and burned them. The little cry came again and the watcher looked up the side of the hill to the dark cave.

"Coyote maybe," he said, and Kino heard the harsh click as he cocked the rifle.

"If it's a coyote, this will stop it," the watcher said as he raised the gun.

Kino was in midleap when the gun crashed and the barrel-flash made a picture on his eyes. The great knife swung and crunched hollowly. It bit through neck and deep into chest, and Kino was a terrible machine now. He grasped the rifle even as he wrenched free his knife. His strength and his movement and his speed were a machine. He whirled and struck the head of the seated man like a melon. The third man scrabbled away like a crab, slipped into the pool, and then he began to climb frantically, to climb up the cliff where the water penciled down. His hands and feet threshed in the tangle of the wild grapevine, and he whimpered and gibbered as he tried to get up. But Kino had become as cold and deadly as steel. Deliberately he threw the lever of the rifle, and then he raised the gun and aimed deliberately and fired. He saw his enemy tumble backward into the pool, and

Kino strode to the water. In the moonlight he could see the frantic frightened eyes, and Kino aimed and fired between the eyes.

And then Kino stood uncertainly. Something was wrong, some signal was trying to get through to his brain. Tree frogs and cicadas were silent now. And then Kino's brain cleared from its red concentration and he knew the sound—the keening, moaning, rising hysterical cry from the little cave in the side of the stone mountain, the cry of death.

Everyone in La Paz remembers the return of the family; there may be some old ones who saw it, but those whose fathers and whose grandfathers told it to them remember it nevertheless. It is an event that happened to everyone.

It was late in the golden afternoon when the first little boys ran hysterically in the town and spread the word that Kino and Juana were coming back. And everyone hurried to see them. The sun was settling toward the western mountains and the shadows on the ground were long. And perhaps that was what left the deep impression on those who saw them.

The two came from the rutted country road into the city, and they were not walking in single file, Kino ahead and Juana behind, as usual, but side by side. The sun was behind them and their long shadows stalked ahead, and they seemed to carry two towers of darkness with them. Kino had a rifle across his arm and Juana carried her shawl like a sack over her shoulder. And in it was a small limp heavy bundle. The shawl was crusted with dried blood, and the bundle swayed a little as she walked. Her face was hard and lined and leathery with fatigue and with the tightness with which she fought fatigue. And her wide eyes stared inward on herself. She was as remote and as removed as Heaven. Kino's lips were thin and his jaws tight, and the people say that he carried fear with him, that he was as dangerous as a rising storm. The people say that the two seemed to be removed from human experience; that they had gone through pain and had come out on the other side; that there was almost a magical protection about them. And those people who had rushed to see them crowded back and let them pass and did not speak to them.

Kino and Juana walked through the city as though it were not there. Their eyes glanced neither right nor left nor up nor down, but stared only straight ahead. Their legs moved a little jerkily, like well-made wooden dolls, and they carried pillars of black fear about them. And as they walked through the stone and plaster city brokers peered at them from barred windows and servants put one eye to a slitted gate and mothers turned the faces of their youngest children inward against their skirts. Kino and Juana strode side by side through the stone and plaster city and down among the brush houses, and the neighbors stood back and let them pass. Juan Tomás raised his hand in greeting and did not say the greeting and left his hand in the air for a moment uncertainly.

In Kino's ears the Song of the Family was as fierce as a cry. He was immune and terrible, and his song had become a battle cry. They trudged past the burned square where their house had been without even looking at it. They cleared the brush that edged the beach and picked their way down the shore toward the water. And they did not look toward Kino's broken canoe.

And when they came to the water's edge they stopped and stared out over the Gulf. And then Kino laid the rifle down, and he dug among his clothes, and then he held the great pearl in his hand. He looked into its

**THE SOB**
*David Alfaro Siqueiros, 1939*
The Museum of Modern Art, New York

surface and it was gray and ulcerous. Evil faces peered from it into his eyes, and he saw the light of burning. And in the surface of the pearl he saw the frantic eyes of the man in the pool. And in the surface of the pearl he saw Coyotito lying in the little cave with the top of his head shot away. And the pearl was ugly; it was gray, like a malignant growth. And Kino heard the music of the pearl, distorted and insane. Kino's hand shook a little, and he turned slowly to Juana and held the pearl out to her. She stood beside him, still holding her dead bundle over her shoulder. She looked at the pearl in his hand for a moment and then she looked into Kino's eyes and said softly, "No, you."

And Kino drew back his arm and flung the pearl with all his might. Kino and Juana watched it go, winking and glimmering under the setting sun. They saw the little splash in the distance, and they stood side by side watching the place for a long time.

And the pearl settled into the lovely green water and dropped toward the bottom. The waving branches of the algae called to it and beckoned to it. The lights on its surface were green and lovely. It settled down to the sand bottom among the fernlike plants. Above, the surface of the water was a green mirror. And the pearl lay on the floor of the sea. A crab scampering over the bottom raised a little cloud of sand, and when it settled the pearl was gone.

And the music of the pearl drifted to a whisper and disappeared.

## THINKING ABOUT THE SELECTION

### Recalling

1. What do the pearl dealers tell Kino about his pearl? Explain Kino's decision after visiting the pearl dealers.
2. For what reason does Kino fear the trackers? What sound does Kino hear after he kills the trackers?
3. What does Kino do with the pearl at the end of the story?

### Interpreting

4. Why does Kino hear "evil music" after the pearl dealer names his price?
5. Compare and contrast reactions to Kino's turning down the 1500 pesos.
6. Explain the implication of Kino's statement at the end of Chapter 4: "I am a man."
7. Why does Kino say, "This pearl has become my soul. If I give it up I shall lose my soul"?
8. When Kino and Juana return to the village, why do they walk side-by-side?

### Applying

9. Do you agree with Kino's decision to go to the capital to sell his pearl instead of accepting one of the pearl dealers' offers? Give reasons for your answer.
10. If Kino and Juana had never found the pearl, their life probably would not have changed. Do you think any good came of their discovery? Give reasons for your answer.

## ANALYZING LITERATURE

### Understanding Plot and Theme

**Plot,** the sequence of related events or incidents that make up a literary work, usually involves conflict, climax, and resolution. The climax, or the story's highest point of interest, comes near the end of the novel. It is followed by the resolution, or the outcome of the plot.

**Theme** is the general idea or insight about life that a story reveals. A novel may have several themes. Analyzing the plot can often lead you to a better understanding of these themes.

1. List the major events that make up the plot in Chapters 4 to 6 of *The Pearl.*
2. What is the major conflict in *The Pearl?*
3. What is the climax in Chapters 4 to 6?
4. How is the conflict resolved?
5. Kino and Juana hear in their minds the "song" of the family, of evil, and of the pearl. How does the writer use these "songs" to give clues to the theme?
6. When Kino and Juana set out to sell the pearl, what do they feel? How does this feeling turn out to be ironic? How does the use of irony help reveal theme?
7. What do you think is the main theme of *The Pearl?* What minor themes can you identify?

## CRITICAL THINKING AND READING

### Recognizing Cause and Effect

Writing about cause and effect is an attempt to explain relationships. A **cause** makes something occur; an **effect** is the outcome of the cause.

To identify an effect, ask yourself "What happened?" To identify its cause, ask "Why?"

1. What causes the following events?
   a. Kino decides to go to the capital.
   b. The watcher shoots into the cave.
2. What are the effects of the following events?
   a. Juana returns the pearl to Kino after he has knocked it from her hand onto the pathway by the beach.
   b. Kino kills a man in self-defense.

## UNDERSTANDING LANGUAGE

### Appreciating Vivid Verbs

Vivid verbs can help you see, hear, smell, taste, and feel what the characters do and experience in the story. For example, in *The Pearl,* "The coyotes cried and laughed in the brush, the owls screeched and hissed over their heads. And once some large animal lumbered away, crackling the undergrowth as it went." Such vivid verbs can make the action in a story come alive.

The following vivid verbs are from the last three chapters of *The Pearl*. Use each word correctly in a sentence.

1. clambered
2. glinted
3. wavered
4. whisked

## THINKING AND WRITING
### Responding to Literary Criticism

It has been said of Steinbeck, "He wanted to be an individualist; he admired individualists; yet he also had a strong social conscience and a strong sense of right and wrong."

Write an essay for a literary magazine explaining how this quotation is true of Steinbeck's writing in *The Pearl*. First list the ways in which Steinbeck shows his admiration for individualists, or people who choose to go their own way; then describe his strong social conscience—his caring for people who are downtrodden—and his strong sense of right and wrong. Then use this information in writing your essay. Revise your essay to include examples that support your statements. Proofread for errors in spelling, grammar, and punctuation.

# A Separate Peace

**TREE TRUNKS, 1913**
*André Derain*
*Moscow, Pushkin Museum/Roos/Art Resource*

# GUIDE FOR READING

## A Separate Peace, Chapters 1–4

**John Knowles** (1926–    ) was born in Fairmont, West Virginia. At the age of fifteen, as World War II raged, he left home to attend Phillips Exeter Academy in New Hampshire. Later he served briefly in the armed services. After graduating from Yale University in 1949, Knowles worked at various writing and editing jobs. He modeled the setting for *A Separate Peace,* his first published novel, after Phillips Exeter. *A Separate Peace* has become one of the most widely read American postwar novels.

### Characters and Verisimilitude

Novels are about people, or **characters.** In fact, you probably could not have a novel without characters. It is the novelist's job to give these characters **verisimilitude.** This means that the novelist creates characters who, although fictional, feel like real-life human beings. In a modern novel, the hero, or protagonist, is usually presented as a fallable creature capable of making mistakes.

### Look For

Carl Sandburg has written, "Time is a great teacher." At the start of *A Separate Peace,* Gene returns to the school he left fifteen years earlier. As you read the novel, look for the things Gene has learned over the passage of time. Why is it necessary for him to find "a separate peace"?

### Writing

Prepare a chart with the headings Personal Qualities, Motives, Feelings Toward Others, Attitudes, Influences. As you read, complete this chart for Gene and Finny.

### Vocabulary

Knowing the following words will help you as you read Chapters 1–4 of *A Separate Peace.*

**capacious** (kə pā'shəs) *adj.*: Roomy; spacious (p. 831)
**contentious** (kən ten'shəs) *adj.*: Quarrelsome (p. 832)
**droll** (drōl) *adj.*: Amusing in an odd or ironic way (p. 833)
**prodigious** (prə dij'əs) *adj.*: Huge or powerful (p. 834)
**rhetorically** (ri tôr' i k'lē) *adv.*: As if asking a question only for effect, without expecting an answer (p. 834)
**anarchy** (an'ər kē) *n.*: Lawlessness; disorder (p. 844)
**solace** (säl'is) *n.*: Something that comforts (p. 854)
**vulnerable** (vul'nər ə b'l) *adj.*: Sensitive (p. 855)

# A Separate Peace

## John Knowles

### Chapter 1

I went back to the Devon School not long ago, and found it looking oddly newer than when I was a student there fifteen years before. It seemed more sedate than I remembered it, more perpendicular and strait-laced, with narrower windows and shinier woodwork, as though a coat of varnish had been put over everything for better preservation. But, of course, fifteen years before there had been a war going on. Perhaps the school wasn't as well kept up in those days; perhaps varnish, along with everything else, had gone to war.

I didn't entirely like this glossy new surface, because it made the school look like a museum, and that's exactly what it was to me, and what I did not want it to be. In the deep, tacit way in which feeling becomes stronger than thought, I had always felt that the Devon School came into existence the day I entered it, was vibrantly real while I was a student there, and then blinked out like a candle the day I left.

Now here it was after all, preserved by some considerate hand with varnish and wax. Preserved along with it, like stale air in an unopened room, was the well-known fear which had surrounded and filled those days, so much of it that I hadn't even known it was there. Because, unfamiliar with the absence of fear and what that was like, I had not been able to identify its presence.

Looking back now across fifteen years, I could see with great clarity the fear I had lived in, which must mean that in the interval I had succeeded in a very important undertaking: I must have made my escape from it.

I felt fear's echo, and along with that I felt the unhinged, uncontrollable joy which had been its accompaniment and opposite face, joy which had broken out sometimes in those days like Northern Lights across black sky.

There were a couple of places now which I wanted to see. Both were fearful sites, and that was why I wanted to see them. So after lunch at the Devon Inn I walked back toward the school. It was a raw, nondescript time of year, toward the end of November, the kind of wet, self-pitying November day when every speck of dirt stands out clearly. Devon luckily had very little of such weather—the icy clamp of winter, or the radiant New Hampshire summers, were more characteristic of it—but this day it blew wet, moody gusts all around me.

I walked along Gilman Street, the best street in town. The houses were as handsome and as unusual as I remembered. Clever modernizations of old Colonial manses,[1] extensions in Victorian wood, capacious Greek Revival temples lined the street, as impressive and just as forbidding as ever. I had rarely seen anyone go into one of them,

---

**1. manses** (mans' əz) n.: Large, imposing houses; ministers' houses.

or anyone playing on a lawn, or even an open window. Today with their failing ivy and stripped, moaning trees the houses looked both more elegant and more lifeless than ever.

Like all old, good schools, Devon did not stand isolated behind walls and gates but emerged naturally from the town which had produced it. So there was no sudden moment of encounter as I approached it; the houses along Gilman Street began to look more defensive, which meant that I was near the school, and then more exhausted, which meant that I was in it.

It was early afternoon and the grounds and buildings were deserted, since everyone was at sports. There was nothing to distract me as I made my way across a wide yard, called the Far Common, and up to a building as red brick and balanced as the other major buildings, but with a large cupola and a bell and a clock and Latin over the doorway —the First Academy Building.

In through swinging doors I reached a marble foyer, and stopped at the foot of a long white marble flight of stairs. Although they were old stairs, the worn moons in the middle of each step were not very deep. The marble must be unusually hard. That seemed very likely, only too likely, although with all my thought about these stairs this exceptional hardness had not occurred to me. It was surprising that I had overlooked that, that crucial fact.

There was nothing else to notice; they of course were the same stairs I had walked up and down at least once every day of my Devon life. They were the same as ever. And I? Well, I naturally felt older—I began at that point the emotional examination to note how far my convalescence had gone—I was taller, bigger generally in relation to these stairs. I had more money and success and "security" than in the days when specters seemed to go up and down them with me.

I turned away and went back outside. The Far Common was still empty, and I walked alone down the wide gravel paths among those most Republican, bankerish of trees, New England elms, toward the far side of the school.

Devon is sometimes considered the most beautiful school in New England, and even on this dismal afternoon its power was asserted. It is the beauty of small areas of order—a large yard, a group of trees, three similar dormitories, a circle of old houses —living together in contentious harmony. You felt that an argument might begin again any time; in fact it had: out of the Dean's Residence, a pure and authentic Colonial house, there now sprouted an ell with a big bare picture window. Some day the Dean[2] would probably live entirely encased in a house of glass and be happy as a sandpiper. Everything at Devon slowly changed and slowly harmonized with what had gone before. So it was logical to hope that since the buildings and the Deans and the curriculum could achieve this, I could achieve, perhaps unknowingly already had achieved, this growth and harmony myself.

I would know more about that when I had seen the second place I had come to see. So I roamed on past the balanced red brick dormitories with webs of leafless ivy clinging to them, through a ramshackle salient[3] of the town which invaded the school for a hundred yards, past the solid gymnasium, full of students at this hour but silent as a monument on the outside, past the Field House, called The Cage—I remembered now what a mystery references to "The Cage" had been during my first weeks at Devon, I had thought it must be a place of severe punishment—and I reached the

---

**2. Dean** (dēn) *n.*: Head of the school administration.
**3. salient** (sāl′ yənt) *n.*: A projecting part or angle.

huge open sweep of ground known as the Playing Fields.

Devon was both scholarly and very athletic, so the playing fields were vast and, except at such a time of year, constantly in use. Now they reached soggily and emptily away from me, forlorn tennis courts on the left, enormous football and soccer and lacrosse fields in the center, woods on the right, and at the far end a small river detectable from this distance by the few bare trees along its banks. It was such a gray and misty day that I could not see the other side of the river, where there was a small stadium.

I started the long trudge across the fields and had gone some distance before I paid any attention to the soft and muddy ground, which was dooming my city shoes. I didn't stop. Near the center of the fields there were thin lakes of muddy water which I had to make my way around, my unrecognizable shoes making noises as I lifted them out of the mire. With nothing to block it the wind flung wet gusts at me; at any other time I would have felt like a fool slogging through mud and rain, only to look at a tree.

A little fog hung over the river so that as I neared it I felt myself becoming isolated from everything except the river and the few trees beside it. The wind was blowing more steadily here, and I was beginning to feel cold. I never wore a hat, and had forgotten gloves. There were several trees bleakly reaching into the fog. Any one of them might have been the one I was looking for. Unbelievable that there were other trees which looked like it here. It had loomed in my memory as a huge lone spike dominating the riverbank, forbidding as an artillery piece, high as the beanstalk. Yet here was a scattered grove of trees, none of them of any particular grandeur.

Moving through the soaked, coarse grass I began to examine each one closely, and finally identified the tree I was looking for by means of certain small scars rising along its trunk, and by a limb extending over the river, and another thinner limb growing near it. This was the tree, and it seemed to me standing there to resemble those men, the giants of your childhood, whom you encounter years later and find that they are not merely smaller in relation to your growth, but that they are absolutely smaller, shrunken by age. In this double demotion the old giants have become pigmies while you were looking the other way.

The tree was not only stripped by the cold season, it seemed weary from age, enfeebled, dry. I was thankful, very thankful that I had seen it. So the more things remain the same, the more they change after all —plus c'est la même chose, plus ça change. Nothing endures, not a tree, not love, not even a death by violence.

Changed, I headed back through the mud. I was drenched; anybody could see it was time to come in out of the rain.

The tree was tremendous, an irate, steely black steeple beside the river. I wasn't going to climb it. No one but Phineas could think up such a crazy idea.

He of course saw nothing the slightest bit intimidating about it. He wouldn't, or wouldn't admit it if he did. Not Phineas.

"What I like best about this tree," he said in that voice of his, the equivalent in sound of a hypnotist's eyes, "what I like is that it's such a cinch!" He opened his green eyes wider and gave us his maniac look, and only the smirk on his wide mouth with its droll, slightly protruding upper lip reassured us that he wasn't completely goofy.

"Is that what you like best?" I said sarcastically. I said a lot of things sarcastically that summer; that was my sarcastic summer, 1942.

"Aey-uh," he said. This weird New England affirmative—maybe it is spelled "aiehuh"—always made me laugh, as Finny knew, so I had to laugh, which made me feel less sarcastic and less scared.

There were three others with us —Phineas in those days almost always moved in groups the size of a hockey team —and they stood with me looking with masked apprehension from him to the tree. Its soaring black trunk was set with rough wooden pegs leading up to a substantial limb which extended farther toward the water. Standing on this limb, you could by a prodigious effort jump far enough out into the river for safety. So we had heard. At least the seventeen-year-old bunch could do it; but they had a crucial year's advantage over us. No Upper Middler, which was the name for our class in the Devon School, had ever tried. Naturally Finny was going to be the first to try, and just as naturally he was going to inveigle[4] others, us, into trying it with him.

We were not even Upper Middler exactly. For this was the Summer Session, just established to keep up with the pace of the war. We were in shaky transit that summer from the groveling[5] status of Lower Middlers to the near-respectability of Upper Middlers. The class above, seniors, draft-bait,[6] practically soldiers, rushed ahead of us toward the war. They were caught up in accelerated courses and first-aid programs and a physical hardening regimen,[7] which included jumping from this tree. We were still calmly, numbly reading Virgil and playing tag in the river farther downstream. Until Finny thought of the tree.

We stood looking up at it, four looks of consternation,[8] one of excitement. "Do you want to go first?" Finny asked us, rhetorically. We just looked quietly back at him, and so he began taking off his clothes, stripping down to his underpants. For such an extraordinary athlete—even as a Lower Middler Phineas had been the best athlete in the school—he was not spectacularly built. He was my height—five feet eight and a half inches (I had been claiming five feet nine inches before he became my roommate, but he had said in public with that simple, shocking self-acceptance of his, "No, you're the same height I am, five-eight and a half. We're on the short side"). He weighed a hundred and fifty pounds, a galling ten pounds more than I did, which flowed from his legs to torso around shoulders to arms and full strong neck in an uninterrupted, unemphatic unity of strength.

He began scrambling up the wooden pegs nailed to the side of the tree, his back muscles working like a panther's. The pegs didn't seem strong enough to hold his weight. At last he stepped onto the branch which reached a little farther toward the water. "Is this the one they jump from?" None of us knew. "If I do it, you're all going to do it, aren't you?" We didn't say anything very clearly. "Well," he cried out, "here's my contribution to the war effort!" and he sprang out, fell through the tops of some lower branches, and smashed into the water.

"Great!" he said, bobbing instantly to the surface again, his wet hair plastered in droll bangs on his forehead. "That's the most fun I've had this week. Who's next?"

I was. This tree flooded me with a sensation of alarm all the way to my tingling fingers. My head began to feel unnaturally

---

**4. inveigle** (in vē' g'l) *v.*: Entice into doing something.
**5. groveling** (gruv' liŋ) *adj.*: Crawling, humbling.
**6. draft-bait** *n.*: Age to be drafted, or called up into the army.
**7. regimen** (rej' ə mən) *n.*: System.

**8. consternation** (kän' stər nā' shən) *n.*: Fear or shock.

light, and the vague rustling sounds from the nearby woods came to me as though muffled and filtered. I must have been entering a mild state of shock. Insulated by this, I took off my clothes and started to climb the pegs. I don't remember saying anything. The branch he had jumped from was slenderer than it looked from the ground and much

higher. It was impossible to walk out on it far enough to be well over the river. I would have to spring far out or risk falling into the shallow water next to the bank. "Come on," drawled Finny from below, "stop standing there showing off." I recognized with automatic tenseness that the view was very impressive from here. "When they torpedo the troopship," he shouted, "you can't stand around admiring the view. Jump!"

What was I doing here anyway? Why did I let Finny talk me into stupid things like this? Was he getting some kind of hold over me?

"Jump!"

With the sensation that I was throwing my life away, I jumped into space. Some tips of branches snapped past me and then I crashed into the water. My legs hit the soft mud of the bottom, and immediately I was on the surface being congratulated. I felt fine.

"I think that was better than Finny's," said Elwin—better known as Leper—Lepellier, who was bidding for an ally in the dispute he foresaw.

"All right, pal," Finny spoke in his cordial, penetrating voice, that reverberant[9] instrument in his chest, "don't start awarding prizes until you've passed the course. The tree is waiting."

Leper closed his mouth as though forever. He didn't argue or refuse. He didn't back away. He became inanimate.[10] But the other two, Chet Douglass and Bobby Zane, were vocal enough, complaining shrilly about school regulations, the danger of stomach cramps, physical disabilities they had never mentioned before.

"It's you, pal," Finny said to me at last, "just you and me." He and I started back across the fields, preceding the others like two seigneurs.[11]

We were the best of friends at that moment.

"You were very good," said Finny good-humoredly, "once I shamed you into it."

"You didn't shame anybody into anything."

"Oh yes I did. I'm good for you that way. You have a tendency to back away from things otherwise."

"I never backed away from anything in my life!" I cried, my indignation at this charge naturally stronger because it was so true. "You're goofy!"

Phineas just walked serenely on, or rather flowed on, rolling forward in his white sneakers with such unthinking unity of movement that "walk" didn't describe it.

I went along beside him across the enormous playing fields toward the gym. Underfoot the healthy green turf was brushed with dew, and ahead of us we could see a faint green haze hanging above the grass, shot through with the twilight sun. Phineas stopped talking for once, so that now I could hear cricket noises and bird cries of dusk, a gymnasium truck gunning along an empty athletic road a quarter of a mile away, a burst of faint, isolated laughter carried to us from the back door of the gym, and then over all, cool and matriarchal,[12] the six o'clock bell from the Academy Building cupola, the calmest, most carrying bell toll in the world, civilized, calm, invincible, and final.

The toll sailed over the expansive tops of all the elms, the great slanting roofs and formidable chimneys of the dormitories, the narrow and brittle old housetops, across the open New Hampshire sky to us coming back from the river. "We'd better hurry or we'll be late for dinner," I said, breaking into what Finny called my "West Point stride." Phineas didn't really dislike West Point in particular or authority in general, but just considered authority the necessary evil against which happiness was achieved by reaction, the backboard which returned all the insults he threw at it. My "West Point stride" was intolerable; his right foot flashed into the middle of my fast walk and I went pitching forward into the grass. "Get those hundred and fifty pounds off me!" I

---

**9. reverberant** (ri vûr′ bər ənt) *adj.:* Reechoing.

**10. inanimate** (in an′ ə mit) *adj.:* Dull; spiritless; not alive.

**11. seigneurs** (sēn yūrz′) *n.:* Men of rank; feudal lords.

**12. matriarchal** (mā′ trē är′ k'l) *n.:* Motherly.

shouted, because he was sitting on my back. Finny got up, patted my head genially, and moved on across the field, not deigning to glance around for my counterattack, but relying on his extrasensory ears, his ability to feel in the air someone coming on him from behind. As I sprang at him he side-stepped easily, but I just managed to kick him as I shot past. He caught my leg and there was a brief wrestling match on the turf which he won. "Better hurry," he said, "or they'll put you in the guardhouse." We were walking again, faster; Bobby and Leper and Chet were urging us from ahead to hurry up, and then Finny trapped me again in his strongest trap, that is, I suddenly became his collaborator. As we walked rapidly along I abruptly resented the bell and my West Point stride and hurrying and conforming. Finny was right. And there was only one way to show him this. I threw my hip against his, catching him by surprise, and he was instantly down, definitely pleased. This was why he liked me so much. When I jumped on top of him, my knees on his chest, he couldn't ask for anything better. We struggled in some equality for a while, and then when we were sure we were too late for dinner, we broke off.

He and I passed the gym and came on toward the first group of dormitories, which were dark and silent. There were only two hundred of us at Devon in the summer, not enough to fill most of the school. We passed the sprawling Headmaster's house—empty, he was doing something for the government in Washington; past the Chapel—empty again, used only for a short time in the mornings; past the First Academy Building, where there were some dim lights shining from a few of its many windows, Masters[13] at work in their classrooms there; down a short slope into the broad and well-clipped

Common, on which light fell from the big surrounding Georgian buildings. A dozen boys were loafing there on the grass after dinner, and a kitchen rattle from the wing of one of the buildings accompanied their talk. The sky was darkening steadily, which brought up the lights in the dormitories and the old houses; a loud phonograph a long way off played "Don't Sit Under the Apple Tree," rejected that and played "They're Either Too Young or Too Old," grew more ambitious with *The Warsaw Concerto*, mellower with *The Nutcracker Suite*, and then stopped.

Finny and I went to our room. Under the yellow study lights we read our Hardy assignments; I was halfway through *Tess of the D'Urbervilles*, he carried on his baffled struggle with *Far from the Madding Crowd*, amused that there should be people named Gabriel Oak and Bathsheba Everdene. Our illegal radio, turned too low to be intelligible, was broadcasting the news. Outside there was a rustling early summer movement of the wind; the seniors, allowed out later than we were, came fairly quietly back as the bell sounded ten stately times. Boys ambled past our door toward the bathroom, and there was a period of steadily pouring shower water. Then lights began to snap out all over the school. We undressed, and I put on some pajamas, but Phineas, who had heard they were unmilitary, didn't; there was the silence in which it was understood we were saying some prayers, and then that summer school day came to an end.

## Chapter 2

Our absence from dinner had been noticed. The following morning—the clean-washed shine of summer mornings in the north country—Mr. Prud'homme stopped at our door. He was broad-shouldered, grave, and he wore a gray business suit. He did not

---

**13. masters:** Teachers.

have the careless, almost British look of most of the Devon Masters, because he was a substitute for the summer. He enforced such rules as he knew; missing dinner was one of them.

We had been swimming in the river, Finny explained; then there had been a wrestling match, then there was that sunset that anybody would want to watch, then there'd been several friends we had to see on business—he rambled on, his voice soaring and plunging in its vibrant sound box, his eyes now and then widening to fire a flash of green across the room. Standing in the shadows, with the bright window behind him, he blazed with sunburned health. As Mr. Prud'homme looked at him and listened to the scatterbrained eloquence of his explanation, he could be seen rapidly losing his grip on sternness.

"If you hadn't already missed nine meals in the last two weeks . . ." he broke in.

But Finny pressed his advantage. Not because he wanted to be forgiven for missing the meal—that didn't interest him at all, he might have rather enjoyed the punishment if it was done in some novel[1] and unknown way. He pressed his advantage because he saw that Mr. Prud'homme was pleased, won over in spite of himself. The Master was slipping from his official position momentarily, and it was just possible, if Phineas pressed hard enough, that there might be a flow of simple, unregulated friendliness between them, and such flows were one of Finny's reasons for living.

"The real reason, sir, was that we just had to jump out of that tree. You know that tree . . ." I knew, Mr. Prud'homme must have known, Finny knew, if he stopped to think, that jumping out of the tree was even more forbidden than missing a meal. "We

---

1. **novel** (näv′ 'l) *adj.*: New and unusual.

had to do that, naturally," he went on, "because we're all getting ready for the war. What if they lower the draft age to seventeen? Gene and I are both going to be seventeen at the end of the summer, which is a very convenient time since it's the start of the academic year and there's never any doubt about which class you should be in. Leper Lepellier is already seventeen, and if I'm not mistaken he will be draftable before the end of this next academic year, and so conceivably he ought to have been in the class ahead, he ought to have been a senior now, if you see what I mean, so that he would have been graduated and been all set to be drafted. But we're all right, Gene and I are perfectly all right. There isn't any question that we are conforming in every possible way to everything that's happening and everything that's going to happen. It's all a question of birthdays." Everything he said was true and sincere; Finny always said what he happened to be thinking, and if this stunned people then he was surprised.

Mr. Prud'homme released his breath with a sort of amazed laugh, stared at Finny for a while, and that was all there was to it.

This was the way the Masters tended to treat us that summer. They seemed to be modifying their usual attitude of floating, chronic disapproval. During the winter most of them regarded anything unexpected in a student with suspicion, seeming to feel that anything we said or did was potentially illegal. Now on these clear June days in New Hampshire they appeared to uncoil, they seemed to believe that we were with them about half the time, and only spent the other half trying to make fools of them. A streak of tolerance was detectable; Finny decided that they were beginning to show commendable signs of maturity.

It was partly his doing. The Devon faculty had never before experienced a student who combined a calm ignorance of the rules with a winning urge to be good, who seemed to love the school truly and deeply, and never more than when he was breaking the regulations, a model boy who was most comfortable in the truant's corner. The faculty threw up its hands over Phineas, and so loosened its grip on all of us.

But there was another reason. I think we reminded them of what peace was like, we boys of sixteen. We were registered with no draft board, we had taken no physical examinations. No one had ever tested us for hernia or color blindness. Trick knees and punctured eardrums were minor complaints and not yet disabilities which would separate a few from the fate of the rest. We were careless and wild, and I suppose we could be thought of as a sign of the life the war was being fought to preserve. Anyway, they were more indulgent toward us than at any other time; they snapped at the heels of the seniors, driving and molding and arming them for the war. They noticed our games tolerantly. We reminded them of what peace was like, of lives which were not bound up with destruction.

Phineas was the essence of this careless peace. Not that he was unconcerned about the war. After Mr. Prud'homme left he began to dress, that is he began reaching for whatever clothes were nearest, some of them mine. Then he stopped to consider, and went over to the dresser. Out of one of the drawers he lifted a finely woven broadcloth shirt, carefully cut, and very pink.

"What's *that* thing?"

"This is a tablecloth," he said out of the side of his mouth.

"No, cut it out. What is it?"

"This," he then answered with some pride, "is going to be my emblem. Ma sent it up last week. Did you ever see stuff like this, and a color like this? It doesn't even button all the way down. You have to pull it over your head, like this."

"Over your head? Pink! It makes you look ridiculous!"

"Does it?" He used this preoccupied tone when he was thinking of something more interesting than what you had said. But his mind always recorded what was said and played it back to him when there was time, so as he was buttoning the high collar in front of the mirror he said mildly, "I wonder what would happen if I looked ridiculous to everyone."

"You're nuts."

"Well, in case suitors begin clamoring at the door, you can tell them I'm wearing this as an emblem." He turned around to let me admire it. "I was reading in the paper that we bombed Central Europe for the first time the other day." Only someone who knew Phineas as well as I did could realize that he was not changing the subject. I waited quietly for him to make whatever fantastic connection there might be between this and his shirt. "Well, we've got to do something to *celebrate*. We haven't got a flag, we can't float Old Glory proudly out the window. So I'm going to wear this, as an emblem."

He did wear it. No one else in the school could have done so without some risk of having it torn from his back. When the sternest of the Summer Sessions Masters, old Mr. Patch-Withers, came up to him after history class and asked about it, I watched his drawn but pink face become pinker with amusement as Finny politely explained the meaning of the shirt.

It was hypnotism. I was beginning to see that Phineas could get away with anything. I couldn't help envying him that a little, which was perfectly normal. There was no harm in envying even your best friend a little.

In the afternoon Mr. Patch-Withers, who was substitute Headmaster for the summer, offered the traditional term tea to the Upper Middle class. It was held in the deserted

Headmaster's house, and Mr. Patch-Withers' wife trembled at every cup tinkle. We were in a kind of sun porch and conservatory[2] combined, spacious and damp and without many plants. Those there were had large nonflowering stalks, with big barbaric[3] leaves. The chocolate brown wicker furniture shot out menacing twigs, and three dozen of us stood tensely teetering our cups amid the wicker and leaves, trying hard not to sound as inane[4] in our conversation with the four present Masters and their wives as they sounded to us.

Phineas had soaked and brushed his hair for the occasion. This gave his head a sleek look, which was contradicted by the surprised, honest expression which he wore on his face. His ears, I had never noticed before, were fairly small and set close to his head, and combined with his plastered hair they now gave his bold nose and cheekbones the sharp look of a prow.

He alone talked easily. He discussed the bombing of Central Europe. No one else happened to have seen the story, and since Phineas could not recall exactly what target in which country had been hit, or whether it was the American, British, or even Russian air force which had hit it, or what day he read it in which newspaper, the discussion was one-sided.

That didn't matter. It was the event which counted. But after a while Finny felt he should carry the discussion to others. "I think we ought to bomb the daylights out of them, as long as we don't hit any women or children or old people, don't you?" he was saying to Mrs. Patch-Withers, perched nervously behind her urn. "Or hospitals," he went on. "And naturally no schools. Or churches."

"We must also be careful about works of art," she put in, "if they are of permanent value."

"A lot of nonsense," Mr. Patch-Withers grumbled, with a flushed face. "How do you expect our boys to be as precise as that thousands of feet up with bombs weighing tons! Look at what the Germans did to Amsterdam![5] Look at what they did to Coventry!"[6]

"The Germans aren't the Central Europeans, dear," his wife said very gently.

He didn't like being brought up short. But he seemed to be just able to bear it, from his wife. After a temperamental pause he said gruffly, "There isn't any 'permanent art' in Central Europe anyway."

Finny was enjoying this. He unbuttoned his seersucker jacket, as though he needed greater body freedom for the discussion. Mrs. Patch-Withers' glance then happened to fall on his belt. In a tentative voice she said, "Isn't that the . . . our . . ." Her husband looked; I panicked. In his haste that morning Finny had not unexpectedly used a tie for a belt. But this morning the first tie at hand had been the Devon School tie.

This time he wasn't going to get away with it. I could feel myself becoming unexpectedly excited at that. Mr. Patch-Withers' face was reaching a brilliant shade, and his wife's head fell as though before the guillotine. Even Finny seemed to color a little, unless it was the reflection from his pink shirt. But his expression was composed, and he said in his resonant voice, "I wore this, you see, because it goes with the shirt and it all ties in together—I didn't mean that to be a pun, I don't think they're very funny, especially in polite company, do you?—it all ties in together with what we've been talking about, this bombing in Central Europe, because when you come right down to it the

---

**2. conservatory** (kən sûr′ və tôr′ ē) n.: Greenhouse.
**3. barbaric** (bär ber′ ik) adj.: Uncivilized; wild.
**4. inane** (in ān′) adj.: Empty; foolish; silly.

**5. Amsterdam** (am′ stər dam′): Capital city of the Netherlands.
**6. Coventry** (kuv′ ən trē): City in central England.

school
is involved in
everything that hap-
pens in the war, it's all
the same war and the same
world, and I think Devon ought to
be included. I don't know whether you think
the way I do on that.''

Mr. Patch-Withers' face had been shifting expressions and changing colors continuously, and now it settled into fixed
surprise. "I never heard anything so illogical as that in my life!" He didn't sound very
indignant, though. "That's probably the

strangest
tribute this school has
had in a hundred and sixty
years.'' He seemed pleased or
amused in some unknown cor-
ner of his mind. Phineas was going to get
away with even this.

His eyes gave their wider, magical gleam
and his voice continued on a more compelling level, "Although I have to admit I didn't
think of that when I put it on this morning."
He smiled pleasantly after supplying this
interesting additional information. Mr.

Patch-Withers settled into a hearty silence at this, and so Finny added, "I'm glad I put on *something* for a belt! I certainly would hate the embarrassment of having my pants fall down at the Headmaster's tea. Of course he isn't here. But it would be just as embarrassing in front of you and Mrs. Patch-Withers," and he smiled politely down at her.

Mr. Patch-Withers' laughter surprised us all, including himself. His face, whose shades we had often labeled, now achieved a new one. Phineas was very happy; sour and stern Mr. Patch-Withers had been given a good laugh for once, and he had done it! He broke into the charmed, thoughtless grin of a man fulfilled.

He had gotten away with everything. I felt a sudden stab of disappointment. That was because I just wanted to see some more excitement; that must have been it.

We left the party, both of us feeling fine. I laughed along with Finny, my best friend, and also unique, able to get away with anything at all. And not because he was a conniver either; I was sure of that. He got away with everything because of the extraordinary kind of person he was. It was quite a compliment to me, as a matter of fact, to have such a person choose me for his best friend.

Finny never left anything alone, not when it was well enough, not when it was perfect. "Let's go jump in the river," he said under his breath as we went out of the sun porch. He forced compliance by leaning against me as we walked along, changing my direction; like a police car squeezing me to the side of the road, he directed me unwillingly toward the gym and the river. "We need to clear our heads of that party," he said, "all that talk!"

"Yes. It sure was boring. Who did most of the talking anyway?"

Finny concentrated. "Mr. Patch-With-ers was pretty gassy, and his wife, and . . ."

"Yeah. And?"

Turning a look of mock shock on me, "You don't mean to infer that *I* talked too much!"

Returning, with interest, his gaping shock, "You? Talk too much? How can you accuse me of accusing you of that!" As I said, this was my sarcastic summer. It was only long after that I recognized sarcasm as the protest of people who are weak.

We walked along through the shining afternoon to the river. "I don't really believe we bombed Central Europe, do you?" said Finny thoughtfully. The dormitories we passed were massive and almost anonymous behind their thick layers of ivy, big, old-looking leaves you would have thought stayed there winter and summer, permanent hanging gardens in New Hampshire. Between the buildings, elms curved so high that you ceased to remember their height until you looked above the familiar trunks and the lowest umbrellas of leaves and took in the lofty complex they held high above, branches and branches of branches, a world of branches with an infinity of leaves. They too seemed permanent and never-changing, an untouched, unreachable world high in space, like the ornamental towers and spires of a great church, too high to be enjoyed, too high for anything, great and remote and never useful. "No, I don't think I believe it either," I answered.

Far ahead of us four boys, looking like white flags on the endless green playing fields, crossed toward the tennis courts. To the right of them the gym meditated behind its gray walls, the high, wide, oval-topped windows shining back at the sun. Beyond the gym and the fields began the woods, our, the Devon School's woods, which in my imagination were the beginning of the great northern forests. I thought that, from the

Devon Woods, trees reached in an unbroken, widening corridor so far to the north that no one had ever seen the other end, somewhere up in the far unorganized tips of Canada. We seemed to be playing on the tame fringe of the last and greatest wilderness. I never found out whether this is so and perhaps it is.

Bombs in Central Europe were completely unreal to us here, not because we couldn't imagine it—a thousand newspaper photographs and newsreels had given us a pretty accurate idea of such a sight—but because our place here was too fair for us to accept something like that. We spent that summer in complete selfishness, I'm happy to say. The people in the world who could be selfish in the summer of 1942 were a small band, and I'm glad we took advantage of it.

"The first person who says anything unpleasant will get a swift kick," said Finny reflectively as we came to the river.

"All right."

"Are you still afraid to jump out of the tree?"

"There's something unpleasant about that question, isn't there?"

"That question? No, of course not. It depends on how you answer it."

"Afraid to jump out of that tree? I expect it'll be a very pleasant jump."

After we had swum around in the water for a while Finny said, "Will you do me the pleasure of jumping out of the tree first?"

"My pleasure."

Rigid, I began climbing the rungs, slightly reassured by having Finny right behind me. "We'll jump together to cement our partnership," he said. "We'll form a suicide society, and the membership requirement is one jump out of this tree."

"A suicide society," I said stiffly. "The Suicide Society of the Summer Session."

"Good! The *Super* Suicide Society of the Summer Session! How's that?"

"That's fine, that's okay."

We were standing on a limb, I a little farther out than Finny. I turned to say something else, some stalling remark, something to delay even a few seconds more, and then I realized that in turning I had begun to lose my balance. There was a moment of total, impersonal panic, and then Finny's hand shot out and grabbed my arm, and with my balance restored, the panic immediately disappeared. I turned back toward the river, moved a few more steps along the limb, sprang far out and fell into the deep water. Finny also made a good jump, and the Super Suicide Society of the Summer Session was officially established.

It was only after dinner, when I was on my way alone to the library, that the full danger I had brushed on the limb shook me again. If Finny hadn't come up right behind me . . . if he hadn't been there . . . I could have fallen on the bank and broken my back! If I had fallen awkwardly enough I could have been killed. Finny had practically saved my life.

## Chapter 3

Yes, he had practically saved my life. He had also practically lost it for me. I wouldn't have been on that limb except for him. I wouldn't have turned around, and so lost my balance, if he hadn't been there. I didn't need to feel any tremendous rush of gratitude toward Phineas.

The Super Suicide Society of the Summer Session was a success from the start. That night Finny began to talk abstractedly[1] about it, as though it were a venerable,[2] entrenched institution of the Devon School.

---

**1. abstractedly** (ab strak′ tid lē) *adv.*: Absent-mindedly.
**2. venerable** (ven′ ər ə b′l) *adj.*: Impressive on account of age.

The half-dozen friends who were there in our room listening began to bring up small questions on details without ever quite saying that they had never heard of such a club. Schools are supposed to be catacombed[3] with secret societies and underground brotherhoods, and as far as they knew here was one which had just come to the surface. They signed up as "trainees" on the spot.

We began to meet every night to initiate them. The Charter Members, he and I, had to open every meeting by jumping ourselves. This was the first of the many rules which Finny created without notice during the summer. I hated it. I never got inured[4] to the jumping. At every meeting the limb seemed higher, thinner, the deeper water harder to reach. Every time, when I got myself into position to jump, I felt a flash of disbelief that I was doing anything so perilous. But I always jumped. Otherwise I would have lost face with Phineas, and that would have been unthinkable.

We met every night, because Finny's life was ruled by inspiration and anarchy, and so he prized a set of rules. His own, not those imposed on him by other people, such as the faculty of the Devon School. The Super Suicide Society of the Summer Session was a club; clubs by definition met regularly; we met every night. Nothing could be more regular than that. To meet once a week seemed to him much less regular, entirely too haphazard, bordering on carelessness.

I went along; I never missed a meeting. At that time it would never have occurred to me to say, "I don't feel like it tonight," which was the plain truth every night. I was subject to the dictates of my mind, which gave me the maneuverability of a strait jacket.

"We're off, pal," Finny would call out, and acting against every instinct of my nature, I went without a thought of protest.

As we drifted on through the summer, with this one inflexible appointment every day—classes could be cut, meals missed, Chapel skipped—I noticed something about Finny's own mind, which was such an opposite from mine. It wasn't completely unleashed after all. I noticed that he did abide by certain rules, which he seemed to cast in the form of Commandments. "Never say you are five feet nine when you are five feet eight and a half" was the first one I encountered. Another was, "Always say some prayers at night."

But the one which had the most urgent influence in his life was, "You always win at sports." This "you" was collective. Everyone always won at sports. When you played a game you won, in the same way as when you sat down to a meal you ate it. It inevitably and naturally followed. Finny never permitted himself to realize that when you won they lost. That would have destroyed the perfect beauty which was sport. Nothing bad ever happened in sports; they were the absolute good.

He was disgusted with that summer's athletic program—a little tennis, some swimming, clumsy softball games, badminton. "Badminton!" he exploded the day it entered the schedule. He said nothing else, but the shocked, outraged, despairing note of anguish in the word said all the rest. *"Badminton!"*

"At least it's not as bad as the seniors," I said, handing him the fragile racquet and the fey shuttlecock. "They're doing calisthenics."

"What are they trying to do?" He swatted the shuttlecock the length of the locker room. "Destroy us?" Humor infiltrated the outrage in his voice, which meant that he was thinking of a way out.

---

**3. catacombed** (kat′ ə kōm′′d) *adj.*: Full of; riddled with.
**4. inured to** (in yŏŏr′d′ tŏŏ): Accustomed to; used to.

We went outside into the cordial afternoon sunshine. The playing fields were optimistically green and empty before us. The tennis courts were full. The softball diamond was busy. A pattern of badminton nets swayed sensually in the breeze. Finny eyed them with quiet astonishment. Far down the fields toward the river there was a wooden tower about ten feet high where the instructor had stood to direct the senior calisthenics. It was empty now. The seniors had been trotted off to the improvised obstacle course in the woods, or to have their blood pressure taken again, or to undergo an insidious[5] exercise in The Cage which consisted in stepping up on a box and down again in rapid rhythm for five minutes. They were off somewhere, shaping up for the war. All of the fields were ours.

Finny began to walk slowly in the direction of the tower. Perhaps he was thinking that we might carry it the rest of the way to the river and throw it in; perhaps he was just interested in looking at it, as he was in everything. Whatever he thought, he forgot it when we reached the tower. Beside it someone had left a large and heavy leather-covered ball, a medicine ball.

He picked it up. "Now this, you see, is everything in the world you need for sports. When they discovered the circle they created sports. As for this thing," embracing the medicine ball in his left arm he held up the shuttlecock, contaminated, in his outstretched right, "this idiot tickler, the only thing it's good for is eeny-meeny-miney-mo." He dropped the ball and proceeded to pick the feathers out of the shuttlecock, distastefully, as though removing ticks from a dog. The remaining rubber plug he then threw out of sight down the field, with a single lunge ending in a powerful downward thrust of his wrist. Badminton was gone.

He stood balancing the medicine ball, enjoying the feel of it. "All you really need is a round ball."

Although he was rarely conscious of it, Phineas was always being watched, like the weather. Up the field the others at badminton sensed a shift in the wind; their voices carried down to us, calling us. When we didn't come, they began gradually to come down to us.

"I think it's about time we started to get a little *exercise* around here, don't you?" he said, cocking his head at me. Then he slowly looked around at the others with the expression of dazed determination he used when the object was to carry people along with his latest idea. He blinked twice, and then said, "We can always start with this ball."

"Let's make it have something to do with the war," suggested Bobby Zane. "Like a blitzkrieg[6] or something."

"Blitzkrieg," repeated Finny doubtfully.

"We could figure out some kind of blitzkrieg baseball," I said.

"We'll call it blitzkrieg ball," said Bobby.

"Or just blitzball," reflected Finny. "Yes, blitzball." Then, with an expectant glance around, "Well, let's get started," he threw the big, heavy ball at me. I grasped it against my chest with both arms. "Well, run!" ordered Finny. "No, not *that* way! Toward the river! Run!" I headed toward the river surrounded by the others in a hesitant herd; they sensed that in all probability they were my adversaries in blitzball. "Don't hog it!" Finny yelled. "Throw it to somebody else. Otherwise, naturally," he talked steadily as he ran along beside me, "now that we've got you surrounded, one of us will knock you down."

"Do what!" I veered away from him,

---

**5. insidious** (in sid′ ē əs) *adj.*: Treacherous.

**6. blitzkrieg** (blits′ krēg′) *n.*: Sudden, overwhelming attack.

hanging on to the clumsy ball. "What kind of a game is that?"

"Blitzball!" Chet Douglass shouted, throwing himself around my legs, knocking me down.

"That naturally was completely illegal," said Finny. "You don't use your *arms* when you knock the ball carrier down."

"You don't?" mumbled Chet from on top of me.

"No. You keep your arms crossed like this on your chest, and you just butt the ball carrier. No elbowing allowed either. All right, Gene, start again."

I began quickly, "Wouldn't somebody else have possession of the ball after——"

"Not when you've been knocked down illegally. The ball carrier retains possession in a case like that. So it's perfectly okay, you still have the ball. Go ahead."

There was nothing to do but start running again, with the others trampling with stronger will around me. "Throw it!" ordered Phineas. Bobby Zane was more or less in the clear and so I threw it at him; it was so heavy that he had to scoop my throw up from the ground. "Perfectly okay," commented Finny, running forward at top speed, "perfectly okay for the ball to touch the ground when it is being passed." Bobby doubled back closer to me for protection. "Knock him down," Finny yelled at me.

"Knock him down! Are you crazy? He's on my team!"

"There aren't any teams in blitzball," he yelled somewhat irritably, "we're all enemies. Knock him down!"

I knocked him down. "All right," said Finny as he disentangled us. "Now you have possession again." He handed the leaden ball to me.

"I would have thought that possession passed——"

"Naturally you gained possession of the ball when you knocked him down. Run."

So I began running again. Leper Lepellier was loping along outside my perimeter, not noticing the game, taggling along without reason, like a porpoise escorting a passing ship. "Leper!" I threw the ball past a few heads at him.

Taken by surprise, Leper looked up in anguish, shrank away from the ball, and voiced his first thought, a typical one. "I don't want it!"

"Stop, stop!" cried Finny in a referee's tone. Everybody halted, and Finny retrieved the ball; he talked better holding it. "Now Leper has just brought out a really important fine point of the game. The receiver can *refuse* a pass if he happens to choose to. Since we're all enemies, we can and will turn on each other all the time. We call that the Lepellier Refusal." We all nodded without speaking. "Here, Gene, the ball is of course still yours."

"Still mine? Nobody else has had the ball but me, for God sakes!"

"They'll get their chance. Now if you are refused three times in the course of running from the tower to the river, you go all the way back to the tower and start over. Naturally."

Blitzball was the surprise of the summer. Everybody played it; I believe a form of it is still popular at Devon. But nobody can be playing it as it was played by Phineas. He had unconsciously invented a game which brought his own athletic gifts to their highest pitch. The odds were tremendously against the ball carrier, so that Phineas was driven to exceed himself practically every day when he carried the ball. To escape the wolf pack which all the other players became he created reverses and deceptions and acts of sheer mass hypnotism which were so extraordinary that they surprised even him; after some of these plays I would notice him chuckling quietly to himself, in a kind of happy disbelief. In such a nonstop

game he
also had the natural
advantage of a flow of energy
which I never saw interrupted. I
never saw him tired, never really winded, never overcharged and never restless. At
dawn, all day long, and at midnight, Phineas
always had a steady and formidable flow of
usable energy.

Right from the start, it was clear that no
one had ever been better adapted to a sport
than Finny was to blitzball. I saw that right
away. Why not? He had made it up, hadn't
he? It needn't be surprising that he was
sensationally good at it, and that the rest of
us were more or less bumblers in our different ways. I suppose it served us right for
letting him do all the planning. I didn't

really think about it myself. What difference did it make? It was just a game. It was good that Finny could shine at it. He could also shine at many other things, with people for instance, the others in our dormitory, the faculty; in fact, if you stopped to think about it, Finny could shine with everyone, he attracted everyone he met. I was glad of that too. Naturally. He was my roommate and my best friend.

Everyone has a moment in history which belongs particularly to him. It is the moment when his emotions achieve their most powerful sway over him, and afterward when you say to this person "the world today" or "life" or "reality" he will assume that you mean this moment, even if it is fifty years past. The world, through his unleashed emotions, imprinted itself upon him, and he carries the stamp of that passing moment forever.

For me, this moment—four years is a moment in history—was the war. The war was and is reality for me. I still instinctively live and think in its atmosphere. These are some of its characteristics: Franklin Delano Roosevelt is the President of the United States, and he always has been. The other two eternal world leaders are Winston Churchill[7] and Josef Stalin.[8] America is not, never has been, and never will be what the songs and poems call it, a land of plenty. Nylon, meat, gasoline, and steel are rare. There are too many jobs and not enough workers. Money is very easy to earn but rather hard to spend, because there isn't very much to buy. Trains are always late and always crowded with "servicemen." The war will always be fought very far from America and it will never end. Nothing in America stands still for very long, including the people, who are always either leaving or on leave. People in America cry often. Sixteen is the key and crucial and natural age for a human being to be, and people of all other ages are ranged in an orderly manner ahead of and behind you as a harmonious setting for the sixteen-year-olds of this world. When you are sixteen, adults are slightly impressed and almost intimidated by you. This is a puzzle, finally solved by the realization that they foresee your military future, fighting for them. You do not foresee it. To waste anything in America is immoral. String and tinfoil are treasures. Newspapers are always crowded with strange maps and names of towns, and every few months the earth seems to lurch from its path when you see something in the newspapers, such as the time Mussolini,[9] who had almost seemed one of the eternal leaders, is photographed hanging upside down on a meathook. Everyone listens to news broadcasts five or six times every day. All pleasurable things, all travel and sports and entertainment and good food and fine clothes, are in the very shortest supply, always were and always will be. There are just tiny fragments of pleasure and luxury in the world, and there is something unpatriotic about enjoying them. All foreign lands are inaccessible except to servicemen; they are vague, distant, and sealed off as though behind a curtain of plastic. The prevailing color of life in America is a dull, dark green called olive drab. That color is always respectable and always important. Most other colors risk being unpatriotic.

It is this special America, a very untypical one I guess, an unfamiliar transitional blur in the memories of most people, which is the real America for me. In that short-

---

**7. Winston Churchill** (1871–1947): Prime Minister of Great Britain during World War II.
**8. Josef Stalin** (1879–1953): Premier of the Soviet Union during World War II.

**9. Mussolini:** Benito Mussolini (1883–1945), dictator of Italy during World War II.

lived and special country we spent this summer at Devon when Finny achieved certain feats as an athlete. In such a period no one notices or rewards any achievements involving the body unless the result is to kill it or save it on the battlefield, so that there were only a few of us to applaud and wonder at what he was able to do.

One day he broke the school swimming record. He and I were fooling around in the pool, near a big bronze plaque marked with events for which the school kept records —50 yards, 100 yards, 220 yards. Under each was a slot with a marker fitted into it, showing the name of the record-holder, his year, and his time. Under "100 Yards Free Style" there was "A. Hopkins Parker —1940—53.0 seconds."

"A. Hopkins Parker?" Finny squinted up at the name. "I don't remember any A. Hopkins Parker."

"He graduated before we got here."

"You mean that record has been up there the *whole time* we've been at Devon and nobody's busted it yet?" It was an insult to the class, and Finny had tremendous loyalty to the class, as he did to any group he belonged to, beginning with him and me and radiating outward past the limits of humanity toward spirits and clouds and stars.

No one else happened to be in the pool. Around us gleamed white tile and glass brick; the green, artificial-looking water rocked gently in its shining basin, releasing vague chemical smells and a sense of many pipes and filters; even Finny's voice, trapped in this closed, high-ceilinged room, lost its special resonance and blurred into a general well of noise gathered up toward the ceiling. He said blurringly, "I have a feeling *I* can swim faster than A. Hopkins Parker."

We found a stopwatch in the office. He mounted a starting box, leaned forward from the waist as he had seen racing swimmers do but never had occasion to do himself—I noticed a preparatory looseness coming into his shoulders and arms, a controlled ease about his stance which was unexpected in anyone trying to break a record. I said, "On your mark—Go!" There was a complex moment when his body uncoiled and shot forward with sudden metallic tension. He planed up the pool, his shoulders dominating the water while his legs and feet rode so low that I couldn't distinguish them; a wake rippled hurriedly by him and then at the end of the pool his position broke, he relaxed, dived, an instant's confusion and then his suddenly and metallically tense body shot back toward the other end of the pool. Another turn and up the pool again—I noticed no particular slackening of his pace—another turn, down the pool again, his hand touched the end, and he looked up at me with a composed, interested expression. "Well, how did I do?" I looked at the watch; he had broken A. Hopkins Parker's record by .7 second.

"So I really did it. You know what? I thought I was going to do it. It felt as though I had that stopwatch in my head and I could hear myself going just a little bit faster than A. Hopkins Parker."

"The worst thing is there weren't any witnesses. And I'm no official timekeeper. I don't think it will count."

"Well of course it won't *count*."

"You can try it again and break it again. Tomorrow. We'll get the coach in here, and all the official timekeepers and I'll call up *The Devonian* to send a reporter and a photographer—"

He climbed out of the pool. "I'm not going to do it again," he said quietly.

"Of course you are!"

"No, I just wanted to see if I could do it. Now I know. But I don't want to do it in public." Some other swimmers drifted in through the door. Finny glanced sharply at them. "By the way," he said in an even more subdued voice, "we aren't going to talk about this. It's just between you and me. Don't say anything about it, to . . . anyone."

"Not say anything about it! When you broke the school record!"

"Sh-h-h-h!" He shot a blazing, agitated glance at me.

I stopped and looked at him up and down. He didn't look directly back at me. "You're too good to be true," I said after a while.

He glanced at me, and then said, "Thanks a lot" in a somewhat expressionless voice.

Was he trying to impress me or something? Not tell anybody? When he had broken a school record without a day of practice? I knew he was serious about it, so I didn't tell anybody. Perhaps for that reason his accomplishment took root in my mind and grew rapidly in the darkness where I was forced to hide it. The Devon School record books contained a mistake, a lie, and nobody knew it but Finny and me. A. Hopkins Parker was living in a fool's paradise, wherever he was. His defeated name remained in bronze on the school record plaque, while Finny deliberately evaded an athletic honor. It was true that he had many already—the Winslow Galbraith Memorial Football Trophy for having brought the most Christian sportsmanship to the game during the 1941–1942 season, the Margaret Duke Bonaventura ribbon and prize for the student who conducted himself at hockey most like the way her son had done, the Devon School Contact Sport Award, Presented Each Year to That Student Who in the Opinion of the Athletic Advisors Excels His Fellows in the Sportsmanlike Performance of Any Game Involving Bodily Contact. But these were in the past, and they were prizes, not school records. The sports Finny played officially—football, hockey, baseball, lacrosse—didn't have school re-

cords. To switch to a new sport suddenly, just for a day, and immediately break a record in it—that was about as neat a trick, as dazzling a reversal as I could, to be perfectly honest, possibly imagine. There was something inebriating[10] in the suppleness[11] of this feat. When I thought about it my head felt a little dizzy and my stomach began to tingle. It had, in one word, glamour, absolute schoolboy glamour. When I looked down at that stopwatch and realized a split second before I permitted my face to show it or my voice to announce it that Finny had broken a school record, I had experienced a feeling that also can be described in one word —shock.

To keep silent about this amazing happening deepened the shock for me. It made Finny seem too unusual for—not friendship, but too unusual for rivalry. And there were few relationships among us at Devon not based on rivalry.

"Swimming in pools is screwy anyway," he said after a long, unusual silence as we walked toward the dormitory. "The only real swimming is in the ocean." Then in the everyday, mediocre tone he used when he was proposing something really outrageous, he added, "Let's go to the beach."

The beach was hours away by bicycle, forbidden, completely out of all bounds. Going there risked expulsion, destroyed the studying I was going to do for an important test the next morning, blasted the reasonable amount of order I wanted to maintain in my life, and it also involved the kind of long, labored bicycle ride I hated. "All right," I said.

We got our bikes and slipped away from Devon along a back road. Having invited me Finny now felt he had to keep me enter-

---

**10. inebriating** (in ēb′ rē āt iŋ) *adj.*: Intoxicating; exciting.

**11. suppleness** (sup′ ′l nes) *n.*: Flexibility; resilience.

tained. He told long, wild stories about his childhood; as I pumped panting up steep hills he glided along beside me, joking steadily. He analyzed my character, and he insisted on knowing what I disliked most about him ("You're too conventional," I said). He rode backward with no hands, he rode on his own handlebars, he jumped off and back on his moving bike as he had seen trick horseback riders do in the movies. He sang. Despite the steady musical undertone in his speaking voice Finny couldn't carry a tune, and he couldn't remember the melody or the words to any song. But he loved listening to music, any music, and he liked to sing.

We reached the beach late in the afternoon. The tide was high and the surf was heavy. I dived in and rode a couple of waves, but they had reached that stage of power in which you could feel the whole strength of the ocean in them. The second wave, as it tore toward the beach with me, spewed[12] me a little ahead of it, encroaching[13] rapidly; suddenly it was immeasurably bigger than I was, it rushed me from the control of gravity and took control of me itself; the wave threw me down in a primitive plunge without a bottom, then there was a bottom, grinding sand, and I skidded onto the shore. The wave hesitated, balanced there, and then hissed back toward the deep water, its tentacles not quite interested enough in me to drag me with it.

I made my way up on the beach and lay down. Finny came, ceremoniously took my pulse, and then went back into the ocean. He stayed in an hour, breaking off every few minutes to come back to me and talk. The sand was so hot from the all-day sunshine that I had to brush the top layer away in order to lie down on it, and Finny's progress across the beach became a series of high, startled leaps.

The ocean, throwing up foaming sun-sprays across some nearby rocks, was winter cold. This kind of sunshine and ocean, with the accumulating roar of the surf and the salty, adventurous, flirting wind from the sea, always intoxicated Phineas. He was everywhere, he enjoyed himself hugely, he laughed out loud at passing sea gulls. And he did everything he could think of for me.

We had dinner at a hot dog stand, with our backs to the ocean and its now cooler wind, our faces toward the heat of the cooking range. Then we walked on toward the center of the beach, where there was a subdued New England strip of honky-tonks. The Boardwalk lights against the deepening blue sky gained an ideal, starry beauty and the lights from the belt of honky-tonks and shooting galleries gleamed with a quiet purity in the clear twilight.

Finny and I went along the Boardwalk in our sneakers and white slacks, Finny in a light blue polo shirt and I in a T-shirt. I noticed that people were looking fixedly at him, so I took a look myself to see why. His skin radiated a reddish copper glow of tan, his brown hair had been a little bleached by the sun, and I noticed that the tan made his eyes shine with a cool blue-green fire.

"Everybody's staring at you," he suddenly said to me. "It's because of that movie-star tan you picked up this afternoon . . . showing off again."

Enough broken rules were enough that night. Neither of us suggested going into any of the honky-tonks. Then we found a good spot among some sand dunes at the lonely end of the beach, and there we settled down to sleep for the night. The last words of Finny's usual nighttime monologue were, "I hope you're having a pretty good time here. I know I kind of dragged you away at the point of a gun, but after all you can't come to the

---

**12. spewed** (spyōod) v.: Ejected; forced out.
**13. encroaching** (in krōch′ iŋ) adj.: Intruding; advancing.

shore with just anybody and you can't come by yourself, and at this teen-age period in life the proper person is your best pal." He hesitated and then added, "which is what you are," and there was silence on his dune.

It was a courageous thing to say. Exposing a sincere emotion nakedly like that at the Devon School was the next thing to suicide. I should have told him then that he was my best friend also and rounded off what he had said. I started to; I nearly did. But something held me back. Perhaps I was stopped by that level of feeling, deeper than thought, which contains the truth.

## Chapter 4

The next morning I saw dawn for the first time. It began not as the gorgeous fanfare over the ocean I had expected, but as a strange gray thing, like sunshine seen through burlap. I looked over to see if Phineas was awake. He was still asleep, although in this drained light he looked more dead than asleep. The ocean looked dead too, dead gray waves hissing mordantly[1] along the beach, which was gray and dead-looking itself.

I turned over and tried to sleep again but couldn't, and so lay on my back looking at this gray burlap sky. Very gradually, like one instrument after another being tentatively rehearsed, beacons of color began to pierce the sky. The ocean perked up a little from the reflection of these colored slivers in the sky. Bright highlights shone on the tips of waves, and beneath its gray surface I could see lurking a deep midnight green. The beach shed its deadness and became a spectral gray-white, then more white than gray, and finally it was totally white and stainless, as pure as the shores of Eden.

Phineas, still asleep on his dune, made me think of Lazarus,[2] brought back to life by the touch of God.

I didn't contemplate this transformation for long. Inside my head, for as long as I could remember, there had always been a sense of time ticking steadily. I looked at the sky and the ocean and knew that it was around six-thirty. The ride back to Devon would take three hours at least. My important test, trigonometry, was going to be held at ten o'clock.

Phineas woke up talking. "That was one of the best night's sleep I ever had."

"When did you ever have a bad one?"

"The time I broke my ankle in football. I like the way this beach looks now. Shall we have a morning swim?"

"Are you crazy? It's too late for that."

"What time is it anyway?" Finny knew I was a walking clock.

"It's going on seven o'clock."

"There's time for just a short swim," and before I could say anything he was trotting down the beach, shedding clothes as he went, and into the ocean. I waited for him where I was. He came back after a while full of chilly glow and energy and talk. I didn't have much to say. "Do you have the money?" I asked once, suddenly suspecting that he had lost our joint seventy-five cents during the night. There was a search, a hopeless one, in the sand, and so we set off on the long ride back without any breakfast, and got to Devon just in time for my test. I flunked it; I knew I was going to as soon as I looked at the test problems. It was the first test I had ever flunked.

But Finny gave me little time to worry about that. Right after lunch there was a game of blitzball which took most of the

---

**1. mordantly** (môr′ dənt lē) adv.: Bitingly; sarcastically.

**2. Lazarus** (laz′ ə rəs): A young man raised from the dead by Jesus, in the New Testament book of John, Chapter 11.

afternoon, and right after dinner there was the meeting of the Super Suicide Society of the Summer Session.

That night in our room, even though I was worn out from all the exercise, I tried to catch up to what had been happening in trigonometry.

"You work too hard," Finny said, sitting opposite me at the table where we read. The study lamp cast a round yellow pool between

us. "You know all about History and English and French and everything else. What good will Trigonometry do you?"

"I'll have to pass it to graduate, for one thing."

"Don't give me that line. Nobody at Devon has ever been surer of graduating than you are. You aren't working for *that*. You want to be head of the class, valedictorian, so you can make a speech on Graduation

Day—in Latin or something boring like that probably—and be the boy wonder of the school. I know you.''

''Don't be stupid. I wouldn't waste my time on anything like that.''

''You never waste your time. That's why I have to do it for you.''

''Anyway,'' I grudgingly added, ''somebody's got to be the head of the class.''

''You see, I knew that's what you were aiming at,'' he concluded quietly.

''Fooey.''

What if I was. It was a pretty good goal to have, it seemed to me. After all, he should talk. He had won and been proud to win the Galbraith Football Trophy and the Contact Sport Award, and there were two or three other athletic prizes he was sure to get this year or next. If I was head of the class on Graduation Day and made a speech and won the Ne Plus Ultra Scholastic Achievement Citation, then we would both have come out on top, we would be even, that was all. We would be even. . . .

*Was that it!* My eyes snapped from the textbook toward him. Did he notice this sudden glance shot across the pool of light? He didn't seem to; he went on writing down his strange curlicue notes about Thomas Hardy in Phineas Shorthand. *Was that it!* With his head bent over in the lamplight I could discern a slight mound in his brow above the eyebrows, the faint bulge which is usually believed to indicate mental power. Phineas would be the first to disclaim any great mental power in himself. But what did go on in his mind? If I was the head of the class and won that prize, then we would be even. . . .

His head started to come up, and mine snapped down. I glared at the textbook. ''Relax,'' he said. ''Your brain'll explode if you keep this up.''

''You don't need to worry about me, Finny.''

''I'm not worried.''

''You wouldn't—'' I wasn't sure I had the control to put this question—''mind if I wound up head of the class, would you?''

''Mind?'' Two clear green-blue eyes looked at me. ''Fat chance you've got, anyway, with Chet Douglass around.''

''But you wouldn't mind, would you?'' I repeated in a lower and more distinct voice.

He gave me that half-smile of his, which had won him a thousand conflicts. ''I'd kill myself out of jealous envy.''

I believed him. The joking manner was a screen; I believed him. In front of my eyes the trigonometry textbook blurred into a jumble. I couldn't see. My brain exploded. He minded, despised the possibility that I might be the head of the school. There was a swift chain of explosions in my brain, one certainty after another blasted —up like a detonation went the idea of any best friend, up went affection and partnership and sticking by someone and relying on someone absolutely in the jungle of a boys' school, up went the hope that there was anyone in this school—in this world—whom I could trust. ''Chet Douglass,'' I said uncertainly, ''is a sure thing for it.''

My misery was too deep to speak any more. I scanned the page; I was having trouble breathing, as though the oxygen were leaving the room. Amid its devastation my mind flashed from thought to thought, despairingly in search of something left which it could rely on. Not rely on absolutely, that was obliterated as a possibility, just rely on a little, some solace, something surviving in the ruins.

I found it. I found a single sustaining thought. The thought was, You and Phineas are even already. You are even in enmity. You are both coldly driving ahead for yourselves alone. You did hate him for breaking that school swimming record, but so what?

He hated you for getting an A in every course but one last term. You would have had an A in that one except for him. Except for him.

Then a second realization broke as clearly and bleakly as dawn at the beach. Finny had deliberately set out to wreck my studies. That explained blitzball, that explained the nightly meetings of the Super Suicide Society, that explained his insistence that I share all his diversions. The way I believed that you're-my-best-friend blabber! The shadow falling across his face if I didn't want to do something with him! His instinct for sharing everything with me? Sure, he wanted to share everything with me, especially his procession of D's in every subject. That way he, the great athlete, would be way ahead of me. It was all cold trickery, it was all calculated, it was all enmity.

I felt better. Yes, I sensed it like the sweat of relief when nausea passes away; I felt better. We were even after all, even in enmity. The deadly rivalry was on both sides after all.

I became quite a student after that. I had always been a good one, although I wasn't really interested and excited by learning itself, the way Chet Douglass was. Now I became not just good but exceptional, with Chet Douglass my only rival in sight. But I began to see that Chet was weakened by the very genuineness of his interest in learning. He got carried away by things; for example, he was so fascinated by the tilting planes of solid geometry that he did almost as badly in trigonometry as I did myself. When we read *Candide* it opened up a new way of looking at the world to Chet, and he continued hungrily reading Voltaire, in French, while the class went on to other people. He was vulnerable there, because to me they were all pretty much alike—Voltaire and Molière and the laws of motion and the Magna Carta and the Pathetic Fallacy and *Tess of the*

*D'Urbervilles*—and I worked indiscriminately on all of them.

Finny had no way of knowing this, because it all happened so far ahead of him scholastically. In class he generally sat slouched in his chair, his alert face following the discussion with an expression of philosophical comprehension, and when he was forced to speak himself the hypnotic power of his voice combined with the singularity of his mind to produce answers which were often not right but could rarely be branded as wrong. Written tests were his downfall because he could not speak them, and as a result he got grades which were barely passing. It wasn't that he never worked, because he did work, in short, intense bouts now and then. As that crucial summer wore on and I tightened the discipline on myself Phineas increased his bouts of studying.

I could see through that. I was more and more certainly becoming the best student in the school; Phineas was without question the best athlete, so in that way we were even. But while he was a very poor student I was a pretty good athlete, and when everything was thrown into the scales they would in the end tilt definitely toward me. The new attacks of studying were his emergency measures to save himself. I redoubled my effort.

It was surprising how well we got along in these weeks. Sometimes I found it hard to remember his treachery, sometimes I discovered myself thoughtlessly slipping back into affection for him again. It was hard to remember when one summer day after another broke with a cool effulgence[3] over us, and there was a breath of widening life in the morning air—something hard to describe—an oxygen intoxicant, a shining northern paganism,[4] some odor, some feel-

---

**3. effulgence** (e ful′ jəns) *n.*: Radiance; brilliance.
**4. paganism** (pā′ gən iz′m) *n.*: Lack of any religion.

ing so hopelessly promising that I would fall back in my bed on guard against it. It was hard to remember in the heady and sensual clarity of these mornings; I forgot whom I hated and who hated me. I wanted to break out crying from stabs of hopeless joy, or intolerable promise, or because these mornings were too full of beauty for me, because I knew of too much hate to be contained in a world like this.

Summer lazed on. No one paid any attention to us. One day I found myself describing to Mr. Prud'homme how Phineas and I had slept on the beach, and he seemed to be quite interested in it, in all the details, so much so that he missed the point: that we had flatly broken a basic rule.

No one cared, no one exercised any real discipline over us; we were on our own.

August arrived with a deepening of all the summertime splendors of New Hampshire. Early in the month we had two days of light, steady rain which aroused a final fullness everywhere. The branches of the old trees, which had been familiar to me either half-denuded or completely gaunt during the winter terms at Devon, now seemed about to break from their storms of leaves. Little disregarded patches of ground revealed that they had been gardens all along, and nondescript underbrush around the gymnasium and the river broke into color. There was a latent[5] freshness in the air, as though spring were returning in the middle of the summer.

But examinations were at hand. I wasn't as ready for them as I wanted to be. The Suicide Society continued to meet every evening, and I continued to attend, because I didn't want Finny to understand me as I understood him.

And also I didn't want to let him excel me in this, even though I knew that it didn't matter whether he showed me up at the tree or not. Because it was what you had in your heart that counted. And I had detected that Finny's was a den of lonely, selfish ambition. He was no better than I was, no matter who won all the contests.

A French examination was announced for one Friday late in August. Finny and I studied for it in the library Thursday afternoon; I went over vocabulary lists, and he wrote messages and passed them with great seriousness to me, as *aide-mémoire*.[6] Of course I didn't get any work done. After supper I went to our room to try again. Phineas came in a couple of minutes later.

"Arise," he began airily, "Senior Overseer Charter Member! Elwin 'Leper' Lepellier has announced his intention to make the leap this very night, to qualify, to save his face at last."

I didn't believe it for a second. Leper Lepellier would go down paralyzed with panic on any sinking troopship before making such a jump. Finny had put him up to it, to finish me for good on the exam. I turned around with elaborate resignation. "If he jumps out of that tree I'm Mahatma Gandhi."[7]

"All right," agreed Finny absently. He had a way of turning clichés[8] inside out like that. "Come on, let's go. We've got to be there. You never know, maybe he *will* do it this time."

I slammed closed the French book.

"What's the matter?"

What a performance! His face was completely questioning and candid.

---

**5. latent** (lāt′ 'nt) *adj.*: Hidden.

**6. aide-mémoire** (ed mā mwar′) *n.*: French for "memory aid."

**7. Mahatma Gandhi** (mä hät′ mä gän′ dē) (1869–1948): Hindu leader of India during India's struggle for independence from British rule.

**8. clichés** (klē shāz′) *n.*: Trite, worn-out expressions.

"Studying!" I snarled. "Studying! You know, books. Work. Examinations."

"Yeah . . ." He waited for me to go on, as though he didn't see what I was getting at.

"Oh! You don't know what I'm talking about. No, of course not. Not you." I stood up and slammed the chair against the desk. "Okay, we go. We watch little lily-liver Lepellier not jump from the tree, and I ruin my grade."

He looked at me with an interested, surprised expression. "You want to study?"

I began to feel a little uneasy at this mildness of his, so I sighed heavily. "Never mind, forget it. I know, I joined the club, I'm going. What else can I do?"

"Don't go." He said it very simply and casually, as though he were saying, "Nice day." He shrugged, "Don't go. It's only a game."

I had stopped halfway across the room, and now I just looked at him. "What d'you mean?" I muttered. What he meant was clear enough, but I was groping for what lay behind his words, for what his thoughts could possibly be. I might have asked, "Who are you, then?" instead. I was facing a total stranger.

"I didn't know you needed to *study*," he said simply, "I didn't think you ever did. I thought it just came to you."

It seemed that he had made some kind of parallel between my studies and his sports. He probably thought anything you were good at came without effort. He didn't know yet that he was unique.

I couldn't quite achieve a normal speaking voice. "If I need to study, then so do you."

"Me?" He smiled faintly. "Listen, I could study forever and I'd never break C. But it's different for you, you're good. You really are. If I had a brain like that, I'd—I'd have my head cut open so people could look at it."

"Now wait a second . . ."

He put his hands on the back of a chair and leaned toward me. "I know. We kid around a lot and everything, but you have to be serious sometime, about something. If you're really good at something, I mean if there's nobody, or hardly anybody, who's as good as you are, then you've got to be serious about that. Don't mess around, for crying out loud." He frowned disapprovingly at me. "Why didn't you say you had to study before? Don't move from that desk. It's going to be all A's for you."

"Wait a minute," I said, without any reason.

"It's okay. I'll oversee old Leper. I know he's not going to do it." He was at the door.

"Wait a minute," I said more sharply. "Wait just a minute. I'm coming."

"No you aren't, pal, you're going to study."

"Never mind my studying."

"You think you've done enough already?"

"Yes." I let this drop curtly to bar him from telling me what to do about my work. He let it go at that, and went out the door ahead of me, whistling off key.

We followed our gigantic shadows across the campus, and Phineas began talking in wild French, to give me a little extra practice. I said nothing, my mind exploring the new dimensions of isolation around me. Any fear I had ever had of the tree was nothing beside this. It wasn't my neck, but my understanding which was menaced. He had never been jealous of me for a second. Now I knew that there never was and never could have been any rivalry between us. I was not of the same quality as he.

I couldn't stand this. We reached the others loitering around the base of the tree, and Phineas began exuberantly to throw off his clothes, delighted by the fading glow of the day, the challenge of the tree, the competitive tension of all of us. He lived and flourished in such moments. "Let's go, you and me," he called. A new idea struck him. "We'll go together, a double jump! Neat, eh?"

None of this mattered now; I would have listlessly agreed to anything. He started up the wooden rungs and I began climbing behind, up to the limb high over the bank. Phineas ventured a little way along it, holding a thin nearby branch for support. "Come out a little way," he said, "and then we'll jump side by side." The countryside was striking from here, a deep green sweep of playing fields and bordering shrubbery, with the school stadium white and miniature-looking across the river. From behind us the last long rays of light played across the campus, accenting every slight undulation[9] of the land, emphasizing the separateness of each bush.

Holding firmly to the trunk, I took a step toward him, and then my knees bent and I jounced the limb. Finny, his balance gone, swung his head around to look at me for an instant with extreme interest, and then he tumbled sideways, broke through the little branches below and hit the bank with a sickening, unnatural thud. It was the first clumsy physical action I had ever seen him make. With unthinking sureness I moved out on the limb and jumped into the river, every trace of my fear of this forgotten.

---

**9. undulation** (un' joo lā' shən) n.: Wavy, curving form.

## THINKING ABOUT THE SELECTION

### Recalling

1. Give three examples of Finny's luring Gene into breaking the rules.
2. Explain the Super Suicide Society of the Summer Session.
3. Describe the events leading to Finny's accident at the tree.

### Interpreting

4. Describe the relationship between Gene and Finny. Explain how the relationship would appear from the outside and the undercurrents at work in it that might not be apparent from the outside.
5. Explain how the setting of this novel—a private school, summer, the war—directly affect the events.

## Applying

6. Do you accept that people can be friends but still harbor jealousy and resentment toward one another? Explain your answer.

## ANALYZING LITERATURE
### Understanding Characters

Novelists try to give their **characters** verisimilitude, or a lifelike quality. When you read a novel, ask questions about the characters based on your experience with real people. For example, how did Gene's relationship to Finny develop? First, Gene followed Finny out of loyalty and rivalry; later, he became bitter from a sense of betrayal; finally, he acted cruelly from a sense of inferiority to Finny. Use examples from the novel to support your answers to these questions.

1. How does Finny view the world; that is, what seem to be his attitudes toward important issues of life?
2. Do you think the novelist achieved verisimilitude in creating the characters of Gene and Finny? Find evidence from the novel to support your answer.

## CRITICAL THINKING AND READING
### Contrasting Characters

Gene and Finny are different from each other in a number of ways. For example, Gene is a good, diligent student, while Finny is an indifferent one. Finny is the best athlete in the school, while Gene is only adequate in sports.

1. What are Gene's and Finny's attitudes toward school authority and rules?

2. What are Gene's and Finny's feelings about the jump from the tree?
3. What qualities does each boy have that explain why he is the leader or the follower.

## UNDERSTANDING LANGUAGE
### Identifying Antonyms

A **synonym** is a word that has the same meaning as another word. An **antonym** is a word that is the opposite of another word. Identify the pairs of synonyms or antonyms in each sentence.

1. "In this double demotion the old giants have become pigmies while you were looking the other way."
2. "Phineas was the essence of this careless peace, not that he was unconcerned about the war."
3. "From behind us the last long rays of light played across the campus, accenting every slight undulation of the land, emphasizing the separateness of each bush."

## THINKING AND WRITING
### Presenting a Point of View

Choose one incident from Chapters 1–4, such as the first jump from the tree or the invention of blitzball. List the main events of the incident. Beside each event, note how Finny probably felt about it or would relate it to others. Then retell the incident from Finny's point of view. Revise your story, making sure you have maintained Finny's point of view throughout. Then proofread it and share it with your classmates.

# GUIDE FOR READING

## Conflict

## A Separate Peace, Chapters 5–10

The sequence of related events that make up a novel is called the **plot.** Often the plot centers on a struggle or problem, called the **conflict,** involving the main character. The conflict might be external, that is, a struggle with another person, an animal, or a force of nature, or it may be internal, or within the character. As the conflict develops toward a pitch, the plot reaches its **climax.** Finally, the plot contains a **resolution;** that is, the story winds down as the conflict is resolved or the struggle ends in some way.

An important external conflict in *A Separate Peace* is the competition between Gene and Finny. Gene also experiences internal conflict, particularly as he tries to understand his friendship with Finny and his feelings about himself.

## Look For

As you read Chapters 5–10 of *A Separate Peace,* look for examples of conflict and the ways in which the conflict is building toward the climax.

## Writing

Imagine that you are Gene talking to Finny for the first time after his accident in the tree. How would you feel about what happened? What would you say to him? Write the conversation that might take place between you and Finny.

## Vocabulary

Knowing the following words will help you as you read Chapters 5–10 of *A Separate Peace.*

**ludicrous** (loo′di krəs) *adj.:* Laughably absurd (p. 864)

**erratic** (i rat′ik) *adj.:* Irregular; not following a normal pattern (p. 864)

**discern** (di surn′) *v.:* To recognize (p. 879)

**contemptuously** (kən temp′ choo wəs lē) *adv.:* Scornfully (p. 880)

**vagaries** (və ger′ēz) *n.:* Odd or unexpected actions or ideas (p. 892)

**culminate** (kul′mə nāt′) *v.:* To bring to its highest point of interest (p. 900)

**aesthete** (es′thēt′) *n.:* Someone highly sensitive to art and beauty; someone who puts on such a sensitivity (p. 901)

**querulous** (kwer′ə ləs) *adj.:* Inclined to find fault; complaining (p. 903)

## Chapter 5

None of us was allowed near the infirmary during the next days, but I heard all the rumors that came out of it. Eventually a fact emerged; it was one of his legs, which had been "shattered." I couldn't figure out exactly what this word meant, whether it meant broken in one or several places, cleanly or badly, and I didn't ask. I learned no more, although the subject was discussed endlessly. Out of my hearing people must have talked of other things, but everyone talked about Phineas to me. I suppose this was only natural. I had been right beside him when it happened, I was his roommate.

The effect of his injury on the masters seemed deeper than after other disasters I remembered there. It was as though they felt it was especially unfair that it should strike one of the sixteen-year-olds, one of the few young men who could be free and happy in the summer of 1942.

I couldn't go on hearing about it much longer. If anyone had been suspicious of me, I might have developed some strength to defend myself. But there was nothing. No one suspected. Phineas must still be too sick, or too noble, to tell them.

I spent as much time as I could alone in our room, trying to empty my mind of every thought, to forget where I was, even who I was. One evening when I was dressing for dinner in this numbed frame of mind, an idea occurred to me, the first with any energy behind it since Finny fell from the tree. I decided to put on his clothes. We wore the same size, and although he always criticized mine he used to wear them frequently, quickly forgetting what belonged to him and what to me. I never forgot, and that evening I put on his cordovan shoes, his pants, and I looked for and finally found his pink shirt, neatly laundered in a drawer. Its high, somewhat stiff collar against my neck, the wide cuffs touching my wrists, the rich material against my skin excited a sense of strangeness and distinction; I felt like some nobleman, some Spanish grandee.[1]

But when I looked in the mirror it was no remote aristocrat I had become, no character out of daydreams. I was Phineas, Phineas to the life. I even had his humorous expression in my face, his sharp, optimistic awareness. I had no idea why this gave me such intense relief, but it seemed, standing there in Finny's triumphant shirt, that I would never stumble through the confusions of my own character again.

I didn't go down to dinner. The sense of transformation stayed with me throughout the evening, and even when I undressed and went to bed. That night I slept easily, and it was only on waking up that this illusion was gone, and I was confronted with myself, and what I had done to Finny.

Sooner or later it had to happen, and that morning it did. "Finny's better!" Dr. Stanpole called to me on the chapel steps over the organ recessional[2] thundering behind us. I made my way haltingly past the members of the choir with their black robes flapping in the morning breeze, the doctor's words reverberating around me. He might denounce me there before the whole school. Instead he steered me amiably into the lane leading toward the infirmary. "He could stand a visitor or two now, after these very nasty few days."

"You don't think I'll upset him or anything?"

"You? No, why? I don't want any of these teachers flapping around him. But a pal or two, it'll do him good."

---

**1. grandee** (gran dē′) *n.*: Nobleman.
**2. recessional** (ri sesh′ ə n'l) *n.*: Music played while people are leaving a church service or ceremony.

"I suppose he's still pretty sick."

"It was a messy break."

"But how does he—how is he feeling? I mean, is he cheerful at all, or—"

"Oh, you know Finny." I didn't, I was pretty sure I didn't know Finny at all. "It was a messy break," he went on, "but we'll have him out of it eventually. He'll be walking again."

"*Walking* again!"

"Yes." The doctor didn't look at me, and barely changed his tone of voice. "Sports are finished for him, after an accident like that. Of course."

"But he must be able to," I burst out, "if his leg's still there, if you aren't going to amputate it—you aren't, are you?—then if it isn't amputated and the bones are still there, then it must come back the way it was, why wouldn't it? Of course it will."

Dr. Stanpole hesitated, and I think glanced at me for a moment. "Sports are finished. As a friend you ought to help him face that and accept it. The sooner he does the better off he'll be. If I had the slightest hope that he could do more than walk I'd be all for trying for everything. There is no such hope. I'm sorry, as of course everyone is. It's a tragedy, but there it is."

I grabbed my head, fingers digging into my skin, and the doctor, thinking to be kind, put his hand on my shoulder. At his touch I lost all hope of controlling myself. I burst out crying into my hands; I cried for Phineas and for myself and for this doctor who believed in facing things. Most of all I cried because of kindness, which I had not expected.

"Now that's no good. You've got to be cheerful and hopeful. He needs that from you. He wanted especially to see you. You were the one person he asked for."

That stopped my tears. I brought my hands down and watched the red brick exte-

rior of the infirmary, a cheerful building, coming closer. Of course I was the first person he wanted to see. Phineas would say nothing behind my back; he would accuse me, face to face.

We were walking up the steps of the infirmary, everything was very swift, and next I was in a corridor being nudged by Dr. Stanpole toward a door. "He's in there. I'll be with you in a minute."

The door was slightly ajar, and I pushed it back and stood transfixed on the threshold. Phineas lay among pillows and sheets, his left leg, enormous in its white bindings, suspended a little above the bed. A tube led from a glass bottle into his right arm. Some channel began to close inside me and I knew I was about to black out.

"Come on in," I heard him say. "You look worse than I do." The fact that he could still make a light remark pulled me back a little, and I went to a chair beside his bed. He seemed to have diminished physically in the few days which had passed, and to have lost his tan. His eyes studied me as though I were the patient. They no longer had their sharp good humor, but had become clouded and visionary. After a while I realized he had been given a drug. "What are *you* looking so sick about?" he went on.

"Finny, I—" there was no controlling what I said, the words were instinctive, like the reactions of someone cornered. "What happened there at the tree? That tree, I'm going to cut down that tree. Who cares who can jump out of it. What happened, what happened? How did you fall, how could you fall off like that?"

"I just fell," his eyes were vaguely on my face, "something jiggled and I fell over. I remember I turned around to look at you, it was like I had all the time in the world. I thought I could reach out and get hold of you."

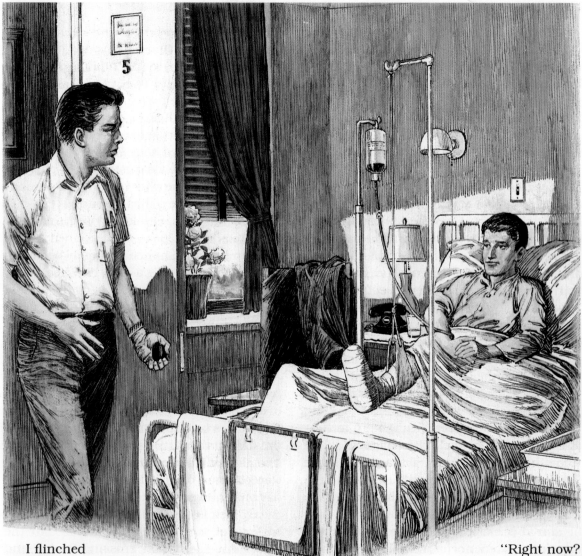

I flinched violently away from him. "To drag me down too!"

He kept looking vaguely over my face. "To get hold of you, so I wouldn't fall off."

"Yes, naturally." I was fighting for air in this close room. "I tried, you remember? I reached out but you were gone, you went down through those little branches underneath, and when I reached out there was only air."

"I just remember looking at your face for a second. Awfully funny expression you had. Very shocked, like you have right now."

"Right now? Well, of course, I *am* shocked. Who wouldn't be shocked. It's terrible, everything's terrible."

"But I don't see why you should look so *personally* shocked. You look like it happened to you or something."

"It's almost like it did! I was right there, right on the limb beside you."

"Yes, I know. I remember it all."

There was a hard block of silence, and then I said quietly, as though my words might detonate the room, "Do you remember what made you fall?"

His eyes continued their roaming across my face. "I don't know, I must have just lost my balance. It must have been that. I did have this idea, this feeling that when you were standing there beside me, y— I don't know, I had a kind of feeling. But you can't say anything for sure from just feelings. And this feeling doesn't make any sense. It was a crazy idea, I must have been delirious.[3] So I just have to forget it. I just fell," he turned away to grope for something among the pillows, "that's all." Then he glanced back at me, "I'm sorry about that feeling I had."

I couldn't say anything to this sincere, drugged apology for having suspected the truth. He was never going to accuse me. It was only a feeling he had, and at this moment he must have been formulating a new commandment in his personal decalogue:[4] Never accuse a friend of a crime if you only have a feeling he did it.

And I thought we were competitors! It was so ludicrous I wanted to cry.

If Phineas had been sitting here in this pool of guilt, how would he have felt, what would he have done?

He would have told me the truth.

I got up so suddenly that the chair overturned. I stared at him in amazement, and he stared back, his mouth breaking into a grin as the moments passed. "Well," he said at last in his friendly, knowing voice, "what are you going to do, hypnotize me?"

"Finny, I've got something to tell you. You're going to hate it, but there's something I've got to tell you."

"What energy," he said, falling back against the pillows. "You sound like General MacArthur."[5]

"I don't care who I sound like, and you won't think so when I tell you. This is the worst thing in the world, and I'm sorry and I hate to tell you but I've got to tell you."

But I didn't tell him. Dr. Stanpole came in before I was able to, and then a nurse came in, and I was sent away. The next day the doctor decided that Finny was not yet well enough to see visitors, even old pals like me. Soon after he was taken in an ambulance to his home outside Boston.

The Summer Session closed, officially came to an end. But to me it seemed irresolutely suspended, halted strangely before its time. I went south for a month's vacation in my home town and spent it in an atmosphere of reverie[6] and unreality, as though I had lived that month once already and had not been interested by it the first time either.

At the end of September I started back toward Devon on the jammed, erratic trains of September, 1942. I reached Boston seventeen hours behind schedule; there would be prestige in that at Devon, where those of us from long distances with travel adventures to report or invent held the floor for several days after a vacation.

By luck I got a taxi at South Station, and instead of saying "North Station" to the driver, instead of just crossing Boston and catching the final train for the short last leg of the trip to Devon, instead of that I sat back in the seat and heard myself give the address of Finny's house on the outskirts.

We found it fairly easily, on a street with a nave[7] of ancient elms branching over it. The house itself was high, white, and oddly proper to be the home of Phineas. It presented a face of definite elegance to the street, although behind that wings and ells

---

**3. delirious** (di lir' ē əs) *adj.*: Raving incoherently.
**4. decalogue** (dek' ə lôg') *n.*: Ten Commandments.
**5. General MacArthur:** Douglas MacArthur (1880–1964), U.S. general and commander in chief of Allied forces in the Pacific during World War II.

**6. reverie** (rev' ər ē) *n.*: Dreamy thinking or imagining.
**7. nave** (nāv) *n.*: Aisle.

dwindled quickly in formality until the house ended in a big plain barn.

Nothing surprised Phineas. A cleaning woman answered the door, and when I came into the room where he was sitting, he looked very pleased and not at all surprised.

"So you *are* going to show up!" his voice took off in one of its flights, "and you brought me something to eat from down South, didn't you? Honeysuckle and molasses or something like that?" I tried to think of something funny. "Corn bread? You did bring something. You didn't go all the way to Dixie and then come back with nothing but your dismal face to show for it." His talk rolled on, ignoring and covering my look of shock and clumsiness. I was silenced by the sight of him propped by white hospital-looking pillows in a big armchair. Despite everything at the Devon Infirmary, he had seemed an athlete there, temporarily injured in a game; as though the trainer would come in any minute and tape him up. Propped now before a great New England fireplace, on this quiet old street, he looked to me like an invalid, house-bound.

"I brought . . . Well I never remember to bring anyone anything." I struggled to get my voice above this self-accusing murmur. "I'll send you something. Flowers or something."

"Flowers! What happened to you in Dixie anyway?"

"Well then," there was no light remark anywhere in my head, "I'll get you some books."

"Never mind about books. I'd rather have some talk. What happened down South?"

"As a matter of fact," I brought out all the cheerfulness I could find for this, "there was a fire. It was just a grass fire out behind our house. We . . . took some brooms and beat it. I guess what we really did was fan it

because it just kept getting bigger until the Fire Department finally came. They could tell where it was because of all the flaming brooms we were waving around in the air, trying to put them out."

Finny liked that story. But it put us on the familiar friendly level, pals trading stories. How was I going to begin talking about it? It would not be just a thunderbolt. It wouldn't even seem real.

Not in this conversation, not in this room. I wished I had met him in a railroad station, or at some highway intersection. Not here. Here the small window panes shone from much polishing and the walls were hung with miniatures and old portraits. The chairs were either heavily upholstered and too comfortable to stay awake in or Early American and never used. There were several square, solid tables covered with family pictures and random books and magazines, and also three small, elegant tables not used for anything. It was a compromise of a room, with a few good "pieces" for guests to look at, and the rest of it for people to use.

But I had known Finny in an impersonal dormitory, a gym, a playing field. In the room we shared at Devon many strangers had lived before us, and many would afterward. It was there that I had done it, but it was here that I would have to tell it. I felt like a wild man who had stumbled in from the jungle to tear the place apart.

I moved back in the Early American chair. Its rigid back and high armrests immediately forced me into a righteous[8] posture. My blood could start to pound if it wanted to; let it. I was going ahead. "I was thinking about you most of the trip up."

"Oh yeah?" He glanced briefly into my eyes.

---

**8. righteous** (rī′ chəs) *adj.*: Just; upright.

"I was thinking about you . . . and the accident."

"There's loyalty for you. To think about me when you were on a vacation."

"I was thinking about it . . . about you because—I was thinking about you and the accident because I caused it."

Finny looked steadily at me, his face very handsome and expressionless. "What do you mean, you caused it?" his voice was as steady as his eyes.

My own voice sounded quiet and foreign. "I jounced the limb. I caused it." One more sentence. "I deliberately jounced the limb so you would fall off."

He looked older than I had ever seen him. "Of course you didn't."

"Yes I did. I did!"

"Of course you didn't do it. You fool. Sit down, you fool."

"Of course I did!"

"I'm going to hit you if you don't sit down."

"*Hit* me!" I looked at him. "*Hit* me! You can't even get up! You can't even come near me!"

"I'll kill you if you don't shut up."

"You see! Kill me! Now you know what it is! I did it because I felt like that! Now you know yourself!"

"I don't know anything. Go away. I'm tired and you make me sick. Go away." He held his forehead wearily, an unlikely way.

It struck me then that I was injuring him again. It occurred to me that this could be an even deeper injury than what I had done before. I would have to back out of it, I would have to disown it. Could it be that he might even be right? Had I really and definitely and knowingly done it to him after all? I couldn't remember, I couldn't think. However it was, it was worse for him to know it. I had to take it back.

But not here. "You'll be back at Devon in a few weeks, won't you?" I muttered after both of us had sat in silence for a while.

"Sure, I'll be there by Thanksgiving anyway."

At Devon, where every stick of furniture didn't assert that Finny was a part of it, I could make it up to him.

Now I had to get out of there. There was only one way to do it; I would have to make every move false. "I've had an awfully long trip," I said, "I never sleep much on trains. I guess I'm not making too much sense today."

"Don't worry about it."

"I think I'd better get to the station. I'm already a day late at Devon."

"You aren't going to start living by the rules, are you?"

I grinned at him. "Oh no, I wouldn't do that," and that was the most false thing, the biggest lie of all.

## Chapter 6

Peace had deserted Devon. Although not in the look of the campus and village; they retained much of their dreaming summer calm. Fall had barely touched the full splendor of the trees, and during the height of the day the sun briefly regained its summertime power. In the air there was only an edge of coolness to imply the coming winter.

But all had been caught up, like the first fallen leaves, by a new and energetic wind. The Summer Session—a few dozen boys being force-fed education, a stopgap while most of the masters were away and most of the traditions stored against sultriness[1]— the Summer Session was over. It had been the school's first, but this was its one hundred and sixty-third Winter Session, and the forces reassembled for it scattered the

---

**1. sultriness** (sul' tri nəs) *n.*: Oppressive heat.

easygoing summer spirit like so many fallen leaves.

The masters were in their places for the first Chapel, seated in stalls in front of and at right angles to us, suggesting by their worn expressions and careless postures that they had never been away at all.

In an apse of the church sat their wives and children, the objects during the tedious winter months of our ceaseless, ritual speculation (Why did he ever marry *her*? What in the world ever made her marry *him*? How could the two of them ever have produced *those* little monsters?). The masters favored seersucker on this mild first day, the wives broke out their hats. Five of the younger teachers were missing, gone into the war. Mr. Pike had come in his Naval ensign's uniform; some reflex must have survived Midshipman's School and brought him back to Devon for the day. His face was as mild and hopeless as ever; mooning above the snappy, rigid blouse, it gave him the air of an impostor.

Continuity was the keynote. The same hymns were played, the same sermon given, the same announcements made. There was one surprise; maids had disappeared "for the Duration,"[2] a new phase then. But continuity was stressed, not beginning again but continuing the education of young men according to the unbroken traditions of Devon.

I knew, perhaps I alone knew, that this was false. Devon had slipped through their fingers during the warm overlooked months. The traditions had been broken, the standards let down, all rules forgotten. In those bright days of truancy we had never thought of What We Owed Devon, as the sermon this opening day exhorted us to do. We had thought of ourselves, of what Devon owed us, and we had taken all of that and much more. Today's hymn was "Dear Lord and Father of Mankind Forgive Our Foolish Ways"; we had never heard that during the summer either. Ours had been a wayward gypsy music, leading us down all kinds of foolish gypsy ways, unforgiven. I was glad of it, I had almost caught the rhythm of it, the dancing, clicking jangle of it during the summer.

Still it had come to an end, in the last long rays of daylight at the tree, when Phineas fell. It was forced on me as I sat chilled through the Chapel service, that this probably vindicated[3] the rules of Devon after all, wintery Devon. If you broke the rules, then they broke you. That, I think, was the real point of the sermon on this first morning.

After the service ended we set out seven hundred strong, the regular winter throng of the Devon School, to hustle through our lists of appointments. All classrooms were crowded, swarms were on the crosswalks, the dormitories were as noisy as factories, every bulletin board was a forest of notices.

We had been an idiosyncratic,[4] leaderless band in the summer, undirected except by the eccentric notions of Phineas. Now the official class leaders and politicians could be seen taking charge, assuming as a matter of course their control of these walks and fields which had belonged only to us. I had the same room which Finny and I had shared during the summer, but across the hall, in the large suite where Leper Lepellier had dreamed his way through July and August amid sunshine and dust motes and windows through which the ivy had reached tentatively into the room, here Brinker Hadley had established his headquarters. Emis-

---

**2. Duration** (dσο rā′ shən) *n.*: In this case, the time until the war is over.

**3. vindicated** (vin′ də kāt əd) *v.*: Upheld; defended.

**4. idiosyncratic** (id′ ē ə sin krat′ ik) *adj.*: Peculiar.

saries were already dropping in to confer with him. Leper, luckless in his last year as all the others, had been moved to a room lost in an old building off somewhere in the trees toward the gym.

After morning classes and lunch I went across to see Brinker, started into the room and then stopped. Suddenly I did not want to see the trays of snails which Leper had passed the summer collecting replaced by Brinker's files. Not yet. Although it was something to have this year's dominant student across the way. Ordinarily he should have been a magnet for me, the center of all the excitement and influences in the class. Ordinarily this would have been so—if the summer, the gypsy days, had not intervened. Now Brinker, with his steady wit and ceaseless plans, Brinker had nothing to offer in place of Leper's dust motes and creeping ivy and snails.

I didn't go in. In any case I was late for my afternoon appointment. I never used to be late. But today I was, later even than I had to be. I was supposed to report to the Crew House, down on the banks of the lower river. There are two rivers at Devon, divided by a small dam. On my way I stopped on the footbridge which crosses the top of the dam separating them and looked upstream, at the narrow little Devon River sliding toward me between its thick fringe of pine and birch.

As I had to do whenever I glimpsed this river, I thought of Phineas. Not of the tree and pain, but of one of his favorite tricks, Phineas in exaltation,[5] balancing on one foot on the prow of a canoe like a river god, his raised arms invoking the air to support him, face transfigured, body a complex set of balances and compensations, each muscle aligned in perfection with all the others to maintain this supreme fantasy of achievement, his skin glowing from immersions,[6] his whole body hanging between river and sky as though he had transcended gravity and might by gently pushing upward with his foot glide a little way higher and remain suspended in space, encompassing all the glory of the summer and offering it to the sky.

Then, an infinitesimal veering of the canoe, and the line of his body would break, the soaring arms collapse, up shoot an uncontrollable leg, and Phineas would tumble into the water, roaring with rage.

I stopped in the middle of this hurrying day to remember him like that, and then, feeling refreshed, I went on to the Crew House beside the tidewater river below the dam.

We had never used this lower river, the Naguamsett, during the summer. It was ugly, saline,[7] fringed with marsh, mud and seaweed. A few miles away it was joined to the ocean, so that its movements were governed by unimaginable factors like the Gulf Stream, the Polar Ice Cap, and the moon. It was nothing like the fresh-water Devon above the dam where we'd had so much fun, all the summer. The Devon's course was determined by some familiar hills a little inland; it rose among highland farms and forests which we knew, passed at the end of its course through the school grounds, and then threw itself with little spectacle over a small waterfall beside the diving dam, and into the turbid Naguamsett.

The Devon School was astride these two rivers.

At the Crew House, Quackenbush, in the midst of some milling oarsmen in the damp main room, spotted me the instant I came in, with his dark expressionless

---

**5. exaltation** (eg′ zôl tā′ s·hən) *n.*: A feeling of great joy, pride, or power.

**6. immersions** (i mʉr′ s·hənz) *n.*: Plunges into water.
**7. saline** (sā′ lēn) *adj.*: Salty.

eyes. Quackenbush was the crew manager, and there was something wrong about him. I didn't know exactly what it was. In the throng of the winter terms at Devon we were at opposite extremities of the class, and to me there only came the disliked edge of Quackenbush's reputation. A clue to it was that his first name was never used—I didn't even know what it was—and he had no nickname, not even an unfriendly one.

"Late, Forrester," he said in his already-matured voice. He was a firmly masculine type; perhaps he was disliked only because he had matured before the rest of us.

"Yes, sorry, I got held up."

"The crew waits for no man." He didn't seem to think this was a funny thing to say. I did, and had to chuckle.

"Well, if you think it's all a joke . . ."

"I didn't say it was a joke."

"I've got to have some real help around here. This crew is going to win the New England scholastics, or my name isn't Cliff Quackenbush."

With that blank filled, I took up my duties as assistant senior crew manager. There is no such position officially, but it sometimes came into existence through necessity, and was the opposite of a sinecure.[8] It was all work and no advantages. The official assistant to the crew manager was a member of the class below, and the following year he could come into the senior managership with its rights and status. An assistant who was already a senior ranked nowhere. Since I had applied for such a nonentity[9] of a job, Quackenbush, who had known as little about me as I had about him, knew now.

_____
**8. sinecure** (sī′ nə kyσσr′) _n._: A position that brings advantage but involves little or no work.
**9. nonentity** (nän en′ tə tē) _n._: A thing of little or no importance.

"Get some towels," he said without looking at me, pointing at a door.

"How many?"

"Who knows? Get some. As many as you can carry. _That_ won't be too many."

Jobs like mine were usually taken by boys with some physical disability, since everyone had to take part in sports and this was all disabled boys could do. As I walked toward the door I supposed that Quackenbush was studying me to see if he could detect a limp. But I knew that his flat black eyes would never detect my trouble.

Quackenbush felt mellower by the end of the afternoon as we stood on the float in front of the Crew House, gathering up towels.

"You never rowed did you." He opened the conversation like that, without pause or question mark. His voice sounded almost too mature, as though he were putting it on a little; he sounded as though he were speaking through a tube.

"No, I never did."

"I rowed on the lightweight crew for two years."

He had a tough bantam body, easily detectable under the tight sweat shirt he wore. "I wrestle in the winter," he went on. "What are you doing in the winter?"

"I don't know, manage something else."

"You're a senior aren't you?"

He knew that I was a senior. "Yeah."

"Starting a little late to manage teams aren't you?"

"Am I?"

"Darn right you are!" He put indignant conviction into this, pouncing on the first sprig of assertiveness in me.

"Well, it doesn't matter."

"Yes it matters."

"I don't think it does."

"Who do you think you are anyway."

I turned with an inward groan to look at him. Quackenbush wasn't going to let me just do the work for him like the automaton[10] I wished to be. We were going to have to be pitted against each other. It was easy enough now to see why. For Quackenbush had been systematically disliked since he first set foot in Devon, with careless, disinterested insults coming at him from the beginning, voting for and applauding the class leaders through years of attaining nothing he wanted for himself. I didn't want to add to his humiliations; I even sympathized with his trembling, goaded egotism[11] he could no longer contain, the furious arrogance which sprang out now at the mere hint of opposition from someone he had at last found whom he could consider inferior to himself. I realized that all this explained him, and it wasn't the words he said which angered me. It was only that he was so ignorant, that he knew nothing of the gypsy summer, nothing of the loss I was fighting to endure, of skylarks and splashes and petal-bearing breezes, he had not seen Leper's snails or the Charter of the Super Suicide Society; he shared nothing, knew nothing, felt nothing as Phineas had done.

"You, Quackenbush, don't know anything about who I am." That launched me, and I had to go on and say, "or anything else."

"Listen you maimed . . ."

I hit him hard across the face. I didn't know why for an instant; it was almost as though I were maimed. Then the realization that there was someone who was flashed over me.

Quackenbush had clamped his arm in some kind of tight wrestling grip around my neck, and I was glad in this moment not to be a cripple. I reached over, grasped the back of his sweat shirt, wrenched, and it came away in my hand. I tried to throw him off, he lunged at the same time, and we catapulted into the water.

The dousing extinguished Quackenbush's rage, and he let go of me. I scrambled back onto the float, still seared by what he had said. "The next time you call anybody maimed," I bit off the words harshly so he would understand all of them, "you better make sure they are first."

"Get out of here, Forrester," he said bitterly from the water, "you're not wanted around here, Forrester. Get out of here."

I fought that battle, that first skirmish of a long campaign, for Finny. Until the back of my hand cracked against Quackenbush's face I had never pictured myself in the role of Finny's defender, and I didn't suppose that he would have thanked me for it now. He was too loyal to anything connected with himself—his roommate, his dormitory, his class, his school, outward in vastly expanded circles of loyalty until I couldn't imagine who would be excluded. But it didn't feel exactly as though I had done it for Phineas. It felt as though I had done it for myself.

If so I had little profit to show as I straggled back toward the dormitory dripping wet, with the job I had wanted gone, temper gone, mind circling over and over through the whole soured afternoon. I knew now that it was fall all right; I could feel it pressing clammily against my wet clothes, an unfriendly, discomforting breath in the air, an edge of wintery chill, air that shriveled, soon to put out the lights on the countryside. One of my legs wouldn't stop trembling, whether from cold or anger I couldn't tell. I wished I had hit him harder.

Someone was coming toward me along the bent, broken lane which led to the dormitory, a lane out of old London, ancient houses on either side leaning as though soon to tumble into it, cobblestones heaving underfoot like a bricked-over ocean squall

---

**10. automaton** (ô täm′ ə tän′) *n.*: A person acting in an automatic or mechanical way.

**11. goaded egotism** (gōd′′d ē′ gə tiz′m): Driven selfishness or conceit.

—a figure of great height advanced down them toward me. It could only be Mr. Ludsbury; no one else could pass over these stones with such contempt for the idea of tripping.

The houses on either side were inhabited by I didn't know who; wispy, fragile old ladies seemed most likely. I couldn't duck into one of them. There were angles and bumps and bends everywhere, but none big enough to conceal me. Mr. Ludsbury loomed on like a high-masted clipper ship in this rocking passage, and I tried to go stealthily by him on my watery, squeaking sneakers.

"Just one moment, Forrester, if you please." Mr. Ludsbury's voice was bass, British, and his Adam's apple seemed to move as much as his mouth when he spoke. "Has there been a cloudburst in your part of town?"

"No, sir. I'm sorry, sir, I fell into the river." I apologized by instinct to him for this mishap which discomforted only me.

"And could you tell me how and why you fell into the river?"

"I slipped."

"Yes." After a pause he went on. "I think you have slipped in any number of ways since last year. I understand for example that there was gaming in my dormitory this summer while you were living there." He was in charge of the dormitory; one of the dispensations[12] of those days of deliverance, I realized now, had been his absence.

"Gaming? What kind of gaming, sir?"

"Cards, dice," he shook his long hand

---

**12. dispensations** (dis′ pən sā′ s⁄hənz) n.: Releases; exemptions.

dismissingly, "I didn't inquire. It didn't matter. There won't be any more of it."

"I don't know who that would have been." Nights of black-jack and poker and unpredictable games invented by Phineas rose up in my mind; the back room of Leper's suite, a lamp hung with a blanket so that only a small blazing circle of light fell sharply amid the surrounding darkness; Phineas losing even in those games he invented, betting always for what *should* win, for what would have been the most brilliant successes of all, if only the cards hadn't betrayed him. Finny finally betting his icebox and losing it, that contraption, to me.

I thought of it because Mr. Ludsbury was just then saying, "And while I'm putting the dormitory back together I'd better tell you to get rid of that leaking icebox. Nothing like that is ever permitted in the dormitory, of course. I notice that everything went straight to seed during the summer and that none of you old boys who knew our standards so much as lifted a finger to help Mr. Prud'homme maintain order. As a substitute for the summer he couldn't have been expected to know everything there was to be known at once. You old boys simply took advantage of the situation."

I stood there shaking in my wet sneakers. If only I had truly taken advantage of the situation, seized and held and prized the multitudes of advantages the summer offered me; if only I had.

I said nothing, on my face I registered the bleak look of a defendant who knows the court will never be swayed by all the favorable evidence he has. It was a schoolboy look; Mr. Ludsbury knew it well.

"There's a long-distance call for you," he continued in the tone of the judge performing the disagreeable duty of telling the defendant his right. "I've written the operator's number on the pad beside the telephone in my study. You may go in and call."

"Thank you very much, sir."

He sailed on down the lane without further reference to me, and I wondered who was sick at home.

But when I reached his study—low-ceilinged, gloomy with books, black leather chairs, a pipe rack, frayed brown rug, a room which students rarely entered except for a reprimand—I saw on the pad not an operator's number from my home town, but one which seemed to interrupt the beating of my heart.

I called this operator, and listened in wonder while she went through her routine as though this were just any long-distance call, and then her voice left the line and it was pre-empted, and charged, by the voice of Phineas. "Happy first day of the new academic year!"

"Thanks, thanks a lot, it's a—you sound—I'm glad to hear your—"

"Stop stuttering, I'm paying for this. Who're you rooming with?"

"Nobody. They didn't put anyone else in the room."

"Saving my place for me! Good old Devon. But anyway, you wouldn't have let them put anyone else in there, would you?" Friendliness, simple outgoing affection, that was all I could hear in his voice.

"No, of course not."

"I didn't think you would. Roommates are roommates. Even if they do have an occasional fight. You were crazy when you were here."

"I guess I was. I guess I must have been."

"Completely over the falls. I wanted to be sure you'd recovered. That's why I called up. I knew that if you'd let them put anybody else in the room in my place, then you really *were* crazy. But you didn't, I knew you wouldn't. Well, I did have just a *trace* of doubt, that was because you talked so crazy here. I have to admit I had just a *second* when I wondered. I'm sorry about that, Gene. Naturally I was completely wrong. You didn't let them put anyone else in my spot.''

"No, I didn't let them.''

"I could shoot myself for thinking you might. I really knew you wouldn't.''

"No, I wouldn't.''

"And I spent my money on a long-distance call! All for nothing. Well, it's spent, on you too. So start talking, pal. And it better be good. Start with sports. What are you going out for?''

"Crew. Well, not exactly crew. Managing crew. Assistant crew manager.''

"Assistant *crew* manager!''

"I don't think I've got the job—''

"Assistant crew *manager!*''

"I got in a fight this after—''

"*Assistant crew manager!*'' No voice could course with dumfoundment like Finny's "You *are* crazy!''

"Listen, Finny, I don't care about being a big man on the campus or anything.''

"Whaaat?'' Much more clearly than anything in Mr. Ludsbury's study I could see his face now, grimacing in wide, obsessed stupefaction.[13] "Who said anything about whoever *they* are!''

"Well then what are you so worked up for?''

"What do you want to manage crew for? What do you want to *manage* for? What's that got to do with sports?''

The point was, the grace of it was, that it had nothing to do with sports. For I wanted no more of sports. They were barred from me, as though when Dr. Stanpole said, "Sports are finished'' he had been speaking of me. I didn't trust myself in them, and I didn't trust anyone else. It was as though football players were really bent on crushing the life out of each other, as though boxers

were in combat to the death, as though even a tennis ball might turn into a bullet. This didn't seem completely crazy imagination in 1942, when jumping out of trees stood for abandoning a torpedoed ship. Later, in the school swimming pool, we were given the second stage in that rehearsal: after you hit the water you made big splashes with your hands, to scatter the flaming oil which would be on the surface.

So to Phineas I said, "I'm too busy for sports,'' and he went into his incoherent groans and jumbles of words, and I thought the issue was settled until at the end he said, "Listen, pal, if *I* can't play sports, *you're* going to play them for me,'' and I lost part of myself to him then, and a soaring sense of freedom revealed that this must have been my purpose from the first: to become a part of Phineas.

## Chapter 7

Brinker Hadley came across to see me late that afternoon. I had taken a shower to wash off the sticky salt of the Naguamsett River—going into the Devon was like taking a refreshing shower itself, you never had to clean up after it, but the Naguamsett was something else entirely. I had never been in it before; it seemed appropriate that my baptism there had taken place on the first day of this winter session, and that I had been thrown into it, in the middle of a fight.

I washed the traces off me and then put on a pair of chocolate brown slacks, a pair which Phineas had been particularly critical of when he wasn't wearing them, and a blue flannel shirt. Then, with nothing to do until my French class at five o'clock, I began turning over in my mind this question of sports.

But Brinker came in. I think he made a point of visiting all the rooms near him the first day. "Well, Gene,'' his beaming face

---

**13. stupefaction** (stoo′ pə fak′ shən) *n.*: Stunned amazement; utter bewilderment.

appeared around the door. Brinker looked the standard preparatory school article in his gray gabardine suit with square, hand-sewn-looking jacket pockets, a conservative necktie, and dark brown cordovan shoes. His face was all straight lines—eyebrows, mouth, nose, everything—and he carried his six feet of height straight as well. He looked but happened not to be athletic, being too busy with politics, arrangements, and offices.

"Here you are in your solitary splendor," he went on genially. "I can see you have real influence around here. This big room all to yourself. I wish I knew how to manage things like you." He grinned confidingly and sank down on my cot, leaning on his elbow in a relaxed, at-home way.

It didn't seem fitting for Brinker Hadley, the hub of the class, to be congratulating me on influence. I was going to say that while he had a roommate it was frightened Brownie Perkins, who would never impinge[1] on Brinker's comfort in any way, and that they had two rooms, the front one with a fireplace. Not that I grudged him any of this. I liked Brinker in spite of his Winter Session efficiency; almost everyone liked Brinker.

But in the pause I took before replying he started talking in his lighthearted way again. He never let a dull spot appear in conversation if he could help it.

"I'll bet you knew all the time Finny wouldn't be back this fall. That's why you picked him for a roommate, right?"

"What?" I pulled quickly around in my chair, away from the desk, and faced him. "No, of course not. How could I know a thing like that in advance?"

Brinker glanced swiftly at me. "You fixed it," he smiled widely. "You knew all the time. I'll bet it was *all* your doing."

––––––––––
1. **impinge** (im pinj') *v.*: Intrude.

"Don't be nutty, Brinker," I turned back toward the desk and began moving books with rapid pointlessness, "what a crazy thing to say." My voice sounded too strained even to my own blood-pounded ears.

"Ah-h-h. The truth hurts, eh?"

I looked at him as sharply as eyes can look. He had struck an accusing pose.

"Sure," I gave a short laugh, "sure." Then these words came out of me by themselves, "But the truth will out."

His hand fell leadenly on my shoulder. "Rest assured of that, my son. In our free democracy, even fighting for its life, the truth will out."

I got up. "I feel like a smoke, don't you? Let's go down to the Butt Room."

"Yes, yes. To the dungeon with you."

The Butt Room was something like a dungeon. It was in the basement, or the bowels, of the dormitory. There were about ten smokers already there. Everyone at Devon had many public faces; in class we looked, if not exactly scholarly, at least respectably alert; on the playing fields we looked like innocent extroverts; and in the Butt Room we looked, very strongly, like criminals. The school's policy, in order to discourage smoking, was to make these rooms as depressing as possible. The windows near the ceiling were small and dirty, the old leather furniture spilled its innards, the tables were mutilated, the walls ash-colored, the floor concrete. A radio with a faulty connection played loud and rasping for a while, then suddenly quiet and insinuating.

"Here's your prisoner, gentlemen," announced Brinker, seizing my neck and pushing me into the Butt Room ahead of him, "I'm turning him over to the proper authorities."

High spirits came hard in the haze of the Butt Room. A slumped figure near the radio, which happened to be playing loud at the moment, finally roused himself to say, "What's the charge?"

"Doing away with his roommate so he could have a whole room to himself. Rankest treachery." He paused impressively. "Practically fratricide."[2]

With a snap of the neck I shook his hand off me, my teeth set, "Brinker . . ."

He raised an arresting hand. "Not a word. Not a sound. You'll have your day in court."

"Shut up! I swear you ride a joke longer than anybody I know."

It was a mistake; the radio had suddenly gone quiet, and my voice ringing in the abrupt, releasing hush galvanized them all.

"So, you killed him, did you?" A boy uncoiled tensely from the couch.

"Well," Brinker qualified judiciously, "not actually killed. Finny's hanging between life and death at home, in the arms of his grief-stricken old mother."

I had to take part in this, or risk losing control completely. "I didn't do hardly a thing," I began as easily as it was possible for me to do, "I—all I did was drop a little bit . . . a little pinch of arsenic in his morning coffee."

"Liar!" Brinker glowered at me. "Trying to weasel out of it with a false confession, eh?"

I laughed at that, laughed uncontrollably for a moment at that.

"We know the scene of the crime," Brinker went on, "high in that . . . that *funereal* tree by the river. There wasn't any poison, nothing as subtle as that."

"Oh, you know about the tree," I tried to let my face fall guiltily, but it felt instead as though it were being dragged downward.

"Yes, huh, yes there was a small, a little *contretemps*[3] at the tree."

No one was diverted from the issue by this try at a funny French pronunciation.

"Tell us everything," a younger boy at the table said huskily. There was an unsettling current in his voice, a genuinely conspiratorial note, as though he believed literally everything that had been said. His attitude seemed to be the attitude of someone who discovers a secret of yours and promises not to tell a soul if you will describe it in detail to him.

"Well," I replied in a stronger voice, "first I stole all his money. Then I found that he cheated on his entrance tests to Devon and I blackmailed his parents about that, then I . . ." it was going well, faint grins were appearing around the room, even the younger boy seemed to suspect that he was being "sincere" about a joke, a bad mistake to make at Devon, "then I . . ." I only had to add, "pushed him out of the tree" and the chain of implausibility would be complete, "then I . . ." just those few words and perhaps this dungeon nightmare would end.

But I could feel my throat closing on them; I could never say them, never.

I swung on the younger boy. "What did I do then?" I demanded. "I'll bet you've got a lot of theories. Come on, reconstruct the crime. There we were at the tree. Then what happened, Sherlock Holmes?"

His eyes swung guiltily back and forth. "Then you just pushed him off, I'll bet."

"Lousy bet," I said offhandedly, falling into a chair as though losing interest in the game. "You lose. I guess you're Dr. Watson, after all."

They laughed at him a little, and he squirmed and looked guiltier than ever. He

---

**2. fratricide** (frat′ rə sīd′) *n*.: The killing of one's brother or sister.

**3. contretemps** (kōn trə tän′) *n*.: French for "an awkward mishap."

had a very weak foothold among the Butt Room crowd, and I had pretty well pushed him off it. His glance flickered out at me from his defeat, and I saw to my surprise that I had, by making a little fun of him, brought upon myself his unmixed hatred. For my escape this was a price I was willing to pay.

"French, French," I exclaimed. "Enough of this *contretemps.* I've got to study my French." And I went out.

Going up the stairs I heard a voice from the Butt Room say, "Funny, he came all the way down here and didn't even have a smoke."

But this was a clue they soon seemed to forget. I detected no Sherlock Holmes among them, nor even a Dr. Watson. No one showed any interest in tracking me, no one pried, no one insinuated.[4] The daily lists of appointments lengthened with the rays of the receding autumn sun until the summer, the opening day, even yesterday became by the middle of October something gotten out of the way and forgotten, because tomorrow bristled with so much to do.

In addition to classes and sports and clubs, there was the war. Brinker Hadley could compose his Shortest War Poem Ever Written

The War
Is a bore

if he wanted to, but all of us had to take stronger action than that. First there was the local apple crop, threatening to rot because the harvesters had all gone into the army or war factories. We spent several shining days picking them and were paid in cash for it. Brinker was inspired to write his Apple Ode

Our chore
Is the core
of the war

and the novelty and money of these days excited us. Life at Devon was revealed as still very close to the ways of peace; the war was at worst only a bore, as Brinker said, no more taxing to us than a day spent at harvesting in an apple orchard.

Not long afterward, early even for New Hampshire, snow came. It came theatrically, late one afternoon; I looked up from my desk and saw that suddenly there were big flakes twirling down into the quadrangle, settling on the carefully pruned shrubbery bordering the crosswalks, the three elms still holding many of their leaves, the still-green lawns. They gathered there thicker by the minute, like noiseless invaders conquering because they took possession so gently. I watched them whirl past my window —don't take this seriously, the playful way they fell seemed to imply, this little show, this harmless trick.

It seemed to be true. The school was thinly blanketed that night, but the next morning, a bright, almost balmy day, every flake disappeared. The following weekend, however, it snowed again, then two days later much harder, and by the end of that week the ground had been clamped under snow for the winter.

In the same way the war, beginning almost humorously with announcements about maids and days spent at apple-picking, commenced its invasion of the school. The early snow was commandeered[5] as its advance guard.

Leper Lepellier didn't suspect this. It was not in fact evident to anyone at first. But Leper stands out for me as the person who

---

**4. insinuated** (in sin′ yōō wāt′′d) *v.*: Hinted; suggested indirectly.

**5. commandeered** (käm′ ən dir′′d) *adj.*: Forced into service.

was most often and most emphatically taken by surprise, by this and every other shift in our life at Devon.

The heavy snow paralyzed the railroad yards of one of the large towns south of us on the Boston and Maine line. At chapel the day following the heaviest snowfall, two hundred volunteers were solicited[6] to spend the day shoveling them out, as part of the Emergency Usefulness policy adopted by the faculty that fall. Again we would be paid. So we all volunteered, Brinker and I and Chet Douglass and even I noticed, Quackenbush.

But not Leper. He generally made little sketches of birds and trees in the back of his notebook during chapel, so that he had probably not heard the announcement. The train to take us south to the work did not arrive until after lunch, and on my way to the station, taking a short cut through a meadow not far from the river, I met Leper. I had hardly seen him all fall, and I hardly recognized him now. He was standing motionless on the top of a small ridge, and he seemed from a distance to be a scarecrow left over from the growing season. As I plodded toward him through the snow I began to differentiate items of clothing—a dull green deer-stalker's cap, brown ear muffs, a thick gray woolen scarf—then at last I recognized the face in the midst of them, Leper's, pinched and pink, his eyes peering curiously toward some distant woods through steel-rimmed glasses. As I got nearer I noticed that below his long tan canvas coat with sagging pockets, below the red and black plaid woolen knickers and green puttees,[7] he was wearing skis. They were very long, wooden and battered, and had two decorative, old-fashioned knobs on their tips.

"You think there's a path through those woods?" he asked in his mild tentative voice when I got near. Leper did not switch easily from one train of thought to another, and even though I was an old friend whom he had not talked to in months I didn't mind his taking me for granted now, even at this improbable meeting in a wide, empty field of snow.

"I'm not sure, Leper, but I think there's one at the bottom of the slope."

"Oh yeah, I guess there is." We always called him Leper to his face; he wouldn't have remembered to respond to any other name.

I couldn't keep from staring at him, at the burlesque[8] explorer look of him. "What are you," I asked at last, "um, what are you doing, anyway?"

"I'm touring."

"Touring." I examined the long bamboo ski poles he held. "How do you mean, touring?"

"Touring. It's the way you get around the countryside in the winter. Touring skiing. It's how you go overland in the snow."

"Where are you going?"

"Well, I'm not *going* anywhere." He bent down to tighten the lacings on a puttee. "I'm just touring around."

"There's that place across the river where you could ski. The place where they have the rope tow on that steep hill across from the railroad station. You could go over there."

"No, I don't think so." He surveyed the woods again, although his breath had fogged his glasses. "That's not skiing."

"Why sure that's skiing. It's a good little run, you can get going pretty fast on that hill."

"Yeah but that's it, that's why it isn't skiing. Skiing isn't supposed to be fast. Skis are for useful locomotion." He turned his

---

**6. solicited** (sə lis′ it əd) *adj.*: Asked.
**7. puttees** (pu tēz′) *n.*: Coverings for the lower leg.

**8. burlesque** (bər lesk′) *adj.*: Comic imitation of.

inquiring eyes on me. "You can break a leg with that downhill stuff."

"Not on that little hill."

"Well, it's the same thing. It's part of the whole wrong idea. They're ruining skiing in this country, rope tows and chair lifts and all that stuff. You get carted up, and then you whizz down. You never get to see the trees or anything. Oh you see a lot of trees shoot by, but you never get to really look at trees, at a tree.

I just like to go along and see

what I'm passing and enjoy myself." He had come to the end of his thought, and now he slowly took me in, noticing my layers of old clothes. "What are you doing, anyway?" he asked mildly and curiously.

"Going to work on the railroad." He kept gazing mildly and curiously at me. "Shovel out those tracks. That work they talked about in chapel this morning. You remember."

"Have a nice day at it, anyway," he said.

"I will. You too."

"I will if I find what I'm looking for—a

beaver dam. It used to be up the Devon a ways, in a little stream that flows into the Devon. It's interesting to see the way beavers adapt to the winter. Have you ever seen it?"

"No, I never have seen that."

"Well, you might want to come sometime, if I find the place."

"Tell me if you find it."

With Leper it was always a fight, a hard fight to win when you were seventeen years old and lived in a keyed-up, competing school, to avoid making fun of him. But as I had gotten to know him better this fight had been easier to win.

Shoving in his long bamboo poles he pushed deliberately forward and slid slowly away from me down the gradual slope, standing very upright, his skis far apart to guard against any threat to his balance, his poles sticking out on either side of him, as though to ward off any interference.

I turned and trudged off to help shovel out New England for the war.

We spent an odd day, toiling in that railroad yard. By the time we arrived there the snow had become drab and sooted, wet and heavy. We were divided into gangs, each under an old railroad man. Brinker, Chet and I managed to be in the same group, but the playful atmosphere of the apple orchard was gone. Of the town we could only see some dull red brick mills and warehouses surrounding the yards, and we labored away among what the old man directing us called "rolling stock"—grim freight cars from many parts of the country immobilized in the snow. Brinker asked him if it shouldn't be called "unrolling stock" now, and the old man looked back at him with bleary dislike and didn't reply. Nothing was very funny that day, the work became hard and unvarying; I began to sweat under my layers of clothes. By the middle of the afternoon we had lost our fresh volunteer look, the grime

of the railroad and the exhaustion of manual laborers were on us all; we seemed of a piece with the railroad yards and the mills and warehouses. The old man resented us, or we made him nervous, or maybe he was as sick as he looked. For whatever reason he grumbled and spat and alternated between growling orders and rubbing his big, unhealthy belly.

Around 4:30 there was a moment of cheer. The main line had been cleared and the first train rattled slowly through. We watched it advance toward us, the engine throwing up balls of steam to add to the heavy overcast.

All of us lined both sides of the track and got ready to cheer the engineer and passengers. The coach windows were open and the passengers surprisingly were hanging out; they were all men, I could discern, all young, all alike. It was a troop train.

Over the clatter and banging of the wheels and couplings we cheered and they yelled back, both sides taken by surprise. They were not much older than we were and although probably just recruits, they gave the impression of being an elite as they were carried past our drab ranks. They seemed to be having a wonderful time, their uniforms looked new and good; they were clean and energetic; they were going places.

After they had gone we laborers looked rather emptily across the newly cleared rails at each other, at ourselves, and not even Brinker thought of the timely remark. We turned away. The old man told us to go back to other parts of the yard, but there was no more real work done that afternoon. Stranded in this mill town railroad yard while the whole world was converging elsewhere, we seemed to be nothing but children playing among heroic men.

The day ended at last. Gray from the beginning, its end was announced by a deepening gray, of sky, snow, faces, spirits.

We piled back into the old, dispiritedly lit coaches waiting for us, slumped into the uncomfortable green seats, and no one said much until we were miles away.

When we did speak it was about aviation training programs and brothers in the service and requirements for enlistment and the futility of Devon and how we would never have war stories to tell our grandchildren and how long the war might last and who ever heard of studying dead languages at a time like this.

Quackenbush took advantage of a break in this line of conversation to announce that he would certainly stay at Devon through the year, however half-cocked others might rush off. He elaborated without encouragement, citing the advantages of Devon's physical hardening program and of a high school diploma when he did in good time reach basic training. He for one would advance into the army step by step.

"You for one," echoed someone contemptuously.

"You *are* one," someone else said.

"Which army, Quackenbush? Mussolini's?"

"Naw, he's a Kraut."[9]

"He's a Kraut spy."

"How many rails did you sabotage today, Quackenbush?"

"I thought they interned all Quackenbushes the day after Pearl Harbor."[10]

To which Brinker added: "They didn't find him. He hid his light under a Quackenbush."

We were all tired at the end of that day. Walking back to the school grounds from the railroad station in the descending darkness we overtook a lone figure sliding along the snow-covered edge of the street.

"Will you look at Lepellier," began Brinker irritably. "Who does he think he is, the Abominable Snowman?"

"He's just been out skiing around," I said quickly. I didn't want to see today's strained tempers exploding on Leper. Then as we came up beside him, "Did you find the dam, Leper?"

He turned his head slowly, without breaking his forward movement of alternately planted poles and thrust skis, rhythmically but feebly continuous like a homemade piston engine's. "You know what? I did find it," his smile was wide and unfocused, as though not for me alone but for anyone and anything which wished to share this pleasure with him, "and it was really interesting to see. I took some pictures of it, and if they come out I'll bring them over and show you."

"What dam is that?" Brinker asked me.

"It's a . . . well a little dam up the river he knows about," I said.

"I don't know of any dam up the river."

"Well, it's not in the Devon itself, it's in one of the . . . tributaries."

"Tributaries! To the *Devon?*"

"You know, a little creek or something."

He knit his brows in mystification. "What kind of a dam is this, anyway?"

"Well," he couldn't be put off with half a story, "it's a beaver dam."

Brinker's shoulders fell under the weight of this news. "That's the kind of a place I'm in with a world war going on. A school for photographers of beaver dams."

"The beaver never appeared himself," Leper offered.

Brinker turned elaborately toward him. "Didn't he really?"

"No. But I guess I was pretty clumsy

---

**9. Kraut:** Derogatory term used during World War II for a German.

**10. Pearl Harbor:** U.S. naval base in Hawaii that was attacked by the Japanese, causing the United States to enter World War II.

getting close to it, so he might have heard me and been frightened."

"Well." Brinker's expansive, dazed tone suggested that here was one of life's giant ironies, "There you are!"

"Yes," agreed Leper after a thoughtful pause, "there you are."

"Here we are," I said, pulling Brinker around the corner we had reached which led to our dormitory. "So long, Leper. Glad you found it."

"Oh," he raised his voice after us, "how was your day? How did the work go?"

"Just like a stag at eve," Brinker roared back. "It was a winter wonderland, every minute." And out of the side of his mouth, to me, "Everybody in this place is either a draft-dodging Kraut or a . . . a . . ." the scornful force of his tone turned the word into a curse, "a *nat-u-ral-ist!*" He grabbed my arm agitatedly. "I'm giving it up, I'm going to enlist. Tomorrow."

I felt a thrill when he said it. This was the logical climax of the whole misbegotten[11] day, this whole out-of-joint term at Devon. I think I had been waiting for a long time for someone to say this so that I could entertain these decisive words myself.

To enlist. To slam the door impulsively on the past, to shed everything down to my last bit of clothing, to break the pattern of my life—that complex design I had been weaving since birth with all its dark threads, its unexplainable symbols set against a conventional background of domestic white and schoolboy blue, all those tangled strands which required the dexterity of a virtuoso[12] to keep flowing—I yearned to take giant military shears to it, snap!

bitten off in an instant, and nothing left in my hands but spools of khaki which could weave only a plain, flat, khaki design, however twisted they might be.

Not that it would be a good life. The war would be deadly all right. But I was used to finding something deadly in things that attracted me; there was always something deadly lurking in anything I wanted, anything I loved. And if it wasn't there, as for example with Phineas, then I put it there myself.

But in the war, there was no question about it at all; it was there.

I separated from Brinker in the quadrangle, since one of his clubs was meeting and he could not go back to the dormitory yet —"I've got to preside at a meeting of the Golden Fleece Debating Society tonight," he said in a tone of amazed contempt, "the Golden Fleece Debating Society! We're mad here, all mad," and he went off raving to himself in the dark.

It was a night made for hard thoughts. Sharp stars pierced singly through the blackness, not sweeps of them or clusters or Milky Ways as there might have been in the South, but single, chilled points of light, as unromantic as knife blades. Devon, muffled under the gentle occupation of the snow, was dominated by them; the cold Yankee stars ruled this night. They did not invoke in me thoughts of God, or sailing before the mast, or some great love as crowded night skies at home had done; I thought instead, in the light of those cold points, of the decision facing me.

Why go through the motions of getting an education and watch the war slowly chip away at the one thing I had loved here, the peace, the measureless, careless peace of the Devon summer? Others, the Quackenbushes of this world, could calmly watch the war approach them and jump into it at the

---

**11. misbegotten** (mis′ bi gät′′n) *adj.*: Wrongly or unlawfully produced.

**12. virtuoso** (vɜr′ ch̄o͞o wō′ sō) *n.*: Person displaying great technical skill in any field.

last and most advantageous instant, as though buying into the stock market. But I couldn't.

There was no one to stop me but myself. Putting aside soft reservations about What I Owed Devon and my duty to my parents and so on, I reckoned my responsibilities by the light of the unsentimental night sky and knew that I owed no one anything. I owed it to myself to meet this crisis in my life when I chose, and I chose now.

I bounced zestfully up the dormitory stairs. Perhaps because my mind still retained the image of the sharp night stars, those few fixed points of light in the darkness, perhaps because of that the warm yellow light streaming from under my own door came as such a shock. It was a simple case of a change of expectation. The light should have been off. Instead, as though alive itself, it poured in a thin yellow slab of brightness from under the door, illuminating the dust and splinters of the hall floor.

I grabbed the knob and swung open the door. He was seated in my chair at the desk, bending down to adjust the gross encumbrance of his leg, so that only the familiar ears set close against his head were visible, and his short-cut brown hair. He looked up with a provocative grin, "Hi pal, where's the brass band?"

Everything that had happened throughout the day faded like that first false snowfall of the winter. Phineas was back.

## Chapter 8

"I can see I never should have left you alone," Phineas went on before I could recover from the impact of finding him there, "Where did you get *those* clothes!" His bright, indignant eyes swept from my battered gray cap, down the frayed sweater and paint-stained pants to a pair of clodhoppers.

"You don't have to advertise like that, we all know you're the worst dressed man in the class."

"I've been working, that's all. These are just work clothes."

"In the boiler room?"

"On the railroad. Shoveling snow."

He sat back in the chair. "Shoveling railroad snow. Well that makes sense, we always did that the first term."

I pulled off the sweater, under which I was wearing a rain slicker I used to go sailing in, a kind of canvas sack. Phineas just studied it in wordless absorption. "I like the cut of it," he finally murmured. I pulled that off revealing an Army fatigue shirt my brother had given me. "Very topical," said Phineas through his teeth. After that came off there was just my undershirt, stained with sweat. He smiled at it for a while and then said as he heaved himself out of the chair, "There. You should have worn that all day, just that. That has real taste. The rest of your outfit was just gilding that lily of a sweat shirt."

"Glad to hear you like it."

"Not at all," he replied ambiguously, reaching for a pair of crutches which leaned against the desk.

I took the sight of this all right, I had seen him on crutches the year before when he broke his ankle playing football. At Devon crutches had almost as many athletic associations as shoulder pads. And I had never seen an invalid whose skin glowed with such health, accenting the sharp clarity of his eyes, or one who used his arms and shoulders on crutches as though on parallel bars, as though he would do a somersault on them if he felt like it. Phineas vaulted across the room to his cot, yanked back the spread and then groaned. "Oh, it's not made up. What is all this about no maids?"

"No maids," I said. "After all, there's a

war on. It's not much of a sacrifice, when you think of people starving and being bombed and all the other things." My unselfishness was responding properly to the influences of 1942. In these past months Phineas and I had grown apart on this; I felt a certain disapproval of him for grumbling about a lost luxury, with a war on. "After all," I repeated, "there is a war on."

"Is there?" he murmured absently. I didn't pay any attention; he was always speaking when his thoughts were somewhere else, asking rhetorical questions and echoing other people's words.

I found some sheets and made up his bed for him. He wasn't a bit sensitive about being helped, not a bit like an invalid striving to seem independent. I put this on the list of things to include when I said some prayers, the first in a long time, that night in bed. Now that Phineas was back it seemed time to start saying prayers again.

After the lights went out the special quality of my silence let him know that I was saying them, and he kept quiet for approximately three minutes. Then he began to talk; he never went to sleep without talking first and he seemed to feel that prayers lasting more than three minutes were showing off. God was always unoccupied in Finny's universe, ready to lend an ear any time at all. Anyone who failed to get his message through in three minutes, as I sometimes failed to do when trying to impress him, Phineas, with my sanctity, wasn't trying.

He was still talking when I fell asleep, and the next morning, through the icy atmosphere which one window raised an inch had admitted to our room, he woke me with the overindignant shout, "What *is* all this about no maids!" He was sitting up in bed, as though ready to spring out of it, totally and energetically awake. I had to laugh at this indignant athlete, with the strength of

five people, complaining about the service. He threw back his bedclothes and said, "Hand me my crutches, will you?"

Until now, in spite of everything, I had welcomed each new day as though it were a new life, where all past failures and problems were erased, and all future possibilities and joys open and available, to be achieved probably before night fell again. Now, in this winter of snow and crutches with Phineas, I began to know that each morning reasserted the problems of the night before, that sleep suspended all but changed nothing, that you couldn't make yourself over between dawn and dusk. Phineas however did not believe this. I'm sure that he looked down at his leg every morning first thing, as soon as he remembered it, to see if it had not been totally restored while he slept. When he found on this first morning back at Devon that it happened still to be crippled and in a cast, he said in his usual self-contained way, "Hand me my crutches, will you?"

Brinker Hadley, next door, always awoke like an express train. There was a gathering rumble through the wall, as Brinker reared up in bed, coughed hoarsely, slammed his feet on the floor, pounded through the freezing air to the closet for something in the way of clothes, and thundered down the hall to the bathroom. Today, however, he veered and broke into our room instead.

"Ready to sign up?" he shouted before he was through the door. "You ready to en—Finny!"

"You ready to en—what?" pursued Finny from his bed. "Who's ready to sign and en what?"

"Finny, you're back!"

"Sure," confirmed Finny with a slight, pleased grin.

"So," Brinker curled his lip at me, "your little plot didn't work so well after all."

"What's he talking about?" said Finny

as I thrust his crutches beneath his shoulders.

"Just talking," I said shortly. "What does Brinker ever talk about?"

"*You* know what I'm talking about well enough."

"No I don't."

"Oh yes you do."

"Are you telling me what I know?"

"I am."

"What's he *talking* about," said Finny.

The room was bitterly cold. I stood trembling in front of Phineas, still holding his crutches in place, unable to turn and face Brinker and this joke he had gotten into his head, this catastrophic joke.

"He wants to know if I'll sign up with him," I said, "enlist." It was the ultimate question for all seventeen-year-olds that year, and it drove Brinker's insinuations from every mind but mine.

"Yeah," said Brinker.

"Enlist!" cried Finny at the same time. His large and clear eyes turned with an odd expression on me. I had never seen such a look in them before. After looking at me closely he said, "You're going to enlist?"

"Well I just thought—last night after the railroad work—"

"You thought you might sign up?" he went on, looking carefully away.

Brinker drew one of his deep senatorial breaths, but he found nothing to say. We three stood shivering in the thin New Hampshire morning light, Finny and I in pajamas, Brinker in a blue flannel bathrobe and ripped moccasins. "When will you?" Finny went on.

"Oh, I don't know," I said. "It was just something Brinker happened to say last night, that's all."

"I said," Brinker began in an unusually guarded voice, glancing quickly at Phineas, "I said something about enlisting today."

Finny hobbled over to the dresser and took up his soap dish. "I'm first in the shower," he said.

"You can't get that cast wet, can you?" asked Brinker.

"No, I'll keep it outside the curtain."

"I'll help," said Brinker.

"No," said Finny without looking at him, "I can manage all right."

"How can you manage all right?" Brinker persisted aggressively.

"I can *manage* all right," Finny repeated with a set face.

I could hardly believe it, but it was too plainly printed in the closed expression of his face to mistake, too discernible[1] beneath the even tone of his voice: Phineas was shocked at the idea of my leaving. In some way he needed me. He needed me. I was the least trustworthy person he had ever met. I knew that; he knew or should know that too. I had even told him. I had told him. But there was no mistaking the shield of remoteness in his face and voice. He wanted me around. The war then passed away from me, and dreams of enlistment and escape and a clean start lost their meaning for me.

"Sure you can manage the shower all right," I said, "but what difference does it make? Come on. Brinker's always . . . Brinker's always getting there first. Enlist! What a nutty idea. It's just Brinker wanting to get there first again. I wouldn't enlist with you if you were General MacArthur's eldest son."

Brinker reared back arrogantly. "And who do you think I am!" But Finny hadn't heard that. His face had broken into a wide and dazzled smile at what I had said, lighting up his whole face. "Enlist!" I drove on, "I

---

**1. discernible** (di sʉrn′ ə b'l) *adj.*: Clearly recognizable.

wouldn't enlist with you if you were Elliott Roosevelt."[2]

"First cousin," said Brinker over his chin, "once removed."

"He wouldn't enlist with you," Finny plunged in, "if you were Madame Chiang Kai-shek."[3]

"Well," I qualified in an undertone, "he really *is* Madame Chiang Kai-shek."

"Well fan my brow," cried Finny, giving us his stunned look of total appalled horrified amazement, "who would have thought that!"

But in a week I had forgotten that, and I have never since forgotten the dazed look on Finny's face when he thought that on the first day of his return to Devon I was going to desert him. I didn't know why he had chosen me, why it was only to me that he could show the most humbling sides of his handicap. I didn't care. For the war was no longer eroding the peaceful summertime stillness I had prized so much at Devon, and although the playing fields were crusted under a foot of congealed snow and the river was now a hard gray-white lane of ice between gaunt trees, peace had come back to Devon for me.

So the war swept over like a wave at the seashore, gathering power and size as it bore on us, overwhelming in its rush, seemingly inescapable, and then at the last moment eluded by a word from Phineas; I had simply ducked, that was all, and the wave's concentrated power had hurtled harmlessly overhead, no doubt throwing others roughly up on the beach, but leaving me peaceably treading water as before. I did not stop to think that one wave is inevitably followed by another even larger and more powerful, when the tide is coming in.

"I *like* the winter," Finny assured me for the fourth time, as we came back from chapel that morning.

"Well, it doesn't like you." Wooden plank walks had been placed on many of the school paths for better footing, but there were icy patches everywhere on them. A crutch misplaced and he could be thrown down upon the frozen wooden planking, or into the ice-encrusted snow.

Even indoors Devon was a nest of traps for him. The school had been largely rebuilt with a massive bequest from an oil family some years before in a peculiar style of Puritan grandeur, as though Versailles[4] had been modified for the needs of a Sunday school. This opulent sobriety[5] betrayed the divided nature of the school, just as in a different way the two rivers that it straddled did. From the outside the buildings were reticent,[6] severe straight lines of red brick or white clapboard, with shutters standing sentinel beside each window, and a few unassuming white cupolas placed here and there on the roofs because they were expected and not pretty, like Pilgrim bonnets.

But once you passed through the Colonial doorways, with only an occasional fan window or low relief pillar to suggest that a certain muted adornment was permissible, you entered an extravaganza of Pompadour splendor. Pink marble walls and white marble floors were enclosed by arched and vaulted ceilings; an assembly room had been done in the manner of the High Italian

---

**2. Elliott Roosevelt:** A son of President Franklin D. Roosevelt.
**3. Madame Chiang Kai-shek** (chäŋ′ kī shek′): The wife of the head of the Chinese government during World War II.

**4. Versailles** (vər sī′) n.: Magnificent French palace.
**5. opulent sobriety** (äp′yə lənt sə brī′ ə tē): Plush or extravagant seriousness.
**6. reticent** (ret′ ə s'nt) adj.: Having a restrained, quiet or understated quality.

Renaissance, another was illuminated by chandeliers flashing with crystal teardrops; there was a wall of fragile French windows overlooking an Italian garden of marble bric-à-brac; the library was Provençal on the first floor, rococo on the second. And everywhere, except in the dormitories, the floors and stairs were of smooth, slick marble, more treacherous even than the icy walks.

"The winter loves me," he retorted, and then, disliking the whimsical[7] sound of that, added, "I mean as much as you can say a season can love. What I mean is, I love winter, and when you really love something, then it loves you back, in whatever way it has to love." I didn't think that this was true, my seventeen years of experience had shown this to be much more false than true, but it was like every other thought and belief of Finny's: it should have been true. So I didn't argue.

The board walk ended and he moved a little ahead of me as we descended a sloping path toward our first class. He picked his way with surprising care, surprising in anyone who before had used the ground mainly as a point of departure, as the given element in a suspended world of leaps in space. And now I remembered what I had never taken any special note of before: how Phineas used to walk. Around Devon we had gaits of every description; gangling shuffles from boys who had suddenly grown a foot taller, swinging cowboy lopes from those thinking of how wide their shoulders had become, ambles, waddles, light trippings, gigantic Bunyan strides. But Phineas had moved in continuous flowing balance, so that he had seemed to drift along with no effort at all, relaxation on the move. He hobbled now among the patches of ice. There was the one certainty that Dr. Stanpole had given

—Phineas would walk again. But the thought was there before me that he would never walk like that again.

"Do you have a class?" he said as we reached the steps of the building.

"Yes."

"So do I. Let's not go."

"Not go? But what'll we use for an excuse?"

"We'll say I fainted from exertion on the way from chapel," he looked at me with a phantom's smile, "and you had to tend me."

"This is your first day back, Finny. You're no one to cut classes."

"I know, I know. I'm going to work. I really am going to work. You're going to pull me through mostly, but I *am* going to work as hard as I can. Only not today, not the first thing. *Not* now, not conjugating verbs when I haven't even looked at the school yet. I want to see this place, I haven't seen anything except the inside of our room, and the inside of chapel. I don't feel like seeing the inside of a classroom. Not now. Not yet."

"What do you want to see?"

He had started to turn around so that his back was to me. "Let's go to the gym," he said shortly.

The gym was at the other end of the school, a quarter of a mile away at least, separated from us by a field of ice. We set off without saying anything else.

By the time we had reached it sweat was running like oil from Finny's face, and when he paused involuntary tremors shook his hands and arms. The leg in its cast was like a sea anchor dragged behind. The illusion of strength I had seen in our room that morning must have been the same illusion he had used at home to deceive his doctor and his family into sending him back to Devon.

We stood on the ice-coated lawn in front of the gym while he got ready to enter it, resting himself so that he could go in with a

---

**7. whimsical** (hwim′ zi k'l) *adj.*: Playful; odd.

show of energy. Later this became his habit; I often caught up with him standing in front of a building pretending to be thinking or examining the sky or taking off gloves, but it was never a convincing show. Phineas was a poor deceiver, having had no practice.

We went into the gym, along a marble hallway, and to my surprise we went on past the Trophy Room, where his name was already inscribed on one cup, one banner, and one embalmed football. I was sure that this was his goal, to mull over these lost glories. I had prepared myself for that, and even thought of several positive, uplifting aphorisms[8] to cheer him up. But he went by it without a thought, down a stairway, steep and marble, and into the locker room. I went along mystified beside him. There was a pile of dirty towels in a corner. Finny shoved them with a crutch. "What is all this," he muttered with a little smile, "about no maids?"

The locker room was empty at this hour, row after row of dull green lockers separated by wide wooden benches. The ceiling was hung with pipes. It was a drab room for Devon, dull green and brown and gray, but at the far end there was a big marble archway, glisteningly white, which led to the pool.

Finny sat down on a bench, struggled out of his sheep-lined winter coat, and took a deep breath of gymnasium air. No locker room could have more pungent air than Devon's; sweat predominated, but it was richly mingled with smells of paraffin and singed rubber, of soaked wool and liniment, and for those who could interpret it, of exhaustion, lost hope and triumph and bodies battling against each other. I thought it anything but a bad smell. It was preemi-nently the smell of the human body after it had been used to the limit, such a smell as has meaning and poignance[9] for any athlete.

Phineas looked down here and there, at the exercise bar over a sand pit next to the wall, at a set of weights on the floor, at the rolled-up wrestling mat, at a pair of spiked shoes kicked under a locker.

"Same old place, isn't it?" he said, turning to me and nodding slightly.

After a moment I answered in a quiet voice, "Not exactly."

He made no pretense of not understanding me. After a pause he said, "You're going to be the big star now," in an optimistic tone, and then added with some embarrassment, "You can fill any gaps or anything." He slapped me on the back, "Get over there and chin yourself a few dozen times. What did you finally go out for anyway?"

"I finally didn't go out."

"You aren't," his eyes burned at me from his grimacing face, "still the assistant senior crew manager!"

"No, I quit that. I've just been going to gym classes. The ones they have for guys who aren't going out for anything."

He wrenched himself around on the bench. Joking was past; his mouth widened irritably. "What," his voice bounded on the word in a sudden rich descent, "did you do that for?"

"It was too late to sign up for anything else," and seeing the energy to blast this excuse rushing to his face and neck I stumbled on, "and anyway with the war on there won't be many trips for the teams. I don't know, sports don't seem so important with the war on."

"Have you swallowed all that war stuff?"

"No, of course I—" I was so committed

---

**8. aphorisms** (af′ ə riz′mz) *n.*: Short sentences expressing wise or clever observations.

**9. poignance** (poin′ yəns) *n.*: A feeling that is emotionally touching or moving.

to refuting him that I had half-denied the charge before I understood it; now my eyes swung back to his face. "All what war stuff?"

"All that stuff about there being a war."

"I don't think I get what you mean."

"Do you really think that the United States of America is in a state of war with Nazi Germany and Imperial Japan?"

"Do I really think . . ." My voice trailed off.

He stood up, his weight on the good leg, the other resting lightly on the floor in front of him. "Don't be a sap," he gazed with cool self-possession at me, "there isn't any war."

"I know why you're talking like this," I said, struggling to keep up with him. "Now I understand. You're still under the influence of some medicinal drug."

"No, you are. Everybody is." He pivoted so that he was facing directly at me. "That's what this whole war story is. A medicinal drug. Listen, did you ever hear of the 'Roaring Twenties'?" I nodded very slowly and cautiously. "When everybody who was young did just what they wanted?"

"Yes."

"Well what happened was that they didn't like that, all the stuffed shirts. So then they tried Prohibition and arranged the Depression. That kept the people who were young in the thirties in their places. But they couldn't use that trick forever, so for us in the forties they've cooked up this war fake."

"Who are 'they,' anyway?"

"The fat old men who don't want us crowding them out of their jobs. They've made it all up. There isn't any real food shortage, for instance. The men have all the best steaks delivered to their clubs now. You've noticed how they've been getting fatter lately, haven't you?"

His tone took it thoroughly for granted that I had. For a moment I was almost taken in by it. Then my eyes fell on the bound and cast white mass pointing at me, and as it was always to do, it brought me down out of Finny's world of invention, down again as I had fallen after awakening that morning, down to reality, to the facts.

"Phineas, this is all pretty amusing and everything, but I hope you don't play this game too much with yourself. You might start to believe it and then I'd have to make a reservation for you at the Funny Farm."

"In a way," deep in argument, his eyes never wavered from mine, "the whole world is on a Funny Farm now. But it's only the fat old men who get the joke."

"And you."

"Yes, and me."

"What makes you so special? Why should you get it and all the rest of us be in the dark?"

The momentum of the argument abruptly broke from his control. His face froze. "Because I've suffered," he burst out.

We drew back in amazement from this. In the silence all the flighty spirits of the morning ended between us. He sat down and turned his flushed face away from me. I sat next to him without moving for as long as my beating nerves would permit, and then I stood up and walked slowly toward anything which presented itself. It turned out to be the exercise bar. I sprang up, grabbed it, and then, in a fumbling and perhaps grotesque[10] offering to Phineas, I chinned myself. I couldn't think of anything else, not the right words, not the right gesture. I did what I could think of.

"Do thirty of them," he mumbled in a bored voice.

I had never done ten of them. At the twelfth I discovered that he had been counting to himself because he began to count

---

**10. grotesque** (grō tesk´) *adj.*: Ridiculous or distorted.

aloud in a noncommittal, half-heard voice. At eighteen there was a certain enlargement in his tone, and at twenty-three the last edges of boredom left it; he stood up, and the urgency with which he brought out the next numbers was like an invisible boost lifting me the distance of my arms, until he sang out "thirty!" with a flare of pleasure.

The moment was past. Phineas I know had been even more startled than I to discover this bitterness in himself. Neither of us ever mentioned it again, and neither of us ever forgot that it was there.

He sat down and studied his clenched hands. "Did I ever tell you," he began in a husky tone, "that I used to be aiming for the Olympics?" He wouldn't have mentioned it except that after what he had said he had to say something very personal, something deeply held. To do otherwise, to begin joking, would have been a hypocritical denial of what had happened, and Phineas was not capable of that.

I was still hanging from the bar; my hands felt as though they had sunk into it. "No, you never told me that," I mumbled into my arm.

"Well I was. And now I'm not sure, not a hundred per cent sure I'll be completely, you know, in shape by 1944. So I'm going to coach you for them instead."

"But there isn't going to be any Olympics in '44. That's only a couple of years away. The war——"

"Leave your fantasy life out of this. We're grooming you for the Olympics, pal, in 1944."

And not believing him, not forgetting that troops were being shuttled toward battlefields all over the world, I went along, as I always did, with any new invention of Finny's. There was no harm in taking aim, even if the target was a dream.

But since we were so far out of the line of fire, the chief sustenance[11] for any sense of the war was mental. We saw nothing real of it; all our impressions of the war were in the false medium of two dimensions —photographs in the papers and magazines, newsreels, posters—or artificially conveyed to us by a voice on the radio, or headlines across the top of a newspaper. I found that only through a continuous use of the imagination could I hold out against Finny's driving offensive in favor of peace.

And now when we were served chicken livers for dinner I couldn't help conceiving a mental picture of President Roosevelt and my father and Finny's father and numbers of other large old men sitting down to porterhouse steak in some elaborate but secluded men's secret society room. When a letter from home told me that a trip to visit relatives had been canceled because of gas rationing it was easy to visualize my father smiling silently with knowing eyes—at least as easy as it was to imagine an American force crawling through the jungles of a place called Guadalcanal[12]—"Wherever that is," as Phineas said.

And when in chapel day after day we were exhorted to new levels of self-deprivation and hard work, with the war as their justification, it was impossible not to see that the faculty were using this excuse to drive us as they had always wanted to drive us, regardless of any war or peace.

What a joke if Finny was right after all!

But of course I didn't believe him. I was too well protected against the great fear of boys' school life, which is to be "taken in." Along with everyone else except a few professional gulls[13] such as Leper, I rejected anything which had the smallest possibility

---

**11. sustenance** (sus' ti nəns) n.: Maintenance, support.

**12. Guadalcanal** (gwä' d'l kə nal') n.: Largest island of the Solomon Islands in the southwest Pacific.

**13. gulls** (gulz) n.: People who are easily cheated or tricked.

of doubt about it. So of course I didn't believe him. But one day after our chaplain, Mr. Carhart, had become very moved by his own sermon in chapel about God in the Foxholes,[14] I came away thinking that if Finny's opinion of the war was unreal, Mr. Carhart's was at least as unreal. But of course I didn't believe him.

And anyway I was too occupied to think about it all. In addition to my own work, I was dividing my time between tutoring Finny in studies and being tutored by him in sports. Since so much of learning anything depends on the atmosphere in which it is taught, Finny and I, to our joint double amazement, began to make flashing progress where we had been bumblers before.

Mornings we got up at six to run. I dressed in a gym sweat suit with a towel tucked around my throat, and Finny in pajamas, ski boots and his sheep-lined coat.

A morning shortly before Christmas vacation brought my reward. I was to run the course Finny had laid out, four times around an oval walk which circled the Headmaster's home, a large rambling, doubtfully Colonial white mansion. Next to the house there was a patriarchal[15] elm tree, against the trunk of which Finny leaned and shouted at me as I ran a large circle around him.

This plain of snow shone a powdery white that morning; the sun blazed icily somewhere too low on the horizon to be seen directly, but its clean rays shed a blue-white glimmer all around us. The northern sunshine seemed to pick up faint particles of whiteness floating in the air and powdering the sleek blue sky. Nothing stirred. The bare arching branches of the elm seemed laid into this motionless sky. As I ran the sound of my footfalls was pitched off short in the vast immobile dawn, as though there was no room amid so many glittering sights for any sound to intrude. The figure of Phineas was set against the bulk of the tree; he shouted now and then, but these sounds too were quickly absorbed and dispelled.

And he needed to give no advice that morning. After making two circuits of the walk every trace of energy was as usual completely used up, and as I drove myself on all my scattered aches found their usual way to a profound seat of pain in my side. My lungs as usual were fed up with all this work, and from now on would only go rackingly through the motions. My knees were boneless again, ready any minute to let my lower legs telescope up into the thighs. My head felt as though different sections of the cranium were grinding into each other.

Then, for no reason at all, I felt magnificent. It was as though my body until that instant had simply been lazy, as though the aches and exhaustion were all imagined, created from nothing in order to keep me from truly exerting myself. Now my body seemed at last to say, "Well, if you must have it, here!" and an accession of strength came flooding through me. Buoyed up, I forgot my usual feeling of routine self-pity when working out, I lost myself, oppressed mind along with aching body; all entanglements were shed, I broke into the clear.

After the fourth circuit, like sitting in a chair, I pulled up in front of Phineas.

"You're not even winded," he said.

"I know."

"You found your rhythm, didn't you, that third time around. Just as you came into that straight part there."

"Yes, right there."

"You've been pretty lazy all along, haven't you?"

"Yes, I guess I have been."

"You didn't even know anything about yourself."

---

**14. foxholes** (fäks hōlz´) *n.*: Holes dug in the ground as temporary protection for soldiers against enemy gunfire.

**15. patriarchal** (pā´ trē ärk´ 'l) *adj.*: Fatherly.

"I don't guess I did, in a way."

"Well," he gathered the sheepskin collar around his throat, "now you know. And stop talking like that—'don't guess I did'!" Despite this gibe he was rather impersonal toward me. He seemed older that morning, and leaning quietly against that great tree wrapped in his heavy coat, he seemed smaller too. Or perhaps it was only that I, inside the same body, had felt myself all at once grown bigger.

We proceeded slowly back to the dormitory. On the steps going in we met Mr. Ludsbury coming out.

"I've been watching you from my window," he said in his hooting voice with a rare trace of personal interest. "What are you up to, Forrester, training for the Commandos?" There was no rule explicitly forbidding exercise at such an hour, but it was not expected; ordinarily therefore Mr. Ludsbury would have disapproved. But the war had modified even his standards; all forms of physical exercise had become conventional for the Duration.

I mumbled some abashed[16] answer, but

---

**16. abashed** (ə bashʹ 'd) *adj.*: Self-conscious, ashamed.

it was Phineas who made the clear response.

"He's developing into a real athlete," he said matter-of-factly. "We're aiming for the '44 Olympics."

Mr. Ludsbury emitted a single chuckle from deep in his throat, then his face turned brick red momentarily and he assumed his customary sententiousness.[17] "Games are all right in their place," he said, "and I won't bore you with the Eton Playing Fields observation, but all exercise today is aimed of course at the approaching Waterloo.[18] Keep that in your sights at all times, won't you."

Finny's face set in determination, with the older look I had just detected in him. "No," he said.

I don't believe any student had ever said "No" flatly to Mr. Ludsbury before. It flustered him uncontrollably. His face turned brick red again, and for a moment I thought he was going to run away. Then he said something so rapid, throaty, and clipped that neither of us understood it, turned quickly and strode off across the quadrangle.

"He's really sincere, he thinks there's a war on," said Finny in simple wonder. "Now why wouldn't he know?" He pondered Mr. Ludsbury's exclusion from the plot of the fat old men as we watched his figure, reedy even in his winter wraps, move away from us. Then the light broke. "Oh, of course!" he cried. "Too thin. Of course."

I stood there pitying Mr. Ludsbury for his fatal thinness and reflecting that after all he had always had a gullible side.

---

**17. sententiousness** (sen ten′ shəs nəs) *n.*: Manner of using pithy sayings in a moralizing way.
**18. Waterloo** (wôt′ er lōō′) *n.*: Any disastrous or decisive defeat.

## Chapter 9

This was my first but not my last lapse into Finny's vision of peace. For hours, and sometimes for days, I fell without realizing it into the private explanation of the world. Not that I ever believed that the whole production of World War II was a trick of the eye manipulated by a bunch of calculating fat old men, appealing though this idea was. What deceived me was my own happiness; for peace is indivisible, and the surrounding world confusion found no reflection inside me. So I ceased to have any real sense of it.

This was not shaken even by the enlistment of Leper Lepellier. In fact that made the war seem more unreal than ever. No real war could draw Leper voluntarily away from his snails and beaver dams. His enlistment seemed just another of Leper's vagaries, such as the time he slept on top of Mount Katahdin in Maine where each morning the sun first strikes United States territory. On that morning, satisfying one of his urges to participate in nature, Leper Lepellier was the first thing the rising sun struck in the United States.

Early in January, when we had all just returned from the Christmas holidays, a recruiter from the United States ski troops showed a film to the senior class in the Renaissance Room. To Leper it revealed what all of us were seeking: a recognizable and friendly face to the war. Skiers in white shrouds[1] winged down virgin slopes, silent as angels, and then, realistically, herringboned up again, but herringboned in cheerful, sunburned bands, with clear eyes and white teeth and chests full of vigor-laden mountain air. It was the cleanest image of war I had ever seen; even the Air Force, reputedly so high above the infantry's mud,

---

**1. shrouds** (shroudz) *n.*: Clothes that conceal.

was stained with axle grease by comparison, and the Navy was vulnerable to scurvy. Nothing tainted these white warriors of winter as they swooped down their spotless mountainsides, and this cool, clean response to war glided straight into Leper's Vermont heart.

"How do you like that!" he whispered to me in a wondering voice during these scenes. "How do you like that!"

"You know, I think these are pictures of Finnish ski troops," Phineas whispered on the other side, "and I want to know when they start shooting our allies the Bolsheviks.[2] Unless that war between them was a fake too, which I'm pretty sure it was."

After the movie ended and the lights came on to illuminate the murals of Tuscany and the painted classical galleries around us, Leper still sat amazed in his folding chair. Ordinarily he talked little, and the number of words which came from him now indicated that this was a turning point in his life.

"You know what? Now I see what racing skiing is all about. It's all right to miss seeing the trees and the countryside and all the other things when you've got to be in a hurry. And when you're in a War you've got to be in a hurry. Don't you? So I guess maybe racing skiers weren't ruining the sport after all. They were preparing it, if you see what I mean, for the future. Everything has to evolve or else it perishes." Finny and I had stood up, and Leper looked earnestly from one to the other of us from his chair. "Take the housefly. If it hadn't developed all those split-second reflexes it would have become extinct long ago."

"You mean it adapted itself to the fly swatter?" queried Phineas.

_____

**2. Bolsheviks** (bōl′ shə viks′) _n._: Russian Communists.

"That's right. And skiing had to learn to move just as fast or it would have been wiped out by this war. Yes, sir. You know what? I'm almost glad this war came along. It's like a test, isn't it, and only the things and the people who've been evolving the right way survive."

You usually listened to Leper's quiet talking with half a mind, but this theory of his brought me to close attention. How did it apply to me, and to Phineas? How, most of all, did it apply to Leper?

"I'm going to enlist in these ski troops," he went on mildly, so unemphatically that my mind went back to half-listening. Threats to enlist that winter were always declaimed like Brinker's, with a grinding of back teeth and a flashing of eyes; I had already heard plenty of them. But only Leper's was serious.

A week later he was gone. He had been within a few weeks of his eighteenth birthday, and with it all chance of enlistment, of choosing a service rather than being drafted into one, would have disappeared. The ski movie had decided him. "I always thought the war would come for me when it wanted me," he said when he came to say goodbye the last day. "I never thought I'd be going to it. I'm really glad I saw that movie in time, you bet I am." Then, as the Devon School's first recruit to World War II, he went out my doorway with his white stocking cap bobbing behind.

It probably would have been better for all of us if someone like Brinker had been the first to go. He could have been depended upon to take a loud dramatic departure, so that the school would have reverberated for weeks afterward with Brinker's Last Words, Brinker's Military Bearing, Brinker's Sense of Duty. And all of us, influenced by the vacuum of his absence, would have felt the touch of war as a daily fact.

But the disappearing tail of Leper's cap inspired none of this. For a few days the war was more unimaginable than ever. We didn't mention it and we didn't mention Leper, until at last Brinker found a workable point of view. One day in the Butt Room he read aloud a rumor in a newspaper about an attempt on Hitler's life. He lowered the paper, gazed in a visionary way in front of him, and then remarked, "That was Leper, of course."

This established our liaison[3] with World War II. The Tunisian campaign became "Leper's liberation"; the bombing of the Ruhr was greeted by Brinker with hurt surprise: "He didn't tell us he'd left the ski troops"; the torpedoing of the *Scharnhorst:* "At it again." Leper sprang up all over the world at the core of every Allied success. We talked about Leper's stand at Stalingrad, Leper on the Burma Road, Leper's convoy to Archangel; we surmised that the crisis over the leadership of the Free French[4] would be resolved by the appointment of neither de Gaulle[5] nor Giraud but Lepellier; we knew, better than the newspapers, that it was not the Big Three[6] but the Big Four who were running the war.

In the silences between jokes about Leper's glories we wondered whether we ourselves would measure up to the humblest minimum standard of the army. I did not know everything there was to know about myself, and I knew that I did not know it; I wondered in the silences between jokes about Leper whether the still hidden parts of myself might contain the Sad Sack, the out-cast, or the coward. We were all at our funniest about Leper, and we all secretly hoped that Leper, that incompetent, was as heroic as we said.

Everyone contributed to this legend except Phineas. At the outset, with the attempt on Hitler's life, Finny had said, "If someone gave Leper a loaded gun and put it at Hitler's temple, he'd miss." There was a general shout of outrage, and then we recommended the building of Leper's triumphal arch around Brinker's keystone. Phineas took no part in it, and since little else was talked about in the Butt Room he soon stopped going there and stopped me from going as well—"How do you expect to be an athlete if you smoke like a forest fire?" He drew me increasingly away from the Butt Room crowd, away from Brinker and Chet and all other friends, into a world inhabited by just himself and me, where there was no war at all, just Phineas and me alone among all the people of the world, training for the Olympics of 1944.

Saturday afternoons are terrible in a boys' school, especially in the winter. There is no football game; it is not possible, as it is in the spring, to take bicycle trips into the surrounding country. Not even the most grinding student can feel required to lose himself in his books, since there is Sunday ahead, long, lazy, quiet Sunday, to do any homework.

And these Saturdays are worst in the late winter when the snow has lost its novelty and its shine, and the school seems to have been reduced to only a network of drains. During the brief thaw in the early afternoon there is a dismal gurgling of dirty water seeping down pipes and along gutters, a gray seamy shifting beneath the crust of snow, which cracks to show patches of frozen mud beneath. Shrubbery loses its bright snow headgear and stands bare and frail,

---

**3. liaison** (lē′ə zän′) *n.*: A link or connection.
**4. Free French:** French military forces that continued to fight the Germans after France's surrender.
**5. de Gaulle:** Charles de Gaulle (1890–1970), leader of the Free French, general, and president of France from 1959 to 1969.
**6. Big Three:** United States, Great Britain, and the Soviet Union.

too undernourished to hide the drains it was intended to hide. These are the days when going into any building you cross a mat of dirt and cinders led in by others before you, thinning and finally trailing off in the corridors. The sky is an empty hopeless gray and gives the impression that this is its eternal shade. Winter's occupation seems to have conquered, overrun and destroyed everything, so that now there is no longer any resistance movement left in nature; all the juices are dead, every sprig of vitality snapped, and now winter itself, an old, corrupt, tired conqueror, loosens its grip on the desolation, recedes a little, grows careless in its watch; sick of victory and enfeebled by the absence of challenge, it begins itself to withdraw from the ruined countryside. The drains alone are active, and on these Saturdays their noises sound a dull recessional to winter.

Only Phineas failed to see what was so depressing. Just as there was no war in his philosophy, there was also no dreary weather. As I have said, all weathers delighted Phineas. "You know what we'd better do next Saturday?" he began in one of his voices, the low-pitched and evenly melodic one which for some reason always reminded me of a Rolls-Royce moving along a highway. "We'd better organize the Winter Carnival."

We were sitting in our room, on either side of the single large window framing a square of featureless gray sky. Phineas was resting his cast, which was a considerably smaller one now, on the desk and thoughtfully pressing designs into it with a pocket knife. "What Winter Carnival?" I asked.

"*The* Winter Carnival. The Devon Winter Carnival."

"There isn't any Devon Winter Carnival and never has been."

"There is now. We'll have it in that park next to the Naguamsett. The main attrac-tion will be sports, naturally, featuring I expect a ski jump—"

"A ski jump! That park's as flat as a pancake."

"—and some slalom races, and I think a little track. But we've got to have some snow statues too, and a little music, and something to eat. Now, which committee do you want to head?"

I gave him a wintry smile. "The snow statues committee."

"I knew you would. You always were secretly arty, weren't you? I'll organize the sports, Brinker can handle the music and food, and then we need somebody to kind of beautify the place, a few holly wreaths and things like that. Someone good with plants and shrubbery. I know. Leper."

From looking at the star he was imprinting in his cast I looked quickly up at his face. "Leper's gone."

"Oh yeah, so he is. Leper *would* be gone. Well, somebody else then."

And because it was Finny's idea, it happened as he said, although not as easily as some of his earlier inspirations. For our dormitory was less enthusiastic about almost everything with each succeeding week. Brinker for example had begun a long, decisive sequence of withdrawals from school activity ever since the morning I deserted his enlistment plan. He had not resented my change of heart, and in fact had immediately undergone one himself. If he could not enlist —and for all his self-sufficiency Brinker could not do much without company—he could at least cease to be so multifariously[7] civilian. So he resigned the presidency of the Golden Fleece Debating Society, stopped writing his school spirit column for the newspaper, dropped the chairmanship of the Underprivileged Local Children subcommittee of the Good Samaritan Confraternity,

---

7. **multifariously** (mul'tə far'ē əs lē) *adv.*: Diversely.

stilled his baritone in the chapel choir, and even, in his most impressive burst of irresponsibility, resigned from the Student Advisory Committee to the Headmaster's Discretionary Benevolent Fund. His well-bred clothes had disappeared; these days he wore khaki pants supported by a garrison belt, and boots which rattled when he walked.

"Who wants a Winter Carnival?" he said in the disillusioned way he had lately developed when I brought it up. "What are we supposed to be celebrating?"

"Winter, I guess."

"Winter!" He gazed out of his window at the vacant sky and seeping ground. "Frankly, I just don't see anything to celebrate, winter or spring or anything else."

"This is the first time Finny's gotten going on anything since . . . he came back."

"He has been kind of nonfunctional, hasn't he? He isn't *brooding,* is he?"

"No, he wouldn't brood."

"No, I don't suppose he would. Well, if you think it's something Finny really wants. Still, there's never been a Winter Carnival here. I think there's probably a rule against it."

"I see," I said in a tone which made Brinker raise his eyes and lock them with mine. In that plotters' glance all his doubts vanished, for Brinker the Lawgiver had turned rebel for the Duration.

The Saturday was battleship gray. Throughout the morning equipment for the Winter Carnival had been spirited out of the dormitory and down to the small incomplete public park on the bank of the Naguamsett River. Brinker supervised the transfer, rattling up and down the stairwell and giving orders. He made me think of a pirate captain disposing of the booty. Several jugs of cider which he had browbeaten away from some lowerclassmen were the most cautiously guarded treasure. They were buried in the snow near a clump of evergreens in the center of the park, and Brinker stationed his roommate, Brownie Perkins, to guard them with his life. He meant this literally, and Brownie knew it. So he trembled alone there in the middle of the park for hours, wondering what would happen if he had an attack of appendicitis, unnerved by the thoughts of a fainting spell, until at last we came. Then Brownie crept back to the dormitory, too exhausted to enjoy the carnival at all. On this day of high illegal competitiveness, no one noticed.

The buried cider was half-consciously plotted at the hub of the carnival. Around it sprang up large, sloppy statues, easily modeled because of the snow's dampness. Nearby, entirely out of place in this snowscape, like a dowager[8] in a saloon, there was a heavy circular classroom table, carried there by superhuman exertions the night before on Finny's insistence that he had to have *something* to display the prizes on. On it rested the prizes—Finny's icebox, hidden all these months in the dormitory basement, a set of York barbells, the *Iliad*[9] with the English translation of each sentence written above it, Brinker's file of Betty Grable[10] photographs, a lock of hair cut under duress from the head of Hazel Brewster, the town belle, a handwoven rope ladder with the proviso[11] that it should be awarded to someone occupying a room on the third floor or higher, a forged draft registration card, and $4.13 from the Headmaster's Discretionary Benevolent Fund. Brinker placed this last prize on the table with such silent dignity that we all thought it was better not to ask any questions about it.

---

**8. dowager** (douʹə jər) *n.*: An elderly woman of wealth and dignity.

**9. Iliad** (ilʹē əd) *n.*: A Greek epic poem by Homer set in the tenth year of the Trojan War.

**10. Betty Grable:** Movie star popular during World War II.

**11. proviso** (prə vīʹzō) *n.*: A condition.

Phineas sat behind the table in a heavily carved black walnut chair; the arms ended in two lions' heads, and the legs ended in paws gripping wheels now sunk in the snow. He had made the purchase that morning. Phineas bought things only on impulse and only when he had the money, and since the two states rarely coincided his purchases were few and strange.

Chet Douglass stood next to him holding his trumpet. Finny had regretfully given up the plan of inviting the school band to supply music, since it would have spread news of our carnival to every corner of the campus. Chet in any case was an improvement over that cacaphony.[12] He was a slim, fair-skinned boy with a ball of curly auburn hair curving over his forehead, and he devoted himself to playing two things, tennis and the trumpet. He did both with such easy, inborn skill that after observing him I had begun to think that I could master either one any weekend I tried. Much like the rest of us on the surface, he had an underlying obliging and considerate strain which barred him from being a really important member of the class. You had to be rude at least sometimes and edgy often to be credited with "personality," and without that accolade[13] no one at Devon could be anyone. No one, with the exception of course of Phineas.

To the left of the Prize Table Brinker straddled his cache[14] of cider; behind him was the clump of evergreens, and behind them there was after all a gentle rise, where the Ski Jump Committee was pounding snow into a little take-off ramp whose lip was perhaps a foot higher than the slope of the rise. From there our line of snow statues, unrecognizable artistic attacks on the Headmaster, Mr. Ludsbury, Mr. Patch-

Withers, Dr. Stanpole, the new dietitian, and Hazel Brewster curved in an enclosing half-circle to the icy, muddy, lisping edge of the tidewater Naguamsett and back to the other side of the Prize Table.

When the ski jump was ready there was a certain amount of milling around; twenty boys, tightly reined in all winter, stood now as though with the bit firmly clamped between their teeth, ready to stampede. Phineas should have started the sports events but he was absorbed in cataloguing the prizes. All eyes swung next upon Brinker. He had been holding a pose above his cider of Gibraltar invulnerability; he continued to gaze challengingly around him until he began to realize that wherever he looked, calculating eyes looked back.

"All right, all right," he said roughly, "let's get started."

The ragged circle around him moved perceptibly closer.

"Let's get going," he yelled. "Come on, Finny. What's first?"

Phineas had one of those minds which could record what is happening in the background and do nothing about it because something else was preoccupying him. He seemed to sink deeper into his list.

"Phineas!" Brinker pronounced his name with a maximum use of the teeth. "What is next?"

Still the sleek brown head bent mesmerized over the list.

"What's the big hurry, Brinker?" someone from the tightening circle asked with dangerous gentleness. "What's the big rush?"

"We can't stand here all day," he blurted. "We've got to get started if we're going to have this thing. What's *next*? Phineas!"

At last the recording in Finny's mind reached its climax. He looked vaguely up, studied the straddling, at-bay figure of Brinker at the core of the poised perimeter of

---

**12. cacaphony** (kə käf′ə nē) *n.*: Harsh sound.

**13. accolade** (ak′ə lād′) *n.*: Approval.

**14. cache** (kash) *n.*: Anything stored or hidden in a secret or safe place.

boys, hesitated, blinked, and then in his organ voice said good-naturedly, "Next? Well that's pretty clear. You are."

Chet released from his trumpet the opening, lifting, barbaric call of a bullfight, and the circle of boys broke wildly over Brinker. He flailed back against the evergreens, and the jugs appeared to spring out of the snow. "What," he kept yelling, off balance among the branches. "What . . ." By then his cider, which he had apparently expected to dole out according to his own governing whim, was disappearing. There was going to be no government, even by whim, even by Brinker's whim, on this Saturday at Devon.

From a scramble of contenders I got one of the jugs, elbowed off a counterattack, opened it, sampled it, choked, and then went through with my original plan by stopping Brinker's mouth with it. His eyes bulged, and blood vessels in his throat began to pulsate, until at length I lowered the jug.

He gave me a long, pondering look, his face closed and concentrating while behind it his mind plainly teetered between fury and hilarity; I think if I had batted an eye he would have hit me. The carnival's breaking apart into a riot hung like a bomb between us. I kept on looking expressionlessly back at him until beneath a blackening scowl his mouth opened enough to fire out the words, "I've been abused."

I jerked the jug to my mouth and took a huge gulp of cider in relief, and the violence latent in the day drifted away; perhaps the Naguamsett carried it out on the receding tide. Brinker strode through the swirl of boys to Phineas. "I formally declare," he bellowed, "that these Games are open."

"You can't do that," Finny said rebukingly. "Who ever heard of opening the Games without the sacred fire from Olympus?"

Sensing that I must act as the Chorus, I registered on my face the universally unheard-of quality of the Games without fire. "Fire, fire," I said across the damp snow.

"We'll sacrifice one of the prizes," said Phineas, seizing the *Iliad.* He touched a match to the pages, and a little jet of flame curled upward. The Games, alight with Homer and cider, were open.

Chet Douglass, leaning against the side of the Prize Table, continued to blow musical figures for his own enlightenment. Forgetful of us and the athletic programing Finny now put into motion, he strolled here and there, sometimes at the start of the ski jump competition, blowing an appropriate call, more often invoking the serene order of Haydn, or a high, remote, arrogant Spanish world, or the cheerful, lowdown carelessness of New Orleans.

Our own exuberance intoxicated us, sent restraint flying, causing Brinker to throw the football block on the statue of the Headmaster, giving me, as I put on the skis and slid down the small slope and off the miniature ski jump a sensation of soaring flight, of hurtling high and far through space; inspiring Phineas, during one of Chet's Spanish inventions, to climb onto the Prize Table and with only one leg to create a droll dance among the prizes, springing and spinning from one bare space to another, cleanly missing Hazel Brewster's hair, never marring by a misstep the pictures of Betty Grable. Under the influence of his own inner joy at life for a moment as it should be, as it was meant to be in his nature, Phineas recaptured that magic gift for existing primarily in space, one foot conceding briefly to gravity its rights before spinning him off again into the air. It was his wildest demonstration of himself, of himself in the kind of world he loved; it was his choreography of peace.

And when he stopped and sat down among the prizes and said, "Now we're going to have the Decathlon. Quiet everybody, our Olympic candidate Gene Forrester, is now going to qualify," what made me in this moment champion of everything he ordered, to run as though I were the abstraction of speed, to walk the half-circle of statues on my hands, to balance on my head on top of the icebox on top of the Prize Table, to jump if he had asked it across the Naguamsett and land crashing in the middle of Quackenbush's boathouse, to accept at the end of it amid a clatter of applause—for on this day even the schoolboy egotism of Devon was conjured[15] away—a wreath made from the evergreen trees which Phineas placed on my head? What made me surpass myself was this liberation we had torn from the gray encroachments of 1943, the escape we had concocted, this afternoon of momentary, illusory, special and separate peace.

And it was this which caused me not to notice Brownie Perkins rejoin us from the dormitory, and not to hear what he was saying until Finny cried hilariously, "A telegram for Gene? It's the Olympic Committee. They want you! Of course they want you! Give it to me, Brownie, I'll read it aloud to this assembled host." And it was this which drained away as I watched Finny's face pass through all the gradations between uproariousness and shock.

I took the telegram from Phineas, facing in advance whatever the destruction was. That was what I learned to do that winter.

I HAVE ESCAPED AND NEED HELP. I AM AT CRISTMAS LOCATION. YOU UNDERSTAND. NO NEED TO RISK ADDRESS HERE. MY SAFETY DEPENDS ON YOU COMING AT ONCE.

(signed)   YOUR BEST FRIEND,

ELWIN LEPER LEPELLIER.

---

**15. conjured** (kän′ jərd) *v*.: Removed as if by magic.

## Chapter 10

That night I made for the first time the kind of journey which later became the monotonous routine of my life: traveling through an unknown countryside from one unknown settlement to another. The next year this became the dominant activity, or rather passivity, of my army career, not fighting, not marching, but this kind of nighttime ricochet;[1] for as it turned out I never got to the war.

I went into uniform at the time when our enemies began to recede so fast that there had to be a hurried telescoping of military training plans. Programs scheduled to culminate in two years became outmoded in six months, and crowds of men gathered for them in one place were dispersed to twenty others. A new weapon appeared and those of us who had traveled to three or four bases mastering the old one were sent on to a fifth, sixth, and seventh to master the new. The closer victory came the faster we were shuttled around America in pursuit of a role to play in a drama which suddenly, underpopulated from the first, now had too many actors. Or so it seemed. In reality there would have been, as always, too few, except that the last act, a mass assault against suicidally-defended Japan, never took place. I and my year—not "my generation" for destiny now cut too finely for that old phrase—I and those of my year were preeminently eligible for that. Most of us, so it was estimated, would be killed. But the men a little bit older closed in on the enemy faster than predicted, and then there was the final holocaust of the Bomb.[2] It seemed to have saved our lives.

So journeys through unknown parts of America became my chief war memory, and

---

**1. ricochet** (rik′ə s·hā′) *n*.: Bouncing from one thing to another.
**2. the Bomb:** The atomic bomb.

I think of the first of them as this nighttime trip to Leper's. There was no question of where to find him; "I am at Christmas location" meant that he was at home. He lived far up in Vermont, where at this season of the year even the paved main highways are bumpy and buckling from the freezing weather, and each house executes a lonely holding action against the cold. The natural state of things is coldness, and houses are fragile havens, holdouts in a death landscape, unforgettably comfortable, simple though they are, just because of their warmth.

Leper's was one of these hearths perched by itself on a frozen hillside. I reached it in the early morning after this night which presaged my war; a bleak, drafty train ride, a damp depot seemingly near no town whatever, a bus station in which none of the people were fully awake, or seemed clean, or looked as though they had homes anywhere; a bus which passengers entered and left at desolate stopping places in the blackness; a chilled nighttime wandering in which I tried to decipher[3] between lapses into stale sleep, the meaning of Leper's telegram.

I reached the town at dawn, and encouraged by the returning light, and coffee in a thick white cup, I accepted a hopeful interpretation. Leper had "escaped." You didn't "escape" from the army, so he must have escaped from something else. The most logical thing a soldier escapes from is danger, death, the enemy. Since Leper hadn't been overseas the enemy must have been in this country. And the only enemies in this country would be spies. Leper had escaped from spies.

I seized this conclusion and didn't try to go beyond it. I suppose all our Butt Room stories about him intriguing around the

world had made me half-ready to half-believe something like this. I felt a measureless relief when it occurred to me. There was some color, some hope, some life in this war after all. The first friend of mine who ever went into it tangled almost immediately with spies. I began to hope that after all this wasn't going to be such a bad war.

The Lepellier house was not far out of town, I was told. There was no taxi, I was also told, and there was no one, I did not need to be told, who would offer to drive me out there. This was Vermont. But if that meant austerity[4] toward strangers it also meant mornings of glory such as this one, in which the snow, white almost to blueness, lay like a soft comforter over the hills, and birches and pines indestructibly held their ground, rigid lines against the snow and sky, very thin and very strong like Vermonters.

The sun was the blessing of the morning, the one celebrating element, an aesthete with no purpose except to shed radiance. Everything else was sharp and hard, but this Grecian sun evoked joy from every angularity and blurred with brightness the stiff face of the countryside. As I walked briskly out the road the wind knifed at my face, but this sun caressed the back of my neck.

The road led out along the side of a ridge, and after a mile or so I saw the house that must be Leper's, riding the top of the slope. It was another brittle-looking Vermont house, white of course, with long and narrow windows like New England faces. Behind one of them hung a star which announced that a son of the house was serving the country, and behind another stood Leper.

Although I was walking straight toward his front door he beckoned me on several

---

**3. decipher** (di sī′fər) *v.*: Figure out the meaning of.

**4. austerity** (ô ster′ə tē) *n.*: Severity.

times, and he never took his eyes from me, as though it was they which held me to my course. He was still at this ground-floor window when I reached the door and so I opened it myself and stepped into the hallway. Leper had come to the entrance of the room on the right, the dining room.

"Come in here," he said, "I spend most of my time in here."

As usual there were no preliminaries. "What do you do that for, Leper? It's not very comfortable, is it?"

"Well, it's a useful room."

"Yes, I guess it's useful, all right."

"You aren't lost for something to do in dining rooms. It's in the living room where people can't figure out what to do with themselves. People get problems in living rooms."

"Bedrooms too." It was a try toward relieving the foreboding[5] in his manner; it only worked to deepen it.

He turned away, and I followed him into an under-furnished dining room of high-backed chairs, rugless floor, and cold fireplace. "If you want to be in a really functional room," I began with false heartiness, "you ought to spend your time in the bathroom then."

He looked at me, and I noticed the left side of his upper lip lift once or twice as though he was about to snarl or cry. Then I realized that this had nothing to do with his mood, that it was involuntary.

He sat down at the head of the table in the only chair with arms, his father's chair I supposed. I took off my coat and sat in a place at the middle of the table, with my back to the fireplace. There at least I could look at the sun rejoicing on the snow.

"In here you never wonder what's going to happen. You know the meals will come in three times a day for instance."

"I'll bet your mother isn't too pleased when she's trying to get one ready."

Force sprang into his expression for the first time. "What's she got to be pleased about!" He glared challengingly into my startled face. "I'm pleasing *myself!*" he cried fervently, and I saw tears trembling in his eyes.

"Well, she's probably pleased." Any words would serve, the more irrelevant and superficial the better, any words which would stop him; I didn't want to see this. "She's probably pleased to have you home again."

His face resumed its dull expression. The responsibility for continuing the conversation, since I had forced it to be superficial, was mine. "How long'll you be here?"

He shrugged, a look of disgust with my question crossing his face. The careful politeness he had always had was gone.

"Well, if you're on furlough you must know when you have to be back." I said this in what I thought of at the time as my older voice, a little businesslike and experienced. "The army doesn't give out passes and then say 'Come back when you've had enough, hear?'"

"I didn't get any pass," he groaned; with the sliding despair of his face and his clenched hands, that's what it was; a groan.

"I know you said," I spoke in short, expressionless syllables, "that you 'escaped.'" I no longer wanted this to be true, I no longer wanted it to be connected with spies or desertion or anything out of the ordinary. I knew it was going to be, and I no longer wanted it to be.

"I *escaped!*" the word surging out in a voice and intensity that was not Leper's. His face was furious, but his eyes denied the fury; instead they saw it before them. They were filled with terror.

---

**5. foreboding** (fôr bōd′iŋ) *n.*: Prediction of something bad or harmful.

"What do you mean, you escaped?" I said sharply. "You don't escape from the army."

"That's what you say. But that's because you're talking through your hat." His eyes were furious now too, glaring blindly at me. "What do you know about it, anyway?" None of this could have been said by the Leper of the beaver dam.

"Well I—how am I supposed to answer that? I know what's normal in the army, that's all."

"Normal," he repeated bitterly. "What a stupid word that is. I suppose that's what you're thinking about, isn't it? That's what you would be thinking about, somebody like you. You're thinking I'm not normal, aren't you? I can see what you're thinking—I see a lot I never saw before" —his voice fell to a querulous whisper —"you're thinking I'm psycho."

I gathered what the word meant. I hated the sound of it at once. It opened up a world I had not known existed—"mad" or "crazy" or "a screw loose," those were the familiar words. "Psycho" had a sudden mental-ward reality about it, a systematic, diagnostic sound. It was as though Leper had learned it while in captivity, far from Devon or Vermont or any experience we had in common, as though it were in Japanese.

Fear seized my stomach like a cramp. I didn't care what I said to him now; it was myself I was worried about. For if Leper was psycho it was the army which had done it to him, and I and all of us were on the brink of the army. "You make me sick, you and your army words."

"They were going to give me," he was almost laughing, everywhere but in his eyes which continued to oppose all he said, "they were going to give me a discharge, a Section Eight discharge."

As a last defense I had always taken refuge in a scornful superiority, based on nothing. I sank back in the chair, eyebrows up, shoulders shrugging. "I don't even know what you're talking about. You just don't make any sense at all. It's all Japanese to me."

"A Section Eight discharge is for the nuts in the service, the psychos, the Funny Farm candidates. Now do you know what I'm talking about? They give you a Section Eight discharge, like a dishonorable discharge only worse. You can't get a job after that. Everybody wants to see your discharge, and when they see a Section Eight they look at you kind of funny—the kind of expression you've got on your face, like you were looking at someone with their nose blown off but don't want them to know you're disgusted—they look at you that way and then they say, 'Well, there doesn't seem to be an opening here at present.' You're ruined for life, that's what a Section Eight discharge means."

"You don't have to yell at me, there's nothing wrong with my hearing."

"Then that's tough for you, Buster. Then they've got you."

"Nobody's *got* me."

"Oh they've got you all right."

"Don't tell me who's got me and who hasn't got me. Who do you think you're talking to? Stick to your snails, Lepellier."

He began to laugh again. "You always were a lord of the manor, weren't you? A swell guy, except when the chips were down. You always were a savage underneath. I always knew that only I never admitted it. But in the last few weeks," despair broke into his face again, "I admitted a lot to myself. Not about you. Don't flatter yourself. I wasn't thinking about you. Why should I think about you? Did you ever think about me? I thought about myself, and Ma, and the old man, and *pleasing* them all the time. Well, never mind about that now. It's you we happen to be talking about now. Like a savage underneath. Like," now there was the blind confusion in his eyes again, a wild slyness around his mouth, "like that time you knocked Finny out of the tree."

I sprang out of the chair. "You stupid crazy . . ."

Still laughing, "Like that time you crippled him for life."

I shoved my foot against the rung of his chair and kicked. Leper went over in his chair and collapsed against the floor. Laughing and crying he lay with his head on the floor and his knees up, ". . . always were a savage underneath."

Quick heels coming down the stairs, and his mother, large, soft, and gentle-looking, quivered at the entrance. "What on earth happened? Elwin!"

"I'm terribly—it was a mistake," I listened objectively to my own voice, "he said something crazy. I forgot myself—I forgot that he's, there's something the matter with his nerves, isn't there? He didn't know what he was saying."

"Well, good heaven, the boy is ill." We both moved swiftly to help up the chuckling Leper. "Did you come here to abuse him?"

"I'm terribly sorry," I muttered. "I'd better get going."

Mrs. Lepellier was helping Leper toward the stairs. "Don't go," he said between chuckles, "stay for lunch. You can count on it. Always three meals a day, war or peace, in this room."

And I did stay. Sometimes you are too ashamed to leave. That was true now. And sometimes you need too much to know the facts, and so humbly and stupidly you stay. That was true now too.

It was an abundant Vermont lunch, more like a dinner, and at first it had no more reality than a meal in the theater. Leper ate almost nothing, but my own appetite deepened my disgrace. I ate everything within reach, and then had to ask, face aflame with embarrassment, for more to be passed to me. But that led to this hard-to-believe transformation: Mrs. Lepellier began to be reconciled to me because I liked her cooking. Toward the end of the meal she became able to speak to me directly, in her high but gentle and modulated voice, and I was so clumsy and fumbling and embarrassed that my behavior throughout lunch amounted to one long and elaborate apology which, when she offered me a second dessert, I saw she had accepted. "He's a good boy underneath," she must have thought, "a terrible temper, no self-control, but he's sorry, and he is a good boy underneath." Leper was closer to the truth.

She suggested he and I take a walk after lunch. Leper now seemed all obedience, and except for the fact that he never looked at his mother, the ideal son. So he put on some odds and ends of clothing, some canvas and woolen and flannel pulled on to form a patchwork against the cutting wind, and we trailed out the back door into the splendor of the failing sunshine. I did not have New England in my bones; I was a guest in this country, even though by now a familiar one, and I could never see a totally extinguished winter field without thinking it unnatural. I would tramp along trying to decide whether corn had grown there in the summer, or whether it had been a pasture, or what it could ever have been, and in that deep layer of the mind where all is judged by the five senses and primitive expectation, I knew that nothing would ever grow there again. We roamed across one of these wastes, our feet breaking through at each step the thin surface crust of ice into a layer of soft snow underneath, and I waited for Leper, in this wintery outdoors he loved, to come to himself again. Just as I knew the field could never grow again, I knew that Leper could not be wild or bitter or psycho tramping across the hills of Vermont.

"Is there an army camp in Vermont?" I asked, so sure in my illusion that I risked making him talk, risked even making him talk about the army.

"I don't think there is."

"There ought to be. That's where they should have sent you. Then you wouldn't have gotten nervous."

"Yeah." A half chuckle. "I was what they call 'nervous in the service.'"

Exaggerated laughter from me. "Is that what they call it?"

Leper didn't bother to make a rejoinder.[6] Before there had always been his polite capping of remarks like this: "Yes, they do, that's what they call it"—but today he glanced speculatively at me and said nothing.

We walked on, the crust cracking uneasily under us. "Nervous in the service," I said. "That sounds like one of Brinker's poems."

"That Brinker!"

"You wouldn't know Brinker these days the way he's changed—"

"I'd know him if he'd changed into Snow White."

"Well. He hasn't changed into Snow White."

"That's too bad," the strained laughter was back in his voice, "Snow White with Brinker's face on her. There's a picture," then he broke into sobs.

"Leper! What is it? What's the matter, Leper? Leper!"

Hoarse, cracking sobs broke from him; another ounce of grief and he would have begun tearing his country-store clothes. "Leper! Leper!" This exposure drew us violently together; I was the closest person in the world to him now, and he to me. "Leper, Leper." I was about to cry myself. "Stop

that, now just stop. Don't do that. Stop doing that, Leper."

When he became quieter, not less despairing but too exhausted to keep on, I said, "I'm sorry I brought up Brinker. I didn't know you hated him so much." Leper didn't look capable of such hates. Especially now, with his rapid plumes of breath puffing out as from a toiling steam engine, his nose and eyes gone red, and his cheeks red too, in large, irregular blotches—Leper had the kind of fragile fair skin given to high, unhealthy coloring. He was all color, painted at random, but none of it highlighted his grief. Instead of desperate and hate-filled, he looked, with his checkered outfit and blotchy face, like a half-prepared clown.

"I don't really hate Brinker, I don't really hate him, not any more than anybody else." His swimming eyes cautiously explored me. The wind lifted a sail of snow and billowed it past us. "It was only—" he drew in his breath so sharply that it made a whistling sound—"the idea of *his* face on a *woman's* body. That's what made me psycho. Ideas like that. I don't know. I guess they must be right. I guess I am psycho. I guess I must be. I must be. Did you ever have ideas like that?"

"No."

"Would they bother you if you did, if you happened to keep imagining a man's head on a woman's body, or if sometimes the arm of a chair turned into a human arm if you looked at it too long, things like that? Would they bother you?"

I didn't say anything.

"Maybe everybody imagines things like that when they're away from home, really far away, for the first time. Do you think so? The camp I went to first, they called it a 'Reception center,' got us up every morning when it was pitch black, and there was food like the kind we throw out here, and all my clothes were gone and I got this uniform that didn't even smell familiar. All day I wanted

---

**6. rejoinder** (ri join'dər) *n.*: A reply or answer.

to sleep, after we got to Basic Training. I kept falling asleep, all day long, at the lectures we went to, and on the firing range, and everywhere else. But not at night. Next to me there was a man who had a cough that sounded like his stomach was going to come up, one of these times, it sounded like it would come up through his mouth and land with a splatter on the floor. He always faced my way. We did sleep head to foot, but I knew it would land near me. I never slept at night. During the day I couldn't eat this food that should have been thrown away, so I was always hungry except in the Mess Hall. The Mess Hall. The army has the perfect word for everything, did you ever think of that?"

I imperceptibly nodded and shook my head, yes-and-no.

"And the perfect word for me," he added in a distorted voice, as though his tongue had swollen, "psycho. I guess I am. I must be. Am I, though, or is the army? Because they turned everything inside out. I couldn't sleep in bed, I had to sleep everywhere else. I couldn't eat in the Mess Hall, I had to eat everywhere else. Everything began to be inside out. And the man next to me at night, coughing himself inside out. That was when things began to change. One day I couldn't make out what was happening to the corporal's face. It kept changing into faces I knew from somewhere else, and then I began to think he looked like me, and then he . . ." Leper's voice had thickened unrecognizably, "he changed into a woman, I was looking at him as close as I'm looking at you and his face turned into a woman's face and I started to yell for everybody, I began to yell so that everyone would see it too, I didn't want to be the only one to see a thing like that, I yelled louder and louder to make sure everyone within reach of my voice would hear —you can see there wasn't anything crazy in the way I was thinking, can't you, I had a

good reason for everything I did, didn't I—but I couldn't yell soon enough, or loud enough, and when somebody did finally come up to me, it was this man with the cough who slept in the next cot, and he was holding a broom because we had been sweeping out the barracks, but I saw right away that it wasn't a broom, it was a man's leg which had been cut off. I remember thinking that he must have been at the hospital helping with an amputation when he heard my yell. You can see there's logic in that." The crust beneath us continued to crack and as we reached the border of the field the frigid trees also were cracking with the cold. The two sharp groups of noises sounded to my ears like rifles being fired in the distance.

I said nothing, and Leper, having said so much, went on to say more, to speak above the wind and crackings as though his story would never be finished. "Then they grabbed me and there were arms and legs and heads everywhere and I couldn't tell when any minute—"

"Shut up!"

Softer, more timidly, "—when any minute—"

"Do you think I want to hear every gory detail! Shut up! I don't care! I don't care what happened to you, Leper. I don't care! Do you understand that? This has nothing to do with me! Nothing at all! I don't care!"

I turned around and began a clumsy run across the field in a line which avoided his house and aimed toward the road leading back into the town. I left Leper telling his story into the wind. He might tell it forever, I didn't care. I didn't want to hear any more of it. I had already heard too much. What did he mean by telling me a story like that! I didn't want to hear any more of it. Not now or ever. I didn't care because it had nothing to do with me. And I didn't want to hear any more of it. Ever.

## THINKING ABOUT THE SELECTION

### Recalling

1. Why does Gene decide to tell Finny the truth and then feel sorry about doing so?
2. How does Finny's injury affect Gene's plans for participation in sports?
3. How does the war affect life at Devon?
4. Describe the Winter Carnival.

### Interpreting

5. Explain what enlisting means to Gene. What does the army come to mean to Leper?
6. What is Finny's theory about the war and how is it typical of his way of thinking?
7. After Finny's accident, Gene's purpose was "to become a part of Phineas." What does he mean? Does he accomplish this?
8. Leper tells Gene, "You always were a savage underneath." How valid is that analysis of Gene? Give specific examples.

### Applying

9. Gene tries to decide whether or not to enlist. How do you think a person should go about reaching such a major decision?

## ANALYZING LITERATURE

### Analyzing Conflict

A novel may have more than one conflict. To analyze conflicts ask yourself questions: What makes the conflict build? How will it be resolved? For example, Gene's internal conflict continues as he is torn between enlisting, thus entering the adult world, and his need to stay near Finny.

1. Describe the conflict between Gene and Brinker.
2. Explain how Gene's reaction to Leper when he goes to see him in his home is related to his internal conflict.

## CRITICAL THINKING AND READING

### Recognizing Symbols

A **symbol** is something that stands for something else. For example, the American flag is a symbol of the United States. In literature, authors use symbols to make a point or to present their ideas. Rain might symbolize a character's sadness, for example.

1. What do you think the tree symbolizes?
2. What might the Winter Carnival symbolize?
3. What do the Quackenbushes of the world symbolize?
4. John Ruskin has written, "At least be sure that you go to the author to get at *his* meaning, not to find yours." First discuss the meaning of the quotation. Then explain why a reader must be careful when reading a novel with symbols.

## UNDERSTANDING LANGUAGE

### Understanding Abstract Terms

**Abstract terms** name qualities, ideas, actions, and conditions that cannot be recognized by the five senses. *Health* and *love* are abstract words. Explain the meaning of each of the following abstract terms from the novel.

1. patriotism    2. peace    3. school spirit

## THINKING AND WRITING

### Analyzing a Symbol

Write an essay about the war as a symbol in this novel. Begin by listing different ideas about its symbolism. Then choose the idea best supported by evidence in the novel. Present this idea and the supporting evidence in your essay. When you revise, add one additional idea about the war as a symbol. Then write a final draft and proofread your essay.

# GUIDE FOR READING

## A Separate Peace, Chapters 11–13

**Theme**

The **theme** of a novel is the insight into life that it reveals. Sometimes, the theme is stated directly. More often, it is implied. The author may give hints about the theme while stepping away from the novel momentarily to address the reader. Such hints in key passages help a thoughtful reader identify the theme of the novel.

The theme will not always be easy for you to state. It may take a sentence, a paragraph, or even a whole essay. After identifying and stating the theme, it is important to test your understanding against actions of the characters and events of the plot. You will know if you have found the theme because events of the story will relate logically to it.

**Look For**

Try to understand the theme of *A Separate Peace* as you read by identifying key passages that direct you toward it. Test your understanding by seeing if events and actions of the characters relate to the theme you have identified.

**Writing**

Begin to reach a personal evaluation of *A Separate Peace* by making notes that will answer questions such as these: Is the novel involving? Do I care about the characters? Are the setting and plot logically consistent? What is the author trying to say?

**Vocabulary**

Knowing the following words will help you as you read Chapters 11–13 of *A Separate Peace*.

**surmise** (sər mīz') *v.*: To guess; to imagine or infer something without conclusive evidence (p. 917)

**guileful** (gīl'fəl) *adj.*: Deceitful; tricky (p. 921)

**incongruity** (in'kən grōō'ə tē) *n.*: Lack of fitness or appropriateness (p. 923)

**decrepit** (di krep'it) *adj.*: Broken down or worn out by old age or long use (p. 924)

**impervious** (im pur'vē əs) *adj.*: Not affected by (p. 927)

**parody** (par'ə dē) *n.*: Poor or weak imitation (p. 928)

**assimilate** (ə sim'ə lāt') *v.*: To absorb into one's thinking (p. 935)

## Chapter 11

I wanted to see Phineas, and Phineas only. With him there was no conflict except between athletes, something Greek-inspired and Olympian in which victory would go to whoever was the strongest in body and heart. This was the only conflict he had ever believed in.

When I got back I found him in the middle of a snowball fight in a place called the Fields Beyond. At Devon the open ground among the buildings had been given carefully English names—the Center Common, the Far Common, the Fields, and the Fields Beyond. These last were past the gym, the tennis courts, the river and the stadium, on the edge of the woods which, however English in name, were in my mind primevally[1] American, reaching in unbroken forests far to the north, into the great northern wilderness. I found Finny beside the woods playing and fighting—the two were approximately the same thing to him—and I stood there wondering whether things weren't simpler and better at the northern terminus[2] of these woods, a thousand miles due north into the wilderness, somewhere deep in the Arctic, where the peninsula of trees which began at Devon would end at last in an untouched grove of pine, austere and beautiful.

There is no such grove, I know now, but the morning of my return to Devon I imagined that it might be just over the visible horizon, or the horizon after that.

A few of the fighters paused to yell a greeting at me, but no one broke off to ask about Leper. But I knew it was a mistake for me to stay there; at any moment someone might.

This gathering had obviously been Finny's work. Who else could have inveigled twenty people to the farthest extremity of the school to throw snowballs at each other? I could just picture him, at the end of his ten o'clock class, organizing it with the easy authority which always came into his manner when he had an idea which was particularly preposterous. There they all were now, the cream of the school, the lights and leaders of the senior class, with their high I.Q.'s and expensive shoes, as Brinker had said, pasting each other with snowballs.

I hesitated on the edge of the fight and the edge of the woods, too tangled in my mind to enter either one or the other. So I glanced at my wrist watch, brought my hand dramatically to my mouth as though remembering something urgent and important, repeated the pantomime in case anybody had missed it, and with this tacit explanation started briskly back toward the center of the school. A snowball caught me on the back of the head. Finny's voice followed it. "You're on our side, even if you do have a lousy aim. We need *somebody* else. Even you." He came toward me, without his cane at the moment, his new walking cast so much smaller and lighter that an ordinary person could have managed it with hardly a limp noticeable. Finny's coordination, however, was such that any slight flaw became obvious; there was an interruption, brief as a drum beat, in the continuous flow of his walk, as though with each step he forgot for a split-second where he was going.

"How's Leper?" he asked in an offhand way.

"Oh Leper's—how would he be? You know Leper—" The fight was moving toward us; I stalled a little more, a stray snowball caught Finny on the side of the face, he shot one back, I seized some ammunition from the ground and we were engulfed.

---

**1. primevally** (prī mē′ v'l lē), *adv.*: Belonging to earliest times.
**2. terminus** (tŭr′mə nəs), *n.*: End, boundary.

Someone knocked me down; I pushed Brinker over a small slope; someone was trying to tackle me from behind. Everywhere there was the smell of vitality in clothes, the vital something in wool and flannel and corduroy which spring releases. I had forgotten that this existed, this smell which instead of the first robin, or the first bud or leaf, means to me that spring has come. I had always welcomed vitality and energy and warmth radiating from thick and sturdy winter clothes. It made me happy, but I kept wondering about next spring, about whether khaki, or suntans or whatever the uniform of the season was, had this aura of promise in it. I felt fairly sure it didn't.

The fight veered. Finny had recruited me and others as allies, so that two sides fighting it out had been taking form. Suddenly he turned his fire against me, he betrayed several of his other friends; he went over to the other, to Brinker's side for a short time, enough to ensure that his betrayal of them would heighten the disorder. Loyalties became hopelessly entangled. No one was going to win or lose after all. Somewhere in the maze Brinker's sense of generalship disappeared, and he too became slippery. We ended the fight in the only way possible; all of us turned on Phineas. Slowly, with a steadily widening grin, he was driven down beneath a blizzard of snowballs.

When he had surrendered I bent cheerfully over to help him up, seizing his wrist to stop the final treacherous snowball he had ready, and he remarked, "Well I guess that takes care of the Hitler Youth[3] outing for one day." All of us laughed. On the way back to the gym he said, "That was a good fight. I thought it was pretty funny, didn't you?"

Hours later it occurred to me to ask him, "Do you think you ought to get into fights like that? After all, there's your leg—"

"Stanpole said something about not falling again, but I'm very careful."

"Oh, don't break it again!"

"No, of course I won't break it again. Isn't the bone supposed to be stronger when it grows together over a place where it's been broken once?"

"Yes, I think it is."

"I think so too. In fact I think I can feel it getting stronger."

"You think you can? Can you feel it?"

"Yes, I think so."

"Thank goodness."

"What?"

"I said that's good."

"Yes, I guess it is. I guess that's good, all right."

After dinner that night Brinker came to our room to pay us one of his formal calls. Our room had by this time of year the exhausted look of a place where two people had lived too long without taking any interest in their surroundings. Our cots at either end of the room were sway-backed beneath their pink and brown cotton spreads. The walls, which were much farther off white than normal, expressed two forgotten interests: Finny had scotch-taped newspaper pictures of the Roosevelt-Churchill meeting above his cot ("They're the two most important of the old men," he had explained, "getting together to make up what to tell us next about the war"). Over my cot I had long ago taped pictures which together amounted to a barefaced lie about my background —weepingly romantic views of plantation

---

**3. Hitler Youth:** An organization of boys and girls who supported Adolf Hitler, dictator of Germany from 1933 to 1945.

mansions, moss-hung trees by moonlight, lazy roads winding dustily past cabins. When asked about them I had acquired an accent appropriate to a town three states south of my own, and I had transmitted the impression, without actually stating it, that this was the old family place. But by now I no longer needed this vivid false identity; now I was acquiring, I felt, a sense of my own real authority and worth, I had had many new experiences and I was growing up.

"How's Leper?" said Brinker as he came in.

"Yeah," said Phineas, "I meant to ask you before."

"Leper? Why he's—he's on leave." But my resentment against having to mislead people seemed to be growing stronger every day. "As a matter of fact Leper is 'Absent Without Leave,' he just took off by himself."

"Leper?" both of them exclaimed together.

"Yes," I shrugged, "Leper. Leper's not the little rabbit we used to know any more."

"Nobody can change *that* much," said Brinker in his new tough-minded way.

Finny said, "He just didn't like the army, I bet. Why should he? What's the point of it anyway?"

"Phineas," Brinker said with dignity, "please don't give us your infantile[4] lecture on world affairs at this time." And to me, "He was too scared to stay, wasn't he?"

I narrowed my eyes as though thinking hard about that. Finally I said, "Yes, I think you could put it that way."

"He panicked."

I didn't say anything.

"He must be out of his mind," said Brinker energetically, "to do a thing like that. I'll bet he cracked up, didn't he? That's what happened. Leper found out that the army was just too much for him. I've heard about guys like that. Some morning they don't get out of bed with everybody else. They just lie there crying. I'll bet something like that happened to Leper." He looked at me. "Didn't it?"

"Yes. It did."

Brinker had closed with such energy, almost enthusiasm, on the truth that I gave it to him without many misgivings. The moment he had it he crumbled. "Well I'll be. I'll be. Old Leper. Quiet old Leper. Quiet old Leper from Vermont. He never could fight. You'd think somebody would have realized that when he tried to enlist. Poor old Leper. What's he act like?"

"He cries a lot of the time."

"Oh. What's the matter with our class anyway? It isn't even June yet and we've already got two men sidelined for the Duration."

"Two?"

Brinker hesitated briefly. "Well there's Finny here."

"Yes," agreed Phineas in his deepest and most musical tone, "there's me."

"Finny isn't out of it," I said.

"Of course he is."

"Yes, I'm out of it."

"Not that there's anything to be out of!" I wondered if my face matched the heartiness of my voice. "Just this dizzy war, this fake, this thing with the old men making . . ." I couldn't help watching Finny as I spoke, and so I ran out of momentum. I waited for him to take it up, to unravel once again his tale of plotting statesmen and deluded public, his great joke, his private toe hold on the world. He was sitting on his cot, elbows on knees, looking down. He brought his wideset eyes up, his grin flashed and

---

**4. infantile** (in′fən tīl′) *adj.*: Characteristic of an infant; immature.

faded, and then he murmured, "Sure. There isn't any war."

It was one of the few ironic remarks Phineas ever made, and with it he quietly brought to a close all his special inventions which had carried us through the winter. Now the facts were re-established, and gone were all the fantasies, such as the Olympic Games for A.D. 1944, closed before they had ever been opened.

There was little left at Devon any more which had not been recruited for the war. The few stray activities and dreamy people not caught up in it were being systematically corralled by Brinker. And every day in chapel there was some announcement about qualifying for "V-12," an officer-training program the Navy had set up in many colleges and universities. It sounded very safe, almost like peacetime, almost like just going normally on to college. It was also very popular; groups the size of LST crews[5] joined it, almost everyone who could qualify, except for a few who "wanted to fly" and so chose the Army Air Force, or something called V-5 instead. There were also a special few with energetic fathers who were expecting appointments to Annapolis or West Point or the Coast Guard Academy or even —this alternative had been unexpectedly stumbled on—the Merchant Marine Academy. Devon was by tradition and choice the most civilian of schools, and there was a certain strained hospitality in the way both the faculty and students worked to get along with the leathery recruiting officers who kept appearing on the campus. There was no latent snobbery in us; we didn't find any in them. It was only that we could feel a deep and sincere difference between us and them, a difference which everyone struggled with awkward fortitude to bridge. It was as though Athens and Sparta[6] were trying to establish not just a truce but an alliance —although we were not as civilized as Athens and they were not as brave as Sparta.

Neither were we. There was no rush to get into the fighting; no one seemed to feel the need to get into the infantry, and only a few were talking about the Marines. The thing to be was careful and self-preserving. It was going to be a long war. Quackenbush, I heard, had two possible appointments to the Military Academy, with carefully prepared positions in V-12 and dentistry school to fall back on if necessary.

I myself took no action. I didn't feel free to, and I didn't know why this was so. Brinker, in his accelerating change from absolute to relative virtue, came up with plan after plan, each more insulated from the fighting than the last. But I did nothing.

One morning, after a Naval officer had turned many heads in chapel with an address on convoy duty, Brinker put his hand on the back of my neck in the vestibule outside and steered me into a room used for piano practice near the entrance. It was soundproofed, and he swung the vaultlike door closed behind us.

"You've been putting off enlisting in something for only one reason," he said at once. "You know that, don't you?"

"No, I don't know that."

"Well, I know, and I'll tell you what it is. It's Finny. You pity him."

"Pity him!"

"Yes, pity him. And if you don't watch out he's going to start pitying himself. Nobody ever mentions his leg to him except me.

---

5. **LST crews:** Sailors who manned landing craft during invasions.

6. **Athens and Sparta:** Ancient Greek city-states always at war with each other.

Keep that up and he'll be sloppy with self-pity any day now. What's everybody beating around the bush for? He's crippled and that's that. He's got to accept it and unless we start acting perfectly natural about it, even kid him about it once in a while, he never will."

"You're so wrong I can't even—I can't even *hear* you, you're so wrong."

"Well, I'm going to do it anyway."

"No. You're not."

"Yes I am. I don't have to have your approval, do I?"

"I'm his roommate, and I'm his best friend—"

"And you were there when it happened. I know. And I don't care. And don't forget," he looked at me sharply, "you've got a little personal stake in this. What I mean is it wouldn't do you any harm, you know, if everything about Finny's accident was cleared up and forgotten."

I felt my face grimacing in the way Finny's did when he was really irritated. "What do you mean by that?"

"I don't know," he shrugged and chuckled in his best manner, "nobody knows." Then the charm disappeared and he added, "unless you know," and his mouth closed in its straight expressionless line, and that was all that was said.

I had no idea what Brinker might say or do. Before he had always known and done whatever occurred to him because he was certain that whatever occurred to him was right. In the world of the Golden Fleece Debating Society and the Underprivileged Local Children subcommittee of the Good Samaritan Confraternity, this had created no problems. But I was afraid of that simple executive directness now.

I walked back from Chapel and found Finny in our dormitory, blocking the stair-case until the others who wanted to go up sang "A Mighty Fortress Is Our God" under his direction. No one who was tone deaf ever loved music so much. I think his shortcoming increased his appreciation; he loved it all indiscriminately—Beethoven, the latest love ditty, jazz, a hymn—it was all profoundly musical to Phineas.

". . . Our helper He a-mid the floods," wafted out across the Common in the tempo of a football march, "Of mortal ills prevailing!"

"Everything was all right," said Finny at the end, "phrasing, rhythm, all that. But I'm not sure about your pitch. Half a tone off, I would estimate offhand."

We went on to our room. I sat down at the translation of Caesar I was doing for him, since he had to pass Latin at last this year or fail to graduate. I thought I was doing a pretty good job of it.

"Is anything exciting happening now?"

"This part is pretty interesting," I said, "if I understand it right. About a surprise attack."

"Read me that."

"Well let's see. It begins, 'When Caesar noticed that the enemy was remaining for several days at the camp fortified by a swamp and by the nature of the terrain, he sent a letter to Trebonius instructing him' —'instructing him' isn't actually in the text but it's understood; you know about that."

"Sure. Go on."

"'Instructing him to come as quickly as possible by long forced marches to him' —this 'him' refers to Caesar of course."

Finny looked at me with glazed interest and said, "Of course."

"'Instructing him to come as quickly as possible by long forced marches to him with three legions; he himself'—Caesar, that is —'sent cavalry to withstand any sudden attacks of the enemy. Now when the Gauls learned what was going on, they scattered a selected band of foot soldiers in ambushes; who, overtaking our horsemen after the leader Vertiscus had been killed, followed our disorderly men up to our camp.' "

"I have a feeling that's what Mr. Horn is going to call a 'muddy translation.' What's it mean?"

"Caesar isn't doing so well."

"But he won it in the end."

"Sure. If you mean the whole campaign —" I broke off. "He won it, if you really think there was a Gallic War . . ." Caesar, from the first, had been the one historical figure Phineas refused absolutely to believe in. Lost two thousand years in the past, master of a dead language and a dead empire, the bane and bore of schoolboys, Caesar he believed to be more of a tyrant at Devon than he had ever been in Rome. Phineas felt a personal and sincere grudge against Caesar, and he was outraged most by his conviction that Caesar and Rome and Latin had never been alive at all . . . "If you really think there ever was a Caesar," I said.

Finny got up from the cot, picking up his cane as an afterthought. He looked oddly at me, his face set to burst out laughing I thought. "Naturally I don't believe books and I don't believe teachers," he came across a few paces, "but I do believe—it's important after all for me to believe *you*. I've got to believe you, at least. I know you better than anybody." I waited without saying anything. "And you told me about Leper, that he's gone crazy. That's the word, we might as well admit it. Leper's gone crazy. When I heard that about Leper, then I knew that the war was real, this war and all the wars. If a war can drive somebody crazy, then it's real all right. Oh I guess I always *knew*, but I didn't have to admit it." He perched his foot, small cast with metal bar across the bottom to walk on, next to where I was sitting on the cot. "To tell you the truth, I wasn't too

completely sure about *you*, when you told me how Leper was. Of course I believed you," he added hurriedly, "but you're the nervous type, you know, and I thought maybe your imagination got a little inflamed up there in Vermont. I thought he might not be quite as mixed up as you made out." Finny's face tried to prepare me for what came next. "Then I saw him myself."

I turned incredulously. "You saw Leper?"

"I saw him here this morning, after chapel. He was—well, there's nothing inflamed about my imagination and I saw Leper *hiding* in the shrubbery next to the chapel. I slipped out the side door the way I always do—to miss the rush—and I saw Leper and he must have seen me. He didn't say a word. He looked at me like I was a gorilla or something and then he ducked into Mr. Carhart's office."

"He must be crazy," I said automatically, and then my eyes involuntarily met Finny's. We both broke into sudden laughter.

"We can't do a thing about it," he said ruefully.

"I don't want to see him," I muttered. Then, trying to be more responsible, "Who else knows he's here."

"No one, I would think."

"There's nothing for us to do, maybe Carhart or Dr. Stanpole can do something. We won't tell anybody about it because . . . because they would just scare Leper, and he would scare them."

"Anyway," said Finny, "then I knew there was a real war on."

"Yes, I guess it's a real war all right. But I liked yours a lot better."

"So did I."

"I wish you hadn't found out. What did you have to find out for!" We started to laugh again, with a half-guilty exchange of glances, in the way that two people who had gone on a gigantic binge when they were last together would laugh when they met again at the parson's tea. "Well," he said, "you did a beautiful job in the Olympics."

"And you were the greatest news analyst who ever lived."

"Do you realize you won every gold medal in every Olympic event? No one's ever done anything like that in history."

"And you scooped every newspaper in the world on every story." The sun was doing antics among the million specks of dust hanging between us and casting a brilliant, unstable pool of light on the floor. "No one's ever done anything like that before."

Brinker and three cohorts[7] came with much commotion into our room at 10:05 P.M. that night. "We're taking you out," he said flatly.

"It's after hours," I said. "Where?" said Finny with interest at the same time.

"You'll see. Get them." His friends half-lifted us half-roughly, and we were hustled down the stairs. I thought it must be some kind of culminating prank, the senior class leaving Devon with a flourish. Were we going to steal the clapper of the school bell, or would we tether a cow in chapel?

They steered us toward the First Building—burned down and rebuilt several times but still known as the First Building of the Devon School. It contained only classrooms and so at this hour was perfectly empty, which made us stealthier than ever. Brinker's many keys, surviving from his class-officer period, jingled softly as we reached the main door. Above us in Latin flowed the inscription, Here Boys Come to Be Made Men.

The lock turned; we went in, entering the doubtful reality of a hallway familiar only in daylight and bustle. Our footsteps fell guiltily on the marble floor. We continued across the foyer to a dreamlike bank of windows, turned left up a pale flight of marble steps, left again, through two doorways, and into the Assembly Room. From the high ceiling one of the celebrated Devon chandeliers, all glittering tears, scattered thin illumination. Row after row of black Early American benches spread emptily back through the shadows to long, vague windows. At the front of the room there was a raised platform with a balustrade[8] in front of it. About ten members of the senior class sat on the platform; all of them were wearing their black graduation robes. This is going to be some kind of schoolboy masquerade, I thought, some masquerade with masks and candles.

"You see how Phineas limps," said Brinker loudly as we walked in. It was too coarse and too loud; I wanted to hit him for shocking me like that. Phineas looked perplexed. "Sit down," he went on, "take a load off your feet." We sat in the front row of the benches where eight or ten others were sitting, smirking uneasily at the students on the platform.

Whatever Brinker had in his mind to do, I thought he had chosen a terrible place for it. There was nothing funny about the Assembly Room. I could remember staring torpidly[9] through these windows a hundred times out at the elms of the Center Common. The windows now had the closed blankness of night, a deadened look about them, a look of being blind or deaf. The great expanses of wall space were opaque with canvas, portraits in oil of deceased headmasters, a founder or two, forgotten leaders of the faculty, a beloved athletic coach none of us had ever heard of, a lady we could not identify —her fortune had largely rebuilt the school;

---

7. **cohorts** (kō′ hôrts) n.: Companions; supporters.

8. **balustrade** (bal′ə strād′) n.: A railing held up by small posts.

9. **torpidly** (tôr′ pid lē) adv.: Sluggishly, slowly.

a nameless poet who was thought when under the school's protection to be destined primarily for future generations; a young hero now anonymous who looked theatrical in the First World War uniform in which he had died.

I thought any prank was bound to fall flat here.

The Assembly Hall was used for large lectures, debates, plays, and concerts; it had the worst acoustics in the school. I couldn't make out what Brinker was saying. He stood on the polished marble floor in front of us,

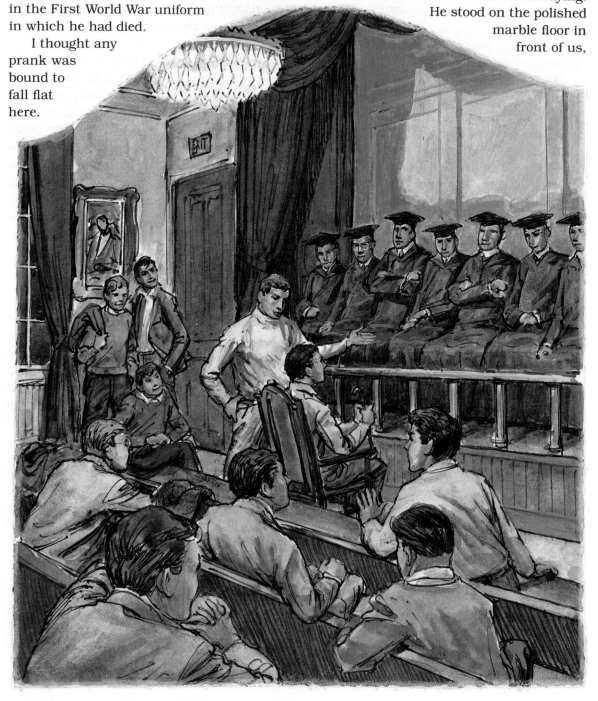

but facing the platform, talking to the boys behind the balustrade. I heard him say the word "inquiry" to them, and something about "the country demands. . . ."

"What is all this hot air?" I said into the blur.

"I don't know," Phineas answered shortly.

As he turned toward us Brinker was saying ". . . blame on the responsible party. We will begin with a brief prayer." He paused, surveying us with the kind of wide-eyed surmise Mr. Carhart always used at this point, and then added in Mr. Carhart's urbane murmur, "Let us pray."

We all slumped immediately and unthinkingly into the awkward crouch in which God was addressed at Devon, leaning forward with elbows on knees. Brinker had caught us, and in a moment it was too late to escape, for he had moved swiftly into the Lord's Prayer. If when Brinker had said "Let us pray" I had said "No" everything might have been saved.

At the end there was an indecisive, semiserious silence and then Brinker said, "Phineas, if you please." Finny got up with a shrug and walked to the center of the floor, between us and the platform. Brinker got an armchair from behind the balustrade, and seated Finny on it with courtly politeness. "Now just in your own words," he said.

"What own words?" said Phineas, grimacing up at him with his best you-are-an-idiot expression.

"I know you haven't got many of your own," said Brinker with a charitable smile. "Use some of Gene's then."

"What shall I talk about? You? I've got plenty of words of my own for that."

"*I'm* all right," Brinker glanced gravely around the room for confirmation, "you're the casualty."

"Brinker," began Finny in a constricted voice I did not recognize, "are you off your head or what?"

"No," said Brinker evenly, "that's Leper, our other casualty. Tonight we're investigating you."

"What are you talking about!" I cut in suddenly.

"Investigating Finny's accident!" He spoke as though this was the most natural and self-evident and inevitable thing we could be doing.

I felt the blood flooding into my head. "After all," Brinker continued, "there *is* a war on. Here's one soldier our side has already lost. We've got to find out what happened."

"Just for the record," said someone from the platform. "You agree, don't you, Gene?"

"I told Brinker this morning," I began in a voice treacherously shaking, "that I thought this was the worst—"

"And I said," Brinker's voice was full of authority and perfectly under control, "that for Finny's good," and with an additional timbre[10] of sincerity, "and for your own good too, by the way, Gene, that we should get all this out into the open. We don't want any mysteries or any stray rumors and suspicions left in the air at the end of the year, do we?"

A collective assent to this rumbled through the blurring atmosphere of the Assembly Room.

"What are you talking about!" Finny's voice was full of contemptuous music. "What rumors and suspicions?"

"Never mind about that," said Brinker with his face responsibly grave. He's enjoying this, I thought bitterly, he's imagining himself Justice incarnate, balancing the

---

**10. timbre** (tam′ bər) *n*.: The distinctive tone of a voice.

scales. He's forgotten that Justice incarnate is not only balancing the scales but also blindfolded. "Why don't you just tell us in your words what happened?" Brinker continued. "Just humor us, if you want to think of it that way. We aren't trying to make you feel bad. Just tell us. You know we wouldn't ask you if we didn't have a good reason . . . good reasons."

"There's nothing to tell."

"Nothing to tell?" Brinker looked pointedly at the small cast around Finny's lower leg and the cane he held between his knees.

"Well then, I fell out of a tree."

"Why?" said someone on the platform. The acoustics were so bad and the light so dim that I could rarely tell who was speaking, except for Finny and Brinker who were isolated on the wide strip of marble floor between us in the seats and the others on the platform.

"Why?" repeated Phineas. "Because I took a wrong step."

"Did you lose your balance?" continued the voice.

"Yes," echoed Finny grimly, "I lost my balance."

"You had better balance than anyone in the school."

"Thanks a lot."

"I didn't say it for a compliment."

"Well then, no thanks."

"Have you ever thought that you didn't just fall out of that tree?"

This touched an interesting point Phineas had been turning over in his mind for a long time. I could tell that because the obstinate, competitive look left his face as his mind became engaged for the first time. "It's very funny," he said, "but ever since then I've had a feeling that the tree did it by itself. It's an impression I've had. Almost as though the tree shook me out by itself."

The acoustics in the Assembly Room were so poor that silences there had a heavy hum of their own.

"Someone else was in the tree, isn't that so?"

"No," said Finny spontaneously, "I don't think so." He looked at the ceiling. "Or was there? Maybe there was somebody climbing up the rungs of the trunk. I kind of forget."

This time the hum of silence was prolonged to a point where I would be forced to fill it with some kind of sound if it didn't end. Then someone else on the platform spoke up. "I thought somebody told me that Gene Forrester was—"

"Finny was there," Brinker interrupted commandingly, "he knows better than anyone."

"You were there too, weren't you, Gene?" this new voice from the platform continued.

"Yes," I said with interest, "yes, I was there too."

"Were you—near the tree?"

Finny turned toward me. "You were down at the bottom, weren't you?" he asked, not in the official courtroom tone he had used before, but in a friend's voice.

I had been studying very carefully the way my hands wrinkled when tightly clenched, but I was able to bring my head up and return his inquiring look. "Down at the bottom, yes."

Finny went on. "Did you see the tree shake or anything?" He flushed faintly at what seemed to him the absurdity of his own question. "I've always meant to ask you, just for the hell of it."

I took this under consideration. "I don't recall anything like that . . ."

"Nutty question," he muttered.

"I thought you were in the tree," the platform voice cut in.

"Well of course," Finny said with an

exasperated chuckle, "of course *I* was in the tree—oh you mean Gene?—he wasn't in—is that what you mean, or—" Finny floundered with muddled honesty between me and my questioner.

"I meant Gene," the voice said.

"Of course Finny was in the tree," I said. But I couldn't make the confusion last, "and I was down at the bottom, or climbing the rungs I think . . ."

"How do you expect him to remember?" said Finny sharply. "There was a lot of confusion right then."

"A kid I used to play with was hit by a car once when I was about eleven years old," said Brinker seriously, "and I remember every single thing about it, exactly where I was standing, the color of the sky, the noise the brakes of the car made—I never will forget anything about it."

"You and I are two different people," I said.

"No one's accusing you of anything," Brinker responded in an odd tone.

"Well of course no one's *accusing* me—"

"Don't argue so much," his voice tried for a hard compromise, full of warning and yet striving to pass unnoticed by the others.

"No, we're not accusing you," a boy on the platform said evenly, and then I stood accused.

"I think I remember now!" Finny broke in, his eyes bright and relieved. "Yes, I remember seeing you standing on the bank. You were looking up and your hair was plastered down over your forehead so that you had that dumb look you always have when you've been in the water—what was it you said? 'Stop posing up there' or one of those best-pal cracks you're always making." He was very happy. "And I think I did start to pose just to make you madder, and I said, what did I say? something about the

two of us . . . yes, I said 'Let's make a double jump,' because I thought if we went together it would be something that had never been done before, holding hands in a jump—" Then it was as though someone suddenly slapped him. "No, that was on the ground when I said that to you. I said that to you on the ground, and then the two of us started to climb . . ." he broke off.

"The two of you," the boy on the platform went on harshly for him, "started to climb up the tree together, was that it? And he's just said he was on the ground!"

"Or on the rungs!" I burst out. "I said I might have been on the rungs!"

"Who else was there?" said Brinker quietly. "Leper Lepellier was there, wasn't he?"

"Yes," someone said, "Leper was there."

"Leper always was the exact type when it came to details," continued Brinker. "He could have told us where everybody was standing, what everybody was wearing, the whole conversation that day, and what the temperature was. He could have cleared the whole thing up. Too bad."

No one said anything. Phineas had been sitting motionless, leaning slightly forward, not far from the position in which we prayed at Devon. After a long time he turned and reluctantly looked at me. I did not return his look or move or speak. Then at last Finny straightened from this prayerful position slowly, as though it was painful for him. "Leper's here," he said in a voice so quiet, and with such quiet unconscious dignity, that he was suddenly terrifyingly strange to me. "I saw him go into Dr. Carhart's office this morning."

"Here! Go get him," said Brinker immediately to the two boys who had come with us. "He must be in Carhart's rooms if he hasn't gone back home."

I kept quiet. To myself, however, I made a number of swift, automatic calculations: that Leper was no threat, no one would ever believe Leper; Leper was deranged, he was not of sound mind and if people couldn't make out their own wills when not in sound mind certainly they couldn't testify in something like this.

The two boys left and the atmosphere immediately cleared. Action had been taken, so the whole issue was dropped for now. Someone began making fun of "Captain Marvel,"[11] the head of the football team, saying how girlish he looked in his graduation gown. Captain Marvel minced for us in his size 12 shoes, the sides of his gown swaying drunkenly back and forth from his big hips. Someone wound himself in the folds of the red velvet curtain and peered out from it like an exotic spy. Someone made a long speech listing every infraction[12] of the rules we were committing that night. Someone else made a speech showing how by careful planning we could break all the others before dawn.

But although the acoustics in the Assembly Hall were poor, those outside the room were admirable. All the talk and horseplay ended within a few seconds of the instant when the first person, that is myself, heard the footsteps returning along the marble stairway and corridors toward us. I knew with absolute certainty moments before they came in that there were three sets of footsteps coming.

Leper entered ahead of the other two. He looked unusually well; his face was glowing, his eyes were bright, his manner was all energy. "Yes?" he said in a clear voice, resonant even in this room, "what can I do for you?" He made this confident remark almost but not quite to Phineas, who was still sitting alone in the middle of the room. Finny muttered something which was too indecisive for Leper, who turned with a cleanly energetic gesture toward Brinker. Brinker began talking to him in the elaborately casual manner of someone being watched. Gradually the noise in the room, which had revived when the three of them came in, subsided again.

Brinker managed it. He never raised his voice, but instead he let the noise surrounding it gradually sink so that his voice emerged in the ensuing silence without any emphasis on his part—"so that you were standing next to the river bank, watching Phineas climb the tree?" he was saying, and had waited, I knew, until this silence to say.

"Sure. Right there by the trunk of the tree. I was looking up. It was almost sunset, and I remember the way the sun was shining in my eyes."

"So you couldn't . . ." I began before I could stop myself.

There was a short pause during which every ear and no eyes were directed toward me, and then Brinker went on. "And what did you see? Could you see anything with the sun in your eyes?"

"Oh sure," said Leper in his new, confident, false voice. "I just shaded my eyes a little, like this," he demonstrated how a hand shades the eyes, "and then I could see. I could see both of them clearly enough because the sun was blazing all around them," a certain singsong sincerity was developing in his voice, as though he were trying to hold the interest of young children, "and the rays of the sun were shooting past them, millions of rays shooting past them like—like golden machine-gun fire." He paused to let us consider the profoundly

11. **Captain Marvel:** Comic book hero.
12. **infraction** (in frak′ shen) *n.:* Violation.

revealing exactness of this phrase. "That's what it was like, if you want to know. The two of them looked as black as—as black as death standing up there with this fire burning all around them."

Everyone could hear, couldn't they? the derangement in his voice. Everyone must be able to see how false his confidence was. Any fool could see that. But whatever I said would be a self-indictment;[13] others would have to fight for me.

"Up there where?" said Brinker brusquely. "Where were the two of them standing up there?"

"On the limb!" Leper's annoyed, this-is-obvious tone would discount what he said in their minds; they would know that he had never been like this before, that he had changed and was not responsible.

"Who was where on the limb? Was one of them ahead of the other?"

"Well of course."

"Who was ahead?"

Leper smiled waggishly. "I couldn't see *that*. There were just two shapes, and with that fire shooting past them they looked as black as—"

"You've already told us that. You couldn't see who was ahead?"

"No, naturally I couldn't."

"But you could see how they were standing. Where were they exactly?"

"One of them was next to the trunk, holding the trunk of the tree. I'll never forget that because the tree was a huge black shape too, and his hand touching the black trunk anchored him, if you see what I mean, to something solid in all the bright fire they were standing in up there. And the other one was a little farther out on the limb."

"Then what happened?"

"Then they both moved."

"How did they move?"

"They moved," now Leper was smiling, a charming and slightly arch[14] smile, like a child who knows he is going to say something clever, "they moved like an engine."

In the baffled silence I began to uncoil slowly.

"Like an engine!" Brinker's expression was a struggle between surprise and disgust.

"I can't think of the name of the engine. But it has two pistons. What is that engine? Well anyway, in this engine first one piston sinks, and then the next one sinks. The one holding on to the trunk sank for a second, up and down like a piston, and then the other one sank and fell."

Someone on the platform exclaimed, "The one who moved first shook the other one's balance!"

"I suppose so." Leper seemed to be rapidly losing interest.

"Was the one who fell," Brinker said slowly, "was Phineas, in other words the one who moved first or second?"

Leper's face became guileful, his voice flat and impersonal. "I don't intend to implicate myself. I'm no fool, you know. I'm not going to tell you everything and then have it used against me later. You always did take me for a fool, didn't you? But I'm no fool any more. I know when I have information that might be dangerous." He was working himself up to indignation. "Why should I tell you! Just because it happens to suit you!"

"Leper," Brinker pleaded, "Leper, this is very important—"

"So am I," he said thinly, "I'm important. You've never realized it, but I'm impor-

---

**13. self-indictment** (self in dīt′ mənt) *n.*: An accusation of oneself.

**14. arch** (ärch) *adj.*: Mischievous.

tant too. You be the fool," he gazed shrewdly at Brinker, "you do whatever anyone wants whenever they want it. You be the fool now."

Phineas had gotten up unnoticed from his chair. "I don't care," he interrupted in an even voice, so full of richness that it overrode all the others. "I don't care."

I tore myself from the bench toward him. "Phineas—!"

He shook his head sharply, closing his eyes, and then he turned to regard me with a handsome mask of face. "I just don't care. Never mind," and he started across the marble floor toward the doors.

"Wait a minute!" cried Brinker. "We haven't heard everything yet. We haven't got all the facts!"

The words shocked Phineas into awareness. He whirled as though being attacked from behind. "You get the rest of the facts, Brinker!" he cried. "You get all your facts!" I had never seen Finny crying, "You collect every fact there is in the world!" He plunged out the doors.

The excellent exterior acoustics recorded his rushing steps and the quick rapping of his cane along the corridor and on the first steps of the marble stairway. Then these separate sounds collided into the general tumult of his body falling clumsily down the white marble stairs.

## Chapter 12

Everyone behaved with complete presence of mind. Brinker shouted that Phineas must not be moved; someone else, realizing that only a night nurse would be at the Infirmary, did not waste time going there but rushed to bring Dr. Stanpole from his house. Others remembered that Phil Latham, the wrestling coach, lived just across the Common and that he was an expert in first aid. It was Phil who made Finny stretch out on one of the wide shallow steps of the staircase, and kept him still until Dr. Stanpole arrived.

The foyer and the staircase of the First Building were soon as crowded as at midday. Phil Latham found the main light switch, and all the marble blazed up under full illumination. But surrounding it was the stillness of near-midnight in a country town, so that the hurrying feet and the repressed voices had a hollow reverberance. The windows, blind and black, retained their look of dull emptiness.

Once Brinker turned to me and said, "Go back to the Assembly Room and see if there's any kind of blanket on the platform." I dashed back up the stairs, found a blanket and gave it to Phil Latham. He carefully wrapped it around Phineas.

I would have liked very much to have done that myself; it would have meant a lot to me. But Phineas might begin to curse me with every word he knew, he might lose his head completely, he would certainly be worse off for it. So I kept out of the way.

He was entirely conscious and from the glimpses I caught of his face seemed to be fairly calm. Everyone behaved with complete presence of mind, and that included Phineas.

When Dr. Stanpole arrived there was silence on the stairs. Wrapped tightly in his blanket, with light flooding down on him from the chandelier, Finny lay isolated at the center of a tight circle of faces. The rest of the crowd looked on from above or below on the stairs, and I stood on the lower edge. Behind me the foyer was now empty.

After a short, silent examination Dr. Stanpole had a chair brought from the Assembly Room, and Finny was lifted cautiously into it. People aren't ordinarily carried in chairs in New Hampshire, and as they raised him up he looked very strange to me, like some tragic and exalted personage, a stricken pontiff.[1] Once again I had the desolating sense of having all along ignored what was finest in him. Perhaps it was just the incongruity of seeing him aloft and stricken, since he was by nature someone who carried others. I didn't think he knew how to act or even how to feel as the object of help. He went past with his eyes closed and his mouth tense. I knew that normally I would have been one of those carrying the chair, saying something into his ear as we went along. My aid alone had never seemed to him in the category of help. The reason for this occurred to me as the procession moved slowly across the brilliant foyer to the doors; Phineas had thought of me as an extension of himself.

Dr. Stanpole stopped near the doors, looking for the light switch. There was an interval of a few seconds when no one was near him. I came up to him and tried to phrase my question but nothing came out, I couldn't find the word to begin. I was being torn irreconcilably between "Is he" and "What is" when Dr. Stanpole, without appearing to notice my tangle, said conversationally, "It's the leg again. Broken again. But a much cleaner break I think, much cleaner. A simple fracture." He found the light switch and the foyer was plunged into darkness.

Outside, the doctor's car was surrounded by boys while Finny was being lifted inside it by Phil Latham. Phil and Dr. Stanpole then got into the car and drove slowly away, the headlights forming a bright parallel as they receded down the road, and then swinging into another parallel at right angles to the first as they turned into the Infirmary driveway. The crowd began to thin

rapidly; the faculty had at last heard that something was amiss in the night, and several alarmed and alarming masters materialized in the darkness and ordered the students to their dormitories.

Mr. Ludsbury loomed abruptly out of a background of shrubbery. "Get along to the dormitory, Forrester," he said with a dry certainty in my obedience which suddenly struck me as funny, definitely funny. Since it was beneath his dignity to wait and see that I actually followed his order, I was able to budge free of him a moment later. I walked into the bank of shrubbery, circled past trees in the direction of the chapel, doubled back along a large building donated by the alumni which no one had ever been able to put to use, recrossed the street and walked noiselessly up the emerging grass next to the Infirmary driveway.

Dr. Stanpole's car was at the top of it, headlights on and motor running, empty. I idly considered stealing it, in the way that people idly consider many crimes it would be possible for them to commit. I took an academic interest in the thought of stealing the car, knowing all the time that it would be not so much criminal as meaningless, a lapse into nothing, an escape into nowhere. As I walked past it the motor was throbbing with wheezy reluctance—prep school doctors don't own very desirable getaway cars, I remember thinking to myself—and then I turned the corner of the building and began to creep along behind it. There was only one window lighted, at the far end, and opposite it I found some thin shrubbery which provided enough cover for me to study the window. It was too high for me to see directly into the room, but after I made sure that the ground had softened enough so that I could jump without making much noise, I sprang as high as I could. I had a flashing glimpse of a door at the other end of the room, opening

---

**1. pontiff** (pän' tif) *n.*: A high priest, bishop.

on the corridor. I jumped again; someone's back. Again; nothing new. I jumped again and saw a head and shoulders partially turned away from me; Phil Latham's. This was the room.

The ground was too damp to sit on, so I crouched down and waited. I could hear their blurred voices droning monotonously through the window. If they do nothing worse, they're going to bore Finny to death, I said to myself. My head seemed to be full of bright remarks this evening. It was cold crouching motionless next to the ground. I stood up and jumped several times, not so much to see into the room as to warm up. The only sounds were occasional snorts from the engine of Dr. Stanpole's car when it turned over with special reluctance, and a thin, lonely whistling the wind sometimes made high in the still-bare trees. These formed the background for the dull hum of talk in Finny's room as Phil Latham, Dr. Stanpole and the night nurse worked over him.

What could they be talking about? The night nurse had always been the biggest windbag in the school. Miss Windbag, R.N. Phil Latham, on the other hand, hardly ever spoke. One of the few things he said was "Give it the old college try"—he thought of everything in terms of the old college try, and he had told students to attack their studies, their sports, religious waverings, physical handicaps and a constellation of other problems with the old college try. I listened tensely for his voice. I listened so hard that I nearly differentiated it from the others, and it seemed to be saying, "Finny, give that bone the old college try."

I was quite a card tonight myself.

Phil Latham's college was Harvard, although I had heard that he only lasted there a year. Probably he had said to someone to give something the old college try, and that had finished him; that would probably be grounds for expulsion at Harvard. There couldn't possibly be such a thing as the old Harvard try. Could there be the old Devon try? The old Devon endeavor? The decrepit Devon endeavor? That was good, the decrepit Devon endeavor. I'd use that some time in the Butt Room. That was pretty funny. I'll bet I could get a rise out of Finny with—

Dr. Stanpole was fairly gabby too. What was he always saying. Nothing. Nothing? Well there must be something he was always saying. Everybody had something, some word, some phrase that they were always saying. The trouble with Dr. Stanpole was that his vocabulary was too large. He talked in a huge circle, he probably had a million words in his vocabulary and he had to use them all before he started over again.

That's probably the way they were talking in there now. Dr. Stanpole was working his way as fast as possible around his big circle, Miss Windbag was gasping out something or other all the time, and Phil Latham was saying, "Give 'er the old college try, Finny." Phineas of course was answering them only in Latin.

I nearly laughed out loud at that.

*Gallia est omnis divisa in partes tres*[2]—Finny probably answered that whenever Phil Latham spoke. Phil Latham would look rather blank at that.

Did Finny like Phil Latham? Yes, of course he did. But wouldn't it be funny if he suddenly turned to him and said, "Phil Latham, you're a boob." That would be funny in a way. And what about if he said, "Dr. Stanpole, old pal, you're the most long-winded licensed medical man alive." And it would be even funnier if he interrupted that night nurse and said, "Miss Windbag, you're rotten, rotten to the core. I just thought I ought to tell you." It would never

---

2. *Gallia est omnis divisa in partes tres*: Latin for "All Gaul is divided into three parts."

occur to Finny to say any of these things, but they struck me as so outrageous that I couldn't stop myself from laughing. I put my hand over my mouth; then I tried to stop my mouth with my fist; if I couldn't get control of this laughing they would hear me in the room. I was laughing so hard it hurt my stomach and I could feel my face getting more and more flushed; I dug my teeth into my fist to try to gain control and then I noticed that there were tears all over my hand.

The engine of Dr. Stanpole's car roared exhaustedly. The headlights turned in an erratic arc away from me, and then I heard the engine laboriously recede into the distance, and I continued to listen until not only had it ceased but my memory of how it sounded had also ceased. The light had gone out in the room and there was no sound coming from it. The only noise was the peculiarly bleak whistling of the wind through the upper branches.

There was a street light behind me somewhere through the trees and the windows of the Infirmary dimly reflected it. I came up close beneath the window of Finny's room, found a foothold on a grating beneath it, straightened up so that my shoulders were at a level with the window sill, reached up with both hands, and since I was convinced that the window would be stuck shut I pushed it hard. The window shot up and there was a startled rustling from the bed in the shadows. I whispered, "Finny!" sharply into the black room.

"Who is it!" he demanded, leaning out from the bed so that the light fell waveringly on his face. Then he recognized me and I thought at first he was going to get out of bed and help me through the window. He struggled clumsily for such a length of time that even my mind, shocked and slowed as it had been, was able to formulate two realizations: that his leg was bound so that he could not

move very well, and that he was struggling to unleash his hate against me.

"I came to—"

"You want to break something else in me! Is that why you're here!" He thrashed wildly in the darkness, the bed groaning under him and the sheets hissing as he fought against them. But he was not going to be able to get to me, because his matchless coordination was gone. He could not even get up from the bed.

"I want to fix your leg up," I said crazily but in a perfectly natural tone of voice which made my words sound even crazier, even to me.

"You'll fix my . . ." and he arched out, lunging hopelessly into the space between us. He arched out and then fell, his legs still on the bed, his hands falling with a loud slap against the floor. Then after a pause all the tension drained out of him, and he let his head come slowly down between his hands. He had not hurt himself. But he brought his head slowly down between his hands and rested it against the floor, not moving, not making any sound.

"I'm sorry," I said blindly, "I'm sorry, I'm sorry."

I had just control enough to stay out of his room, to let him struggle back into the bed by himself. I slid down from the window, and I remember lying on the ground staring up at the night sky, which was neither clear nor overcast. And I remember later walking alone down a rather aimless road which leads past the gym to an old water hole. I was trying to cope with something that might be called double vision. I saw the gym in the glow of a couple of outside lights near it and I knew of course that it was the Devon gym which I entered every day. It was and it wasn't. There was something innately[3]

---

**3. innately** (i nāt′ lē) *adv*.: Existing naturally rather than acquired.

strange about it, as though there had always been an inner core to the gym which I had never perceived before, quite different from its generally accepted appearance. It seemed to alter moment by moment before my eyes, becoming for brief flashes a totally

unknown building with a significance much deeper and far more real than any I had noticed before. The same was true of the water hole, where unauthorized games of hockey were played during the winter. The ice was breaking up on it now, with just a few glazed islands of ice remaining in the center and a fringe of hard surface glinting along the banks. The old trees surrounding it all were intensely meaningful, with a message that was very pressing and entirely indecipherable. Here the road turned to the left and became dirt. It proceeded along the lower end of the playing fields, and under the pale night glow the playing fields swept away from me in slight frosty undulations which bespoke meanings upon meanings, levels of reality I had never suspected before, a kind of thronging and epic grandeur which my superficial eyes and cluttered mind had been blind to before. They unrolled away impervious to me as though I were a roaming ghost, not only tonight but always, as though I had never played on them a hundred times, as though my feet had never touched them, as though my whole life at Devon had been a dream, or rather that everything at Devon, the playing fields, the gym, the water hole, and all the other buildings and all the people there were intensely real, wildly alive and totally meaningful, and I alone was a dream, a figment[4] which had never really touched anything. I felt that I was not, never had been and never would be a living part of this overpoweringly solid and deeply meaningful world around me.

I reached the bridge which arches over the little Devon River and beyond it the dirt track which curves toward the stadium. The stadium itself, two white concrete banks of seats, was as powerful and alien to me as an Aztec ruin, filled with the traces of vanished people and vanished rites, of supreme emotions and supreme tragedies. The old phrase about "If these walls could only speak" occurred to me and I felt it more deeply than anyone has ever felt it, I felt that the stadium could not only speak but that its words could hold me spellbound. In fact the stadium did speak powerfully and at all times, including this moment. But I could not hear, and that was because I did not exist.

I awoke the next morning in a dry and fairly sheltered corner of the ramp underneath the stadium. My neck was stiff from sleeping in an awkward position. The sun was high and the air freshened.

I walked back to the center of the school and had breakfast and then went to my room to get a notebook, because this was Wednesday and I had a class at 9:10. But at the door of the room I found a note from Dr. Stanpole. "Please bring some of Finny's clothes and his toilet things to the Infirmary."

I took his suitcase from the corner where it had been accumulating dust and put what he would need into it. I didn't know what I was going to say at the Infirmary. I couldn't escape a confusing sense of having lived through all of this before—Phineas in the Infirmary, and myself responsible. I seemed to be less shocked by it now than I had the first time last August, when it had broken over our heads like a thunderclap in a flawless sky. There were hints of much worse things around us now like a faint odor in the air, evoked by words like "plasma" and "psycho" and "sulfa," strange words like that with endings like Latin nouns. The newsreels and magazines were choked with images of blazing artillery and bodies half sunk in the sand of a beach somewhere. We members of the Class of 1943 were moving very fast toward the war now, so fast that there were casualties even before we reached it, a mind was clouded and a leg was broken—maybe these should be thought of as minor and inevitable mishaps in the accelerating rush. The air around us was filled with much worse things.

In this way I tried to calm myself as I walked with Finny's suitcase toward the

---

4. **figment** (fig' mənt) *n.*: Something merely imagined.

Infirmary. After all, I reflected to myself, people were shooting flames into caves and grilling other people alive, ships were being torpedoed and dropping thousands of men in the icy ocean, whole city blocks were exploding into flame in an instant. My brief burst of animosity, lasting only a second, a part of a second, something which came before I could recognize it and was gone before I knew it had possessed me, what was that in the midst of this holocaust?

I reached the Infirmary with Finny's suitcase and went inside. The air was laden with hospital smells, not unlike those of the gym except that the Infirmary lacked that sense of spent human vitality. This was becoming the new background of Finny's life, this purely medical element from which bodily health was absent.

The corridor happened to be empty, and I walked along it in the grip of a kind of fatal exhilaration. All doubt had been resolved at last. There was a wartime phrase coming into style just then—"this is it"—and although it later became a parody of itself, it had a final flat accuracy which was all that could be said at certain times. This was one of the times: this was it.

I knocked and went in. He was stripped to the waist, sitting up in bed leafing through a magazine. I carried my head low by instinct, and I had the courage for only a short glance at him before I said quietly, "I've brought your stuff."

"Put the suitcase on the bed here, will you?" The tone of his words fell dead center, without a trace of friendliness or unfriendliness, not interested and not bored, not energetic and not languid.[5]

I put it down beside him, and he opened it and began to look through the extra underwear and shirts and socks I had packed. I

stood precariously[6] in the middle of the room, trying to find somewhere to look and something to say, wanting desperately to leave and powerless to do so. Phineas went carefully over his clothes, apparently very calm. But it wasn't like him to check with such care, not like him at all. He was taking a long time at it, and then I noticed that as he tried to slide a hairbrush out from under a flap holding it in the case his hands were shaking so badly that he couldn't get it out. Seeing that released me on the spot.

"Finny, I tried to tell you before, I tried to tell you when I came to Boston that time—"

"I know, I remember that." He couldn't, after all, always keep his voice under control. "What'd you come around here for last night?"

"I don't know." I went over to the window and placed my hands on the sill. I looked down at them with a sense of detachment, as though they were hands somebody had sculptured and put on exhibition somewhere. "I had to." Then I added, with great difficulty, "I thought I belonged here."

I felt him turning to look at me, and so I looked up. He had a particular expression which his face assumed when he understood but didn't think he should show it, a settled, enlightened look; its appearance now was the first decent thing I had seen in a long time.

He suddenly slammed his fist against the suitcase. "I wish there wasn't any war."

I looked sharply at him. "What made you say that?"

"I don't know if I can take this with a war on. I don't know."

"If you can take—"

"What good are you in a war with a busted leg!"

---

**5. languid** (lan′ gwid) adj.: Without vitality.

**6. precariously** (pri ker′ ē əs lē) adj.: Dependent upon the will or favor of another person.

"Well you—why there are lots—you can—"

He bent over the suitcase again. "I've been writing to the Army and the Navy and the Marines and the Canadians and everybody else all winter. Did you know that? No, you didn't know that. I used the Post Office in town for my return address. They all gave me the same answer after they saw the medical report on me. The answer was no soap. We can't use you. I also wrote the Coast Guard, the Merchant Marine, I wrote to General de Gaulle personally, I also wrote Chiang Kai-shek, and I was about ready to write somebody in Russia."

I made an attempt at a grin. "You wouldn't like it in Russia."

"I'll *hate* it *everywhere* if I'm not in this war! Why do you think I kept saying there wasn't any war all winter? I was going to keep on saying it until two seconds after I got a letter from Ottawa[7] or Chungking[8] or some place saying, 'Yes, you can enlist with us.'" A look of pleased achievement flickered over his face momentarily, as though he had really gotten such a letter. "Then there would have been a war."

"Finny," my voice broke but I went on, "Phineas, you wouldn't be any good in the war, even if nothing had happened to your leg."

A look of amazement fell over him. It scared me, but I knew what I said was important and right, and my voice found that full tone voices have when they are expressing something long-felt and long-understood and released at last. "They'd get you some place at the front and there'd be a lull in the fighting, and the next thing anyone knew you'd be over with the Germans or the Japs, asking if they'd like to field a baseball team against our side. You'd be sitting in one of their command posts, teaching them English. Yes, you'd get confused and borrow one of their uniforms, and you'd lend them one of yours. Sure, that's just what would happen. You'd get things so scrambled up nobody would know who to fight any more. You'd make a mess, a terrible mess, Finny, out of the war."

His face had been struggling to stay calm as he listened to me, but now he was crying but trying to control himself. "It was just some kind of blind impulse you had in the tree there, you didn't know what you were doing. Was that it?"

"Yes, yes, that was it. Oh that was it, but how can you believe that? How can you believe that? I can't even make myself pretend that you could believe that."

"I do, I think I can believe that. I've gotten awfully mad sometimes and almost forgotten what I was doing. I think I believe you, I think I can believe that. Then that was it. Something just seized you. It wasn't anything you really felt against me, it wasn't some kind of hate you've felt all along. It wasn't anything personal."

"No, I don't know how to show you, how can I show you, Finny? Tell me how to show you. It was just some ignorance inside me, some crazy thing inside me, something blind, that's all it was."

He was nodding his head, his jaw tightening and his eyes closed on the tears. "I believe you. It's okay because I understand and I believe you. You've already shown me and I believe you."

The rest of the day passed quickly. Dr. Stanpole had told me in the corridor that he was going to set the bone that afternoon. Come back around 5 o'clock, he had said,

---

**7. Ottawa** (ät′ ə wə) *n.*: Capital of Canada.
**8. Chungking** (choong′ kiŋ′) *n.*: Capital of China during World War II.

when Finny should be coming out of the anaesthesia.

I left the Infirmary and went to my 10:10 class, which was on American history. Mr. Patch-Withers gave us a five-minute written quiz on the "necessary and proper" clause of the Constitution. At 11 o'clock I left that building and crossed the Center Common where a few students were already lounging although it was still a little early in the season for that. I went into the First Building, walked up the stairs where Finny had fallen, and joined my 11:10 class, which was in mathematics. We were given a ten-minute trigonometry problem which appeared to solve itself on my paper.

At 12 I left the First Building, recrossed the Common and went into the Jared Potter Building for lunch. It was a breaded veal cutlet, spinach, mashed potatoes, and prune whip.

After lunch I walked back to the dormitory with Brinker. He alluded to last night only by asking how Phineas was; I said he seemed to be in good spirits. I went on to my room and read the assigned pages of *Le bourgeois gentilhomme*. At 2:30 I left my room, and walking along one side of the oval Finny had used for my track workouts during the winter, I reached the Far Common and beyond it the gym. I went past the Trophy Room, downstairs into the pungent air of the locker room, changed into gym pants, and spent an hour wrestling. I pinned my opponent once and he pinned me once. Phil Latham showed me an involved method of escape in which you executed a modified somersault over your opponent's back. He started to talk about the accident but I concentrated on the escape method and the subject was dropped. Then I took a shower, dressed, and went back to the dormitory, reread part of *Le bourgeois gentil-homme*, and at 4:45, instead of going to a scheduled meeting of the Commencement Arrangements Committee, on which I had been persuaded to take Brinker's place, I went to the Infirmary.

Dr. Stanpole was not patrolling the corridor as he habitually did when he was not busy, so I sat down on a bench amid the medical smells and waited. After about ten minutes he came walking rapidly out of his office, his head down and his hands sunk in the pockets of his white smock. He didn't notice me until he was almost past me, and then he stopped short. His eyes met mine carefully, and I said, "Well, how is he, sir?" in a calm voice which, the moment after I had spoken, alarmed me unreasonably.

Dr. Stanpole sat down next to me and put his capable-looking hand on my leg. "This is something I think boys of your generation are going to see a lot of," he said quietly, "and I will have to tell you about it now. Your friend is dead."

He was incomprehensible. I felt an extremely cold chill along my back and neck, that was all. Dr. Stanpole went on talking incomprehensibly. "It was such a simple, clean break. Anyone could have set it. Of course, I didn't send him to Boston. Why should I?"

He seemed to expect an answer from me, so I shook my head and repeated, "Why should you?"

"In the middle of it his heart simply stopped, without warning. I can't explain it. Yes, I can. There is only one explanation. As I was moving the bone some of the marrow must have escaped into his blood stream and gone directly to his heart and stopped it. That's the only possible explanation. The only one. There are risks, there are always risks. An operating room is a place where the risks are just more formal than in other places. An operating room and a war." And I noticed that his self-control was breaking up. "Why did it have to happen to you boys so soon, here at Devon?"

"The marrow of his bone . . ." I repeated aimlessly. This at last penetrated my mind. Phineas had died from the marrow of his bone flowing down his blood stream to his heart.

I did not cry then or ever about Finny. I did not cry even when I stood watching him being lowered into his family's strait-laced burial ground outside of Boston. I could not escape a feeling that this was my own funeral, and you do not cry in that case.

## Chapter 13

The quadrangle surrounding the Far Common was never considered absolutely essential to the Devon School. The essence was elsewhere, in the older, uglier, more comfortable halls enclosing the Center Common. There the School's history had unrolled, the fabled riot scenes and Presidential visits and Civil War musterings, if not in these buildings then in their predecessors on the same site. The upperclassmen and the faculty met there, the budget was compiled there, and there students were expelled. When you said "Devon" to an alumnus ten years after graduation he visualized the Center Common.

The Far Common was different, a gift of the rich lady benefactress. It was Georgian like the rest of the school, and it combined scholasticism[1] with grace in the way which made Devon architecturally interesting. But the bricks had been laid a little too skillfully, and the woodwork was not as brittle and chipped as it should have been. It was not the essence of Devon, and so it was donated, without too serious a wrench, to the war.

The Far Common could be seen from the

window of my room, and early in June I stood at the window and watched the war moving in to occupy it. The advance guard which came down the street from the railroad station consisted of a number of Jeeps, being driven with a certain restraint, their gyration-prone[2] wheels inactive on these old ways which offered nothing bumpier than a few cobblestones. I thought the Jeeps looked noticeably uncomfortable from all the power they were not being allowed to use. There is no stage you comprehend better than the one you have just left, and as I watched the Jeeps almost asserting a wish to bounce up the side of Mount Washington at eighty miles an hour instead of rolling along this dull street, they reminded me, in a comical and a poignant way, of adolescents.

Following them there were some heavy trucks painted olive drab, and behind them came the troops. They were not very bellicose-looking;[3] their columns were straggling, their suntan uniforms had gotten rumpled in the train, and they were singing "Roll Out the Barrel."

"What's that?" Brinker said from behind me, pointing across my shoulder at some open trucks bringing up the rear. "What's in those trucks?"

"They look like sewing machines."

"They *are* sewing machines!"

"I guess a Parachute Riggers' school has to have sewing machines."

"If only Leper had enlisted in the Army Air Force and been assigned to Parachute Riggers' school . . ."

"I don't think it would have made any difference," I said. "Let's not talk about Leper."

"Leper'll be all right. There's nothing like

---

1. **scholasticism** (skə las′ tə siz′m) *n.*: Tradition.

2. **gyration-prone** (jī ra′shən prōn) *adj.*: Inclined to spin.
3. **bellicose-looking** (bel′ ə kōs′) *adj.*: Appearing warlike; eager to fight.

a discharge. Two years after the war's over people will think a Section Eight means a berth on a Pullman car."[4]

"Right. Now do you mind? Why talk about something you can't do anything about?"

"Right."

I had to be right in never talking about

4. **Pullman-car** (pool′ mən kär) *n.*: A railroad car with private compartments for sleeping.

what you could not change, and I had to make many people agree that I was right. None of them ever accused me of being responsible for what had happened to Phineas, either because they could not believe it or else because they could not understand it. I would have talked about that, but they would not, and I would not talk about Phineas in any other way.

The Jeeps, troops, and sewing machines were now drawn up next to the Far Common quadrangle. There was some kind of consultation or ceremony under way on the steps of one of the buildings, Veazy Hall. The Headmaster and a few of the senior members of the faculty stood in a group before

the door, and a number of Army Air Force officers stood in another group within easy speaking distance of them. Then the Headmaster advanced several steps and enlarged his gestures; he was apparently addressing the troops. Then an officer took his place and spoke longer and louder; we could hear his voice fairly well but not make out the words.

Around them spread a beautiful New England day. Peace lay on Devon like a blessing, the summer's peace, the reprieve,[5] New Hampshire's response to all the cogitation[6] and deadness of winter. There could be no urgency in work during such summers; any parachutes rigged would be no more effective than napkins.

Or perhaps that was only true for me and a few others, our gypsy band of the summer before. Or was it rarer even than that; had Chet and Bobby sensed it then, for instance? Had Leper, despite his trays of snails? I could be certain of only two people, Phineas and myself. So now it might be true only for me.

The company fell out and began scattering through the Far Common. Dormitory windows began to fly open and olive drab blankets were hung over the sills by the dozens to air. The sewing machines were carried with considerable exertion into Veazy Hall.

"Dad's here," said Brinker. "I told him to take his cigar down to the Butt Room. He wants to meet you."

We went downstairs and found Mr. Hadley sitting in one of the lumpy chairs, trying not to look offended by the surroundings. But he stood up and shook my hand with genuine cordiality when we came in. He was a distinguished-looking man, taller than Brinker so that his portliness[7] was not very noticeable. His hair was white, thick, and healthy-looking and his face was healthily pink.

"You boys look fine, fine," he said in his full and cordial voice, "better I would say than those doughboys—G.I.'s—I saw marching in. And how about their artillery! Sewing machines!"

Brinker slid his fingers into the back pockets of his slacks. "This war's so technical they've got to use all kinds of machines, even sewing machines, don't you think so, Gene?"

"Well," Mr. Hadley went on emphatically, "I can't imagine any man in my time settling for duty on a sewing machine. I can't picture that at all." Then his temper switched tracks and he smiled cordially again. "But then times change, and wars change. But men don't change, do they? You boys are the image of me and my gang in the old days. It does me good to see you. What are you enlisting in, son," he said, meaning me, "the Marines, the Paratroops? There are doggone many exciting things to enlist in these days. There's that bunch they call the Frogmen, underwater demolition stuff. I'd give something to be a kid again with all that to choose from."

"I was going to wait and be drafted," I replied, trying to be polite and answer his question honestly, "but if I did that they might put me straight in the infantry, and that's not only the dirtiest but also the most dangerous branch of all, the worst branch of all. So I've joined the Navy and they're sending me to Pensacola.[8] I'll probably have a lot of training, and I'll never see a foxhole. I hope."

---

5. **reprieve** (ri prēv′) n.: A temporary relief or escape.
6. **cogitation** (käj′ ə tā′ shən) n.: Meditation; seriousness.

7. **portliness** (pôrt′ lē nes) n.: Stoutness; heaviness.
8. **Pensacola** (pen′ sə kō′ lə) n.: Seaport and site of a naval base in northwest Florida, on an inlet of the Gulf of Mexico.

"Foxhole" was still a fairly new term and I wasn't sure Mr. Hadley knew what it meant. But I saw that he didn't care for the sound of what I said. "And then Brinker," I added, "is all set for the Coast Guard, which is good too." Mr. Hadley's scowl deepened, although his experienced face partially masked it.

"You know, Dad," Brinker broke in, "the Coast Guard does some very rough stuff, putting the men on the beaches, all that dangerous amphibious[9] stuff."

His father nodded slightly, looking at the floor, and then said, "You have to do what you think is the right thing, but just make sure it's the right thing in the long run, and not just for the moment. Your war memories will be with you forever, you'll be asked about them thousands of times after the war is over. People will get their respect for you from that—*partly* from that, don't get me wrong—but if you can say that you were up front where there was some real shooting going on, then that will mean a whole lot to you in years to come. I know you boys want to see plenty of action, but don't go around talking too much about being comfortable, and which branch of the service has too much dirt and stuff like that. Now I know you—I feel I know you, Gene, as well as I know Brink here—but other people might misunderstand you. You want to serve, that's all. It's your greatest moment, greatest privilege, to serve your country. We're all proud of you, and we're all—old guys like me—we're all darn jealous of you too."

I could see that Brinker was more embarrassed by this than I was, but I felt it was his responsibility to answer it. "Well, Dad," he mumbled, "we'll do what we have to."

"That's not a very good answer, Brink," he said in a tone struggling to remain reasonable.

"After all that's all we can do."

"You can do more! A lot more. If you want a military record you can be proud of, you'll do a heck of a lot more than just what you have to. Believe me."

Brinker sighed under his breath, his father stiffened, paused, then relaxed with an effort. "Your mother's out in the car. I'd better get back to her. You boys clean up—ah, those shoes," he added reluctantly, in spite of himself, having to, "those shoes, Brink, a little polish?—and we'll see you at the Inn at six."

"Okay, Dad."

His father, left, trailing the faint, unfamiliar, prosperous aroma of his cigar.

"Dad keeps making that speech about serving the country," Brinker said apologetically, "I wish he wouldn't."

"That's all right." I knew that part of friendship consisted in accepting a friend's shortcomings, which sometimes included his parents.

"I'm enlisting," he went on, "I'm going to 'serve' as he puts it, I may even get killed. But I won't have that Nathan Hale[10] attitude of his about it. It's all that World War I malarkey that gets me. They're all children about that war, did you never notice?" He flopped comfortably into the chair which had been disconcerting[11] his father. "It gives me a pain, personally. I'm not any kind of hero, and neither are you. And neither is the old man, and he never was, and I don't care

---

**9. amphibious** (am fib′ē əs) *adj.*: That can operate or travel on both land and water.

**10. Nathan Hale** (hāl) *n.*: American soldier (1755–76) in the Revolutionary War who just before being hanged by the British as a spy said, "I only regret that I have but one life to lose for my country."

**11. disconcerting** (dis′ kən surt′ iŋ) *adj.*: Upsetting the composure of; confusing.

what he says he almost did at Château-Thierry."[12]

"He's just trying to keep up with the times. He probably feels left out, being too old this time."

"Left out!" Brinker's eyes lighted up. "Left out! He and his crowd are responsible for it! And *we're* going to fight it!"

I had heard this generation-complaint from Brinker before, so often that I finally identified this as the source of his disillusionment during the winter, this generalized, faintly self-pitying resentment against millions of people he did not know. He did know his father, however, and so they were not getting along well now. In a way this was Finny's view, except that naturally he saw it comically, as a huge and intensely practical joke, played by fat and foolish old men bungling away behind the scenes.

I could never agree with either of them. It would have been comfortable, but I could not believe it. Because it seemed clear that wars were not made by generations and their special stupidities, but that wars were made instead by something ignorant in the human heart.

Brinker went upstairs to continue his packing, and I walked over to the gym to clean out my locker. As I crossed the Far Common I saw that it was rapidly becoming unrecognizable, with huge green barrels placed at many strategic points, the ground punctuated by white markers identifying offices and areas, and also certain less tangible things: a kind of snap in the atmosphere, a professional optimism, a conscious maintenance of high morale. I myself had often been happy at Devon, but such times it seemed to me that afternoon were over now.

Happiness had disappeared along with rubber, silk, and many other staples, to be replaced by the wartime synthetic, high morale, for the Duration.

At the gym a platoon was undressing in the locker room. The best that could be said for them physically was that they looked wiry in their startling sets of underwear, which were the color of moss.

I never talked about Phineas and neither did anyone else; he was, however, present in every moment of every day since Dr. Stanpole had told me. Finny had a vitality which could not be quenched so suddenly, even by the marrow of his bone. That was why I couldn't say anything or listen to anything about him, because he endured so forcefully that what I had to say would have seemed crazy to anyone else—I could not use the past tense, for instance—and what they had to say would be incomprehensible to me. During the time I was with him, Phineas created an atmosphere in which I continued now to live, a way of sizing up the world with erratic and entirely personal reservations, letting its rocklike facts sift through and be accepted only a little at a time, only as much as he could assimilate without a sense of chaos and loss.

No one else I have ever met could do this. All others at some point found something in themselves pitted violently against something in the world around them. With those of my year this point often came when they grasped the fact of the war. When they began to feel that there was this overwhelmingly hostile thing in the world with them, then the simplicity and unity of their characters broke and they were not the same again.

Phineas alone had escaped this. He possessed an extra vigor, a heightened confidence in himself, a serene capacity for affection which saved him. Nothing as he

---

**12. Château-Thierry** (shȧ tŏ tye rē') *n.*: Town in northern France that was the site of a famous battle in World War I.

was growing up at home, nothing at Devon, nothing even about the war had broken his harmonious and natural unity. So at last I had.

The parachute riggers sprinted out of the hallway toward the playing fields. From my locker I collected my sneakers and gym pants and then turned away, leaving the door ajar for the first time, forlornly open and abandoned, the locker unlocked. This was more final than the moment when the Headmaster handed me my diploma. My schooling was over now.

I walked down the aisle past the rows of lockers, and instead of turning left toward the exit leading back to my dormitory, I turned right and followed the Army Air Force out onto the playing fields of Devon. A high wooden platform had been erected there and on it stood a barking instructor, giving the rows of men below him calisthenics by the numbers.

This kind of regimentation would fasten itself on me in a few weeks. I no longer had any qualms[13] about that, although I couldn't help being glad that it would not be at Devon, at anywhere like Devon, that I would have that. I had no qualms at all; in fact I could feel now the gathering, glowing sense of sureness in the face of it. I was ready for the war, now that I no longer had any hatred to contribute to it. My fury was gone, I felt it gone, dried up at the source, withered and lifeless. Phineas had absorbed it and taken it with him, and I was rid of it forever.

The P.T. instructor's voice, like a frog's croak amplified a hundred times, blared out the Army's numerals, "Hut! Hew! Hee! Hore!" behind me as I started back toward the dormitory, and my feet of course could not help but begin to fall involuntarily into step with that coarse, compelling voice, which carried to me like an air-raid siren across the fields and commons.

They fell into step then, as they fell into step a few weeks later under the influence of an even louder voice and a stronger sun. Down there I fell into step as well as my nature, Phineas-filled, would allow.

I never killed anybody and I never developed an intense level of hatred for the enemy. Because my war ended before I ever put on a uniform; I was on active duty all my time at school; I killed my enemy there.

Only Phineas never was afraid, only Phineas never hated anyone. Other people experienced this fearful shock somewhere, this sighting of the enemy, and so began an obsessive labor of defense, began to parry[14] the menace they saw facing them by developing a particular frame of mind, "You see," their behavior toward everything and everyone proclaimed, "I am a humble ant, I am nothing, I am not worthy of this menace," or else, like Mr. Ludsbury, "How dare this threaten me, I am much too good for this sort of handling, I shall rise above this," or else, like Quackenbush, strike out at it always and everywhere, or else, like Brinker, develop a careless general resentment against it, or else, like Leper, emerge from a protective cloud of vagueness only to meet it, the horror, face to face, just as he had always feared, and so give up the struggle absolutely.

All of them, all except Phineas, constructed at infinite cost to themselves these Maginot Lines[15] against this enemy they thought they saw across the frontier, this enemy who never attacked that way—if he ever attacked at all; if he was indeed the enemy.

---

**13. qualms:** (kwämz) *n.:* Feelings of doubt or uneasiness; misgivings.

**14. parry** (par′ ē) *v.:* Ward off.
**15. Maginot Lines** (mazh′ ə nō′ līnz′): A system of fortifications built before World War II on the eastern frontier of France to prevent invasion that were by-passed by German armies and thus proved useless.

# THINKING ABOUT THE SELECTION
## Recalling

1. Why did Finny give up his theory about there being no war?
2. What is Brinker investigating, and who are the witnesses?
3. What happens to Finny after his fall down the staircase?
4. Explain the understanding Finny and Gene reach about the original accident?

## Interpreting

5. How has Gene changed during the novel?
6. In what way was Finny a war casualty?
7. Interpret the last line of the novel.

## Applying

8. Comment on Gene's view that "wars were not made by generations and their special stupidities, but . . . instead by something ignorant in the human heart."
9. Why do you think people set up Maginot Lines?

# ANALYZING LITERATURE
## Identifying a Theme

The **theme** of a novel is its insight into life. The main events in the plot usually reveal the theme. In addition, the novelist may include symbols that suggest thematic concerns.

1. State the theme of *A Separate Peace.*
2. Give a quotation that hints at the theme.
3. Name events in the story that relate to the theme and that support your idea about it.

# CRITICAL THINKING AND READING
## Evaluating the Novel

When **critics** evaluate the work of other writers, they consider many factors in their criticisms, including use of language and imagery, fullness of characterization, and logical consistency of plot.

1. How does Knowles use language to describe the setting or explain ideas?
2. Explain if and how the author makes you understand and care about the characters.
3. Is the plot logically consistent? (If not, what events seem out of place?) Explain.

# THINKING AND WRITING
## Responding to Criticism

Read the excerpt from a critic's evaluation of *A Separate Peace.* Make notes about whether you agree or disagree with the critic's points. Then draft a response, adding your own evaluation of the novel. Proofread carefully.

I make no reservations whatever about this book. It is a beautifully written story. For style and imagery *A Separate Peace* ranks with the work of the very best young American novelists, such as William Styron. At the same time it has none of the false symbolism which so many Americans employ in an attempt to add depth to their work. But style and imagery are only the writer's tools; if a work of fiction has only these, it becomes mere decoration, with an immediate impact, but no depth. Here we may read messages which only become clear much later, after we have pondered long over the disturbing allegories. The interpretation of the messages must be highly subjective, which holds true of all major works of art. It is a fine first novel, one that should be read by every person who likes to think about a book after reading it.

Douglas Aitken
*San Francisco Chronicle*
June 26, 1960

# Making Generalizations

A general statement or rule drawn from specific facts or cases is called **a generalization.** For a generalization to be considered valid, it must apply to more than one case or situation. Form generalizations based on the information provided in order to read with deeper insight and greater appreciation.

**Evaluating Generalizations**

Evaluate the generalizations you form as you read by being aware of how many situations your generalization encompasses. Remember that a sound generalization must apply to a number of situations, but it does not have to apply to all cases.

**Overgeneralizations**

An **overgeneralization** is a generalization that is invalid because it is too broad. There are words that tip you off to overgeneralizations. Some of these words are "always," "everyone," "all," "must," "no one," and "never." Using these words may make a generalization too broad. On the other hand, using qualifying words such as "several," "many," "most," "usually," "often," and "sometimes" will help you avoid making overgeneralizations.

**Activity**

Think about *A Separate Peace*. Decide which of the following generalizations are sound and which are overgeneralizations. Explain your answers.

1. All school boys are reckless.
2. Some school boys are reckless.
3. All roommates at boarding school become best friends.
4. Sometimes roommates at boarding school become best friends.
5. A person's guilt often makes him or her act strangely.

You should have selected sentences 2, 4, and 5 as sound. The facts in the novel support them, and they apply to a broad number of cases. Sentences 1 and 3 are too broad. From this novel, which follows the lives of only a handful of boys, you cannot conclude that all boys are reckless or that all roommates become best friends.

**Hasty Generalizations**

A **hasty generalization** is a generalization that is made prematurely because it is based on too little evidence. For example, imagine that on your first visit to a school, you heard some students shouting in the hallways. You then said, "Students in this school are unruly." Your generalization would be hasty, since you were basing it on only one experience. Perhaps you caught the students on a bad day. Normally, they are quite well behaved.

## Guidelines

- Make sure you understand the main idea and supporting details of the material.
- Make sure the conclusions you draw are adequately supported by facts or evidence.
- Make sure the generalization you draw applies to many different cases or situations.
- Make sure you do not use words such as "always" or "must," which do not allow for any exceptions and which make the generalizations too broad.

## Activity

Read each of the following sentences based on *The Pearl*. Tell whether or not the generalization is sound. Explain your answers.
1. All pearl dealers are greedy and evil.
2. Sudden wealth can mean new and unforeseen problems for the recipients.
3. At the time of this novel, many Mexican pearl divers had to work very hard to earn a living.
4. All pearl divers have to work very hard to earn a living.
5. Some pearl dealers do not offer fair prices to divers.
6. The more money you have, the more money you want.
7. Sudden wealth makes other people both envious and suspicious.
8. No one ever gained happiness from sudden wealth.

## Activity

Think about *The Pearl* and *A Separate Peace*.
1. What generalizations can you make about the lives of pearl divers in Mexico in the early 1900's? Support your generalizations with evidence from the novel.
2. What generalizations can you make about the lives of high school boys going to private school during World War II? Support your answers with evidence from the novel.

# YOU THE WRITER

**Assignment**

**1.** Imagine that you meet one of the characters in *The Pearl* or *A Separate Peace*. Which character would you like to meet? What would you discuss? What would you like to ask? Write a dialogue between you and this character.

    **Prewriting.** Write a list of all the characters in one of the novels. Circle the name of the character you would most like to meet. Freewrite about what you would like to talk about.

    **Writing.** Write your dialogue. Try to focus your dialogue around one topic. Use appropriate language that is consistent with the way this character speaks in the novel.

    **Revising.** Make certain that your dialogue is believable and interesting. Have you used quotation marks to indicate when each speaker is talking?

**Assignment**

**2.** You are a world-renowned film producer and have been hired to film either *The Pearl* or *A Separate Peace*. Choose one of the novels, and select one powerful scene from it. Write a description of how you will film the scene—either at an on-location shoot or a studio set.

    **Prewriting.** Skim through the novel you have chosen to find a scene you would like to film. Brainstorm about how you would film it effectively, and jot down notes about the setting.

    **Writing.** Use your prewriting notes to write a description of your studio or on-location set. Make certain that you explain which scene you are going to film in your introductory sentence.

    **Revising.** Make certain that you have explained what you are going to film and how you plan to do so. Have you used vivid sensory details?

**Assignment**

**3.** Rewrite the ending of either *The Pearl* or *A Separate Peace*, providing an outcome different from the one in the novel.

    **Prewriting.** Make a semantic map to explain what happens and identify who is involved.

    **Writing.** Write your own ending to one of the novels, using the map you made as a guideline. Make certain that your ending differs significantly from the novel's ending.

    **Revising.** Although your ending is new, it should result logically from the previous events. Check to see that it does. If not, make changes in it now.

# YOU THE CRITIC

**Assignment**

**1.** Write an essay comparing and contrasting two characters in two of the novels.

**Prewriting.** Prepare a chart showing the similarities and differences between the two characters.

**Writing.** Write the first draft of your essay. Begin by showing how the characters are alike. Then show how they differ. Finally, explain the effects the similarities and differences have on their relationship.

**Revising.** When you revise, make sure you have included enough details to reveal the similarities and differences.

**Assignment**

**2.** Imagine that you are in a book club that meets every week. Interpret the theme of either *The Pearl* or *A Separate Peace* for club members. Write a summary of the novel's theme that you will present to the club.

**Prewriting.** Skim one of the novels to remind you of its theme. In your own words, jot down your thoughts about the theme of the novel.

**Writing.** Use your prewriting notes as the basis for your interpretation. Write an introduction and a conclusion. Include evidence from the novel that supports your interpretation.

**Revising.** Make certain that your interpretation includes a strong introduction, a conclusion, and details and examples to support your interpretation.

**Assignment**

**3.** As the new book reviewer for the *Sunday Pen and Ink,* you will review either *The Pearl* or *A Separate Peace*. Write a review that discusses your positive and negative reactions. Discuss why you would or would not recommend the novel to your readers.

**Prewriting.** Make two lists of your impressions, one noting what you liked about the novel and the other noting what you did not like.

**Writing.** Write your book review. Begin by stating the title and author of the novel; then give your negative reactions in one paragraph and your positive reactions in the other. Summarize your feelings about the novel in your conclusion.

**Revising.** Make certain that your book review has a strong introduction and conclusion. Does it include reasons and examples from the novel that support your opinions?

# HANDBOOK OF WRITING ABOUT LITERATURE

**SECTION 1:**    **UNDERSTANDING THE WRITING PROCESS** . . . . . . . . . . . . . **944**

  **Lesson 1:**    **Prewriting** . . . . . . . . . . . . . . . . . . . . . . . . . . . . . . . . . . . . . . . . . . . **944**

       *CASE STUDY*   *945*
       *ACTIVITIES AND ASSIGNMENTS*   *946*

  **Lesson 2:**    **Drafting and Revising** . . . . . . . . . . . . . . . . . . . . . . . . . . . . . . **947**

       *CASE STUDY*   *948*
       *ACTIVITIES AND ASSIGNMENTS*   *948*

  **Lesson 3:**    **Proofreading and Publishing** . . . . . . . . . . . . . . . . . . . . . . . **950**

       *CASE STUDY*   *951*
       *ACTIVITIES AND ASSIGNMENTS*   *951*

**SECTION 2:**    **UNDERSTANDING THE PARTS OF A LITERARY WORK: ANALYSIS AND INTERPRETATION** . . . . . . . . . . . . . . . . . . . . **952**

  **Lesson 4:**    **Writing About Images** . . . . . . . . . . . . . . . . . . . . . . . . . . . . . . . **952**

       *CASE STUDY*   *952*
       *ACTIVITIES AND ASSIGNMENTS*   *954*

  **Lesson 5:**    **Writing About Sound** . . . . . . . . . . . . . . . . . . . . . . . . . . . . . . . . **955**

       *CASE STUDY*   *955*
       *ACTIVITIES AND ASSIGNMENTS*   *956*

  **Lesson 6:**    **Writing About Figures of Speech** . . . . . . . . . . . . . . . . . . . **958**

       *CASE STUDY*   *958*
       *ACTIVITIES AND ASSIGNMENTS*   *959*

  **Lesson 7:**    **Writing About Setting** . . . . . . . . . . . . . . . . . . . . . . . . . . . . . . . **960**

       *CASE STUDY*   *960*
       *ACTIVITIES AND ASSIGNMENTS*   *961*

  **Lesson 8:**    **Writing About Plot** . . . . . . . . . . . . . . . . . . . . . . . . . . . . . . . . . . **963**

       *CASE STUDY*   *963*
       *ACTIVITIES AND ASSIGNMENTS*   *964*

  **Lesson 9:**    **Writing About Character** . . . . . . . . . . . . . . . . . . . . . . . . . . . . **966**

       *CASE STUDY*   *966*
       *ACTIVITIES AND ASSIGNMENTS*   *967*

  **Lesson 10:**    **Writing About Point of View** . . . . . . . . . . . . . . . . . . . . . . . . **969**

       *CASE STUDY*   *969*
       *ACTIVITIES AND ASSIGNMENTS*   *970*

**Lesson 11:**   **Writing About Theme** . . . . . . . . . . . . . . . . . . . . . . . . . . . . . . . . . . . **972**

        *CASE STUDY*   *972*
        *ACTIVITIES AND ASSIGNMENTS*   *973*

**SECTION 3:**   **UNDERSTANDING THE WORK AS A WHOLE:**
                   **INTERPRETATION AND SYNTHESIS** . . . . . . . . . . . . . . . . . . . **975**

**Lesson 12:**   **Writing About Fiction** . . . . . . . . . . . . . . . . . . . . . . . . . . . . . . . . . . . . **975**

        *CASE STUDY*   *975*
        *ACTIVITIES AND ASSIGNMENTS*   *976*

**Lesson 13:**   **Writing About a Poem** . . . . . . . . . . . . . . . . . . . . . . . . . . . . . . . . . . . **978**

        *CASE STUDY*   *978*
        *ACTIVITIES AND ASSIGNMENTS*   *979*

**Lesson 14:**   **Writing About Drama** . . . . . . . . . . . . . . . . . . . . . . . . . . . . . . . . . . . . **981**

        *CASE STUDY*   *981*
        *ACTIVITIES AND ASSIGNMENTS*   *982*

**SECTION 4:**   **JUDGING A LITERARY WORK, EVALUATION** . . . . . . . . . . . **984**

**Lesson 15:**   **Evaluating a Literary Work** . . . . . . . . . . . . . . . . . . . . . . . . . . . . . . . **984**

        *CASE STUDY*   *985*
        *ACTIVITIES AND ASSIGNMENTS*   *985*

**Lesson 16:**   **Writing a Comparative Evaluation** . . . . . . . . . . . . . . . . . . . . . . . . **987**

        *CASE STUDY*   *987*
        *ACTIVITIES AND ASSIGNMENTS*   *988*

**SECTION 5:**   **WRITING CREATIVELY** . . . . . . . . . . . . . . . . . . . . . . . . . . . . . . . **990**

**Lesson 17:**   **Writing a Short Story** . . . . . . . . . . . . . . . . . . . . . . . . . . . . . . . . . . . **990**

        *CASE STUDY*   *991*
        *ACTIVITIES AND ASSIGNMENTS*   *992*

**Lesson 18:**   **Writing a Poem** . . . . . . . . . . . . . . . . . . . . . . . . . . . . . . . . . . . . . . . . **993**

        *CASE STUDY*   *994*
        *ACTIVITIES AND ASSIGNMENTS*   *994*

**Lesson 19:**   **Writing a Short Dramatic Sketch** . . . . . . . . . . . . . . . . . . . . . . . . . **996**

        *CASE STUDY*   *996*
        *ACTIVITIES AND ASSIGNMENTS*   *998*

**Lesson 20:**   **Writing a Personal Essay** . . . . . . . . . . . . . . . . . . . . . . . . . . . . . . . **999**

        *CASE STUDY*   *999*
        *ACTIVITIES AND ASSIGNMENTS*   *1001*

# SECTION 1: UNDERSTANDING THE WRITING PROCESS

## Lesson 1: Prewriting

The process of writing involves five major stages. In the *prewriting* stage you plan the work to be done. In the *drafting* stage, you get your ideas down on paper. In the *revising* stage, you rework your written draft. In the *proofreading* stage, you check your final draft for errors in spelling and mechanics. Finally, in the *publishing* stage, you share your work with others. This lesson will explain the steps you should take during the prewriting stage.

### STEP 1: ANALYZE THE SITUATION

*Analysis* is the process of dividing something into parts and then studying these parts to see what they are and how they are related. When you are given a writing assignment, begin by analyzing the situation in the following parts.

1. *Topic* (the subject you will be writing about): What, exactly, is this subject? Can you state it in a sentence? Is your subject too broad or too narrow?
2. *Purpose* (what you want your writing to accomplish): Is your purpose to tell a story? To describe? To explain? To persuade? To entertain?
3. *Audience* (the people for whom you are writing): What are the backgrounds of these people? Do they already know a great deal about your topic? Will you have to provide basic background information?
4. *Voice* (the way the writing will sound to the reader): What impressions do you want to make on your readers? What tone should your writing have? Should the writing be formal or informal? Should it be objective or subjective?
5. *Content* (the subject and all the information

provided about it): How much do you already know about your subject? What will you have to find out? Will you have to do some research? If so, what sources can you use? Can you use books? Magazines? Newspapers? Reference works? Interviews with other people? Your own memories and experiences?
6. *Form* (the shape the writing will take, including its length and organization): What will the final piece of writing look like? How long will it be? Will it be written in one or more paragraphs? Will it have a distinct introduction, body, and conclusion? What method of organization will you use?

Asking questions such as these will help you to clarify the writing task. In the course of asking and answering these questions, you will have to make many decisions. These decisions will determine what your writing will be like and what steps you will have to take to produce it.

### STEP 2: MAKE A PLAN

After analyzing the writing situation, you will probably find that some of your questions remain unanswered. For example, you might know what your topic, purpose, audience, voice, and form will be, but you might be unsure about your content. The next step in prewriting is to make a plan for answering your unanswered questions. For example, you might plan to do some research in the library to gather content information.

### STEP 3: GATHER INFORMATION

There are many possible sources of information for use in writing. The following methods are useful for gathering the information you need.

1. *Freewriting:* Without stopping to punctuate or to think about spelling or form, write everything that comes into your mind as you think about your topic.

2. *Clustering:* Write your topic in the center of a sheet of blank paper. Then think about the topic and jot down other ideas that occur to you. Draw lines connecting these ideas to your topic. Then think about each of these ideas, write down new ideas, and connect them with lines. Continue until your paper is full.

3. *Questioning:* Make a list of *who, what, where, when, why,* and *how* questions related to your topic. Use your own knowledge or outside sources to answer these questions.

4. *Charting* or *listing:* Make lists of key ideas or concepts related to your topic. List the parts of your topic. If appropriate, make a chart of pros and cons, a time line, a tree diagram, or some other type of chart of information related to your topic.

5. *Researching:* Check outside sources of information such as books, magazines, and reference works. Interview people who are knowledgeable about your topic.

6. *Analyzing:* Break your topic down into its parts, study these parts, and think about how they are related.

Each of these techniques can also be used to generate a topic idea.

## STEP 4: ORGANIZE YOUR NOTES

After you have gathered the information you will use, organize this information in a logical way. Some common methods of organization include *chronological order, spatial order, degree order* (less to more or more to less), and *order of importance, value, utility,* or *familiarity.* Once you have organized your information, you may want to make a rough outline.

## CASE STUDY: PREWRITING

Anthony's English teacher told the students to write descriptive paragraphs about their neighborhood or environment.

Anthony, a city-dweller, wanted to make the city his topic, but he wasn't sure about what to focus on. He tried clustering to come up with ideas.

As he worked, Anthony realized that by focusing on his own street, he was able to say something about the city as a whole. Then he was able to prepare the following plan.

- Topic: my street in the city
- Purpose: to describe and to inform
- Audience: the teacher and the class
- Voice: informal but positive; I want readers to like the street I describe

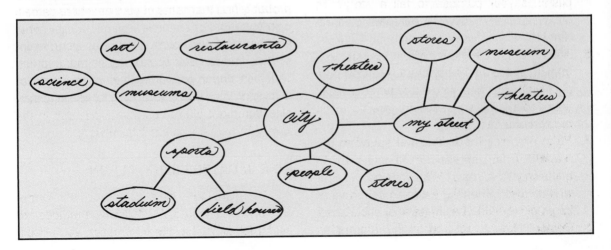

- Form: paragraph
- Content: information on the things that are within walking distance of my apartment

Anthony decided to gather information in list form. He made his preliminary list in study hall. On his way home, he kept his eyes open and was able to add to his list as a result of his observations. Here is a portion of Anthony's list.

- Jade Pavilion Chinese restaurant
- small museum—1820 house
- all three- and four-story buildings
- people everywhere
- the Palace movie theater
- a college playhouse
- Yesteryear Antiques
- Sweaterville
- a video rental store
- Pop's Pop-In (convenience store)
- parking on just one side
- Gino's Pizza
- the park around the corner

When Anthony looked over his list, he realized that he had far too much information for a paragraph. He decided to focus on this main idea.

Living in the city is very convenient. Within a few blocks of my house, I can find almost anything I could ever need or want.

Anthony crossed out the items on his list that did not fit this idea. Then he organized his remaining ideas under three supporting points:

1. Shops for any need
2. Entertainment of every type
3. Food for any taste

Anthony grouped his details under these points and ended up with an outline that he could use as he began to write.

## ACTIVITIES AND ASSIGNMENTS

A. Answer the following questions about the case study:
1. For what purpose did Anthony use clustering? For what purpose did he make a list?
2. Which items on Anthony's list did he probably cross out as he worked on Step 3?
3. Which items on his list did he include under each of his planned supporting points?

B. Do prewriting for a paragraph of your own. Follow these steps:
1. Choose one of the following topics or one of your own:

  your neighborhood    sports
  student concerns    music

2. Prepare a planning chart. Take notes about the topic, purpose, audience, voice, form, and content of your paragraph.
3. Use a prewriting technique—freewriting, clustering, questioning, making a list or chart, using outside sources, or outlining—to narrow your topic to a manageable size and to gather information.
4. Organize your notes. Decide on your main idea, find the key supporting points, and list details under supporting points to create a rough outline. Save your notes for use in a later lesson.

# Lesson 2: Drafting and Revising

## WRITING A DRAFT

Once you have found a topic, taken notes, and organized them, you are ready to write a preliminary version, or *draft*, of your paper. Keep the following points in mind as you draft a piece of writing:

1. Write the draft in a way that feels comfortable to you. Some writers like to dash off a draft as fast as possible, to keep their pens going as fast as their ideas flow. Others prefer to draft more slowly, considering how each idea should be presented and doing some revision as they go. Whichever way works best for you is the method you should use. You may find that the fast method works well in some writing situations while the slow method works better in other situations.

2. Do not aim for perfection in the draft. If you work fast, you won't have time to worry; but even if you work slowly, do not get too caught up in any section. Move on; get something on paper. Some writers use codes: They underline words or sections they want to work on further, or put a small question mark above words they're not sure how to spell. These techniques are fine because they do not unduly interrupt the flow of writing.

3. Keep your notes beside you as you write, and keep your purpose and audience in mind. Doing so will guide you as you move from idea to idea.

4. As you draft, feel free to change your original plan. Remember that writing is a form of thinking. If you think of new ideas, add them. If you discover that some ideas in your rough outline don't seem to work after all, eliminate them.

5. If you discover a better approach as you are writing, feel free to start a new draft at any time. Some writers discard many drafts before they are happy with one. If the piece you are working on just doesn't seem right, start again.

## REVISING THE DRAFT

Once you have completed your draft, you can begin revising it. This is the stage during which you work on your draft to make it as good as possible. If time permits, put your draft aside for a day before you revise; doing so will allow you to bring a fresh eye to your work.

Keep in mind that while some drafts may need very little revision, some will require major reworking.

Use the Checklist for Revision on page 948 as you revise your work.

The symbols in the following chart can be helpful when revising a piece of writing:

| EDITORIAL SYMBOLS | | |
|---|---|---|
| *Symbol* | *Meaning* | *Example* |
| ↻ | move text | ˅screams suddenly |
| ℒ℘ — | delete | the silent, quiet room |
| ∧ | insert | a ⌃yellow dress *(lovely)* |
| ⌢ ⌣ | close up; no space | sun shine |
| ⊙ | insert period | the end⌄ knew |
| ⋏ | insert comma | left⌄but they |
| ˅ | add apostrophe | Rons contribution |
| ˅ ˅ | add quotation marks | Chee's Daughter |
| ∿ | transpose | to quietly leave |
| ⫲ | begin paragraph | trees. ⫫Next we |
| / | make lower case | the Main Street in the town |
| ≡ | capitalize | on main street |

## CHECKLIST FOR REVISION

*Topic and Purpose*
- ☐ Is my main idea clear?
- ☐ Does the writing achieve its purpose?

*Content and Development*
- ☐ Have I developed the main idea completely?
- ☐ Have I provided examples or details that support the statements I have made?
- ☐ Are my sources of information unbiased, up-to-date, and authoritative?
- ☐ Have I avoided including unnecessary or unrelated ideas?
- ☐ If I have used quotations, are these quotations verbatim, or word-for-word?

*Form*
- ☐ Have I following a logical method of organization?
- ☐ Have I used transitions to make the connections between ideas clear?
- ☐ Does the writing have a clear introduction, body, and conclusion?

*Audience*
- ☐ Will my audience understand what I have said?
- ☐ Will my audience find the writing interesting?
- ☐ Will my audience respond in the way I have intended?

*Voice and Word Choice*
- ☐ Does the writing convey the impression I have intended it to convey?
- ☐ Is my language appropriate?
- ☐ Have I avoided vague, undefined terms?
- ☐ Have I used vivid, specific nouns, verbs, and adjectives?
- ☐ Have I avoided jargon?
- ☐ Have I avoided clichés, slang, euphemisms, and gobbledygook except for humorous effect?

Life at 132 Lincoln Street

~~Why where I live~~ is very convenient.

Whatever I need to buy is very close. Just

next door is Pops Pop-In where I can get
*paper and pens.* *a new sweater or a gift,*
snacks and ~~supplies.~~ If I need ~~something,~~

there's two shops within a block of my apart-

ment. ~~I can get antiques at Yesteryear.~~ I can

*find*
~~get~~ records and tapes just down the street at
*outland event entertainment, that's close by, too.*
Rockys music land. The Theater around the
*prefer*
corner has first-run movies, if I ~~want to get~~ a

home movie there's a video store downstairs.

Three or four times a year the local colledge

puts on plays at there play house down the

street. The minipark in the next block has a
*As for food,*
basketball court and a bocche court. I can

walk to almost anything my heart desires ~~for~~ *or*
~~food.~~ The Jade Pavilion chinese restaurant,

Gino's Pizza, Hamburger Heaven, the Deli
*All of this is within two blocks of*
Delight. ~~I call that convenient.~~
*my apartment—Now that's what I call*
*convenient*

## CASE STUDY: DRAFTING AND REVISING

Anthony kept his notes from the previous lesson next to him as he began drafting his paragraph. Then, as he worked on his draft, he used

## ACTIVITIES AND ASSIGNMENTS

A. Answer the following questions about Anthony's draft:

1. Which sentence is Anthony's topic sentence? Why did he change the wording of this sentence?

2. What sentence did Anthony eliminate? Why did he do so?

3. What is the purpose of the sentence Anthony added between sentences 6 and 7?
4. Why did Anthony change the wording in the next-to-last sentence?
5. Why did Anthony change his last sentence?
6. In which sentences did Anthony replace general words with specific words?

B. Use the notes you prepared in the previous lesson to draft and revise a paragaph. Follow these steps:

1. If you have not already done so, prepare a rough outline. Indicate your main idea, group your notes into several subtopics, and list your details under each subtopic.
2. Write an introductory, or topic, sentence that states your main idea.
3. Keep your notes next to you as you draft the body of your paragraph.
4. Draft a conclusion that ties your ideas together.
5. Use the checklist in this lesson to revise your paragraph. Work until you can answer "yes" to each question. Use editorial symbols to indicate changes.

# Lesson 3: Proofreading and Publishing

## Proofreading

After you have revised your draft, you must proofread it to eliminate errors. Use the Checklist for Proofreading as you work:

---

### CHECKLIST FOR PROOFREADING

*Grammar and Usage*
- ☐ Are all my sentences complete? That is, have I avoided sentence fragments?
- ☐ Do all my sentences express just one complete thought? That is, have I avoided run-on sentences?
- ☐ Do my verbs agree with their subjects?
- ☐ Have I used all the words in my paper correctly? Am I sure the meaning and connotation of each word fits the writing?
- ☐ Does each pronoun clearly refer to something?
- ☐ Have I used adjectives and adverbs correctly?

*Spelling*
- ☐ Is every word correctly spelled?
- ☐ Have I double-checked the spelling of proper nouns?

*Punctuation*
- ☐ Does each sentence end with a punctuation mark?
- ☐ Have I used commas, semicolons, colons, hyphens, dashes, parentheses, quotation marks, and apostrophes correctly?

*Capitalization*
- ☐ Have I eliminated unnecessary capital letters?
- ☐ Have I correctly capitalized all words that need capital letters?

---

If your answer to any of these questions is "no," make the necessary corrections on your paper. Consult a dictionary, writing textbook, or handbook of style as necessary.

When you are satisfied with the grammar and mechanics of your paper, neatly recopy or type it. Use correct manuscript form:
1. Indent the first line(s) of the paragraph(s).
2. Write your name and the page number in the top right-hand corner of each page.
3. If you type, double-space the manuscript.

Finally, proofread the final copy of your paper one more time, checking to make sure that it is free of errors.

## PROOFREADING AND PUBLISHING

Some writing, such as diaries or journals, is intended to be kept private; other writing should be shared. You will, of course, submit most writing you do in school to your teachers. There are, however, other ways to publish it as well. Here are a few ideas:
1. Read your work to your family, or give it to family members to read.
2. Make a second copy of your work and send it to a relative or friend.
3. Trade papers with a friend and read each other's writing.
4. Read your paper aloud in class.
5. Share your work with a small group of classmates.
6. Post your paper on the bulletin board.
7. Recast your ideas in the form of a letter, and send it to an appropriate recipient.
8. Submit your work to the school newspaper or to the school literary magazine.
9. Work with your classmates to put together a class magazine.
10. Submit your writing to a local newspaper or newsletter.
11. Enter your writing in a literary contest for student writers.
12. Submit your writing to a magazine that publishes work by young writers.

13. Save your writing in a folder and bind appropriate pieces together to create your own book.

## CASE STUDY: PROOFREADING AND PUBLISHING

After Anthony revised his draft for content, form, and word choice, he used the Checklist for Proofreading in this lesson to find and correct errors in his paragraph. On the right is Anthony's paragraph with his corrections marked.

Anthony made two clean final copies of his paragraph and proofread them one last time. One copy he submitted in class; the other he sent to a cousin with whom he has a running argument: Anthony claims city life is best, while Ricky prefers suburban or country life.

## ACTIVITIES AND ASSIGNMENTS

A. Answer the following questions about the case study in this lesson.
1. What run-on sentence did Anthony correct? How did he correct it?
2. What sentence fragment did Anthony find and correct? How did he correct it?
3. What errors in subject-verb agreement did Anthony correct?
4. What spelling errors did Anthony correct?
5. What punctuation errors did Anthony correct?
6. What errors in capitalization did Anthony correct?

B. Proofread and publish the paragraph you revised in the previous lesson. Follow these steps:
1. Use the Checklist for Proofreading as you work on your paragraph. Evaluate and correct your grammar and usage, spelling, punctuation, and capitalization. Consult reference books as necessary.

Life at 1302 Lincoln Street is very convenient. Whatever I need to buy is very close. Just next door is Pop's Pop-In where I can get snacks and soda, paper and pens. If I need a new sweater or a gift, there *are* two shops within a block of my apartment. Records and tapes I can find just down the street at Rocky's music land. The *T*heater around the corner has first-run movies, *but* if I prefer a home mov*i*e there's a video store downstairs. Three or four times a year the local *college* puts on plays at its play house down the street. The minipark in the next block has a basketball court and a *bocce* court. As for food, I can walk to almost anything my heart desires. *T*he Jade Pavilion *c*hinese restaurant, Gino's Pizza, Hamburger Heaven, the Deli Delight. All of these are within two blocks of my apartment—now that's what I'd call a convenient neighborhood.

2. Write or type a clean final copy of your paragraph. Proofread this copy to be sure you have not introduced any new errors. Make any corrections very neatly.
3. Share your paragraph with a friend before you submit it in class.

# SECTION 2: UNDERSTANDING THE PARTS OF A LITERARY WORK: ANALYSIS AND INTERPRETATION

## Lesson 4: Writing About Images

### WHAT IS AN IMAGE?

An *image* is a word or a phrase that appeals to one or more of the five senses—sight, hearing, touch, taste, or smell. The following lines contain images of sight:

GARDEN

Ho-O

Mossbound and weatherworn,
the boulders stand:
Around them flows a stream
of silver sand.

The third line of the following stanza, from Theodore Roethke's "The Heron," contains an image of sound:

He jerks a frog across his bony lip,
Then points his heavy bill above the
wood.
The wide wings flap but once to lift him
up.
A single ripple starts from where he
stood.

Some poems also contain images of touch, taste, and smell.

### WHY WRITERS USE IMAGES

Writers use images for two reasons:
1. to create pictures of people, places, and things,
2. to create moods, or feelings.
The images in the following poem are used both to create a picture of a person in a frozen landscape and to create a mood of fear:

COLD FEAR

Elizabeth Madox Roberts

As I came home through Drury's Woods,

My face stung in the hard sleet.
The rough ground kept its frozen tracks;
They stumbled my feet.
The trees shook off the blowing frost.
The wind found out my coat was thin.
It tried to tear my clothes away.
And the cold came in.

The following images create a picture:
1. (stinging) face
2. "hard sleet"
3. "frozen tracks"
4. "blowing frost"
5. "cold"
These images create a feeling of fear:
1. "Drury's woods"
2. "rough ground"
3. "(tracks) stumbled my feet"
4. (wind) "found out" (blows through) my thin coat
5. (wind) "tried to tear my clothes"

### CASE STUDY: WRITING ABOUT IMAGES

#### Prewriting

Lisa and her classmates were directed to find a poem rich in sensory images and to write a paragraph analyzing the effects of those images. Lisa chose the following poem:

KNOXVILLE, TENNESSEE

Nikki Giovanni

I always like summer
best
you can eat fresh corn
from daddy's garden
and okra
and greens

and cabbage
and lots of
barbecue
and buttermilk
and homemade ice-cream
at the church picnic
and listen to
gospel music
outside
at the church
homecoming
and go to the mountains with
your grandmother
and go barefooted
and be warm
all the time
not only when you go to bed
and asleep

Lisa knew that she must check the definitions of unfamiliar words in the poem. She suspected that okra is a vegetable and confirmed it by checking a dictionary. (She was surprised to learn that okra is the "gumbo" in chicken gumbo soup.) She also learned that gospel music is a kind of folk singing associated with spirited religious gatherings.

Next, Lisa made a list of images in the poem:

- Images of sight:
   the summer garden
   the churchyard
   the mountains

- Images of sound:
   the gospel music

- Images of touch:
   being barefooted
   feeling warm

- Images of taste:
   corn, okra, greens, cabbage, barbecue,
   buttermilk, ice-cream

- Images of smell:
   none

As Lisa prepared and thought about her list, she asked herself what overall effect was created by these images and what mood was evoked by them.

- Picture: the rich pleasures of summer days in Knoxville; carefree childhood

- Mood: the warmth of summer that comes from more than the sun

Lisa planned to mention the title and subject of the poem in her topic sentence. In the body of the paragraph, she decided to discuss the images used in the poem to describe the garden, the churchyard, and the mountains. In her conclusion Lisa planned to show how the word *warm*, near the end of the poem, tied the images together and expressed the mood created by them.

### Drafting and Revising

Lisa kept the poem and her notes handy as she wrote the first draft of her paragraph. Then she revised her draft, checking its organization, content, and wording. Here is Lisa's revised draft:

---

In Nikki Giovanni's poem "Knoxville, Tennessee," the speaker ~~describes~~ uses imagery to describe several *carefree* scenes from her youth. The poem begins with a ~~bunch~~ *series* of visual images describing products from a country garden: *okra, greens, cabbage and cabbage*. This section is followed by a description of a church picnic ~~described~~ *presented* with images of sight ~~and~~ *sound* ~~taste~~: "buttermilk, "homemade ice-cream," and "gospel music." The poem ends with images of touch that convey a sense of warmth and freedom. The speaker describes *being* "warm all the time not only when you go to bed." going barefoot and ~~stuff~~. These references to warmth and freedom sum up the feeling *a mood,* of the poem as a whole

---

## Proofreading and Publishing

When she was satisfied with her paragraph, Lisa recopied it neatly. Then she showed the paragraph to her brother, who seemed to hibernate in the winter and come alive in the summer. She also volunteered to read the paragraph aloud in class.

## ACTIVITIES AND ASSIGNMENTS

A. Analyze Lisa's paragraph and answer the following questions:

1. Which sentence is her topic sentence?
2. Where does she identify the title and author of the poem?
3. The body of Lisa's paragraph develops three ideas. Where does each idea begin and end?
4. How does Lisa pull her paragraph together in the final sentence?
5. What revisions did Lisa make in her paragraph? Why did she make each revision?

B. Choose a poem rich in sensory images from the poetry unit of your anthology. Possibilities include "La Belle Dame sans Merci," on page 591; "Eldorado," on page 615; and "Shall I Compare Thee to a Summer's Day?" on page 686. Write a paragraph about the poem's images and its overall effect. Follow these steps:

1. Read the poem carefully. Find out the meaning of unfamiliar words or concepts.
2. Make a chart listing the images of sight, sound, touch, taste, and smell in the poem.
3. Make notes about the pictures and moods created by the images.
4. Determine your main idea, decide how you will organize supporting ideas, and plan the conclusion of your paragraph.
5. Draft your paragraph. In the topic sentence, identify the poem and its author, and state the overall effect of the poem. Write the body of your paragraph, showing how the images contribute to this effect. Write a conclusion that ties the ideas in the paragraph to the topic sentence.
6. Revise and proofread your paragraph. Check it for organization, completeness, and wording. Use the Checklist for Revision on page 948.
7. After revising your paragraph, make a clean final copy and proofread it, using the Checklist for Proofreading on page 950. Finally, give a dramatic reading or oral interpretation of the poem, followed by the reading of your paragraph.

# Lesson 5:  Writing About Sound

## UNDERSTANDING SOUND EFFECTS

Writers, especially poets, often work deliberately to achieve a certain sound in a piece of writing. They choose words with particular sounds to please the ear, to echo the meaning, or to emphasize certain ideas. The following special techniques of sound are commonly used.

## CASE STUDY: WRITING ABOUT SOUND

### Prewriting

Rico's English teacher asked him to choose a poem with striking sound effects, to write a paragraph about these effects, and to prepare an oral reading for the class. Rico chose the poem on the following page.

---

### SOUND DEVICES

*Rhyme:* the repetition of sounds at the ends of words. If the repeated sounds occur at the ends of lines, the repetition is called *end rhyme*. If the repeated sounds occur within lines, the repetition is called *internal rhyme*. *Friend* and *end* rhyme in the lines below, from William Shakespeare's "Sonnet 30":

> But if the while I think on thee, dear
> *friend,*
> All losses are restored and sorrows *end*

*Rhythm:* the beat, the way stress falls on certain accented syllables when something is read. Some poems have a fixed rhythm. In the lines from Shakespeare's "Sonnet 30," for example, every other syllable is stressed, and there are five stressed syllables per line. Fixed patterns of stress can create various kinds of rhythms—musical rhythms, marching rhythms, and the like.

Many contemporary poets do not use fixed rhythmical patterns. Instead, they use the natural rhythms of everyday speech. The following lines, from Diane Wakorski's "Thanking My Mother for Piano Lessons," are from this kind of poem, which is called free verse:

> I want to thank
> my mother for working and always
> paying for
> my piano lessons
> before she paid the Bank of America loan
> or bought the groceries
> or had our old rattling Ford repaired.

*Alliteration:* the repetition of initial consonant sounds. Notice the repetition of consonant sounds in the following lines from "Break, Break, Break," by Alfred, Lord Tennyson:

> And the *s*tately *s*hips go on
> To their *h*aven under the *h*ill;
> But O for a touch of a vanished hand,
> And the *s*ound of a voice that is *s*till!

*Assonance:* the repetition of vowel sounds. Listen to the long *i*'s in these lines from "The Collar," by George Herbert:

> What, shall *I* s*i*gh and p*i*ne?
> My l*i*nes and l*i*fe are free; free as
> the road

All the techniques discussed above involve *repetition* of sound or pattern. In their crafting of sound effects, writers can also repeat a word, a phrase, or a sentence. A *refrain* is a line or group of lines that is repeated at regular intervals in a poem or song.

*Onomatopoeia:* the use of words that imitate sounds. *Hiss* and *gurgle* are onomatopoeic words. Similarly, words with the ending -*atter*, including *clatter*, *shatter*, *batter*, and *tatter*, suggest a violent breaking apart.

*Consonance*: the close repetition of consonants. These consonants are not necessarily at the beginnings of words. For example, notice the repetition of *t* and *d* sounds in the first line of Robert Frost's poem "Once By the Pacific":

> The shattered water made a misty din.

---

## RHAPSODY

### WILLIAM STANLEY BRAITHWAITE

I am glad daylong for the gift of song,
For time and change and sorrow;
For the sunset wings and the world-end
   things
Which hang on the edge of tomorrow,
I am glad for my heart whose gates apart
Are the entrance-place of wonders,
Where dreams come in from the rush and
   din
Like sheep from the rains and thunders.

When Rico looked up the word *rhapsody*, he found that it means both "a free-flowing, emotional piece of music" and "a speech or a piece of writing that is full of feeling or enthusiasm." Rico decided that both these definitions fit the pem. Next he made an outline categorizing the sound effects:

- Topic sentence: Rhyme and consonance, the two dominant sound effects used by William Stanley Braithwaite in his poem "Rhapsody," reflect the joy that is the subject of his poem.

- Rhyme:
     end rhyme: (sorrow–tomorrow; wonders–thunders)
     internal rhyme: (daylong–song; wings–things; heart–apart; in–din)

- Rhythm: alternating 4 beats and 3 beats

- Alliteration: *d*reams, *d*in

- Assonance: none

- Onomatopoeia: din, thunders

- Consonance: drea*m*s, co*m*e; ru*sh*, *sh*eep; rai*n*s, thu*n*der

- Conclusion: Although there are three repetitions of consonants in the last two lines, the major sound device that Braithwaite employs is rhyme, especially internal rhyme, in all four of the four-beat lines. In their stressed echoes of sound, these internal rhymes reinforce the

speaker's joy in his emotions and dreams.

### Drafting and Revising

Using his notes, Rico wrote a draft of his paragraph. However, when he started going over the draft, he realized that he needed to add evidence from the poem to support his statements. Therefore, he added specific quotations from the poem, and he also revised his topic sentence. Here is Rico's final topic sentence:

> In the poem entitled "Rhapsody," William Stanley Braithwaite uses the sound effects of rhyme and consonance to sing about the things that make him glad.

### Proofreading and Publishing

After he recopied his final version, Rico read both the poem and his paragraph to his parents. After his classmates heard his oral reading of the poem, they also asked to hear his analysis.

### ACTIVITIES AND ASSIGNMENTS

A. Write a paragraph based on the outline given in the case study.
1. Use Rico's topic sentence for your paragraph.
2. In the body of the paragraph, discuss the devices of sound used in the poem and give examples, quoting from the poem as necessary.
3. Write a concluding sentence.
4. Revise and proofread your paragraph. Then exchange papers with a classmate. Discuss with this classmate the differences in your papers.

B. Choose a poem with striking sound effects from the poetry unit of your anthology. Possibilities include "O What Is That Sound," on page 611; "Big Wind," on page 658; "Reapers," on page 664; and "The Splendor Falls," on page 676. Write a paragraph about how sound effects contribute to the poem's overall effect. Follow these steps:
1. Read the poem carefully. Look up any unfamiliar words in a dictionary.

2. Make a chart listing the sound effects in the poem.
3. Makes notes on the purpose that the poet wishes to accomplish and on how the sound effects contribute to accomplishing this purpose.
4. Determine your main idea. Decide how you will organize your supporting ideas. Plan the conclusion of your paragraph.
5. Draft your paragraph. In the topic sentence, identify the poem and its author, and state the overall effect of the devices of sound used in the poem. In the body of your paragraph, refer to specific examples of sound effects used in the poem. Write a conclusion that ties the ideas in the paragraph to the topic sentence.
6. Revise and proofread your paragraph. Use the Checklist for Revision on page 948 and the Checklist for Proofreading on page 950.
7. Make a clean final copy and share both the poem and your paragraph with a classmate.

# Lesson 6: Writing About Figures of Speech

## UNDERSTANDING FIGURES OF SPEECH

*Figurative* language is writing or speech not meant to be interpreted literally. One common figure of speech is *metaphor*, in which a thing is described as though it were something else. In the lines below, from Georgia Douglas Johnson's "Your World," the speaker describes herself as though she were a bird. The metaphor is not meant to be taken literally. Instead, the speaker uses the metaphor to suggest characteristics that she and a bird have in common.

> Your world is as big as you make it.
> I know, for I used to abide
> In the narrowest nest in a corner,
> My wings pressing close to my side.

A *simile* is a figure of speech that makes a direct comparison between two subjects using either *like* or *as*. In the following lines, from Jesse Stuart's "Our Heritage," the speaker compares Americans to trees. The simile suggests that both Americans and trees are dependent on and rooted in the land.

> We are part of this rough land
> Deep-rooted like the tree.

*Personification* is a figure of speech in which a nonhuman subject is described as having human characteristics. In the following lines from Owen Dodson's "Faithful One," sorrow is personified as a faithful companion:

> Sorrow is the only faithful one:
> The lone companion clinging like a season
> To its original skin no matter what the variations.

## CASE STUDY: WRITING ABOUT FIGURES OF SPEECH

Sarah's class was told to find a poem with dramatic figures of speech and to write a paragraph analyzing their meaning and purpose. Sarah chose the following:

### A WISH
#### Fanny Kemble

> Let me not die for ever, when I'm gone
>   To the cold earth! but let my memory
> Live like the gorgeous western light that shone
>   Over the clouds where sank day's majesty.
> Let me not be forgotten; though the grave
>   Has clasped its hideous arms around my brow.
> Let me not be forgotten; though the wave
>   Of time's dark current rolls above me now.
> Yet not in tears remembered by my name;
>   Weep over those ye loved; for me, for me,
> Give me the wreath of glory, and let fame
>   Over my tomb spread immortality!

### Prewriting

Sarah read the poem carefully to see if there were any words she did not understand. She double-checked *immortality* and was glad she did. Besides meaning "living forever," which she knew, it also means "enduring for a long time" or "lasting fame." She made a note of the fact that this word was probably deliberately chosen.

Next Sarah made a list of the figures of speech in the poem and their meaning:

- Metaphors:
  "the wave/Of Time's dark current"—compares the passage of time to the ocean current pulling one away into nothingness
  "the wreath of glory"—compares fame to a traditional funeral wreath

- Simile:
  "let my memory/Live like the gorgeous western light"—compares the reputation she wants to the beautiful glow of a sunset

- Personification:
  "where sank day's majesty"—compares the sun to a ruler, the ruler of the day
  "though the grave/Has clasped its hideous arms around my brow"—compares

death to a person holding someone against his or her will.

As Sarah considered these figures of speech, she realized that they were important to the poem's overall effect. She took these notes:

- Negative characterizations of death and being forgotten: "cold earth," "hideous arms," "time's dark current"
- Positive characterizations of being remembered: "gorgeous western light," "the wreath of glory"
- Double meaning of *immortality*

Sarah planned to include her understanding of the word *immortality* in her topic sentence and to develop her paragraph around the contrast in the poem between dying and being forgotten, on the one hand, and being remembered, on the other. She was not sure yet how she would conclude her paragraph.

### Drafting and Revising

Using the poem and her notes, Sarah wrote the following draft:

The speaker in A Wish has a very special wish: immortality. However, she does not literally want to live forever, instead she wants to be remembered forever, she does not want to be forgotten. Death and being forgotten are ugly things to the speaker. She pictures "the cold earth." She personifies death as someone with "hideous arms" clasping her. She pictures time as "a dark current" that threatens to pull her into nothingness. The speaker sees fame as something beautiful. She uses this simile: "Let my memory/Live like the gorgeus western light that shone/Over the clouds where sank day's majesty." When she dies, the speaker does not want traditional floral wreaths. She also doesn't want tears shed for her. Instead, she wants a "wreath of glory," and it is this glory that will give her immortality.

As Sarah considered her draft, she was satisfied with the basic organization and with her conclusion, which seemed to flow naturally from her paragraph. However, she worked extensively on the structure of her sentences to make them flow more smoothly.

### Proofreading and Publishing

Sarah neatly recopied her final paragraph. Then she proofread the paragraph carefully and gave it to her English teacher.

## ACTIVITIES AND ASSIGNMENTS

A. Revise and proofread Sarah's paragraph. Follow these steps:
1. Include the poet's name in the first sentence.
2. Correct the run-on sentence with which the paragraph begins.
3. Combine sentences where possible.
4. Proofread the revised draft carefully. Correct any errors that you find in spelling, in punctuation, or in the use of quotation marks.

B. Choose from your anthology a poem that uses figures of speech, such as "The Wreck of the Hesperus," on page 601; "Generations," on page 632; or "The Fish," on page 665. Write a paragraph analyzing the figures of speech in the poem. Follow these steps:
1. Read the poem carefully. Check the meanings of any unfamiliar words.
2. Make a chart, listing the metaphors, similes, and personifications in the poem.
3. State how these figures of speech contribute to the overall effect.
4. First determine your main idea. Then decide how you will organize supporting ideas. Finally, plan the conclusion of your paragraph.
5. Draft your paragraph. In the topic sentence identify the name of the poem and its author and state your main idea. In the body of your paragraph, show how the figures of speech in the poem relate to the main idea. Write a conclusion that ties your paragraph together.
6. Revise your paragraph. Make sure that the paragraph is well organized and that your main idea is fully developed. Use the Checklist for Revision on page 948.
7. Make a clean final copy and proofread it for errors in spelling, grammar, punctuation, capitalization, and manuscript form.

# Lesson 7: Writing About Setting

## UNDERSTANDING SETTING

The *setting* of a literary work is the time and place in which the action occurs. A writer can develop a setting by describing any or all of the following:

1. Historical period (past, present, or future)
2. Season of the year
3. Year, month, day, or time of day
4. Geographical location
5. Physical environment
6. Weather
7. Clothing, habits, customs, or dialects of the characters

## THE FUNCTIONS OF SETTING

In some stories the setting is fairly unimportant. The same or similar events could take place at any time or in any place. In most stories, however, setting is a key element. The primary purpose of a historical novel, for example, might be to provide a glimpse of an earlier time. The primary purpose of a science-fiction story might be to make predictions about a time in the future.

Often the action, or plot, of a story results from a conflict created by the setting. For example, a character may struggle against a force of nature or against other elements in his or her environment. Sometimes, too, the setting is important in establishing the mood, or atmosphere, of a work. Notice, for instance, how the setting of W. W. Jacobs's "The Monkey's Paw," on page 29, establishes a mood of loneliness and impending horror:

> "That's the worst of living so far out," bawled Mr. White, with sudden and unlooked-for violence; "of all the beastly, slushy, out-of-the-way places to live, this is the worst. Pathway's a bog, and the road's a torrent."

## CASE STUDY: WRITING ABOUT SETTING

After Li-Chiang's class had read Ray Bradbury's "There Will Come Soft Rains," on page 133, his teacher directed the students to write a paragraph analyzing its setting and mood.

### Prewriting

To prepare for the assignment, Li-Chiang reread the story, paying close attention to details used to describe the setting. The following are Li-Chiang's notes:

- Time: Aug. 4 and 5, A.D. 2026
  after a nuclear war (the house "stood alone in a city of rubble and ashes," a city that "gave off a radioactive glow")

- Place: Allendale, California.
  a house with very advanced features (computer brain in attic, voice that gives information and reminders, robot mice that do cleaning, automatic food-preparation center)
  a rainy day; rain also mentioned in Teasdale poem (source of title) and in three other places "the gentle sprinkler rain" in the garden; "the quenching rain ceased" (meaning the house sprinkler system); and "rain of fire and timber" (when house collapses)

- Mood:
  gentle sadness, first at the loneliness and then at the destruction
  regret that there is no one who minds that the people have "perished utterly"

irony that the house mindlessly continues to work

Li-Chiang planned to state in his topic sentence the relationship between the story's mood and its theme: the possible effects of nuclear war. In his paragraph he would use details of the setting to show how this mood is created. Since the image of the rain seemed so important, he decided to use it in the clincher sentence at the end of his paragraph.

### Drafting and Revising

Li-Chiang used his prewriting notes to create the following rough draft:

> Ray Bradbury's ''There Will Come Soft Rains'' expresses gentle regret and sadness. About the possibility of humanitys destroying itself through nucular conflict. It does so by picturing a world without people, where things people have built live on for a while and then die, with no one to care. The setting is a house in Allendale, California, in August 2026 the house stands ''alone in a city of rubble and ashes,'' a city that gives off ''a radioactive glow.'' A computer within the house directs machines to prepare food to dust and vacuum and to set up tables and refreshments for a bridge game. But despite all this automation stuff, the house is mindless. It creates fantasys that no child will enjoy it lights a cigar that no one will smoke. When a fire starts accidentally, the house cannot save itself, and it, too, dies. However, as the house itself says,
>
> And not one will know of the war, not one
> Will care at last when it is done.
>
> Not one would care, neither bird nor tree,
> If mankind perished utterly.
>
> The gentle rains come down, gently washing humanity and its words from the earth.

After finishing his draft, Li-Chiang reread it carefully. He had organized his paper well, expressed his ideas clearly, and supported his topic

sentence. All in all, it seemed an excellent draft. Therefore, Li-Chiang decided to move immediately to the proofreading stage.

### Proofreading and Publishing

As Li-Chiang proofread his paragraph, he found and corrected a sentence fragment, three spelling errors, and several errors in punctuation. He also checked the Teasdale quotation against the text, and found that he had misquoted one of the lines. After correcting this misquotation, he borrowed a recording of Bradbury's story from his teacher, played this recording to his family, and shared his paragraph with them. Finally, he submitted his paragraph to his teacher for grading.

### ACTIVITIES AND ASSIGNMENTS

A. If you have not already done so, read Ray Bradbury's ''There Will Come Soft Rains,'' on page 133. Then proofread Li-Chiang's paragraph and correct the following errors:

1. The sentence fragment at the beginning of the paragraph
2. The three spelling errors in the paragraph
3. The punctuation errors throughout the paragraph
4. The misquotation from Teasdale's poem ''There Will Come Soft Rains''
5. The vague, slangy word *stuff* in the sentence that begins, ''But despite all this automation stuff''

B. Find a story in your anthology in which setting plays an important role in establishing mood. Write a paragraph discussing the mood created by the setting. Follow these steps:

1. Reread the story, paying close attention to the setting details.

2. Take notes on the time, place, and mood of the story. For each, list key details or quotations.
3. Take notes on the overall relationship between setting and mood.
4. Draft a topic sentence that states this relationship.
5. Draft the rest of your paragraph, showing how details of setting create the mood. Write a conclusion that ties the ideas in the paragraph to the topic sentence.
6. Revise your paragraph. Make sure that the paragraph is well organized, clearly worded, and graceful.
7. Make a clean final copy and proofread it, using the Checklist for Proofreading on page 950. Share your paragraph in a small-group discussion in class.

# Lesson 8: Writing About Plot

## UNDERSTANDING PLOT

Short stories, novels, and plays are built around characters in conflict. That conflict might be within a character or between a character and an outside force—another character, society, or nature. What happens as a result of this conflict—the sequence of events in the story—is the plot.

## ANALYZING PLOT

The plot of many stories can be analyzed in the following.

Plot is sometimes charted like this:

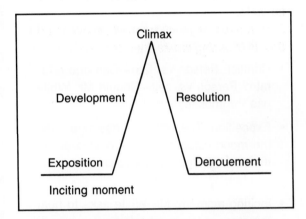

## RECOGNIZING PLOT DEVICES

To structure the plot or to maintain interest, writers will frequently use one or more of the following techniques:

1. *Suspense:* Suspense is a feeling of anxious uncertainty about the outcome of events. It is created by raising questions in the reader's mind.
2. *Foreshadowing:* Using this technique, an author hints at what is to come. The title of a story, a detail, or an action can foreshadow future events. Sometimes readers may not notice foreshadowing until they think back on a story or reread it.
3. *Flashback:* A writer using flashback breaks away from the current action of a story to recount events that happened earlier.
4. *Surprise ending:* When something unexpected happens at the end of a story, the story has a surprise ending.

## CASE STUDY: WRITING ABOUT PLOT

Becky's English class analyzed the plot of

---

### PARTS OF A PLOT

*Exposition or introduction:* In this section the author provides background information, establishes the setting, and introduces the characters.

*Inciting moment:* This is the first important event of the story. Something happens that causes or leads to the central conflict. The inciting moment may come before the exposition. Some writers like to open the story with the inciting moment to attract the reader's attention.

*Development:* This section includes the key events of the story between the inciting moment and the climax.

*Climax:* This is the high point of interest or suspense in the story. The climax may coincide with the resolution.

*Resolution:* This is the event or series of events that ends the central conflict.

*Denouement:* This section tells of any events after the main action of the story is complete; it ties up loose ends. Many stories have no denouement.

one short story in class. When her teacher directed the class to write a one-paragraph analysis of another story, Becky chose W. W. Jacobs' "The Monkey's Paw," on page 29, which she had already read.

## Prewriting

To prepare for writing, Becky reread the story and then took the following notes:

- Conflict: Person vs. fate—Can one affect fate? Person *vs.* self—Should Mr. White use the monkey's paw?

- Exposition: The setting is described and the mood established; the Whites are introduced; Sergeant Morris arrives; they all chat.

- Inciting moment: Mr. White asks to hear the story of the monkey's paw.

- Development: Sergeant Morris tells his story; Mr. White retrieves the paw from the fire; Mr. White wishes for 200 pounds; a company representative arrives with news of Herbert's death and 200 pounds as compensation; Mrs. White persuades Mr. White to wish their son alive again; a knock comes at the door.

- Climax and resolution: Mr. White gropes for the paw and makes his third wish.

- Denouement: The knocking ceases; the Whites look down the deserted road.

Becky also took notes on the use of special techniques in the story:

- Great suspense: gloomy setting, supernatural details, rising tension in details and action.

- Foreshadowing:
  Mr. White says, "I don't know what to wish for. . . . It seems to me I've got all I want."
  Mrs. White says, "How could 200 pounds hurt you, Father?"
  Herbert comments, "Well, I don't see

the money, and I bet I never shall."
After Herbert's death the Whites "remained in a state of expectation as though of something else to happen."

Becky debated whether to focus her paragraph on the story's suspense or on its conflict. She decided to focus on the suspense.

## Drafting and Revising

Becky used her notes to draft her paragraph. When she began to revise it, she realized that it sounded too much like a mere summary. To emphasize the fact that she was analyzing the plot, she introduced formal terminology: exposition, inciting moment, development, climax, resolution, and denouement. She also added details that emphasized the rising tension in the story. Finally, she worked on her sentence structure and wording.

## Proofreading and Publishing

When Becky was satisfied with her paragraph, she recopied it neatly and proofread it. A friend of hers had also analyzed "The Monkey's Paw," and the two girls read and discussed one another's paragraphs before submitting them in class.

## ACTIVITIES AND ASSIGNMENTS

A. If you have not already done so, read "The Monkey's Paw," on page 29. Then use Becky's notes to write a paragraph analyzing the story's plot. Follow these steps:
1. If, as Becky did, you want to focus on the story's suspense, use this topic sentence:

> Suspense builds all through the plot of W. W. Jacobs's story "The Monkey's Paw."

If, instead, you want to focus on the story's conflicts, use this introduction:

> Does fate rule our lives? Will we regret it if we try to interfere with fate? These are the questions Mr. White grapples with in W. W. Jacobs' story "The Monkey's Paw."

2. In the body of your paragraph, develop your topic sentence by referring to specific parts of the story. Use formal terminology as you identify the exposition, inciting moment, development, climax, resolution, and denouement. Use specific details and quotations that emphasize your unifying idea, either suspense or conflict.

3. As you revise your paragraph, make sure that it reads like an analysis, not merely a summary. Recopy and proofread your paragraph.

B. Choose a story from your anthology and write a paragraph analyzing its plot. Follow these steps:

1. Reread the story, paying close attention to the development of the plot.

2. Take notes on the conflict and on the parts of the plot.

3. Take notes on special techniques of plot used by the author. Note dramatic details or quotations.

4. Decide whether to focus on the conflict or on some other aspect of the plot. Write a topic sentence that presents your main idea.

5. Draft the body of your paragraph, showing how the plot confirms your topic sentence. Use specific details and quotations that prove your point.

6. Revise your paragraph. Make sure that it reads like an analysis. Work on your sentence structure and wording. Check your mechanics.

7. Make a clean final copy and proofread it. Share your paragraph with a classmate before submitting it in class.

# Lesson 9: Writing About Character

## UNDERSTANDING CHARACTER

A *character* is a person in a story. The main character is called the *protagonist*; if that character is in conflict with another character, the opposing character is called the *antagonist*. *Major characters* are important to the story, while *minor characters* play less important roles. Characters can be described as round or flat—*round* if they are fully developed, *flat* if readers see only one side of them. Characters can also be described as dynamic or static—*dynamic* if they change during the course of the story, *static* if they do not.

## UNDERSTANDING CHARACTERIZATION

Writers reveal their characters in a variety of ways:

1. *Direct statement:* The author can tell readers that a character is, for example, "a foolish man."
2. *Description of characters and their backgrounds:* Knowing what people look like, how they dress, and where they come from helps readers begin to know them.
3. *Narration of characters' actions, words, and thoughts:* Seeing how characters behave, reading what they say, sharing their thoughts—all these help readers to know them.
4. *Record of others' reaction:* Learning how others treat someone or what they think about that person helps us understand both that person and the ones reacting.

## COMING TO CONCLUSIONS ABOUT A CHARACTER

In general, if you are to write a short paper about a character, you will want to concentrate on one aspect of the character. Ask yourself the following questions to discover the key aspect that you want to concentrate on:

1. *Appearance:* What do the character's appearance and clothes reveal?
2. *Background:* What significant things have happened in the character's past? How does the character live and work?
3. *Personality and motivation:* What kind of person is this, based on how he or she behaves, speaks, and thinks? Why does the character behave as he or she does?
4. *Relationships:* How do other characters react to this character? Why? What effect do these reactions have on him or her?
5. *Conflict:* What problems does the character face? Are the conflicts faced by the character external or internal?
6. *Change:* Does the character change because of what happens in the story?

## CASE STUDY: WRITING ABOUT CHARACTER

After Louis and his class had written descriptive papers about people they know, they turned their attention to characters in stories. Since Louis had very much enjoyed "Chee's Daughter," on page 73, he decided to write about Old Man Fat, a character in that story.

### Prewriting

First Louis reread the story, paying particular attention to any scene in which Old Man Fat is mentioned or in which he appears. Louis decided that he would concentrate on Old Man Fat's selfishness. Louis kept that idea in mind as he took the following notes:

- Appearance:
    fat, especially around the middle
    has a lazy walk, lazy eyes
    Chee's mother: "When you see a fat Navajo, you see one who hasn't worked for what he has."

at end: his face sags and his cheeks are no longer full

- Background:
  lives in a garish, pseudo-Navajo hogan with a blue door facing the wrong direction
  Chee believes he is thriftless and greedy.

- Personality and motivation:
  likes money: lets people see his home for money, collects money from people who see the Little One
  is proud that he lives by the new ways, not by digging in the dirt
  likes an easy life

- Relationships:
  looks down on Chee for farming
  is willing to take in the Little One as custom dictates

- Conflict:
  Should he keep the Little One or give her up?

- Change:
  When things are going well, he doesn't want Chee's help because that might disrupt the Little One, but at end he tries to get Chee's sympathy and then gives the Little One up.

Reviewing his notes, Louis decided that the words *lazy* and *greedy* describe Old Man Fat better than the word *selfish*. He also decided to use Old Man Fat's final conflict in his concluding sentence.

## Drafting and Revising

Louis wrote his paragraph, using his notes to provide support for his main idea about Old Man Fat's greed and laziness. Then he revised his paragraph, eliminating some details that did not relate to the main idea, reorganizing some information, and improving his sentence structure. Here is Louis's draft, before he worked on grammar and mechanics:

Old Man Fat, a character in Juanita Platero and Siyowin Miller's story "Chee's Daughter" is a lazy greedy man. Chee's mother knows what Old Man Fat is like. "When you see a fat Navajo, you see one who has'nt worked for what he has," she says. Old Man Fat indeed likes life to be easy, he boasts to Chee about how easy he has it. Living near the trading post, selling rugs and letting turists see his home for money. In many ways, Old Man Fat rejects trudition, but he does take in Chee's daughter after the childs mother dies. (By custom the wifes family cares for a motherless child.) When Old Man Fat starts collecting money from turists who are admiring the Little One, however he shows that greed was at least part of his motivation. At the end of the story, when Old Man Fat's easy life is over, he at first resists giving the Little One up just because Chee has brought him food. But when he looks at the Little One eating some of it, she "became just another mouth to feed" and he lets Chee take her. Old Man Fat is to lazy to work to keep his grandaughter and to greedy to share with her the little he now has.

## Proofreading and Publishing

After Louis was satisfied with his paragraph, he neatly recopied it and proofread it. As he proofread, he corrected many errors in spelling and in punctuation. He also corrected sentence fragments and run-on sentences. He shared his paragraph with his sister, who had read "Chee's Daughter" the previous year in her English class.

## ACTIVITIES AND ASSIGNMENTS

A. If you have not already done so, read "Chee's Daughter," beginning on page 73. Then answer the following questions about the case study:
1. Where does Louis identify the story he is writing about and its author?
2. Where does Louis state his main idea?
3. How many of his notes did Louis use in his paragraph? Did he use too many? Did he leave out anything important?
4. Where does Louis restate his main idea? Does he do so effectively?
5. Copy Louis's final paragraph. As you do so, revise to eliminate one run-on sentence, one

fragment, and many errors in spelling and punctuation. Proofread your final copy.

B. Choose a character in one of the stories in your anthology and write a paragraph discussing one aspect of the character. Follow these steps:

1. Reread the story, paying close attention to details of character.

2. Take notes on the character's appearance, background, personality and motivation, relationships, conflicts, and changes.

3. Review your notes to identify the one aspect of the character that you will deal with in your paper. State this idea in a topic sentence that identifies the story and its author.

4. Check your notes to pinpoint those that support your topic sentence. Use these details as you draft the body of your paragraph. In your concluding sentence, restate your main idea, but word it differently than you did at the beginning of your paper.

5. Revise your paragraph. Be sure every detail you included relates to the one aspect of the character that you are focusing on. Ask yourself if you have included enough detail to illustrate your point. Work on your sentence structure and wording. Check your mechanics.

6. Make a clean final copy and proofread it. Share your paragraph with your classmates and with your teacher.

# Lesson 10:  Writing About Point of View

## UNDERSTANDING POINT OF VIEW

The point of view of a story is the perspective from which it is told. The narrator of the story, the one who tells it, may or may not be a character in the story.

When a character in the story tells it, the point of view is said to be *first person*. The first-person narrator refers to himself or herself as *I* or *me*, even outside of quotations.

When someone outside the action tells the story, the point of view is said to be *third person*. Outside of quotations, a third-person narrator refers to all characters as *he* or *him*, *she* or *her*. In stories written from the *third-person limited point of view*, the narrator reveals only one character's thoughts, usually the main character's. In stories written from the *third-person omniscient point of view*, the narrator reveals several characters' thoughts and can record several characters' internal experiences. The term *omniscient* is therefore appropriate; it means "all-knowing."

## UNDERSTANDING THE EFFECT OF POINT OF VIEW

The choice of point of view is very important to the overall effect of a story. A story told in the first person has a sense of immediacy and authenticity. On the other hand, the author is restricted: The narrator can tell us his or her own thoughts but can only guess about other characters' thoughts. Furthermore, readers must determine whether the narrator is reliable or not. Is the narrator telling the truth? Does the narrator truly understand what is happening?

A story told from the third-person limited point of view also has a sense of immediacy. Readers tend to identify with the focus character and to see the world of the story as he or she does. Readers themselves must still judge the character: Does the narrator approve or disapprove of the character's behavior? Does the character make wise or unwise choices?

A story told from the third-person omniscient point of view gives readers a feeling of power since they see not everything, perhaps, but a great deal. They can learn directly about the thoughts and other internal states of several or all of the characters.

## CASE STUDY: WRITING ABOUT POINT OF VIEW

Claudia's English class had discussed how literature allows readers to share other people's worlds. As a follow-up, Mr. Kowalski, her teacher, told the class to examine the effect of point of view in Gwendolyn Brooks's sketch "Maud Martha Spares the Mouse," on page 119.

### Prewriting

Claudia read the story several times. She knew the story was told from a third-person limited point of view, but she also noticed that within the story, Maud Martha tries to see the mouse's point of view. Claudia took these notes:

- Point of view:
  third-person limited, though Maud Martha's eyes

- Effect of point of view:
  shows Maud Martha's thoughts directly, just as she thinks them
  allows Maud Martha to think about mouse's point of view
  shows how imaginative and softhearted Maud Martha is
  author-narrator doesn't comment on Maud Martha's behavior, but seems kindly disposed toward her

## Drafting and Revising

Claudia kept both the story and her notes handy as she wrote her draft. Then she revised it as shown in the chart on the right.

## Proofreading and Publishing

After Claudia had revised her paragraph to her satisfaction, she recopied it neatly and proofed it. The next day, she volunteered to read it in class.

## ACTIVITIES AND ASSIGNMENTS

A. If you have not yet done so, read "Maud Martha Spares the Mouse," on page 119. Then answer the following questions about the case study:

1. What sentences did Claudia combine to make one more forceful sentence?
2. What repetitive words did Claudia eliminate?
3. What transition words did Claudia add?
4. Where did Claudia improve her word choice?
5. Where did Claudia discover that she had drifted into the past tense?
6. Where did Claudia spot and fix a sentence fragment?
7. What spelling and punctuation errors did Claudia spot and fix?

B. Choose a story from your anthology and write a paragraph analyzing its point of view. Follow these steps:

1. Reread the story. Identify the point of view and pay attention to what advantages and limitations it has in this story.
2. Take notes on the point of view and on its effects.
3. Draft your paragraph. In the topic sentence, identify the story, its author, and the point of view. Write the body of your paragraph, showing the effect of this point of view. Write a conclusion that ties the ideas in the paragraph to the topic sentence.
4. Revise your paragraph. Ask yourself if you have adequately explained the effect of the

Gwendolyn Brooks's "Maud Martha Spares the Mouse" is a good example of point of view. ~~It has~~ third-person limited ~~point of view. The interesting thing~~ *What is intriguing, however,* is that within the story Maud Martha puts herself in a mouse's position and in *her* imagination sees the mouse's point of view. *At first* Maud Martha ~~was~~ *is* happy that she *has* caught the mouse at last, but suddenly she ~~started~~ *starts* wondering what the mouse ~~was~~ *is* thinking. In this paragraph, the author continues to record Maud Martha's thoughts, but Maud Martha's thoughts are what she imagines the mouse is thinking: "Perhaps that there was not enough food in its locker. Maud Martha is very ~~imaginative~~ *imaginative* and very ~~unreal~~ *unscientific* in her ~~thoughts,~~ *musings,* but the result is that she ~~becomes so sympathetic that~~ she feels sorry for the mouse and she lets it loose. Now readers see Maud Martha feeling very good about herself. She feels she has done a godlike thing because instead of destroying, she preserved. And in preserving, created. Gwendolyn Brooks gives readers a ~~third-person limited point of view inside a~~ third-person limited point of view. The inside point of view may not be accurate. *but* It lets

> readers see Maud Martha as an imaginative,
>
> soft-hearted woman.

point of view. Check to make sure that your organization is clear. Also check to make sure

that your sentence structure is correct and that your wording is clear and graceful. Check your mechanics.

5. Make a clean final copy and proofread it. If your teacher asks for volunteers, offer to share your paper with the class.

# Lesson 11: Writing About Theme

## UNDERSTANDING THEME

The *theme* of a poem, story, or drama is its central idea or insight into life. The theme is not equivalent to a summary of the work; it is a generalizaton that can be drawn from the work. For example, "Mr. Bigelow refuses to be defeated by his blindness, and in the end he defeats his problem" is not a statement of theme. However, "If we refuse to be defeated by our limitations, we can defeat them" is a statement of theme.

A poem, short story, or one-act play usually develops only one theme, while a novel or full-length play may develop several. Different readers will word a statement of theme differently, perhaps with slightly different emphasis, but it is not true that any statement is correct. Your statement of theme must reflect the work as the author wrote it, not your opinion of the characters or events.

Some works of literature, notably those meant solely for entertainment, have no real theme.

## DISCOVERING THEME

Sometimes the author states the theme directly. In the poem below, author Naomi Long Madgett states the theme in the last line:

### WOMAN WITH FLOWER
### Naomi Long Madgett

I wouldn't coax the plant if I were you.
Such watchful nurturing may do it harm.
Let the soil rest from so much digging
And wait until it's dry before you water
  it.
The leaf's inclined to find its own
  direction;
Give it a chance to seek the sunlight for
  itself.

Much growth is stunted by too careful
  prodding,
Too eager tenderness.

The things we love we have to learn to
  leave alone.

Notice that by "things" Madgett does not mean *plants*. From the images in the poem, a reader can conclude that she is talking about parents and children. The theme is that parents must not try to control their children's lives; they must learn to leave them alone. If you were to write a paragraph analyzing the theme of this poem, you would show how the various images of plants could be understood in terms of parents and children.

Writers of fiction, too, sometimes state the theme within the story. More often, however, the author suggests or implies the theme. Asking yourself the following questions will help you discover the theme of a work of literature:

1. Does the title of the work suggest the theme?
2. What is the conflict? How is it resolved? What does the result seem to say about how people face similar conflicts?
3. In what ways does the main character change? Why does the character change? Does this change reflect the theme?
4. Do any significant details seem to suggest theme, either through repetition or intensity?
5. Considering all of the above, what, overall, does the work seem to be saying?

## CASE STUDY: WRITING ABOUT THEME

After Malcolm's English class read Doris Lessing's short story "Through the Tunnel," on page 159, they discussed the concept of theme and applied that concept to the story. Then they each wrote a paragraph analyzing the theme.

### Prewriting

As Malcolm reread the story, he kept this question in the back of his mind: What, overall, is the story saying? Then he reviewed his notes from class and added the following:

- Title: Is significant; Jerry literally goes through the tunnel, but also passes from one stage of life to another.

- Conflicts: Jerry faces both physical and psychological internal conflicts: Can he train himself to hold his breath? Does he dare face the tunnel?
  Jerry also faces external conflicts: Can he free himself from his mother's control? Can he win the approval of the local boys?

- Resolution of conflicts: Jerry overcomes his physical limitations and his fear and gains independence from his mother and from the boys.

- Change: Early in the story Jerry wants to be independent but checks frequently to see if his mother is near. In the middle he simply takes his independence. At the end he realizes that he does not have to "win" against his mother. (Maybe quote last paragraph.)
  Early in the story Jerry wants the local boys to accept him, but at the end "He could see the local boys diving and playing half a mile away. He did not want them."

- Significant details: The contrast between the "safe beach" and the "wild bay."

Malcolm then read over his notes and asked himself, "Overall, what does this add up to?" Here is the statement of theme that Jerry formulated:

Part of growing up is gaining confidence in ourselves. Once we have done so, especially through our own efforts, we do not depend so much on the approval of others.

## DRAFTING AND REVISING

Malcolm built his statement of theme into a topic sentence. In the body of his paragraph, he demonstrated how the conflicts led to Jerry's gaining self-confidence and independence. Malcolm used his idea about the title of the story in his concluding sentence to tie his paragraph together.

Then Malcolm revised his paragraph. He removed some details, added others, and did minor reorganization. He improved his sentence structure and checked for correctness of expression.

## PROOFREADING AND PUBLISHING

Malcolm preprared a clean final copy of his paragraph and proofread it. When his teacher divided the class into small groups to compare paragraphs, Malcolm volunteered to read his first.

## ACTIVITIES AND ASSIGNMENTS

A. If you have not already done so, read "Through the Tunnel," on page 159. Then do the following activities:

1. Reread the story, asking yourself if you agree with Malcolm's interpretations of the theme.
2. Review Malcolm's notes. Are there any that you would eliminate? Are there any you would add?
3. "Adopt" Malcolm's statement of theme or formulate your own.
4. Using Malcolm's notes, along with your changes, write a paragraph analyzing the theme of "Through the Tunnel." Mention the title, the author, and the theme in your topic sentence. Draft and revise your paragraph.
5. Recopy your paragraph neatly and proofread it. Compare your version with those of your classmates.

B. Choose a story from your anthology and write a paragraph analyzing its theme. Follow these steps:

1. Reread the story, keeping in the back of your mind the question, "What, overall, is the story saying?"
2. Take notes on those aspects of the story that are relevant to its theme: the title, the conflicts

and their resolution, the changes that characters undergo, and any other significant details. Include in your notes any direct quotations that you believe point to the story's theme.

3. Consider your notes and formulate a statement of theme. Be sure it is stated as a generalization and in the form of a sentence.

4. Draft your paragraph. In your topic sentence, identify the story, the author, and the theme. In the body of your paragraph, point out those aspects of the story that demonstrate this theme. In your concluding sentence, restate the theme, but word it differently than you did in the topic sentence.

5. Revise your paragraph. Check its organization. Improve your sentence structure and wording. Correct any grammatical or mechanical errors.

6. Copy your paragraph neatly and proofread it. If an opportunity is provided, offer to read your paragraph in class.

# SECTION 3: UNDERSTANDING THE WORK AS A WHOLE: INTERPRETATION AND SYNTHESIS

## Lesson 12: Writing About Fiction

*Fiction* includes both short stories and novels. In a short paper you cannot say everything there is to say about a work of fiction; instead, through your reading and prewriting activities you must discover some point that you want to analyze in detail. Perhaps it will be one aspect of the work—the characters, the plot, the setting. More often, however, you will want to discuss the overall effect of the story—its purpose, or its theme.

You must begin with an in-depth analysis of the story. Reread it at least once. Keep your copy of the story handy as you take notes on the following points:

1. Note the title and author and the significance of the title.
2. Note the setting and its significance: Does it establish mood? Does it play a role in the central conflict or plot?
3. Note the point of view: first person, third person limited, or third person omniscient. Identify the narrator, and note whether he or she is reliable.
4. Identify the major character, and take notes on his or her personality and motivations. Examine how this character deals with the central conflict and how he or she changes as a result.
5. Identify other major and minor characters and explain their roles in the story.
6. Note the major conflicts in the story: Does the major character struggle against another person? Against society? Against nature? Against a supernatural force? Or against something within himself or herself?
7. Identify the key events in the plot: the inciting moment, the development, the climax, the resolution, and the denouement. Note whether the author has used any special plot techniques such as foreshadowing, flashbacks, suspense, or a surprise ending.
8. Note any other special techniques that the author has used. Perhaps an object or a setting has symbolic value. Perhaps the whole story is ironic. Perhaps the story sounds poetic because of the author's use of sound or figures of speech.
9. Note the theme of the story—the central idea that the story conveys. Take all your notes into account as you consider the overall effect and point of the story.

### CASE STUDY: WRITING ABOUT FICTION

Chuck's class had already written several paragraphs about various aspects of fiction. Now their teacher told them to demonstrate their overall understanding by writing an analysis of a story.

**Prewriting**

Chuck chose to work with Saki's story "The Open Window," on page 195. After his second reading, Chuck felt he understood the story well enough to begin a thorough analysis. One thing that puzzled him, however, was the last line: "Romance at short notice was her specialty." Chuck could not see how the idea of *romance* fit the story. However, when he used his dictionary, he found that the word can mean "a story of excitement and adventure" or "any exaggerated, made-up story."

Now Chuck was ready to analyze the story. He took these notes:

- Title and author: "The Open Window," by Saki

- Setting: A country house, October

- Point of View: Third person omniscient, though most of story is third person limited, seen through Framton's eyes

- Major characters: Vera: 15 years old, a very "self-possessed," imaginative practical joker who does not consider others' feelings; Framton Nuttel: a self-involved stranger who came to the country for a cure for his nerves

- Minor character: Mrs. Sappleton: Vera's aunt, who seems unaware of her niece's addiction to stories

- Conflict: Person vs. person

- Plot: [In this section of his notes, Chuck identified the inciting moment, rising action, climax, falling action, and denouement.]

- Special plot techniques: Suspense; surprise ending

- Other techniques:
  Symbol: "open window" represents both horror and imagination
  Irony: contrast between what reader thinks is going on and what is actually going on; contrast between horror in first part and humor of ending; contrast between Vera's name (means "truth") and personality; verbal ironies in some lines

- Theme: With imagination and self-possession, one can create a world that seems real to others.

As Chuck read over his notes, he realized that the symbolism and irony in the story were the keys to understanding it. He decided to build these concepts into his thesis, which he would identify in his introductory paragraph. He planned to have two body paragraphs. In one he would contrast the characters of Vera and Framton. In the next he would briefly summarize the plot of the story, emphasizing the ironic contrast between the first part of the story and the ending. In his conclusion, in order to tie his paper together, he would explain the ironic symbolism of the open window.

**Drafting and Revising**

Chuck discarded two drafts of his paper before he finally wrote one that he felt would work. Here are the first and last paragraphs from his third draft:

> From the title to the last line, "The Open Window" is an ironic story. It was written by Saki (H. H. Munro). Both the reader and Framton Nuttell are led astray. Framton Nuttell is one of the major characters. Neither the reader nor Framton realize until late in the story that Vera has set them up. And that Saki has set them up for a surprise.

· · · · ·

> Thus, it is easy to see the symbolism of the open window. Its use in the title points to its significance. It represents the horror of Vera's first story. In fact, it is a classic symbol of horror: What will come through the window? But it also represents the window of imagination. Almost any kind of romance can come through that window.

When Chuck finished drafting his paper, he worked on it further. He added details that on reflection he believed strengthened his main idea, and he eliminated some unimportant details. When he realized that his paper was rather choppy, he worked extensively on his sentence structure. Finally, he worked on his mechanics.

**Proofreading and Publishing**

When he was satisfied with his draft, Chuck neatly typed it and then proofread the typed copy. In class the next day, he shared his paper with his classmates and then submitted it to his teacher.

**ACTIVITIES AND ASSIGNMENTS**

A. If you have not already done so, read "The

Open Window," on page 195. Then consider the case study in this lesson as you do the following activities:

1. Analyze the plot of "The Open Window." Identify the inciting moment, the events of the rising action, the climax, the events of the falling action, and the denouement.
2. Evaluate the rest of Chuck's prewriting notes. Is there anything you would add, change, or delete?
3. Revise Chuck's introduction and conclusion. Combine some of his sentences to make the paper less choppy.
4. Write two body paragraphs for the paper. Develop them as Chuck planned or in a way that seems appropriate to you.

B. Write a paper analyzing a story in your anthology. Follow these steps:

1. Read and reread the story, checking any key words or concepts that are unfamiliar to you.
2. Take notes on setting, point of view, characters, conflict, plot, other techniques, and theme.
3. Consider the overall effect of the story and how it is achieved. Plan to state this effect in your introduction.
4. Identify the story, the author, and your thesis in your introduction. Write two or three body paragraphs that develop your thesis. Write a conclusion that ties your ideas together.
5. Revise your paper and proofread it.
6. Make a clean final copy and proofread that. Volunteer to read your paper in class.

# Lesson 13: Writing About a Poem

## UNDERSTANDING A POEM

A poet, more than any other writer, considers each word very carefully, trying to choose the ones that are exactly right. The effect of this effort is to condense a complex experience into a simple, short work. When reading a poem, you must be just as careful in identifying how the poet achieved the overall effect. Follow these steps:

1. Read and reread the poem to be sure you understand what it means, what it is describing, what idea it conveys, and what emotion it is expressing.
2. Read the poem aloud and listen carefully to its music.
3. Use your dictionary or other sources to find the meanings of unfamiliar words.
4. Try paraphrasing the poem, or restating it in your own words.

## ANALYZING A POEM

As you begin analyzing the poem, take notes on the following points:

1. Note the title and author and the significance of the title.
2. Note what type of poem it is: lyric, narrative, dramatic, or concrete.
3. Note the stanza form. If the poem uses a standard form, note what it is. Examine the purpose of stanza breaks.
4. Note the sensory images in the poem, the details that appeal to sight, hearing , smell, taste, and touch. Consider the purpose of these.
5. Note the figures of speech used in the poem: the metaphors, the similes, the personification. Consider the meaning and purpose of each.
6. Note the sound effects in the poem, particularly the rhythm. See if the poem uses other techniques such as alliteration, assonance, onomatopoeia, or rhyme. Note whether it repeats words, lines, or stanzas. Then consider

the purpose of these sound effects.
7. Note other important aspects. Identify the speaker, the mood, and the theme. Note any special techniques the author used, such as unusual punctuation or spacing.
8. Reconsider your preliminary ideas about the poem as a whole. Perhaps the notes you took reinforce your original ideas. Perhaps they have given you a different or a deeper understanding of the poem. Take notes on your conclusions and on how the various techniques contribute to the poem as a whole.

## CASE STUDY: WRITING ABOUT A POEM

After working with poetry for several weeks, the students in Laureen's English class were asked to write an essay analyzing the following poem:

THE VOYAGE OF JIMMY POO

James A. Emanuel

A soapship went a-rocking
Upon a bathtub sea.
The sailor crouched a-smiling
Upon a dimpled knee.

Young Neptune dashed the waters
Against enamel shore,
And kept the air a-tumbling
With bubble-clouds galore.

But soon the voyage ended.
The ship was swept away
By a hand that seemed to whisper
"There'll be no more games today."

The ship lay dry and stranded
On a shiny metal tray,
And a voice was giving orders
That a sailor must obey.

Oh captain, little captain,
Make room for just one more
The next time you go sailing
Beyond enamel shore.

## Prewriting

Laureen was puzzled by the title at first, but after she had read the poem a couple times, she realized that "Jimmy Poo" must be a pet name that the speaker in the poem uses for his or her son. When Laureen checked her dictionary, she found out that Neptune was the Roman god of the sea and that "enamel" refers to a glassy surface fused to metal or pottery, as on a bathtub. Her first impression of the poem was that it conveyed a charming picture of a common childhood game.

Then Laureen began her close analysis of the poem. She first examined the images in the poem, noting that it is highly visual, containing images such as the rocking soapship, the crouching sailor with his dimpled knee, and the bubble clouds. As she worked, Laureen realized, too, that the soapship is actually a bar of soap, not a toy boat as she first thought, and that the "shiny metal tray" is the soap dish.

Then Laureen took notes on the figures of speech: picturing the little boy as a sailor and as Neptune are metaphors. The sea is the bathwater, and the shore is the tub itself. The third stanza puzzled Laureen for a while until she realized that the hand represents the whole person, the father or mother, who lets the water out and thus says, in effect, "the fun's over."

Next Laureen considered the sound effects in the poem. She noted the rhyme in lines 2 and 4 of each stanza and the definite one-two rhythm, three stressed syllables per line, seven syllables in odd-numbered lines, six in even-numbered lines. She noted the repetition of s sounds in the first, third, and fourth stanzas.

As Laureen looked over her notes and thought about the poem as a whole, she came to several realizations:

- How is poem organized?
  First two stanzas picture a cheerful childhood game of imagination
  Next two stanzas picture the adult world intruding on and ending the game
  Last two stanzas express an adult yearning for the lost joys of imagination

- How is effect achieved?
  Rhyme and rhythm made poem sound like a childhood song
  s sounds are soft like the water
  Sea images, not just a metaphor describing bath, are also metaphors for imagination itself

Laureen decided to use her conclusion about rhyme and rhythm in the introduction to her essay, which she would organize around the poem's organization. She would devote one paragraph to the first two stanzas, one to the second two stanzas, and one to the last stanza. In her conclusion she would show how a closer analysis reveals the deeper meaning of the metaphors in the poem.

## Drafting and Revising

After Laureen wrote her draft, she worked on it further. She added to her introduction a reference to the soft s sounds. She also worked on her sentence structure, wording, and mechanics.

## Proofreading and Publishing

When Laureen was satisfied with her work, she neatly recopied and proofread it. Her teacher divided the class into small groups, and Laureen compared her analysis with those of others in her group.

## ACTIVITIES AND ASSIGNMENTS

A. As you do the following acitivities, consider the process that Laureen used to analyze "The Voyage of Jimmy Poo."

1. Recreate Laureen's notes on the images, the figures of speech, and the sound effects in the poem.
2. Prepare an outline for Laureen's paper, following her organizational scheme.
3. Based on the work you did above, write an essay analyzing "The Voyage of Jimmy Poo."

B. Write an essay analyzing a poem in your anthology. Follow these steps:

1. Read and reread the poem to make sure that you understand it thoroughly.
2. Take notes on the poem's genre, stanza form, sensory images, figures of speech, sound effects, and other features.
3. Consider your preliminary ideas and come to some conclusions about the poem as a whole.
4. Look over all your notes and decide on your main idea, your thesis. Perhaps the main idea of your paper will be a statement of main idea. Perhaps your paper will focus on a key feature of the poem.
5. Decide how to organize your paper. Perhaps you will analyze the poem section by section, or perhaps you will devote separate paragraphs to several of the poem's key features.
6. Consider how you will conclude your essay. Perhaps you will restate your main idea, perhaps you will summarize the ideas in your paper, or perhaps you will demonstrate a deeper understanding revealed by your analysis.
7. Draft and revise your essay.
8. Proofread your essay, prepare a final copy, and proofread the paper once again. Read both the poem and your essay to a friend or to a relative.

# Lesson 14: Writing About Drama

## UNDERSTANDING DRAMA

*Drama* is a special form of narrative that is written to be presented on stage. A drama can, however, be read and analyzed just like a work of fiction. As in a short story or a novel, a character in a drama faces a conflict, a plot develops from that conflict, and a theme emerges as a result.

There is, however, an important difference between prose fiction and drama. While writers of prose can state any sort of information directly, a playwright must present all the information by means of the spectacle on a stage. The playwright cannot show characters' thoughts except through dialogue or through the use of special devices such as asides or soliloquies. Nor can the playwright comment on the characters or on their behavior, as can the author of prose. Radio dramatists face one more limitation: They can present only what can be heard.

### Reading a Play

The printed version of a play is presented in script format. The script is made up of dialogue and stage directions. The *dialogue* consists of lines to be delivered by actors. The *stage directions* are the playwright's notes on how the drama is to be staged. These notes tell what the set should look like, what the characters should look like or wear, what actions should take place, how certain lines should be delivered, what lighting and sound effects should be used, and the like. Some playwrights provide extensive stage directions. Others leave almost all staging decisions to directors, technicians, and producers.

The script format requires special cooperation from the reader of a play. As you read a drama, you must stage it in your imagination. Envision the stage, give faces and costumes to the characters, picture the movements of the characters, and imagine hearing their voices.

## WRITING ABOUT DRAMA

You can write about drama in the same way you write about fiction:

1. You can do a character study of one or more characters, analyzing their personality and behavior to explain why they do the things they do and how and why they change.
2. You can analyze the central conflict in the drama, showing how the main character struggles against an external or internal force.
3. You can analyze the plot of the drama, identifying its parts and any special techniques that are used, such as foreshadowing, flashbacks, suspense, or a surprise ending.
4. You can examine the theme of the play, showing how it emerges from the events that occur.
5. You can analyze a special technique used in the play, such as symbolism, irony, or poetic language.

In addition, you can write about a play in terms of performance:

1. You can analyze how a character should be portrayed or how a scene should be staged.
2. You can evaluate the staging direction suggested by the playwright.
3. You can review an actual performance of the play, evaluating not only the play itself, but also this particular production.

## CASE STUDY: WRITING ABOUT DRAMA

After Kate's English class read and discussed Howard Koch's *Invasion from Mars*, on page 289, students were given various assignments. Kate's group was to analyze the techniques the author used to make the play realistic and believable.

### Prewriting

Kate began by rereading the play, watching especially for details that heighten its reality. She kept her copy of the play next to her as she took these notes:

- Frame of first act: Story of invasion given as interruption of radio show

- Use of actual news techniques:
    Interruption for "special bulletin"
    Reports from "official" agencies like the Government Meteorological Bureau and the Princeton Observatory
    Comments from "informed sources" like Professor Richard Pierson
    "On-the-scene" interviews like the one with Mr. Wilmuth
    "Round-up" reports of information from many places
    "Eyewitness" accounts like those of Carl Phillips at Grovers Mill

- Use of scientific jargon: Example: heat guns "able to generate an intense heat in a chamber of practically absolute non-conductivity. This intense heat they project in a parallel beam against any object they choose, by means of a polished parabolic mirror of unknown composition"

- Use of realistic sound effects: Applause during "musical show" frame, crowd noises, police sirens, humming sound coming from airship, clanking metal, etc.

As Kate worked, she notice that while these realistic touches dominate the first act, the second act is a more conventional radio drama: One character "talks" to the audience and engages in normal dialogue with another character. Kate made a note of this observation.

Kate next planned the organization of her paper. She decided to use a straightforward introduction in which she would state her thesis: "The success of Howard Koch's radio drama *Invasion from Mars* can be attributed to his skillful use of techniques that make the play seem real."

Kate planned to have four paragraphs in the body of her paper: a short paragraph on the frame of the first act, one on the use of news techniques, one on the use of scientific commentary and jargon, and one on the sound effects.

In her conclusion, Kate decided, she would mention the panic that actually erupted during the original broadcast of the play.

**Drafting and Revising**

Kate kept her outline, her notes, and the script of the play next to her as she wrote the draft of her paper. Then she revised her draft, replacing general observations with quotations, tightening the wording of her topic sentences, and incorporating transitions to show the connections between her ideas.

Finally, Kate proofread her paper for errors in grammar and mechanics. Here is Kate's concluding paragraph:

> With all these realistic touches, is it any wonder that thousands of listeners panicked when they heard the original 1938 production of *Invasion from Mars*? To be sure, once they heard a commercial after the first act and heard a character supposedly talking to them in the second act, they should have realized the truth. If the purpose of drama is to make an audience react, however, Howard Koch and the producers can certainly be proud of this play.

**Proofreading and Publishing**

Kate neatly copied her paper over and then proofread the copy. She helped her group tape a portion of the play, shared her paper with them, and submitted it to her teacher.

## ACTIVITIES AND ASSIGNMENTS

A. If you have not yet done so, read *Invasion from Mars*, on page 289. Then answer the following questions about the case study:

1. How complete are Kate's notes?
2. How could Kate have enlivened her introduction? That is, what could she have used in addition to her thesis statement to make the introduction more interesting?
3. Is Kate's conclusion effective? Why or why not?

B. Write a paper analyzing a different aspect of Howard Koch's *Invasion from Mars* or some aspect of another drama in your anthology. Follow these steps:

1. Read and reread the play.
2. Decide what aspect of the play you will discuss—the characters, the plot, the theme, some special technique, or some aspect of staging.
3. Take notes that relate to your topic, decide on your main idea, and organize your notes.
4. Draft and revise your paper.
5. Neatly copy your paper, proofread it, and exchange papers with a friend who wrote about the same play you did. Compare your papers.

# SECTION 4: JUDGING A LITERARY WORK, EVALUATION

## Lesson 15: Evaluating a Literary Work

### UNDERSTANDING EVALUATION

To *evaluate* a work of literature is to judge it, to make a statement about its value or quality. Here, for example, is an evaluation of a story in this book:

> Ray Bradbury's short story "There Will Come Soft Rains" gives heartbreaking reality to Sara Teasdale's poem of the same name.

An evaluation expresses an opinion, but it must express a reasonable one. The opinion must be supportable by actual evidence from the work. An evaluation can be rejected as unreasonable if, like the statement below, it cannot be supported by facts from the story:

> Ray Bradbury's short story "There Will Come Soft Rains" is unimaginative.

### USING CRITERIA TO MAKE AN EVALUATION

To evaluate a work of literature, you must judge it against certain standards, or *criteria*. The following evaluative criteria are commonly applied to literature:

1. *Originality or inventiveness:* It is said that there are only a handful of themes to write about, but an infinity of ways to do so. One standard that can be applied to a work of literature, therefore, is originality: To what extent does this work offer a fresh perspective on its theme? A work that does offer something new—an inventive plot, unique characters, fresh language, surprising twists—will be judged favorably. A work that seems too similar to another work or that depends on stereotyped characters, predictable events, or cliquéd observations will be judged unfavorably.

2. *Consistency of effect:* In a given work, an author aims for a particular effect. For example, W. W. Jacobs, in "The Monkey's Paw," wants to initiate and sustain a growing feeling of horror, and Philip Booth, in the poem "First Lesson," aims to create a feeling of gentle trust. Both can be judged on the extent to which every scene, every character, every line, and every word contribute to this effect. If some section of a work seems inappropriate—if it contains inappropriate language, an ill-chosen character, or an unbelievable outcome—the work will be judged unfavorably.

3. *Theme:* The theme of a work is generally an idea or insight into life that can itself be judged. One who accepts the theme will rate the work favorably, while one who objects to it may reject the work itself. For example, a reader who believes that it is dangerous to trust life may criticize Philip Booth's poem "First Lesson" as naive.

4. *Clarity:* While works of literature vary considerably in how difficult they are to read, it is not appropriate to evaluate a work solely on its level of difficulty. It is, however, appropriate to judge how clearly the work is presented. If the ideas become clear once you deal fairly with the work, it deserves a fair evaluation. If it is not clear—if the central idea is fuzzy or if the connections between parts seem random—then the work deserves an unfavorable evaluation.

5. *Completeness of effect:* The intent of a work may be clear and the effort admirable, but the work may yet fail if it seems incomplete. For example, you may see why an author reveals

four different characters' thoughts on a subject, but if these characters are not distinctive or if they all sound alike, you can judge the work unfavorably. By contrast, if the author succeeds in putting together lines or characters or ideas so that readers gain a sense of satisfaction, the work can be favorably judged.

6. *Importance:* Literary works can also be judged on whether or not they are of lasting value. For example, a straight adventure story, while enjoyable to read, may be evaluated as less important than one that causes readers to reflect on human nature.

## CASE STUDY: EVALUATING A SINGLE WORK

Carl's class had written about various aspects of poetry. Now the teacher asked students to apply the standards they had been developing in a written evaluation of a poem.

### Prewriting

Carl chose to write about James Wright's "A Blessing," on page 636. After he considered the various criteria, he decided to focus on consistency of effect in the poem. Although Carl had read the poem before, he reread it several times before formulating this evaluation:

> Every word and every image in James Wright's "A Blessing" contributes to the overall effect, that of reverent joy in nature.

Carl noted a number of striking details in the poem and then organized them as follows:

- Word choice:
  "Twilight bounds softly"
  eyes "darken with kindness"
  the ponies "ripple tensely"
  "I would break/Into bloom"

- Soft sounds:
  "shyly as wet swans"
  "love," "loneliness"
  "munching the young tufts of spring"

  "the slenderer one"
  "muzzled," "caress," "blossom"

- Images:
  twilight "bounds" like horses
  horses bow like wet swans
  horse's ear like skin of a girl's wrist
  the speaker is like a flower blooming

- Title: "blessing" means both divine favor and a source of joy

### Drafting and Revising

Carl used his statement of evaluation in the introduction to his paragraph. Then he used his notes to support his evaluation with evidence from the poem. In his conclusion, he used his understanding of the word *blessing* to tie his observations to the title of the poem.

Once Carl completed his draft, he revised it, changing the order of some details and, in general, strengthening his sentence structure.

### Proofreading and Publishing

Carl proofread his draft, correcting grammatical and mechanical errors. Then he made a clean final copy and proofread that. Carl made a copy of the poem and of his paragraph and sent them to a friend of his who worked during the summers at a riding camp.

### ACTIVITIES AND ASSIGNMENTS

A. If you have not already done so, read James Wright's "A Blessing," on page 636. Then answer the following questions.

1. Evaluate Carl's notes. Are there other or better examples of words, sounds, or images that he should have included? Are there other aspects of the poem that he should have considered?

2. Use your version of Carl's notes to write a paragraph evaluating "A Blessing." You may use Carl's statement of evaluation or you may write your own.

3. Apply a different criterion to "A Blessing." That is, judge the poem on originality, theme, clarity,

completeness of effect, or importance. State your evaluation in a sentence, collect evidence to support this evaluation, and write a paragraph based on your notes.

B. Choose a work in your anthology and write a paragraph evaluating some aspect of that work. Follow these steps:

1. Read the work several times to make sure you understand it.
2. Decide what criterion you will apply to the work: originality, consistency of effect, theme, clarity, completeness of effect, or importance.
3. Judge the work by this criterion, and write a sentence stating your evaluation.
4. Gather evidence from the work to support your opinion.

5. Draft your paragraph. Use your statement of evaluation as your topic sentence, build your evidence into the body of your paragraph, and write a concluding sentence that ties your ideas together.

6. Revise your paragraph. Check to make sure that it is well organized, complete, and convincing. Also check to make sure that your wording is clear and graceful.

7. Proofread the draft of your paragraph. Then make a clean final copy and proofread once more. Compare your evaluation with one a friend has written. See if you agree with your friend's evaluation, and see if he or she agrees with yours.

# Lesson 16: Writing a Comparative Evaluation

## UNDERSTANDING A COMPARATIVE EVALUATION

As you learned in the preceding lesson, an evaluation of a work of literature is a judgment about its value or quality, based on some standard. When you write a *comparative evaluation*, you go one step further: You apply the same standard to two works and then judge which succeeds more completely.

Remember that an evaluation must be supportable by evidence from the story. In a comparative evaluation, you must support your judgment of each work by reference to evidence in each.

Here is an example of a statement that expresses a comparative evaluation:

> Though W. W. Jacobs's "The Monkey's Paw" is a classic horror story, Ray Bradbury's "There Will Come Soft Rains" is actually a story of more chilling horror.

In this comparative evaluation, the standard of completeness of effect has been applied to two stories, one of which was judged superior.

## DEVELOPING A COMPARATIVE EVALUATION

Follow these steps to develop a comparative evaluation:

1. Choose the works to be compared and read them carefully.
2. Decide what aspects you will compare—setting, characters, theme, imagery, ease of staging, and so on—and what standard you will apply.
3. Reread each work carefully, taking notes of the aspect that you are concerned about.
4. Evaluate each on the standard you have decided to apply.
5. Decide which work best meets the standard that you are applying. Take notes on your reasons for thinking so.

6. In your paper, state your main idea—your comparative evaluation of the two works—in an introductory paragraph. Devote at least one paragraph to each of the works. In your conclusion, state your reasons for rating one work above the other.

## CASE STUDY: WRITING A COMPARATIVE EVALUATION

Maggie's English teacher asked the class to choose two poems that deal with the same topic and to write a comparative evaluation of them.

### Prewriting

Maggie chose John Updike's "Ex-Basketball Player," on page 709, and Frank Horne's "To James," on page 702, since both are about athletes. Though she had read both poems before, she reread them several times before she decided to focus on theme—to judge which poem gives a more optimistic view of life to young athletes. Maggie knew that "To James" is far more optimistic, so she was able to state her main idea before she took notes:

> Frank Horne's poem "To James" gives a far more positive, optimistic picture of the value of athletics than does John Updike's "Ex-Basketball Player."

Then Maggie took these notes:

- "Ex-Basketball Player"
    depressing scene, symbolic of dead-end life
    sad contrast between Flick then and now
        positive images of past
        "loser" image now

- "To James"
    proud, exultant images of success
    a race as symbol of proud, joyful approach to life

## Drafting and Revising

Maggie kept her notes and her textbook handy as she wrote her rough draft:

> Frank Horne's poem "To James" gives a far more positive, optomistic picture of the value of atheletics than does John Updike's "Ex-Basketball Player."
>
> Poor Flick Webb, the "hero" of Updike's poem, got zero out of his days as an athlete. He now pumps gas on a street that is "cut off/Before it has a chance to go two blocks." That is just like Flick's life. And it faces west, of course. Flick still has a body that won't quit, he "stands tall" and "his hands are fine and nervous," but his "teamates" are gas pumps and the lug wrench does'nt care about his hands. Flick was good once, he made a record that still stands. But what did it get him? Nothing. Flick remembers his days of glory, in the lunchenett he "sits and nods . . . towards bright applauding tiers," but instead of his memories helping him out, they just remind him of what a loser he is now. Now only "Necco Wafers, Nibs, and Juju Beads" watch Flick.
>
> James is the boy being addressed in Horne's poem. The speaker uses words of joy and exultation to remind James of his race, of each straining, glorius moment, from the starting lunge, through the stretch, and through the tape—a winner! The speaker rejoices with James: "Did not my shout /Tell of the/Triumpant ecstasy/Of victory . . .?" But the speaker doesn't stop their, he goes on to tell James that he should live his life as he ran his race. If he does, the speaker promeses, he will "finish/With an ecstatic burst/That carries you/Hurtling/Through the tape/To victory."
>
> Horne's poem gives a much more positive message to young atheletes: What they learn of striving and winning can help them make it big in life. Updike seems to believe that young athletes will never again make it big and will have to live with the bitter contrast between their winning days and their adult days.

## Drafting and Revising

As Maggie began to revise her draft, she noticed that neither her third nor her fourth paragraph had topic sentences. She corrected this flaw, clarified certain unclear sections, and made her wording more formal.

## Proofreading and Publishing

Maggie also proofread her draft. Since she knows that she is apt to have run-on sentences and spelling errors, she checked carefully for these mistakes. She also picked up several other errors. When she was satisfied with her draft, Maggie recopied it carefully. She showed both the two poems and her paper to her track coach before she submitted her analysis in class.

## ACTIVITIES AND ASSIGNMENTS

A. If you have not already done so, read John Updike's "Ex-Basketball Player," on page 709, and Frank Horne's "To James," on page 702. Then revise Maggie's paper. Follow these steps:

1. The third and fourth sentences of Maggie's second paragraph are vague. Rewrite these sentences so they explain more clearly the symbolism of the setting.

2. The first sentence of Maggie's third paragraph is not really a topic sentence. Reword it or replace it with a better sentence. Include a transition to link the third paragraph to the second.

3. Maggie's conclusion also lacks a topic sentence. Write one. Then reverse the order of her two sentences so that they reflect the order of the treatment in the rest of the paper.

4. Throughout her paper, Maggie uses inappropriately informal expressions. Replace them with more formal words or phrases.

5. Maggie has written a number of run-on sentences. Find and correct them.

6. Find and correct Maggie's spelling errors and her errors in the use of the apostrophe.

7. Make a clean copy of the revised paper.

B. Choose two works from your anthology and write a comparative evaluation. Follow these steps:

1. Read both works carefully and decide what aspect you will explore: imagery, characterization, theme, use of dialogue, use of examples, and so on.

2. Decide what standard you will apply to the works.

3. Reread both works and take notes on the aspect you chose.

4. Evaluate each work according to the standard you are applying.

5. Decide which work better meets this standard, state your opinion in a sentence, and take notes on your reasons.

6. Draft your paper. Use your overall statement of opinion in your introduction. Remember to mention the titles and authors of both works. Write a paragraph devoted to the weaker of the two works. Then write a paragraph devoted to the stronger work. In each of these body paragraphs, use the evidence you collected. Write a concluding paragraph in which you state your overall reasons for rating one above the other.

7. Revise your paper. Check to make sure that it is well organized, complete, and convincing. Also make sure that the wording is clear and graceful. Check your sentence structure and mechanics.

8. Make a clean final copy and proofread it. Share your paper with your family before you submit it in class.

# SECTION 5: WRITING CREATIVELY
## Lesson 17: Writing a Short Story

### FINDING AN IDEA FOR A STORY

Professional writers find ideas for stories from many sources. Some base their stories on personal experiences. Others find ideas in books, magazines, or newspaper articles. Still others start from current local, national, or world events. Such sources provide the seed from which a story grows in the writer's imagination. The following are some starting points that you can work from to come up with an idea for your own short story:

1. Think about a place, real or imagined. The place might be your own home, a summer camp, a city street, a stable, a ship headed for the stars, or a distant planet. What might happen in a place like this?

2. Think about a person, real or imagined. The person might be yourself, a friend or relative, a historical figure, someone in the news, or someone with limited resources or special abilities. What problems might such a person face?

3. Think about a conflict, real or imagined. The conflict might be within a family, between friends, in school, or between a person and members of his or her social group. What might happen as a result of this conflict?

4. Think about an event, real or imagined. The event might be a crime, a sports contest, a holiday celebration, a death, or a move. What conflicts might arise for someone involved in this event?

5. Think of an observation about people or about life that you believe is true. What might someone do or be involved in that would demonstrate the truth of this idea?

### DEVELOPING A STORY

Once you have an idea, plan your story, con-sidering each key aspect: setting, character, conflict, plot, theme, and point of view. Many professional writers take far more notes than they need for a story. Some, for example, write complete biographies for their major characters, even though they may use only part of this information. They want to make sure that they really know their characters before they write about them.

Take notes, then, on the following aspects of your story:

1. *Setting:* When and where will your story take place? Do the events occur in a special kind of house or town or region? Is the time of the year or the time of day important? Do you want to illustrate a particular lifestyle?

2. *Major character:* What is this character's name? What does he or she look like? What is his or her age, background, social position, and lifestyle? How would you describe this character's personality? What does he or she do or say that reveals this personality? What things are important to this character? What does he or she do by necessity? by choice? Who are this character's friends? Is this character sympathetic or unappealing? Will he or she change in the course of the story?

3. *Other characters:* Will there be an antagonist, a key character who opposes the main character? If so, what will this character be like? What other characters will be necessary? What role will each play?

4. *Conflict:* What is the central problem that the main character faces. Is the character in conflict with the physical or social environment, with another character or group, or with something within himself or herself? Does this conflict arise from or generate problems in the character's life?

5. *Plot:* How will the events of the story unfold?

6. *Exposition:* What background information must be revealed about the setting, characters, and basic situation?
7. *Inciting incident:* What event will introduce the central conflict?
8. *Development:* What will happen as the conflict develops? What will happen to the major character? What will he or she do?
9. *Climax:* What will be the high point of interest or suspense in the story?
10. *Resolution:* How will the conflict be ended, or resolved? Will this resolution involve a winner of a struggle or a shift in the thoughts or life of the major character?
11. *Denouement:* What, if anything, will occur after the conflict is resolved?
12. *Theme:* What overall idea do you want the story to convey? What tone should you use as you describe events in order to suggest this theme?
13. *Point of View:* Will a character in the story tell it (first-person narration), or will an outside voice narrate the events (third-person narration)? If you use a third-person narrator, will this narrator's knowledge be limited to the internal states of one character, or will the narrator be omniscient and thus able to reveal several characters' internal states?

## CASE STUDY: WRITING A SHORT STORY

A few weeks after Rena had become a volunteer at a local hospital, her teacher asked the class to write short stories. Rena's work sparked a story idea in her mind.

### Prewriting

Rena thought through her story by asking herself about the various elements of short stories. Here are the notes that she took:

- Setting: A medium-sized hospital, contemporary, with a very dedicated staff.
- Major character: Josephine (Jo) Higgins, a fifteen-year-old sophomore. Jo is a good student, somewhat shy and therefore alone and lonely. She volunteers at the hospital in order to get out and meet people.

- Other characters: Marcy Langtree, also a sophomore but a member of the accepted (or popular) crowd. She's vice president of the class, a student council representative, and a cheerleader. She volunteers in order to get one more plus on her record. Her friends think she's wonderful, but she can be very cutting. There's also Ms. Levin, who trains and supervises volunteers, and Mr. Loman, a patient.

- Conflict: (1) Jo *vs.* Marcy—who will do better at the job? (Marcy starts the conflict; Jo is first dismayed, then angered.) (2) Jo *vs.* herself—how will she resolve an ethical question?

- Plot: The story opens with Jo assigned to take magazines around to patients and Marcy to deliver mail. Then the story backs up to introduce Jo and show why she is working at the hospital. Marcy is cool when she recognizes Jo. At first Jo tries to ignore this and make friends with Marcy, but when Marcy says something cruel, Jo becomes angry and resolves to outdo Marcy. Both girls do well, but both want to win the carnation for Volunteer of the Month. On the last day of the month, Jo arrives early and finds that Ms. Levin has left the assignments for the volunteers on the board. Jo is to straighten up the patient lounges, and Marcy is first to deliver flowers and then read to Mr. Loman. Jo notices that if she cut off the last line of the note, Marcy would never know about the second assignment and would be downgraded. Jo reaches for the sheet but then reconsiders. Mr. Loman is a heart patient and a lonely man; his family lives far away. She shakes her head, leaves the note alone, and even greets Marcy pleasantly when the other girl arrives. The next day when Marcy is given the carnation, Jo shakes her hand. Marcy is startled, but accepts Jo's congratulations graciously. Perhaps on impulse, she says Jo may win next month. Jo smiles.

- Point of view: Third-person limited, from Jo's perspective.

## Drafting and Revising

Rena drafted her story and then revised it, specifically aiming for vivid words, realistic dialogue, and effective description of Jo's thoughts.

## Proofreading and Publishing

Rena proofread her story, copied it neatly, and proofread it again. She read her story to her best friend before she submitted it in class.

## ACTIVITIES AND ASSIGNMENTS

A. Consider the case study as you do the following activities.
1. Write a title for Rena's story.
2. Analyze Rena's plot, identifying the exposition, the inciting incident, the development, the climax, the resolution, and the denouement.
3. In a sentence or two, state the theme of Rena's story.
4. Write a story based on Rena's notes.
B. Write an original story, following the steps outlined in this lesson.

# Lesson 18: Writing a Poem

## FINDING AN IDEA FOR A POEM

Poets conceive and develop ideas in a multitude of ways. You, too, can take many different approaches when writing a lyric poem. Remember that a lyric poem expresses the speaker's thoughts and emotions, usually in a way that recalls the lyric's musical origins.

The sources of poems are endless. Everything you observe, think about, experience, or feel is a possible subject for a poem. Here are some possibilities:

1. A single scene that struck you—its beauty, ugliness, stillness, endurance, movement, or power
2. A person whom you know, an intriguing stranger, someone who conveys a striking impression or who embodies some contradiction, or yourself, the you that others see and the you that they don't know
3. An event or something that moves—a ski run, a ball game, a highway at rush hour, or the halls at change of classes
4. An object, one that holds memories or sparks thoughts—old clothes, a battered hockey puck, or a chair with the springs gone
5. A time of day, a day, a month, or a season— what it is like, how you regard it, and what happens during this time
6. A specific sight—a sunset or a statue, a closed door or one ajar, a campfire or a furnace
7. A sound or a rhythm that moves you, that reflects a feeling or an idea—a line of music, the wind in the trees, or a cat's purr
8. A touch—a first kiss, a parent's hand on the forehead of a sick child, a dog's nuzzling, or a victory hug
9. A taste or smell—rainy air, a beach at low tide, burned toast, or a locker room at half time.

10. A word that you like, a word that you hate, a word that intrigues you, or a word that enrages you.

As you consider possible subjects, also consider the overall impression you might wish to convey about this subject.

## DEVELOPING A POEM

Once you have discovered a subject for your poem and, possibly, the overall impression you wish to convey, follow these steps to develop it into a poem:

1. Collect a list of words, phrases, or lines you might use. Consciously consider what sensory images you can include: sights, sounds, smells, tastes, and touches. Also consider what figures of speech, such as metaphor or personification, might heighten the experience. Finally, consider what special effects of sound you can use to mirror your ideas. Possibilities include alliteration, assonance, consonance, repetition. If you prefer, do freewriting or clustering to collect ideas. See page 945 for a description of these techniques.
2. If you have not already done so, decide on the single impression that you want the poem to convey. Cross out those notes that do not contribute to creating this impression. Add others as they occur to you.
3. Begin to organize the ideas into lines of poetry. Will you move from the center outward? convey different sense impressions in order? develop a single metaphor in detail?
4. Decide whether you will use rhyme or a fixed rhythmical pattern. If you decide to do so, begin to work on finding rhymes and words that fit the rhythm. Even if you choose not to use a fixed rhythm, see if you can make the poem sound like what you mean—slow and meditative, perhaps, or fast-paced and energetic.

5. Work on every word in every line of your poem. Make sure that each is highly precise—not a *bird*, but a *swallow*; not *loud* but *screeching*. Make sure that each word fits the rhythm and the tone that are emerging in your poem.

## CASE STUDY: WRITING A POEM

After Terry's class had read and studied lyric poetry, the class was assigned to write original poems.

### Prewriting

Terry considered several possible subjects for his poem—his grandfather, now helpless but once a laughing giant; a canoe trip that he took one summer; his yard just after a heavy snow; his varsity sweater. For each subject, Terry jotted down a few ideas, but he finally settled on his sweater. As he wrote down phrases to describe it, a contrast occurred to him. This sweater was very different from his old practice sweater. Terry decided that he wanted to convey just that contrast in his poem. He then noted additional words and phrases that described his old sweater.

### Drafting and Revising

Terry used his notes to write a draft of his poem, which he wrote as free verse—a poem with no regular rhythm or rhyme scheme. Then he worked extensively on each word and line, sharpening his images and searching for words that both sounded right and expressed what he wanted to say. On the right is Terry's draft, along with his revisions.

### Proofreading and Publishing

As Terry proofread his poem, he made final decisions about how he would punctuate it. Then he recopied his poem and proofread this final copy. Terry read his poem in class and also submitted it to the school literary magazine.

## ACTIVITIES AND ASSIGNMENTS

A. Consider Terry's poem as you answer the following questions.

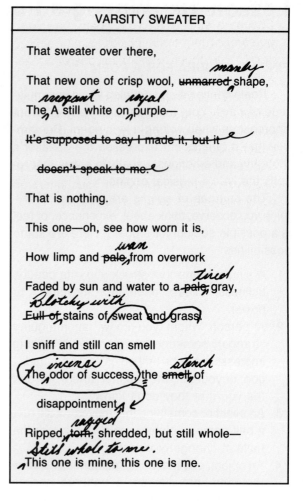

### VARSITY SWEATER

That sweater over there,

That new one of crisp wool, ~~unmarred~~ *manly* shape,

The *arrogant* *royal* ~~A~~ still white on, purple—

~~It's supposed to say I made it, but it~~

~~doesn't speak to me.~~

That is nothing.

This one—oh, see how worn it is,

How limp and ~~pale~~ *wan*, from overwork

Faded by sun and water to a ~~pale~~ *tired* gray,

*Blotchy with* ~~Full of~~ stains of sweat and grass.

I sniff and still can smell

The *incense* odor of success, the ~~smell~~ *stench* of

disappointment,

Ripped, ~~torn~~ *ragged*, shredded, but still whole—

*Still whole to me.*

This one is mine, this one is me.

1. Terry eliminated one line entirely. Did he make the right decision? Why?
2. Terry added two words to line 3. Explain the metaphor created by these words. How do they contribute to Terry's theme?
3. Terry made many changes in individual words. In each case, explain why the new word is better than his original word.
4. Terry added a line near the end of his poem, one that creates repetition. Did the addition strengthen his poem? Explain.
5. Why did Terry reverse the order of the two phrases near the end of his poem?
6. Can you make any additional suggestions to Terry about how to improve his poem still further? How would you rate his poem?

B. Write your own lyric poem. Follow these steps.

1. Choose a subject for your poem—a scene, person, event, time, object, sight, sound, smell, taste, touch, or word that sparks a reaction in you.

2. Make a list of images, figures of speech, and sound effects associated with this subject. If you prefer, use freewriting or clustering to generate ideas.

3. Decide on the overall impression that you want to convey. Eliminate items from your notes that do not contribute to this impression.

4. Use your notes to write a draft of your poem. If you want to do so, use rhyme or a fixed rhythmical pattern.

5. Work on every word and line to make the poem vivid and precise.

6. Proofread your poem. Make final decisions about how you will use capital letters and punctuation, and correct any errors in spelling or punctuation. Prepare a clean final copy of the poem. Then read your poem aloud in class or share it with other students in a discussion group.

# Lesson 19: Writing a Short Dramatic Sketch

## UNDERSTANDING THE DRAMATIC SKETCH

A *dramatic sketch* is a short scene that makes a single point, either serious or humorous. Just like a longer play, a dramatic sketch is written in script format and contains both dialogue and stage directions. *Dialogue* is the actual speech of the characters, while *stage directions* present information about the set, costumes, entrances and exits, actions, delivery of lines, lighting and sound effects—any directions, in fact, that the playwright wants to give to the director, the cast, and the crew. Look at the opening section of the script of *Twelve Angry Men*, from page 312:

> [*Fade in on a jury box: Twelve men are seated in it, listening intently to the voice of the JUDGE as he charges them. . . .*]
> JUDGE. Murder in the first degree—premeditated homicide—is the most serious charge tried in our criminal courts.

Notice that stage directions are italicized and enclosed in square brackets. The name of each speaker is indicated by capital letters.

## DEVELOPING A DRAMATIC SKETCH

You can discover ideas for a dramatic sketch in the same way you find them for short stories: by imagining a setting, character, conflict, plot, or theme and seeing where this starting idea leads you.

You can use the same planning method for a dramatic sketch, too, but keep the following points in mind:

1. *Setting:* In a short dramatic sketch, use only one setting, one that can be reproduced on stage.
2. *Characters:* Remember that characters are revealed through what they say and do and how they speak and act; the playwright cannot comment on the characters or reveal their thoughts directly. You can let characters speak their thoughts by using an aside (a brief remark that other characters on stage do not hear) or a soliloquy (a longer speech made by a character alone on stage).
3. *Conflict and plot:* A short sketch can develop a true conflict and plot, or it may do so only loosely: The conflict may involve no more than a misunderstanding and the action may consist of only one event.
4. *Theme:* A serious sketch will have a theme, or insight into life. However, the point of a humorous sketch may simply be to make people laugh or to poke good-natured fun at a group, an institution, or a custom.

## WRITING THE SKETCH

Begin with the title and list of characters. Use stage directions to describe the characters and the set. Then present the dialogue, using stage directions to specify actions. Keep stage directions brief. You need not specify each action in detail, nor should you give directions on how each speech should be delivered.

Try to develop a distinctive speech pattern for each character. Also, be sure that each speech sounds natural. As you revise, read your work aloud to check the naturalness of the lines.

## CASE STUDY: WRITING A DRAMATIC SKETCH

Every year Phil's school puts on a program for Parents' Night, at which each class presents a dramatic sketch. Phil decided to submit a sketch to the script committee.

### Prewriting

Phil thought of using Sophomore Slump— a disease afflicting several of his friends—as a medical case for experts to solve. Phil made a list of characters and of the events in his plot.

## Drafting, Revising, and Publishing

Phil drafted his sketch quickly, and then revised it extensively. He read the entire sketch aloud, checking to make sure that each speech sounded natural and advanced the action. Phil recopied and proofread his sketch and then submitted it to the committee. He was very proud when his script was selected for presentation on Parents' Night. The following is Phil's sketch, up to the climax:

Down in the Slumps

CHARACTERS

| | |
|---|---|
| Sammy | Dr. Schoolman |
| Nurse | Dr. Joiner |
| Dr. Worriman | Dr. Love |
| Dr. Lord | SuperSophomore |

[*Sammy is a typical sophomore. The doctors can be male or female. All have stethoscopes around their necks. Dr. Worriman wears the traditional white jacket, Dr. Lord a leather jacket, Dr. Schoolman a prim and proper outfit, Dr. Joiner a football or cheerleading uniform, and Dr. Love a soft suit or dress. SuperSophomore wears a Superman-type outfit.*]

[*The curtain opens on a typical hospital room, with a window at center rear and a door at stage right. Sammy is in bed, stage left, groaning loudly. Nurse and Dr. Worriman stand on either side of bed.*]

WORRIMAN. [*Checking chart in his hand*] I just can't understand it. You've checked his temperature? Blood pressure? White cell count? Red cell count?

[*Nurse nods at each question.*]

WORRIMAN. Then I can't figure it out. There seems to be nothing wrong with this young man and yet he complains that—

SAMMY. [*In a macabre voice*] Everything! Everything is wrong!

NURSE. Doctor, if I may make a suggestion—

WORRIMAN. Yes, yes, anything!

NURSE: Do you suppose it's [*She lowers her voice to an eerie stage whisper*] Sophomore Slump?

SAMMY. Aaaah! Ooooh! Aaaah!

WORRIMAN: Listen to him! You must be right. Cer-

tainly all the signs are there—grades down, skipping practices, no interest in anything, grumpy at home, even complains about hamburgers again for lunch. But I'm not equipped to deal with such a problem. We're going to have to call in the experts.

NURSE. Ah, Dr. Worriman, forgive me, but I took the liberty of calling for you. Four of our best people are just outside.

WORRIMAN. You're a wonder! You should be a doctor!

NURSE. [*Crossing to door*] I know.

[*She opens door and four experts enter, chattering among themselves: "Yes, it's sure to be," "No, but what of the Dalton case?" etc.*]

WORRIMAN. Come, come my friends, we have a serious case here. Please examine the patient.

[*He and Nurse retire to stage right while experts move around bed, examine the chart, lift Sammy's arm, poke him, etc. Sammy continues to groan. As each expert gives his or her speech, he or she moves away from the bed a bit and addresses the other experts, Dr. Worriman, and the Nurse.*]

LORD. [*In a gloating voice*] Ah ha! I have it! The lad is suffering from having eaten too much humble pie! For a year and a half he's had to look up to those juniors and seniors, feeling like a nothing himself. It's time he developed a little pride. He's got to begin lording it over the freshmen, ordering them around, giving them wrong information. He needs to feel BIG!

JOINER. [*In a rah-rah voice*] No, no, Dr. Lord! Wrong, I say! This boy doesn't have enough interests! He must get into things—football, hockey, basketball, baseball, the school newspaper, student council, Boy Scouts, the drama club! *That's* what he needs—a lively dose of activity!

SCHOOLMAN. [*Primly*] Tsk, tsk, Dr. Joiner, you forget that Sammy is a student. He has to hit those books! Study! Cram it in! Stay up all night with his nose in a book!

LOVE. [*Romantically*] Aren't you forgetting, Dr. Schoolman, that this boy is fifteen years old? He needs love, my friends, a girlfriend who will understand him, who will run a cool hand over his fevered brow. I tell you this: Love conquers all.

WORRIMAN. [*More worried than ever*] But—but you can't all be right! Why, poor Sammy would be dead if we prescribed all that. [*The window suddenly opens and SuperSophomore bursts in, a spotlight thrown on him.*]

NURSE. At last! SuperSophomore! I knew you wouldn't fail us!

[*Sammy takes one look and dives under the covers, visibly shaking and groaning louder.*]

SUPERSOPHOMORE. Yes, I am here. Now let me see.

[*He goes to bed and throws off covers. He walks around, chin in hand, and then returns to center stage, where he faces out. The spotlight follows him.*]

SUPERSOPHOMORE. The answer is clear. [*All, including Sammy, lean forward expectantly.*]

## ACTIVITIES AND ASSIGNMENTS

A.  Use the case study to complete the following activities.

1.  Point out where Phil used stage directions to establish a setting, describe characters, specify action, and suggest how lines should be delivered.

2.  Write the climax and resolution of Phil's sketch.

B.  Write a short dramatic sketch of your own, following the steps outlined in this lesson.

# Lesson 20: Writing a Personal Essay

## FINDING A SUBJECT FOR AN ESSAY

An *essay* allows a writer to express his or her thoughts on almost any subject imaginable. Writers use essays to share experiences they have had, opinions they have come to, and observations they have made.

When planning a personal essay, choose a topic that is important to you, one about which you have strong feelings or ideas. If a subject does not immediately occur to you, try the techniques of freewriting or clustering described on page 945 to help you focus on an idea.

Once you have chosen a topic, decide what your purpose will be: Do you intend to describe something, to tell a story, to share some information, to entertain, or to persuade others to believe or do something? With your topic and purpose in mind, you should be able to formulate a thesis statement, a sentence or two stating the overall point of your essay. The following are examples of thesis statements for various kinds of essays:

1. *Descriptive essay:* The field house was a scene of orderly chaos on the night of the semifinal basketball championship game.
2. *Narrative essay:* Lincoln High School showed its best and its worst during the semifinal playoff game for the state basketball championship.
3. *Expository essay:* Participation in a championship playoff can have unexpected side benefits, no matter how the score comes out.
4. *Entertainment essay:* Which would be more disastrous, the end of the world or losing a basketball championship game?
5. *Persuasive essay:* Lincoln High School needs to purchase new basketball uniforms before the championships.

## DEVELOPING THE ESSAY

If you have not already done so, identify the audience you want to address in your essay. Keeping your purpose and audience in mind can help you as you begin to gather ideas and information. Use whatever technique for collecting information works best for you—freewriting, clustering, making lists or charts, writing and answering questions, taking notes from books or interviews, or outlining.

The type of essay you want to write can guide your selection of details: For a descriptive essay, note sensory details. For a narrative essay, jot down events in chronological order. For an expository essay, note key facts or ideas. For a persuasive essay, make a chart of reasons, facts, and examples that support your case.

Next organize your information. Decide how long your essay will be—one paragraph? Three? Five? Group the information you have into related sections and decide what information you will present in the introduction, body, and conclusion of your essay. If you intend to write several body paragraphs, decide on the key idea that each paragraph will develop.

Then make a rough outline that you can refer to as you draft your essay. Keep your purpose and audience in mind as you write, but feel free to add, eliminate, or change ideas as you go.

After you complete your draft, revise and proofread it, and prepare your final copy. Share your essay with your teacher and with friends, relatives, or classmates.

## CASE STUDY: WRITING A PERSONAL ESSAY

Jean's class had practiced writing various kinds of paragraphs. The teacher then asked the class to write personal essays of three-to-five paragraphs on topics of their choice.

### Prewriting

Jean's basketball team had just lost the semifinal playoff game for the state championship, and Jean knew that she wanted to write about this loss. Several ideas occurred to her: She could tell the story of what happened, or she could express her anger about the way some people in the school had acted before, during, and after the game. However, since several of Jean's teammates were in the same class, she decided to take a different approach. She would write a descriptive essay about the locker room, using this description to reflect on athletes' attitudes and feelings. She tried this thesis statement:

The locker room is symbolic of the athletes.

Jean thought that this was too vague, so she rewrote it as follows:

The locker room before and after a game vibrates with the players' feelings.

Wording it this way helped Jean decide to make a list of her notes:

- Before a game:
  clean uniforms
  clean faces, tidy hair
  lockers open and shut jauntily
  voices sing
  clothes hung up
  banners and signs crisp and
  encouraging
  hope and confidence pervade the air

- After a victory:
  Lockers ring with joy
  whoops of laughter
  towels whistle
  sweaty faces and hair
  signs taken down and paraded around
  uniforms waved proudly

- After a defeat:
  sweaty faces and hair
  uniforms in sodden heap
  lockers left open, silent
  every sound an insult
  signs ripped down and crumpled
  players dejected like wet towels

As Jean surveyed her notes, she realized that she could use her three charts as the basis for three paragraphs in the body of her essay.

**Drafting and Revising**

Jean kept her notes next to her as she drafted her essay. She wrote five paragraphs as she had planned to do, but she included many extra details as one idea led to another. When she began to revise, she found that the paragraphs in the body of her essay were now rich in detail but poorly organized. She wrote another draft of her paper, concentrating especially on internal organization. She revised this draft for sentence structure, wording, and tone.

**Proofreading and Publishing**

Jean proofread her draft and made two clean copies. One she submitted to her English teacher, and the other she submitted to the school newspaper as a possible guest editorial.

The following are the introduction and conclusion from Jean's final essay:

*Introduction:*
An empty locker room has little personality. The lockers and benches look neutral, institutional. The floor looks cold, and the lights glare. But just fill that room with fifteen girls, two coaches, and a trainer, and watch how, like magic, the room changes. Now it vibrates with the players' feelings.

*Conclusion:*
And that's how the locker room at Lincoln High School felt after last week's bitter defeat in the semifinal state championship game: damp, muted, crumpled. But not completely—no, not completely. You see, these fifteen girls, two coaches, and a trainer had come through a Cinderella season, winning game after game that all the experts said they would lose. As clean clothes were donned, so was a fresh spirit. Those people looked at each other, and while they still felt the pain of their defeat, they could smile a little, too. For a few minutes after they left, the locker room vibrated with new hope.

## ACTIVITIES AND ASSIGNMENTS

**A.** Answer the following questions based on the case study.

1. How did Jean's restatement of her thesis improve it?

2. Where in Jean's introduction is her thesis statement? What other information does her introduction include? Is the introduction effective?

3. In her conclusion, Jean uses the championship game to tie the body of her essay to her thesis. Did she do so effectively? Is the conclusion too long?

4. Jean saw the sentence fragment in her conclusion but deliberately left it in. Should she have rewritten it as a complete sentence?

5. Use Jean's prewriting notes to write the body of her essay.

**B.** Follow these steps to write a personal essay of your own:

1. Choose a subject, or discover one through freewriting or clustering.

2. Identify your purpose—description, narration, exposition, or persuasion—and your audience.

3. Formulate a thesis statement that expresses the overall idea you want to convey.

4. Gather information in a way that works for you.

5. Organize your information and draft your essay. Write a clear introduction in which you state your thesis. Also write one or more body paragraphs and a solid conclusion.

6. Revise, recopy, and proofread your essay. Submit your essay to a school publication or to some person to whom it would be meaningful.

# HANDBOOK OF LITERARY TERMS AND TECHNIQUES

**ACT**   See *Drama*.

**ALLEGORY**   An *allegory* is a story with more than one level of meaning—a literal and one or more symbolic levels. Allegory allows a writer both to tell a story about literal characters and to make a moral, religious, or political point. Besides having a literal surface meaning, the events, settings, or characters in an allegory also stand for ideas or qualities and have a second meaning on that level. Edgar Allan Poe's story, "The Masque of the Red Death," on page 173, allegorically shows the inevitable arrival of death no matter how people try to avoid it.

**ALLITERATION**   *Alliteration* is the repetition of initial consonant sounds. Writers and poets use alliteration to create pleasing musical effects. Alma Villanueva uses alliteration in these lines from "I Was a Skinny Tomboy Kid,"

I grew like a thin, stubborn *w*eed
*w*atering myself *w*hatever *w*ay I could.

See *Assonance*, *Consonance*, and *Rhyme*.

**ALLUSION**   An *allusion* is a reference to a well-known person, place, event, literary work, or work of art. Writers often make allusions to famous works such as the Bible or William Shakespeare's plays. They also make allusions to mythology, politics, current events, or other fields familiar to readers. For example, the title of John Steinbeck's novel *The Pearl*, on page 779, may remind readers of the Biblical "pearl of great price." A writer may use allusions as a sort of shorthand, briefly suggesting specific ideas or views.

**ANACHRONISM**   An *anachronism* is something presented out of its actual chronological time. For example, the events in *Julius Caesar* take place

in 44 B.C. However, Shakespeare probably wrote the play in A.D. 1599. In the play, William Shakespeare naturally includes many Roman customs, but he also mentions Elizabethan doublets, striking clocks, and chimney tops. These items from Shakespeare's time did not exist in Caesar's day and are therefore anachronisms.

**ANALOGY**   An *analogy* compares two different things to point out how they are similar. In "Some Remarks on Humor," on page 535, E. B. White writes about seeing a man blowing gigantic soap bubbles that are so big that they are no longer pretty. He then uses an analogy to explain that humor, like a bubble, is fragile and should not be overblown. White's analogy shows that a writer may use an analogy to explain the unfamiliar by comparing it with the familiar.

**ANAPEST**   See *Meter*.

**ANECDOTE**   An *anecdote* is a brief story about an amusing, or strange event. James Thurber, for example, fills "The Dog That Bit People," on page 441, with humorous anecdotes about his family and about the dog Muggs. In the essay on page 451, Van Wyck Brooks presents anecdotes about Emily Dickinson's experiences and about her reactions to events.

**ANTAGONIST**   An *antagonist* is a character or force in conflict with the main character, or protagonist. In John Steinbeck's *The Pearl*, on page 779, Kino and his family, threatened by all those who want the pearl, try to escape from the trackers, their antagonists. In Carl Stephenson's short story on page 41, "Leiningen Versus the Ants," Leiningen battles nonhuman antagonists, the ants. A story does not have to have an antagonist, as Toshio Mori's "Abalone, Abalone,

Abalone,'' on page 169, illustrates. Nevertheless, the conflict between the protagonist and an antagonist is often the basis for the plot.
See *Conflict* and *Protagonist*.

**APHORISM**  An *aphorism* is a general truth or observation about life, usually stated concisely and pointedly. Some writers have an aphoristic style, using many witty or wise statements to sum up their essays or to reinforce points or arguments. Once written, aphorisms may become part of our ordinary language, as Calvin Trillin humorously illustrates in "Rural Literalism," on page 539.

**APOSTROPHE**  An *apostrophe* is a figure of speech in which a writer speaks directly to an idea, to a quality, to an object, or to a person who is not present. In the following lines Emily Dickinson addresses a month of the year:

> Dear March—come in—
> How glad I am—
> I hoped for you before—
> Put down your Hat—
> You must have walked—
> How out of Breath you are—

Apostrophe is most often used in poetry and in speeches to add emotional intensity.
See *Figurative Language*.

**ARGUMENTATION**  *Argumentation* is the type of writing that presents and logically supports the writer's views about an issue. Argumentation is one of the forms of discourse, or formal discussion of a subject. It includes persuasive writing that not only presents the writer's opinion but also tries to move the reader to take some action or to adopt some way of thinking. Lorraine Hansberry's, "On Summer," on page 529, is a *persuasive essay*.
See *Forms of Discourse* and *Persuasion*.

**ASIDE**  An *aside* is a short speech delivered to the audience by an actor in a play and spoken in an undertone to suggest that the rest of the characters on stage are unable to hear it. In William Shakespeare's *Julius Caesar*, which begins on page 345, Caesar says, "and we (like friends) will straightway go together." Then Brutus says in an aside, "That every like is not the same, O Caesar,/The heart of Brutus earns to think upon." Brutus makes this comment in an aside so that Caesar will not hear it. The comment is heard, however, by the audience. An aside allows the writer to reveal a character's private thoughts, reactions, or motivations to the audience without making these known to the other characters.

**ASSONANCE**  *Assonance* is the close repetition of similar vowels in conjunction with dissimilar consonant sounds. Used particularly in poetry, assonance differs from rhyme because only the vowel sounds are repeated. For example, *at* and *bat* rhyme, but *at* and *ask* illustrate assonance. These lines from "Alli por la calle San Luis," by Carmen Taffolla, use assonance to describe the cooking of corn tortillas:

> Cooked on the homeblack of a flat stove,
> Flipped to slap the birth awake.
> Wrapped by corn hands.

Here the repeated *a* sounds contribute to the poem's music and unity, enriching the description of the cooking process.
See *Consonance*.

**ATMOSPHERE**  See *Mood*.

**AUTOBIOGRAPHY**  An *autobiography* is a form of nonfiction in which a person tells his or her own life story. An autobiography may record personal thoughts as well as narrate events. Its focus is the individual, not the times or public incidents, though these of course play a part in anyone's life story. Unlike a journal, a collection of letters, or a diary, an autobiography is written and organized for a public audience. Notable examples of the genre include the autobiographies of Benjamin Franklin and Frederick Douglass, as well

as Dylan Thomas's "A Child's Christmas in Wales," which appears on page 469.
See *Biography*.

**BALLAD**     A *ballad* is a songlike poem that tells a story, often one dealing with adventure or romance. Ballads tell their stories with simple language, dramatic action, dialogue, and repetition, often in a refrain. Most ballads are about ordinary people and everyday life. Most deal with adventure, disaster, disappointment, love, tragedy, or other emotional themes.

This very old type of narrative poetry generally follows a traditional form called the *ballad stanza*. A ballad stanza may have four or six rhyming lines.

A *folk ballad* is passed along orally from generation to generation. Its writer is not known. Examples include the ballads of Robin Hood, Casey Jones, and John Henry. In contrast, a *literary ballad* is written by a specific person, following the model of the folk ballad. An example is Longfellow's "The Wreck of the Hesperus," on page 601.
See *Narrative Poem, Oral Tradition*, and *Refrain*.

**BIOGRAPHY**     A *biography* is a form of nonfiction in which a writer tells the life story of another person. A biographer uses the subject's letters or writings, interviews, personal knowledge, and other books or materials to find details about the main events of the subject's life. After gathering this information, the biographer generally selects a particular focus to concentrate on in the essay or book. For example, in "Marian Anderson: Famous Concert Singer," on page 463, Langston Hughes focuses on Marian Anderson's career as a singer.
See *Autobiography*.

**BLANK VERSE**     *Blank verse* is poetry written in unrhymed iambic pentameter lines. Each iambic foot has an unstressed syllable followed by a stressed syllable. A pentameter line has five of these feet. Robert Frost uses blank verse in "Birches":

When Í | see bírch|es bénd | tŏ léft | and right
Acróss | the lines ŏf straight|er dárk|er trées,
Ĭ líke | tŏ think | some bóy's | béen swing|ǐng thém.

Because blank verse sounds like ordinary spoken English, it has been used in much famous poetry and drama, including William Shakespeare's *Julius Caesar*.
See *Iambic Pentameter* and *Meter*.

**CAESURA**     A *caesura* is a pause or break in the middle of a line of poetry. Often, a caesura is indicated by punctuation. Double slash marks (*//*) have been used to indicate the caesuras in these lines from Paul Laurence Dunbar's "We Wear the Mask":

We wear the mask//that grins and lies,
It hides our cheeks//and shades our eyes,—
This debt we pay//to human guile;
With torn and bleeding//hearts we smile.

Poets use caesuras to reflect the ordinary sound patterns of English, to keep the rhythm from becoming monotonous, to emphasize certain words, and to create special effects.

**CHARACTER**     A *character* is a person or animal who takes part in the action of a literary work. Characters are called round or flat, depending on how they are developed. *Round characters* are complicated and exhibit numerous qualities or traits. As a result, they seem like real people, as does Chee in "Chee's Daughter," on page 73. In contrast, *flat characters* have only one or two characteristics. For example, all that the reader learns about Chee's father-in-law, Old Man Fat, is that he is thriftless and greedy. Character types that readers easily recognize, such as the hard-boiled detective or the wicked stepmother, are called *stereotypes* or *stock characters*. Usually writers try to develop their main characters as lifelike, round characters. Other characters, however, may be flat because they are less important to the story and to readers.

Throughout the action of a story, a *static character* stays essentially the same. Scoresby

in Mark Twain's "Luck," on page 99, is a static character. In contrast, a *dynamic character* is changed by events or by interactions with other characters, as is Tom Benecke in Jack Finney's "Contents of the Dead Man's Pocket," on page 15. Novels and plays often contain many dynamic characters. Short stories often have several static characters and only one or two dynamic characters.
See *Characterization* and *Motivation*.

**CHARACTERIZATION**   *Characterization* is the act of creating and developing a character. A writer uses *direct characterization* when stating or describing a character's traits. For example, in William Melvin Kelley's "A Visit to Grandmother," on page 65, GL is described as "part con man, part practical joker and part Don Juan." A writer uses *indirect characterization* when showing a character's personality through his or her actions, thoughts, feelings, words, and appearance, or through another character's observations and reactions. In the same story, Kelley presents Chig's observations and memories of his father. Kelley also shows the actions and words of Chig's father during the emotional scene with Chig's grandmother. Such indirect characterization relies on the reader to put together the clues in order to figure out the character's personality.
See *Character*.

**CINQUAIN**   See *Stanza*.

**CLIMAX**   The *climax* in a story or play is the high point of interest or suspense in a literary work. The climax generally occurs near the end of the work. In "Chee's Daughter," on page 73, the climax occurs when Chee takes the food to his in-laws at the trading post. At this point, readers sympathize with Chee and feel great suspense, wondering whether he will succeed in getting back his daughter.
See *Plot*.

**COMEDY**   A *comedy* is a work of literature, es-pecially a play, that is less serious than a trage-dy and that has a happy ending. Comedies often show ordinary people in conflict with their socie-ties. Comedies may feature humorous physical action or witty dialogue.
See *Drama* and *Tragedy*.

**CONCRETE POETRY**   A *concrete poem* is one with a shape that suggests its subject. "A Christmas Tree," by William Burfors, is one example:

Star
If you are
A love compassionate,
You will walk with us this year.
We face a glacial distance, who are here
Huddled
At your feet.

**CONFLICT**   A *conflict* is a struggle between op-posing forces. Sometimes this struggle is *inter-nal*, or inside a character, as when a character strives to meet a self-imposed challenge. At other times the struggle is *external* and involves a force outside the character. This force may be another character, the antagonist; a force of nature; or a social convention or custom.
    Many stories involve several types of conflict. In Kay Boyle's "The Soldier Ran Away," on page 85, Colonel Wheeler faces both a conflict within himself and a conflict with his son.
See *Antagonist, Plot*, and *Protagonist*.

**CONNOTATION**   The *connotation* of a word is the set of associations that the word calls to mind. For example, most people would prefer a "vin-tage automobile" to an "old wreck." In fact, some car dealers think a buyer would rather look at a "previously owned vehicle" than at a "used car." As these examples illustrate, words with similar *denotations*, or literal, dictionary meanings, often have very different connotations. As a result, the words can create different emotional reactions and feelings. Careful writing involves choosing words with appropriate connotations as well as denotations.
See *Denotation*.

**CONSONANCE**    *Consonance* is the repetition of consonant sounds in conjunction with dissimilar vowel sounds. The following word pairs illustrate consonance: *will–wall, flip–flop,* and *hid–head.* In "I Want to Write," Margaret Walker uses consonance within a line:

> I want to catch their sunshine laughter in a bowl:
> fling dark hands to a darker sky
> and *fill* them *full* of stars.

Consonance is used to create musical effects, to link ideas, and to emphasize particular words.
See *Assonance.*

**CONVENTION**    A *convention* is an artificial or unrealistic literary technique, form, or style that is nonetheless accepted by the audience or reader. For example, in a story or a play, a writer may jump backward in time by using the convention known as the *flashback,* even though such movement in time doesn't occur in real life. Similarly, a story or play may contain an all-knowing narrator, even though such a person could not actually exist. Common conventions in drama include asides, sound effects, and the use of a stage to represent a place other than a stage. Common conventions in poetry include rhyme, stanzas, and regular meters.

**COUPLET**    A *couplet* is a pair of consecutive rhyming lines. These lines usually are of the same length and rhythmical pattern. Kathleen Raine's poem "in the Beck" describes "a fish, that quivers in [a] pool." The poem ends with this couplet:

> It lives unmoved, equated with the stream,
> as flowers are fit for air, man for his dream.

See *Stanza.*

**CRISIS**    The *crisis* in the plot of a story or play is the turning point for the protagonist. At this point the protagonist changes his or her situation or reaches some new understanding. Often the crisis and the climax coincide. In Arnold Perl's "Tev-

ya and the First Daughter," on page 271, the crisis comes when Tevya learns why Tzeitl does not want to marry Lazar Wolf. The crisis in John Steinbeck's *The Pearl,* on page 779, takes place when Coyotito is killed, thus totally changing Kino and Juana's situation and motivation.
See *Climax* and *Plot.*

**DACTYL**    See *Meter.*

**DEAD METAPHOR**    See *Metaphor.*

**DENOTATION**    A *denotation* is the literal or exact meaning of a word. The denotation, or dictionary meaning, includes none of the feelings or suggestions that are part of a word's *connotations.*
See *Connotation.*

**DENOUEMENT**    See *Plot.*

**DESCRIPTION**    A *description* is a portrait, in words, of a person, place, or object. Its purpose is to provide the concrete details and lively images that make the appearance of people, places, and things easy for the reader to envision. For example, Bienvenido Santos uses description to set the scene in his essay "Scent of Apples":

> In a backyard an old man burned leaves and twigs while a gray-haired woman sat on the porch, her red hands quiet on her lap, watching the smoke rising above the elms, both of them thinking the same thought, perhaps, about a tall, grinning boy with blue eyes and flying hair who went out to war; where could he be now this month when leaves were turning into gold and the fragrance of gathered apples was in the wind?

As this passage shows, vivid description uses details that appeal to the senses so that the reader can easily imagine how something looks, sounds, feels, tastes, or smells. Such details can also help to define the characters or to suggest the mood, or feeling, of the work.
See *Forms of Discourse.*

**DEVELOPMENT**  See *Plot*.

**DIALECT**  A *dialect* is the form of a language spoken by people in a particular region or group. Everyone speaks some dialect, usually that of the place where he or she grew up. Dialects differ in vocabulary, in grammar, and in pronunciation. In Willa Cather's ''The Sentimentality of William Tavener,'' on page 255, the characters speak in a western dialect. Writers use dialect to make their characters sound realistic and to create local color.
See *Local Color* and *Vernacular*.

**DIALOGUE**  A *dialogue* is a conversation between characters. Writers use dialogue to reveal character, to present events, to add variety to a narrative, and to interest readers.

**DICTION**  *Diction* is word choice. A writer chooses specific words to suit his or her audience, purpose, and subject. Diction is part of a writer's style and may be described in many ways—as formal or informal, as ordinary or technical, as abstract or concrete. In ''Flood,'' on page 509, Annie Dillard's diction is both informal and exact. She chooses words that are fairly simple but that create a precise picture of the flood so that readers can share her experience.
See *Connotation, Denotation*, and *Style*.

**DIMETER**  See *Meter*.

**DRAMA**  A *drama* is a story written to be performed by actors. The playwright, or author, of a drama creates dialogue, or words for the actors to speak, and stage directions, or notes about elements of staging and performance. The audience accepts as believable the presentation on stage as well as whatever dramatic conventions are used, such as soliloquies, asides, poetic language, or the passage of time between acts or scenes. This text contains several dramas, including William Shakespeare's *The Tragedy of Julius Caesar*, on page 345. A drama is often divided into long sections called *acts* and into shorter sections called *scenes*. Types of drama include comedy, tragedy, melodrama, and farce.
See *Genre*.

**DRAMATIC IRONY**  See *Irony*.

**DRAMATIC POEM**  A *dramatic poem* is a verse that presents the speech of one or more characters. In a *dramatic monologue*, only one character speaks. In a *dramatic dialogue*, two or more characters speak. Dramatic poems are like little plays and usually involve many narrative elements such as setting, conflict, and plot. Such elements may be found in Rudyard Kipling's ''Danny Deever,'' on page 607, and in W. H. Auden's ''O What Is That Sound,'' on page 611.

**DYNAMIC CHARACTER**  See *Character*.

**END-STOPPED LINE**  An *end-stopped line* is a line, in a poem, that ends with a major pause. The pause is often punctuated by a comma, dash, colon, semicolon, or period. The following lines from ''Beneath the Shadow of the Freeway,'' by Lorna Dee Cervantes, are end-stopped:

> Before rain I notice seagulls.
> They walk in flocks,
> cautious across lawns:
> splayed toes, indecisive beaks.
> Grandma says seagulls mean a storm.

The pauses concluding end-stopped lines may vary in degree in order to vary the poem's emphasis and rhythm.
See *Run-on Line*.

**EPIC**  An *epic* is a long narrative poem about the exploits of a hero or a god. Because of its length and its loftiness of theme, an epic usually presents a telling portrait of the culture in which it was produced. The ancient *folk epics* were recited aloud as entertainment at feasts and were not written down until long after they were composed.

The English poem *Beowulf* is a folk epic, as are the two classical Greek poems, *the Odyssey* and *The Iliad*. The *art epic* is modeled on the folk epic but has a known author and is written down as it is composed. Examples include the *Aeneid*, by the Roman poet Virgil, and *Paradise Lost*, by the English poet John Milton.
See *Narrative Poem*

**EPITHET** An *epithet* is a brief descriptive phrase that is used like a name. Eve Merriam uses epithets such as "bright words" and "dark words" in "Metaphor," on page 646. *Homeric epithets*, such as "rosy-fingered Dawn," are common in epic poems, and descriptive epithets such as "land of liberty" are part of everyday speech and writing.

**ESSAY** An *essay* is a short, nonfiction work about a particular subject. Essays are of many types but may be grouped on the basis of tone, style, and structure as informal or formal.

The *informal essay* is generally brief, relaxed, and entertaining. It may be humorous, conversational, or unconventional. Whatever the subject or approach, an informal essay usually reveals the writer's character, as if the writer and the reader were sitting and talking together. James Thurber's "The Dog That Bit People," on page 441 and Calvin Trillin's "Rural Literalism," on page 539, show how playful and entertaining informal essays can be.

In contrast, the *formal essay* is longer, more serious, and less personal. It is also organized more strictly according to some logical pattern. An example in this text of the formal essay is Theodore H. White's "The American Idea," on page 549.

An essay also may be categorized by its main purpose—to portray a person, place, or thing through description; to tell a story through narration; to explain and inform through exposition; or to support an opinion through persuasion or argumentation.

See *Argumentation, Description, Exposition, Forms of Discourse, Narration*, and *Persuasion*.

**EXACT RHYME** See *Rhyme*.

**EXAGGERATION** See *Hyperbole*.

**EXPOSITION** *Exposition* is writing or speech that explains, informs, or presents information. The main methods used in expository writing are illustration, classification, definition, comparison and contrast, and analysis. Examples of expository essays in this text are Annie Dillard's "Flood," on page 509; Lorraine Hansberry's "On Summer," on page 529; and Rachel Carson's "The Marginal World," on page 565.

In the plot of a story or drama, the exposition is the part of the work that introduces the characters, the setting, and the basic situation. Such information is typically presented at the beginning. The opening scene in Reginald Rose's *Twelve Angry Men*, on page 311, shows the jury sitting in the jury box, listening to the judge's instructions before going out to reach a verdict. The judge's speech immediately tells the viewer where the characters are, why they are there, and what they are going to do.
See *Forms of Discourse*.

**EXTENDED METAPHOR** In an *extended metaphor*, as in a regular metaphor, a subject is spoken or written of as though it were something else. However, extended metaphor differs from regular metaphor in that several comparisons are made. Marcie Hans uses extended metaphor in her poem "Fueled," on page 652, to compare a flower to a rocket.
See *Metaphor*.

**FABLE** A *fable* is a brief story, usually with animal characters, that teaches a lesson, or moral. The fable is an ancient literary form found in many cultures. The fables of Aesop, a Greek slave who lived in the sixth century B.C., are still popular with children. Other famous writers of fables include La Fontaine, a seventeenth-century Frenchman, and James Thurber, a twentieth-century American.

**FANTASY** *Fantasy* is highly imaginative writing that contains elements not found in real life. A writer of fantasy presents improbable characters, places, and events, often ones involving magic or the supernatural. Many science-fiction stories, such as Ray Bradbury's "There Will Come Soft Rains," on page 133, contain elements of fantasy.

**FARCE** *Farce* is a kind of comedy that features physical humor, stereotyped characters, and improbable plots. Writers of farces make considerable use of such literary devices as hyperbole, irony of situation, and surprising twists of the plot. Many farces involve mistaken identity and contain recognition scenes in which the true identities of characters are revealed. A farce may be a complete play or a scene within a play. William Shakespeare often used farce for contrast or for comic relief within his serious works. An example can be found in Act I, Scene i of *Julius Caesar*. See *Comedy* and *Drama*.

**FICTION** *Fiction* is prose writing that tells about imaginary characters and events. The term is generally used to refer to narrative prose, to novels and short stories, rather than to poetry and drama. Fictional writing is sometimes based on real people, places, and events. However, the fiction writer reshapes these realistic elements, placing them in an imaginary or invented context. Doris Lessing's "Through the Tunnel," on page 159, and John Knowles's *A Separate Peace*, on page 831, are examples of fiction.
See *Genre*, *Novel*, and *Short Story*.

**FIGURATIVE LANGUAGE** *Figurative language* is writing or speech not meant to be interpreted literally. Most writers, and especially poets, use figurative language to help readers to see things

in new ways. For example, Naomi Long Madgett begins her poem "Black Woman" with these examples of figurative language:

> My hair is springy like the forest grasses
> That cushion the feet of squirrels—
> Crinkled and blown in a south breeze
> Like the small leaves of native bushes.
>
> My black eyes are coals burning
> Like a low, full jungle moon
> Through the darkness of being.

Madgett does not mean, literally, that forest grasses grow from her head or that she has coals for eyes. Instead, she means her language to be interpreted figuratively. She is using types of figurative language known as simile and metaphor to describe herself imaginatively.

The many types of figurative language are called *figures of speech*. Poets and other writers use figurative language to create vivid word pictures, to make their writing emotionally intense and concentrated, and to state their ideas in new and unusual ways.
See *Figure of Speech* and *Literal Language*.

**FIGURE OF SPEECH** A *figure of speech* is an expression or a word used imaginatively rather than literally. Types of figurative language include apostrophe, hyperbole, irony, metaphor, metonymy, oxymoron, paradox, personification, simile, synecdoche, and understatement.
See *Figurative Language*.

**FIRST-PERSON POINT OF VIEW** See *Point of View*.

**FLASHBACK** A *flashback* is a section of a literary work that interrupts the sequence of events to relate an event from an earlier time. The events in a work are usually presented in chronological order, the order of their occurrence in time. However, a writer may present a flashback that describes an earlier event in order to shed light on the present situation. A flashback is often presented as a character's memory or recollection. For example, in William Melvin Kelley's "A Visit to Grandmother," on page 65, the grandmother tells about events that took place at least twenty-five years earlier. Writers often use flashbacks to show what motivates a character or to supply background information in a dramatic way. See *Foreshadowing*.

**FOIL**  A *foil* is a character who provides a contrast to another character. In William Shakespeare's *Julius Caesar*, for example, both the ambitious Cassius and the shrewd Antony are foils for the idealistic Brutus.

**FOLK BALLAD**  See *Ballad*.

**FOLKLORE**  *Folklore* includes the stories, legends, myths, ballads, riddles, sayings, and other traditions handed down orally by ordinary people. Folklore reveals a great deal about the culture in which it originates. Folklore also influences written literature in many ways. John Keats's "La Belle Dame sans Merci," on page 591, draws on British fairy lore, while Edgar Allan Poe's "Eldorado," on page 615, draws on a folk legend of the Americas.
See *Oral Tradition*.

**FOLK TALE**  A *folk tale* is a story composed orally and then passed from person to person by word of mouth. Folk tales originated among people who could not read and write. These people told the tales aloud. The tales were passed from generation to generation and then, in the modern era, were collected and written down by scholars. The well-known *Grimm's Fairy Tales* is a collection of European folk tales.
See *Oral Tradition*.

**FOOT**  A *foot* is a group of two or three syllables with a particular pattern of stresses. Poets often create rhythmical patterns, or meters, by repeating specific types of feet. The most common feet in English poetry are iambs, trochees, anapests, and dactyls.
See *Meter* and *Scansion*.

**FORESHADOWING**  *Foreshadowing* is the use, in a literary work, of clues that suggest events that have yet to occur. In W. W. Jacobs's "The Monkey's Paw," on page 29, many clues suggest what wishing on the monkey's paw will bring. For example, Mr. White's son says that he bets he never will see the money wished for by his father. This guess, of course, proves true and foreshadows the death of the son. Writers use foreshadowing to create suspense and to prepare readers for the outcome of the plot.
See *Flashback*.

**FORM**  The *form* of a literary work is its structure, shape, pattern, organization, or style. A work's form is often distinguished from its content, or subject matter.

**FORMS OF DISCOURSE**  The *forms of discourse* are the main types of writing, classified by purpose. Common forms of discourse include description, narration, exposition, persuasion, and argumentation. Sometimes a work is written entirely in one of these forms. More often, however, the forms of discourse are used together to support each other. For instance, a narrative story may include description, or an argument may begin with an expository section that explains key terms or that presents background information. See *Argumentation, Description, Exposition, Narration,* and *Persuasion*.

**FREE VERSE**  *Free verse* is poetry not written in a regular, rhythmical pattern, or meter. Instead of having metrical feet and lines, free verse has a varying rhythm that suits its meaning and that uses the sounds of spoken language in lines of different lengths. Ana Castillo begins her free-verse poem "Napa, California" this way:

> We pick
>     the bittersweet grapes
>     at harvest
>     one
>         by
>             one
> with leather worn hands.

Free verse is one of the most common forms in twentieth-century poetry.
See *Meter* and *Rhythm*.

**GENRE**   A *genre* is a division or type of literature. Literature is commonly divided into three major genres: poetry, prose, and drama, Each major genre is in turn divided into smaller genres, as follows:

1. *Poetry*: Lyric Poetry, Concrete Poetry, Dramatic Poetry, Narrative Poetry, and Epic Poetry
2. *Prose*: Fiction (Novels and Short Stories) and Nonfiction (Biography, Autobiography, Letters, Essays, and Reports)
3. *Drama*: Serious Drama and Tragedy, Comic Drama, Melodrama, and Farce

See *Drama, Poetry,* and *Prose*.

**HAIKU**   *Haiku* is a three-line Japanese verse form. The first and third lines of a haiku have five syllables. The second line has seven syllables. See the examples of haiku on pages 691 and 692.

**HEPTAMETER**   See *Meter*.

**HEPTASTICH**   See *Stanza*.

**HERO/HEROINE**   A *hero* or *heroine* is a character whose actions are inspiring or noble. Often heroes struggle to overcome foes or to escape difficulties. The most obvious examples of heroes and heroines are the larger-than-life characters in myths and legends. However, more ordinary characters can, and often do, perform heroic deeds.

**HEXAMETER**   See *Meter*.

**HYPERBOLE**   *Hyperbole* is deliberate exaggeration or overstatement that is not meant to be taken literally. For example, as bad as Muggs is in James Thurber's "The Dog That Bit People," on page 441, a reader may suspect exaggeration when Thurber says, "He gave me more trouble than all the other fifty-four or -five [dogs] put together."
See *Figurative Language*.

**IAMB**   See *Meter*.

**IAMBIC PENTAMETER**   *Iambic pentameter* is a line of poetry with five iambic feet, each with one unstressed syllable followed by one stressed syllable ( ˘ ´ ). Iambic pentameter may be rhymed or unrhymed. Unrhymed iambic pentameter is called *blank verse*. These opening lines from Arna Bontemps's "A Note of Humility" are in iambic pentameter:

> Whĕn áll | oŭr hópĕs | ărĕ sówn | ŏn stŏn|y̆ ground
> ănd wĕ | hăve yíeld|ĕd úp | thĕ thought | ŏf gaín,
> lŏng aft|ĕr oŭr | lăst sóngs | hăve lóst|
>    theĭr sound
> wĕ máy | cŏme báck, | wĕ máy | cŏme báck |
>    ăgaín.

Because iambic pentameter sounds like ordinary spoken language, it is one of the most commonly used rhythmical patterns.
See *Blank Verse* and *Meter*.

**IMAGE**   An *image* is a word or phrase that appeals to one or more of the five senses—sight, hearing, touch, taste, or smell.
See *Imagery*.

**IMAGERY**   *Imagery* is the descriptive language used in literature to re-create sensory experiences. The images in a work supply details of sight, sound, taste, touch, smell, or movement and help the reader to sense the experience being described. In her poem "Living Tenderly," May Swenson uses imagery of sight to describe a turtle:

> My body a rounded stone
> with a pattern of smooth seams.
> My head a short snake,
> retractive, projective.
> My legs come out of their sleeves
> or shrink within,
> and so does my chin.
> My eyelids are quick clamps.

**INCITING INCIDENT**   See *Plot*.

**INCONGRUITY**   *Incongruity* is the combination of incompatible or opposite elements. Sometimes a writer's wording may not match the subject. In Mark Twain's "Luck," on page 99, the speaker admires Scoresby as "that demigod," noting "the noble gravity of his countenance; the simple honesty that expressed itself all over him; the sweet unconsciousness of his greatness" only to hear from another guest that "Privately—he's an absolute fool." When a writer talks about something trivial in formal language, the surprise of the incongruity may create a comic or humorous effect.

**INVERSION**   An *inversion* is a reversal of the regular word order in a sentence. For instance, Humbert Wolfe begins his poem "The Gray Squirrel" with "Like a small gray/coffeepot/sits the squirrel." These lines reverse the usual subject–predicate order, "The squirrel sits like a small gray coffeepot." Poets often use inversion to emphasize certain words and sometimes to fit them into the meter of a poem.

**IRONY**   *Irony* is the general name given to literary techniques that involve surprising, interesting, or amusing contradictions. In *verbal irony* words are used to suggest the opposite of their usual meaning. In *dramatic irony* there is a contradiction between what a character thinks and what the reader or audience knows to be true. In *irony of situation* an event occurs that directly contradicts the expectations of the reader or the audience.

During the funeral in William Shakespeare's *Julius Caesar*, on page 345, Antony calls Brutus "an honorable man" when, in fact, he wants the people to think just the opposite. This is an example of verbal irony.

In the same play, dramatic irony occurs when the audience knowing that Caesar will be assassinated, watches him set out on the Ides of March.

In John Steinbeck's *the Pearl*, on page 779, Kino expects the pearl to bring Coyotito a good future. Instead, it brings the baby's death. This is an example of irony of situation.

**IRONY OF SITUATION**   See *Irony*.

**LEGEND**   A *legend* is a widely told story about the past, one that may or may not have a foundation in fact. One example, retold in many versions, is the legend of King Arthur. A legend often reflects a people's identity or cultural values. It generally has more historical truth and less emphasis on the supernatural than does a myth. See *Oral Tradition*.

**LIMITED POINT OF VIEW**   See *Point of View*.

**LITERAL LANGUAGE**   *Literal language* is language not meant to be interpreted figuratively. Calvin Trillin's "Rural Literalism, on page 539, points out how many of our ordinary expressions are used figuratively rather than literally. See *Figurative Language*.

**LOCAL COLOR**   *Local color* is the use of characters and details from a specific geographic region. Local color suggests the special features of the area through the regional dialect, customs, clothing, manners, attitudes, scenery, and landscape. Josephina Niggli's "The Street of the Cannon," on page 139, uses local color to present Mexican village life, while Juanita Platero and Siyowin Miller's "Chee's Daughter," on page 73, uses local color to portray Navaho life.

**LYRIC POEM**   A *lyric poem* is a highly musical verse that expresses the observations and feelings of a single speaker. A lyric may follow a traditional pattern, as does a sonnet, or it may be in free verse. Unlike a narrative poem, a lyric presents an experience or creates a single effect, but it does not tell a full story. An example is Sara Teasdale's "There Will come Soft Rains":

There will come soft rains and the smell
   of the ground,
And swallows circling with their
   shimmering sound;
And frogs in the pools singing at night,
And wild plum-trees in tremulous white.

Robins will wear their feathery fire
Whistling their whims on a low fence-wire;
And not one will know of the war, not one
Will care at last when it is done.

Not one would mind, neither bird nor tree,
If mankind perished utterly;

And Spring herself, when she woke at dawn,
Would scarcely know that we were gone.

This lyric poem concentrates on describing a particular moment, not on telling how it came about or why or what might happen next. In contrast, Ray Bradbury's story on page 133, which has the same title as the poem, shows how this theme can be treated in a short story. Among contemporary American poets, the lyric is the most common poetic form.

**MAIN CHARACTER**   See *Character.*

**METAPHOR**   A *metaphor* is a figure of speech in which one thing is spoken of as though it were something else. In a metaphor, a comparison is suggested or implied through identification, as in "death *is* a long sleep" or "the sleeping dead." In contrast, "death is *like* a long sleep" is a *simile.* A simile uses *like, as, than,* or similar phrasing to make a comparison.

A metaphor may be brief, as in Simon J. Ortiz's "A Pretty Woman." He describes looking over the edge of a mesa and finding that "the land was a pretty woman/smiling at us." An *extended metaphor,* however, is developed at length, as in the third section of "Four Glimpses of Night," by Frank Marshall Davis:

Peddling
From door to door
Night sells
Black bags of peppermint stars
Heaping cones of vanilla moon

Until
His wares are gone
Then shuffles homeward
Jingling the gray coins
Of daybreak.

A *mixed metaphor* occurs when two metaphors are jumbled together. For example, thorns and rain are illogically mixed in "The thorns of life rained down on him." Because a mixed metaphor does not consistently stick to one idea, it is not clear and may even be funny. A *dead metaphor* is one that is not effective because it has been used too often. Many common expressions, such as "the foot of the stairs" or "toe the line" are dead metaphors because they have lost their freshness. They contrast with the metaphors used to make writing, especially poetry, more imaginative and more meaningful.
See *Figurative Language.*

**METER**   The *meter* of a poem is its rhythmical pattern. This pattern is determined by the number and types of stresses, or beats, in each line. To describe the meter of a poem, you must *scan* its lines. *Scanning* involves marking the stressed and unstressed syllables, as follows:

When Í | am áll | alŏne
Envy | me then,
For Í | have béttĕr friends
Than wŏ|mĕn and men.
          —Sara Teasdale, "Thoughts"

Each strong stress is marked with a slanted line ( ΄ ), and each weak stress is marked with a horseshoe symbol ( ˘ ). The weak and strong stresses are then divided by vertical lines ( | ) into groups called *feet.* The following types of feet are common in English poetry:

1. *Iamb:* a foot with one weak stress followed by one strong stress, as in the word "around"
2. *Trochee:* a foot with one strong stress followed by one weak stress, as in he word "flutter"
3. *Anapest:* a foot with two weak stresses followed by one strong stress, as in the phrase "in a car"

4. *Dactyl:* a foot with one strong stress followed by two weak stresses, as in the word "glimmering"

5. *Spondee:* a foot with two strong stresses, as in the word "nightfall"

6. *Pyrrhic:* a foot with two weak stresses, as in the last foot of the word "exhaust|ively"

7. *Amphibrach:* a foot with a weak syllable, one strong syllable, and another weak syllable, as in "a wonder|ful poem"

8. *Amphimacer:* a foot with a strong syllable, one weak syllable, and another strong syllable, as in "back and forth"

Depending on the type of foot that is most common in them, lines of poetry are described as *iambic, trochaic, anapestic,* or *dactylic.*

Lines are also described in terms of the number of feet that occur in them, as follows:

1. *Monometer:* verse written in one-foot lines

    All things
    Are a
    Becoming
        —Heraclitus

2. *Dimeter:* verse written in two-foot lines

    Your grief | and mine
    Must in|tertwine
    Like sea | and river
        —Countee Cullen, "Any Human to
        Another"

3. *Trimeter:* verse written in three-foot lines

    Tell me no sec|ret, friend,
    My heart | will not | sustain
    Its load, | too heav|ily
        —Francesca Yetunde Pereira, "The
        Burden"

4. *Tetrameter:* verse written in four-foot lines

    Wood of | popple | pale as | moonbeam
    Wood of | oak for | yoke and | barn-beam
        —Edna St. Vincent Millay, "Counting-
        Out Rhyme"

5. *Pentameter:* verse written in five-foot lines

    I scatt|ered seed | enough | to plant | the
    land

In rows | from Can|ada | to Mex|ico
But for | my reap|ing on|ly what | the
hand
Can hold | at once | is all | that I | can
show.
    —Arna Bontemps, "A Black Man
    Talks of Reaping"

A six-foot line is called a *hexameter.* A line with seven feet is a *heptameter.*

A complete description of the meter of a line tells both how many feet there are in the line and what kind of foot is most common. Thus the lines from Bontemps's poem would be described as *iambic pentameter. Blank verse* is poetry written in unrhymed iambic pentameter. Poetry that does not have a regular meter is called *free verse.*

**METONYMY**   *Metonymy* is a figure of speech that substitutes something closely related for the thing actually meant. In his poem "Spring," Richard Hovey says,

    I said in my heart, "I am sick of four
        walls and a ceiling.
    I have need of the sky. . . ."

Here "sky" stands for open air and space, expressing the speaker's need for outdoor activity and change, and "four walls and a ceiling" stands for both a room and a claustrophobic feeling. People use metonymy in everyday speech when they refer to the executive branch of government as "The White House."
See *Figurative Language* and *Synecdoche.*

**MINOR CHARACTER**   See *Character.*

**MIXED METAPHOR**   See *Metaphor.*

**MONOLOGUE**   A *monologue* is a speech made entirely by one person or character. A monologue may be addressed to another character or to the audience, or it may be a *soliloquy*—a speech that presents the character's thoughts as though the character were overheard when alone. In Howard Koch's *Invasion from Mars,* on page 289, Profes-

sor Richard Pierson's long monologue tells about his trip from Grovers Mill to Newark after the Martian attack.
See *Soliloquy*.

**MONOMETER**  See *Meter*.

**MOOD**  *Mood*, or atmosphere, is the feeling created in the reader by a literary work or passage. The mood may be suggested by the writer's choice of words, by events in the work, or by the physical setting. For example, the first paragraph in Juanita Platero and Siyowin Miller's "Chee's Daughter," on page 73, describes the angle of Chee's hat and his songless ride home, despite a fine horse and a sunny winter's day. The passage suggests Chee's unhappiness and grief as well as the power of the natural world to restore a person's spirit.
See *Setting* and *Tone*.

**MORAL**  A *moral* is a lesson taught by a literary work. Fables present morals that are directly stated. Poems, novels, short stories, and plays often present morals that are not directly stated but must be inferred by the reader.

**MOTIVATION**  A *motivation* is a reason that explains or partially explains a character's thoughts, feelings, actions, or speech. Convincing motivation usually combines outside forces with inside forces, linking events in the plot with the character's personality and needs. The more effectively and persuasively a writer presents a character's motivations, the more realistic and believable the character will seem.
See *Character*.

**MYTH**  A *myth* is a fictional tale that explains the actions of gods or heroes or the causes of natural phenomena. The *mythology* of a people or of a society is the group of myths created by them to explain where the world came from, why certain events occur, and what life means. Literary works often allude to or adapt stories from Greek, Roman, or Norse mythologies.
See *Oral Tradition*.

**NARRATION**  *Narration* is writing that tells a story. The act of telling a story is also called narration. The *narrative*, or story, is told by a storyteller called the *narrator*. The story generally is told chronologically, in time order, but it may include flashbacks and foreshadowing. Narratives may be either fiction or nonfiction. Narration is one of the forms of discourse and is used in such works as novels, short stories, plays, narrative poems, essays, anecdotes, and newspaper reports.
See *Forms of Discourse, Narrative, Narrative Poem,* and *Narrator*.

**NARRATIVE**  A *narrative* is a story told in fiction, nonfiction, poetry, or drama.
See *Narration*.

**NARRATIVE POEM**  A *narrative poem* tells a story in verse. There are many types of narrative poems. Ballads use four- or six-line stanzas to tell of dramatic events involving ordinary people. *Epics* tell of the adventures of heroes or gods. *Metrical romances* tell tales of love and chivalry. Although ballads are still popular, especially when sung to music, narrative poetry now is less common than lyric poetry or narrative prose fiction. Examples of narrative poems in the text are John Keats's "La Belle Dame sans Merci," on page 591; Robert Frost's "Two Tramps in Mud Time," on page 595; and Henry Wadsworth Longfellow's "The Wreck of the Hesperus," on page 601.
See *Ballad, Epic, Lyric, Narrative,* and *Romance*.

**NARRATOR**  A *narrator* is a speaker or character who tells a story. A story or novel may be narrated by a main character, by a minor character, or by someone uninvolved in the story. The narrator may speak in the first person (using *I* or *we*), or in the third person (using *he, she, it,* or *they*). The third-person narrator may have an *omniscient*

point of view, and know everything, or a *limited point of view*, and know only what one character knows. Because the writer's choice of narrator helps determine the point of view, this decision affects what version of a story is told and how readers will react to it.
See *Point of View*.

**NONFICTION**  *Nonfiction* is prose writing that presents and explains ideas or that tells about real people, places, objects, or events. The nonfiction writer tries to present what is true and accurate, without imaginary or invented additions. Nonfiction includes biography, autobiography, historical accounts, essays, and other writings about real people, places, events, or subjects.
See *Fiction*.

**NOVEL**  A *novel* is a long work of fiction. As a long narrative, a novel often has a complicated plot, many major and minor characters, several interrelated themes, and several settings. Novels can be grouped in many ways, based on the historical periods in which they were written, on the subjects and themes they treat, on the techniques the writers use, or on the literary movements that influenced them. Popular types of novels are historical novels, mysteries, science fiction novels, and thrillers.
See *Fiction* and *Genre*.

**OCTAVE**  See *Stanza*.

**OMNISCIENT POINT OF VIEW**  See *Point of View*.

**ONOMATOPOEIA**  *Onomatopoeia* is the use of words that imitate sounds. Examples of such words include *hiss, hum, murmur*, and *rustle*. Robert Frost uses onomatopoeia in this line: "The *buzz* saw *snarled* and *rattled* in the yard." Onomatopoeia is used to create musical effects and to reinforce meaning, especially in poetry.

**ORAL TRADITION**  The *oral tradition* is the passing of songs, stories, and poems from generation to generation by word of mouth. The oral traditions of peoples around the globe have given us many myths, legends, spirituals, folk ballads, fairy tales, and other stories or songs.
See *Ballad, Folklore, Folk tale, Legend*, and *Myth*.

**OVERSTATEMENT**  See *Hyperbole*.

**OXYMORON**  An *oxymoron* is a figure of speech that puts together two opposing or contradictory ideas. An oxymoron, such as "freezing fire," thus suggests a *paradox* in just a few words.
See *Figurative Language* and *Paradox*.

**PARABLE**  A *parable* is a brief story, usually with human characters, that is told to teach a moral lesson. The most famous parables are those told by Christ in the Bible. Many writers make allusions to these famous Biblical parables.

**PARADOX**  A *paradox* is a statement that seems to be contradictory but that actually presents a truth. Dorothy Donnelly uses paradox in "Glass World" when she says, "Ice/is setting the world on fire." Because a paradox is surprising or even shocking, it draws the reader's attention to what is being said.
See *Figurative Language* and *Oxymoron*.

**PARALLELISM**  *Parallelism* is the repetition of a sentence pattern, or grammatical structure. Elizabeth Barrett Browning uses parallelism in her "Sonnet 43," as the opening octave shows:

How do I love thee? Let me count the ways.
I love thee to the depth and breadth and height
My soul can reach, when feeling out of sight
For the ends of Being and ideal Grace.
I love thee to the level of everyday's
Most quiet need, by sun and candle light.
I love thee freely, as men strive for Right;
I love thee purely, as they turn from Praise.

Parallelism is used in poetry and in other writing to emphasize and to link related ideas.
See *Repetition*.

**PARODY**   A *parody* is an imitation of another work that exaggerates or distorts features of the work to make fun of it or simply to amuse readers. Christopher Morley's "Nursery Rhymes for the Tender-Hearted," on page 678, parodies "Twinkle, Twinkle, Little Star."

**PERSONIFICATION**   *Personification* is a type of figurative language in which a nonhuman subject is given human qualities. In "Moonlight Night: Carmel," Langston Hughes personifies ocean waves:

> Tonight the waves march
> In long ranks
> Cutting the darkness
> With their silver shanks,
>
> Cutting the darkness
> And kissing the moon
> And beating the land's
> Edge into a swoon.

Effective personification of things or ideas makes them seem vital and alive, as if they were human.
See *Figurative Language.*

**PERSUASION**   *Persuasion* is writing or speech that attempts to convince the reader to adopt a particular opinion or course of action. Persuasion is used in advertising, editorials, sermons, political speeches, and in other writing and speech that urges people to think or act in certain ways. Lorraine Hansberry's essay "On Summer," on page 529, is a persuasive essay. Some critics and scholars make a distinction between persuasion and argumentation, reserving the former for emotional appeals and the latter for appeals to reason.
See *Argumentation* and *Forms of Discourse.*

**PETRARCHAN SONNET**   The *Petrarchan,* or *Italian, sonnet* is a fourteen-line lyric poem. It is named for the Italian poet Francesco Petrarca, who wrote sonnets about his beloved Laura. The Petrarchan sonnet has no more than five rhymes, usually is written in iambic pentameter, and generally follows a traditional rhyme scheme. This type of sonnet has two parts. First is the eight-line *octave,* traditionally rhymed *abba abba.* This section asks a question, reveals a problem, or tells a brief story. Next comes the six-line *sestet,* generally rhymed *cde cde* or with some combination of *cd* rhymes. The sestet answers the question, solves the problem, or comments on the story in the octave. In this way, the two parts of the Petrarchan sonnet work together to form a whole. "I Shall Go Back Again to the Bleak Shore," by Edna St. Vincent Millay, illustrates this sonnet pattern:

> I shall go back again to the bleak shore   *a*
> And build a little shanty on the sand,   *b*
> In such a way that the extremest band   *b*
> Of brittle seaweed will escape my door   *a*
> But by a yard or two; and nevermore   *a*
> Shall I return to take you by the hand;   *b*
> I shall be gone to what I understand,   *b*
> And happier than I ever was before.   *a*
>
> The love that stood a moment in your eyes,   *c*
> The words that lay a moment on your tongue,   *d*
> Are one with all that in a moment dies,   *c*
> A little under-said and over-sung.   *d*
> But I shall find the sullen rocks and skies   *c*
> Unchanged from what they were when I
> was young.   *d*

See *Lyric, Shakespearean Sonnet,* and *Sonnet.*

**PLOT**   *Plot* is the sequence of events in a literary work. In most novels, dramas, short stories, and narrative poems, the plot involves both characters and a central conflict. The plot usually begins with an *exposition* that introduces the setting, the characters, and the basic situation. This is followed by the *inciting incident,* which introduces the central conflict. The conflict then increases during the *development* until it reaches a high point of interest or suspense, the *climax.* The climax is followed by the *resolution,* or, end, of the central conflict. Any events that occur after the resolution make up the *denouement.* The *rising action* consists of all the events that precede the climax. The *falling action* consists of all the events that follow the climax.

See *Climax*, *Conflict*, and *Crisis*.

**POETRY**   *Poetry* is one of the three major types of literature, the others being prose and drama. Defining poetry more precisely isn't easy, for there is no single, unique characteristic that all poems share. Poems are often divided into lines and stanzas and often employ regular rhythmical patterns, or meters. However, some poems are written out like prose, and some are written in free verse. Most poems make use of highly concise, musical, and emotionally charged language. Many also make use of imagery, figurative language, and special devices such as rhyme.
See *Genre*.

**POINT OF VIEW**   The *point of view* is the perspective, or vantage point, from which a story is told. A story may be told by a narrator who supplies more information about all the characters and events than any one character could know. Such a narrator has an *omniscient*, or all-knowing, point of view. For example, Virginia Woolf's "The Widow and the Parrot," on page 123, includes Mrs. Gage's thoughts, her dead brother's motives, background information about crossing the river Ouse, and other information that could be known only by an omniscient narrator.

Instead of knowing everything, the narrator may know only what one character knows. This character may or may not personally tell the story. If the character tells the story directly using *I*, *me*, and *we*, the writer has chosen a *limited first-person* point of view. For example, the narrator in Heinrich Böll's "The Laugher," on page 107, speaks in the first person, and the story is limited to his own words and knowledge.

If the narrator reveals only one character's inner thoughts and is not himself or herself a character in the story, then the story is told from a *limited third-person* point of view. Like an omniscient narrator, this narrator speaks in the third person, using *he*, *she*, *it*, and *they*. However, like a first-person narrator, this narrator reveals the inner life of only one character. Gwendolyn Brooks uses a limited third-person point of view in "Maud Martha Spares the Mouse," on page 119.

Each point of view creates a different story with a different account of events. When the writer chooses a particular point of view and narrator, that choice affects both the nature of the story and the reader's understanding of the story.
See *Narrator* and *Speaker*.

**PROSE**   *Prose* is the ordinary form of written language. Most writing that is not poetry, drama, or song is considered prose. Prose is one of the major genres of literature and occurs in two forms: fiction and nonfiction.
See *Fiction*, *Genre*, and *Nonfiction*.

**PROTAGONIST**   The *protagonist* is the main character in a literary work. The protagonist is at the center of the action, often in conflict with an external antagonist or with internal forces. In Anne Tyler's "With All Flags Flying," on page 181, Mr. Carpenter is the protagonist. He struggles to keep his independence, against his family's good intentions and against his own physical weakness.
See *Antagonist* and *Conflict*.

**PUN**   A *pun* is a play on words. Some puns involve a single word or phrase that has two different meanings. Others involve two different words or phrases with the same sound, such as in words *awl* and *all* in the scene from William Shakespeare's *Julius Caesar* on page 345. Puns are often humorous but also have serious purposes.

**PYRRHIC**   See *Meter*.

**QUATRAIN**   A *quatrain* is a four-line poem or a stanza with four lines. If a quatrain is rhymed, it usually uses one of these rhyme schemes: *abab*, *aabb*, *abba*, or *abcb*. "For My Grandmother", by Countee Cullen, is a quatrain with the rhyme scheme *abcb*:

This lovely flower fell to see;      a
Work gently sun and rain;            b
She held it as her dying creed       c
That she would grow again.           b

See *Rhyme Scheme* and *Stanza*.

**REFRAIN**   A *refrain* is a regularly repeated line or group of lines in a poem or song. Most refrains come at the ends of stanzas, as does "An' they're hangin' Danny Deever in the mornin' " in Rudyard Kipling's "Danny Deever," on page 607. See *Repetition*.

**REPETITION**   *Repetition* is the use, more than once, of any element of language—a sound, a word, a phrase, a clause, a sentence, or a rhythmical or grammatical pattern. In "The Marginal World," on page 565, Rachel Carson uses repetition to connect her points and to unify her writing. When she describes the pool within the cave, she repeats the key word *beauty* and the idea of "exquisite beauty" through related words like *magical*, *fragile*, *delicate*, and *enchanted*. Careless repetition bores a reader, but successful repetition links ideas, emphasizes main points, and makes the language forceful and musical. See *Alliteration*, *Assonance*, *Consonance*, *Parallelism* and *Rhyme*.

**RESOLUTION**   See *Plot*.

**RHYME**   *Rhyme* is the repetition of sounds at the ends of words. Rhymed words have the same vowel sounds in their accented syllables. The consonants before the vowels may be different, but the consonants after them are the same. Examples of rhyming words are *frog* and *bog*, and *willow* and *pillow*. The type of rhyme used most often is *end rhyme*, in which the rhyming words are repeated at the ends of lines. *Internal rhyme* occurs when the rhyming words fall within a line. In the first stanza of Edgar Allan Poe's "The Raven," rhymes link words at the ends of lines, within lines, and in different lines:

Once upon a midnight *dreary*, while I pondered, weak and *weary*,
Over may a quaint and curious volume of forgotten *lore*—
While I nodded, nearly *napping*, suddenly there came a *tapping*,
As of some one gently *rapping*, *rapping* at my chamber *door*,
" 'Tis some visitor," I muttered, *tapping* at my chamber *door*—
Only this and nothing *more*.

*Exact rhyme* is present when the rhyming sounds are identical, as in *love* and *dove*. *Approximate*, or *slant*, *rhyme* is present when the sounds are similar, as in *prove* and *glove*. Both exact and approximate rhymes are illustated in this stanza from "Mind," by Richard Wilbur:

Mind in the purest play is like some *bat*
That beats about in caverns all *alone*,
Contriving by a kind of senseless *wit*
Not to conclude against a wall of *stone*.

*Bat* and *wit* illustrate approximate or slant rhyme, while *alone* and *stone* illustrate exact rhyme. See *Rhyme Scheme*.

**RHYME SCHEME**   A *rhyme scheme* is a regular pattern of rhyming words in a poem. To describe a rhyme scheme, use different letters of the alphabet for the different sounds at the ends of the lines. For example, next to the lines of "Fire and Ice" by Robert Frost, *a* stands for the first sound, *b* for the next, and *c* for the third:

Some say the world will end in fire,      a
Some say in ice.                          b
From what I've tasted of desire           a
I hold with those who favor fire.         a
But if it had to perish twice,            b
I think I know enough of hate             c
To say that for destruction ice           b
Is also great                             c
And would suffice.                        b

The rhyme scheme here is *abaabcbcb*. In this poem, the rhyme scheme directly reinforces the meaning. Each *a* rhyme has to do with fire, each *b* with ice.

In many poems with more than one stanza,

the pattern of the first stanza is repeated in each of the next two stanzas. As a result, each new stanza seems consistent with the others. Each also seems different because it uses its own rhyming sounds.

See *Rhyme* and *Stanza*.

**RHYTHM**   *Rhythm* is the pattern of beats, or stresses, in spoken or written language. In prose, this pattern is often irregular. In traditional poetry, regular rhythmical pattern, or meter, is used. Poetry that is rhythmic but that does not have a regular pattern is called *free verse*. Instead of following a set metrical pattern, a poem in free verse has its own rhythm that suits its meaning.

In both poetry and prose, writers use rhythm to emphasize their ideas and feelings. In addition, the musical quality of rhythm is appealing because people enjoy expecting and finding a pattern.

See *Foot*, *Free Verse*, *Meter*, and *Scansion*.

**RISING ACTION**   See *Plot*.

**ROMANCE**   A *romance* is a story that presents fantastic events, especially ones involving love or chivalry. When written in verse, such a story is called a *metrical romance*. Traditional medieval romances, such as Sir Thomas Malory's tales of King Arthur, tell of the deeds and loves of noble knights and ladies. These stories are full of idealized characters, faraway settings, and mysterious or magical elements. In loosely structured, entertaining incidents, the heroic characters bravely battle their evil antagonists. During the nineteenth century, a revitalized romance tradition was opposed by the more realistic novel. This return to romance influenced many writers, including Alfred, Lord Tennyson, who retold the Arthurian legends in his long narrative poem *Idylls of the King*.

See *Narrative Poem*.

**ROUND CHARACTER**   See *Character*.

**RUN-ON LINE**   A *run-on line* is one that does not end with a pause. Instead, the idea is continued on the next line. Naoshi Koriyama's "Unfolding Bud" shows how one line can move to the next:

> One is amazed
> By a water-lily bud
> Unfolding
> With each passing day,
> Taking on a richer color
> And new dimensions.

Three run-on lines begin the poem, each leading the reader on to the next line. Thus the poem unfolds, line by line, just as a water-lily bud does. In contrast, lines four and six are end-stopped, as their punctuation shows. They stop the poem's movement after the unfolding and after the comment on its meaning. Besides reinforcing meaning, run-on lines can change a poem's rhythm, adding variety and helping the writer to avoid monotony.

See *Caesura*, *End-Stopped Line*, and *Rhythm*.

**SATIRE**   *Satire* is a type of writing that ridicules or criticizes the faults of individuals or groups. The satirist may use a tolerant, sympathetic tone or an angry, bitter tone. Some satire is written in poetry and some in prose.

Although a satire may be humorous, its purpose is not simply to make readers laugh but to correct, through laughter, the flaws and shortcomings it points out.

**SCANSION**   *Scansion* is the process of figuring out a poem's metrical pattern. When a poem is scanned, its stressed and unstressed syllables are marked. Their pattern shows what poetic foot is used and how many feet appear in each line. See *Meter*.

**SCENE**   See *Drama*.

**SCIENCE FICTION**   *Science fiction* is writing that tells about imaginary events that involve science or technology. Many science-fiction stories are set in the future. Ray Bradbury's "There Will Come Soft Rains," on page 133, is an example of science fiction.

**SCRIPT**   A *script* is the written version of a play, a movie, a radio program, or a television show. The script provides the information needed to produce the work—the list of characters, the stage directions, the speaking parts for the characters, and any other directions the writer decides to include.

**SENSORY LANGUAGE**   *Sensory language* is writing or speech that appeals to one or more of the senses.
See *Image*.

**SESTET**   See *Stanza*.

**SETTING**   The *setting* of a literary work is the time and place of the action. A setting provides the location and background for the characters and plot and may help to create a particular atmosphere, or mood. Sometimes the central conflict of a story is a struggle against some element of the setting.

**SHAKESPEAREAN SONNET**   The *Shakespearean*, or *English*, *sonnet* is a fourteen-line lyric poem. It follows a traditional rhyme scheme and usually is written in iambic pentameter. It is named for William Shakespeare, who perfected the form in a series of sonnets that he wrote in his youth. This type of sonnet developed after English poets brought the Petrarchan sonnet home from Italy and changed its form.

The typical Shakespearean sonnet is made up of three quatrains and a couplet and follows the rhyme scheme *abab cdcd efef gg*. See William Shakespeare's sonnet "Shall I Compare Thee to a Summer's Day?" on page 686.
See *Lyric*, *Petrarchan Sonnet*, and *Sonnet*.

**SHORT STORY** A *short story* is a brief work of fiction. The short story resembles the longer novel but generally has a simpler plot and setting. In addition, the short story tends to reveal character at a crucial moment rather than to develop it through many incidents. For example, Doris Lessing's "Through the Tunnel," on page 159, concentrates on what happens as Jerry learns to swim the tunnel.
See *Fiction*, *Genre*, and *Novel*.

**SIMILE**   A *simile* is a figure of speech that makes a direct comparison between two subjects using either *like* or *as*. In "Tiger Year," Laura Tokunaga uses this simile:

> planets circle in the gathering
> dark like pale insects
> around the opened throats of flowers.

By drawing together different things, effective similes make vivid and meaningful comparisons that enrich what the writer has to say.
See *Figurative Language*.

**SLANT RHYME**   See *Rhyme*.

**SOLILOQUY**   A *soliloquy* is a long speech made by a character who is alone. The character thus reveals his or her private thoughts and feelings to the audience. In William Shakespeare's *Julius Caesar*, on page 365, Brutus begins a soliloquy that is spoken while he is alone in his orchard. This soliloquy reveals Brutus's fears about how Caesar might change were he crowned as king.
See *Monologue*.

**SONNET**   The *sonnet* is a fourteen-line lyric poem focused on a single theme. Sonnets have many variations, but they are usually written in iambic pentameter, following either the Petrarchan or Shakespearean form.
See *Lyric*, *Petrarchan Sonnet*, and *Shakespearean Sonnet*.

**SPEAKER**   The *speaker* is the imaginary voice assumed by the writer of a poem. In other words, the speaker is the character who says the poem. This character often is not identified by name. The speaker in May Swenson's "The Centaur," on page 585, is a woman who is recalling the summer when she was ten years old.

**SPONDEE** See *Meter*.

**STAGE DIRECTIONS** *Stage directions* are notes included in a drama to describe how the work is to be performed or staged. Stage directions are usually printed in italics and enclosed within brackets or parentheses. They may mention how the characters should speak or move, what the costumes or any scenery should look like, how the set should be arranged, how the lighting should work, and so on.

**STANZA** A *stanza* is a group of lines in a poem, considered as a unit. Many poems are divided into stanzas that are separated by spaces. Stanzas often function just as paragraphs do in prose. Each stanza states and develops a single main idea.

Stanzas are commonly named according to the number of lines found in them, as follows:
1. *Couplet:* a two-line stanza
2. *Tercet:* a three-line stanza
3. *Quatrain:* a four-line stanza
4. *Cinquain:* a five-line stanza
5. *Sestet:* a six-line stanza
6. *Heptastich:* a seven-line stanza
7. *Octave:* an eight-line stanza

A *sonnet* is a fourteen-line poem that is composed either of an octave and a sestet or of three quatrains and a couplet.

**STATIC CHARACTER** See *Character*.

**STEREOTYPE** See *Character*.

**STOCK CHARACTER** See *Character*.

**STYLE** A writer's *style* is his or her typical way of writing. Style includes word choice, tone, degree of formality, figurative language, rhythm, grammatical structure, sentence length, organization—in short, every feature of a writer's use of language.

**SUBPLOT** A *subplot* is a second, less important plot within a story. A subplot may add to, reflect, vary, or contrast with the main plot. See *Plot*.

**SURPRISE ENDING** A *surprise ending* is a conclusion that violates the expectations of the reader. Especially in a short story, the plot may take a sudden twist or turn when something crucial is revealed or concealed. An example in this text of a story with a surprise ending is O. Henry's "Hearts and Hands," on page 59.

**SUSPENSE** *Suspense* is a feeling of growing curiosity or anxious uncertainty about the outcome of events in a literary work. Writers create suspense by raising questions in the minds of their readers.

**SYMBOL** A *symbol* is anything that stands for or represents something else. A *conventional symbol* is one that is widely known and accepted, such as a voyage symbolizing life or a skull symbolizing death. A *personal symbol* is one created for a particular work by a particular author.

**SYNECDOCHE** *Synecdoche* is a figure of speech that uses a part of something to stand for the whole thing. In "February Evening in New York," Denise Levertov uses feet, heads, and bodies to refer to the human beings in the impersonal city crowds:

> As the buildings close, released autonomous
> feet pattern the streets
> in hurry and stroll; balloon heads
> drift and dive above them; the bodies
> aren't really there.

See *Figurative Language* and *Metonymy*.

**TERCET**  See *Stanza*.

**TETRAMETER**  See *Meter*.

**THEME**  A *theme* is a central idea, concern, or purpose in a literary work. An essay's theme might be its thesis, its point about the topic. The theme of a story, play, or poem might be its point about life—the insight that the writer wants to pass along to the reader. A light work, one meant strictly for entertainment, may not have a theme. In most serious poems, stories, and plays, the theme is expressed indirectly rather than directly. For example, in Juanita Platero and Siyowin Miller's "Chee's Daughter," on page 73, the authors do not directly say that Chee's actions show the power of love and the importance of one's values, but readers understand that this idea is the theme of the story.

**THIRD-PERSON POINT OF VIEW**  See *Point of View*.

**TONE**  The *tone* of a literary work is the writer's attitude toward the readers and toward the subject. A writer's tone may be formal or informal, friendly or distant, personal or impersonal. For example, although Lewis Thomas's advice is serious in "Notes on Punctuation," on page 545, his tone is lighthearted and amusing. Rachel Carson's awed and respectful tone in "The Marginal World," on page 565, expresses her intensity as she seeks the meaning behind the beauty of the natural world.
See *Mood*.

**TRAGEDY**  *Tragedy* is a type of drama or literature that shows the downfall or destruction of a noble or outstanding person. Traditionally this person has a character weakness called a *tragic flaw* that accounts for his or her fall. In William Shakespeare's *Julius Caesar*, on page 345, Brutus is a brave and noble figure who is guilty of the tragic flaw of assuming that honorable ends justify dishonorable means. Such a tragic hero, through choice or circumstance, is caught up in a sequence of events that inevitably result in disaster. Because this hero is neither purely wicked nor purely innocent, the audience reacts with mixed emotions—both pity and fear. The outcome of a tragedy—the downfall of the tragic hero— contrasts with the happy ending found in a comedy. Thus tragedies tend to end with funerals and comedies with weddings.
See *Comedy* and *Drama*.

**TRIMETER**  See *Meter*.

**TROCHEE**  See *Meter*.

**UNDERSTATEMENT**  *Understatement* means saying less than is actually meant, generally in an ironic way. An example of understatement is the description of a flooded area as "slightly soggy" or of weather during a heat wave as "a bit warm."
See *Figurative Language* and *Hyperbole*.

**VERBAL IRONY**  See *Irony*.

**VERNACULAR**  The *vernacular* is the ordinary language used by the people in a particular place. Instead of using more formal literary language, writers may use the vernacular to create realistic characters or to approach readers informally.
See *Dialect*.

# HANDBOOK OF CRITICAL THINKING AND READING TERMS

**ABSTRACT** *adj.* Anything that is not concrete or definite is *abstract*. Literature often deals with abstract ideas such as justice, truth, beauty, love, hope, or peace. Writers attempt to make these abstract ideas clear by using specific examples and illustrations. Suppose, for instance, that a writer wants to convey the abstract idea that a character is worried. The writer might do this by concretely describing the character as having a furrowed brow or by showing him pacing back and forth.

Another way to express an abstract idea clearly is to use a figure of speech, such as a simile, a metaphor, or a personification. For example, the simile "soft as a kitten" uses a concrete image—a kitten—to express an abstract idea—softness.

**ANALOGY** *n.* An *analogy* is a comparison that explains one subject by pointing out its similarities to another subject. In his poem "The End of the World," for example, Archibald MacLeish imagines that the end of the world will be much like a circus. Analogies usually differ from mere comparisons in that the subjects being compared are, on the surface, quite different. Thus comparing one automobile to another is not an analogy, but comparing an automobile to a person is.

To understand an analogy, a reader matches characteristics of the first subject with similar characteristics of the second subject. Writers make this matching process easier by devising analogies that are likely to fall within the experience of the reader. Archibald MacLeish, for example, can reasonably assume that his readers will know what a circus is like.

An analogy may be expressed using a variety of literary techniques, such as simile, meta-

phor, and extended metaphor. See the definitions of these terms in the Handbook of Literary Terms and Techniques.

**ANALYSIS** *n.* *Analysis* is the process of studying the parts of a whole. To conduct an analysis, follow these steps:
1. Separate the whole into its individual parts.
2. Describe each part.
3. Look for relationships among the parts and between each part and the whole.

As part of the analysis, you might ask yourself questions such as these:
1. How are the parts similar to one another?
2. How are they different?
3. How would the whole be affected if the parts were arranged differently?

When you analyze a literary work, you break it down into parts, observe the characteristics of these parts, and think about how they are related. For example, you might analyze Edgar Allan Poe's "The Masque of the Red Death," on page 173, by dividing it into its beginning, middle, and end. You would then find the points at which the story moves from the beginning to the middle and from the middle to the end. In this way you could identify the parts of the work that create, increase, and resolve the suspense.

**ARGUMENT** *n.* An *argument* is a set of statements consisting of a conclusion and one or more premises, or reasons, for accepting the conclusion. The Declaration of Independence, for example, argues that the American Colonies are justified in separating from England, and it supports this claim with a long series of facts and reasons. People also present arguments when writing about literature. They use the various elements of a literary work—plot, characters, images, dialogue—as reasons, or evidence, to support their analysis or interpretation. For example, on the basis of the elements in Shakespeare's *The Tragedy of Julius Caesar*, on page 345, you could argue that Brutus is a tragic hero. You would then cite various actions and statements in the play to support this argument.

The term *argument* is also used to describe a brief summary, or synopsis, of a literary work. Thus a paragraph summarizing the plot of *Tevya and the First Daughter*, on page 271, might be described as presenting the "argument of the play."
See *Conclusion, Deduction, Evidence, Induction*, and *Inference*.

**BANDWAGON**   See *Propaganda Technique*.

**BEGGING THE QUESTION**   See *Logical Fallacy*.

**CATEGORIZATION** *n.*   *Categorization* is the process of placing objects or ideas into groups or classes. Objects or ideas possessing similar characteristics may be placed in the same category. To categorize something, follow these steps:
1. Note the characteristics of the object you are studying.
2. Think of other subjects that share these characteristics.
3. Select a name or phrase to describe the group.

Categorizing literary works can be a useful technique in literary study. It is often helpful to begin consideration of a work by thinking about other works that are similar in subject, style, or structure. Normally, specific categories are more helpful than very general ones. Prose and poetry, for instance, are the two basic categories into which all writing can be grouped, but each can be divided further into more specific and more useful categories. For example, John Steinbeck's *The Pearl* and John Knowles's *A Separate Peace* are both long fictional narratives in prose. Thus, they can be put into the category, *novel*. A standard literary category such as the novel, the autobiography, the lyric poem, and the short story is called a *genre*, from the French word for "a kind."

**CAUSE AND EFFECT** *n. phrase*   When one event precedes and brings about another event, the first is said to be a *cause* and the second an *effect*. In literature, *cause-and-effect* relationships can exist between the characters and events in a plot and between the literary work and the reader. For example, in "The Monkey's Paw," on page 29, Mrs. White removes her apron and stuffs it under the cushion of her chair because a strange man is coming up the path to the house. The impending arrival of a well-dressed stranger is the cause. The hiding of the apron is the effect. Cause and effect is the technique that keeps the plot of a narrative work moving: The *inciting incident* leads to one or more effects, which, in turn, cause other effects, and so on, to the end of the story.

The second type of cause-and-effect relationship involves the reader or listener. Writers choose their language carefully in order to create certain effects on their readers. Howard Koch's *Invasion from Mars* tries to create an effect of immediacy by presenting the main action of the play as if it were a currently breaking news story.

**CIRCULAR REASONING**   See *Logical Fallacy*.

**COMPARISON** *n.*   *Comparison* is the process of observing and pointing out similarities. For example, a comparison of James Thurber and E. B. White might note the following similarities: each wrote for *The New Yorker* magazine; each tended to write humorous, informal essays and stories; and each writer used a simple yet sophisticated style.
See *Contrast*.

**CONCLUSION** *n.*   A *conclusion* is an idea that follows reasonably from one or more other ideas. In an argument, the conclusion follows from supporting statements, facts, and reasons. For example, each of E. B. White's remarks about the nature of humor, in "Some Remarks on Humor," on page 535, is a conclusion, and each is supported by specific reasons or illustrations.

The *conclusion* of a literary work is its ending. The conclusion of *The Tragedy of Julius Caesar* is the death of Brutus and the triumph of Octavius. In works of the imagination as well as in formal arguments, the effectiveness of a conclusion is judged on the basis of what has come before it.

**CONTRAST** *n.* *Contrast* is the process of observing and pointing out differences. In any kind of analysis, differences can often be more useful than similarities. Contrast, therefore, is an important technique in literary study.
See *Comparison*.

**DEDUCTION** *n.* *Deduction* is a form of argument in which the conclusion has to be true if the premises are true. It is a thinking process by which general, related principles are used to support specific conclusions. The following is an example of a deductive argument:

Premise: All hockey players know how to skate.
Premise: Maurice is a hockey player.
Conclusion: Maurice knows how to skate.

The premises are related because the second premise provides an example—Maurice the hockey player—of the first element in the first premise—hockey players. If you accept these premises, then you must also accept the conclusion. Therefore, the argument is a deduction.

**DEFINITION** *n.* *Definition* is the process of explaining the meaning of a word or phrase. Definition makes communication possible by establishing agreed-upon meanings for words. The simplest type of definition, *ostensive definition*, involves pointing to something and saying its name. For example, if you point to an object and say, "television," you are giving an ostensive definition of the word *television*. Only other objects that share the characteristics of the object you pointed to can share that definition. The most common type of definition is that found in dictionaries, *lexical definition*. Lexical definition uses words to explain the meanings of other words and phrases.

Definition by synonym, by antonym, by example, and by genus and differentia are all types of lexical definition.

In a *definition by synonym*, you use a word or phrase that has the same meaning: *Sloth* is "laziness."

In *definition by antonym*, you use a word or phrase that has an opposite meaning: A *fool* is one who is "not wise."

In *definition by example*, you list things to which the term being defined applies: *Stringed instruments* include the violin, the cello, the guitar, and the bass.

In a *genus and differentia definition*, you place the thing to be defined into a general category, or *genus*. Then you tell how it differs from other members of the group:

To be defined: lion
Genus, or group: cats
Differentia: very large
 indigenous to Africa
 eats meat
 yellowish mane of hair
Definition: A lion is "a very large, meat-eating cat that is indigenous to Africa and is distinguished by a yellow mane."

The purpose of definition is to make your reader understand your meaning as exactly as possible. Whenever you write about literature, make sure you define your key terms. Use the methods of lexical definition explained here.

**EITHER/OR FALLACY** See *Logical Fallacy*.

**EVALUATION** *n.* *Evaluation* is the process of making judgments about the quality or value of something. The statement " 'There Will Come Soft Rains' is one of the best stories I've ever read" is an evaluation. Before you can fairly and accurately evaluate a literary work, you must first analyze it. Once you have identified the parts of a work—subject, form, characters, plot, language—and have understood how these components contribute to the whole, you can evaluate it. Tastes may vary from one person to the next, and intelligent readers can disagree on the merits of a work. Still, appropriate standards, or criteria, are necessary to make sensible judgments. Most readers agree that literary works should contain believable plots, imaginative language, and interesting, convincing characters. Standards such as these should be used to evaluate literary works. Convincing evaluations use elements in the work—plot details, characters, descriptions—as supporting evidence. Judgments such as "I hated it" or "I think it's stupid" or "It's great" are unacceptable because they are too vague. See *Opinion* and *Judgment*.

**EVIDENCE** *n.* *Evidence* is factual information presented to support an argument. An argument is only as good as its evidence. In literary analysis or evaluation, the elements of a work—language, plot, characters, tone—are the evidence that must be used to support an interpretation or judgment. For example, consider the statement, "The twelve angry men of Reginald Rose's play are meant to symbolize American society." You might support this interpretation with the following evidence: The twelve jurors of the play represent a cross-section of ages, educational backgrounds, professions, and social views.
See *Fact, Reason*, and *Support*.

**FALSE ANALOGY** See *Logical Fallacy*.

**FACT** *n.* A *fact* is a statement that is true or false by evidence. For example, the following facts are true by definition:

Twelve inches equal one foot.
A *sonnet* is a fourteen-line poem in iambic pentameter.

The following facts are true by observation:

John Updike grew up in Shillington, Pennsylvania.
Little is known about the historical King Arthur.

Facts are extremely important in literary works. An author uses facts to develop characters, settings, and plots. A reader uses them as the evidence with which to make predictions and inferences about and evaluations of the work. See *Opinion*.

**GENERALIZATION** *n.* A *generalization* is a statement that applies to more than one thing. The following are generalizations:

James Wright often writes about his native Ohio.
Robert Frost's poems usually rhyme.

The first statement applies to more than one of Wright's works, and the second to more than one of Frost's.

*Deductive arguments* usually begin with generalizations. Consider the following deductive argument:

Premise: (generalization) You enjoy stories about King Arthur.
Conclusion: You will enjoy T. H. White's "Arthur Becomes King."

*Inductive arguments*, on the other hand, often end with generalizations. Consider the following:

Premise: Thomas Malory wrote about King Arthur.
Premise: Alfred, Lord Tennyson wrote about King Arthur.
Premise: Edwin Muir wrote about King Arthur.
Conclusion: (generalization) Many people have written about the legend of King Arthur.

Like categories, generalizations are useful for sorting or summarizing observations. Most true generalizations assert only that something is frequently or usually the case, not that it is always so. Be careful not to overgeneralize. For example, the statement "All of Truman Capote's stories are set in the South" is an overgeneralization because many exceptions could be found. One way to avoid overgeneralizing is to limit your statement by using qualifiers, such as *usually, often, generally, a few*, and *many*.
See *Conclusion* and *Stereotype*.

**INDUCTION** *n.* *Induction* is a form of argument in which the conclusion is probably, but not necessarily, true. For example, if you read several works by Mark Twain and find that each is humorous, then you might conclude, "All of Mark Twain's writings are humorous." This conclusion may be true, but it is not necessarily true because you have not read all of Twain's stories. You should probably limit your conclusion to something like, "Many of Mark Twain's works are humorous."

Scientists, it is worth noting, depend heavily on inductive reasoning. Indeed, most of the laws of science are the product of induction. A scientist observes something—the sun rising in the east and setting in the west, for example—and draws a conclusion: The sun always rises in the east and sets in the west. It is possible, however, that changes in the orbit of the earth could alter this pattern, in which case this law would be invalid. The possibility of such exceptions or alterations is what makes inductive conclusions only probably or temporarily true.

See *Generalization* and *Inference*.


**INFERENCE** n.  An *inference* is any logical or reasonable conclusion based on known facts or accepted premises. The conclusions of both inductive and deductive arguments are inferences. When you read something or listen to someone, the words of the author or speaker are the facts from which you must continually draw inferences. This process of drawing inferences is sometimes called "reading between the lines."

For example, if you read the sentence, "John was in an automobile accident Sunday, so he has had to take the bus to work this week," you can draw inferences such as the following: John owns a car; he was not seriously injured in the accident; John has a job; and he usually drives to work.

The number of inferences you can draw is limited only by your thoughtfulness and by the information supplied in the material you are studying. Whenever you read or listen, think about the language that is used and draw conclusions, or inferences, from it.


**INTERPRETATION** n.  *Interpretation* is the pro-cess of determining the meaning or significance of speech, writing, art, music, or actions. The interpretation of a literary work involves many different processes. These include the following:

1. Reading carefully and actively and responding to each new detail, character, or plot incident
2. Breaking down the work into its parts, describing each part, and looking for patterns and connections among them
3. Examining your own responses to the work and identifying the details that help to create these responses
4. Pulling together your observations to make generalizations about the meaning or purpose of the work

Interpretation usually aims at making clear the theme of a literary work. For example, your reading of Robert Frost's "Two Tramps in Mud Time," on page 595, might lead you to this statement of theme: "The ideal life is one in which what one does to support oneself and what one does for pleasure are one and the same." Credible interpretations will take into account, directly or indirectly, all important parts of a work.

See *Analysis*.


**JUDGMENT** n.  A *judgment* is a statement about the quality or value of something. Like arguments, judgments must be supported by facts and reasons. A sound judgment of a literary work, therefore, must be based on evidence from the text.

See *Evaluation* and *Opinion*.


**LOADED WORDS**  See *Propaganda Technique*.


**LOGICAL FALLACY** n. phrase  A *logical fallacy* is an error in reasoning. People often commit such errors when they are attempting to persuade others to adopt some opinion or to take some action. The following logical fallacies are quite common:

1. *Begging the question:* This fallacy occurs when someone assumes the truth of the statement to be proved without providing any sup-

porting evidence. For example: "Of course, everyone knows it is easier to do math while listening to one of Beethoven's symphonies." (No evidence is given to support the claim.)

2. *Circular reasoning:* This fallacy occurs when the evidence given to support a claim is simply a restatement of the claim in other words. For example: "In Shakespeare's *Macbeth*, there is bad weather in some scenes because it is stormy." (The second part of the sentence simply restates the original claim without supplying any new evidence.)

3. *Either/or fallacy:* This fallacy occurs when someone claims that there are only two alternatives when there are actually more. For example: "You either have to go to the dance Friday evening or you have to stay home." (The statement ignores another possibility: A person may want to do something else.)

4. *False analogy:* This fallacy occurs when someone falsely assumes that two subjects are similar in some respect just because they are similar in some other respect. For example: "Psychology and sociology both study human behavior. Therefore they must be the same." (The false assumption is made that these sciences study the same aspects of human behavior.)

5. *Overgeneralization:* This fallacy occurs when someone makes a statement that is too broad or too inclusive. For example: "All tall people make good basketball players." (This statement may be true of some tall people; it is certainly not true of all tall people.)

6. *Post hoc, ergo propter hoc:* (a Latin phrase meaning "After this, therefore because of this") This fallacy occurs when someone falsely assumes that an event is caused by another event simply because of the order of the events in time. For example: "Because northern abolitionists were opposed to slavery, the American Civil War broke out." (Although the abolition movement may have been a factor, it was only one of a great many causes.)

When you do persuasive writing or speaking, try to avoid these logical fallacies. Also be on guard against these fallacies in the speech and writing of others.

**MAIN IDEA** *n. phrase*   The *main idea* is the central point a speaker or writer wants to communicate. The main idea of an essay might be its thesis statement. The main idea of an argument might be its conclusion. For example, the main idea of Lewis Thomas's essay "Notes on Punctuation" is this: Punctuation is not a dry, lifeless subject but rather a rich and subtle element of creative written communication. In most works of poetry and fiction, the main idea is implied rather than stated directly. When you write an essay that analyzes or interprets a literary work, always state your main idea clearly.
See *Purpose*.

**OBJECTIVE** *adj.*   Something is *objective* if it has to do with a reality that is independent of any particular person's mind or of any personal, internal experiences. Statements of fact are objective because anyone, at least in theory, can determine whether they are true. For example, the statement, "Lucille Clifton wrote 'Miss Rosie'," is objective because it deals with an impersonal, external reality. On the other hand, the statement, "Miss Rosie is a touching, poignant poem," is subjective because it reports one individual's personal, internal experience of the work.

Aside from statements of fact, total objectivity is impossible. In practice, then, to be objective is to be fair. In writing about literature, a subjective statement will seem fair if it takes into account the important facts and details contained within the work.
See *Subjective*.

**OPINION** *n.*   An *opinion* is a statement that can be supported by facts but is not itself a fact. An opinion is usually one of three types: the evaluation, the prediction, and the statement of obligation or necessity. Here are examples of each:

Octavio Paz is one of the greatest writers of our time. (evaluation)
Poetry will reach new audiences in the coming years. (prediction)
We must seek to eradicate illiteracy in our country. (obligation/necessity)

Opinions are subjective, so whenever you express an opinion, you should be prepared to support it with facts or with reasoned arguments. A statement that you cannot back up is merely a prejudice.
See *Fact*, *Judgment*, and *Prediction*.

**OVERGENERALIZATION**  See *Logical Fallacy.*

**PARAPHRASE** *n.*  A *paraphrase* is a restatement in different words. A paraphrase can be used to support an interpretive argument when the exact words of the original are not essential to the argument. Be careful not to alter the meaning of the original passage. Simply put into your own words what the writer has said. You can also test your understanding of a literary work by attempting to paraphrase key passages. Never paraphrase another writer without identifying the original source.

**POST HOC, ERGO PROPTER HOC**  See *Logical Fallacy.*

**PREDICTION** *n.*  *Prediction* is the act of making statements about the future. Like inference, prediction is important to active reading, especially of narrative works. As an active reader, you make predictions about what will happen in a literary work on the basis of the details in the work and your own knowledge about the world and about how people act.

When you read a novel, for instance, you are continually predicting subsequent developments as each new detail presents itself—a plot twist, a new character, or an unusually long description. Authors often signal or hint at future plot developments by means of images, incidents, and characters introduced early in their works. This technique is called *foreshadowing*. Repeated references to weather, for example, might lead you to predict that weather will play a crucial role later in the story. Sometimes authors intentionally mislead readers into making predictions that will later prove false. This often happens in mysteries and in stories with surprise endings.
See *Opinion.*

**PROBLEM SOLVING** *n. phrase*  *Problem solving* is the process by which a person comes up with a solution to some difficulty. Advances in medicine and in technology always involve problem solving. NASA's space program, for example, is a team effort in problem solving. The following steps can be used in any situation that requires problem solving:
1. Define the problem as exactly as possible.
2. Identify your goal.
3. List the details that prevent you from reaching the goal.
4. Think of partial solutions—ones that eliminate parts of the problem.
5. Combine the successful elements from your partial solutions to form a solution that resolves the difficulty completely.

The following rules of thumb are useful in solving many problems:
1. Break the problem down into parts and solve the parts separately.
2. Think of similar problems you have solved before. Use part or all of those solutions to solve the current problem.
3. Restate the problem in various ways or from several points of view.
4. Ask someone to help you with parts of the problem that are especially difficult.
5. Use general thinking strategies such as brainstorming, freewriting, and diagraming.

People who study literature also engage in

problem solving. Literary problems might include determining the meaning or significance of a work, or the meaning of an individual plot detail. Actual examples of literary problems include the following: What does Rainy Mountain mean to N. Scott Momaday? What is "the Red Death" in Poe's tale? Why is Brutus more prominent in Shakespeare's play than is Julius Caesar, for whom the play is named?

When solving such literary problems, draw upon evidence from the works you are examining.

**PROPAGANDA TECHNIQUE** *n. phrase* A *propaganda technique* is an improper appeal to emotion for the purpose of swaying the opinions of an audience. Propaganda techniques are often used in politics and in advertising. The following propaganda techniques are quite common:

1. *Bandwagon:* This technique involves encouraging people to think or act in some way simply because other people are doing so. For example: "All of your friends have bought computers. Isn't it about time that you did, too?"
2. *Loaded words:* This technique involves the use of words with strong positive or negative connotations. Name-calling is an example of the use of loaded words. So is any use of words that are charged with emotional associations. For example: "No good American will vote for this evil man."
3. *Snob appeal:* This technique involves making a direct or implied claim that one should act or think in a certain way because of the high social status associated with the act or thought. For example: "When only the best will do, buy Charm perfume."
4. *Transfer:* This technique involves making an illogical association between one thing and something else that is generally viewed as positive or negative. For example: "As the son of the actor who plays the good guy in cowboy movies, I can help bring justice to your town. So, vote for me."

5. *Unreliable testimonial:* This technique involves having someone who is unqualified to do so endorse a product, an action, or an opinion. For example: "You know me. I play a policeman on television. I'd like to talk to you about home security."
6. *Vague, undefined terms:* This technique involves promoting or challenging an opinion by using words that are so vague or so poorly defined as to be almost meaningless. For example: "Be an aware consumer, and buy this product."

Try to avoid propaganda techniques in your own speech and writing, and be on guard against these techniques in the speech and writing of others.

**PURPOSE** *n.* The *purpose* is the goal or aim of a literary work. Aaron Copland's purpose in "The Creative Process in Music," on page 553, is to explain how a piece of music comes into being. The purpose of a work might be to persuade the reader to act and think a certain way, to inform the reader, to tell a story, to describe something, or simply to entertain. A writer often may have more than one purpose. For example, Calvin Trillin's essay "Rural Literalism," on page 539, both informs and entertains.
See *Main Idea.*

**REALISTIC DETAILS/FANTASTIC DETAILS** *n. phrases* A *realistic detail* is one that is drawn from actual or possible experience; a *fantastic detail* is one that is not based on actual experience and is improbable or imaginary. Realistic details make plots, characters, descriptions, and statements seem true to life or believable. They make the reader think that the people, places, and events in the work could actually exist in real life. Willa Cather, in "The Sentimentality of William Tavener," uses realistic details exclusively. Some writers, such as Edgar Allan Poe and Ray Bradbury, mix fantastic details with realistic details to capture their readers' imaginations. For example, in "There Will Come Soft Rains," on page 133,

Bradbury uses realistic details about a house and fantastic details about the future.

**REASON** *n.*   A *reason* is a statement in support of some conclusion. A writer must state a reason clearly and carefully for it to support a conclusion effectively. The term *reason* is also used as a verb to signify the human ability to think logically and rationally.
See *Argument* and *Conclusion*.

**SNOB APPEAL**   See *Propaganda Technique*.

**SOURCE** *n.*   A *source* is anything from which ideas and information are taken. Books, magazines, speeches, television programs, conversations, and personal experience may all serve as sources. Some books, such as dictionaries, encyclopedias, almanacs, and atlases, are designed to be used as sources. However, not all sources are of equal value. Good sources are thorough, objective, and up-to-date.

There are two types of sources, primary sources and secondary sources. *Primary sources* are first hand accounts. Conversations, speeches, documents, and letters are examples of primary sources. *Secondary sources* are accounts written by others, after the fact. For example, Emily Dickinson's personal letters are a primary source of information about her life and writings. Van Wyck Brooks's "Emily Dickinson," on the other hand, is a secondary source because it relies on his reading of other sources of information about Dickinson. Brooks himself never met her.

Whenever you borrow facts and ideas from other sources, be sure to credit your sources by means of footnotes or end notes. If you do not credit them, you are committing the dishonest act called *plagiarism*.

**STEREOTYPE** *n.*   A *stereotype* is a fixed or conventional notion or characterization. It is a type of overgeneralization or oversimplification. Some examples include the dumb blond, the jolly fat man, the absent-minded professor, and the cigar-smoking politician. Relying on stereotypes is intellectual laziness. Although writers occasionally use stereotypes when they do not have sufficient time to develop a character fully, good writers generally avoid stereotyping. They know that carefully drawn characters and situations are more interesting to read about than tired, simplistic stereotypes.
See *Generalization*.

**SUBJECTIVE** *adj.*   Something is *subjective* if it is based on personal reactions or emotions rather than on some objective reality. A reader's reaction to a work of literature—"I think it is terrific," for example—is subjective because another reader may have a different reaction. Opinions are subjective statements, but not all opinions are equally valid. Sensible subjective statements about a literary work are based on evidence from the text. For example, if you find N. Scott Momaday's essay "The Way To Rainy Mountain" to be beautiful and moving, you should be able to identify some of the details in it that make you feel this way.

Writers often try to recreate subjective experiences in their works. Dylan Thomas's "A Child's Christmas in Wales," for example, richly recreates subjective feelings and experiences from Thomas's childhood, such as his feelings about cats, uncles, snowballs, and Christmas jellies.
See *Objective*.

**SUMMARIZE** *v.*   To *summarize* something is to restate it briefly in different words. A brief summary of O. Henry's story "Hearts and Hands" might be as follows:

A young, pretty women is sitting alone on a train. At the next stop, two men in handcuffs board the train and take seats across from the woman. Only after she recognizes and speaks to the younger man does she notice the handcuffs. The young man apologizes for his inability to shake her hand, since his right hand is chained to the older man. This companion breaks into the conversation to explain that the younger man is a marshall taking him to Leavenworth prison for counterfeiting. Later, at the older man's insistence, the pair leaves for the smoking car. When they are gone, a discussion ensues among two other passengers, and the young man is identified as the prisoner, for as a passenger notes: "Did you ever know an officer to handcuff a prisoner to his right hand?"

**SUPPORT** *v.* To *support* something is to provide evidence for it.
See *Argument* and *Evidence*.

**TIME ORDER** *n. phrase* *Time order* is organization by order of occurrence, that is, by chronological order. Both fiction and nonfiction narratives usually use *time order* to organize and present the events they describe.

**TRANSFER** See *Propaganda Technique*.

**UNRELIABLE TESTIMONIAL** See *Propaganda Technique*.

**VAGUE, UNDEFINED TERMS** See *Propaganda Technique*.

# GLOSSARY

## READING THE GLOSSARY ENTRIES

The words in this glossary are from selections appearing in your textbook. Each entry in the glossary contains the following parts:

**1. Entry Word.** This word appears at the beginning of the entry, in boldface type.

**2. Pronunciation.** The symbols in parentheses tell how the entry word is pronounced. If a word has more than one possible pronunciation, the most common of these pronunciations is given first.

**3. Part of Speech.** Appearing after the pronunciation, in italics, is an abbreviation that tells the part of speech of the entry word. The following abbreviations have been used:

| | | |
|---|---|---|
| **n.** noun | **p.** pronoun | **v.** verb |
| **adj.** adjective | **adv.** adverb | **conj.** conjunction |

**4. Definition.** This part of the entry follows the part-of-speech abbreviation and gives the meaning of the entry word as used in the selection in which it appears.

## KEY TO PRONUNCIATION SYMBOLS USED IN THE GLOSSARY

The following symbols are used in the pronunciations that follow the entry words:

| Symbol | Key Words | Symbol | Key Words |
|---|---|---|---|
| a | asp, fat, parrot | b | bed, fable, dub |
| ā | ape, date, play | d | dip, beadle, had |
| ä | ah, car, father | f | fall, after, off |
| | | g | get, haggle, dog |
| e | elf, ten, berry | h | he, ahead, hotel |
| ē | even, meet, money | j | joy, agile, badge |
| | | k | kill, tackle, bake |
| i | is, hit, mirror | l | let, yellow, ball |
| ī | ice, bite, high | m | met, camel, trim |
| | | n | not, flannel, ton |
| ō | open, tone, go | p | put, apple, tap |
| ô | all, horn, law | r | red, port, dear |
| o͞o | ooze, tool, crew | s | sell, castle, pass |
| oo | look, pull, moor | t | top, cattle, hat |
| yo͞o | use, cute, few | v | vat, hovel, have |
| yoo | united, cure, globule | w | will, always, swear |
| oi | oil, point, toy | y | yet, onion, yard |
| ou | out, crowd, plow | z | zebra, dazzle, haze |
| u | up, cut, color | ch | chin, catcher, arch |
| ʉr | urn, fur, deter | sh | she, cushion, dash |
| | | th | thin, nothing, truth |
| ə | a in ago | t͟h | then, father, lathe |
| | e in agent | zh | azure, leisure |
| | i in sanity | ŋ | ring, anger, drink |
| | o in comply | | [see explanatory note |
| | u in focus | | below and also *Foreign sounds* below] |
| ər | perhaps, murder | | |

This pronunciation key is from *Webster's New World Dictionary*, Second College Edition. Copyright © 1986 by Simon & Schuster. Used by permission.

## A

**abalone** (ab′ ə lō′ nē) *n.* A shellfish with a flat shell and a pearly lining

**abandonment** (ə ban′ dən mənt) *n.* Freedom from restraint

**abash** (ə basht′) *adj.* Self-conscious, ashamed

**abate** (ə bāt′) *v.* To lessen; to put an end to

**aberration** (ab′ ər ā′ shən) *n.* Something that differs from the norm

**abhorrently** (əb hôr′ ənt lē) *adv.* Frighteningly; disgustingly; hatefully

**abstain** (əb stān′) *v.* Voluntarily refrain from

**abstract** (ab strakt′) *adj.* Apart from any particular example; theoretical

**accolade** (ak′ ə lād′) *n.* Approval

**accompaniment** (ə kump′ ni mənt) *n.* A part, usually instrumental, performed together with the main part for richer effect

**acquittal** (ə kwit′ ′l) *n.* The judgment of a judge or jury that a person is not guilty of a crime as charged

**ad-lib** (ad′ lib) *v.* To add words not in the script

**adobe** (ə dō′ bē) *n.* Unburnt, sun-dried brick

**aesthete** (es′ thēt′) *n.* Someone highly sensitive to art and beauty; someone who puts on such a sensitivity

**affiliate** (ə fil′ ē āt) *v.* To associate

**akin** (ə kin′) *adj.* Having a similar quality or character

**albatross** (al′ bə trôs′) *n.* A large sea bird often used as a symbol of a burden or source of distress

**albino** (al bī′ nō) *n.* People who because of a genetic factor have unusually pale skin and white hair

**alchemy** (al′ kə mē) *n.* An early form of chemistry in which the goal was to change baser metals into gold

**alluvium** (ə lo͞o′ vē əm) *n.* Material such as sand or gravel deposited by moving water

**aloofness** (ə lo͞of′ nəs) *n.* The state of being distant, removed, or uninvolved

**ambiguity** (am′bə gyo͞o′ ə tē) *n.* Uncertainty

**amphibious** (am fib′ ē əs) *adj.* That can operate or travel on both land and water

**amulet** (am′ yə lit) *adj.* Charm worn to protect against evil

**anarchy** (an′ ər kē) *n.* Lawlessness; disorder

**Angelus** (an′ jə ləs) *n.* Bell rung to announce the time for a prayer said at morning, noon, and evening

**antimacassar** (an′ ti mə kas′ ər) *n.* A small cover on the arms or back of a chair or sofa to prevent soiling

**anvil** (an′ vəl) *n.* An iron or steel block

**aphorism** (af′ ə riz′m) *n.* Short sentence expressing wise or clever observation

**apocryphal** (ə pä′ krə f′l) *adj.* Fictitious; false

**apoplexy** (ap′ ə plek′ sē) *n.* A stroke

**appertain** (ap′ ər tān′) *v.* Belong

**appurtenance** (ə pur′ t′n əns) *n.* Accessory

**apropos** (ap′ rə pō′) *adv.* Aptly; fittingly for the occasion

**arabesque** (ar′ ə besk′) *adj.* Elaborately designed

**arch** (ärch) *adj.* Mischievous

**arias** (är′ ē əz) *n.* Melodies in an opera, especially for solo voice with instrumental accompaniment

**armada** (är mä′ də) *n.* A fleet of warships

**arnica** (är′ ni kə) *n.* A preparation made from certain plants, once used for treating sprains, bruises, and so forth

**arrant** (ar′ ənt) *adj.* Extreme

**arrogance** (ar′ ə gəns) *n.* Pride; self-importance

**arsenic** (är′ s′n ik′) *n.* A poison

**assimilate**   (ə sim′ ə lāt′)   *v.* To absorb into one's thinking

**assumption**   (ə sump′ shən)   *n.* Idea accepted as true without proof

**assurance**   (ə shoor′ əns)   *n.* Sureness, confidence

**audaciously**   (ô dā′ shəs lē)   *adv.* In a bold manner

**augment**   (ôg ment′)   *v.* To make greater

**august**   (ô gust′)   *adj.* Imposing and magnificent

**austerity**   (ô ster′ ə tē)   *n.* Severity

**automation**   (ô täm′ ə tän′)   *n.* A person acting in an automatic or mechanical way

**avail**   (ə vāl′)   *n.* Usefulness; advantage

**avarice**   (av′ ər is)   *n.* Greediness

**avaricious**   (av′ ə rish′ əs)   *adj.* Greedy for riches

**avenge**   (ə venj′)   *v.* To get revenge for an injury

**avert**   (ə vurt′)   *v.* To turn away

**avocation**   (a və kā′ shən)   *n.* Hobby

**avowal**   (ə vou′ əl)   *n.* Declaration

**awl**   (ôl)   *n.* A small, pointed tool for making holes in leather

**B**

**bailer**   (bā′ lər)   *n.* A scoop for removing water from a boat

**balustrade**   (bal′ ə strād′)   *n.* A railing held up by small posts

**banal**   (bā′ n'l)   *adj.* Without originality or freshness; stale from overuse; commonplace

**barbaric**   (bär ber′ ik)   *adj.* Uncivilized; wild

**barrow**   (bar′ ō)   *n.* Ancient grave

**bedight**   (bi dīt′)   *adj.* Adorned

**bevel**   (bev′ 'l)   *v.* To cut to an angle other than a right angle

**bibulous**   (bib′ yoo ləs)   *adj.* Given to drinking alcoholic beverages

**bifocal**   (bī fō′ k'l)   *n.* A pair of glasses with one part of each lens for close focus and the other part of each lens for distant focus

**bigot**   (big′ ət)   *n.* A person who holds blindly and intolerantly to a particular opinion

**bilge**   (bilj)   *n.* Dirty water in the bottom of a boat

**billet**   (bil′ it)   *v.* To assigned quarters

**billow**   (bil′ ō)   *v.* To surge; swell

**blitzkreig**   (blits′ krēg)   *n.* Sudden, overwhelming attack

**boast**   (bōst′)   *v.* To show too much pride; brag

**bounty**   (boun′ tē)   *n.* Generosity

**bouquet**   (bō kā′)   *n.* Fragrance

**bowel**   (bou′ əl)   *n.* Intestine; gut

**bower**   (bou′ ər)   *n.* Private chamber

**brackish**   (brak′ ish)   *adj.* Salty and marshy

**brandish**   (bran′ dish)   *v.* To wave or flourish menacingly

**brazier**   (brā′ zhər)   *n.* A metal pan or bowl to hold burning coals or charcoal

**brittle**   (brit′ 'l)   *adj.* Stiff and unbending; easily broken or shattered

**buffet**   (buf′ it)   *n.* A blow or cuff with, or as if with, the hand

**bundling**   (bun′ d'lin)   *v.* Moving quickly; bustling

**burgh**   (berg)   *n.* Small town

**burlesque**   (bər lesk′)   *adj.* Comic imitation of

**butte**   (byoot)   *n.* Flat-topped rock formation

**C**

**cacaphony**   (kə käf′ ə nē)   *n.* Harsh sound

**cache**   (kash)   *n.* Anything stored or hidden in a secret or safe place

**cairn**   (kern)   *n.* A cone-shaped heap of stones used as a marker or monument

**caldron**   (kôl′ drən)   *n.* Heat like that of a boiling kettle

**calico**   (kal′ ə kō)   *adj.* Made of cotton cloth, usually printed

**cameo**   (kam′ ē ō′)   *n.* A shell or stone carved with a head in profile and used as jewelry

**candelabrum**   (kan′ də lä′ brəm)   *n.* A large branched candlestick

**cantor**   (kan′ tər)   *n.* A singer of solos in a synagogue, who leads the congregation in prayer

**capacious**   (kə pā′ shəs)   *adj.* Roomy; spacious

**capricious**   (ka prish′ əs)   *adj.* Without apparent reason

**caress**   (kə res′)   *v.* To touch or stroke lightly or lovingly

**carnage**   (kär′ nij)   *n.* Slaughter; massacre

**cavort**   (kə vôrt′)   *v.* To leap or prance about

**cerement**   (sir′ mənt)   *n.* Wrapping or shroud

**chafer**   (chāf′ ər)   *n.* An insect that feeds on plants

**chamiso**   (chə mē′ sō)   *n.* Densely growing desert shrub

**chamois**   (sham′ ē)   *n.* A small, goatlike antelope

**chastisement**   (chas tīz′ mənt)   *n.* Punishment; severe criticism

**check**   (chek)   *n.* A move in chess that threatens to capture the king

**chitinous**   (kī′ tən əs)   *adj.* Of a material which forms the tough outer covering of insects, crustaceans, and so on

**choleric**   (käl′ ər ik)   *adj.* Quick-tempered

**circumvent**   (sur′ kəm vent′)   *v.* To prevent from happening

**citable**   (sīt′ ə b'l)   *adj.* Able to be named

**citron**   (si′ trən)   *n.* A yellow, thick-skinned, lemonlike fruit

**claque**   (klak)   *n.* A group paid to applaud a performance

**cliché**   (klē shā′)   *n.* An overused phrase or expression

**coaster**   (kōs′ tər)   *n.* A ship that carries cargo or passengers from port to port along a coast

**cogitation**   (käj′ ə tā′ shən)   *n.* Meditation; seriousness

**coherent**   (kō hir′ ənt)   *adj.* Logically connected or ordered

**cohort**   (kō′ hôrt)   *n.* Companion; supporter

**collusion**   (kə loo′ zhən)   *n.* A secret agreement for an illegal purpose

**commandeer**   (käm′ ən dir′)   *adj.* To force into service

**complacence**   (kəm plās′ 'ns)   *n.* Self-satisfaction

**confounded**   (kən found′ id)   *adj.* Confused

**conjecture**   (kən jek′ chər)   *n.* An inference based on incomplete or inconclusive evidence

**conjunction**   (kən junk′ shən)   *n.* Union

**conjure**   (kän′ jər)   *v.* To remove as if by magic

**consecrated**   (kän′ sə krāt′ əd)   *adj.* Dedicated

**conservatory**   (kən sur′ və tôr′ ē)   *n.* Greenhouse

**consort** (kän′ sôrt)   *n.* Harmony of sounds

**conspicuous** (kən spik′ yoo wəs)   *adj.* Attracting attention by being unexpected

**conspiracy** (kən spir′ ə sē)   *n.* 1. A group of people plotting an illegal or evil act 2. Such a plot itself

**constancy** (kän′ stən sē)   *n.* Firmness of mind or purpose; resoluteness

**consternation** (kän′ stər nā′ shən)   *n.* Fear or shock

**constrained** (kən strānd′)   *adj.* Compelled

**contemptuous** (kən temp′ choo wəs)   *adj.* Full of contempt; scornful

**contentious** (kən ten′ shəs)   *adj.* Quarrelsome

**contretemps** (kōn trə tän′)   *n.* French for "an awkward mishap."

**contrition** (kən trish′ ən)   *n.* A feeling of remorse for having done something wrong

**conventional** (kən ven′ shən l)   *adj.* Of the usual kind; customary

**convoluted** (kän və loot′ id)   *adj.* Intricate; twisted

**convulsive** (kən vul′ siv)   *adj.* Marked by an involuntary, muscular contraction

**coquettish** (kō ket′ ish)   *adj.* Flirtatious

**coral** (kôr′ əl)   *n.* An animal with tentacles at the top of a tubelike body

**cordon** (kôr′ d′n)   *n.* A line or circle of police stationed around an area to guard it

**coroner** (kôr′ ə nər)   *n.* A public official whose chief duty is to determine the cause of a death

**cosmic** (käz′ mik)   *adj.* Relating to the universe

**counsel** (koun s′l)   *n.* Lawyer

**countenance** (koun′ tə nəns)   *n.* The expression of a person's face; facial feature

**counterfeit** (koun′ tər fit′)   *v.* To make imitation money to pass off as real money

**covert** (kuv′ ərt)   *n.* A hiding place

**cowlish** (koul ish)   *adj.* Hood-shaped

**cozen** (kuz′ ən)   *v.* To deceive

**credence** (krēd′ əns)   *n.* Belief

**credulity** (krə doo′ lə tē)   *n.* A tendency to believe too readily, especially without proof

**criterion** (krī tir′ ē ən)   *n.* A standard or rule for making a judgment

**crocheted** (krō shā′ d)   *adj.* Made with thread or yarn woven together with hooked needles

**crofter** (krôft′ ər)   *n.* Tenant farmer

**cryptic** (krip′ tik)   *adj.* Having a hidden or mysterious meaning

**culminate** (kul′ mə nāt′)   *v.* To bring to its highest point of interest

**czar** (zär)   *n.* The emperor of Russia

## D

**dacha** (dä′ chə)   *n.* In Russia, a country house or cottage

**damsel** (dam′ zəl)   *n.* A young woman or girl; maiden

**damson** (dam′ z′n)   *n.* Small purple plum

**davenport** (dav′ ən pôrt′)   *n.* A large couch or sofa

**Dean** (dēn)   *n.* Head of the school administration

**decalogue** (dek′ ə lôg′)   *n.* The Ten Commandments

**decipher** (di sī′ fər)   *v.* To figure out the meaning of

**decora** (di kor′ ə)   *n.* Requirements of good taste

**decrepit** (di krep′ it)   *adj.* Broken down or worn out by old age or long use

**defendant** (di fen′ dənt)   *n.* In law, the person accused

**deference** (def′ ər əns)   *n.* Respect and consideration

**deftness** (deft′ nis)   *adj.* Skillfulness

**delirious** (di lir′ ē əs)   *adj.* Raving incoherently

**delirium** (di lir′ ē əm)   *n.* State of extreme mental confusion

**delusion** (di loo′ zhən)   *n.* A false belief held in spite of evidence to the contrary

**dematerialize** (dē′ mə tir′ ē ə līz′)   *v.* To lose or cause to lose physical form ~

**dementia** (di men′ shə)   *n.* Insanity or madness

**denouement** (dā′ nü män′)   *n.* Outcome or the end

**density** (den′ sə tē)   *n.* Thickness

**deploy** (dē ploi′)   *v.* To spread out

**depravity** (di prav′ ə tē)   *n.* Wickedness

**deranged** (di rānjd′)   *adj.* Disturbed out of the normal way of acting

**desolate** (des′ ə lit)   *adj.* Deserted; gloomy; lifeless

**desolation** (des′ ə la′ shən)   *n.* Wretchedness; loneliness

**diffuse** (di fyoos′)   *adj.* Widely spread or scattered

**dilapidated** (di lap′ ə dāt′ id)   *adj.* Fallen into a shabby and neglected state

**dilettante** (dil′ ə tänt′)   *n.* An amateur or dabbler in the arts

**disapprobation** (dis ap′ rə bā′ shən)   *n.* Disapproval

**discern** (di surn′)   *v.* To recognize

**discernible** (di surn′ ə b′l)   *adj.* Clearly recognizable

**disconcerting** (dis′ kən surt′ iŋ)   *adj.* Upsetting the composure of; confusing

**discourse** (dis′ kôrs)   *v.* To speak formally and at length

**disdain** (dis dān′)   *n.* Scorn; lofty contempt

**disillusionment** (dis′ i loo′ zhən mənt)   *n.* Disappointment

**disown** (dis ōn′)   *v.* To deny ownership of or responsibility for

**dispensation** (dis′ pən sā′ shən)   *n.* Release; exemption

**disposition** (dis pə zish′ ən)   *n.* Inclination; tendency; choice

**dissect** (di sekt′)   *v.* To cut up into parts

**dissemble** (di sem′ b′l)   *v.* To conceal the real feelings by a pretense

**dissipate** (dis′ ə pāt′)   *v.* To scatter

**distemper** (dis tem′ pər)   *n.* An infectious virus disease of young dogs

**divination** (div′ ə nā′ shən)   *n.* Guessing correctly

**docile** (däs′ ′l)   *adj.* Easy to teach or manage

**dogged** (dôg′ id)   *adj.* Persistent; stubborn

**doleful** (dōl′ fəl)   *adj.* Full of sadness

**dominion** (də min′ yən)   *n.* Rule or power to rule

**douche** (doosh′)   *v.* To wash or flush away

**doughty** (dout′ ē)   *adj.* Brave; valiant

**dowager** (dou′ ə jər)   *n.* An elderly woman of wealth and dignity

**dower** (dou′ ər)   *v.* To endow

**dowry** (dou′ rē)   *n.* Money or property brought by a bride to her husband at marriage

**drayman** (drā′ mən)   *n.* The driver of a horse-drawn cart with detachable sides for carrying heavy loads

**droll**  (drōl)  *adj.* Amusing in an odd or ironic way

**drollery**  (drōl′ ər ē)  *n.* Wry humor

**Dryad**  (drī əd)  *n.* A nature goddess who lives in a tree

# E

**edelweiss**  (ā′ d'l vīs′)  *n.* A small, flowering alpine plant

**effulgence**  (e ful′ jəns)  *n.* Radiance; brilliance

**egress**  (ē′ gres)  *n.* Leaving

**elocution**  (el′ ə kyü′ shən)  *n.* The art of clear and effective public speaking

**emaciated**  (i mā′ shē āt əd)  *adj.* Abnormally thin because of starvation or illness

**embryo**  (em′ brē ō)  *n.* Anything in an early stage of development

**emulation**  (em′ yə lā′ shən)  *n.* Old word for envy, jealousy

**enchantment**  (en chant′ mənt)  *n.* An act of casting under a spell

**encroaching**  (in krōch′ iŋ)  *adj.* Intruding; advancing

**engender**  (in jen′ dər)  *v.* To bring about; cause; produce

**enigmatic**  (en′ ig mat′ ik)  *adj.* Baffling

**ensign**  (en′ s'n)  *n.* Old word for a standard bearer; one who carries a flag

**entrail**  (en′ trāl)  *n.* Intestine, gut

**entreat**  (in trēt′)  *v.* To beg; plead with

**envy**  (en′ vē)  *n.* Feeling of desire for another's possessions or qualities and jealousy at not having them

**ephemeral**  (i fem′ ə rəl)  *adj.* Passing quickly

**Epicurus**  (ep′ ə kyoor′ əs)  *n.* A Greek philosopher who tried to find freedom from physical pain and emotional disturbance

**ermine**  (ur′ mən)  *adj.* Of the soft, white, black-tipped fur of a weasel

**errant**  (er′ ənt)  *adj.* Straying outside the proper path or bounds

**erratic**  (i rat′ ik)  *adj.* Irregular; not following a normal pattern

**escarpment**  (e skärp′ mənt)  *n.* A steep cliff

**essence**  (es′ 'ns)  *n.* Real nature of something

**esthetically**  (es thet′ ik lē)  *adv.* Artistically

**estuary**  (es′ choo wer′ ē)  *n.* An inlet formed where a river enters the ocean

**ethereal**  (i thir′ ē əl)  *adj.* Of the upper regions of space

**eulogy**  (yoo′ lə jē)  *n.* A formal speech in praise of someone who has recently died

**evanescent**  (ev′ ə nes′ 'nt)  *adj.* Tending to fade from sight

**evasion**  (i vā′ zhən)  *n.* The tendency to avoid or escape something

**evocative**  (i väk′ ə tiv)  *adj.* Having the power to bring forth

**exaltation**  (eg′ zôl tā′ shən)  *n.* A feeling of great joy, pride, or power

**excursion**  (ik skur′ zhən)  *n.* A short trip

**executive**  (ig zek′ yə tiv)  *adj.* Capable of carrying out duties

**exertion**  (ig zur′ shən)  *n.* The active use of strength or power

**exhilarate**  (ig zil′ ə rāt)  *v.* To make cheerful, lively

**exorcist**  (ek′ sôr sist)  *n.* One who calls up spirits

**expedient**  (ik spē′ dē ənt)  *adj.* Useful; convenient

**exploit**  (eks′ ploit)  *n.* Act or deed, especially a heroic achievement

**exquisite**  (eks′ kwi zit)  *adj.* Delicately beautiful

**extenuating**  (ik sten′ yoo wāt iŋ′)  *adj.* Serving as an excuse

# F

**fagot**  (fag′ ət)  *n.* A bundle of sticks used for fuel

**falconry**  (fal′ kən rē)  *n.* The training of falcons to hunt game

**fathomless**  (fath′ əm lis)  *adj.* Too deep to be measured

**feint**  (fānt)  *v.* To make a pretense of attack

**feisty**  (fīst′ ē)  *adj.* Spunky; touchy and quarrelsome

**fieldpiece**  (fēld′ pēs)  *n.* Mobile artillery

**figment**  (fig′ mənt)  *n.* Something merely imagined

**fillet**  (fi lā′)  *n.* Boned and sliced fish

**flailing**  (flāl′ iŋ)  *adj.* Beating or striking with a thrashing movement

**flank**  (flaŋk)  *n.* Side

**flicker**  (flik′ ər)  *n.* A species of woodpecker

**flout**  (flout)  *v.* To show contempt for

**floweret**  (flou′ ər it)  *n.* A small flower

**fluctuating**  (fluk′ choo wāt′ iŋ)  *adj.* Moving in a wavelike manner

**fluke**  (flook)  *n.* 1. A flounder or other flatfish 2. Successful result brought about by accident; stroke of luck

**flurriedly**  (flur′ əd lē)  *adv.* In a flustered, agitated way

**fomentation**  (fō′ mən tā′ shən)  *n.* An application of warm, moist substances in the treatment of an injury

**ford**  (fôrd)  *n.* A shallow place in a body of water, such as a river, where a crossing can be made

**foreboding**  (fôr bōd′ iŋ)  *n.* Prediction of something bad or harmful

**forestall**  (fôr stôl′)  *v.* To prevent by doing something ahead of time

**forfeiture**  (fôr′ fi chər)  *n.* The act of giving up something as punishment for a crime

**forlorn**  (fər lôrn′)  *adj.* Abandoned; deserted

**foxhole**  (fäks hōl′)  *n.* A hole dug in the ground as temporary protection for soldiers against enemy gunfire

**fragility**  (frə jil′ ə tē)  *n.* State of being easily broken or damaged

**franc**  (fraŋk)  *n.* Unit of money in France

**fratricide**  (frat′ rə sīd′)  *n.* The killing of one's brother or sister

**friction**  (frik′ shən)  *n.* Resistance

**frond**  (fränd)  *n.* A leaflike shoot of seaweed

**furrow**  (fur′ ō)  *n.* A narrow groove or rut

**furtive**  (fur′ tiv)  *adj.* Sneaky; secretive

**fusillade**  (fyoo′ sə läd′)  *n.* Something that is like the rapid firing of many firearms

# G

**gait**  (gāt)  *n.* Way of moving

**galleon**  (gal′ yən)  *n.* A large Spanish ship of the fifteenth and sixteenth centuries

**gargoyle**  (gär′ goil)  *n.* A projecting ornament, usually a grotesquely carved animal or fantastic creature, on a building

**gauche** (gōsh) *adj.* Awkward

**gendarme** (zhän′ därm) *n.* A French policeman

**giddy** (gid′ e) *adj.* Mad or foolish

**glen** (glen) *n.* A secluded, narrow valley between mountains

**goad** (gōd) *n.* To urge

**gourd** (gôrd) *n.* The dried, hollowed-out shell of a squash, used to hold the shape of the sock

**gout** (gσut) *n.* A spurt, splash, or glob

**grace** (grās) *n.* Seemingly effortless beauty or charm of movement, form, or proportion

**grimace** (gri mās′) *n.* A twisted facial expression

**grandee** (gran dē′) *n.* Nobleman

**grisly** (griz′ lē) *adj.* Horrifying; gruesome

**grotesque** (grō tesk′) *adj.* Ridiculous or distorted

**groveling** (gruv′ liŋ) *adj.* Crawling; humbling

**gunnel** (gun′ ′l) *n.* The upper edges of the sides of a boat

**guileful** (gīl′ fəl) *adj.* Deceitful; tricky

**guileless** (gīl′ lis) *adj.* Without slyness or cunning; frank

# H

**habiliment** (hə bil′ ə ment) *n.* Clothing

**hale** (hāl) *adj.* Vigorous; healthy

**harmony** (här′ mə nē) *n.* The study of chords in music; chords are combinations of tones sounded together

**headstall** (hed′ stôl′) *n.* The part of a bridle that fits over a horse's head

**heirloom** (er′ lōōm) *n.* A treasured possession handed down from generation to generation

**hogan** (hō′ gôn) *n.* A traditional Navaho dwelling, built of wood and adobe

**homage** (häm′ ij) *n.* Public show of honor and allegiance

**Homo sapiens** (hō′ mō sā′ pē ənz) *n.* A human being

**hone** (hōn) *n.* A stone used for sharpening cutting tools

**horoscope** (hôr′ ə skōp′) *n.* The position of the planets and stars with relation to one another at a given time, especially at the time of a person's birth

**hue** (hyōō) *n.* Color; shade of a given color

**hulking** (hul′ kiŋ) *adj.* Large; heavy; clumsy

**hull** (hul′) *v.* To take the shells off nuts

**hummock** (hum′ ək) *n.* A low, rounded hill

**hurdy-gurdy** (hʉr′ dē gʉr′ dē) *n.* A musical instrument, like a barrel organ, played by turning a crank

**husbandman** (huz′ bənd mən) *n.* A farmer

# I

**ichthyologist** (ik′ thē äl′ ə jist) *n.* One who studies fish

**idiom** (id′ ē əm) *n.* Meaning different from the literal; the style of artistic expression characteristic of an individual

**idiosyncratic** (id′ ē ə sin krat′ ik) *adj.* Peculiar

**idyllic** (ī dil′ ik) *adj.* Pleasing and simple

**Iliad** (il′ ē əd) *n.* A Greek epic poem by Homer set in the tenth year of the Trojan War

**immersion** (i mʉr′ shən) *n.* A plunge into water

**imminent** (im′ ə nənt) *adj.* Likely to happen presently; threatening

**impalpable** (im pal′ pə b′l) *adj.* That which cannot be felt by touching

**impassive** (im pas′ iv) *adj.* Showing no emotion

**imperatrix** (im′ pə rā′ triks) *n.* A woman emperor

**imperceptibly** (im pər sep′ tə blē) *adv.* In such a slight way as to be almost unnoticeable

**imperiously** (im pir′ ē əs lē) *adv.* Arrogantly

**imperturbable** (im′ pər tʉr′bə b′l) *adj.* Unable to be excited or disturbed

**impervious** (im pʉr′vē əs) *adj.* Not affected by

**impinge** (im pinj′) *v.* To intrude

**implication** (im ′plə kā′ shən) *n.* A suggestion

**impregnable** (im preg′ nə b′l) *adj.* Not capable of being entered by force

**impudent** (im′ pyōō dənt) *adj.* Shamelessly bold or disrespectful

**inane** (in ān′) *adj.* Empty; foolish; silly

**inanimate** (in an′ ə mit) *adj.* Dull; spiritless; not alive

**inaugurate** (in ô′ gyə rāt) *v.* To make a formal beginning; celebrate the opening of

**incapacitated** (in kə pas′ ə tāt′ ed) *adj.* Disabled

**incessant** (in ses′ ′nt) *adj.* Never ceasing; continual

**incongruity** (in′ kən grōō′ ə tē) *n.* Something lacking harmony or agreement; inconsistency; lack of fitness or appropriateness

**incorporate** (in kôr′ pər it) *adj.* United

**indigent** (in′ di jənt) *adj.* Needy; poor

**indolence** (in′ də ləns) *n.* Idleness; a dislike for work

**indulgence** (in dul′ jəns) *n.* Leniency; forgiveness

**inebriating** (in ēb′ rē āt iŋ) *adj.* Intoxicating; exciting

**inert** (in ʉrt′) *adj.* Unable to move or act

**inevitable** (in ev′ ə tə b′l) *adj.* Certain to occur

**inexplicability** (in eks′ pli kə bil′ ə tē) *n.* A condition that cannot be explained

**infantile** (in′fən tīl′) *adj.* Characteristic of an infant; immature

**infectious** (in fek′ shəs) *adj.* Tending to spread; catching

**infirm** (in fʉrm′) *adj.* Weak; feeble

**infirmity** (in fʉr′mə tē) *n.* A bodily weakness

**influx** (in′ fluks′) *n.* A coming in

**infraction** (in frak′ shən) *n.* A violation

**ingress** (in′ gres) *n.* Entering

**inherently** (in hir′ənt lē) *adv.* Basically; by its very nature

**innately** (i nāt′ lē) *adv.* Existing naturally rather than acquired

**insidious** (in sid′ ē əs) *adj.* Treacherous

**insignificant** (in′sig nif′ ə kənt) *adj.* Having little or no importance

**insinuate** (in sin′ yōō wāt) *v.* To hint; suggest indirectly

**insurrection** (in′ sə rek′ shən) *n.* A revolt

**intercession** (in ′tər sesh′ ən) *n.* A prayer said on behalf of another person

**interminable** (in tʉr′ mi nə b′l) *adj.* Seemingly endless

**intimidate** (in tim′ ə dāt′) *v.* To discourage or inhibit by making threats

**inveigle** (in vē′ g′l) *v.* To entice into doing something

**iris** (ī′ ris) *n.* The iris is the round, colored part of an eye

**isinglass** (ī′ z′n glas′)  *n.* A semitransparent substance obtained from fish bladders and sometimes used for windows

## J

**jerked** (jʉrkt)  *adj.* Preserved by cutting into strips and drying in the sun

**jostling** (jäs′ liŋ)  *adj.* Bumping; pushing

**juxtapose** (juk′ stə pōz′)  *v.* Put side by side to show contrast

## K

**keening** (kēn′ iŋ)  *adj.* Wailing for the dead

**knave** (nāv)  *n.* A tricky rascal; a rogue

## L

**laconic** (lə kän′ ik)  *adj.* Using few words; terse

**lacquer** (lak′ər)  *v.* To give a hard, highly polished finish

**lament** (lə ment′)  *v.* To feel or express great sorrow

**lamentation** (lam′ən ta′ shən)  *n.* Mourning

**languid** (laŋ′ gwid)  *adj.* Weak; listless; without vitality

**latent** (lāt′ nt)  *adj.* Hidden

**lather** (lath′ər)  *n.* An excited or disturbed state (Slang)

**layman** (lā′ mən)  *n.* A person not belonging to or skilled in a given profession

**legacy** (leg′ə sē)  *n.* Money, property, or position left in a will to someone

**legerdemain** (lej′ ər di mān′)  *n.* Trickery; tricks with the hand

**lethargy** (leth′ər jē)  *n.* Laziness or indifference

**liaison** (lē′ə zän′)  *n.* A link or connection

**libation** (lī bā′ shən)  *n.* A liquid poured as an offering in a religious ritual

**limpid** (lim′ pid)  *adj.* Clear

**literalism** (lit′ər əl izm)  *n.* Tendency to take things according to their dictionary definitions, instead of figuratively

**logistics** (lō jis′tiks)  *n.* The providing and transporting of people and equipment

**lucent** (lōo′ sənt)  *adj.* Shining

**ludicrous** (lōo′ di krəs)  *adj.* Laughably absurd

**luminous** (lōo′ mə nəs)  *adj.* Giving off light

**lure** (lʊr)  *v.* To attract or entice

**luster** (lus′tər)  *n.* Soft, reflected light; brilliance

## M

**mackintosh** (mak′ in täsh′)  *n.* A waterproof raincoat

**maitre** (me′ trə)  *n.* Mister, a term of address

**malevolent** (mə lev′ə lənt)  *adj.* Intended as evil or harmful

**malice** (mal′ is)  *n.* A desire to harm or see harm done to others

**malign** (mə līn′)  *adj.* Evil; harmful

**mandible** (man′ də b′l)  *n.* Biting jaw

**mangrove** (maŋ′ grōv)  *n.* A tropical tree that grows in swampy ground with spreading branches that send down roots and thus form more trunks

**manifestation** (man′ə fes tā′ shən)  *n.* An appearance or evidence

**manor** (man′ər)  *n.* The district over which a lord had domain in medieval western Europe

**manse** (mans)  *n.* A large, imposing house; minister's house

**marginal** (mär′jən 'l)  *adj.* Occupying the borderland of a stable area

**martial law** (mär′ shəl lô′)  *n.* Temporary rule by the military authorities

**marzipan** (mär′ zi pan′)  *n.* A candy made from almonds, sugar, and egg whites

**masque** (mask)  *n.* A costume ball or masquerade theme

**mate** (māt)  *n.* Checkmate, a chess move in which the king is captured and the game is over

**matriarchal** (mā′ trē är′ k'l)  *n.* Motherly

**maul** (môl)  *v.* To handle roughly or clumsily

**mead** (mēd)  *n.* A drink made of honey and water, often with spices or fruit added

**melancholy** (mel′ən käl′ ē)  *adj.* Sadness; gloominess; depression

**mellifluous** (mə lif′ lōo wəs)  *adj.* Sweet and smooth

**mesa** (mā′ sə)  *n.* A flattened hill with steep sides

**metal** (met′ 'l)  *n.* Basic character; mettle

**metamorphosis** (met′ə môr′fə sis)  *n.* A change in form, structure, or substance

**meteorite** (mēt′ ē ə rīt′)  *n.* Part of a heavenly body that passes through the atmosphere and falls to earth

**mettle** (met′ 'l)  *n.* Basic character

**militia** (mə lish′ ə)  *n.* An army of citizens rather than professional soldiers, called out in time of emergency

**millinery** (mil′ ə ner′ ē)  *n.* Women's hats

**mime** (mīm)  *n.* Pantomime

**ministration** (min′is trā′shən)  *n.* The act of serving as a minister or clergyman

**minute** (mī nōot′)  *adj.* Tiny

**misbegotten** (mis′bi gät′ 'n)  *adj.* Wrongly or unlawfully produced

**moidore** (mɔi′ dor)  *n.* Gold coin of Portugal and Brazil

**monolithic** (män′ə lith′ik)  *adj.* Formed from a single block

**monopoly** (mə näp′ ə lē)  *n.* Exclusive control

**mordantly** (môr′ dənt lē)  *adv.* Bitingly; sarcastically

**mortal** (môr′ tul)  *adj.* That eventually must die

**mortgage** (môr′ gij)  *n.* The pledging of property for money

**motive** (mōt′iv)  *n.* The emotion or impulse that causes a person to act in a certain way

**mottled** (mät′ 'ld)  *adj.* Marked with spots of different shades

**multifariously** (mul′tə far′ē əs lē)  *adv.* Diversely

**mummer** (mum′ ər)  *n.* A masked and costumed person who acts out pantomimes

**muse** (myōoz)  *v.* To think deeply; to meditate

**mutable** (myōot′ə b'l)  *adj.* Capable of change

**mutiny** (myōot′'n ē)  *n.* Open rebellion against authority

## N

**naive** (nä ēv′)  *adj.* Unsophisticated; lacking in worldly wisdom

**nave** (nāv)  *n.* Aisle

**negotiate** (ni gō′shē āt)  *v.* To master or successfully move through a situation

**nonchalantly** (nän shə länt′ lē)  *adv.* Casually; indifferently

**nonconductivity** (nän kən duk tiv′ə tē)  *n.* The ability to contain and not transmit heat

**nonentity**   (nän en′ tə tē)   *n.* A thing of little or no importance

**novel**   (näv′ 'l)   *adj.* New and unusual

**nursery**   (nʉr′ sə rē)   *n.* A place where young trees and plants are grown

# O

**obligatory**   (ə blig′ə tôr ē)   *adj.* Required; necessary

**obliterate**   (ə blit′ə rāt)   *v.* To destroy; erase without a trace

**occult**   (ə kult′)   *adj.* Having to do with so-called mystic arts such as alchemy and astrology

**officious**   (ə fish′əs)   *adj.* Overly ready to serve; obliging

**okapi**   (ō kä′ pē)   *n.* An African animal related to the giraffe but with a much shorter neck

**ominous**   (äm′ ə nəs)   *adj.* Threatening; sinister

**opacity**   (ō pas′ə tē)   *n.* The quality of not letting light pass through

**opaque**   (ō pāk′)   *adj.* Not letting light pass through

**oracle**   (ôr′ə k′l)   *n.* A source of knowledge or wise counsel

**oration**   (ô rā shən)   *n.* A formal speech, especially one given at a state occasion, ceremony, or funeral

**orthodox**   (ôr′ thə däks′)   *adj.* Conforming to the usual beliefs

**outstrip**   (out strip′)   *v.* To move ahead of

# P

**paddock**   (pad′ ək)   *n.* A small enclosed field

**paganism**   (pā′ gən iz′m)   *n.* Lack of any religion

**palfrey**   (pôl′frē)   *n.* A saddle horse, especially one for a woman

**palmetto**   (pal met′ō)   *n.* A palm tree with fan-shaped leaves

**palpable**   (pal′ pə b′l)   *adj.* Able to be perceived by the senses

**pampas**   (pam′pəz)   *n.* Treeless plains in South America

**parable**   (par′ə b′l)   *n.* A short story that illustrates a spiritual truth

**parabolic**   (par′ə bäl′ ik)   *adj.* Bowl-shaped

**paranoia**   (par′ə noi′ ə)   *n.* A mental disorder characterized by delusions of persecution

**paraphernalia**   (par′ə fər nāl′yə)   *n.* Collection of articles, gear necessary for some activity; personal belongings

**pariah**   (pə rī′ ə)   *n.* A social outcast

**parody**   (par′ə dē)   *n.* Poor or weak imitation

**parry**   (par′ē)   *v.* Ward off

**parsimonious**   (pär′sə mō′nē əs)   *adj.* Stingy

**particularization**   (pər tik′yə lə rīz ā′ shən)   *n.* Presentation in minute detail

**patriarchal**   (pā′ trē ärk′′l)   *adj.* Fatherly

**peon**   (pē′ än)   *n.* A laborer in Spanish America

**peony**   (pē′ ə nē)   *n.* A plant with large, showy flowers often red or pink in color

**perceive**   (pər sēv′)   *v.* To become aware of

**perplexing**   (pər pleks′in)   *adj.* Puzzling; difficult to understand

**perspective**   (pər spek′tiv)   *n.* Point of view

**perverse**   (pər vʉrs′)   *adj.* Wicked, wrong, improper

**peso**   (pā sō)   *n.* Mexican unit of money

**phantasm**   (fan′ taz′m)   *n.* Something apparently seen but having no physical reality

**philosophy**   (fil äs′ə fē)   *n.* A system of values

**phosphorescence**   (fäs′ fə res′ ′ns)   *n.* Light

**pillage**   (pil′ij)   *n.* The act of robbing and destroying, especially during wartime

**pinnacled**   (pin′ə kəld)   *adj.* Decorated with turrets or spires, like a high tower

**piquancy**   (pē′ kan sē)   *n.* A pleasantly sharp quality

**pique**   (pēk)   *v.* To provoke

**pith**   (pith)   *n.* Force or strength

**plague**   (plāg)   *n.* A contagious epidemic disease

**plaintive**   (plān′ tiv)   *adj.* Mournful; sad

**plausibility**   (plô′zə bil′ it ē)   *n.* Believability

**poignancy**   (poin′ yən sē)   *n.* 1. A feeling that is emotionally touching or moving 2. The quality of being deeply affecting

**poise**   (poiz)   *n.* Self assurance; ease of manner

**pommel**   (pum′′l)   *n.* The round knob on the end of the hilt of some swords

**pontiff**   (pän′ tif)   *n.* A high priest, bishop

**portentous**   (pôr ten′təs)   *adj.* Foreboding; full of unspecified meaning

**portliness**   (pôrt′ lē nes)   *n.* Stoutness; heaviness

**potent**   (pōt′ ′nt)   *adj.* Powerful

**poultice**   (pōl′ tis)   *n.* An absorbent mass applied to a sore or inflamed part of the body

**pragmatic**   (prag mat′ik)   *adj.* Practical

**precariously**   (pri ker′ ē əs lē)   *adv.* Dependent upon the will or favor of another person

**predator**   (pred′ə tər)   *n.* An animal that eats other animals

**predestined**   (prē des′ tin′d)   *adj.* Decreed beforehand; foreordained

**predilection**   (pred′l ek′shən)   *n.* An inclination to like something; a special fondness

**prelude**   (prel′ yōōd)   *n.* Introduction

**presuppose**   (prē′ sə pōz′)   *v.* To assume beforehand

**prey**   (prā)   *n.* An animal hunted or killed for food

**prime**   (prīm)   *v.* 1. To prepare a water pump for operation by pouring in water 2. To prepare a person or thing for work or action

**primeval**   (prī mē′v′l)   *adj.* Ancient or primitive

**primevally**   (prī mē′ v′l lē)   *adv.* Belonging to earliest times

**prodigious**   (prə dij′əs)   *adj.* Impressively forceful; huge or powerful

**proffer**   (prof′ ər)   *v.* To offer or tender

**promontory**   (präm′ ən tôr′ ē)   *n.* A high place extending out over a body of water

**propriety**   (prə prī′ ə tē)   *n.* The quality of being proper, fitting, or suitable fitness

**prosaic**   (prō zā′ik)   *adj.* Commonplace; dull; ordinary

**prosecution**   (präs′ ə kyōō′ sh ən)   *n.* The conducting of criminal proceedings in court against a person

**prosperous**   (präs′ pər əs)   *adj.* Having continued success

**provender**   (präv′ən dər)   *n.* Food

**proviso**   (prə vī′ zō)   *n.* A condition

**provocativeness**   (prə väk′ə tiv nis)   *n.* Stimulation; incitement

**prowess**   (prou′ is)   *n.* Skill; bravery

**propriety**   (prə prī′ə tē)   *n.* The quality of being proper, fitting, or suitable

**psychopathic**   (sī kə path′ ik)   *adj.* With a mental disorder

**punctilious** (puŋk til′ē əs) *adj.* Very careful about every detail of behavior

**purify** (pyʊr′ ə fī) *v.* To cleanse; rid of impurity

**putrefactive** (pyoo′ trə fak′ tiv) *adj.* Rotting; decomposing

## Q

**qualm** (kwäm) *n.* Feelings of doubt or uneasiness; misgiving

**querulous** (kwer′ə ləs) *adj.* Inclined to find fault; complaining

**queue** (kyoo) *n.* A braid or pigtail worn down one's back

**quickstep** (kwik′ step′) *n.* The pace used in normal military marching, as contrasted with slower pace of the dead march

**quince** (kwins′) *n.* Hard, green-yellow, apple-shaped fruit

**quinquireme** (kwin′ kwī rēm) *n.* An ancient ship propelled by sails and oars

## R

**raftered** (raf′tərd) *adj.* Supported by horizontal beams

**rebuke** (ri byook′) *n.* Reproof; disapproving statement

**recessional** (ri sesh′ ə n'l) *n.* Music played while people are leaving a church service or ceremony

**redeem** (ri dēm′) *v.* To rescue or save

**refuge** (ref′ yooj) *n.* Shelter or protection from danger

**regimen** (rej′ ə mən) *n.* System

**rejoinder** (ri join′ dər) *n.* A reply or answer

**relief** (ri lēf′) *n.* The projection of shapes from a flat surface, so that they stand out

**repast** (ri past′) *n.* A meal, or the food eaten or provided at a meal

**repealing** (ri pēl′iŋ) *n.* Old word for "recalling," especially from exile

**repertoire** (rep′ər twär) *n.* The stock of songs that a singer is familiar with and is ready to perform

**replication** (rep′lə kā′shən) *n.* Echo or reverberation

**repository** (ri päz′ə tôr′ē) *n.* A place where things are stored and saved

**repress** (ri pres′) *v.* To hold back; restrain

**reprieve** (ri prēv′) *n.* 1. Postponement, 2. A temporary relief or escape

**repulsive** (ri pul′ siv) *adj.* Disgusting or offensive

**resolution** (rez′ə loo′shən) *n.* Strong determination

**reticent** (ret′ə s'nt) *adj.* Having a restrained, quiet, or understated quality

**revel** (rev′ 'l) *v.* To take great pleasure in

**reverberant** (re vʉr′ bər ənt) *adj.* Reechoing

**reverie** (rev′ ər ē) *n.* Dreamy thinking or imagining

**rhetorical** (ri tôr′ i k'l) *adj.* Elaborate in style

**ribald** (rib′əld) *adj.* Characterized by coarse or vulgar joking

**ricochet** (rik′ə shā′) *n.* Bouncing from one thing to another

**righteous** (rī′ chəs) *adj.* Just; upright

**rigorous** (rig′ ər əs) *adj.* Precisely accurate; strict

**rile** (rīl) *v.* To irritate; anger

**rime** (rīm) *n.* Another spelling for rhyme; poetry or verse in general

**rime** (rīm) *n.* Frost

**rind** (rīnd) *n.* The skin of oranges or lemons

**roadster** (rōd′ stər) *n.* An early sportscar with an open cab and a "rumble seat" in the rear

**rosette** (rō zet′) *n.* Pattern suggesting a rose

**ruble** (roo′ b'l) *n.* The monetary unit of Russia

**rueful** (roo′ fəl) *adj.* Causing sorrow or pity

**rural** (roor′əl) *adj.* Having to do with country, farming

## S

**sacrilegious** (sak′ rə lij′ əs) *adj.* Disrespectful or irreverent toward anything regarded as sacred

**sadist** (sad′ ist) *n.* One who gets pleasure from inflicting physical or psychological pain on others

**sagacity** (sə gas′ ə tē) *n.* Wisdom

**salient** (sāl′ yənt) *n.* A projecting part or angle

**saline** (sā′ lēn) *adj.* Salty

**sacrophagus** (sär käf′ə gəs) *n.* A stone coffin

**sastrugus** (sas′ troo gəs) *n.* A wavelike ridge of hard snow formed by the wind and common in polar regions

**saurian** (sôr′ ē ən) *n.* A lizardlike animal

**scholasticism** (skə las′ tə siz′m) *n.* Tradition

**schooner** (skoo′ nər) *n.* A ship with two or more masts, or supports for sails

**scorpion** (skôr′pē ən) *n.* Any of a group of arachnids found in warm regions, with a long tail ending in a curved, poisonous sting

**scroll** (skrōl) *n.* A roll of parchment used for writing a document

**scrupulously** (skroo′ pyə ləs lē) *adv.* Conscientiously; painstakingly

**scrutinize** (skroot′ 'n īz) *v.* To examine closely

**scythe** (sīth) *n.* A tool with a long curving blade, used for mowing grass or grain

**sedate** (si dāt′) *adj.* Quiet; composed; serious

**sedge** (sej) *n.* A grassy plant that grows in wet areas

**seigneur** (sen yʉr′) *n.* A man of rank; feudal lord

**seismograph** (sīz′ mə graf′) *n.* An instrument that records the intensity and duration of earthquakes

**selectmen** (sə lekt′ mən) *n.* Board of officials who manage local affairs in many New England towns

**self-indictment** (self in dīt′ mənt) *n.* An accusation of oneself

**sensible** (sen′sə b'l) *adj.* Emotionally or intellectually aware

**sententiousness** (sen ten′ shəs nəs) *n.* Manner of using pithy sayings in a moralizing way

**serene** (sə rēn′) *adj.* Undisturbed

**serenely** (sə rēn′ lē) *adv.* In a calm, untroubled way

**shackly** (shak′ lē) *adj.* Dialect expression meaning "ramshackle," or falling apart

**sheath** (shēth) *n.* A case or covering

**sheave** (shēv) *n.* A bunch of cut stalks of grain bound up in a bundle

**shilling** (shil′ iŋ) *n.* A British silver coin

**shimmy** (shim′ ē) *n.* A jazz dance popular in the early 1920s involving shaking the body

**shroud** (shroud) *n.* Clothes that conceal

**shrouds** (shroudz) *n.* A set of ropes used to tie a mast to the side of a ship

**sidereal** (sī dir′ ē əl) *adj.* Of the star

**sidle** (sī′d'l) *v.* To move sideways in a sneaky manner

**silhouette** (sil′ ōō wet′)   *n.* An outline of something that appears dark against a light background
**simian** (sim′ ē ən)   *adj.* Monkeylike
**simulated** (sim′yōō lāt′ id)   *adj.* Taking on the appearance of
**sinecure** (sī′ nə kyōōr′)   *n.* A position that brings advantage but involves little or no work
**sinew** (sin′ yōō)   *n.* Tendon—the fibrous cord attaching muscle to bone
**skinflint** (skin′ flint′)   *adj.* Miserly
**slain** (slān)   *adj.* Killed
**slanderous** (slan′dər əs)   *adj.* Damaging to a person's reputation
**sloth** (slôth)   *n.* A two-toed mammal that hangs from trees
**smite** (smīt)   *v.* To strike strongly and suddenly
**sobriety** (sə brī′ ə tē)   *n.* Seriousness
**sojourn** (sō′ jurn)   *n.* A temporary stay
**solace** (säl′ is)   *n.* Something that comforts
**soldering** (säd′ər iŋ)   *n.* Piecing together; uniting
**solicited** (sə lis′ it əd)   *adj.* Asked
**solicitor** (sə lis′ it ər)   *n.* British legal representative
**solicitude** (sə lis′ ə tōōd′)   *n.* Caring or concern
**sovereign** (säv′ rən)   *n.* A British gold coin worth one pound
**spar** (spär)   *n.* A pole that supports a sail
**spare** (sper)   *adj.* Lean or thin
**spectroscope** (spek′ trə skōp′)   *n.* A scientific instrument used to identify substances
**spew** (spyōō)   *v.* 1. To throw up from, or as from, the stomach 2. To eject; force out
**spoor** (spōōr)   *n.* The dropping of a wild animal
**spurn** (spurn)   *v.* 1. Old word for "to kick disdainfully" 2. reject
**stalwart** (stôl wərt)   *adj.* Strong; with unwavering determination
**stately** (stāt′le)   *adj.* Majestic
**staunch** (stônch)   *adj.* Steadfast; loyal
**stickler** (stik′lər)   *n.* A person who insists uncompromisingly on the observance of something specified
**stimulate** (stim′yə lāt′)   *v.* To rouse or excite to action
**straightaway** (strāt′ ə wa′)   *n.* A straight course
**stricken** (strik′ ′n)   *adj.* Hit or wounded, as if by a missile
**stripling** (strip′ liŋ)   *adj.* Young or youthful
**stupefaction** (stōō′ pə fak′ shən)   *n.* Stunned amazement; utter bewilderment
**sturgeon** (stur′ jən)   *n.* A large fish
**suave** (swäv)   *adj.* Smoothly polite; polished
**subjectively** (səb jek′tiv lē)   *adv.* Personally
**sublimity** (sə blim′ ə tē)   *n.* A noble or exalted state
**subsequently** (sub′si kwənt lē)   *adv.* After; following
**subservient** (səb sur′ vē ənt)   *adj.* Submissive
**subsidiary** (səb sid′ē er ē)   *adj.* Secondary; supporting
**subtle** (sut′ ′l)   *adj.* Showing fine distinctions in meaning
**subtlety** (sut′ ′l tē)   *n.* A fine quality that is not immediately obvious
**subversion** (səb vur′ zhən)   *n.* A systematic attempt to overthrow a government from within

**suit** (sōōt)   *n.* Old word for "petition"
**sultriness** (sul′ tri nəs)   *n.* Oppressive heat
**sumac** (shōō′ mak)   *n.* Small tree or shrub with compound flowers and clusters of small greenish flowers followed by hairy fruits. Some varieties cause an itching rash.
**summit** (sum′ it)   *n.* The highest point of a mountain
**sumptuous** (sump′ chōō wəs)   *adj.* Magnificent
**sundry** (sun′ drē)   *adj.* Various; several; miscellaneous
**superfluity** (sōō′ pər flōō′ ə tē)   *n.* An excess
**suppleness** (sup′ ′l nes)   *n.* Flexibility; resilience
**supplication** (sup′ lə kā′ shən)   *n.* The act of asking humbly and earnestly
**surcease** (sur sēs′)   *n.* An end
**surly** (sur′lē)   *adj.* Proud; commanding
**surmise** (sər mīz′)   *v.* To guess; to imagine or infer something
**surreptitious** (sur′əp tish′ əs)   *adj.* Done in a secret way
**sustenance** (sus′ ti nəns)   *n.* Maintenance; support
**swarthy** (swor′ *the*)   *adj.* Having a dark complexion
**syringa** (sə riŋ′ gə)   *n.* A hardy shrub with tiny fragrant flowers, also known as lilac

# T

**taciturn** (tas′ ə turn′)   *adj.* Not talkative
**talisman** (tal′ is mən)   *n.* Anything believed to have magical power
**temperate** (tem′ pər it)   *adj.* Moderate in degree or quality
**tempest** (tem′pist)   *n.* A violent windstorm often with rain, snow, or hail
**temporal** (tem′ pər əl)   *adj.* Lasting only for a time, not eternal; worldly, not spiritual
**tenuous** (ten′yōō wəs)   *adj.* Slight; flimsy; not substantial or strong
**tepid** (tep′ id)   *adj.* Barely warm; lukewarm
**terminus** (tur′mə nəs)   *n.* End, boundary
**terse** (turs)   *adj.* Concise; polished
**thrall** (thrôl)   *n.* Complete control; slavery
**throe** (thrō)   *n.* A spasm or pang of pain
**thwart** (th wôrt)   *n.* A rower's seat lying across a boat
**timbre** (tam′ bər)   *n.* The distinctive tone of a voice
**Titan** (tī′ tən)   *n.* Giant; any of a race of giant deities
**titanic** (tī tan′ik)   *adj.* Having great power
**tithe** (ti *th*)   *n.* One tenth of one's income; here, a small amount given to charity
**torpidly** (tôr′ pid lē)   *adv.* Sluggishly; slowly
**tortuous** (tôr′ chōō wəs)   *adj.* Full of twists and turns
**tourniquet** (tur′ nə ket)   *n.* A bandage to stop bleeding by compressing a blood vessel
**transcendental** (tran sen dent′t′l)   *adj.* Supernatural; not concrete
**transient** (tran′ shənt)   *adj.* Not permanent; passing quickly
**transverse** (trans vurs′)   *adj.* Crossing from side to side
**traverse** (tra vurs′)   *v.* To travel over, across, or through
**travesty** (trav′ is tē)   *v.* To ridicule; represent in a crude, distorted, or ridiculous way

**treason** (trē′zən)    *n.* Betrayal of trust or confidence; treachery

**trek** (trek)    *v.* To journey

**tremulous** (trem′ yŏŏ ləs)    *adj.* Trembling; quivering

**tripod** (trī päd)    *n.* A three-legged support

**trod** (träd)    *v.* Walked

**tureen** (tŏŏ rēn′)    *n.* A deep dish with a cover

# U

**unanimous** (yŏŏ nan′ə məs)    *adj.* Showing complete agreement

**undulation** (un′ jŏŏ lā′ shən)    *n.* A wavy, curving form

**unethical** (un eth′ik′ l)    *adj.* Not moral; not conforming to certain rules

**unkempt** (un kempt′)    *adj.* Untidy; rough

**usurer** (yŏŏ′ zhŏŏ rər)    *n.* A person who lends money at a high rate of interest

**usurp** (yŏŏ sŭrp′)    *v.* To take power over; hold by force

**utilitarian** (yŏŏ til′ə ter′ē ən)    *adj.* Meant to be useful

# V

**vagary** (və ger′ ē)    *n.* Odd or unexpected action or idea

**vanguard** (van′ gärd)    *n.* The part of an army that goes ahead of the main body in an advance

**venerable** (ven′ər ə b′l)    *adj.* Worthy of respect because of age and character; impressive on account of age

**venison** (ven′ i s′n)    *n.* The flesh of a game animal, now especially the deer, used as food

**veracity** (və ras′ə tē)    *n.* Truthfulness; honesty

**vermilion** (vər mil′yən)    *adj.* Bright red or reddish orange in color

**vermin** (vŭr′min)    *n.* Small animals that are offensive to humans

**victrola** (vic trōl′ ə)    *n.* A record player

**vigorous** (vig′ ər əs)    *adj.* Living or growing with full vital strength

**vile** (vīl)    *adj.* Depraved; ignoble; evil; wicked

**vindicate** (vin′ də kāt)    *v.* To uphold; defend

**virtuoso** (vŭr′ chŏŏ wō′ sō)    *n.* Person displaying great technical skill in any field

**vocation** (vō kā′ shən)    *n.* Occupation

**void** (void)    *adj.* Containing no matter; empty

**vouchsafe** (vouch′ sāf)    *v.* To grant a reply

**vulnerable** (vul′ nər ə b′l)    *adj.* Sensitive

# W

**wallow** (wäl′ō)    *v.* To enjoy completely; take great pleasure

**waning** (wān′ iŋ)    *adj.* A full moon shrinking to a new moon

**wariness** (war′ē nis)    *n.* Caution

**warren** (wôr′ ən)    *n.* A crowded, mazelike passage

**wattle** (wät′ 'l)    *n.* A small, flowering tree

**weir** (wir)    *n.* A low dam

**wheeling** (hwēl′ iŋ)    *adj.* Changing direction suddenly

**whimper** (hwim′ pər)    *v.* Make a low, whining sound as in crying or in fear

**whimsical** (hwim′ zi k′l)    *adj.* Playful; odd

**willet** (wil′ it)    *n.* A large, gray and white, long-legged wading bird

**windfall** (wind′fôl)    *n.* 1. A thing blown down by the wind 2. An unexpected profit or gain

**wistfully** (wist′ fəl ē)    *adv.* Longingly

**withered** (with′ərd)    *adj.* Weakened; dried up

**worthy** (wûr′ thē)    *adj.* Honorable; admirable

**wrath** (rath)    *n.* Intense anger, rage, or fury

**writhe** (rīth)    *v.* To twist in pain and agony

**wroth** (rôth)    *adj.* Archaic form of wrathful; angry

# Y

**yew** (yŏŏ)    *n.* An evergreen shrub and tree of the yew family

# Z

**zenith** (zē′ nith)    *n.* The highest point

# INDEX OF FINE ART

| | |
|---|---|
| Cover | *Indian in Canoe.* Frank Schoonover |
| 1 | *Girls on the Jetty.* Edvard Munch |
| 4 | *The Marketplace in Front of the Town Hall at Pointoise.* Ludovic Piette |
| 9 | *Road to Sin le Noble.* Jean Baptiste Corot |
| 13 | *Regattas at Argenteuil.* Claude Monet |
| 59 | *The "Lightning Express" Trains: "Leaving the Junction."* F. F. Palmer (Currier & Ives) |
| 63 | *Evening, Monhegan Island.* Samuel Reindorf |
| 73 | *The Canyon.* Jack Dudley |
| 75 | *Carmen.* James Asher |
| 81 | *Private Performance.* Lois Johnson |
| 100 | *Hint to Modern Sculptors as an Ornament to a Future Square.* James Gillray |
| 102–103 | *Scotland Forever.* Elizabeth Butler |
| 105 | *Stairway.* Edward Hopper |
| 131 | *Road with Cypress and Star.* Vincent van Gogh |
| 140 | *Evening View, San Miguel.* Samuel Reindorf |
| 143 | *Señora Sabasa Garcia.* Francisco José de Goya |
| 148 | *Red Hills and Bones.* Georgia O'Keeffe |
| 155 | *City Night.* Georgia O' Keeffe |
| 160 | *The Beach Treat* (detail). Suzanne Nagler |
| 165 | *Coast Scene, Isle of Shoals.* Childe Hassam |
| 167 | *Street Scene in Lower New York.* Glenn O. Coleman |
| 189 | *Telephone Booths.* Richard Estes |
| 192 | *Unicorn.* Jonathan Meader |
| 210 | *Melancholy.* Edvard Munch |
| 215 | *Girl Looking at Landscape.* Richard Diebenkorn |
| 218 | *Orchard with Flowering Fruit Trees in Springtime, Pontoise.* Camille Pissaro |
| 220 | *Apple Plenty.* Herbert Shuptrine |
| 228 | *Simone in a White Bonnet.* Mary Cassatt |
| 234 | *Bennington.* Grandma Moses |
| 237 | *Henry Look Unhitching.* Thomas Hart Benton |
| 242 | Etruscan Flute Player. |
| 247 | Greek Pottery, mid-sixth century B.C. |
| 250 | *Flora de Stabia.* |
| 258 | *The Circus.* A. Logan |
| 266–267 | *Raised Stage with Masks, Narrator, and Auditorium.* David Hockney |
| 343 | Johannes DeWitt's drawing of the Swan Theatre, London |
| 438–439 | Untitled. Robert Rauschenberg |
| 443 | Drawing by James Thurber |
| 445 | Drawing by James Thurber |
| 449 | *Diego Martelli.* Edgar Degas |
| 471 | Etching by Fritz Eichenberg |
| 474 | Etching by Fritz Eichenberg |
| 476 | Etching by Fritz Eichenberg |
| 491 | *A Young Girl Reading.* Jean-Honoré Fragonard |
| 493 | *One Wing Above Dream or Hunger.* Richard Casey |
| 497 | *Soaring.* Andrew Wyeth |
| 504 | *Annie Old Crow.* James Bama |
| 506 | *Old Ones Talking.* R. Brownell McGrew |
| 540 | *Around the Fish.* Paul Klee |
| 543 | *Song.* Ben Shahn |
| 549 | *Statue of Liberty.* Pete Turner |
| 557 | *Beethoven's Sterbezimmer in Schwarzpanierhaus.* Johann Nepomuk Hoechle |
| 562 | *The Table.* Alex Katz |

| | |
|---|---|
| 582–584 | *Red Poppies*. Georgia O'Keeffe |
| 589 | *Central Park*. Maurice Prendergast |
| 591 | *La Belle Dame sans Merci*. T. W. Waterhouse |
| 601 | *The Wreck of a Transport Ship*. J. M. W. Turner |
| 605 | *Portrait of Kitty Jagger, the Artist's Wife*. David Jagger |
| 607 | *The Battle of Bunker Hill*. Howard Pyle |
| 615 | *The Battle of Life (The Golden Knight)*. Gustav Klimt |
| 617 | *Couple*. Kees Van Dongen |
| 625 | *Violinist at the Window*. Henri Matisse |
| 628 | *Ground Hog Day*. Andrew Wyeth |
| 630 | *Impressions of Hands*. Antoni Tapies |
| 641 | *Mediterranean Landscape*. Pablo Picasso |
| 647 | *Melanie and Me Swimming*. Michael Andrews |
| 650 | *Toilers of the Sea*. Albert Pinkham Ryder |
| 652 | *Apollo 13 Launch*. Fletcher Martin |
| 652 | *Christmas Rose (Helleborus niger)*. Crispin de Passe |
| 655 | *Memory*. Elihu Vedder |
| 671 | *Swinging Landscape*. Stuart Davis |
| 676 | *Cochem on Mosel River*. John Lewis Stage |
| 683 | *Still Life with Magnolia*. Henri Matisse |
| 686 | *Frances Howard*. Isaac Oliver |
| 691 | *Snow-laden Camellia and Sparrow*. Ando Hiroshige |
| 692 | *A Sudden Shower at Ohashi*. Ando Hiroshige |
| 699 | *Girl with Cat*. Franz Marc |
| 716–717 | *Miniature of the Round Table* from *Le Roman de Lancelot du Lac*. |
| 721 | *Crowning of Arthur* |
| 729 | *Galahad and Sword in Stone* |
| 739 | How Four Queens Found Launcelot Sleeping. Aubrey Beardsley |
| 744 | ''Sir Mador's Spear Brake all to pieces.'' N. C. Wyeth |
| 751 | *Death of Arthur* |
| 756 | How Sir Bedivere Cast the Sword Excalibur into the Water. Aubrey Beardsley |
| 758 | *Arthur in Avalon*. T. Archer, R.S.A. |
| 764 | *The Astrologer*. N. C. Wyeth |
| 772–773 | *Hyde Park*. André Derain |
| 777 | *La Molendera*. Diego Rivera |
| 780 | *Peasant with Sombrero (Peon)*. Diego Rivera |
| 783 | *Delfina and Dimas*. Diego Rivera |
| 790 | *Two Mexican Women and a Child*. Diego Rivera |
| 802 | *Group*. Jesus Guerrero Galvan |
| 809 | *Mexican Peasant with Sombrero and Serape (Peon)*. Diego Rivera |
| 819 | *Cactus on the Plains (Hands)*. Diego Rivera |
| 825 | *The Sob*. David Alfaro Siqueiros |
| 829 | *Tree Trunks*. André Derain |

# INDEX OF SKILLS

## ANALYZING LITERATURE

Act (*See* Drama)

Allegory, *172, 179, 1002*

Alliteration, *673, 677, 1002*

Allusion, *588, 1002*

Anachronism, *1002*

Analogy, *1002*

Anapest, *612* (*See also* Meter)

Anecdote, *1002*

Antagonist, *322, 331, 1002–03*

Aphorism, *1003*

Apostrophe, *1003*

Argumentation, *1003*

Aside, *382, 403, 1003*

Assonance, *673, 679, 1003*

Atmosphere, *158, 166* (*See also* Mood)

Autobiography, *468, 477, 1003–04*

Ballad, *1004*

Biography, *450, 462, 467, 1004*

Blank Verse, *344, 363, 1004*

Caesura, *1004*

Character, *254, 461, 830, 859, 1004–05*

   dynamic, *98, 104*

   flat, *72, 83*

   round, *72, 83*

   static, *98, 104*

   as symbol, *180, 188*

Character Flaw, *420*

Characterization, *1005*

   in biography, *450, 461*

   direct, *64, 71*

   indirect, *64, 71*

Chivalry, *732, 735*

Cinquain (*See* Stanza)

Classification, *544, 547*

Climax, *14, 27, 860, 1005*

Comedy, *1005*

Complications, *14*

Concrete Poetry, *695, 696, 1005*

Conflict, *14, 27, 40, 57, 404, 419, 860, 907, 1005*

   external, *40, 57*

   internal, *40, 57*

Connotation, *1005*

Consonance, *1006*

Convention, *1006*

Couplet, *1006*

Crisis, *1006*

Dactyl, *613* (*See also* Meter)

Dead Metaphor (*See* Metaphor)

Definition, *548, 551*

Denotation, *1006*

Denouement (*See* Plot)

Description, *1006*

Descriptive Essay (*See* Essay)

Development (*See* Plot)

Dialect, *1007*

Dialogue, *614, 616, 1007* (*See also* Tone)

Diction, *1007*

Dimeter (*See* Meter)

Direct Characterization (*See* Characterization)

Drama, *267, 268–69, 1007*

   clarify, *269*

   plot, *332, 341*

Dramatic Irony, *208, 214, 364* (*See also* Irony)

Dramatic Poem, *606, 609, 1007*

Dynamic Character (*See* Character)

End-Stopped Line, *1007*

English Sonnet (*See* Shakespearean Sonnet)

Epic, *748, 761, 1007–8*

Epithet, *1008*

Essay, *1008*

   descriptive, *508, 515*

   expository, *516, 527*

   imagery, *500, 507*

   narrative, *492, 498–99*

   persuasive, *528, 533*

   tone, *538, 542*

Exact Rhyme (*See* Rhyme)

Exaggeration (*See* Hyperbole)

Exposition, *14, 27, 1008*

Expositor Essay (*See* Essay)

Extended Definition, *534, 537*

Extended Metaphor, *1008*

External Conflict (*See* Conflict)

Fable, *1008–9*

Fantasy, *1009*

Farce, *1009*

Feminine Rhyme (*See* Rhyme)

Fiction, *1009*

Figurative Language, *649, 1009*

Figure of Speech, *1009*

First-person Point of View (*See* Point of View)

Flashback, *1009–10*

Flat Character (*See* Character)

Foil, *1010*

Folk Ballad (*See* Ballad)

Folklore, *1010*

Folk tale, *1010*

Foot, *1010*

Foreshadowing, *28, 600, 604, 1010*

Form, *1010*

Forms of Discourse, *1010*

Free Verse, *635, 637, 711, 1010–11*
Genre, *1011*
Haiku, *690, 693, 1011*
Heptameter (*See* Meter)
Heptastich (*See* Stanza)
Hero, *736*
Hero/Heroine, *1011*
Heroic Tradition, *736, 747*
Hexameter (*See* Meter)
Humorous Essay, *448*
Hyperbole, *1011*
Iamb, *612* (*See also* Meter)
Iambic Pentameter, *1011* (*See also* Blank Verse)
Image, *1011*
Imagery, *500, 507, 657, 658, 661, 1011*
Inciting Incident (*See* Plot)
Incongruity, *1012*
Indirect Characterization (*See* Charaterization)
Inference, *564, 571*
Internal Conflict (*See* Conflict)
Internal Rhyme, *677*
Inversion, *1012*
Irony, *200, 206, 208, 214, 381, 1012*
    dramatic, *208, 214, 364*
    and sarcasm, *622*
    verbal, *200, 206, 208, 214*
Irony of Situation, *200, 206* (*See also* Irony)
Key Statement, *240, 253*
Legend, *717, 718–19, 720, 731, 1012*
    background, *718*
    character, *719*
    reading strategy, *718*
    theme, *719*
Limited Point of View (*See* Point of View)
Literal Language, *1012*
Local Color, *138, 145, 1012*
Lyric Poem, *627, 629, 1012–13*
Main Character (*See* Character)
Masculine Rhyme (*See* Rhyme)
Metaphor, *643, 646, 1013*
Meter, *612, 673, 682, 1013–14*
Metonymy, *1014*
Metrical Foot, *612*
Minor Character (*See* Character)
Mixed Metaphor (*See* Metaphor)
Monologue, *382, 403, 1014–1015*
Monometer (*See* Meter)
Mood, *663, 664, 1015*
Moral, *1015*
Motivation, *84, 97, 1015*
Myth, *1015*
Narration, *1015*
Narrative, *1015*
    essay, *492, 498–99, 577*
    poetry, *590, 593*
Narrative Poem, *1015*
Narrator, *1015–16*

Nonfiction, *439, 440, 572, 1016*
Novel, *773, 774–76, 1016*
    background, *774, 775*
    reading strategy, *774, 776*
    theme, *775, 776*
Observation, *564, 571*
Octave (*See* Stanza)
Omniscient Point of View (*See* Point of View)
One–act Play, *270, 287*
Onomatopoeia, *673, 681, 1016*
Oral Tradition, *1016*
Overstatement (*See* Hyperbole)
Oxymoron, *1016*
Parable, *778, 799, 1016*
Paradox, *12, 1016*
Parallelism, *675, 1016*
Parody, *1017*
Personification, *654, 1017*
Persuasion, *1017*
Persuasive Essay, *528, 533*
Petrarchan Sonnet, *689, 1017*
Plot, *14, 27, 254, 332, 800, 827–28, 860, 1017*
Plot Structure, *341*
Poetry, *583, 584, 708, 1018*
    concrete, *695, 696*
    dramatic, *606, 609*
    epic, *748, 761*
    free verse, *635, 637, 711*
    Haiku, *690, 693*
    lyric, *627, 629*
    narrative, *590, 593*
    type of, *708*
Point of View, *106, 254, 1018*
    first–person, *106, 109*
    third-person, *110*
    third-person limited, *110, 117, 118, 121,*
    third-person omniscient, *122, 130*
Process analysis, *552*
Prose, *1018*
Protagonist, *322, 331, 1018*
Pun, *1018*
Pyrrhic (*See* Meter)
Quatrain, *1018–19*
Radio Play, *288, 308–9*
Refrain, *1019*
Reminiscence, *478, 490*
Repetition, *673, 675, 1019*
Resolution, *14, 27, 860* (*See also* Plot)
Rhyme, *610, 612–13, 1019*
    feminine, *610, 613*
    masculine, *610*
Rhyme Scheme, *1019–20*
Rhythm, *610, 612–13, 1020*
Rising Action (*See* Plot)
Romance, *1020*
Round Character (*See* Character)
Run-on Line, *1020*
Satire, *1020*

Scansion, *1020*
Scene (*See* Drama)
Science Fiction, *1020–21*
Script, *1021*
Sensory Language, *1021*
Sestet (*See* Stanza)
Setting, *132, 137, 146, 254, 1021*
   time and place, *146, 157*
Shakespearean Sonnet, *687, 1021*
Short Story, *1, 2, 254, 1021*
Simile, *643, 1021*
Slant Rhyme (*See* Rhyme)
Soliloquy, *382, 403, 1021*
Sonnet, *685, 1021*
  Petrarchan, *689*
Speaker, *594, 598, 619, 621, 1021–22*
Spondee (*See* Meter)
Stage Directions, *1022*
Staging, *310, 321*
Stanza, *1022*
Static Character (*See* Character)
Stereotype (*See* Character)
Stock Character (*See* Character)
Style, *1022*
Subplot, *1022*
Surprise Ending, *58, 61, 1022*
Suspense, *28, 39, 600, 1022*
Symbol, *168, 171, 188, 222, 225, 254, 653, 1022*
Synecdoche, *1022*
Tercet (*See* Stanza)
Tetrameter (*See* Stanza)
Theme, *216, 221, 222, 225, 226, 239, 240, 254, 701, 703, 763,*
    *767, 800, 827–28, 908, 937, 1023*
Third-person limited point of view (*See* Point of View)
Third-person Omniscient Point of View (*See* Point of View)
Third-person Point of View (*See* Point of View)
Tone, *190, 193, 194, 199, 538, 542, 619, 621, 1023*
  in dialogue, *194, 199*
  and irony, *254*
  in narration, *190*
Total Effect, *261*
Tragedy, *420, 433, 1023*
Tragic flaw, *420*
Trimeter (*See* Meter)
Trochee, *612* (*See also* Meter)
Understatement, *1023*
Unexpected Combinations, *660*
Verbal Irony (*See* Irony)
Verisimilitude, *830*
Vernacular, *1023*

## CRITICAL THINKING AND READING

Abstract, *1024*
Analogy, *1024*
Analysis, *1024*
Argument, *419, 1024–25*
  sound, *331*
  unsound, *331*
Bandwagon (*See* Propaganda Technique)
Begging the question (*See* Logical Fallacy)
Categorization, *1025*
Cause and Effect, *57, 262, 571, 828, 1025*
Circular Reasoning (*See* Logical Fallacy)
Classifying, *711*
Comparison, *1025*
Comparison and Contrasting, *262, 527*
  characters, *239*
Conclusion, *461, 1025–26*
Contrast, *1026*
Contrasting Characters, *859*
Creating Mood, *638*
Deduction, *1026*
Defending a Character, *97*
Definition, *1026*
Either/Or Fallacy (*See* Logical Fallacy)
Emotive Language, *225, 490*
Evaluation, *1026–27*
  critic, *937*
  technique, *309*
Evidence, *1027*
Fact, *1027*
False Analogy (*See* Logical Fallacy)
Generalization, *188, 938, 1027*
  hasty, *341, 938*
  overgeneralization, *938*
Induction, *1027–28*
Inference, *712, 1028*
  about author, *577*
  about character, *71, 130, 145, 199, 287, 598–99, 712*
  events, past and present, *712*
  from evidence, *61–62*
  from stage directions, *321*
  theme, *631*
  tone, *712*
Interpretation, *1028*
  of connotative meaning, *117, 171, 179, 221*
  of imagery, *363*
  of metaphorical meaning, *761*
Inversion, *735*
Judgment, *563, 1028*
Loaded Words (*See* Propaganda Technique)
Logical Fallacy, *1028–29*
Main Idea, *448, 547, 559, 1029*
Objective, *1029*
  details, *477*
Opinion, *515, 1029–30*
Order of importance, *263*
Overgeneralization, *938*, (*See also* Logical Fallacy)
Paraphrase, *1030*
*Post Hoc, Ergo Propter Hoc* (*See* Logical Fallacy)
Prediction, *1030*
  outcome, *39, 214, 381*
Persuasive Technique, *533*
Problem Solving, *1030–31*
Propaganda Technique, *1031*
Purpose, *109, 121, 1031*
  biographer's, *467*

Realistic Details/Fantastic Details, *1031–32*
Reading a Map, *434, 507, 768*
  guidelines, *768–69*
  information, *768*
  key, *768*
  layout, *768*
  symbols, *768*
Reading Charts and Tables, *578–79*
Reading Poetry, *588*
Reason, *537, 1032*
Recognizing Humor, *104*
Recognizing Symbols, *907*
Recognizing Tone, *731*
Relationship, *262*
  cause and effect, *262*
  comparison and contrast, *262*
  order of importance, *263*
Relevant Details, *193, 206–7*
Responding
  to parody, *679*
  tetrameter, *679*
  trochee, *679*
Sematic Map, *434*
Separating Fact from Opinion, *515*
Sequence of Events, *499*
Snob Appeal (*See* Propaganda Technique)
Sound Argument (*See* Argument)
Source, *1032*
Stereotype, *12, 83, 1032*
Subjective, *1032*
  details, *477*
Summarize, *253, 1032–33*
Support, *559, 1033*
Time Order, *1033*
Transfer (*See* Propaganda Technique)
Understanding
  figurative meaning, *542*
  metaphorical language, *433*
  setting, *137*
  tone, *403*
Unreliable Testimonial (*See* Propaganda Technique)
Unsound Argument (*See* Argument)
Vague, Undefined Terms (*See* Propaganda Technique)
Valid Conclusion, *261*

### READING IN THE ARTS AND SCIENCES

Classification, *544, 547*
Critical writing, *560, 563*
Definition, *548, 551*
Inference, *564, 571*
Observation, *564, 571*
Process analysis, *552, 559*

### SPEAKING AND LISTENING

Debating the Premise, *533*

Oral Presentation
  dramatic reading, *121*
  funeral oration, *403*
  radio play, *309*
Reading Dramatic Poetry Aloud, *609*
Reading a Selection Aloud, *199*
Reader's Theater, *62*
Shakespearean Theater, *342–43*
Speaking Blank Verse, *363*

### STUDY AND RESEARCH

Analyzing Situation, *944*
Charts and Tables, *578–79*
Classifying, *711*
Gathering Ideas and Information
  analyzing, *945*
  charting or listing, *945*
  clustering, *945*
  freewriting, *945*
  questioning, *945*
  research, *945*
Making a Plan, *944*
Mapping, *434*
Organizing Notes, *945*
Reading a Map, *768–69*
Semantic Map, *434*

### THINKING AND WRITING

Analyzing a Symbol, *907*
Comparing and Contrasting
  characters, *83*
  memories, *490*
  poems, *767*
  sonnets, *689*
  tones, *624*
Description
  of a pet, *448*
  of a place, *145*
Drafting, *947*
Editorial Symbols, *947*
Evaluating a literary work, *984–85*
Parodying a Nursery Rhyme, *679*
Patterning a Poem, *707*
Patterning the Style of the Poem, *613*
Preparing an Argument, *433*
Presenting a Point of View, *859*
Prewriting, *944–45*
Proofreading, *950*
Proofreading Checklist, *950*
Publishing, *950–51*
Responding to Criticism, *937*
Responding to Literary Criticism, *828*
Responding to Meaning, *121*
Revising, *947*
Revision Checklist, *948*
Rewriting in Contemporary Language, *419*

Sound devices, *955*
Summarizing an Essay, *533*
Writing a Biography, *467*
Writing About a Code of Conduct, *735*
Writing About a Descriptive Essay, *515*
Writing About a Journey, *507*
Writing About Allegory, *179*
Writing About an Expository Essay, *527*
Writing About a Person, *104*
Writing About a Place, *137*
Writing About a Play, *331*
Writing About a Poem, *978*
Writing About Art, *166, 261, 563*
Writing About a Symbol, *171*
Writing About a Title, *207*
Writing About Background Music, *403*
Writing About Character, *966*
Writing About Character and Theme, *239*
Writing About Characters in a Play, *287*
Writing About Conflict, *57*
Writing About Drama, *981*
Writing About Emily Dickinson's Poetry, *461*
Writing About Epic Poetry, *761*
Writing About Fiction, *975*
Writing About Figures of Speech, *958*
Writing About Humor, *130*
Writing About Imagery, *661*
Writing About Images, *952*
Writing About Irony, *214*
Writing About Language Arts, *547*
Writing About Lyric Poetry, *633*
Writing About Meaning in Free Verse, *640*
Writing About Metaphors, *647*
Writing About Mood, *39, 667*
Writing About Motivation, *97*
Writing About Music, *253*
Writing About Point of View, *969*
Writing About Plot, *27, 963*
Writing About Science, *571*
Writing About Setting, *960*
Writing About Simile, *645*
Writing About Staging, *321*
Writing About Sound, *955*
Writing About Suspense and Foreshadowing, *604*
Writing About Symbols, *225*
Writing About the Heroic Tradition, *747*
Writing About Theme, *972*
Writing About the Speaker, *599*
Writing About Tone, *199*
Writing a Character Sketch, *71*
Writing a Comparative Evaluation, *987*
Writing a Different Ending, *341*
Writing a Drama Review, *309*
Writing a Journal Entry About History, *551*
Writing an Account, *12*
Writing a Narrative Essay, *499*
Writing a Narrative Poem, *593*
Writing an Autobiographical Sketch, *477*

Writing an Essay About Music, *559*
Writing an Extended Definition, *537*
Writing a Paraphrase of a Poem, *698*
Writing a Personal Essay, *999*
Writing a Personal Narrative Essay, *577*
Writing a Poem, *588, 993*
Writing a Poem with a Metaphor, *651*
Writing a Poem with Imagery, *670*
Writing a Short Dramatic Sketch, *996*
Writing a Short Story, *990–1*
Writing a Summary, *221*
Writing a Surprise Ending, *62*
Writing Blank Verse, *363*
Writing Concrete Poetry, *696*
Writing Couplets, *668*
Writing Free Verse, *711*
Writing from a Different Point of View, *117*
Writing from Character's Point of View, *799*
Writing Haiku, *693*
Writing in the First Person, *109*
Writing Process
    drafting, *947*
    proofreading, *950*
    prewriting, *944–945*
    publishing, *950–51*
    revision, *947–48*
Writing to Contrast Settings, *157*
Writing to Convey a Tone, *193*
Writing with a Symbol, *188*
Writing with Dramatic Irony, *381*

## UNDERSTANDING LANGUAGE

Abstract Terms, *907*
Allusions, *193, 221*
Antonyms, *537, 859*
Aphorism, *542*
Archaic words, *381, 735*
Colloquial Language, *711*
Completing Sentences, *467*
Compound Adjective, *490*
Context Clue, *39, 57, 179, 461*
Dialect, *71, 130, 239*
Elizabethan Words, *343*
Etymology (*See* Word Origin)
Figurative Language
    metaphor, *419*
Glossary, *261*
Jargon, *499*
Meaning
    multiple, *157, 599*
    right, *616*
Metaphor, *419*
Precise Words, *433*
Prefix, *97, 207, 507*
Reading a Dictionary Entry, *27*
Roots, *12, 97*
    from Latin, *225*

Sensory Language, *166*
Simile, *477, 577*
  and Metaphor, *477*
Specific Words, *188, 670*
Suffix, *97, 507*
Synonym, *109, 214, 448*
Terms
  science, *571*
  aft, *563*

Verb, *137, 588, 828*
Verbal Analogy, *527*
Vivid Writing, *747*
Word Origin, *83, 171*
  from Greek myths, *253*
  from Old English, *731*
  from Spanish, *145, 799*
Word Parts, *97*

# INDEX OF TITLES BY THEMES

## SEARCH FOR JUSTICE AND DIGNITY

*Adventures of Sir Launcelot, The,* 737
*American Idea, The,* 549
*Arthur Becomes King of Britain,* 721
*Brothers, The,* 209
*Chee's Daughter,* 73
*Christmas Memory, A,* 479
*Danny Deever,* 607
*Hawk Is Flying, The,* 493
*Hearts and Hands,* 59
*In Flanders Fields,* 682
*Julius Caesar, The Tragedy of,* 345
*Laugher, The,* 107
*Making a Fist,* 630
*Marian Anderson: Famous Concert Singer,* 463
*Miss Rosie,* 644
*Old Pipes and the Dryad,* 241
*Pearl, The,* 779
*Piece of String, The,* 3
*Sentimentality of William Tavener, The,* 255
*Soldier Ran Away, The,* 85
*Tevya and the First Daughter,* 271
*Through the Tunnel,* 159
*Twelve Angry Men,* 311
*Two Tramps in Mud Time,* 595
*Visit to Grandmother, A,* 65
*Way to Rainy Mountain,* from *The,* 501
*Widow and the Parrot, The,* 123
*With All Flags Flying,* 181

## NEW AMERICANS AND
## THE IMMIGRATION EXPERIENCE

*American Idea, The,* 549

## EXPERIENCES WITH WAR AND PEACE

*Adventures of Sir Launcelot, The,* 737
*By the Waters of Babylon,* 147
*Danny Deever,* 607
*In Flanders Fields,* 682
*Invasion from Mars,* 289
*La Belle Dame sans Merci,* 591
*Luck,* 99
*Machine That Won the War, The,* 201
*Morte d'Arthur,* 749
*O What Is That Sound,* 611
*Separate Peace, A,* 831
*Soldier Ran Away, The,* 85
*Sonnet-Ballad, The,* 620
*There Will Come Soft Rains,* 133

## INDIVIDUALS AND
## THE NEED FOR ACCEPTANCE

*Alex Katz's* The Table, 561
*American Idea, The,* 549
*Apple Tree, The,* 217
*Blessing, A,* 636
*Brothers, The,* 209
*Chee's Daughter,* 73
*Child's Christmas in Wales, A,* 469
*Christmas Memory, A,* 479
*Constantly Risking Absurdity,* 697
*Contents of the Dead Man's Pocket,* 15
*Creative Process in Music, The,* 553
*Ebb,* 707
*Emily Dickinson,* 451
*Ex-Basketball Player,* 709
*Generations,* 632
*Glove's Labor Lost,* 573
*Hearts and Hands,* 59
*Jazz Fantasia,* 680
*Julius Caesar, The Tragedy of,* 345
*Laugher, The,* 107
*Letter from Home, A,* 639
*Marian Anderson: Famous Concert Singer,* 463
*Maud Martha Spares the Mouse,* 119
*Miss Rosie,* 644
*Old Pipes and the Dryad,* 241
*On Summer,* 529
*One Perfect Rose,* 622
*Pearl, The,* 779
*Sentimentality of William Tavener, The,* 255
*Separate Peace, A,* 831
*Shaving,* 111
*Soldier Ran Away, The,* 85
*Some Remarks on Humor,* from, 535
*Street of the Cañon, The,* 139
*Tevya and the First Daughter,* 271
*Through the Tunnel,* 159
*To James,* 702
*To Satch,* 623
*Twelve Angry Men,* 311
*Two Tramps in Mud Time,* 595
*Visit to Grandmother, A,* 65
*Way to Rainy Mountain,* from *The,* 501
*Widow and the Parrot, The,* 123
*With All Flags Flying,* 181

## PASSAGES AND TRANSFORMATIONS

*Abalone, Abalone, Abalone,* 169
*Adventures of Sir Launcelot, The,* 737
*Alex Katz's* The Table, 561

American Idea, The, 549
Apple Tree, The, 217
Arthur Becomes King of Britain, 721
Auto Wreck, 704
Blessing, A, 636
Brothers, The, 209
By the Waters of Babylon, 147
Cargoes, 669
Centaur, The, 585
Chee's Daughter, 73
Child's Christmas in Wales, A, 469
Christmas Memory, A, 479
Contents of the Dead Man's Pocket, 15
Creative Process in Music, The, 553
Danny Deever, 607
Ebb, 707
Eldorado, 615
Emily Dickinson, 451
Ex-Basketball Player, 709
First Lesson, 647
Generations, 632
Glove's Labor Lost, 573
Hawk Is Flying, The, 493
Hiltons' Holiday, The, 227
In Flanders Fields, 682
Julius Caesar, The Tragedy of, 345
La Belle Dame sans Merci, 591
Leiningen Versus the Ants, 41
Making a Fist, 630
Marginal World, The, 565
Marian Anderson: Famous Concert Singer, 463
Marriage of King Arthur, The, 733
Merlin, 764
Merlin, 766
Morte d'Arthur, 749
Music I Heard, 628
Old Pipes and the Dryad, 241
On Summer, 529
Oxen, The, 706
Pearl, The, 779
Pitcher, 668
Sentimentality of William Tavener, The, 255
Separate Peace, A, 831
Shaving, 111
Soldier Ran Away, The, 85
Sonnet-Ballad, The, 620
Street, The, 638
Street of the Cañon, The, 139
Tevya and the First Daughter, 271
Through the Tunnel, 159
To James, 702
To Satch, 623
Twelve Angry Men, 311
Visit to Grandmother, A, 65
Way to Rainy Mountain, from The, 501
Widow and the Parrot, The, 123
With All Flags Flying, 181
White Gardens, 223

White Lantern, from The, 517
Wreck of the Hesperus, The, 601

## THE INDIVIDUAL AND SOCIETY

Adventures of Sir Launcelot, The, 737
American Idea, The, 549
Arthur Becomes King of Britain, 721
By the Waters of Babylon, 147
Child's Christmas in Wales, A, 469
Christmas Memory, A, 479
Danny Deever, 607
Emily Dickinson, 451
Ex-Basketball Player, 709
Flood, 509
Glove's Labor Lost, 595
Hearts and Hands, 59
Hiltons' Holiday, The, 227
Invasion from Mars, 289
Julius Caesar, The Tragedy of, 345
Laugher, The, 107
Letter Slot, 696
Luck, 99
Machine That Won the War, The, 201
Marginal World, The, 565
Marian Anderson: Famous Concert Singer, 463
Marriage of King Arthur, The, 733
Masque of the Red Death, The, 173
Miss Rosie, 644
My Heart's in the Highlands, 674
Notes on Punctuation, 545
O What Is That Sound, 611
Old Pipes and the Dryad, 241
Pearl, The, 779
Piece of String, The, 3
Separate Peace, A, 831
Soldier Ran Away, The, 85
Some Remarks on Humor, from, 535
Street of the Cañon, The, 139
Tevya and the First Daughter, 271
To James, 702
Twelve Angry Men, 311
Two Tramps in Mud Time, 595
Way to Rainy Mountain, from The, 501
White Gardens, 223
White Lantern, from The, 517
Widow and the Parrot, The, 123
With All Flags Flying, 181

## JOURNEY TO PERSONAL FULFILLLMENT

Abalone, Abalone, Abalone, 169
Adventures of Sir Launcelot, The, 737
Alex Katz's The Table, 561
American Idea, The, 549
Apple Tree, The, 217
Arthur Become King of Britain, 721
Brothers, The, 209

By the Waters of Babylon, 147
Centaur, The, 585
Chee's Daughter, 73
Christmas Memory, A, 479
Constantly Risking Absurdity, 697
Contents of the Dead Man's Pocket, 15
Creative Process in Music, The, 553
Eldorado, 615
Emily Dickinson, 451
Ex-Basketball Player, 709
First Lesson, 647
Generations, 632
Glove's Labor Lost, 573
Hawk Is Flying, The, 493
Hiltons' Holiday, The, 227
Jazz Fantasia, 680
Julius Caesar, The Tragedy of, 345
Laugher, The, 107
Leiningen Versus the Ants, 41
Luck, 99
Marginal World, The, 565
Marian Anderson: Famous Concert Singer, 463
Marriage of King Arthur, The, 733
Old Pipes and the Dryad, 241
On Summer, 529
Pearl, The, 779
Sentimentality of William Tavener, The, 255
Separate Peace, A, 831
Shaving, 111
Soldier Ran Away, The, 85
Sonnet-Ballad, The, 620
Street, The, 638
Tevya and the First Daughter, 271
Through the Tunnel, 159
To James, 702
To Satch, 623
Two Tramps in Mud Time, 595
Visit to Grandmother, A, 65
Way to Rainy Mountian, from The, 501
Widow and the Parrot, The, 123
With All Flags Flying, 181
White Lantern, from The, 517

## A TIME FOR COURAGE

Adventures of Sir Launcelot, The, 737
By the Waters of Babylon, 147
Chee's Daughter, 73
Contents of the Dead Man's Pocket, 15
First Lesson, 647
La Belle Dame sans Merci, 591
Leiningen Versus the Ants, 41
Luck, 99
Making a Fist, 630
Marian Anderson: Famous Concert Singer, 463
Miss Rosie, 644
O What Is That Sound, 611
On Summer, 529

Pearl, The, 779
Separate Peace, A, 831
Shaving, 111
Sonnet-Ballad, The, 620
Through the Tunnel, 159
To James, 702
White Lantern, from The, 517
Wreck of the Hesperus, The, 601

## FANTASY AND THE UNEXPLAINED

Adventures of Sir Launcelot, The, 737
Arthur Becomes King of Britain, 721
Invasion from Mars, 289
La Belle Dame sans Merci, 591
Last Unicorns, The, 191
Marriage of King Arthur, The, 733
Masque of the Red Death, The, 173
Merlin, 764
Merlin, 766
Monkey's Paw, The, 29
Morte d'Arthur, 749
Old Pipes and the Dryad, 241
Open Window, The, 195
There Will Come Soft Rains, 133
Widow and the Parrot, The, 123

## THE ENVIRONMENT AND
## THE TOUCHED AND UNTOUCHED EARTH

Abalone, Abalone, Abalone, 169
Apple Tree, The, 217
Auto Wreck, 704
Big Wind, 658
Blessing, A, 636
By the Waters of Babylon, 147
Cargoes, 669
Chee's Daughter, 73
Ebb, 707
Fish, The, 665
Flood, 509
Four Haiku, 691
Fueled, 652
Generations, 632
Hawk Is Flying, The, 493
In Flanders Fields, 682
Jelly-Fish, A, 651
July Storm, 645
Last Unicorns, The, 191
Leiningen Versus the Ants, 41
Letter from Home, A, 639
Loss, 659
Marginal World, The, 565
Metaphor, 646
My Heart's in the Highlands, 674
Night Clouds, 650
Nursery Rhymes for the Tender-Hearted, 678
On Summer, 529

Oxen, The, 706
Puritan Sonnet, 688
Reapers, 664
Shall I Compare Thee to a Summer's Day? 686
Splendor Falls, The, 676
There Will Come Soft Rains, 133
Through the Tunnel, 159
Way to Rainy Mountain, from The, 501
White Lantern, from The, 517
Wind—tapped like a tired Man, The, 654
Wreck of the Hesperus, The, 601

## A TIME FOR LAUGHTER

Child's Christmas in Wales, A, 469
Dog That Bit People, The, 441
Letter Slot, 696
Luck, 99
Notes on Punctuation, 545
Nursery Rhymes for the Tender-Hearted, 678
One Perfect Rose, 622
Open Window, The, 195
Rural Literalism, 539
Some Remarks on Humor, from, 535

# INDEX OF AUTHORS AND TITLES

*Page numbers in italics refer to biographical information.*

*Abalone, Abalone, Abalone*, 169
*Adventures of Sir Launcelot, The*, 737
Aiken, Conrad, *626*, 629
Aleichem, Sholom, *270*, 271
*Alex Katz's* The Table, 561
Allen, Samuel (Paul Vesey), *618*, 623
*American Idea, The*, 549
Ammons, A. R., *656*, 659
*Apple Tree, The*, 217
*Arthur Becomes King of Britain*, 721
Asimov, Isaac, *200*, 201
Auden, Wystan Hugh, *610*, 611
*Auto Wreck*, 704

Bashō, *690*, 691
Beattie, Ann, *560*, 561
Benét, Stephen Vincent, *146*, 147
*Big Wind*, 658
Bishop, Elizabeth, *662*, 665
Björnson, Björnstjerne, *208*, 209
*Blessing, A*, 636
Böll, Heinrich, *106*, 107
Booth, Philip, *642*, 647
Boswell, Thomas, *573*, 573
Boyle, Kay, *84*, 85
Bradbury, Ray, *132*, 133
Brooks, Gwendolyn, *118*, 119, 618, 620
Brooks, Van Wyck, *450*, 451
*Brothers, The*, 209
Burns, Robert, *672*, 674
*By the Waters of Babylon*, 147

Capote, Truman, *478*, 479
*Cargoes*, 669
Carson, Rachel, *564*, 565
Cather, Willa, 255, *260*
*Centaur, The*, 585
*Chee's Daughter*, 73
*Child's Christmas in Wales, A*, 469
*Chiyojo*, *690*, 691
*Christmas Memory, A*, 479
Ciardi, John, *656*, 660
Clemens, Samuel Langhorne (*See* Twain, Mark)
Clifton, Lucille, *642*, 644
Coatsworth, Elizabeth, *642*, 645
Connell, Evan S., *516*, 517
Copland, Aaron, *552*, 553
*Constantly Risking Absurdity*, 698
*Contents of the Dead Man's Pocket*, 15
*Creative Process in Music, The*, 553

Crews, Harry, *492*, 493

*Danny Deever*, 607
de Maupassant, Guy, *3*, 3
Dickinson, Emily, *648*, 654
Dillard, Annie, *508*, 509
*Dog That Bit People, The*, 441

*Ebb*, 707
*Eldorado*, 615
*Emily Dickinson*, 451
*Ex-Basketball Player*, 709

Ferlinghetti, Lawrence, *694*, 697
Finney, Jack, *14*, 15
*First Lesson*, 647
*Fish, The*, 665
*Flanders Fields, In*, 682
*Flood*, 509
*Four Haiku*, 691
Francis, Robert, *662*, 668
Frost, Robert, *594*, 595
*Fueled*, 652

*Generations*, 632
*Glove's Labor Lost*, 573

Hans, Marcie, *648*, 652
Hansberry, Lorraine, *528*, 529
Hardy, Thomas, *700*, 706
*Hawk Is Flying, The*, 493
*Hearts and Hands*, 59
Helprin, Mark, *222*, 223
Henry, O., *58*, 59
Hill, Geoffrey, *762*, 764
*Hiltons' Holiday, The*, 227
Hoch, Edward D., *190*, 191
Horne, Frank, *700*, 702
Hughes, Langston, *462*, 463
*Hyakuchi*, *690*, 691

*Invasion form Mars*, 289
*Issa*, *690*, 692

Jacobs, W. W., *28*, 29
*Jazz Fantasia*, 680
*Jelly-Fish, A*, 651
Jewett, Sarah Orne, *226*, 227
*Julius Caesar* (*See* Tragedy of Julius Caesar, The)
*July Storm*, 645

Keats, John, *590*, 591
Kelley, William Melvin, *64*, 65
Kipling, Rudyard, *606*, 607
Knowles, John, *830*, 831
Koch, Howard, *288*, 289

*La Belle Dame sans Merci*, 591
*Last Unicorns*, The, 191
*Laugher, The*, 107
*Legend of King Arthur, The*, 718
*Leiningen Versus the Ants*, 41
Lessing, Doris, *158*, 159
*Letter from Home, A*, 639
*Letter Slot*, 696
Longfellow, Henry Wadsworth, *600*, 601
*Loss*, 659
Lowell, Amy, *626*, 632, 648, 650
*Luck*, 99

*Machine That Won the War, The*, 201
*Making a Fist*, 630
Malory, Sir Thomas, *732*, 733, 737
Mansfield, Katherine, *216*, 217
*Marginal World, The*, 565
*Marian Anderson: Famous Concert Singer*, 463
*Marriage of King Arthur, The*, 733
Masefield, John, *662*, 669
*Masque of the Red Death, The*, 173
*Maud Martha Spares the Mouse*, 119
Maupassant, Guy de (*See* de Maupassant, Guy)
McCrae, John, *672*, 682
*Merlin*, 764, 766
Merriam, Eve, *642*, 646
*Metaphor*, 646
Millay, Edna St. Vincent, *700*, 707
Miller, Siyowin, *72*, 73
*Miss Rosie*, 644
Momaday, N. Scott, *500*, 501
*Monkey's Paw, The*, 29
Moore, Marianne, *648*, 651
Mori, Toshio, *168*, 169
Morley, Christopher, *672*, 678
*Morte d'Arthur*, 749
Muir, Edwin, *762*, 766
*Music I Heard*, 628
*My Heart's in the Highlands*, 674

Niggli, Josephina, *138*, 139
*Night Clouds*, 650
Norris, Leslie, *110*, 111
*Notes on Punctuation*, 545
*Nursery Rhymes for the Tender-Hearted*, 678
Nye, Naomi Shihab, *626*, 630

*Old Pipes and the Dryad*, 241
Oliver, Mary, *634*, 639

*One Morning*, 660
*One Perfect Rose*, 622
*On Summer*, 529
*Open Window, The*, 195
*O What Is That Sound*, 611
Orbeck, Anders, (translator), 209
*Oxen, The*, 706

Parker, Dorothy, *618*, 622
Paz, Octavio, *634*, 638
*Pearl, The*, 779
Perl, Arnold, *270*, 271
*Piece of String, The*, 3
*Pitcher*, 668
Platero, Juanita, *72*, 73
Poe, Edgar Allan, *172*, 173, 614, 615
*Puritan Ballad, A*, 688

*Reapers*, 664
Roethke, Theodore, *656*, 658
Rose, Reginald, *310*, 311
Rukeyser, Muriel, (translator), 638
*Rural Literalism*, 539

Saki, *194*, 195
Sandburg, Carl, *672*, 680
*Sentimentality of William Tavener, The*, 255
*Separate Peace, A*, 831
Shakespeare, William, *344*, 345, 684, 686
*Shall I Compare Thee to a Summer's Day?*, 686
Shapiro, Karl, *700*, 704
*Shaving*, 111
*Soldier Ran Away, The*, 85
*Some Remarks on Humor*, from, 535
*Sonnet-Ballad, The*, 620
*Splendor Falls, The*, 676
Steinbeck, John Ernst, *778*, 779
Stephenson, Carl, *40*, 41
Stockton, Frank R., *240*, 241
*Street, The*, 638
*Street of the Cañon, The*, 139
Swenson, May, 585, *587*

Tennyson, Alfred, Lord, *672*, 676, 748, 749
*Tevya and the First Daughter*, 271
*There Will Come Soft Rains*, 133
Thomas, Dylan, *468*, 469
Thomas, Lewis, *544*, 545
*Through the Tunnel*, 159
Thurber, James, 441, *447*
*To James*, 702
Toomer, Jean, *662*, 664
*Tragedy of Julius Caesar, The*, 345
Trillin, Calvin, *538*, 539
Twain, Mark, *98*, 99
*Twelve Angry Men*, 311
*Two Tramps in Mud Time*, 595
Tyler, Anne, *180*, 181

Updike, John, *694*, 696, 709
Vesey, Paul (*See* Allen, Samuel)
*Visit to Grandmother, A,* 65

*Way to Rainy Mountain,* from *The,* 501
White, E. B. (Elwyn Brooks), *534,* 535
*White Gardens,* 223
*White Lantern* from *The,* 517

White, Theodore H., *548,* 549
White, Terence Hanbury, *720,* 721
*Widow and the Parrot, The,* 123
*Wind—tapped like a tired Man, The,* 654
*With All Flags Flying,* 181
Woolf, Virginia, *122,* 123
*Wreck of the Hesperus, The,* 601
Wright, James, *634,* 636
Wylie, Elinor, *684,* 688

# ACKNOWLEDGMENTS (continued)

**Don Congdon Associates, Inc.**
"There Will Come Soft Rains" by Ray Bradbury, published in *Collier's National Weekly Magazine*, 1950. Copyright 1950 by Ray Bradbury; renewed © 1977 by Ray Bradbury. "Contents of the Dead Man's Pocket" by Jack Finney, published in *Collier's*, 1956. Copyright © 1956 by Crowell-Collier Publishing Co; renewed 1984 by Jack Finney. Reprinted by permission of Don Congdon Associates, Inc.

**Molly Malone Cook Literary Agency**
"A Letter from Home" by Mary Oliver, published in *Mademoiselle*, 1964. Copyright © 1964 by Mary Oliver.

**Curtis Brown Ltd.**
*A Separate Peace* by John Knowles. Copyright © 1959 by John Knowles. Copyright renewed 1987 by John Knowles. Reprinted by permission of Curtis Brown Ltd.

**The Curtis Publishing Company**
"The Soldier Ran Away" by Kay Boyle. Reprinted from *The Saturday Evening Post*, copyright 1953 The Curtis Publishing Company.

**Delacorte Press/Seymour Lawrence**
"White Gardens" excerpted from *Ellis Island & Other Stories* by Mark Helprin. Copyright © 1976, 1977, 1979, 1980, 1981 by Mark Helprin. Reprinted by permission of Delacorte Press/Seymour Lawrence.

**Dodd, Mead & Company, Inc.**
"The Sentimentality of William Tavener" reprinted by permission of Dodd, Mead & Company, Inc. from *The Early Stories of Willa Cather* edited by Mildred R. Bennett. Copyright © 1957 by Mildred R. Bennett; copyright renewed 1985 by Mildred R. Bennett. Lines from "We Wear the Mask" from *The Complete Poems of Paul Laurence Dunbar*. Lines from "Spring" reprinted by permission of Dodd, Mead & Company, Inc. from *Poems* by Richard Hovey. "Marian Anderson: Famous Concert Singer" reprinted by permission of Dodd, Mead & Company, Inc. from *Famous American Negroes* by Langston Hughes. Copyright 1954 by Langston Hughes; copyright renewed 1982 by George Houston Bass.

**Doubleday, a division of Bantam, Doubleday, Dell Publishing Group, Inc.**
"The Machine That Won the War" by Isaac Asimov. Copyright © 1961 by Mercury Press, Inc. From the book *Nightfall and Other Stories* by Isaac Asimov. "Glove's Labor Lost" from *How Life Imitates the World Series* by Thomas Boswell. Copyright © 1982 by Washington Post's Writers Group. "Hearts and Hands" by O. Henry from *Waifs and Strays*, published by Doubleday & Company, Inc. "A Visit to Grandmother" by William Melvin Kelley. Copyright © 1964 by William Melvin Kelley. From the book *Dancers on the Shore*. "Big Wind" by Theodore Roethke. Copyright 1947 by United Chapters of Phi Beta Kappa. From *The Collected Poems of Theodore Roethke*. Lines from "The Heron" copyright 1937 by Theodore Roethke from *The Collected Poems of Theodore Roethke*. Reprinted by permission of Doubleday, a division of Bantam, Doubleday, Dell Publishing Group, Inc.

**E. P. Dutton, a division of NAL Penguin Inc.**
"Emily Dickinson" from *New England: Indian Summer, 1865–1915* by Van Wyck Brooks. Copyright 1940, 1950 by Van Wyck Brooks, renewed 1968, 1978 by Gladys Brooks. Reprinted by permission of the publisher, E. P. Dutton, a division of NAL Penguin Inc.

**Ann Elmo Agency, Inc.**
"Leiningen Versus the Ants" by Carl Stephenson. Reprinted by permission of Ann Elmo Agency, Inc., 60 East 42nd Street, New York, NY 10165.

**Estate of John Ciardi**
"One Morning" from *Person to Person* by John Ciardi, Rutgers University Press, 1964. Permission granted by the Estate of John Ciardi on the advice of John L. Ciardi, personal representative.

**Farrar, Straus and Giroux, Inc.**
"The Fish" from *The Complete Poems 1927–1979* by Elizabeth Bishop. Copyright © 1983 by Alice Helen Methfessel. Copyright 1940 by Elizabeth Bishop. Excerpt from "Sorrow Is the Only Faithful One" from *Powerful Long Ladder* by Owen Dodson. Copyright © 1946 by Owen Dodson, renewed copyright © 1974 by Owen Dodson. Reprinted by permission of Farrar, Straus and Giroux, Inc.

**Harcourt Brace Jovanovich, Inc.**
Lines from "anyone lived in a pretty how town" copyright 1940 by E. E. Cummings; renewed 1968 by Marion Morehouse Cummings. Reprinted from his volume *Complete Poems 1913–1962* by E. E. Cummings. "Fueled" from *Serve Me a Slice of Moon*, copyright © 1965 by Marcie Hans. "Jazz Fantasia" from *Smoke and Steel* by Carl Sandburg, copyright 1920 by Harcourt Brace Jovanovich, Inc.; renewed 1948 by Carl Sandburg. Lines from "Mind" from *Things of This World*, copyright © 1956, 1984 by Richard Wilbur. Reprinted by permission of Harcourt Brace Jovanovich, Inc.

**Harcourt Brace Jovanovich, Inc., Quentin Bell, Angelica Garnett, Julian Bell, and The Hogarth Press Ltd.**
"The Widow and the Parrot" from *The Complete Shorter Fiction of Virginia Woolf* edited by Susan Dick, copyright © 1985 by Quentin Bell and Angelica Garnett. Reprinted by permission.

**Harper & Row, Publishers, Inc.**
"The Hawk Is Flying" from *Blood and Grits* by Harry Crews, copyright © 1979 by Harry Crews. Lines from "Any Human to Another" from *On These I Stand: An Anthology of the Best-Loved Poems by Countee Cullen*. Copyright 1935 by Harper & Row, Publishers, Inc.; renewed 1963 by Ida M. Cullen. Chapter 9, "Flood," from *Pilgrim at Tinker Creek* by Annie Dillard, copyright © 1974 by Annie Dillard. "Nursery Rhymes for the Tender-Hearted" from *Poems* by Christopher Morley (J. B. Lippincott), copyright 1920, renewed 1948 by George H. Doran Company. From "Some Remarks on Humor" from *Essays of E. B. White*, copyright 1941, renewed 1969 by E. B. White. Reprinted by permission of Harper & Row, Publishers, Inc.

**Harper & Row, Publishers, Inc. and Jonathan Clowes Ltd., London, on behalf of Doris Lessing**
"Through the Tunnel" from *The Habit of Loving* by Doris Lessing (Thomas Y. Crowell). Copyright 1954, © 1955 by Doris Lessing. Reprinted by permission.

**Harvard University Press and the Trustees of Amherst College**
Lines from "Dear March, come in" reprinted by permission of the publishers and the Trustees of Amherst College from *The Poems of Emily Dickinson* edited by Thomas H. Johnson, Cambridge, Mass.: The Belknap Press of Harvard University Press, copyright 1951, © 1955, 1979, 1983 by The President and Fellows of Harvard College. "The Wind—tapped like a tired Man—" reprinted by permission of the publishers and the Trustees of Amherst College from *The Poems of Emily Dickinson* edited by Thomas H. Johnson, Cambridge, Mass.: The Belknap Press of Harvard University Press, copyright 1951, © 1955, 1979, 1983 by The President and Fellows of Harvard College.

**Edward D. Hoch**
"The Last Unicorns" by Edward D. Hoch. Copyright © 1958 by Columbia Publications, Inc.; © renewed 1986 by Edward D. Hoch. Reprinted by permission of the author.

**Henry Holt and Company, Inc.**
"Fire and Ice," "Once by the Pacific," and lines from "Birches" from *The Poetry of Robert Frost* edited by Edward Connery Lathem. Copyright © 1969 by Holt, Rinehart and Winston, Inc.; copyright © 1962 by Robert Frost; copyright © 1975 by Lesley Frost Ballantine. "Two Tramps in Mud Time" copyright 1936 by Robert Frost. Copyright © 1964 by Lesley Frost Ballantine. Copyright © 1969 by Holt, Rinehart and Winston, Inc. Reprinted from *The Poetry of Robert Frost* edited by Edward Connery Lathem, by permission of Henry Holt and Company, Inc.

**Houghton Mifflin Company**
"The Marginal World" from *The Edge of the Sea* by Rachel Carson. Copyright © 1955 by Rachel L. Carson. Copyright © renewed 1983 by Roger Christie. "The Hiltons' Holiday" from *Life of Nancy* by Sarah Orne Jewett. "Generations" and "Night Clouds" from *The Complete Poetical Works of Amy Lowell*. Copyright © 1955 by Houghton Mifflin Company. Copyright © renewed 1983 by Houghton Mifflin Company, Brinton P. Roberts, Esquire, and G. D'Andelot Belin, Esquire. Reprinted by permission of Houghton Mifflin Company.

**International Creative Management, Inc.**
"Alex Katz's *The Table*" from *Alex Katz* by Ann Beattie. Text copyright © 1987 by Ann Beattie. "Invasion from Mars" from *The Panic Broadcast: Portrait of an Event* by Howard Koch. Copyright 1940 by Princeton University Press; (c) 1968 by Howard Koch. "Twelve Angry Men" from *Six Television Plays* by Reginald Rose. Copyright © 1956 by Reginald Rose. Reprinted by permission of International Creative Management, Inc.

**Japan Publications, Inc.**
"Falling upon earth" by Bashō, "Having viewed the moon" by Chiyojo, "With one who muses" by Hyakuchi, and "A gentle spring rain" by Issa, reprinted from *One Hundred Famous Haiku* translated by Daniel C. Buchanan, with permission from Japan Publications, Inc., © 1973.

**Alfred A. Knopf, Inc.**
"Moonlight Night: Carmel" copyright 1947 by Langston Hughes. Reprinted from *Selected Poems of Langston Hughes*, by Langston Hughes. "Ex-Basketball Player" copyright © 1957, 1982 by John Updike. Reprinted from *The Carpentered Hen and Other Tame Creatures* by John Updike. "Letter Slot" from *Verse* by John Updike. Copyright 1952 and renewed 1982 by John Updike. "Puritan Sonnet" from "Wild Peaches" in *Collected Poems of Elinor Wylie*. Copyright 1921 by Alfred A. Knopf, Inc. and renewed 1949 by William Rose Benét. Reprinted by permission of Alfred A. Knopf, Inc.

**Alfred A. Knopf, Inc. and The Society of Authors as the literary representative of the Estate of Katherine Mansfield**
"The Apple Tree" copyright 1939 by Alfred A. Knopf, Inc. and renewed 1967 by Mrs. Mary Middleton Murry. Reprinted from *The Scrapbook of Katherine Mansfield* by Katherine Mansfield, by permission.

**Latin American Review**
Lines from "Beneath the Shadow of the Freeway" by Lorna Dee Cervantes, published in *Latin American Review* (Spring-Summer 1977). Copyright © 1977 by Lorna Dee Cervantes. Reprinted by permission of the editors of *Latin American Review*.

**Liveright Publishing Corporation**
"Reapers" is reprinted from *Cane* by Jean Toomer by permission of Liveright Publishing Corporation. Copyright 1923 by Boni & Liveright. Copyright renewed 1951 by Jean Toomer.

**Macmillan Publishing Company**
"July Storm" reprinted with permission of Macmillan Publishing Company from *Down Half the World* by Elizabeth Coatsworth. Copyright 1924, 1926, 1946, 1949, 1950, 1952, 1953, 1954, © 1955, 1956, 1957, 1958, 1959, 1963, 1964, 1968 by Elizabeth Coatsworth Beston. Originally appeared in *Down East* Magazine. "The Oxen" from *The Complete Poems of Thomas Hardy* edited by James Gibson (New York: Macmillan, 1978). "Cargoes" reprinted with permission of Macmillan Publishing Company from *Poems* by John Masefield (New York: Macmillan, 1953). "There Will Come Soft Rains" reprinted with permission of Macmillan Publishing Company from *Collected Poems* by Sara Teasdale. Copyright 1920 by Macmillan Publishing Company, renewed 1948 by Mamie T. Wheless. Lines from "Thoughts" reprinted with permission of Macmillan Publishing Company from *Collected Poems* by Sara Teasdale. Copyright 1920 by Macmillan Publishing Company, Inc.; renewed 1948 by Mamie T. Wheless.

**Naomi Long Madgett**
Lines from "Black Woman" from *Pink Ladies in the Afternoon* by Naomi Long Madgett. Copyright © 1972 by Naomi Long Madgett. "Woman with Flower" from *Star by Star* by Naomi Long Madgett. Copyright © 1965, 1970 by Naomi Long Madgett.

**McGraw-Hill Book Company**
"The Creative Process in Music" from *What to Listen for in Music* by Aaron Copland. Copyright © 1957 by the McGraw-Hill Book Company, Inc. Reprinted with permission.

**McGraw-Hill Book Company and Joan Daves**
"The Laugher" from *18 Stories* by Heinrich Böll, translated by Leila Vennewitz. Copyright © 1966 by Heinrich Böll. Reprinted by permission.

**William Morrow & Company, Inc.**
''Knoxville, Tennessee'' from *Black Feeling, Black Talk, Black Judgment* by Nikki Giovanni; copyright © 1968, 1970 by Nikki Giovanni. Reprinted by permission.

**NAL Penguin Inc.**
''Eldorado'' from *The Complete Poetry and Selected Criticism of Edgar Allan Poe* edited by Allen Tate. From *The Tragedy of Julius Caesar* by William Shakespeare, edited by William and Barbara Rosen. Copyright © 1963 by William and Barbara Rosen. Reprinted by arrangement with NAL Penguin Inc., New York, New York.

**The Nation Magazine/The Nation Company, Inc.**
''Variations'' (''Rural Literalism'') by Calvin Trillin, from *The Nation*, September 12, 1981, © 1981.

**New Directions Publishing Corporation**
''Constantly Risking Absurdity'' from Lawrence Ferlinghetti, *Endless Life*. Copyright © 1981 by Lawrence Ferlinghetti. Lines from ''February Evening in New York'' from Denise Levertov, *Collected Earlier Poems 1940–1960*. Copyright © 1959 by Denise Levertov Goodman. ''The Street'' from Octavio Paz, *Selected Poems*. Copyright © 1963 by Octavio Paz and Muriel Rukeyser. Reprinted by permission of New Directions Publishing Corporation.

**New Directions Publishing Corporation and David Higham Associates Ltd.**
Dylan Thomas, *A Child's Christmas in Wales*. Copyright 1954 by New Directions Publishing Corporation. Published in Great Britain by J. M. Dent & Sons Ltd.

**The New Yorker**
Lines from ''Glass World'' by Dorothy Donnelly. From the March 12, 1960 issue of *The New Yorker*. Copyright © 1960, 1988 by The New Yorker Magazine, Inc. Reprinted by permission.

**The New York Times**
''The American Idea'' by Theodore H. White from *The New York Times Magazine*, July 6, 1986. Copyright © 1986 by The New York Times Company. Reprinted by permission.

**North Point Press**
Excerpted from *The White Lantern*, copyright © 1980, 1988 by North Point Press, by Evan S. Connell. Published by North Point Press and reprinted by permission.

**W. W. Norton & Company, Inc.**
''Loss'' is reprinted from *Collected Poems, 1951–1971* by A. R. Ammons, by permission of W. W. Norton & Company, Inc. Copyright © 1972 by A. R. Ammons.

**Naomi Shihab Nye**
''Making a Fist'' from *Hugging the Jukebox* by Naomi Shihab Nye. Copyright © Naomi Shihab Nye, 1982. Reprinted by permission of the author.

**Harold Ober Associates, Inc.**
Lines from ''A Black Man Talks of Reaping'' and lines from ''A Note of Humility'' from *Personals* by Arna Bontemps. Copyright © 1963 by Arna Bontemps. Reprinted by permission of Harold Ober Associates, Inc.

**Oxford University Press, Inc.**
''Music I Heard'' (from ''Discordants'') from *Collected Poems* by Conrad Aiken. Copyright © 1953, 1970 by Conrad Aiken; renewed 1981 by Mary Aiken. ''Merlin'' from *Collected Poems* by Geoffrey Hill. Copyright © 1985 by Geoffrey Hill. Reprinted by permission of Oxford University Press, Inc.

**Oxford University Press, Inc. and Faber and Faber Ltd.**
''Merlin'' from *Collected Poems* by Edwin Muir. Copyright © 1960 by Willa Muir. Reprinted by permission.

**Mrs. Nancy Perl**
''Tevya and the First Daughter'' by Arnold Perl, published in *The Best Short Plays 1959–1960* edited by Margaret Mayorga, Beacon Press.

**Playbill Magazine**
''On Summer'' by Lorraine Hansberry, reprinted from *Playbill* Magazine, June 1960. Playbill® is a registered trademark of Playbill Incorporated, NYC. All rights reserved. Used by permission.

**The Putnam Publishing Group**
''Rhapsody'' reprinted by the permission of The Putnam Publishing Group from *Selected Poems* by William Stanley Braithwaite. Copyright 1948 by William Stanley Braithwaite. ''In Flanders Fields'' reprinted by permission of The Putnam Publishing Group from *In Flanders Fields* by John McCrae. Copyright 1919 by G. P. Putnam's Sons. Renewed.

**The Putnam Publishing Group and Watkins/Loomis Agency, Inc.**
Excerpt (titled, ''Arthur Becomes King'') reprinted by permission from *The Once and Future King* by T. H. White. Copyright 1939, 1940, and © 1958 by T. H. White. Renewed.

**Random House, Inc.**
''A Christmas Memory'' copyright © 1956 by Truman Capote. Reprinted from *Breakfast at Tiffany's* by Truman Capote. ''Miss Rosie'' from *Good Times* by Lucille Clifton. Copyright © 1969 by Lucille Clifton. ''Auto Wreck'' copyright 1942 and renewed 1970 by Karl Shapiro. Reprinted from *Collected Poems 1940–1978* by Karl Shapiro. Reprinted by permission of Random House, Inc.

**Random House, Inc. and Faber and Faber Ltd.**
''O What Is That Sound'' copyright 1937 and renewed 1967 by W. H. Auden. Reprinted from *W. H. Auden: Collected Poems* by W. H. Auden, edited by Edward Mendelson. Reprinted by permission.

**Marian Reiner for Eve Merriam**
''Metaphor'' from *It Doesn't Always Have to Rhyme* by Eve Merriam. Copyright © 1964 by Eve Merriam. All Rights Reserved. Reprinted by permission of Marian Reiner for the author.

**Russell and Volkening, Inc., as agents for the author**
''With All Flags Flying'' by Anne Tyler, published in *Redbook* Magazine, June 1971. Copyright © 1971 by Anne Tyler. Reprinted by permission of Russell and Volkening, Inc., as agents for the author.

**Simon & Schuster, Inc.**
Pronunciation key from *Webster's New World Dictionary—Second College Edition*. Copyright © 1984 by Simon & Schuster, Inc. Reprinted by permission.

**Southern Methodist University Press**
''A Christmas Tree'' by William Burford from *Man Now*, 1954, Southern Methodist University Press.

**The Jesse Stuart Foundation**
Lines from ''Our Heritage'' from *A Jesse Stuart Reader* by Jesse Stuart, published by McGraw-Hill Book Company, 1963.

**May Swenson**
''The Centaur'' by May Swenson is reprinted by permission of the author, copyright © 1956, renewed © 1984 by May Swenson. Lines from ''Living Tenderly'' by May Swenson are reprinted by permission of the author, copyright © 1963 by May Swenson.

**Carmen Tafolla**
Lines from ''Alli por la Calle San Luis'' copyright © 1977 by Carmen Tafolla. Reprinted by permission of the author.

**Rosemary A. Thurber**
''The Dog That Bit People'' copyright 1933, © 1961 by James Thurber. From *My Life and Hard Times*, published by Harper & Row.

**University Books, Inc.**
''The Adventures of Sir Launcelot'' and ''The Marriage of King Arthur'' from *Le Morte d'Arthur* by Sir Thomas Malory. Reprinted with permission of University Books, Inc., 120 Enterprise Avenue, Secaucus, NJ 07094.

**University of New Mexico Press**
From *The Way to Rainy Mountain* by N. Scott Momaday. First published in *The Reporter*, January 26, 1967. Reprinted from *The Way to Rainy Mountain*, © 1969, the University of New Mexico Press.

**The University of North Carolina Press**
''The Street of the Cañon'' from *Mexican Village* by Josephina Niggli. Copyright 1945 The University of North Carolina Press. Reprinted by permission of the publisher.

**Unwin Hyman Ltd.**
Lines from ''In the Beck'' from *The Collected Poems of Kathleen Raine* by Kathleen Raine. © Copyright 1956 by Kathleen Raine. Reprinted by permission of Unwin Hyman Ltd.

**Viking Penguin Inc.**
''First Lesson'' from *Relations* by Phillip Booth. Copyright 1957, renewed © 1985 by Philip Booth. ''A Jelly-Fish'' from *The Complete Poems of Marianne Moore* by Marianne Moore. Copyright © 1959 by Marianne Moore. ''One Perfect Rose'' from *The Portable Dorothy Parker* edited by Brendan Gill. Copyright 1926, renewed 1954 by Dorothy Parker. Lines from ''Cold Fear'' from *Under the Tree* by Elizabeth Madox Roberts. Copyright 1922 by B. W. Huebsch, Inc.; copyright renewed 1950 by Ivor S. Roberts. Copyright 1930 by the Viking Press, Inc.; renewed © 1958 by Ivor S. Roberts and The Viking Press, Inc. ''The Open Window'' from *The Complete Short Stories of Saki* by Saki (H. H. Munro). Copyright 1930, renewed 1958 by The Viking Press, Inc. *The Pearl* by John Steinbeck. Copyright 1945 by John Steinbeck; copyright renewed © 1973 by Elaine Steinbeck, Thom Steinbeck, and John Steinbeck IV. ''Notes on Punctuation'' from *The Medusa and the Snail* by Lewis Thomas. Copyright © 1979 by Lewis Thomas. Reprinted by permission of Viking Penguin Inc.

**Alma Villanueva**
Lines from ''I Was a Skinny Tomboy Kid'' from *Bloodroot* by Alma Villanueva. Copyright © 1977 by Alma Villanueva. Reprinted by permission of the author.

**Diane Wakoski**
Lines from ''Thanking My Mother for Piano Lessons'' from *The Motorcycle Betrayal Poems* by Diane Wakoski (Simon & Schuster). Copyright © 1971 by Diane Wakoski. Reprinted by permission of the author.

**Wesleyan University Press**
''Pitcher'' copyright 1953 by Robert Francis, reprinted from *The Orb Weaver* by permission of Wesleyan University Press. ''A Blessing'' copyright © 1961 by James Wright, reprinted from *Collected Poems* by permission of Wesleyan University Press. ''A Blessing'' first appeared in *Poetry*.

**Euphemia Ann Wolfe**
Lines from ''The Gray Squirrel'' from *Kensington Gardens* by Humbert Wolfe. Reprinted by permission.

*Note:* Every effort has been made to locate the copyright owner of material reprinted in this book. Omissions brought to our attention will be corrected in subsequent editions.

## ART CREDITS

Cover and Title Page: Indian in Canoe, 1922, Frank Schoonover, Private Collection; SHORT STORIES. **pp. 0–1**: Girls on the Jetty, Edvard Munch, Three Lions; **p. 4**: The Marketplace in Front of the Town Hall at Pontoise, 1876, Ludovic Piette, Musees de Pontoise; **p. 9**: Road to Sin le Noble, Jean Baptiste Corot, Three Lions; **p. 13**: Régates a Argenteuil, 1875, Claude Monet, Paris, Louvre/Giraudon/Art Resource; **p. 28**: W.W. Jacobs: Carton Moore-Park, 1910, The Granger Collection; **p. 59**: The ''Lightning Express'' Trains: ''Leaving the Junction'', F.F. Palmer, Del/lithography by Currier & Ives, 1863, Harry T. Peters Collection, Museum of the City of New York; **p. 63**: Evening, Monhegan Island, Samuel Reindorf; **p. 73**: The Canyon, Jack Dudley; **p. 75**: Carmen, James Asher, Courtesy of the artist; **p. 81**: Private Performance, Lois Johnson, Courtesy of the artist; **p. 98**: Mark Twain: Frank Edwin Larson, 1935, by E. Mantie, National Portrait Gallery, Smithsonian Institution; **p. 100**: ''Hint to Modern Sculptors as an ornament to a Future Square'', Hand-colored etching by James Gillray, Victoria and Albert Museum Trustees; **pp. 102–103**: Scotland Forever, Elizabeth Butler, Leeds City Art Galleries; **p. 105**: Stairway, 1925, Edward Hopper, Collection of Whitney Museum of American Art, Josephine N. Hopper Bequest; **p. 131**: Road with Cypress and Star, Vincent van Gogh, Collection: State Museum, Kroller-Muller/The Netherlands; **p. 140**: Evening View San Miguel, 1961, Samuel Reindorf, Collection: Robert Smith; **p. 143**: Señora Sabasa Garcia, 1906–07, Francisco Jose de Goya, National Gallery of Art, Washington, Andrew W. Mellon Collection; **p. 148**: Red Hills and Bones, 1941, Georgia O'Keeffe, Philadelphia Museum of Art: The Alfred Stieglitz Collection; **p. 155**: City Night, 1926, Georgia O'Keeffe, **p. 160**: The Beach Treat (detail), Suzanne Nagler, Photographed by © Stephen Tucker, Collection of Mr. and Mrs. X. Daniel Kafcas; **p. 165**: Coast Scene, Isle of Shoals, 1901, Childe Hassam, Metropolitan Museum of Art, Gift of George A. Hearn, 1909; **p. 167**: Street Scene in Lower New York, © 1926 Glenn O. Coleman, Collection of Whitney Museum of American Art, Gift of Mrs. Herbert B. Lazarus; **p. 189**: Telephone Booths, 1967, Richard Estes, Thyssen-Bornemisza Foundation, Lugano, Switzerland; **p. 192**: Unicorn, Jonathan Meader; **p. 210**: Melancholy, Edvard Munch, Rasmus Meyers Samlinger, Bergen; **p. 215**: Girl Looking at Landscape, 1957, Richard Diebenkorn, Collection of Whitney Museum of American Art, Gift of Mr. and Mrs. Alan H. Temple; **p. 218**: Orchard with Flowering Fruit Trees in Springtime, Pontoise, 1877, Camille Pissaro, Paris, Musée d'Orsay, **p. 220**: Apple Plenty, 1970, Herbert Shuptrine, Private Collection. Courtesy New York Graphic Society; **p. 228**: Simone in a White Bonnet, c. 1903, Mary Cassatt, Collection, Dale F. Dorn, San Antonio, Texas; **p. 234**: Bennington, Grandma Moses, © 1988, Grandma Moses Properties Co., NY, Bennington Museum, Bennington, Vermont; **p. 237**: Henry Look Unhitching, Thomas Hart Benton, Indianapolis Museum of Art, Gift of Mr. and Mrs. Joseph Cantor, Carmel, Indiana; **p. 242**: Etruscan Flute Player, Fresco, Tomb of the Leopards, Scala/Art Resource; **p. 247**: Greek Pottery, mid-sixth century B.C., Internal Picture: Man Between Two Trees, Louvre; **p. 240**: Frank R. Stockton: J.W. Alexander, The Bettmann Archive; **p. 250**: Flora de Stabia, Museo Archeologico Nazionale, Naples; **p. 258**: The Circus, 1874, A. Logan, Collection of the Whitney Museum of American Art, Gift of Edgar William and Bernice Chrysler Garbisch; DRAMA. **pp. 266–267**: Raised Stage with Masks, Narrator and Auditorium, 1981, © David Hockney, 1981, David Hockney; **p. 343**: Johannes DeWitt's drawing of the Swan Theatre, London, c. 1596, The Granger Collection; NONFICTION. **pp. 438–439**: Untitled, 1968, Robert Rauschenberg, Collection of Whitney Museum of American Art, Purchased with the aid of funds from the National Endowment for the Arts, **p. 449**: Diego Martelli, Edgar Degas, National Gallery of Scotland, Edinburgh; **p. 443**: Drawing by James Thurber, © 1933, 1961, James Thurber, From *My Life and Hard Times*, published by Harper and Row; **p. 445**: Drawing by James Thurber, © 1933, 1961, James Thurber, From *My Life and Hard Times*, published by Harper and Row; **p. 450**: Van Wyck Brooks; **p. 462**: Langston Hughes: Winold Reiss, 1925, National Portrait Gallery, Smithsonian Institution, gift of W. Tjark Reiss, in memory of his father, Winold Reiss; **p. 471**: Etching by Fritz Eichenberg (child in window, wolf howling); **p. 474**: Etching by Fritz Eichenberg (two children blowing whistles); **p. 476**: Etching by Fritz Eichenberg (three old women having tea/child on floor); **p. 491**: A Young Girl Reading, 1776, Jean-Honoré Fragonard, National Gallery of Art, Washington, Gift of Mrs. Mellon Bruce in memory of her father Andrew W. Mellon; **p. 493**: One Wing Above Dream or Hunger © 1985 Richard Casey, Mill Pond Press, Inc.; **p. 497**: Soaring, Andrew Wyeth, Shelburne Museum; **p. 504**: Annie Old Crow, James Bama, courtesy of the artist; **p. 506**: Old Ones Talking, R. Brownell McGrew, courtesy of the artist; **p. 540**: Around the Fish, 1926, Paul Klee, Collection, Museum of Modern Art, Abby Aldrich Rockefeller Fund; **p. 543**: Song, 1950, Ben Shahn, Hirshhorn Museum and Sculpture Gallery, Smithsonian Institution; **p. 549**: Statue of Liberty, Pete Turner/The Image Bank; **p. 552**: Aaron Copland; **p. 557**: Beethoven's Sterbezimmer in Schwarzpanierhaus, 1827, Johann Nepomuk Hoechle, Historisches Museum der Stadt Wien; **p. 562**: The Table, 1984, Alex Katz, Courtesy of Marlborough Gallery; POETRY. **pp. 582–584**: Red Poppies, Georgia O'Keeffe; **p. 589**: Central Park, 1901, Maurice Prendergast, Collection of Whitney Museum of American Art; **p. 590**: John Keats: The Granger Collection; **p. 591**: La Belle Dame sans Merci, T.W. Waterhouse, Hessisches Landesmuseum, Darmstadt; **p. 600**:

Henry Wadsworth Longfellow: Thomas B. Read, National Portrait Gallery, Smithsonian Institution; **p. 601**: The Wreck of a Transport Ship, 1810, Joseph Mallord William Turner, Calouste Gulbenkian Foundation Museum; **p. 605**: Portrait of Kitty Jagger, the Artist's Wife, David Jagger, The Bridgeman Art Library/Art Resource; **p. 606**: Rudyard Kipling: P. Burne-Jones, 1899, courtesy of the National Portrait Gallery, London; **p. 607**: The Battle of Bunker Hill; Howard Pyle, Delaware Art Museum; **p. 615**: The Battle of Life (The Golden Knight), Gustav Klimt, Private Collection. Courtesy Galerie St. Etienne, New York; **p. 617**: Couple, Kees Van Dongen, Galleria d'Arte Moderna-Parigi/Servizio, Editoriale Fotografico/Art Resource; **p. 625**: Violinist at the Window, 1918, Henri Matisse, Musée Nationale d'Art Moderne; **p. 628**: Ground Hog Day, Andrew Wyeth, Philadelphia Museum of Art, Given by Henry F. Dupont and Mrs. John Wintersteen; **p. 630**: Impressions of Hands, Antoni Tapies, Museum of Modern Art, Donald Karshan Fund; **p. 641**: Mediterranean Landscape, Pablo Picasso, Private Collection, Giraudon/Art Resource; **p. 647**: Melanie and Me Swimming, Michael Andrews, Tate Gallery, London; **p. 650**: Toilers of the Sea, Albert Pinkham Ryder, Metropolitan Museum of Art, George A. Hearn Fund, 1915; **p. 652**: Apollo 13 Launch, Fletcher Martin; **p. 652**: Christmas Rose (*Helleborus niger*), Crispin de Passe, Engraving from *Hortus Floridus* (1614), New York Public Library; **p. 655**: Memory, 1870, Elihu Vedder, Los Angeles County Museum of Art, Mr. and Mrs. William Preston Harrison Collection; **p. 662**: Jean Toomer; **p. 671**: Swing Landscape, 1938, Stuart Davis, Indiana University Art Museum; **p. 672**: Robert Burns: A. Nasmyth, The Granger Collection; **pp. 672, 748**: Alfred, Lord Tennyson: Laurence, c. 1840, courtesy of the National Portrait Gallery, London; **p. 676**: Cochem on Mosel River, John Lewis Stage/The Image Bank; **p. 672**: Carl Sandburg: National Portrait Gallery, Smithsonian Institution; **p. 683**: Still Life with Magnolia, 1941, Henri Matisse, Paris Musée Nationale Art Moderne, Giraudon/Art Resource; **pp. 344, 684**: William Shakespeare: Unknown artist; courtesy of the National Portrait Gallery, London; **p. 686**: Frances Howard, Isaac Oliver, Victoria and Albert Museum Trustees; **p. 691**: Snow-laden Camellia and Sparrow, Ando Hiroshige, Metropolitan Museum of Art, Rogers Fund; **p. 692**: A Sudden Shower at Ohashi, Ando Hiroshige, Metropolitan Museum of Art, Purchase 1918, Joseph Pulitzer Bequest; **p. 699**: Girl with Cat, Franz Marc, Three Lions; **p. 700**: Thomas Hardy: The Granger Collection; **p. 700**: Edna St. Vincent Millay: Charles Ellis, National Portrait Gallery, Smithsonian Institution; THE LEGEND OF KING ARTHUR. **pp. 716–717**: Miniature of the Round Table from *Le Roman de Lancelot du Lac*, 14th Century French Manuscript, Bibliotheque Nationale, Paris; **p. 721**: Crowning of Arthur, The British Library; **p. 729**: Galahad and Sword in Stone, The British Library; **p. 739**: How Four Queens Found Launcelot Sleeping, Aubrey Beardsley, Houghton Reading Room, Houghton Library, Harvard University; **p. 744**: N.C. Wyeth, illustration for *The Boy's King Arthur*, ''Sir Mador's Spear Brake all to pieces,'' Delaware Art Museum; **pp. 672, 748**: Alfred, Lord Tennyson: Laurence, c. 1840, courtesy of the National Portrait Gallery, London; **p. 751**: Death of Arthur, The British Library; **p. 756**: How Sir Bedivere Cast the Sword Excalibur into the Water, Aubrey Beardsley, Houghton Library, Harvard University; **p. 758**: T. Archer R.S.A., Culver Pictures; **p. 764**: The Astrologer, N.C. Wyeth, Diamond M Museum of Fine Art, Texas; NOVEL. **pp. 772–773**: Hyde Park, 1905-06, Andre Derain, Paris, Musée Nationale D'Art Moderne, Giraudon/Art Resource; **p. 777**: La Molendera, 1924, Diego Rivera, Mu de Arte Moderno, Reproduction authorized by El, Instituto Nacional de Bellas Artes y Literatura; **p. 780**: Peasant with Sombrero (Peon), Diego Rivera, Galeria Avril, Mexico City; **p. 783**: Delfina and Dimas, Diego Rivera, Property of Guy Henle; **p. 790**: Two Mexican Women and a Child, Diego Rivera, Fine Arts Museum of San Francisco, M.H. DeYoung Memorial Museum; **p. 802**: ''Group,'' Jesus Guerrero Galvan, Collection IBM Corp., Armonk, NY; **p. 809**: Mexican Peasant with Sombrero and Serape ''Peon,'' Diego Rivera, from the Mr. and Mrs. Dudley Smith Collection, Iconography A/C, Harry Ransom Humanities Research Center, The University of Texas, Austin; **p. 818**: Cactus on the Plains (Hands), Diego Rivera, Edsel & Eleanor Ford House, Grosse Pointe Shores, Michigan; **p. 825**: The Sob, David Alfaro Siqueiros, Collection, Museum of Modern Art; **p. 829**: Tree Trunks, 1913, Andre Derain, Moscow, Pushkin Museum/Roos/Art Resource.

## PHOTOGRAPH CREDITS

**p. 11**: Guy de Maupassant: The Bettmann Archive; **p. 14**: Jack Finney; **p. 15**: NYC looking south on 2nd Ave. from 58th St. at dusk, Joseph Neltis/Stock Boston; **p. 19**: NYC—view of building and street from air, Ken Karp; **p. 23**: apartment windows NYC, Hiroyuki Matsumoto/Black Star; **p. 40**: Carl Stephenson; **p. 58**: O. Henry: UPI/Bettmann Newsphotos; **p. 64**: William Melvin Kelly; **p. 65**: Black woman, David Hundley/The Stock Market; **p. 69**: Amish Buggy, Alvis Upitis/The Image Bank; **p. 72**: Juanita Platero and Siyowin Miller; **p. 84**: Kay Boyle: The Bettmann Archive; **p. 86**: Shadow/windows, Dan McCoy/Rainbow; **p. 93**: stairway, J. Dimaggio/J. Kalish/The Image Bank; **p. 106**: Heinrich Böll: AP/Wide World Photos; **p. 108**: man/microphone, Ken Karp; **p. 110**: Leslie Norris: Brandt & Brandt; **p. 112**: shaving equipment, Ken Karp; **pp. 114–115**: young man in reflection, Herb Snitzer/Stock—Boston; **pp. 118, 618**: Gwendolyn Brooks: UPI/Bettmann Newsphotos; **p. 122**: Virginia Woolf: The Granger Collection; **p. 132**: Ray Bradbury: Thomas Victor; **p. 138**: Josephina Niggli: Gary V. Fields; **p. 146**: Stephen Vincent Benét: AP/Wide World Photos; **p. 158**: Doris Lessing: Thomas Victor; **p. 168**: Toshio Mori: Stephen Y. Mori; **pp. 172, 614**: Edgar Allan Poe: UPI/Bettmann Newsphotos; **p. 169**: elderly Japanese, T. Fujihira/Monkmeyer Press; **p. 170**: abalone shell, Thomas Braise/The Shock Market; **p. 180**: Anne Tyler: Thomas Victor; **p. 182**: John Cherrix, Chincoteague, VA, Michael Ventura/Folio Inc.; **p. 186**: Ken Karp; **p. 190**: Edward D. Hoch: Patricia M. Hoch; **p. 194**: H.H. Munro (Saki): The Granger Collection; **p. 200**: Isaac Asimov: Thomas Victor; **p. 208**: Bjornstjerne Bjornson: The Bettmann Archive; **p. 216**: Katherine Mansfield: The Granger Collection; **p. 222**: Mark Helprin: Thomas Victor; **p. 226**: Sara Orne Jewett: The Granger Collection; **p. 270**: Arnold Perl; **p. 288**: Howard Koch: AP/Wide World Photos; **p. 295**: Phototeque; **pp. 300–301**: spacecraft shooting fire at building, Phototeque; **pp. 302–303**: spacecraft in bubble dome, Phototeque; **p. 310**: Reginald Rose; **p. 315**: Phototeque; **p. 319**: Phototeque; **p. 330**: Phototeque; **p. 337**: Phototeque; **p. 349**: Phototeque; **p. 354**: Phototeque; **p. 369**: Phototeque; **p. 378**: Phototeque; **p. 386**: Phototeque; **p. 395**: Phototeque; **p. 398**: Phototeque; **p. 406**: Phototeque; **p. 412**: Phototeque; **p. 427**: Phototeque; **p. 447**: James Thurber: Bettmann Newsphotos; **p. 451**: tintype of Emily Dickinson, Dan McCoy/Rainbow; **p. 454**: Emily Dickinson's room, McCoy/Rainbow; **p. 459**: Emily Dickinson's home, Coco Rainbow; **p. 464**: singing/piano/accompanist, am Newsphotos; **p. 468**: Dylan Thomas: The Bett-

mann Archive; **p. 492**: Harry Crews: Linda Mathias; **p. 500**: N. Scott Momaday: Thomas Victor; **p. 508**: Annie Dillard: Thomas Victor; **p. 510**: Flood of '86 near Rio Vista, Steve Proehl/Image Bank; **p. 516**: Evan S. Connell: © 1987 by Nancy Crampton; **p. 518**: Captain Amundsen, Library of Congress; **p. 521**: The Five at the Pole, National Archives, Washington, D.C.; **p. 525**: Amundsen taking a sight, Library of Congress; **p. 528**: Lorraine Hansberry: The Bettmann Archive, Inc.; **p. 530**: jumping rope, Enrico Ferorelli/Dot; **p. 532**: Pemaquid Lighthouse, Robert Frerck/Woodfin Camp; **p. 534**: E.B. White: AP/Wide World Photos; **p. 534**: 2 faces/clowns, Paul Barton/Stock Martet; **p. 538**: Calvin Trillin: © 1987 Thomas Victor; **p. 544**: Lewis Thomas: © Thomas Victor; **p. 548**: Theodore H. White: Thomas Victor; **p. 549**: Statue of Liberty, Pete Turner/ The Image Bank; **p. 557**: Beethoven's Sterbezimmer im Schwarzspanierhaus Hoechle, Johann Nepomuk, Historisches Museum der Stadt Wien; **p. 560**: Ann Beattie: Thomas Victor; **p. 564**; Rachel Carson: UPI/Bettmann Newsphotos; **p. 565**: starfish, green sponge, sea anemones, Anne Wertheim/Animals Animals; **pp. 568–569**: yellow-crowned night heron, Breck P. Kent; **p. 570**: ghost crab, Stephen J. Krasemann/DRK Photo; **p. 575**: Baseball (Puerto Rico: people), Stephanie Maze/Woodfin Camp; **p. xxx**: Thomas Boswell: © 1983 by Playboy; **p. 586**: young girl on hilltop/sun, Frank Whitney/The Image Bank; **p. 587**: May Swenson: Thomas Victor; **p. 595**: Robert Frost: Dimitri Kessel/Life Magazine © Time Inc.; **pp. 596–597**: chopping trees for firewood, Philip Jon Bailey/The Picture Cube; **p. 610**: W.H. Auden: The Bettmann Archive/BBC Hulton; **pp. 172, 614**: Edgar Allan Poe: UPI/Bettmann Newsphotos; **pp. 118, 618**: Gwendolyn Brooks: UPI/Bettmann Newsphotos; **p. 620**: Black woman, Richard Nowitz/The Image Bank; **p. 618**: Dorothy Parker: The Granger Collection; **p. 618**: Samuel Allen; **p. 623**: Black baseball pitcher, AP/Wide World Photos; **p. 626**: Conrad Aiken: UPI/Bettmann Newsphotos; **p. 626**: Naomi Shihab Nye: Marjorie Ransom; **pp. 626, 648**: Amy Lowell: The Bettmann Archive; **p. 634**: James Wright: © Thomas Victor; **p. 636**: horses grazing, Bill Weems/Woodfin Camp; **p. 634**: Octavio Paz: © 1987 Thomas Victor; **p. 634**: Mary Oliver: AP/Wide World Photos; **p. 642**: Lucille Clifton; **p. 642**: Elizabeth Coatsworth: AP/Wide World Photos; **p. 645**: summer rain, Grafton Marshall Smith/The Image Bank; **p. 642**: Eve Merriam: James Salzano; **p. 642**: Philip Booth: © Rollie McKenna; **pp. 626, 648**: Amy Lowell: The Bettmann Archive; **p. 648**: Marianne Moore: AP/Wide World Photos; **p. 648**: Marcie Hans; **p. 648**: Emily Dickinson: The Granger Collection; **p. 656**: Theodore Roethke: AP/Wide World Photos; **p. 659**: daisies, Peter Miller/The Image Bank; **p. 656**: A.R. Ammons: © 1987 Thomas Victor; **p. 661**: Jesse Outdoors, Bonnie Rauch/The Image Bank; **p. 656**; John Ciardi: © 1987 Thomas Victor; **p. 665**: Fishing Lake Unbagog, Errol, NH, William Johnson/The Stock Market; **p. 662**: Elizabeth Bishop: © 1983 Thomas Victor; **p. 668**: baseball, David Madison/Duomo; **p. 662**: Robert Francis: AP/Wide World Photos; **p. 662**: John Masefield: The Bettmann Archive; **p. 676**: German Cochem on Mosel River, John Lewis Stage/The Image Bank; **p. 682**: Flanders Fields, Corette Moreau; **p. 672**: Christopher Morley: The Granger Collection; **p. 681**: Musicians, Enrico Ferorelli/Dot; **p. 672**: John McCrae; **p. 684**: Elinor Wylie: The Bettmann Archive; **p. 690**: Bashō, Issa, and Hyakuchi: Japanese Lacquers Meiji Period, Metropolitan Museum of Art, Bequest of Benjamin Altman, 1913; **pp. 694, 700**: John Updike: Thomas Victor; **p. 694**: Lawrence Ferlinghetti: The Bettmann Archive; **p. 700**: Frank Horne: AP/Wide World Photos; **p. 702**: Man in Footrace Track

& Field, C. Rentmeester/The Image Bank; **p. 700**: Karl Shapiro; **p. 700**: Edna St. Vincent Millay: Charles Ellis, National Portrait Gallery, Smithsonian Institution; **p. 707**; Florida West Coast Sunset, Derek Berwin/The Image Bank; **pp. 694, 700**: John Updike: Thomas Victor; **p. 709**: basketball players, Adam J. Stoltman/Duomo; **p. 720**: T.H. White; **p. 732**: Thomas Malory; **p. 736**: Thomas Malory; **p. 762**: Geoffrey Hill: Jerry Bauer; **p. 762**: Edwin Muir: Mark Gerson; **p. 778**: John Steinbeck: UPI/Bettmann Newphotos; **p. 830**: John Knowles.

*Acknowledgments*